TODD McFARLANE AND
IMAGE COMICS PRESENT

SPAWN COLLECTED EDITION
VOLUME THREE

STORY
TODD MCFARLANE

PENCILS
TODD MCFARLANE
GREG CAPULLO
TONY DANIELS

INKS
TODD MCFARLANE
KEVIN CONRAD
CHANCE WOLF
DANNY MIKI

LETTERING
TOM ORZECHOWSKI
LOIS BUHALIS

COLOR
STEVE OLIFF
QUINN SUPPLEE
OLYOPTICS
BRIAN HABERLIN
DAN KEMP
TODD BROEKER
ROY YOUNG
J.D. SMITH
MATT MILLA

COVER
TODD MCFARLANE

EDITOR IN CHIEF
BRIAN HABERLIN

PRESIDENT
MCFARLANE TOYS
LARRY MARDER

PRESIDENT OF
ENTERTAINMENT
TERRY FITZGERALD

EXECUTIVE DIRECTOR
OF SPAWN.COM
TYLER JEFFERS

MANAGER OF
INT'L. PUBLISHING
FOR TMP
SUZY THOMAS

PUBLISHER FOR
IMAGE COMICS
ERIK LARSEN

SPAWN CREATED BY
TODD McFARLANE

Spawn created by
TODD MCFARLANE

TODD McFARLANE
PRODUCTIONS
SPAWN.COM

SPAWN COLLECTION VOL. 3. March 2007. First Printing. Contains issues 35-54 of Spawn. Published by IMAGE COMICS, 1942 University Ave. Berkeley, CA 94704. **PRINTED IN CANADA**

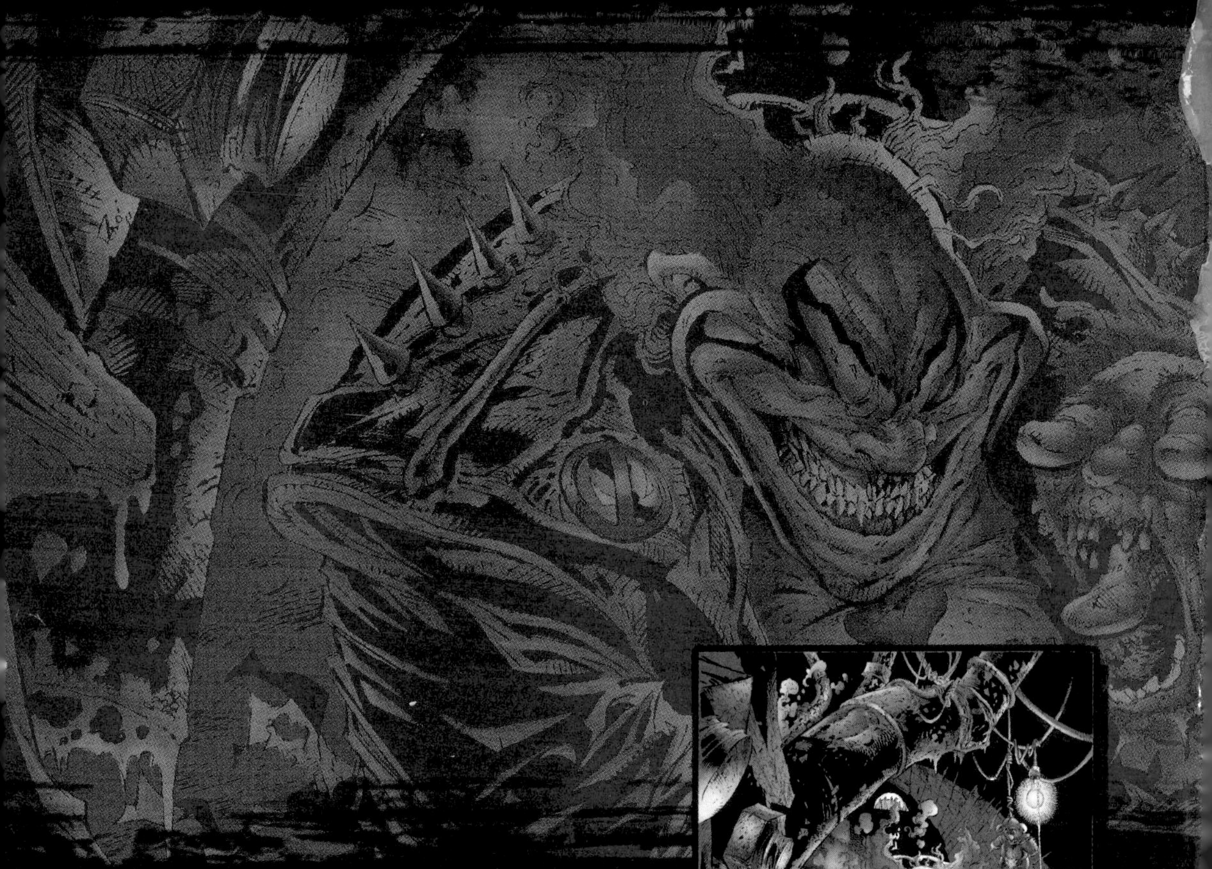

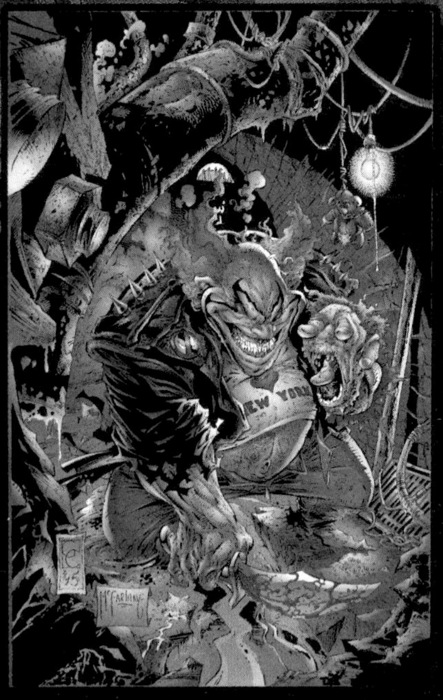

ISSUE THIRTY-FOUR

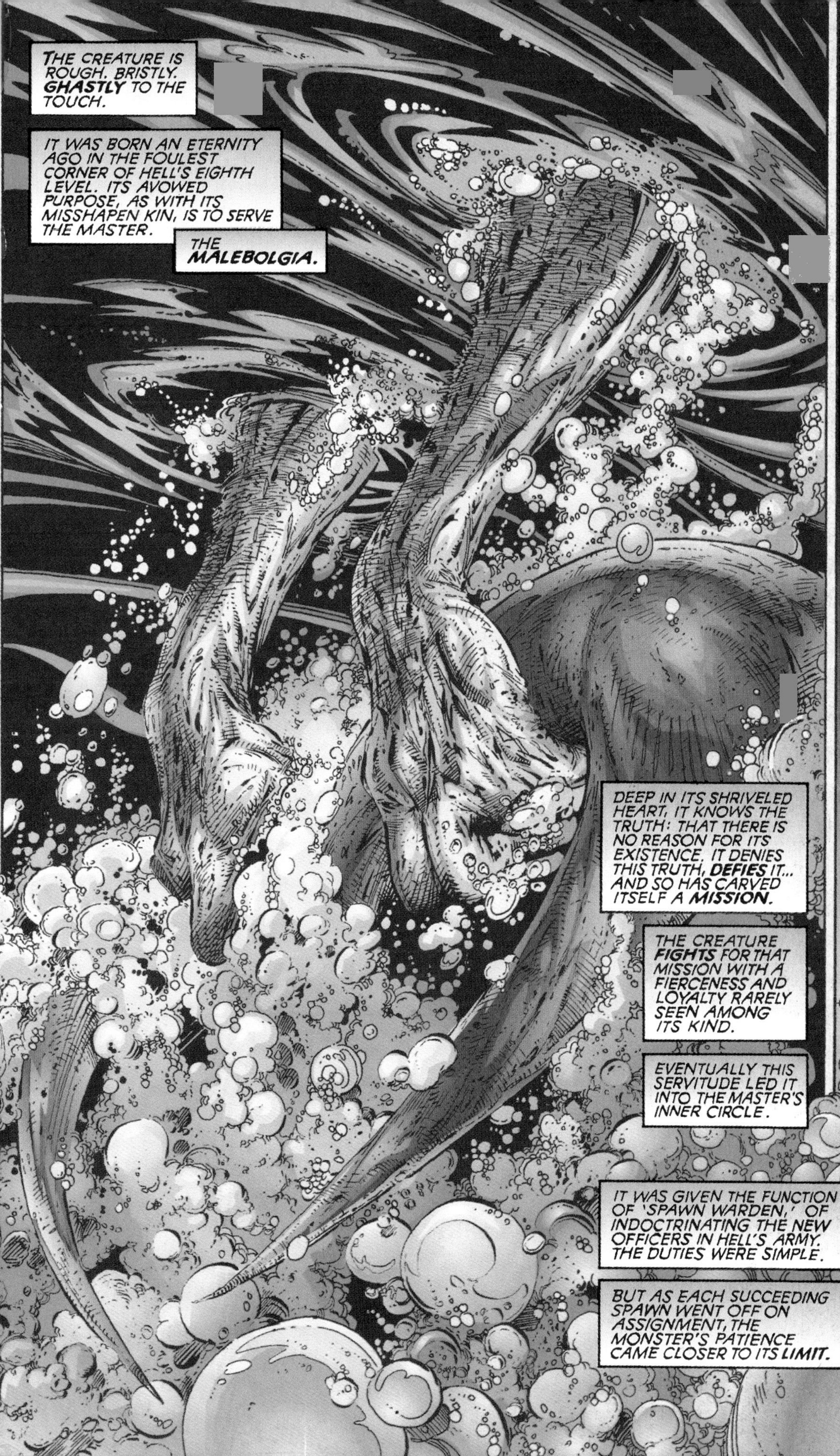
THE CREATURE IS ROUGH. BRISTLY. **GHASTLY** TO THE TOUCH.
IT WAS BORN AN ETERNITY AGO IN THE FOULEST CORNER OF HELL'S EIGHTH LEVEL. ITS AVOWED PURPOSE, AS WITH ITS MISSHAPEN KIN, IS TO SERVE THE MASTER.
THE **MALEBOLGIA.**
DEEP IN ITS SHRIVELED HEART, IT KNOWS THE TRUTH: THAT THERE IS NO REASON FOR ITS EXISTENCE. IT DENIES THIS TRUTH, **DEFIES** IT... AND SO HAS CARVED ITSELF A **MISSION.**
THE CREATURE **FIGHTS** FOR THAT MISSION WITH A FIERCENESS AND LOYALTY RARELY SEEN AMONG ITS KIND.
EVENTUALLY THIS SERVITUDE LED IT INTO THE MASTER'S INNER CIRCLE.
IT WAS GIVEN THE FUNCTION OF 'SPAWN WARDEN,' OF INDOCTRINATING THE NEW OFFICERS IN HELL'S ARMY. THE DUTIES WERE SIMPLE.
BUT AS EACH SUCCEEDING SPAWN WENT OFF ON ASSIGNMENT, THE MONSTER'S PATIENCE CAME CLOSER TO ITS **LIMIT.**

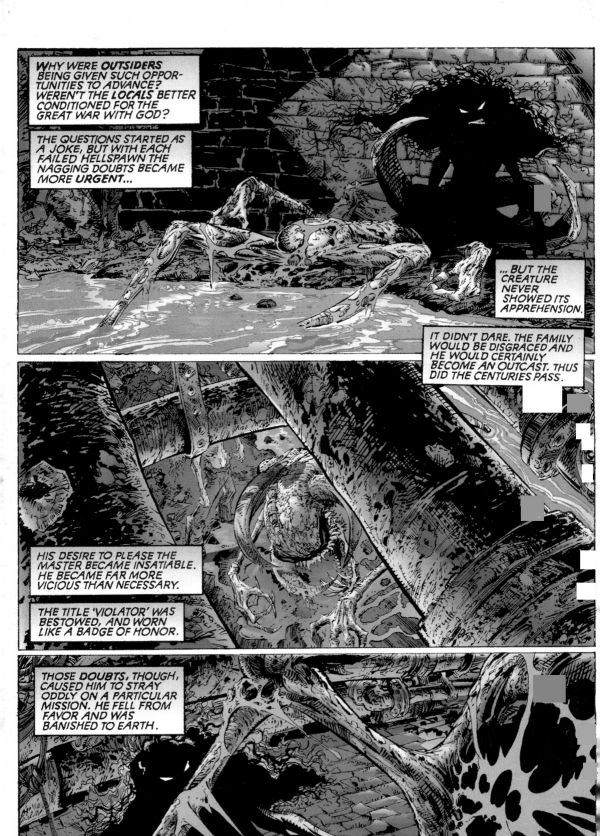

WHY WERE *OUTSIDERS* BEING GIVEN SUCH OPPORTUNITIES TO ADVANCE? WEREN'T THE *LOCALS* BETTER CONDITIONED FOR THE GREAT WAR WITH GOD?

THE QUESTIONS STARTED AS A JOKE, BUT WITH EACH FAILED HELLSPAWN THE NAGGING DOUBTS BECAME MORE *URGENT*...

...BUT THE CREATURE NEVER SHOWED ITS APPREHENSION.

IT DIDN'T DARE. THE FAMILY WOULD BE DISGRACED AND HE WOULD CERTAINLY BECOME AN OUTCAST. THUS DID THE CENTURIES PASS.

HIS DESIRE TO PLEASE THE MASTER BECAME INSATIABLE. HE BECAME FAR MORE VICIOUS THAN NECESSARY.

THE TITLE 'VIOLATOR' WAS BESTOWED, AND WORN LIKE A BADGE OF HONOR.

THOSE *DOUBTS*, THOUGH, CAUSED HIM TO STRAY ODDLY ON A PARTICULAR MISSION. HE FELL FROM FAVOR AND WAS BANISHED TO EARTH.

NOW, VIOLATOR'S ONLY HOPE IS TO *BEAT* THE CURRENT HELL-SPAWN, BOTH *PHYSICALLY* AND *EMOTIONALLY*.

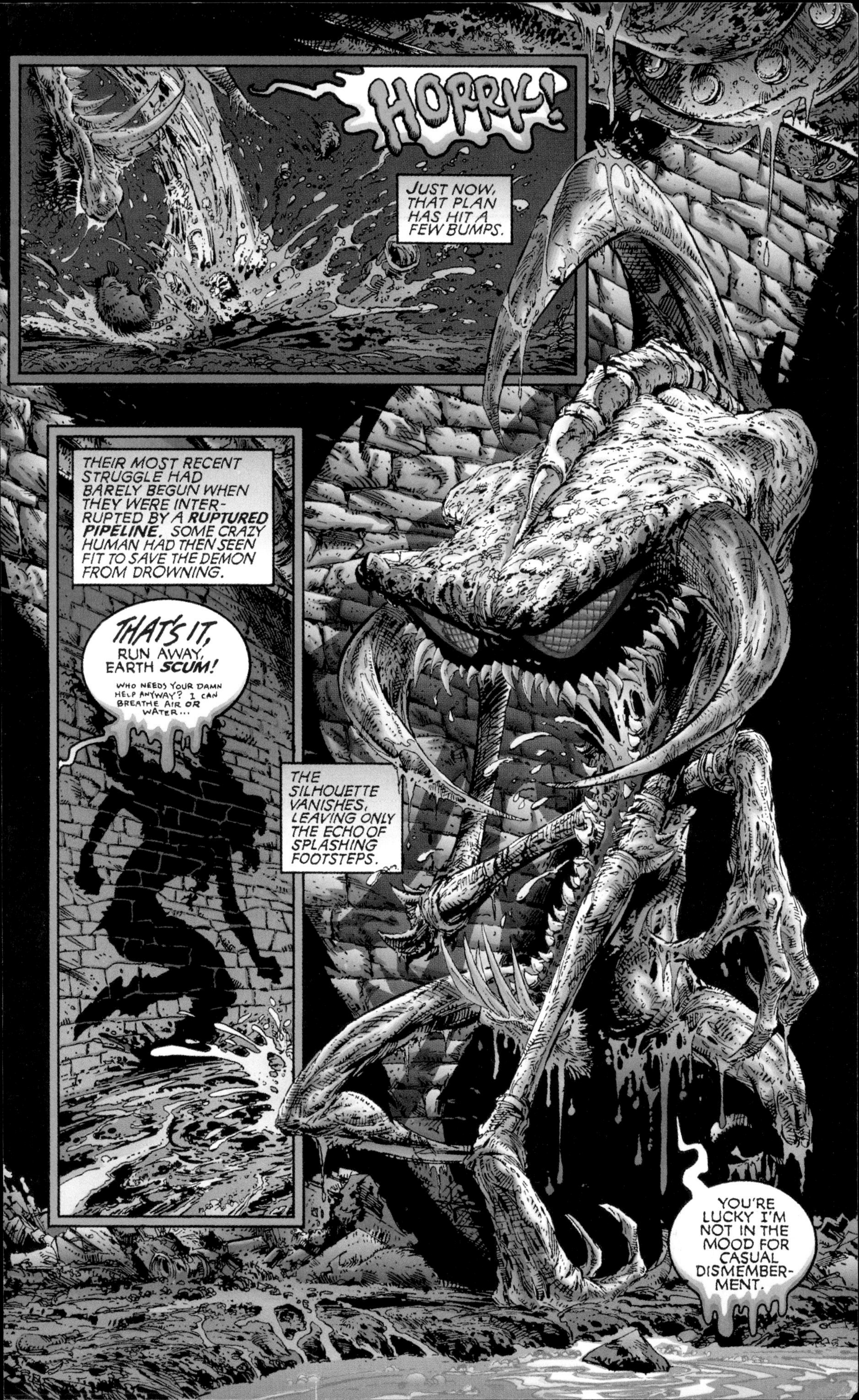
HORRK!
JUST NOW, THAT PLAN HAS HIT A FEW BUMPS.
THEIR MOST RECENT STRUGGLE HAD BARELY BEGUN WHEN THEY WERE INTER-RUPTED BY A **RUPTURED PIPELINE**. SOME CRAZY HUMAN HAD THEN SEEN FIT TO SAVE THE DEMON FROM DROWNING.
THAT'S IT, RUN AWAY, EARTH **SCUM**!
WHO NEEDS YOUR DAMN HELP ANYWAY? I CAN BREATHE AIR **OR** WATER...
THE SILHOUETTE VANISHES, LEAVING ONLY THE ECHO OF SPLASHING FOOTSTEPS.
YOU'RE LUCKY I'M NOT IN THE MOOD FOR CASUAL DISMEMBER-MENT.

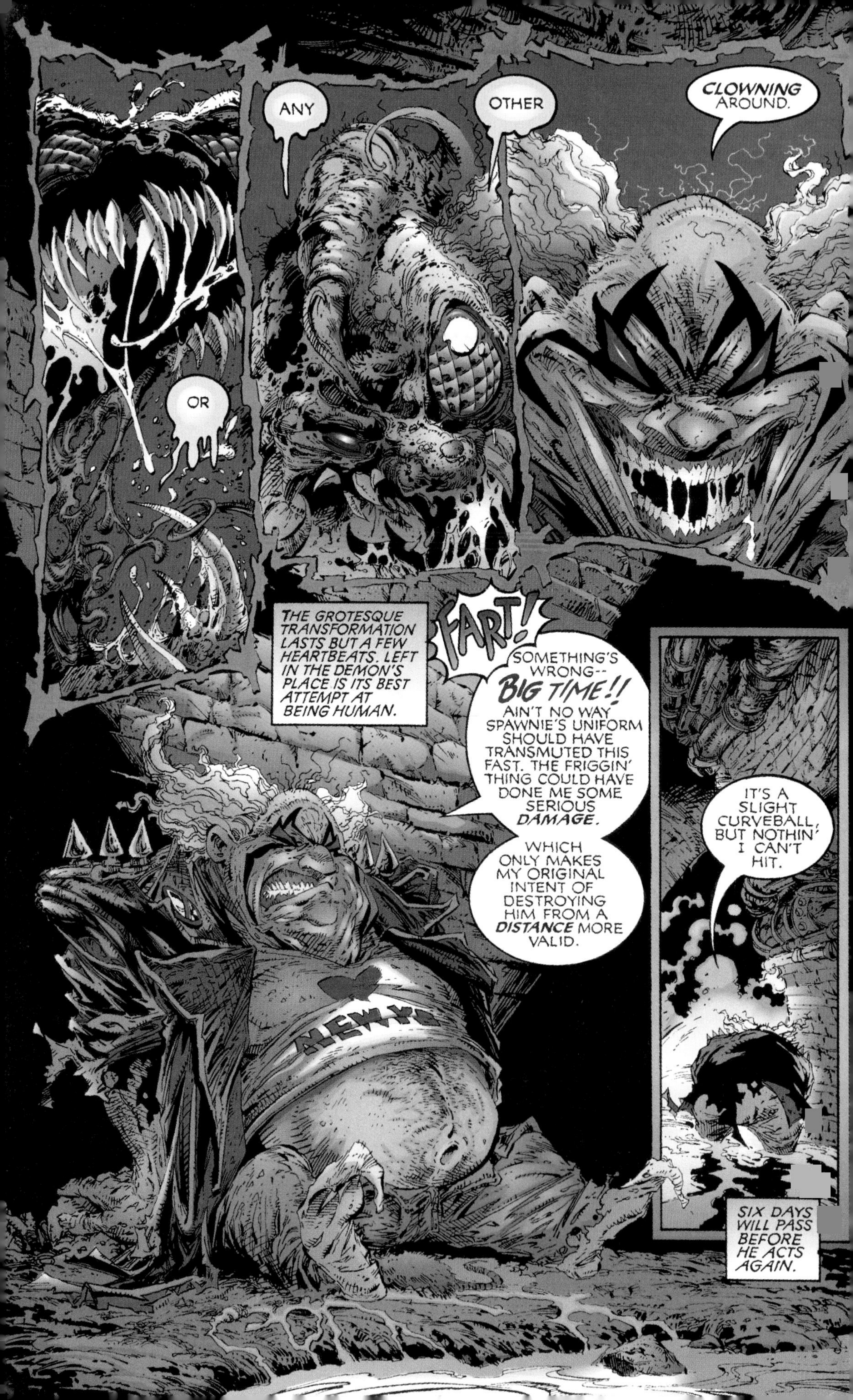
OR
ANY
OTHER
CLOWNING AROUND.
THE GROTESQUE TRANSFORMATION LASTS BUT A FEW HEARTBEATS. LEFT IN THE DEMON'S PLACE IS ITS BEST ATTEMPT AT BEING HUMAN.
FART!
SOMETHING'S WRONG-- BIG TIME!! AIN'T NO WAY SPAWNIE'S UNIFORM SHOULD HAVE TRANSMUTED THIS FAST. THE FRIGGIN' THING COULD HAVE DONE ME SOME SERIOUS DAMAGE.
WHICH ONLY MAKES MY ORIGINAL INTENT OF DESTROYING HIM FROM A DISTANCE MORE VALID.
NEWY'S
IT'S A SLIGHT CURVEBALL, BUT NOTHIN' I CAN'T HIT.
SIX DAYS WILL PASS BEFORE HE ACTS AGAIN.

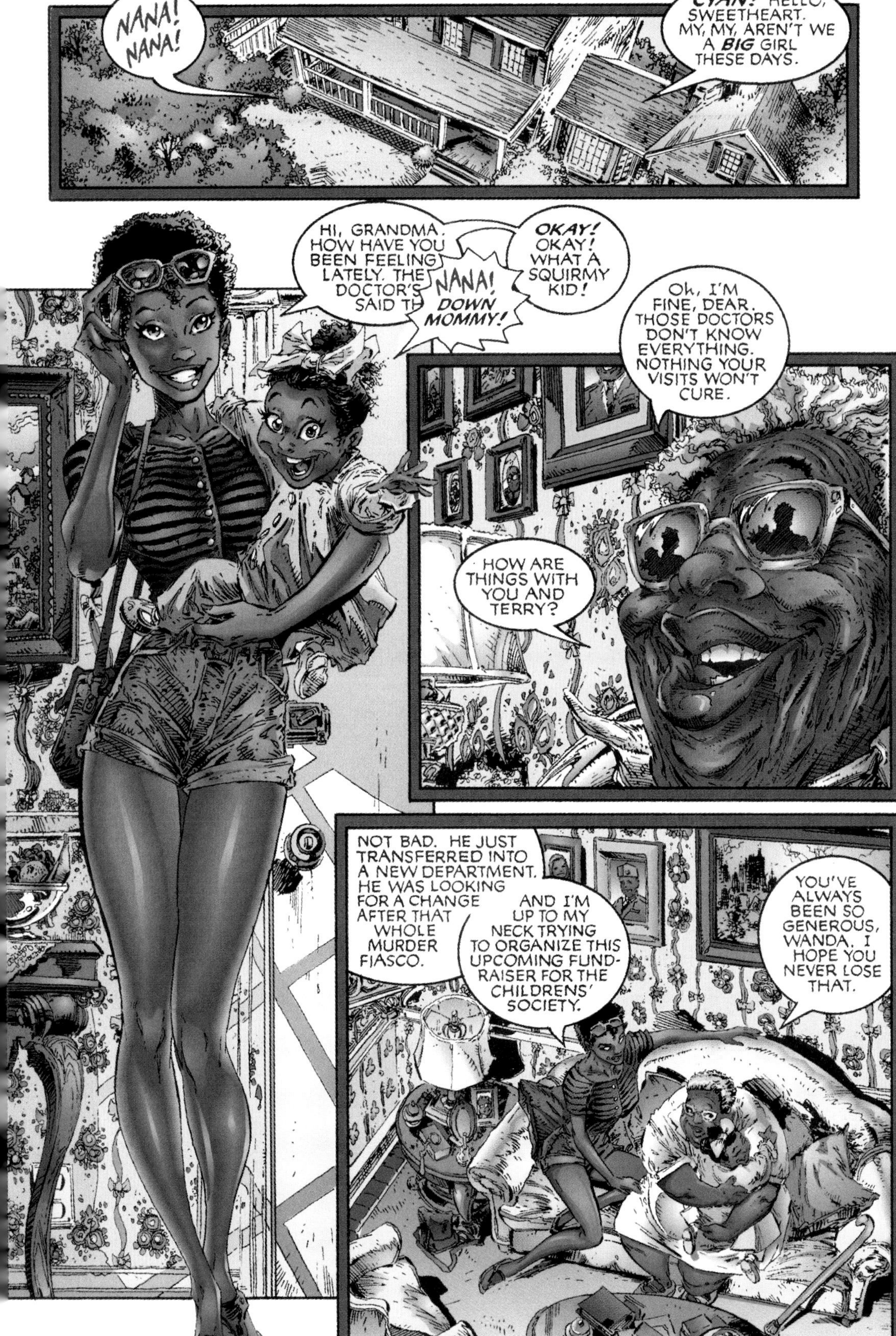
NANA! NANA!
CYAN! HELLO, SWEETHEART. MY, MY, AREN'T WE A BIG GIRL THESE DAYS.
HI, GRANDMA. HOW HAVE YOU BEEN FEELING LATELY. THE DOCTOR'S SAID TH
NANA! DOWN MOMMY!
OKAY! OKAY! WHAT A SQUIRMY KID!
Oh, I'M FINE, DEAR. THOSE DOCTORS DON'T KNOW EVERYTHING. NOTHING YOUR VISITS WON'T CURE.
HOW ARE THINGS WITH YOU AND TERRY?
NOT BAD. HE JUST TRANSFERRED INTO A NEW DEPARTMENT. HE WAS LOOKING FOR A CHANGE AFTER THAT WHOLE MURDER FIASCO.
AND I'M UP TO MY NECK TRYING TO ORGANIZE THIS UPCOMING FUND-RAISER FOR THE CHILDRENS' SOCIETY.
YOU'VE ALWAYS BEEN SO GENEROUS, WANDA. I HOPE YOU NEVER LOSE THAT.

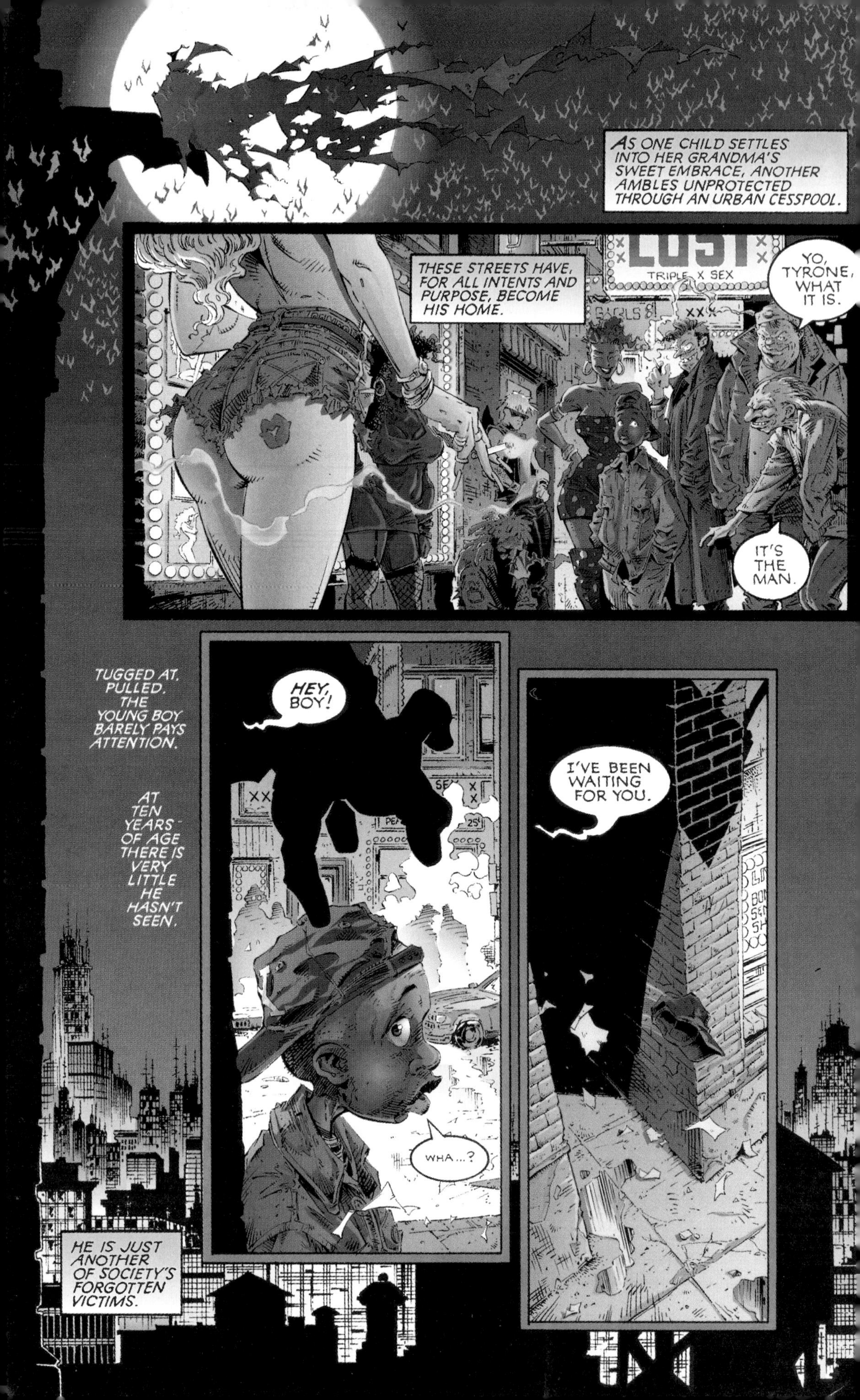
AS ONE CHILD SETTLES INTO HER GRANDMA'S SWEET EMBRACE, ANOTHER AMBLES UNPROTECTED THROUGH AN URBAN CESSPOOL.
THESE STREETS HAVE, FOR ALL INTENTS AND PURPOSE, BECOME HIS HOME.
LOST
TRIPLE X SEX
YO, TYRONE, WHAT IT IS.
IT'S THE MAN.
TUGGED AT. PULLED. THE YOUNG BOY BARELY PAYS ATTENTION.
AT TEN YEARS OF AGE THERE IS VERY LITTLE HE HASN'T SEEN.
HE IS JUST ANOTHER OF SOCIETY'S FORGOTTEN VICTIMS.
HEY, BOY!
WHA...?
I'VE BEEN WAITING FOR YOU.

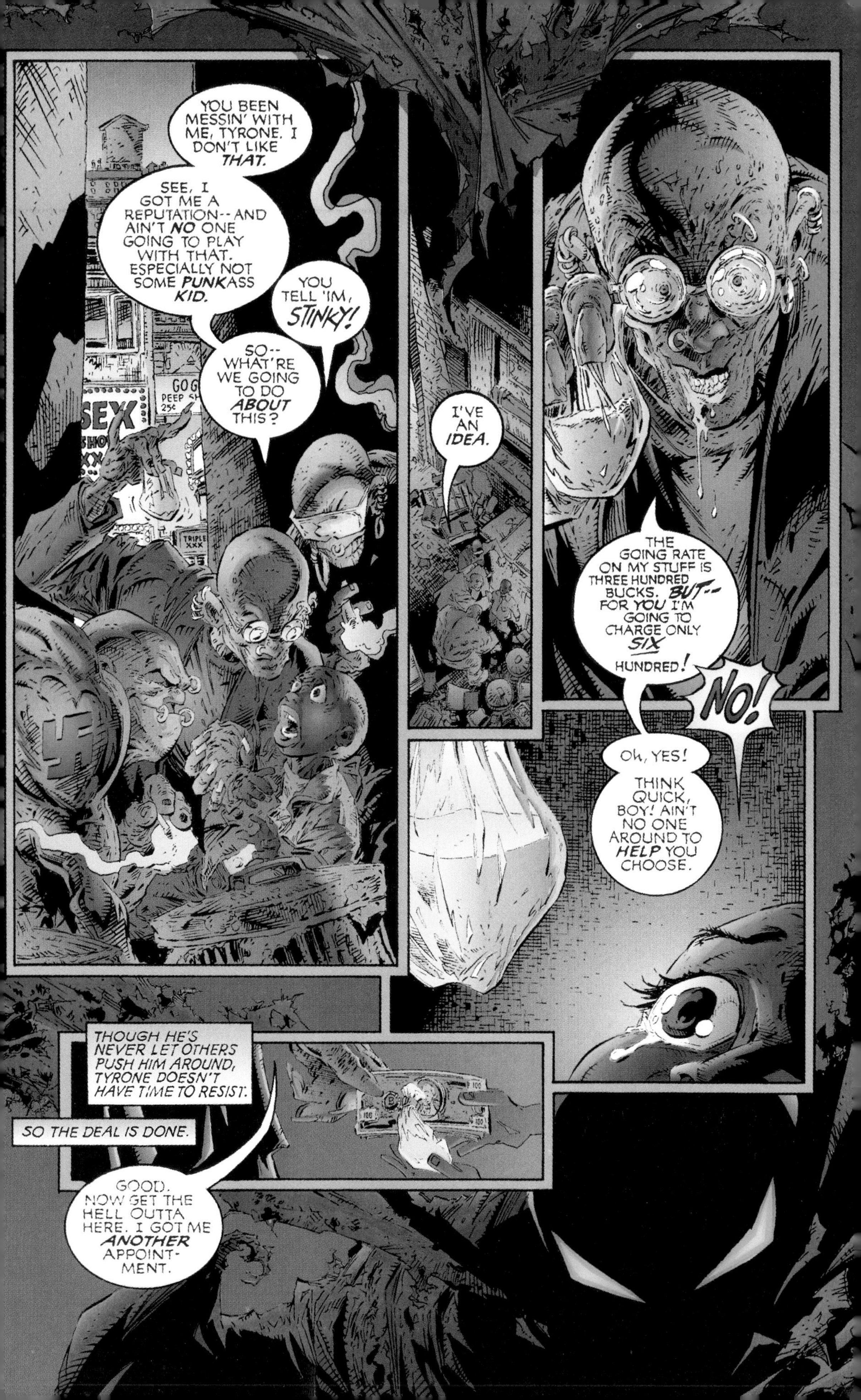
YOU BEEN MESSIN' WITH ME, TYRONE. I DON'T LIKE *THAT.*
SEE, I GOT ME A REPUTATION--AND AIN'T *NO* ONE GOING TO PLAY WITH THAT. ESPECIALLY NOT SOME *PUNK*ASS *KID.*
YOU TELL 'IM, *STINKY!*
SO--WHAT'RE WE GOING TO DO *ABOUT* THIS?
I'VE AN *IDEA.*
THE GOING RATE ON MY STUFF IS THREE HUNDRED BUCKS. *BUT*--FOR *YOU* I'M GOING TO CHARGE ONLY *SIX* HUNDRED!
NO!
Oh, YES!
THINK QUICK, BOY! AIN'T NO ONE AROUND TO *HELP* YOU CHOOSE.
THOUGH HE'S NEVER LET OTHERS PUSH HIM AROUND, TYRONE DOESN'T HAVE TIME TO RESIST.
SO THE DEAL IS DONE.
GOOD. NOW GET THE HELL OUTTA HERE. I GOT ME *ANOTHER* APPOINT-MENT.

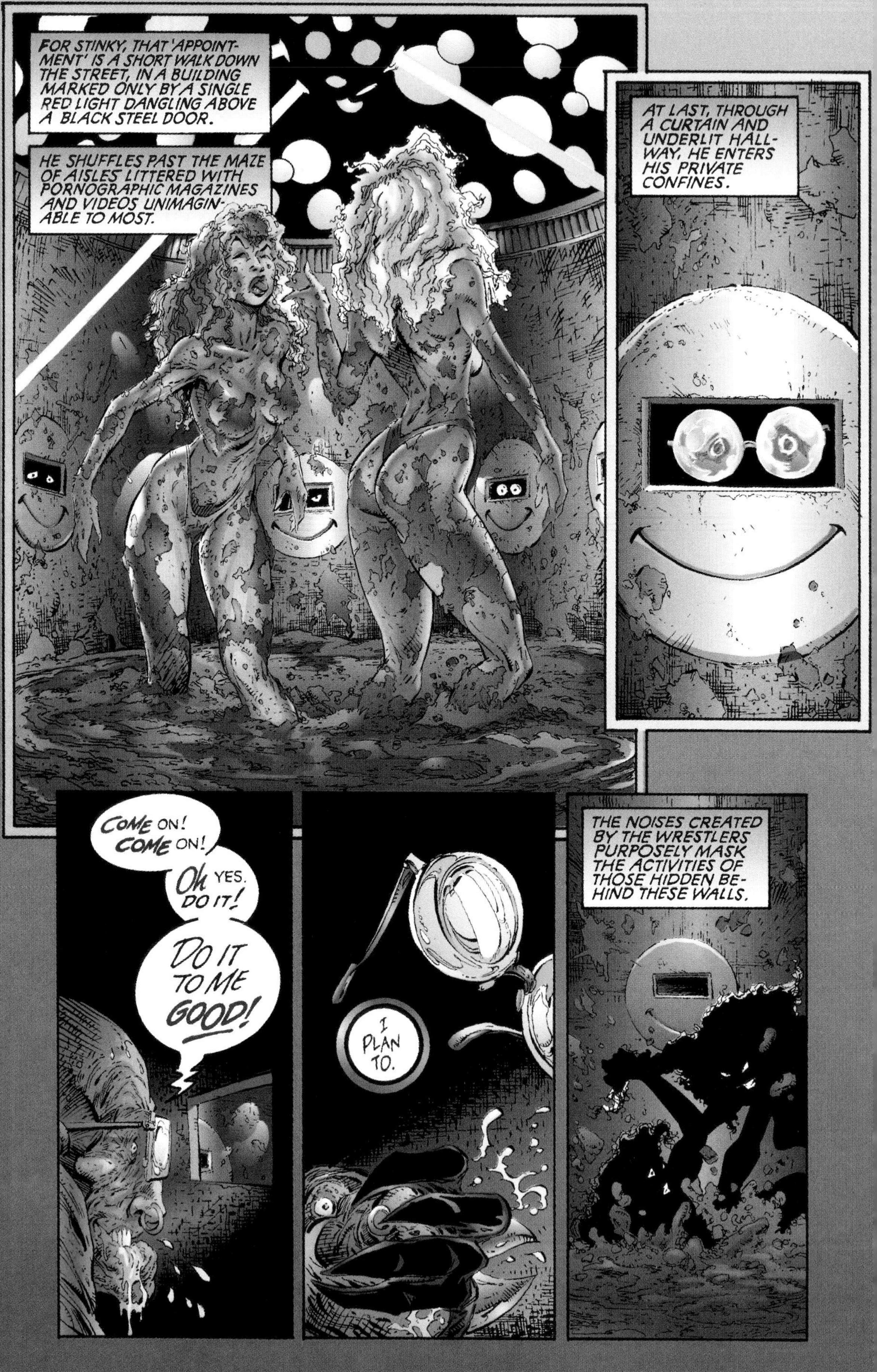
FOR STINKY, THAT 'APPOINTMENT' IS A SHORT WALK DOWN THE STREET, IN A BUILDING MARKED ONLY BY A SINGLE RED LIGHT DANGLING ABOVE A BLACK STEEL DOOR.
HE SHUFFLES PAST THE MAZE OF AISLES LITTERED WITH PORNOGRAPHIC MAGAZINES AND VIDEOS UNIMAGINABLE TO MOST.
AT LAST, THROUGH A CURTAIN AND UNDERLIT HALLWAY, HE ENTERS HIS PRIVATE CONFINES.
COME ON! COME ON!
Oh YES. DO IT!
DO IT TO ME GOOD!
I PLAN TO.
THE NOISES CREATED BY THE WRESTLERS PURPOSELY MASK THE ACTIVITIES OF THOSE HIDDEN BEHIND THESE WALLS.

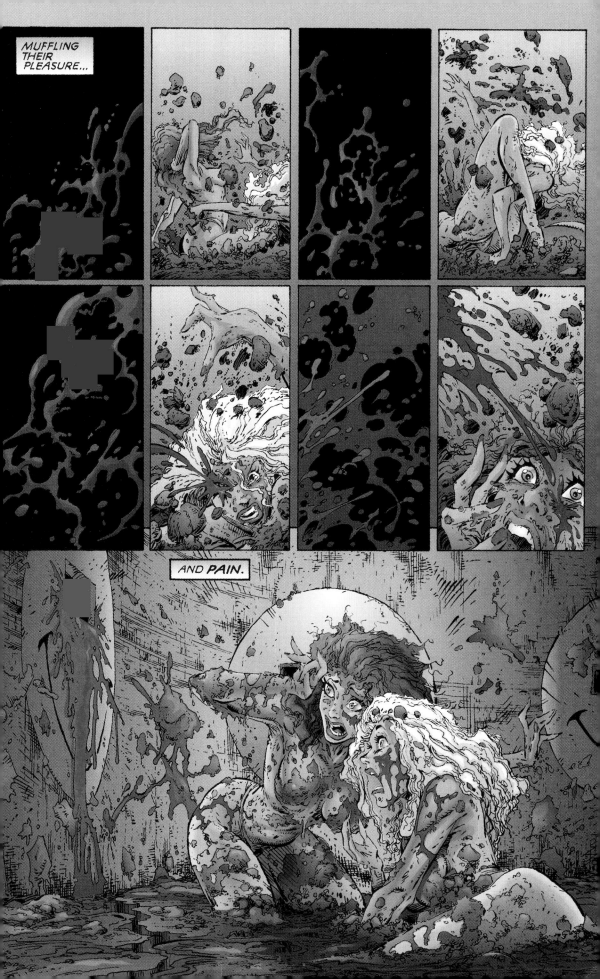

MUFFLING THEIR PLEASURE...

AND PAIN.

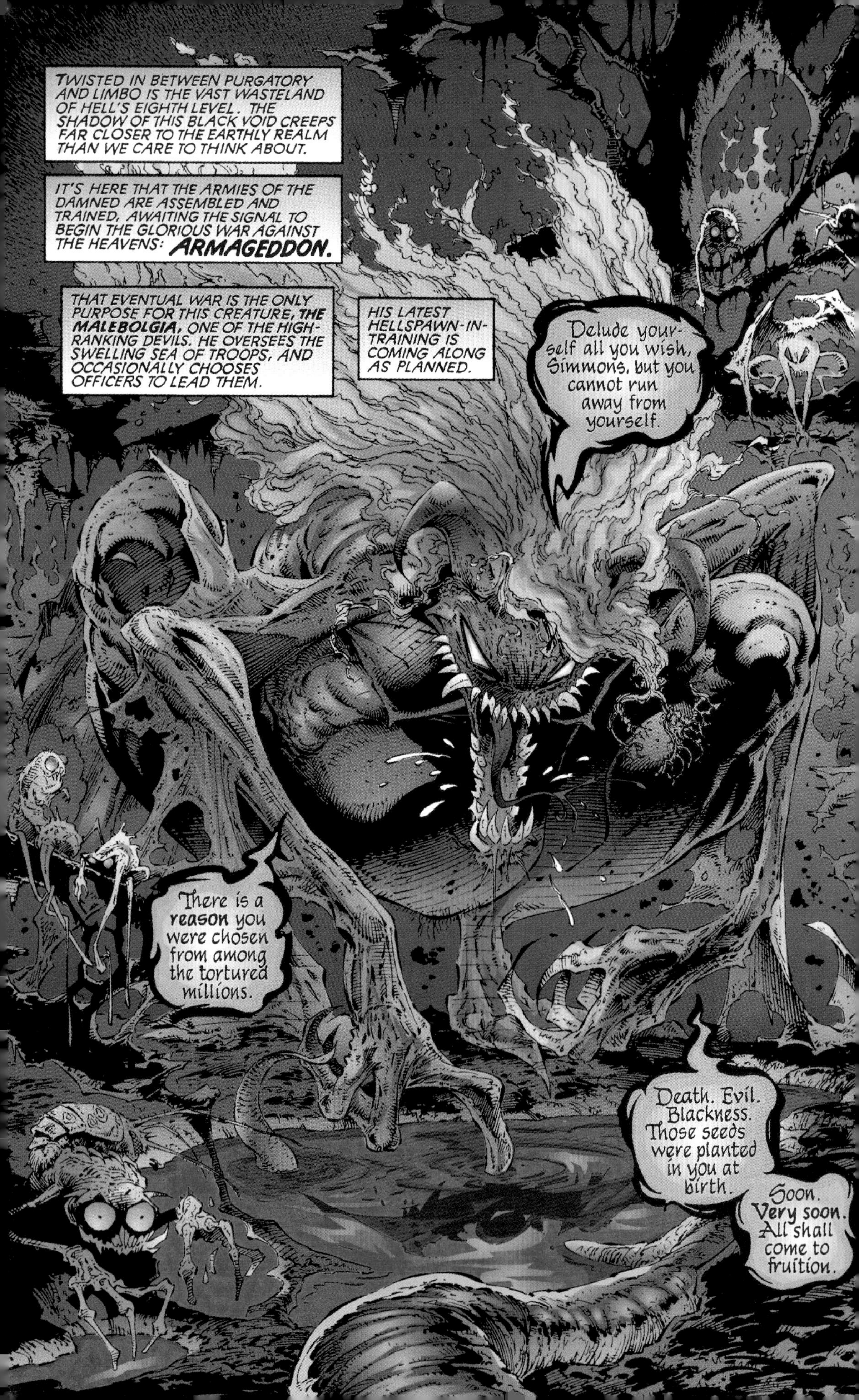
TWISTED IN BETWEEN PURGATORY AND LIMBO IS THE VAST WASTELAND OF HELL'S EIGHTH LEVEL. THE SHADOW OF THIS BLACK VOID CREEPS FAR CLOSER TO THE EARTHLY REALM THAN WE CARE TO THINK ABOUT.
IT'S HERE THAT THE ARMIES OF THE DAMNED ARE ASSEMBLED AND TRAINED, AWAITING THE SIGNAL TO BEGIN THE GLORIOUS WAR AGAINST THE HEAVENS: ARMAGEDDON.
THAT EVENTUAL WAR IS THE ONLY PURPOSE FOR THIS CREATURE, THE MALEBOLGIA, ONE OF THE HIGH-RANKING DEVILS. HE OVERSEES THE SWELLING SEA OF TROOPS, AND OCCASIONALLY CHOOSES OFFICERS TO LEAD THEM.
HIS LATEST HELLSPAWN-IN-TRAINING IS COMING ALONG AS PLANNED.
Delude yourself all you wish, Simmons, but you cannot run away from yourself.
There is a reason you were chosen from among the tortured millions.
Death. Evil. Blackness. Those seeds were planted in you at birth.
Soon. Very soon. All shall come to fruition.

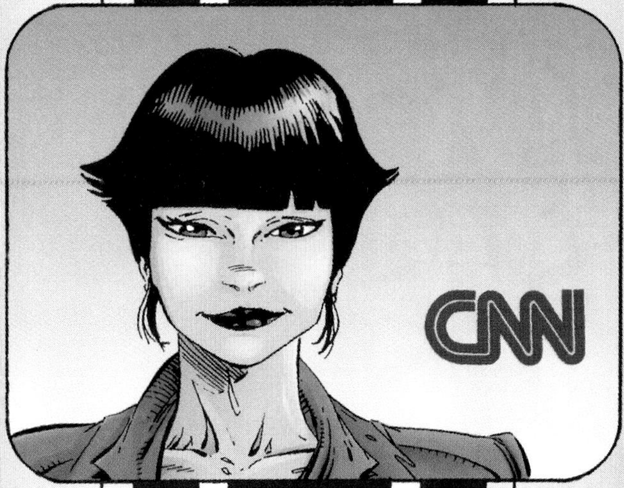
CNN

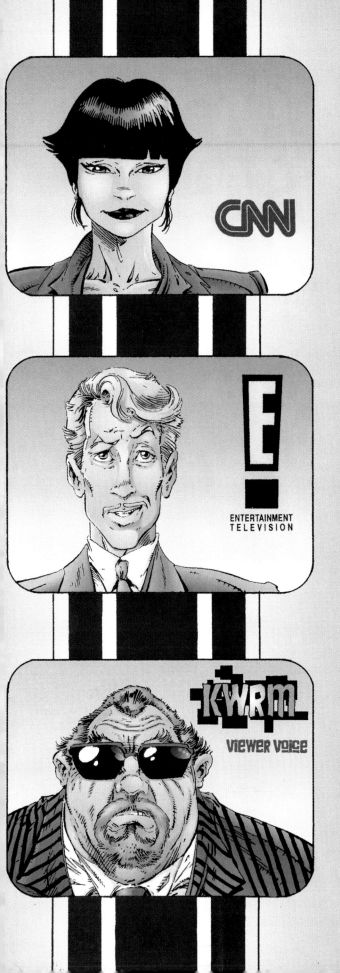

THE SITUATION IN BOSNIA INTENSIFIES AS NEITHER BOSNIAN DIPLOMATS NOR THEIR SERBIAN COUNTERPARTS SEEM WILLING TO RESUME PEACEKEEPING TALKS. THE PRESIDENT'S MUCH-PUBLICIZED VISIT TO BOSNIA WAS CUT UNEXPECTEDLY SHORT, THREE FEWER DAYS THAN PLANNED, AFTER THE BOSNIAN PRESIDENT WALKED OUT DURING OUR PRESIDENT'S PRESENTATION REGARDING THE ONGOING BORDER DISPUTE. CITING FAVORITISM TOWARD THE SERBS, THE BOSNIAN PRESIDENT ADVISED THE COMMITTEE THAT BOSNIAN PARTICIATION WOULD RESUME ONLY IF THE U.S. PRESIDENT WAS REMOVED FROM THE PEACE NEGOTIATIONS. CLOSER TO HOME, POLICE IN NEW YORK CITY ARE STILL INVESTIGATING A GRUESOME MURDER IN THE RED LIGHT DISTRICT. THERE ARE NO REPORTED SUSPECTS AT THIS TIME.

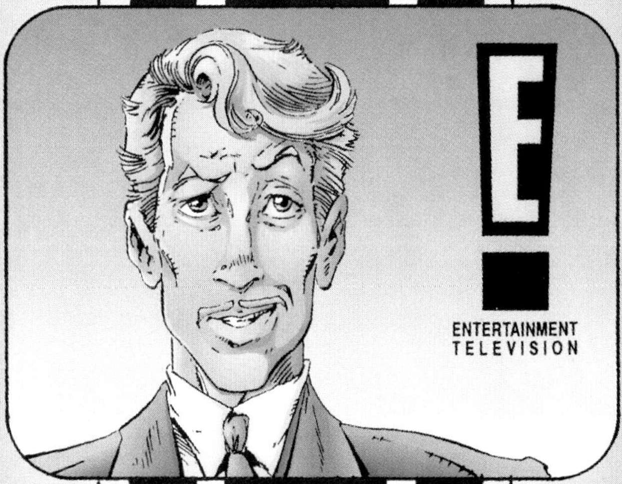
E!
ENTERTAINMENT
TELEVISION

AS THE INTERMINABLE DRUG WAR IN NEW YORK CITY ESCALATES, ANOTHER PAWN FALLS, VICTIM TO A ***GRUESOME*** ATTACK IN A PORN THEATER. POLICE HAD TO RESORT TO DENTAL RECORDS IN AN ATTEMPT TO IDENTIFY THE BODY. SOURCES INDICATE THAT THE VICTIM HAD OVER A ***DOZEN*** BROKEN BONES. A BLOOD SPATTER EXPERT BEGINS HIS INVESTIGATION TODAY IN AN ATTEMPT TO DETERMINE WHAT, IF ***ANY,*** WEAPON WAS USED TO SEVER THE VICTIM'S HEAD. OFFICIALS ARE BAFFLED BY THE EXTENT OF THE MUTILATION, AND CANNOT DETERMINE IF THE ATTACK WAS COMMITTED BY A HUMAN OR SOME WILD ANIMAL. EVEN THOUGH THE RECENT ***VAMPIRE*** CASE HAS BEEN CLOSED, POLICE ARE NOT RULING OUT THE POSSIBILITY OF A CONNECTION. IS THIS JUST ANOTHER MEANINGLESS CRIME, OR A REVENGE HIT FOR A DRUG DEAL GONE BAD? BEFORE A MOTIVE CAN BE SUGGESTED, POLICE SAY THE VICTIM'S IDENTITY MUST FIRST BE DETERIMINED. CREDIT WHERE IT'S DUE. SOUNDS FAIR TO ME.

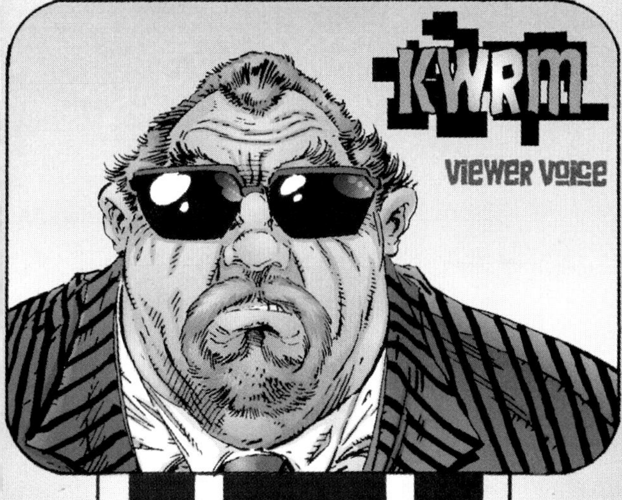
KWRM
VIEWER VOICE

BIG SURPRISE. OUR OVERWHELMINGLY ELECTED PRESIDENT HAS PUT HIS FOOT IN HIS MOUTH ONCE AGAIN, THIS TIME AS HIS PROPOSAL FOR ENDING THE BOSNIAN CONFLICT WENT OVER LIKE A LEAD BALLOON. THE PRESIDENT IS WASTING OUR VALUABLE TIME TRYING TO MAKE HIS MARK IN HISTORY. I GUESS HE'S NOT PLANNING ON RETURNING FOR ANOTHER FOUR YEARS, SO THIS WOULD BE A GOOD OPPORTUNITY. INSTEAD OF GETTING THE JOB DONE, AS ***THIS*** CITIZEN WOULD LIKE TO DO, HE PUSSY-FOOTS AROUND THE ISSUE, ACCOMPLISHING ***NOTHING.*** BACK AT HOME, WE KNOW HOW TO DEAL WITH SIMILAR PROBLEMS. FOR INSTANCE, LAST NIGHT'S GRUESOME MURDER IN NEW YORK. OBVIOUSLY THIS GUY, ANOTHER DRUG-PUSHING PUNK OR MAFIA THUG, GOT WHAT WAS ***COMING*** TO HIM. HE SCREWED SOMEONE OVER AND PAID THE PRICE. SHORT, SWEET, AND TO THE POINT. THE PRESIDENT COULD ***LEARN*** SOMETHING FROM THIS.

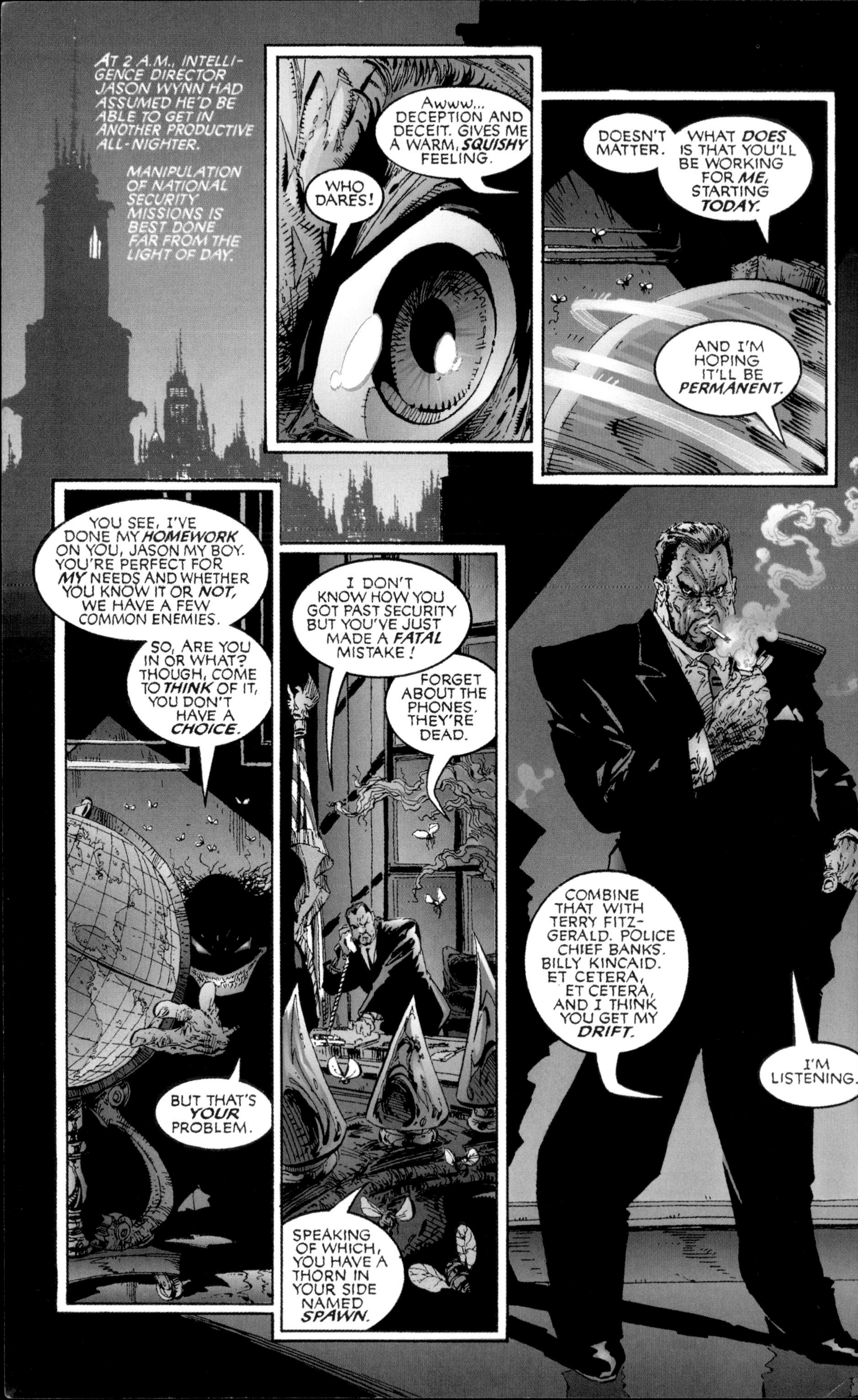
AT 2 A.M., INTELLIGENCE DIRECTOR JASON WYNN HAD ASSUMED HE'D BE ABLE TO GET IN ANOTHER PRODUCTIVE ALL-NIGHTER.
MANIPULATION OF NATIONAL SECURITY MISSIONS IS BEST DONE FAR FROM THE LIGHT OF DAY.
Awww... DECEPTION AND DECEIT. GIVES ME A WARM, SQUISHY FEELING.
WHO DARES!
DOESN'T MATTER.
WHAT DOES IS THAT YOU'LL BE WORKING FOR ME, STARTING TODAY.
AND I'M HOPING IT'LL BE PERMANENT.
YOU SEE, I'VE DONE MY HOMEWORK ON YOU, JASON MY BOY. YOU'RE PERFECT FOR MY NEEDS AND WHETHER YOU KNOW IT OR NOT, WE HAVE A FEW COMMON ENEMIES.
SO, ARE YOU IN OR WHAT? THOUGH, COME TO THINK OF IT, YOU DON'T HAVE A CHOICE.
BUT THAT'S YOUR PROBLEM.
I DON'T KNOW HOW YOU GOT PAST SECURITY BUT YOU'VE JUST MADE A FATAL MISTAKE!
FORGET ABOUT THE PHONES. THEY'RE DEAD.
SPEAKING OF WHICH, YOU HAVE A THORN IN YOUR SIDE NAMED SPAWN.
COMBINE THAT WITH TERRY FITZ-GERALD. POLICE CHIEF BANKS. BILLY KINCAID. ET CETERA, ET CETERA, AND I THINK YOU GET MY DRIFT.
I'M LISTENING.

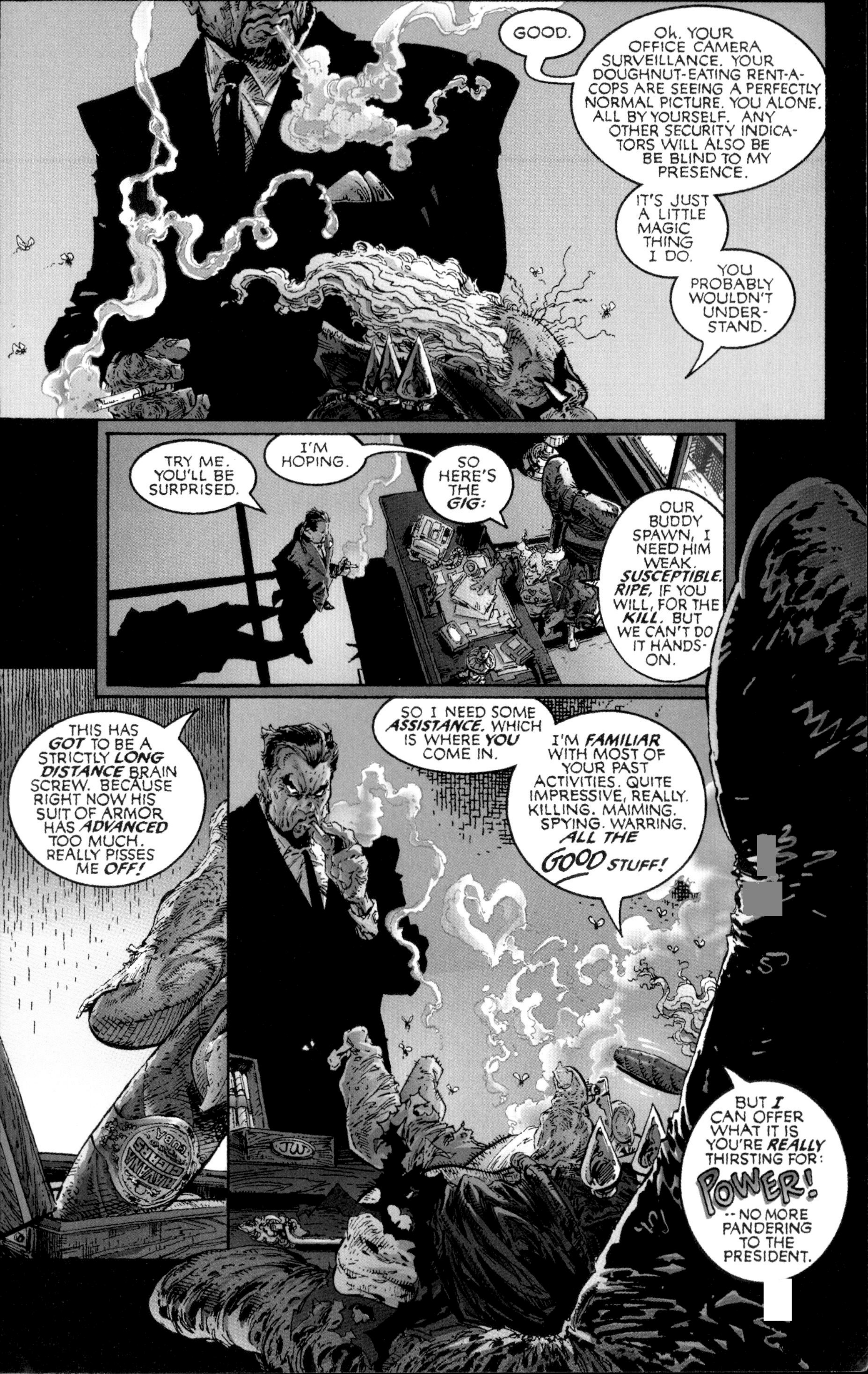
GOOD.
Oh. YOUR OFFICE CAMERA SURVEILLANCE. YOUR DOUGHNUT-EATING RENT-A-COPS ARE SEEING A PERFECTLY NORMAL PICTURE. YOU ALONE. ALL BY YOURSELF. ANY OTHER SECURITY INDICATORS WILL ALSO BE BE BLIND TO MY PRESENCE.
IT'S JUST A LITTLE MAGIC THING I DO.
YOU PROBABLY WOULDN'T UNDERSTAND.
TRY ME. YOU'LL BE SURPRISED.
I'M HOPING.
SO HERE'S THE GIG:
OUR BUDDY SPAWN, I NEED HIM WEAK. SUSCEPTIBLE. RIPE, IF YOU WILL, FOR THE KILL. BUT WE CAN'T DO IT HANDS-ON.
THIS HAS GOT TO BE A STRICTLY LONG DISTANCE BRAIN SCREW. BECAUSE RIGHT NOW HIS SUIT OF ARMOR HAS ADVANCED TOO MUCH. REALLY PISSES ME OFF!
SO I NEED SOME ASSISTANCE. WHICH IS WHERE YOU COME IN.
I'M FAMILIAR WITH MOST OF YOUR PAST ACTIVITIES. QUITE IMPRESSIVE, REALLY. KILLING. MAIMING. SPYING. WARRING. ALL THE GOOD STUFF!
BUT I CAN OFFER WHAT IT IS YOU'RE REALLY THIRSTING FOR: POWER! -- NO MORE PANDERING TO THE PRESIDENT.

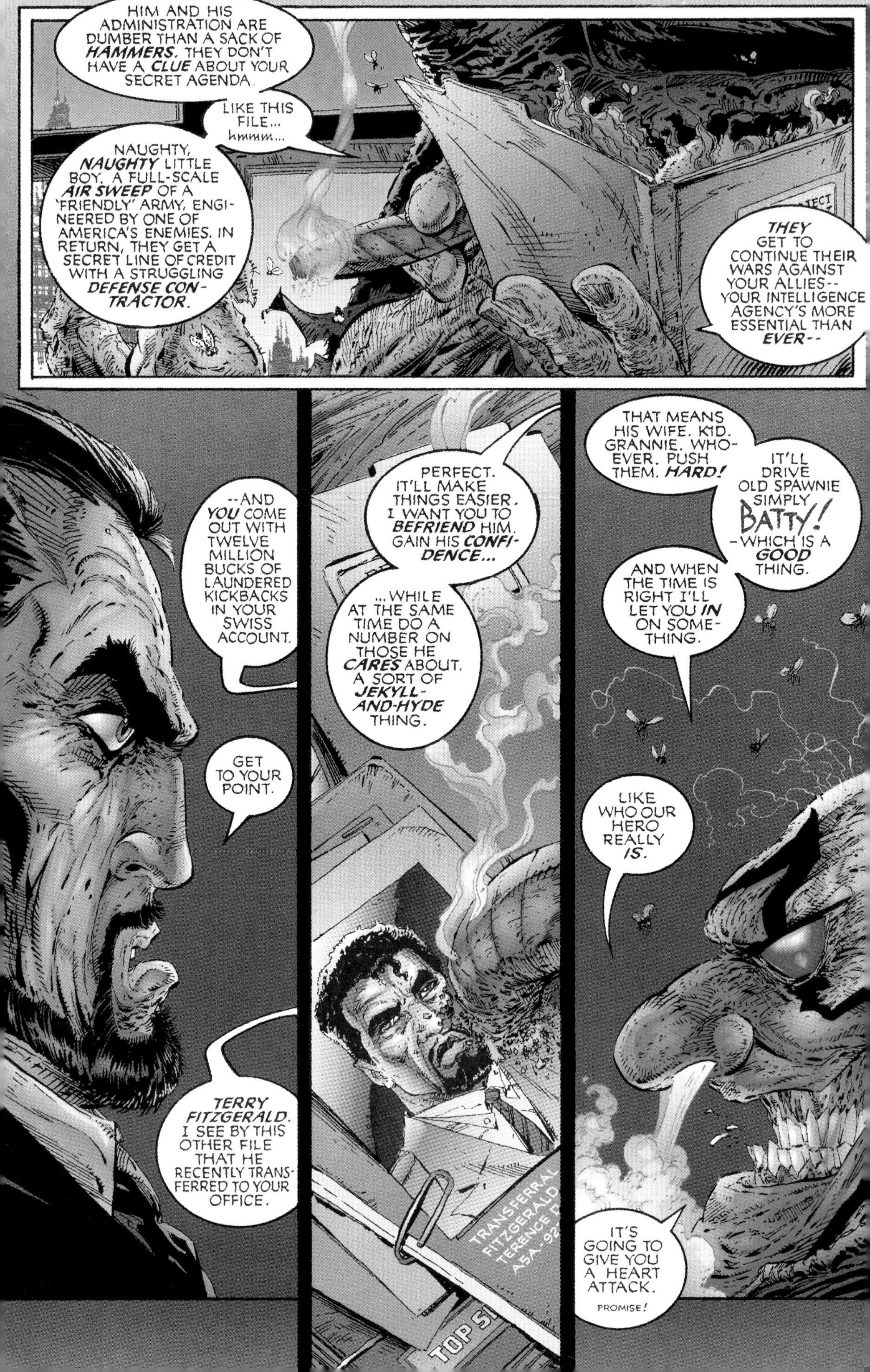
HIM AND HIS ADMINISTRATION ARE DUMBER THAN A SACK OF HAMMERS. THEY DON'T HAVE A CLUE ABOUT YOUR SECRET AGENDA.
LIKE THIS FILE... hmmm...
NAUGHTY, NAUGHTY LITTLE BOY. A FULL-SCALE AIR SWEEP OF A 'FRIENDLY' ARMY, ENGINEERED BY ONE OF AMERICA'S ENEMIES. IN RETURN, THEY GET A SECRET LINE OF CREDIT WITH A STRUGGLING DEFENSE CONTRACTOR.
THEY GET TO CONTINUE THEIR WARS AGAINST YOUR ALLIES-- YOUR INTELLIGENCE AGENCY'S MORE ESSENTIAL THAN EVER--
--AND YOU COME OUT WITH TWELVE MILLION BUCKS OF LAUNDERED KICKBACKS IN YOUR SWISS ACCOUNT.
GET TO YOUR POINT.
TERRY FITZGERALD. I SEE BY THIS OTHER FILE THAT HE RECENTLY TRANSFERRED TO YOUR OFFICE.
PERFECT. IT'LL MAKE THINGS EASIER. I WANT YOU TO BEFRIEND HIM. GAIN HIS CONFIDENCE...
...WHILE AT THE SAME TIME DO A NUMBER ON THOSE HE CARES ABOUT. A SORT OF JEKYLL-AND-HYDE THING.
TRANSFERRAL
FITZGERALD
TERENCE
TOP S
THAT MEANS HIS WIFE. KID. GRANNIE. WHOEVER. PUSH THEM. HARD!
IT'LL DRIVE OLD SPAWNIE SIMPLY BATTY! -WHICH IS A GOOD THING.
AND WHEN THE TIME IS RIGHT I'LL LET YOU IN ON SOMETHING.
LIKE WHO OUR HERO REALLY IS.
IT'S GOING TO GIVE YOU A HEART ATTACK.
PROMISE!

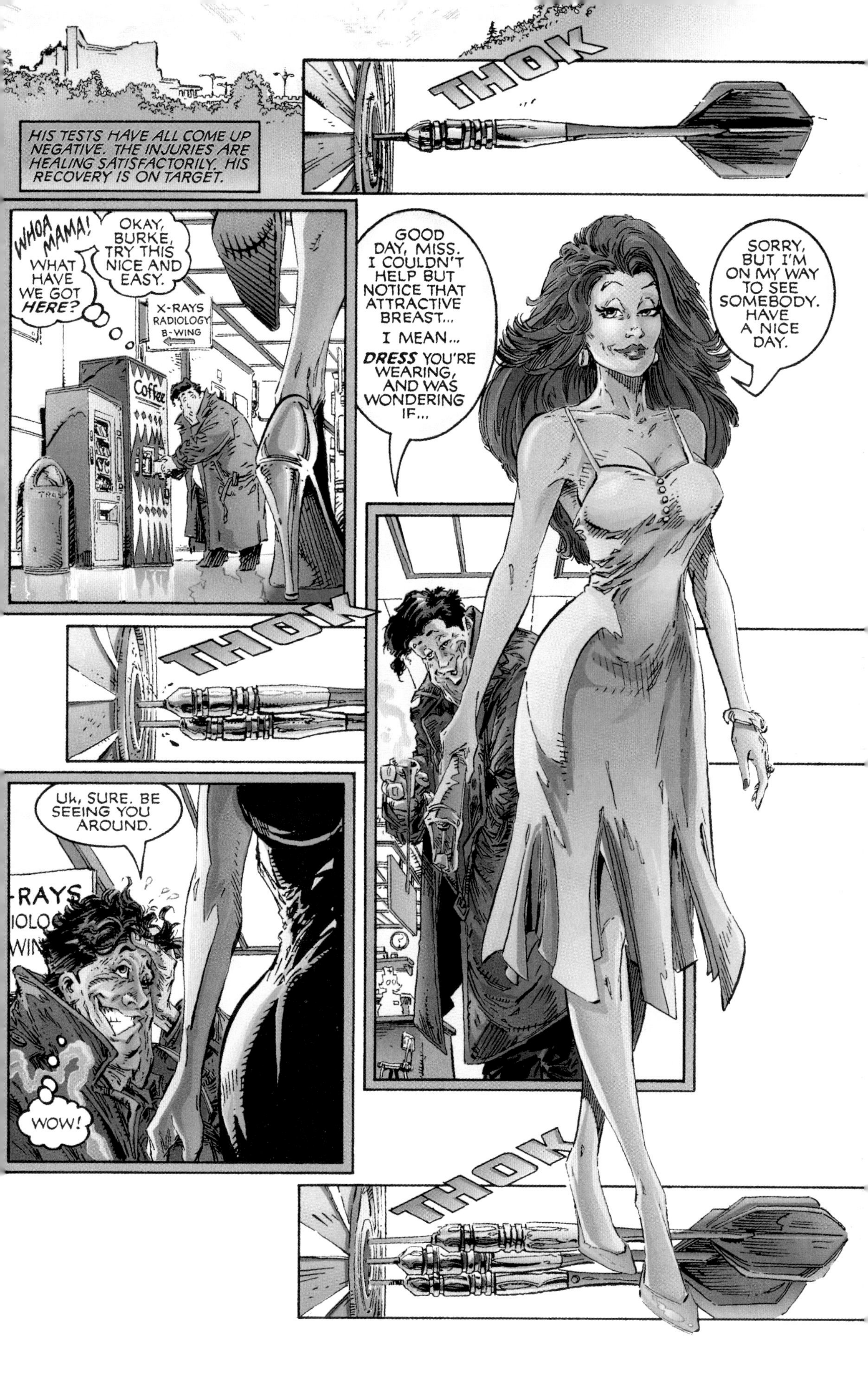

HIS TESTS HAVE ALL COME UP NEGATIVE. THE INJURIES ARE HEALING SATISFACTORILY. HIS RECOVERY IS ON TARGET.
THOK
WHOA MAMA! WHAT HAVE WE GOT HERE?
OKAY, BURKE, TRY THIS NICE AND EASY.
X-RAYS RADIOLOGY B-WING
Coffee
TRASH
GOOD DAY, MISS. I COULDN'T HELP BUT NOTICE THAT ATTRACTIVE BREAST... I MEAN... DRESS YOU'RE WEARING, AND WAS WONDERING IF...
SORRY, BUT I'M ON MY WAY TO SEE SOMEBODY. HAVE A NICE DAY.
THOK
Uh, SURE. BE SEEING YOU AROUND.
WOW!
THOK

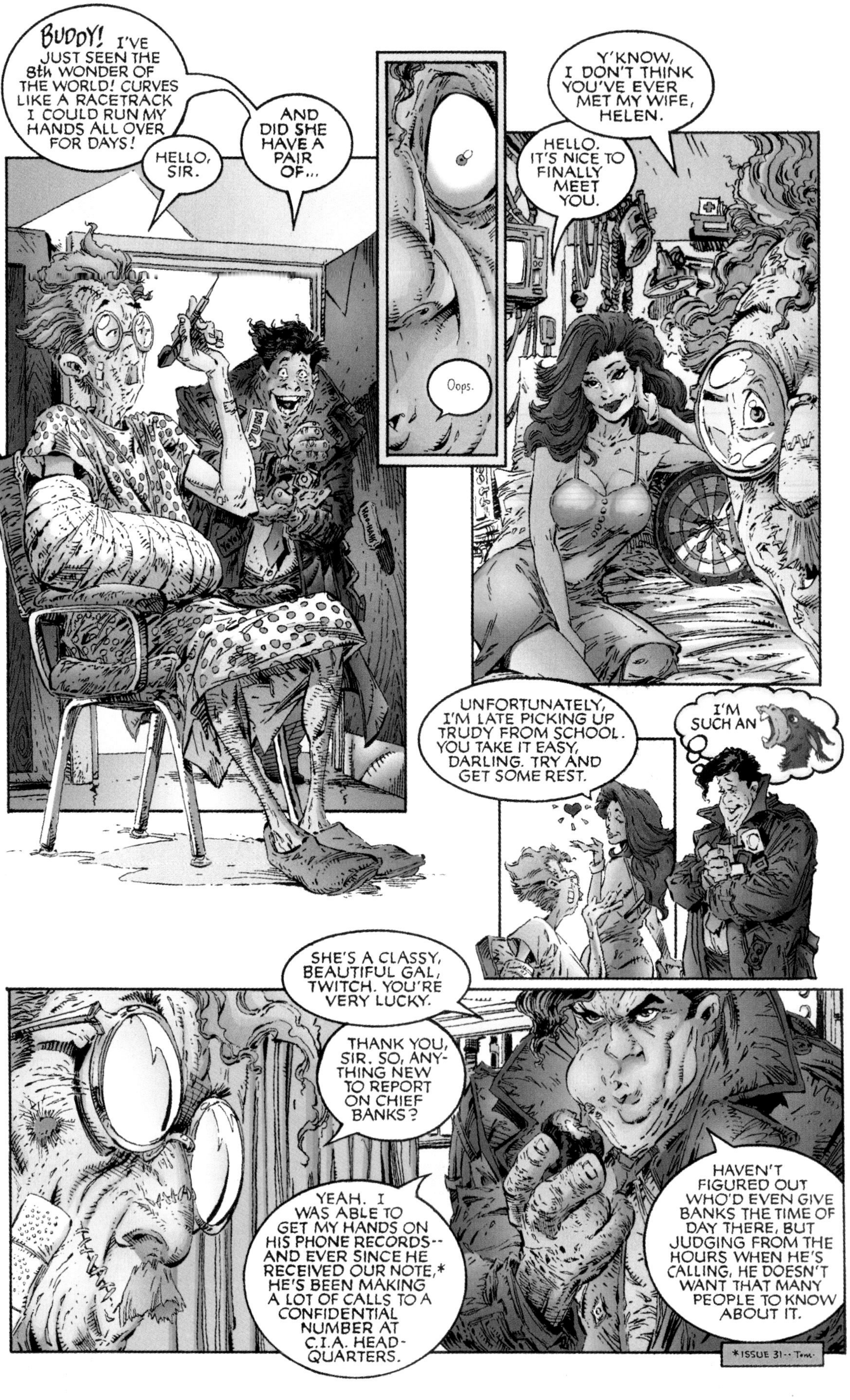
BUDDY! I'VE JUST SEEN THE 8th WONDER OF THE WORLD! CURVES LIKE A RACETRACK I COULD RUN MY HANDS ALL OVER FOR DAYS!
HELLO, SIR.
AND DID SHE HAVE A PAIR OF...
Oops.
Y'KNOW, I DON'T THINK YOU'VE EVER MET MY WIFE, HELEN.
HELLO. IT'S NICE TO FINALLY MEET YOU.
UNFORTUNATELY, I'M LATE PICKING UP TRUDY FROM SCHOOL. YOU TAKE IT EASY, DARLING. TRY AND GET SOME REST.
I'M SUCH AN
SHE'S A CLASSY, BEAUTIFUL GAL, TWITCH. YOU'RE VERY LUCKY.
THANK YOU, SIR. SO, ANYTHING NEW TO REPORT ON CHIEF BANKS?
YEAH. I WAS ABLE TO GET MY HANDS ON HIS PHONE RECORDS-- AND EVER SINCE HE RECEIVED OUR NOTE,* HE'S BEEN MAKING A LOT OF CALLS TO A CONFIDENTIAL NUMBER AT C.I.A. HEAD-QUARTERS.
HAVEN'T FIGURED OUT WHO'D EVEN GIVE BANKS THE TIME OF DAY THERE, BUT JUDGING FROM THE HOURS WHEN HE'S CALLING, HE DOESN'T WANT THAT MANY PEOPLE TO KNOW ABOUT IT.
*ISSUE 31-- Tom.

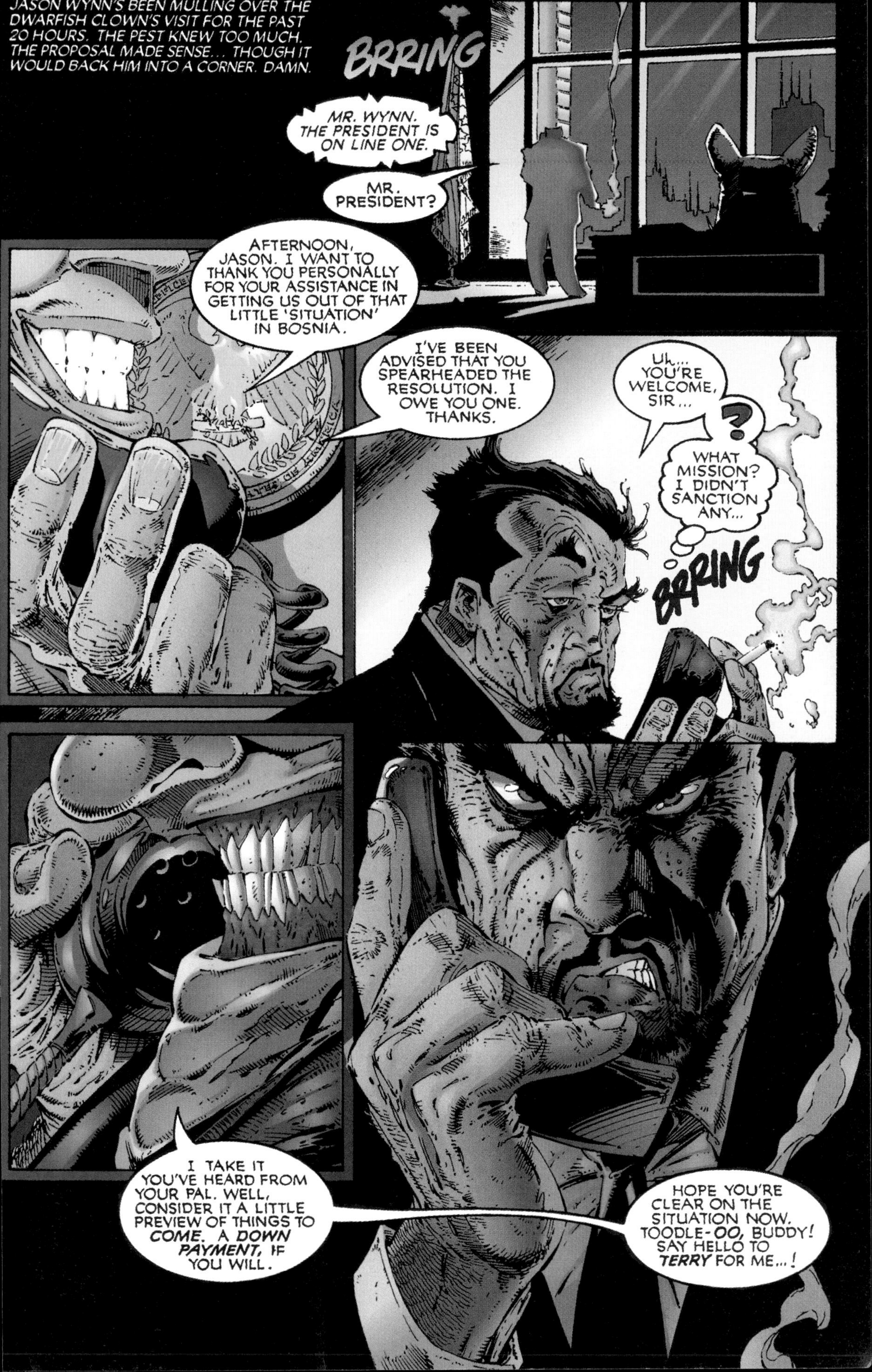
JASON WYNN'S BEEN MULLING OVER THE DWARFISH CLOWN'S VISIT FOR THE PAST 20 HOURS. THE PEST KNEW TOO MUCH. THE PROPOSAL MADE SENSE... THOUGH IT WOULD BACK HIM INTO A CORNER. DAMN.
BRRING
MR. WYNN. THE PRESIDENT IS ON LINE ONE.
MR. PRESIDENT?
AFTERNOON, JASON. I WANT TO THANK YOU PERSONALLY FOR YOUR ASSISTANCE IN GETTING US OUT OF THAT LITTLE 'SITUATION' IN BOSNIA.
I'VE BEEN ADVISED THAT YOU SPEARHEADED THE RESOLUTION. I OWE YOU ONE. THANKS.
UH... YOU'RE WELCOME, SIR...
?
WHAT MISSION? I DIDN'T SANCTION ANY...
BRRING
I TAKE IT YOU'VE HEARD FROM YOUR PAL. WELL, CONSIDER IT A LITTLE PREVIEW OF THINGS TO COME. A DOWN PAYMENT, IF YOU WILL.
HOPE YOU'RE CLEAR ON THE SITUATION NOW. TOODLE-OO, BUDDY! SAY HELLO TO TERRY FOR ME...!

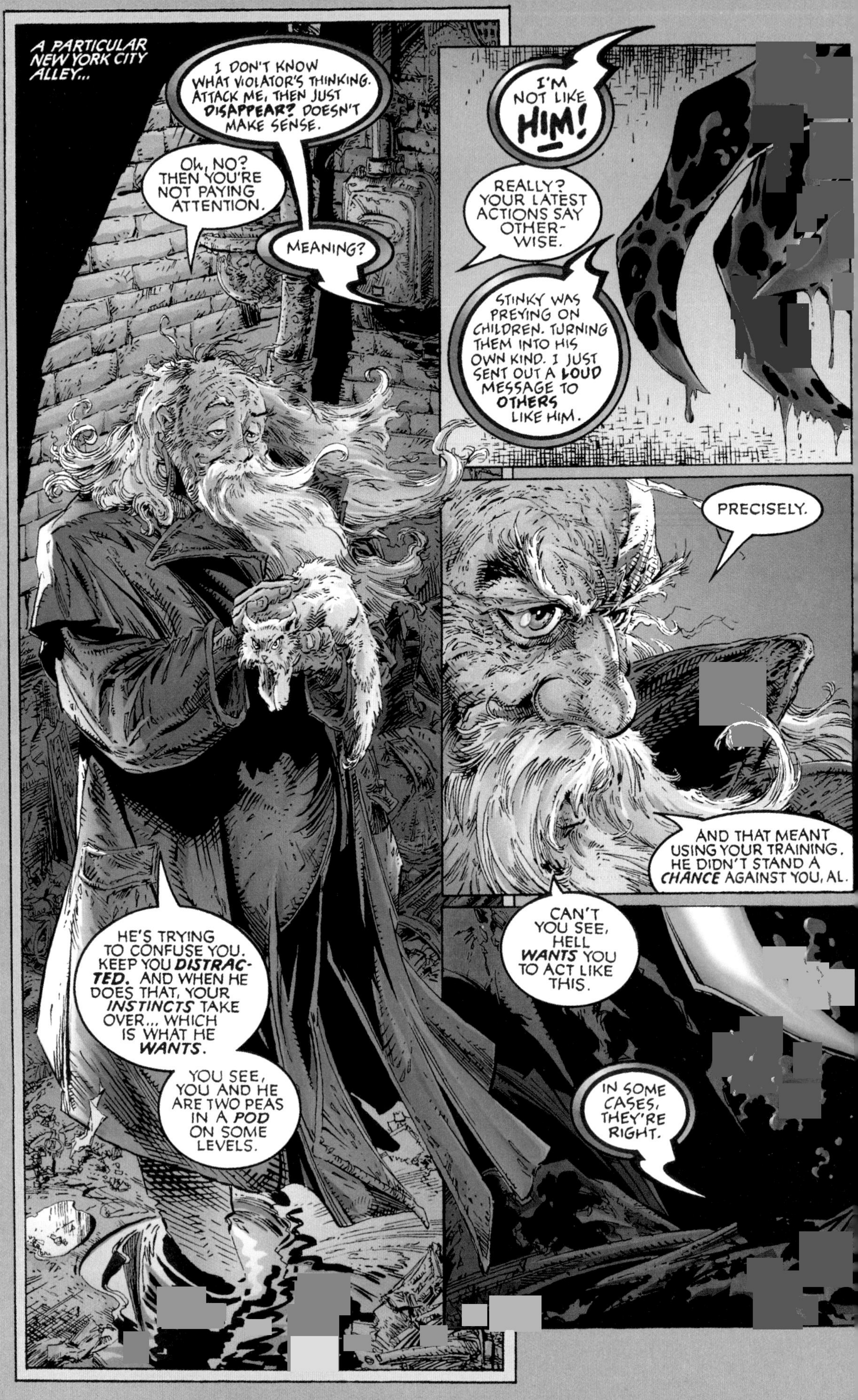

A PARTICULAR NEW YORK CITY ALLEY...
I DON'T KNOW WHAT VIOLATOR'S THINKING. ATTACK ME, THEN JUST DISAPPEAR? DOESN'T MAKE SENSE.
Oh, NO? THEN YOU'RE NOT PAYING ATTENTION.
MEANING?
HE'S TRYING TO CONFUSE YOU. KEEP YOU DISTRACTED. AND WHEN HE DOES THAT, YOUR INSTINCTS TAKE OVER... WHICH IS WHAT HE WANTS.
YOU SEE, YOU AND HE ARE TWO PEAS IN A POD ON SOME LEVELS.
I'M NOT LIKE HIM!
REALLY? YOUR LATEST ACTIONS SAY OTHERWISE.
STINKY WAS PREYING ON CHILDREN. TURNING THEM INTO HIS OWN KIND. I JUST SENT OUT A LOUD MESSAGE TO OTHERS LIKE HIM.
PRECISELY.
AND THAT MEANT USING YOUR TRAINING. HE DIDN'T STAND A CHANCE AGAINST YOU, AL.
CAN'T YOU SEE, HELL WANTS YOU TO ACT LIKE THIS.
IN SOME CASES, THEY'RE RIGHT.

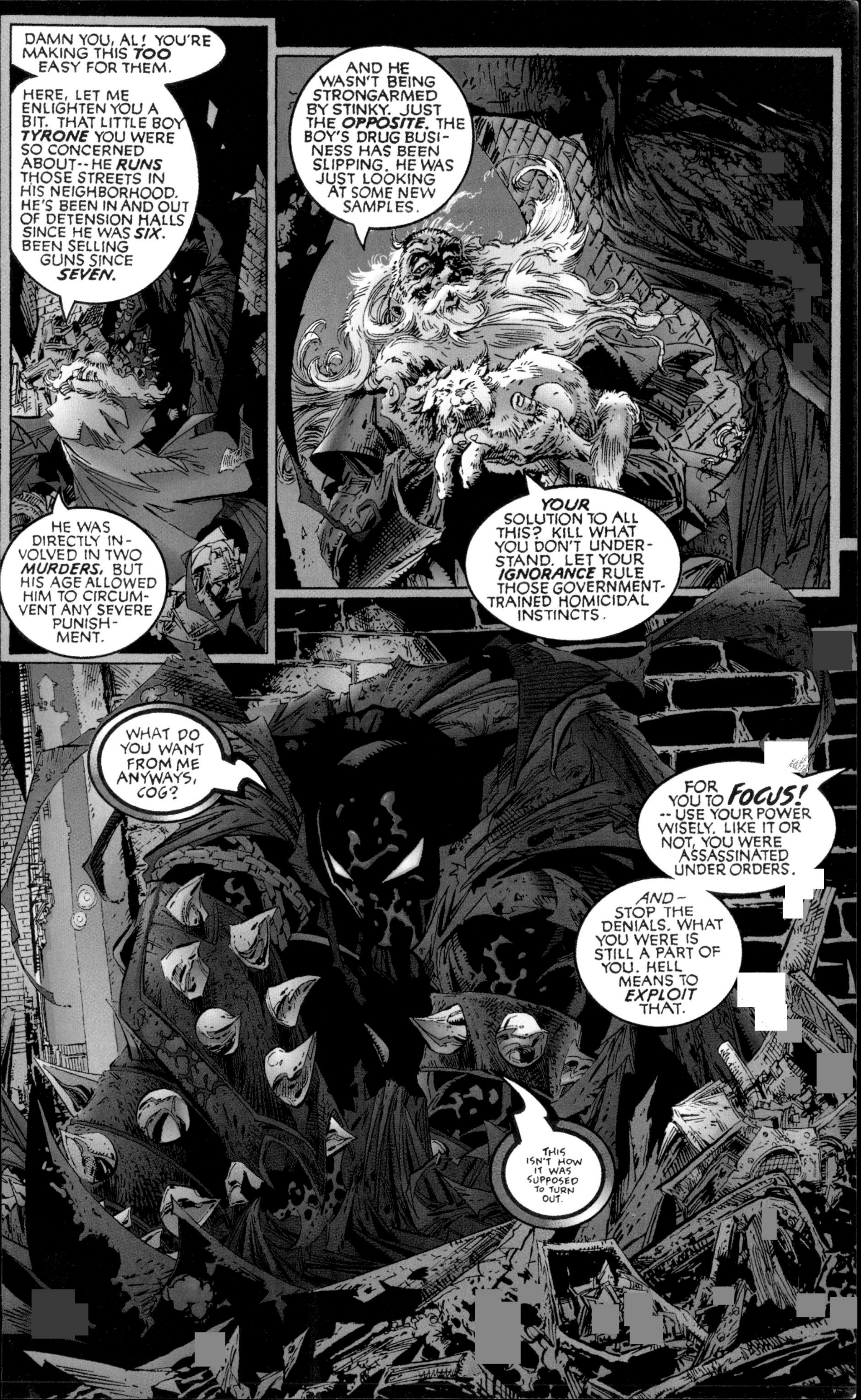
DAMN YOU, AL! YOU'RE MAKING THIS TOO EASY FOR THEM.
HERE, LET ME ENLIGHTEN YOU A BIT. THAT LITTLE BOY TYRONE YOU WERE SO CONCERNED ABOUT-- HE RUNS THOSE STREETS IN HIS NEIGHBORHOOD. HE'S BEEN IN AND OUT OF DETENSION HALLS SINCE HE WAS SIX. BEEN SELLING GUNS SINCE SEVEN.
HE WAS DIRECTLY IN-VOLVED IN TWO MURDERS, BUT HIS AGE ALLOWED HIM TO CIRCUM-VENT ANY SEVERE PUNISH-MENT.
AND HE WASN'T BEING STRONGARMED BY STINKY. JUST THE OPPOSITE. THE BOY'S DRUG BUSI-NESS HAS BEEN SLIPPING. HE WAS JUST LOOKING AT SOME NEW SAMPLES.
YOUR SOLUTION TO ALL THIS? KILL WHAT YOU DON'T UNDER-STAND. LET YOUR IGNORANCE RULE THOSE GOVERNMENT-TRAINED HOMICIDAL INSTINCTS.
WHAT DO YOU WANT FROM ME ANYWAYS, COG?
FOR YOU TO FOCUS! -- USE YOUR POWER WISELY. LIKE IT OR NOT, YOU WERE ASSASSINATED UNDER ORDERS.
AND-- STOP THE DENIALS. WHAT YOU WERE IS STILL A PART OF YOU. HELL MEANS TO EXPLOIT THAT.
THIS ISN'T HOW IT WAS SUPPOSED TO TURN OUT.

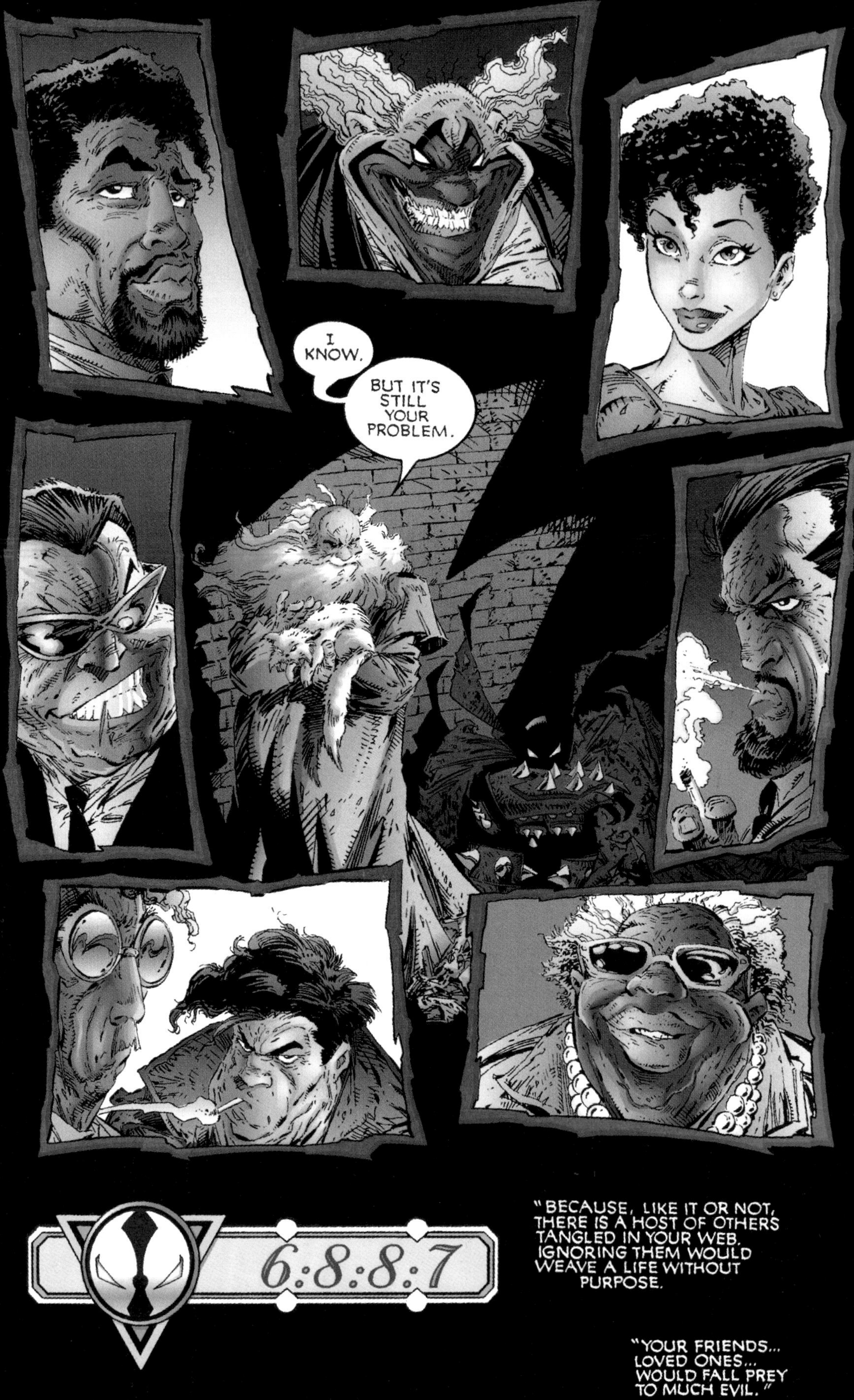
I KNOW.
BUT IT'S STILL YOUR PROBLEM.
6:8:8:7
"BECAUSE, LIKE IT OR NOT, THERE IS A HOST OF OTHERS TANGLED IN YOUR WEB. IGNORING THEM WOULD WEAVE A LIFE WITHOUT PURPOSE.
"YOUR FRIENDS... LOVED ONES... WOULD FALL PREY TO MUCH EVIL."

AS THE DAY COMES TO A CLOSE, **TERRY FITZGERALD** FINDS HIMSELF ALONE AT HIS NEW OFFICE AT C.I.A. HEADQUARTERS.

FINALLY, HE HAS A CHANCE TO PURSUE HIS ONLY REASON FOR REQUESTING A TRANSFER TO JASON WYNN'S DEPARTMENT IN THE FIRST PLACE:

FINDING OUT WHAT HIS NEW DEPARTMENT HEAD IS REALLY UP TO.

THE GUY IS SLICK. RETRACING HIS TRACKS WON'T BE EASY, ESPECIALLY WITH ALL THE SECURITY CHECKS INVOLVED. BUT THERE HAS TO BE *SOMETHING* HERE I CAN USE.

HIS INTERNATIONAL ACTIVITIES LOOK CLEAN. *ALMOST* TOO CLEAN.

THEN, A NOISE BEHIND HIM SNAPS TERRY BACK TO ATTENTION.

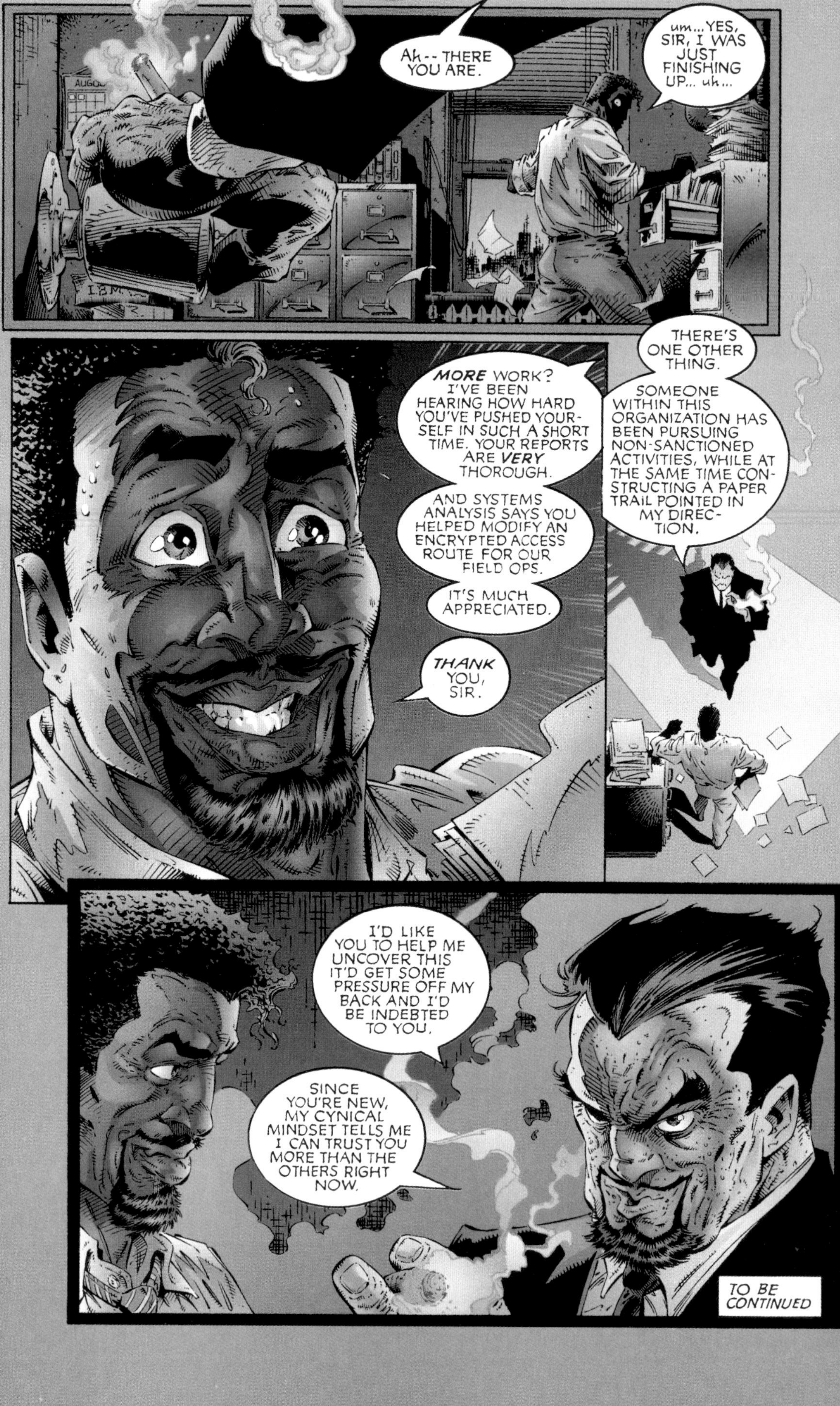

Ah-- THERE YOU ARE.
um... YES, SIR, I WAS JUST FINISHING UP... uh...
MORE WORK? I'VE BEEN HEARING HOW HARD YOU'VE PUSHED YOURSELF IN SUCH A SHORT TIME. YOUR REPORTS ARE VERY THOROUGH.
AND SYSTEMS ANALYSIS SAYS YOU HELPED MODIFY AN ENCRYPTED ACCESS ROUTE FOR OUR FIELD OPS.
IT'S MUCH APPRECIATED.
THANK YOU, SIR.
THERE'S ONE OTHER THING.
SOMEONE WITHIN THIS ORGANIZATION HAS BEEN PURSUING NON-SANCTIONED ACTIVITIES, WHILE AT THE SAME TIME CONSTRUCTING A PAPER TRAIL POINTED IN MY DIRECTION.
I'D LIKE YOU TO HELP ME UNCOVER THIS. IT'D GET SOME PRESSURE OFF MY BACK AND I'D BE INDEBTED TO YOU.
SINCE YOU'RE NEW, MY CYNICAL MINDSET TELLS ME I CAN TRUST YOU MORE THAN THE OTHERS RIGHT NOW.
TO BE CONTINUED

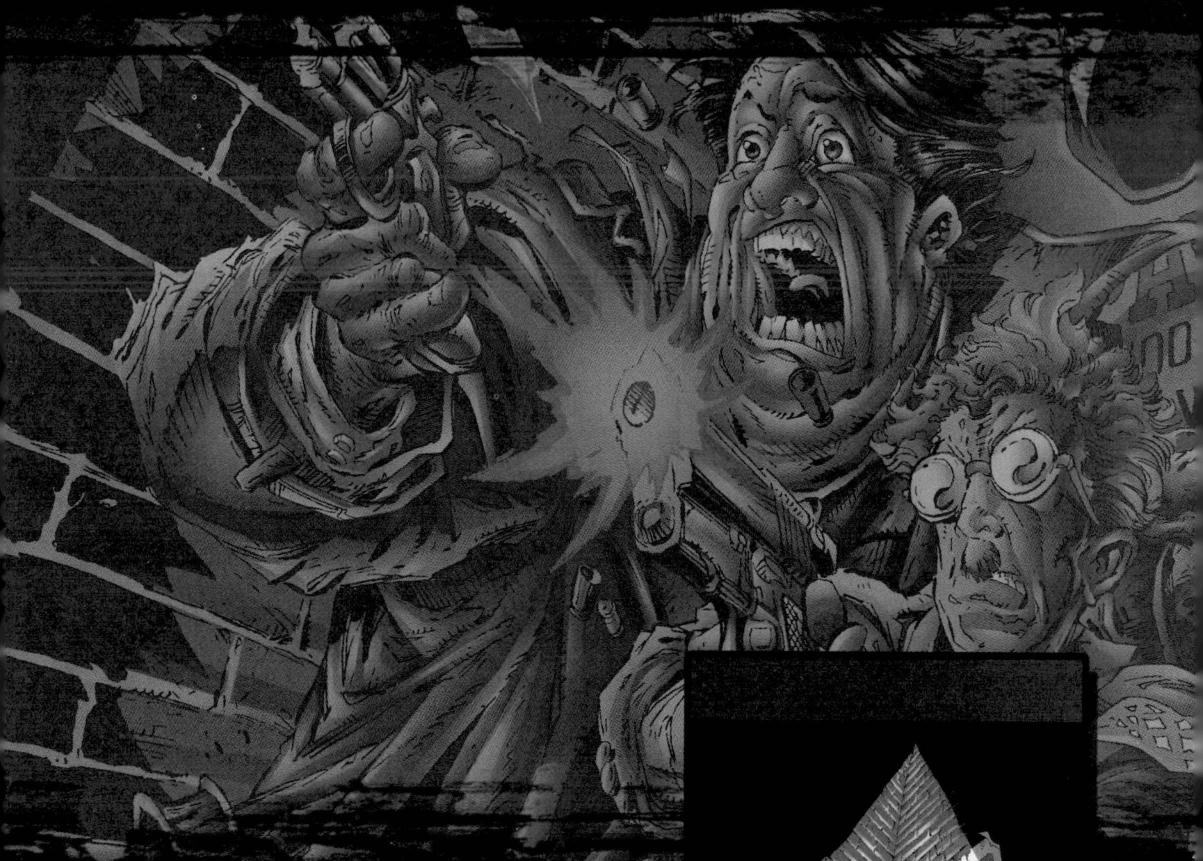

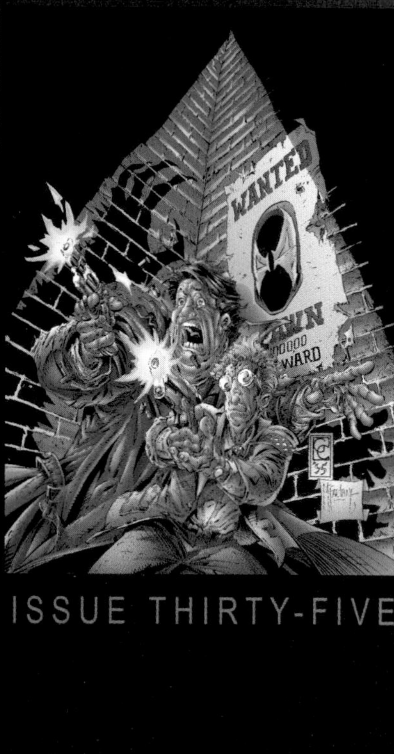
WANTED

ISSUE THIRTY-FIVE

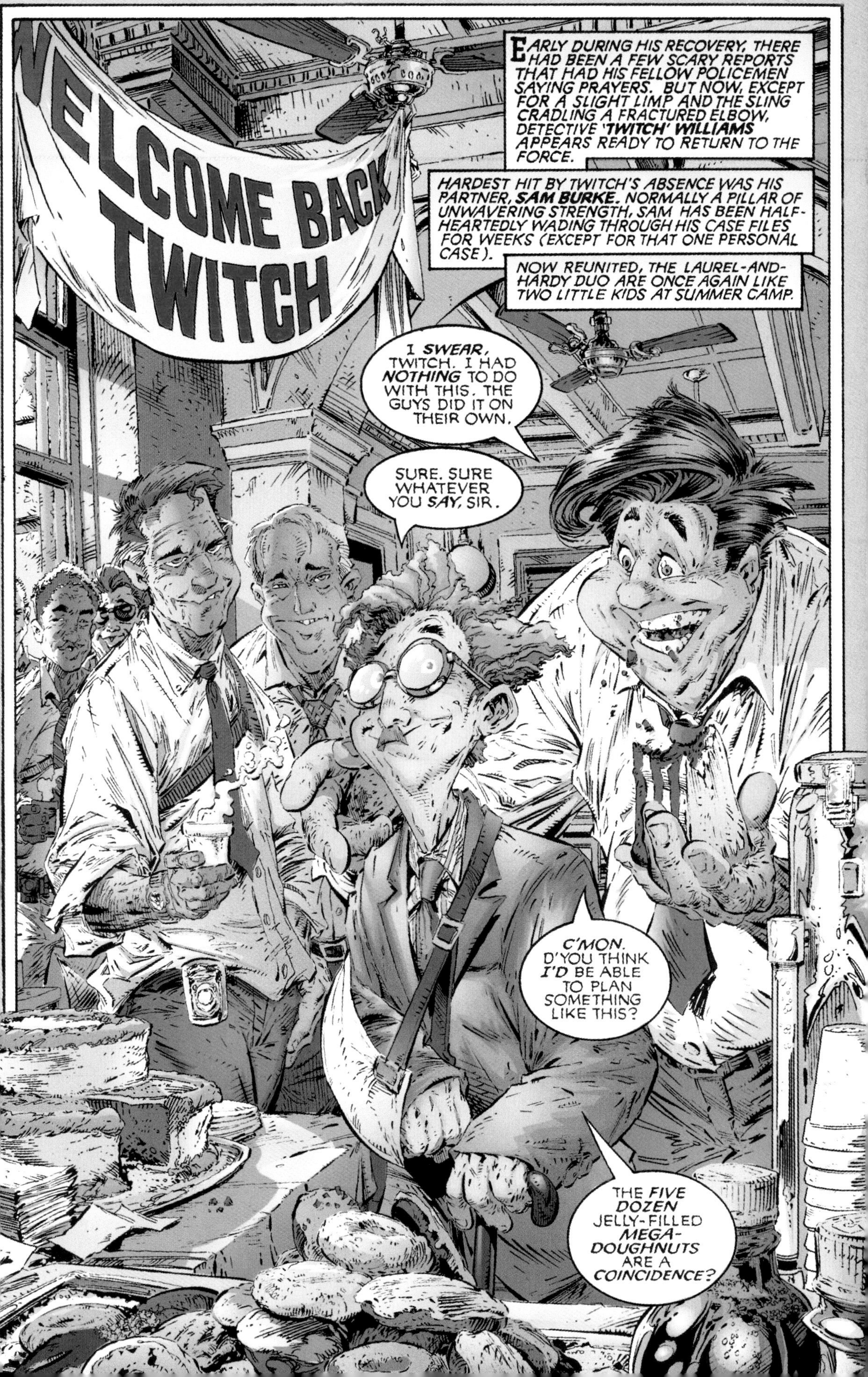

WELCOME BACK TWITCH
EARLY DURING HIS RECOVERY, THERE HAD BEEN A FEW SCARY REPORTS THAT HAD HIS FELLOW POLICEMEN SAYING PRAYERS. BUT NOW, EXCEPT FOR A SLIGHT LIMP AND THE SLING CRADLING A FRACTURED ELBOW, DETECTIVE 'TWITCH' WILLIAMS APPEARS READY TO RETURN TO THE FORCE.
HARDEST HIT BY TWITCH'S ABSENCE WAS HIS PARTNER, SAM BURKE. NORMALLY A PILLAR OF UNWAVERING STRENGTH, SAM HAS BEEN HALF-HEARTEDLY WADING THROUGH HIS CASE FILES FOR WEEKS (EXCEPT FOR THAT ONE PERSONAL CASE).
NOW REUNITED, THE LAUREL-AND-HARDY DUO ARE ONCE AGAIN LIKE TWO LITTLE KIDS AT SUMMER CAMP.
I SWEAR, TWITCH. I HAD NOTHING TO DO WITH THIS. THE GUYS DID IT ON THEIR OWN.
SURE. SURE WHATEVER YOU SAY, SIR.
C'MON. D'YOU THINK I'D BE ABLE TO PLAN SOMETHING LIKE THIS?
THE FIVE DOZEN JELLY-FILLED MEGA-DOUGHNUTS ARE A COINCIDENCE?

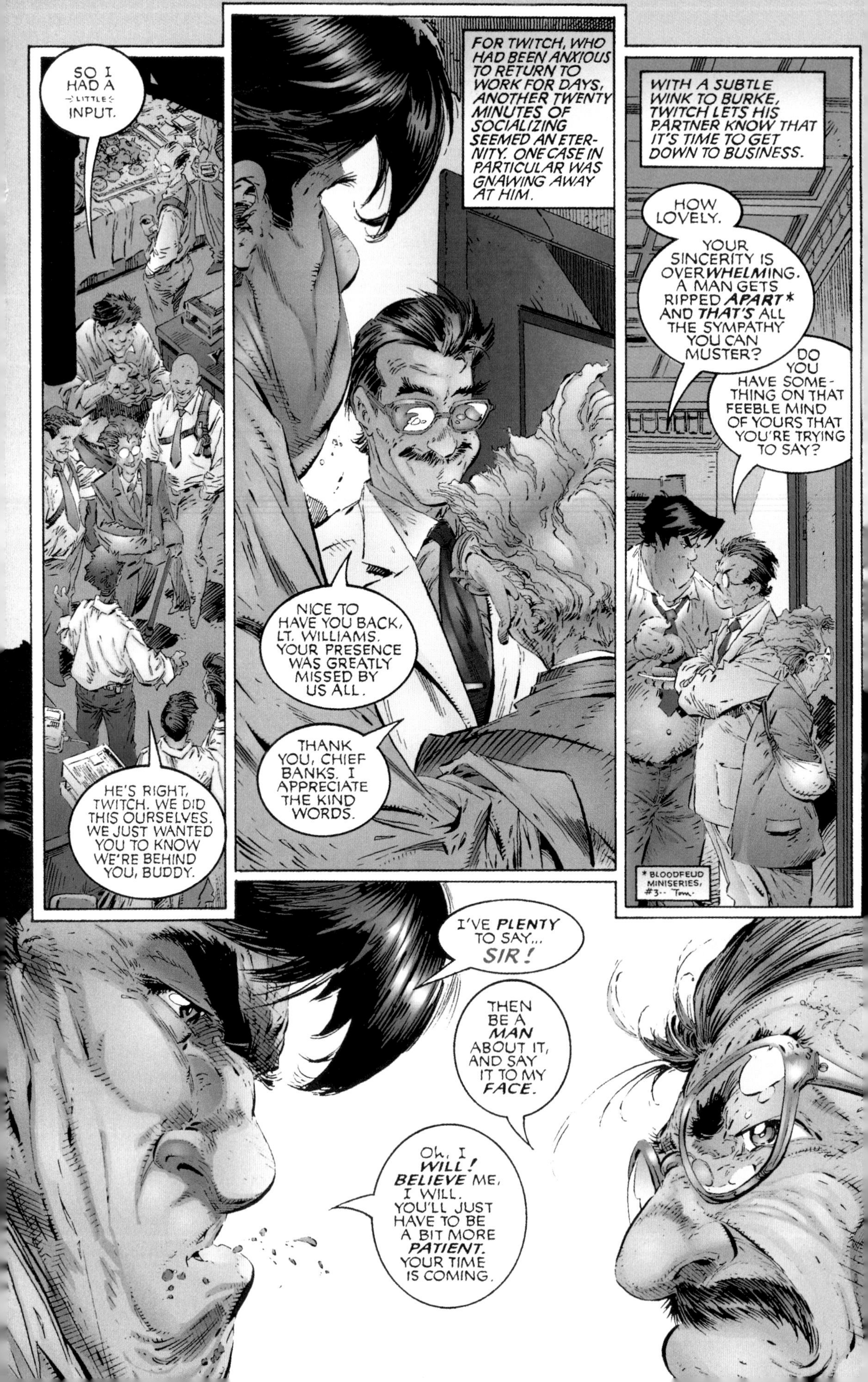
SO I HAD A LITTLE INPUT.
HE'S RIGHT, TWITCH. WE DID THIS OURSELVES. WE JUST WANTED YOU TO KNOW WE'RE BEHIND YOU, BUDDY.
FOR TWITCH, WHO HAD BEEN ANXIOUS TO RETURN TO WORK FOR DAYS, ANOTHER TWENTY MINUTES OF SOCIALIZING SEEMED AN ETERNITY. ONE CASE IN PARTICULAR WAS GNAWING AWAY AT HIM.
NICE TO HAVE YOU BACK, LT. WILLIAMS. YOUR PRESENCE WAS GREATLY MISSED BY US ALL.
THANK YOU, CHIEF BANKS. I APPRECIATE THE KIND WORDS.
WITH A SUBTLE WINK TO BURKE, TWITCH LETS HIS PARTNER KNOW THAT IT'S TIME TO GET DOWN TO BUSINESS.
HOW LOVELY.
YOUR SINCERITY IS OVERWHELMING. A MAN GETS RIPPED APART* AND THAT'S ALL THE SYMPATHY YOU CAN MUSTER?
DO YOU HAVE SOMETHING ON THAT FEEBLE MIND OF YOURS THAT YOU'RE TRYING TO SAY?
* BLOODFEUD MINISERIES, #3-- Tom.
I'VE PLENTY TO SAY... SIR!
THEN BE A MAN ABOUT IT, AND SAY IT TO MY FACE.
Oh, I WILL! BELIEVE ME, I WILL. YOU'LL JUST HAVE TO BE A BIT MORE PATIENT. YOUR TIME IS COMING.

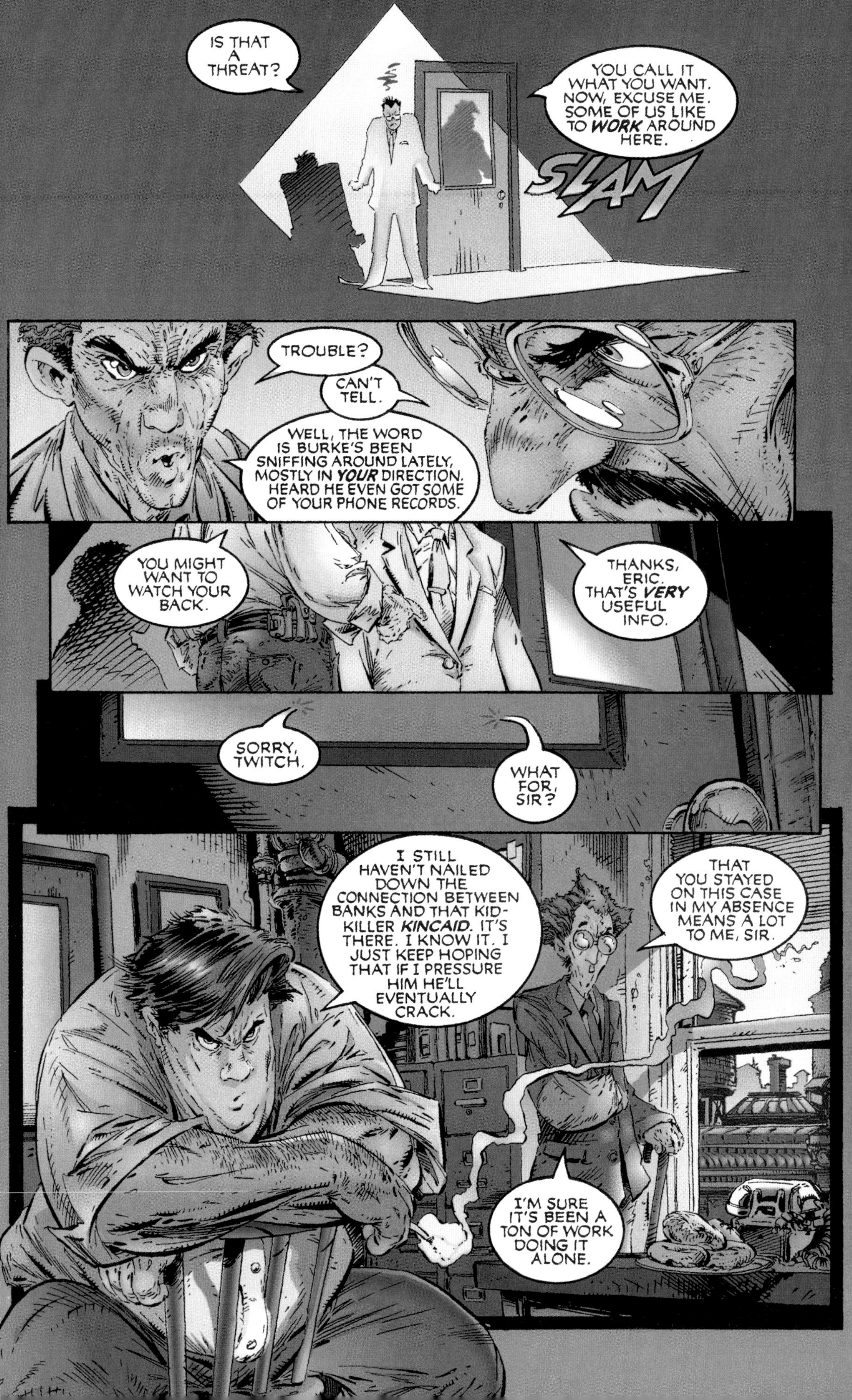
IS THAT A THREAT?
YOU CALL IT WHAT YOU WANT. NOW, EXCUSE ME. SOME OF US LIKE TO *WORK* AROUND HERE.
SLAM
TROUBLE?
CAN'T TELL.
WELL, THE WORD IS BURKE'S BEEN SNIFFING AROUND LATELY, MOSTLY IN *YOUR* DIRECTION. HEARD HE EVEN GOT SOME OF YOUR PHONE RECORDS.
YOU MIGHT WANT TO WATCH YOUR BACK.
THANKS, ERIC. THAT'S *VERY* USEFUL INFO.
SORRY, TWITCH.
WHAT FOR, SIR?
I STILL HAVEN'T NAILED DOWN THE CONNECTION BETWEEN BANKS AND THAT KID-KILLER *KINCAID*. IT'S THERE. I KNOW IT. I JUST KEEP HOPING THAT IF I PRESSURE HIM HE'LL EVENTUALLY CRACK.
THAT YOU STAYED ON THIS CASE IN MY ABSENCE MEANS A LOT TO ME, SIR.
I'M SURE IT'S BEEN A TON OF WORK DOING IT ALONE.

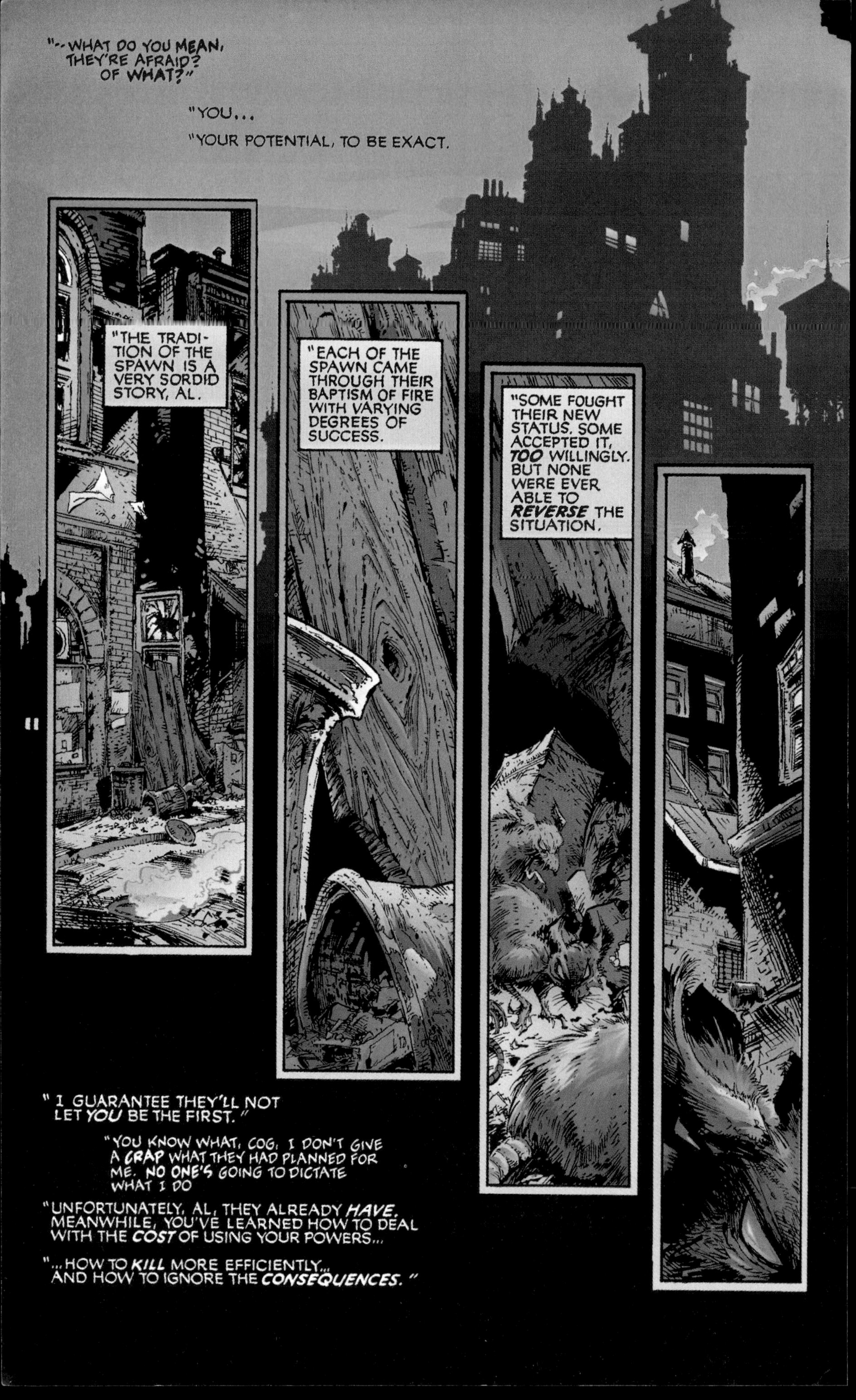
"...WHAT DO YOU MEAN, THEY'RE AFRAID? OF WHAT?"
"YOU...
"YOUR POTENTIAL, TO BE EXACT.
"THE TRADITION OF THE SPAWN IS A VERY SORDID STORY, AL.
"EACH OF THE SPAWN CAME THROUGH THEIR BAPTISM OF FIRE WITH VARYING DEGREES OF SUCCESS.
"SOME FOUGHT THEIR NEW STATUS. SOME ACCEPTED IT, TOO WILLINGLY. BUT NONE WERE EVER ABLE TO REVERSE THE SITUATION.
"I GUARANTEE THEY'LL NOT LET YOU BE THE FIRST."
"YOU KNOW WHAT, COG, I DON'T GIVE A CRAP WHAT THEY HAD PLANNED FOR ME. NO ONE'S GOING TO DICTATE WHAT I DO
"UNFORTUNATELY, AL, THEY ALREADY HAVE. MEANWHILE, YOU'VE LEARNED HOW TO DEAL WITH THE COST OF USING YOUR POWERS...
"...HOW TO KILL MORE EFFICIENTLY... AND HOW TO IGNORE THE CONSEQUENCES."

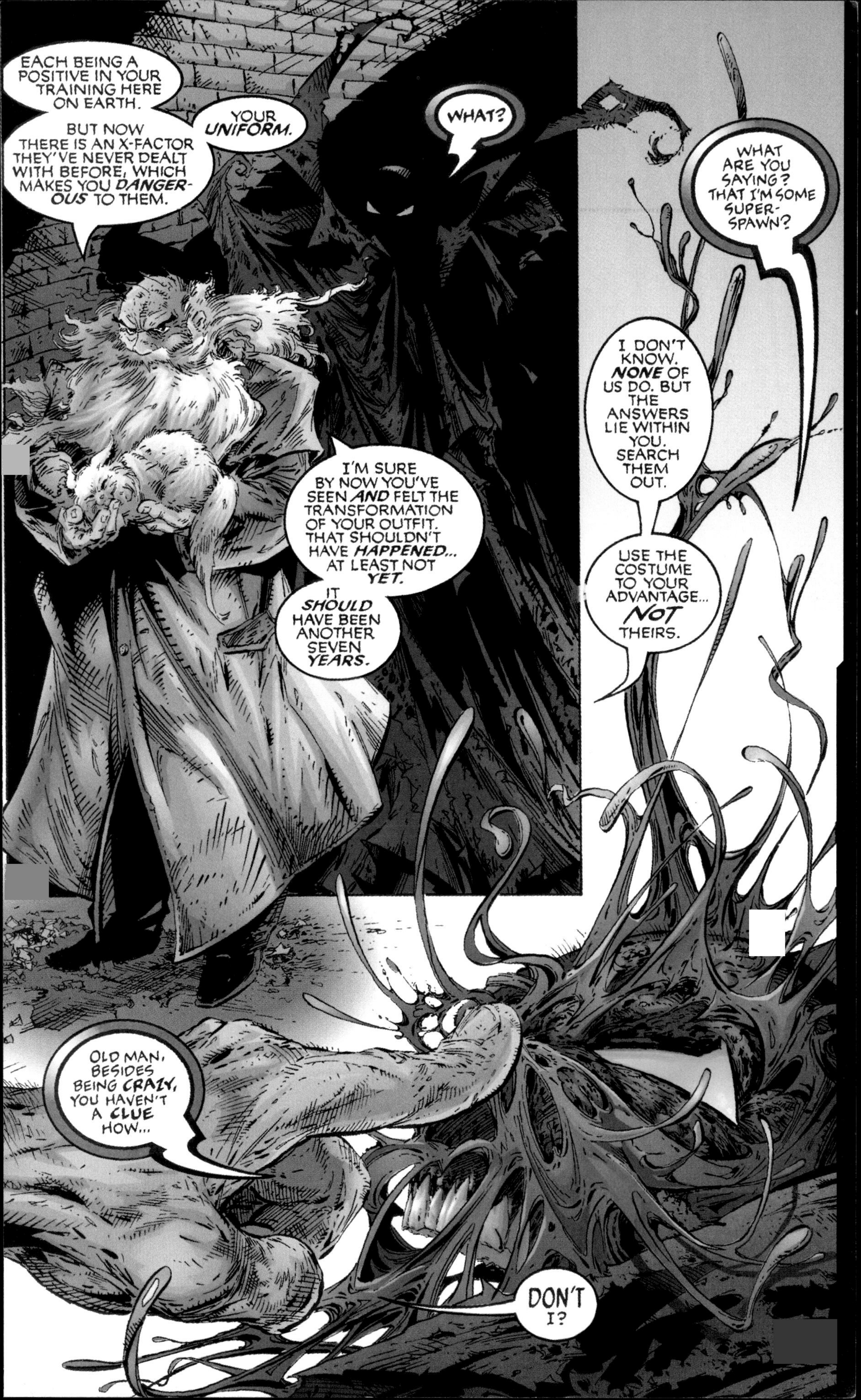
EACH BEING A POSITIVE IN YOUR TRAINING HERE ON EARTH.
BUT NOW THERE IS AN X-FACTOR THEY'VE NEVER DEALT WITH BEFORE, WHICH MAKES YOU *DANGEROUS* TO THEM.
YOUR *UNIFORM*.
WHAT?
WHAT ARE YOU SAYING? THAT I'M SOME SUPER-SPAWN?
I'M SURE BY NOW YOU'VE SEEN *AND* FELT THE TRANSFORMATION OF YOUR OUTFIT. THAT SHOULDN'T HAVE *HAPPENED*... AT LEAST NOT *YET*.
IT *SHOULD* HAVE BEEN ANOTHER SEVEN *YEARS*.
I DON'T KNOW. *NONE* OF US DO. BUT THE ANSWERS LIE WITHIN YOU. SEARCH THEM OUT.
USE THE COSTUME TO YOUR ADVANTAGE... *NOT* THEIRS.
OLD MAN, BESIDES BEING *CRAZY*, YOU HAVEN'T A *CLUE* HOW...
DON'T I?

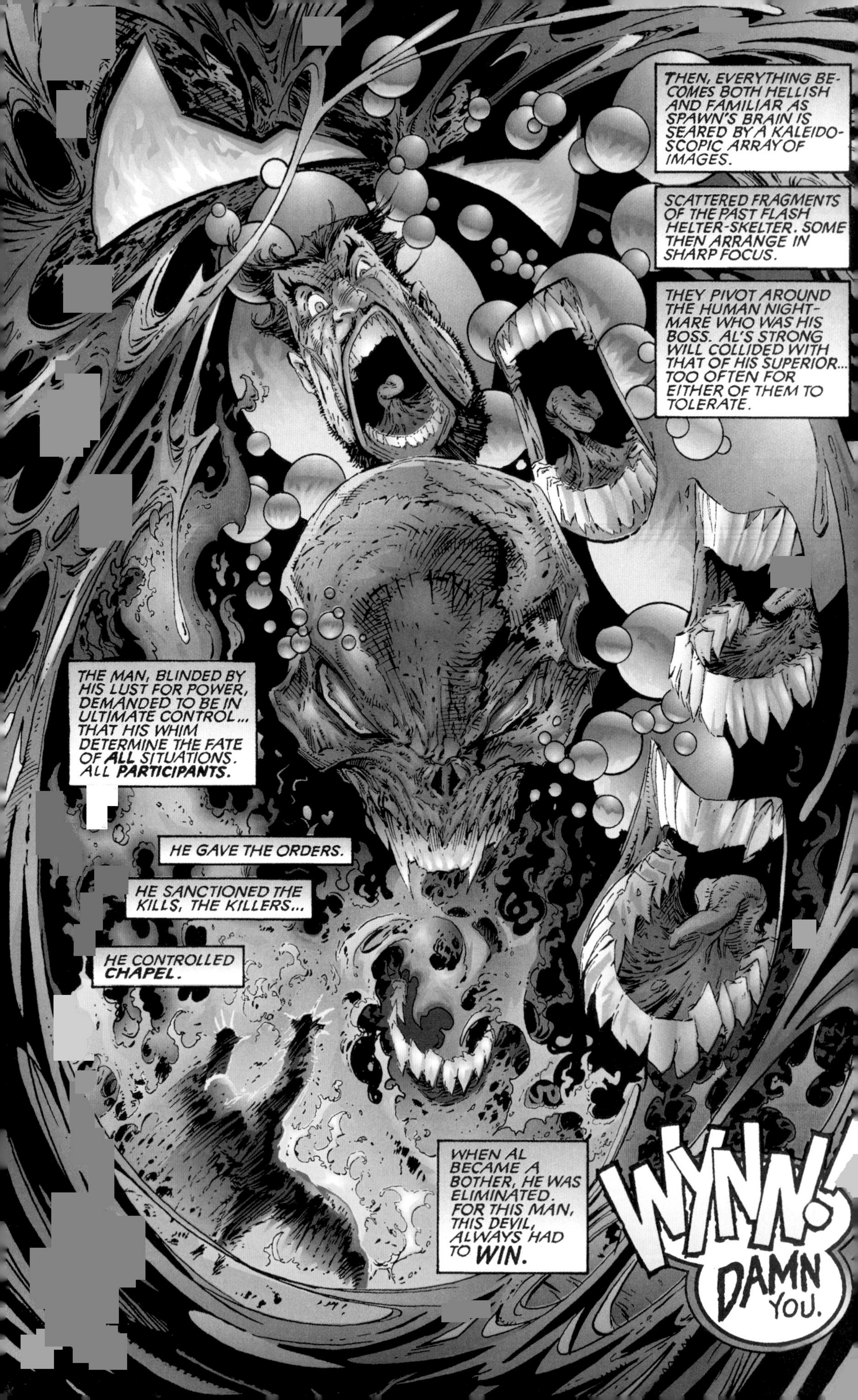
THEN, EVERYTHING BE-COMES BOTH HELLISH AND FAMILIAR AS SPAWN'S BRAIN IS SEARED BY A KALEIDO-SCOPIC ARRAY OF IMAGES.
SCATTERED FRAGMENTS OF THE PAST FLASH HELTER-SKELTER. SOME THEN ARRANGE IN SHARP FOCUS.
THEY PIVOT AROUND THE HUMAN NIGHT-MARE WHO WAS HIS BOSS. AL'S STRONG WILL COLLIDED WITH THAT OF HIS SUPERIOR... TOO OFTEN FOR EITHER OF THEM TO TOLERATE.
THE MAN, BLINDED BY HIS LUST FOR POWER, DEMANDED TO BE IN ULTIMATE CONTROL... THAT HIS WHIM DETERMINE THE FATE OF ALL SITUATIONS. ALL PARTICIPANTS.
HE GAVE THE ORDERS.
HE SANCTIONED THE KILLS, THE KILLERS...
HE CONTROLLED CHAPEL.
WHEN AL BECAME A BOTHER, HE WAS ELIMINATED. FOR THIS MAN, THIS DEVIL, ALWAYS HAD TO WIN.
WYNN. DAMN YOU.

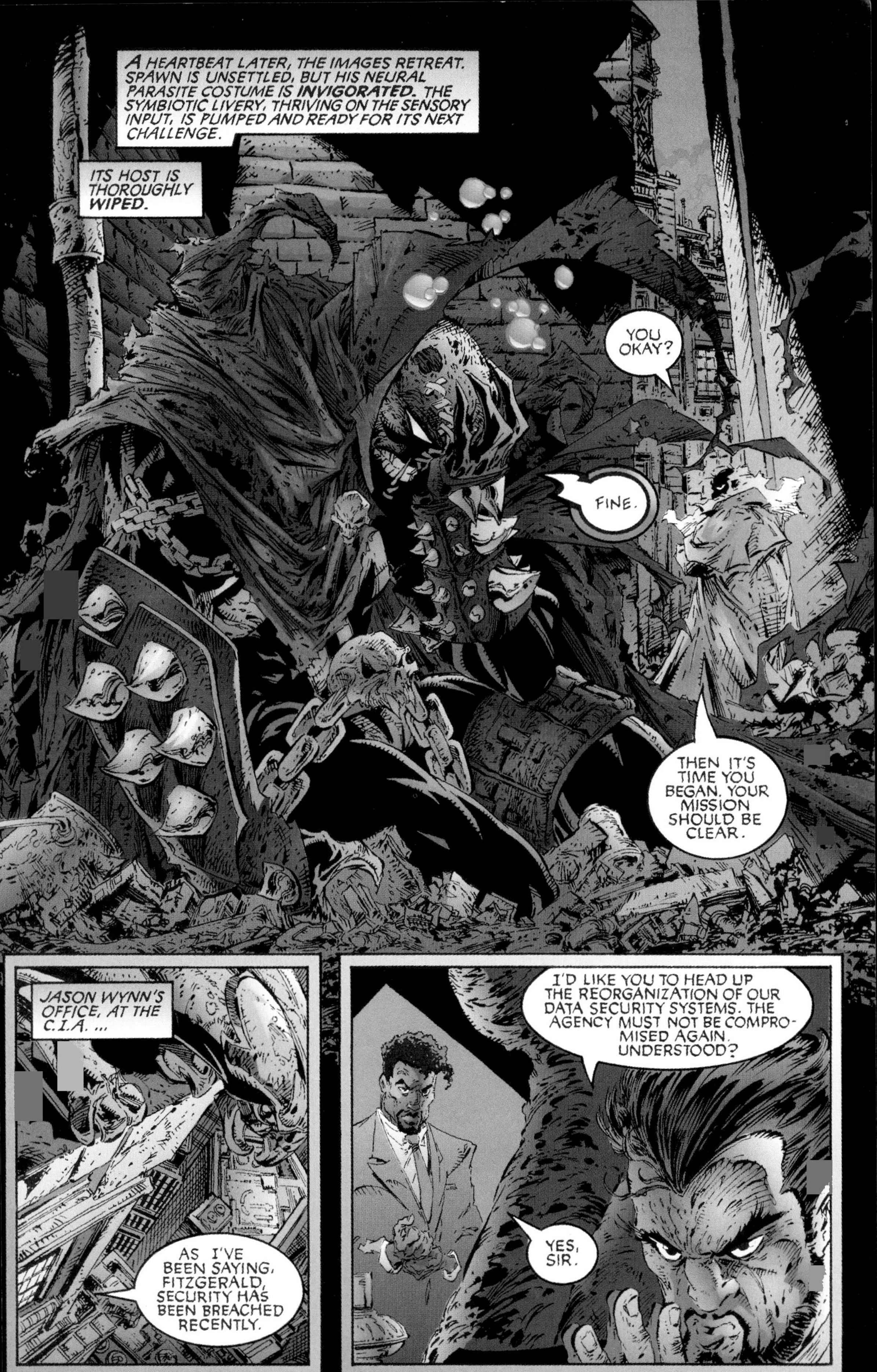
A HEARTBEAT LATER, THE IMAGES RETREAT. SPAWN IS UNSETTLED, BUT HIS NEURAL PARASITE COSTUME IS **INVIGORATED.** THE SYMBIOTIC LIVERY, THRIVING ON THE SENSORY INPUT, IS PUMPED AND READY FOR ITS NEXT CHALLENGE.
ITS HOST IS THOROUGHLY **WIPED.**
YOU OKAY?
FINE.
THEN IT'S TIME YOU BEGAN. YOUR MISSION SHOULD BE CLEAR.
JASON WYNN'S OFFICE, AT THE C.I.A. ...
AS I'VE BEEN SAYING, FITZGERALD, SECURITY HAS BEEN BREACHED RECENTLY.
I'D LIKE YOU TO HEAD UP THE REORGANIZATION OF OUR DATA SECURITY SYSTEMS. THE AGENCY MUST NOT BE COMPROMISED AGAIN. UNDERSTOOD?
YES, SIR.

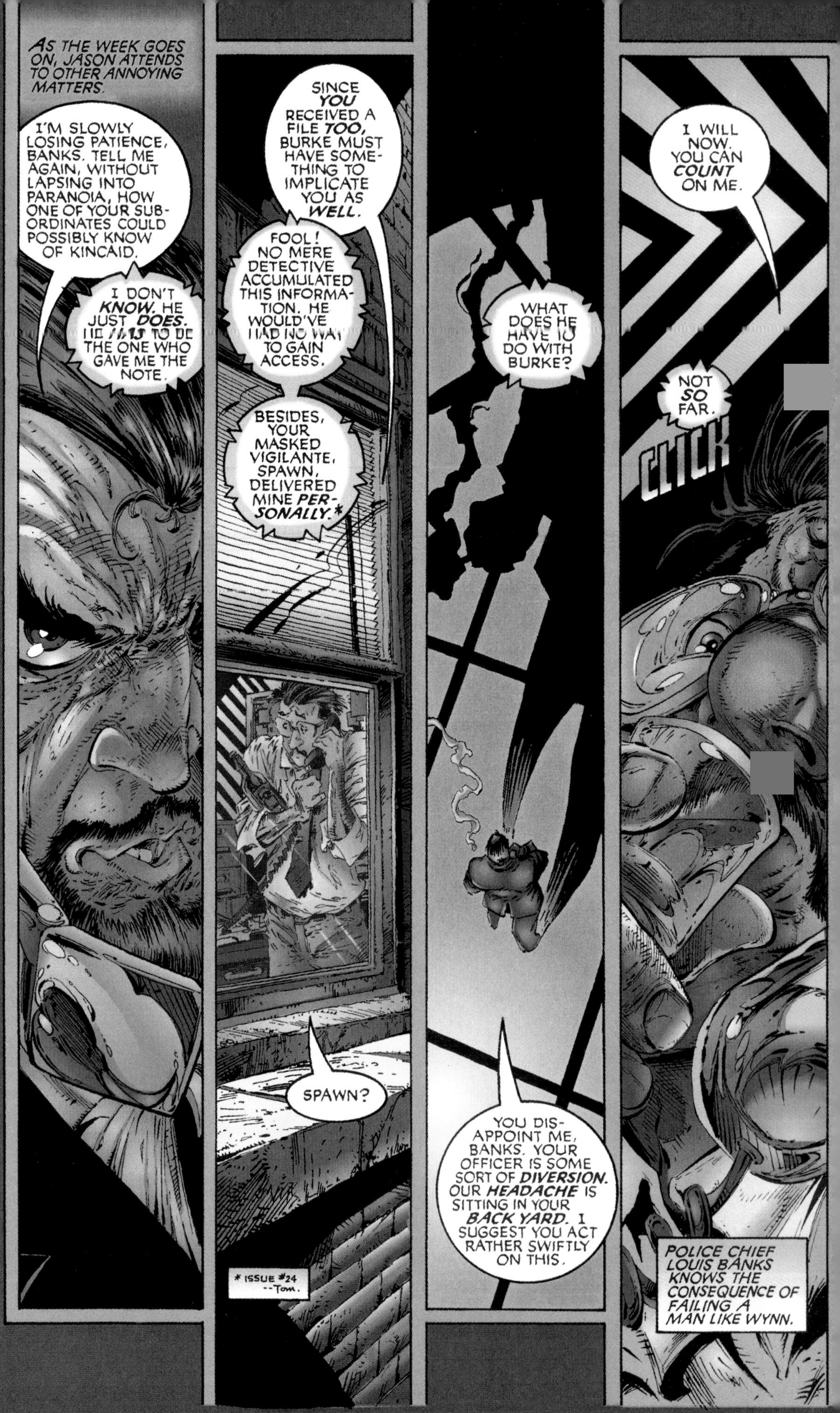

AS THE WEEK GOES ON, JASON ATTENDS TO OTHER ANNOYING MATTERS.
I'M SLOWLY LOSING PATIENCE, BANKS. TELL ME AGAIN, WITHOUT LAPSING INTO PARANOIA, HOW ONE OF YOUR SUBORDINATES COULD POSSIBLY KNOW OF KINCAID.
I DON'T KNOW. HE JUST DOES. HE HAS TO BE THE ONE WHO GAVE ME THE NOTE.
SINCE YOU RECEIVED A FILE TOO, BURKE MUST HAVE SOMETHING TO IMPLICATE YOU AS WELL.
FOOL! NO MERE DETECTIVE ACCUMULATED THIS INFORMATION. HE WOULD'VE HAD NO WAY TO GAIN ACCESS.
BESIDES, YOUR MASKED VIGILANTE, SPAWN, DELIVERED MINE PERSONALLY.*
SPAWN?
* ISSUE #24 --TOM.
WHAT DOES HE HAVE TO DO WITH BURKE?
YOU DISAPPOINT ME, BANKS. YOUR OFFICER IS SOME SORT OF DIVERSION. OUR HEADACHE IS SITTING IN YOUR BACK YARD. I SUGGEST YOU ACT RATHER SWIFTLY ON THIS.
I WILL NOW. YOU CAN COUNT ON ME.
NOT SO FAR.
CLICK
POLICE CHIEF LOUIS BANKS KNOWS THE CONSEQUENCE OF FAILING A MAN LIKE WYNN.

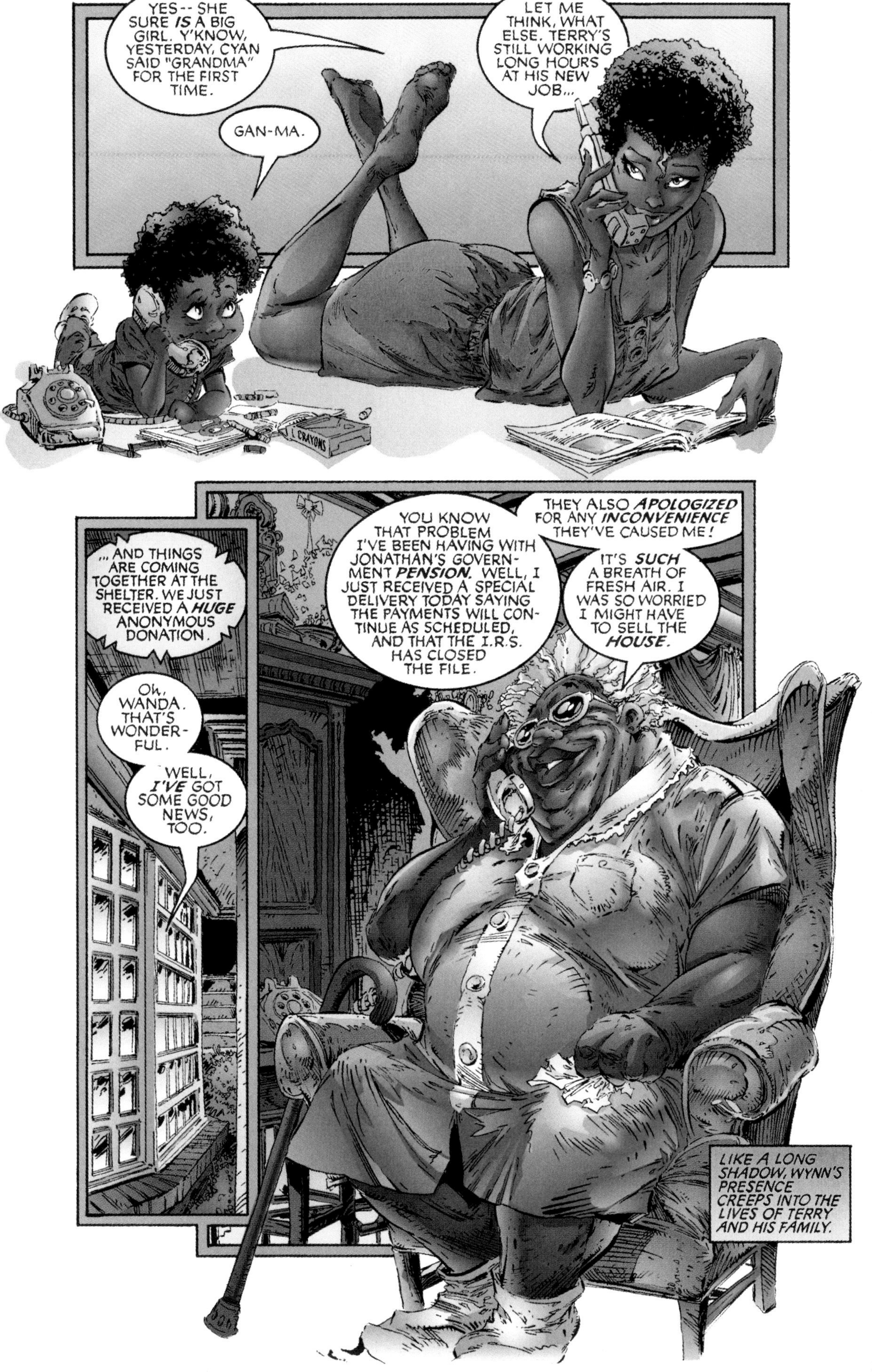
YES-- SHE SURE *IS* A BIG GIRL. Y'KNOW, YESTERDAY, CYAN SAID "GRANDMA" FOR THE FIRST TIME.
GAN-MA.
LET ME THINK, WHAT ELSE. TERRY'S STILL WORKING LONG HOURS AT HIS NEW JOB...
CRAYONS
...AND THINGS ARE COMING TOGETHER AT THE SHELTER. WE JUST RECEIVED A *HUGE* ANONYMOUS DONATION.
Oh, WANDA. THAT'S WONDERFUL.
WELL, *I'VE* GOT SOME GOOD NEWS, TOO.
YOU KNOW THAT PROBLEM I'VE BEEN HAVING WITH JONATHAN'S GOVERNMENT *PENSION.* WELL, I JUST RECEIVED A SPECIAL DELIVERY TODAY SAYING THE PAYMENTS WILL CONTINUE AS SCHEDULED, AND THAT THE I.R.S. HAS CLOSED THE FILE.
THEY ALSO *APOLOGIZED* FOR ANY *INCONVENIENCE* THEY'VE CAUSED ME!
IT'S *SUCH* A BREATH OF FRESH AIR. I WAS SO WORRIED I MIGHT HAVE TO SELL THE *HOUSE.*
LIKE A LONG SHADOW, WYNN'S PRESENCE CREEPS INTO THE LIVES OF TERRY AND HIS FAMILY.

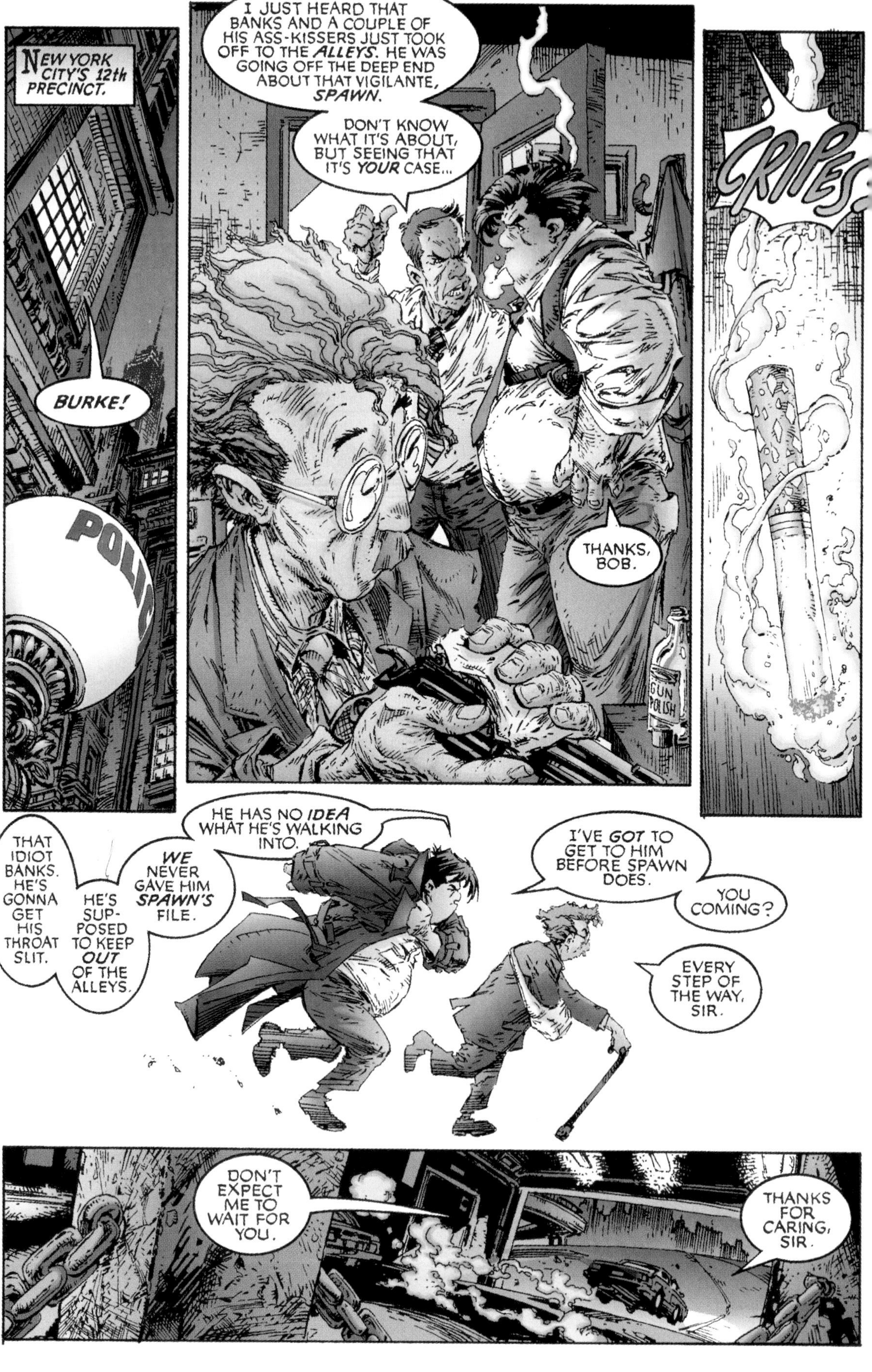
NEW YORK CITY'S 12th PRECINCT.
BURKE!
POLIC
I JUST HEARD THAT BANKS AND A COUPLE OF HIS ASS-KISSERS JUST TOOK OFF TO THE *ALLEYS*. HE WAS GOING OFF THE DEEP END ABOUT THAT VIGILANTE, *SPAWN*.
DON'T KNOW WHAT IT'S ABOUT, BUT SEEING THAT IT'S *YOUR* CASE...
THANKS, BOB.
GUN POLISH
CRIPES!
THAT IDIOT BANKS. HE'S GONNA GET HIS THROAT SLIT.
HE'S SUP-POSED TO KEEP *OUT* OF THE ALLEYS.
WE NEVER GAVE HIM *SPAWN'S* FILE.
HE HAS NO *IDEA* WHAT HE'S WALKING INTO.
I'VE *GOT* TO GET TO HIM BEFORE SPAWN DOES.
YOU COMING?
EVERY STEP OF THE WAY, SIR.
DON'T EXPECT ME TO WAIT FOR YOU.
THANKS FOR CARING, SIR.

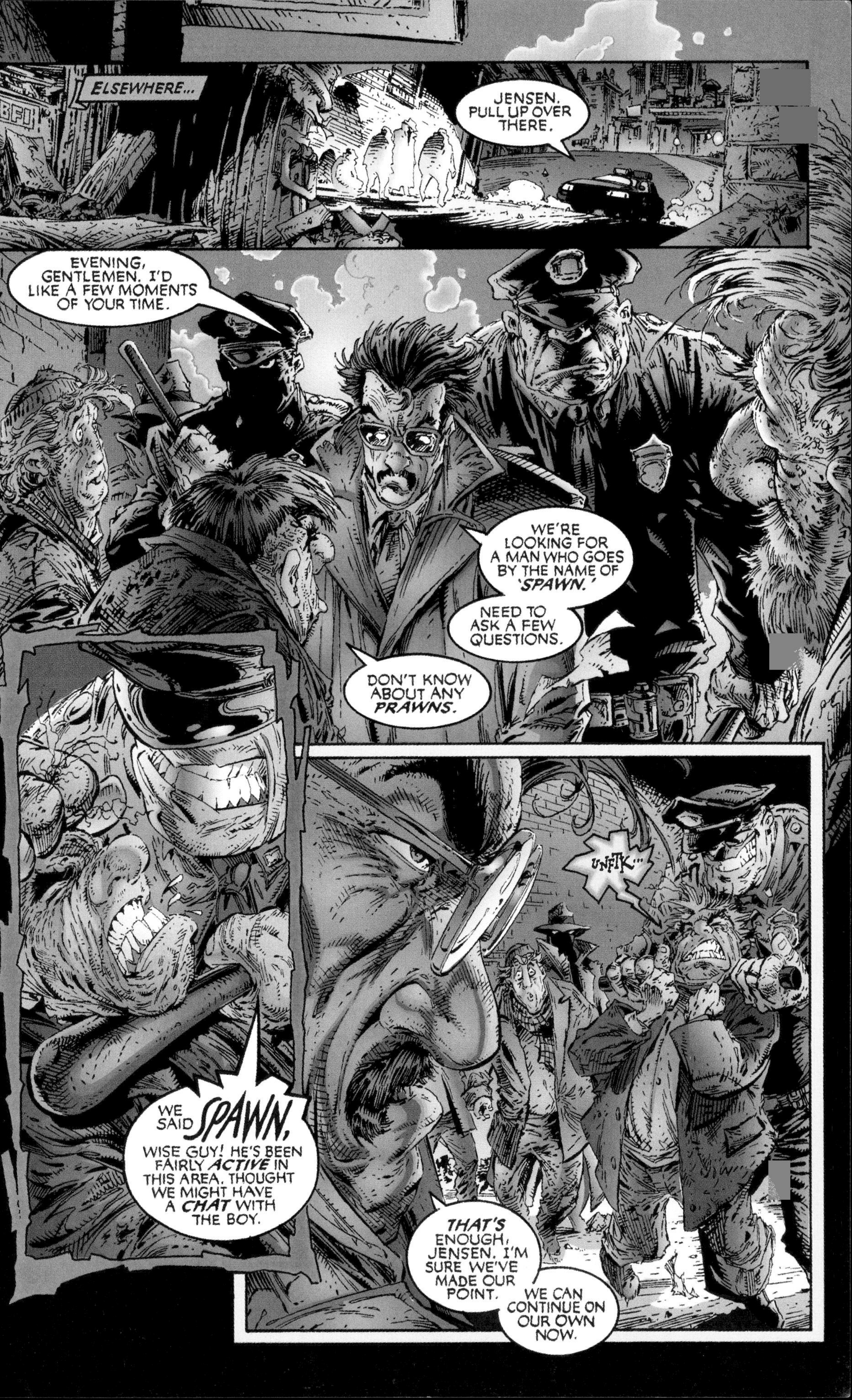
ELSEWHERE...
JENSEN. PULL UP OVER THERE.
EVENING, GENTLEMEN. I'D LIKE A FEW MOMENTS OF YOUR TIME.
WE'RE LOOKING FOR A MAN WHO GOES BY THE NAME OF 'SPAWN.'
NEED TO ASK A FEW QUESTIONS.
DON'T KNOW ABOUT ANY PRAWNS.
WE SAID SPAWN, WISE GUY! HE'S BEEN FAIRLY ACTIVE IN THIS AREA. THOUGHT WE MIGHT HAVE A CHAT WITH THE BOY.
UNFTK...
THAT'S ENOUGH, JENSEN. I'M SURE WE'VE MADE OUR POINT.
WE CAN CONTINUE ON OUR OWN NOW.

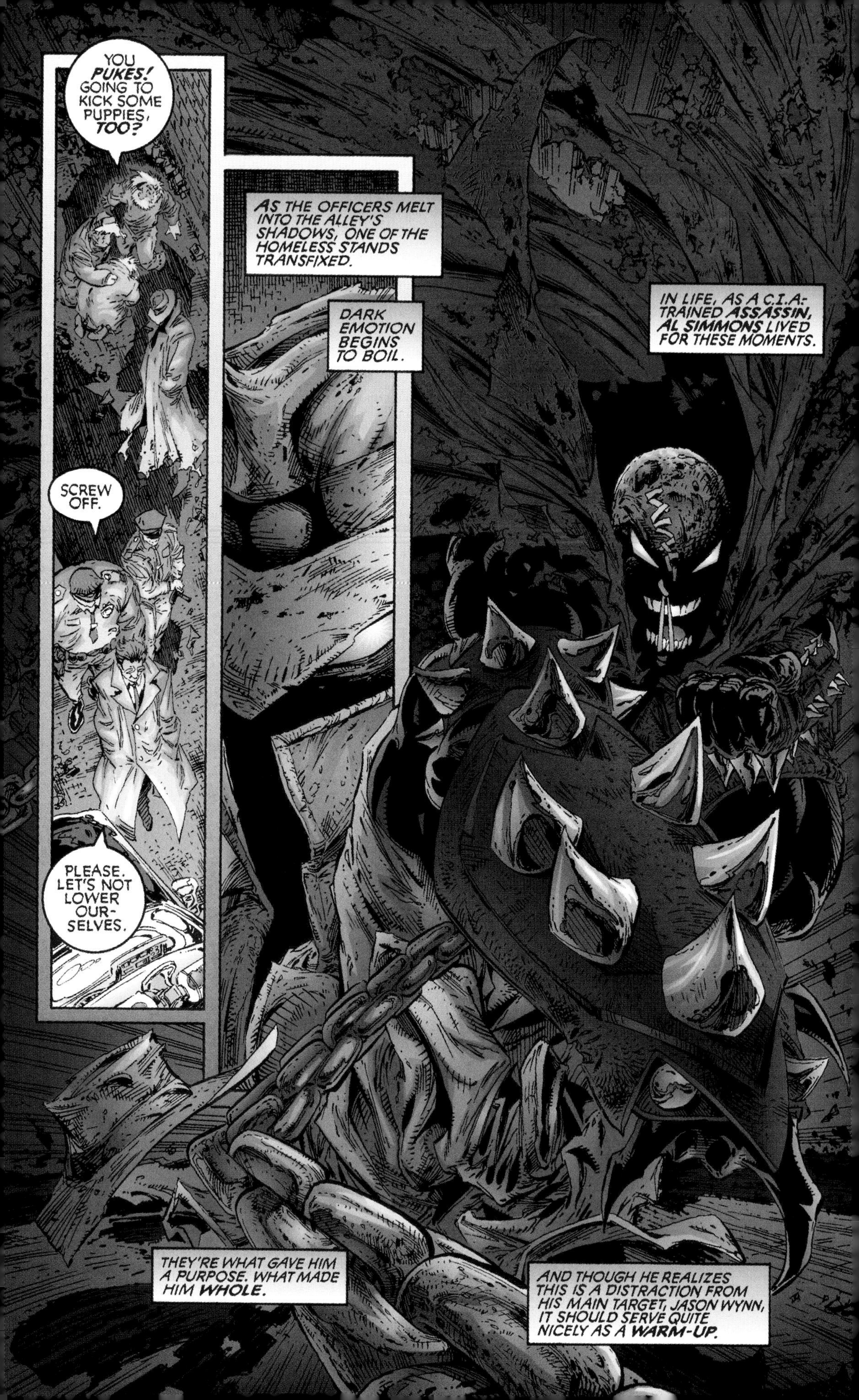
YOU ***PUKES!*** GOING TO KICK SOME PUPPIES, ***TOO?***
SCREW OFF.
PLEASE. LET'S NOT LOWER OUR-SELVES.
AS THE OFFICERS MELT INTO THE ALLEY'S SHADOWS, ONE OF THE HOMELESS STANDS TRANSFIXED.
DARK EMOTION BEGINS TO BOIL.
IN LIFE, AS A C.I.A.-TRAINED ***ASSASSIN, AL SIMMONS*** LIVED FOR THESE MOMENTS.
THEY'RE WHAT GAVE HIM A PURPOSE. WHAT MADE HIM ***WHOLE***.
AND THOUGH HE REALIZES THIS IS A DISTRACTION FROM HIS MAIN TARGET, JASON WYNN, IT SHOULD SERVE QUITE NICELY AS A ***WARM-UP***.

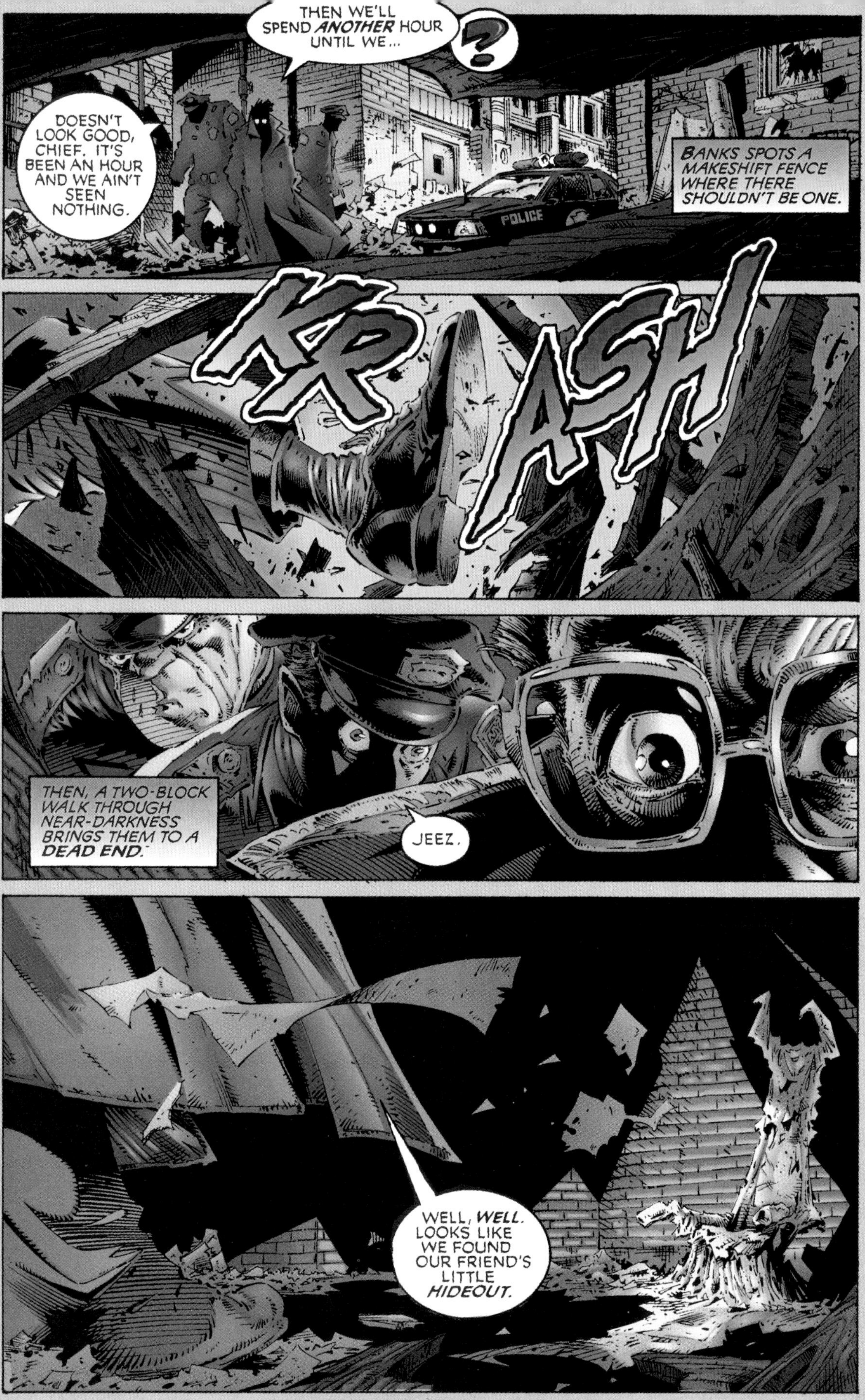
DOESN'T LOOK GOOD, CHIEF. IT'S BEEN AN HOUR AND WE AIN'T SEEN NOTHING.
THEN WE'LL SPEND ANOTHER HOUR UNTIL WE...
?
BANKS SPOTS A MAKESHIFT FENCE WHERE THERE SHOULDN'T BE ONE.
POLICE
KRASH
THEN, A TWO-BLOCK WALK THROUGH NEAR-DARKNESS BRINGS THEM TO A DEAD END.
JEEZ.
WELL, WELL. LOOKS LIKE WE FOUND OUR FRIEND'S LITTLE HIDEOUT.

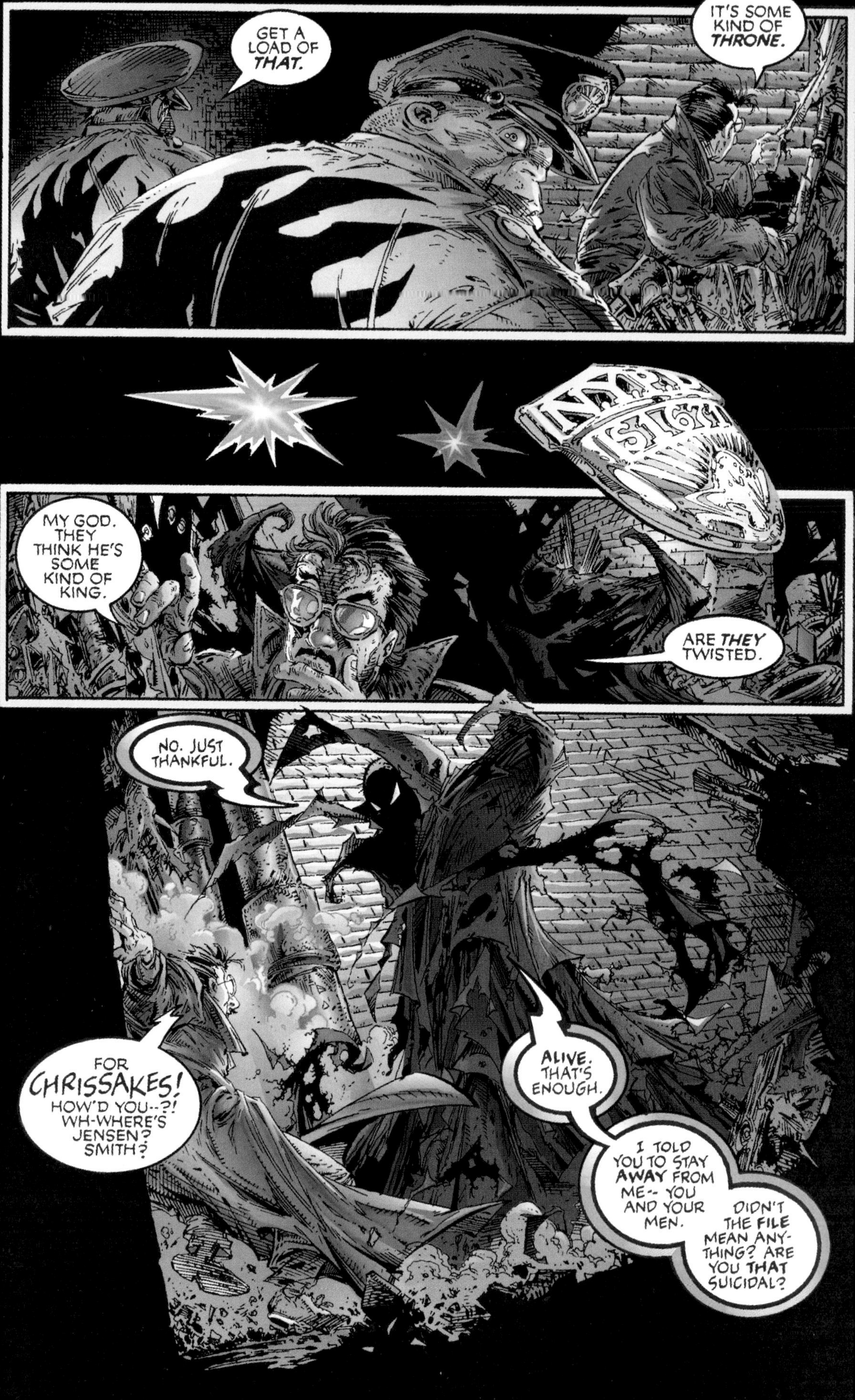
GET A LOAD OF THAT.
IT'S SOME KIND OF THRONE.
MY GOD. THEY THINK HE'S SOME KIND OF KING.
ARE THEY TWISTED.
NO. JUST THANKFUL.
FOR CHRISSAKES! HOW'D YOU--?! WH-WHERE'S JENSEN? SMITH?
ALIVE. THAT'S ENOUGH.
I TOLD YOU TO STAY AWAY FROM ME-- YOU AND YOUR MEN.
DIDN'T THE FILE MEAN ANYTHING? ARE YOU THAT SUICIDAL?

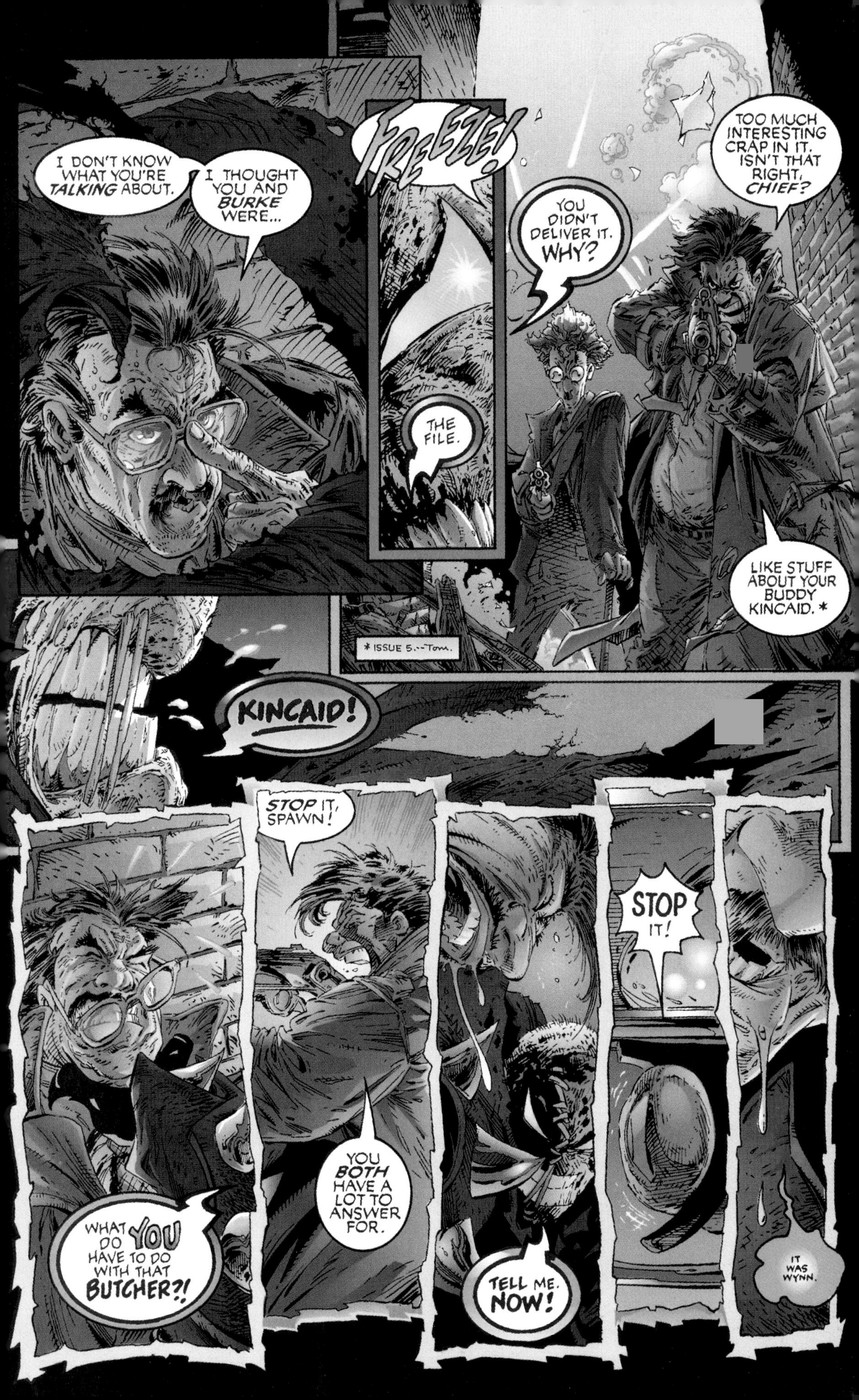
I DON'T KNOW WHAT YOU'RE TALKING ABOUT.
I THOUGHT YOU AND BURKE WERE...
FREEZE!
THE FILE.
YOU DIDN'T DELIVER IT. WHY?
TOO MUCH INTERESTING CRAP IN IT. ISN'T THAT RIGHT, CHIEF?
LIKE STUFF ABOUT YOUR BUDDY KINCAID. *
* ISSUE 5.--Tom.
KINCAID!
WHAT DO YOU HAVE TO DO WITH THAT BUTCHER?!
STOP IT, SPAWN!
YOU BOTH HAVE A LOT TO ANSWER FOR.
TELL ME. NOW!
STOP IT!
IT WAS WYNN.

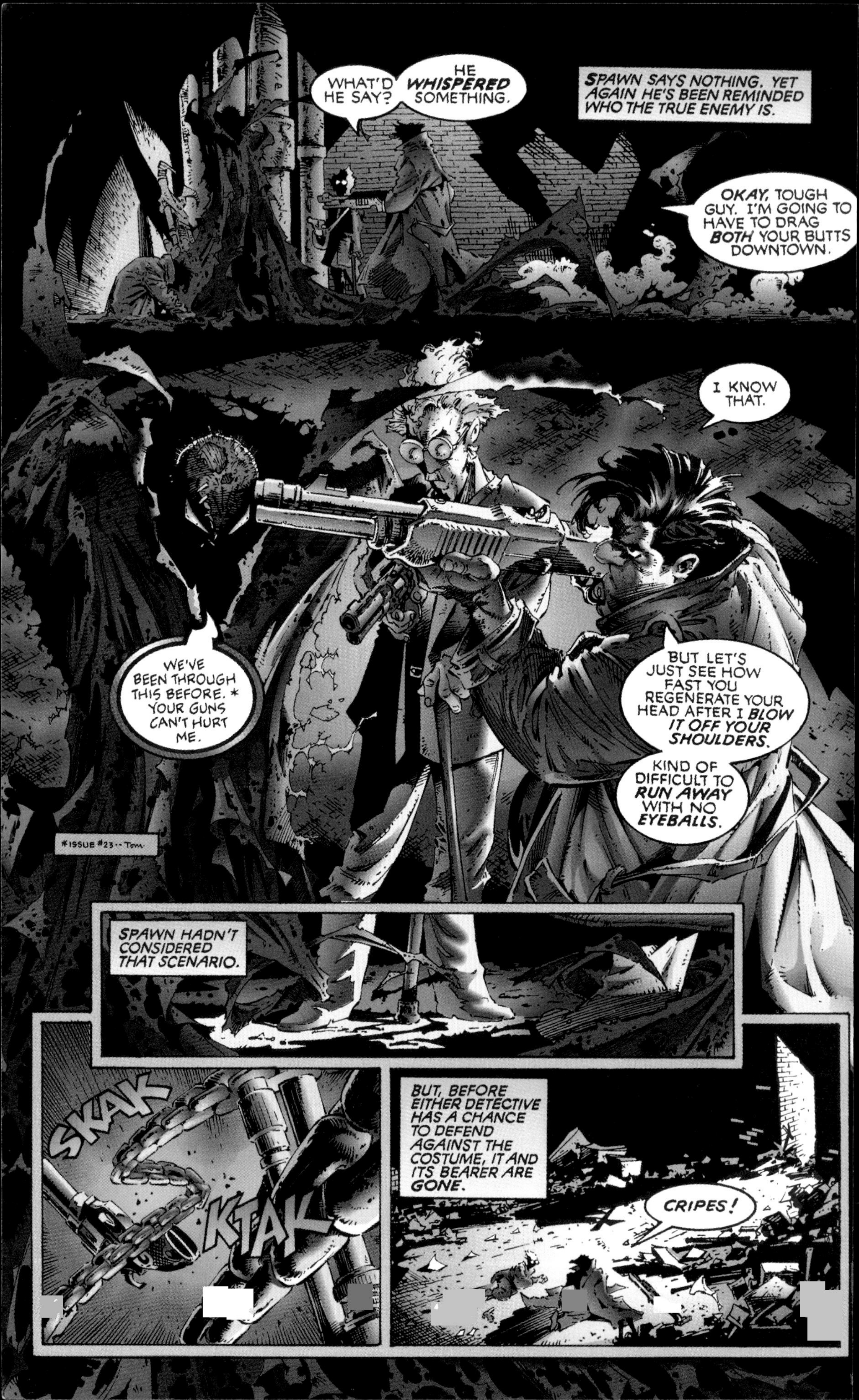
WHAT'D HE SAY?
HE WHISPERED SOMETHING.
SPAWN SAYS NOTHING. YET AGAIN HE'S BEEN REMINDED WHO THE TRUE ENEMY IS.
OKAY, TOUGH GUY. I'M GOING TO HAVE TO DRAG BOTH YOUR BUTTS DOWNTOWN.
I KNOW THAT.
WE'VE BEEN THROUGH THIS BEFORE. * YOUR GUNS CAN'T HURT ME.
BUT LET'S JUST SEE HOW FAST YOU REGENERATE YOUR HEAD AFTER I BLOW IT OFF YOUR SHOULDERS.
KIND OF DIFFICULT TO RUN AWAY WITH NO EYEBALLS.
*ISSUE #23 -- Tom.
SPAWN HADN'T CONSIDERED THAT SCENARIO.
SKAK
KTAK
BUT, BEFORE EITHER DETECTIVE HAS A CHANCE TO DEFEND AGAINST THE COSTUME, IT AND ITS BEARER ARE GONE.
CRIPES!

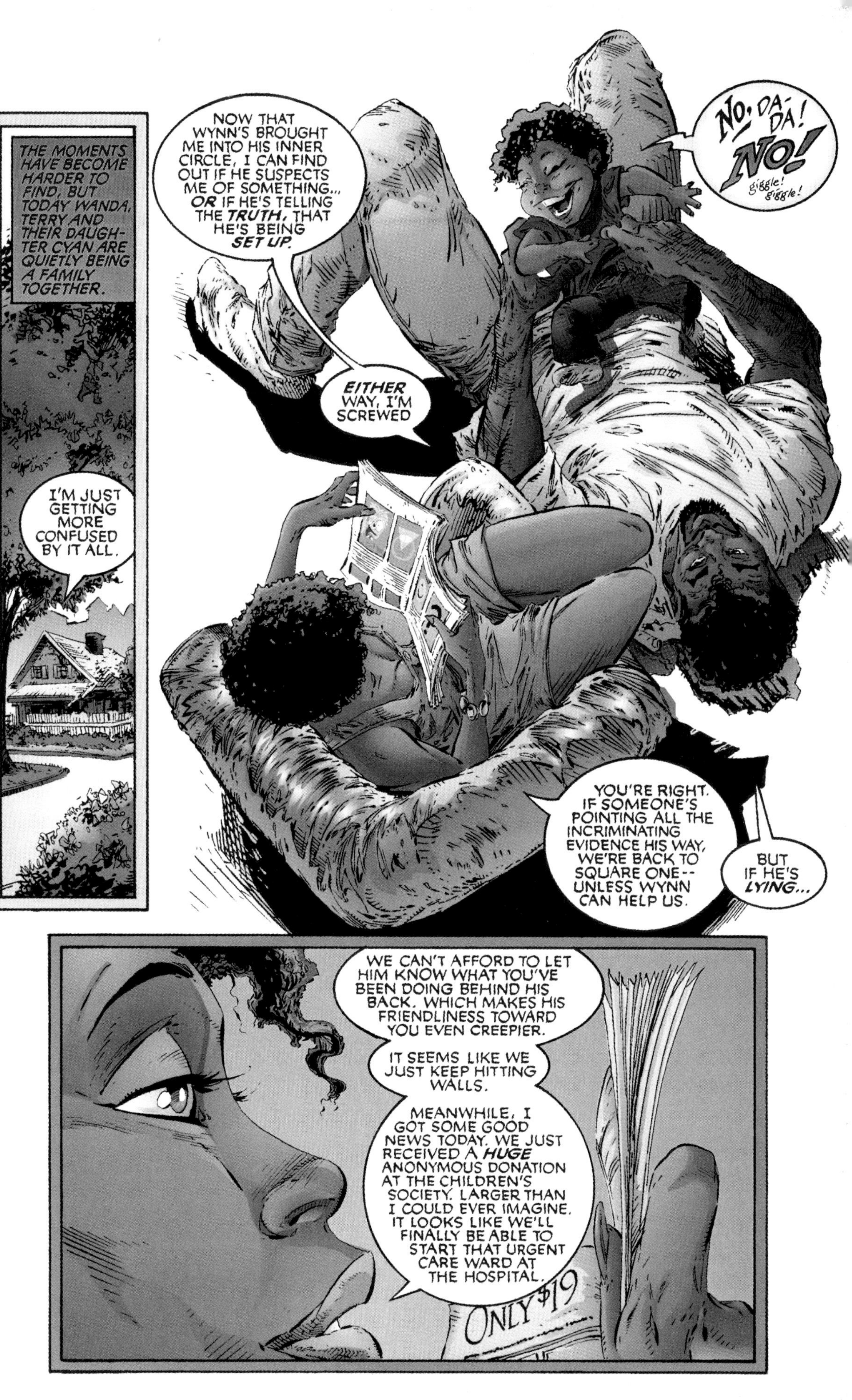
THE MOMENTS HAVE BECOME HARDER TO FIND, BUT TODAY WANDA, TERRY AND THEIR DAUGHTER CYAN ARE QUIETLY BEING A FAMILY TOGETHER.
I'M JUST GETTING MORE CONFUSED BY IT ALL.
NOW THAT WYNN'S BROUGHT ME INTO HIS INNER CIRCLE, I CAN FIND OUT IF HE SUSPECTS ME OF SOMETHING... OR IF HE'S TELLING THE TRUTH, THAT HE'S BEING SET UP.
EITHER WAY, I'M SCREWED
NO, DA-DA! NO!
giggle! giggle!
YOU'RE RIGHT. IF SOMEONE'S POINTING ALL THE INCRIMINATING EVIDENCE HIS WAY, WE'RE BACK TO SQUARE ONE-- UNLESS WYNN CAN HELP US.
BUT IF HE'S LYING...
WE CAN'T AFFORD TO LET HIM KNOW WHAT YOU'VE BEEN DOING BEHIND HIS BACK. WHICH MAKES HIS FRIENDLINESS TOWARD YOU EVEN CREEPIER.
IT SEEMS LIKE WE JUST KEEP HITTING WALLS.
MEANWHILE, I GOT SOME GOOD NEWS TODAY. WE JUST RECEIVED A HUGE ANONYMOUS DONATION AT THE CHILDREN'S SOCIETY. LARGER THAN I COULD EVER IMAGINE. IT LOOKS LIKE WE'LL FINALLY BE ABLE TO START THAT URGENT CARE WARD AT THE HOSPITAL.
ONLY $19

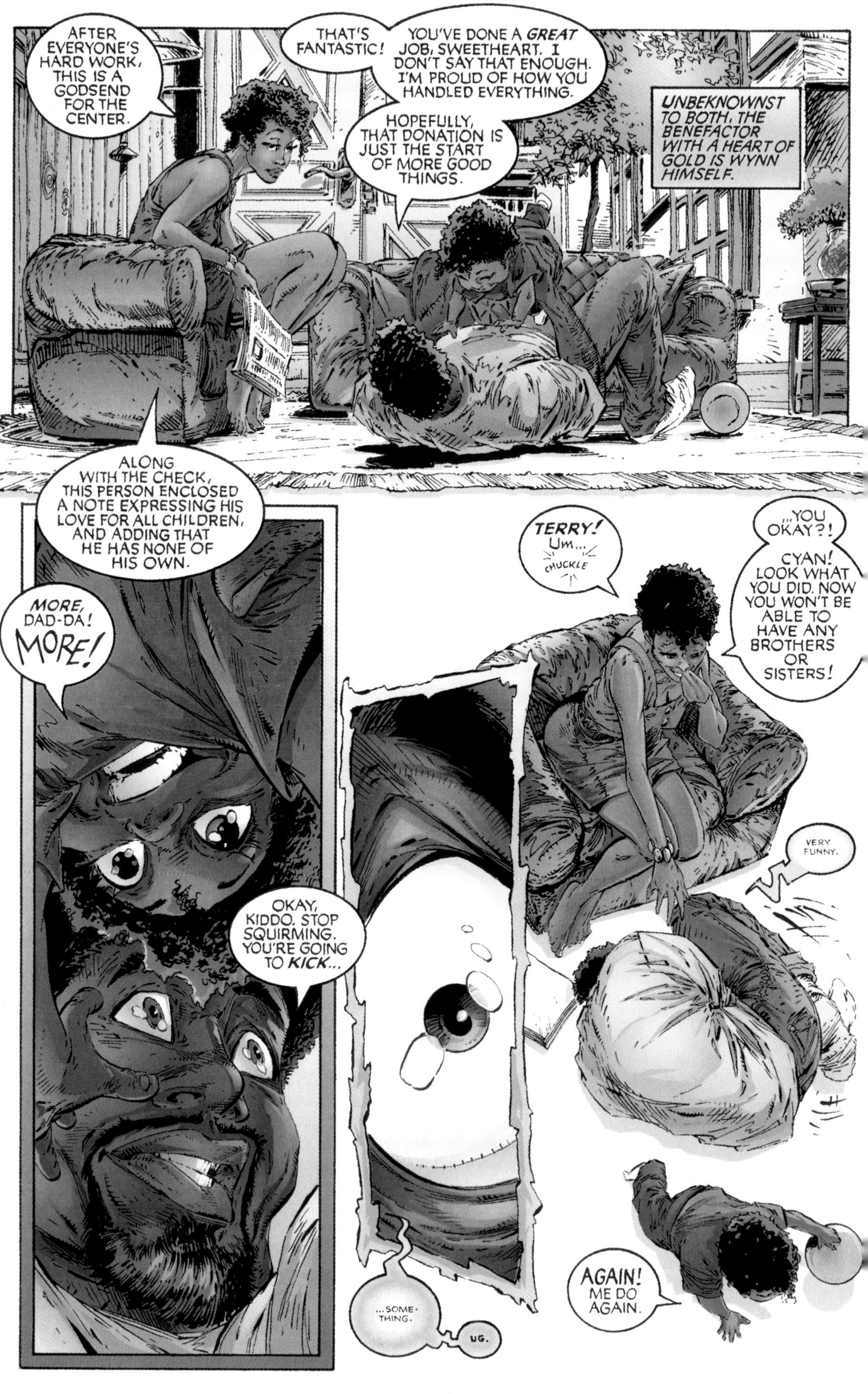
AFTER EVERYONE'S HARD WORK, THIS IS A GODSEND FOR THE CENTER.
THAT'S FANTASTIC!
YOU'VE DONE A GREAT JOB, SWEETHEART. I DON'T SAY THAT ENOUGH. I'M PROUD OF HOW YOU HANDLED EVERYTHING.
HOPEFULLY, THAT DONATION IS JUST THE START OF MORE GOOD THINGS.
UNBEKNOWNST TO BOTH, THE BENEFACTOR WITH A HEART OF GOLD IS WYNN HIMSELF.
ALONG WITH THE CHECK, THIS PERSON ENCLOSED A NOTE EXPRESSING HIS LOVE FOR ALL CHILDREN, AND ADDING THAT HE HAS NONE OF HIS OWN.
MORE, DAD-DA! MORE!
OKAY, KIDDO. STOP SQUIRMING. YOU'RE GOING TO KICK...
...SOME-THING.
UG.
TERRY! Um... CHUCKLE
...YOU OKAY?!
CYAN! LOOK WHAT YOU DID. NOW YOU WON'T BE ABLE TO HAVE ANY BROTHERS OR SISTERS!
VERY FUNNY.
AGAIN! ME DO AGAIN.

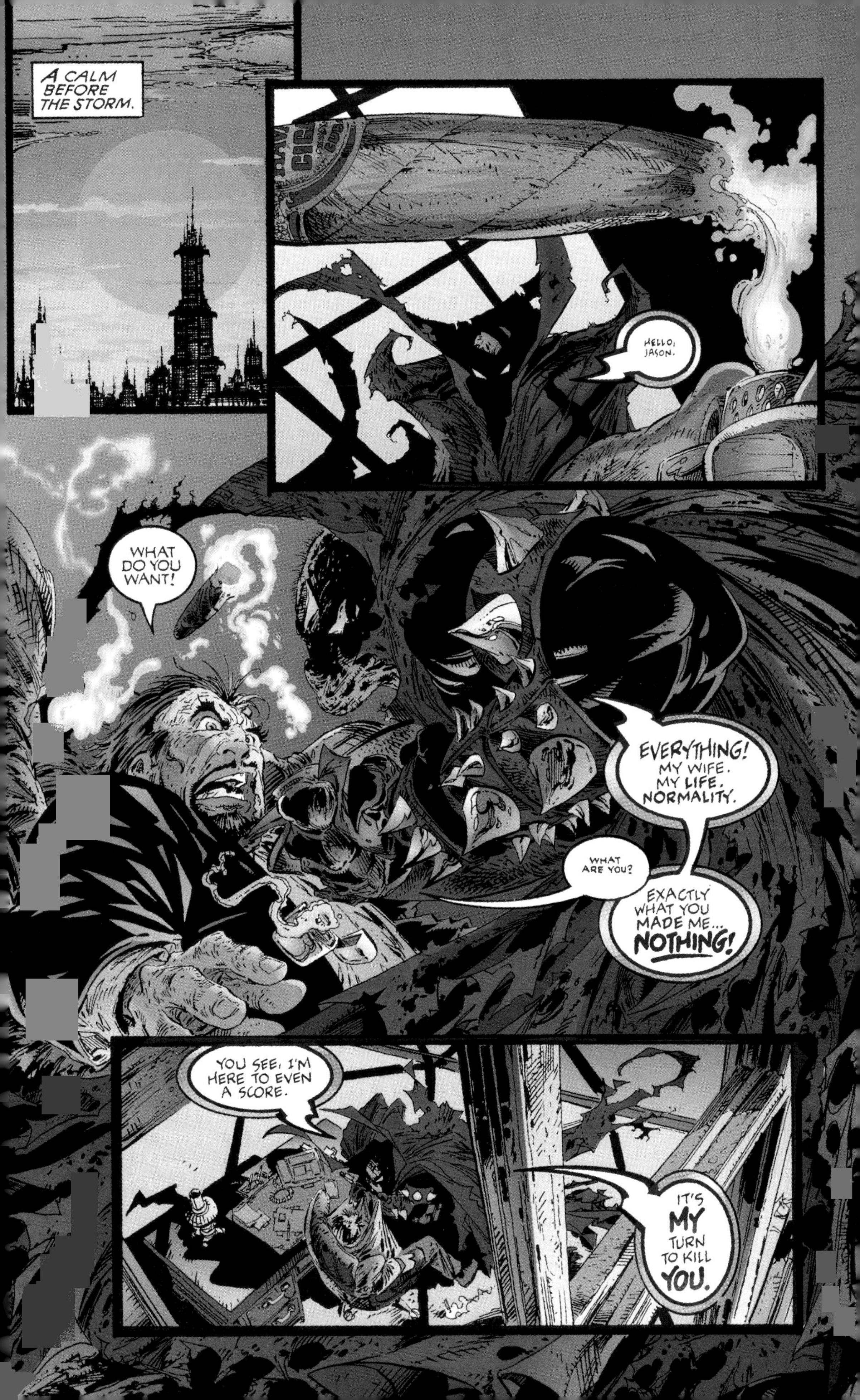
A CALM BEFORE THE STORM.
HELLO, JASON.
WHAT DO YOU WANT!
EVERYTHING! MY WIFE. MY LIFE. NORMALITY.
WHAT ARE YOU?
EXACTLY WHAT YOU MADE ME... NOTHING!
YOU SEE, I'M HERE TO EVEN A SCORE.
IT'S MY TURN TO KILL YOU.

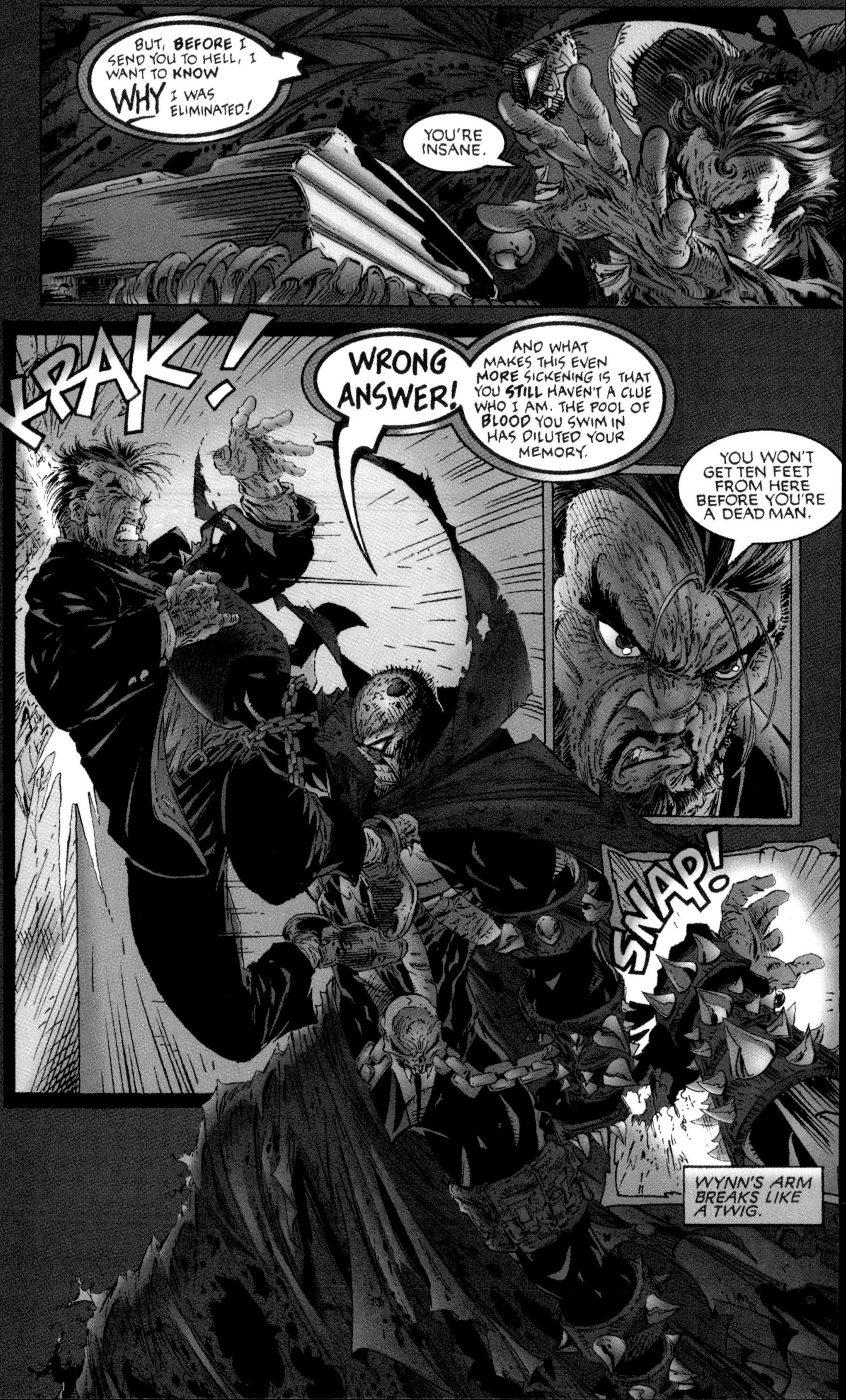
BUT, BEFORE I SEND YOU TO HELL, I WANT TO KNOW WHY I WAS ELIMINATED!
YOU'RE INSANE.
KRAK!
WRONG ANSWER!
AND WHAT MAKES THIS EVEN MORE SICKENING IS THAT YOU STILL HAVEN'T A CLUE WHO I AM. THE POOL OF BLOOD YOU SWIM IN HAS DILUTED YOUR MEMORY.
YOU WON'T GET TEN FEET FROM HERE BEFORE YOU'RE A DEAD MAN.
SNAP!
WYNN'S ARM BREAKS LIKE A TWIG.

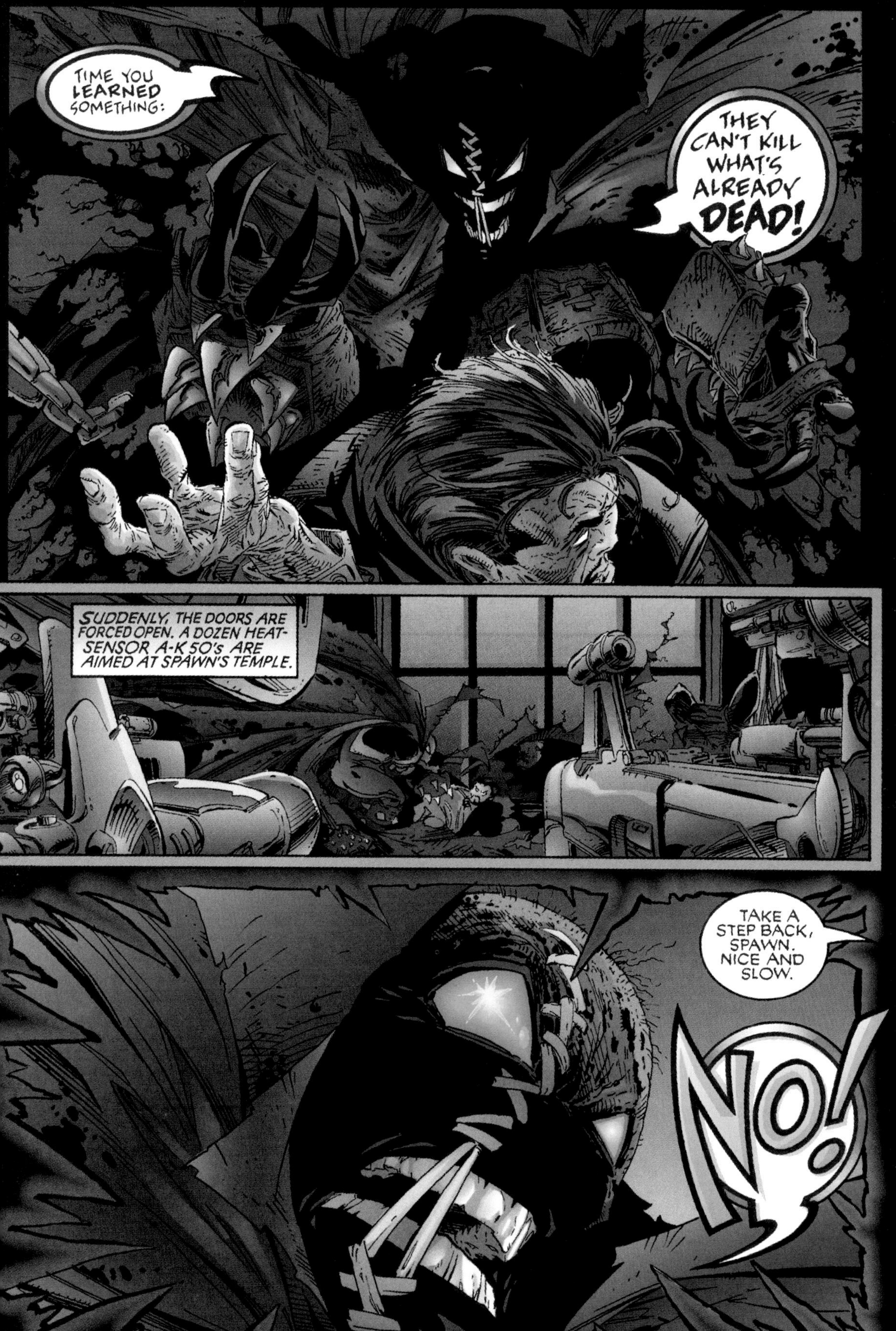
TIME YOU LEARNED SOMETHING:
THEY CAN'T KILL WHAT'S ALREADY DEAD!
SUDDENLY, THE DOORS ARE FORCED OPEN. A DOZEN HEAT-SENSOR A-K 50's ARE AIMED AT SPAWN'S TEMPLE.
TAKE A STEP BACK, SPAWN. NICE AND SLOW.
NO!

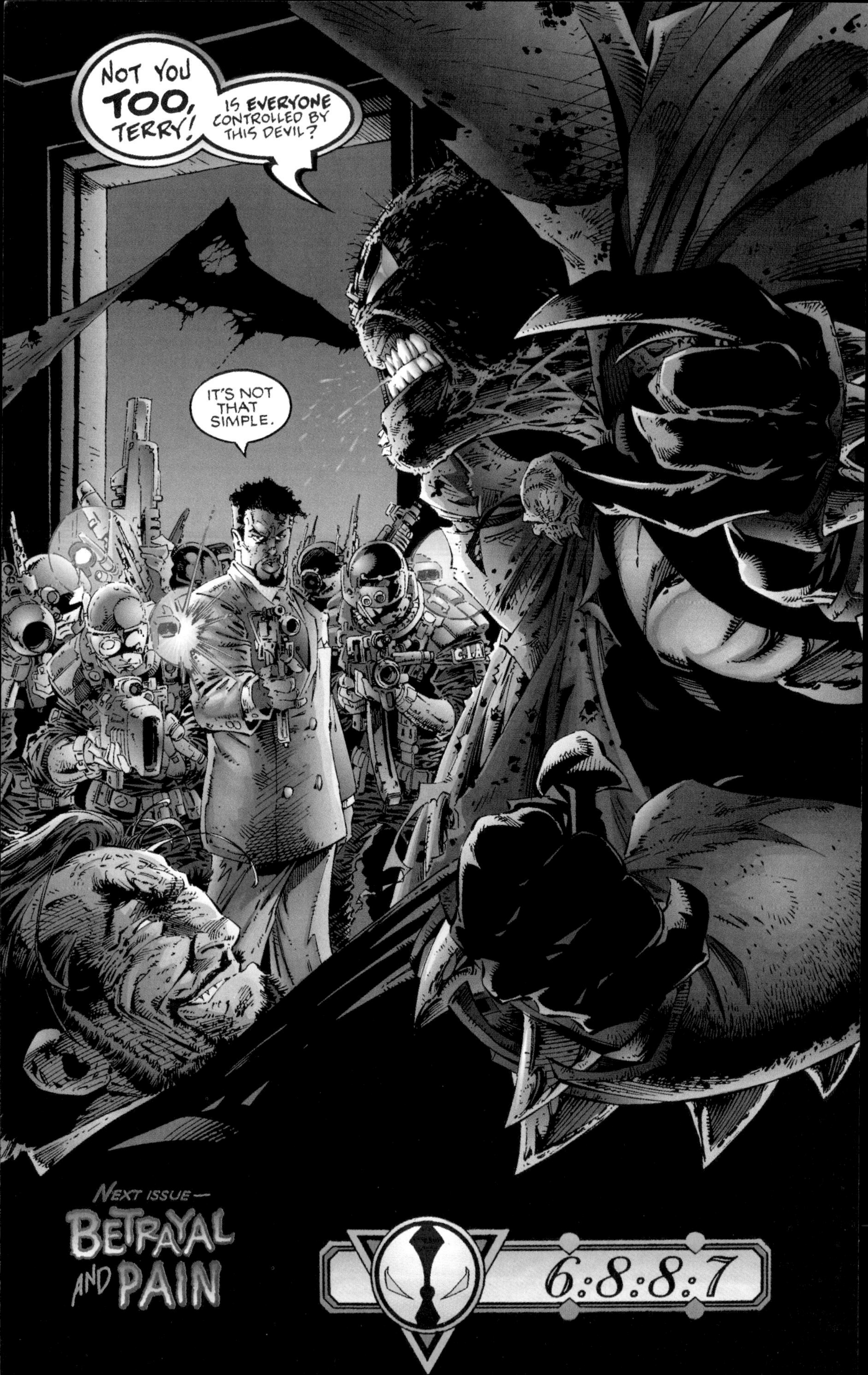

NOT YOU TOO, TERRY!
IS EVERYONE CONTROLLED BY THIS DEVIL?
IT'S NOT THAT SIMPLE.
NEXT ISSUE— BETRAYAL AND PAIN
6:8:8:7

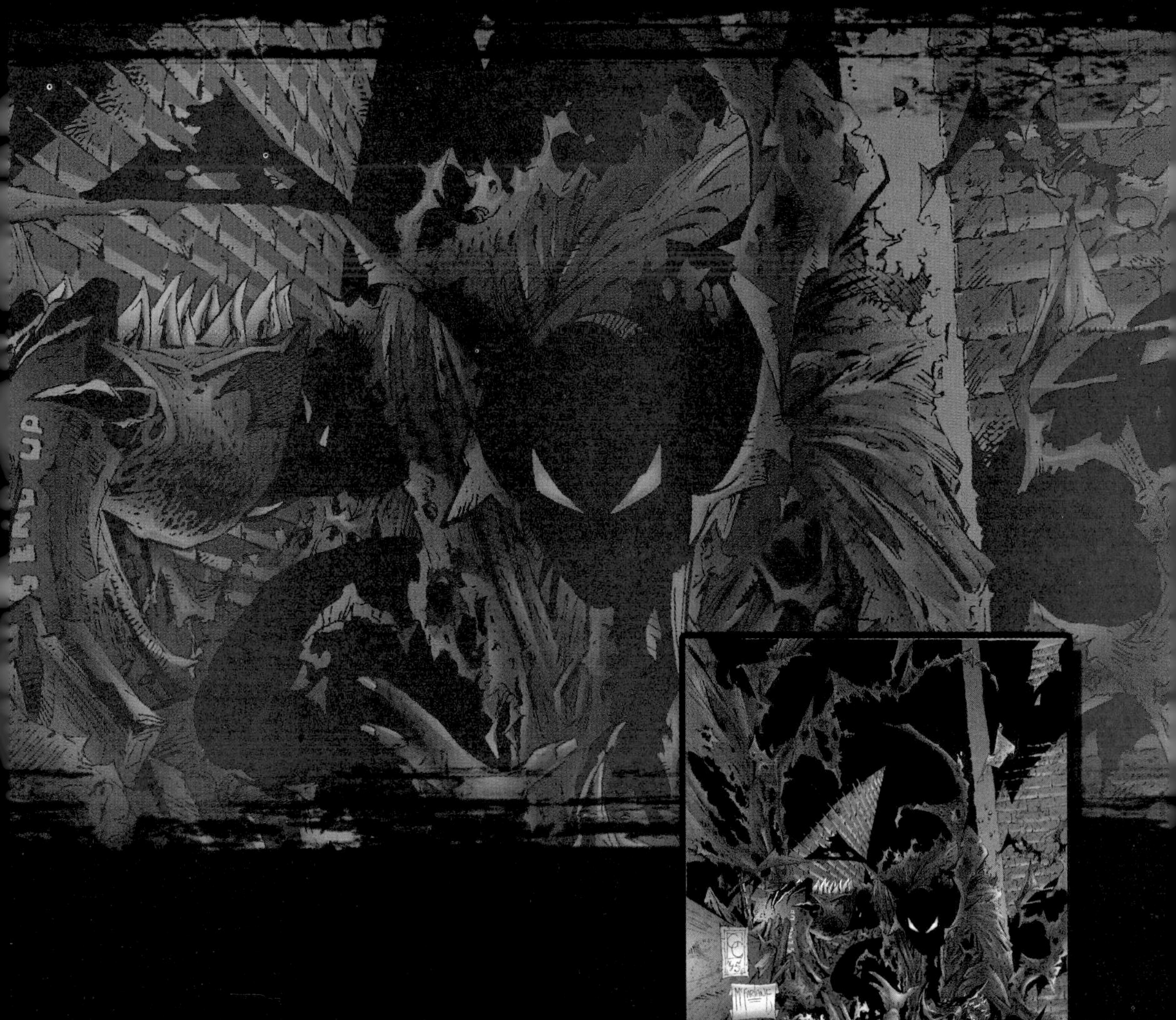

ISSUE THIRTY-SIX

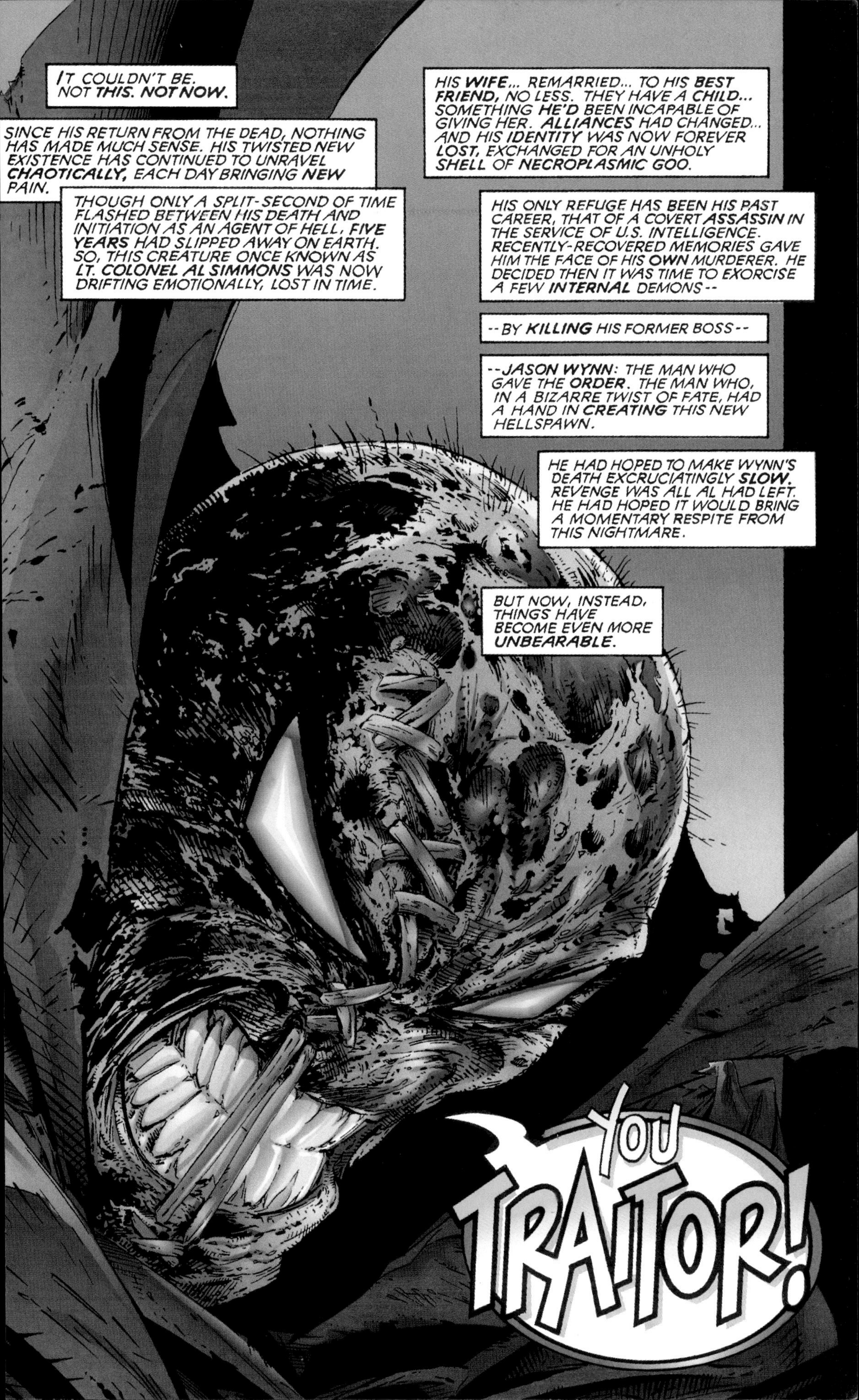
IT COULDN'T BE. NOT THIS. NOT NOW.
SINCE HIS RETURN FROM THE DEAD, NOTHING HAS MADE MUCH SENSE. HIS TWISTED NEW EXISTENCE HAS CONTINUED TO UNRAVEL CHAOTICALLY, EACH DAY BRINGING NEW PAIN.
THOUGH ONLY A SPLIT-SECOND OF TIME FLASHED BETWEEN HIS DEATH AND INITIATION AS AN AGENT OF HELL, FIVE YEARS HAD SLIPPED AWAY ON EARTH. SO, THIS CREATURE ONCE KNOWN AS LT. COLONEL AL SIMMONS WAS NOW DRIFTING EMOTIONALLY, LOST IN TIME.
HIS WIFE... REMARRIED... TO HIS BEST FRIEND, NO LESS. THEY HAVE A CHILD... SOMETHING HE'D BEEN INCAPABLE OF GIVING HER. ALLIANCES HAD CHANGED... AND HIS IDENTITY WAS NOW FOREVER LOST, EXCHANGED FOR AN UNHOLY SHELL OF NECROPLASMIC GOO.
HIS ONLY REFUGE HAS BEEN HIS PAST CAREER, THAT OF A COVERT ASSASSIN IN THE SERVICE OF U.S. INTELLIGENCE. RECENTLY-RECOVERED MEMORIES GAVE HIM THE FACE OF HIS OWN MURDERER. HE DECIDED THEN IT WAS TIME TO EXORCISE A FEW INTERNAL DEMONS--
--BY KILLING HIS FORMER BOSS--
--JASON WYNN: THE MAN WHO GAVE THE ORDER. THE MAN WHO, IN A BIZARRE TWIST OF FATE, HAD A HAND IN CREATING THIS NEW HELLSPAWN.
HE HAD HOPED TO MAKE WYNN'S DEATH EXCRUCIATINGLY SLOW. REVENGE WAS ALL AL HAD LEFT. HE HAD HOPED IT WOULD BRING A MOMENTARY RESPITE FROM THIS NIGHTMARE.
BUT NOW, INSTEAD, THINGS HAVE BECOME EVEN MORE UNBEARABLE.
YOU TRAITOR!

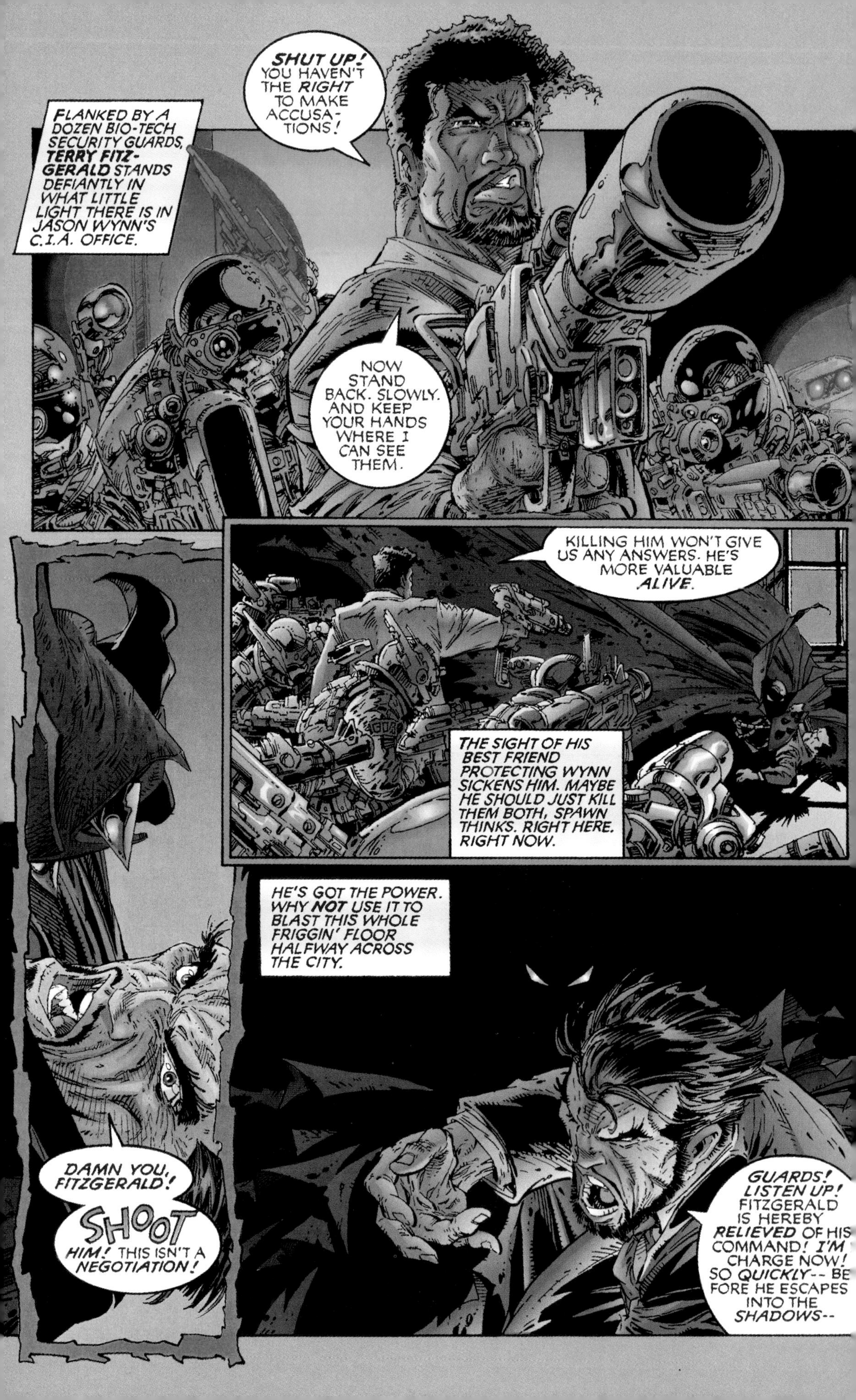
FLANKED BY A DOZEN BIO-TECH SECURITY GUARDS, TERRY FITZ-GERALD STANDS DEFIANTLY IN WHAT LITTLE LIGHT THERE IS IN JASON WYNN'S C.I.A. OFFICE.
SHUT UP! YOU HAVEN'T THE RIGHT TO MAKE ACCUSA-TIONS!
NOW STAND BACK. SLOWLY. AND KEEP YOUR HANDS WHERE I CAN SEE THEM.
KILLING HIM WON'T GIVE US ANY ANSWERS. HE'S MORE VALUABLE ALIVE.
THE SIGHT OF HIS BEST FRIEND PROTECTING WYNN SICKENS HIM. MAYBE HE SHOULD JUST KILL THEM BOTH, SPAWN THINKS. RIGHT HERE. RIGHT NOW.
HE'S GOT THE POWER. WHY NOT USE IT TO BLAST THIS WHOLE FRIGGIN' FLOOR HALFWAY ACROSS THE CITY.
DAMN YOU, FITZGERALD!
SHOOT HIM! THIS ISN'T A NEGOTIATION!
GUARDS! LISTEN UP! FITZGERALD IS HEREBY RELIEVED OF HIS COMMAND! I'M CHARGE NOW! SO QUICKLY-- BE FORE HE ESCAPES INTO THE SHADOWS--

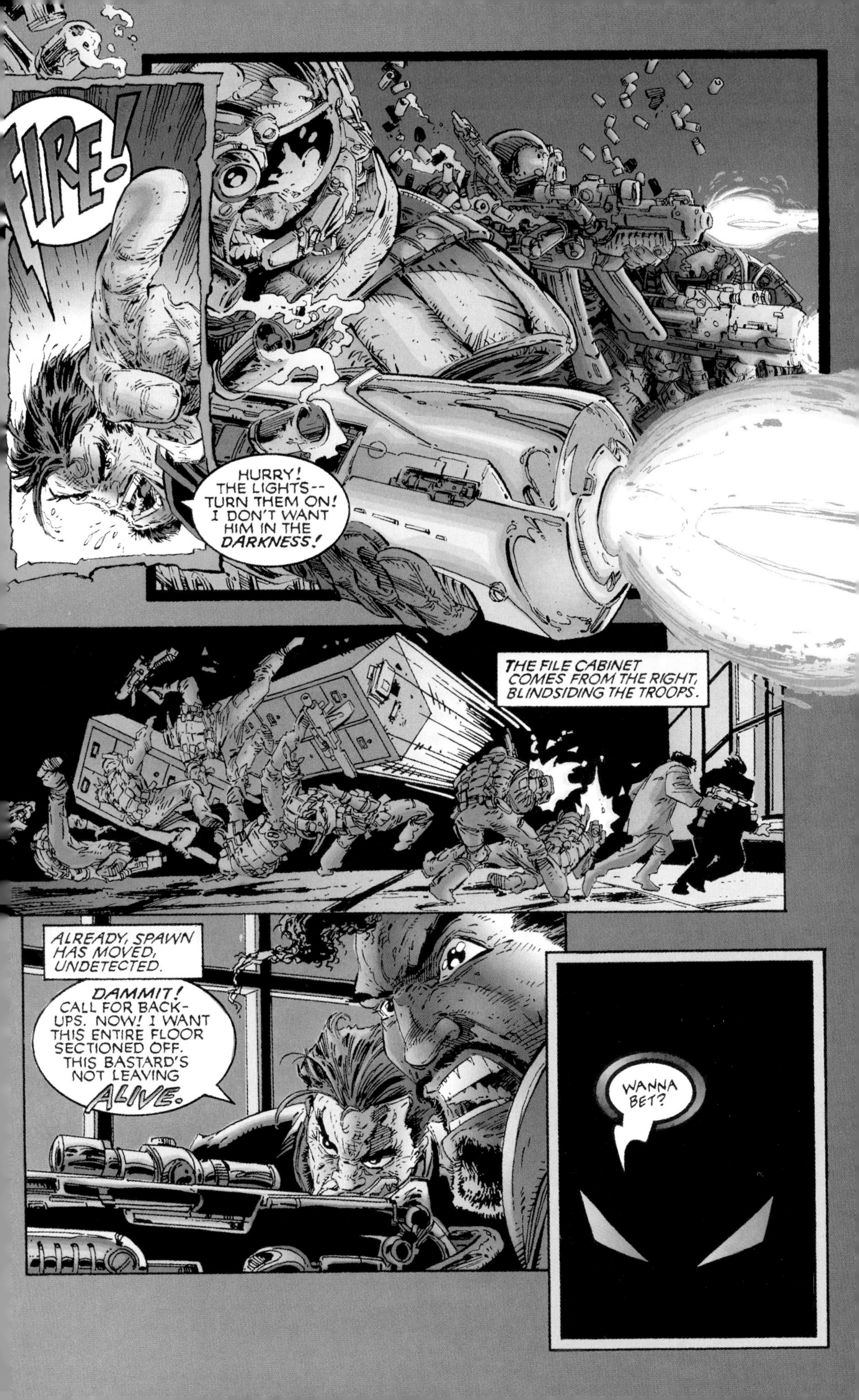
FIRE!
HURRY! THE LIGHTS-- TURN THEM ON! I DON'T WANT HIM IN THE DARKNESS!
THE FILE CABINET COMES FROM THE RIGHT, BLINDSIDING THE TROOPS.
ALREADY, SPAWN HAS MOVED, UNDETECTED.
DAMMIT! CALL FOR BACK-UPS. NOW! I WANT THIS ENTIRE FLOOR SECTIONED OFF. THIS BASTARD'S NOT LEAVING ALIVE.
WANNA BET?

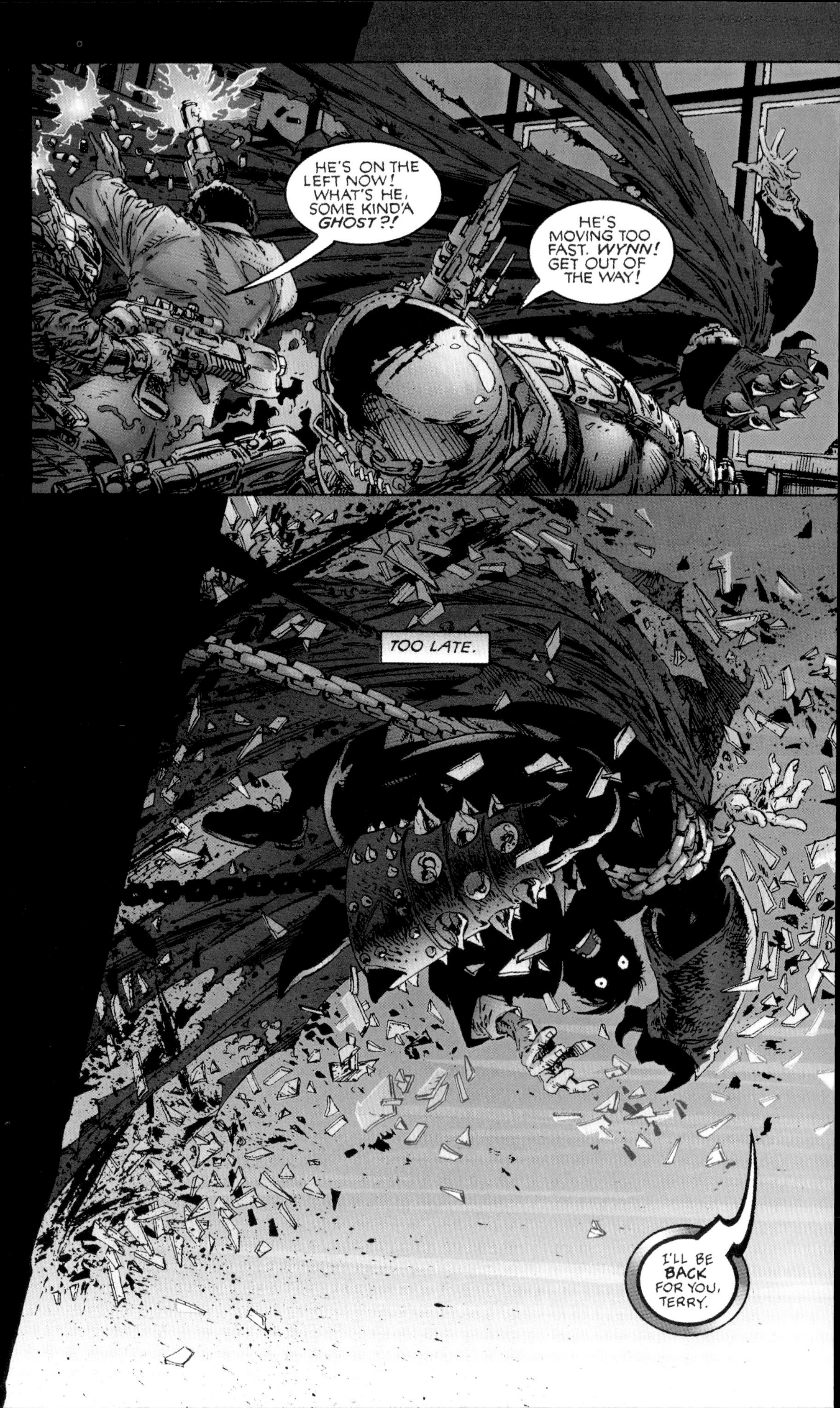

HE'S ON THE LEFT NOW! WHAT'S HE, SOME KIND'A GHOST?!
HE'S MOVING TOO FAST. WYNN! GET OUT OF THE WAY!
TOO LATE.
I'LL BE BACK FOR YOU, TERRY.

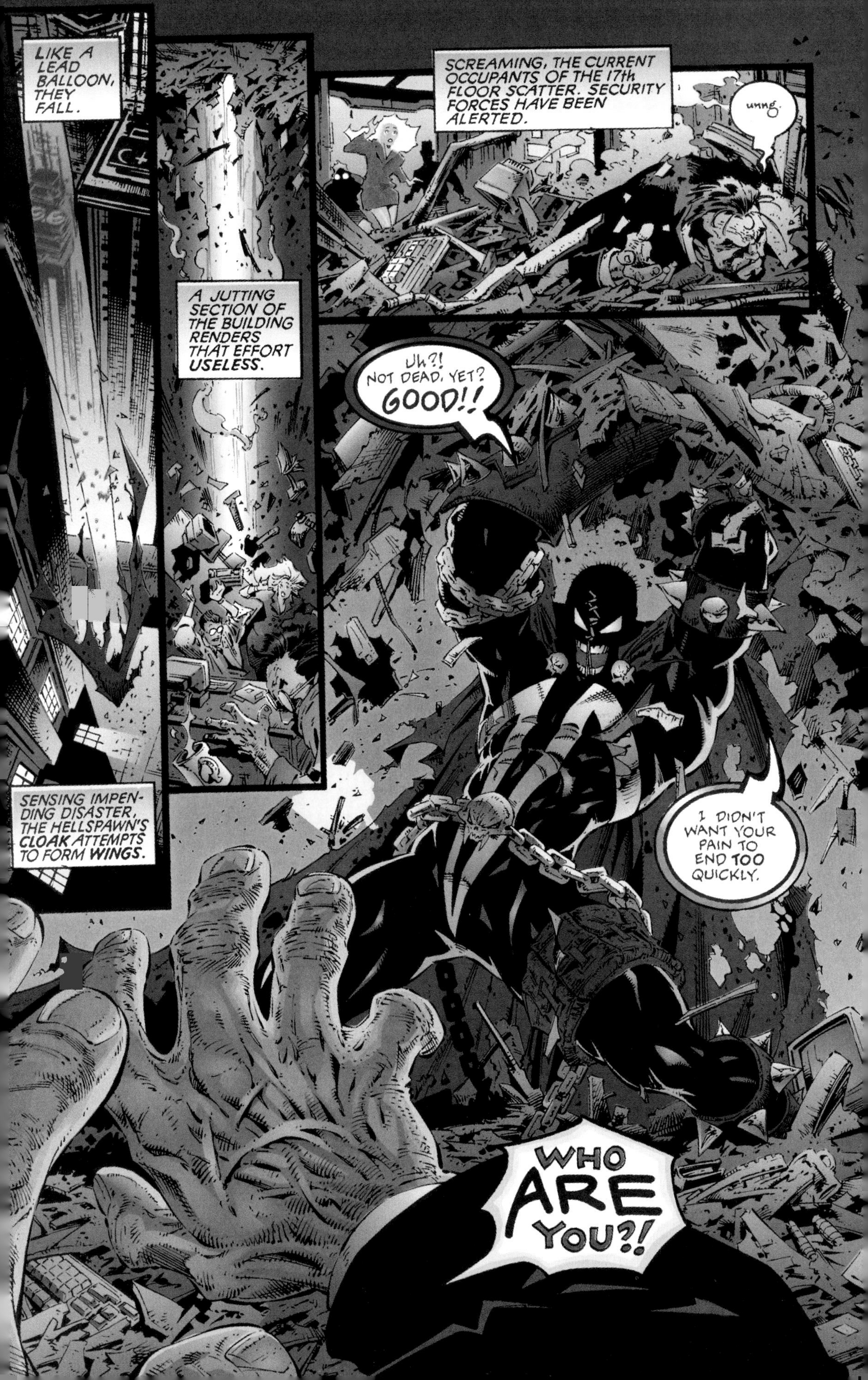
LIKE A LEAD BALLOON, THEY FALL.
A JUTTING SECTION OF THE BUILDING RENDERS THAT EFFORT USELESS.
SCREAMING, THE CURRENT OCCUPANTS OF THE 17th FLOOR SCATTER. SECURITY FORCES HAVE BEEN ALERTED.
unng.
SENSING IMPENDING DISASTER, THE HELLSPAWN'S CLOAK ATTEMPTS TO FORM WINGS.
Uh?! NOT DEAD, YET? GOOD!!
I DIDN'T WANT YOUR PAIN TO END TOO QUICKLY.
WHO ARE YOU?!

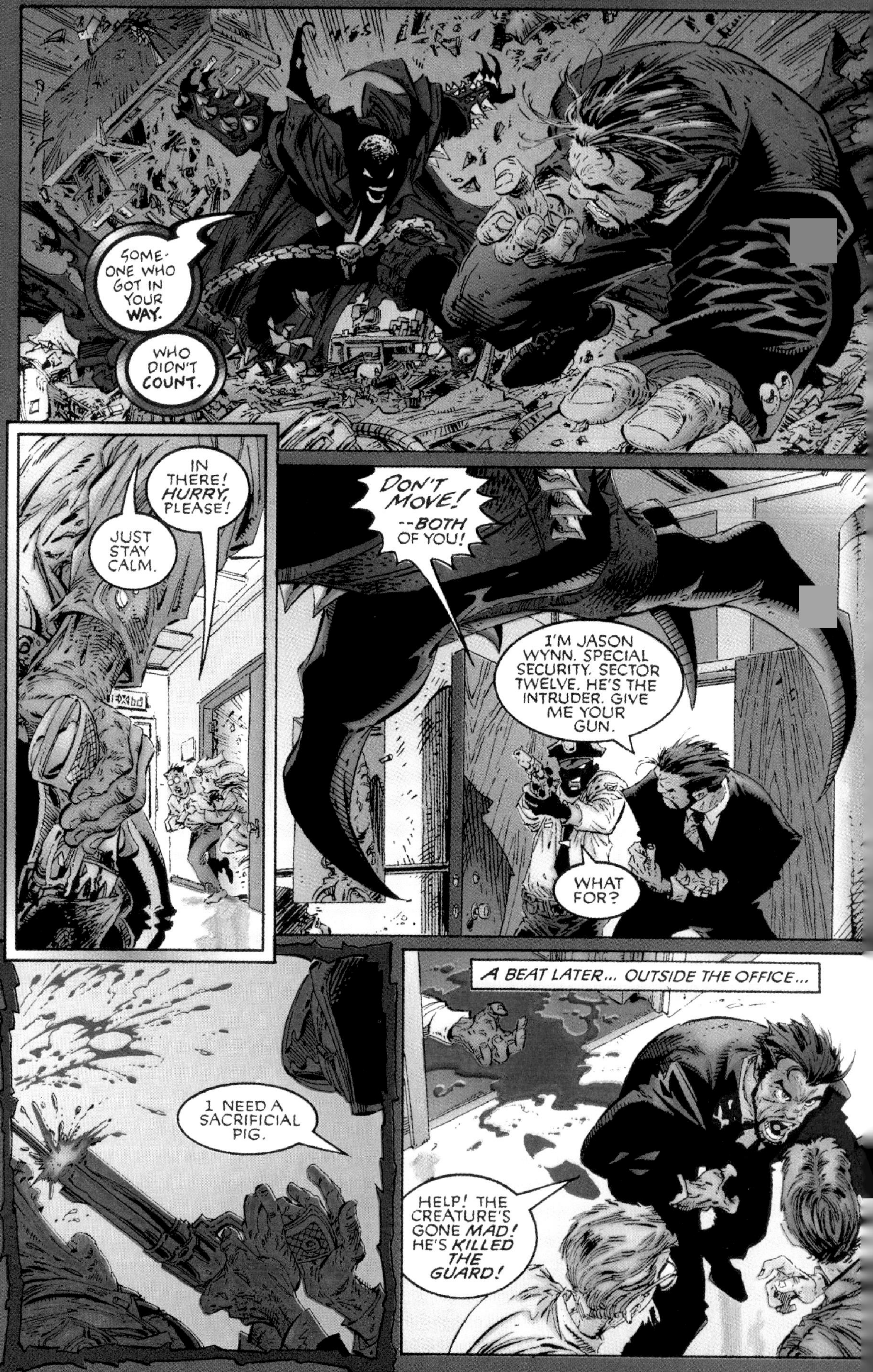
SOME-ONE WHO GOT IN YOUR WAY.
WHO DIDN'T COUNT.
IN THERE! HURRY, PLEASE!
JUST STAY CALM.
DON'T MOVE! --BOTH OF YOU!
I'M JASON WYNN. SPECIAL SECURITY. SECTOR TWELVE. HE'S THE INTRUDER. GIVE ME YOUR GUN.
WHAT FOR?
I NEED A SACRIFICIAL PIG.
A BEAT LATER... OUTSIDE THE OFFICE...
HELP! THE CREATURE'S GONE MAD! HE'S KILLED THE GUARD!

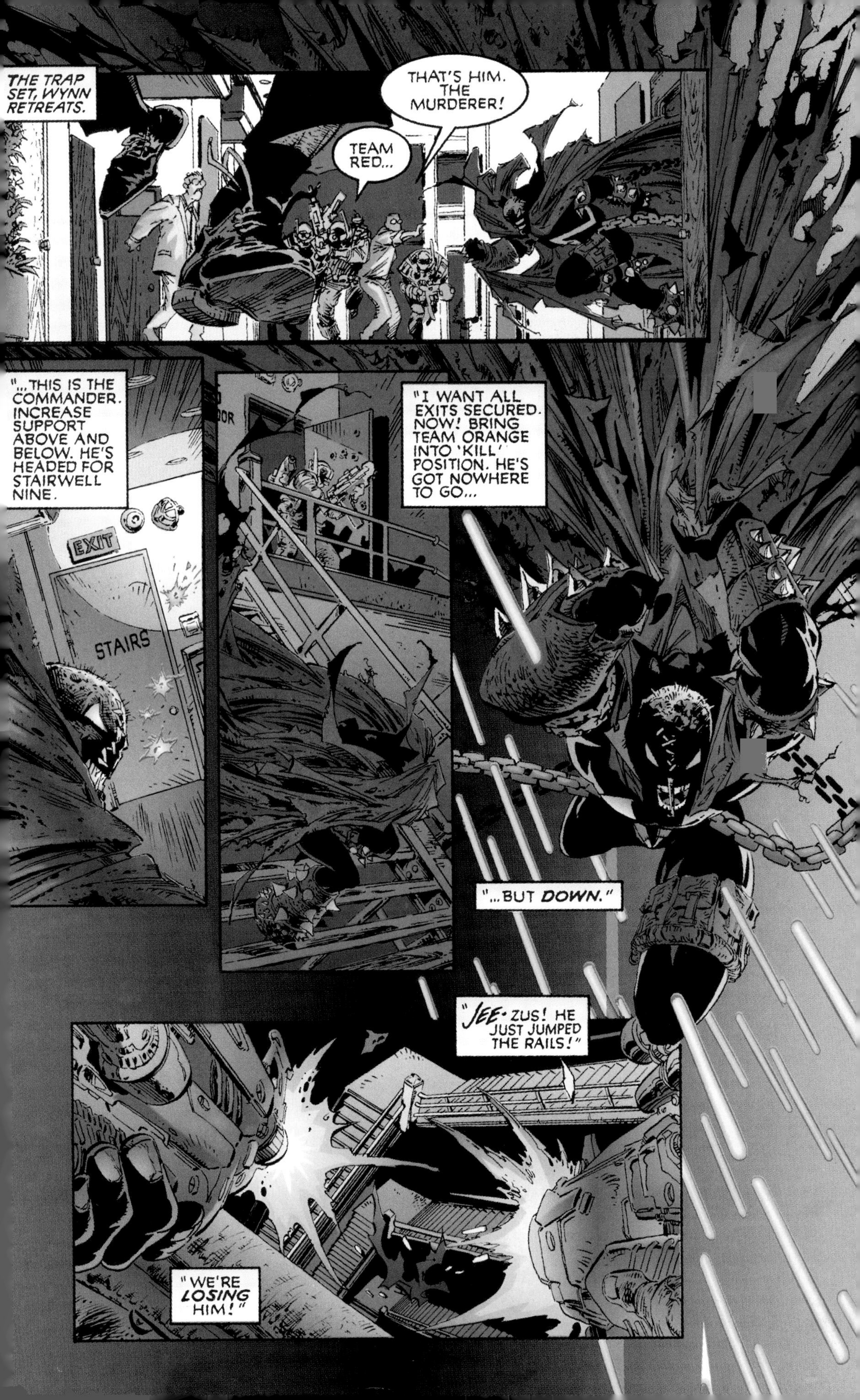
THE TRAP SET, WYNN RETREATS.
THAT'S HIM. THE MURDERER!
TEAM RED...
"...THIS IS THE COMMANDER. INCREASE SUPPORT ABOVE AND BELOW. HE'S HEADED FOR STAIRWELL NINE.
EXIT
STAIRS
"I WANT ALL EXITS SECURED. NOW! BRING TEAM ORANGE INTO 'KILL' POSITION. HE'S GOT NOWHERE TO GO...
"...BUT DOWN."
"JEE-ZUS! HE JUST JUMPED THE RAILS!"
"WE'RE LOSING HIM!"

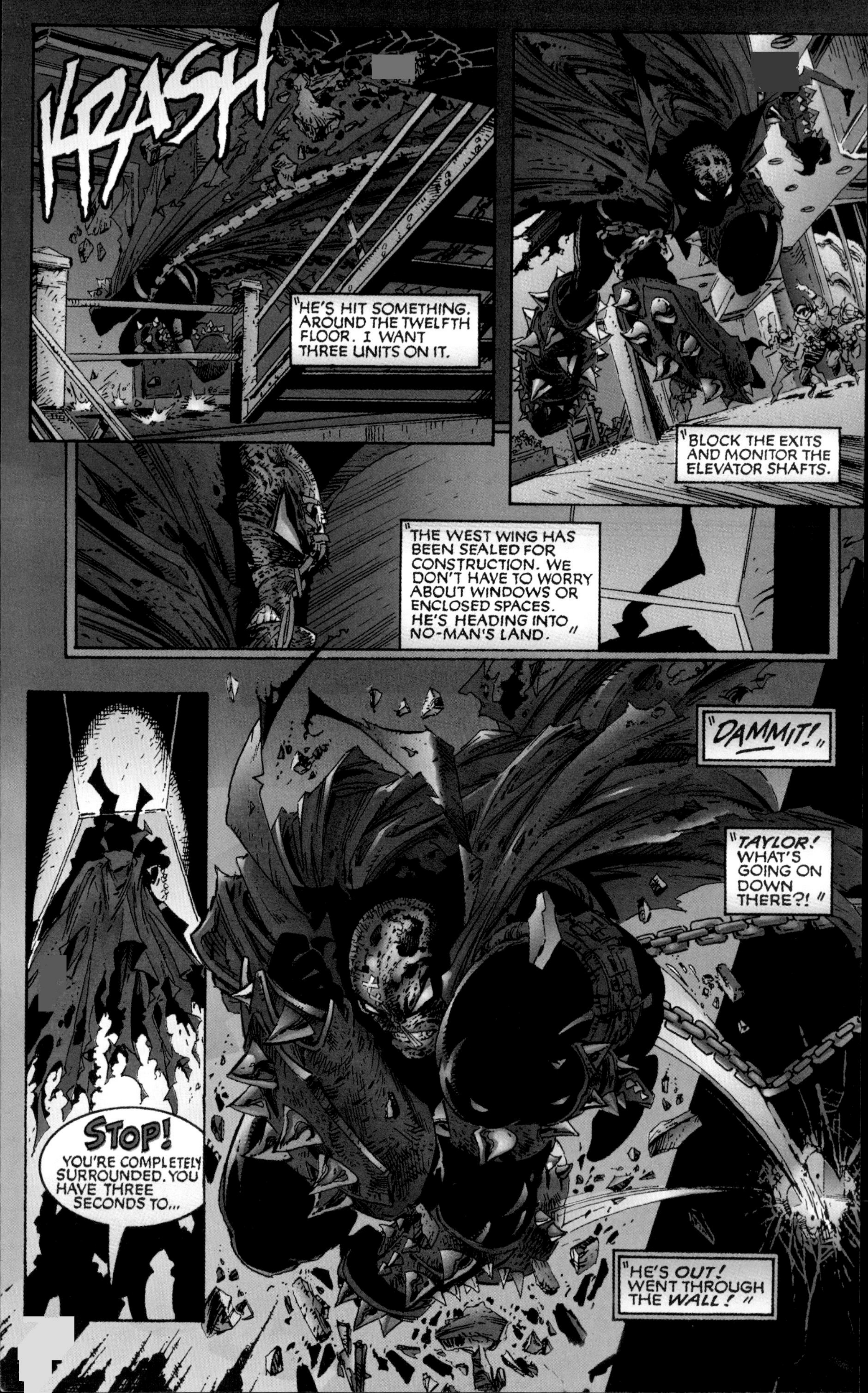
KRASH
"HE'S HIT SOMETHING. AROUND THE TWELFTH FLOOR. I WANT THREE UNITS ON IT.
"BLOCK THE EXITS AND MONITOR THE ELEVATOR SHAFTS.
"THE WEST WING HAS BEEN SEALED FOR CONSTRUCTION. WE DON'T HAVE TO WORRY ABOUT WINDOWS OR ENCLOSED SPACES. HE'S HEADING INTO NO-MAN'S LAND."
STOP! YOU'RE COMPLETELY SURROUNDED. YOU HAVE THREE SECONDS TO...
"DAMMIT!"
"TAYLOR! WHAT'S GOING ON DOWN THERE?!"
"HE'S OUT! WENT THROUGH THE WALL!"

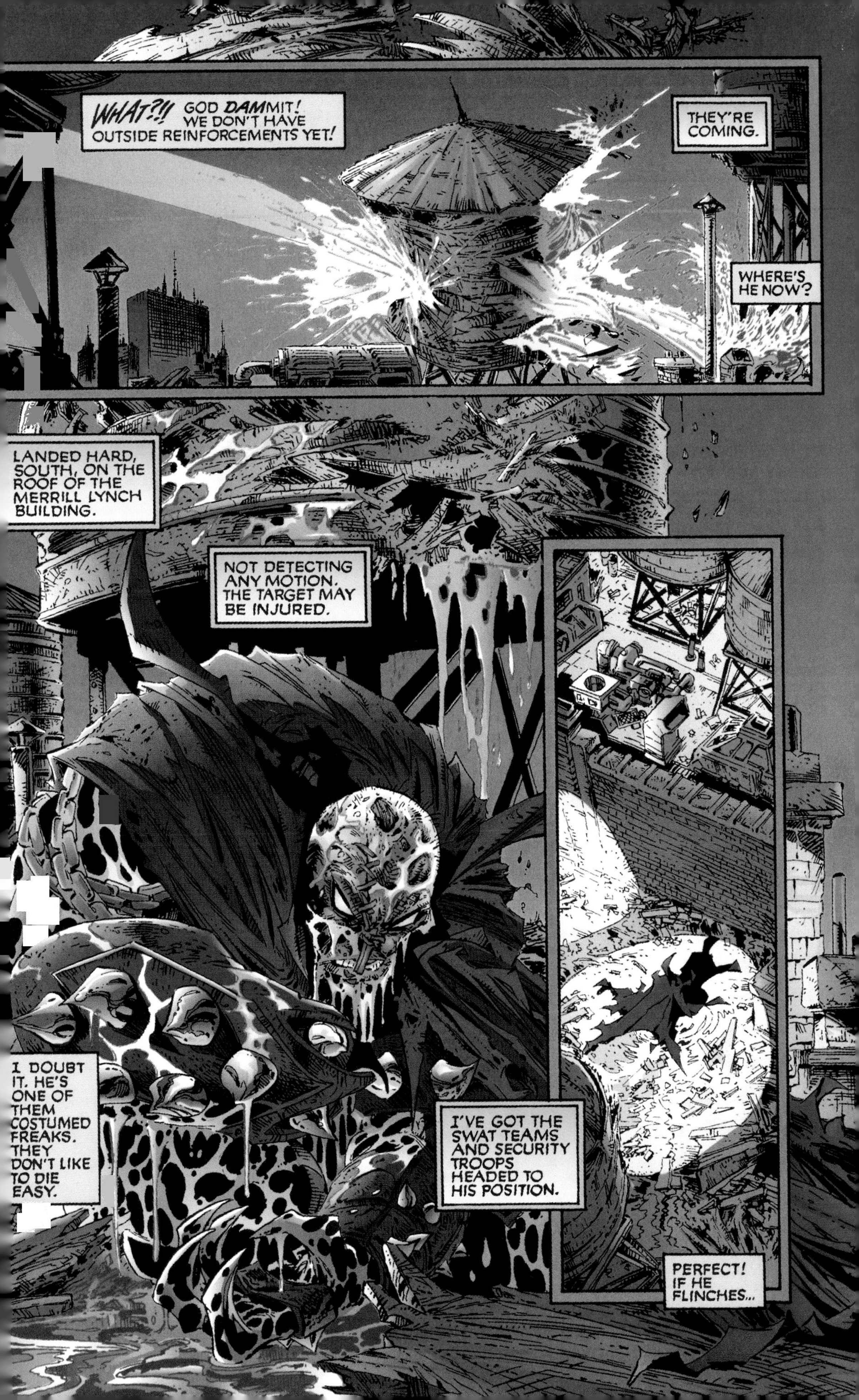

WHAT?!! GOD DAMMIT! WE DON'T HAVE OUTSIDE REINFORCEMENTS YET!
THEY'RE COMING.
WHERE'S HE NOW?
LANDED HARD, SOUTH, ON THE ROOF OF THE MERRILL LYNCH BUILDING.
NOT DETECTING ANY MOTION. THE TARGET MAY BE INJURED.
I DOUBT IT. HE'S ONE OF THEM COSTUMED FREAKS. THEY DON'T LIKE TO DIE EASY.
I'VE GOT THE SWAT TEAMS AND SECURITY TROOPS HEADED TO HIS POSITION.
PERFECT! IF HE FLINCHES...

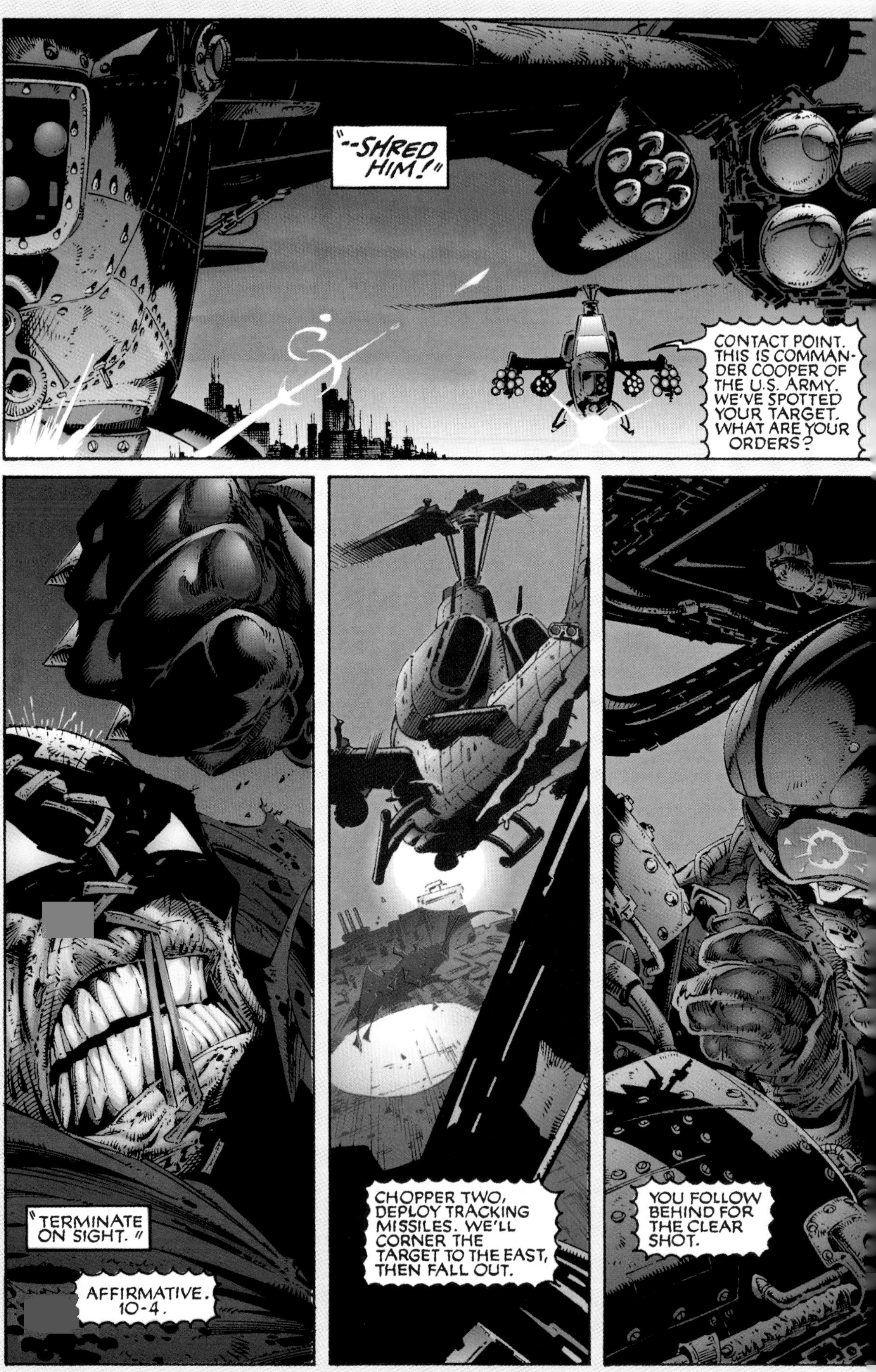
"--SHRED HIM!"
CONTACT POINT. THIS IS COMMANDER COOPER OF THE U.S. ARMY. WE'VE SPOTTED YOUR TARGET. WHAT ARE YOUR ORDERS?
"TERMINATE ON SIGHT."
AFFIRMATIVE. 10-4.
CHOPPER TWO, DEPLOY TRACKING MISSILES. WE'LL CORNER THE TARGET TO THE EAST, THEN FALL OUT.
YOU FOLLOW BEHIND FOR THE CLEAR SHOT.

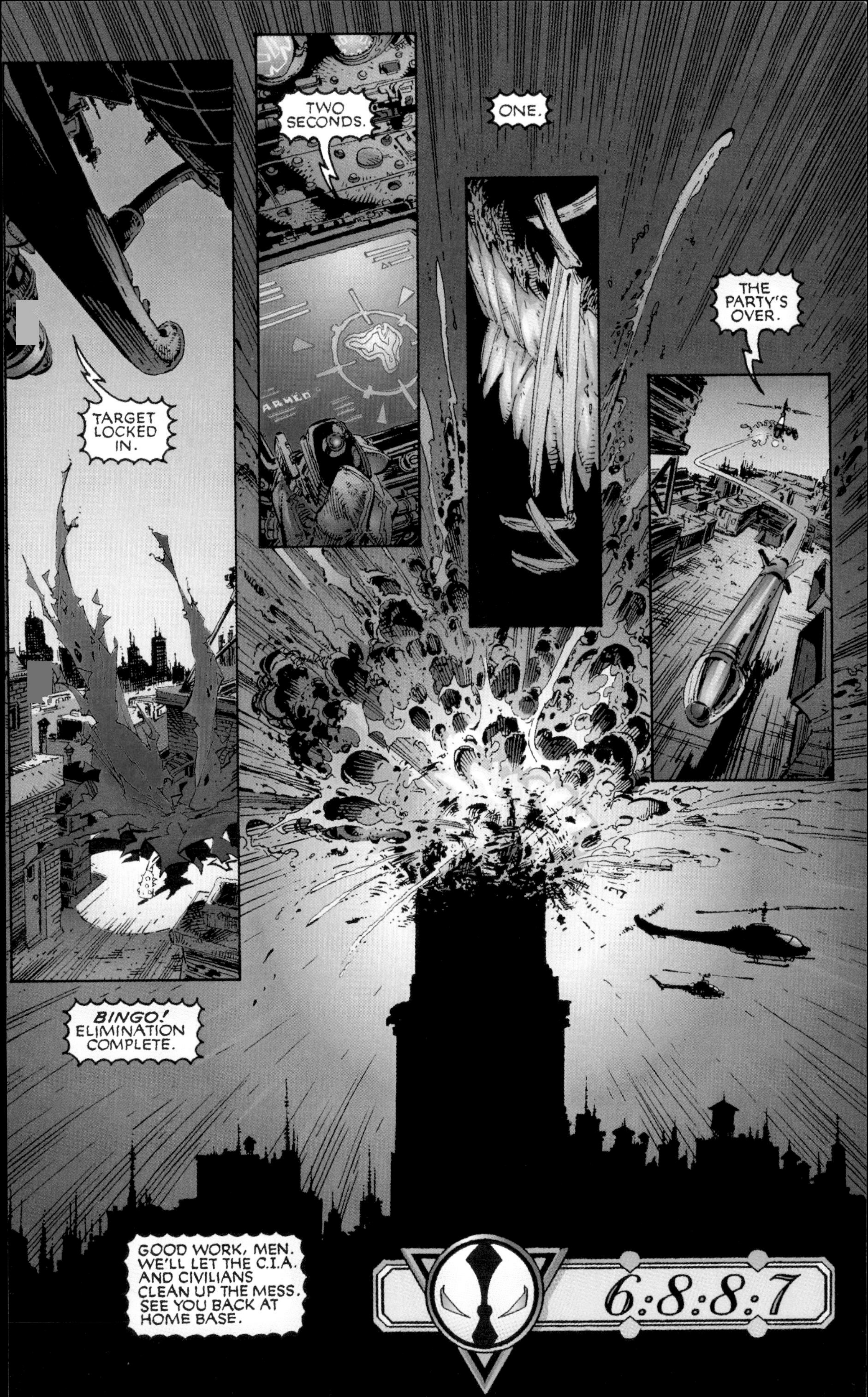
TARGET LOCKED IN.
TWO SECONDS.
ARMED
ONE.
THE PARTY'S OVER.
BINGO! ELIMINATION COMPLETE.
GOOD WORK, MEN. WE'LL LET THE C.I.A. AND CIVILIANS CLEAN UP THE MESS. SEE YOU BACK AT HOME BASE.
6:8:8:7

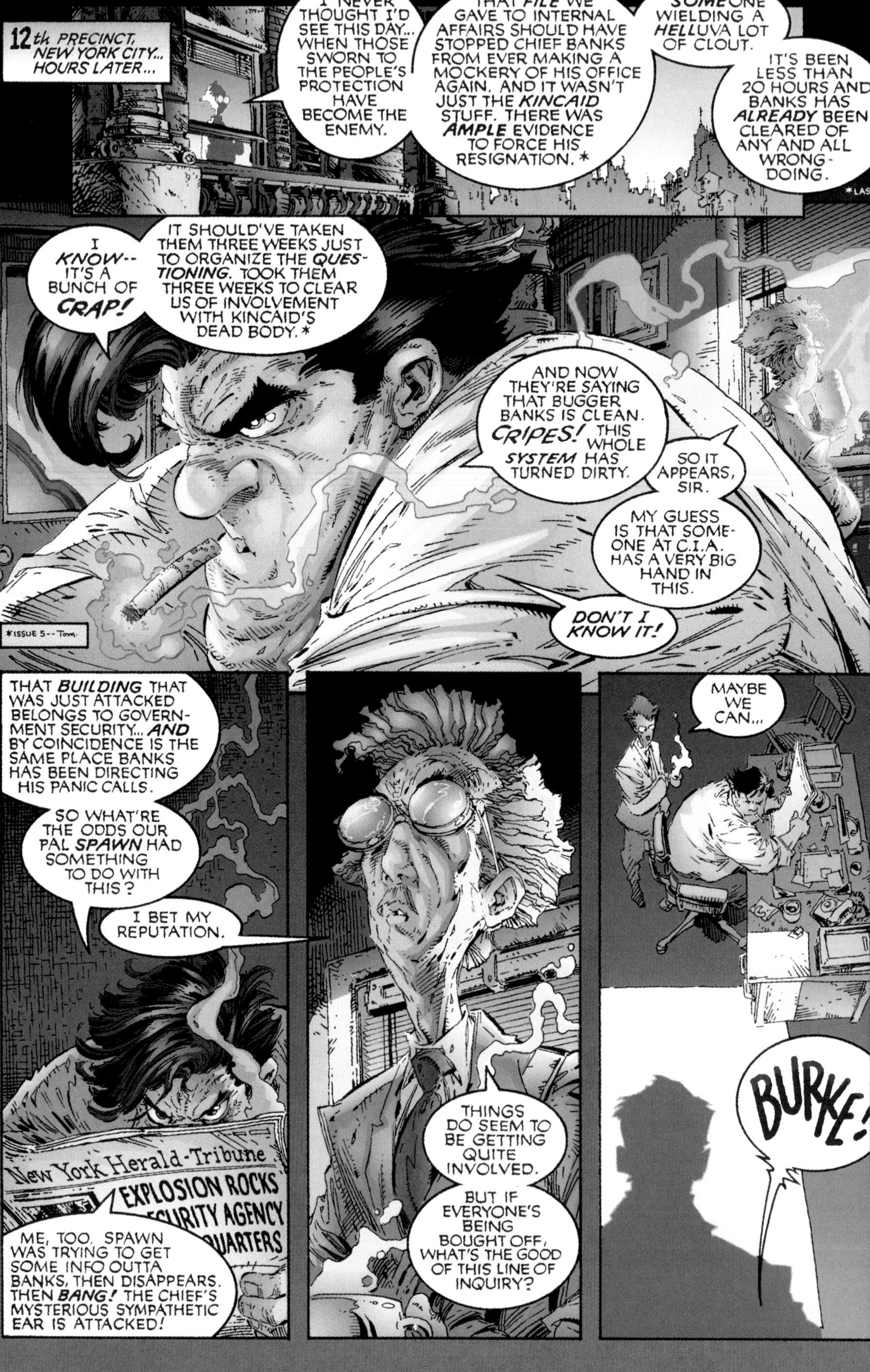
12th PRECINCT, NEW YORK CITY... HOURS LATER...
I NEVER THOUGHT I'D SEE THIS DAY... WHEN THOSE SWORN TO THE PEOPLE'S PROTECTION HAVE BECOME THE ENEMY.
THAT FILE WE GAVE TO INTERNAL AFFAIRS SHOULD HAVE STOPPED CHIEF BANKS FROM EVER MAKING A MOCKERY OF HIS OFFICE AGAIN. AND IT WASN'T JUST THE KINCAID STUFF. THERE WAS AMPLE EVIDENCE TO FORCE HIS RESIGNATION. *
SOMEONE WIELDING A HELLUVA LOT OF CLOUT.
IT'S BEEN LESS THAN 20 HOURS AND BANKS HAS ALREADY BEEN CLEARED OF ANY AND ALL WRONG-DOING.
I KNOW-- IT'S A BUNCH OF CRAP!
IT SHOULD'VE TAKEN THEM THREE WEEKS JUST TO ORGANIZE THE QUESTIONING. TOOK THEM THREE WEEKS TO CLEAR US OF INVOLVEMENT WITH KINCAID'S DEAD BODY. *
AND NOW THEY'RE SAYING THAT BUGGER BANKS IS CLEAN. CRIPES! THIS WHOLE SYSTEM HAS TURNED DIRTY.
SO IT APPEARS, SIR.
MY GUESS IS THAT SOMEONE AT C.I.A. HAS A VERY BIG HAND IN THIS.
DON'T I KNOW IT!
*ISSUE 5--Tom.
THAT BUILDING THAT WAS JUST ATTACKED BELONGS TO GOVERNMENT SECURITY... AND BY COINCIDENCE IS THE SAME PLACE BANKS HAS BEEN DIRECTING HIS PANIC CALLS.
SO WHAT'RE THE ODDS OUR PAL SPAWN HAD SOMETHING TO DO WITH THIS?
I BET MY REPUTATION.
New York Herald-Tribune
EXPLOSION ROCKS
ME, TOO. SPAWN WAS TRYING TO GET SOME INFO OUTTA BANKS, THEN DISAPPEARS. THEN BANG! THE CHIEF'S MYSTERIOUS SYMPATHETIC EAR IS ATTACKED!
THINGS DO SEEM TO BE GETTING QUITE INVOLVED.
BUT IF EVERYONE'S BEING BOUGHT OFF, WHAT'S THE GOOD OF THIS LINE OF INQUIRY?
MAYBE WE CAN...
BURKE!

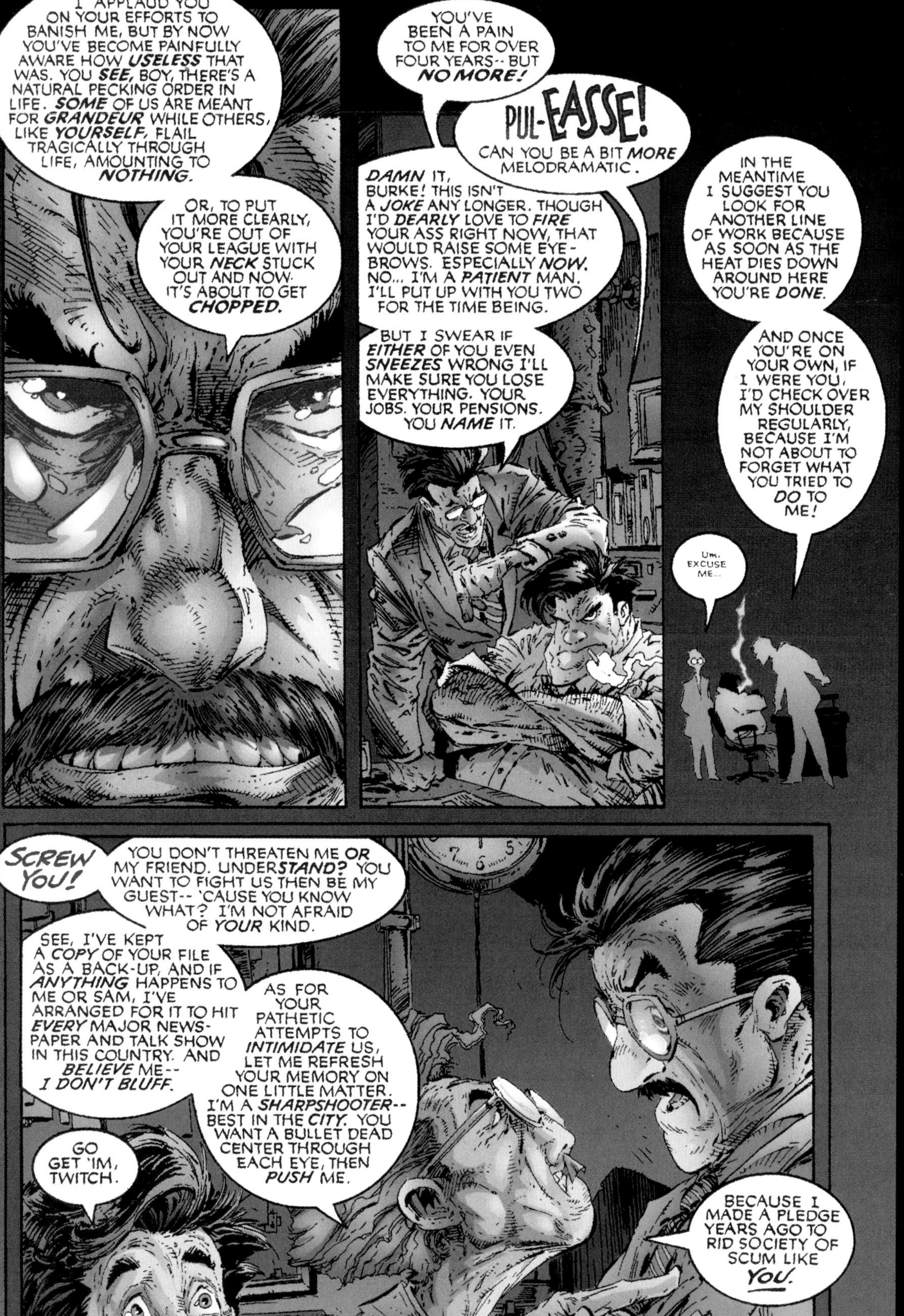
I APPLAUD YOU ON YOUR EFFORTS TO BANISH ME, BUT BY NOW YOU'VE BECOME PAINFULLY AWARE HOW USELESS THAT WAS. YOU SEE, BOY, THERE'S A NATURAL PECKING ORDER IN LIFE. SOME OF US ARE MEANT FOR GRANDEUR WHILE OTHERS, LIKE YOURSELF, FLAIL TRAGICALLY THROUGH LIFE, AMOUNTING TO NOTHING.
OR, TO PUT IT MORE CLEARLY, YOU'RE OUT OF YOUR LEAGUE WITH YOUR NECK STUCK OUT AND NOW IT'S ABOUT TO GET CHOPPED.
YOU'VE BEEN A PAIN TO ME FOR OVER FOUR YEARS-- BUT NO MORE!
PUL-EASSE!
CAN YOU BE A BIT MORE MELODRAMATIC.
DAMN IT, BURKE! THIS ISN'T A JOKE ANY LONGER. THOUGH I'D DEARLY LOVE TO FIRE YOUR ASS RIGHT NOW, THAT WOULD RAISE SOME EYE-BROWS. ESPECIALLY NOW. NO... I'M A PATIENT MAN. I'LL PUT UP WITH YOU TWO FOR THE TIME BEING.
BUT I SWEAR IF EITHER OF YOU EVEN SNEEZES WRONG I'LL MAKE SURE YOU LOSE EVERYTHING. YOUR JOBS. YOUR PENSIONS. YOU NAME IT.
IN THE MEANTIME I SUGGEST YOU LOOK FOR ANOTHER LINE OF WORK BECAUSE AS SOON AS THE HEAT DIES DOWN AROUND HERE YOU'RE DONE.
AND ONCE YOU'RE ON YOUR OWN, IF I WERE YOU, I'D CHECK OVER MY SHOULDER REGULARLY, BECAUSE I'M NOT ABOUT TO FORGET WHAT YOU TRIED TO DO TO ME!
Um, EXCUSE ME...
SCREW YOU!
YOU DON'T THREATEN ME OR MY FRIEND. UNDERSTAND? YOU WANT TO FIGHT US THEN BE MY GUEST-- 'CAUSE YOU KNOW WHAT? I'M NOT AFRAID OF YOUR KIND.
SEE, I'VE KEPT A COPY OF YOUR FILE AS A BACK-UP, AND IF ANYTHING HAPPENS TO ME OR SAM, I'VE ARRANGED FOR IT TO HIT EVERY MAJOR NEWS-PAPER AND TALK SHOW IN THIS COUNTRY. AND BELIEVE ME-- I DON'T BLUFF.
AS FOR YOUR PATHETIC ATTEMPTS TO INTIMIDATE US, LET ME REFRESH YOUR MEMORY ON ONE LITTLE MATTER. I'M A SHARPSHOOTER-- BEST IN THE CITY. YOU WANT A BULLET DEAD CENTER THROUGH EACH EYE, THEN PUSH ME.
GO GET 'IM, TWITCH.
BECAUSE I MADE A PLEDGE YEARS AGO TO RID SOCIETY OF SCUM LIKE YOU.

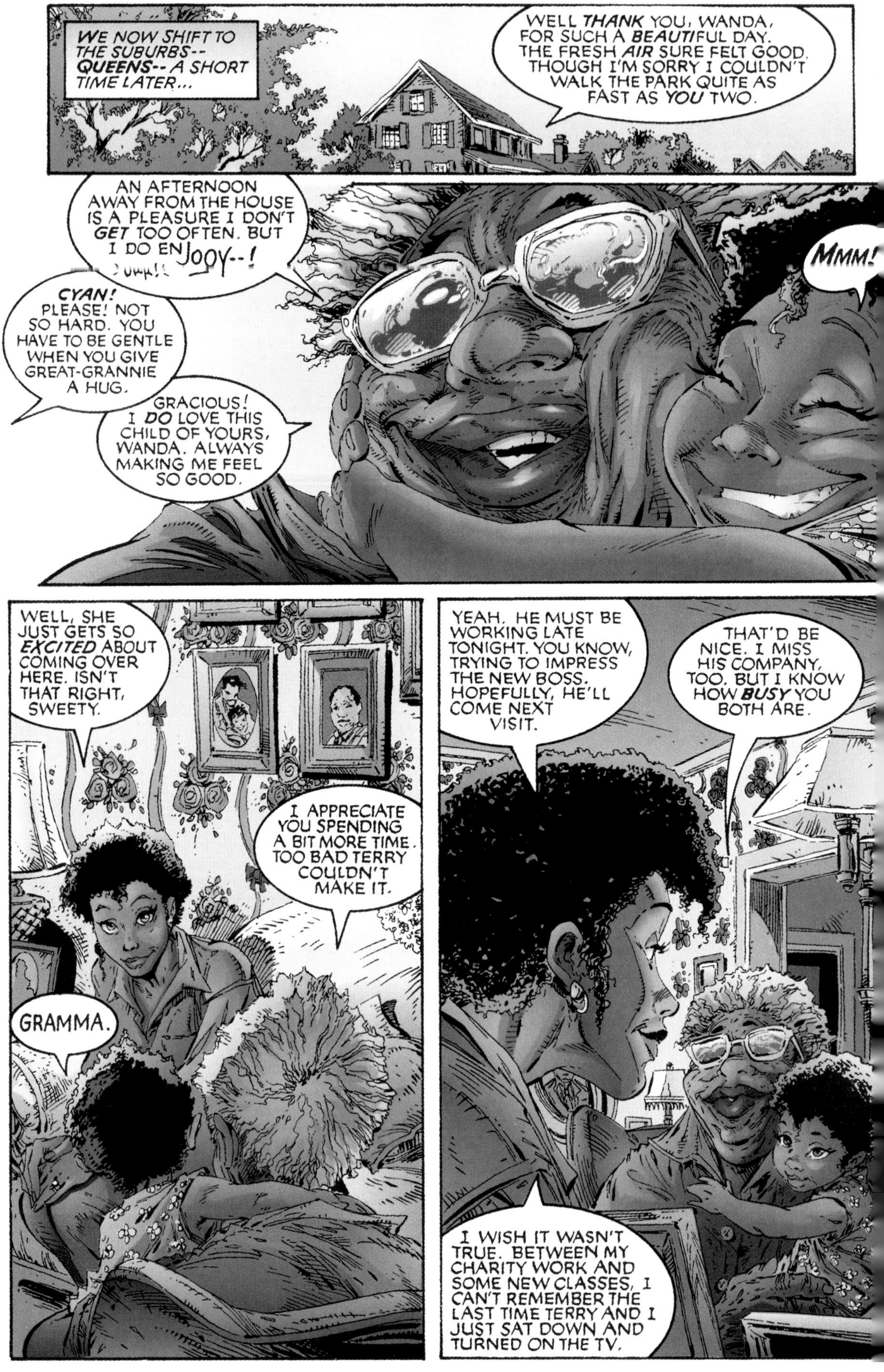
WE NOW SHIFT TO THE SUBURBS-- QUEENS-- A SHORT TIME LATER...
WELL THANK YOU, WANDA, FOR SUCH A BEAUTIFUL DAY. THE FRESH AIR SURE FELT GOOD. THOUGH I'M SORRY I COULDN'T WALK THE PARK QUITE AS FAST AS YOU TWO.
AN AFTERNOON AWAY FROM THE HOUSE IS A PLEASURE I DON'T GET TOO OFTEN. BUT I DO ENJOOY--!
MMM!
CYAN! PLEASE! NOT SO HARD. YOU HAVE TO BE GENTLE WHEN YOU GIVE GREAT-GRANNIE A HUG.
GRACIOUS! I DO LOVE THIS CHILD OF YOURS, WANDA. ALWAYS MAKING ME FEEL SO GOOD.
WELL, SHE JUST GETS SO EXCITED ABOUT COMING OVER HERE. ISN'T THAT RIGHT, SWEETY.
I APPRECIATE YOU SPENDING A BIT MORE TIME. TOO BAD TERRY COULDN'T MAKE IT.
GRAMMA.
YEAH. HE MUST BE WORKING LATE TONIGHT. YOU KNOW, TRYING TO IMPRESS THE NEW BOSS. HOPEFULLY, HE'LL COME NEXT VISIT.
THAT'D BE NICE. I MISS HIS COMPANY, TOO. BUT I KNOW HOW BUSY YOU BOTH ARE.
I WISH IT WASN'T TRUE. BETWEEN MY CHARITY WORK AND SOME NEW CLASSES, I CAN'T REMEMBER THE LAST TIME TERRY AND I JUST SAT DOWN AND TURNED ON THE TV.

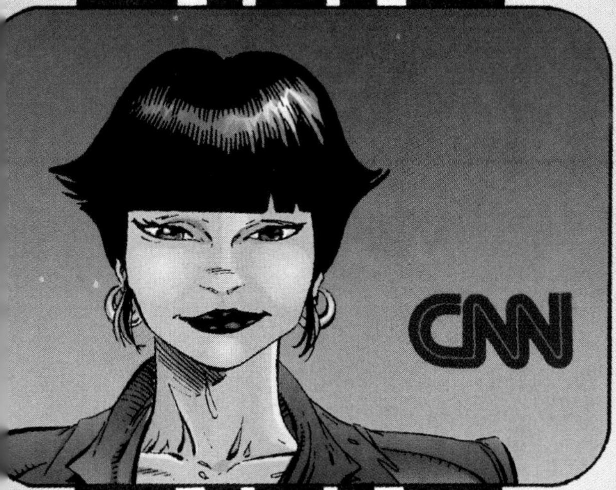
CNN

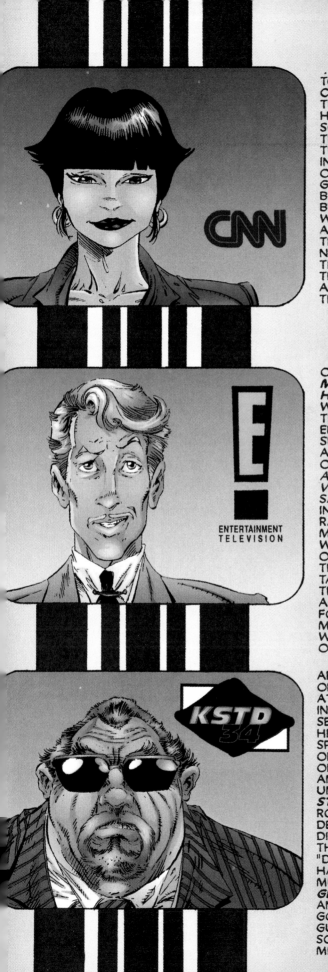

...CONTINUE OUR LIVE COVERAGE OF TONIGHT'S BOMBING AT NEW YORK CITY'S MERRILL LYNCH BUILDING, AND THE REPORTED ASSAULT ON THE C.I.A HEADQUARTERS NEXT DOOR. POLICE SOURCES ARE CAUTIOUSLY OPTIMISTIC THAT NO ONE DIED IN THIS ATTACK ON THE NATION'S LARGEST BROKERAGE INSTITUTION. THE UPPER TWO STORIES OF THIS BUILDING, WHICH HOUSE THE GYM AND CAFETERIA, HAD ALREADY BEEN SECURED FOR THE NIGHT. IT IS BELIEVED THAT NO EMPLOYEES WERE WORKING LATE IN ANY OTHER AREAS, AND MOST HAVE BEEN LOCATED AT THEIR HOMES. THE WHITE HOUSE DENIES REPORTS THAT AN AS-YET UNIDENTIFIED TERRORIST GROUP HAD STAGED THE EVENT AS A REJECTION OF THE ADMINSTRATION'S PEACE NEGOTIATIONS IN THE MIDDLE EAST.

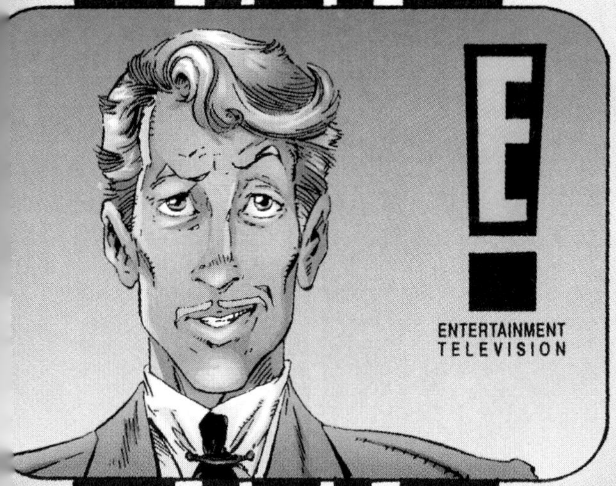
E!
ENTERTAINMENT TELEVISION

OFF THE RECORD SPECULATION FROM ***MY*** ANONYMOUS SOURCES IS THAT A ***HOME-GROWN*** TERRORIST GROUP WAS BLOWING A LOUD RASPBERY AT THE PRESIDENT'S MIDDLE EAST PEACE EFFORT. AT THE SAME TIME, FRENZIED SPIN DOCTORS ARE QUICK TO DISPEL ANY ***HINT*** OF A CONNECTION TO THE OKLAHOMA CITY INCIDENT. ***"JUST THE ACTIONS OF ANOTHER DERANGED INDIVIDUAL"***, THEY TELL US, WHICH IS TO SAY, NOBODY HAS A ***CLUE***. CONFUSING MATTERS EVEN FURTHER IS THE RAPID INVOLVEMENT OF OUR NATION'S MILITARY FORCES. SOME EYEWITNESSES SAY IT WAS THE ***PRESENCE*** OF THE HELICOPTERS THAT TRIGGERED THE BOMBINGS, WHILE OTHERS MAINTAIN THE DAMAGE WAS DONE ***BEFORE*** THEIR ARRIVAL. IN EITHER CASE, EVERY AGENCY IN THE CITY IS NOW ON ALERT FOR POSSIBLE FOLLOW-UP ACTION. MEANWHILE, ALL EYES TURN TO THE WHITE HOUSE FOR SOMEONE -- ***ANYONE*** -- TO EXPLAIN IT ALL FOR US.

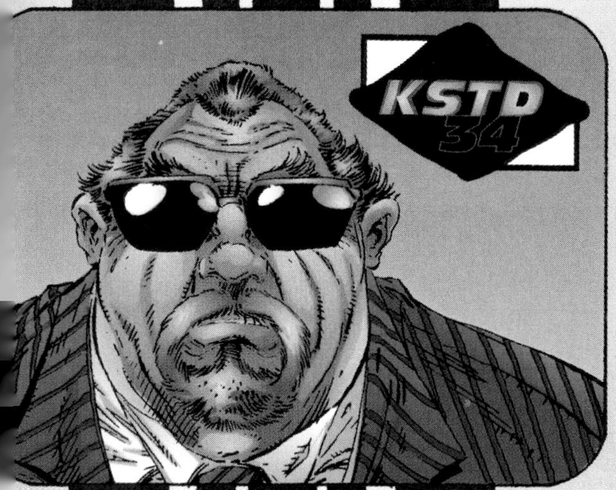
KSTD
34

ARE YOU ***KIDDING*** ME?! THIS ISN'T A CASE OF WHACKED-OUT IDIOTS LOOKING FOR ATTENTION, ***NO*** SIR! WHAT WE'RE LOOKING AT IS ***RETALIATION***. SOME GROUP IS SENDING A MESSAGE TO THOSE WHO HIDE IN THE SHADOWS, PLAYING DOPEY SPY GAMES WITH OUR TAX DOLLARS. NO ONE IS ADMITTING ANYTHING, BUT ANYONE WHO THINKS THE C.I.A. ATTACK AND THE MERRILL-LYNCH BOMBING ARE UNRELATED IS EITHER ***IGNORANT*** OR ***STUPID***. THIS WHOLE ***THING*** SMELLS ROTTEN. WORSE THAN THAT, THE PRESIDENT AND HIS AIDES ARE STONEWALLING. DIDN'T WE ELECT THESE GUYS BECAUSE THE ***PREVIOUS*** BUNCH WERE CLAIMING "DENIABILITY" TOO OFTEN?! SO NOW WE HAVE THE ***ARMY***, THE ***FINANCIAL*** COMMUNITY AND THE ***CENTRAL INTELLIGENCE*** BOYS RUNNING AROUND IN AN ANT FARM, BUT FOR A CHANGE WE'VE GOT A MAGNIFYING GLASS ON 'EM. I GUARANTEE THAT ***SOME***ONE'S HIDING SOMETHING, AND THIS TIME WE JUST MIGHT FIND OUT WHAT IT IS.

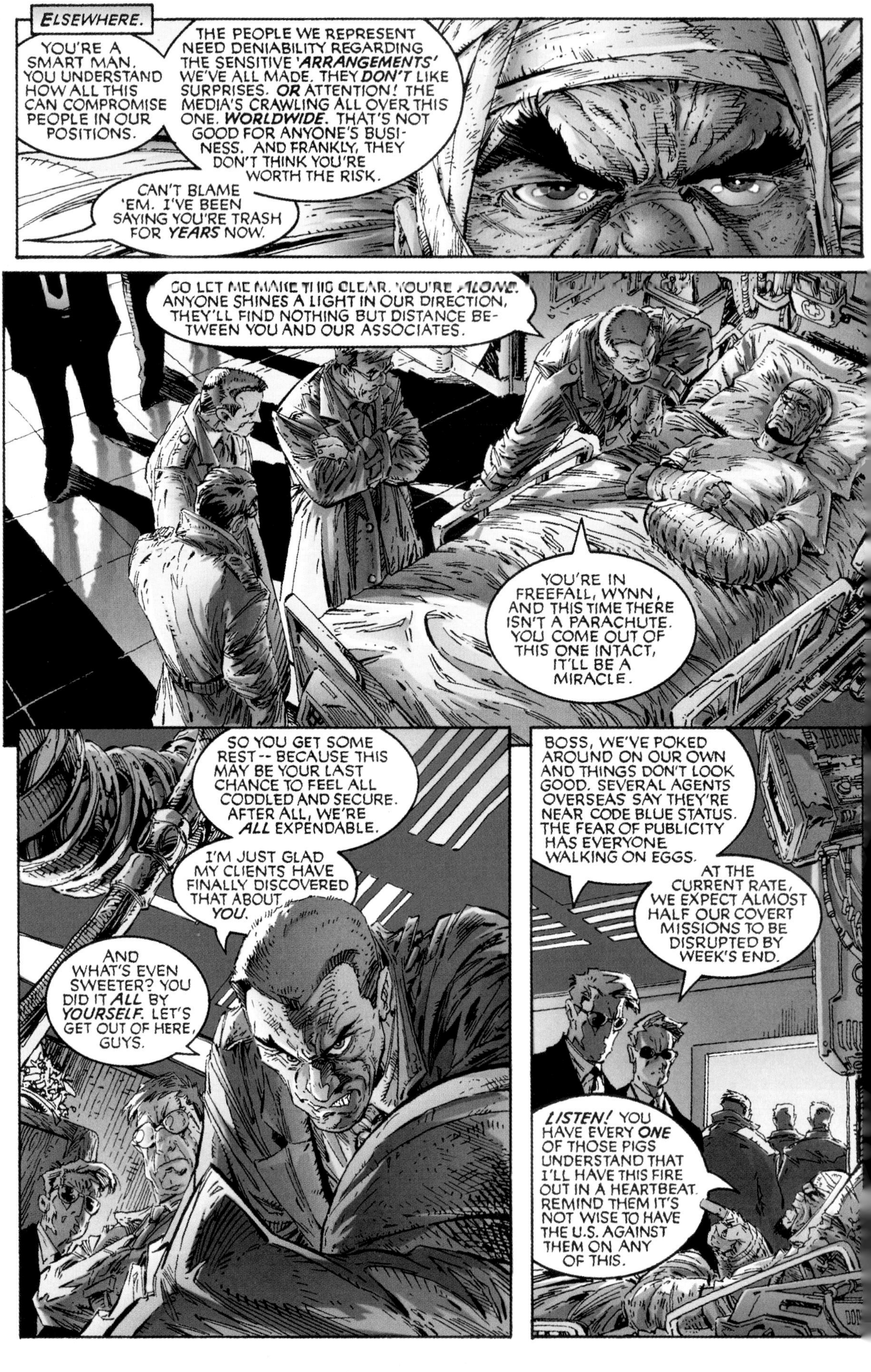
ELSEWHERE.
YOU'RE A SMART MAN. YOU UNDERSTAND HOW ALL THIS CAN COMPROMISE PEOPLE IN OUR POSITIONS.
THE PEOPLE WE REPRESENT NEED DENIABILITY REGARDING THE SENSITIVE 'ARRANGEMENTS' WE'VE ALL MADE. THEY DON'T LIKE SURPRISES. OR ATTENTION! THE MEDIA'S CRAWLING ALL OVER THIS ONE. WORLDWIDE. THAT'S NOT GOOD FOR ANYONE'S BUSI-NESS. AND FRANKLY, THEY DON'T THINK YOU'RE WORTH THE RISK.
CAN'T BLAME 'EM. I'VE BEEN SAYING YOU'RE TRASH FOR YEARS NOW.
SO LET ME MAKE THIS CLEAR. YOU'RE ALONE. ANYONE SHINES A LIGHT IN OUR DIRECTION, THEY'LL FIND NOTHING BUT DISTANCE BE-TWEEN YOU AND OUR ASSOCIATES.
YOU'RE IN FREEFALL, WYNN, AND THIS TIME THERE ISN'T A PARACHUTE. YOU COME OUT OF THIS ONE INTACT, IT'LL BE A MIRACLE.
SO YOU GET SOME REST -- BECAUSE THIS MAY BE YOUR LAST CHANCE TO FEEL ALL CODDLED AND SECURE. AFTER ALL, WE'RE ALL EXPENDABLE.
I'M JUST GLAD MY CLIENTS HAVE FINALLY DISCOVERED THAT ABOUT YOU.
AND WHAT'S EVEN SWEETER? YOU DID IT ALL BY YOURSELF. LET'S GET OUT OF HERE, GUYS.
BOSS, WE'VE POKED AROUND ON OUR OWN AND THINGS DON'T LOOK GOOD. SEVERAL AGENTS OVERSEAS SAY THEY'RE NEAR CODE BLUE STATUS. THE FEAR OF PUBLICITY HAS EVERYONE WALKING ON EGGS.
AT THE CURRENT RATE, WE EXPECT ALMOST HALF OUR COVERT MISSIONS TO BE DISRUPTED BY WEEK'S END.
LISTEN! YOU HAVE EVERY ONE OF THOSE PIGS UNDERSTAND THAT I'LL HAVE THIS FIRE OUT IN A HEARTBEAT. REMIND THEM IT'S NOT WISE TO HAVE THE U.S. AGAINST THEM ON ANY OF THIS.

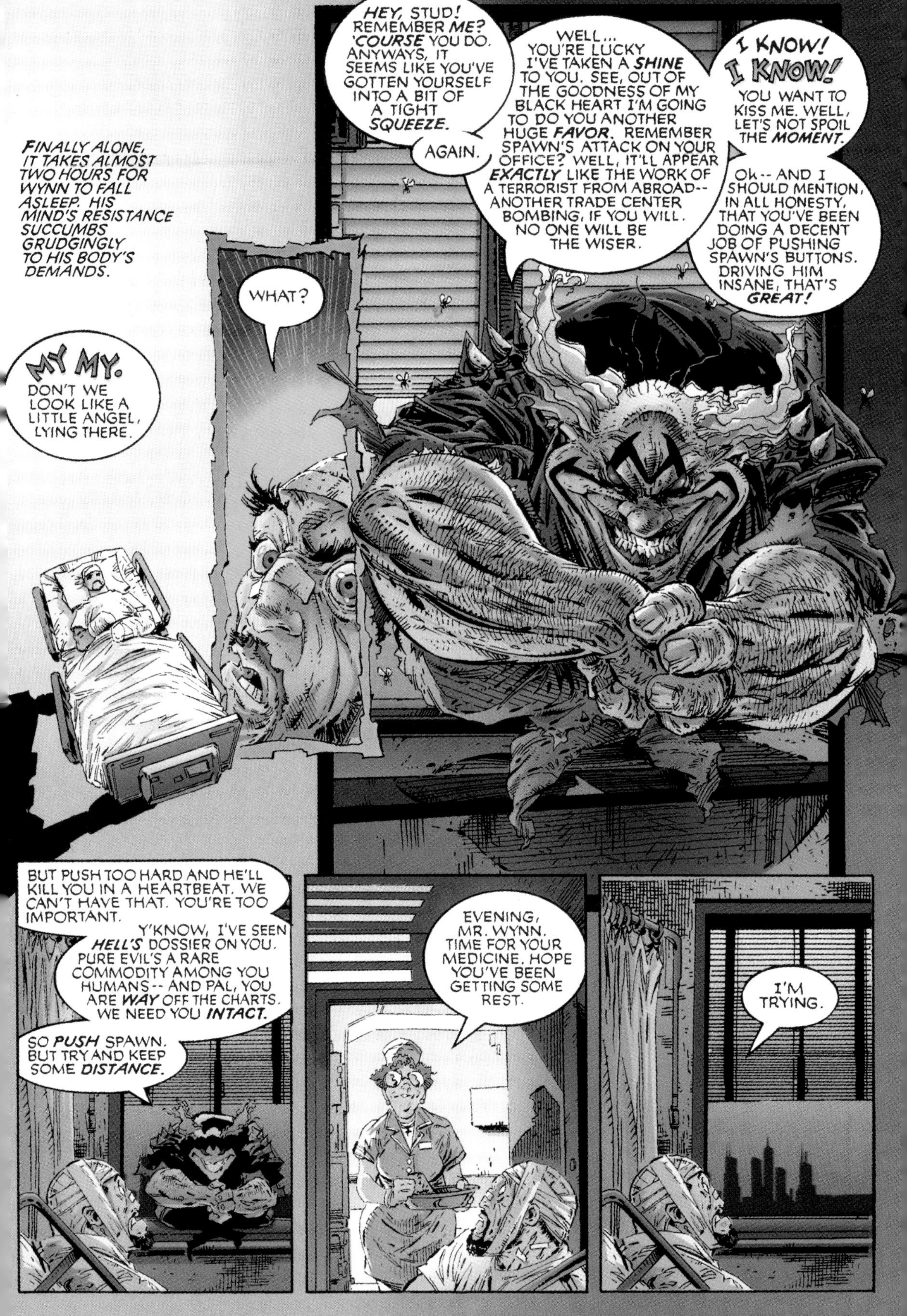
FINALLY ALONE, IT TAKES ALMOST TWO HOURS FOR WYNN TO FALL ASLEEP. HIS MIND'S RESISTANCE SUCCUMBS GRUDGINGLY TO HIS BODY'S DEMANDS.
MY MY. DON'T WE LOOK LIKE A LITTLE ANGEL, LYING THERE.
WHAT?
HEY, STUD! REMEMBER ME? 'COURSE YOU DO. ANYWAYS, IT SEEMS LIKE YOU'VE GOTTEN YOURSELF INTO A BIT OF A TIGHT SQUEEZE.
AGAIN.
WELL... YOU'RE LUCKY I'VE TAKEN A SHINE TO YOU. SEE, OUT OF THE GOODNESS OF MY BLACK HEART I'M GOING TO DO YOU ANOTHER HUGE FAVOR. REMEMBER SPAWN'S ATTACK ON YOUR OFFICE? WELL, IT'LL APPEAR EXACTLY LIKE THE WORK OF A TERRORIST FROM ABROAD-- ANOTHER TRADE CENTER BOMBING, IF YOU WILL. NO ONE WILL BE THE WISER.
I KNOW! I KNOW! YOU WANT TO KISS ME. WELL, LET'S NOT SPOIL THE MOMENT.
Oh -- AND I SHOULD MENTION, IN ALL HONESTY, THAT YOU'VE BEEN DOING A DECENT JOB OF PUSHING SPAWN'S BUTTONS. DRIVING HIM INSANE, THAT'S GREAT!
BUT PUSH TOO HARD AND HE'LL KILL YOU IN A HEARTBEAT. WE CAN'T HAVE THAT. YOU'RE TOO IMPORTANT.
Y'KNOW, I'VE SEEN HELL'S DOSSIER ON YOU. PURE EVIL'S A RARE COMMODITY AMONG YOU HUMANS -- AND PAL, YOU ARE WAY OFF THE CHARTS. WE NEED YOU INTACT.
SO PUSH SPAWN. BUT TRY AND KEEP SOME DISTANCE.
EVENING, MR. WYNN. TIME FOR YOUR MEDICINE. HOPE YOU'VE BEEN GETTING SOME REST.
I'M TRYING.

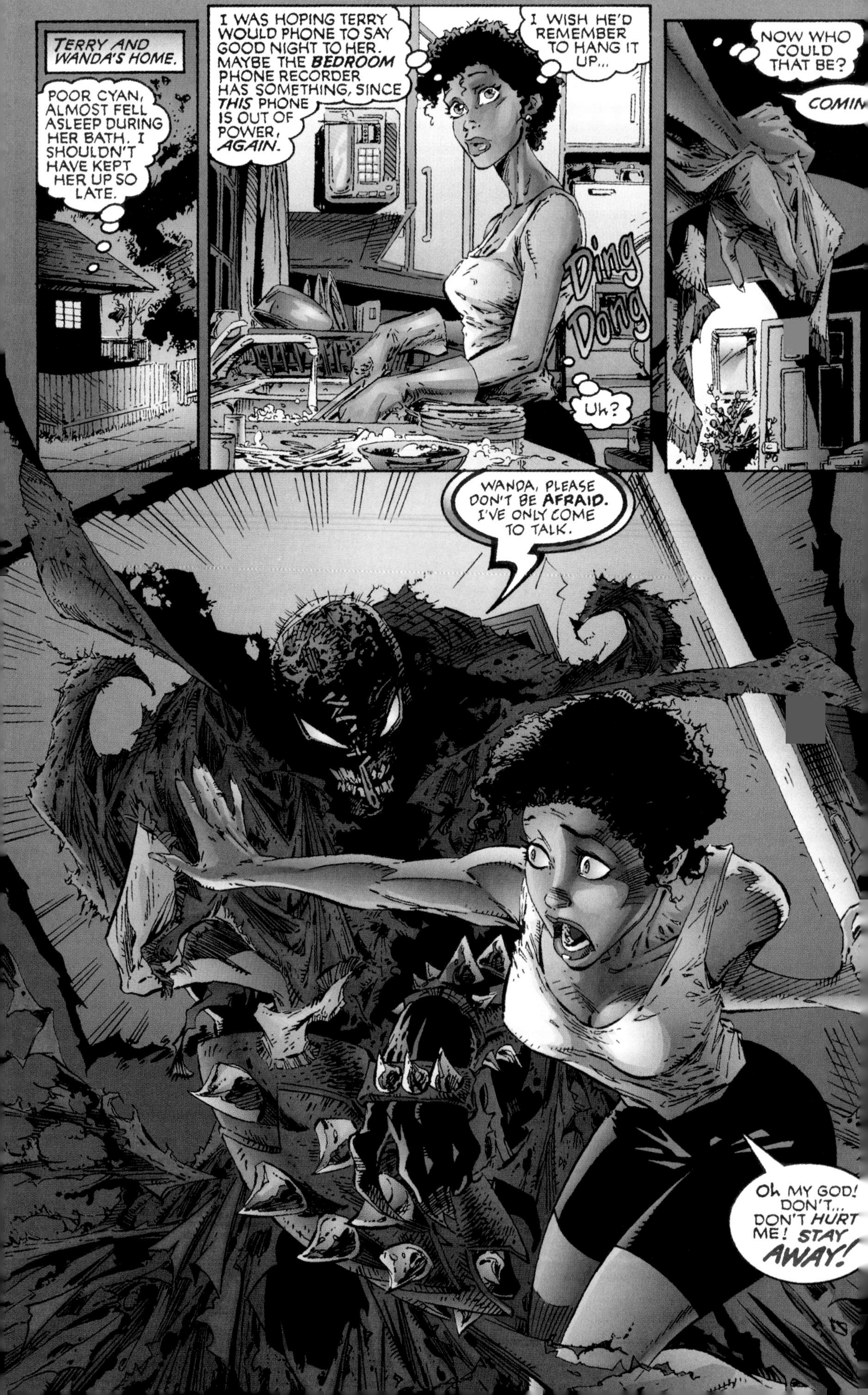
TERRY AND WANDA'S HOME.
POOR CYAN, ALMOST FELL ASLEEP DURING HER BATH. I SHOULDN'T HAVE KEPT HER UP SO LATE.
I WAS HOPING TERRY WOULD PHONE TO SAY GOOD NIGHT TO HER. MAYBE THE BEDROOM PHONE RECORDER HAS SOMETHING, SINCE THIS PHONE IS OUT OF POWER, AGAIN.
I WISH HE'D REMEMBER TO HANG IT UP...
Ding Dong
Uh?
NOW WHO COULD THAT BE?
COMIN
WANDA, PLEASE DON'T BE AFRAID. I'VE ONLY COME TO TALK.
Oh MY GOD! DON'T... DON'T HURT ME! STAY AWAY!

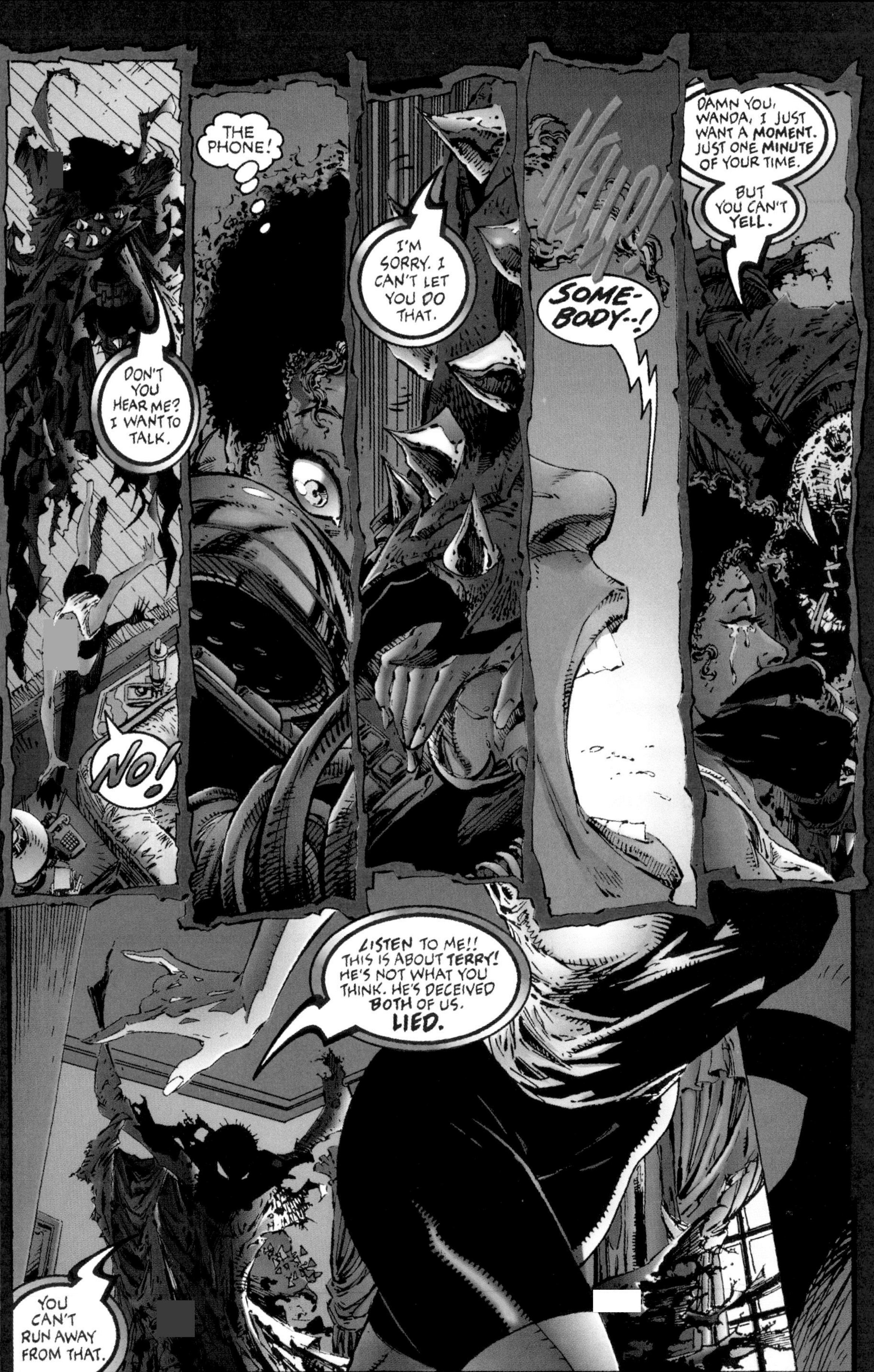
DON'T YOU HEAR ME? I WANT TO TALK.
NO!
THE PHONE!
I'M SORRY. I CAN'T LET YOU DO THAT.
HELP!
SOME-BODY--!
DAMN YOU, WANDA, I JUST WANT A MOMENT. JUST ONE MINUTE OF YOUR TIME.
BUT YOU CAN'T YELL.
LISTEN TO ME!! THIS IS ABOUT TERRY! HE'S NOT WHAT YOU THINK. HE'S DECEIVED BOTH OF US. LIED.
YOU CAN'T RUN AWAY FROM THAT.

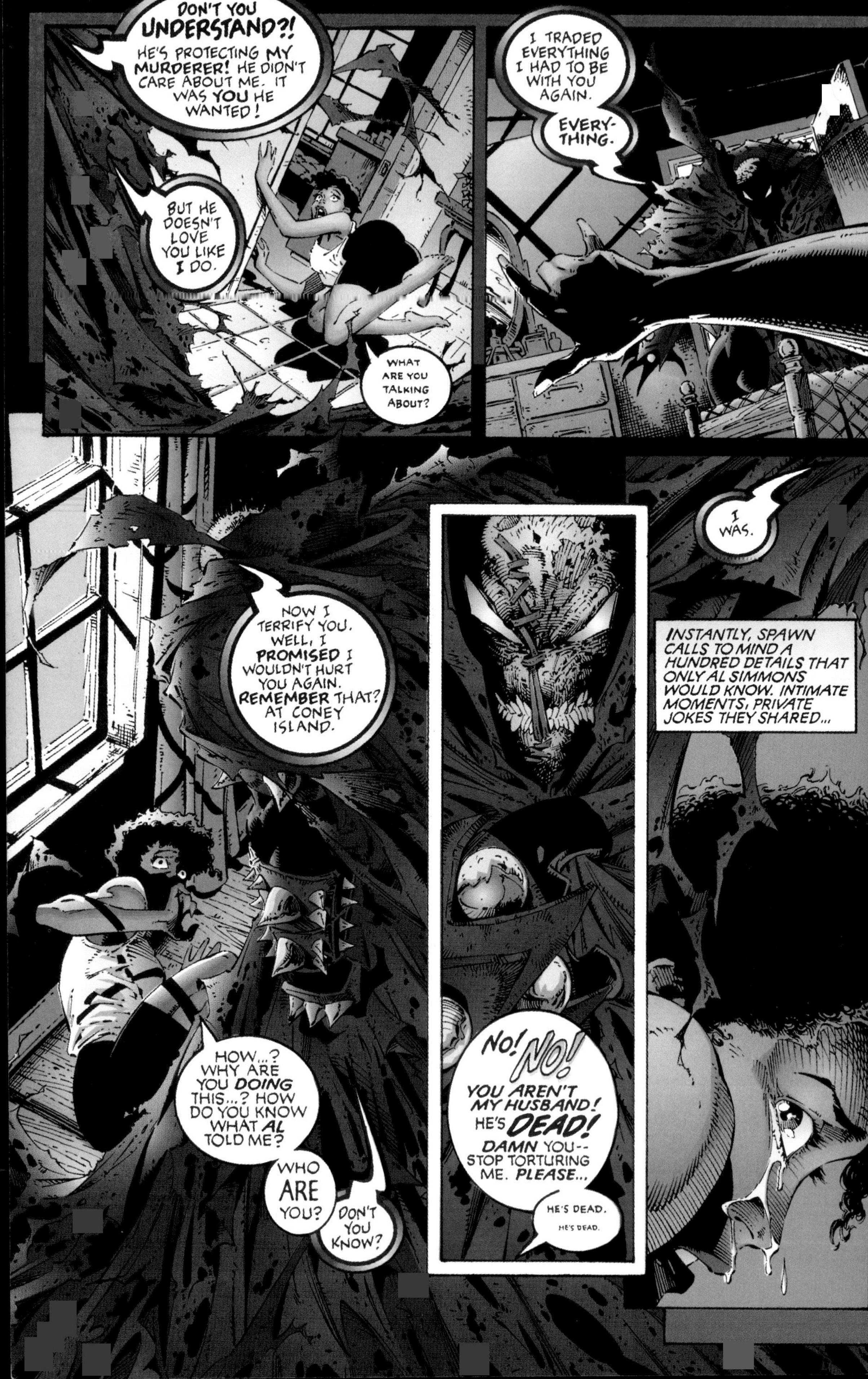
DON'T YOU UNDERSTAND?! HE'S PROTECTING MY MURDERER! HE DIDN'T CARE ABOUT ME. IT WAS YOU HE WANTED!
BUT HE DOESN'T LOVE YOU LIKE I DO.
WHAT ARE YOU TALKING ABOUT?
I TRADED EVERYTHING I HAD TO BE WITH YOU AGAIN.
EVERY-THING.
NOW I TERRIFY YOU. WELL, I PROMISED I WOULDN'T HURT YOU AGAIN. REMEMBER THAT? AT CONEY ISLAND.
HOW...? WHY ARE YOU DOING THIS...? HOW DO YOU KNOW WHAT AL TOLD ME?
WHO ARE YOU?
DON'T YOU KNOW?
NO! NO!
YOU AREN'T MY HUSBAND! HE'S DEAD! DAMN YOU-- STOP TORTURING ME. PLEASE...
HE'S DEAD.
HE'S DEAD.
I WAS.
INSTANTLY, SPAWN CALLS TO MIND A HUNDRED DETAILS THAT ONLY AL SIMMONS WOULD KNOW. INTIMATE MOMENTS, PRIVATE JOKES THEY SHARED...

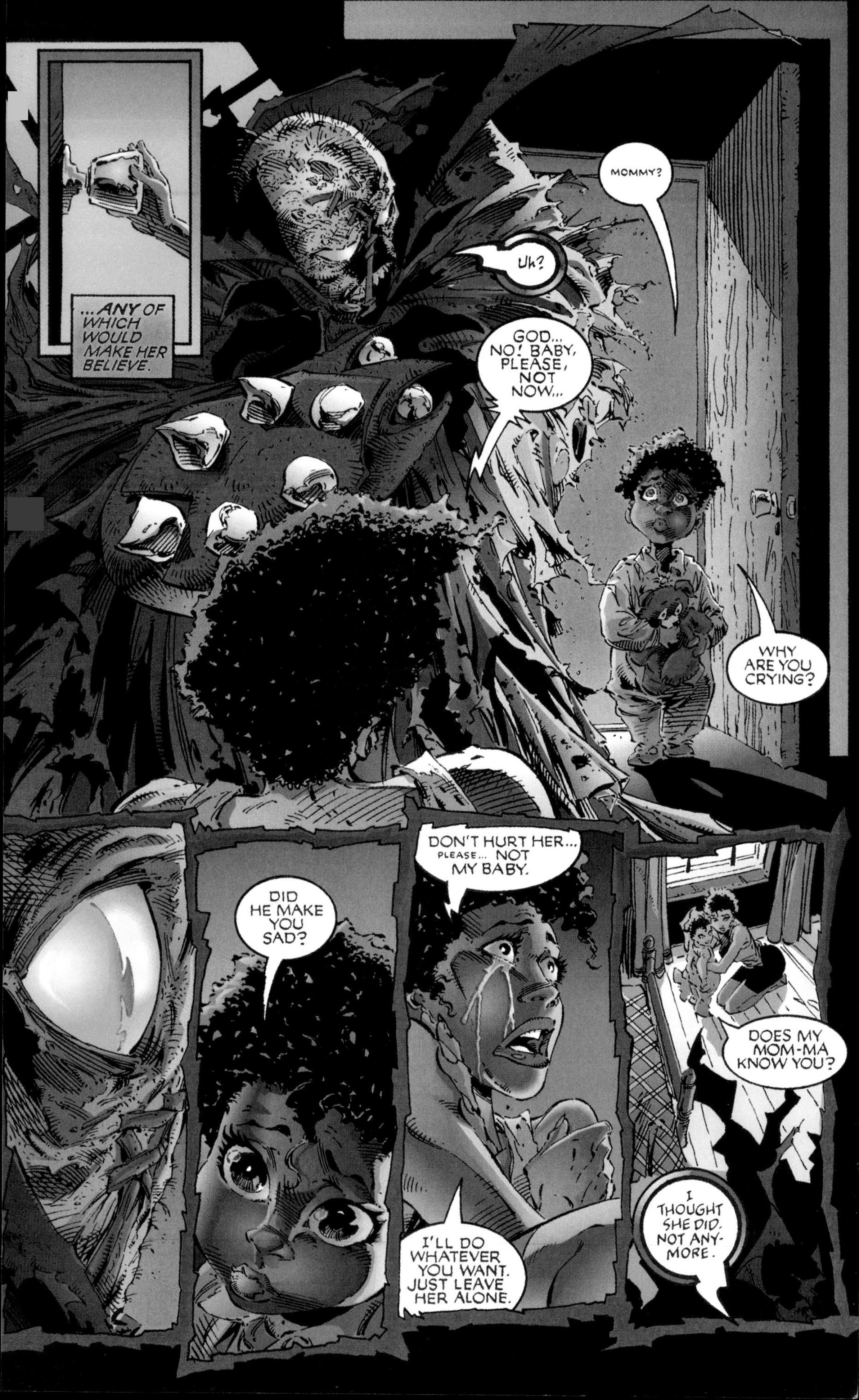
...ANY OF WHICH WOULD MAKE HER BELIEVE.
Uh?
MOMMY?
GOD... NO! BABY, PLEASE, NOT NOW...
WHY ARE YOU CRYING?
DID HE MAKE YOU SAD?
DON'T HURT HER... PLEASE... NOT MY BABY.
I'LL DO WHATEVER YOU WANT. JUST LEAVE HER ALONE.
DOES MY MOM-MA KNOW YOU?
I THOUGHT SHE DID. NOT ANY-MORE.

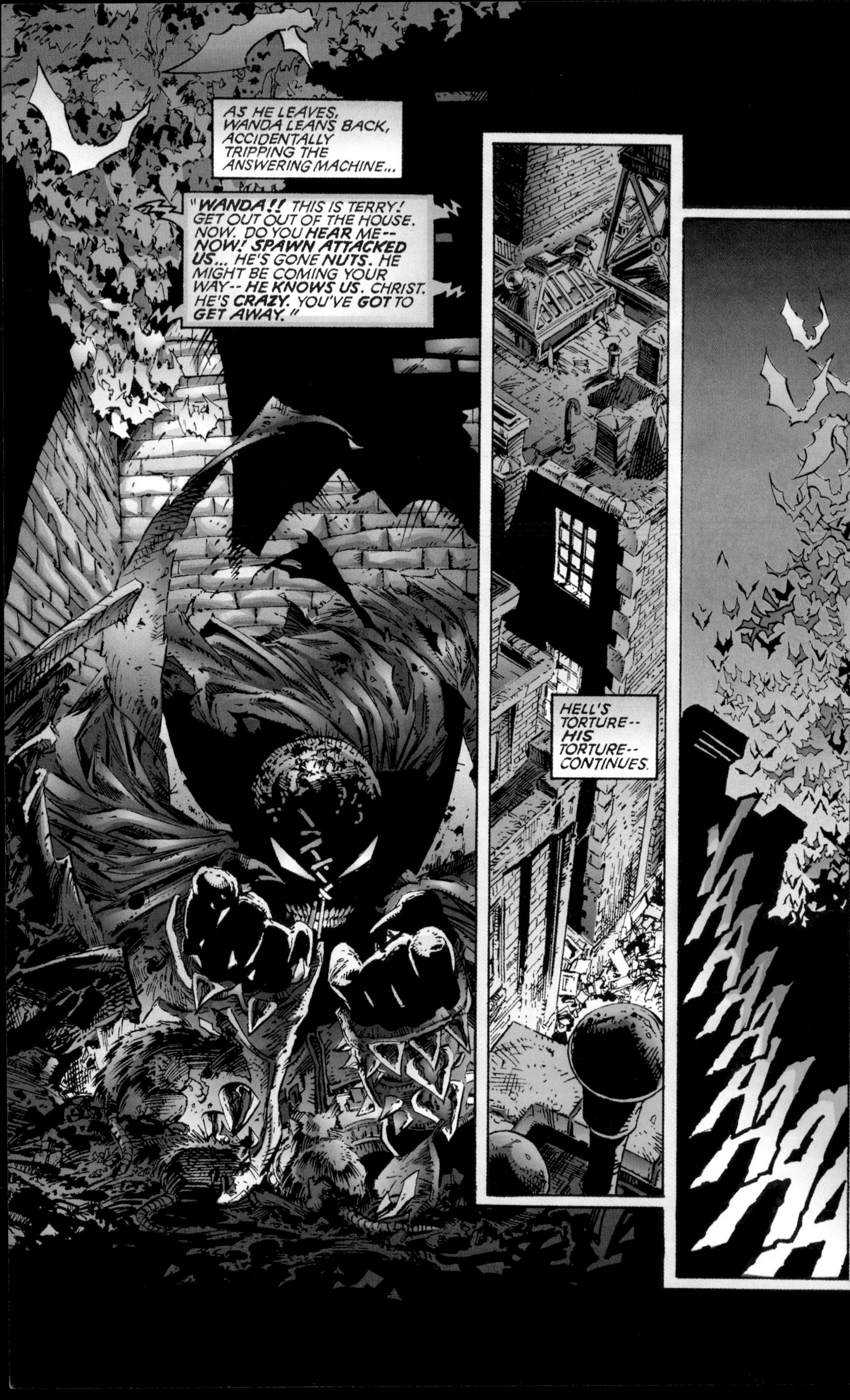
AS HE LEAVES, WANDA LEANS BACK, ACCIDENTALLY TRIPPING THE ANSWERING MACHINE...
"WANDA!! THIS IS TERRY! GET OUT OUT OF THE HOUSE. NOW. DO YOU HEAR ME-- NOW! SPAWN ATTACKED US... HE'S GONE NUTS. HE MIGHT BE COMING YOUR WAY-- HE KNOWS US. CHRIST. HE'S CRAZY. YOU'VE GOT TO GET AWAY."
HELL'S TORTURE-- HIS TORTURE-- CONTINUES.
YAAAAAAAAA

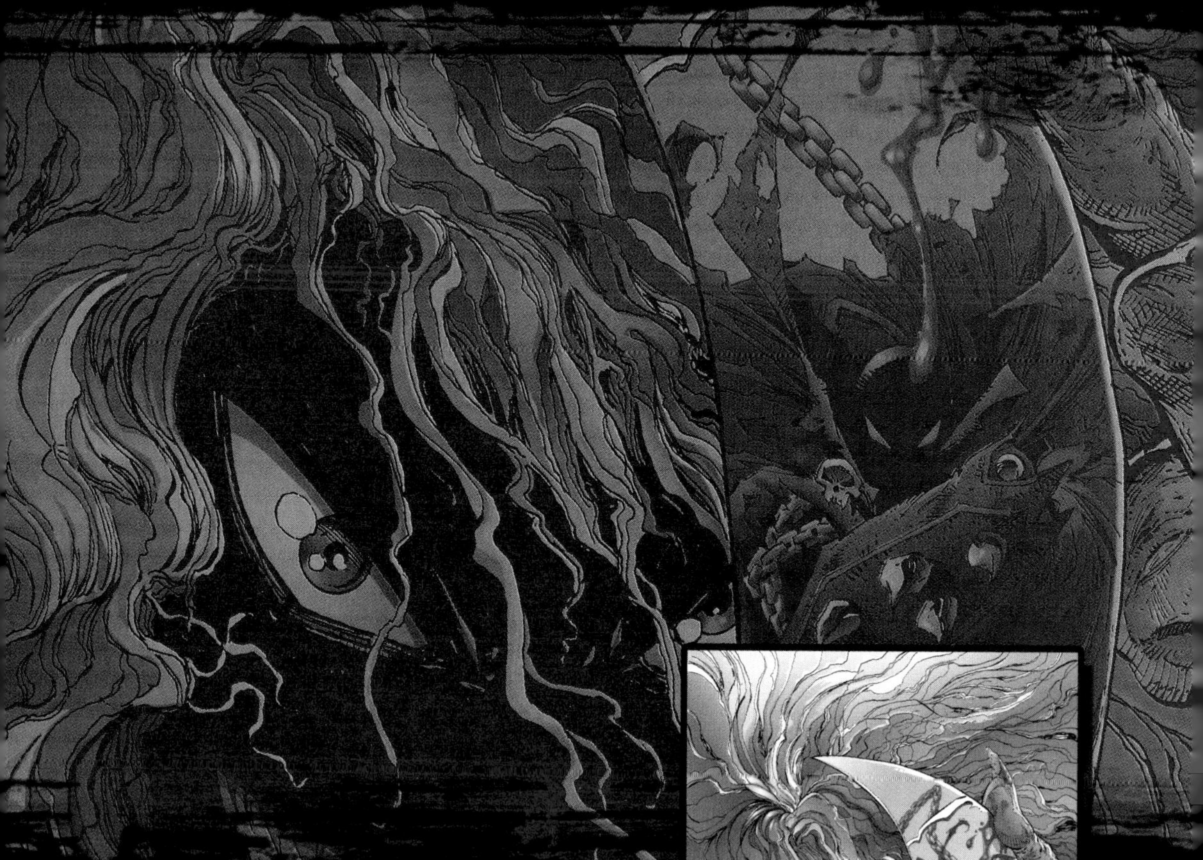

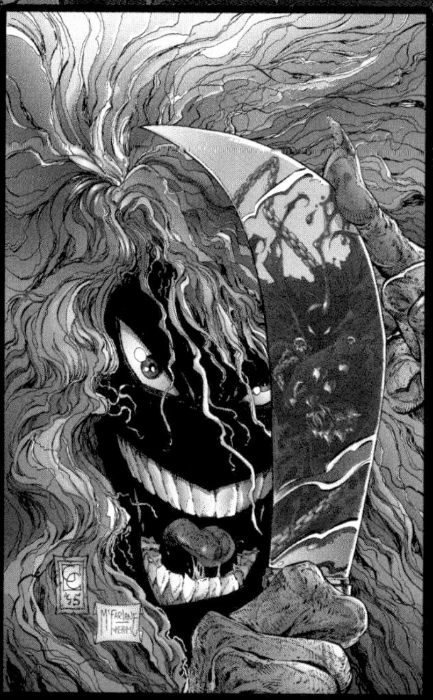

ISSUE THIRTY-SEVEN

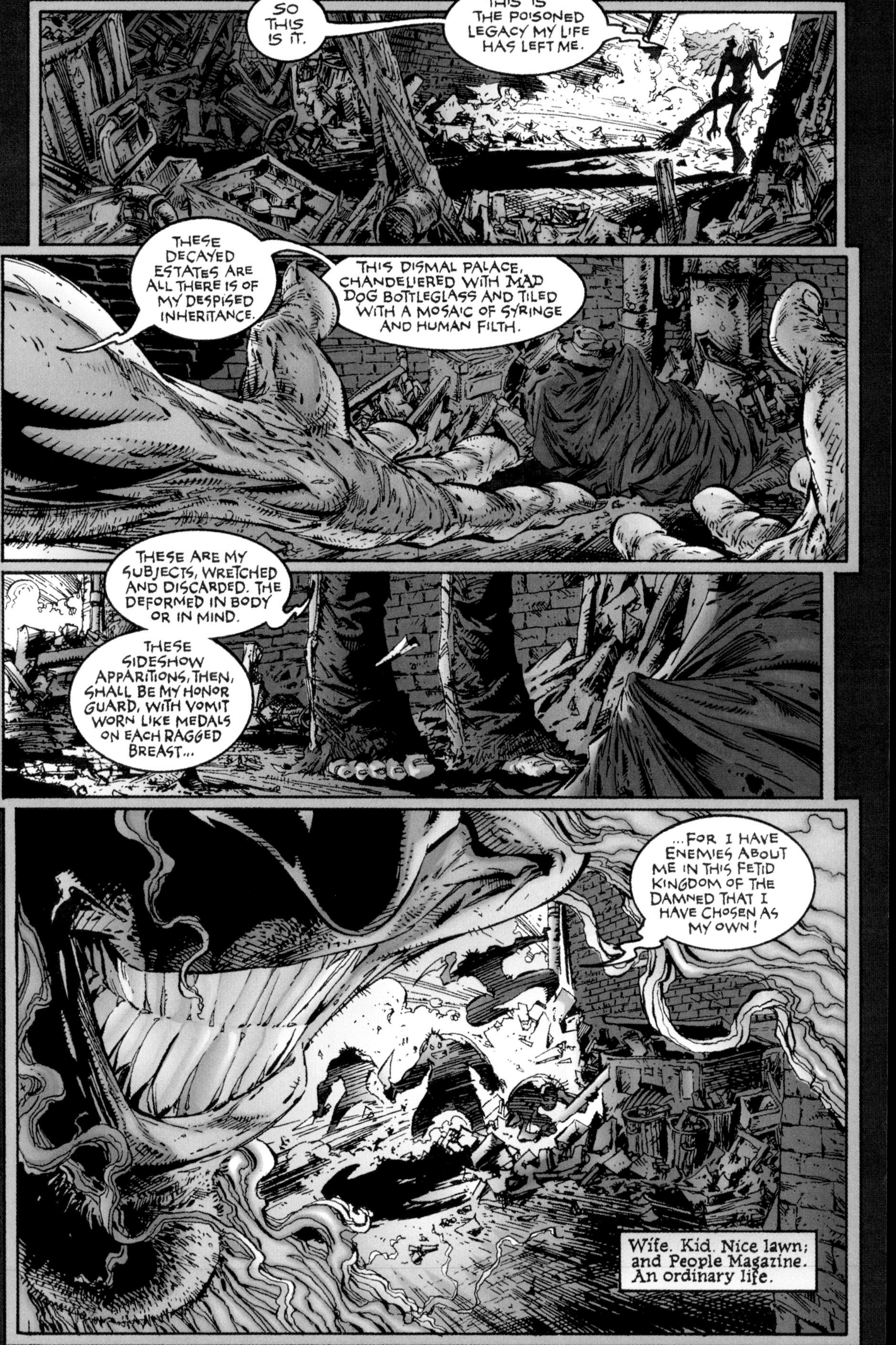
SO THIS IS IT.
THIS IS THE POISONED LEGACY MY LIFE HAS LEFT ME.
THESE DECAYED ESTATES ARE ALL THERE IS OF MY DESPISED INHERITANCE.
THIS DISMAL PALACE, CHANDELIERED WITH MAD DOG BOTTLEGLASS AND TILED WITH A MOSAIC OF SYRINGE AND HUMAN FILTH.
THESE ARE MY SUBJECTS, WRETCHED AND DISCARDED. THE DEFORMED IN BODY OR IN MIND.
THESE SIDESHOW APPARITIONS, THEN, SHALL BE MY HONOR GUARD, WITH VOMIT WORN LIKE MEDALS ON EACH RAGGED BREAST...
...FOR I HAVE ENEMIES ABOUT ME IN THIS FETID KINGDOM OF THE DAMNED THAT I HAVE CHOSEN AS MY OWN!
Wife. Kid. Nice lawn; and People Magazine. An ordinary life.

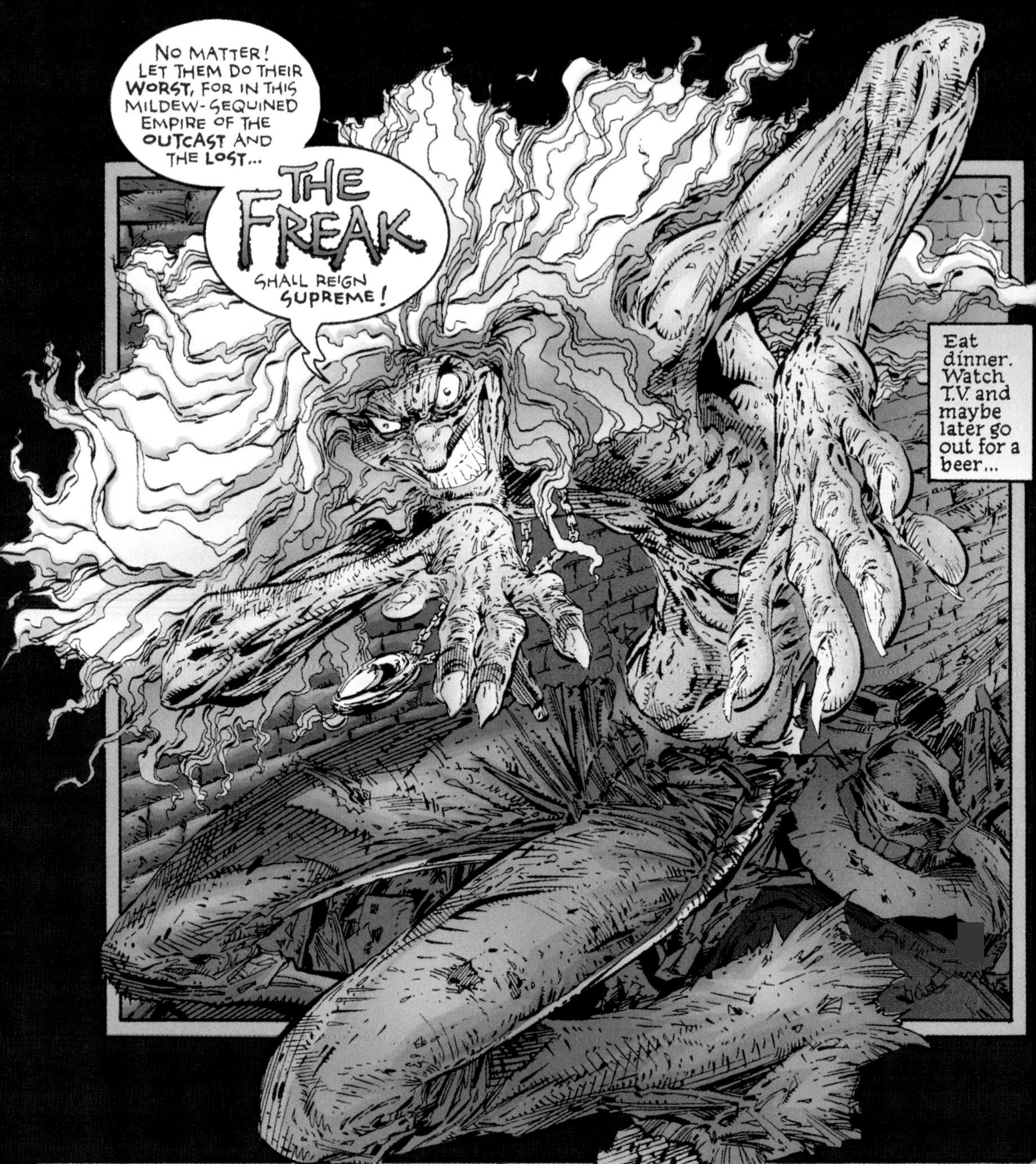
NO MATTER! LET THEM DO THEIR WORST, FOR IN THIS MILDEW-SEQUINED EMPIRE OF THE OUTCAST AND THE LOST...
THE FREAK SHALL REIGN SUPREME!
Eat dinner. Watch T.V. and maybe later go out for a beer...
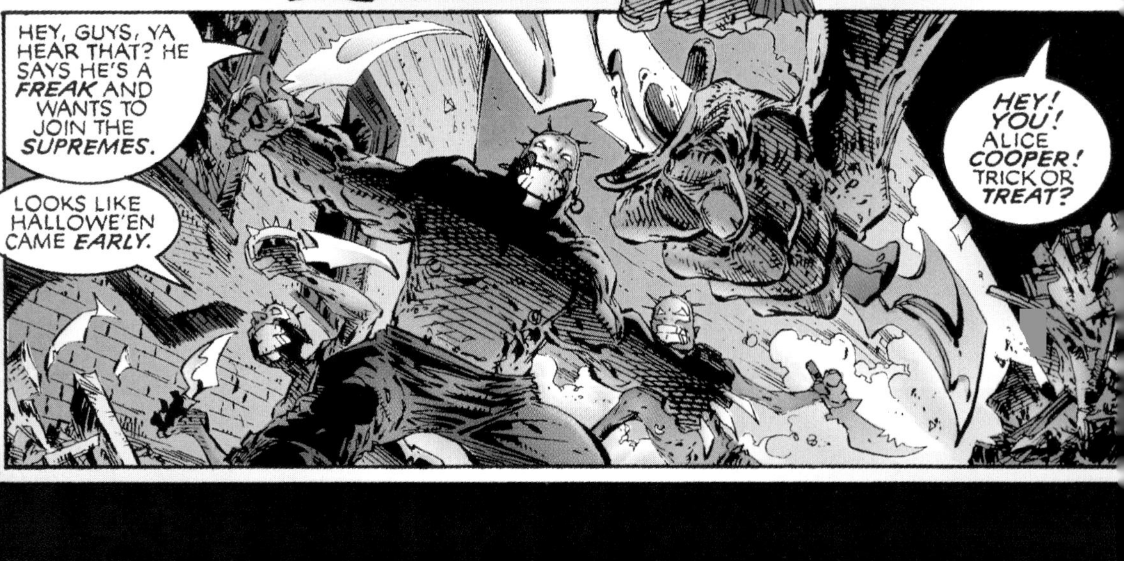
HEY, GUYS, YA HEAR THAT? HE SAYS HE'S A FREAK AND WANTS TO JOIN THE SUPREMES.
LOOKS LIKE HALLOWE'EN CAME EARLY.
HEY! YOU! ALICE COOPER! TRICK OR TREAT?

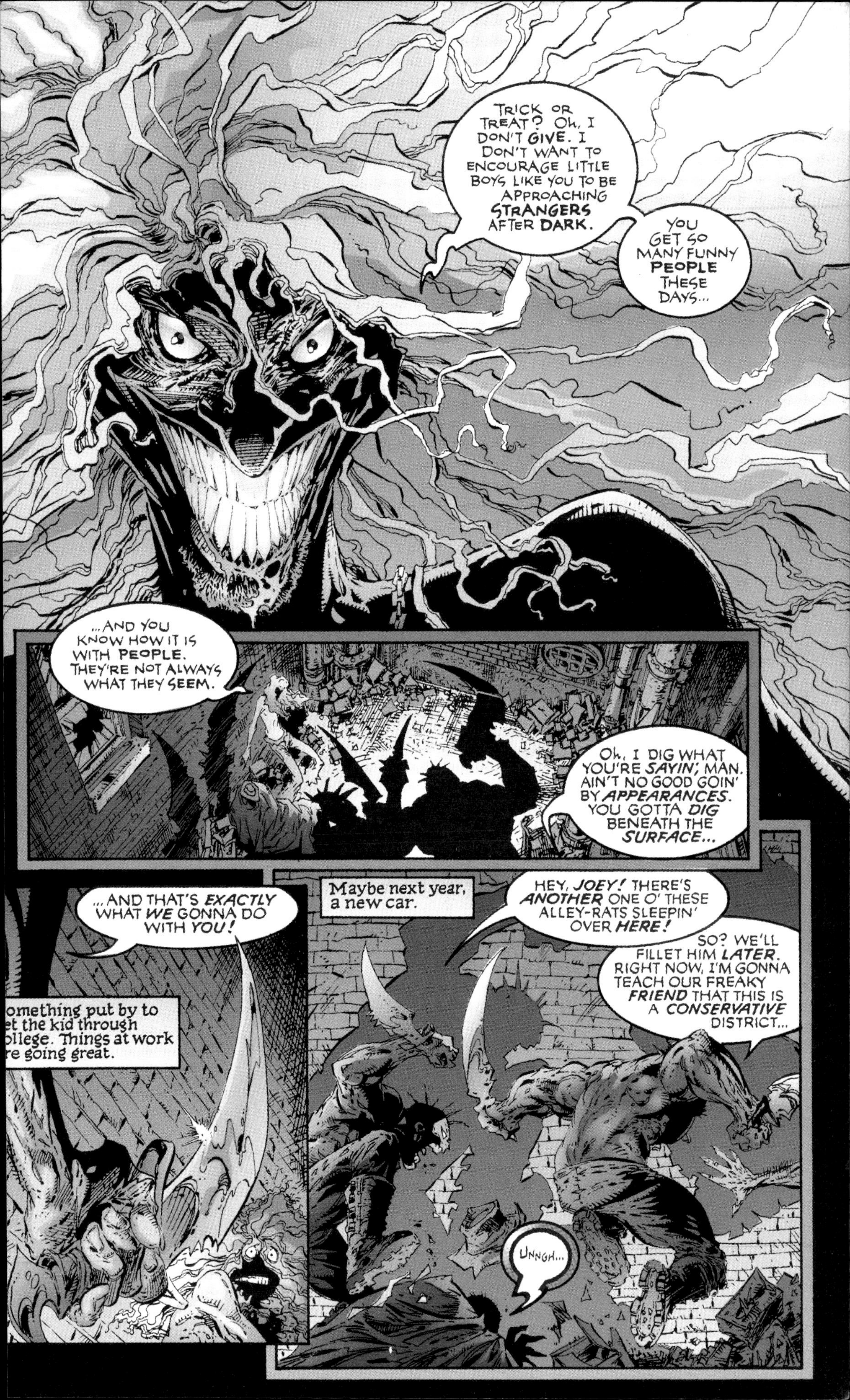
TRICK OR TREAT? Oh, I DON'T GIVE. I DON'T WANT TO ENCOURAGE LITTLE BOYS LIKE YOU TO BE APPROACHING STRANGERS AFTER DARK.
YOU GET SO MANY FUNNY PEOPLE THESE DAYS...
...AND YOU KNOW HOW IT IS WITH PEOPLE. THEY'RE NOT ALWAYS WHAT THEY SEEM.
Oh, I DIG WHAT YOU'RE SAYIN', MAN. AIN'T NO GOOD GOIN' BY APPEARANCES. YOU GOTTA DIG BENEATH THE SURFACE...
...AND THAT'S EXACTLY WHAT WE GONNA DO WITH YOU!
omething put by to et the kid through ollege. Things at work re going great.
Maybe next year, a new car.
HEY, JOEY! THERE'S ANOTHER ONE O' THESE ALLEY-RATS SLEEPIN' OVER HERE!
SO? WE'LL FILLET HIM LATER. RIGHT NOW, I'M GONNA TEACH OUR FREAKY FRIEND THAT THIS IS A CONSERVATIVE DISTRICT...
UNNGH...

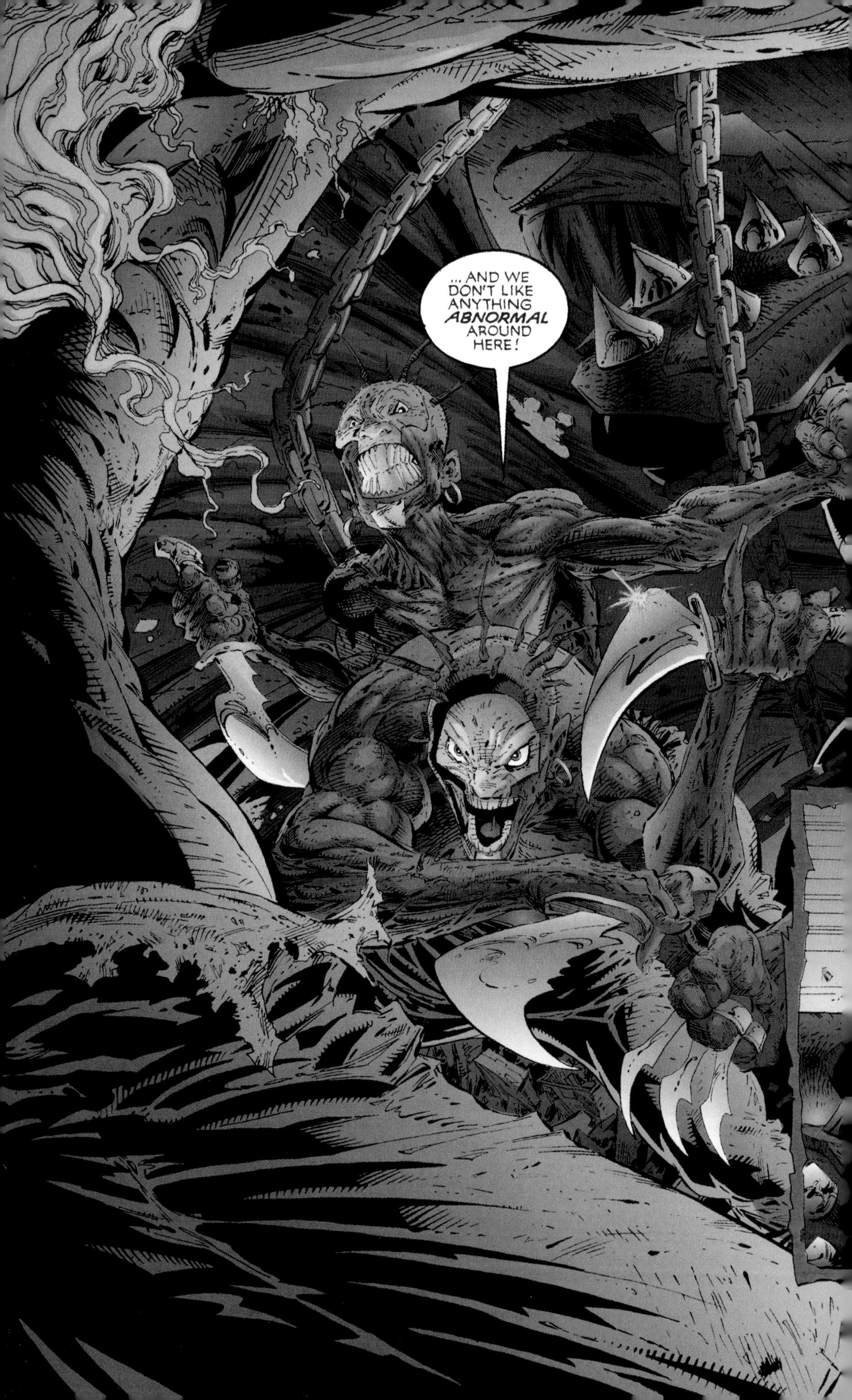
...AND WE DON'T LIKE ANYTHING ABNORMAL AROUND HERE!

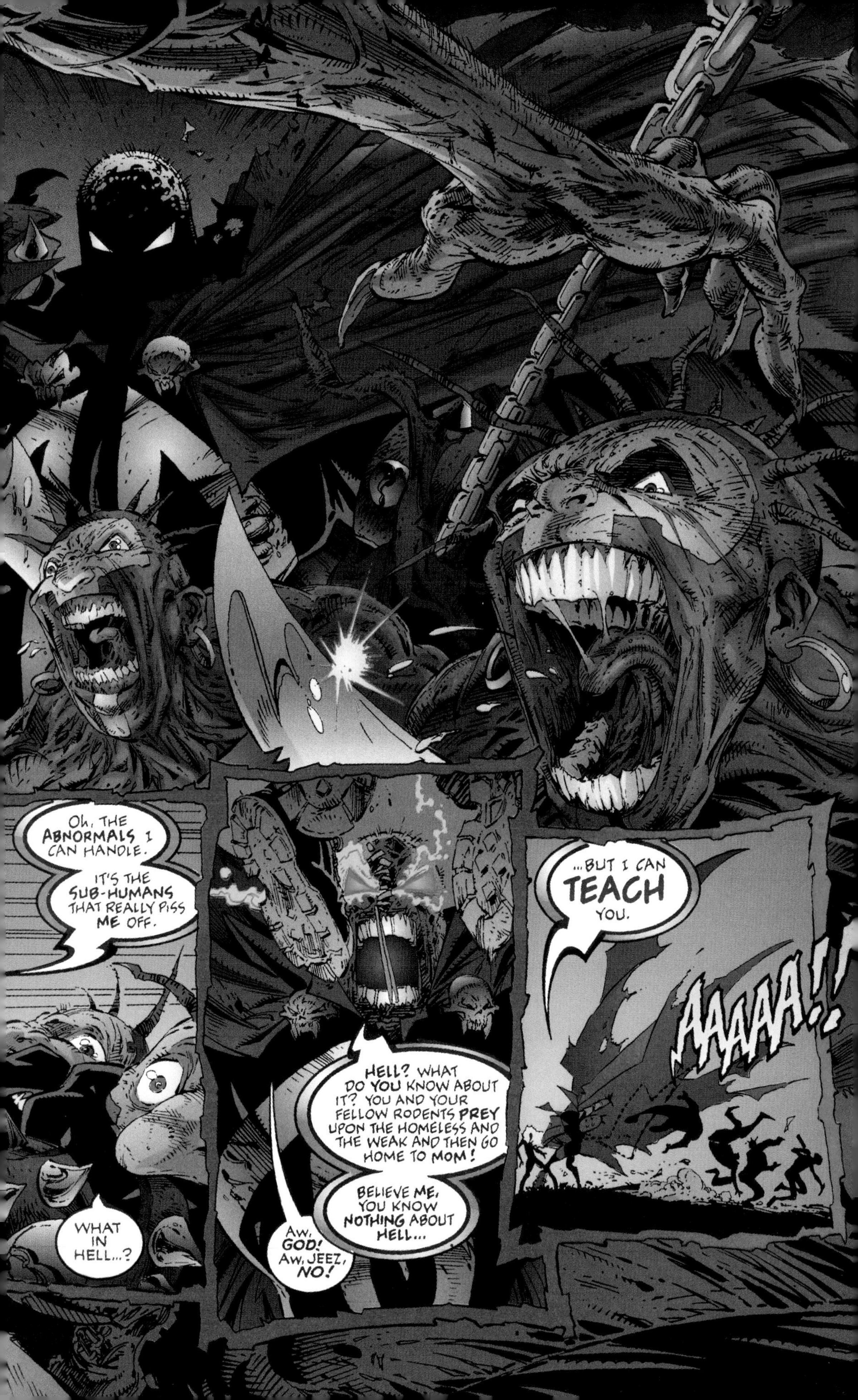
Oh, the **ABNORMALS** I can handle.
It's the **SUB-HUMANS** that really piss **ME** off.
What in hell...?
HELL? What do **YOU** know about it? You and your fellow rodents **PREY** upon the homeless and the weak and then go home to **MOM!**
Believe me, you know **NOTHING** about **HELL...**
Aw, **GOD!** Aw, jeez, **NO!**
...But I can **TEACH** you.
AAAAA!!

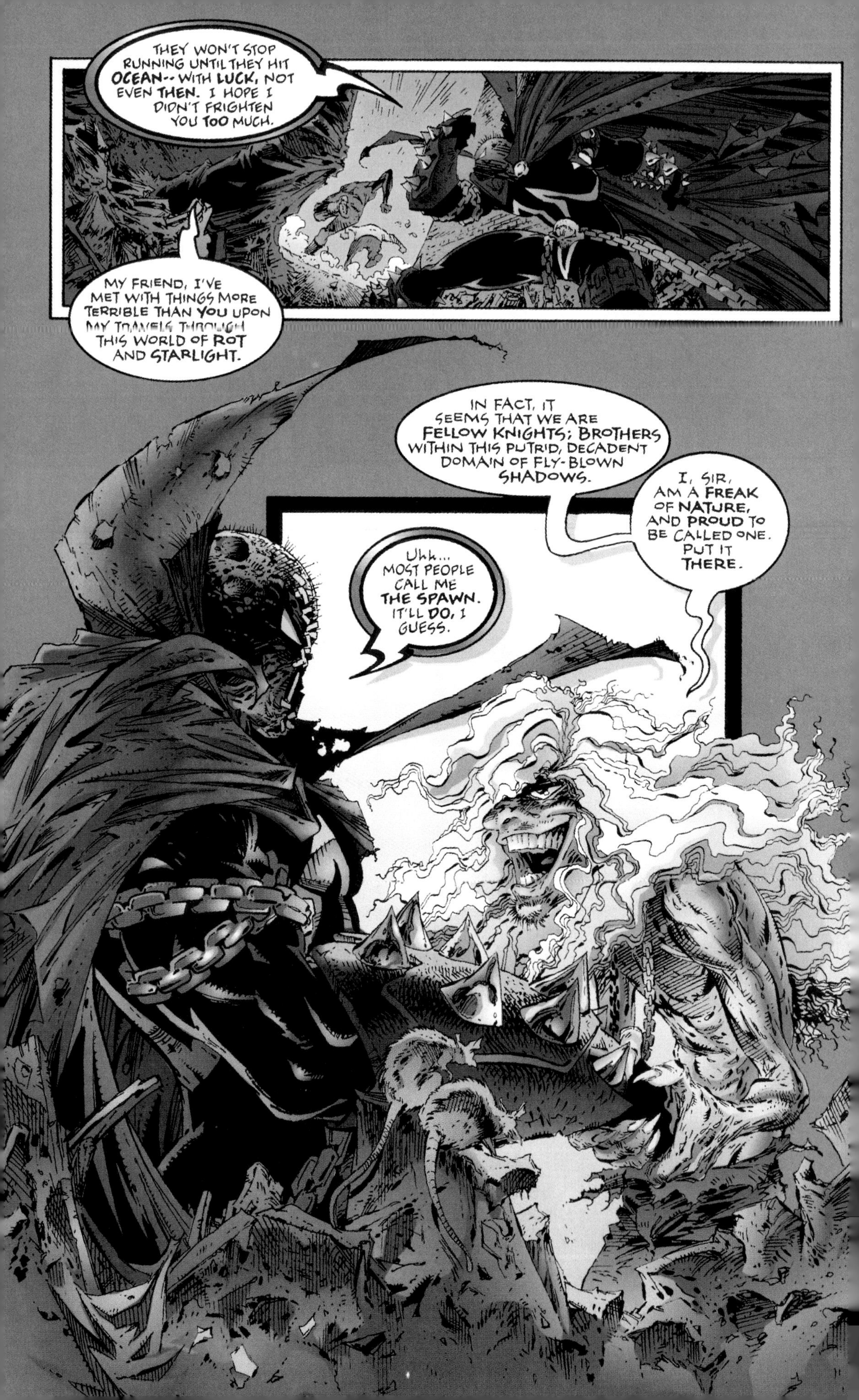
THEY WON'T STOP RUNNING UNTIL THEY HIT OCEAN-- WITH LUCK, NOT EVEN THEN. I HOPE I DIDN'T FRIGHTEN YOU TOO MUCH.
MY FRIEND, I'VE MET WITH THINGS MORE TERRIBLE THAN YOU UPON MY TRAVELS THROUGH THIS WORLD OF ROT AND STARLIGHT.
IN FACT, IT SEEMS THAT WE ARE FELLOW KNIGHTS; BROTHERS WITHIN THIS PUTRID, DECADENT DOMAIN OF FLY-BLOWN SHADOWS.
I, SIR, AM A FREAK OF NATURE, AND PROUD TO BE CALLED ONE. PUT IT THERE.
Uhh... MOST PEOPLE CALL ME THE SPAWN. IT'LL DO, I GUESS.

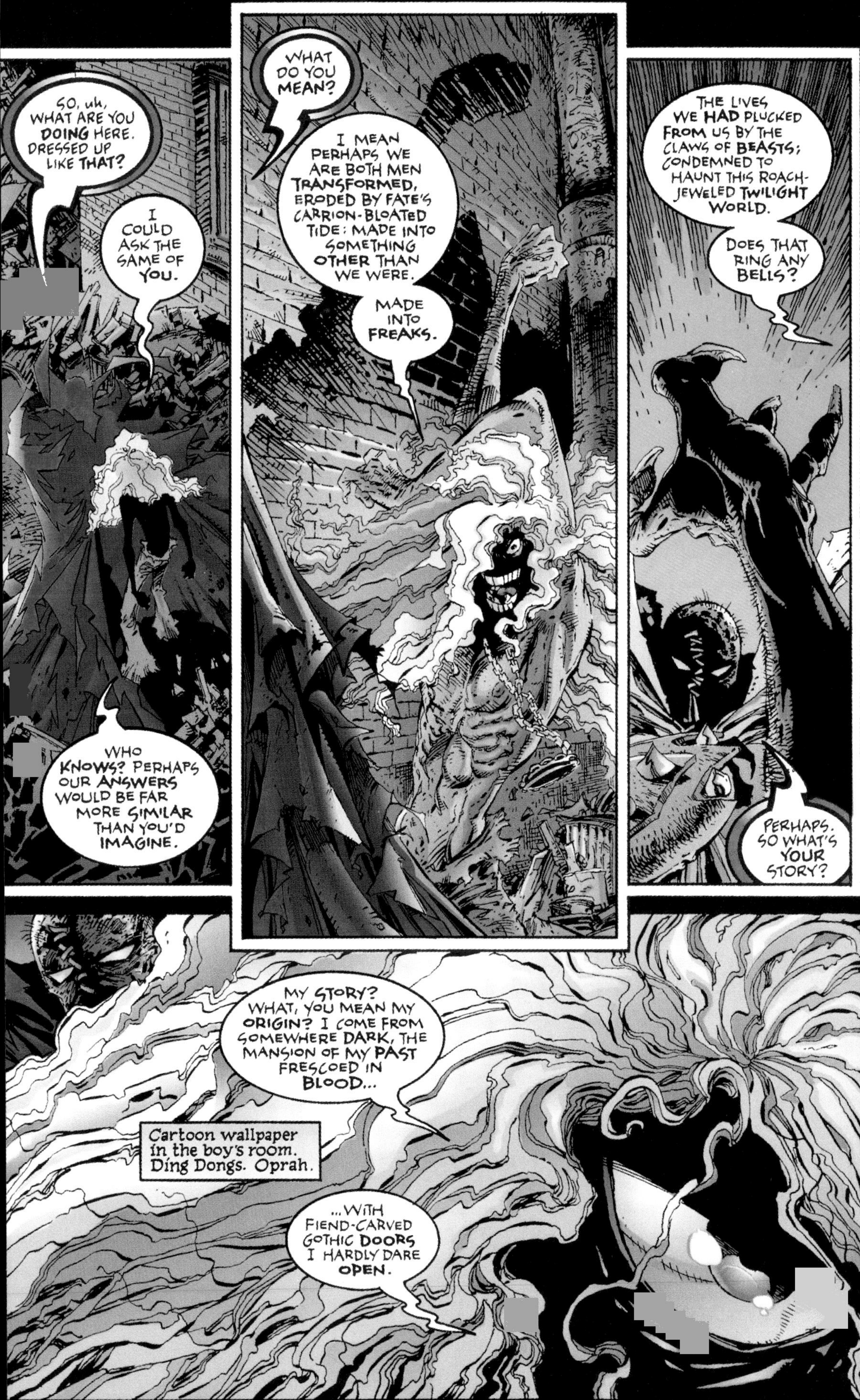
SO, uh, WHAT ARE YOU DOING HERE. DRESSED UP LIKE THAT?
I COULD ASK THE SAME OF YOU.
WHO KNOWS? PERHAPS OUR ANSWERS WOULD BE FAR MORE SIMILAR THAN YOU'D IMAGINE.
WHAT DO YOU MEAN?
I MEAN PERHAPS WE ARE BOTH MEN TRANSFORMED, ERODED BY FATE'S CARRION-BLOATED TIDE: MADE INTO SOMETHING OTHER THAN WE WERE.
MADE INTO FREAKS.
THE LIVES WE HAD PLUCKED FROM US BY THE CLAWS OF BEASTS; CONDEMNED TO HAUNT THIS ROACH-JEWELED TWILIGHT WORLD.
DOES THAT RING ANY BELLS?
PERHAPS. SO WHAT'S YOUR STORY?
MY STORY? WHAT, YOU MEAN MY ORIGIN? I COME FROM SOMEWHERE DARK, THE MANSION OF MY PAST FRESCOED IN BLOOD...
Cartoon wallpaper in the boy's room. Ding Dongs. Oprah.
...WITH FIEND-CARVED GOTHIC DOORS I HARDLY DARE OPEN.

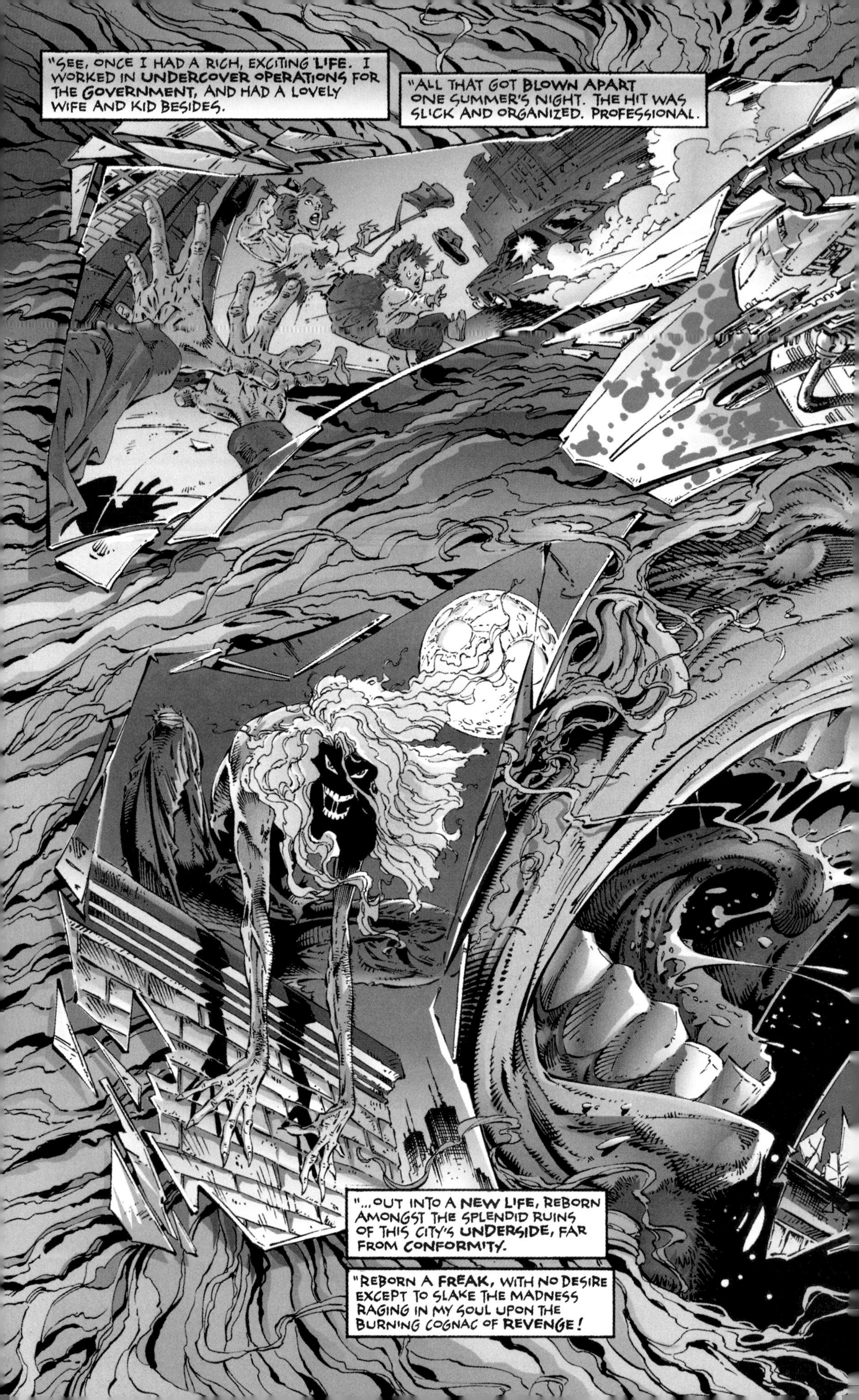
"SEE, ONCE I HAD A RICH, EXCITING LIFE. I WORKED IN UNDERCOVER OPERATIONS FOR THE GOVERNMENT, AND HAD A LOVELY WIFE AND KID BESIDES.
"ALL THAT GOT BLOWN APART ONE SUMMER'S NIGHT. THE HIT WAS SLICK AND ORGANIZED. PROFESSIONAL.
"...OUT INTO A NEW LIFE, REBORN AMONGST THE SPLENDID RUINS OF THIS CITY'S UNDERSIDE, FAR FROM CONFORMITY.
"REBORN A FREAK, WITH NO DESIRE EXCEPT TO SLAKE THE MADNESS RAGING IN MY SOUL UPON THE BURNING COGNAC OF REVENGE!

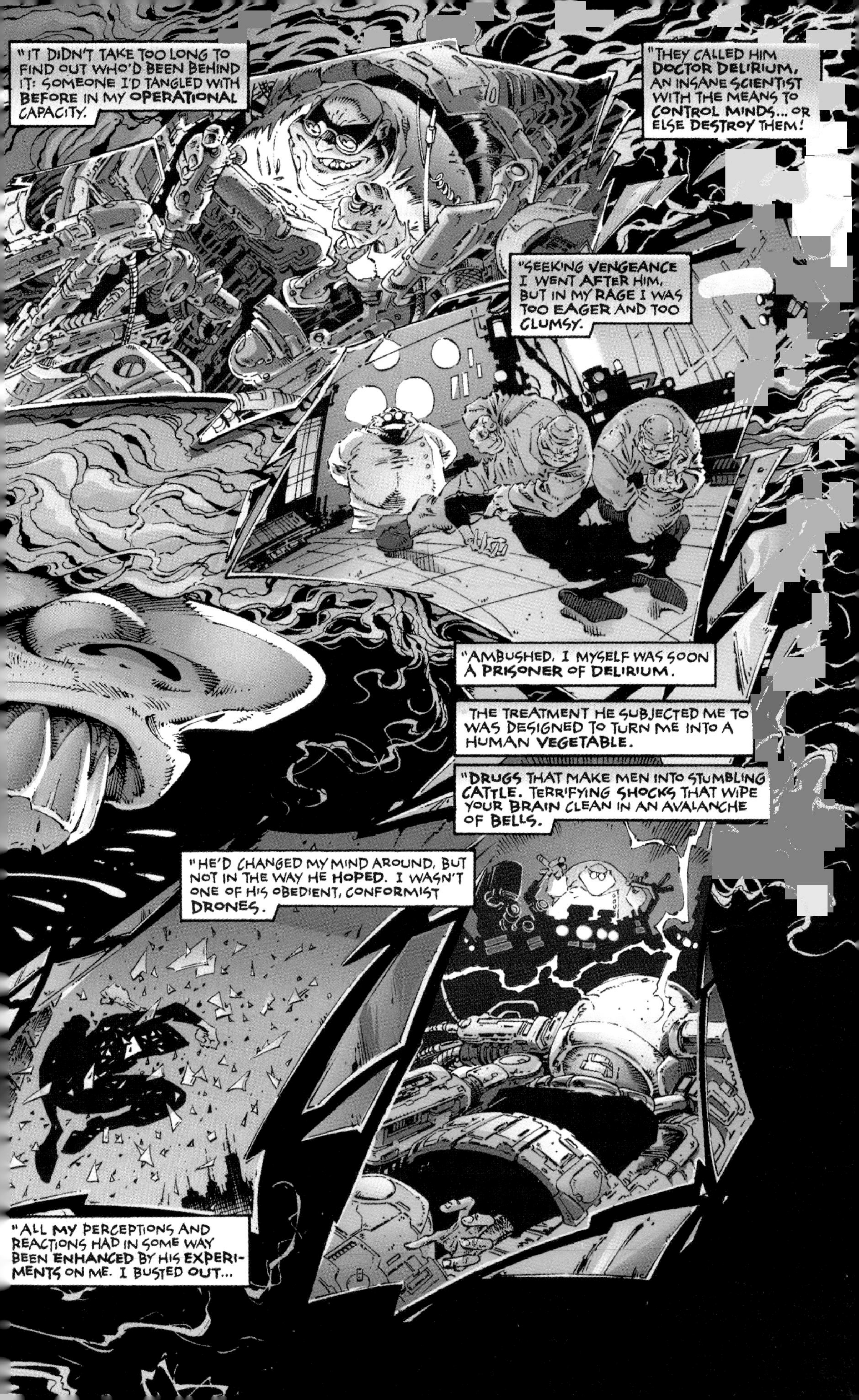
"IT DIDN'T TAKE TOO LONG TO FIND OUT WHO'D BEEN BEHIND IT: SOMEONE I'D TANGLED WITH BEFORE IN MY OPERATIONAL CAPACITY.
"THEY CALLED HIM DOCTOR DELIRIUM, AN INSANE SCIENTIST WITH THE MEANS TO CONTROL MINDS... OR ELSE DESTROY THEM!
"SEEKING VENGEANCE I WENT AFTER HIM, BUT IN MY RAGE I WAS TOO EAGER AND TOO CLUMSY.
"AMBUSHED, I MYSELF WAS SOON A PRISONER OF DELIRIUM.
THE TREATMENT HE SUBJECTED ME TO WAS DESIGNED TO TURN ME INTO A HUMAN VEGETABLE.
"DRUGS THAT MAKE MEN INTO STUMBLING CATTLE. TERRIFYING SHOCKS THAT WIPE YOUR BRAIN CLEAN IN AN AVALANCHE OF BELLS.
"HE'D CHANGED MY MIND AROUND, BUT NOT IN THE WAY HE HOPED. I WASN'T ONE OF HIS OBEDIENT, CONFORMIST DRONES.
"ALL MY PERCEPTIONS AND REACTIONS HAD IN SOME WAY BEEN ENHANCED BY HIS EXPERIMENTS ON ME. I BUSTED OUT...

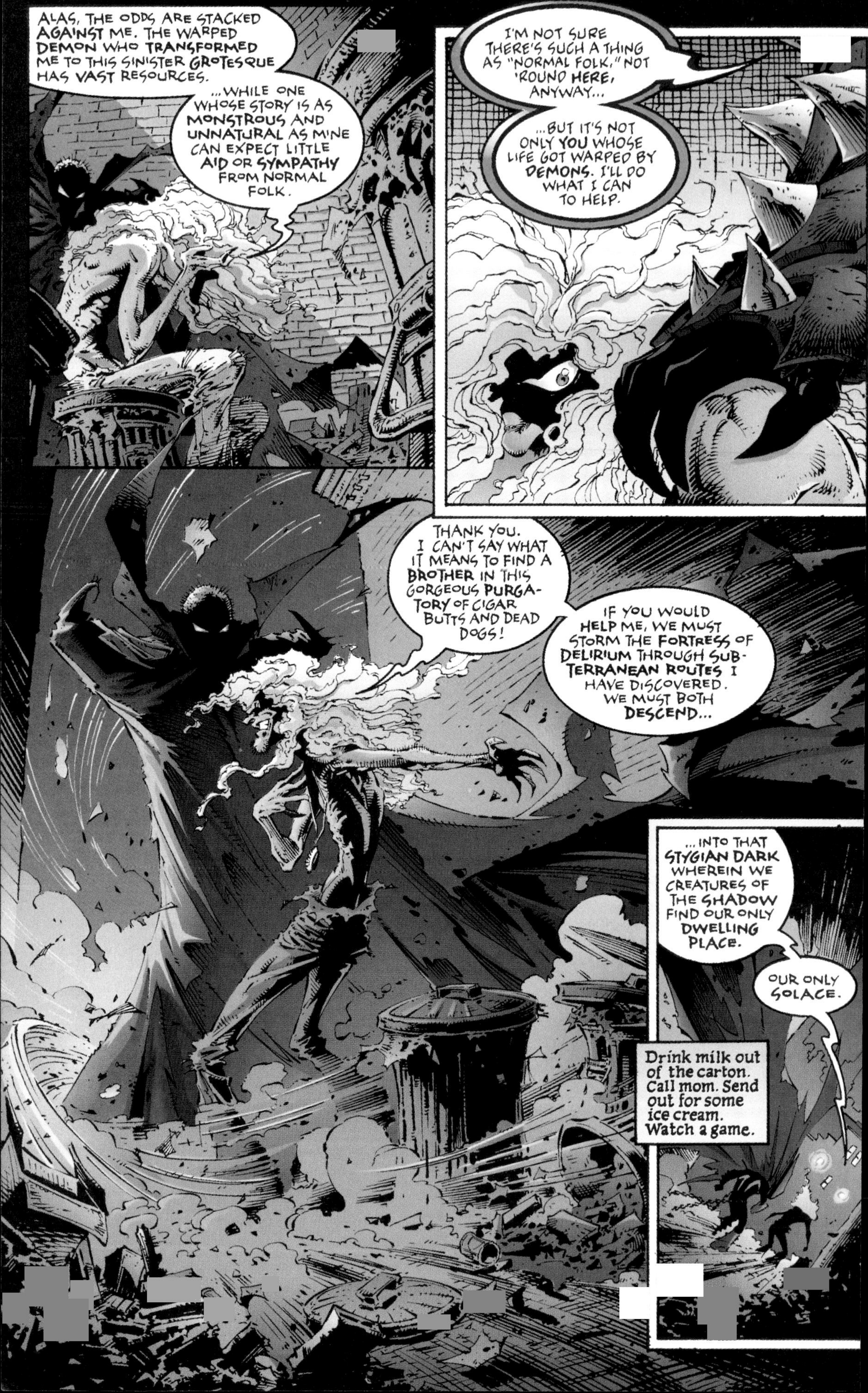

ALAS, THE ODDS ARE STACKED AGAINST ME. THE WARPED DEMON WHO TRANSFORMED ME TO THIS SINISTER GROTESQUE HAS VAST RESOURCES.
...WHILE ONE WHOSE STORY IS AS MONSTROUS AND UNNATURAL AS MINE CAN EXPECT LITTLE AID OR SYMPATHY FROM NORMAL FOLK.
I'M NOT SURE THERE'S SUCH A THING AS "NORMAL FOLK," NOT 'ROUND HERE, ANYWAY...
...BUT IT'S NOT ONLY YOU WHOSE LIFE GOT WARPED BY DEMONS. I'LL DO WHAT I CAN TO HELP.
THANK YOU. I CAN'T SAY WHAT IT MEANS TO FIND A BROTHER IN THIS GORGEOUS PURGATORY OF CIGAR BUTTS AND DEAD DOGS!
IF YOU WOULD HELP ME, WE MUST STORM THE FORTRESS OF DELIRIUM THROUGH SUBTERRANEAN ROUTES I HAVE DISCOVERED. WE MUST BOTH DESCEND...
...INTO THAT STYGIAN DARK WHEREIN WE CREATURES OF THE SHADOW FIND OUR ONLY DWELLING PLACE.
OUR ONLY SOLACE.
Drink milk out of the carton. Call mom. Send out for some ice cream. Watch a game.

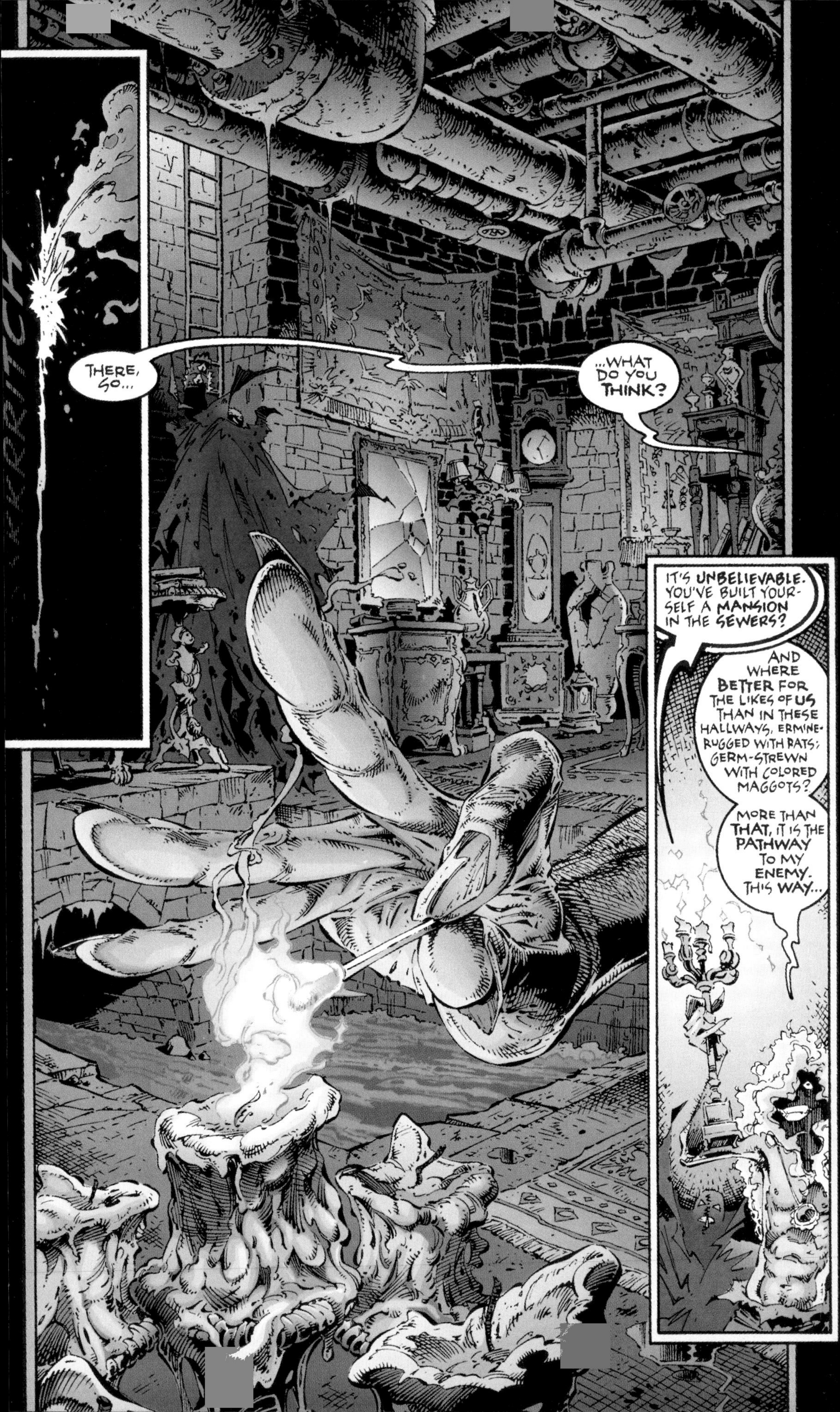
SKKRRITCH
THERE, SO...
...WHAT DO YOU THINK?
IT'S UNBELIEVABLE. YOU'VE BUILT YOURSELF A MANSION IN THE SEWERS?
AND WHERE BETTER FOR THE LIKES OF US THAN IN THESE HALLWAYS, ERMINE-RUGGED WITH RATS; GERM-STREWN WITH COLORED MAGGOTS?
MORE THAN THAT, IT IS THE PATHWAY TO MY ENEMY. THIS WAY...

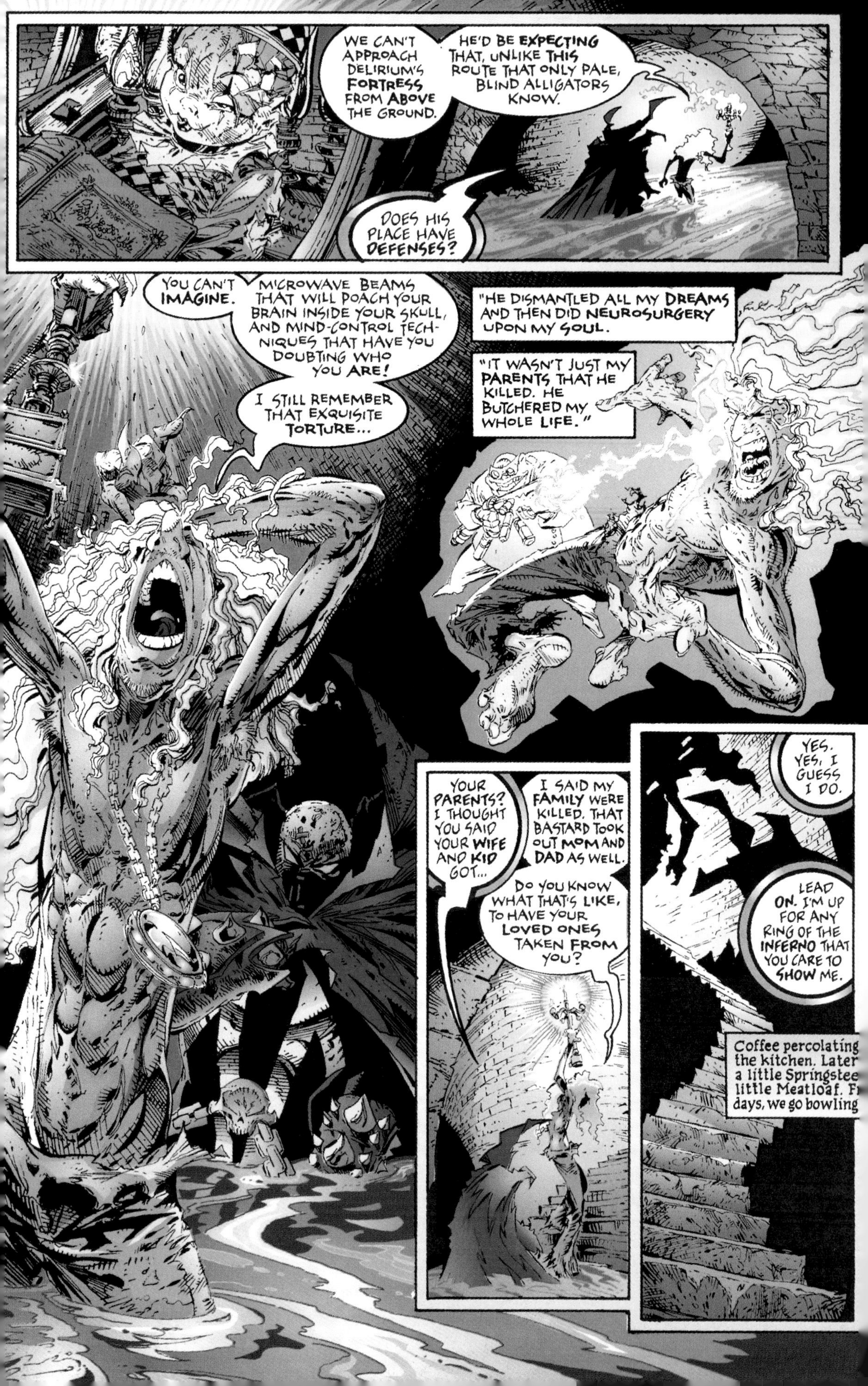
WE CAN'T APPROACH DELIRIUM'S FORTRESS FROM ABOVE THE GROUND.
HE'D BE EXPECTING THAT, UNLIKE THIS ROUTE THAT ONLY PALE, BLIND ALLIGATORS KNOW.
DOES HIS PLACE HAVE DEFENSES?
YOU CAN'T IMAGINE.
MICROWAVE BEAMS THAT WILL POACH YOUR BRAIN INSIDE YOUR SKULL, AND MIND-CONTROL TECHNIQUES THAT HAVE YOU DOUBTING WHO YOU ARE!
I STILL REMEMBER THAT EXQUISITE TORTURE...
"HE DISMANTLED ALL MY DREAMS AND THEN DID NEUROSURGERY UPON MY SOUL.
"IT WASN'T JUST MY PARENTS THAT HE KILLED. HE BUTCHERED MY WHOLE LIFE."
YOUR PARENTS? I THOUGHT YOU SAID YOUR WIFE AND KID GOT...
I SAID MY FAMILY WERE KILLED. THAT BASTARD TOOK OUT MOM AND DAD AS WELL.
DO YOU KNOW WHAT THAT'S LIKE, TO HAVE YOUR LOVED ONES TAKEN FROM YOU?
YES. YES, I GUESS I DO.
LEAD ON. I'M UP FOR ANY RING OF THE INFERNO THAT YOU CARE TO SHOW ME.
Coffee percolating the kitchen. Later a little Springstee little Meatloaf. F days, we go bowling

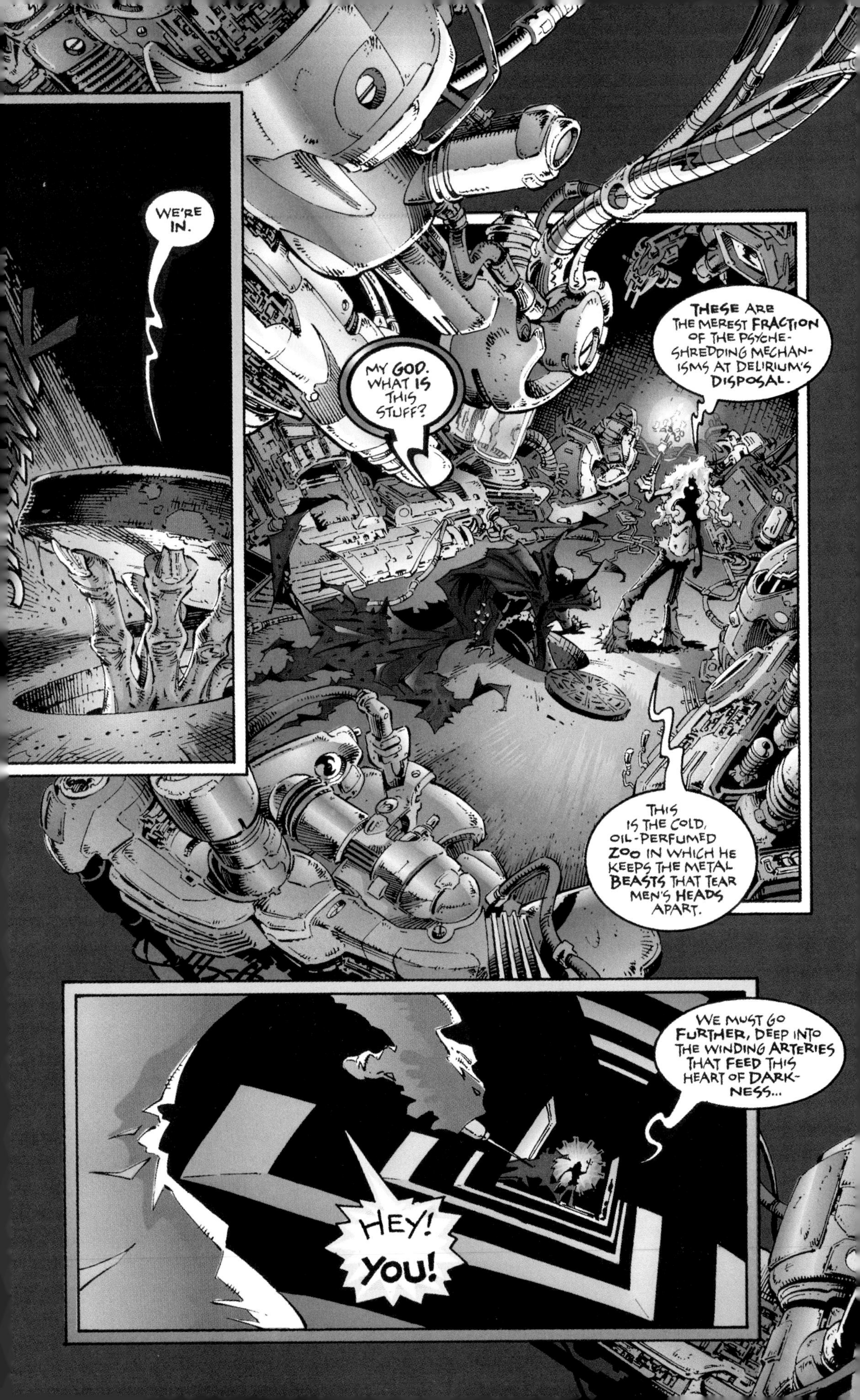
WE'RE IN.
MY GOD. WHAT IS THIS STUFF?
THESE ARE THE MEREST FRACTION OF THE PSYCHE-SHREDDING MECHAN-ISMS AT DELIRIUM'S DISPOSAL.
THIS IS THE COLD, OIL-PERFUMED ZOO IN WHICH HE KEEPS THE METAL BEASTS THAT TEAR MEN'S HEADS APART.
WE MUST GO FURTHER, DEEP INTO THE WINDING ARTERIES THAT FEED THIS HEART OF DARK-NESS...
HEY! YOU!

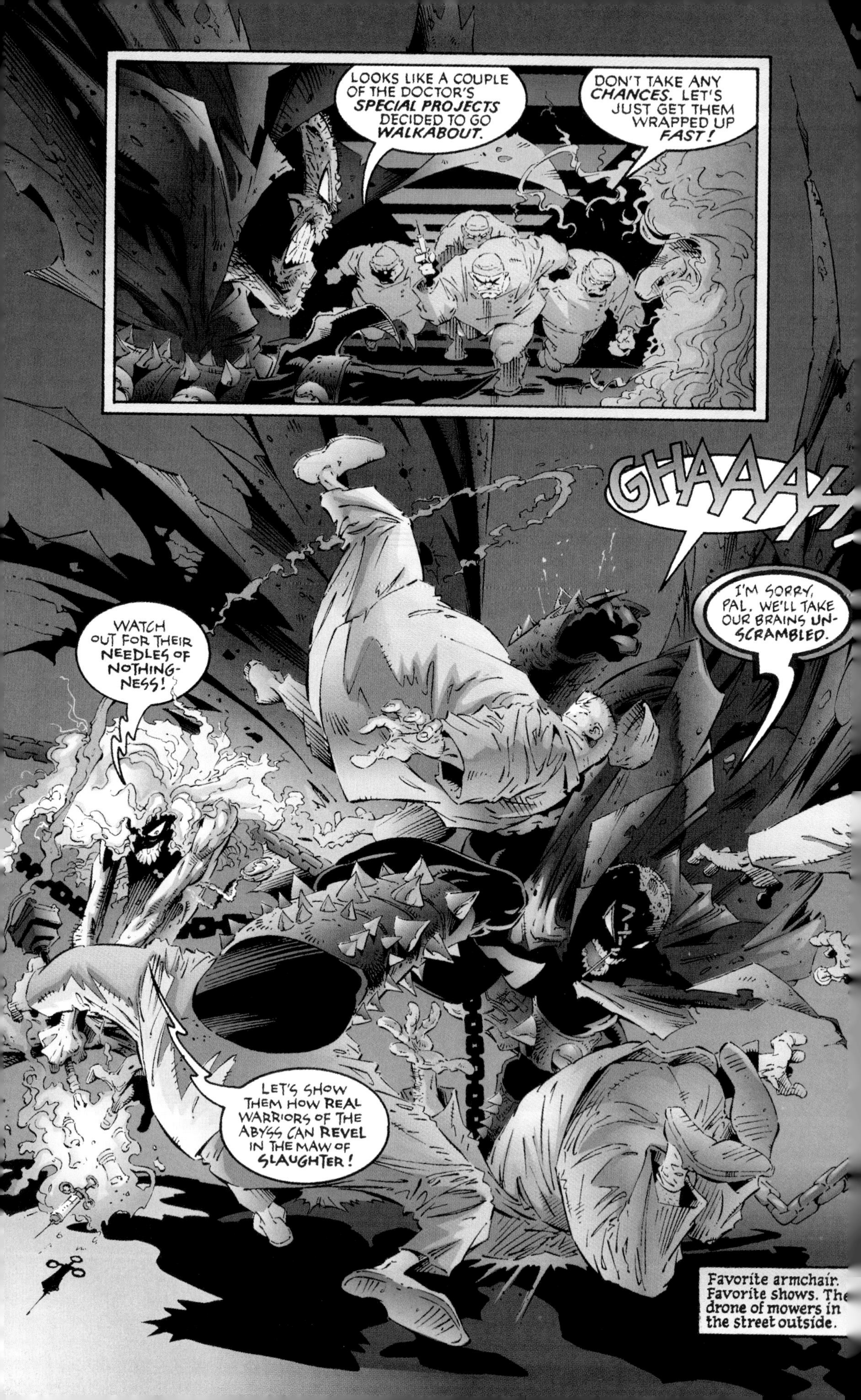
LOOKS LIKE A COUPLE OF THE DOCTOR'S SPECIAL PROJECTS DECIDED TO GO WALKABOUT.
DON'T TAKE ANY CHANCES. LET'S JUST GET THEM WRAPPED UP FAST!
GHAAAA
WATCH OUT FOR THEIR NEEDLES OF NOTHING-NESS!
I'M SORRY, PAL. WE'LL TAKE OUR BRAINS UN-SCRAMBLED.
LET'S SHOW THEM HOW REAL WARRIORS OF THE ABYSS CAN REVEL IN THE MAW OF SLAUGHTER!
Favorite armchair. Favorite shows. The drone of mowers in the street outside.

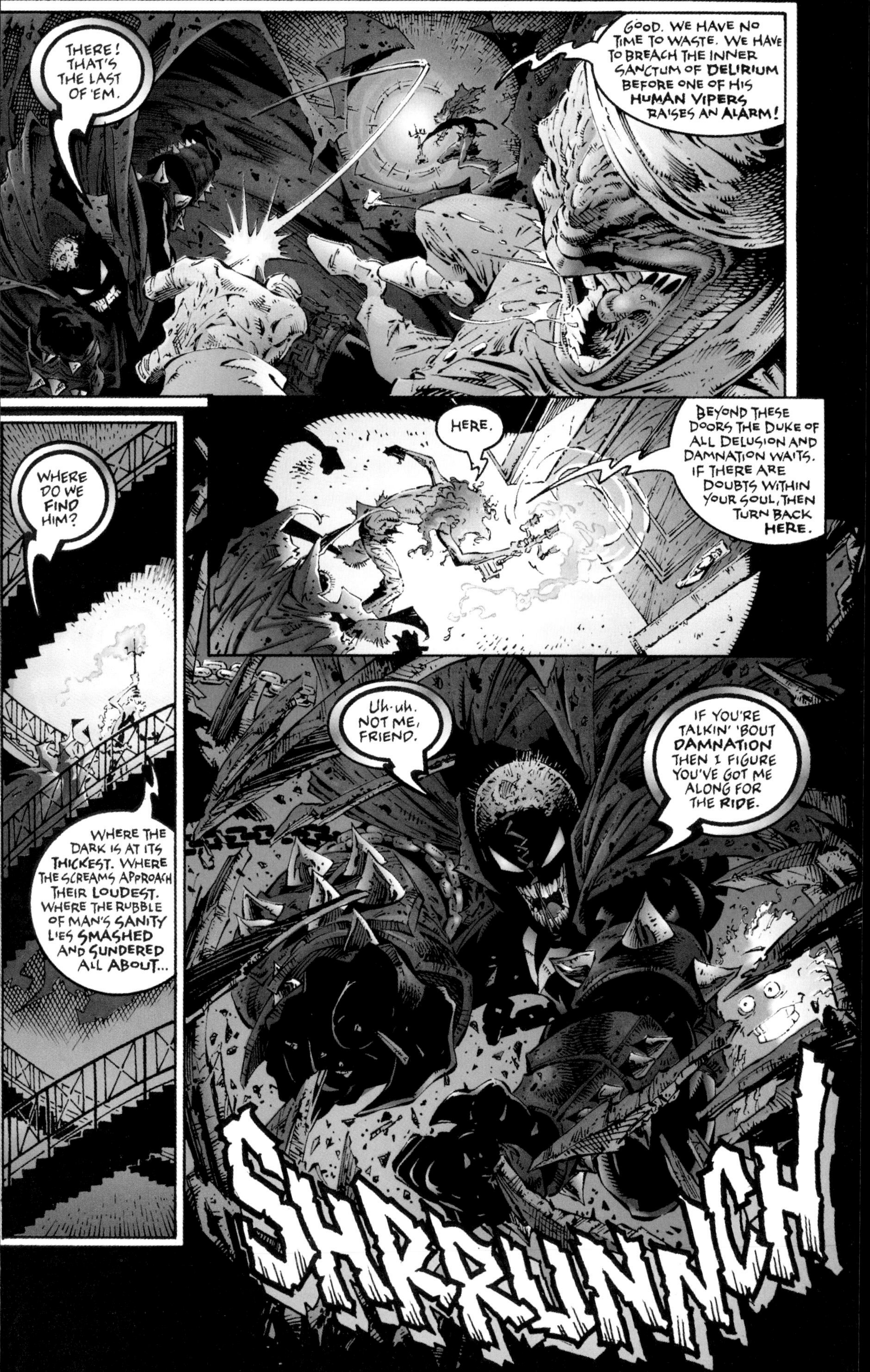
THERE! THAT'S THE LAST OF 'EM.
GOOD. WE HAVE NO TIME TO WASTE. WE HAVE TO BREACH THE INNER SANCTUM OF DELIRIUM BEFORE ONE OF HIS HUMAN VIPERS RAISES AN ALARM!
WHERE DO WE FIND HIM?
WHERE THE DARK IS AT ITS THICKEST. WHERE THE SCREAMS APPROACH THEIR LOUDEST. WHERE THE RUBBLE OF MAN'S SANITY LIES SMASHED AND SUNDERED ALL ABOUT...
HERE.
BEYOND THESE DOORS THE DUKE OF ALL DELUSION AND DAMNATION WAITS. IF THERE ARE DOUBTS WITHIN YOUR SOUL, THEN TURN BACK HERE.
Uh-uh. NOT ME, FRIEND.
IF YOU'RE TALKIN' 'BOUT DAMNATION THEN I FIGURE YOU'VE GOT ME ALONG FOR THE RIDE.
SHRRUNNCH

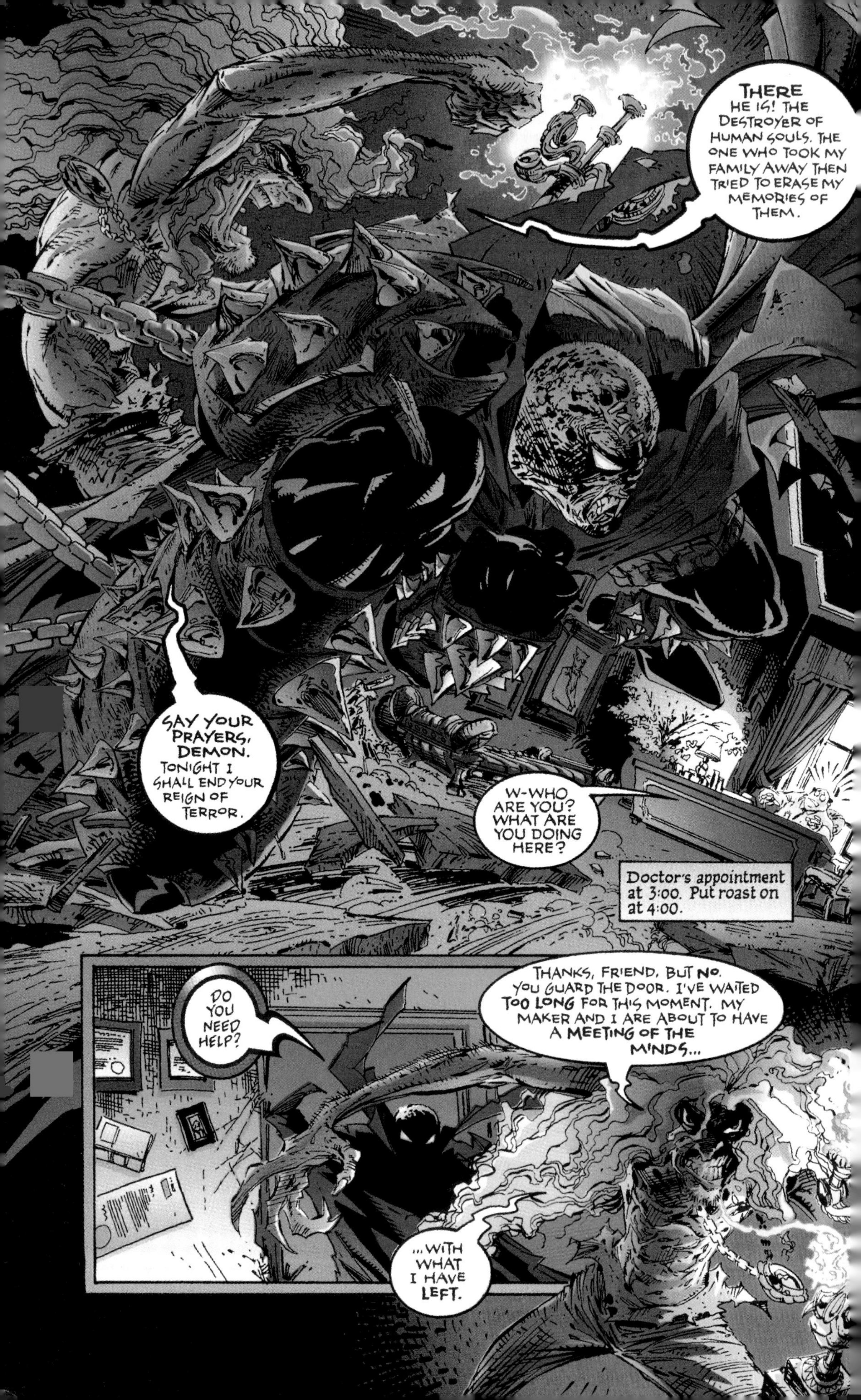
THERE HE IS! THE DESTROYER OF HUMAN SOULS. THE ONE WHO TOOK MY FAMILY AWAY THEN TRIED TO ERASE MY MEMORIES OF THEM.
SAY YOUR PRAYERS, DEMON. TONIGHT I SHALL END YOUR REIGN OF TERROR.
W-WHO ARE YOU? WHAT ARE YOU DOING HERE?
Doctor's appointment at 3:00. Put roast on at 4:00.
DO YOU NEED HELP?
THANKS, FRIEND, BUT NO. YOU GUARD THE DOOR. I'VE WAITED TOO LONG FOR THIS MOMENT. MY MAKER AND I ARE ABOUT TO HAVE A MEETING OF THE MINDS...
...WITH WHAT I HAVE LEFT.

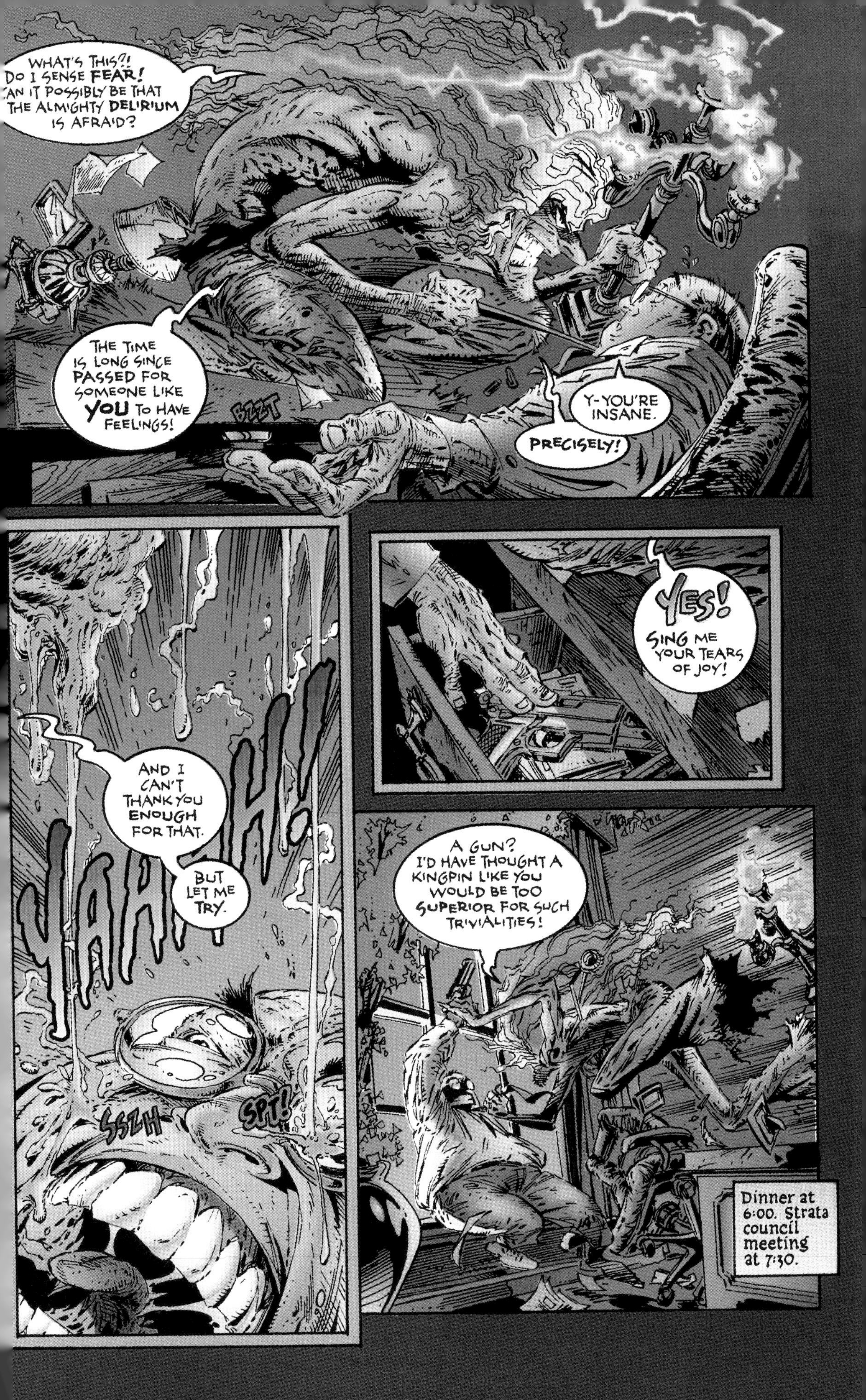
WHAT'S THIS?! DO I SENSE **FEAR**! CAN IT POSSIBLY BE THAT THE ALMIGHTY **DELIRIUM** IS AFRAID?
THE TIME IS LONG SINCE **PASSED** FOR SOMEONE LIKE **YOU** TO HAVE FEELINGS!
BZZT
Y-YOU'RE INSANE.
PRECISELY!
AND I CAN'T THANK YOU **ENOUGH** FOR THAT.
BUT LET ME **TRY**.
SSZH
SPT!
YES!
SING ME YOUR TEARS OF JOY!
A GUN? I'D HAVE THOUGHT A KINGPIN LIKE YOU WOULD BE TOO **SUPERIOR** FOR SUCH TRIVIALITIES!
Dinner at 6:00. Strata council meeting at 7:30.

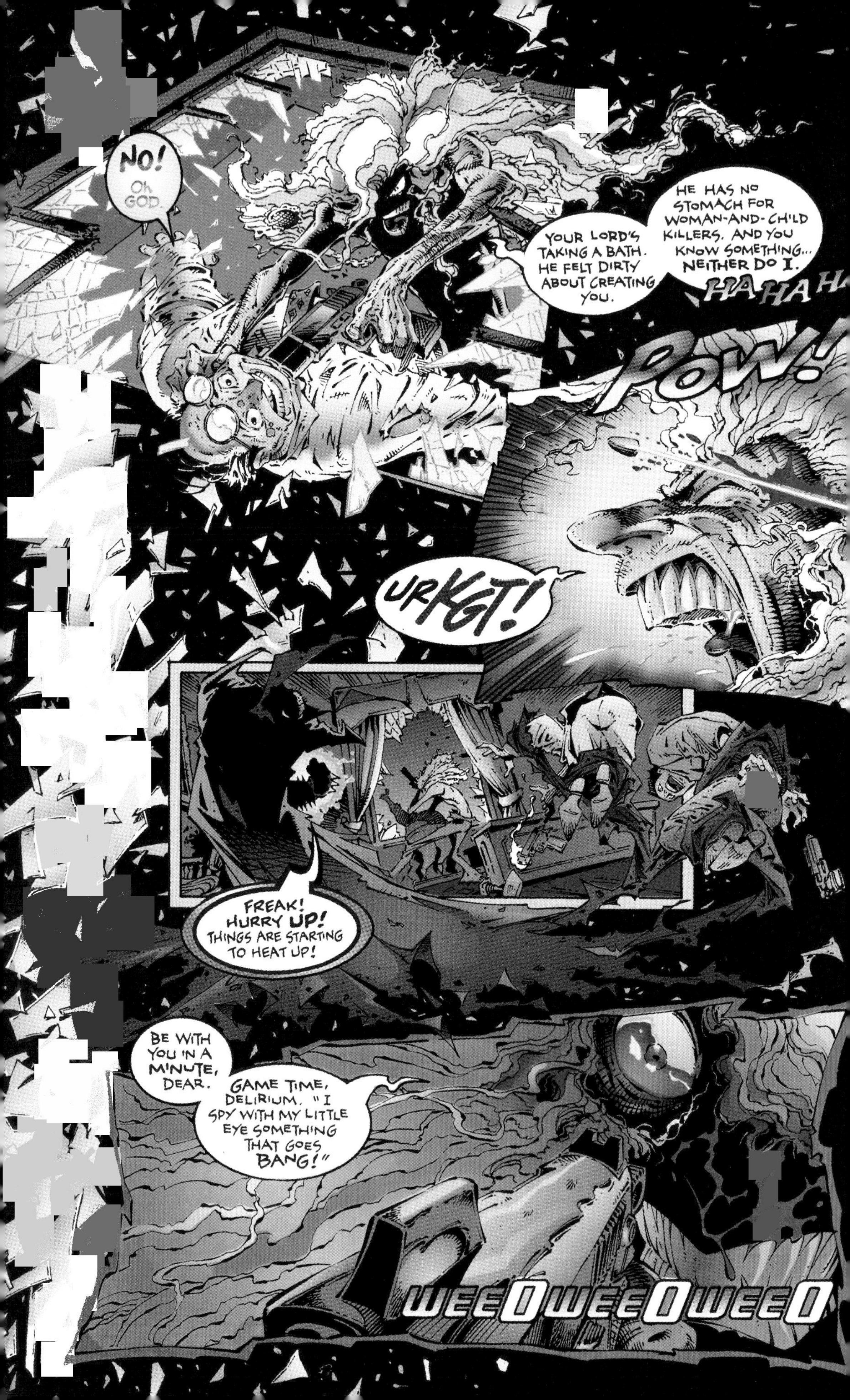
NO! Oh GOD.
YOUR LORD'S TAKING A BATH. HE FELT DIRTY ABOUT CREATING YOU.
HE HAS NO STOMACH FOR WOMAN-AND-CHILD KILLERS. AND YOU KNOW SOMETHING... NEITHER DO I.
HAHAHA
POW!
URKGT!
FREAK! HURRY UP! THINGS ARE STARTING TO HEAT UP!
BE WITH YOU IN A MINUTE, DEAR.
GAME TIME, DELIRIUM. "I SPY WITH MY LITTLE EYE SOMETHING THAT GOES BANG!"
WEEOWEEOWEEO

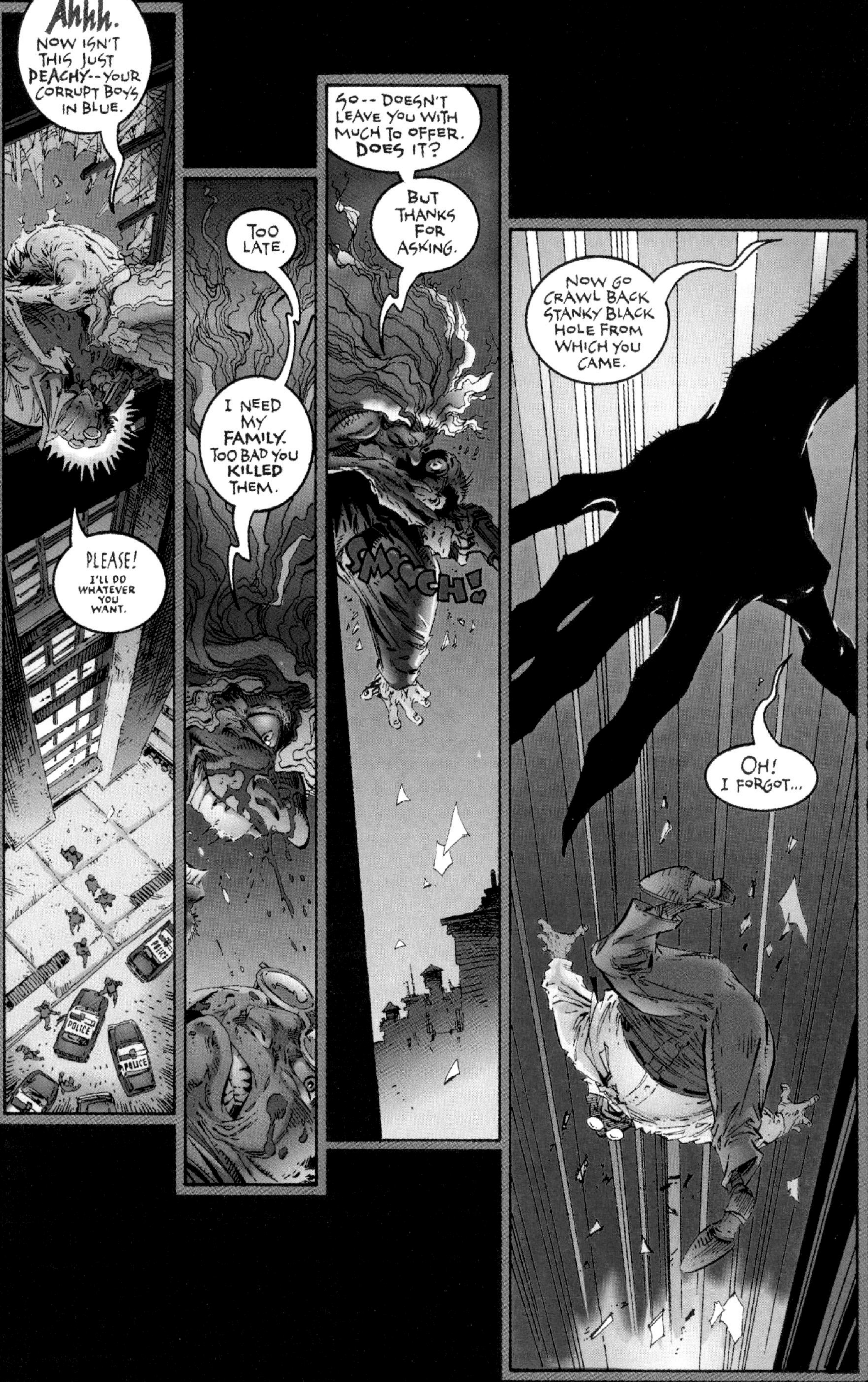
Ahhh. NOW ISN'T THIS JUST PEACHY--YOUR CORRUPT BOYS IN BLUE.
PLEASE! I'LL DO WHATEVER YOU WANT.
TOO LATE.
I NEED MY FAMILY. TOO BAD YOU KILLED THEM.
SO-- DOESN'T LEAVE YOU WITH MUCH TO OFFER. DOES IT?
BUT THANKS FOR ASKING.
SMUCH!
NOW GO CRAWL BACK STANKY BLACK HOLE FROM WHICH YOU CAME.
OH! I FORGOT...

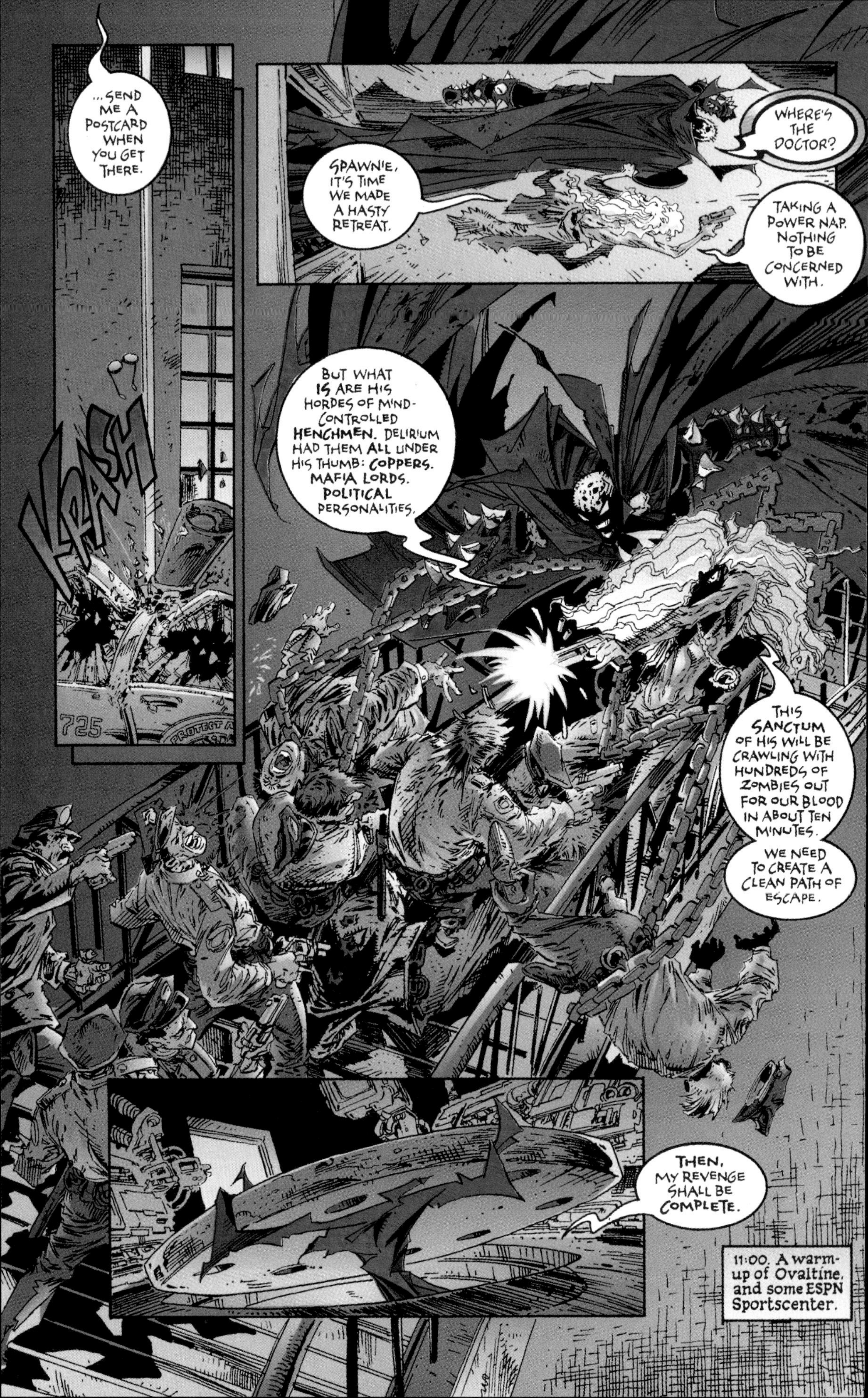
...SEND ME A POSTCARD WHEN YOU GET THERE.
KRASH
725
SPAWNIE, IT'S TIME WE MADE A HASTY RETREAT.
WHERE'S THE DOCTOR?
TAKING A POWER NAP. NOTHING TO BE CONCERNED WITH.
BUT WHAT IS ARE HIS HORDES OF MIND-CONTROLLED HENCHMEN. DELIRIUM HAD THEM ALL UNDER HIS THUMB: COPPERS. MAFIA LORDS. POLITICAL PERSONALITIES.
THIS SANCTUM OF HIS WILL BE CRAWLING WITH HUNDREDS OF ZOMBIES OUT FOR OUR BLOOD IN ABOUT TEN MINUTES.
WE NEED TO CREATE A CLEAN PATH OF ESCAPE.
THEN, MY REVENGE SHALL BE COMPLETE.
11:00. A warm-up of Ovaltine, and some ESPN Sportscenter.

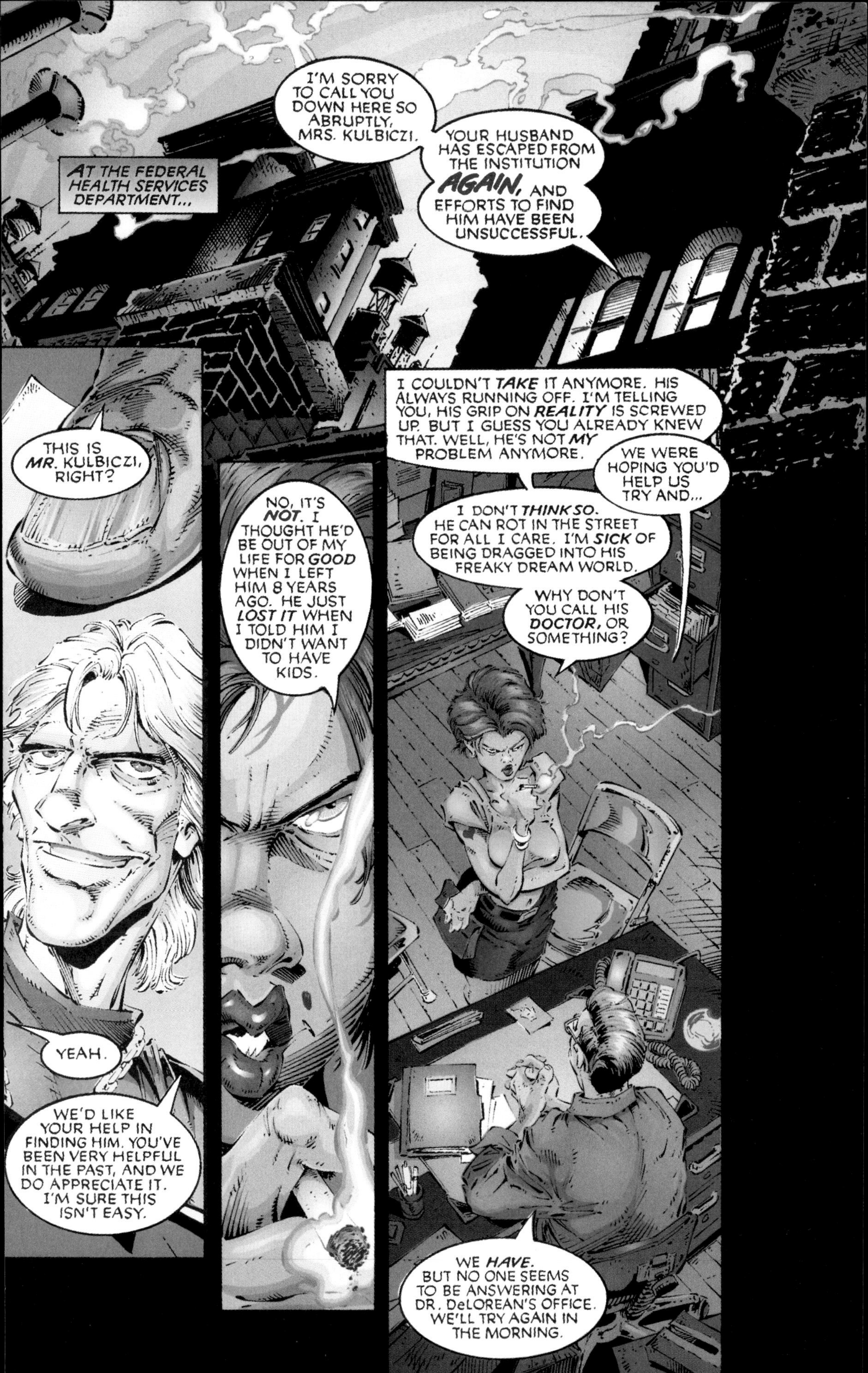

AT THE FEDERAL HEALTH SERVICES DEPARTMENT...
I'M SORRY TO CALL YOU DOWN HERE SO ABRUPTLY, MRS. KULBICZI.
YOUR HUSBAND HAS ESCAPED FROM THE INSTITUTION *AGAIN*, AND EFFORTS TO FIND HIM HAVE BEEN UNSUCCESSFUL.
THIS IS *MR.* KULBICZI, RIGHT?
YEAH.
WE'D LIKE YOUR HELP IN FINDING HIM. YOU'VE BEEN VERY HELPFUL IN THE PAST, AND WE DO APPRECIATE IT. I'M SURE THIS ISN'T EASY.
NO, IT'S *NOT*. I THOUGHT HE'D BE OUT OF MY LIFE FOR *GOOD* WHEN I LEFT HIM 8 YEARS AGO. HE JUST *LOST IT* WHEN I TOLD HIM I DIDN'T WANT TO HAVE KIDS.
I COULDN'T *TAKE* IT ANYMORE. HIS ALWAYS RUNNING OFF. I'M TELLING YOU, HIS GRIP ON *REALITY* IS SCREWED UP. BUT I GUESS YOU ALREADY KNEW THAT. WELL, HE'S NOT *MY* PROBLEM ANYMORE.
WE WERE HOPING YOU'D HELP US TRY AND...
I DON'T *THINK SO*. HE CAN ROT IN THE STREET FOR ALL I CARE. I'M *SICK* OF BEING DRAGGED INTO HIS FREAKY DREAM WORLD.
WHY DON'T YOU CALL HIS *DOCTOR*, OR SOMETHING?
WE *HAVE*. BUT NO ONE SEEMS TO BE ANSWERING AT DR. DeLOREAN'S OFFICE. WE'LL TRY AGAIN IN THE MORNING.

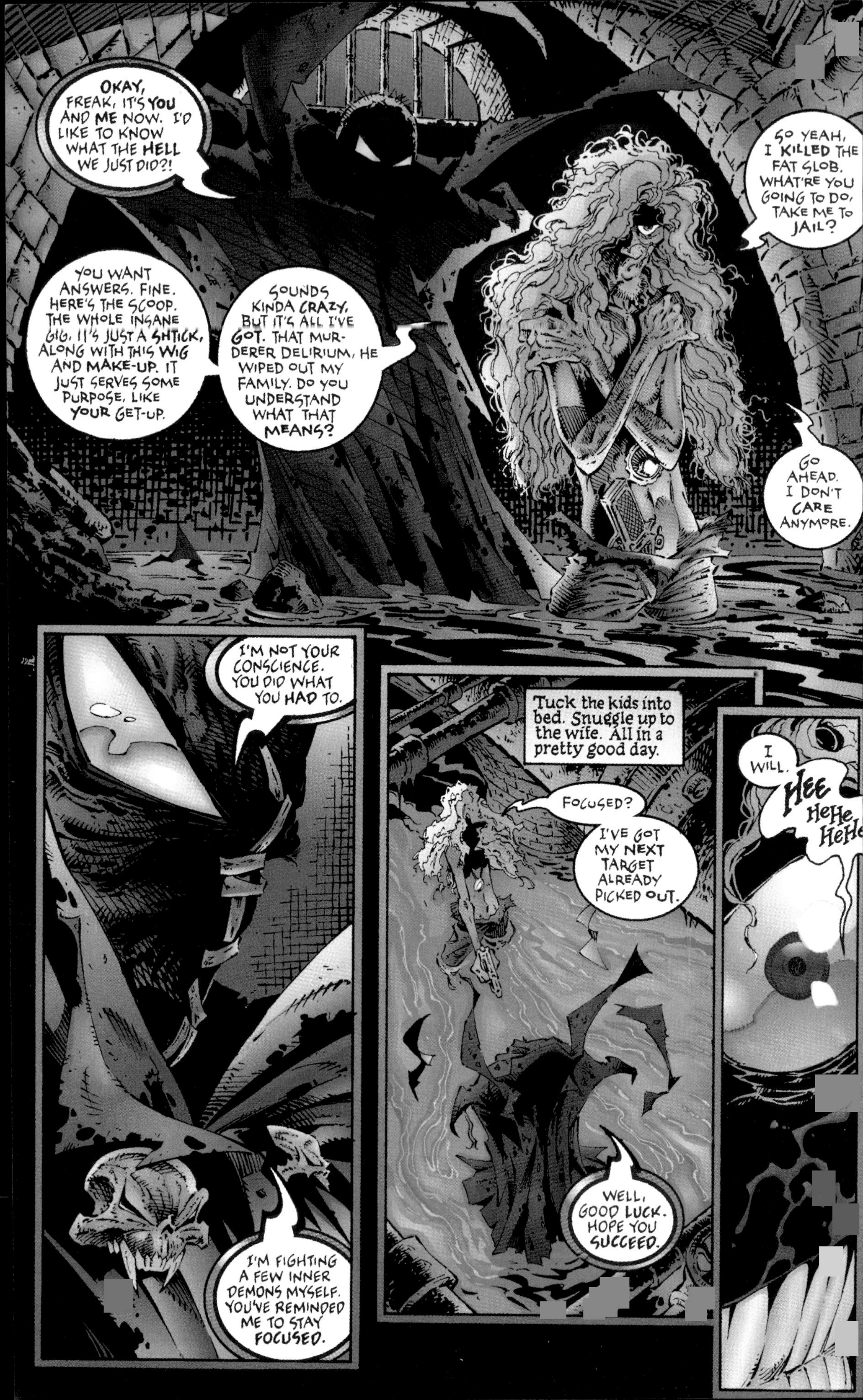
OKAY, FREAK, IT'S YOU AND ME NOW. I'D LIKE TO KNOW WHAT THE HELL WE JUST DID?!
SO YEAH, I KILLED THE FAT SLOB. WHAT'RE YOU GOING TO DO, TAKE ME TO JAIL?
YOU WANT ANSWERS. FINE. HERE'S THE SCOOP. THE WHOLE INSANE GIG, IT'S JUST A SHTICK, ALONG WITH THIS WIG AND MAKE-UP. IT JUST SERVES SOME PURPOSE, LIKE YOUR GET-UP.
SOUNDS KINDA CRAZY, BUT IT'S ALL I'VE GOT. THAT MURDERER DELIRIUM, HE WIPED OUT MY FAMILY. DO YOU UNDERSTAND WHAT THAT MEANS?
GO AHEAD. I DON'T CARE ANYMORE.
I'M NOT YOUR CONSCIENCE. YOU DID WHAT YOU HAD TO.
I'M FIGHTING A FEW INNER DEMONS MYSELF. YOU'VE REMINDED ME TO STAY FOCUSED.
Tuck the kids into bed. Snuggle up to the wife. All in a pretty good day.
FOCUSED?
I'VE GOT MY NEXT TARGET ALREADY PICKED OUT.
WELL, GOOD LUCK. HOPE YOU SUCCEED.
I WILL.
HEE HeHe HeHe

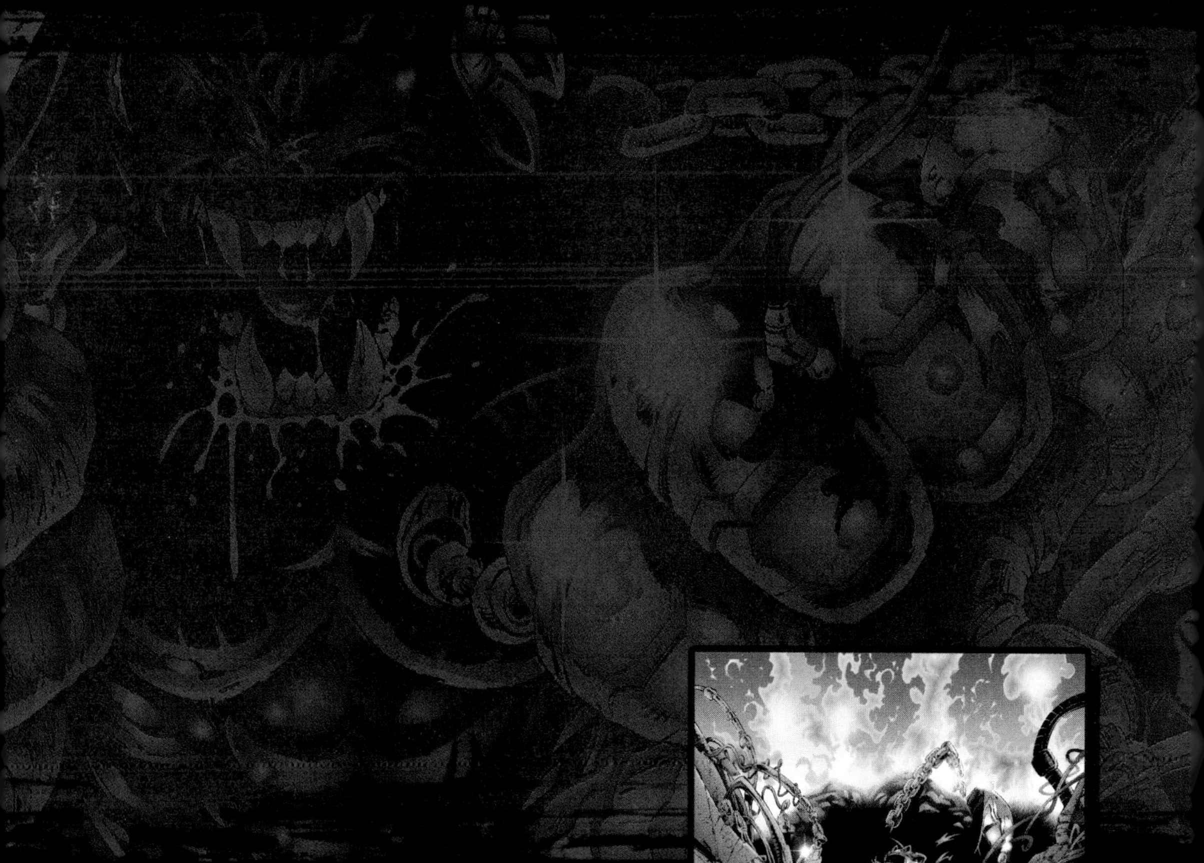

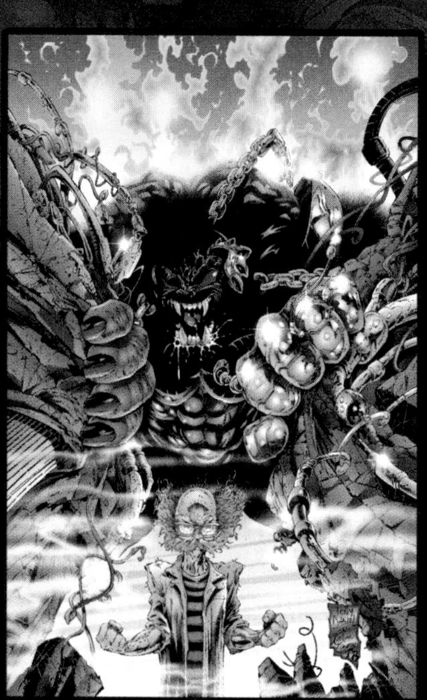

ISSUE THIRTY-EIGHT

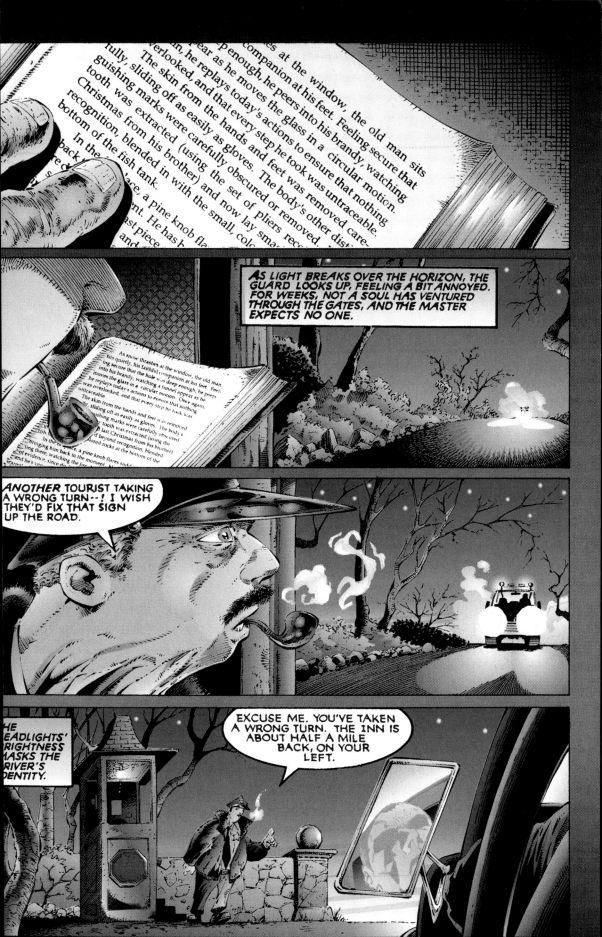

AS LIGHT BREAKS OVER THE HORIZON, THE GUARD LOOKS UP, FEELING A BIT ANNOYED. FOR WEEKS, NOT A SOUL HAS VENTURED THROUGH THE GATES, AND THE MASTER EXPECTS NO ONE.

ANOTHER TOURIST TAKING A WRONG TURN--! I WISH THEY'D FIX THAT SIGN UP THE ROAD.

EXCUSE ME. YOU'VE TAKEN A WRONG TURN. THE INN IS ABOUT HALF A MILE BACK, ON YOUR LEFT.

THE HEADLIGHTS' BRIGHTNESS MASKS THE DRIVER'S IDENTITY.

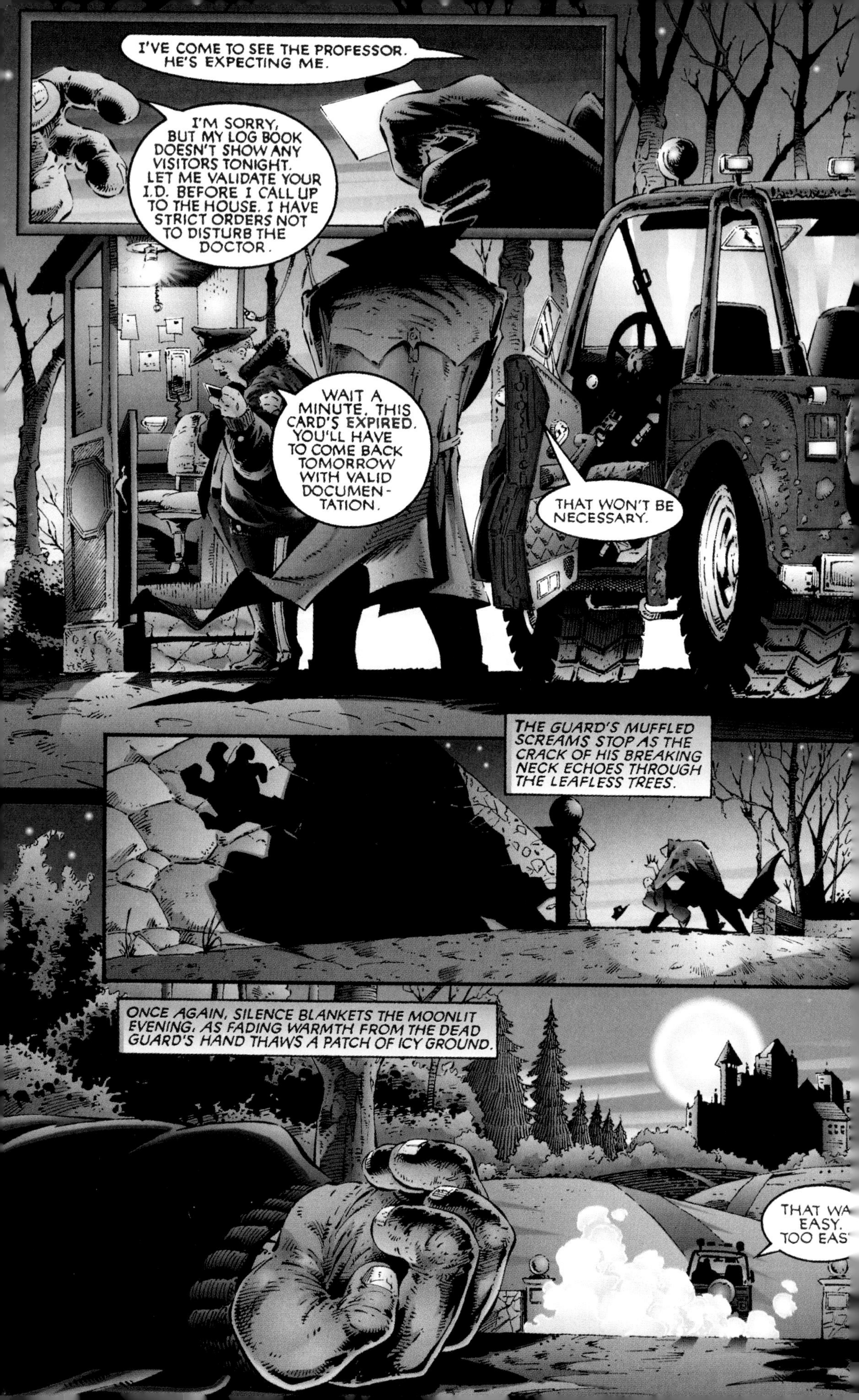
I'VE COME TO SEE THE PROFESSOR. HE'S EXPECTING ME.
I'M SORRY, BUT MY LOG BOOK DOESN'T SHOW ANY VISITORS TONIGHT. LET ME VALIDATE YOUR I.D. BEFORE I CALL UP TO THE HOUSE. I HAVE STRICT ORDERS NOT TO DISTURB THE DOCTOR.
WAIT A MINUTE, THIS CARD'S EXPIRED. YOU'LL HAVE TO COME BACK TOMORROW WITH VALID DOCUMENTATION.
THAT WON'T BE NECESSARY.
THE GUARD'S MUFFLED SCREAMS STOP AS THE CRACK OF HIS BREAKING NECK ECHOES THROUGH THE LEAFLESS TREES.
ONCE AGAIN, SILENCE BLANKETS THE MOONLIT EVENING, AS FADING WARMTH FROM THE DEAD GUARD'S HAND THAWS A PATCH OF ICY GROUND.
THAT WA EASY. TOO EAS

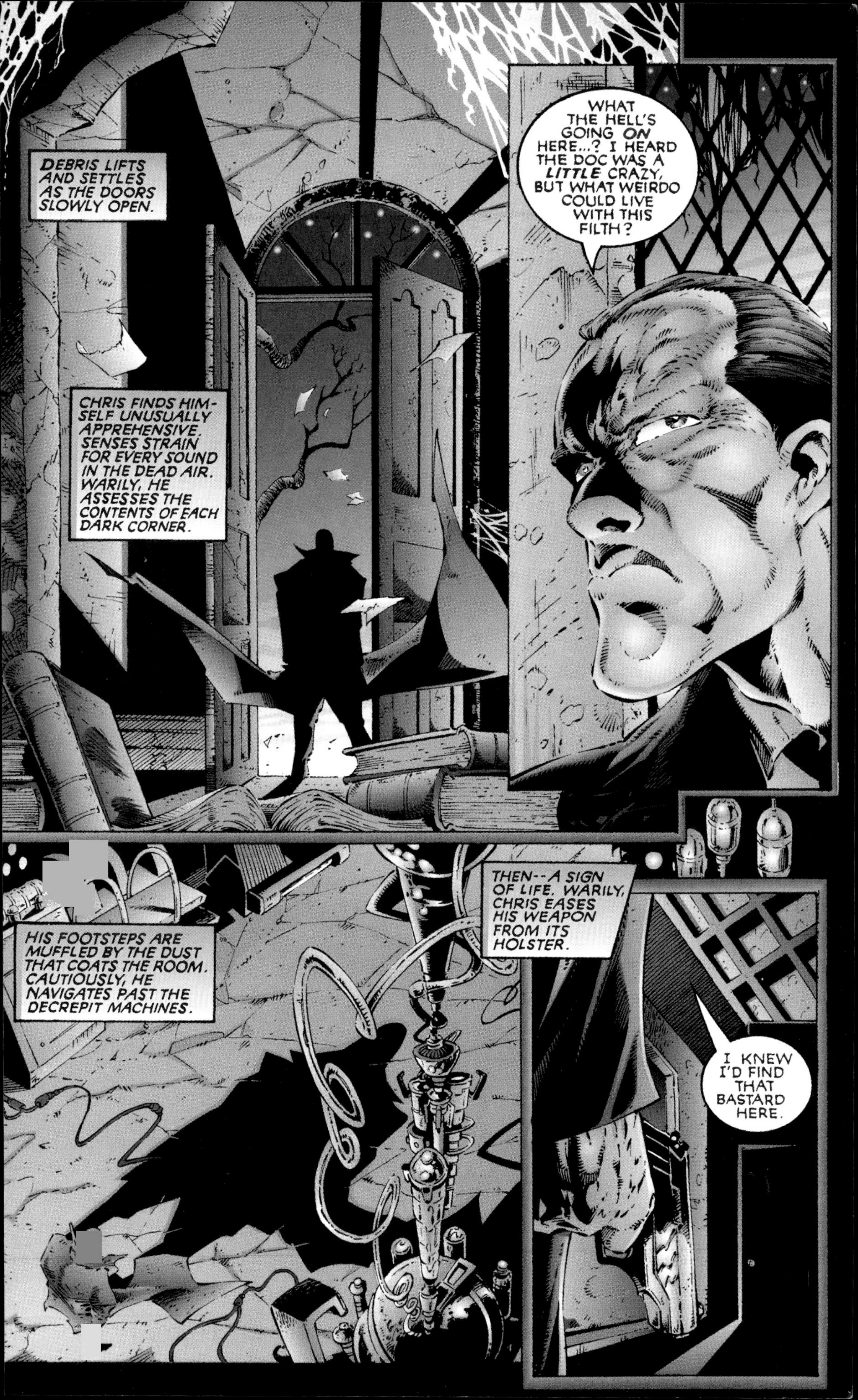
DEBRIS LIFTS AND SETTLES AS THE DOORS SLOWLY OPEN.
CHRIS FINDS HIM-SELF UNUSUALLY APPREHENSIVE. SENSES STRAIN FOR EVERY SOUND IN THE DEAD AIR. WARILY, HE ASSESSES THE CONTENTS OF EACH DARK CORNER.
WHAT THE HELL'S GOING ON HERE...? I HEARD THE DOC WAS A LITTLE CRAZY, BUT WHAT WEIRDO COULD LIVE WITH THIS FILTH?
HIS FOOTSTEPS ARE MUFFLED BY THE DUST THAT COATS THE ROOM. CAUTIOUSLY, HE NAVIGATES PAST THE DECREPIT MACHINES.
THEN--A SIGN OF LIFE. WARILY, CHRIS EASES HIS WEAPON FROM ITS HOLSTER.
I KNEW I'D FIND THAT BASTARD HERE.

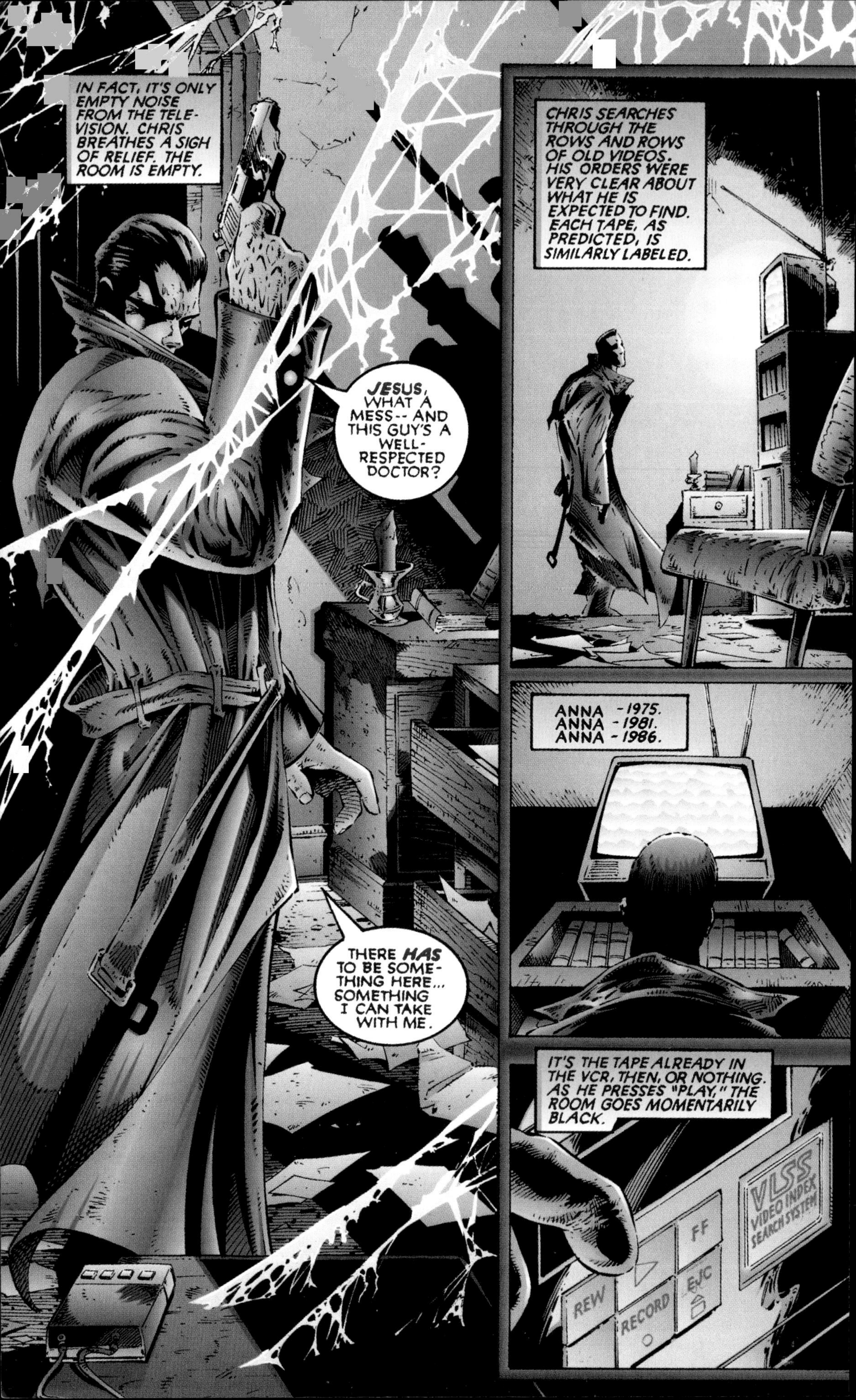
IN FACT, IT'S ONLY EMPTY NOISE FROM THE TELE-VISION. CHRIS BREATHES A SIGH OF RELIEF. THE ROOM IS EMPTY.
JESUS, WHAT A MESS-- AND THIS GUY'S A WELL-RESPECTED DOCTOR?
THERE HAS TO BE SOME-THING HERE... SOMETHING I CAN TAKE WITH ME.
CHRIS SEARCHES THROUGH THE ROWS AND ROWS OF OLD VIDEOS. HIS ORDERS WERE VERY CLEAR ABOUT WHAT HE IS EXPECTED TO FIND. EACH TAPE, AS PREDICTED, IS SIMILARLY LABELED.
ANNA -1975.
ANNA -1981.
ANNA -1986.
IT'S THE TAPE ALREADY IN THE VCR, THEN, OR NOTHING. AS HE PRESSES "PLAY," THE ROOM GOES MOMENTARILY BLACK.
VLSS VIDEO INDEX SEARCH SYSTEM
FF
REW
RECORD
EJC

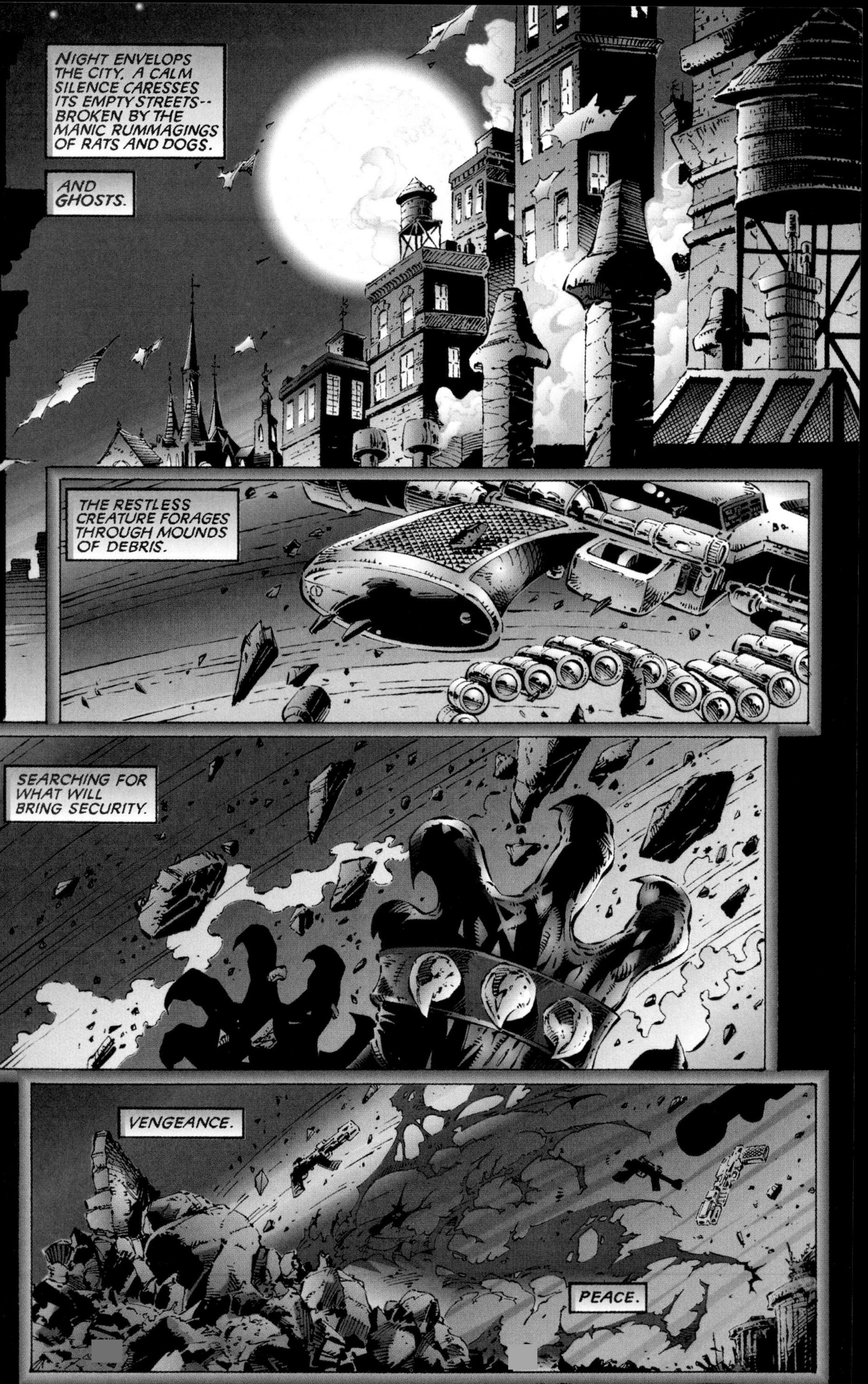
NIGHT ENVELOPS THE CITY. A CALM SILENCE CARESSES ITS EMPTY STREETS-- BROKEN BY THE MANIC RUMMAGINGS OF RATS AND DOGS.
AND GHOSTS.
THE RESTLESS CREATURE FORAGES THROUGH MOUNDS OF DEBRIS.
SEARCHING FOR WHAT WILL BRING SECURITY.
VENGEANCE.
PEACE.

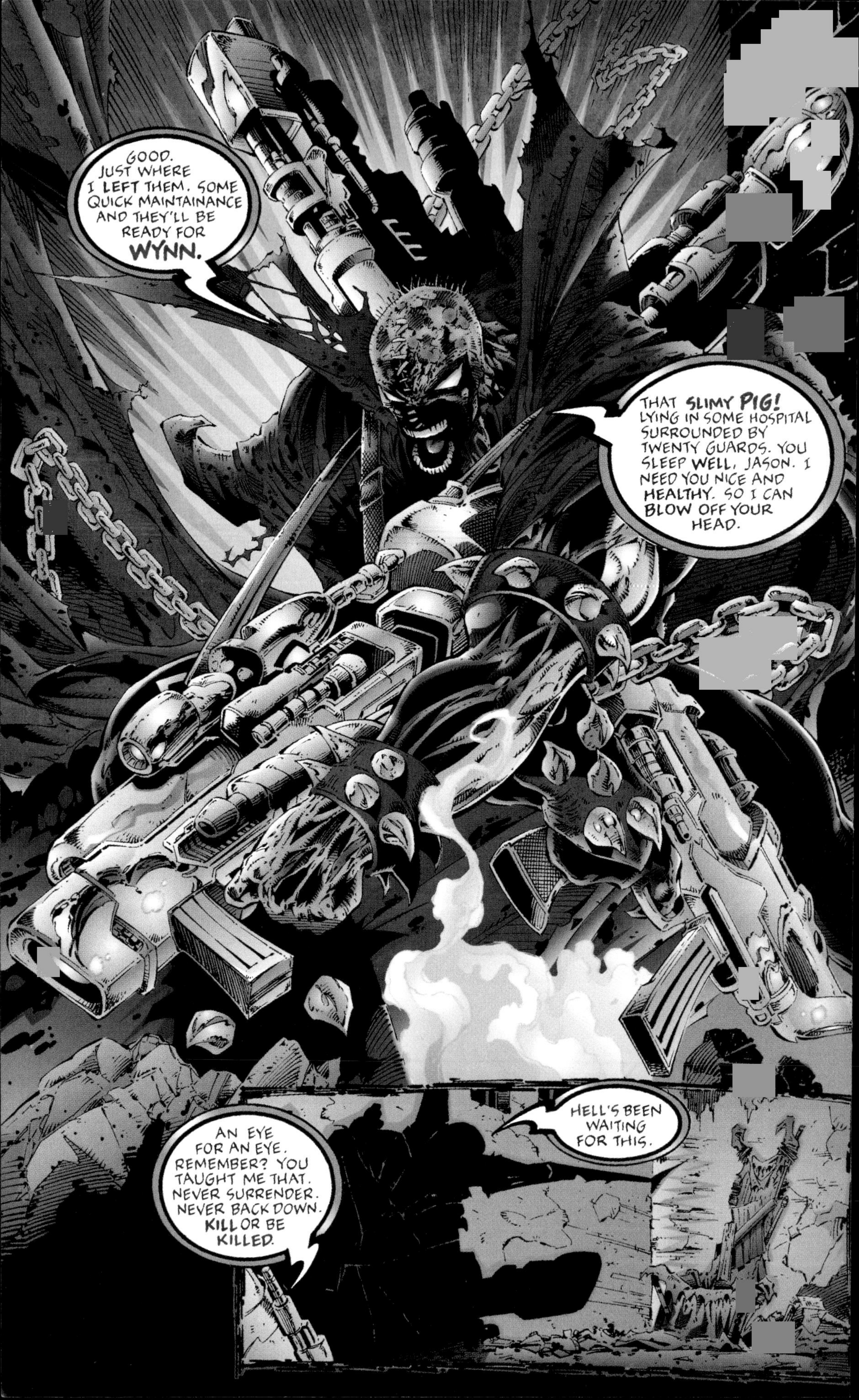
GOOD. JUST WHERE I LEFT THEM. SOME QUICK MAINTAINANCE AND THEY'LL BE READY FOR WYNN.
THAT SLIMY PIG! LYING IN SOME HOSPITAL SURROUNDED BY TWENTY GUARDS. YOU SLEEP WELL, JASON. I NEED YOU NICE AND HEALTHY. SO I CAN BLOW OFF YOUR HEAD.
HELL'S BEEN WAITING FOR THIS.
AN EYE FOR AN EYE. REMEMBER? YOU TAUGHT ME THAT. NEVER SURRENDER. NEVER BACK DOWN. KILL OR BE KILLED.

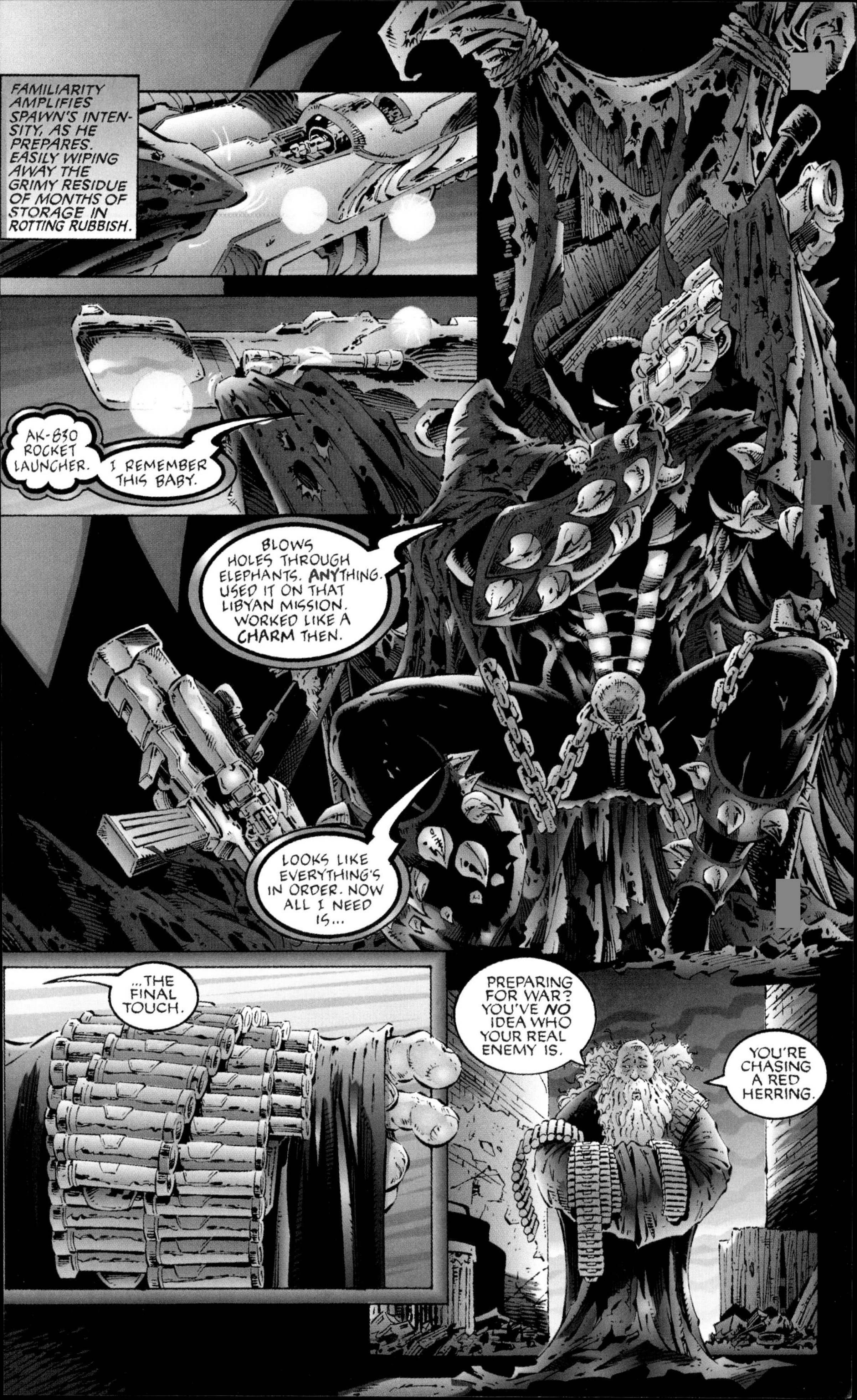
FAMILIARITY AMPLIFIES SPAWN'S INTENSITY, AS HE PREPARES. EASILY WIPING AWAY THE GRIMY RESIDUE OF MONTHS OF STORAGE IN ROTTING RUBBISH.
AK-830 ROCKET LAUNCHER.
I REMEMBER THIS BABY.
BLOWS HOLES THROUGH ELEPHANTS. ANYTHING. USED IT ON THAT LIBYAN MISSION. WORKED LIKE A CHARM THEN.
LOOKS LIKE EVERYTHING'S IN ORDER. NOW ALL I NEED IS...
...THE FINAL TOUCH.
PREPARING FOR WAR? YOU'VE NO IDEA WHO YOUR REAL ENEMY IS.
YOU'RE CHASING A RED HERRING.

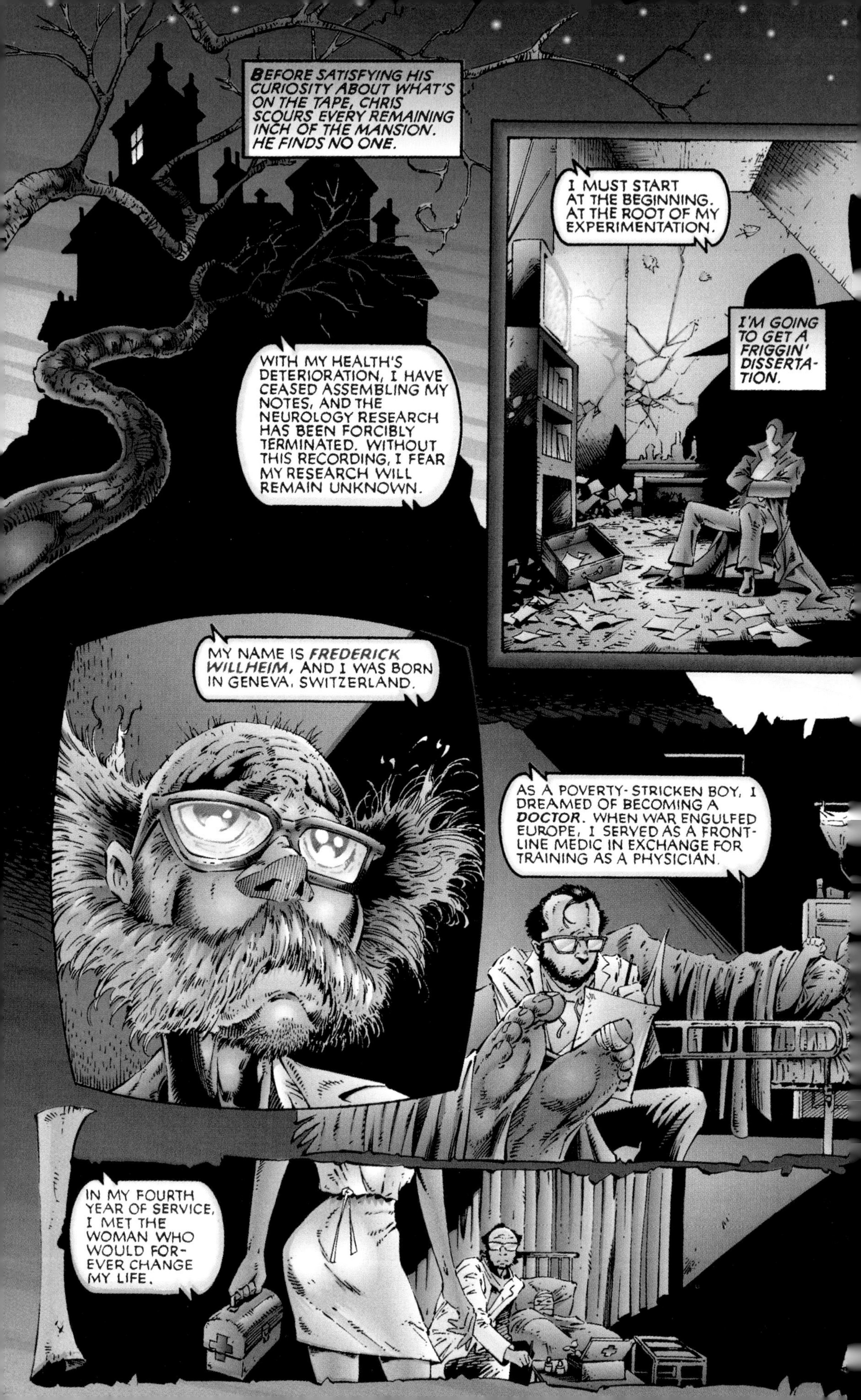
BEFORE SATISFYING HIS CURIOSITY ABOUT WHAT'S ON THE TAPE, CHRIS SCOURS EVERY REMAINING INCH OF THE MANSION. HE FINDS NO ONE.
WITH MY HEALTH'S DETERIORATION, I HAVE CEASED ASSEMBLING MY NOTES, AND THE NEUROLOGY RESEARCH HAS BEEN FORCIBLY TERMINATED. WITHOUT THIS RECORDING, I FEAR MY RESEARCH WILL REMAIN UNKNOWN.
I MUST START AT THE BEGINNING. AT THE ROOT OF MY EXPERIMENTATION.
I'M GOING TO GET A FRIGGIN' DISSERTATION.
MY NAME IS FREDERICK WILLHEIM, AND I WAS BORN IN GENEVA, SWITZERLAND.
AS A POVERTY-STRICKEN BOY, I DREAMED OF BECOMING A DOCTOR. WHEN WAR ENGULFED EUROPE, I SERVED AS A FRONT-LINE MEDIC IN EXCHANGE FOR TRAINING AS A PHYSICIAN.
IN MY FOURTH YEAR OF SERVICE, I MET THE WOMAN WHO WOULD FOREVER CHANGE MY LIFE.

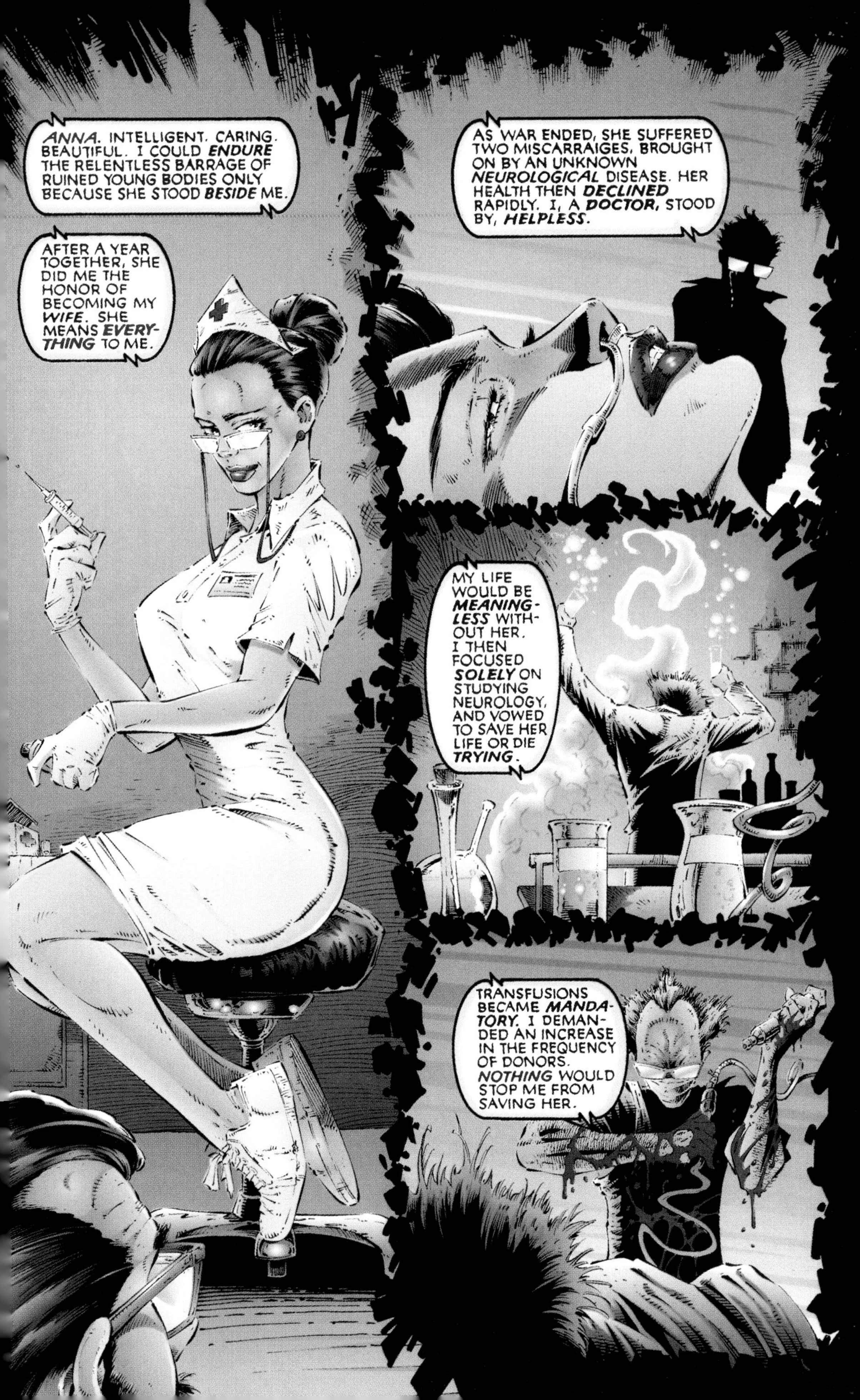
ANNA. INTELLIGENT. CARING. BEAUTIFUL. I COULD ENDURE THE RELENTLESS BARRAGE OF RUINED YOUNG BODIES ONLY BECAUSE SHE STOOD BESIDE ME.
AFTER A YEAR TOGETHER, SHE DID ME THE HONOR OF BECOMING MY WIFE. SHE MEANS EVERYTHING TO ME.
AS WAR ENDED, SHE SUFFERED TWO MISCARRAIGES, BROUGHT ON BY AN UNKNOWN NEUROLOGICAL DISEASE. HER HEALTH THEN DECLINED RAPIDLY. I, A DOCTOR, STOOD BY, HELPLESS.
MY LIFE WOULD BE MEANINGLESS WITHOUT HER. I THEN FOCUSED SOLELY ON STUDYING NEUROLOGY, AND VOWED TO SAVE HER LIFE OR DIE TRYING.
TRANSFUSIONS BECAME MANDATORY. I DEMANDED AN INCREASE IN THE FREQUENCY OF DONORS. NOTHING WOULD STOP ME FROM SAVING HER.

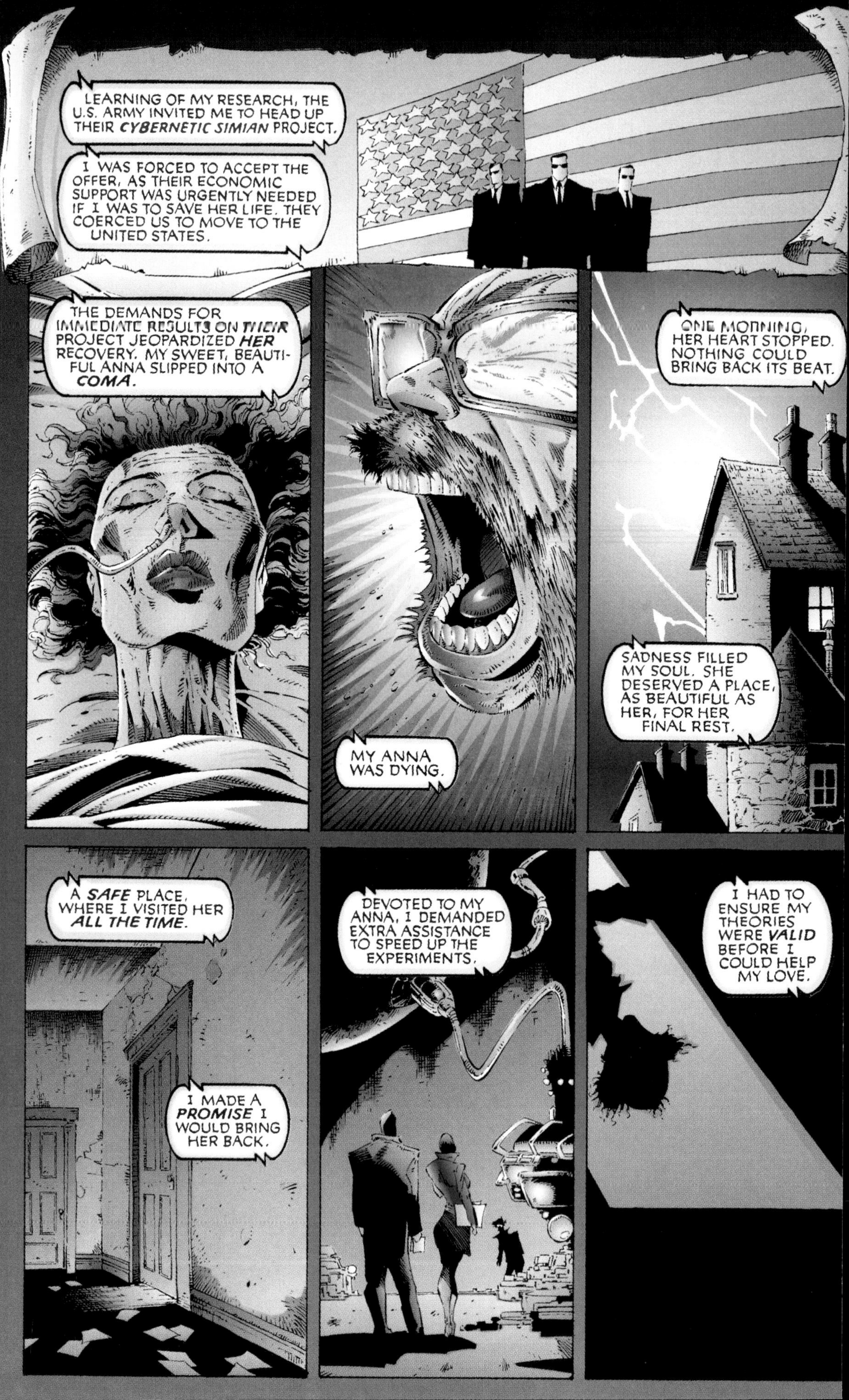
LEARNING OF MY RESEARCH, THE U.S. ARMY INVITED ME TO HEAD UP THEIR CYBERNETIC SIMIAN PROJECT.
I WAS FORCED TO ACCEPT THE OFFER, AS THEIR ECONOMIC SUPPORT WAS URGENTLY NEEDED IF I WAS TO SAVE HER LIFE. THEY COERCED US TO MOVE TO THE UNITED STATES.
THE DEMANDS FOR IMMEDIATE RESULTS ON THEIR PROJECT JEOPARDIZED HER RECOVERY. MY SWEET, BEAUTIFUL ANNA SLIPPED INTO A COMA.
MY ANNA WAS DYING.
ONE MORNING, HER HEART STOPPED. NOTHING COULD BRING BACK ITS BEAT.
SADNESS FILLED MY SOUL. SHE DESERVED A PLACE, AS BEAUTIFUL AS HER, FOR HER FINAL REST.
A SAFE PLACE, WHERE I VISITED HER ALL THE TIME.
I MADE A PROMISE I WOULD BRING HER BACK.
DEVOTED TO MY ANNA, I DEMANDED EXTRA ASSISTANCE TO SPEED UP THE EXPERIMENTS.
I HAD TO ENSURE MY THEORIES WERE VALID BEFORE I COULD HELP MY LOVE.

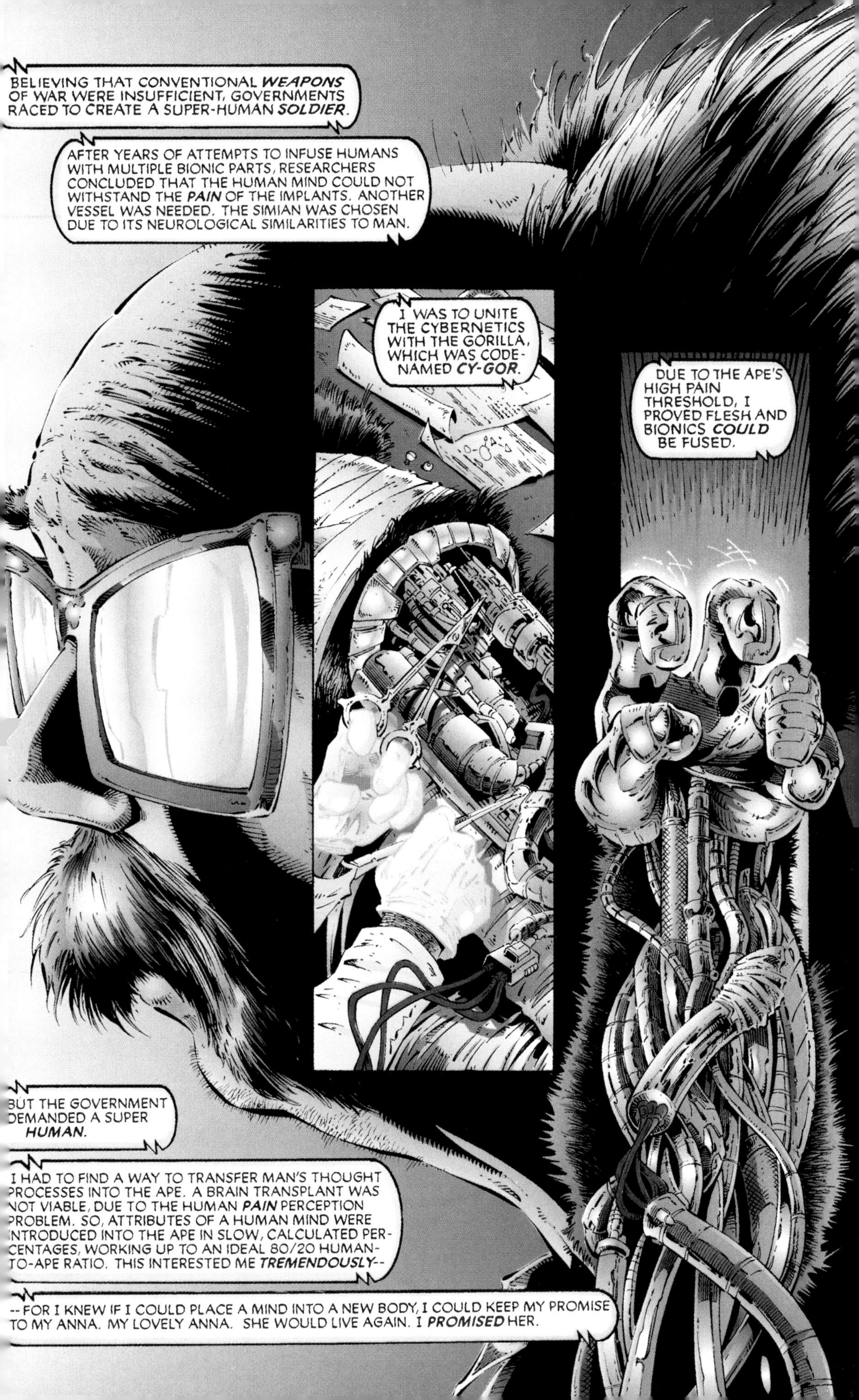
BELIEVING THAT CONVENTIONAL *WEAPONS* OF WAR WERE INSUFFICIENT, GOVERNMENTS RACED TO CREATE A SUPER-HUMAN *SOLDIER*.
AFTER YEARS OF ATTEMPTS TO INFUSE HUMANS WITH MULTIPLE BIONIC PARTS, RESEARCHERS CONCLUDED THAT THE HUMAN MIND COULD NOT WITHSTAND THE *PAIN* OF THE IMPLANTS. ANOTHER VESSEL WAS NEEDED. THE SIMIAN WAS CHOSEN DUE TO ITS NEUROLOGICAL SIMILARITIES TO MAN.
I WAS TO UNITE THE CYBERNETICS WITH THE GORILLA, WHICH WAS CODE-NAMED *CY-GOR*.
DUE TO THE APE'S HIGH PAIN THRESHOLD, I PROVED FLESH AND BIONICS *COULD* BE FUSED.
BUT THE GOVERNMENT DEMANDED A SUPER *HUMAN.*
I HAD TO FIND A WAY TO TRANSFER MAN'S THOUGHT PROCESSES INTO THE APE. A BRAIN TRANSPLANT WAS NOT VIABLE, DUE TO THE HUMAN *PAIN* PERCEPTION PROBLEM. SO, ATTRIBUTES OF A HUMAN MIND WERE INTRODUCED INTO THE APE IN SLOW, CALCULATED PERCENTAGES, WORKING UP TO AN IDEAL 80/20 HUMAN-TO-APE RATIO. THIS INTERESTED ME *TREMENDOUSLY*--
-- FOR I KNEW IF I COULD PLACE A MIND INTO A NEW BODY, I COULD KEEP MY PROMISE TO MY ANNA. MY LOVELY ANNA. SHE WOULD LIVE AGAIN. I *PROMISED* HER.

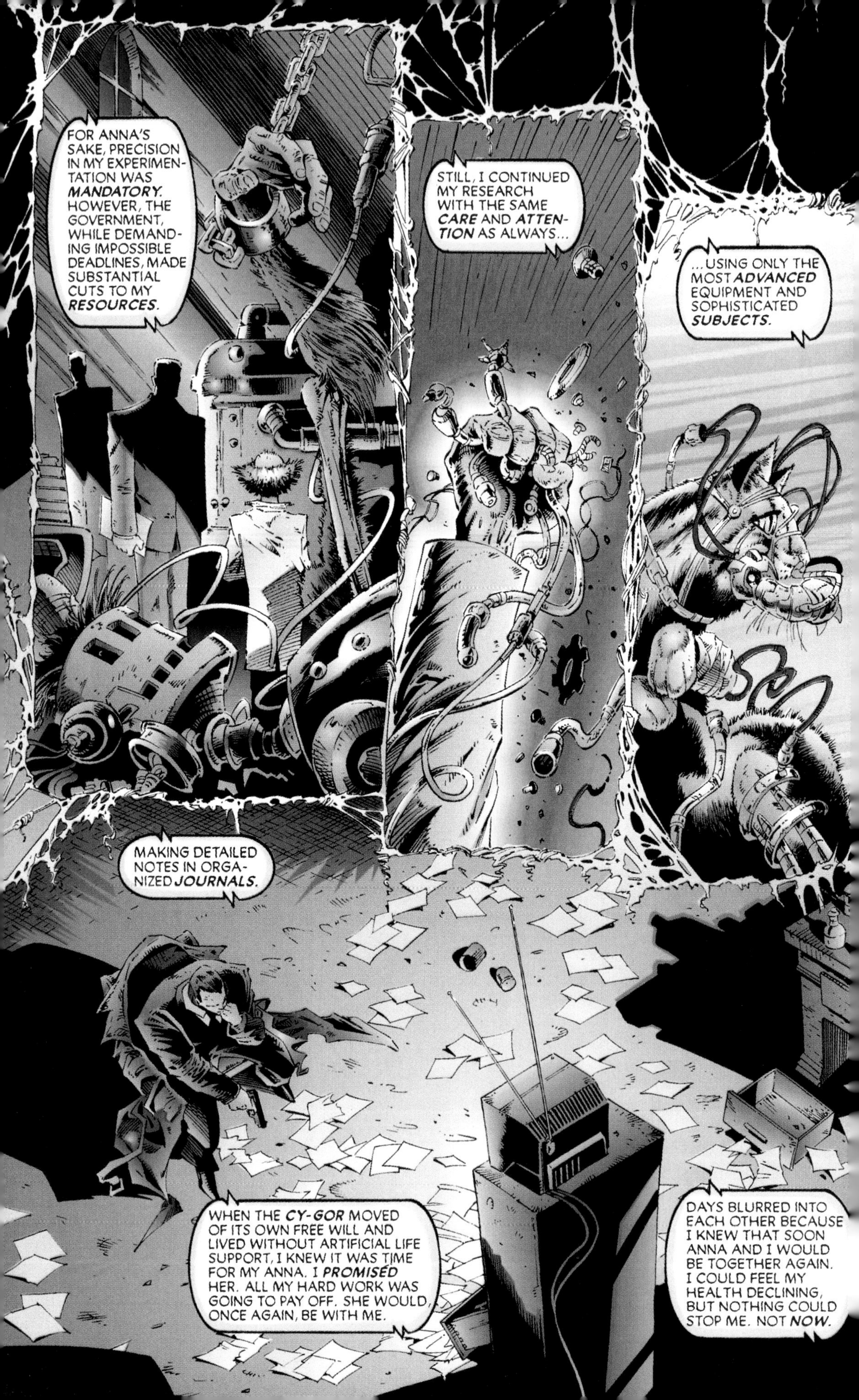
FOR ANNA'S SAKE, PRECISION IN MY EXPERIMENTATION WAS *MANDATORY.* HOWEVER, THE GOVERNMENT, WHILE DEMANDING IMPOSSIBLE DEADLINES, MADE SUBSTANTIAL CUTS TO MY *RESOURCES*.
STILL, I CONTINUED MY RESEARCH WITH THE SAME *CARE* AND *ATTENTION* AS ALWAYS...
...USING ONLY THE MOST *ADVANCED* EQUIPMENT AND SOPHISTICATED *SUBJECTS*.
MAKING DETAILED NOTES IN ORGANIZED *JOURNALS*.
WHEN THE *CY-GOR* MOVED OF ITS OWN FREE WILL AND LIVED WITHOUT ARTIFICIAL LIFE SUPPORT, I KNEW IT WAS TIME FOR MY ANNA. I *PROMISED* HER. ALL MY HARD WORK WAS GOING TO PAY OFF. SHE WOULD, ONCE AGAIN, BE WITH ME.
DAYS BLURRED INTO EACH OTHER BECAUSE I KNEW THAT SOON ANNA AND I WOULD BE TOGETHER AGAIN. I COULD FEEL MY HEALTH DECLINING, BUT NOTHING COULD STOP ME. NOT *NOW*.

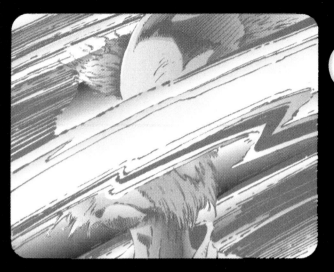

THAT BRINGS ME UP TO DATE.
I MUST CONTINUE MY WORK.
ANNA DEPENDS ON ME.

THE TELEVISION SCREEN FILLS ONCE AGAIN
WITH SNOW, BRINGING CHRIS BACK TO
REALITY. BELIEVING THE TAPE IS OVER, HE
RISES TO REMOVE IT FROM THE VCR, BUT
STOPS WHEN THE PICTURE RESUMES.

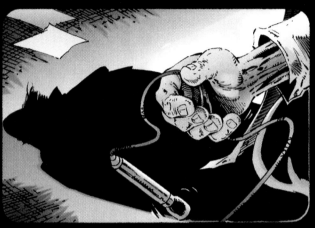

HELP ME. I'VE BEEN LYING HERE
FOR THREE DAYS. I'M WEAK. I
STRUGGLED FOR DAYS TO REACH
THE MICROPHONE.

I CANNOT MOVE MY LEFT ARM,
OR MY LEGS. I'VE HAD A *STROKE*. I
CANNOT REACH HER. MY *ANNA*.

I'M NOT READY, NOT *YET*. THE BEAST.
AT LEAST FOUR *DAYS* HAVE PASSED.
I CAN'T MOVE. IT WILL GET...

A THUNDERING *CRASH* ECHOES THROUGH-
OUT THE MANSION. A POWER FAILURE
SHROUDS THE ROOM IN DARKNESS. CHRIS
REMAINS SEATED, HEARING ONLY HIS OWN
HEART BEATING. FINALLY, THE AUXILIARY
LIGHTS FLICKER ON.

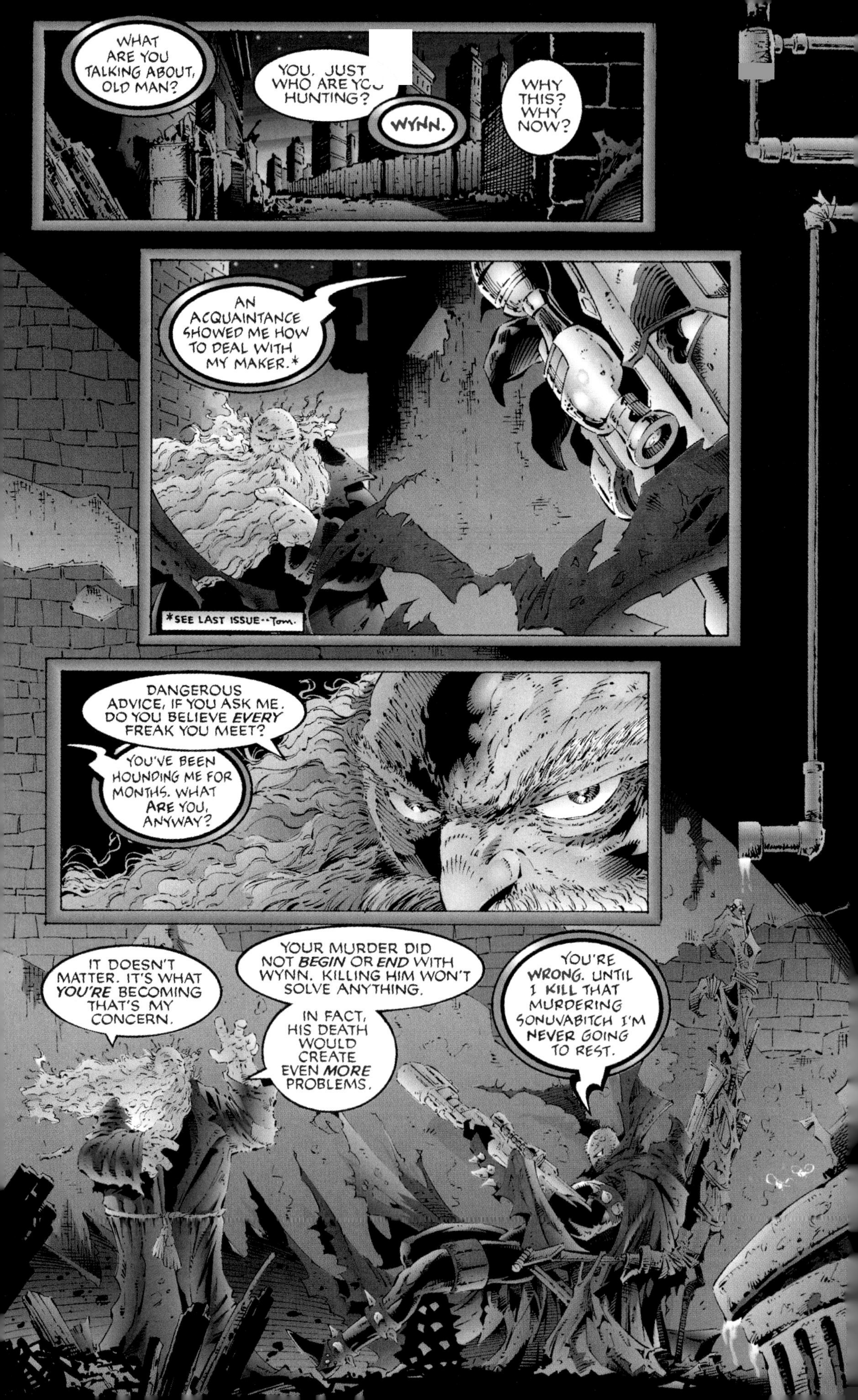
WHAT ARE YOU TALKING ABOUT, OLD MAN?
YOU. JUST WHO ARE YOU HUNTING?
WYNN.
WHY THIS? WHY NOW?
AN ACQUAINTANCE SHOWED ME HOW TO DEAL WITH MY MAKER.*
*SEE LAST ISSUE--Tom.
DANGEROUS ADVICE, IF YOU ASK ME. DO YOU BELIEVE *EVERY* FREAK YOU MEET?
YOU'VE BEEN HOUNDING ME FOR MONTHS. WHAT **ARE** YOU, ANYWAY?
IT DOESN'T MATTER. IT'S WHAT *YOU'RE* BECOMING THAT'S MY CONCERN.
YOUR MURDER DID NOT *BEGIN* OR *END* WITH WYNN. KILLING HIM WON'T SOLVE ANYTHING.
IN FACT, HIS DEATH WOULD CREATE EVEN *MORE* PROBLEMS.
YOU'RE **WRONG**. UNTIL I **KILL** THAT MURDERING SONUVABITCH I'M **NEVER** GOING TO REST.

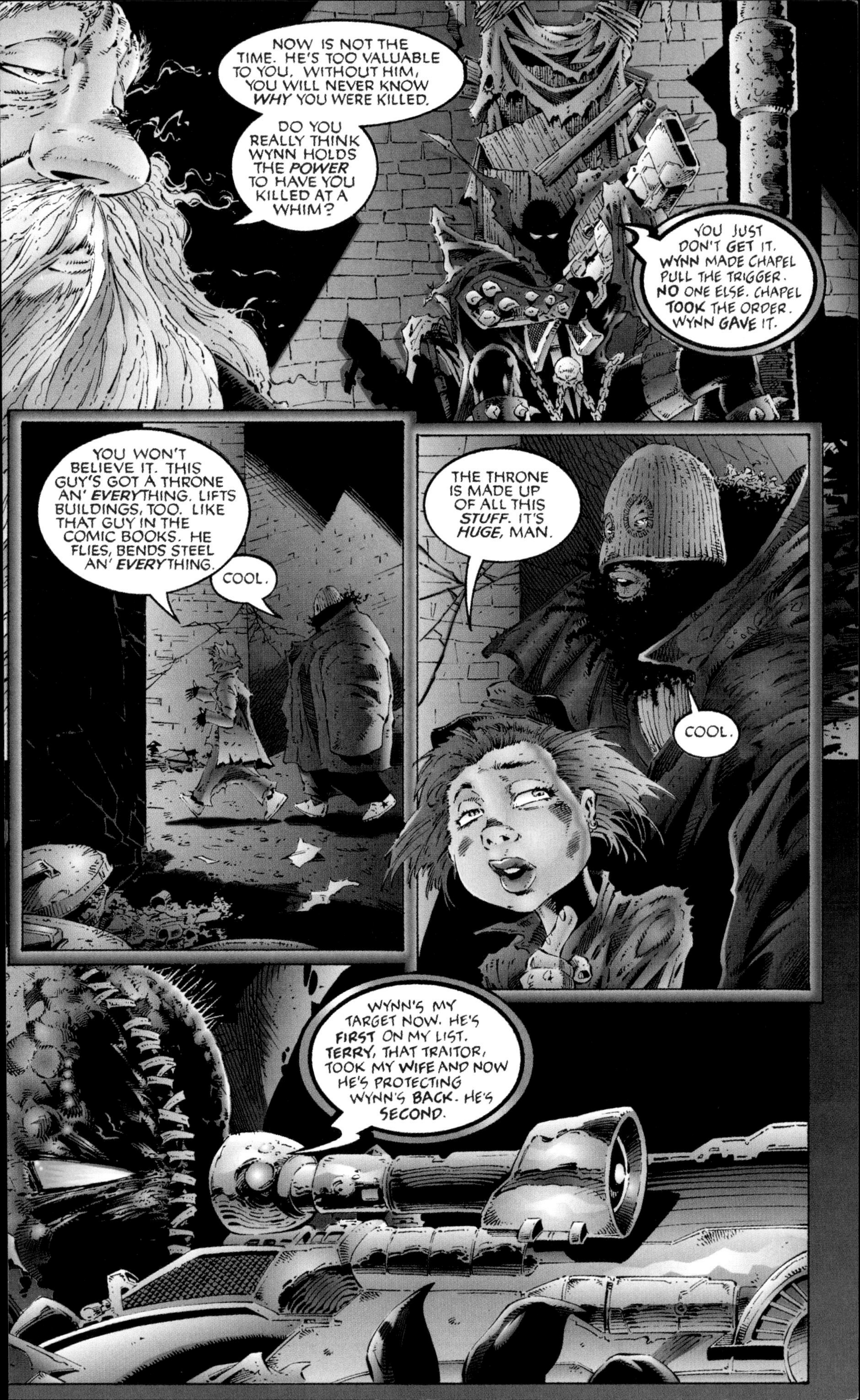
NOW IS NOT THE TIME. HE'S TOO VALUABLE TO YOU. WITHOUT HIM, YOU WILL NEVER KNOW *WHY* YOU WERE KILLED.
DO YOU REALLY THINK WYNN HOLDS THE *POWER* TO HAVE YOU KILLED AT A WHIM?
YOU JUST DON'T **GET** IT. **WYNN** MADE CHAPEL PULL THE TRIGGER. **NO** ONE ELSE. CHAPEL **TOOK** THE ORDER. WYNN **GAVE** IT.
YOU WON'T BELIEVE IT. THIS GUY'S GOT A THRONE AN' *EVERY*THING. LIFTS BUILDINGS, TOO. LIKE THAT GUY IN THE COMIC BOOKS. HE FLIES, BENDS STEEL AN' *EVERY*THING.
COOL.
THE THRONE IS MADE UP OF ALL THIS *STUFF*. IT'S *HUGE*, MAN.
COOL.
WYNN'S MY TARGET NOW. HE'S **FIRST** ON MY LIST. **TERRY**, THAT TRAITOR, TOOK MY **WIFE** AND NOW HE'S PROTECTING WYNN'S **BACK**. HE'S **SECOND**.

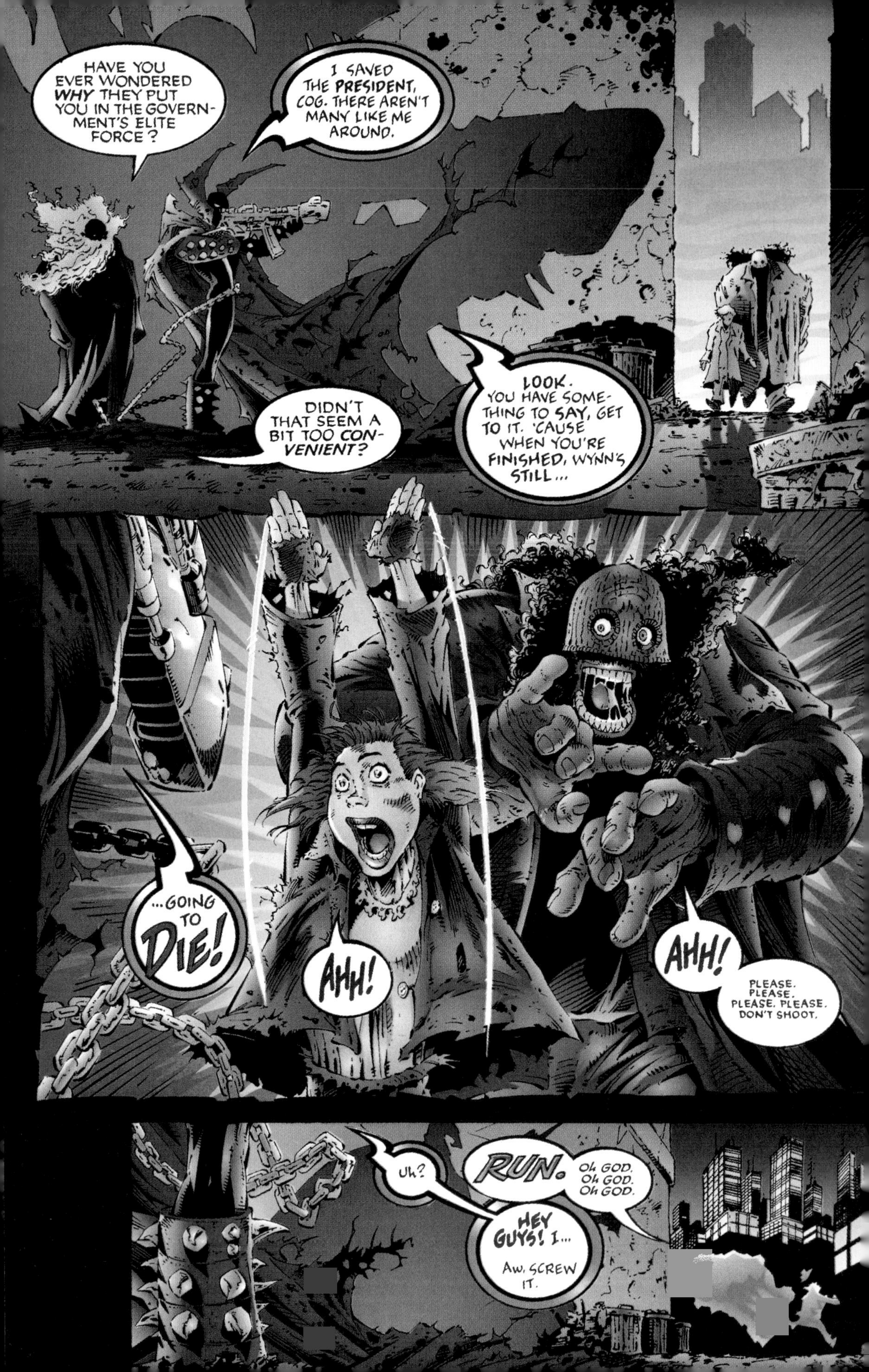
HAVE YOU EVER WONDERED WHY THEY PUT YOU IN THE GOVERNMENT'S ELITE FORCE?
I SAVED THE PRESIDENT, COG. THERE AREN'T MANY LIKE ME AROUND.
DIDN'T THAT SEEM A BIT TOO CONVENIENT?
LOOK. YOU HAVE SOMETHING TO SAY, GET TO IT. 'CAUSE WHEN YOU'RE FINISHED, WYNN'S STILL...
...GOING TO DIE!
AHH!
AHH!
PLEASE. PLEASE. PLEASE. PLEASE. DON'T SHOOT.
Uh?
RUN.
Oh GOD. Oh GOD. Oh GOD.
HEY GUYS! I...
AW, SCREW IT.

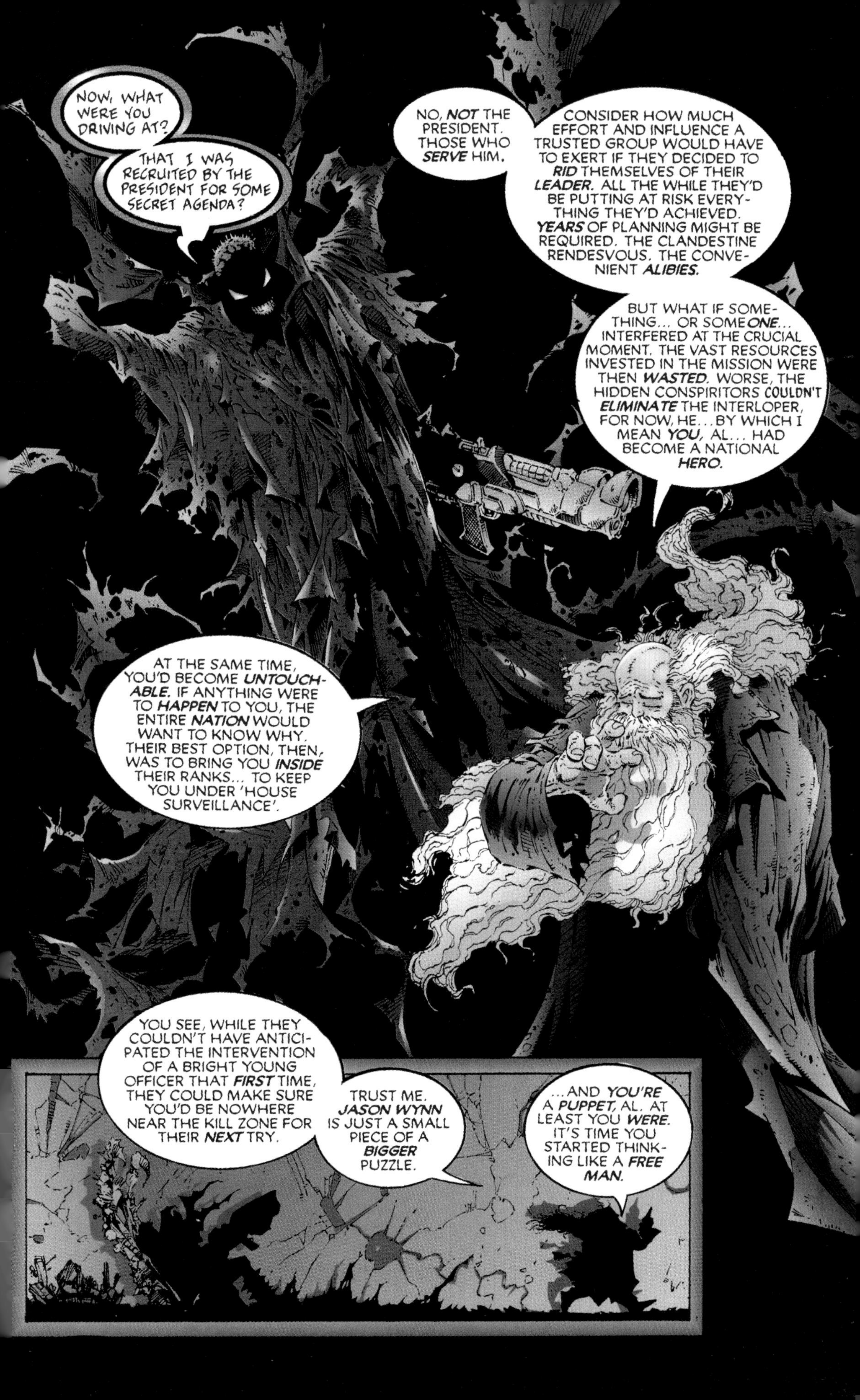
NOW, WHAT WERE YOU DRIVING AT?
THAT I WAS RECRUITED BY THE PRESIDENT FOR SOME SECRET AGENDA?
NO, NOT THE PRESIDENT. THOSE WHO SERVE HIM.
CONSIDER HOW MUCH EFFORT AND INFLUENCE A TRUSTED GROUP WOULD HAVE TO EXERT IF THEY DECIDED TO RID THEMSELVES OF THEIR LEADER. ALL THE WHILE THEY'D BE PUTTING AT RISK EVERYTHING THEY'D ACHIEVED. YEARS OF PLANNING MIGHT BE REQUIRED. THE CLANDESTINE RENDESVOUS. THE CONVENIENT ALIBIES.
BUT WHAT IF SOMETHING... OR SOMEONE... INTERFERED AT THE CRUCIAL MOMENT. THE VAST RESOURCES INVESTED IN THE MISSION WERE THEN WASTED. WORSE, THE HIDDEN CONSPIRITORS COULDN'T ELIMINATE THE INTERLOPER, FOR NOW, HE... BY WHICH I MEAN YOU, AL... HAD BECOME A NATIONAL HERO.
AT THE SAME TIME, YOU'D BECOME UNTOUCHABLE. IF ANYTHING WERE TO HAPPEN TO YOU, THE ENTIRE NATION WOULD WANT TO KNOW WHY. THEIR BEST OPTION, THEN, WAS TO BRING YOU INSIDE THEIR RANKS... TO KEEP YOU UNDER 'HOUSE SURVEILLANCE'.
YOU SEE, WHILE THEY COULDN'T HAVE ANTICIPATED THE INTERVENTION OF A BRIGHT YOUNG OFFICER THAT FIRST TIME, THEY COULD MAKE SURE YOU'D BE NOWHERE NEAR THE KILL ZONE FOR THEIR NEXT TRY.
TRUST ME. JASON WYNN IS JUST A SMALL PIECE OF A BIGGER PUZZLE.
...AND YOU'RE A PUPPET, AL. AT LEAST YOU WERE. IT'S TIME YOU STARTED THINKING LIKE A FREE MAN.

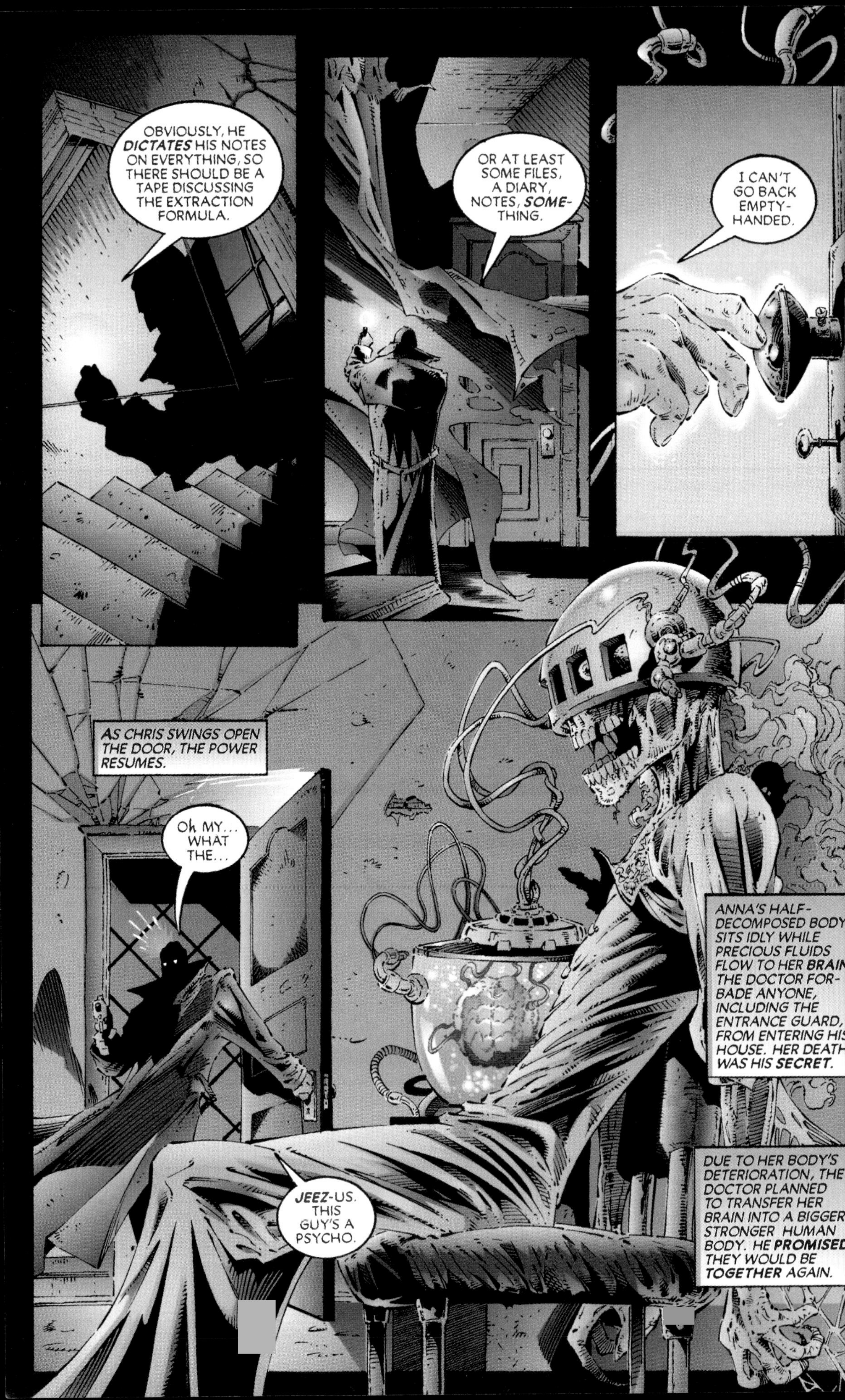
OBVIOUSLY, HE **DICTATES** HIS NOTES ON EVERYTHING, SO THERE SHOULD BE A TAPE DISCUSSING THE EXTRACTION FORMULA.
OR AT LEAST SOME FILES, A DIARY, NOTES, ***SOME-*** THING.
I CAN'T GO BACK EMPTY-HANDED.
AS CHRIS SWINGS OPEN THE DOOR, THE POWER RESUMES.
Oh MY... WHAT THE...
*ANNA'S HALF-DECOMPOSED BODY SITS IDLY WHILE PRECIOUS FLUIDS FLOW TO HER **BRAIN**. THE DOCTOR FORBADE ANYONE, INCLUDING THE ENTRANCE GUARD, FROM ENTERING HIS HOUSE. HER DEATH WAS HIS **SECRET**.*
JEEZ-US. THIS GUY'S A PSYCHO.
*DUE TO HER BODY'S DETERIORATION, THE DOCTOR PLANNED TO TRANSFER HER BRAIN INTO A BIGGER, STRONGER HUMAN BODY. HE **PROMISED** THEY WOULD BE **TOGETHER** AGAIN.*

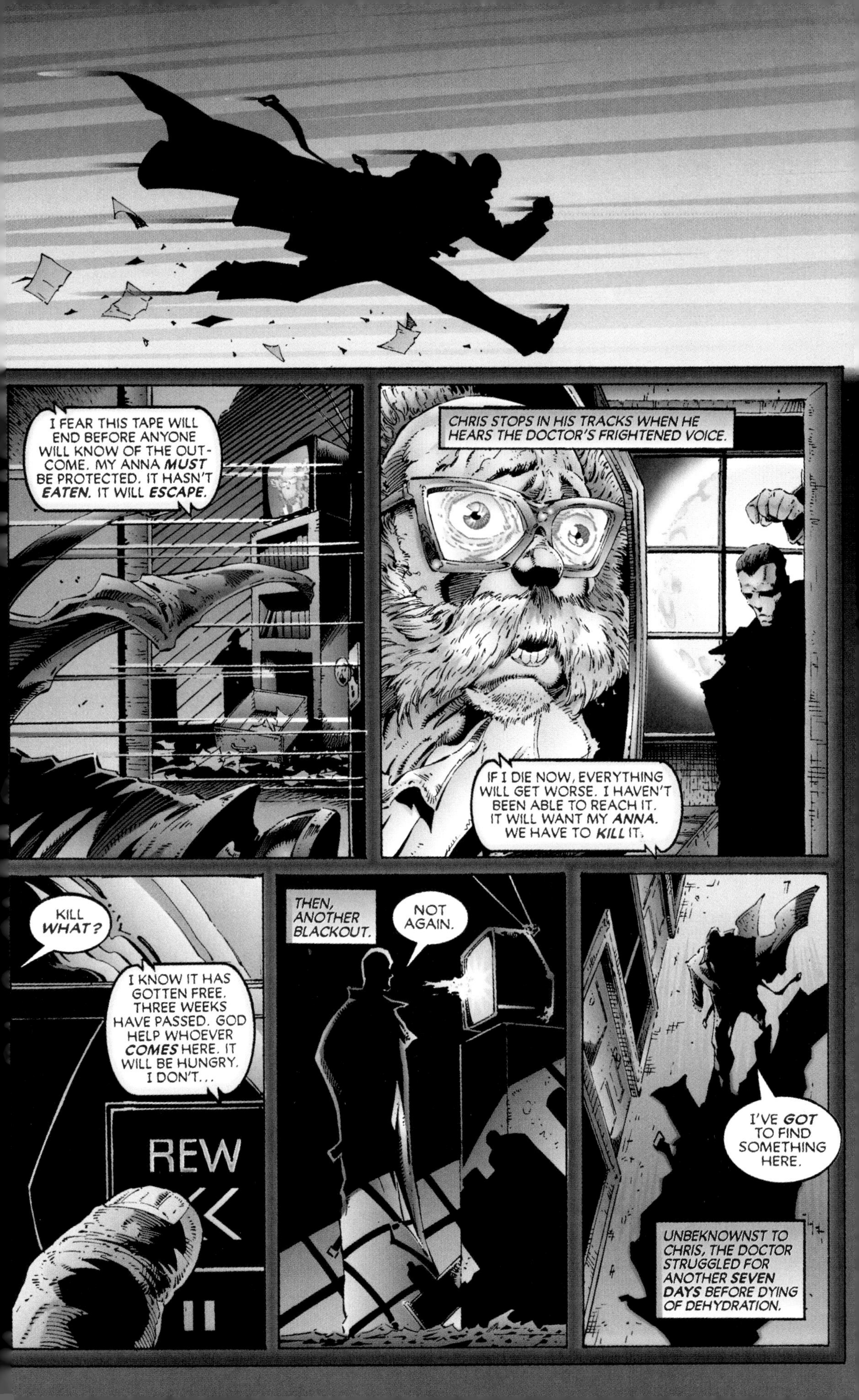
I FEAR THIS TAPE WILL END BEFORE ANYONE WILL KNOW OF THE OUT-COME. MY ANNA MUST BE PROTECTED. IT HASN'T EATEN. IT WILL ESCAPE.
CHRIS STOPS IN HIS TRACKS WHEN HE HEARS THE DOCTOR'S FRIGHTENED VOICE.
IF I DIE NOW, EVERYTHING WILL GET WORSE. I HAVEN'T BEEN ABLE TO REACH IT. IT WILL WANT MY ANNA. WE HAVE TO KILL IT.
KILL WHAT?
I KNOW IT HAS GOTTEN FREE. THREE WEEKS HAVE PASSED. GOD HELP WHOEVER COMES HERE. IT WILL BE HUNGRY. I DON'T...
REW
THEN, ANOTHER BLACKOUT.
NOT AGAIN.
I'VE GOT TO FIND SOMETHING HERE.
UNBEKNOWNST TO CHRIS, THE DOCTOR STRUGGLED FOR ANOTHER SEVEN DAYS BEFORE DYING OF DEHYDRATION.

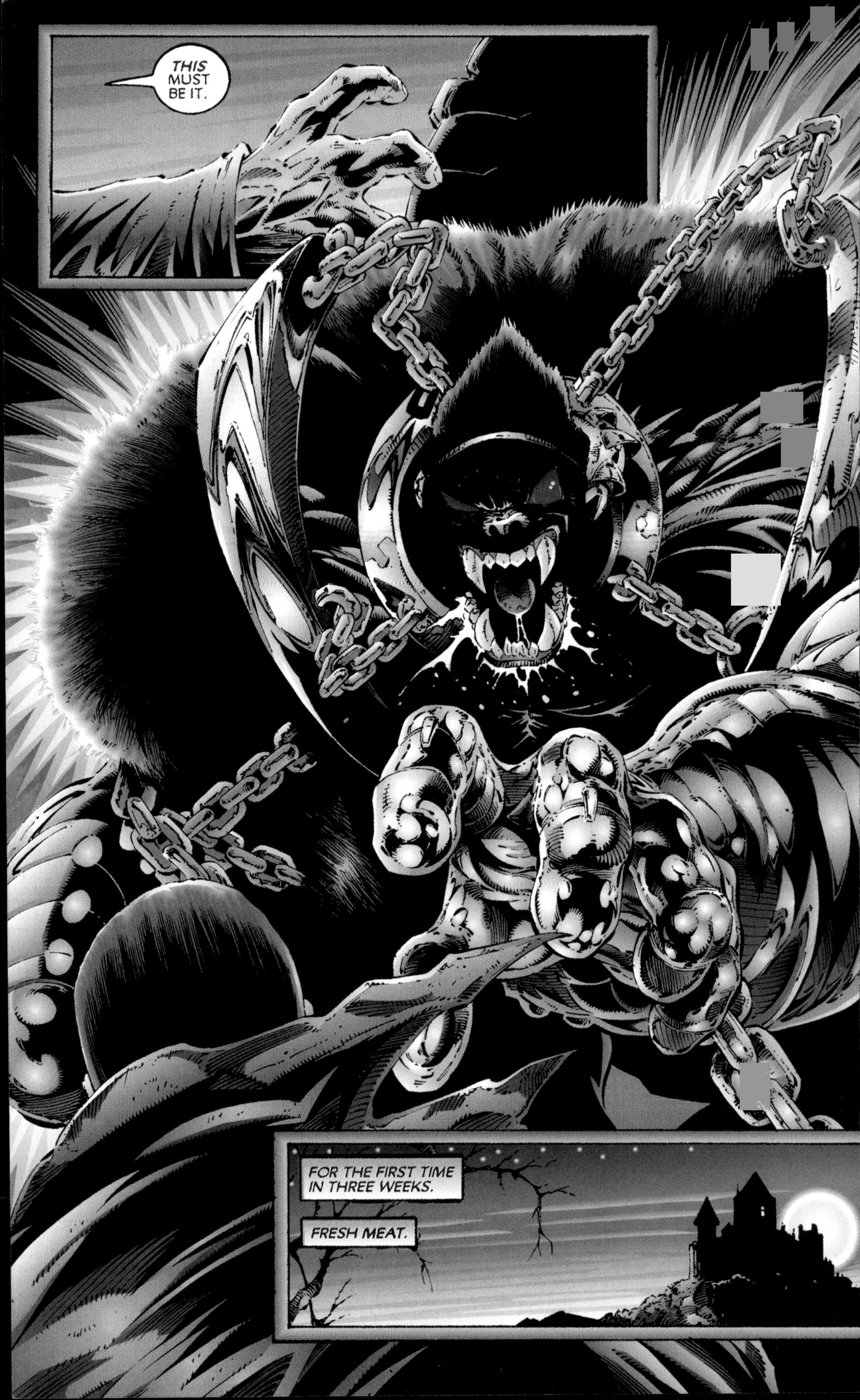
THIS MUST BE IT.
FOR THE FIRST TIME IN THREE WEEKS.
FRESH MEAT.

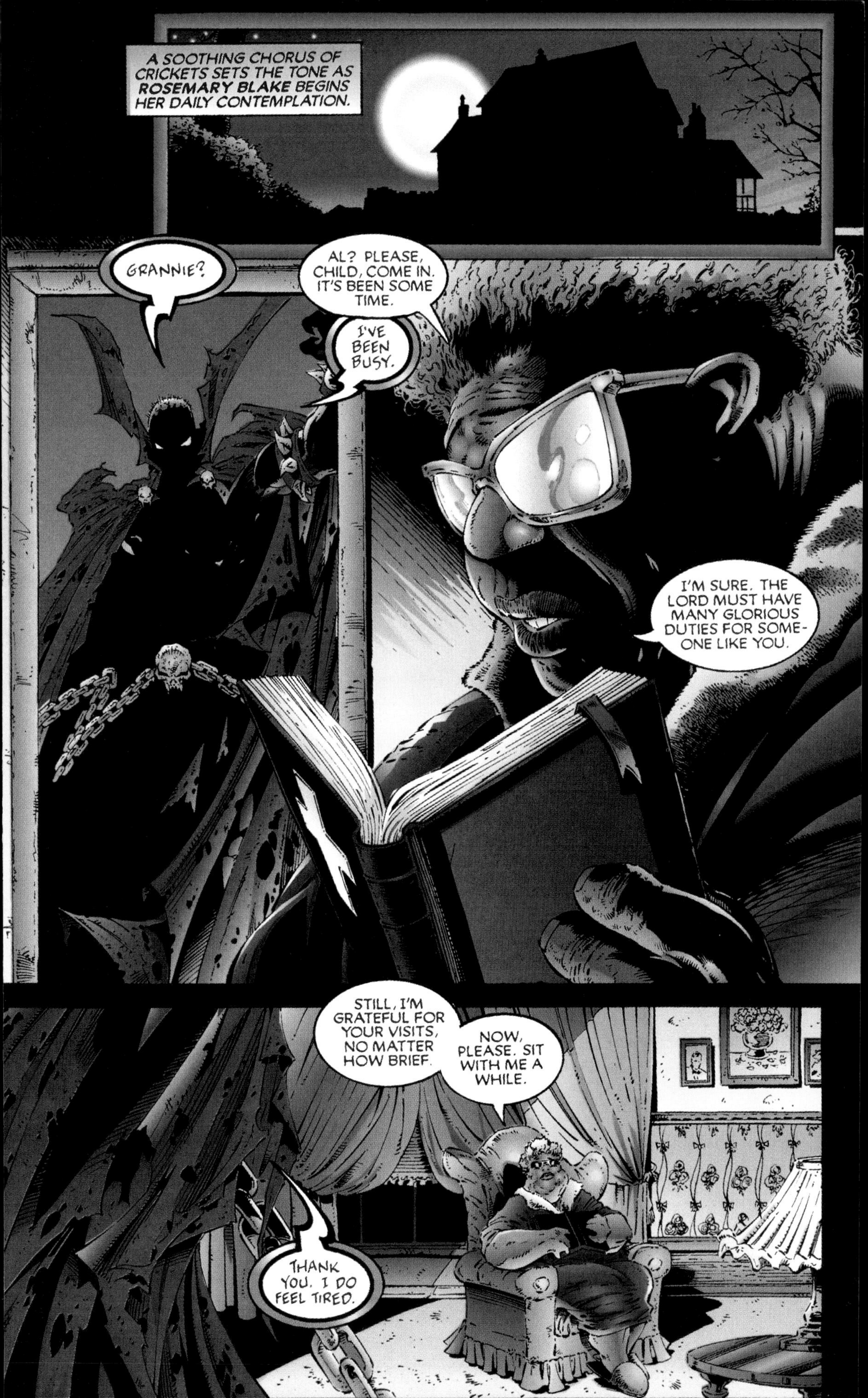
A SOOTHING CHORUS OF CRICKETS SETS THE TONE AS ROSEMARY BLAKE BEGINS HER DAILY CONTEMPLATION.
GRANNIE?
AL? PLEASE, CHILD, COME IN. IT'S BEEN SOME TIME.
I'VE BEEN BUSY.
I'M SURE. THE LORD MUST HAVE MANY GLORIOUS DUTIES FOR SOME-ONE LIKE YOU.
STILL, I'M GRATEFUL FOR YOUR VISITS, NO MATTER HOW BRIEF.
NOW, PLEASE. SIT WITH ME A WHILE.
THANK YOU. I DO FEEL TIRED.

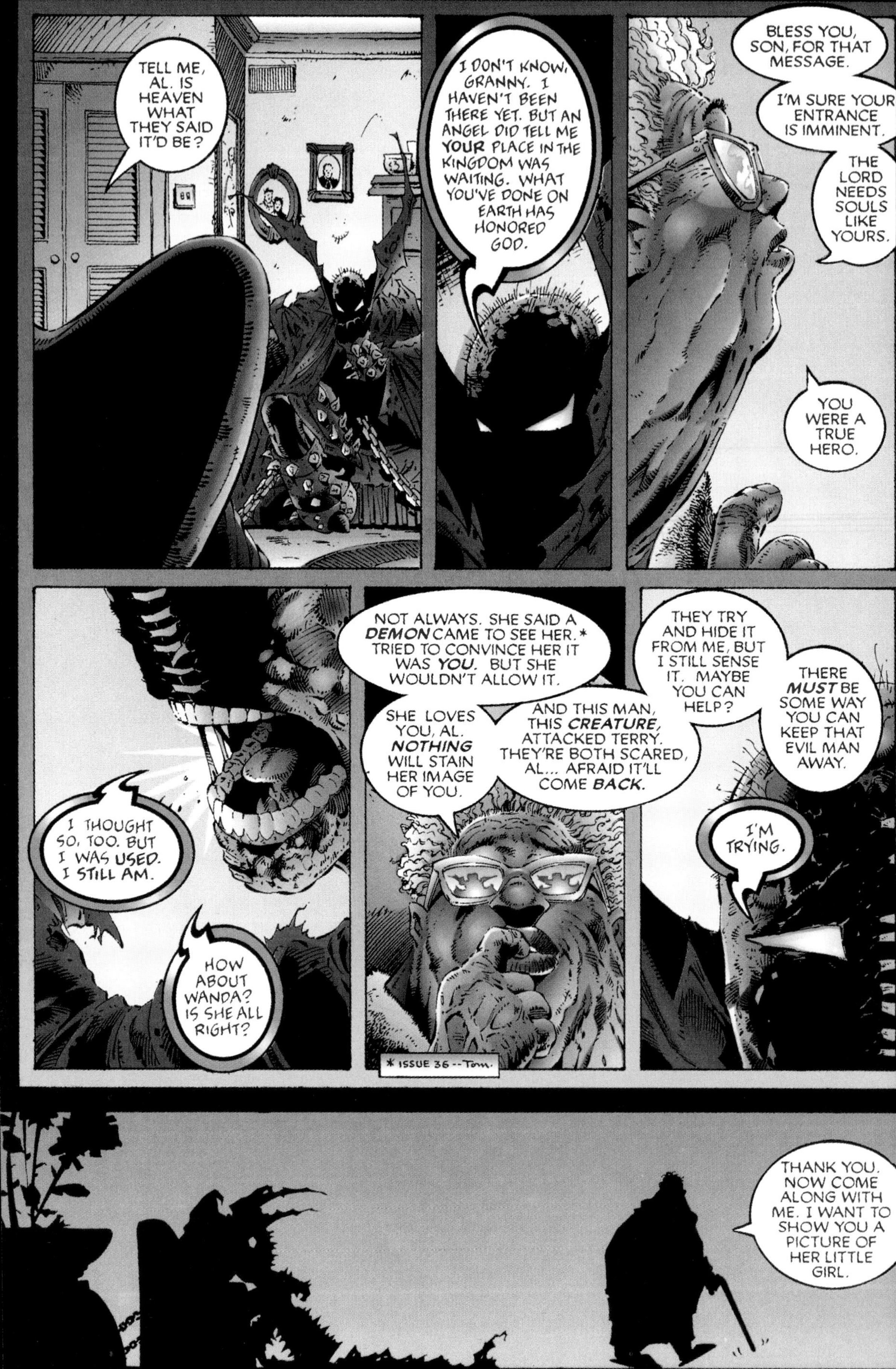
TELL ME, AL. IS HEAVEN WHAT THEY SAID IT'D BE?
I DON'T KNOW, GRANNY. I HAVEN'T BEEN THERE YET. BUT AN ANGEL DID TELL ME YOUR PLACE IN THE KINGDOM WAS WAITING. WHAT YOU'VE DONE ON EARTH HAS HONORED GOD.
BLESS YOU, SON, FOR THAT MESSAGE.
I'M SURE YOUR ENTRANCE IS IMMINENT.
THE LORD NEEDS SOULS LIKE YOURS.
YOU WERE A TRUE HERO.
I THOUGHT SO, TOO. BUT I WAS USED. I STILL AM.
HOW ABOUT WANDA? IS SHE ALL RIGHT?
NOT ALWAYS. SHE SAID A DEMON CAME TO SEE HER.* TRIED TO CONVINCE HER IT WAS YOU. BUT SHE WOULDN'T ALLOW IT.
SHE LOVES YOU, AL. NOTHING WILL STAIN HER IMAGE OF YOU.
AND THIS MAN, THIS CREATURE, ATTACKED TERRY. THEY'RE BOTH SCARED, AL... AFRAID IT'LL COME BACK.
*ISSUE 36 --Tom.
THEY TRY AND HIDE IT FROM ME, BUT I STILL SENSE IT. MAYBE YOU CAN HELP?
THERE MUST BE SOME WAY YOU CAN KEEP THAT EVIL MAN AWAY.
I'M TRYING.
THANK YOU. NOW COME ALONG WITH ME. I WANT TO SHOW YOU A PICTURE OF HER LITTLE GIRL.

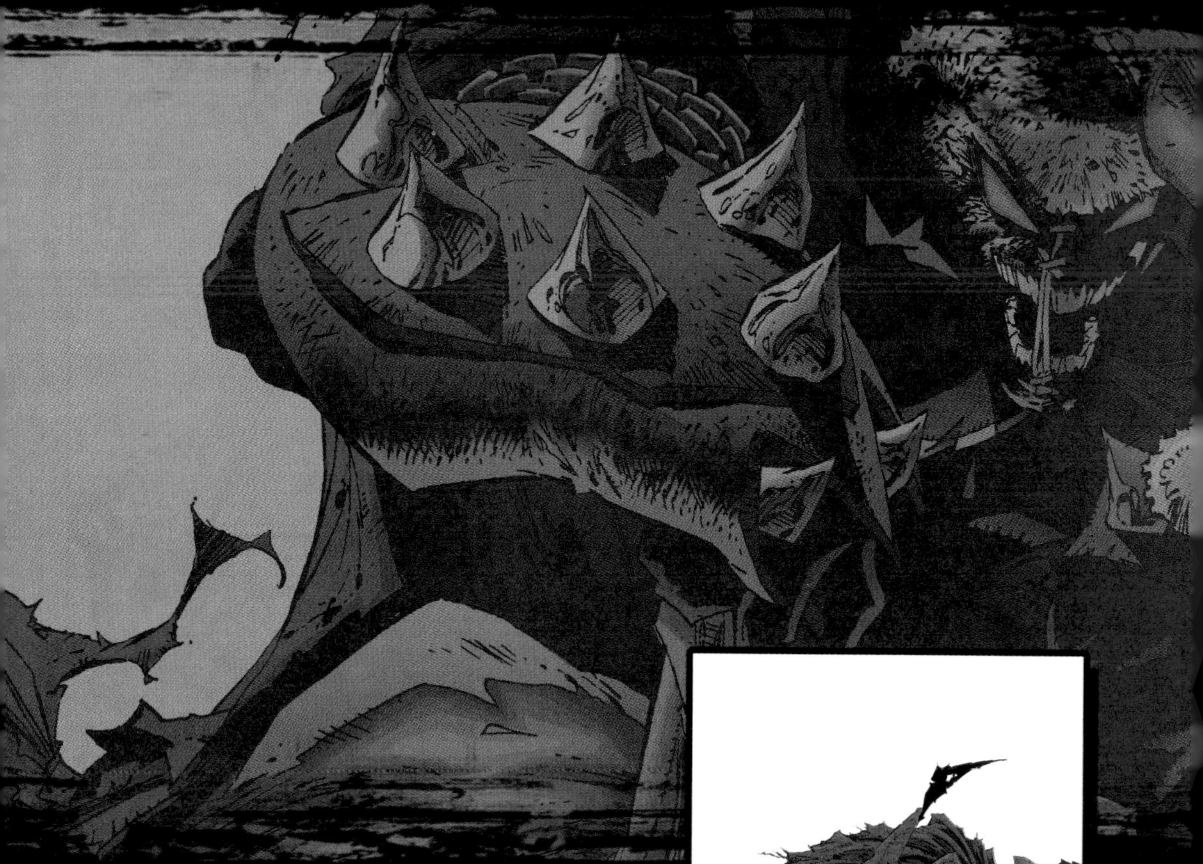
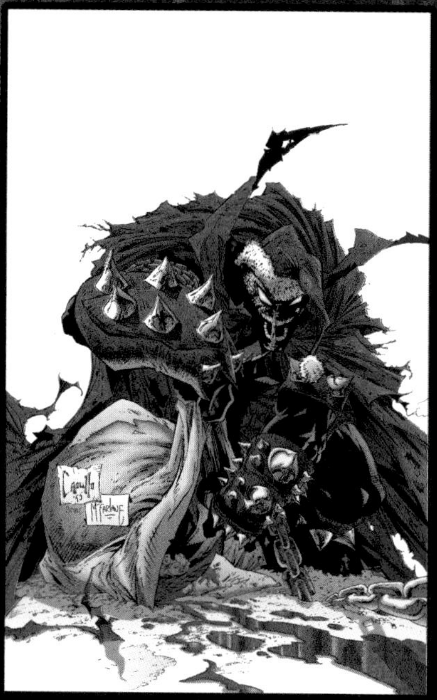

ISSUE THIRTY-EIGHT

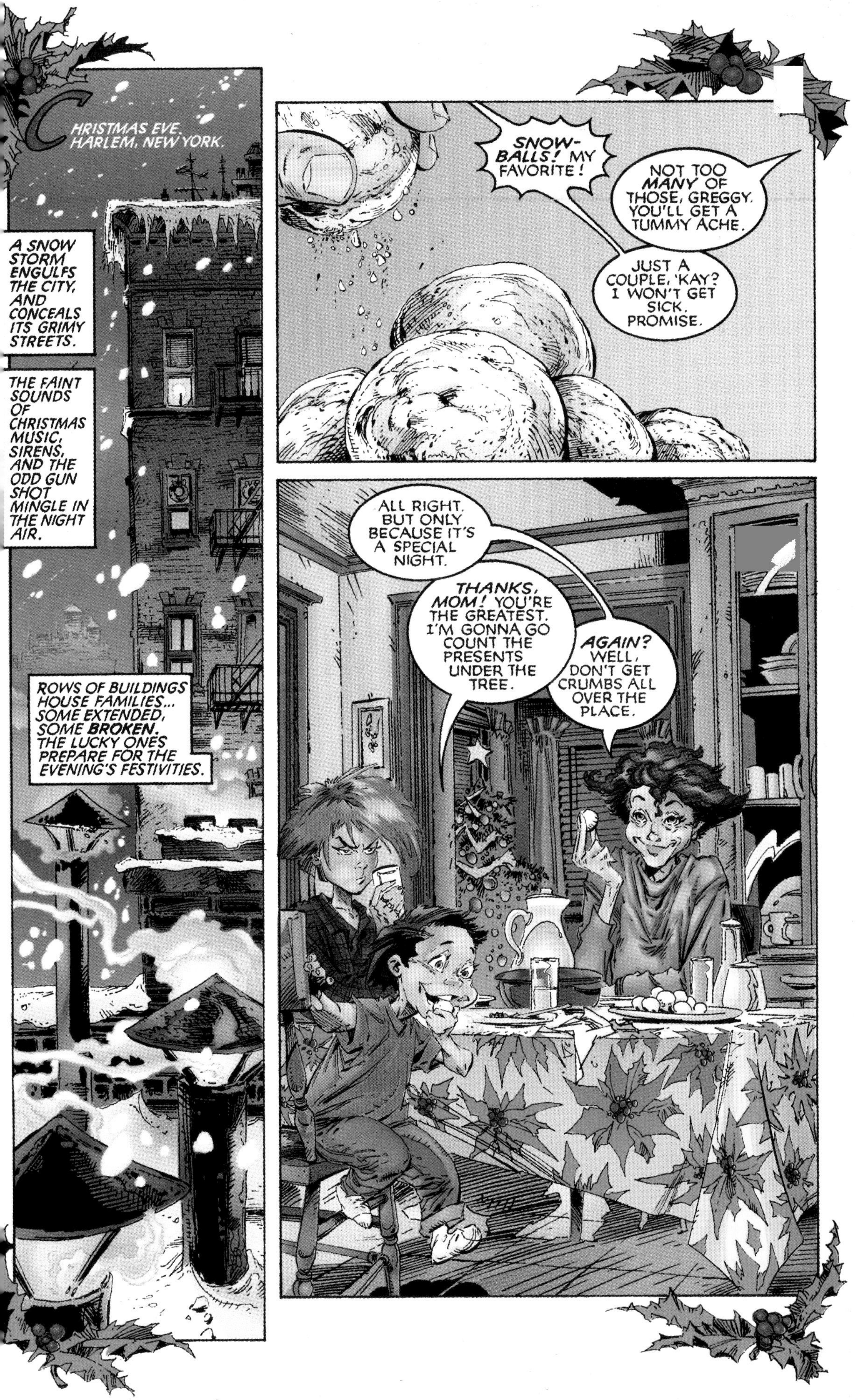

CHRISTMAS EVE.
HARLEM, NEW YORK.
A SNOW STORM ENGULFS THE CITY, AND CONCEALS ITS GRIMY STREETS.
THE FAINT SOUNDS OF CHRISTMAS MUSIC, SIRENS, AND THE ODD GUN SHOT MINGLE IN THE NIGHT AIR.
ROWS OF BUILDINGS HOUSE FAMILIES... SOME EXTENDED, SOME **BROKEN.** THE LUCKY ONES PREPARE FOR THE EVENING'S FESTIVITIES.
SNOW-BALLS! MY FAVORITE!
NOT TOO *MANY* OF THOSE, GREGGY. YOU'LL GET A TUMMY ACHE.
JUST A COUPLE, 'KAY? I WON'T GET SICK. PROMISE.
ALL RIGHT, BUT ONLY BECAUSE IT'S A SPECIAL NIGHT.
THANKS, MOM! YOU'RE THE GREATEST. I'M GONNA GO COUNT THE PRESENTS UNDER THE TREE.
AGAIN? WELL, DON'T GET CRUMBS ALL OVER THE PLACE.

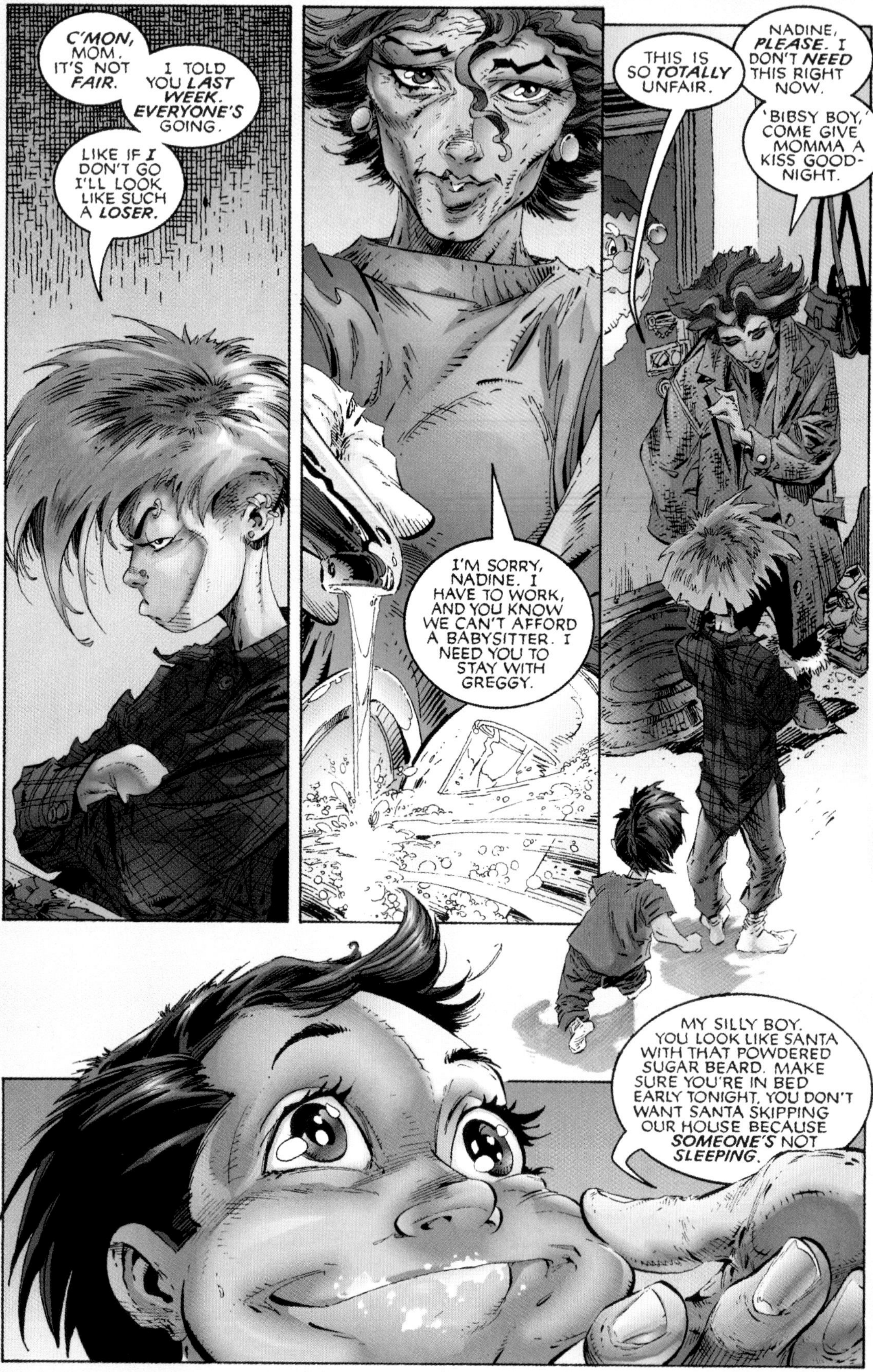

C'MON, MOM. IT'S NOT FAIR.
I TOLD YOU LAST WEEK. EVERYONE'S GOING.
LIKE IF I DON'T GO I'LL LOOK LIKE SUCH A LOSER.
I'M SORRY, NADINE. I HAVE TO WORK, AND YOU KNOW WE CAN'T AFFORD A BABYSITTER. I NEED YOU TO STAY WITH GREGGY.
THIS IS SO TOTALLY UNFAIR.
NADINE, PLEASE. I DON'T NEED THIS RIGHT NOW.
'BIBSY BOY,' COME GIVE MOMMA A KISS GOOD-NIGHT.
MY SILLY BOY. YOU LOOK LIKE SANTA WITH THAT POWDERED SUGAR BEARD. MAKE SURE YOU'RE IN BED EARLY TONIGHT. YOU DON'T WANT SANTA SKIPPING OUR HOUSE BECAUSE SOMEONE'S NOT SLEEPING.

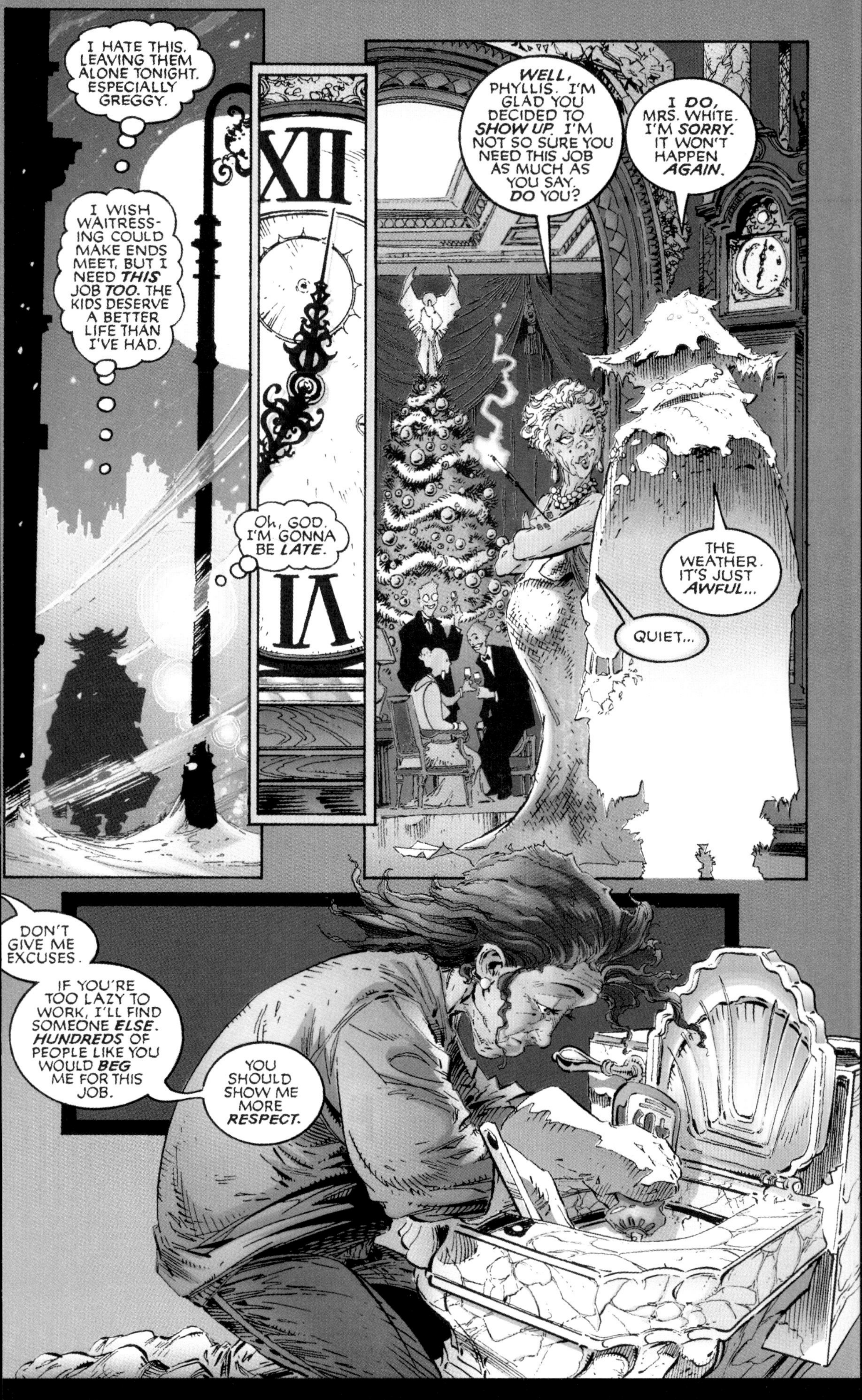
I HATE THIS. LEAVING THEM ALONE TONIGHT. ESPECIALLY GREGGY.
I WISH WAITRESSING COULD MAKE ENDS MEET, BUT I NEED THIS JOB TOO. THE KIDS DESERVE A BETTER LIFE THAN I'VE HAD.
XII
Oh, GOD. I'M GONNA BE LATE.
VI
WELL, PHYLLIS. I'M GLAD YOU DECIDED TO SHOW UP. I'M NOT SO SURE YOU NEED THIS JOB AS MUCH AS YOU SAY. DO YOU?
I DO, MRS. WHITE. I'M SORRY. IT WON'T HAPPEN AGAIN.
THE WEATHER. IT'S JUST AWFUL...
QUIET...
DON'T GIVE ME EXCUSES.
IF YOU'RE TOO LAZY TO WORK, I'LL FIND SOMEONE ELSE. HUNDREDS OF PEOPLE LIKE YOU WOULD BEG ME FOR THIS JOB.
YOU SHOULD SHOW ME MORE RESPECT.

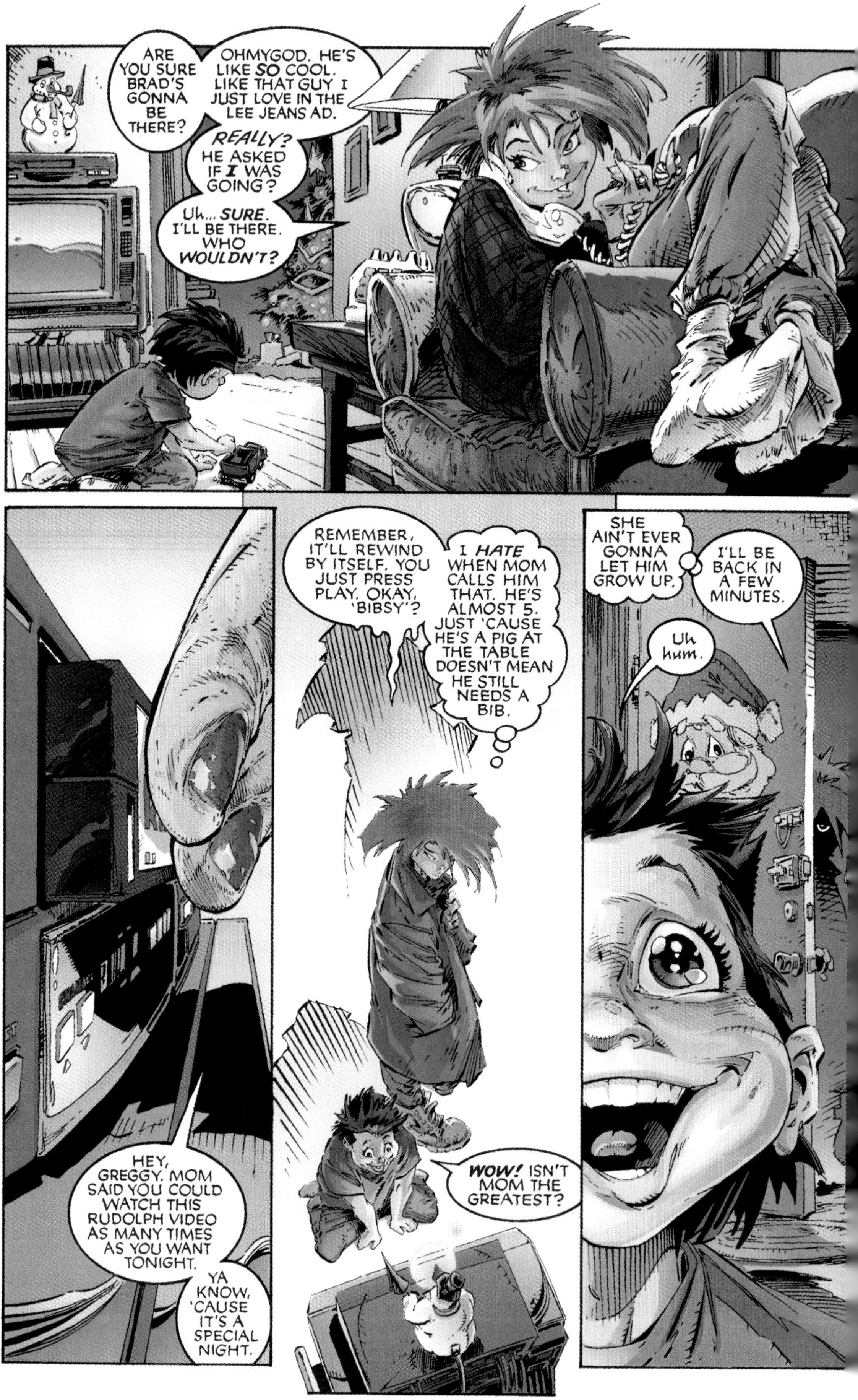

ARE YOU SURE BRAD'S GONNA BE THERE?
OHMYGOD. HE'S LIKE SO COOL. LIKE THAT GUY I JUST LOVE IN THE LEE JEANS AD.
REALLY? HE ASKED IF I WAS GOING?
Uh... SURE. I'LL BE THERE. WHO WOULDN'T?
HEY, GREGGY. MOM SAID YOU COULD WATCH THIS RUDOLPH VIDEO AS MANY TIMES AS YOU WANT TONIGHT.
YA KNOW, 'CAUSE IT'S A SPECIAL NIGHT.
REMEMBER, IT'LL REWIND BY ITSELF. YOU JUST PRESS PLAY, OKAY, 'BIBSY'?
I HATE WHEN MOM CALLS HIM THAT. HE'S ALMOST 5. JUST 'CAUSE HE'S A PIG AT THE TABLE DOESN'T MEAN HE STILL NEEDS A BIB.
WOW! ISN'T MOM THE GREATEST?
SHE AIN'T EVER GONNA LET HIM GROW UP.
I'LL BE BACK IN A FEW MINUTES.
Uh hum.

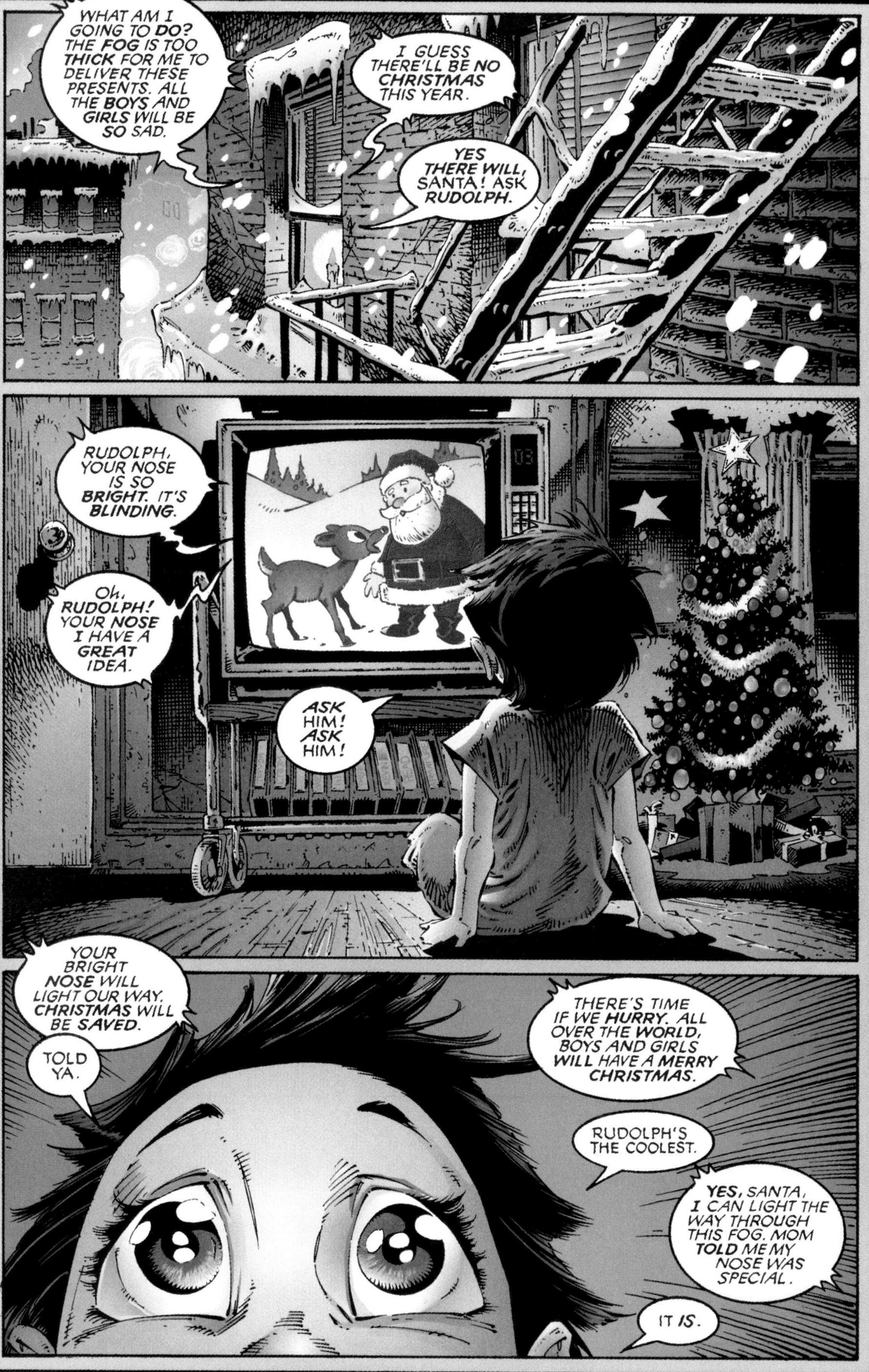
WHAT AM I GOING TO DO? THE FOG IS TOO THICK FOR ME TO DELIVER THESE PRESENTS. ALL THE BOYS AND GIRLS WILL BE SO SAD.
I GUESS THERE'LL BE NO CHRISTMAS THIS YEAR.
YES THERE WILL, SANTA! ASK RUDOLPH.
RUDOLPH, YOUR NOSE IS SO BRIGHT. IT'S BLINDING.
Oh, RUDOLPH! YOUR NOSE I HAVE A GREAT IDEA.
ASK HIM! ASK HIM!
YOUR BRIGHT NOSE WILL LIGHT OUR WAY. CHRISTMAS WILL BE SAVED.
TOLD YA.
THERE'S TIME IF WE HURRY. ALL OVER THE WORLD, BOYS AND GIRLS WILL HAVE A MERRY CHRISTMAS.
RUDOLPH'S THE COOLEST.
YES, SANTA, I CAN LIGHT THE WAY THROUGH THIS FOG. MOM TOLD ME MY NOSE WAS SPECIAL.
IT IS.

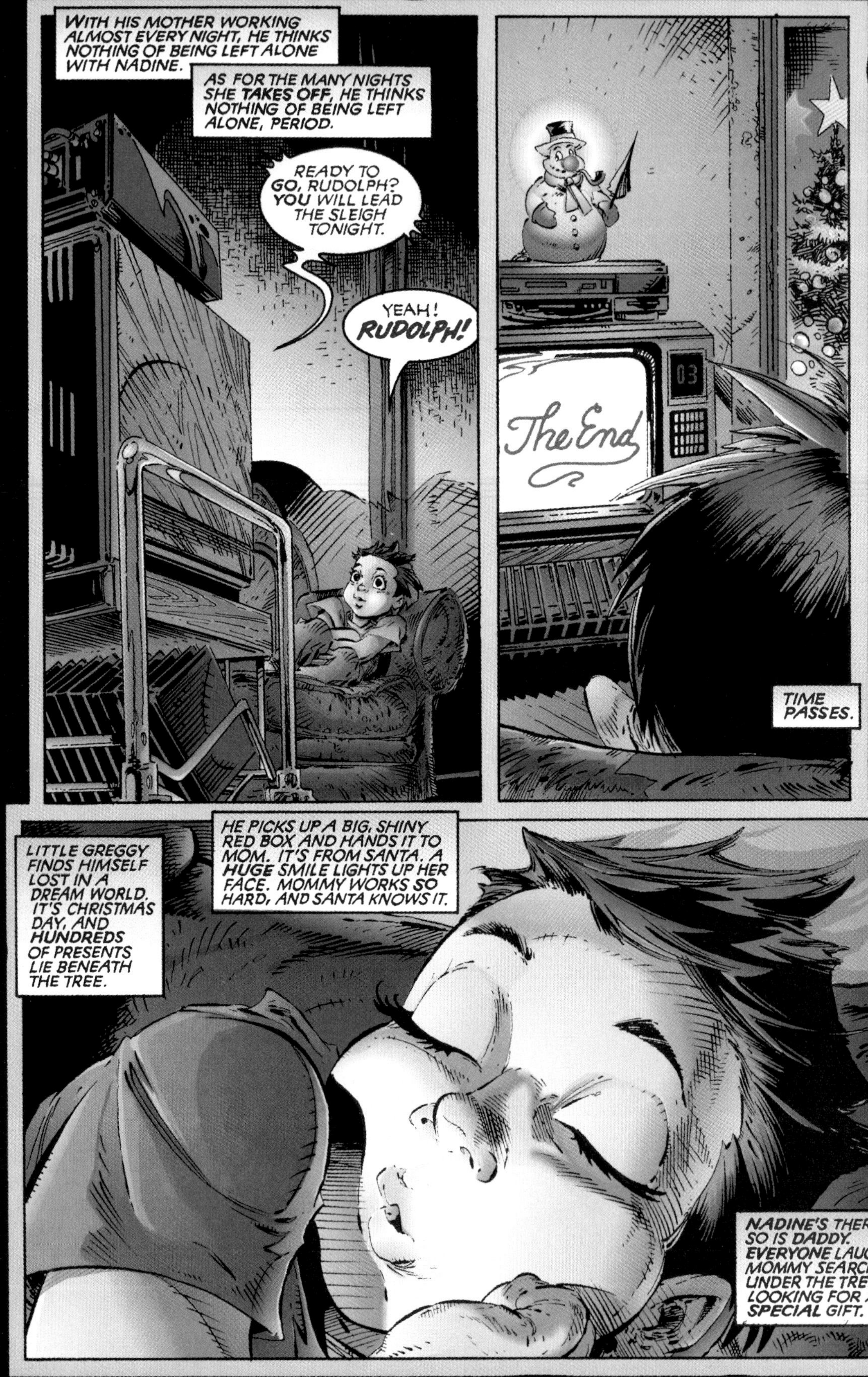
WITH HIS MOTHER WORKING ALMOST EVERY NIGHT, HE THINKS NOTHING OF BEING LEFT ALONE WITH NADINE.
AS FOR THE MANY NIGHTS SHE TAKES OFF, HE THINKS NOTHING OF BEING LEFT ALONE, PERIOD.
READY TO GO, RUDOLPH? YOU WILL LEAD THE SLEIGH TONIGHT.
YEAH! RUDOLPH!
The End
TIME PASSES.
LITTLE GREGGY FINDS HIMSELF LOST IN A DREAM WORLD. IT'S CHRISTMAS DAY, AND HUNDREDS OF PRESENTS LIE BENEATH THE TREE.
HE PICKS UP A BIG, SHINY RED BOX AND HANDS IT TO MOM. IT'S FROM SANTA. A HUGE SMILE LIGHTS UP HER FACE. MOMMY WORKS SO HARD, AND SANTA KNOWS IT.
NADINE'S THER SO IS DADDY. EVERYONE LAU MOMMY SEARC UNDER THE TRE LOOKING FOR SPECIAL GIFT.

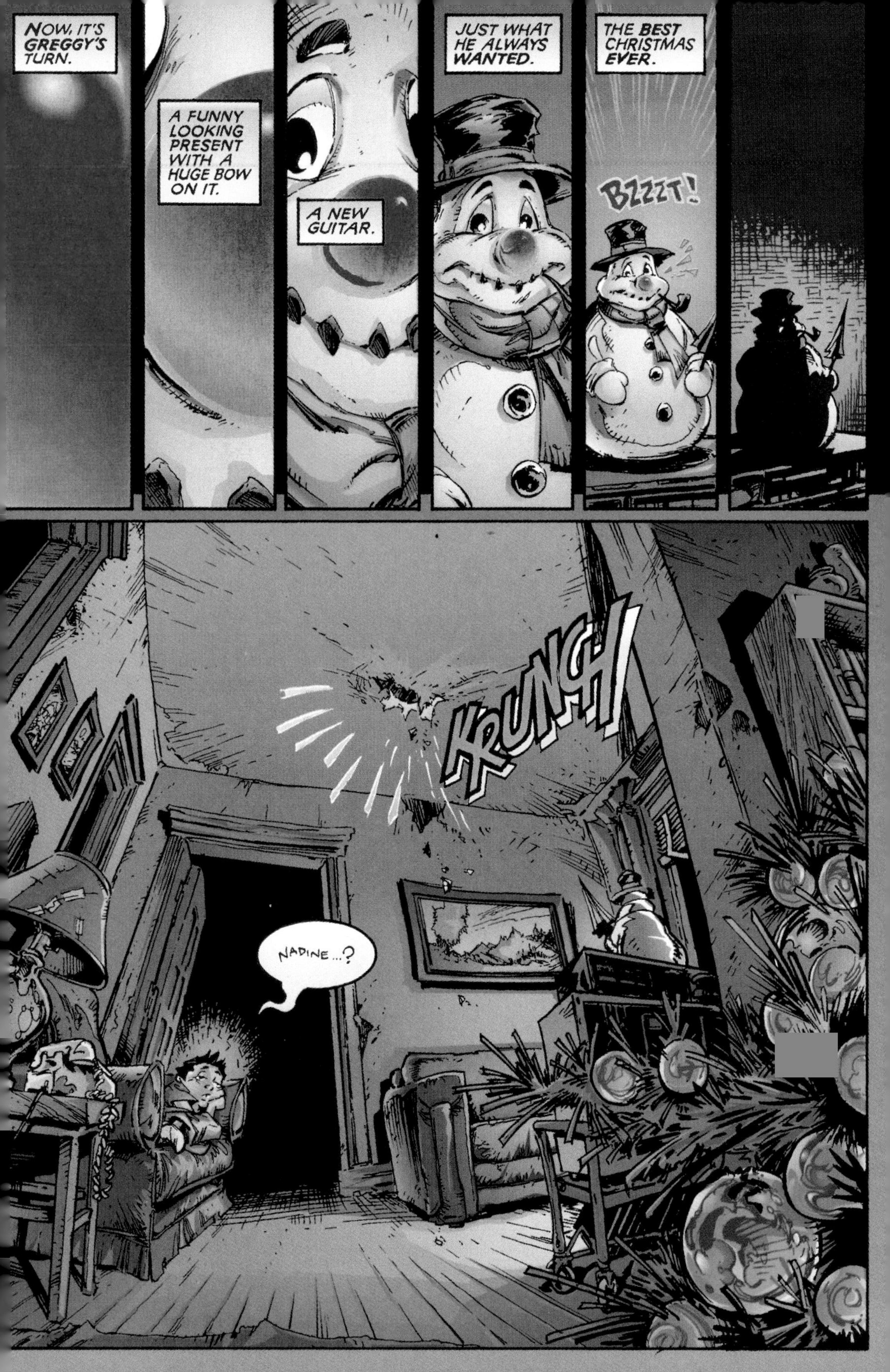
NOW, IT'S GREGGY'S TURN.
A FUNNY LOOKING PRESENT WITH A HUGE BOW ON IT.
A NEW GUITAR.
JUST WHAT HE ALWAYS WANTED.
THE BEST CHRISTMAS EVER.
BZZZT!
KRUNCH
NADINE...?

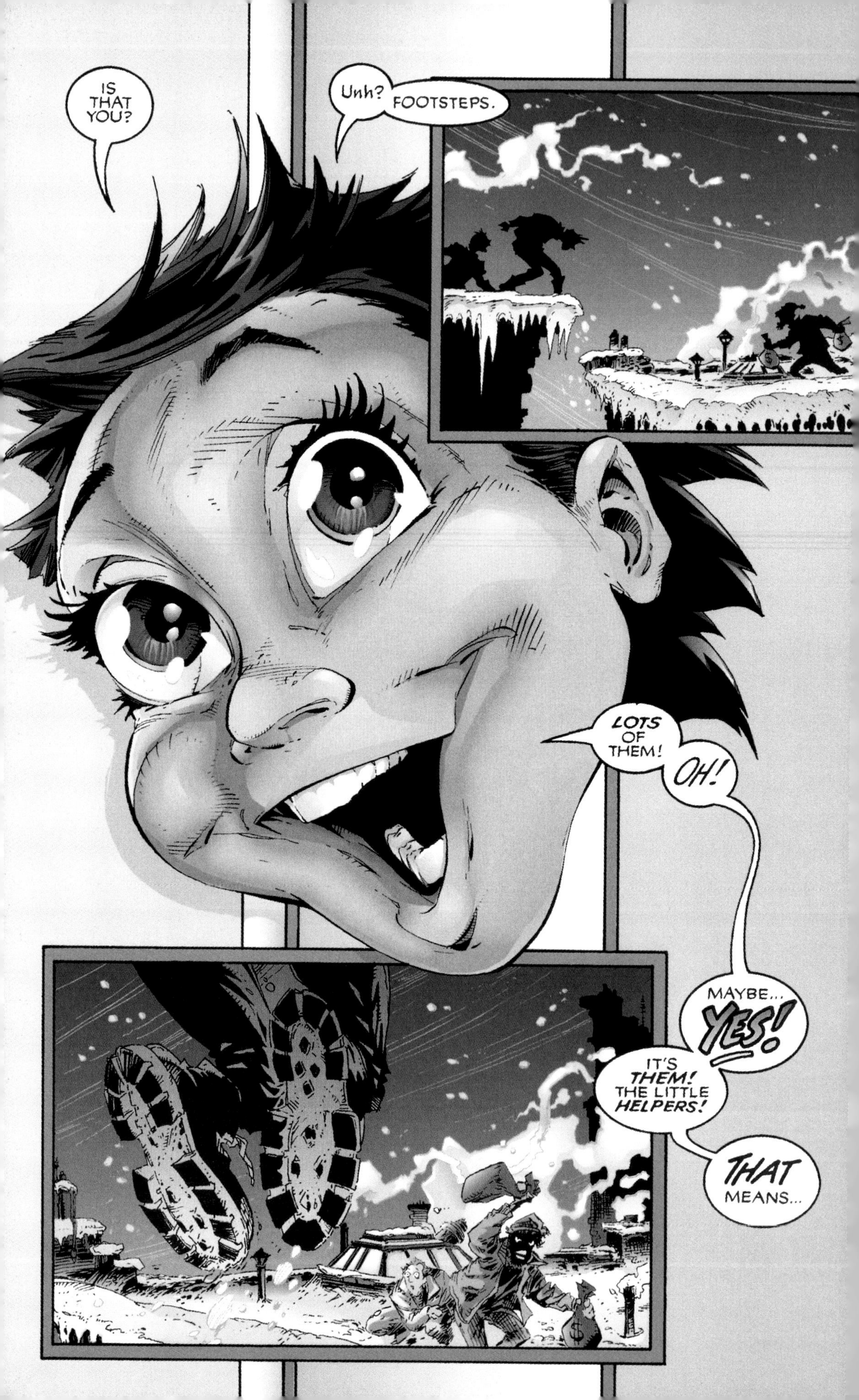

IS THAT YOU?
Unh? FOOTSTEPS.
LOTS OF THEM!
OH!
MAYBE... YES!
IT'S THEM! THE LITTLE HELPERS!
THAT MEANS...

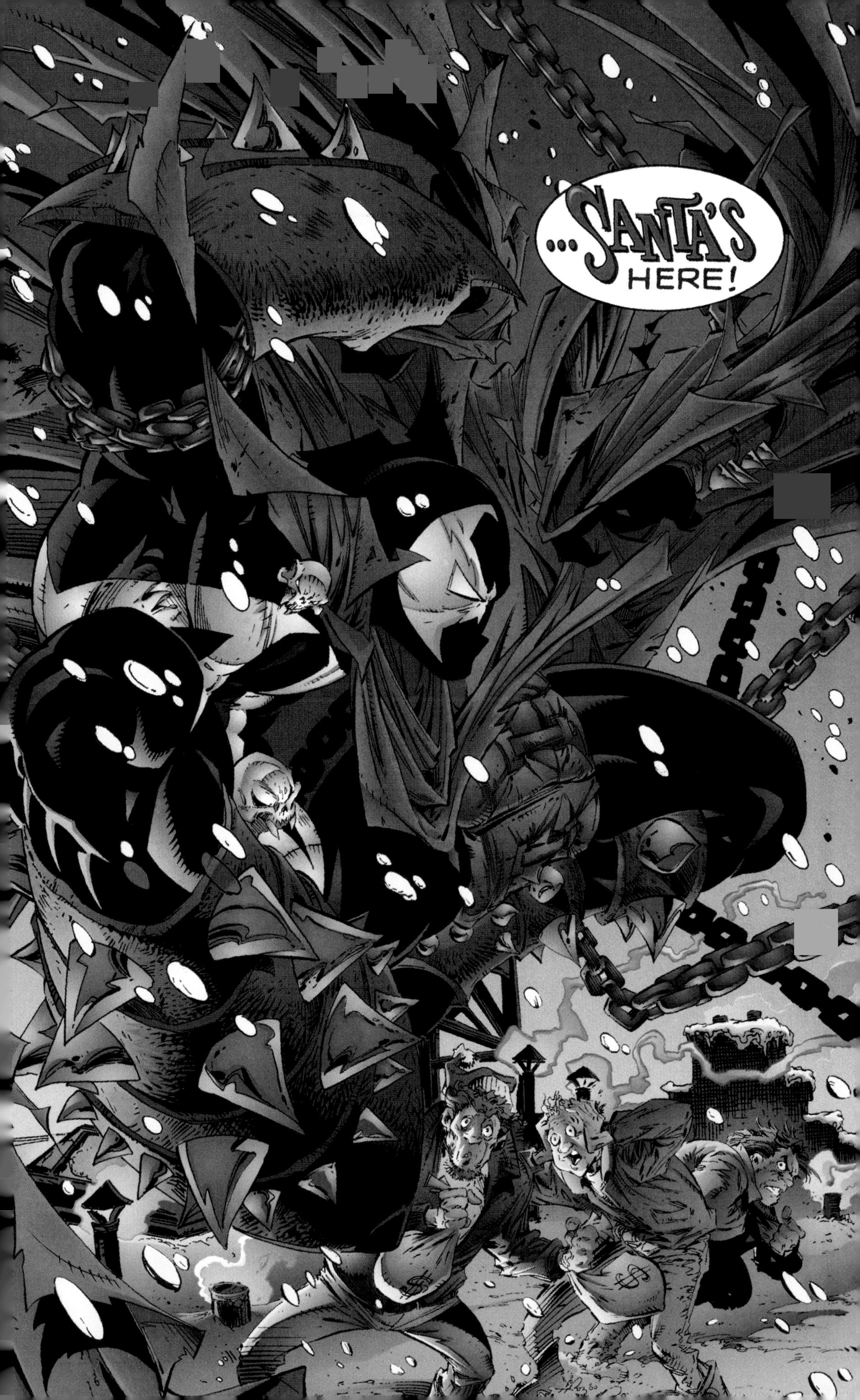
...SANTA'S HERE!

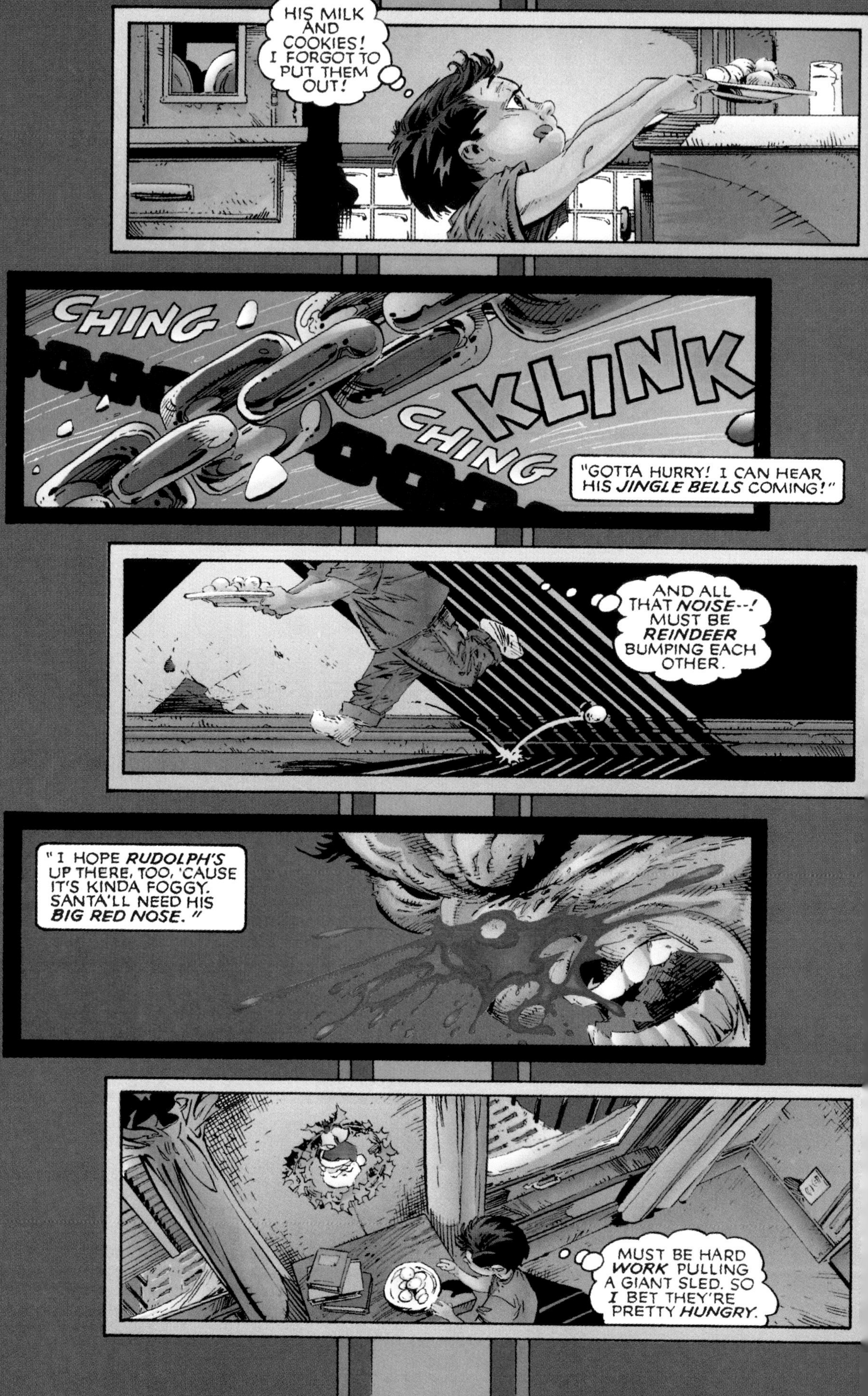
HIS MILK AND COOKIES! I FORGOT TO PUT THEM OUT!
CHING
KLINK
CHING
"GOTTA HURRY! I CAN HEAR HIS JINGLE BELLS COMING!"
AND ALL THAT NOISE--! MUST BE REINDEER BUMPING EACH OTHER.
"I HOPE RUDOLPH'S UP THERE, TOO, 'CAUSE IT'S KINDA FOGGY. SANTA'LL NEED HIS BIG RED NOSE."
MUST BE HARD WORK PULLING A GIANT SLED. SO I BET THEY'RE PRETTY HUNGRY.

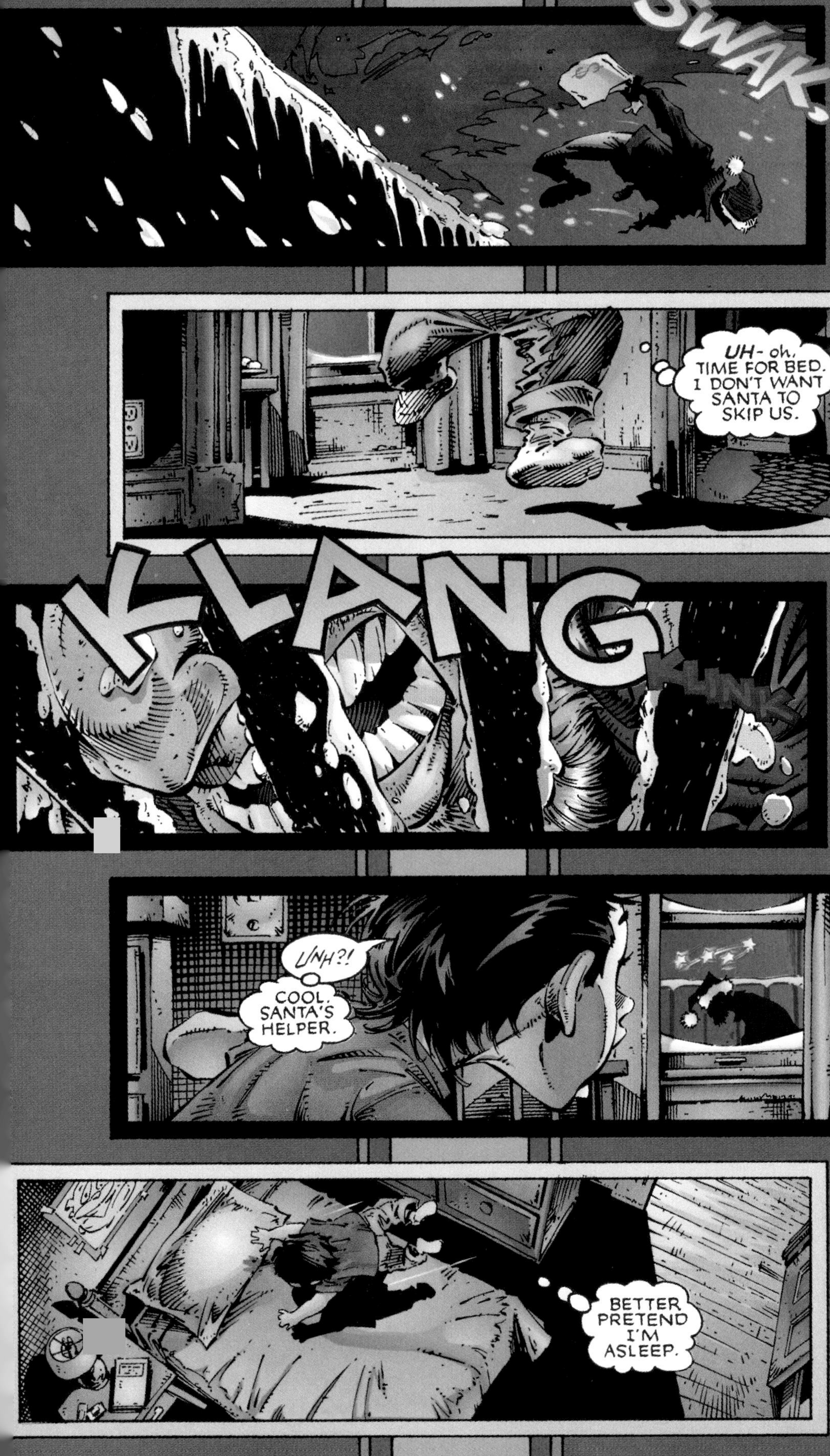
SWAK!
UH- oh, TIME FOR BED. I DON'T WANT SANTA TO SKIP US.
KLANG
KLINK
UNH?!
COOL. SANTA'S HELPER.
BETTER PRETEND I'M ASLEEP.

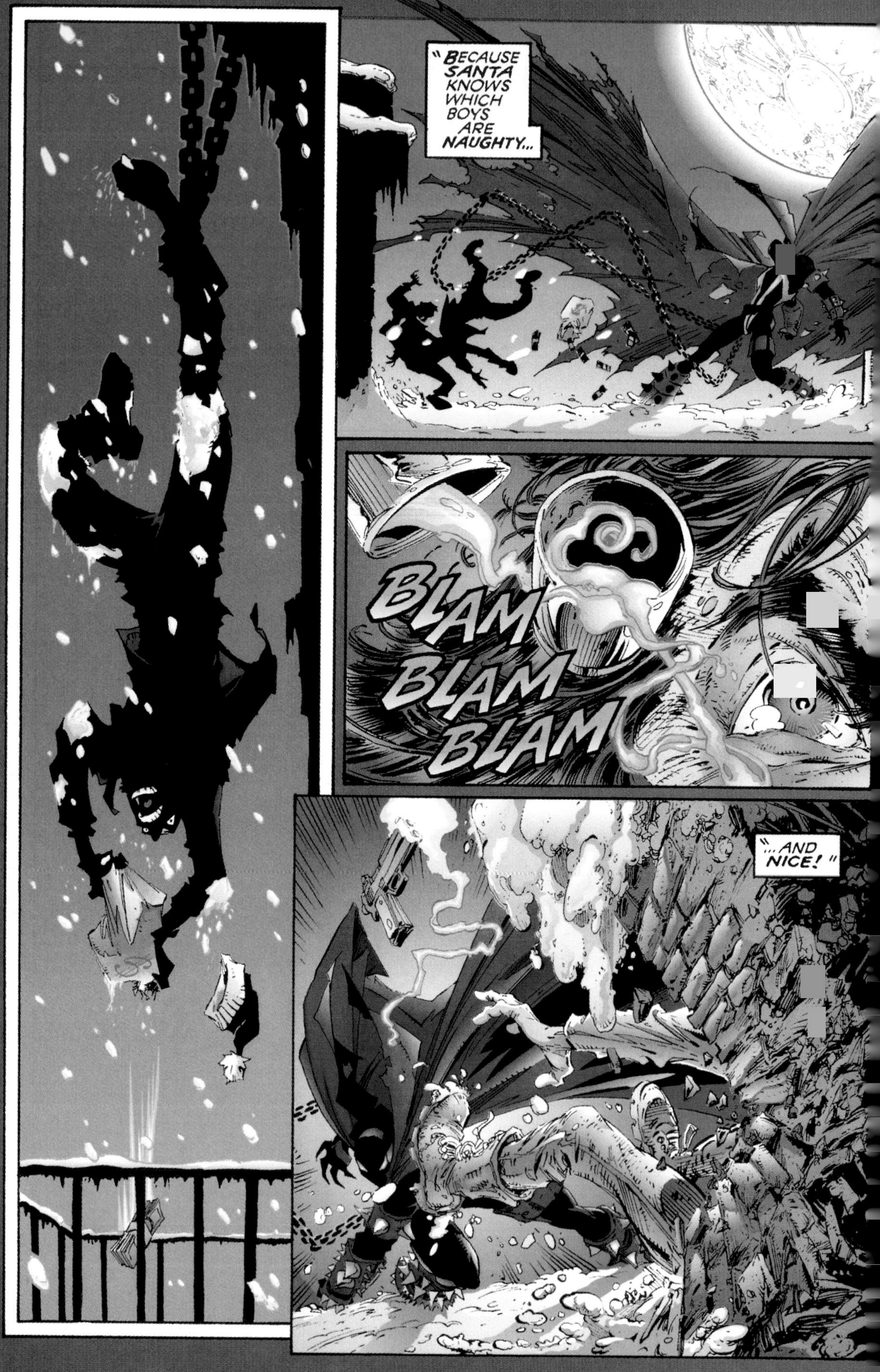
"BECAUSE SANTA KNOWS WHICH BOYS ARE NAUGHTY...
BLAM BLAM BLAM
"...AND NICE!"

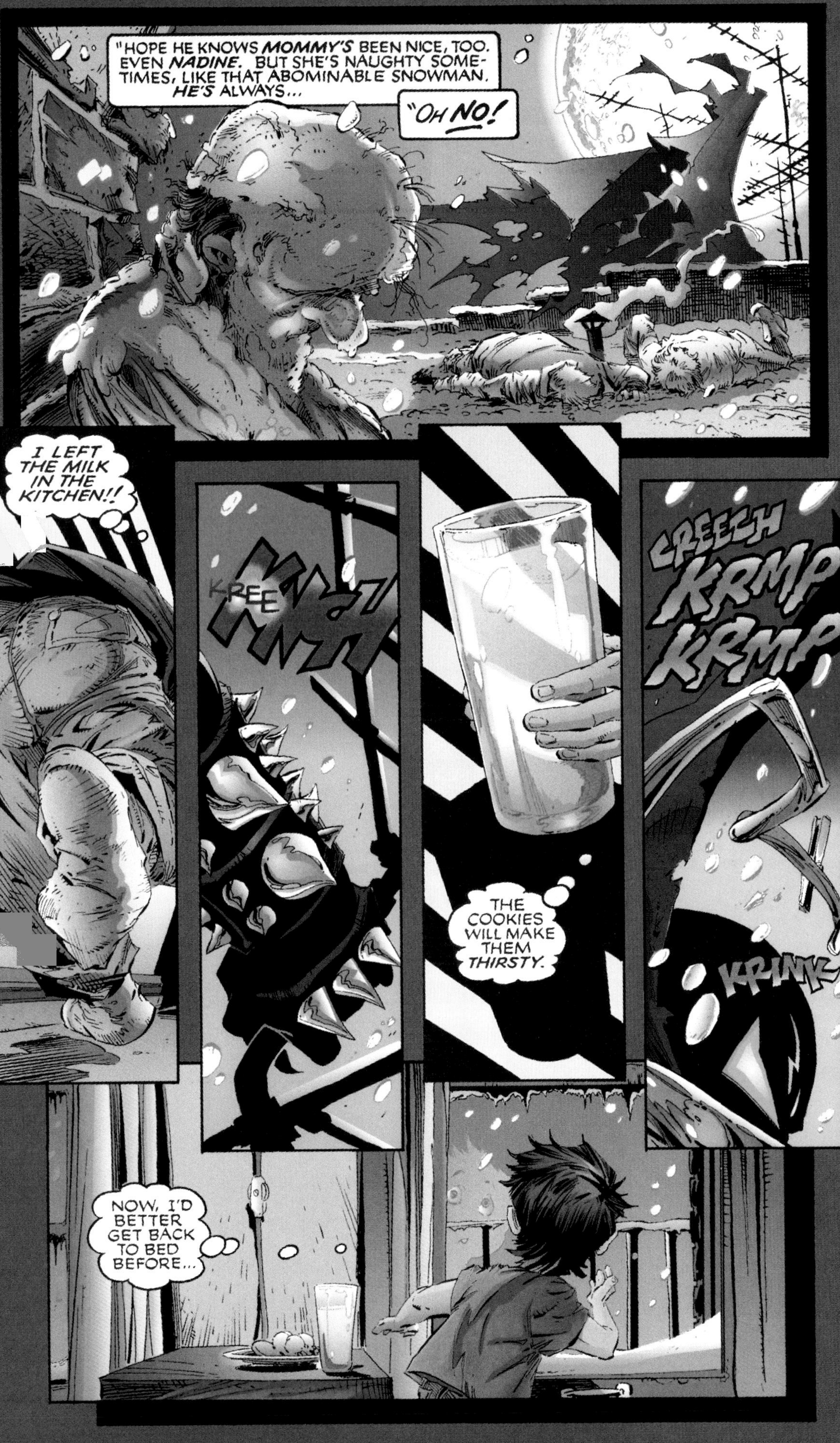
"HOPE HE KNOWS MOMMY'S BEEN NICE, TOO. EVEN NADINE. BUT SHE'S NAUGHTY SOMETIMES, LIKE THAT ABOMINABLE SNOWMAN. HE'S ALWAYS...
"OH NO!
I LEFT THE MILK IN THE KITCHEN!!
KREEE
CREECH
KRMP
KRMP
KRINK
THE COOKIES WILL MAKE THEM THIRSTY.
NOW, I'D BETTER GET BACK TO BED BEFORE...

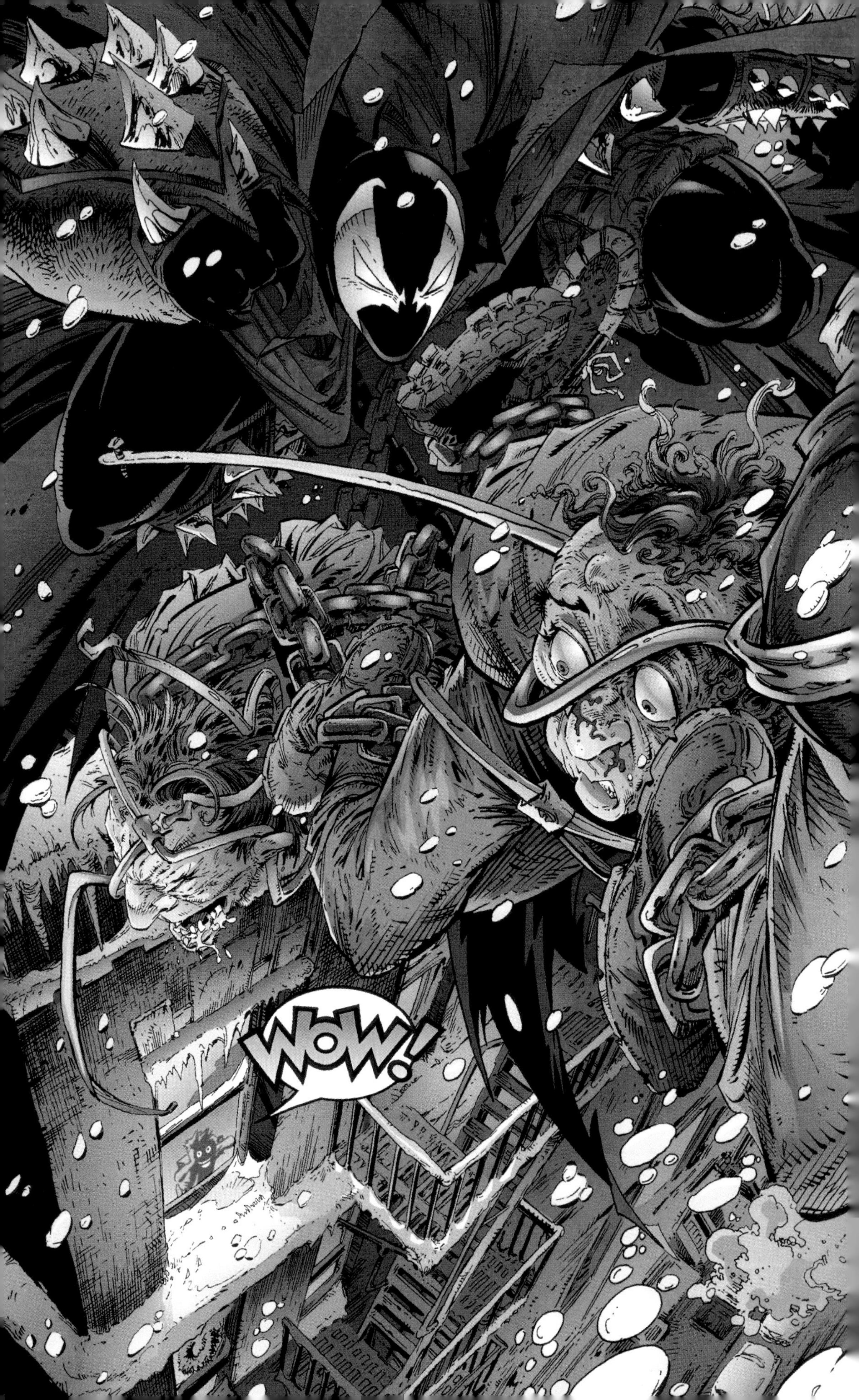
WOW!

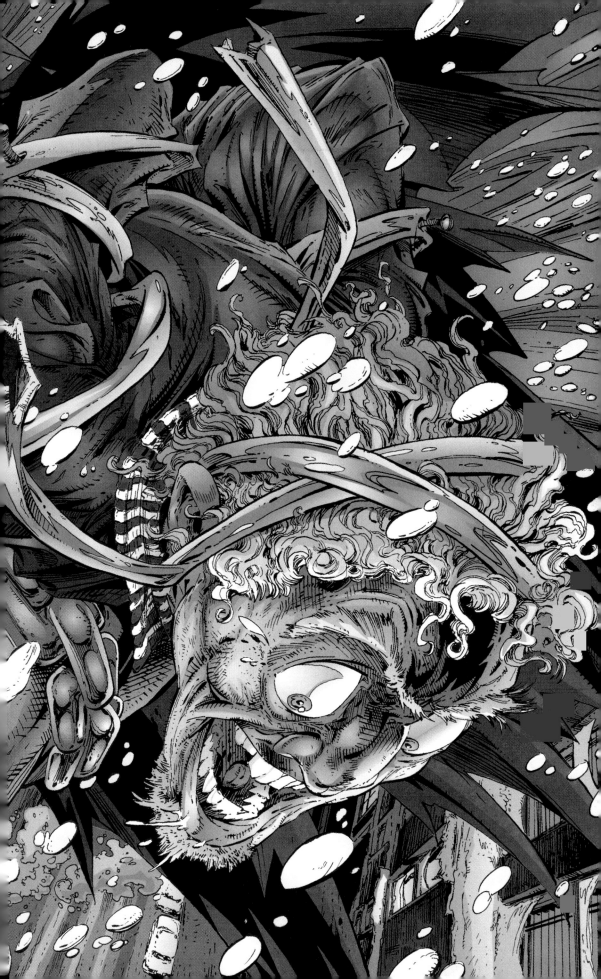

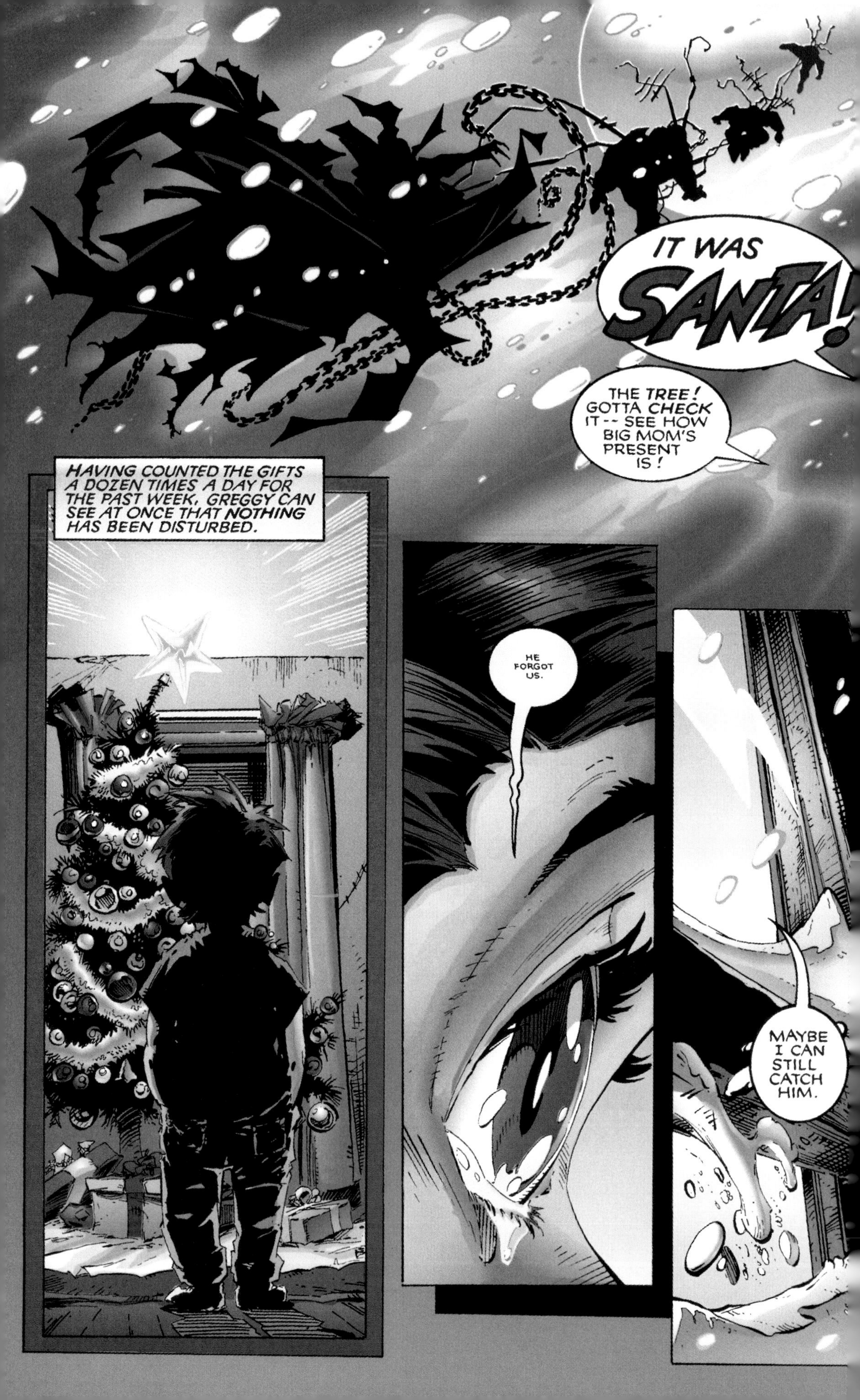
IT WAS SANTA!
THE TREE! GOTTA CHECK IT -- SEE HOW BIG MOM'S PRESENT IS!
HAVING COUNTED THE GIFTS A DOZEN TIMES A DAY FOR THE PAST WEEK, GREGGY CAN SEE AT ONCE THAT NOTHING HAS BEEN DISTURBED.
HE FORGOT US.
MAYBE I CAN STILL CATCH HIM.

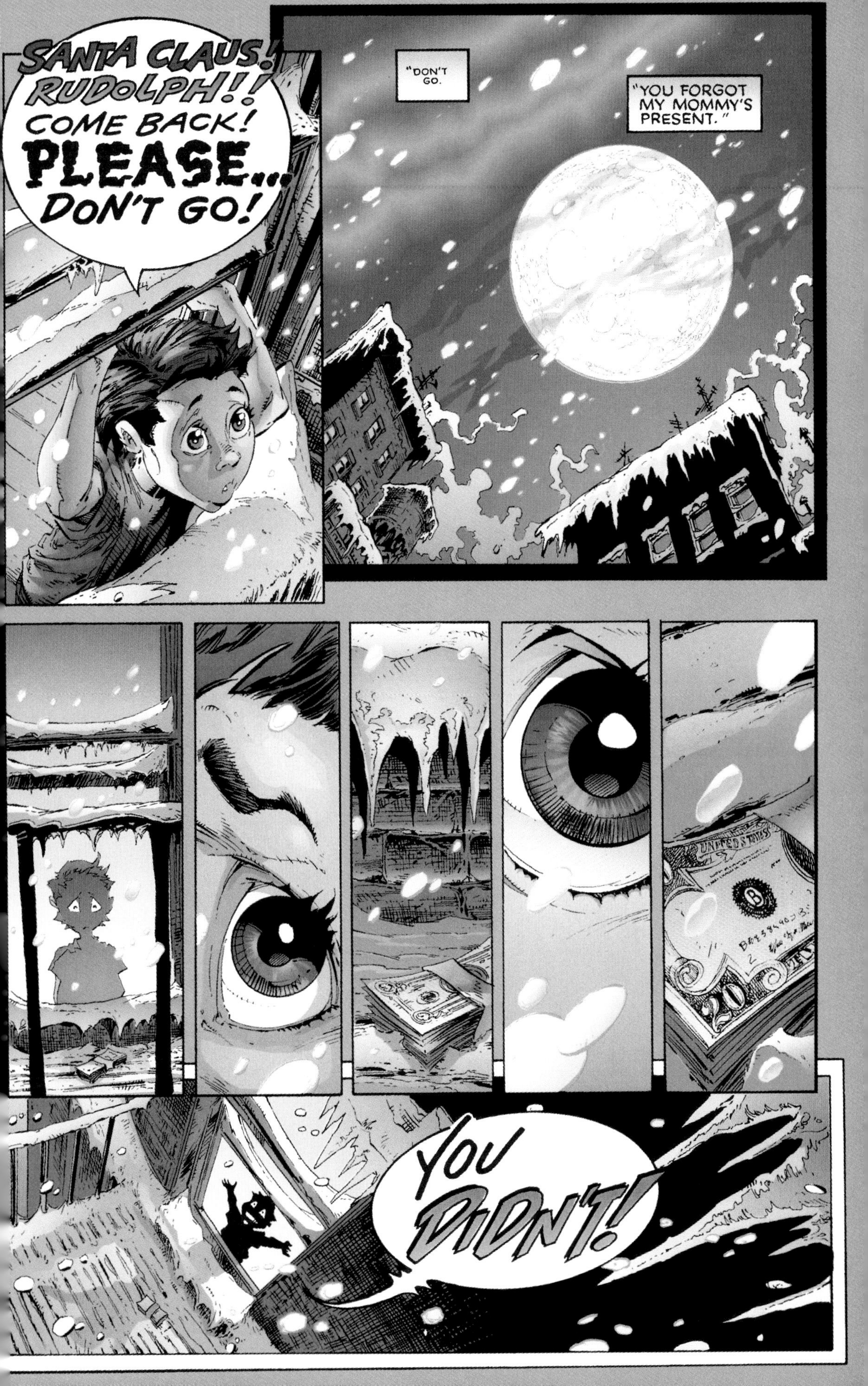
SANTA CLAUS! RUDOLPH!! COME BACK! PLEASE... DON'T GO!
"DON'T GO.
"YOU FORGOT MY MOMMY'S PRESENT."
YOU DIDN'T!

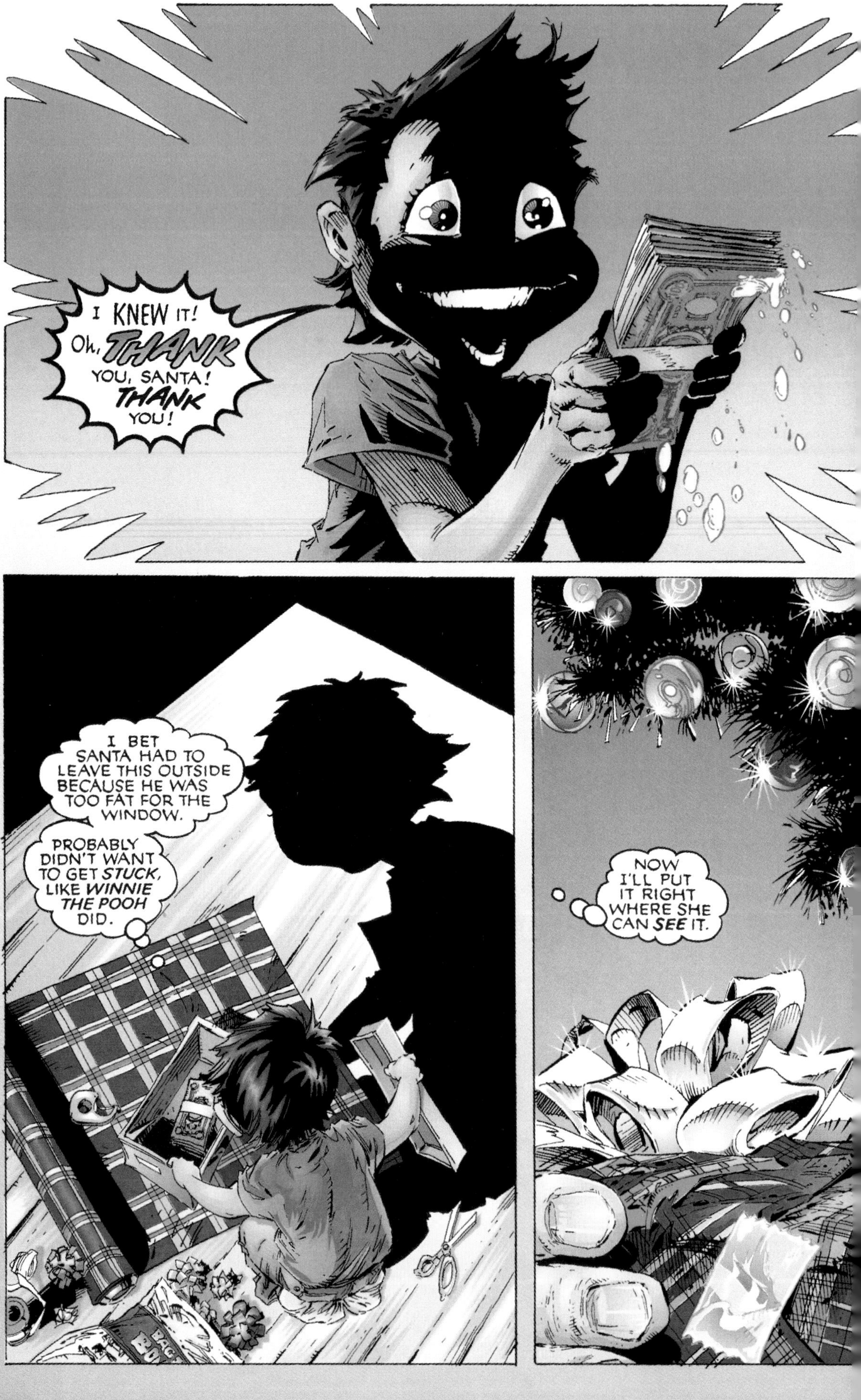
I KNEW IT! Oh, THANK YOU, SANTA! THANK YOU!
I BET SANTA HAD TO LEAVE THIS OUTSIDE BECAUSE HE WAS TOO FAT FOR THE WINDOW.
PROBABLY DIDN'T WANT TO GET STUCK, LIKE WINNIE THE POOH DID.
NOW I'LL PUT IT RIGHT WHERE SHE CAN SEE IT.

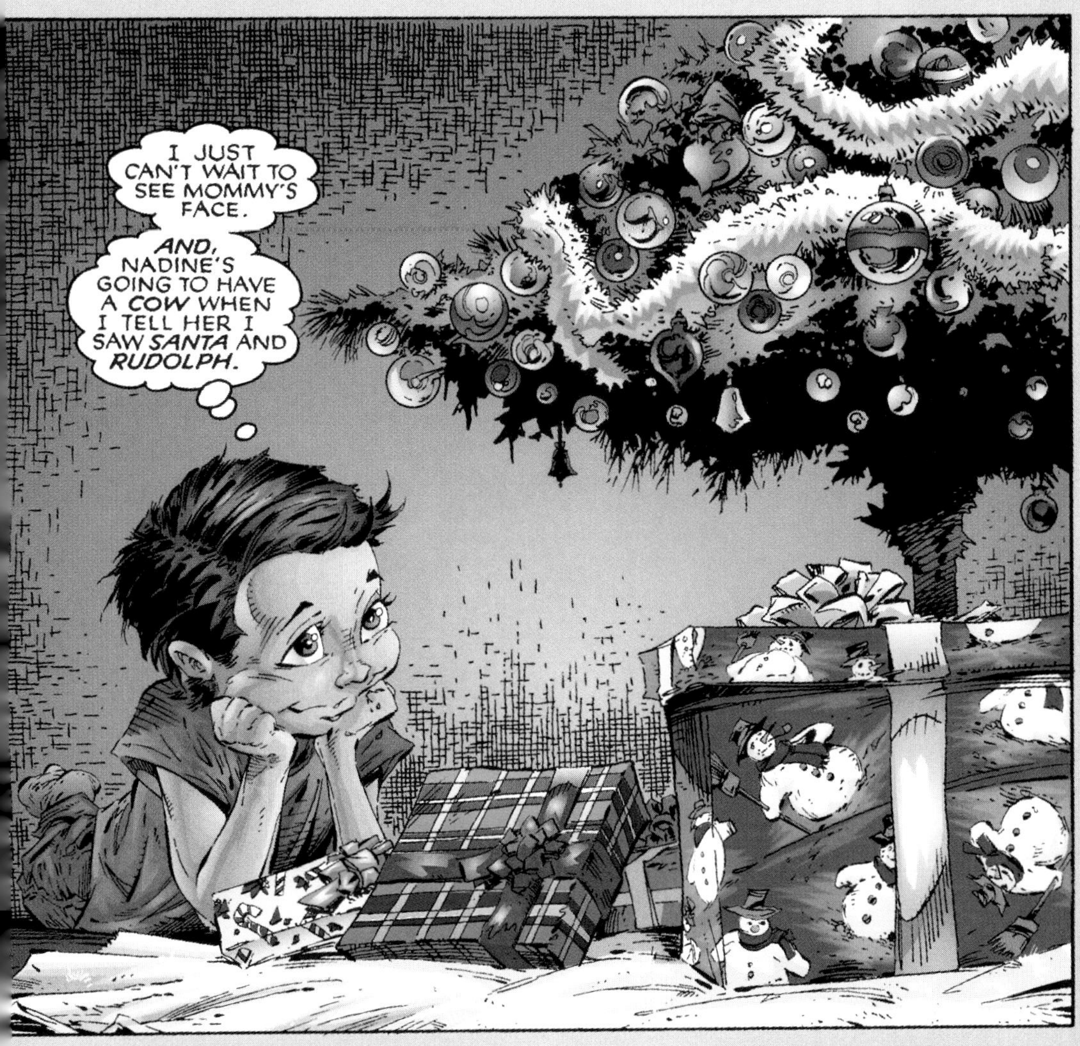
I JUST CAN'T WAIT TO SEE MOMMY'S FACE.
AND, NADINE'S GOING TO HAVE A COW WHEN I TELL HER I SAW SANTA AND RUDOLPH.

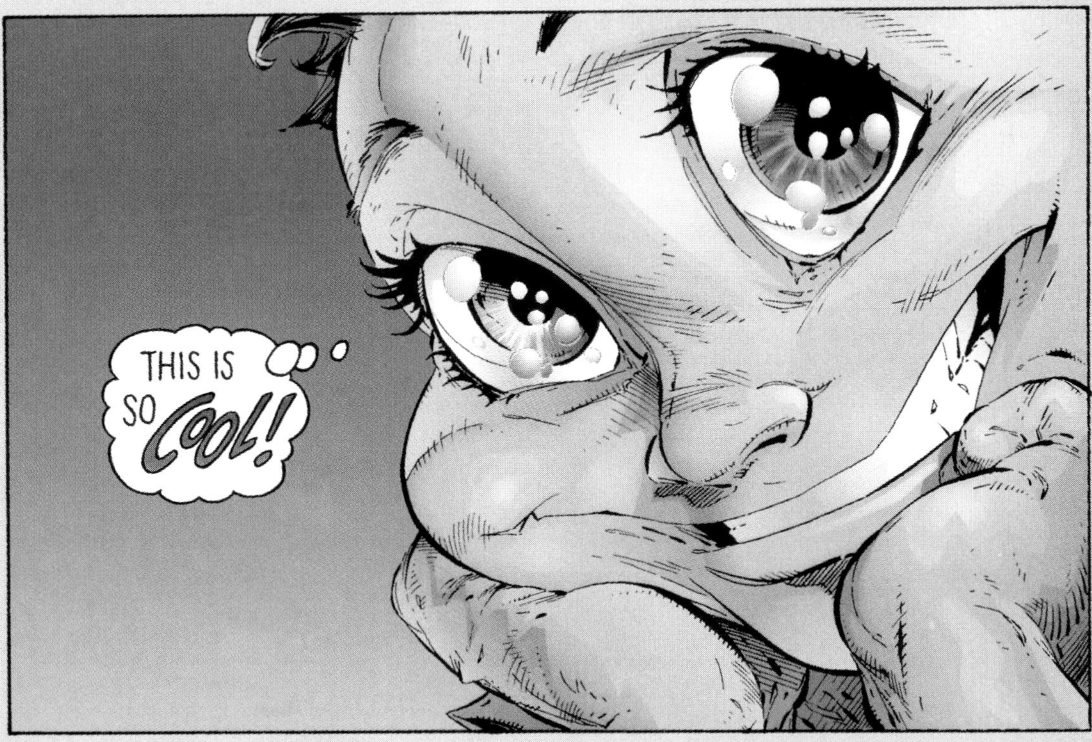
THIS IS SO COOL!

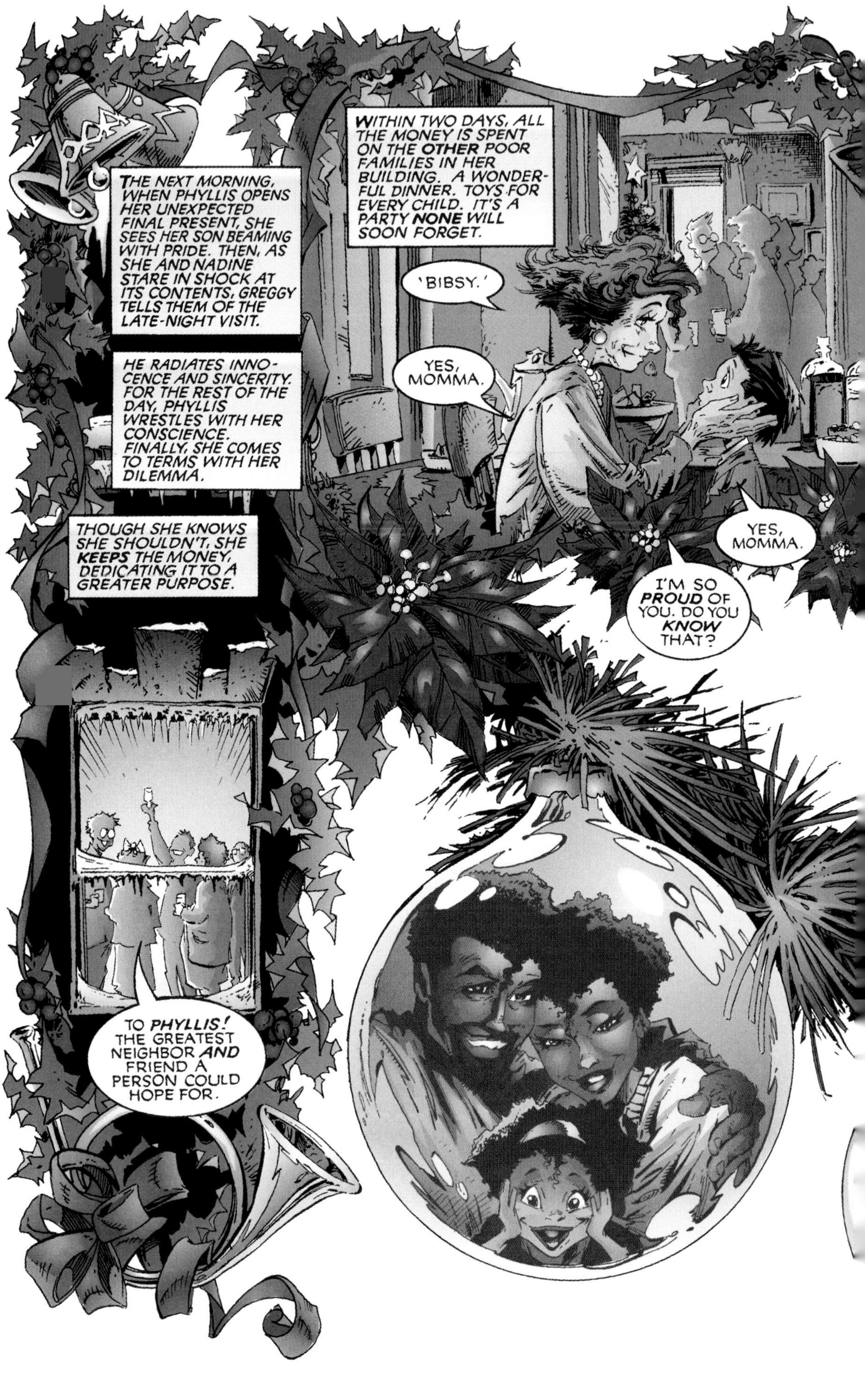
THE NEXT MORNING, WHEN PHYLLIS OPENS HER UNEXPECTED FINAL PRESENT, SHE SEES HER SON BEAMING WITH PRIDE. THEN, AS SHE AND NADINE STARE IN SHOCK AT ITS CONTENTS, GREGGY TELLS THEM OF THE LATE-NIGHT VISIT.
HE RADIATES INNOCENCE AND SINCERITY. FOR THE REST OF THE DAY, PHYLLIS WRESTLES WITH HER CONSCIENCE. FINALLY, SHE COMES TO TERMS WITH HER DILEMMA.
THOUGH SHE KNOWS SHE SHOULDN'T, SHE **KEEPS** THE MONEY, DEDICATING IT TO A GREATER PURPOSE.
TO ***PHYLLIS!*** THE GREATEST NEIGHBOR ***AND*** FRIEND A PERSON COULD HOPE FOR.
WITHIN TWO DAYS, ALL THE MONEY IS SPENT ON THE **OTHER** POOR FAMILIES IN HER BUILDING. A WONDERFUL DINNER. TOYS FOR EVERY CHILD. IT'S A PARTY **NONE** WILL SOON FORGET.
'BIBSY.'
YES, MOMMA.
I'M SO ***PROUD*** OF YOU. DO YOU ***KNOW*** THAT?
YES, MOMMA.

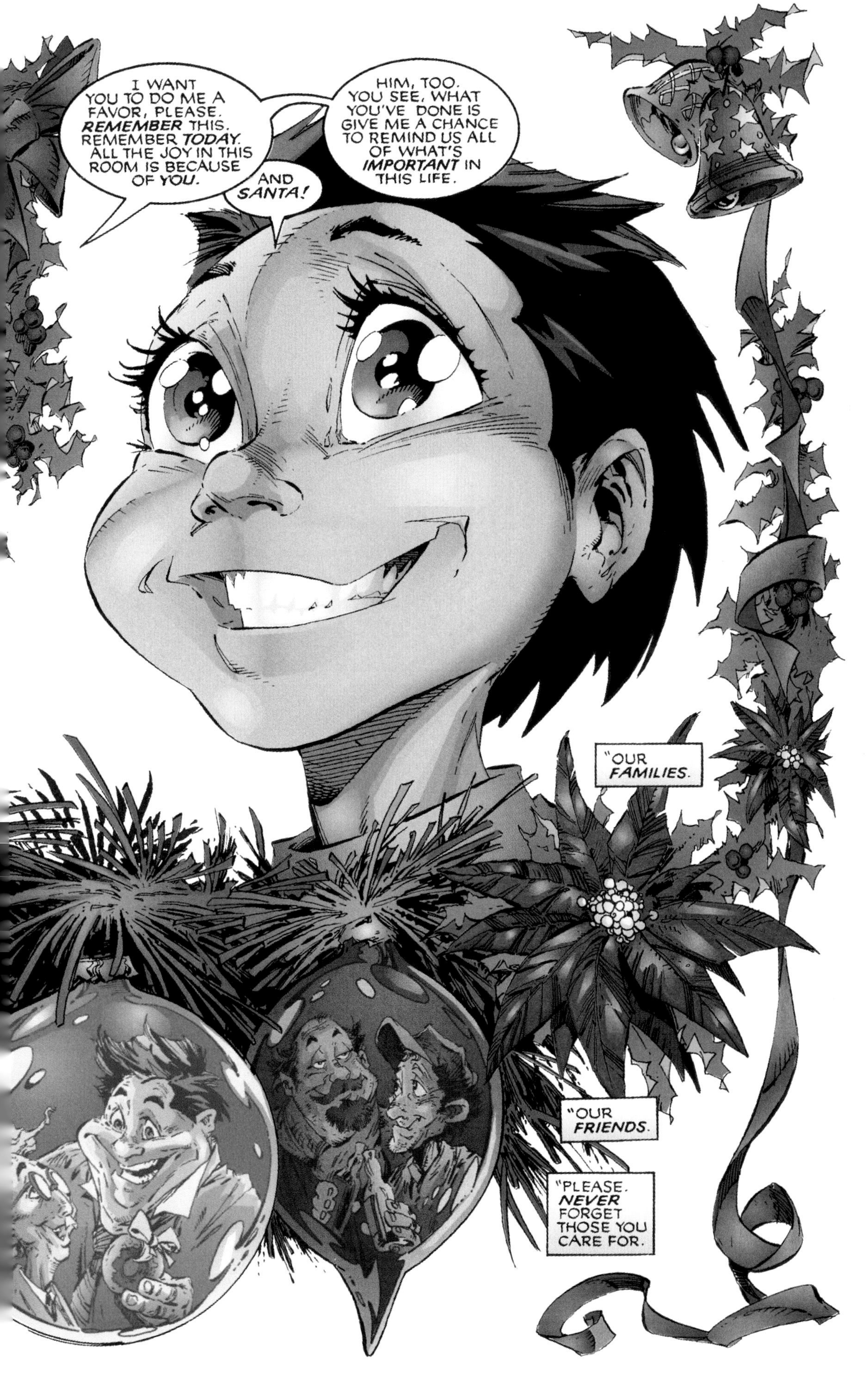
I WANT YOU TO DO ME A FAVOR, PLEASE. REMEMBER THIS. REMEMBER TODAY. ALL THE JOY IN THIS ROOM IS BECAUSE OF YOU.
AND SANTA!
HIM, TOO. YOU SEE, WHAT YOU'VE DONE IS GIVE ME A CHANCE TO REMIND US ALL OF WHAT'S IMPORTANT IN THIS LIFE.
"OUR FAMILIES.
"OUR FRIENDS.
"PLEASE. NEVER FORGET THOSE YOU CARE FOR.

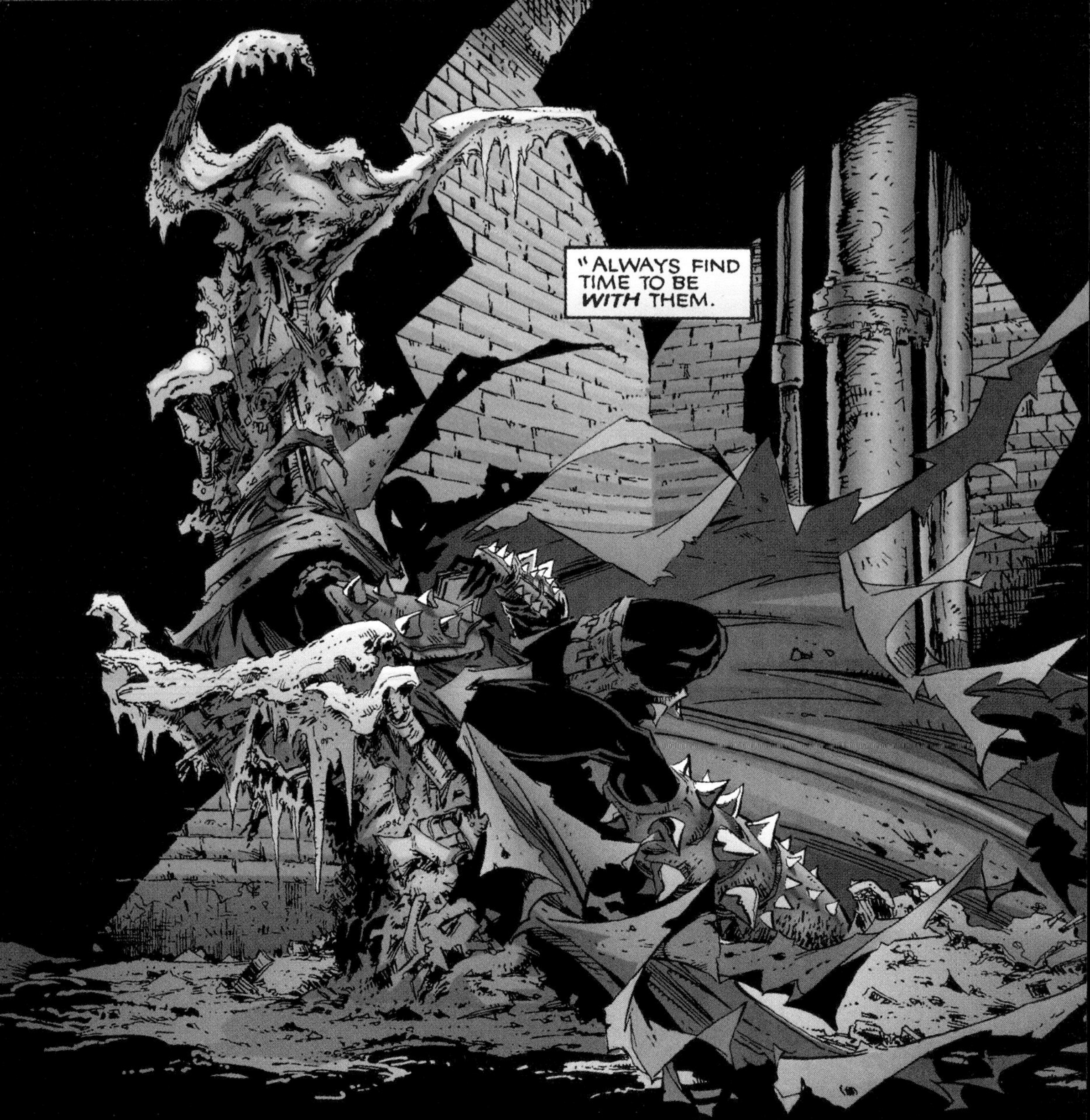
"ALWAYS FIND TIME TO BE *WITH* THEM.

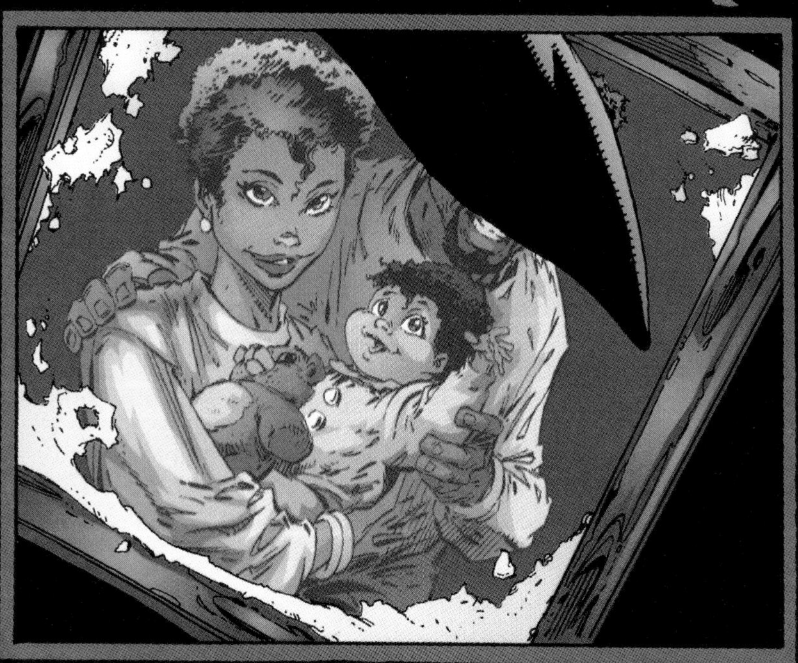

" AND NEVER, ***EVER*** DESERT THEM IN A TIME OF NEED. THAT'S HOW YOU SHOW YOU ***CARE***. HOW PEOPLE KNOW YOU ***LOVE*** THEM."

"I'LL REMEMBER."

"MOMMY?"

"YES, GREGGY?"

"ISN'T THIS THE BEST CHRISTMAS ***EVER?***"

"YES IT IS, SON. YES IT ***IS***."

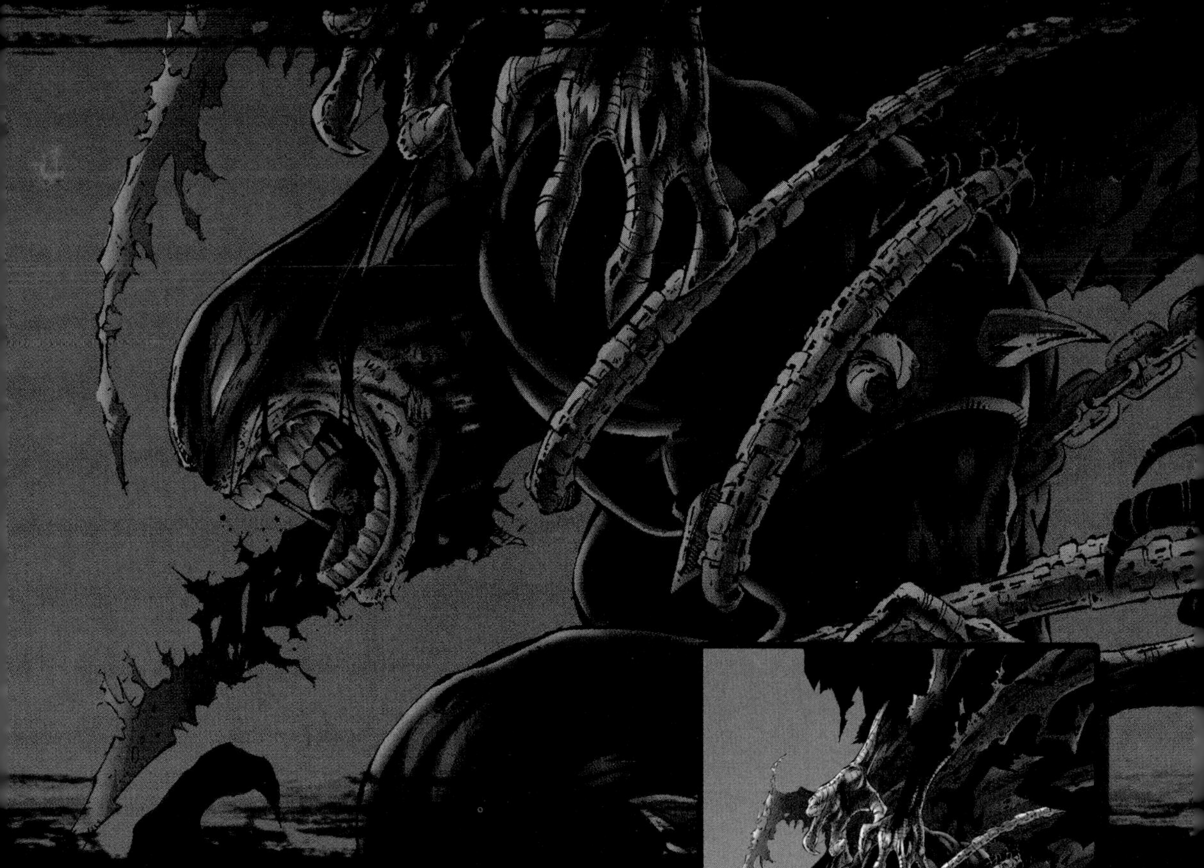

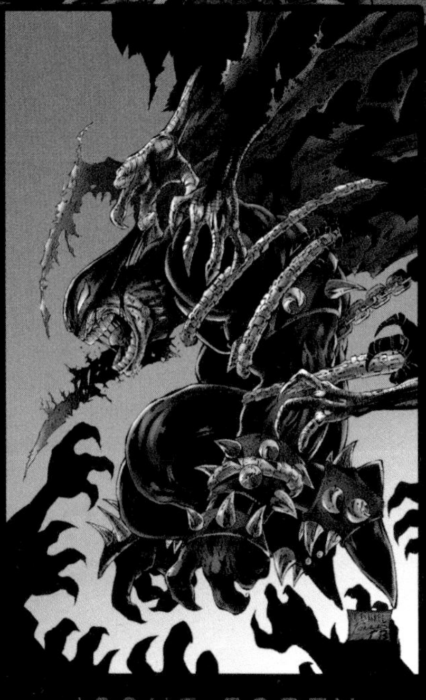

ISSUE FORTY

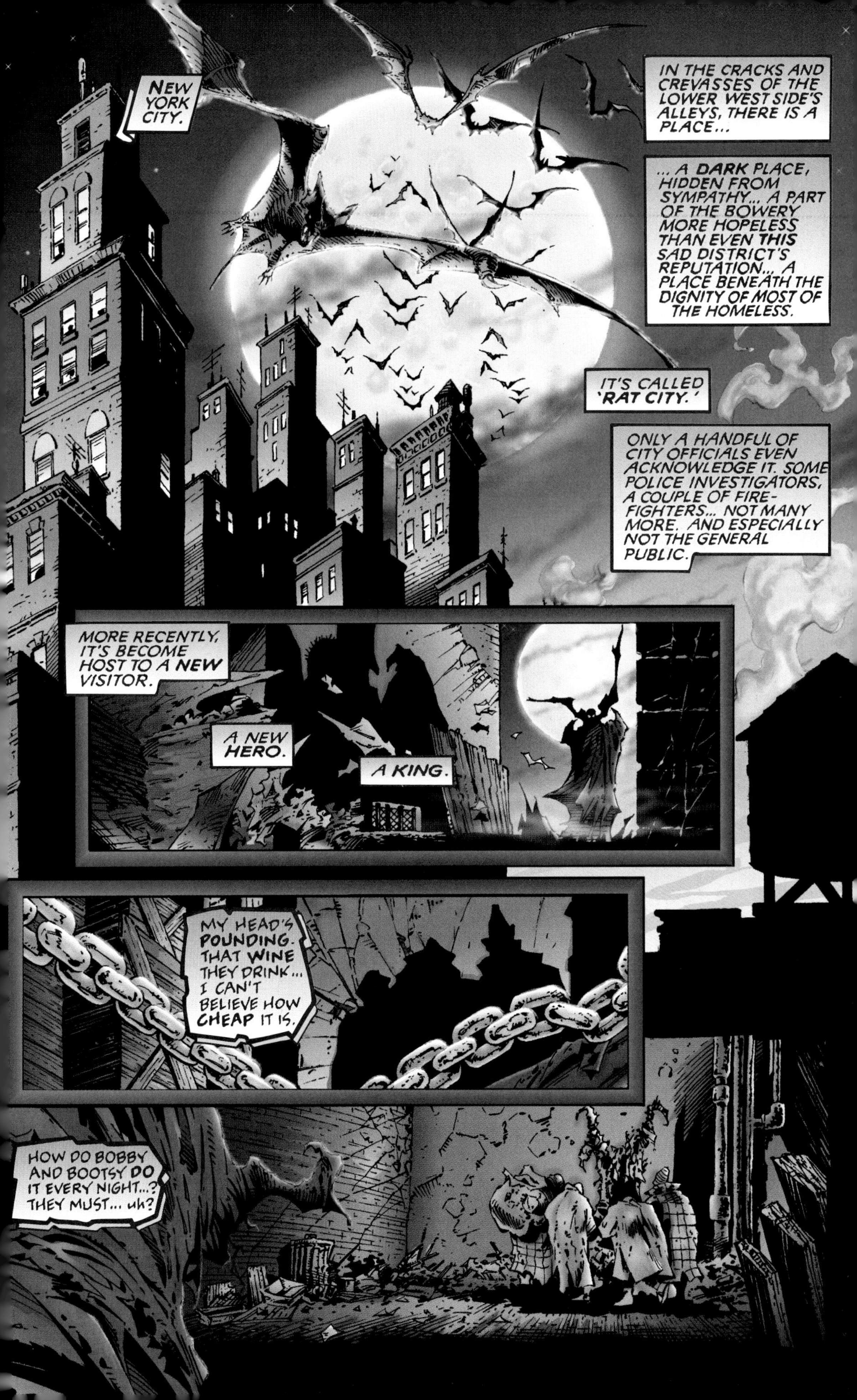
NEW YORK CITY.
IN THE CRACKS AND CREVASSES OF THE LOWER WEST SIDE'S ALLEYS, THERE IS A PLACE...
...A DARK PLACE, HIDDEN FROM SYMPATHY... A PART OF THE BOWERY MORE HOPELESS THAN EVEN THIS SAD DISTRICT'S REPUTATION... A PLACE BENEATH THE DIGNITY OF MOST OF THE HOMELESS.
IT'S CALLED 'RAT CITY.'
ONLY A HANDFUL OF CITY OFFICIALS EVEN ACKNOWLEDGE IT. SOME POLICE INVESTIGATORS, A COUPLE OF FIRE-FIGHTERS... NOT MANY MORE. AND ESPECIALLY NOT THE GENERAL PUBLIC.
MORE RECENTLY, IT'S BECOME HOST TO A NEW VISITOR.
A NEW HERO.
A KING.
MY HEAD'S POUNDING. THAT WINE THEY DRINK... I CAN'T BELIEVE HOW CHEAP IT IS.
HOW DO BOBBY AND BOOTSY DO IT EVERY NIGHT...? THEY MUST... uh?

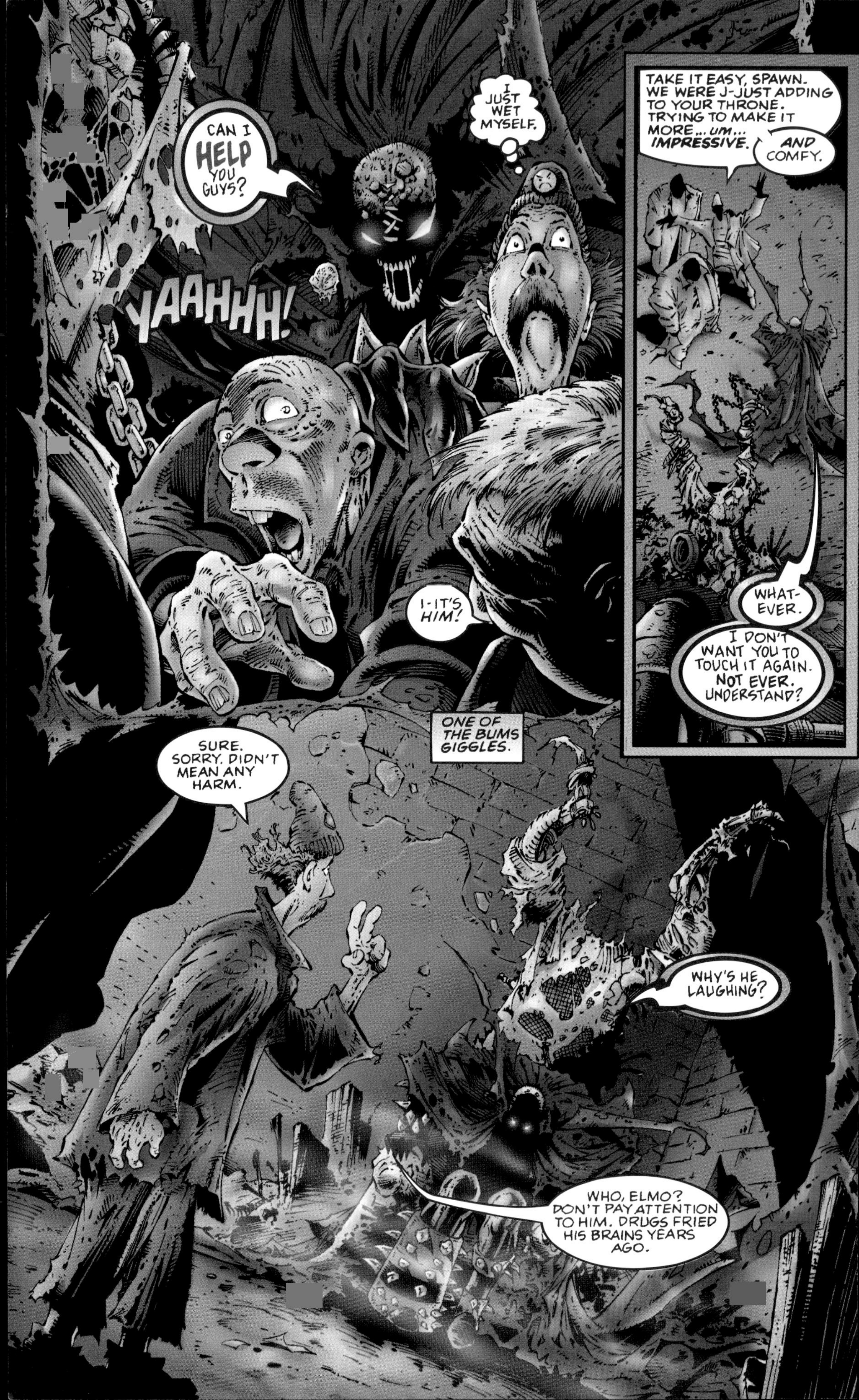
CAN I HELP YOU GUYS?
I JUST WET MYSELF.
YAAHHH!
I-IT'S HIM!
TAKE IT EASY, SPAWN. WE WERE J-JUST ADDING TO YOUR THRONE. TRYING TO MAKE IT MORE... *um...* ***IMPRESSIVE.***
AND COMFY.
WHAT-EVER.
I DON'T WANT YOU TO TOUCH IT AGAIN. **NOT EVER.** UNDERSTAND?
ONE OF THE BUMS GIGGLES.
SURE. SORRY. DIDN'T MEAN ANY HARM.
WHY'S HE LAUGHING?
WHO, ELMO? DON'T PAY ATTENTION TO HIM. DRUGS FRIED HIS BRAINS YEARS AGO.

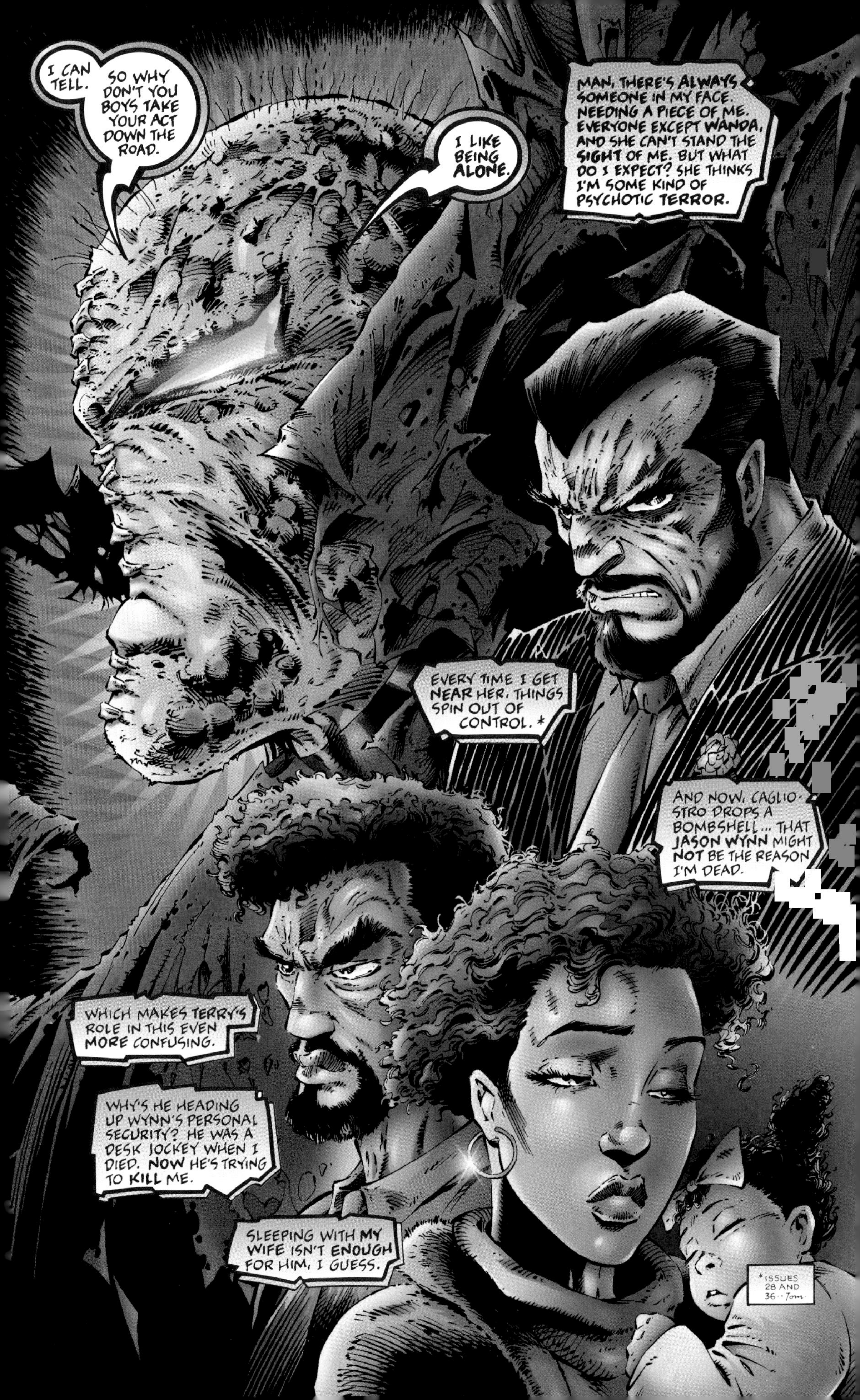

I CAN TELL.
SO WHY DON'T YOU BOYS TAKE YOUR ACT DOWN THE ROAD.
I LIKE BEING ALONE.
MAN, THERE'S ALWAYS SOMEONE IN MY FACE. NEEDING A PIECE OF ME. EVERYONE EXCEPT WANDA, AND SHE CAN'T STAND THE SIGHT OF ME. BUT WHAT DO I EXPECT? SHE THINKS I'M SOME KIND OF PSYCHOTIC TERROR.
EVERY TIME I GET NEAR HER, THINGS SPIN OUT OF CONTROL.*
AND NOW, CAGLIO-STRO DROPS A BOMBSHELL... THAT JASON WYNN MIGHT NOT BE THE REASON I'M DEAD.
WHICH MAKES TERRY'S ROLE IN THIS EVEN MORE CONFUSING.
WHY'S HE HEADING UP WYNN'S PERSONAL SECURITY? HE WAS A DESK JOCKEY WHEN I DIED. NOW HE'S TRYING TO KILL ME.
SLEEPING WITH MY WIFE ISN'T ENOUGH FOR HIM, I GUESS.
*ISSUES 28 AND 36--Tom

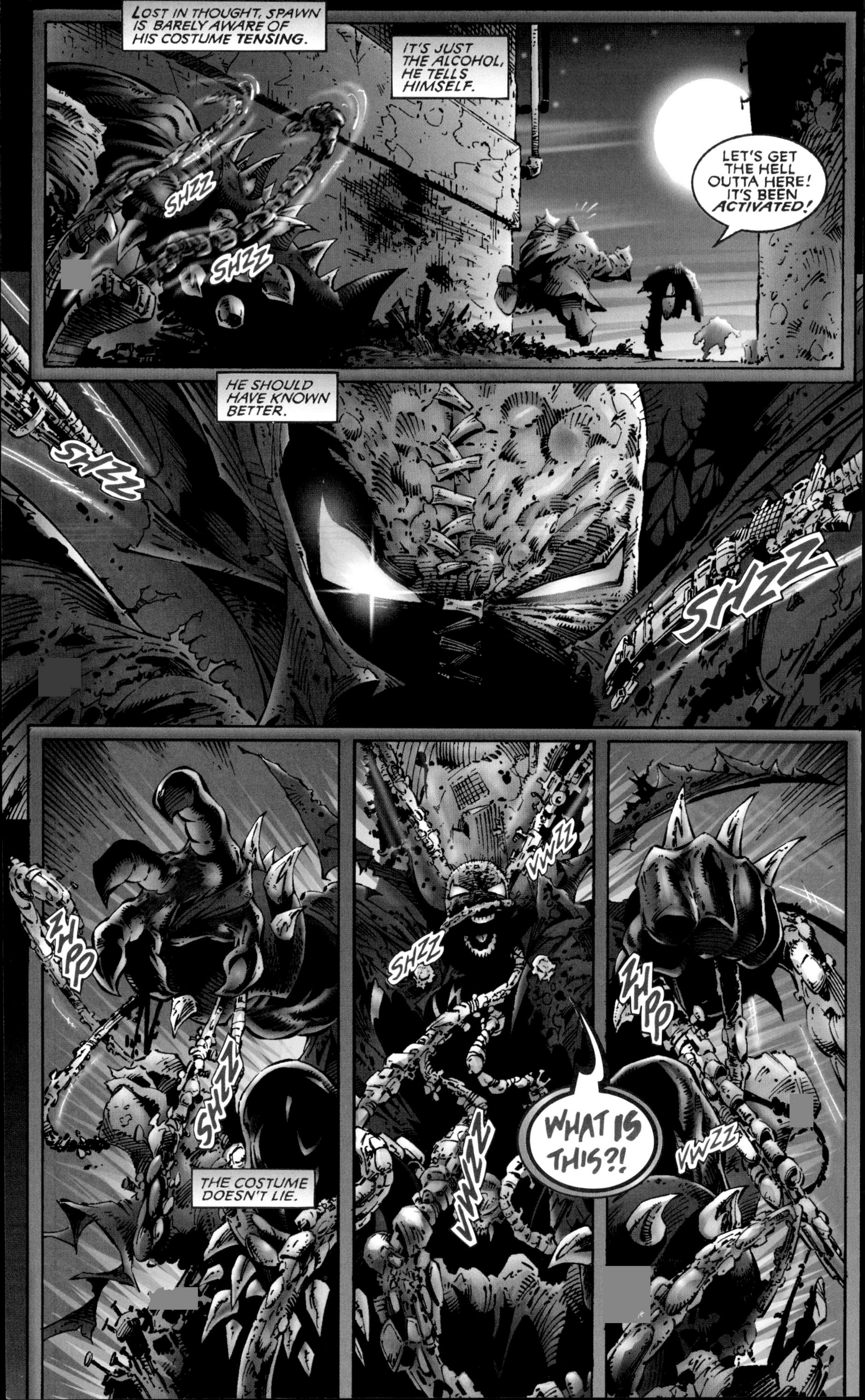
LOST IN THOUGHT, SPAWN IS BARELY AWARE OF HIS COSTUME TENSING.
IT'S JUST THE ALCOHOL, HE TELLS HIMSELF.
SHZZ
SHZZ
LET'S GET THE HELL OUTTA HERE! IT'S BEEN ACTIVATED!
HE SHOULD HAVE KNOWN BETTER.
SHZZ
SHZZ
ZHPP
SHZZ
THE COSTUME DOESN'T LIE.
VWZZ
SHZZ
VWZZ
WHAT IS THIS?!
ZHPP
VWZZ

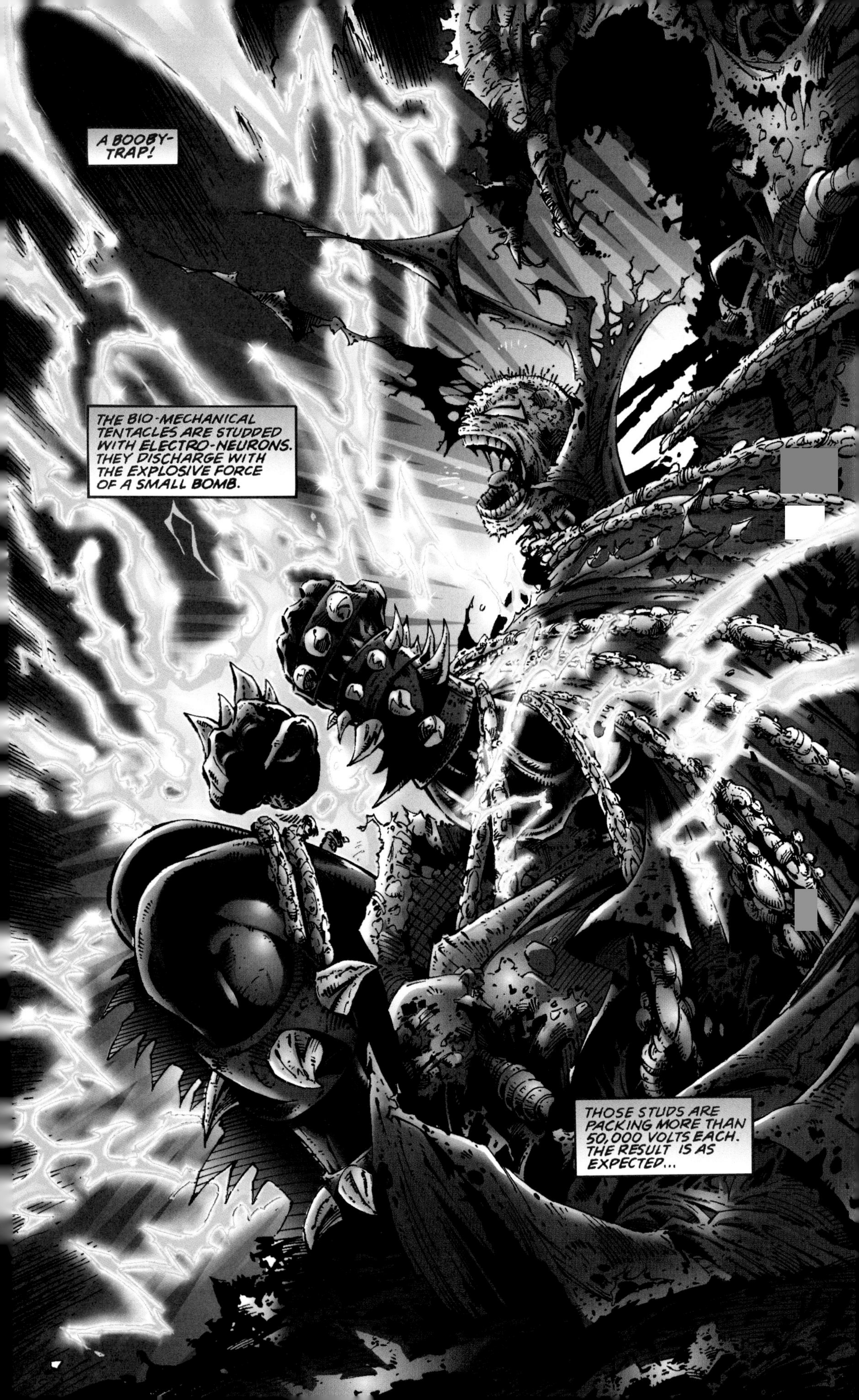
A BOOBY-TRAP!
THE BIO-MECHANICAL TENTACLES ARE STUDDED WITH ELECTRO-NEURONS. THEY DISCHARGE WITH THE EXPLOSIVE FORCE OF A SMALL BOMB.
THOSE STUDS ARE PACKING MORE THAN 50,000 VOLTS EACH. THE RESULT IS AS EXPECTED...

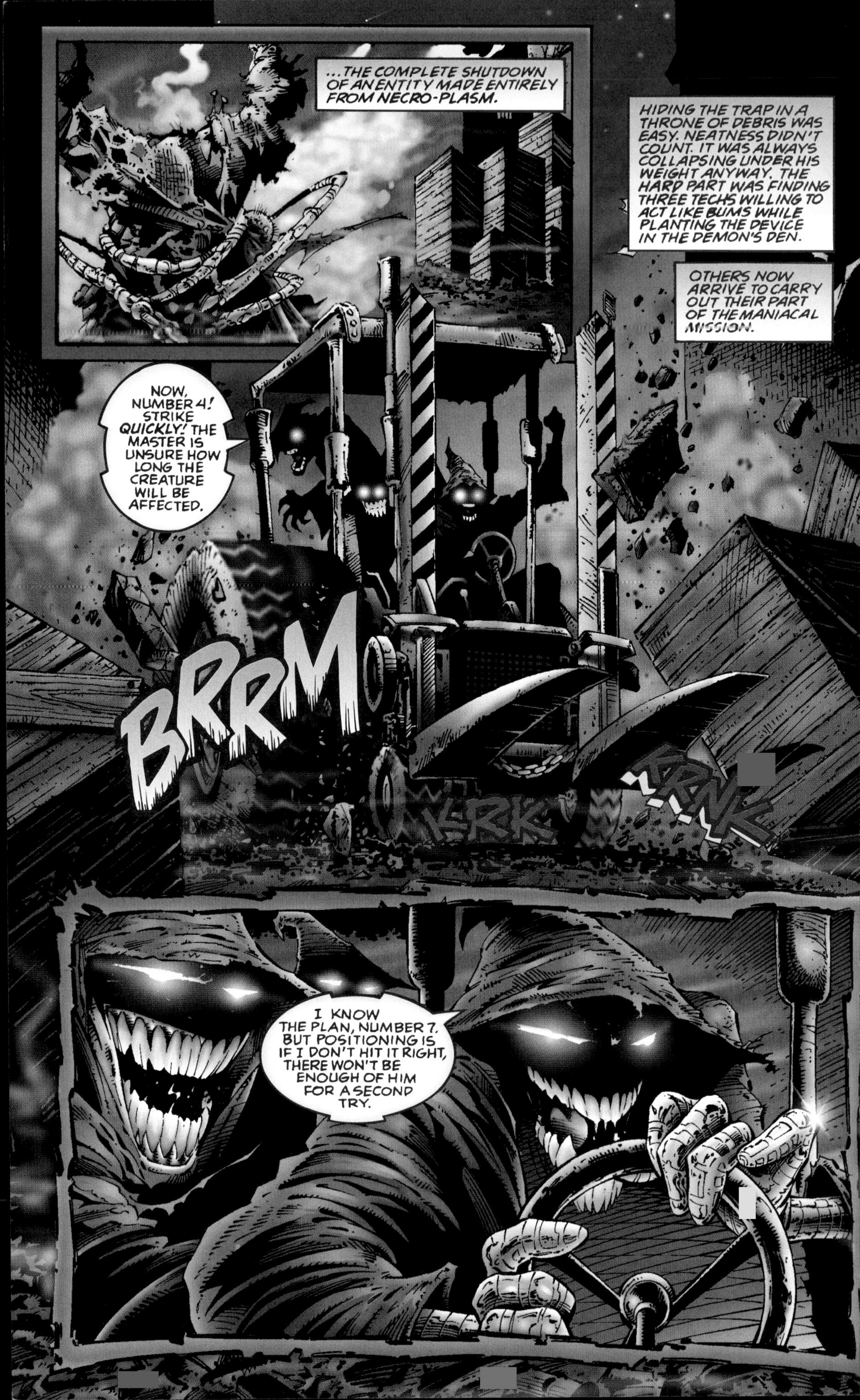
...THE COMPLETE SHUTDOWN OF AN ENTITY MADE ENTIRELY FROM NECRO-PLASM.
HIDING THE TRAP IN A THRONE OF DEBRIS WAS EASY. NEATNESS DIDN'T COUNT. IT WAS ALWAYS COLLAPSING UNDER HIS WEIGHT ANYWAY. THE HARD PART WAS FINDING THREE TECHS WILLING TO ACT LIKE BUMS WHILE PLANTING THE DEVICE IN THE DEMON'S DEN.
OTHERS NOW ARRIVE TO CARRY OUT THEIR PART OF THE MANIACAL MISSION.
NOW, NUMBER 4! STRIKE QUICKLY! THE MASTER IS UNSURE HOW LONG THE CREATURE WILL BE AFFECTED.
BRRM
KRANK
I KNOW THE PLAN, NUMBER 7. BUT POSITIONING IS IF I DON'T HIT IT RIGHT, THERE WON'T BE ENOUGH OF HIM FOR A SECOND TRY.

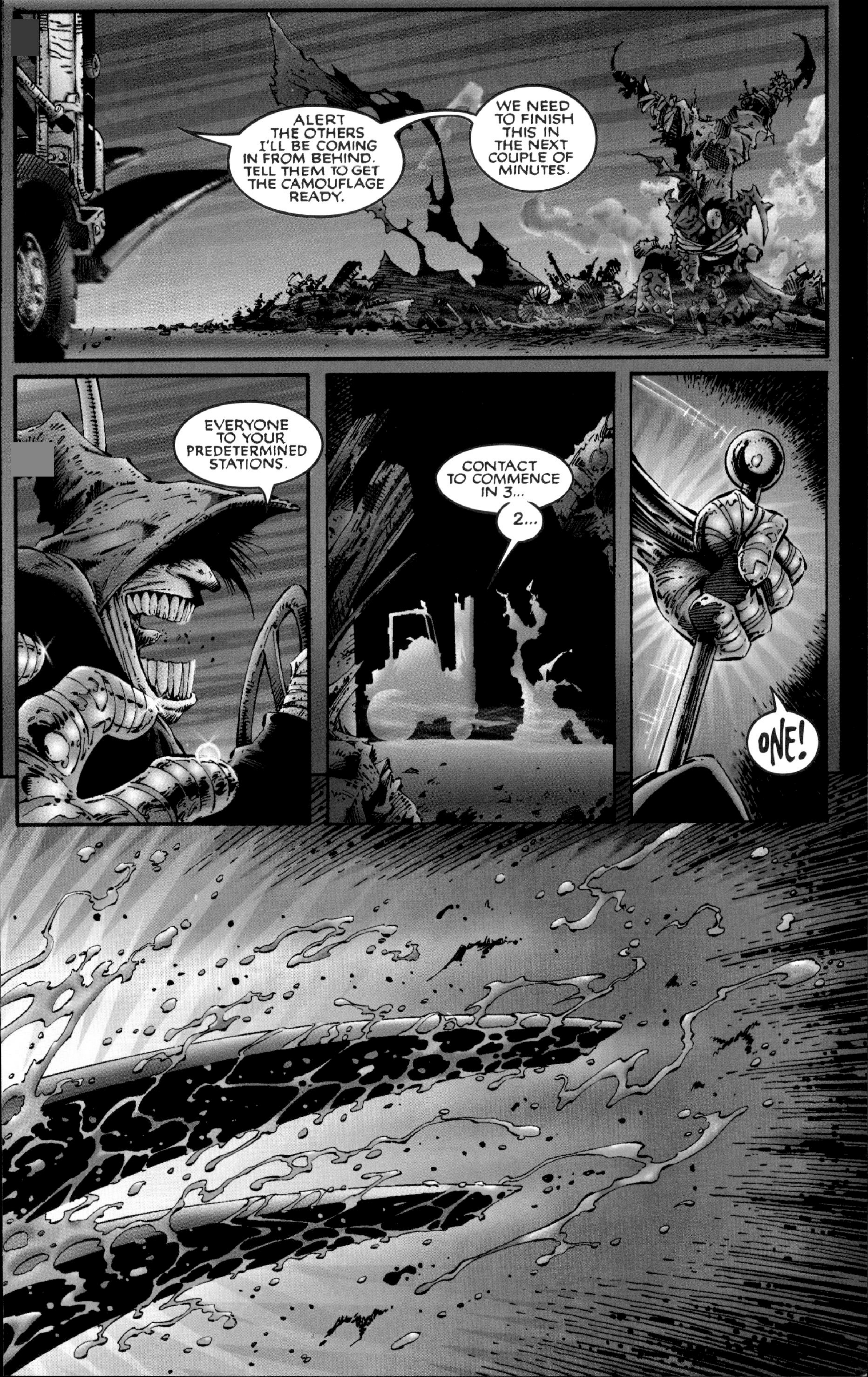
ALERT THE OTHERS I'LL BE COMING IN FROM BEHIND. TELL THEM TO GET THE CAMOUFLAGE READY.
WE NEED TO FINISH THIS IN THE NEXT COUPLE OF MINUTES.
EVERYONE TO YOUR PREDETERMINED STATIONS.
CONTACT TO COMMENCE IN 3...
2...
ONE!

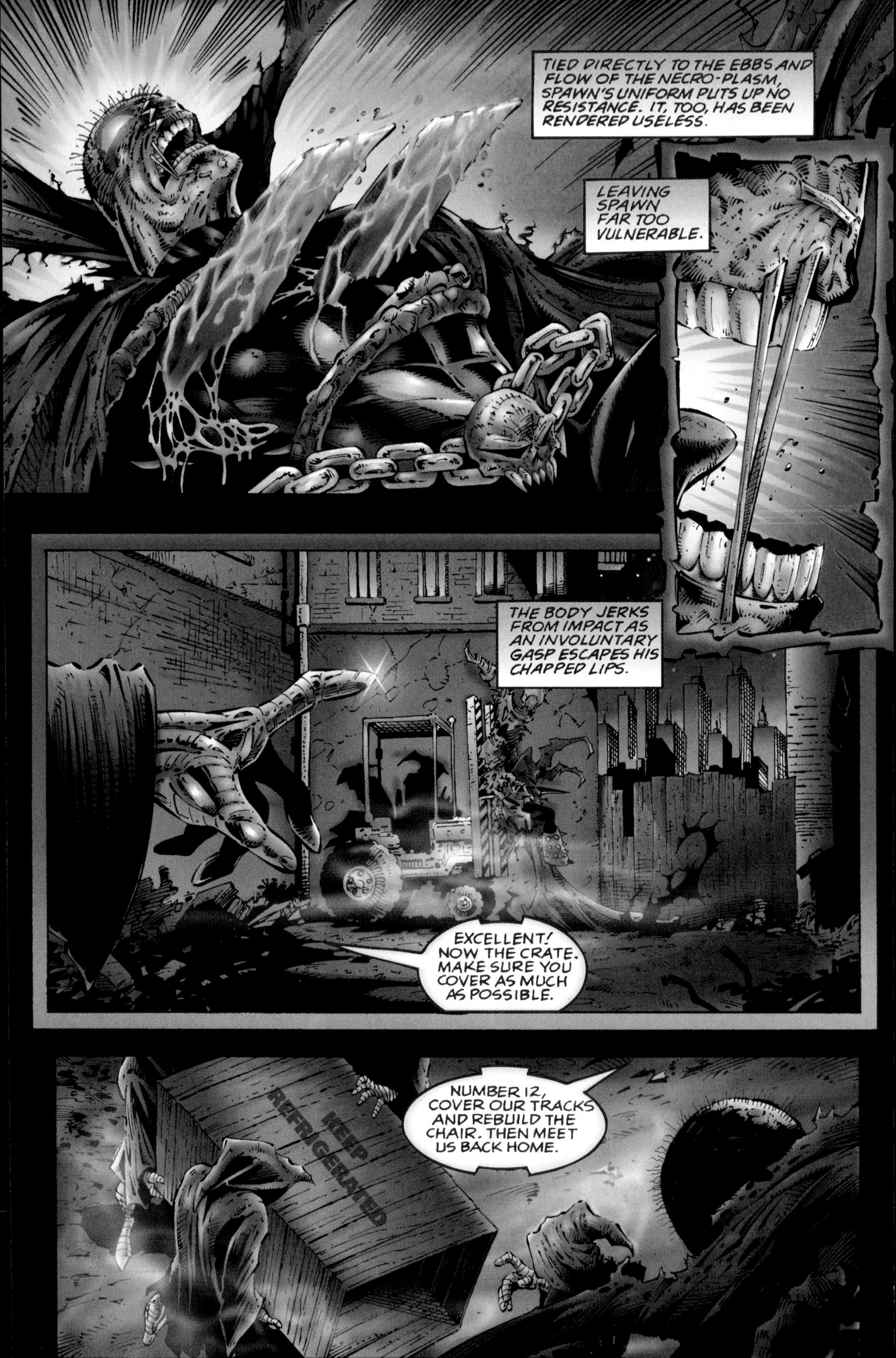
TIED DIRECTLY TO THE EBBS AND FLOW OF THE NECRO-PLASM, SPAWN'S UNIFORM PUTS UP NO RESISTANCE. IT, TOO, HAS BEEN RENDERED USELESS.
LEAVING SPAWN FAR TOO VULNERABLE.
THE BODY JERKS FROM IMPACT AS AN INVOLUNTARY GASP ESCAPES HIS CHAPPED LIPS.
EXCELLENT! NOW THE CRATE. MAKE SURE YOU COVER AS MUCH AS POSSIBLE.
KEEP REFRIGERATED
NUMBER 12, COVER OUR TRACKS AND REBUILD THE CHAIR. THEN MEET US BACK HOME.

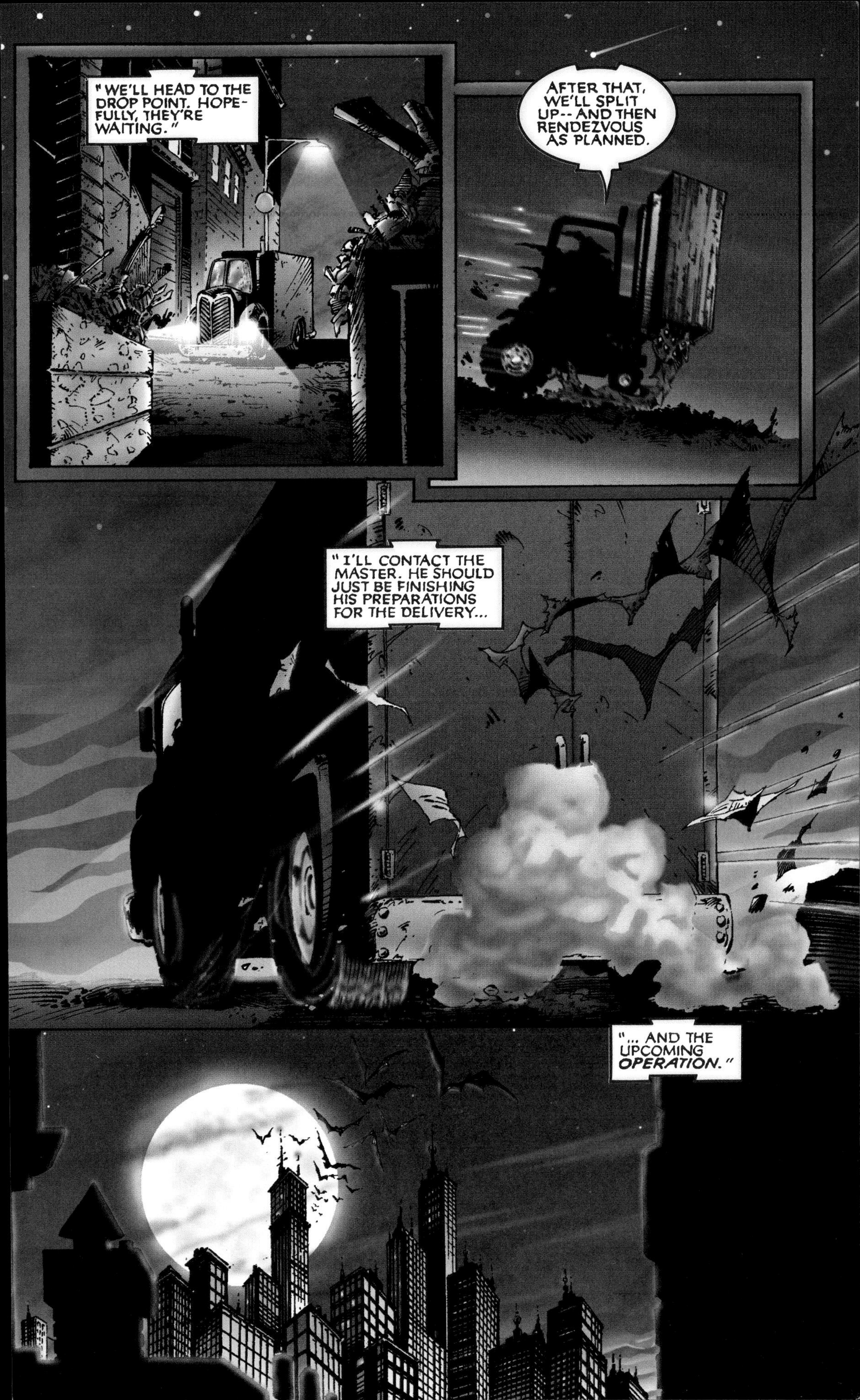
"WE'LL HEAD TO THE DROP POINT. HOPE-FULLY, THEY'RE WAITING."
AFTER THAT, WE'LL SPLIT UP-- AND THEN RENDEZVOUS AS PLANNED.
"I'LL CONTACT THE MASTER. HE SHOULD JUST BE FINISHING HIS PREPARATIONS FOR THE DELIVERY...
"... AND THE UPCOMING *OPERATION.*"

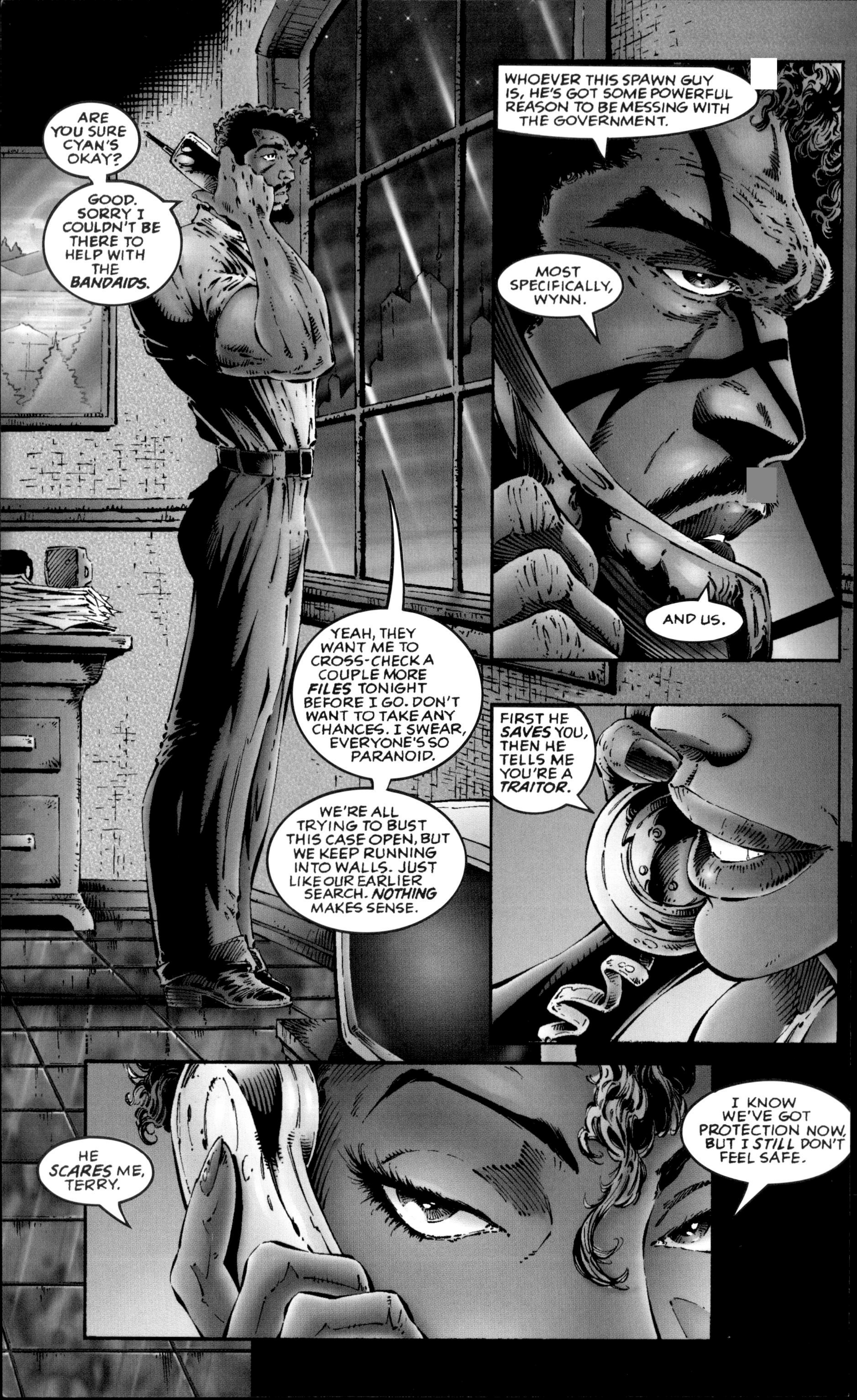
ARE YOU SURE CYAN'S OKAY?
GOOD. SORRY I COULDN'T BE THERE TO HELP WITH THE BANDAIDS.
YEAH, THEY WANT ME TO CROSS-CHECK A COUPLE MORE FILES TONIGHT BEFORE I GO. DON'T WANT TO TAKE ANY CHANCES. I SWEAR, EVERYONE'S SO PARANOID.
WE'RE ALL TRYING TO BUST THIS CASE OPEN, BUT WE KEEP RUNNING INTO WALLS. JUST LIKE OUR EARLIER SEARCH. NOTHING MAKES SENSE.
WHOEVER THIS SPAWN GUY IS, HE'S GOT SOME POWERFUL REASON TO BE MESSING WITH THE GOVERNMENT.
MOST SPECIFICALLY, WYNN.
AND US.
FIRST HE SAVES YOU, THEN HE TELLS ME YOU'RE A TRAITOR.
HE SCARES ME, TERRY.
I KNOW WE'VE GOT PROTECTION NOW, BUT I STILL DON'T FEEL SAFE.

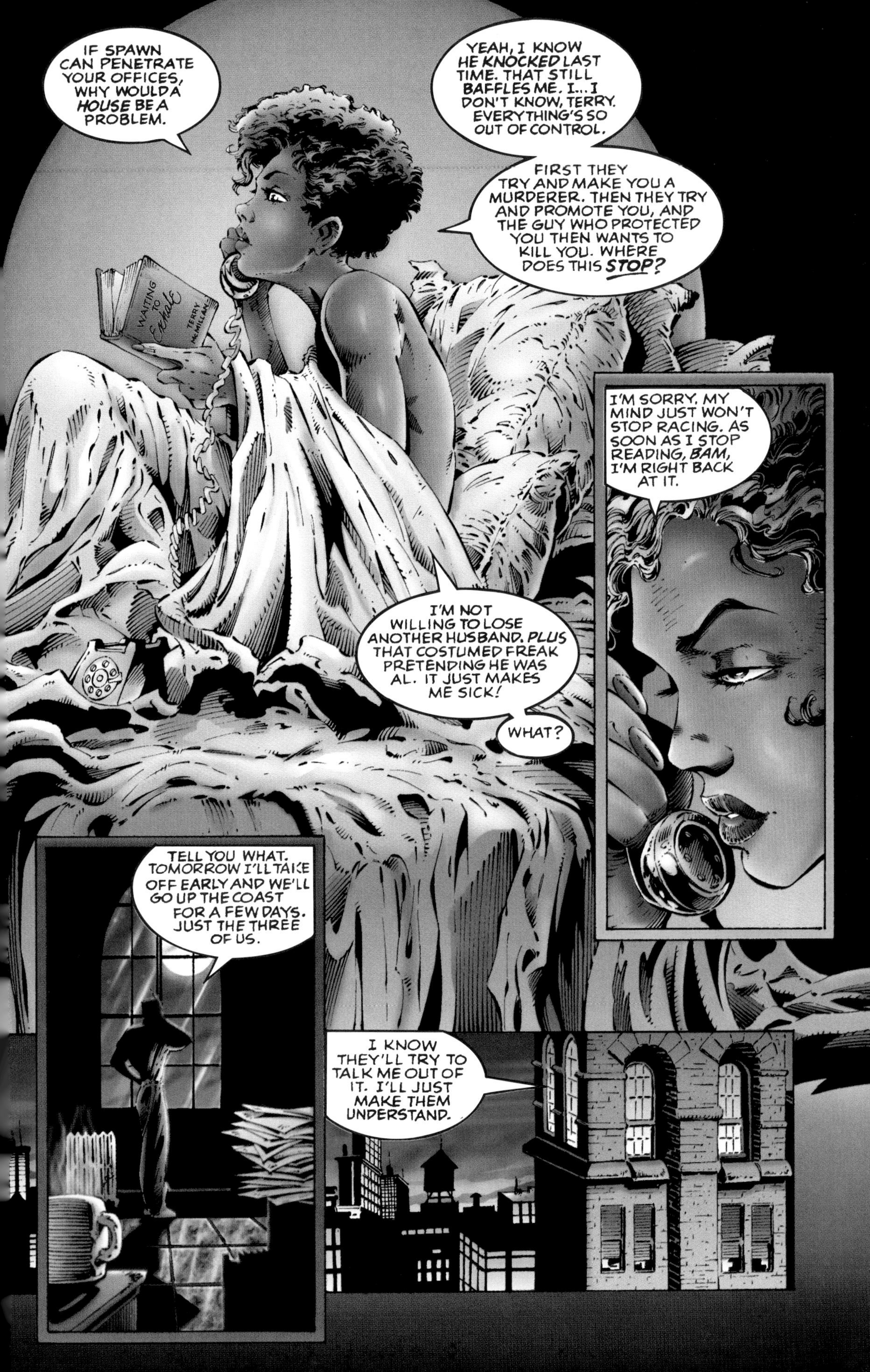
IF SPAWN CAN PENETRATE YOUR OFFICES, WHY WOULD A *HOUSE* BE A PROBLEM.
YEAH, I KNOW HE *KNOCKED* LAST TIME. THAT STILL BAFFLES ME. I... I DON'T KNOW, TERRY. EVERYTHING'S SO OUT OF CONTROL.
FIRST THEY TRY AND MAKE YOU A MURDERER. THEN THEY TRY AND PROMOTE YOU, AND THE GUY WHO PROTECTED YOU THEN WANTS TO KILL YOU. WHERE DOES THIS *STOP?*
WAITING TO Exhale
TERRY McMILLAN
I'M NOT WILLING TO LOSE ANOTHER HUSBAND. *PLUS* THAT COSTUMED FREAK PRETENDING HE WAS AL. IT JUST MAKES ME SICK!
WHAT?
I'M SORRY. MY MIND JUST WON'T STOP RACING. AS SOON AS I STOP READING, *BAM,* I'M RIGHT BACK AT IT.
TELL YOU WHAT. TOMORROW I'LL TAKE OFF EARLY AND WE'LL GO UP THE COAST FOR A FEW DAYS. JUST THE THREE OF US.
I KNOW THEY'LL TRY TO TALK ME OUT OF IT. I'LL JUST MAKE THEM UNDERSTAND.

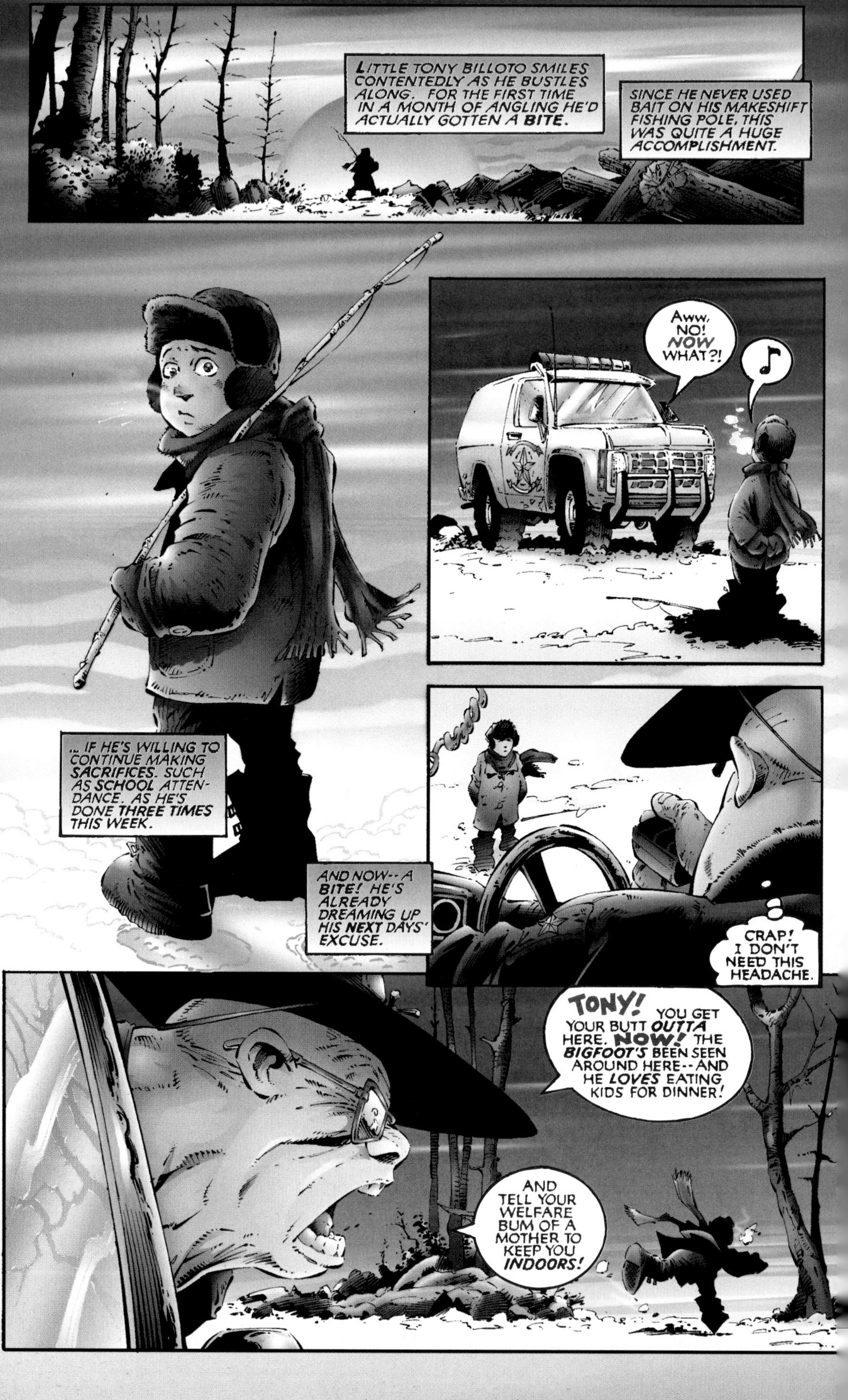
LITTLE TONY BILLOTO SMILES CONTENTEDLY AS HE BUSTLES ALONG. FOR THE FIRST TIME IN A MONTH OF ANGLING HE'D ACTUALLY GOTTEN A BITE.
SINCE HE NEVER USED BAIT ON HIS MAKESHIFT FISHING POLE, THIS WAS QUITE A HUGE ACCOMPLISHMENT.
... IF HE'S WILLING TO CONTINUE MAKING SACRIFICES. SUCH AS SCHOOL ATTENDANCE. AS HE'S DONE THREE TIMES THIS WEEK.
AND NOW-- A BITE! HE'S ALREADY DREAMING UP HIS NEXT DAYS' EXCUSE.
AWW, NO! NOW WHAT?!
♪
CRAP! I DON'T NEED THIS HEADACHE.
TONY! YOU GET YOUR BUTT OUTTA HERE. NOW! THE BIGFOOT'S BEEN SEEN AROUND HERE--AND HE LOVES EATING KIDS FOR DINNER!
AND TELL YOUR WELFARE BUM OF A MOTHER TO KEEP YOU INDOORS!

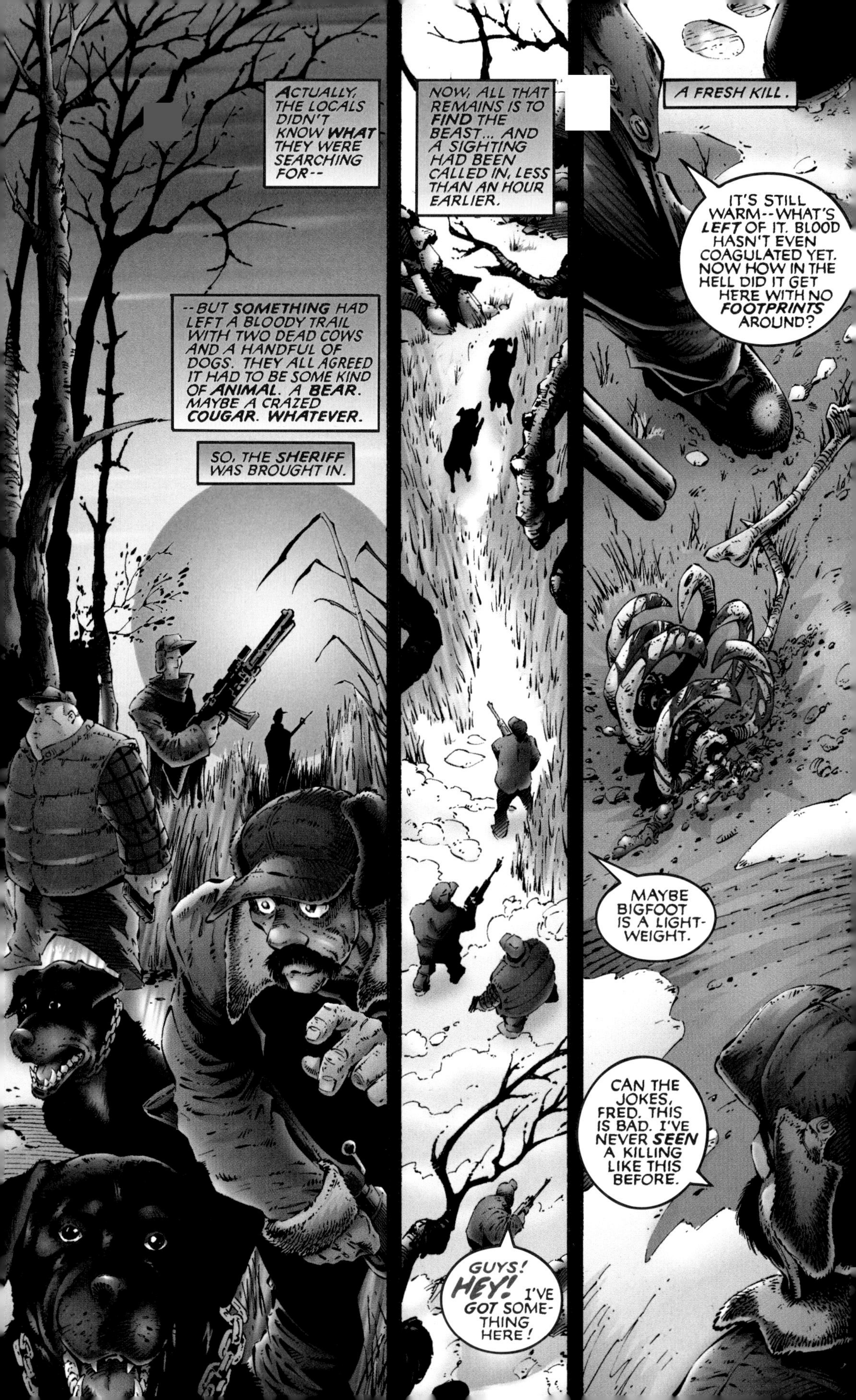
ACTUALLY, THE LOCALS DIDN'T KNOW WHAT THEY WERE SEARCHING FOR--
--BUT SOMETHING HAD LEFT A BLOODY TRAIL WITH TWO DEAD COWS AND A HANDFUL OF DOGS. THEY ALL AGREED IT HAD TO BE SOME KIND OF ANIMAL. A BEAR. MAYBE A CRAZED COUGAR. WHATEVER.
SO, THE SHERIFF WAS BROUGHT IN.
NOW, ALL THAT REMAINS IS TO FIND THE BEAST... AND A SIGHTING HAD BEEN CALLED IN, LESS THAN AN HOUR EARLIER.
GUYS! HEY! I'VE GOT SOMETHING HERE!
A FRESH KILL.
IT'S STILL WARM--WHAT'S LEFT OF IT. BLOOD HASN'T EVEN COAGULATED YET. NOW HOW IN THE HELL DID IT GET HERE WITH NO FOOTPRINTS AROUND?
MAYBE BIGFOOT IS A LIGHTWEIGHT.
CAN THE JOKES, FRED. THIS IS BAD. I'VE NEVER SEEN A KILLING LIKE THIS BEFORE.

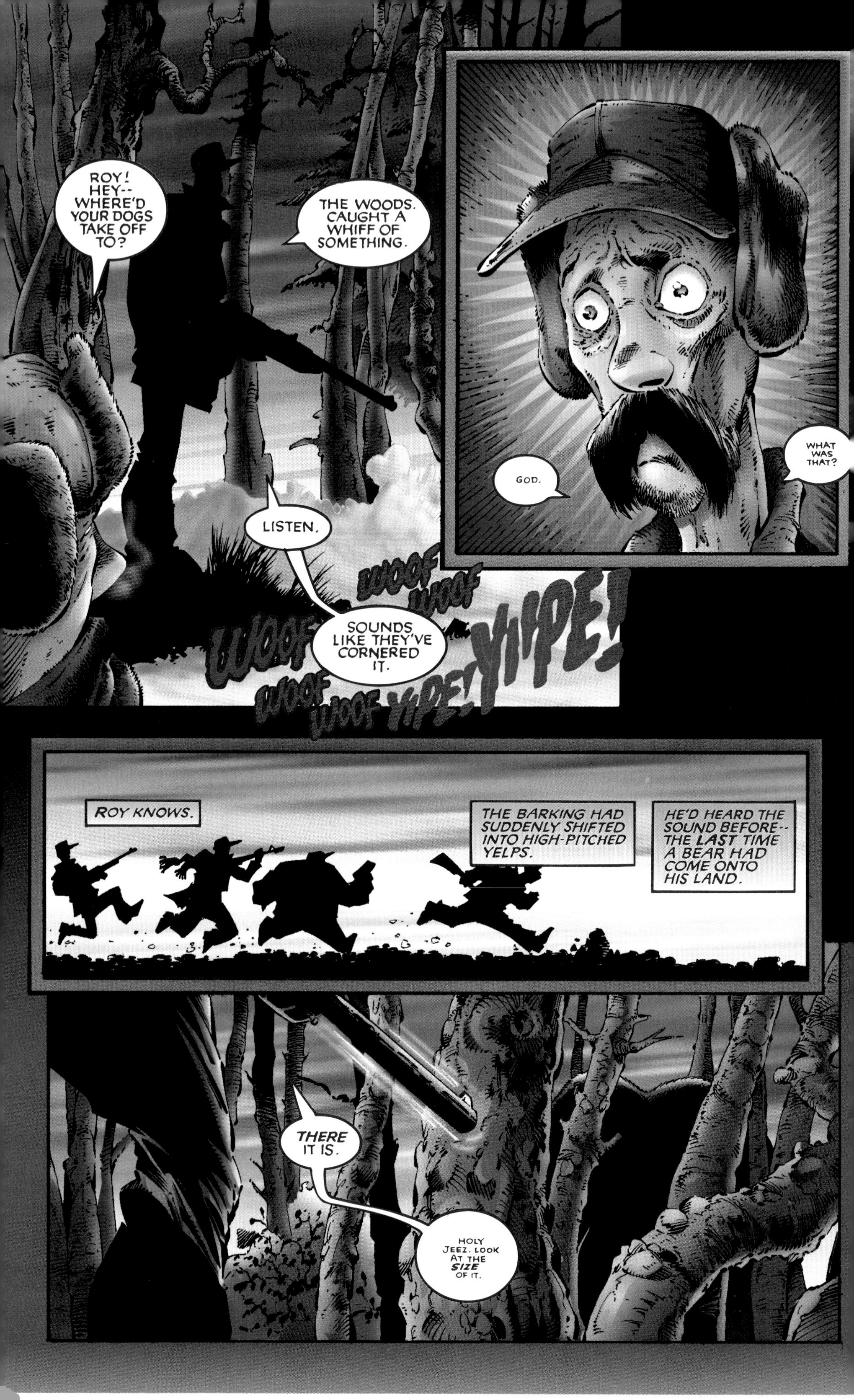
ROY! HEY-- WHERE'D YOUR DOGS TAKE OFF TO?
THE WOODS. CAUGHT A WHIFF OF SOMETHING.
LISTEN.
WOOF WOOF WOOF
SOUNDS LIKE THEY'VE CORNERED IT.
WOOF WOOF YIPE! YIIPE!
GOD.
WHAT WAS THAT?
ROY KNOWS.
THE BARKING HAD SUDDENLY SHIFTED INTO HIGH-PITCHED YELPS.
HE'D HEARD THE SOUND BEFORE-- THE LAST TIME A BEAR HAD COME ONTO HIS LAND.
THERE IT IS.
HOLY JEEZ. LOOK AT THE SIZE OF IT.

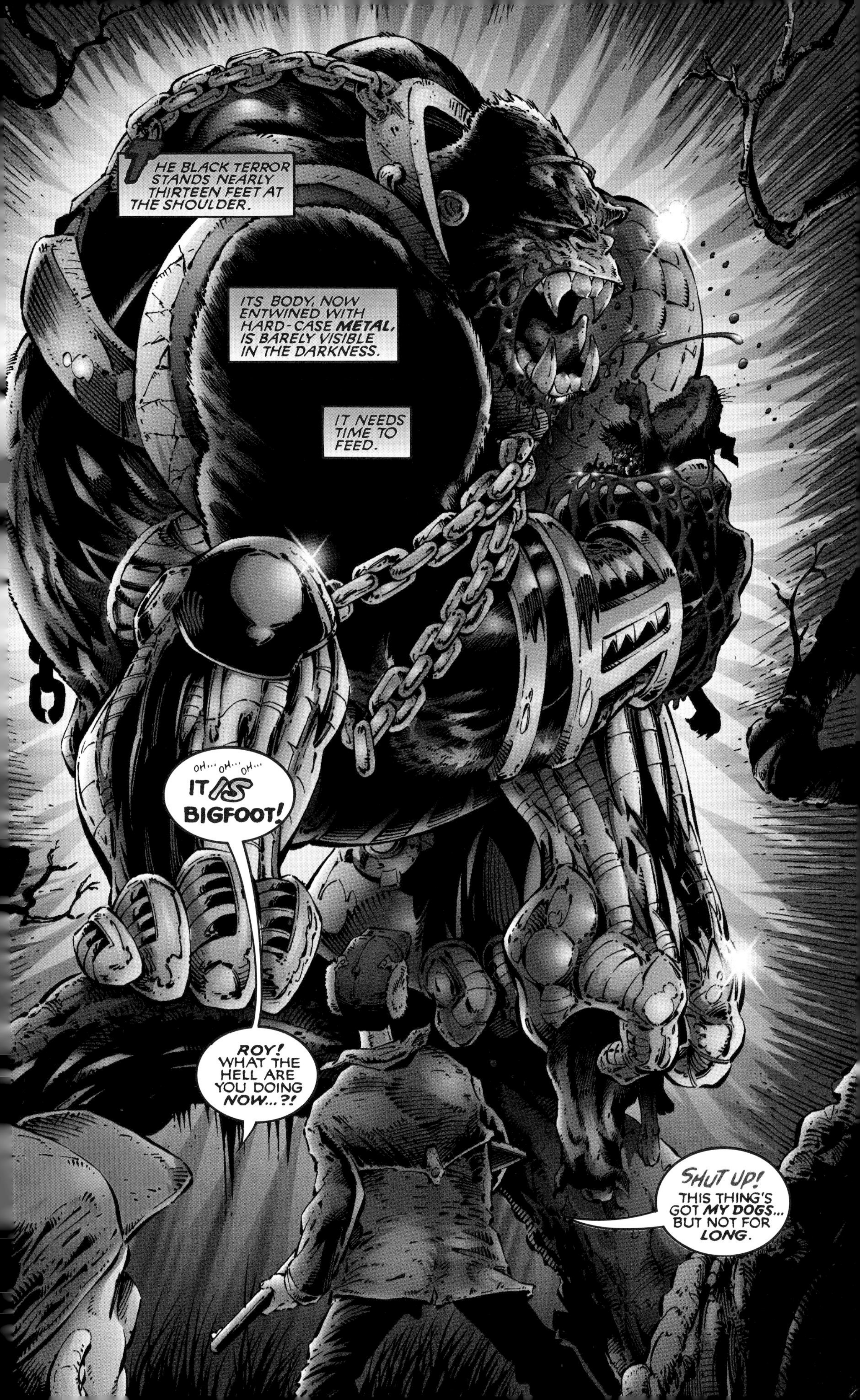
THE BLACK TERROR STANDS NEARLY THIRTEEN FEET AT THE SHOULDER.
ITS BODY, NOW ENTWINED WITH HARD-CASE METAL, IS BARELY VISIBLE IN THE DARKNESS.
IT NEEDS TIME TO FEED.
OH... OH... OH... IT IS BIGFOOT!
ROY! WHAT THE HELL ARE YOU DOING NOW...?!
SHUT UP! THIS THING'S GOT MY DOGS... BUT NOT FOR LONG.

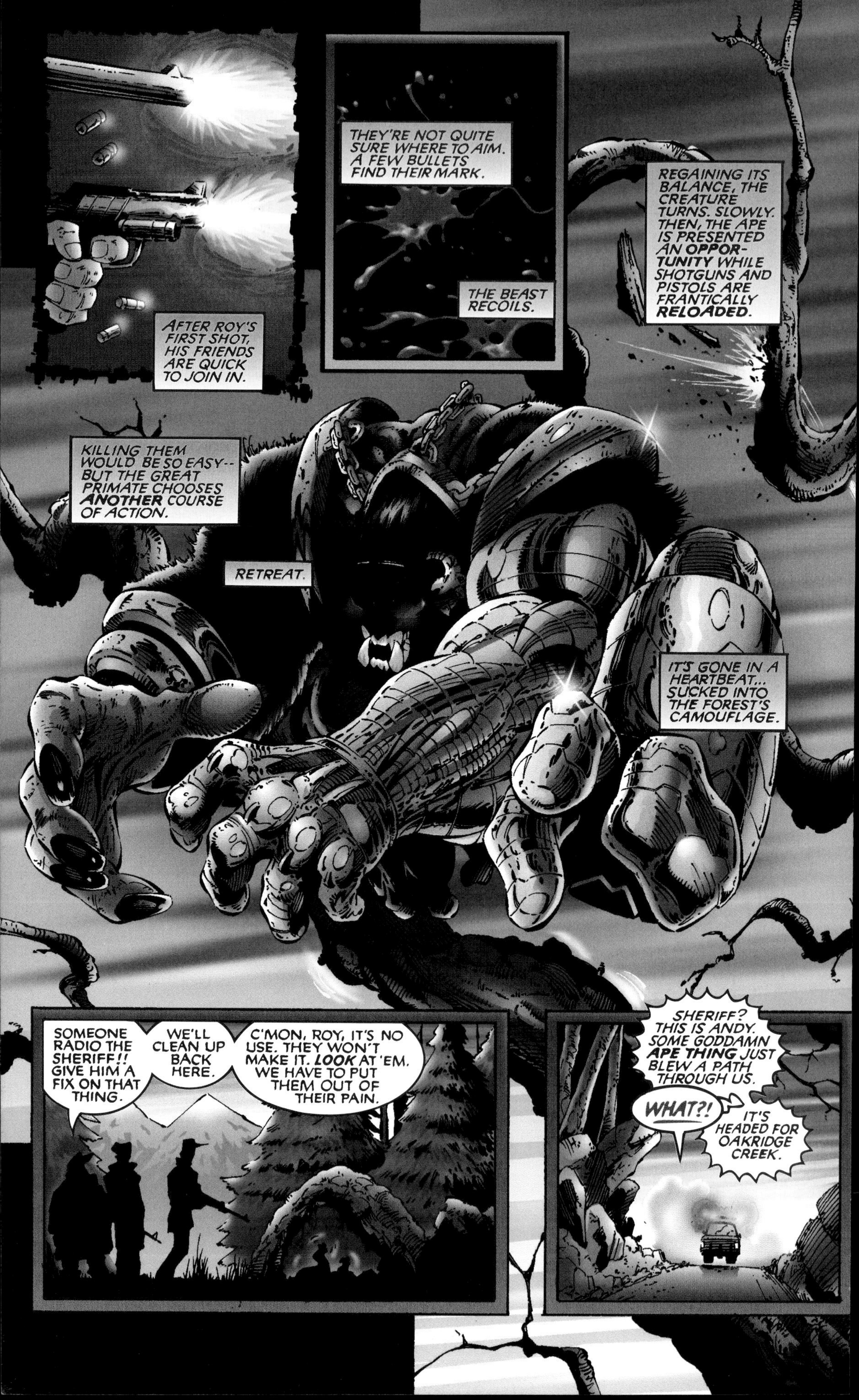
AFTER ROY'S FIRST SHOT, HIS FRIENDS ARE QUICK TO JOIN IN.
THEY'RE NOT QUITE SURE WHERE TO AIM. A FEW BULLETS FIND THEIR MARK.
THE BEAST RECOILS.
REGAINING ITS BALANCE, THE CREATURE TURNS. SLOWLY. THEN, THE APE IS PRESENTED AN **OPPORTUNITY** WHILE SHOTGUNS AND PISTOLS ARE FRANTICALLY **RELOADED**.
KILLING THEM WOULD BE SO EASY-- BUT THE GREAT PRIMATE CHOOSES **ANOTHER** COURSE OF ACTION.
RETREAT.
IT'S GONE IN A HEARTBEAT... SUCKED INTO THE FOREST'S CAMOUFLAGE.
SOMEONE RADIO THE SHERIFF!! GIVE HIM A FIX ON THAT THING.
WE'LL CLEAN UP BACK HERE.
C'MON, ROY, IT'S NO USE. THEY WON'T MAKE IT. ***LOOK*** AT 'EM. WE HAVE TO PUT THEM OUT OF THEIR PAIN.
SHERIFF? THIS IS ANDY. SOME GODDAMN **APE THING** JUST BLEW A PATH THROUGH US.
WHAT?!
IT'S HEADED FOR OAKRIDGE CREEK.

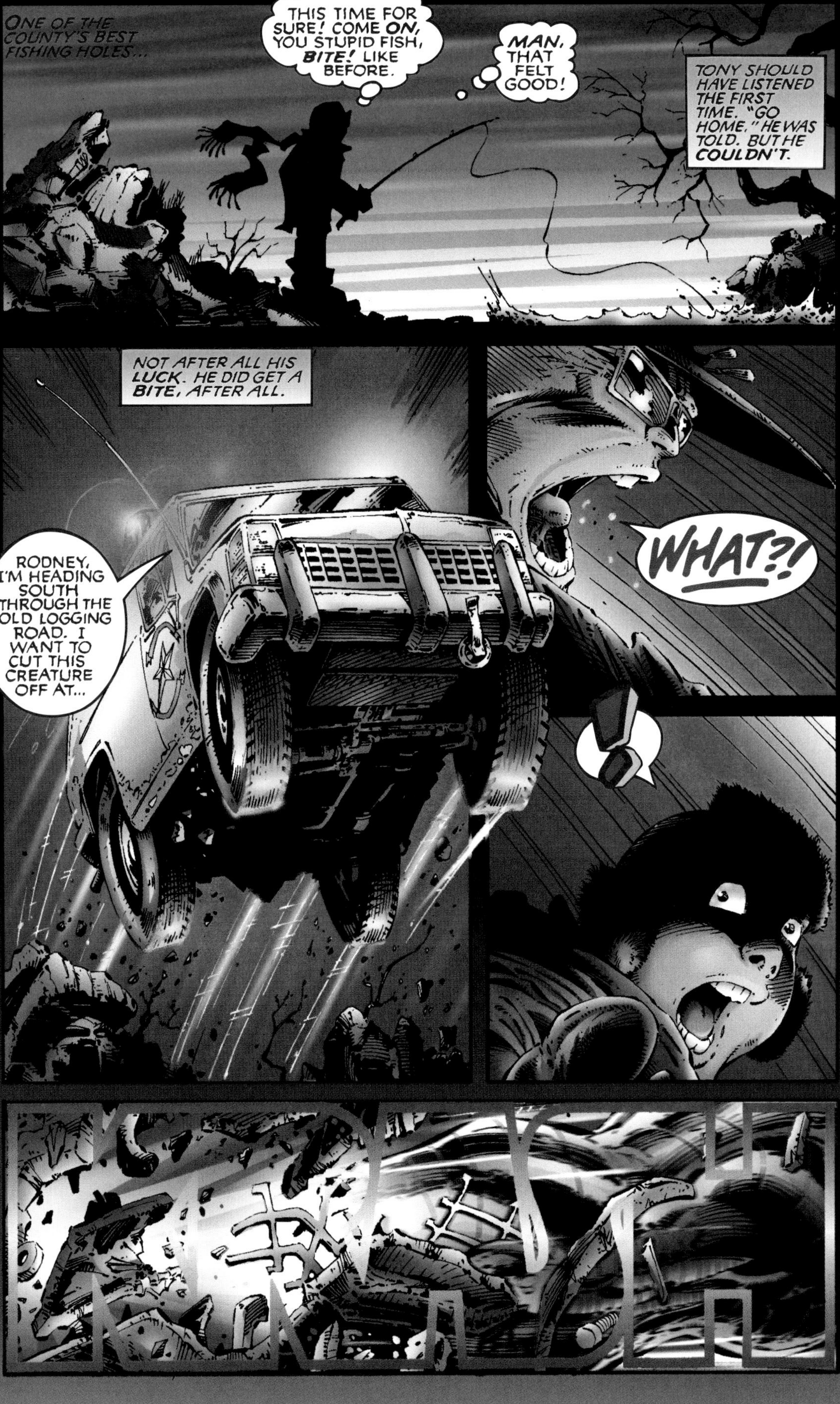
ONE OF THE COUNTY'S BEST FISHING HOLES...
THIS TIME FOR SURE! COME ON, YOU STUPID FISH, BITE! LIKE BEFORE.
MAN, THAT FELT GOOD!
TONY SHOULD HAVE LISTENED THE FIRST TIME. "GO HOME," HE WAS TOLD. BUT HE COULDN'T.
NOT AFTER ALL HIS LUCK. HE DID GET A BITE, AFTER ALL.
RODNEY, I'M HEADING SOUTH THROUGH THE OLD LOGGING ROAD. I WANT TO CUT THIS CREATURE OFF AT...
WHAT?!

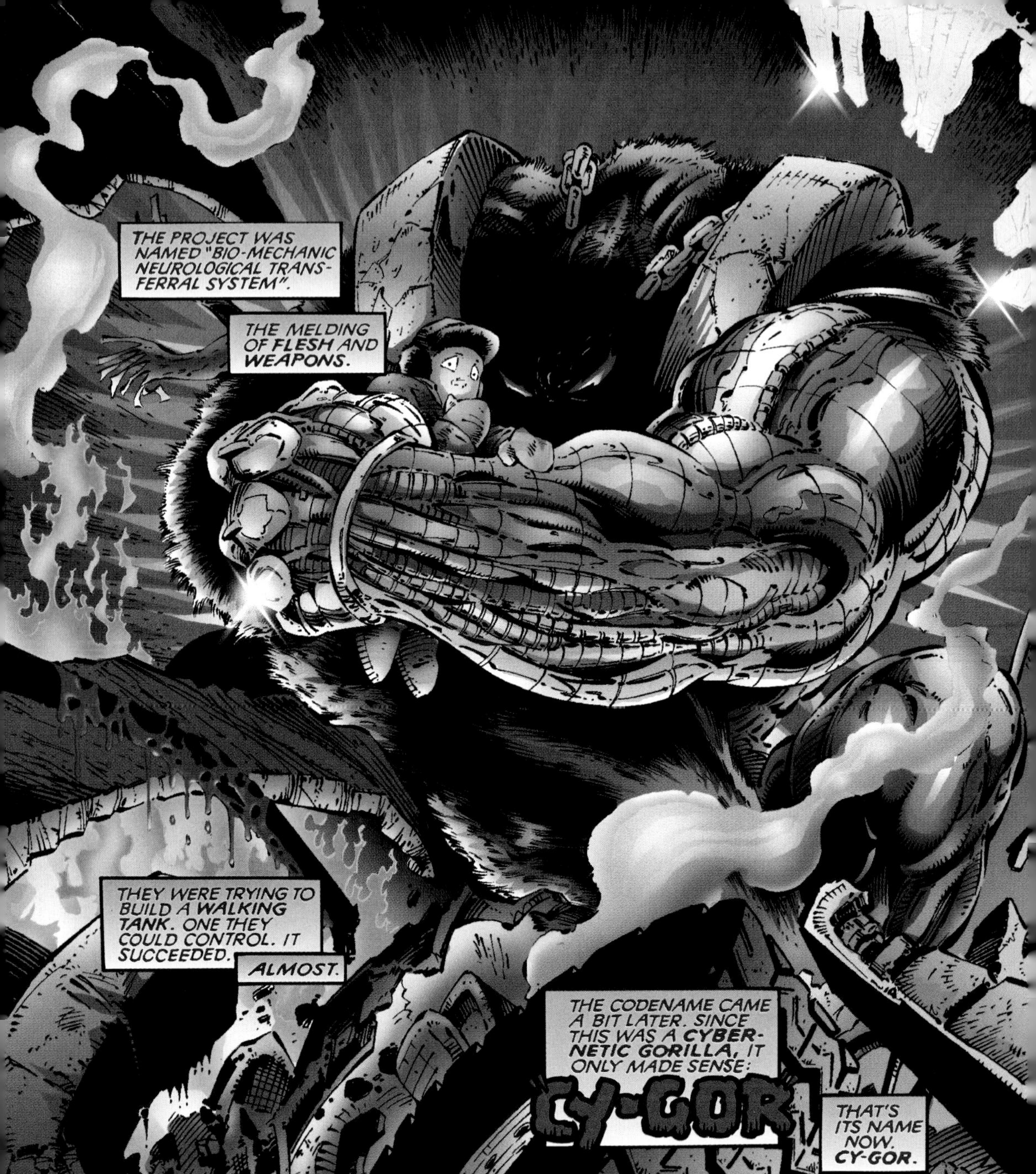
THE PROJECT WAS NAMED "BIO-MECHANIC NEUROLOGICAL TRANS-FERRAL SYSTEM".
THE MELDING OF FLESH AND WEAPONS.
THEY WERE TRYING TO BUILD A WALKING TANK. ONE THEY COULD CONTROL. IT SUCCEEDED.
ALMOST.
THE CODENAME CAME A BIT LATER. SINCE THIS WAS A CYBER-NETIC GORILLA, IT ONLY MADE SENSE:
CY-GOR
THAT'S ITS NAME NOW. CY-GOR.
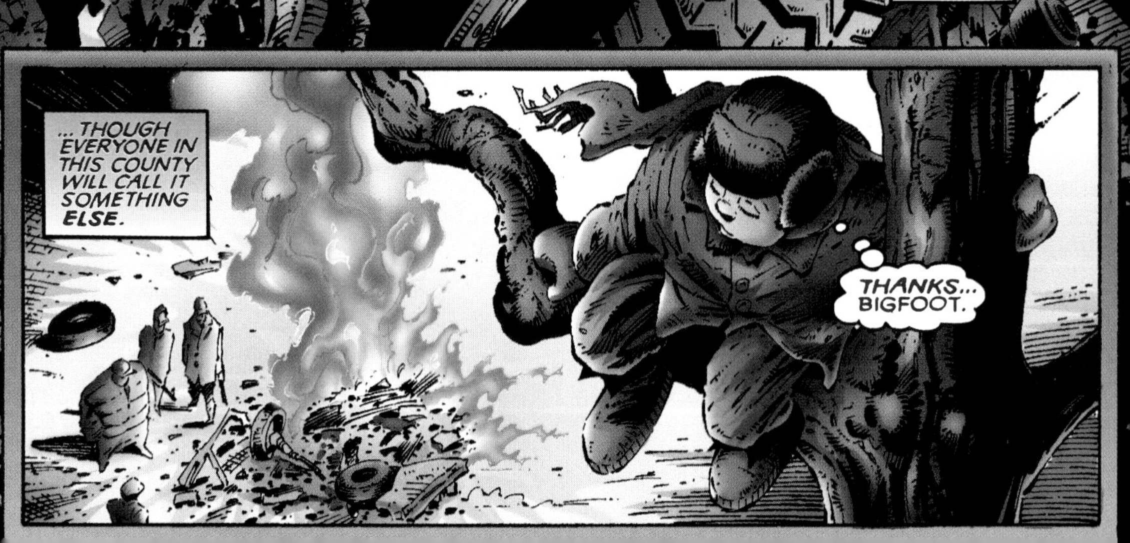
...THOUGH EVERYONE IN THIS COUNTY WILL CALL IT SOMETHING ELSE.
THANKS... BIGFOOT.

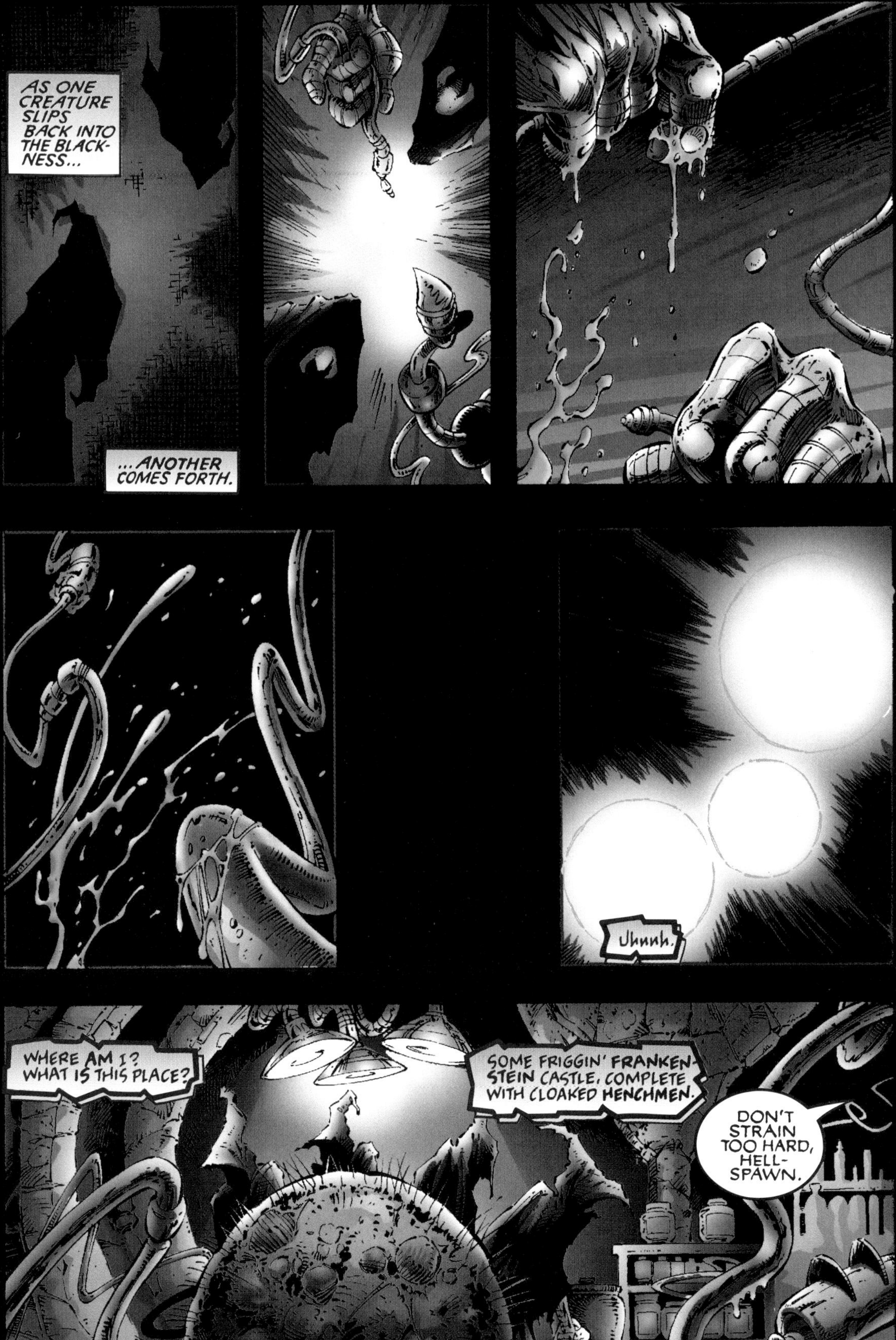
AS ONE CREATURE SLIPS BACK INTO THE BLACKNESS...
...ANOTHER COMES FORTH.
Uhnnh.
WHERE AM I? WHAT IS THIS PLACE?
SOME FRIGGIN' FRANKENSTEIN CASTLE, COMPLETE WITH CLOAKED HENCHMEN.
DON'T STRAIN TOO HARD, HELLSPAWN.

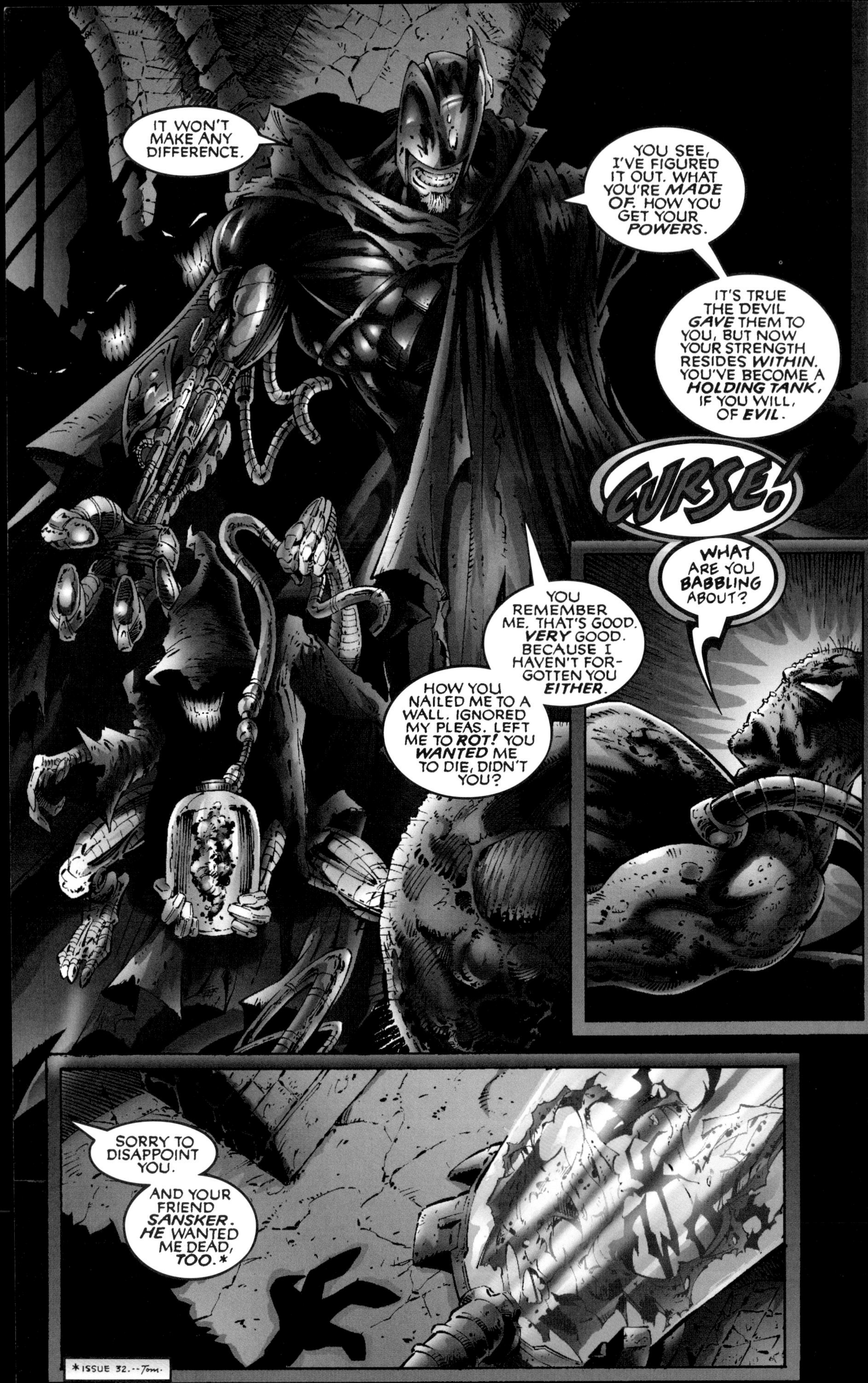
IT WON'T MAKE ANY DIFFERENCE.
YOU SEE, I'VE FIGURED IT OUT. WHAT YOU'RE *MADE OF*. HOW YOU GET YOUR *POWERS*.
IT'S TRUE THE DEVIL *GAVE* THEM TO YOU, BUT NOW YOUR STRENGTH RESIDES *WITHIN*. YOU'VE BECOME A *HOLDING TANK*, IF YOU WILL, OF *EVIL*.
CURSE!
WHAT ARE YOU BABBLING ABOUT?
YOU REMEMBER ME. THAT'S GOOD. *VERY* GOOD. BECAUSE I HAVEN'T FOR-GOTTEN YOU *EITHER*.
HOW YOU NAILED ME TO A WALL. IGNORED MY PLEAS. LEFT ME TO *ROT!* YOU *WANTED* ME TO DIE, DIDN'T YOU?
SORRY TO DISAPPOINT YOU.
AND YOUR FRIEND *SANSKER*. *HE* WANTED ME DEAD, *TOO*.*
*ISSUE 32.--Tom.

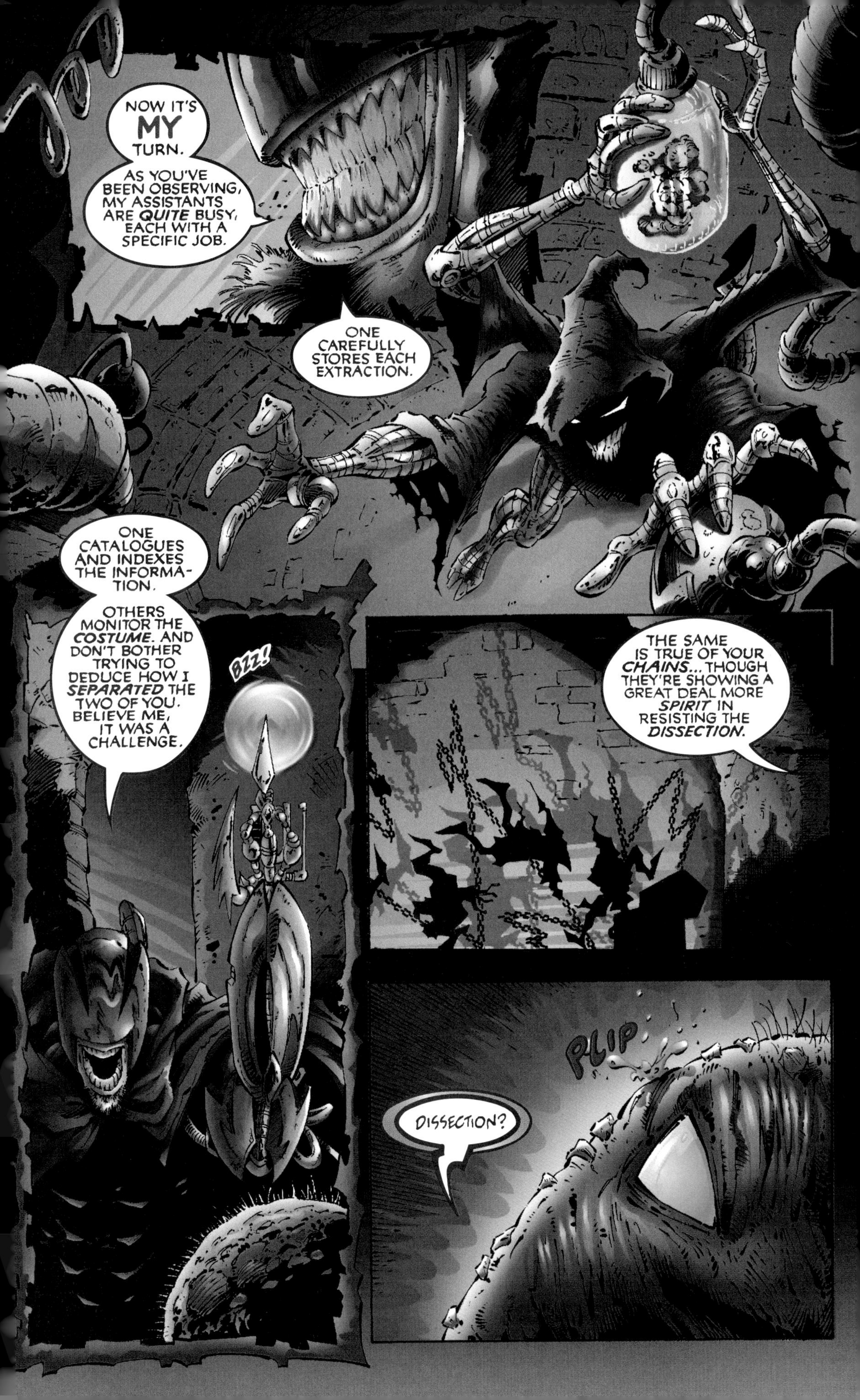
NOW IT'S MY TURN.
AS YOU'VE BEEN OBSERVING, MY ASSISTANTS ARE QUITE BUSY, EACH WITH A SPECIFIC JOB.
ONE CAREFULLY STORES EACH EXTRACTION.
ONE CATALOGUES AND INDEXES THE INFORMATION.
OTHERS MONITOR THE COSTUME. AND DON'T BOTHER TRYING TO DEDUCE HOW I SEPARATED THE TWO OF YOU. BELIEVE ME, IT WAS A CHALLENGE.
BZZ!
THE SAME IS TRUE OF YOUR CHAINS... THOUGH THEY'RE SHOWING A GREAT DEAL MORE SPIRIT IN RESISTING THE DISSECTION.
PLIP
DISSECTION?

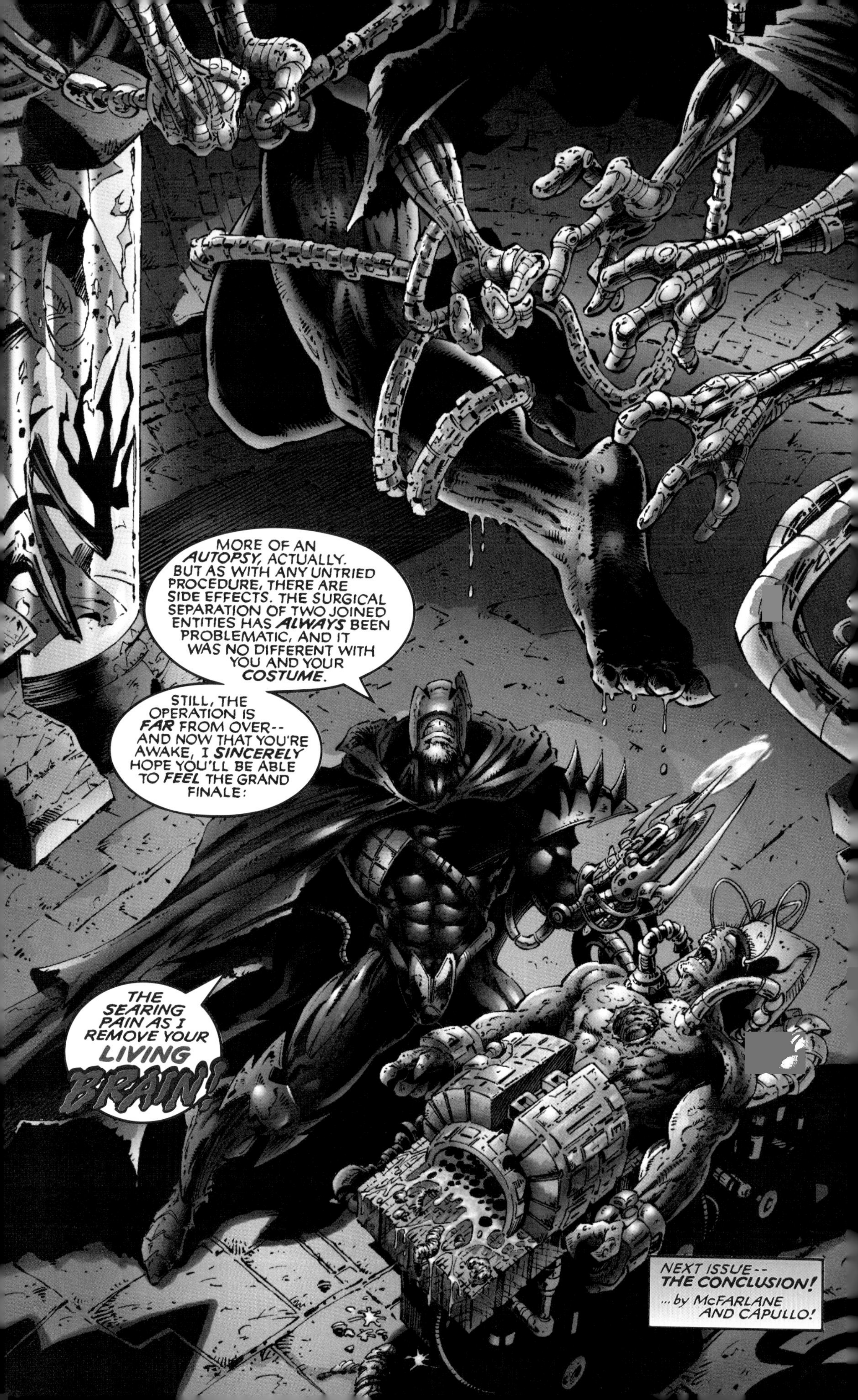
MORE OF AN AUTOPSY, ACTUALLY. BUT AS WITH ANY UNTRIED PROCEDURE, THERE ARE SIDE EFFECTS. THE SURGICAL SEPARATION OF TWO JOINED ENTITIES HAS ALWAYS BEEN PROBLEMATIC, AND IT WAS NO DIFFERENT WITH YOU AND YOUR COSTUME.
STILL, THE OPERATION IS FAR FROM OVER-- AND NOW THAT YOU'RE AWAKE, I SINCERELY HOPE YOU'LL BE ABLE TO FEEL THE GRAND FINALE:
THE SEARING PAIN AS I REMOVE YOUR LIVING BRAIN!
NEXT ISSUE -- THE CONCLUSION!
...by McFARLANE AND CAPULLO!

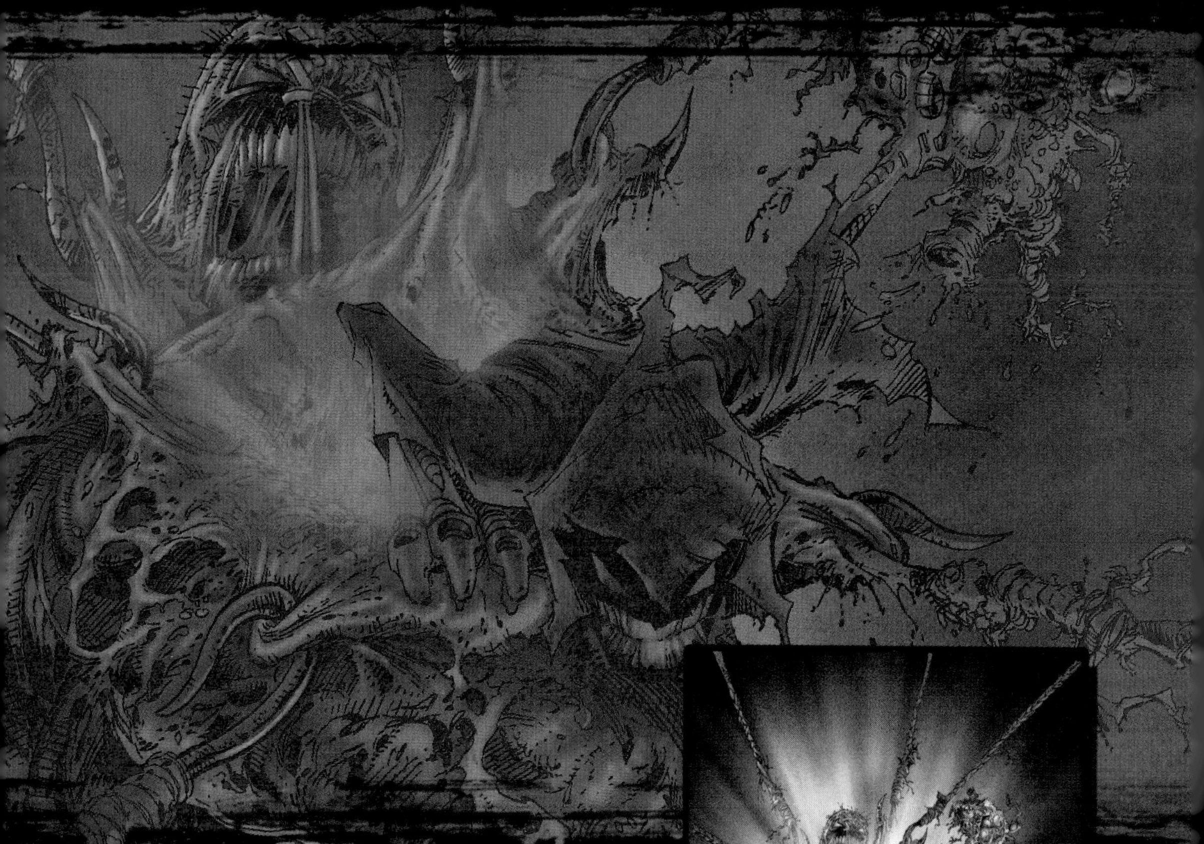

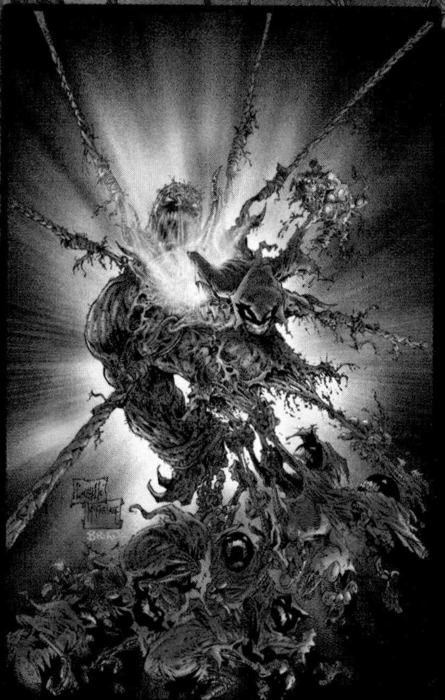

ISSUE FORTY-ONE

ARMAGEDDON.

*THE PLACE WHERE IT ALL ENDS: ULTIMATE **GOOD** VERSUS ULTIMATE **EVIL** IN THE LAST BEST EXAMPLE OF HOLY WARFARE.*

*THE WINNER, IT HAS BEEN PROPHESIED, WILL REIGN ETERNALLY. SUCH A PRIZE IS COVETED BY **BOTH** SIDES, THE SUPERNATURALLY OPPOSING CAMPS WHOSE PHILOSOPHIES INSPIRE US HUMANS. WHILE SOME OF US SEEK HARMONY WITH ALL PEOPLE AND THINGS, OTHERS WOULD LIKE NOTHING BETTER THAN TO THWART AND HUMILIATE THEM. AND DAY BY DAY, HEAVEN AND HELL **NUDGE** US AS THEY'VE DONE FOR UNTOLD CENTURIES... **GROOMING** US INTO ARMIES WHICH WILL CHARGE HEADLONG INTO BATTLE UNTIL THE ENEMY HAS, AT LAST, BEEN **SILENCED.***

*NOW, TODAY, SOME SAY THAT THE **END TIMES** HAVE BEGUN. BEHAVIOR AMONG MANY PEOPLE HAS BECOME MORE **EXTREME**, AND THE RECRUITMENT OF SOULS HAS GAINED A NEW **INTENSITY**. AT THE MOMENT OF DEATH, EACH SOUL IS WELCOMED TO BOTH HEAVEN AND HELL. FROM THIS POOL OF MILLIONS THE TWO SIDES SEEK NEW CANDIDATES. MOST ARE WORTHY BUT **UNREMARKABLE...** ACCEPTED, WELCOMED, ABSORBED INTO THE ASSEMBLED WHOLE. AND OCCASIONALLY, A **JEWEL** WORKS ITS WAY TO THE FORE.*

*THEY ARE GIVEN **POWER**. A NEW **LIFE**. ANOTHER CHANCE TO USE EARTH AS A **LEARNING FACILITY.** IN HEAVEN, THIS SORT ARE CALLED "**ANGELS**". IN HELL, THEY ARE KNOWN AS "**SPAWN**".*

*LIEUTENANT COLONEL **AL SIMMONS** WAS SUCH A FIND. HE HAD THE RIGHT WIRING. THE **GIFT**. HELL COULD ONLY SMILE WHEN HE CAME DOWN THE CHUTE. FOR YOU SEE, A GREAT ARMY DEMANDS GREAT **LEADERS.** AL SIMMONS' LIFE SHOWED HIS POTENTIAL. DUTY FIRST. BLIND OBEDIENCE TO HIS SUPERIORS, WITH A GOOD SENSE OF IMPROVISATION IN THE ACCOMPLISHMENT OF THEIR GOALS. IN ALL, A CREDIT TO HIS OFFICIALLY-SANCTIONED **ASSASSINS' TRAINING.***

*BETTER YET, HE HAD COME **WILLINGLY** INTO THE DOMAIN OF SIN. HIS LOVE FOR HIS WIFE INSPIRED HIS INFERNAL BARGAIN.*

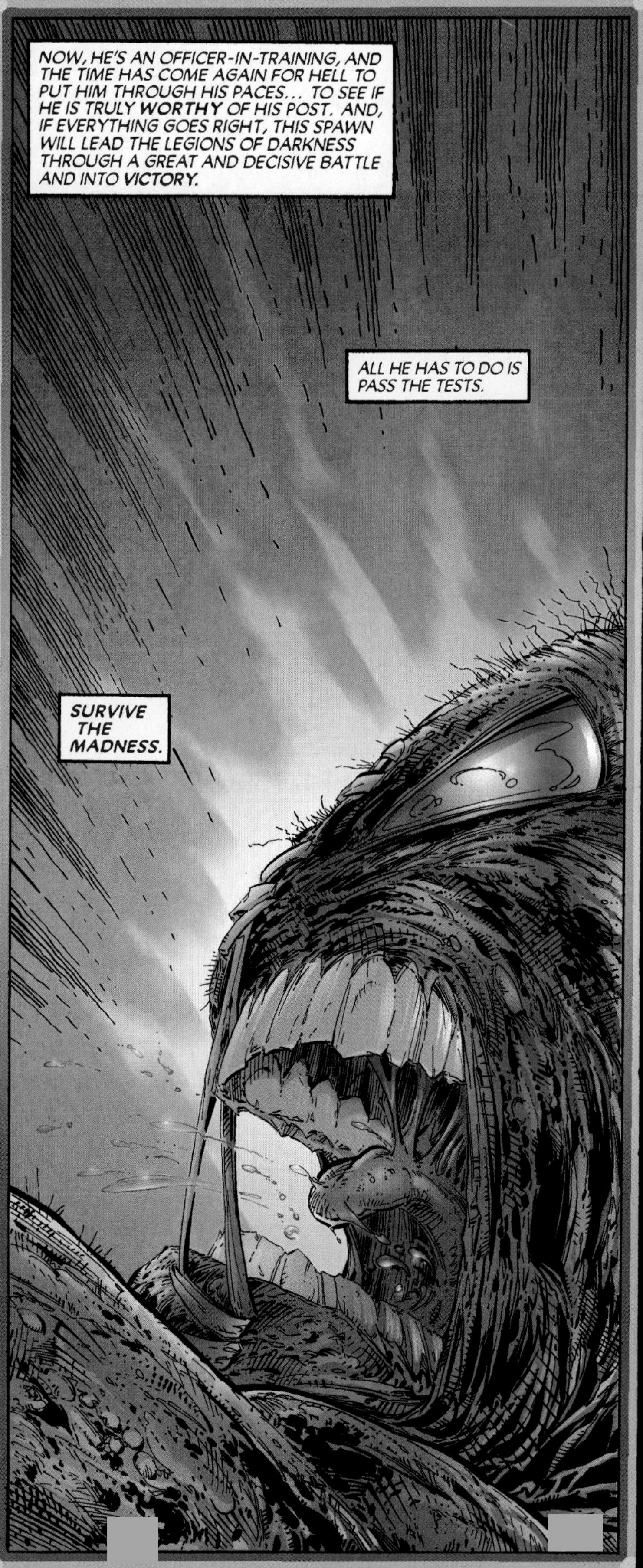
NOW, HE'S AN OFFICER-IN-TRAINING, AND THE TIME HAS COME AGAIN FOR HELL TO PUT HIM THROUGH HIS PACES... TO SEE IF HE IS TRULY WORTHY OF HIS POST. AND, IF EVERYTHING GOES RIGHT, THIS SPAWN WILL LEAD THE LEGIONS OF DARKNESS THROUGH A GREAT AND DECISIVE BATTLE AND INTO VICTORY.
ALL HE HAS TO DO IS PASS THE TESTS.
SURVIVE THE MADNESS.

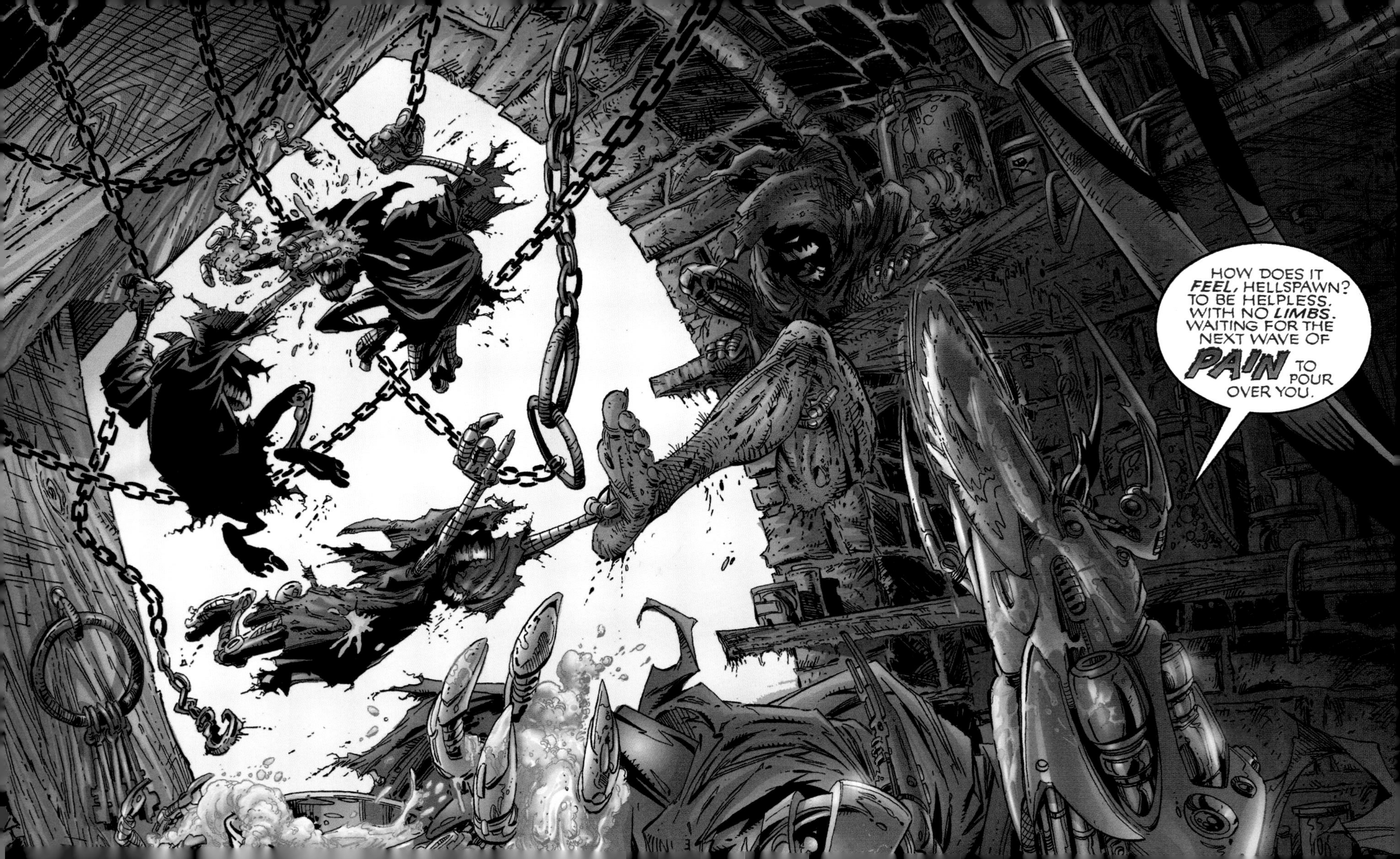
HOW DOES IT FEEL, HELLSPAWN? TO BE HELPLESS. WITH NO LIMBS. WAITING FOR THE NEXT WAVE OF PAIN TO POUR OVER YOU.

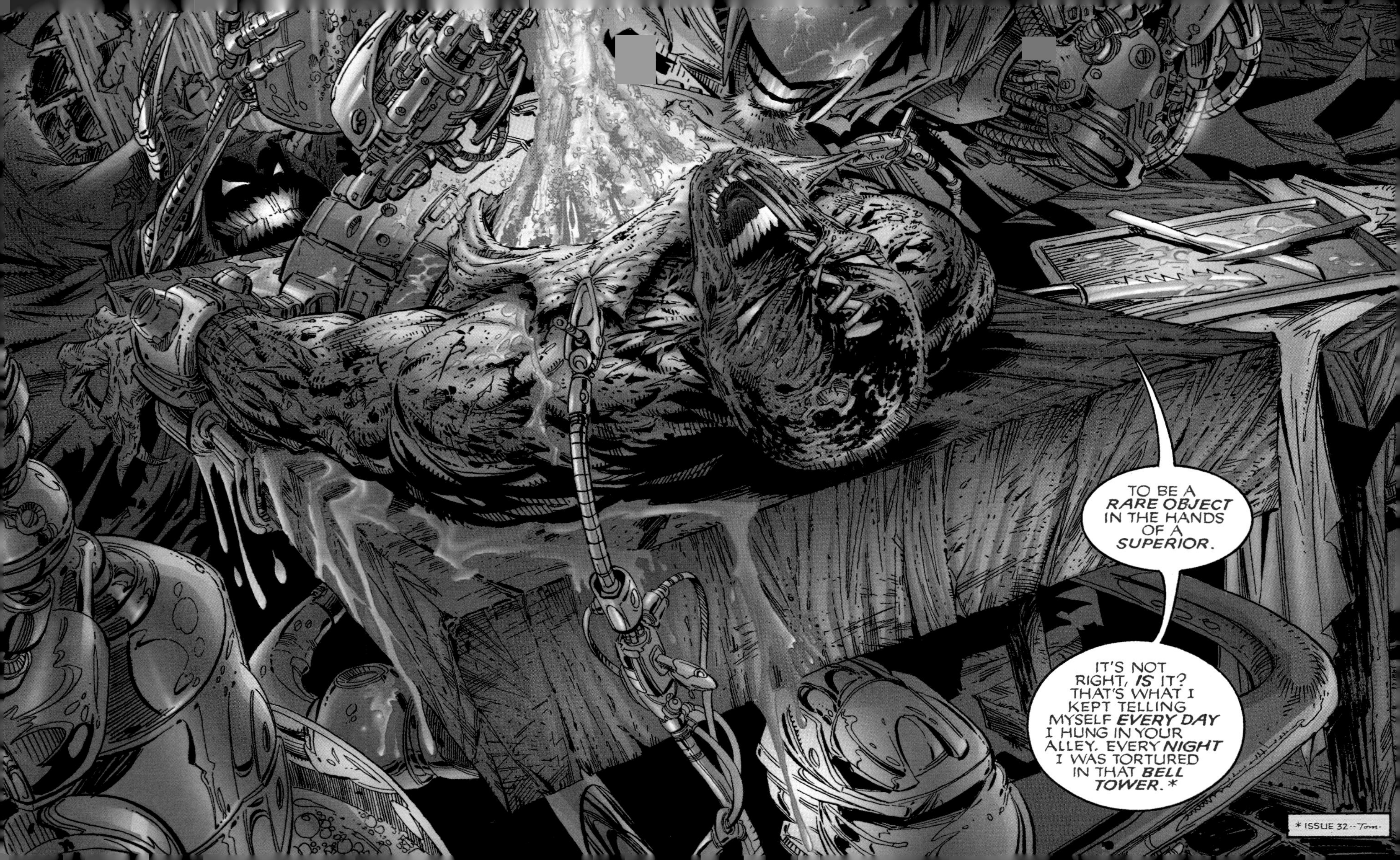
TO BE A *RARE OBJECT* IN THE HANDS OF A *SUPERIOR*.
IT'S NOT RIGHT, *IS* IT? THAT'S WHAT I KEPT TELLING MYSELF *EVERY DAY* I HUNG IN YOUR ALLEY. EVERY *NIGHT* I WAS TORTURED IN THAT *BELL TOWER*.*
* ISSUE 32 -- Tom.

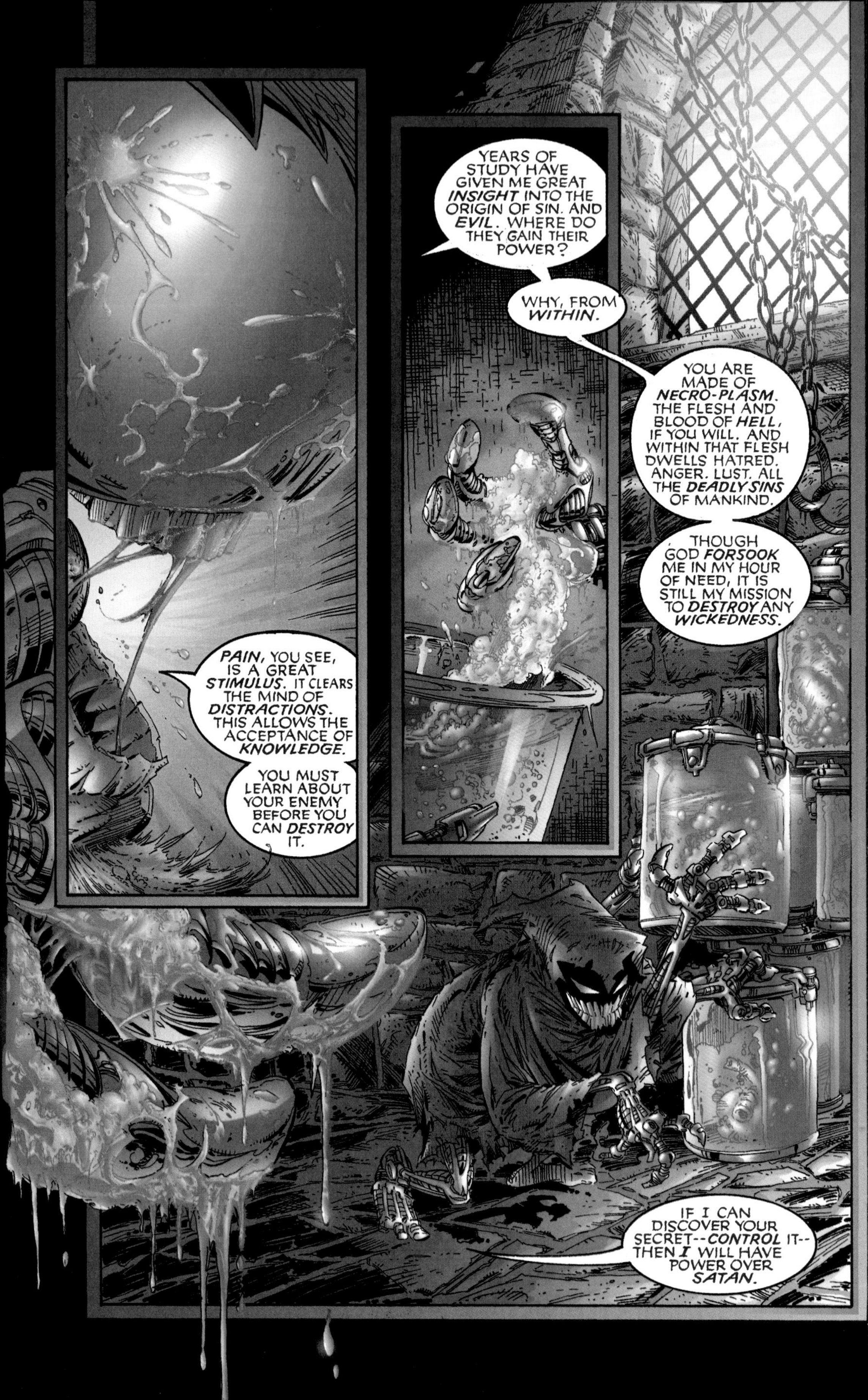
PAIN, YOU SEE, IS A GREAT STIMULUS. IT CLEARS THE MIND OF DISTRACTIONS. THIS ALLOWS THE ACCEPTANCE OF KNOWLEDGE.
YOU MUST LEARN ABOUT YOUR ENEMY BEFORE YOU CAN DESTROY IT.
YEARS OF STUDY HAVE GIVEN ME GREAT INSIGHT INTO THE ORIGIN OF SIN. AND EVIL. WHERE DO THEY GAIN THEIR POWER?
WHY, FROM WITHIN.
YOU ARE MADE OF NECRO-PLASM. THE FLESH AND BLOOD OF HELL, IF YOU WILL. AND WITHIN THAT FLESH DWELLS HATRED. ANGER. LUST. ALL THE DEADLY SINS OF MANKIND.
THOUGH GOD FORSOOK ME IN MY HOUR OF NEED, IT IS STILL MY MISSION TO DESTROY ANY WICKEDNESS.
IF I CAN DISCOVER YOUR SECRET--CONTROL IT--THEN I WILL HAVE POWER OVER SATAN.

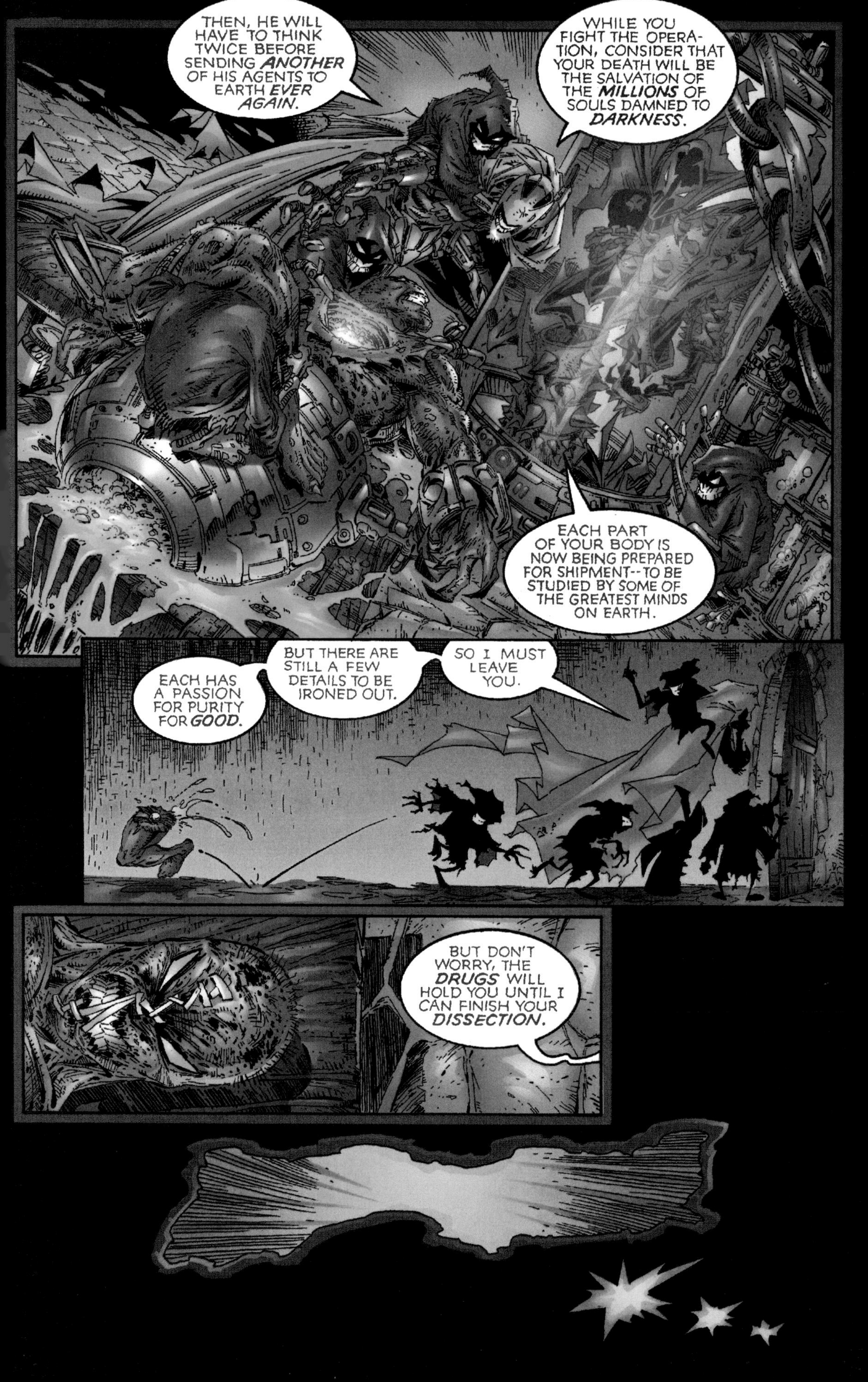
THEN, HE WILL HAVE TO THINK TWICE BEFORE SENDING ***ANOTHER*** OF HIS AGENTS TO EARTH ***EVER AGAIN***.
WHILE YOU FIGHT THE OPERATION, CONSIDER THAT YOUR DEATH WILL BE THE SALVATION OF THE ***MILLIONS*** OF SOULS DAMNED TO ***DARKNESS***.
EACH PART OF YOUR BODY IS NOW BEING PREPARED FOR SHIPMENT-- TO BE STUDIED BY SOME OF THE GREATEST MINDS ON EARTH.
EACH HAS A PASSION FOR PURITY FOR ***GOOD***.
BUT THERE ARE STILL A FEW DETAILS TO BE IRONED OUT.
SO I MUST LEAVE YOU.
BUT DON'T WORRY, THE ***DRUGS*** WILL HOLD YOU UNTIL I CAN FINISH YOUR ***DISSECTION***.

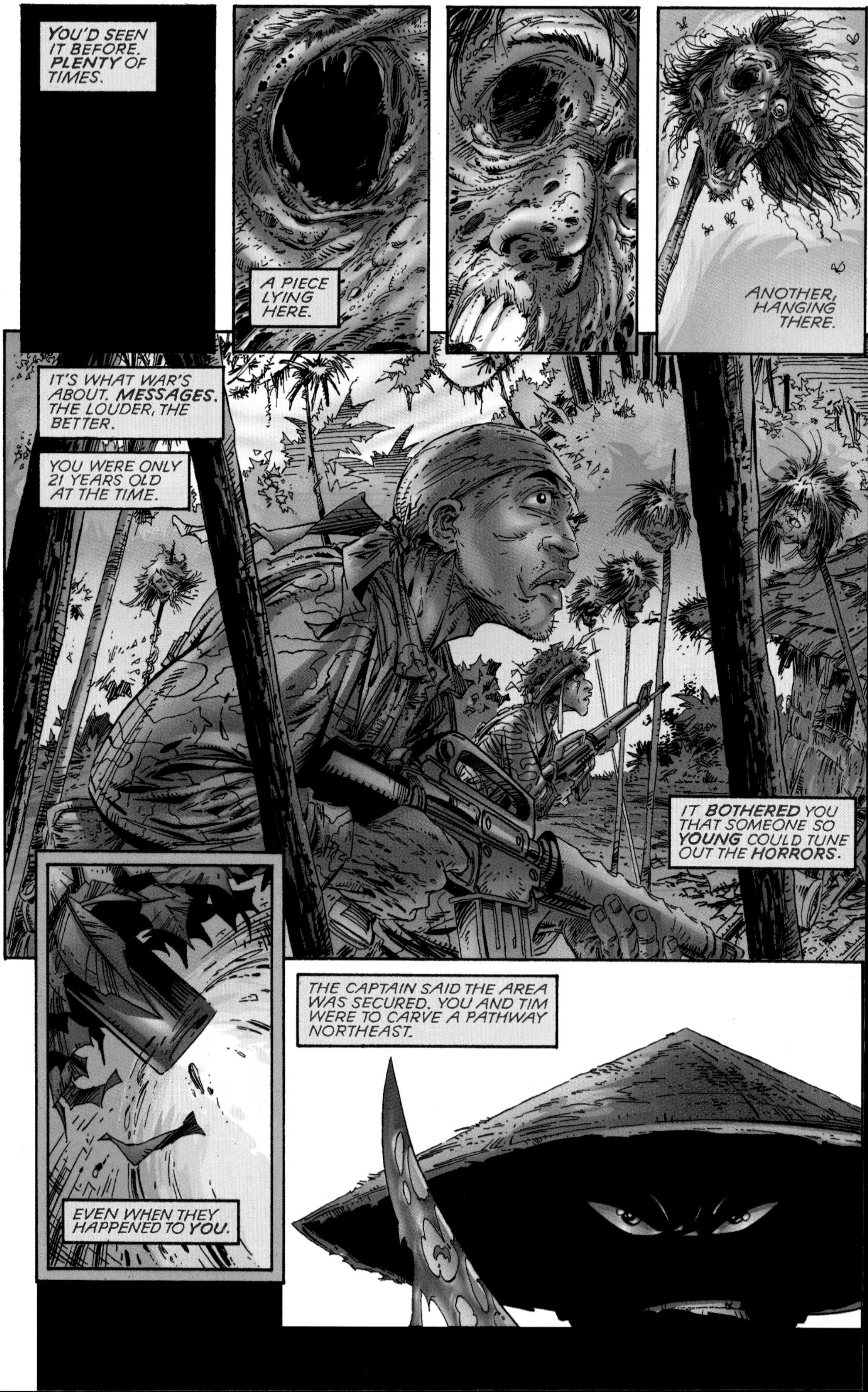
YOU'D SEEN IT BEFORE. PLENTY OF TIMES.
A PIECE LYING HERE.
ANOTHER, HANGING THERE.
IT'S WHAT WAR'S ABOUT. MESSAGES. THE LOUDER, THE BETTER.
YOU WERE ONLY 21 YEARS OLD AT THE TIME.
IT BOTHERED YOU THAT SOMEONE SO YOUNG COULD TUNE OUT THE HORRORS.
EVEN WHEN THEY HAPPENED TO YOU.
THE CAPTAIN SAID THE AREA WAS SECURED. YOU AND TIM WERE TO CARVE A PATHWAY NORTHEAST.

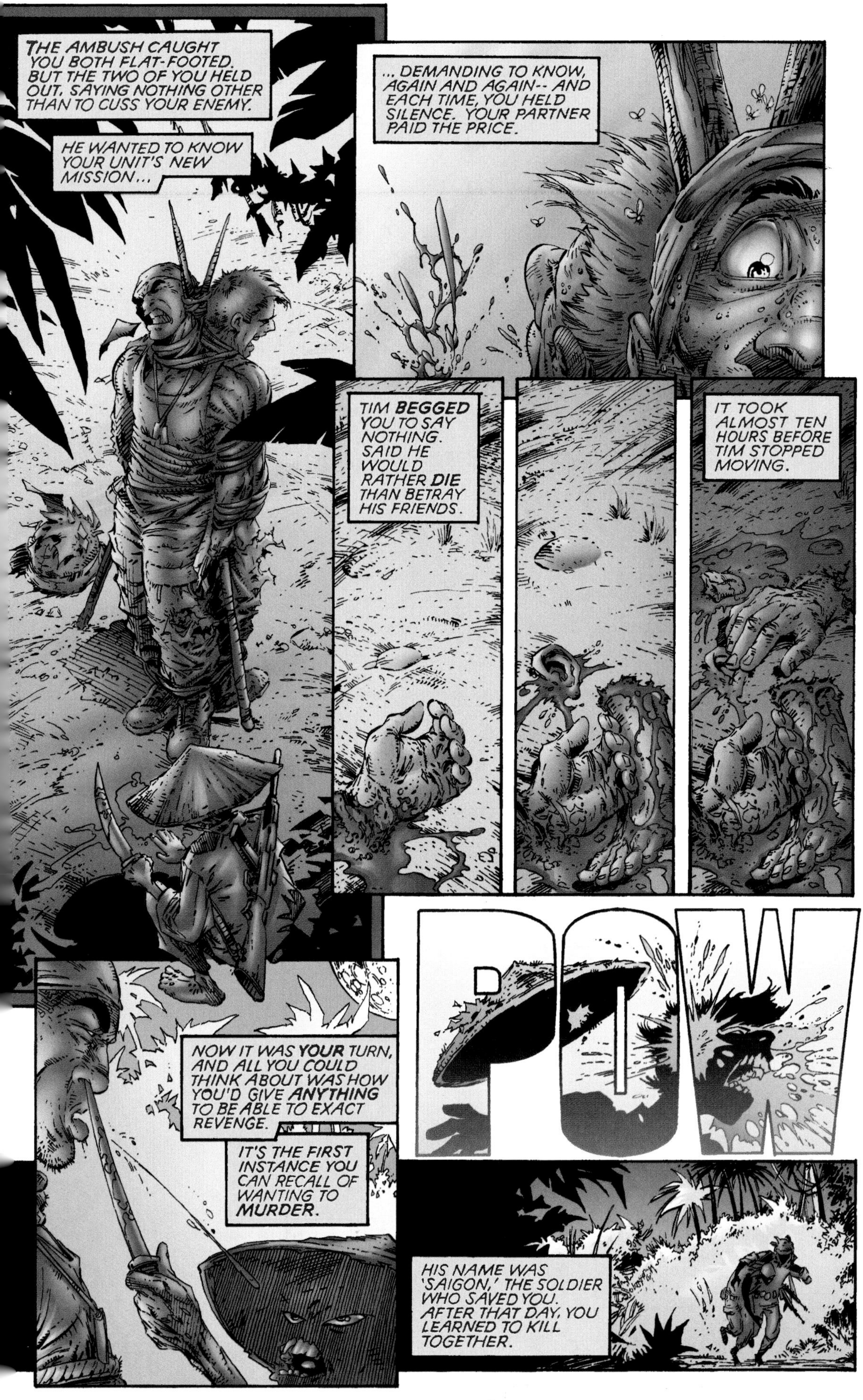
THE AMBUSH CAUGHT YOU BOTH FLAT-FOOTED. BUT THE TWO OF YOU HELD OUT, SAYING NOTHING OTHER THAN TO CUSS YOUR ENEMY.
HE WANTED TO KNOW YOUR UNIT'S NEW MISSION...
... DEMANDING TO KNOW, AGAIN AND AGAIN-- AND EACH TIME, YOU HELD SILENCE. YOUR PARTNER PAID THE PRICE.
TIM **BEGGED** YOU TO SAY NOTHING. SAID HE WOULD RATHER **DIE** THAN BETRAY HIS FRIENDS.
IT TOOK ALMOST TEN HOURS BEFORE TIM STOPPED MOVING.
NOW IT WAS **YOUR** TURN, AND ALL YOU COULD THINK ABOUT WAS HOW YOU'D GIVE **ANYTHING** TO BE ABLE TO EXACT REVENGE.
IT'S THE **FIRST** INSTANCE YOU CAN RECALL OF WANTING TO **MURDER**.
POW
HIS NAME WAS 'SAIGON,' THE SOLDIER WHO SAVED YOU. AFTER THAT DAY, YOU LEARNED TO KILL TOGETHER.

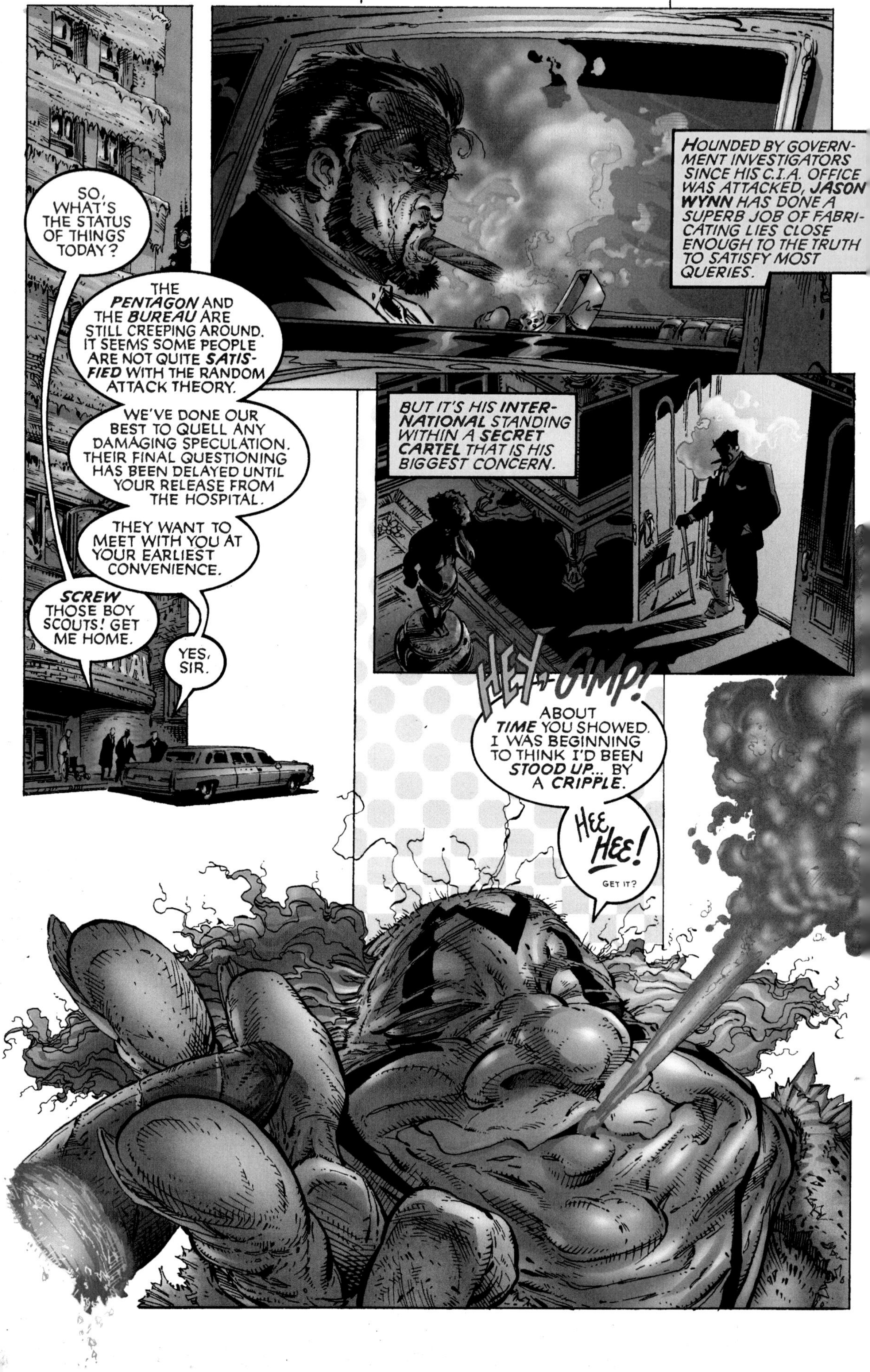

SO, WHAT'S THE STATUS OF THINGS TODAY?
THE PENTAGON AND THE BUREAU ARE STILL CREEPING AROUND. IT SEEMS SOME PEOPLE ARE NOT QUITE SATISFIED WITH THE RANDOM ATTACK THEORY.
WE'VE DONE OUR BEST TO QUELL ANY DAMAGING SPECULATION. THEIR FINAL QUESTIONING HAS BEEN DELAYED UNTIL YOUR RELEASE FROM THE HOSPITAL.
THEY WANT TO MEET WITH YOU AT YOUR EARLIEST CONVENIENCE.
SCREW THOSE BOY SCOUTS! GET ME HOME.
YES, SIR.
HOUNDED BY GOVERNMENT INVESTIGATORS SINCE HIS C.I.A. OFFICE WAS ATTACKED, JASON WYNN HAS DONE A SUPERB JOB OF FABRICATING LIES CLOSE ENOUGH TO THE TRUTH TO SATISFY MOST QUERIES.
BUT IT'S HIS INTERNATIONAL STANDING WITHIN A SECRET CARTEL THAT IS HIS BIGGEST CONCERN.
HEY, GIMP!
ABOUT TIME YOU SHOWED. I WAS BEGINNING TO THINK I'D BEEN STOOD UP... BY A CRIPPLE.
HEE HEE!
GET IT?

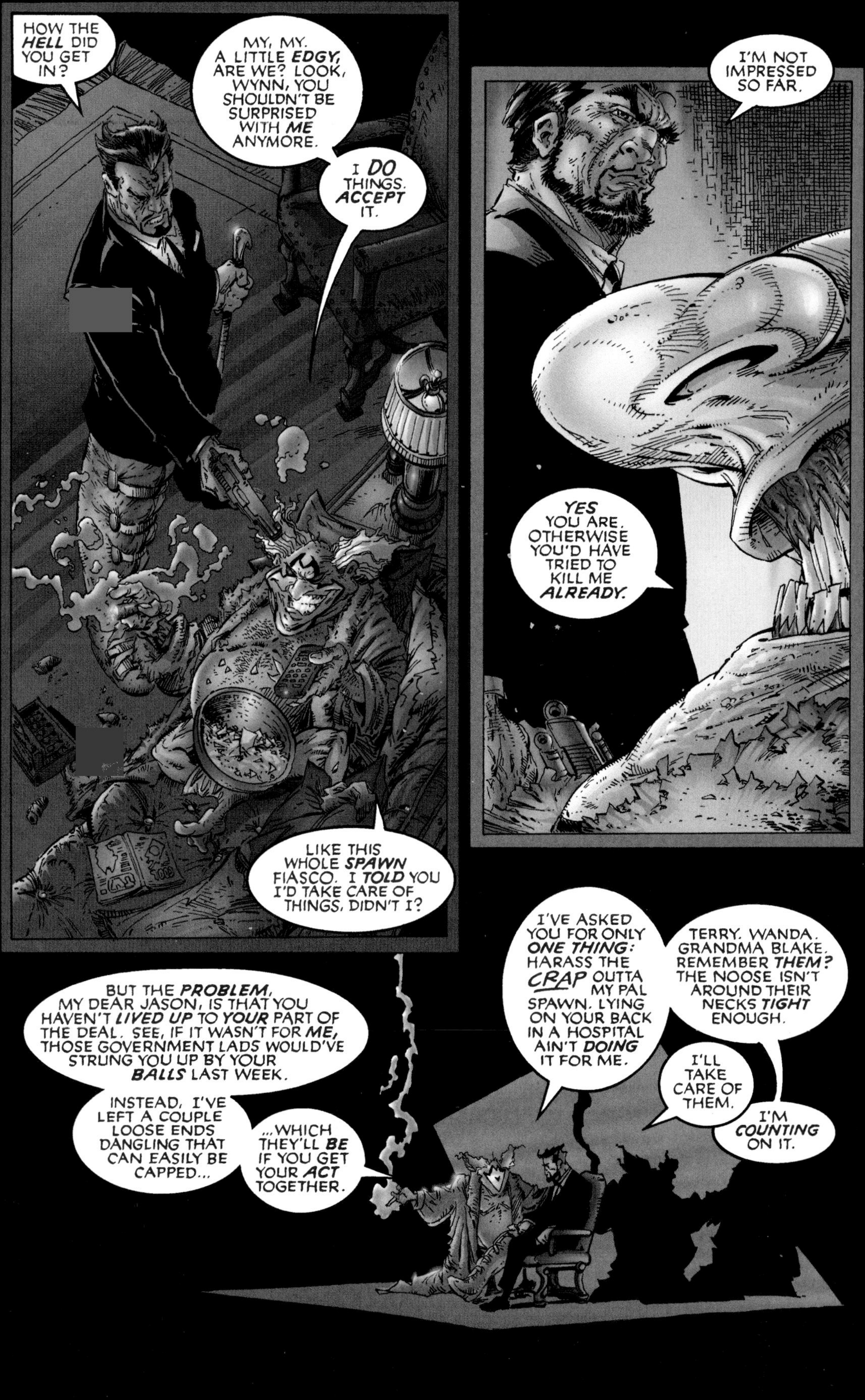
HOW THE HELL DID YOU GET IN?
MY, MY. A LITTLE EDGY, ARE WE? LOOK, WYNN, YOU SHOULDN'T BE SURPRISED WITH ME ANYMORE.
I DO THINGS. ACCEPT IT.
LIKE THIS WHOLE SPAWN FIASCO. I TOLD YOU I'D TAKE CARE OF THINGS, DIDN'T I?
I'M NOT IMPRESSED SO FAR.
YES YOU ARE. OTHERWISE YOU'D HAVE TRIED TO KILL ME ALREADY.
BUT THE PROBLEM, MY DEAR JASON, IS THAT YOU HAVEN'T LIVED UP TO YOUR PART OF THE DEAL. SEE, IF IT WASN'T FOR ME, THOSE GOVERNMENT LADS WOULD'VE STRUNG YOU UP BY YOUR BALLS LAST WEEK.
INSTEAD, I'VE LEFT A COUPLE LOOSE ENDS DANGLING THAT CAN EASILY BE CAPPED...
...WHICH THEY'LL BE IF YOU GET YOUR ACT TOGETHER.
I'VE ASKED YOU FOR ONLY ONE THING: HARASS THE CRAP OUTTA MY PAL SPAWN. LYING ON YOUR BACK IN A HOSPITAL AIN'T DOING IT FOR ME.
TERRY. WANDA. GRANDMA BLAKE. REMEMBER THEM? THE NOOSE ISN'T AROUND THEIR NECKS TIGHT ENOUGH.
I'LL TAKE CARE OF THEM.
I'M COUNTING ON IT.

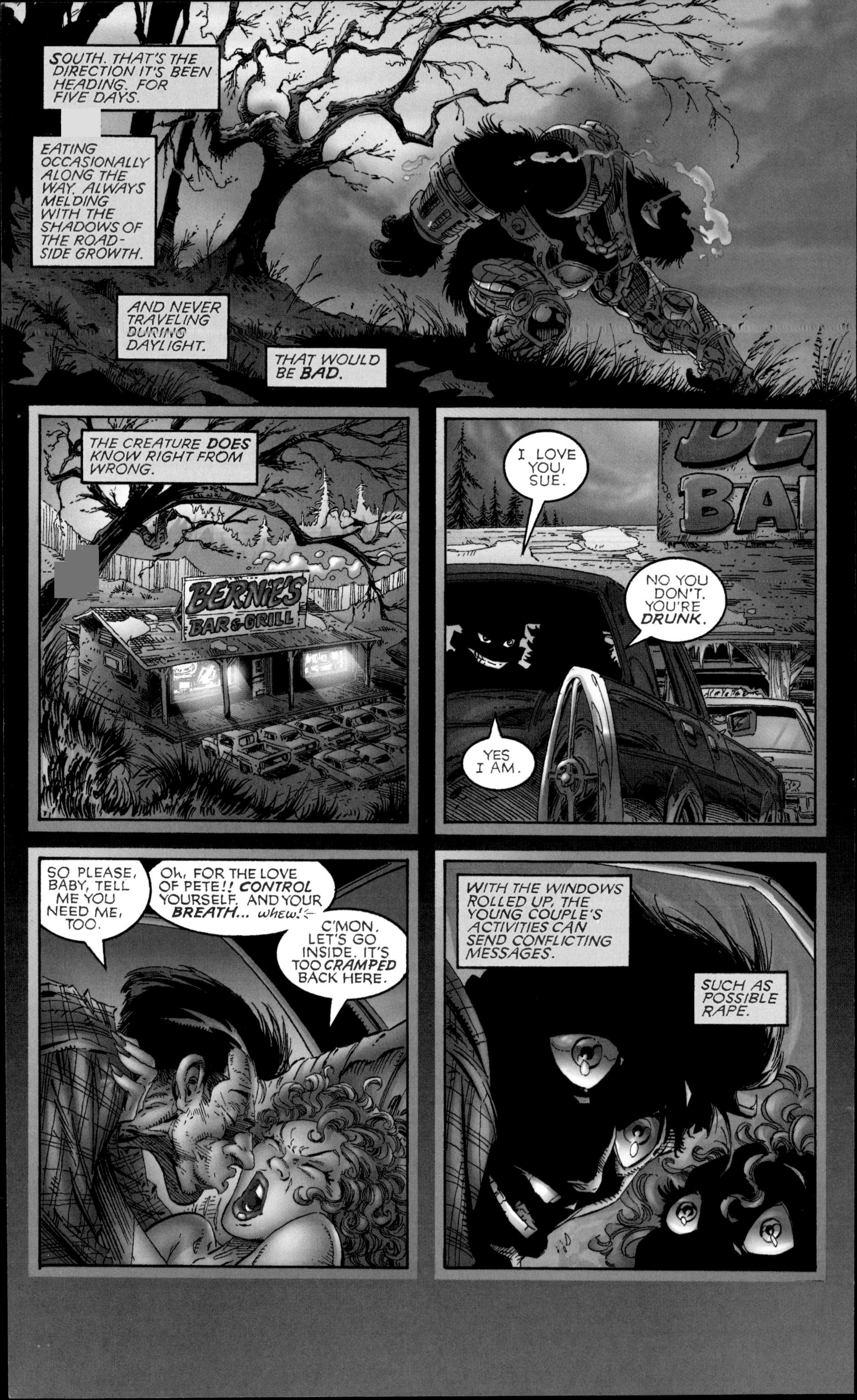
SOUTH. THAT'S THE DIRECTION IT'S BEEN HEADING. FOR FIVE DAYS.
EATING OCCASIONALLY ALONG THE WAY. ALWAYS MELDING WITH THE SHADOWS OF THE ROAD-SIDE GROWTH.
AND NEVER TRAVELING DURING DAYLIGHT.
THAT WOULD BE BAD.
THE CREATURE DOES KNOW RIGHT FROM WRONG.
BERNIE'S
BAR & GRILL
I LOVE YOU, SUE.
NO YOU DON'T. YOU'RE DRUNK.
YES I AM.
SO PLEASE, BABY, TELL ME YOU NEED ME, TOO.
Oh, FOR THE LOVE OF PETE!! CONTROL YOURSELF. AND YOUR BREATH... whew!
C'MON, LET'S GO INSIDE. IT'S TOO CRAMPED BACK HERE.
WITH THE WINDOWS ROLLED UP, THE YOUNG COUPLE'S ACTIVITIES CAN SEND CONFLICTING MESSAGES.
SUCH AS POSSIBLE RAPE.

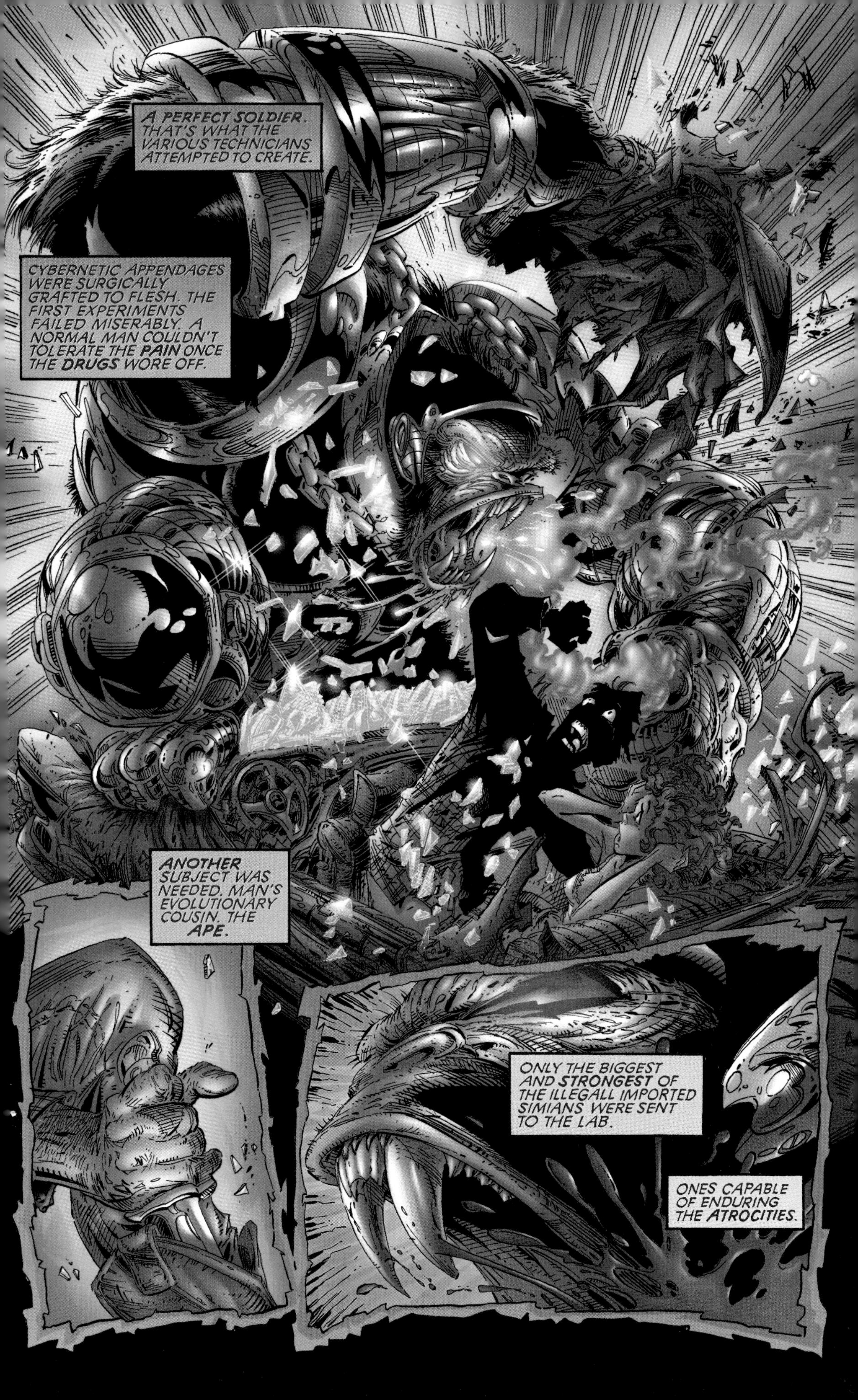
A PERFECT SOLDIER. THAT'S WHAT THE VARIOUS TECHNICIANS ATTEMPTED TO CREATE.
CYBERNETIC APPENDAGES WERE SURGICALLY GRAFTED TO FLESH. THE FIRST EXPERIMENTS FAILED MISERABLY. A NORMAL MAN COULDN'T TOLERATE THE PAIN ONCE THE DRUGS WORE OFF.
ANOTHER SUBJECT WAS NEEDED. MAN'S EVOLUTIONARY COUSIN. THE APE.
ONLY THE BIGGEST AND STRONGEST OF THE ILLEGALL IMPORTED SIMIANS WERE SENT TO THE LAB.
ONES CAPABLE OF ENDURING THE ATROCITIES.

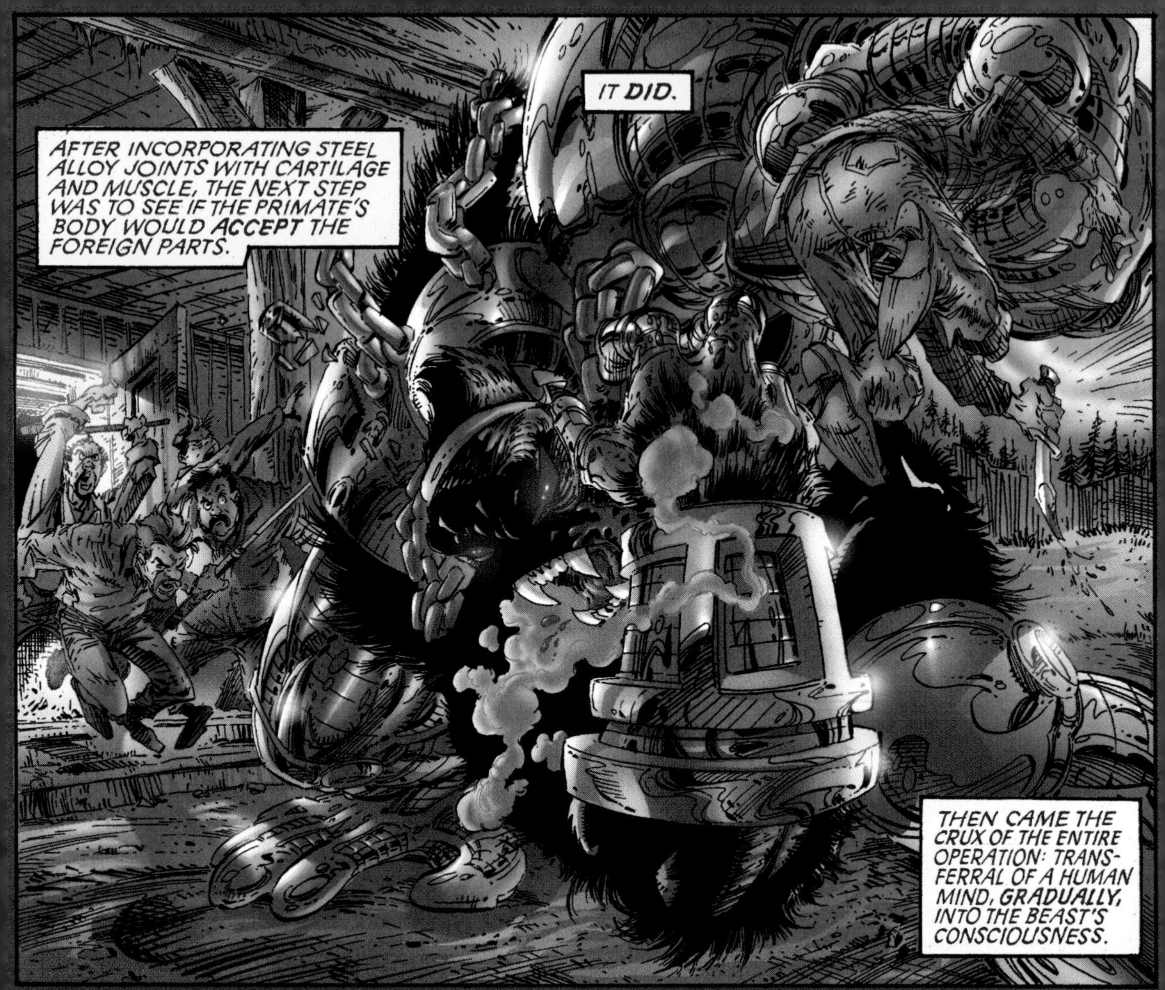
AFTER INCORPORATING STEEL ALLOY JOINTS WITH CARTILAGE AND MUSCLE, THE NEXT STEP WAS TO SEE IF THE PRIMATE'S BODY WOULD ACCEPT THE FOREIGN PARTS.
IT DID.
THEN CAME THE CRUX OF THE ENTIRE OPERATION: TRANS-FERRAL OF A HUMAN MIND, GRADUALLY, INTO THE BEAST'S CONSCIOUSNESS.
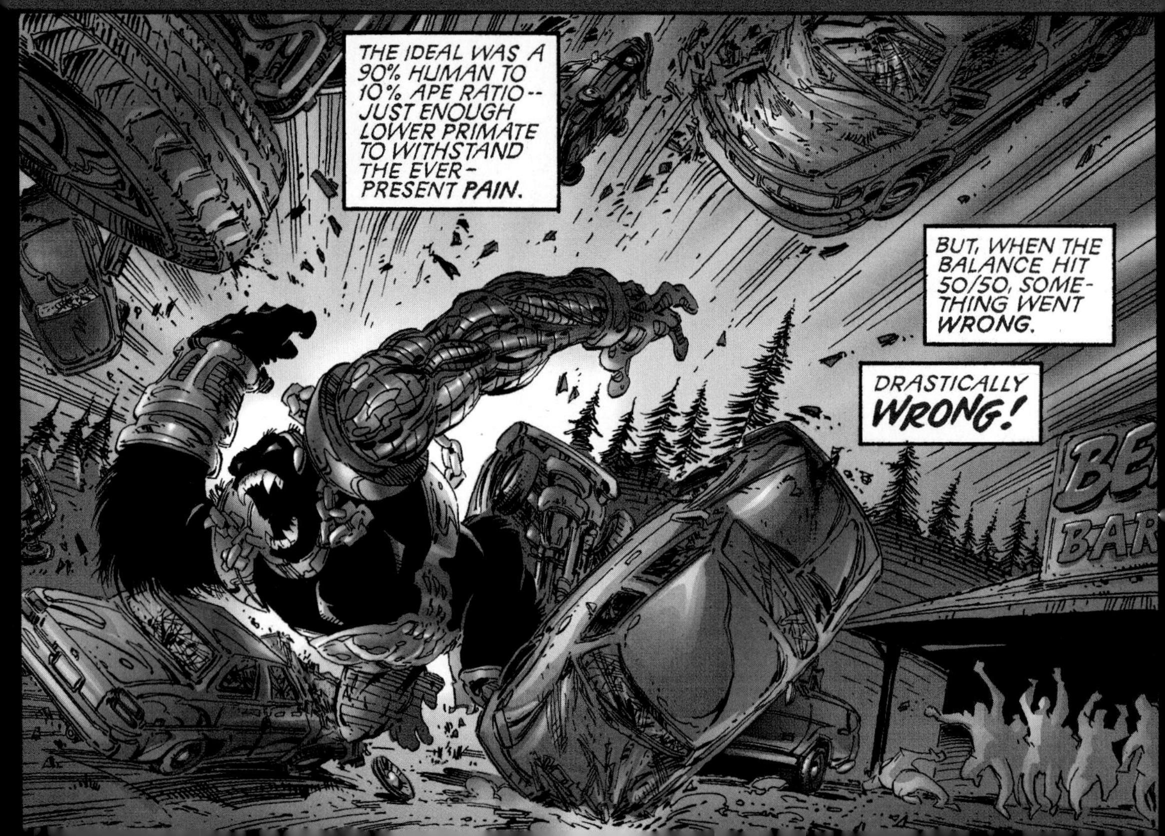
THE IDEAL WAS A 90% HUMAN TO 10% APE RATIO-- JUST ENOUGH LOWER PRIMATE TO WITHSTAND THE EVER-PRESENT PAIN.
BUT, WHEN THE BALANCE HIT 50/50, SOME-THING WENT WRONG.
DRASTICALLY WRONG!

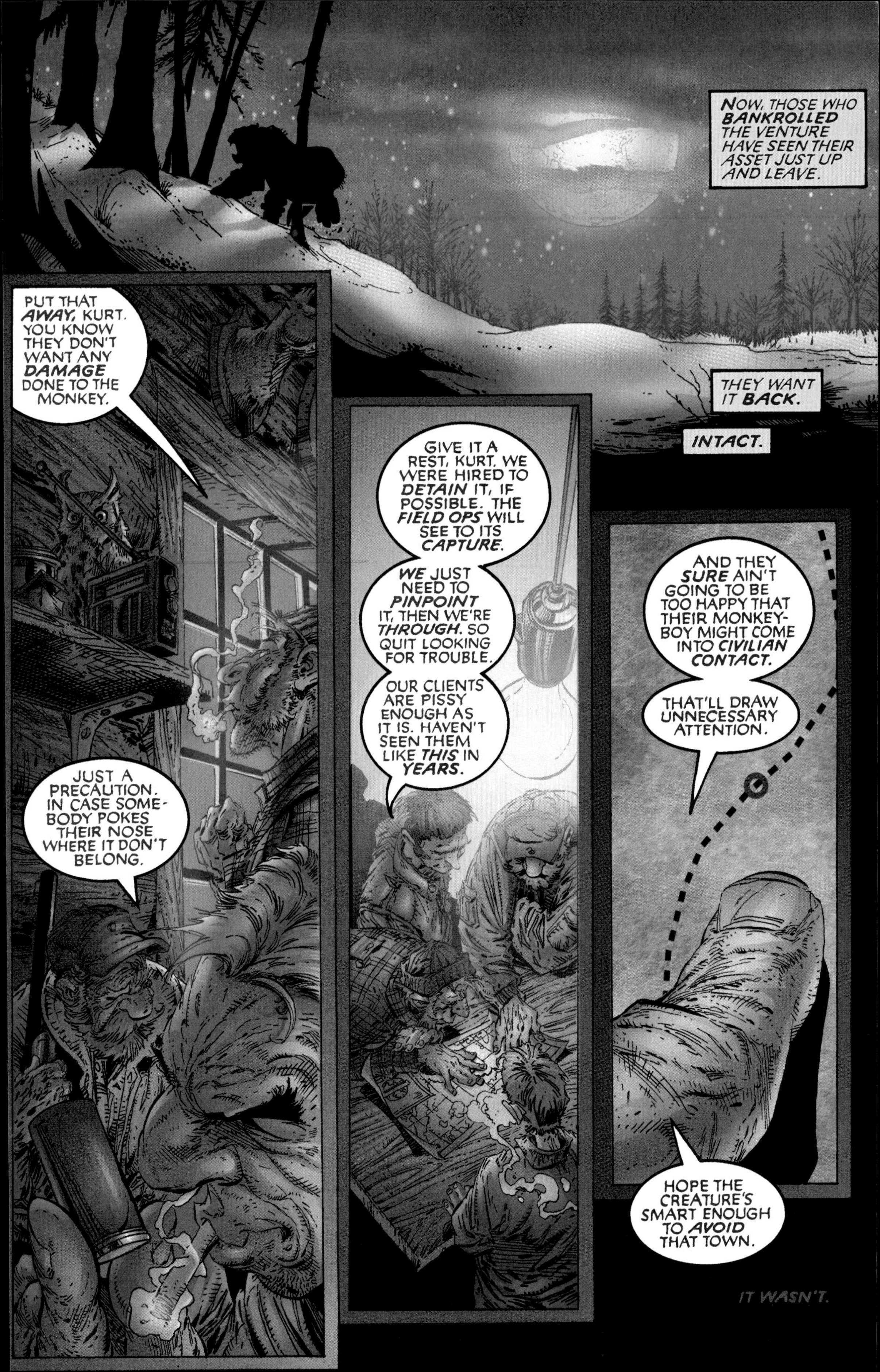
NOW, THOSE WHO BANKROLLED THE VENTURE HAVE SEEN THEIR ASSET JUST UP AND LEAVE.
THEY WANT IT BACK.
INTACT.
PUT THAT AWAY, KURT. YOU KNOW THEY DON'T WANT ANY DAMAGE DONE TO THE MONKEY.
JUST A PRECAUTION. IN CASE SOME-BODY POKES THEIR NOSE WHERE IT DON'T BELONG.
GIVE IT A REST, KURT. WE WERE HIRED TO DETAIN IT, IF POSSIBLE. THE FIELD OPS WILL SEE TO ITS CAPTURE.
WE JUST NEED TO PINPOINT IT, THEN WE'RE THROUGH. SO QUIT LOOKING FOR TROUBLE.
OUR CLIENTS ARE PISSY ENOUGH AS IT IS. HAVEN'T SEEN THEM LIKE THIS IN YEARS.
AND THEY SURE AIN'T GOING TO BE TOO HAPPY THAT THEIR MONKEY-BOY MIGHT COME INTO CIVILIAN CONTACT.
THAT'LL DRAW UNNECESSARY ATTENTION.
HOPE THE CREATURE'S SMART ENOUGH TO AVOID THAT TOWN.
IT WASN'T.

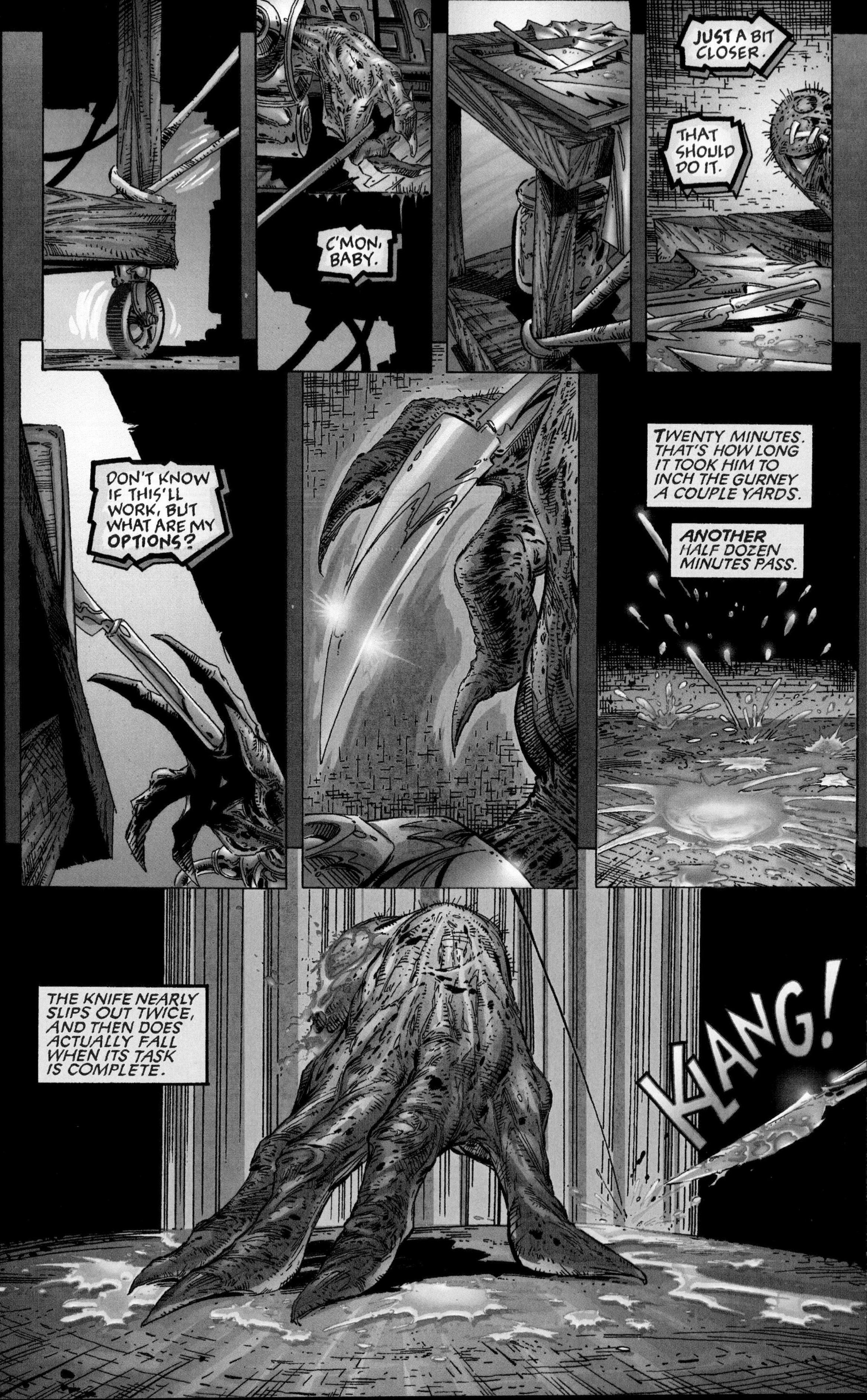
C'MON, BABY.
JUST A BIT CLOSER.
THAT SHOULD DO IT.
DON'T KNOW IF THIS'LL WORK, BUT WHAT ARE MY OPTIONS?
TWENTY MINUTES. THAT'S HOW LONG IT TOOK HIM TO INCH THE GURNEY A COUPLE YARDS.
ANOTHER HALF DOZEN MINUTES PASS.
THE KNIFE NEARLY SLIPS OUT TWICE, AND THEN DOES ACTUALLY FALL WHEN ITS TASK IS COMPLETE.
KLANG!

HAVE TO CONCENTRATE... **NO!** IT'S GOING IN THE **WRONG DIRECTION!**

IT TAKES ANOTHER 3 MINUTES FOR MIND AND LIMBS TO GET IN SYNC.

DAMN!

THUD!

THUK!

DAMN! THE DRUGS MADE ME TOO WEAK!

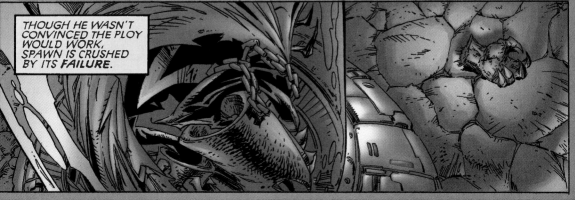

THOUGH HE WASN'T CONVINCED THE PLOY WOULD WORK, SPAWN IS CRUSHED BY ITS *FAILURE.*

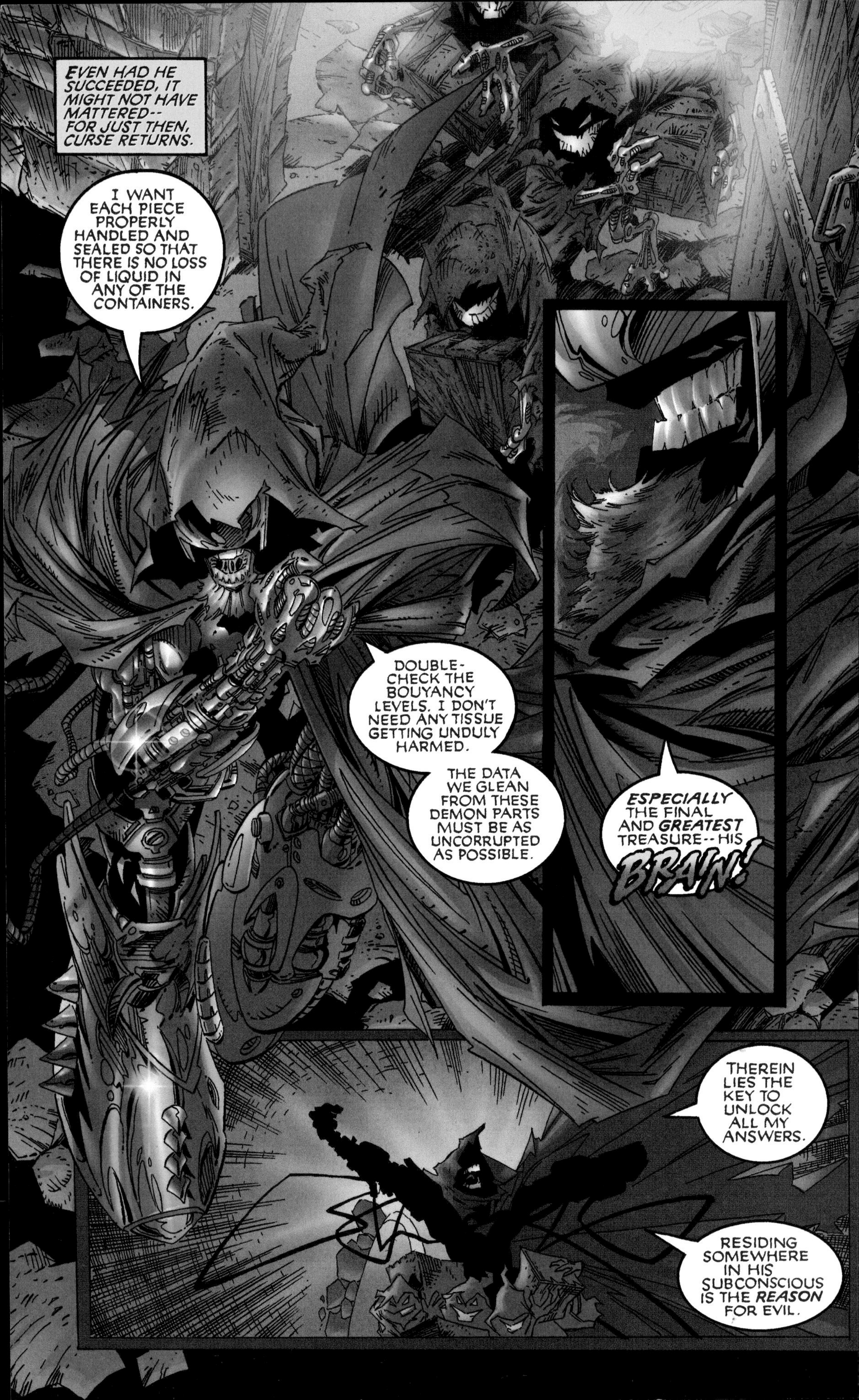
EVEN HAD HE SUCCEEDED, IT MIGHT NOT HAVE MATTERED-- FOR JUST THEN, CURSE RETURNS.
I WANT EACH PIECE PROPERLY HANDLED AND SEALED SO THAT THERE IS NO LOSS OF LIQUID IN ANY OF THE CONTAINERS.
DOUBLE-CHECK THE BOUYANCY LEVELS. I DON'T NEED ANY TISSUE GETTING UNDULY HARMED.
THE DATA WE GLEAN FROM THESE DEMON PARTS MUST BE AS UNCORRUPTED AS POSSIBLE.
ESPECIALLY THE FINAL AND GREATEST TREASURE--HIS BRAIN!
THEREIN LIES THE KEY TO UNLOCK ALL MY ANSWERS.
RESIDING SOMEWHERE IN HIS SUBCONSCIOUS IS THE REASON FOR EVIL.

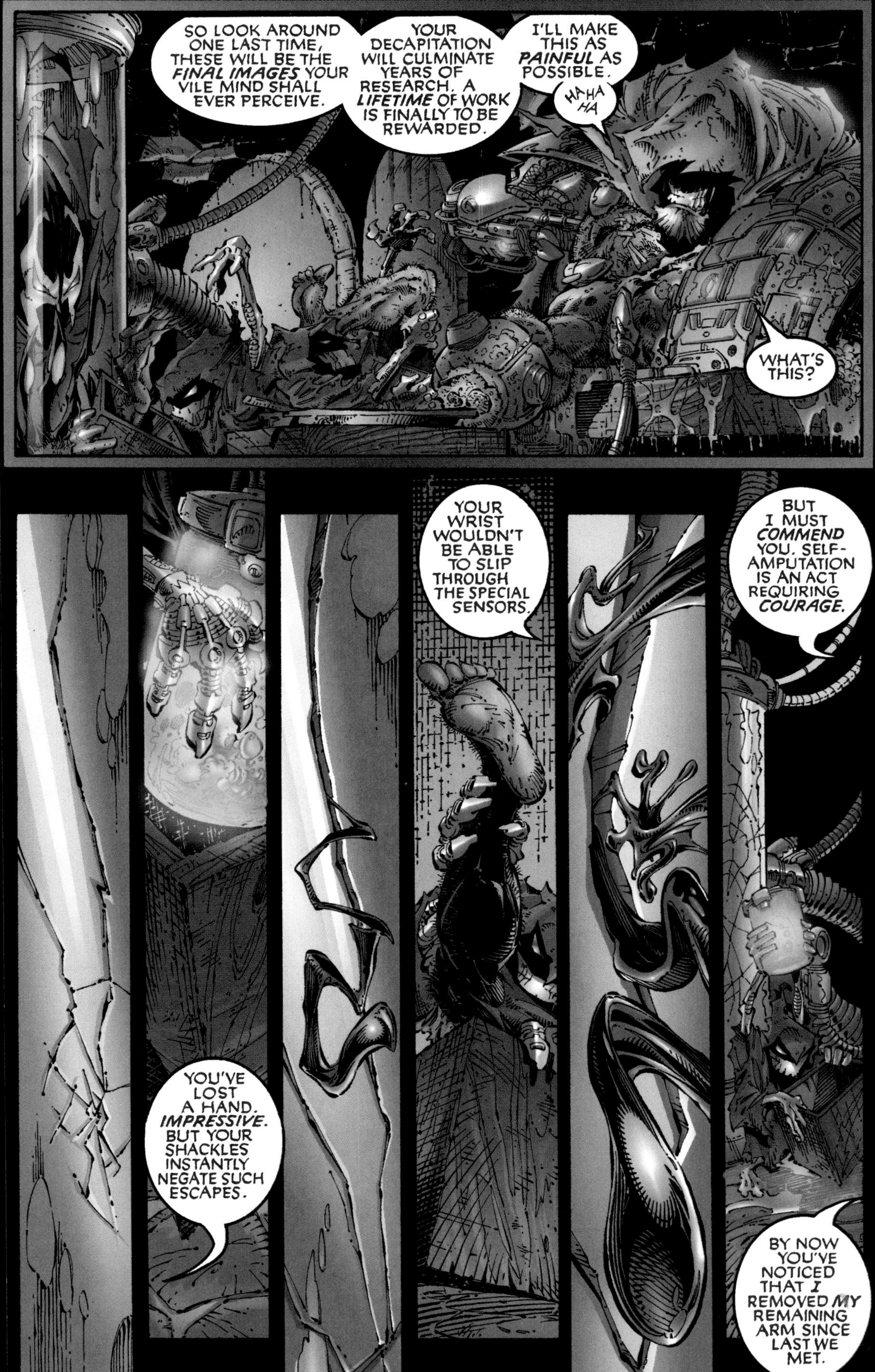
SO LOOK AROUND ONE LAST TIME, THESE WILL BE THE *FINAL IMAGES* YOUR VILE MIND SHALL EVER PERCEIVE.
YOUR DECAPITATION WILL CULMINATE YEARS OF RESEARCH. A *LIFETIME* OF WORK IS FINALLY TO BE REWARDED.
I'LL MAKE THIS AS *PAINFUL* AS POSSIBLE.
HA HA HA
WHAT'S THIS?
YOU'VE LOST A HAND. *IMPRESSIVE*. BUT YOUR SHACKLES INSTANTLY NEGATE SUCH ESCAPES.
YOUR WRIST WOULDN'T BE ABLE TO SLIP THROUGH THE SPECIAL SENSORS.
BUT I MUST *COMMEND* YOU. SELF-AMPUTATION IS AN ACT REQUIRING *COURAGE*.
BY NOW YOU'VE NOTICED THAT *I* REMOVED *MY* REMAINING ARM SINCE LAST WE MET.

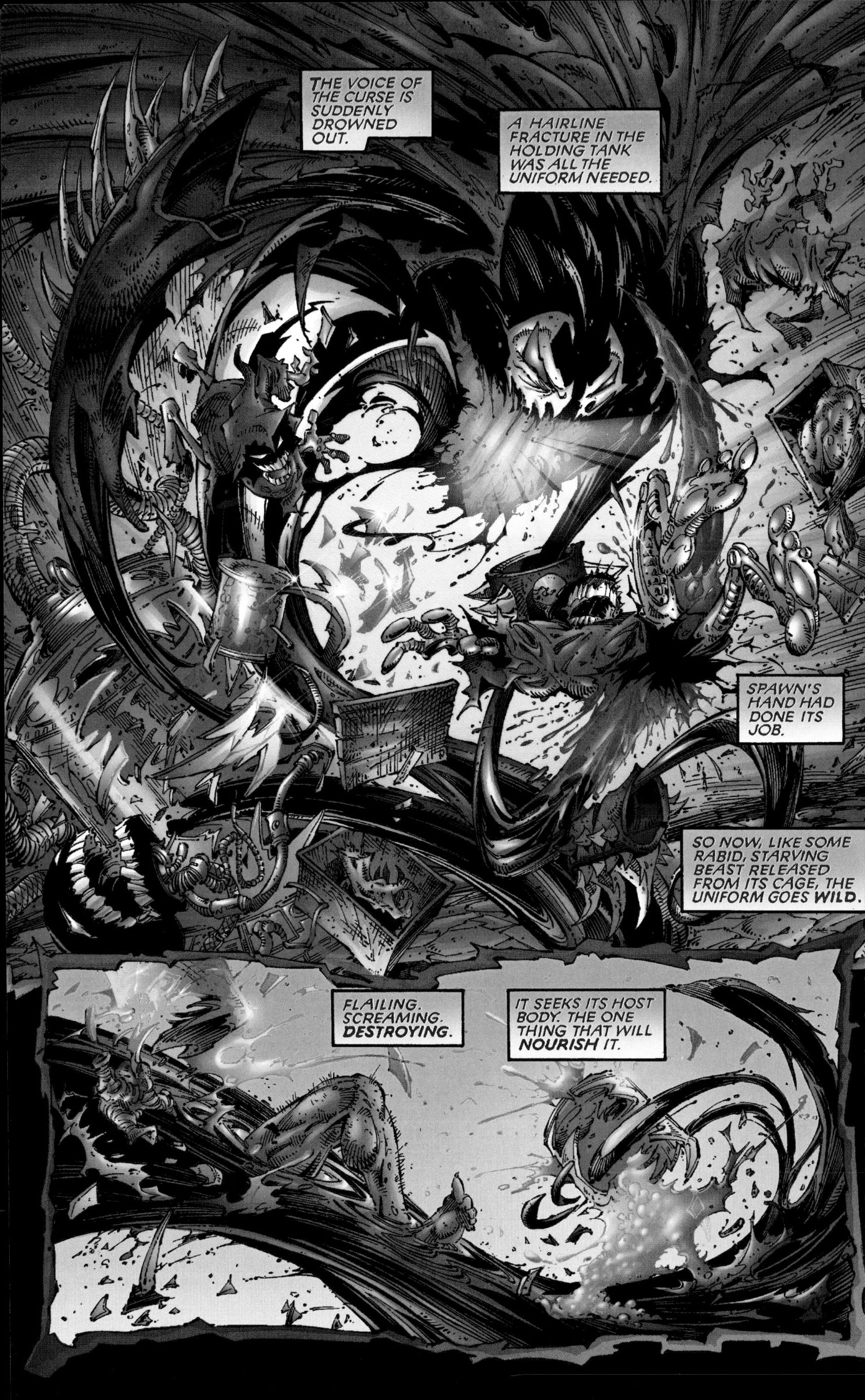
THE VOICE OF THE CURSE IS SUDDENLY DROWNED OUT.
A HAIRLINE FRACTURE IN THE HOLDING TANK WAS ALL THE UNIFORM NEEDED.
SPAWN'S HAND HAD DONE ITS JOB.
SO NOW, LIKE SOME RABID, STARVING BEAST RELEASED FROM ITS CAGE, THE UNIFORM GOES **WILD**.
FLAILING. SCREAMING. **DESTROYING**.
IT SEEKS ITS HOST BODY. THE ONE THING THAT WILL **NOURISH** IT.

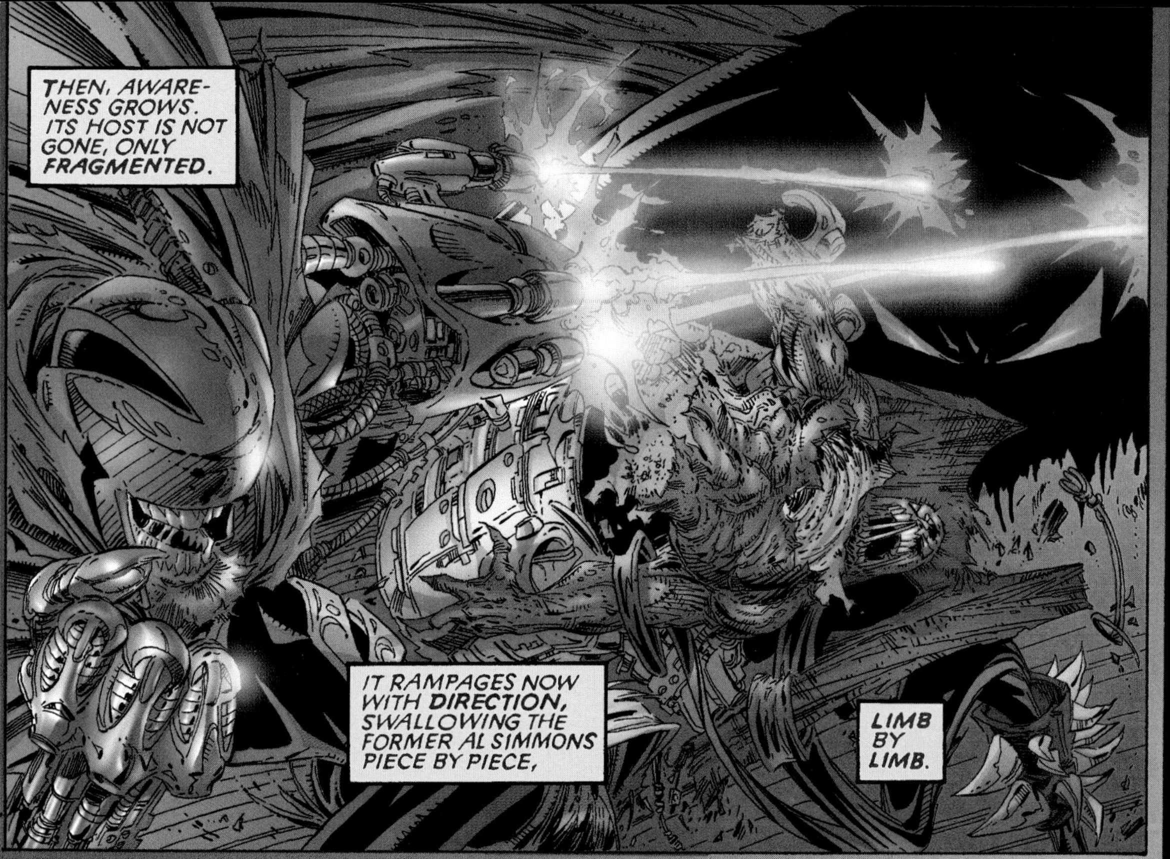
THEN, AWARENESS GROWS. ITS HOST IS NOT GONE, ONLY FRAGMENTED.
IT RAMPAGES NOW WITH DIRECTION, SWALLOWING THE FORMER AL SIMMONS PIECE BY PIECE,
LIMB BY LIMB.
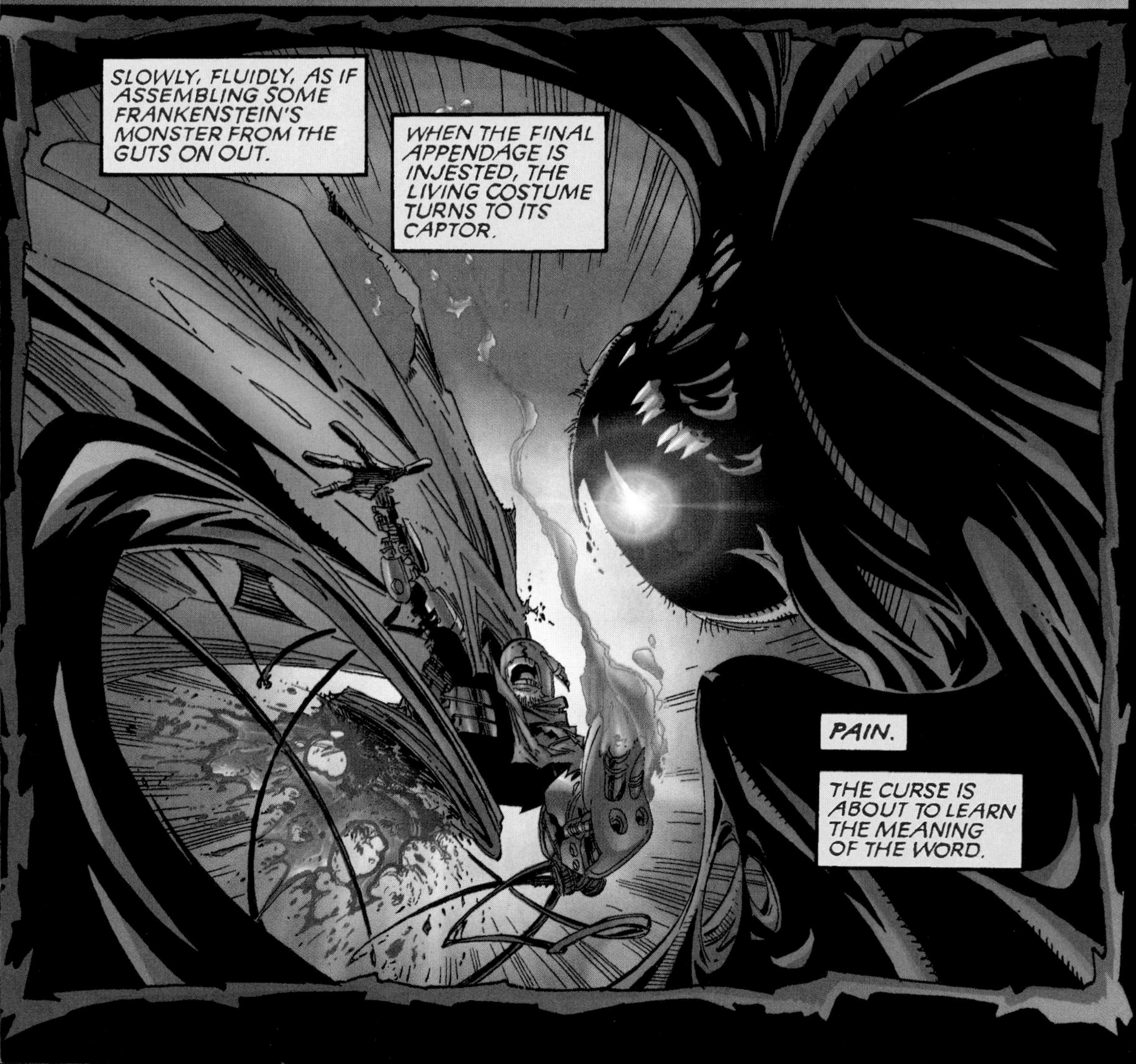
SLOWLY, FLUIDLY, AS IF ASSEMBLING SOME FRANKENSTEIN'S MONSTER FROM THE GUTS ON OUT.
WHEN THE FINAL APPENDAGE IS INJESTED, THE LIVING COSTUME TURNS TO ITS CAPTOR.
PAIN.
THE CURSE IS ABOUT TO LEARN THE MEANING OF THE WORD.

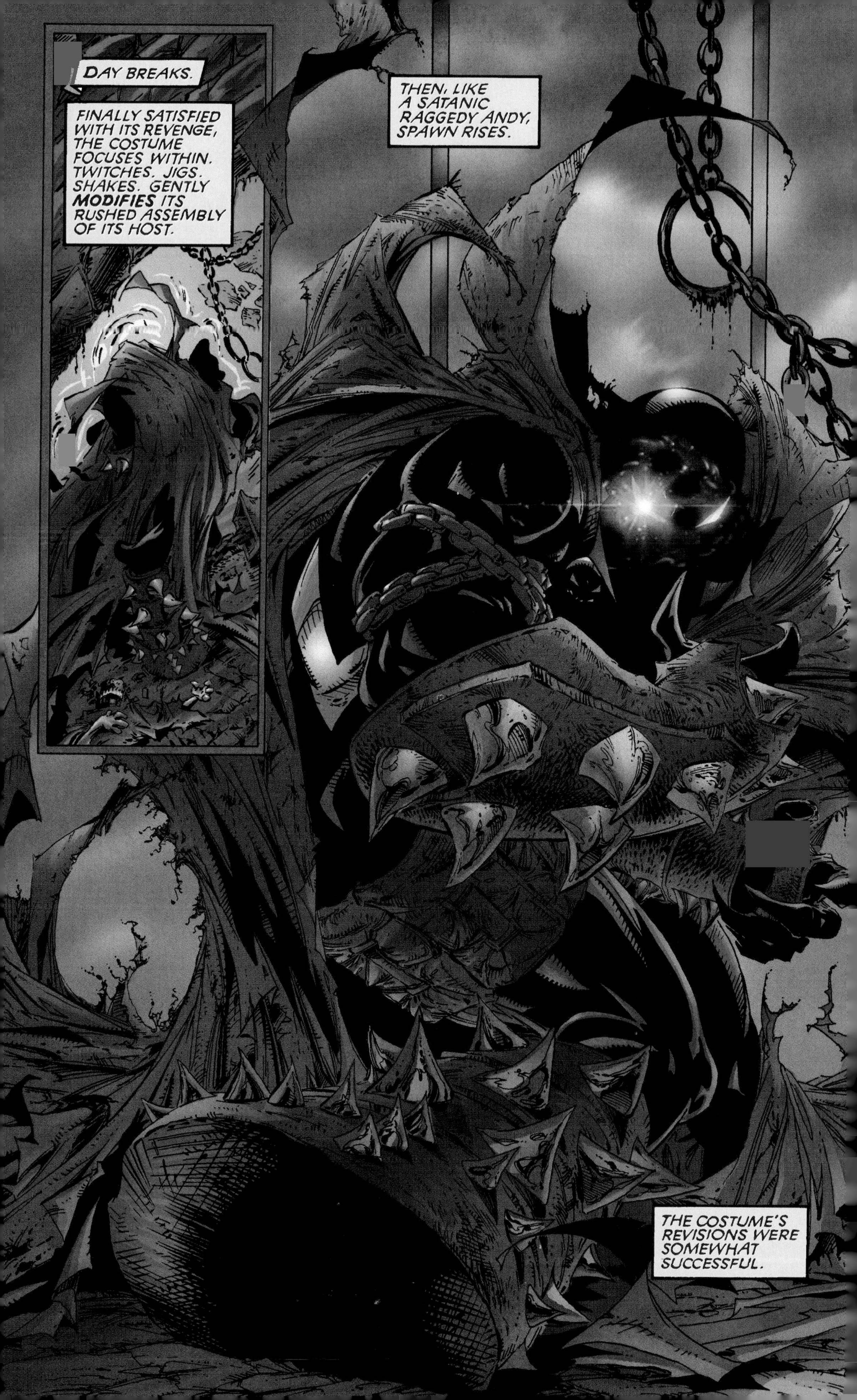
DAY BREAKS.
FINALLY SATISFIED WITH ITS REVENGE, THE COSTUME FOCUSES WITHIN. TWITCHES. JIGS. SHAKES. GENTLY **MODIFIES** ITS RUSHED ASSEMBLY OF ITS HOST.
THEN, LIKE A SATANIC RAGGEDY ANDY, SPAWN RISES.
THE COSTUME'S REVISIONS WERE SOMEWHAT SUCCESSFUL.

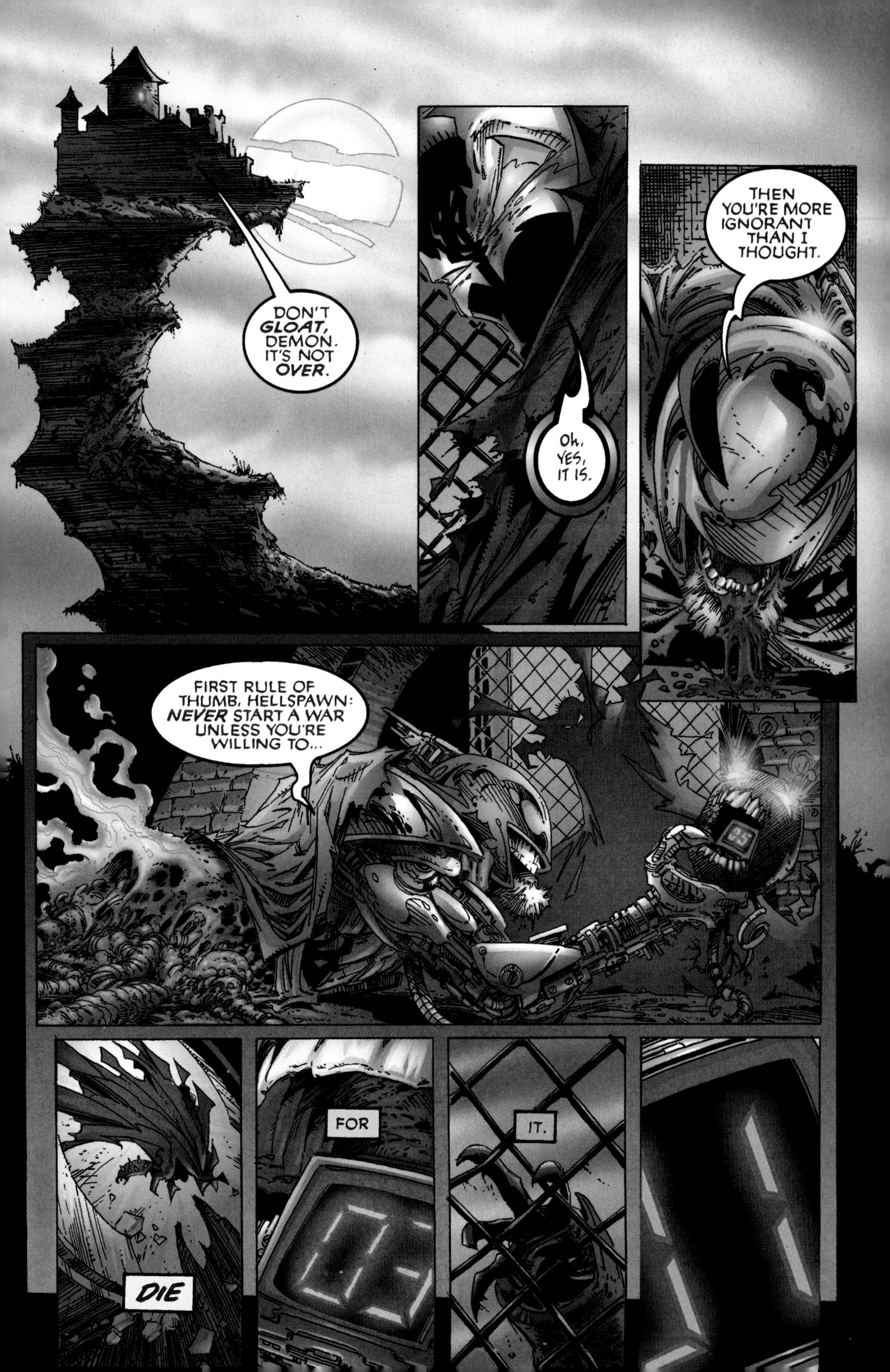
DON'T GLOAT, DEMON. IT'S NOT OVER.
Oh, YES, IT IS.
THEN YOU'RE MORE IGNORANT THAN I THOUGHT.
FIRST RULE OF THUMB, HELLSPAWN: NEVER START A WAR UNLESS YOU'RE WILLING TO...
DIE
FOR
IT.

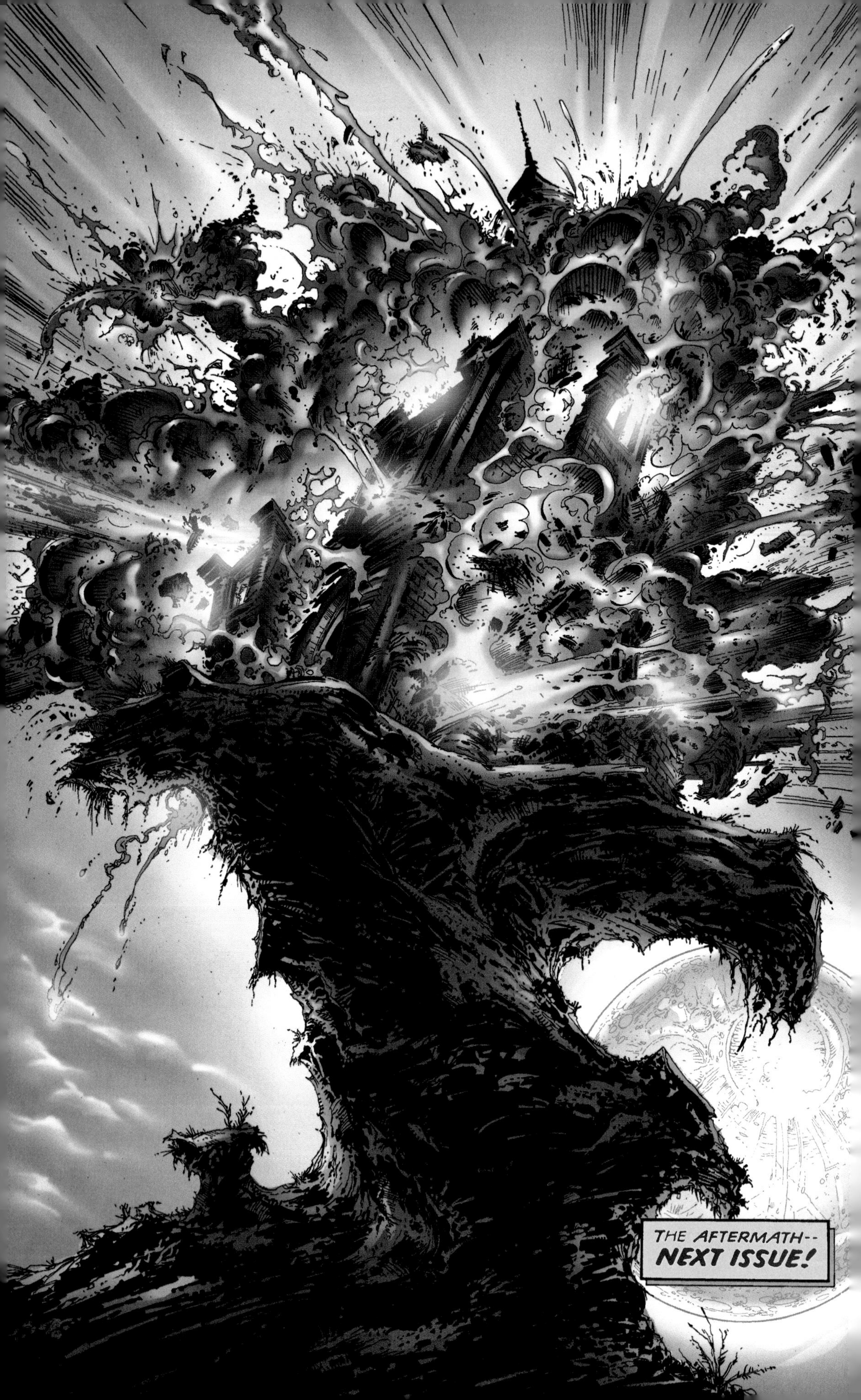
THE AFTERMATH--
NEXT ISSUE!

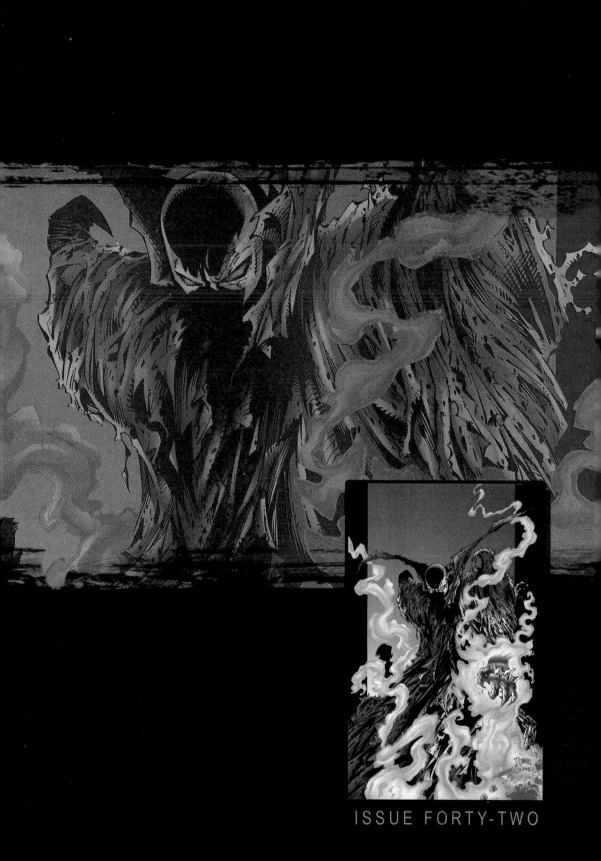

ISSUE FORTY-TWO

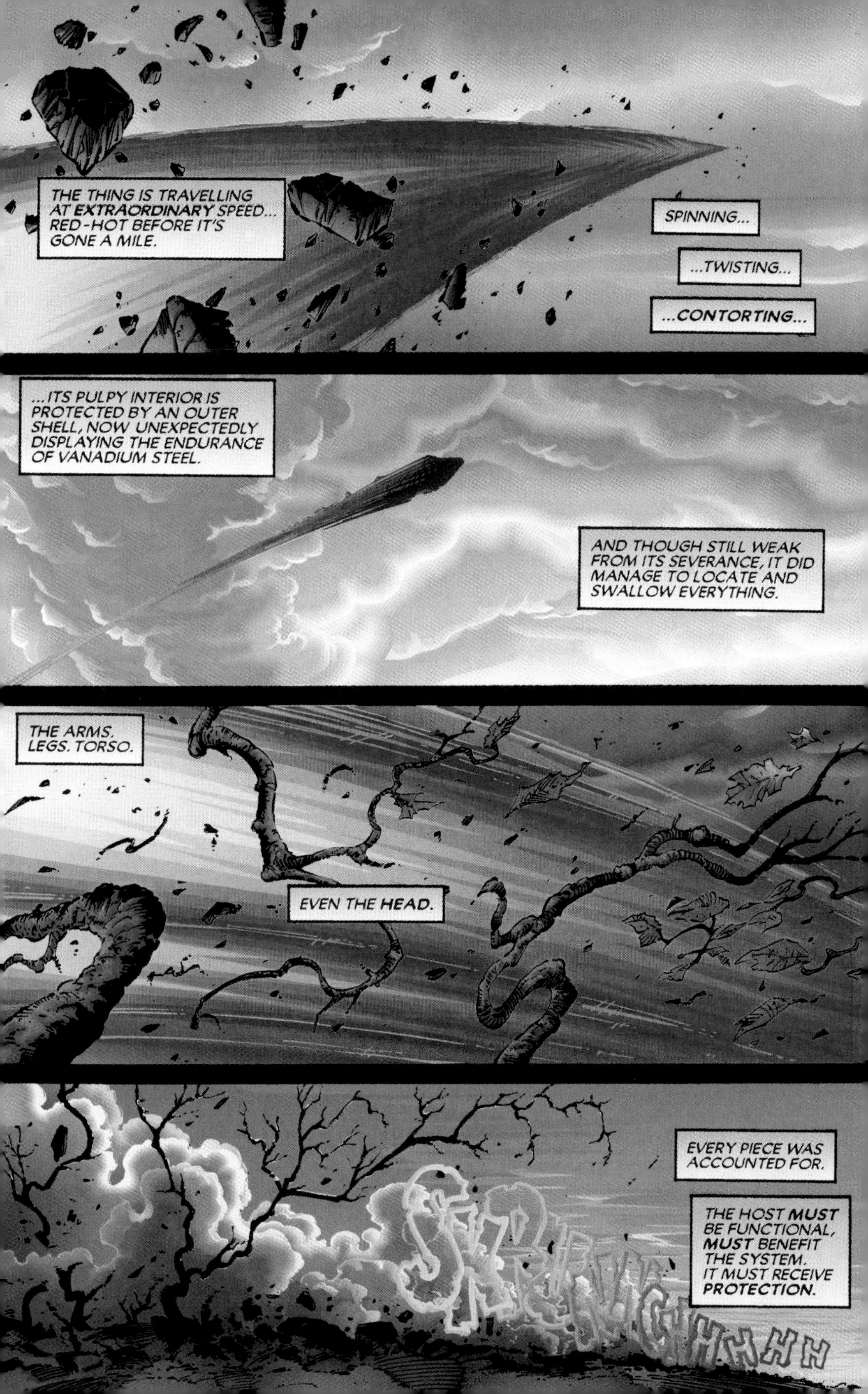
THE THING IS TRAVELLING AT **EXTRAORDINARY** SPEED... RED-HOT BEFORE IT'S GONE A MILE.
SPINNING...
...TWISTING...
...CONTORTING...
...ITS PULPY INTERIOR IS PROTECTED BY AN OUTER SHELL, NOW UNEXPECTEDLY DISPLAYING THE ENDURANCE OF VANADIUM STEEL.
AND THOUGH STILL WEAK FROM ITS SEVERANCE, IT DID MANAGE TO LOCATE AND SWALLOW EVERYTHING.
THE ARMS. LEGS. TORSO.
EVEN THE **HEAD**.
EVERY PIECE WAS ACCOUNTED FOR.
THE HOST **MUST** BE FUNCTIONAL, **MUST** BENEFIT THE SYSTEM. IT MUST RECEIVE **PROTECTION**.

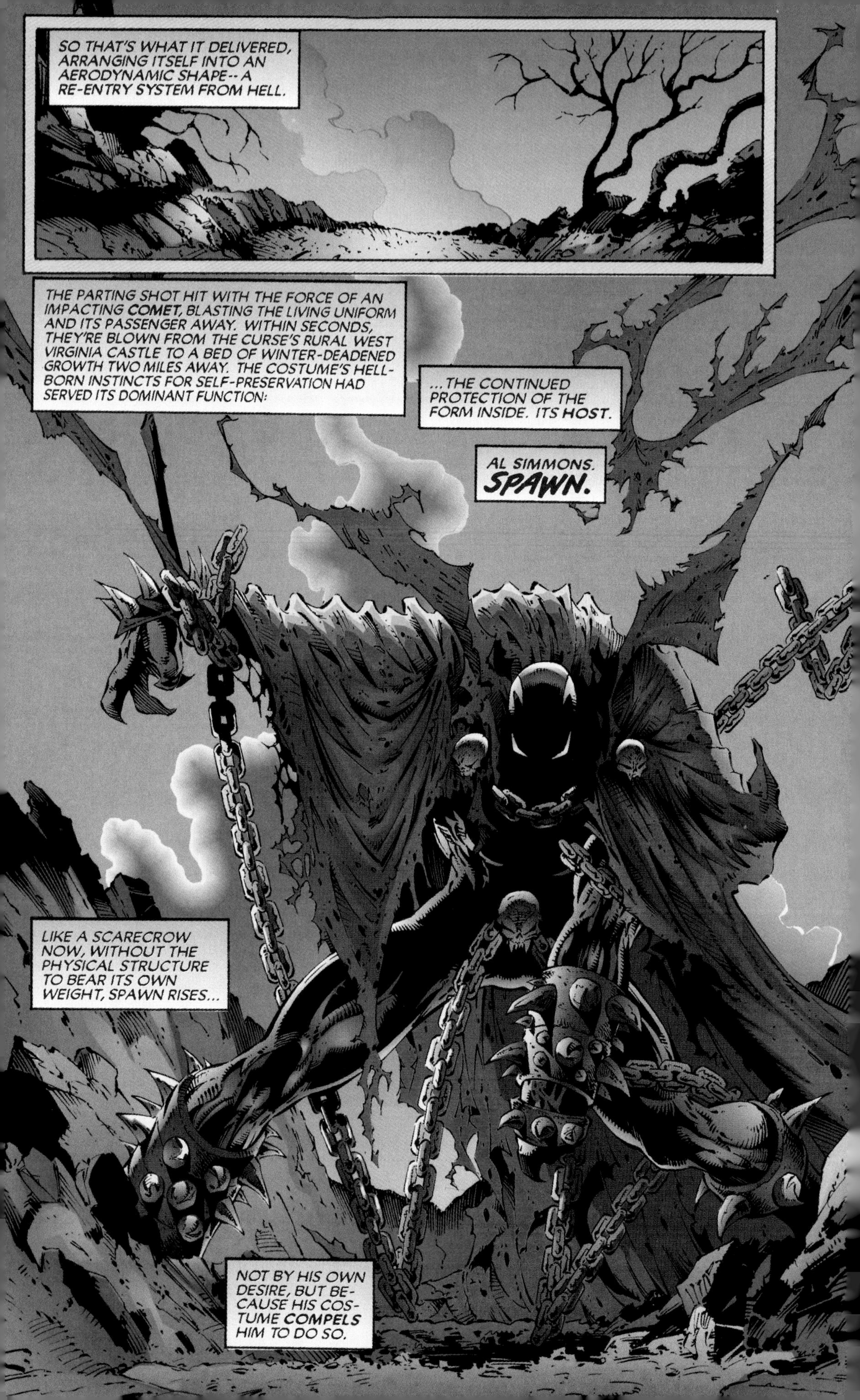
SO THAT'S WHAT IT DELIVERED, ARRANGING ITSELF INTO AN AERODYNAMIC SHAPE-- A RE-ENTRY SYSTEM FROM HELL.
THE PARTING SHOT HIT WITH THE FORCE OF AN IMPACTING COMET, BLASTING THE LIVING UNIFORM AND ITS PASSENGER AWAY. WITHIN SECONDS, THEY'RE BLOWN FROM THE CURSE'S RURAL WEST VIRGINIA CASTLE TO A BED OF WINTER-DEADENED GROWTH TWO MILES AWAY. THE COSTUME'S HELL-BORN INSTINCTS FOR SELF-PRESERVATION HAD SERVED ITS DOMINANT FUNCTION:
...THE CONTINUED PROTECTION OF THE FORM INSIDE. ITS HOST.
AL SIMMONS. SPAWN.
LIKE A SCARECROW NOW, WITHOUT THE PHYSICAL STRUCTURE TO BEAR ITS OWN WEIGHT, SPAWN RISES...
NOT BY HIS OWN DESIRE, BUT BE-CAUSE HIS COS-TUME COMPELS HIM TO DO SO.

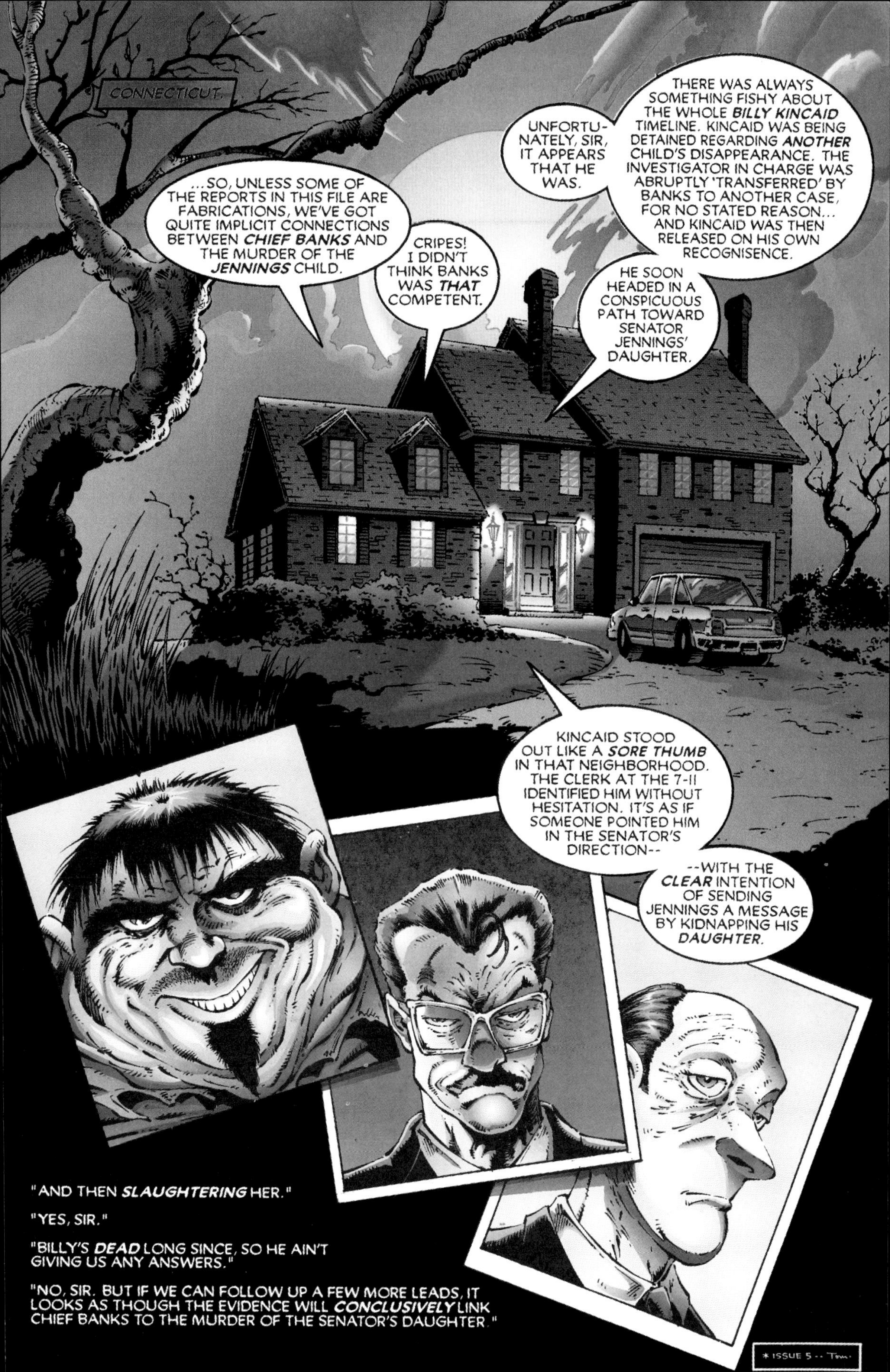
CONNECTICUT.
...SO, UNLESS SOME OF THE REPORTS IN THIS FILE ARE FABRICATIONS, WE'VE GOT QUITE IMPLICIT CONNECTIONS BETWEEN ***CHIEF BANKS*** AND THE MURDER OF THE ***JENNINGS*** CHILD.
CRIPES! I DIDN'T THINK BANKS WAS ***THAT*** COMPETENT.
UNFORTU-NATELY, SIR, IT APPEARS THAT HE WAS.
THERE WAS ALWAYS SOMETHING FISHY ABOUT THE WHOLE ***BILLY KINCAID*** TIMELINE. KINCAID WAS BEING DETAINED REGARDING ***ANOTHER*** CHILD'S DISAPPEARANCE. THE INVESTIGATOR IN CHARGE WAS ABRUPTLY 'TRANSFERRED' BY BANKS TO ANOTHER CASE, FOR NO STATED REASON... AND KINCAID WAS THEN RELEASED ON HIS OWN RECOGNISENCE.
HE SOON HEADED IN A CONSPICUOUS PATH TOWARD SENATOR JENNINGS' DAUGHTER.
KINCAID STOOD OUT LIKE A ***SORE THUMB*** IN THAT NEIGHBORHOOD. THE CLERK AT THE 7-11 IDENTIFIED HIM WITHOUT HESITATION. IT'S AS IF SOMEONE POINTED HIM IN THE SENATOR'S DIRECTION--
--WITH THE ***CLEAR*** INTENTION OF SENDING JENNINGS A MESSAGE BY KIDNAPPING HIS ***DAUGHTER.***
"AND THEN ***SLAUGHTERING*** HER."
"YES, SIR."
"BILLY'S ***DEAD*** LONG SINCE, SO HE AIN'T GIVING US ANY ANSWERS."
"NO, SIR. BUT IF WE CAN FOLLOW UP A FEW MORE LEADS, IT LOOKS AS THOUGH THE EVIDENCE WILL ***CONCLUSIVELY*** LINK CHIEF BANKS TO THE MURDER OF THE SENATOR'S DAUGHTER."
* ISSUE 5 -- Tom.

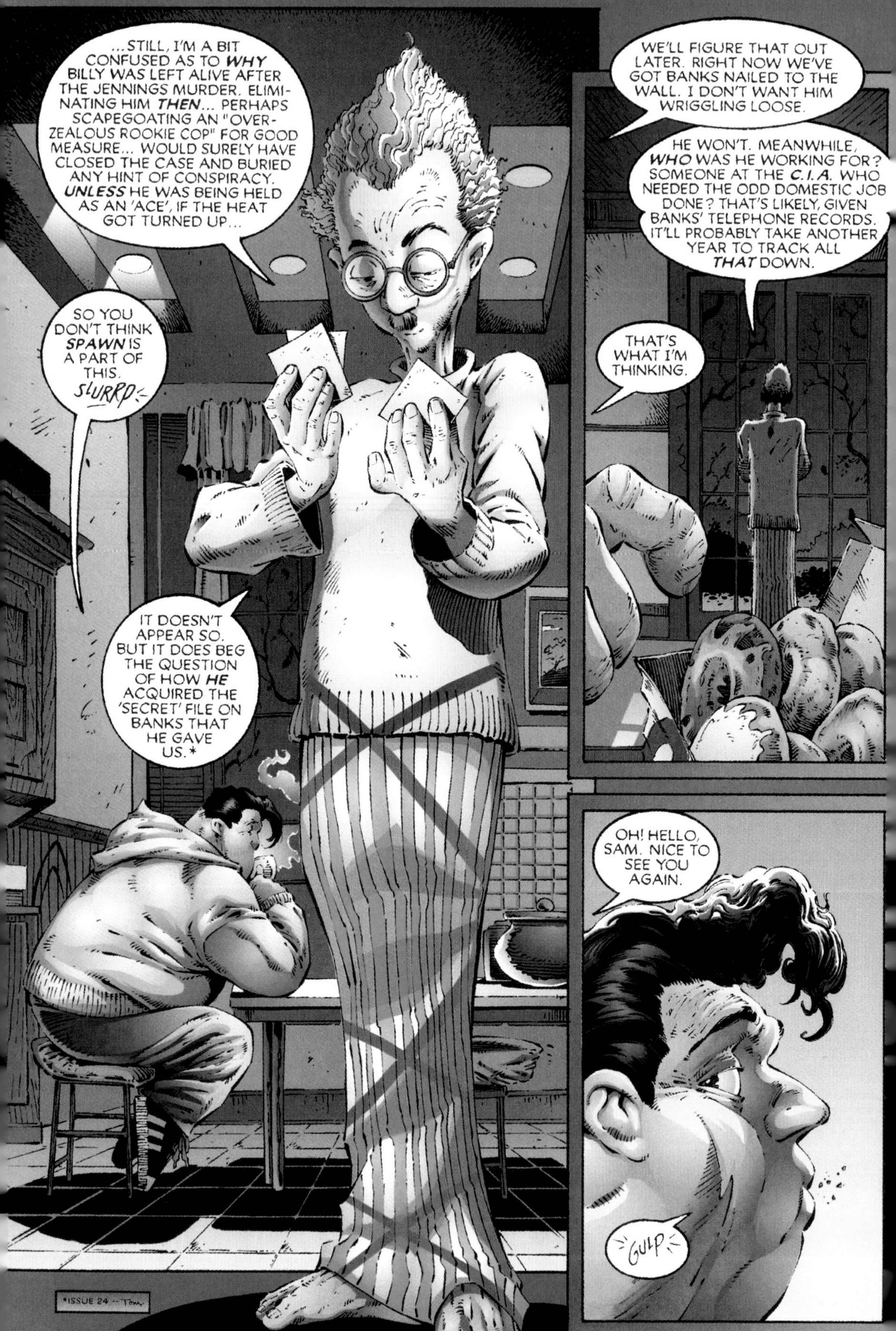
...STILL, I'M A BIT CONFUSED AS TO WHY BILLY WAS LEFT ALIVE AFTER THE JENNINGS MURDER. ELIMINATING HIM THEN... PERHAPS SCAPEGOATING AN "OVER-ZEALOUS ROOKIE COP" FOR GOOD MEASURE... WOULD SURELY HAVE CLOSED THE CASE AND BURIED ANY HINT OF CONSPIRACY. UNLESS HE WAS BEING HELD AS AN 'ACE', IF THE HEAT GOT TURNED UP...
SO YOU DON'T THINK SPAWN IS A PART OF THIS.
SLURRP
IT DOESN'T APPEAR SO. BUT IT DOES BEG THE QUESTION OF HOW HE ACQUIRED THE 'SECRET' FILE ON BANKS THAT HE GAVE US.*
*ISSUE 24 -- Tom.
WE'LL FIGURE THAT OUT LATER. RIGHT NOW WE'VE GOT BANKS NAILED TO THE WALL. I DON'T WANT HIM WRIGGLING LOOSE.
HE WON'T. MEANWHILE, WHO WAS HE WORKING FOR? SOMEONE AT THE C.I.A. WHO NEEDED THE ODD DOMESTIC JOB DONE? THAT'S LIKELY, GIVEN BANKS' TELEPHONE RECORDS. IT'LL PROBABLY TAKE ANOTHER YEAR TO TRACK ALL THAT DOWN.
THAT'S WHAT I'M THINKING.
OH! HELLO, SAM. NICE TO SEE YOU AGAIN.
GULP

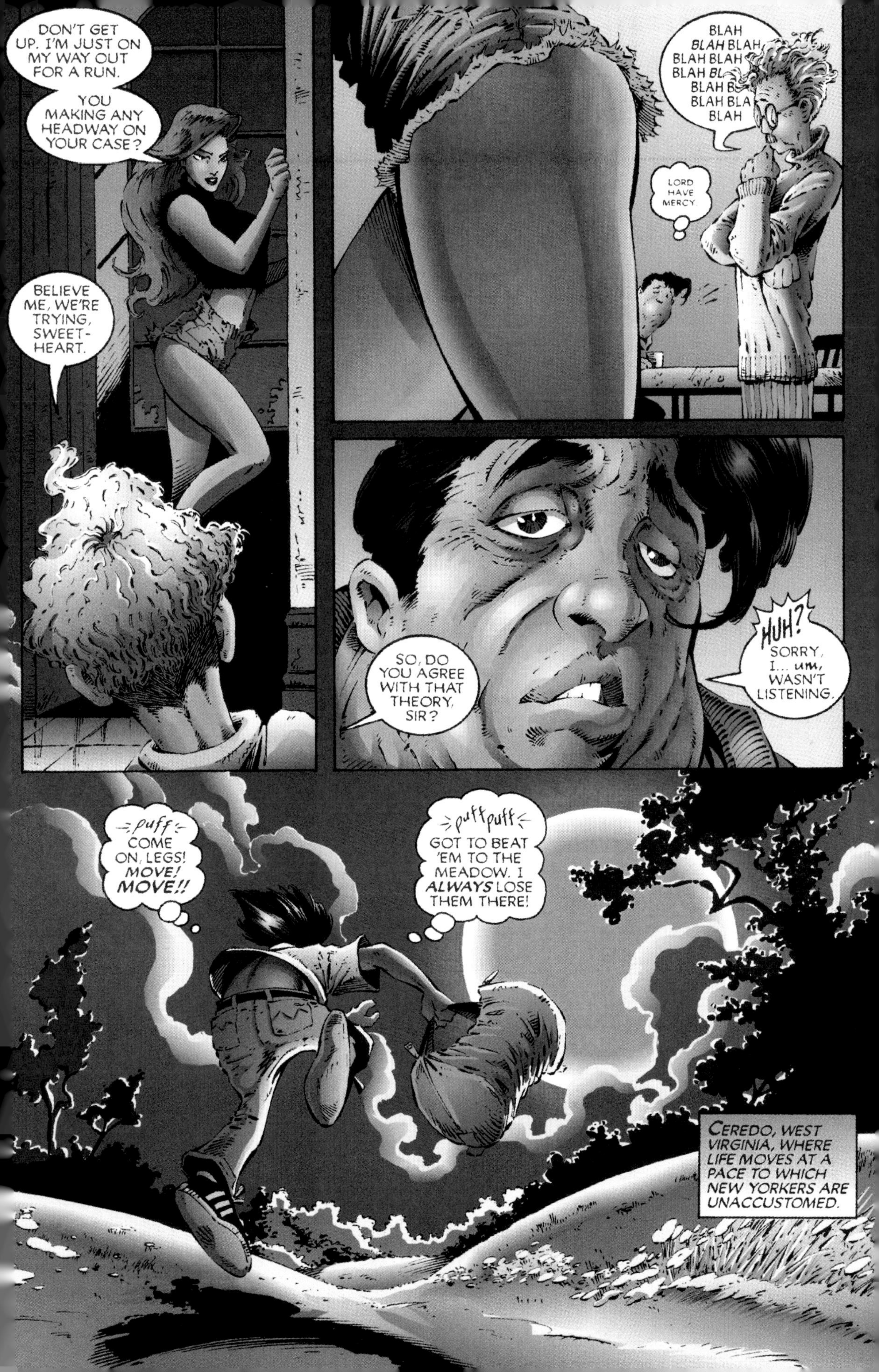
DON'T GET UP. I'M JUST ON MY WAY OUT FOR A RUN.
YOU MAKING ANY HEADWAY ON YOUR CASE?
BELIEVE ME, WE'RE TRYING, SWEET-HEART.
BLAH BLAH BLAH BLAH BLAH BLAH BL BLAH B BLAH BLA BLAH
LORD HAVE MERCY.
SO, DO YOU AGREE WITH THAT THEORY, SIR?
HUH?
SORRY, I... um, WASN'T LISTENING.
puff
COME ON, LEGS! MOVE! MOVE!!
puff puff
GOT TO BEAT 'EM TO THE MEADOW. I ALWAYS LOSE THEM THERE!
CEREDO, WEST VIRGINIA, WHERE LIFE MOVES AT A PACE TO WHICH NEW YORKERS ARE UNACCUSTOMED.

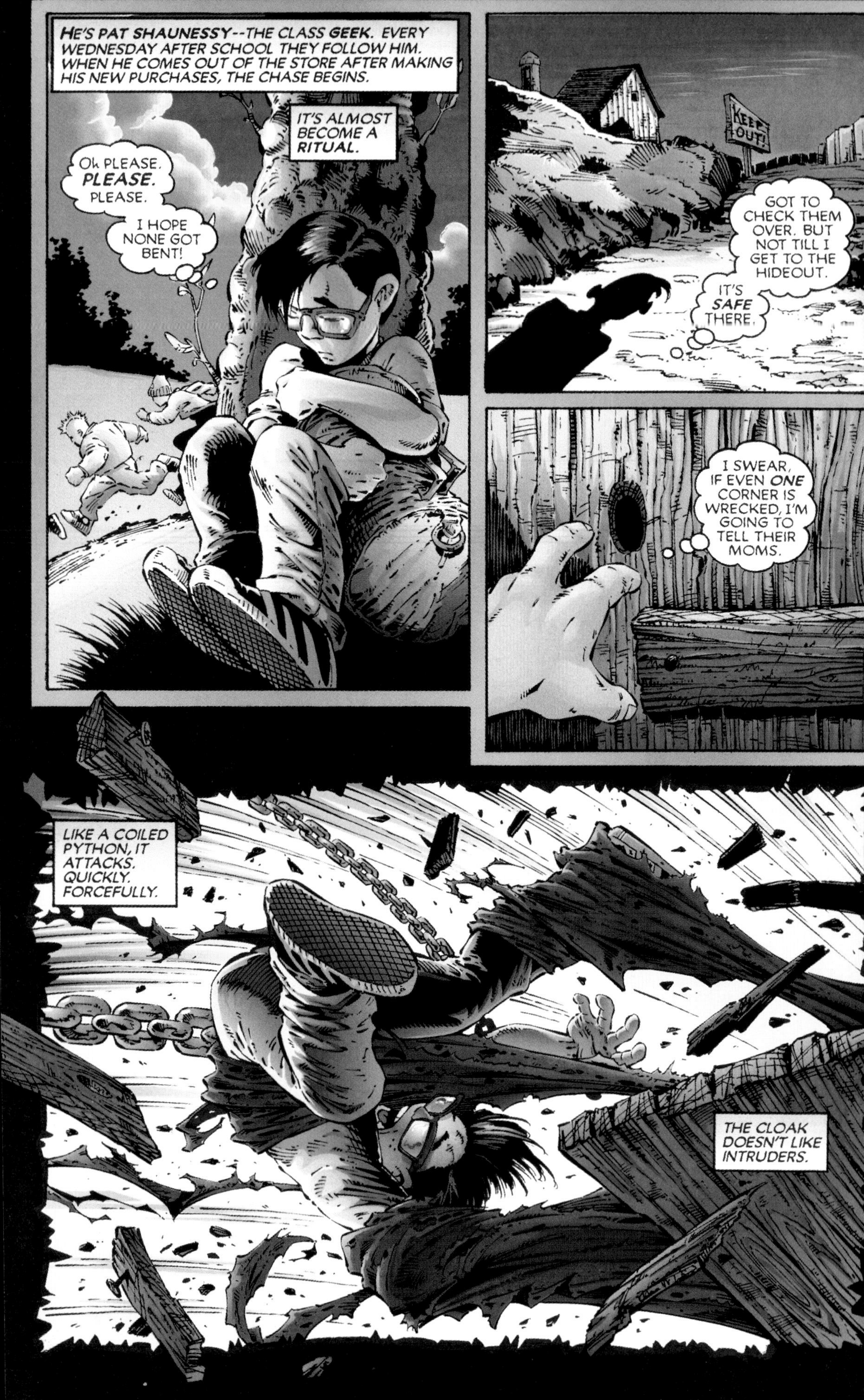

HE'S PAT SHAUNESSY--THE CLASS GEEK. EVERY WEDNESDAY AFTER SCHOOL THEY FOLLOW HIM. WHEN HE COMES OUT OF THE STORE AFTER MAKING HIS NEW PURCHASES, THE CHASE BEGINS.
IT'S ALMOST BECOME A RITUAL.
Oh PLEASE. PLEASE. PLEASE.
I HOPE NONE GOT BENT!
KEEP OUT!
GOT TO CHECK THEM OVER. BUT NOT TILL I GET TO THE HIDEOUT.
IT'S SAFE THERE.
I SWEAR, IF EVEN ONE CORNER IS WRECKED, I'M GOING TO TELL THEIR MOMS.
LIKE A COILED PYTHON, IT ATTACKS. QUICKLY. FORCEFULLY.
THE CLOAK DOESN'T LIKE INTRUDERS.

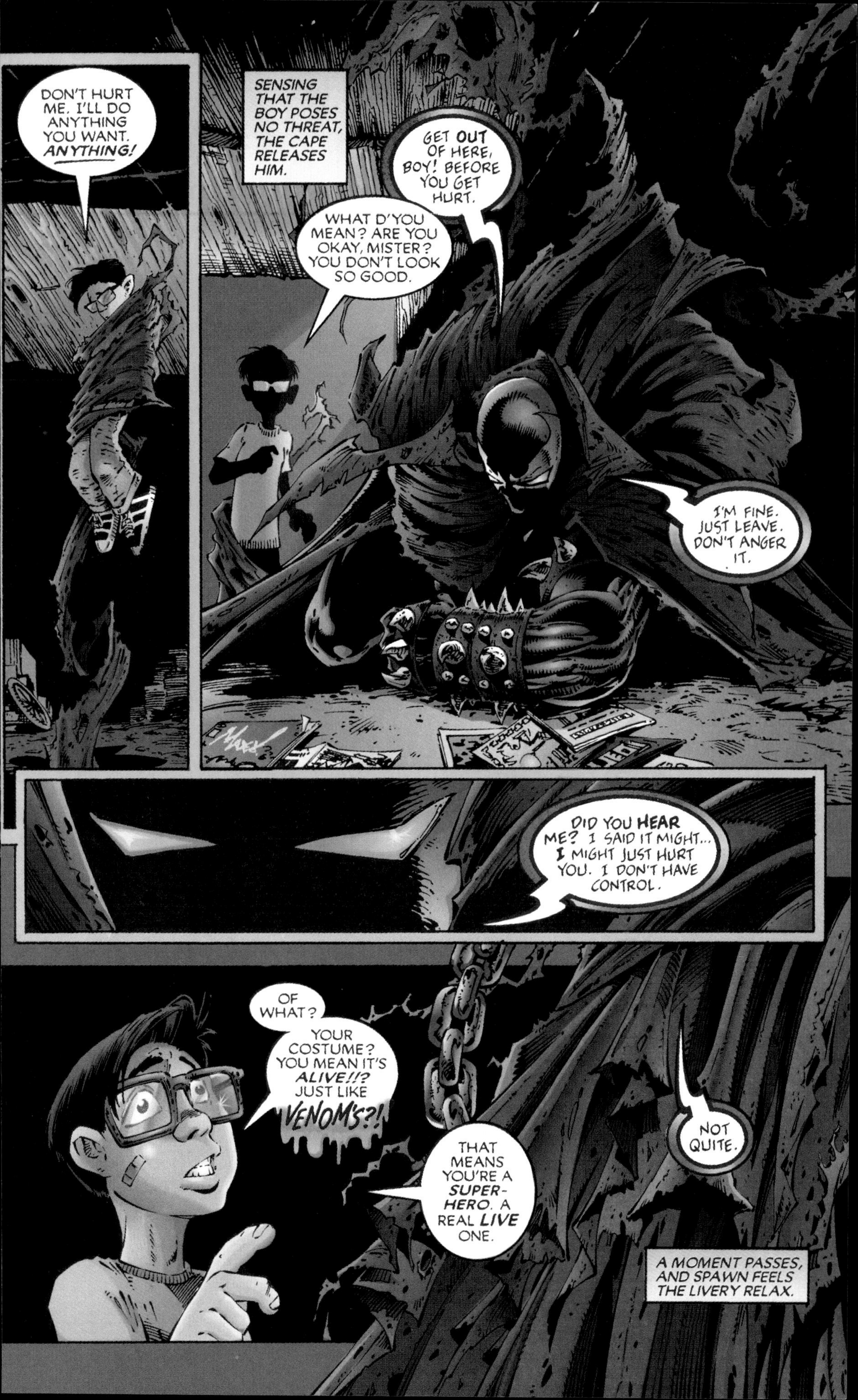
DON'T HURT ME. I'LL DO ANYTHING YOU WANT. ANYTHING!
SENSING THAT THE BOY POSES NO THREAT, THE CAPE RELEASES HIM.
GET OUT OF HERE, BOY! BEFORE YOU GET HURT.
WHAT D'YOU MEAN? ARE YOU OKAY, MISTER? YOU DON'T LOOK SO GOOD.
I'M FINE. JUST LEAVE. DON'T ANGER IT.
DID YOU HEAR ME? I SAID IT MIGHT... I MIGHT JUST HURT YOU. I DON'T HAVE CONTROL.
OF WHAT?
YOUR COSTUME? YOU MEAN IT'S ALIVE!!? JUST LIKE VENOM'S?!
THAT MEANS YOU'RE A SUPER-HERO. A REAL LIVE ONE.
NOT QUITE.
A MOMENT PASSES, AND SPAWN FEELS THE LIVERY RELAX.

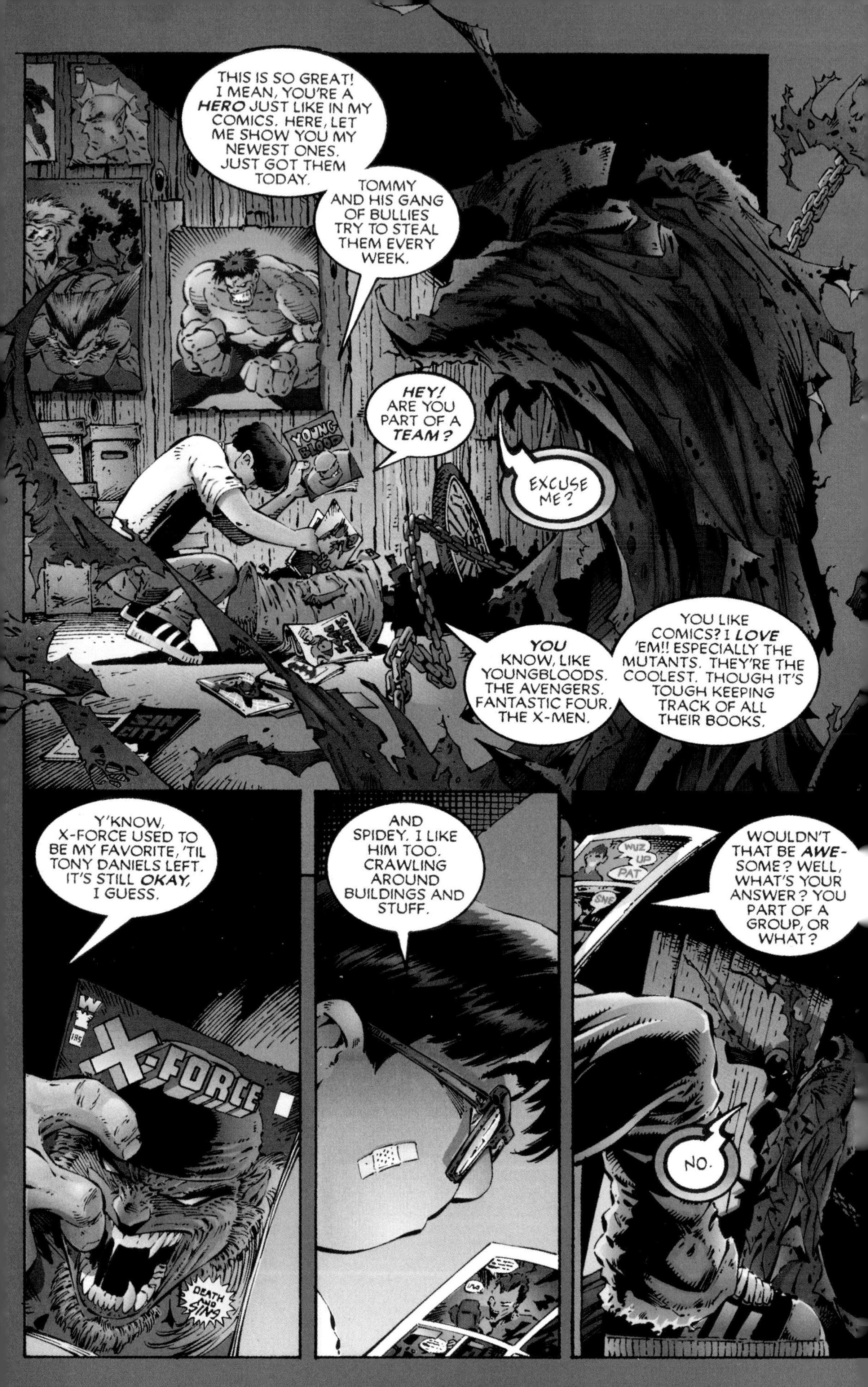
THIS IS SO GREAT! I MEAN, YOU'RE A **HERO** JUST LIKE IN MY COMICS. HERE, LET ME SHOW YOU MY NEWEST ONES. JUST GOT THEM TODAY.
TOMMY AND HIS GANG OF BULLIES TRY TO STEAL THEM EVERY WEEK.
YOUNG BLOOD
HEY! ARE YOU PART OF A ***TEAM?***
EXCUSE ME?
YOU KNOW, LIKE YOUNGBLOODS. THE AVENGERS. FANTASTIC FOUR. THE X-MEN.
YOU LIKE COMICS? I ***LOVE*** 'EM!! ESPECIALLY THE MUTANTS. THEY'RE THE COOLEST. THOUGH IT'S TOUGH KEEPING TRACK OF ALL THEIR BOOKS.
SIN CITY
Y'KNOW, X-FORCE USED TO BE MY FAVORITE, 'TIL TONY DANIELS LEFT. IT'S STILL ***OKAY,*** I GUESS.
X-FORCE
DEATH AND SINS
AND SPIDEY. I LIKE HIM TOO. CRAWLING AROUND BUILDINGS AND STUFF.
WUZ UP PAT
WOULDN'T THAT BE ***AWE***-SOME? WELL, WHAT'S YOUR ANSWER? YOU PART OF A GROUP, OR WHAT?
NO.

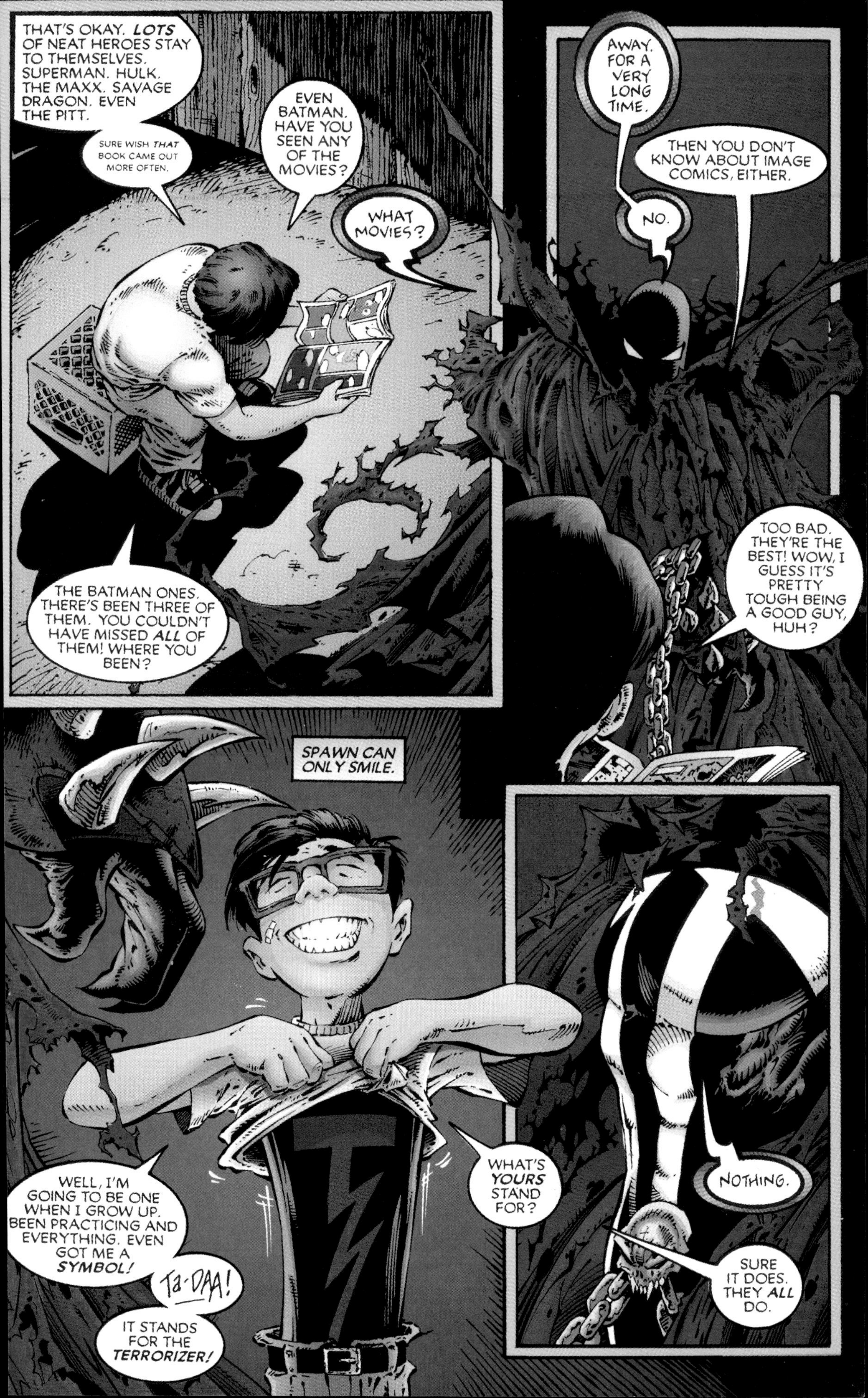
THAT'S OKAY. LOTS OF NEAT HEROES STAY TO THEMSELVES. SUPERMAN. HULK. THE MAXX. SAVAGE DRAGON. EVEN THE PITT.
SURE WISH THAT BOOK CAME OUT MORE OFTEN.
EVEN BATMAN. HAVE YOU SEEN ANY OF THE MOVIES?
WHAT MOVIES?
THE BATMAN ONES. THERE'S BEEN THREE OF THEM. YOU COULDN'T HAVE MISSED ALL OF THEM! WHERE YOU BEEN?
AWAY. FOR A VERY LONG TIME.
THEN YOU DON'T KNOW ABOUT IMAGE COMICS, EITHER.
NO.
TOO BAD. THEY'RE THE BEST! WOW, I GUESS IT'S PRETTY TOUGH BEING A GOOD GUY, HUH?
SPAWN CAN ONLY SMILE.
WELL, I'M GOING TO BE ONE WHEN I GROW UP. BEEN PRACTICING AND EVERYTHING. EVEN GOT ME A SYMBOL!
TA-DAA!
IT STANDS FOR THE TERRORIZER!
WHAT'S YOURS STAND FOR?
NOTHING.
SURE IT DOES. THEY ALL DO.

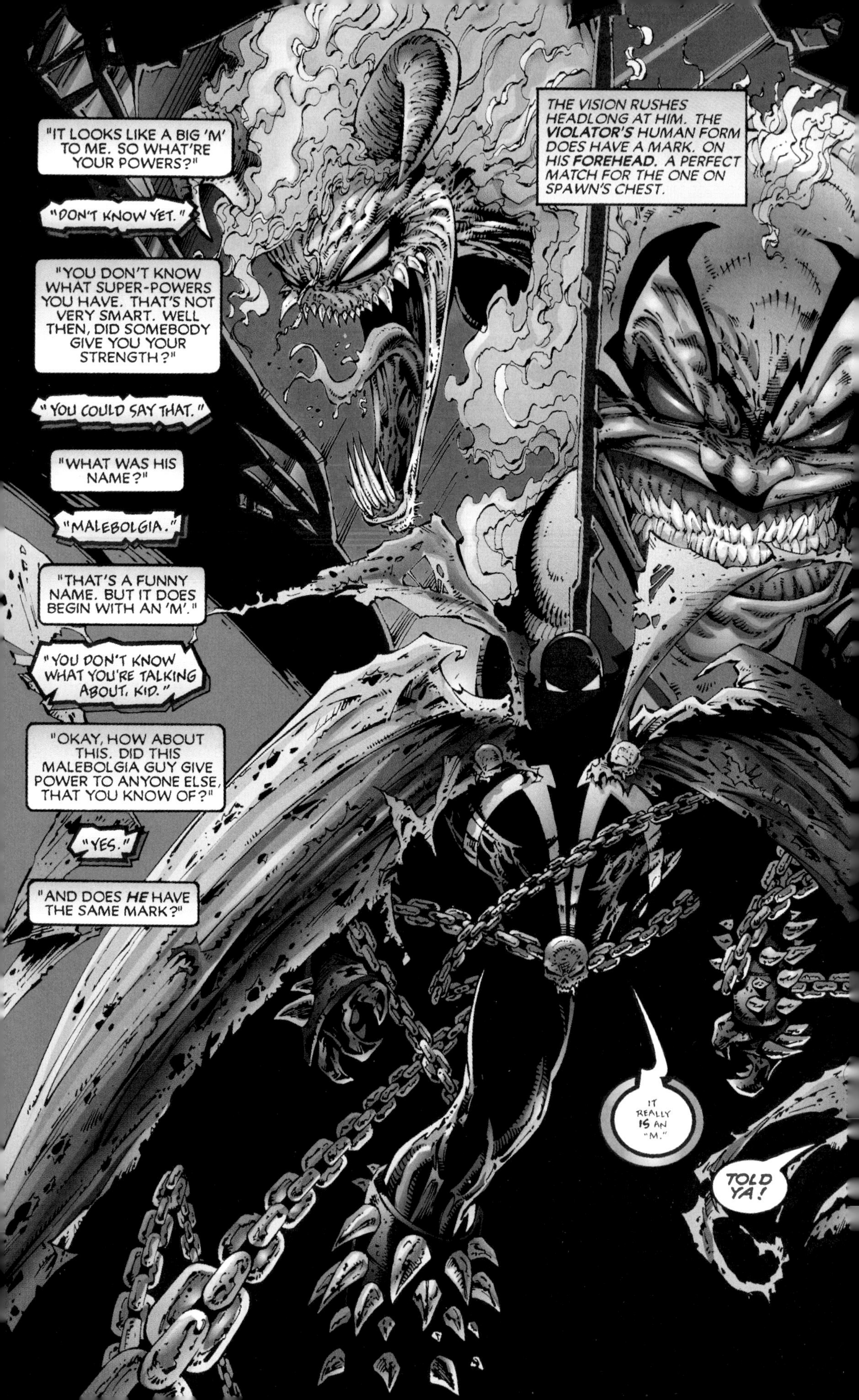
"IT LOOKS LIKE A BIG 'M' TO ME. SO WHAT'RE YOUR POWERS?"
"DON'T KNOW YET."
"YOU DON'T KNOW WHAT SUPER-POWERS YOU HAVE. THAT'S NOT VERY SMART. WELL THEN, DID SOMEBODY GIVE YOU YOUR STRENGTH?"
"YOU COULD SAY THAT."
"WHAT WAS HIS NAME?"
"MALEBOLGIA."
"THAT'S A FUNNY NAME. BUT IT DOES BEGIN WITH AN 'M'."
"YOU DON'T KNOW WHAT YOU'RE TALKING ABOUT, KID."
"OKAY, HOW ABOUT THIS. DID THIS MALEBOLGIA GUY GIVE POWER TO ANYONE ELSE, THAT YOU KNOW OF?"
"YES."
"AND DOES HE HAVE THE SAME MARK?"
THE VISION RUSHES HEADLONG AT HIM. THE VIOLATOR'S HUMAN FORM DOES HAVE A MARK. ON HIS FOREHEAD. A PERFECT MATCH FOR THE ONE ON SPAWN'S CHEST.
IT REALLY IS AN "M."
TOLD YA!

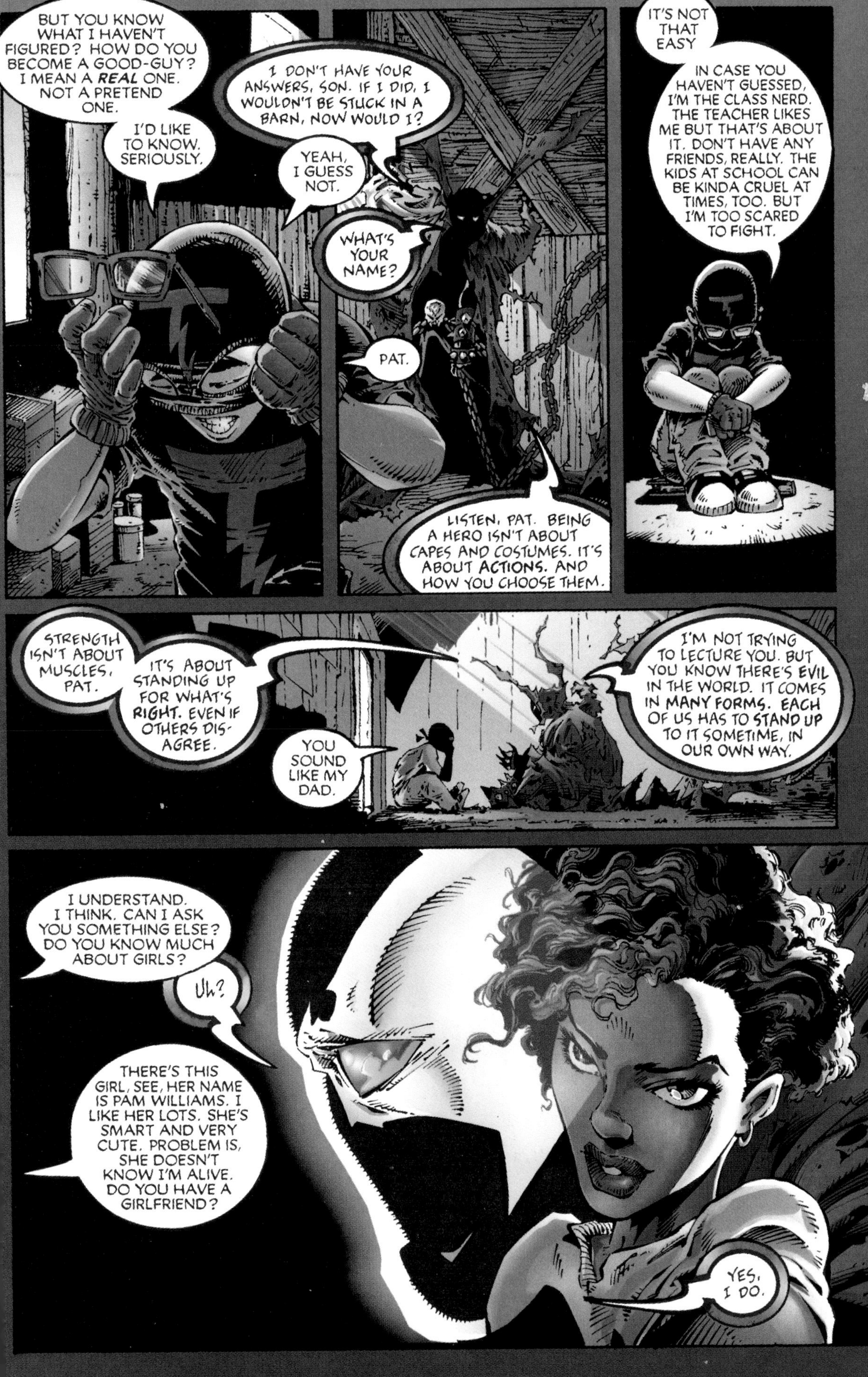
BUT YOU KNOW WHAT I HAVEN'T FIGURED? HOW DO YOU BECOME A GOOD-GUY? I MEAN A **REAL** ONE. NOT A PRETEND ONE.
I'D LIKE TO KNOW. SERIOUSLY.
I DON'T HAVE YOUR ANSWERS, SON. IF I DID, I WOULDN'T BE STUCK IN A BARN, NOW WOULD I?
YEAH, I GUESS NOT.
WHAT'S YOUR NAME?
PAT.
LISTEN, PAT. BEING A HERO ISN'T ABOUT CAPES AND COSTUMES. IT'S ABOUT **ACTIONS.** AND HOW YOU CHOOSE THEM.
IT'S NOT THAT EASY
IN CASE YOU HAVEN'T GUESSED, I'M THE CLASS NERD. THE TEACHER LIKES ME BUT THAT'S ABOUT IT. DON'T HAVE ANY FRIENDS, REALLY. THE KIDS AT SCHOOL CAN BE KINDA CRUEL AT TIMES, TOO. BUT I'M TOO SCARED TO FIGHT.
STRENGTH ISN'T ABOUT MUSCLES, PAT.
IT'S ABOUT STANDING UP FOR WHAT'S **RIGHT.** EVEN IF OTHERS DIS-AGREE.
YOU SOUND LIKE MY DAD.
I'M NOT TRYING TO LECTURE YOU. BUT YOU KNOW THERE'S **EVIL** IN THE WORLD. IT COMES IN **MANY FORMS. EACH** OF US HAS TO **STAND UP** TO IT SOMETIME, IN OUR OWN WAY.
I UNDERSTAND. I THINK. CAN I ASK YOU SOMETHING ELSE? DO YOU KNOW MUCH ABOUT GIRLS?
Uh?
THERE'S THIS GIRL, SEE, HER NAME IS PAM WILLIAMS. I LIKE HER LOTS. SHE'S SMART AND VERY CUTE. PROBLEM IS, SHE DOESN'T KNOW I'M ALIVE. DO YOU HAVE A GIRLFRIEND?
YES, I DO.

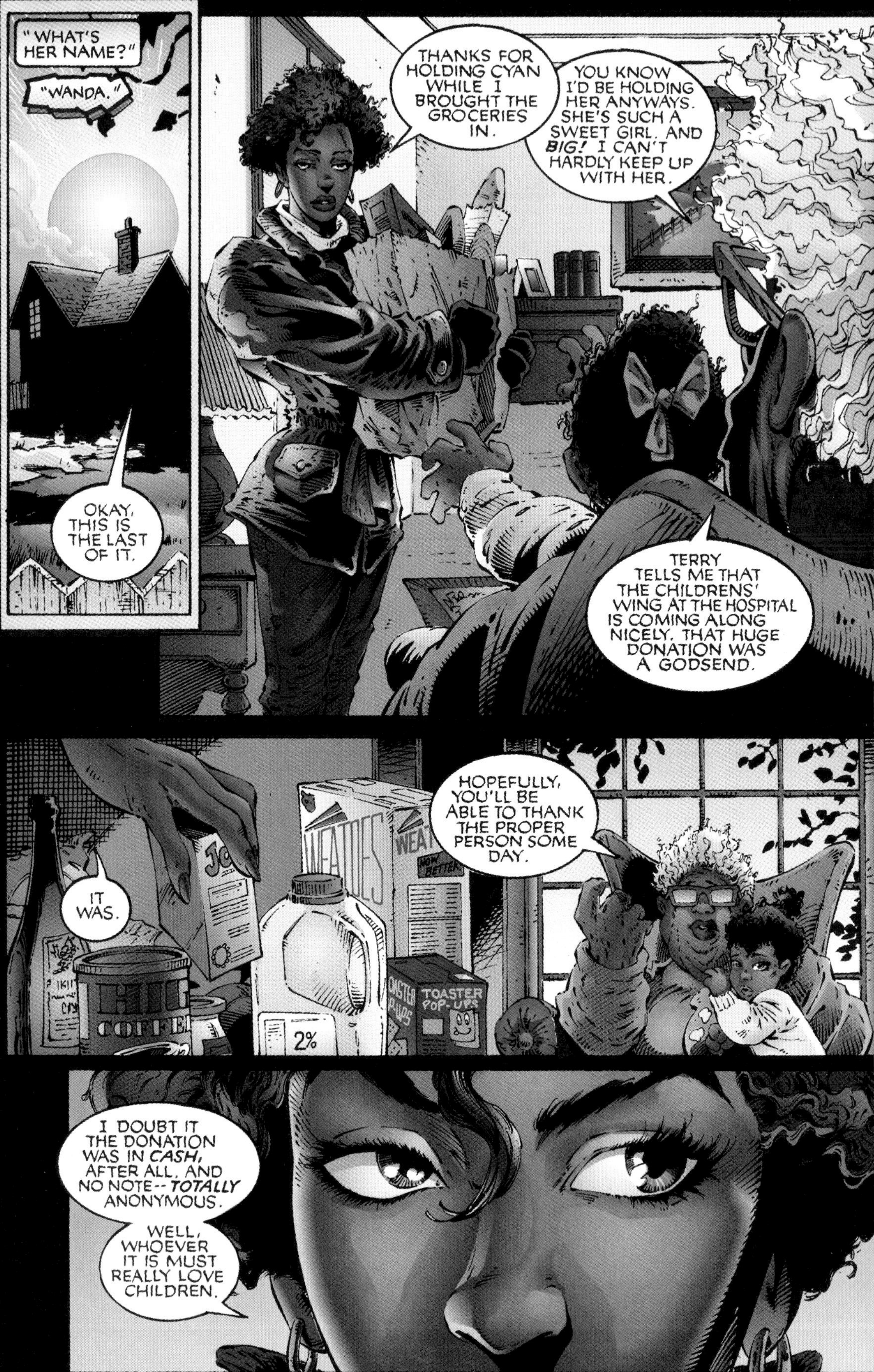

"WHAT'S HER NAME?"
"WANDA."
OKAY, THIS IS THE LAST OF IT.
THANKS FOR HOLDING CYAN WHILE I BROUGHT THE GROCERIES IN.
YOU KNOW I'D BE HOLDING HER ANYWAYS. SHE'S SUCH A SWEET GIRL. AND BIG! I CAN'T HARDLY KEEP UP WITH HER.
TERRY TELLS ME THAT THE CHILDRENS' WING AT THE HOSPITAL IS COMING ALONG NICELY. THAT HUGE DONATION WAS A GODSEND.
IT WAS.
WEATOES
NOW BETTER
2%
COFFEE
TOASTER POP-UPS
HOPEFULLY, YOU'LL BE ABLE TO THANK THE PROPER PERSON SOME DAY.
I DOUBT IT THE DONATION WAS IN CASH, AFTER ALL, AND NO NOTE-- TOTALLY ANONYMOUS.
WELL, WHOEVER IT IS MUST REALLY LOVE CHILDREN.

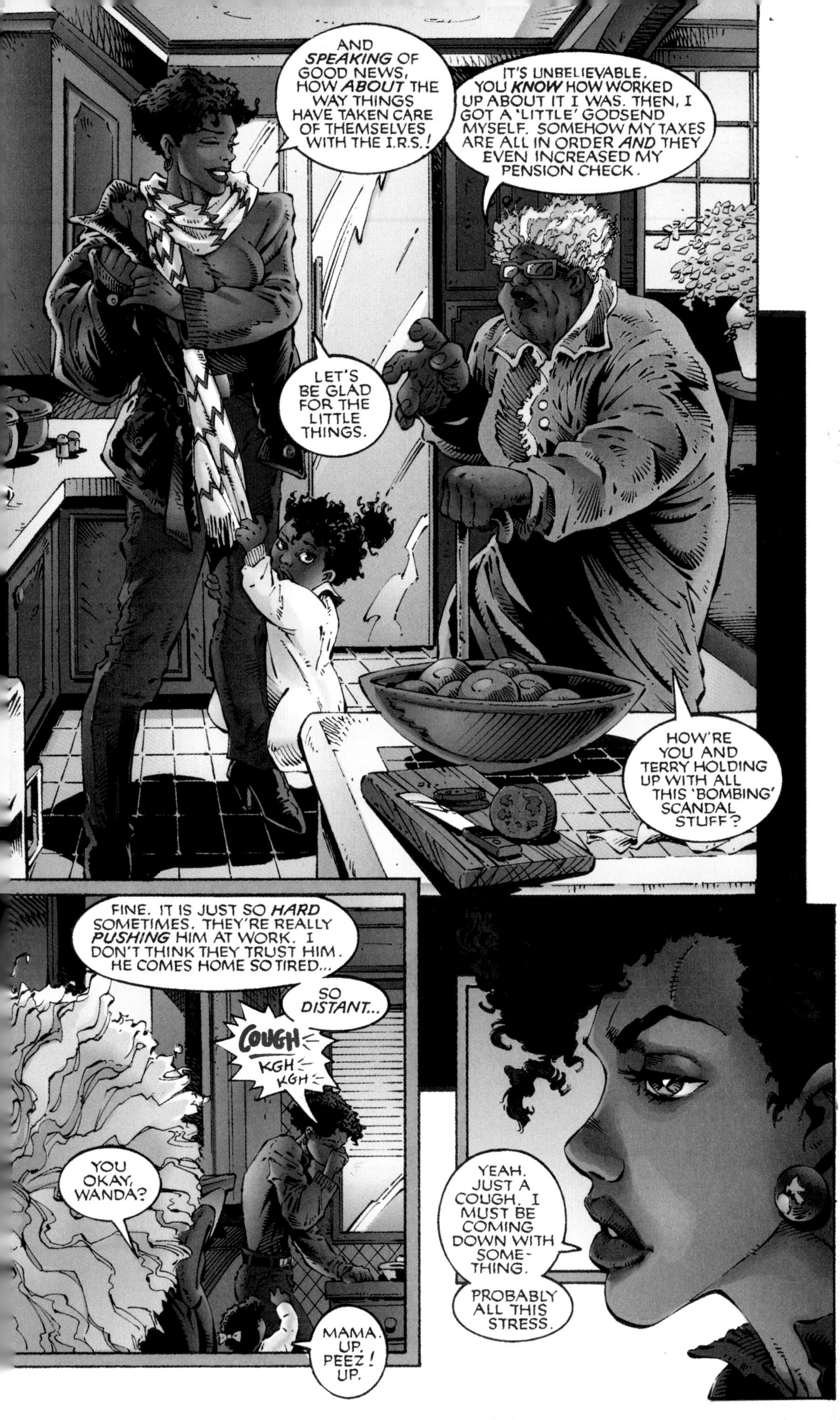
AND SPEAKING OF GOOD NEWS, HOW ABOUT THE WAY THINGS HAVE TAKEN CARE OF THEMSELVES WITH THE I.R.S.!
IT'S UNBELIEVABLE. YOU KNOW HOW WORKED UP ABOUT IT I WAS. THEN, I GOT A 'LITTLE' GODSEND MYSELF. SOMEHOW MY TAXES ARE ALL IN ORDER AND THEY EVEN INCREASED MY PENSION CHECK.
LET'S BE GLAD FOR THE LITTLE THINGS.
HOW'RE YOU AND TERRY HOLDING UP WITH ALL THIS 'BOMBING' SCANDAL STUFF?
FINE. IT IS JUST SO HARD SOMETIMES. THEY'RE REALLY PUSHING HIM AT WORK. I DON'T THINK THEY TRUST HIM. HE COMES HOME SO TIRED...
SO DISTANT...
COUGH
KGH
KGH
YOU OKAY, WANDA?
MAMA. UP. PEEZ! UP.
YEAH. JUST A COUGH. I MUST BE COMING DOWN WITH SOME-THING.
PROBABLY ALL THIS STRESS.

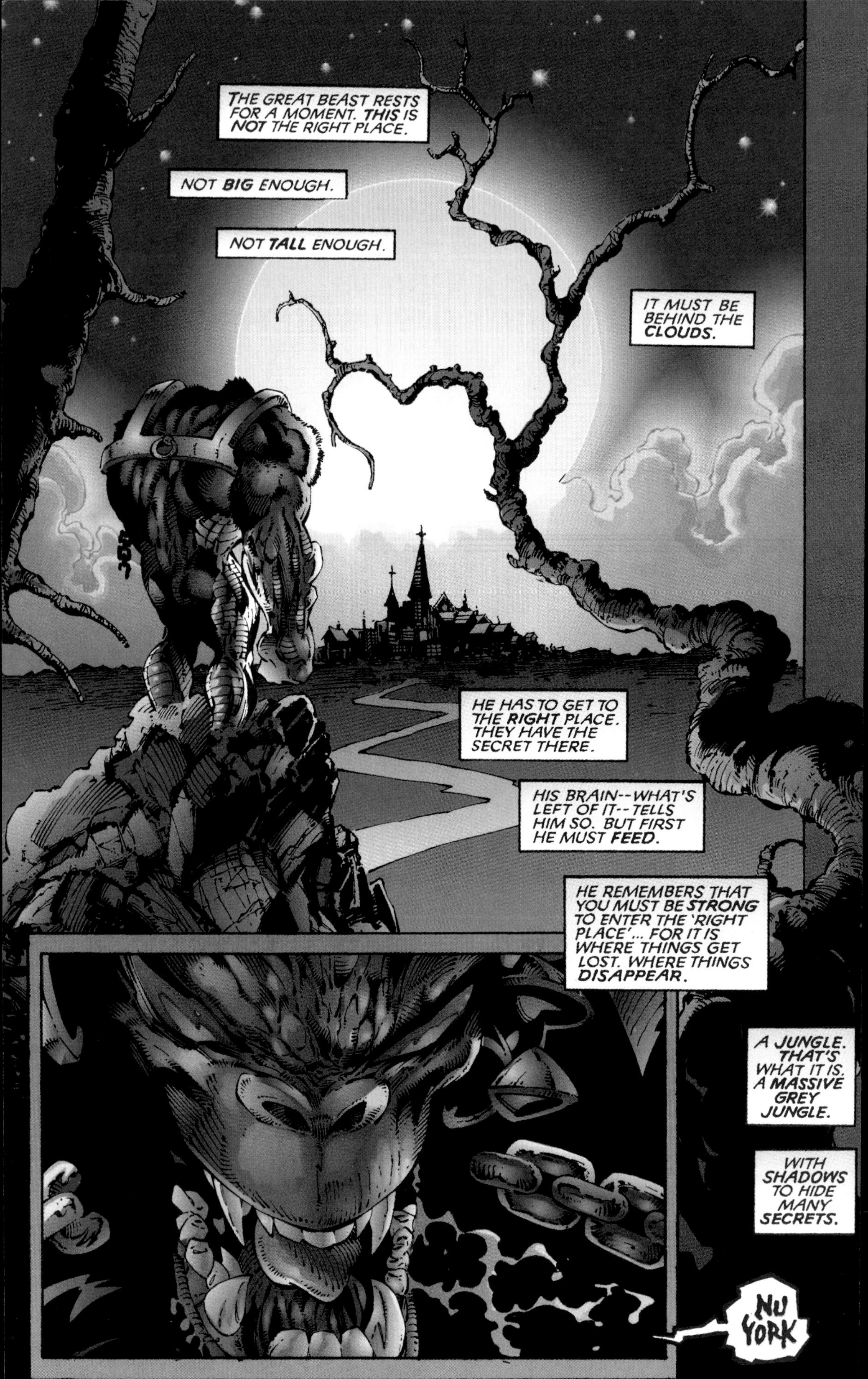
THE GREAT BEAST RESTS FOR A MOMENT. THIS IS NOT THE RIGHT PLACE.
NOT BIG ENOUGH.
NOT TALL ENOUGH.
IT MUST BE BEHIND THE CLOUDS.
HE HAS TO GET TO THE RIGHT PLACE. THEY HAVE THE SECRET THERE.
HIS BRAIN--WHAT'S LEFT OF IT--TELLS HIM SO. BUT FIRST HE MUST FEED.
HE REMEMBERS THAT YOU MUST BE STRONG TO ENTER THE 'RIGHT PLACE'... FOR IT IS WHERE THINGS GET LOST. WHERE THINGS DISAPPEAR.
A JUNGLE. THAT'S WHAT IT IS. A MASSIVE GREY JUNGLE.
WITH SHADOWS TO HIDE MANY SECRETS.
NU YORK

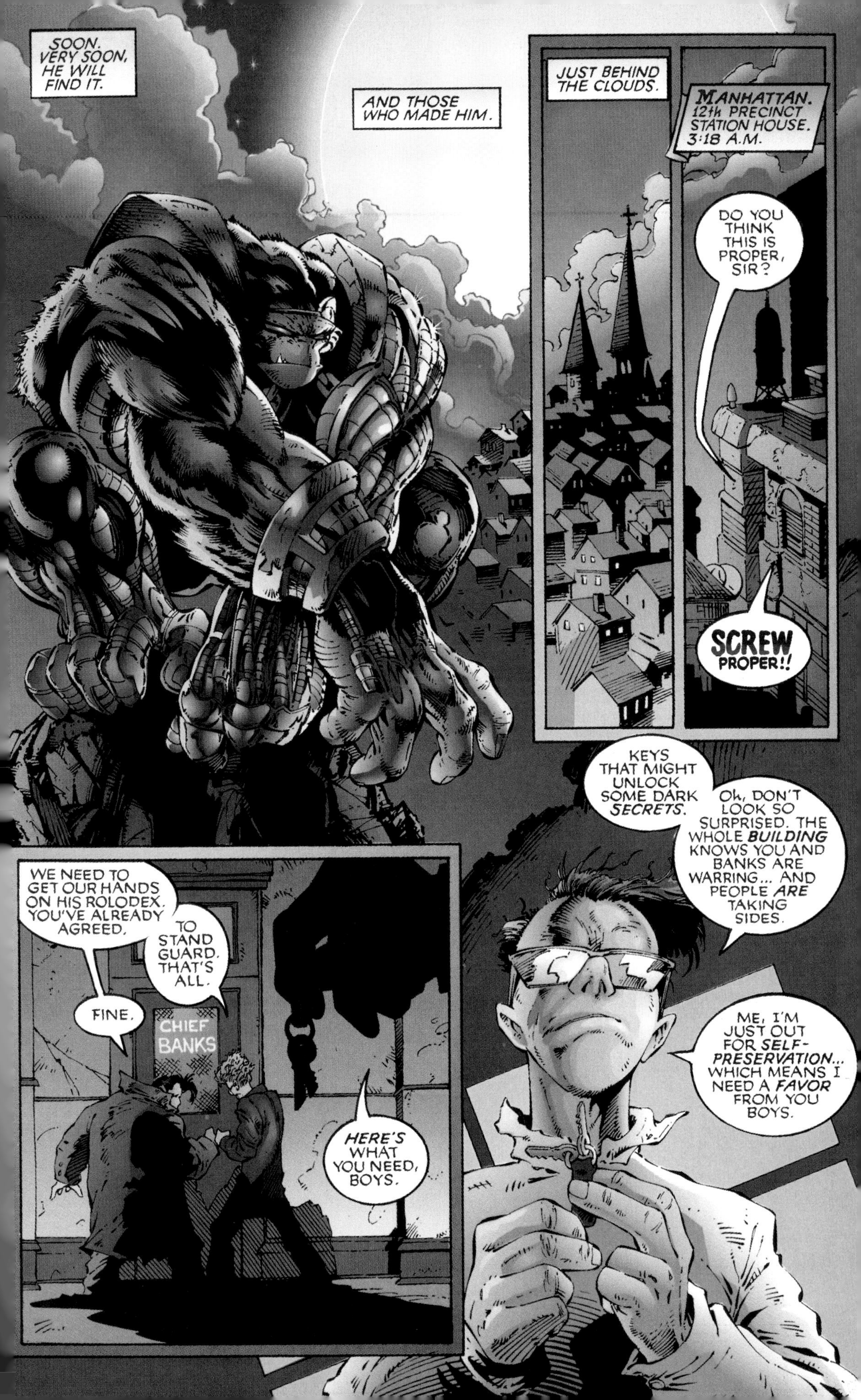
SOON. VERY SOON, HE WILL FIND IT.
AND THOSE WHO MADE HIM.
JUST BEHIND THE CLOUDS.
MANHATTAN. 12th PRECINCT STATION HOUSE. 3:18 A.M.
DO YOU THINK THIS IS PROPER, SIR?
SCREW PROPER!!
WE NEED TO GET OUR HANDS ON HIS ROLODEX. YOU'VE ALREADY AGREED.
TO STAND GUARD. THAT'S ALL.
FINE.
CHIEF BANKS
HERE'S WHAT YOU NEED, BOYS.
KEYS THAT MIGHT UNLOCK SOME DARK SECRETS.
Oh, DON'T LOOK SO SURPRISED. THE WHOLE BUILDING KNOWS YOU AND BANKS ARE WARRING... AND PEOPLE ARE TAKING SIDES.
ME, I'M JUST OUT FOR SELF-PRESERVATION... WHICH MEANS I NEED A FAVOR FROM YOU BOYS.

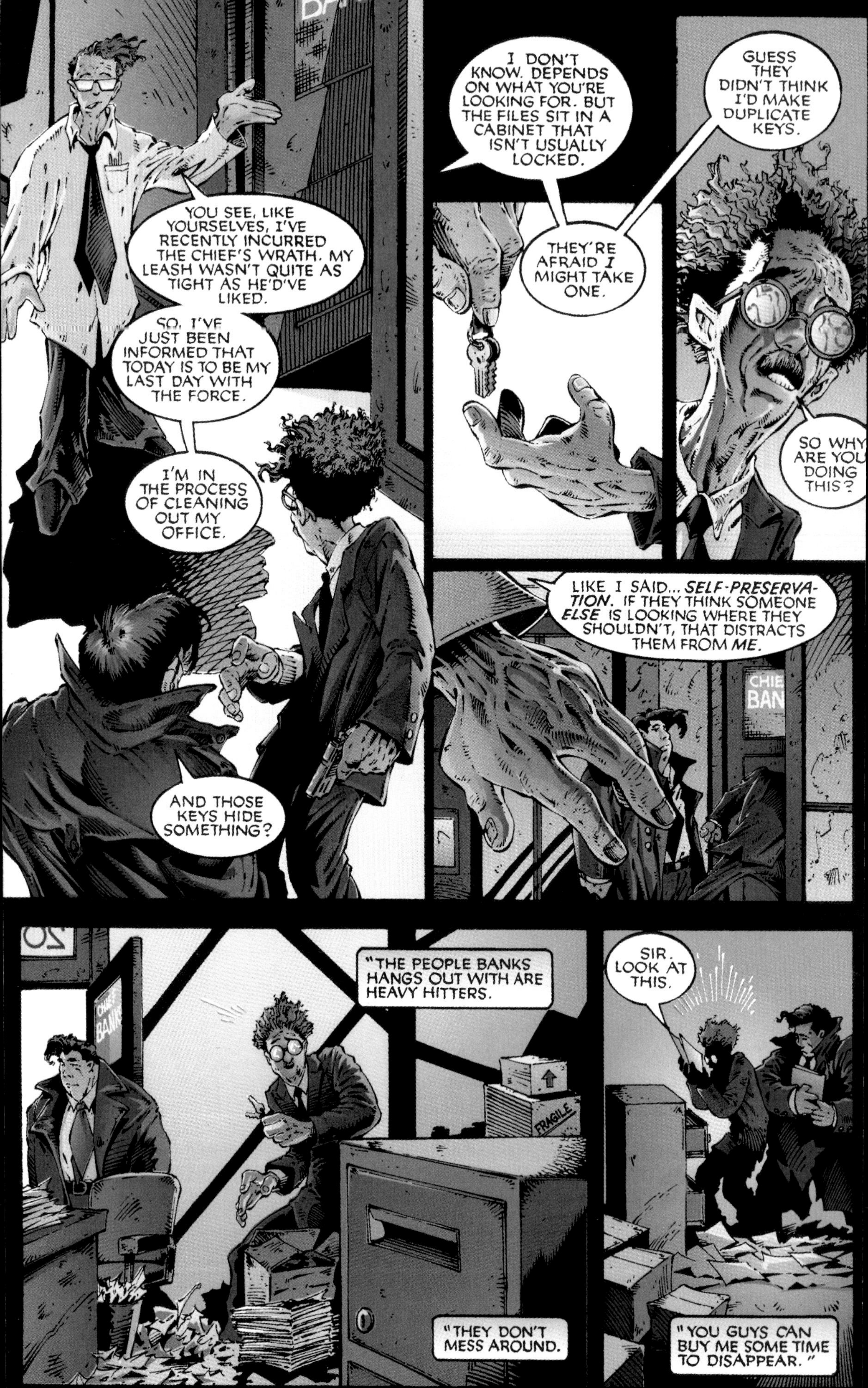
YOU SEE, LIKE YOURSELVES, I'VE RECENTLY INCURRED THE CHIEF'S WRATH. MY LEASH WASN'T QUITE AS TIGHT AS HE'D'VE LIKED.
SO, I'VE JUST BEEN INFORMED THAT TODAY IS TO BE MY LAST DAY WITH THE FORCE.
I'M IN THE PROCESS OF CLEANING OUT MY OFFICE.
AND THOSE KEYS HIDE SOMETHING?
I DON'T KNOW. DEPENDS ON WHAT YOU'RE LOOKING FOR. BUT THE FILES SIT IN A CABINET THAT ISN'T USUALLY LOCKED.
THEY'RE AFRAID *I* MIGHT TAKE ONE.
GUESS THEY DIDN'T THINK I'D MAKE DUPLICATE KEYS.
SO WHY ARE YOU DOING THIS?
LIKE I SAID... *SELF-PRESERVATION*. IF THEY THINK SOMEONE *ELSE* IS LOOKING WHERE THEY SHOULDN'T, THAT DISTRACTS THEM FROM *ME*.
"THE PEOPLE BANKS HANGS OUT WITH ARE HEAVY HITTERS.
FRAGILE
"THEY DON'T MESS AROUND.
SIR. LOOK AT THIS.
"YOU GUYS CAN BUY ME SOME TIME TO DISAPPEAR."

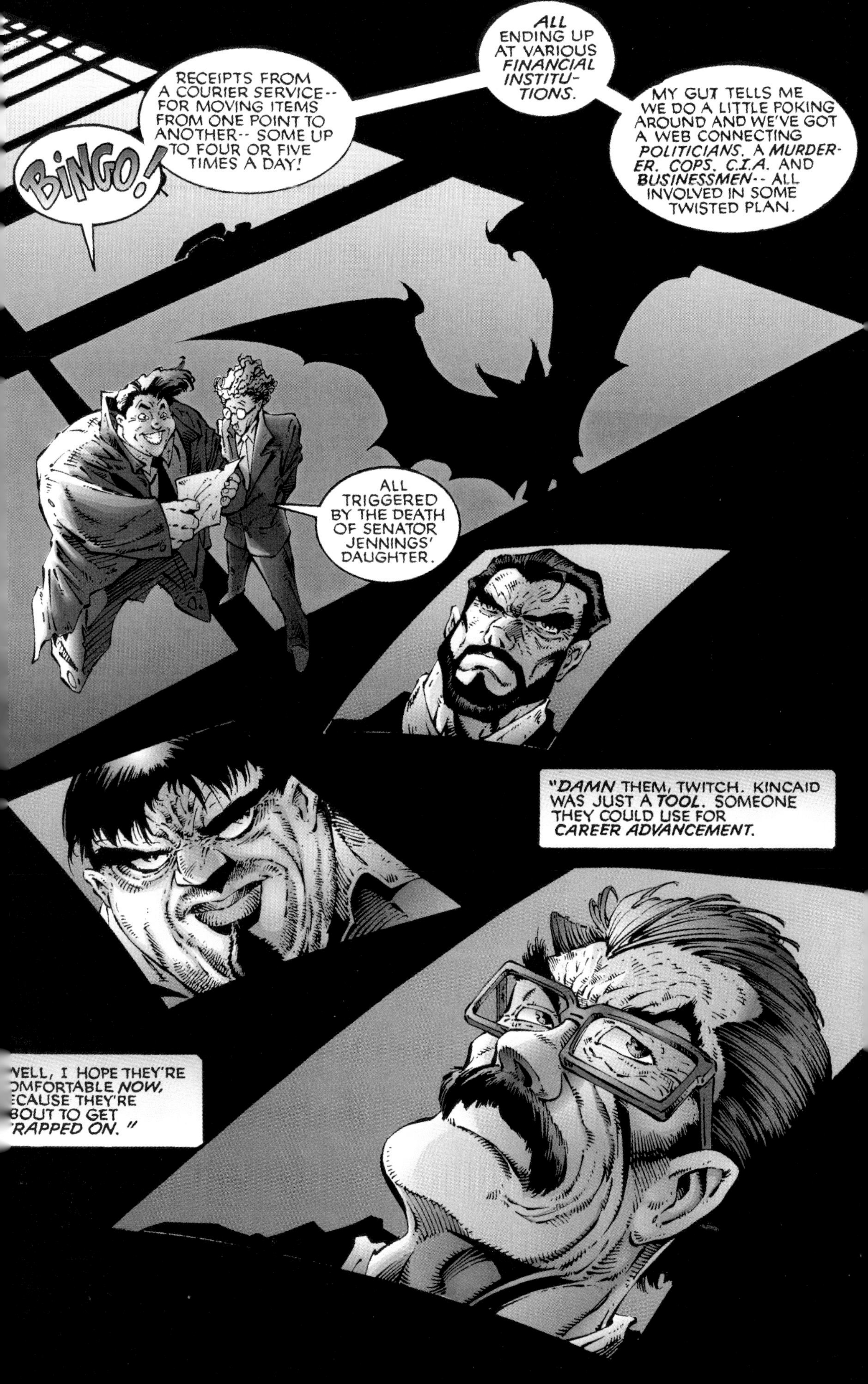
BINGO!
RECEIPTS FROM A COURIER SERVICE-- FOR MOVING ITEMS FROM ONE POINT TO ANOTHER-- SOME UP TO FOUR OR FIVE TIMES A DAY!
ALL ENDING UP AT VARIOUS FINANCIAL INSTITUTIONS.
MY GUT TELLS ME WE DO A LITTLE POKING AROUND AND WE'VE GOT A WEB CONNECTING POLITICIANS, A MURDERER, COPS, C.I.A. AND BUSINESSMEN-- ALL INVOLVED IN SOME TWISTED PLAN.
ALL TRIGGERED BY THE DEATH OF SENATOR JENNINGS' DAUGHTER.
"DAMN THEM, TWITCH. KINCAID WAS JUST A TOOL. SOMEONE THEY COULD USE FOR CAREER ADVANCEMENT.
WELL, I HOPE THEY'RE OMFORTABLE NOW, ECAUSE THEY'RE BOUT TO GET RAPPED ON."

THE MOON SHINES BRIGHT IN WEST VIRGINIA, GUIDING YOUNG PAT'S FOOTSTEPS THROUGH THE DARKNESS.

LOST IN THOUGHT AS HE WALKS HOMEWARD, PAT MULLS OVER EVERYTHING SPAWN TRIED TO TELL HIM.

ABOUT LIFE. GIRLS. HEROISM. AND THE POWER FROM WITHIN.

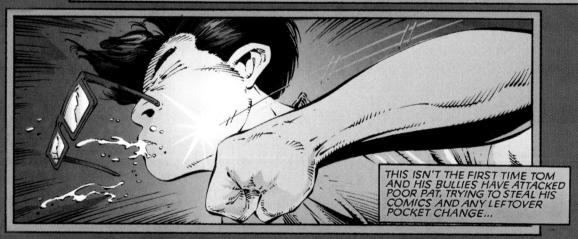

THIS ISN'T THE FIRST TIME TOM AND HIS BULLIES HAVE ATTACKED POOR PAT, TRYING TO STEAL HIS COMICS AND ANY LEFTOVER POCKET CHANGE...

... BUT TONIGHT'S OUTCOME WILL BE THE FIRST THAT THEY COULD NOT HAVE PREDICTED.

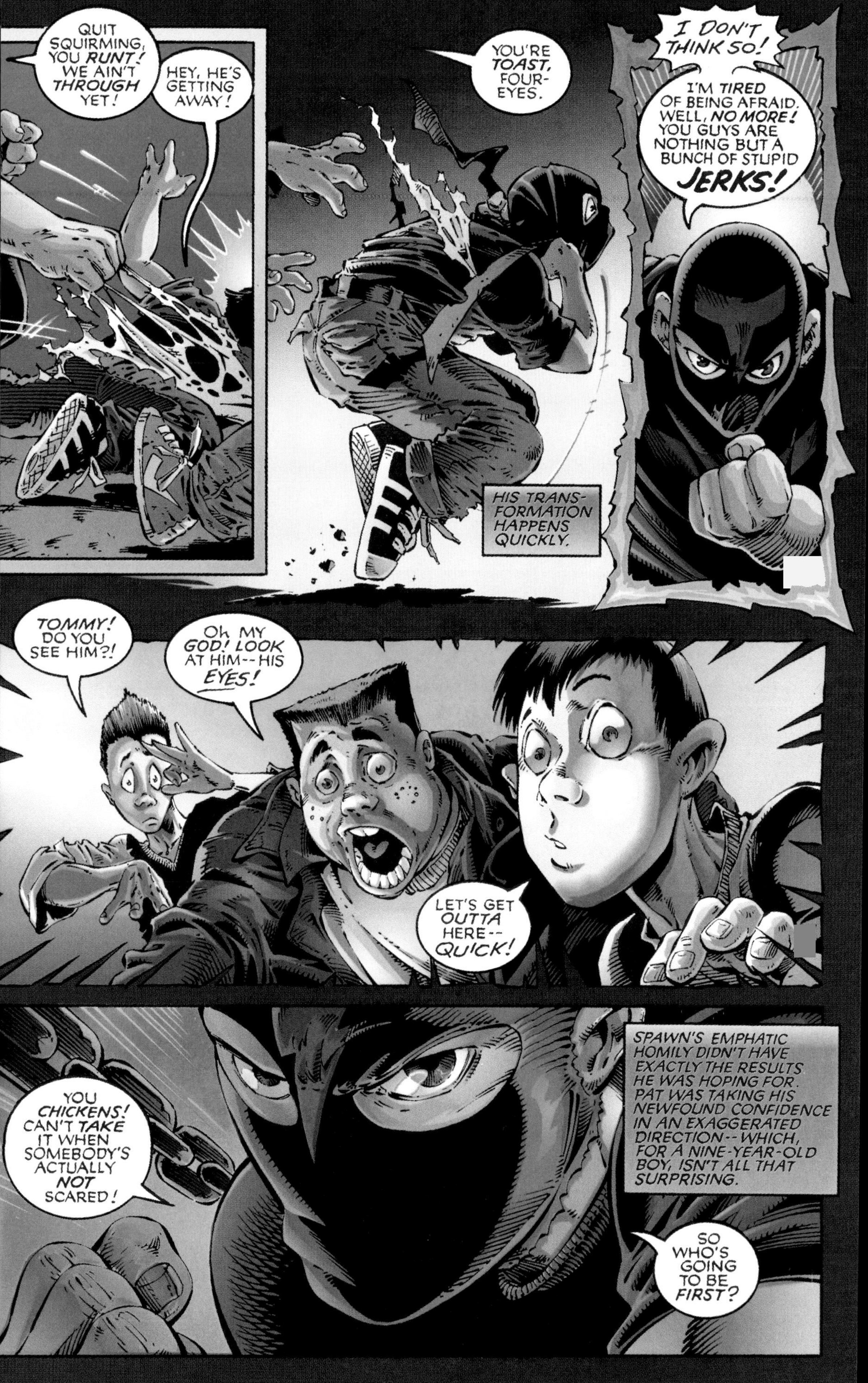
QUIT SQUIRMING, YOU RUNT! WE AIN'T THROUGH YET!
HEY, HE'S GETTING AWAY!
YOU'RE TOAST, FOUR-EYES.
HIS TRANSFORMATION HAPPENS QUICKLY.
I DON'T THINK SO!
I'M TIRED OF BEING AFRAID. WELL, NO MORE! YOU GUYS ARE NOTHING BUT A BUNCH OF STUPID JERKS!
TOMMY! DO YOU SEE HIM?!
Oh MY GOD! LOOK AT HIM--HIS EYES!
LET'S GET OUTTA HERE--QUICK!
YOU CHICKENS! CAN'T TAKE IT WHEN SOMEBODY'S ACTUALLY NOT SCARED!
SPAWN'S EMPHATIC HOMILY DIDN'T HAVE EXACTLY THE RESULTS HE WAS HOPING FOR. PAT WAS TAKING HIS NEWFOUND CONFIDENCE IN AN EXAGGERATED DIRECTION--WHICH, FOR A NINE-YEAR-OLD BOY, ISN'T ALL THAT SURPRISING.
SO WHO'S GOING TO BE FIRST?

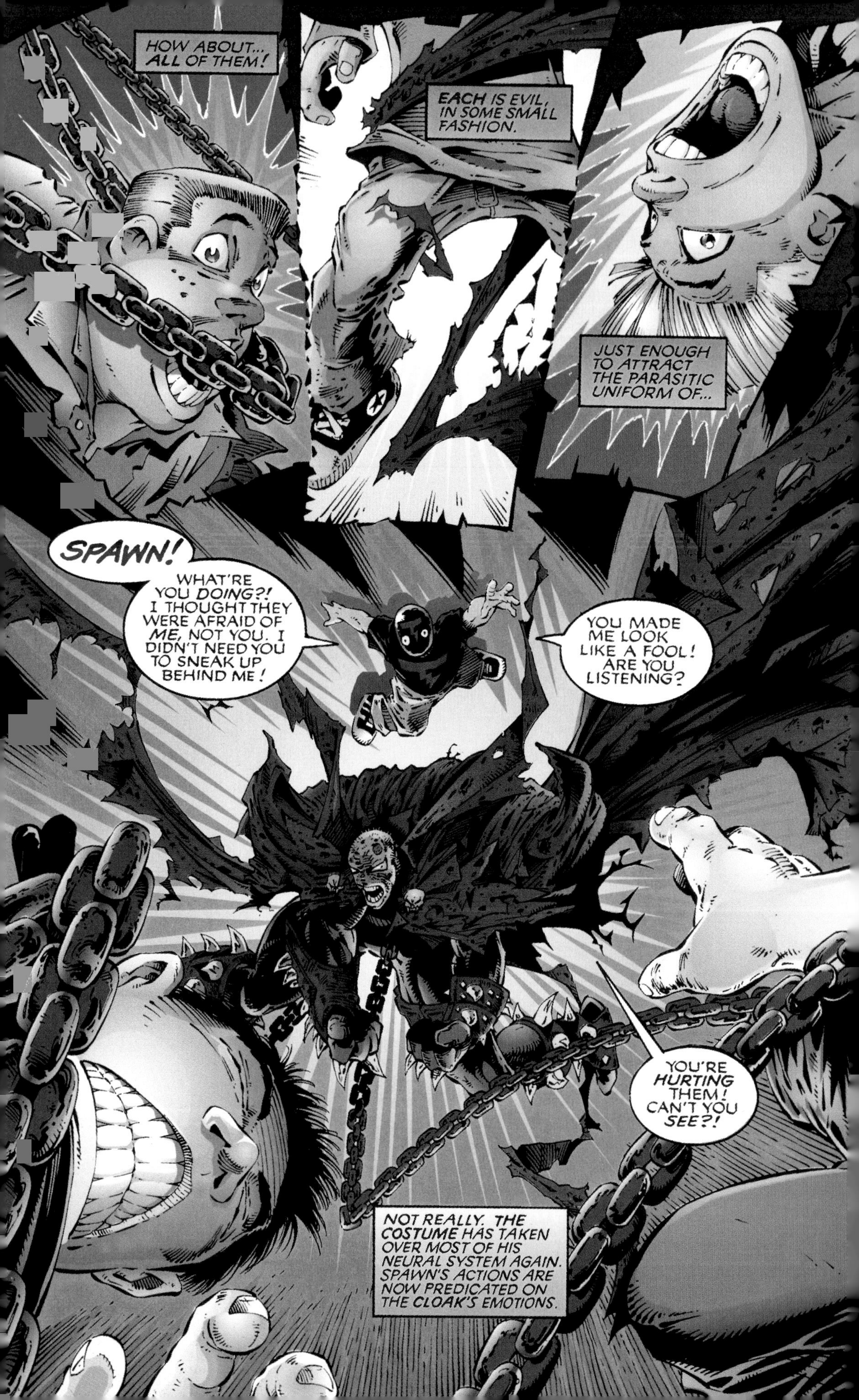
HOW ABOUT... ALL OF THEM!
EACH IS EVIL, IN SOME SMALL FASHION.
JUST ENOUGH TO ATTRACT THE PARASITIC UNIFORM OF...
SPAWN!
WHAT'RE YOU DOING?! I THOUGHT THEY WERE AFRAID OF ME, NOT YOU. I DIDN'T NEED YOU TO SNEAK UP BEHIND ME!
YOU MADE ME LOOK LIKE A FOOL! ARE YOU LISTENING?
YOU'RE HURTING THEM! CAN'T YOU SEE?!
NOT REALLY. THE COSTUME HAS TAKEN OVER MOST OF HIS NEURAL SYSTEM AGAIN. SPAWN'S ACTIONS ARE NOW PREDICATED ON THE CLOAK'S EMOTIONS.

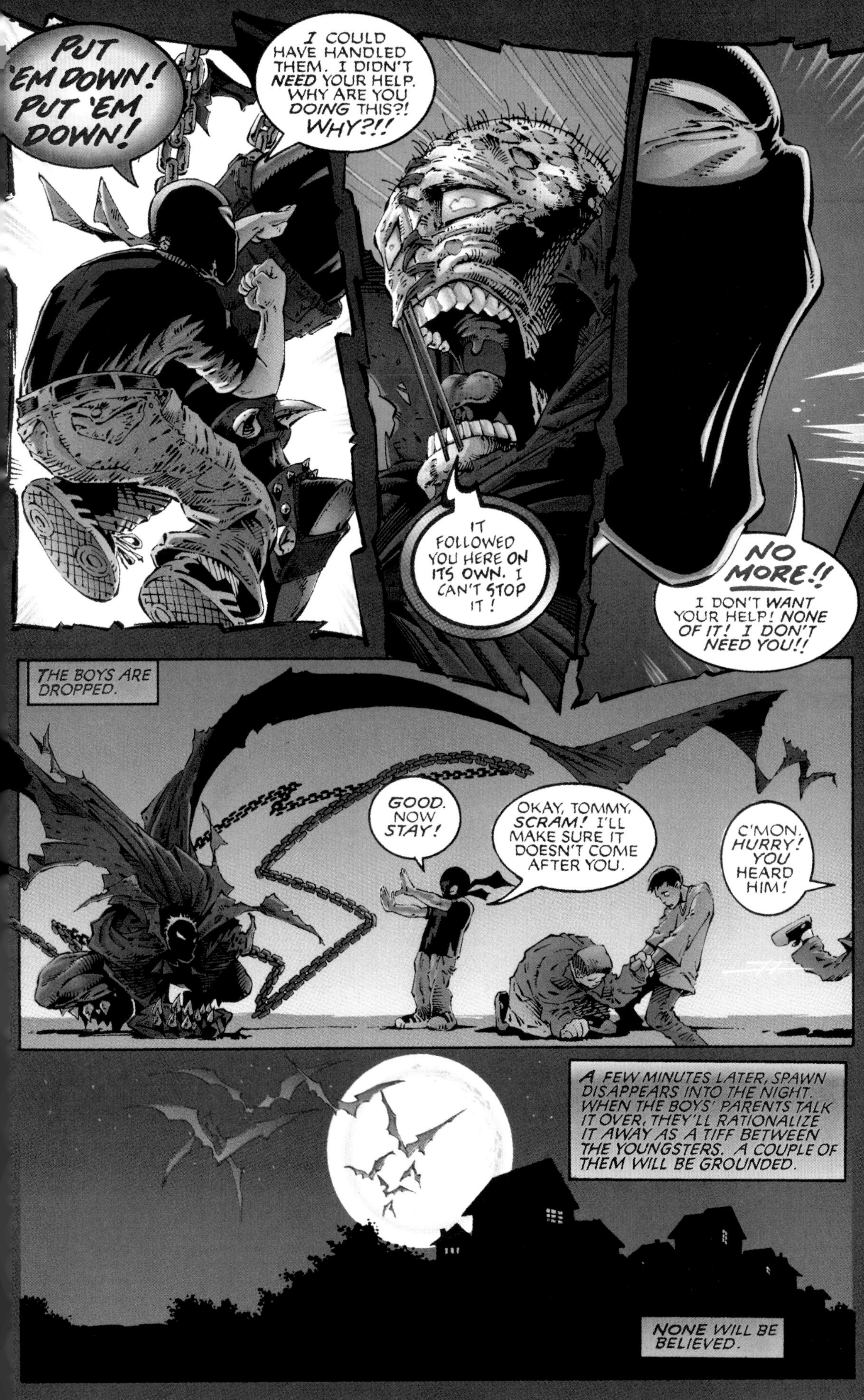
PUT 'EM DOWN! PUT 'EM DOWN!
I COULD HAVE HANDLED THEM. I DIDN'T NEED YOUR HELP. WHY ARE YOU DOING THIS?! WHY?!!
IT FOLLOWED YOU HERE ON ITS OWN. I CAN'T STOP IT!
NO MORE!! I DON'T WANT YOUR HELP! NONE OF IT! I DON'T NEED YOU!!
THE BOYS ARE DROPPED.
GOOD. NOW STAY!
OKAY, TOMMY, SCRAM! I'LL MAKE SURE IT DOESN'T COME AFTER YOU.
C'MON, HURRY! YOU HEARD HIM!
A FEW MINUTES LATER, SPAWN DISAPPEARS INTO THE NIGHT. WHEN THE BOYS' PARENTS TALK IT OVER, THEY'LL RATIONALIZE IT AWAY AS A TIFF BETWEEN THE YOUNGSTERS. A COUPLE OF THEM WILL BE GROUNDED.
NONE WILL BE BELIEVED.

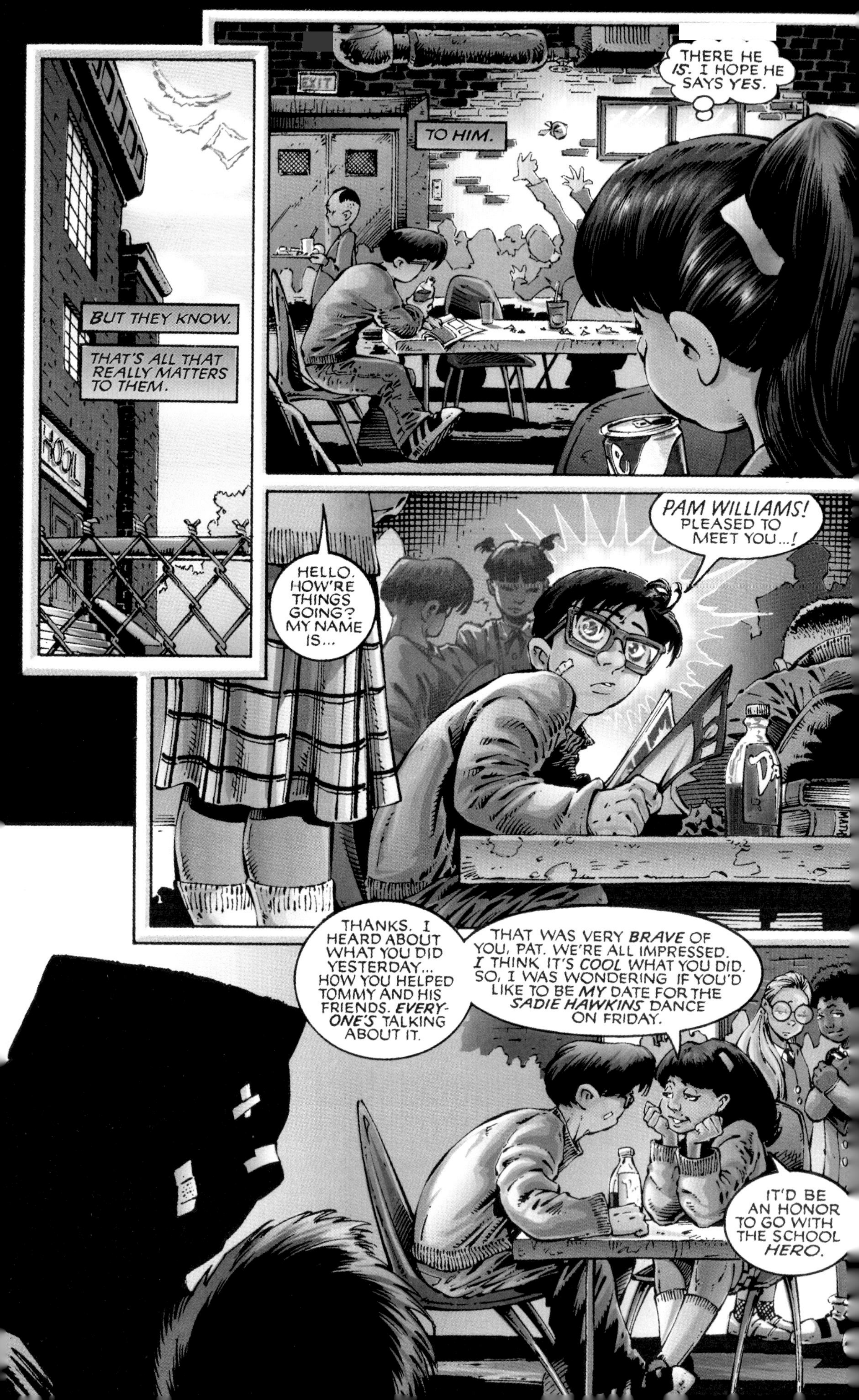
BUT THEY KNOW.
THAT'S ALL THAT REALLY MATTERS TO THEM.
TO HIM.
THERE HE IS. I HOPE HE SAYS YES.
HELLO. HOW'RE THINGS GOING? MY NAME IS...
PAM WILLIAMS! PLEASED TO MEET YOU...!
THANKS. I HEARD ABOUT WHAT YOU DID YESTERDAY... HOW YOU HELPED TOMMY AND HIS FRIENDS. EVERY-ONE'S TALKING ABOUT IT.
THAT WAS VERY BRAVE OF YOU, PAT. WE'RE ALL IMPRESSED. I THINK IT'S COOL WHAT YOU DID. SO, I WAS WONDERING IF YOU'D LIKE TO BE MY DATE FOR THE SADIE HAWKINS DANCE ON FRIDAY.
IT'D BE AN HONOR TO GO WITH THE SCHOOL HERO.

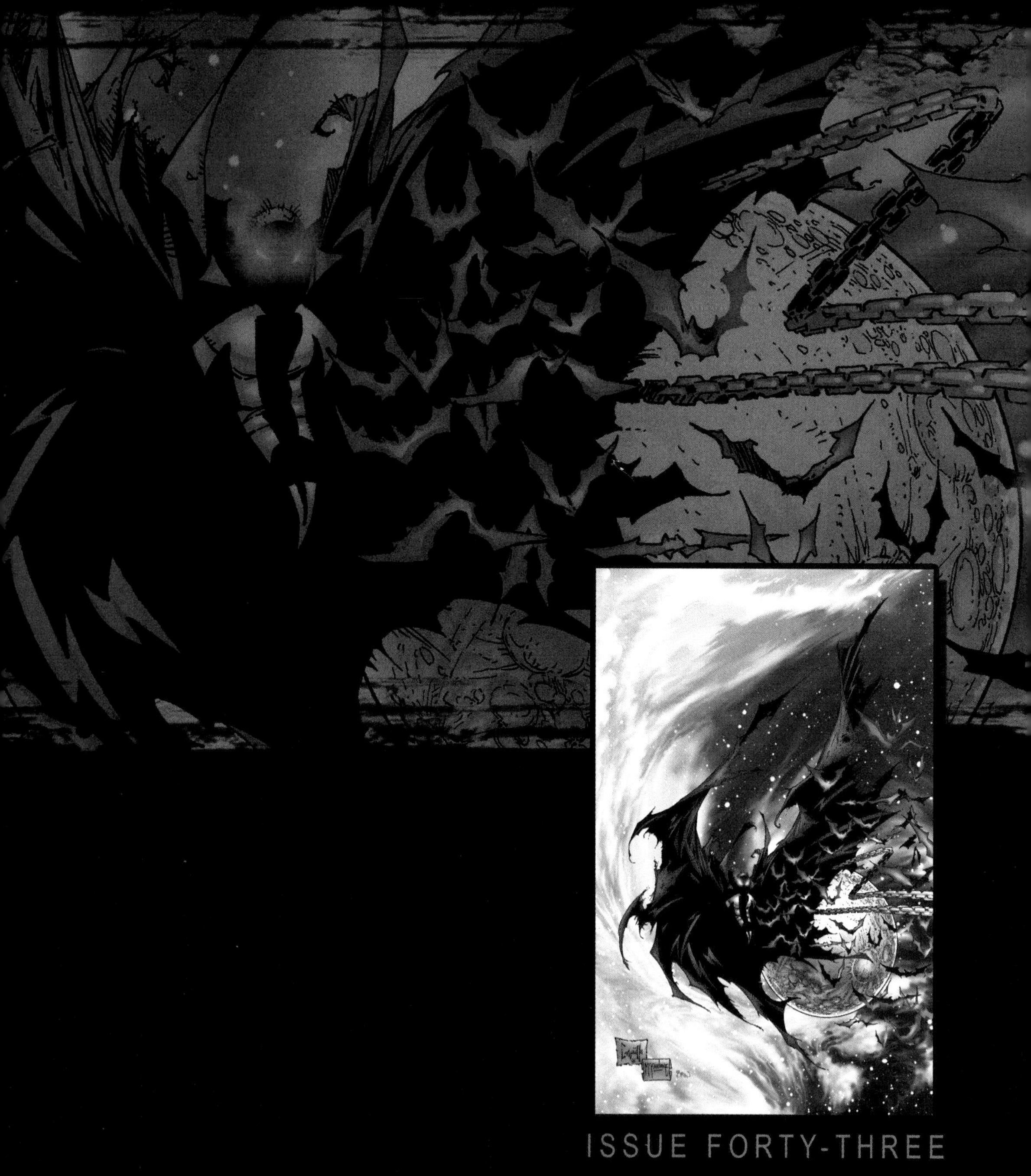

ISSUE FORTY-THREE

5:51 A.M.

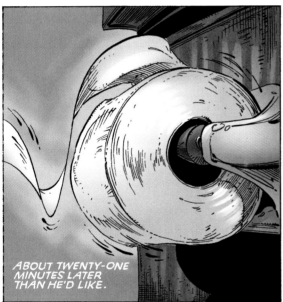

ABOUT TWENTY-ONE MINUTES LATER THAN HE'D LIKE.

CRIPES!

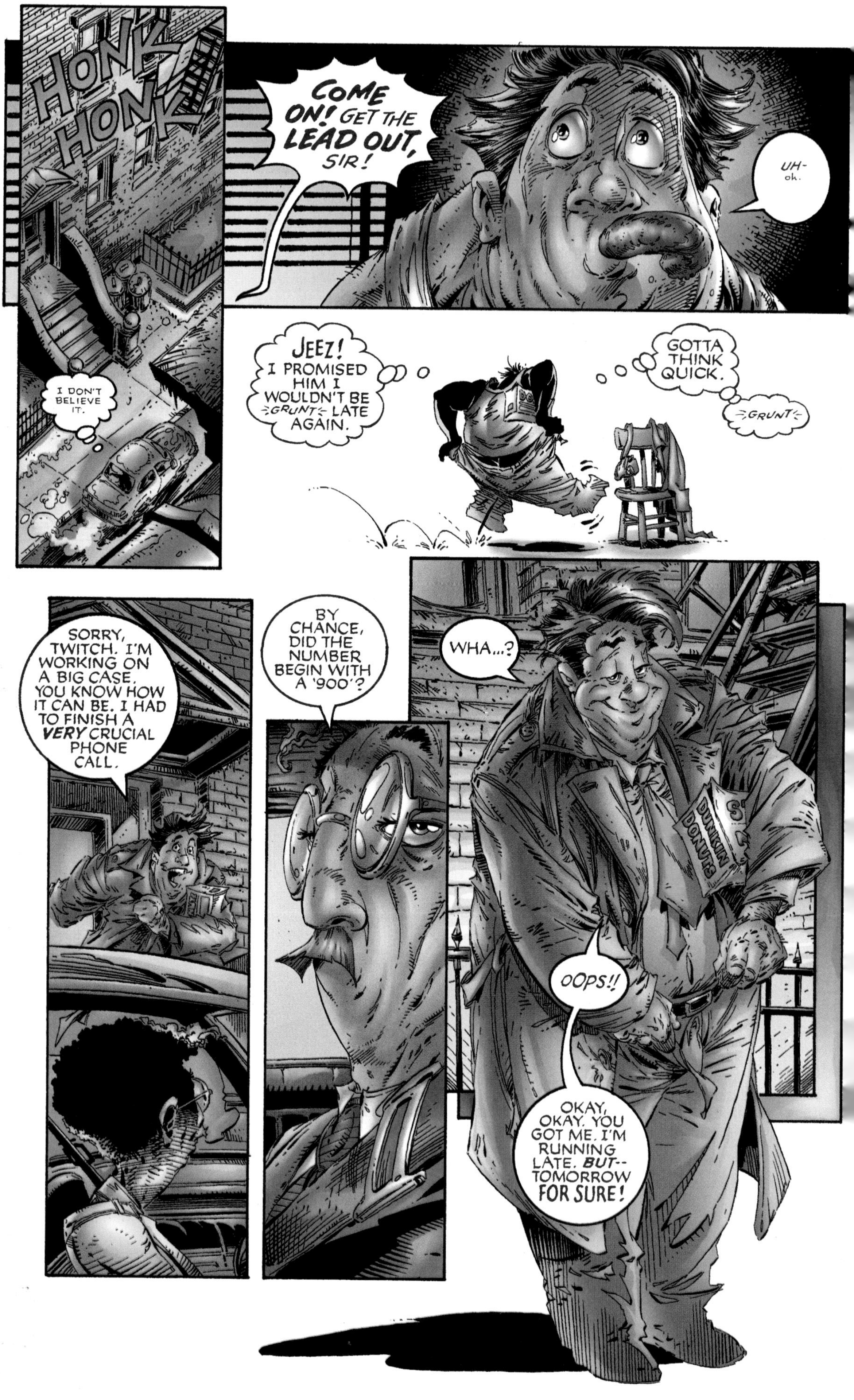
HONK HONK
I DON'T BELIEVE IT.
COME ON! GET THE LEAD OUT, SIR!
UH-oh.
JEEZ! I PROMISED HIM I WOULDN'T BE GRUNT LATE AGAIN.
GOTTA THINK QUICK.
GRUNT
SORRY, TWITCH. I'M WORKING ON A BIG CASE. YOU KNOW HOW IT CAN BE. I HAD TO FINISH A VERY CRUCIAL PHONE CALL.
BY CHANCE, DID THE NUMBER BEGIN WITH A '900'?
WHA...?
OOPS!!
OKAY, OKAY. YOU GOT ME. I'M RUNNING LATE. BUT-- TOMORROW FOR SURE!
DUNKIN DONUTS

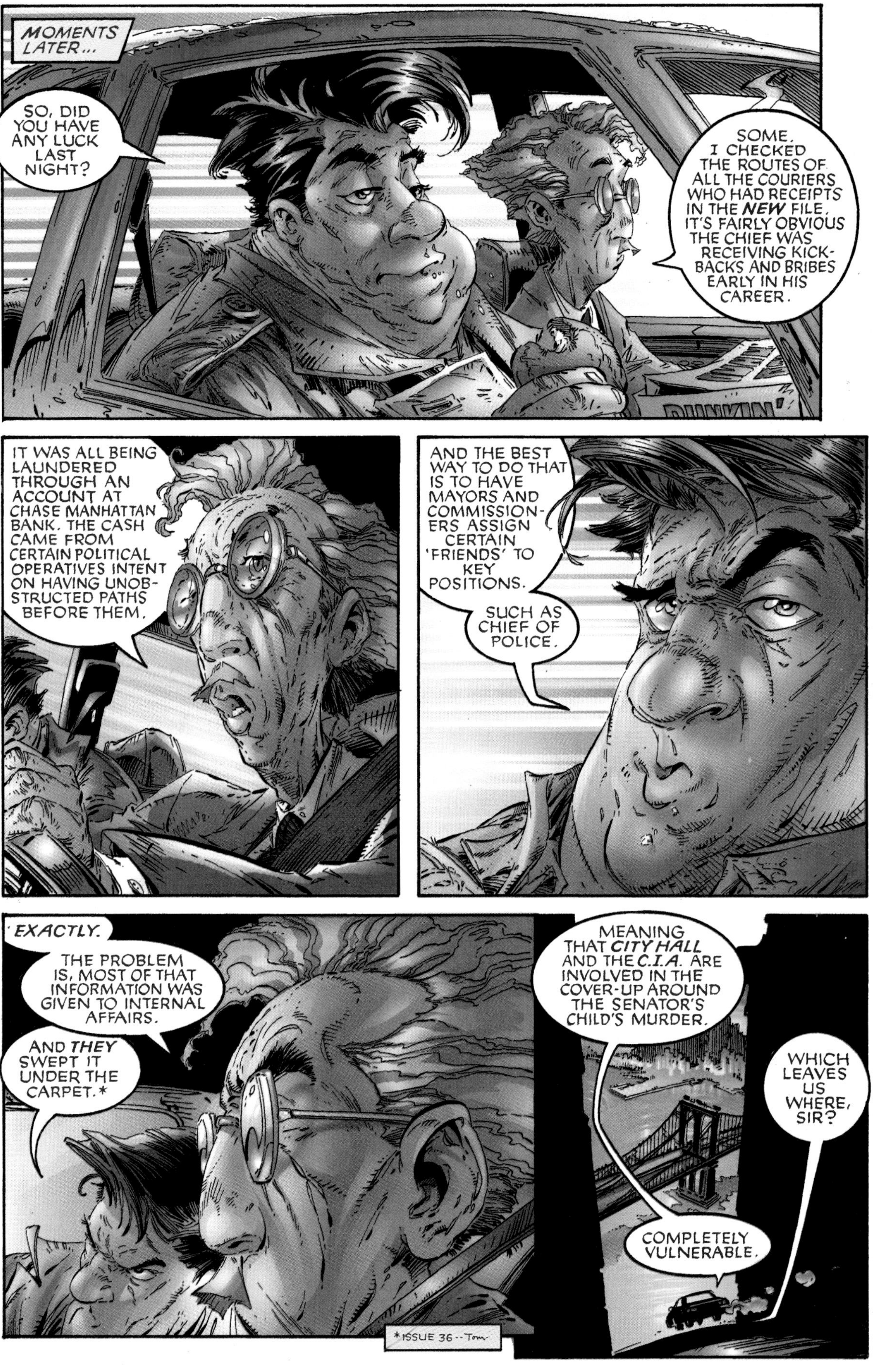
MOMENTS LATER...
SO, DID YOU HAVE ANY LUCK LAST NIGHT?
SOME. I CHECKED THE ROUTES OF ALL THE COURIERS WHO HAD RECEIPTS IN THE *NEW* FILE. IT'S FAIRLY OBVIOUS THE CHIEF WAS RECEIVING KICK-BACKS AND BRIBES EARLY IN HIS CAREER.
DUNKIN'
IT WAS ALL BEING LAUNDERED THROUGH AN ACCOUNT AT CHASE MANHATTAN BANK. THE CASH CAME FROM CERTAIN POLITICAL OPERATIVES INTENT ON HAVING UNOB-STRUCTED PATHS BEFORE THEM.
AND THE BEST WAY TO DO THAT IS TO HAVE MAYORS AND COMMISSION-ERS ASSIGN CERTAIN 'FRIENDS' TO KEY POSITIONS.
SUCH AS CHIEF OF POLICE.
EXACTLY.
THE PROBLEM IS, MOST OF THAT INFORMATION WAS GIVEN TO INTERNAL AFFAIRS.
AND *THEY* SWEPT IT UNDER THE CARPET.*
*ISSUE 36 --Tom
MEANING THAT *CITY HALL* AND THE *C.I.A.* ARE INVOLVED IN THE COVER-UP AROUND THE SENATOR'S CHILD'S MURDER.
WHICH LEAVES US WHERE, SIR?
COMPLETELY VULNERABLE.

THE FINAL TWENTY MINUTES OF THEIR DRIVE IS *SILENT.* EACH IS PAINFULLY AWARE THEY'RE SITTING ON A TIME BOMB...

...ONE THAT'S ALREADY BEGUN TICKING.

'MORNING, JOE! SO WHAT'S THE GOOD WORD?

Um... I CAN'T LET YOU PARK IN THE COMPOUND.

WHY?

GOT SOME PAPERWORK REVOKING YOUR PARKING SPACE. I DOUBLE-CHECKED. IT'S ALL OFFICIAL. SORRY.

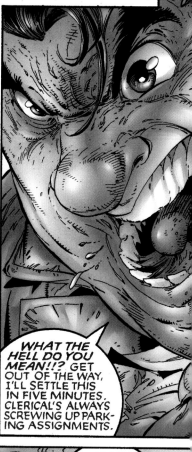

WHAT THE HELL DO YOU MEAN!!? GET OUT OF THE WAY, I'LL SETTLE THIS IN FIVE MINUTES. CLERICAL'S ALWAYS SCREWING UP PARK-ING ASSIGNMENTS.

YOU HEARD JOE. YOU'RE NOT WELCOME ANYMORE. NOW BACK THIS PIECE OF CRAP OUTTA HERE.

WHERE *CAN* THEY PARK?

WHO CARES? AS LONG AS IT AIN'T *HERE.*

CAPICE, BOYS?

EIGHT BLOCKS AWAY. THAT WAS THE CLOSEST SPOT THEY COULD FIND. AFTER A 25-MINUTE WALK IN FREEZING WEATHER, DETECTIVE SAM BURKE IS ABOUT TO BURST.

SOMEONE'S DEAD! AND I DON'T MEAN PRETTY DEAD. I MEAN UGLY, WRETCHED DEAD.

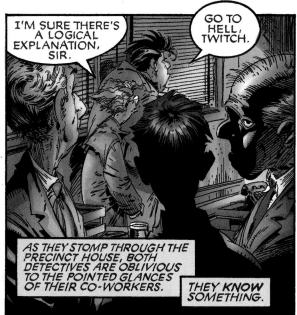

I'M SURE THERE'S A LOGICAL EXPLANATION, SIR.

GO TO HELL, TWITCH.

AS THEY STOMP THROUGH THE PRECINCT HOUSE, BOTH DETECTIVES ARE OBLIVIOUS TO THE POINTED GLANCES OF THEIR CO-WORKERS.

THEY KNOW SOMETHING.

HEY! WHAT'S GOING ON HERE? WHO ARE YOU?

AND WHAT ARE YOU DOING IN MY OFFICE?!

I... I...

TALK FAST! WHO SAID YOU COULD DO THIS WITH MY FILES?

I DID.

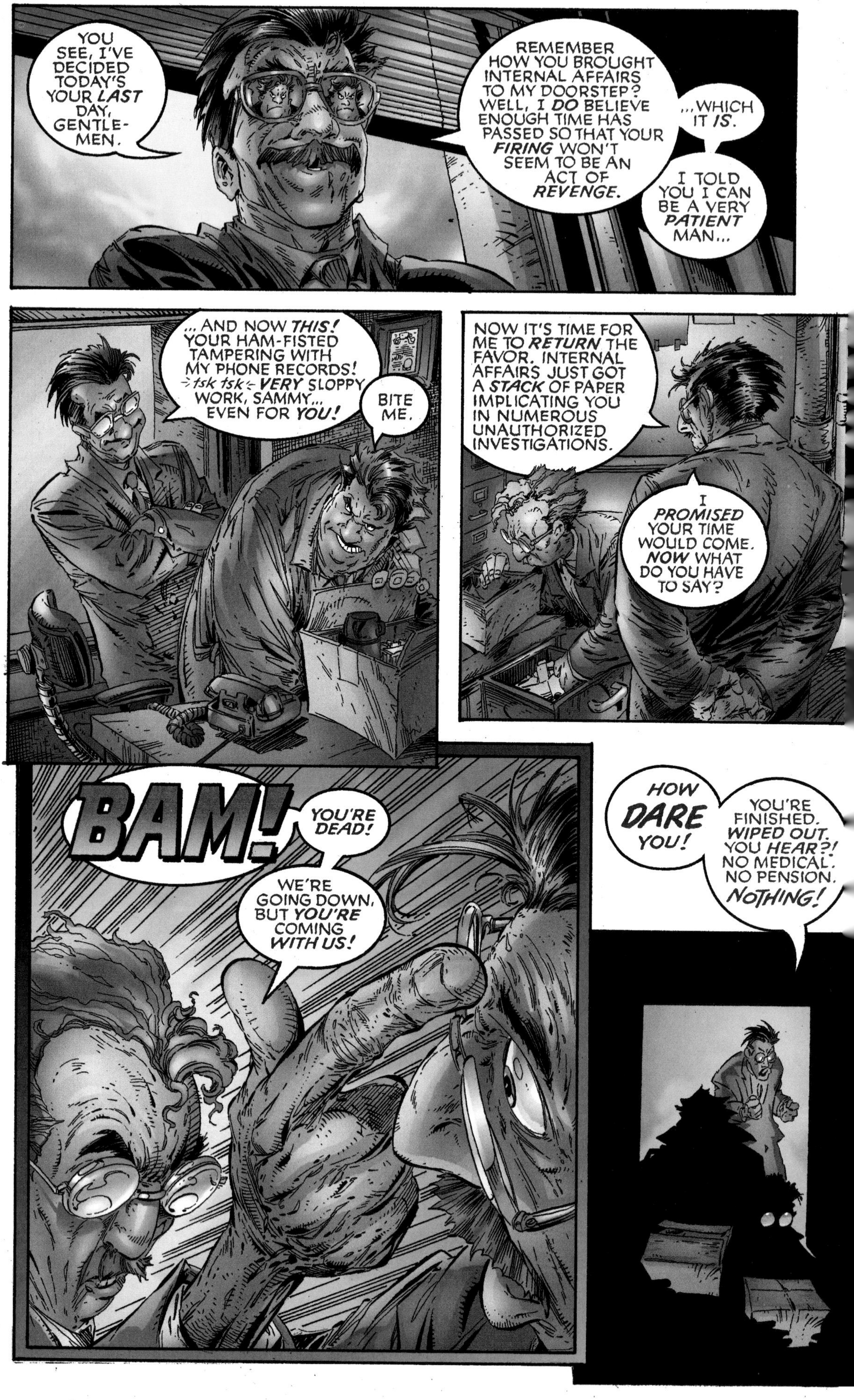
YOU SEE, I'VE DECIDED TODAY'S YOUR LAST DAY, GENTLEMEN.
REMEMBER HOW YOU BROUGHT INTERNAL AFFAIRS TO MY DOORSTEP? WELL, I DO BELIEVE ENOUGH TIME HAS PASSED SO THAT YOUR FIRING WON'T SEEM TO BE AN ACT OF REVENGE.
...WHICH IT IS.
I TOLD YOU I CAN BE A VERY PATIENT MAN...
...AND NOW THIS! YOUR HAM-FISTED TAMPERING WITH MY PHONE RECORDS! tsk tsk VERY SLOPPY WORK, SAMMY... EVEN FOR YOU!
BITE ME.
NOW IT'S TIME FOR ME TO RETURN THE FAVOR. INTERNAL AFFAIRS JUST GOT A STACK OF PAPER IMPLICATING YOU IN NUMEROUS UNAUTHORIZED INVESTIGATIONS.
I PROMISED YOUR TIME WOULD COME. NOW WHAT DO YOU HAVE TO SAY?
BAM!
YOU'RE DEAD!
WE'RE GOING DOWN, BUT YOU'RE COMING WITH US!
HOW DARE YOU!
YOU'RE FINISHED. WIPED OUT. YOU HEAR?! NO MEDICAL. NO PENSION. NOTHING!

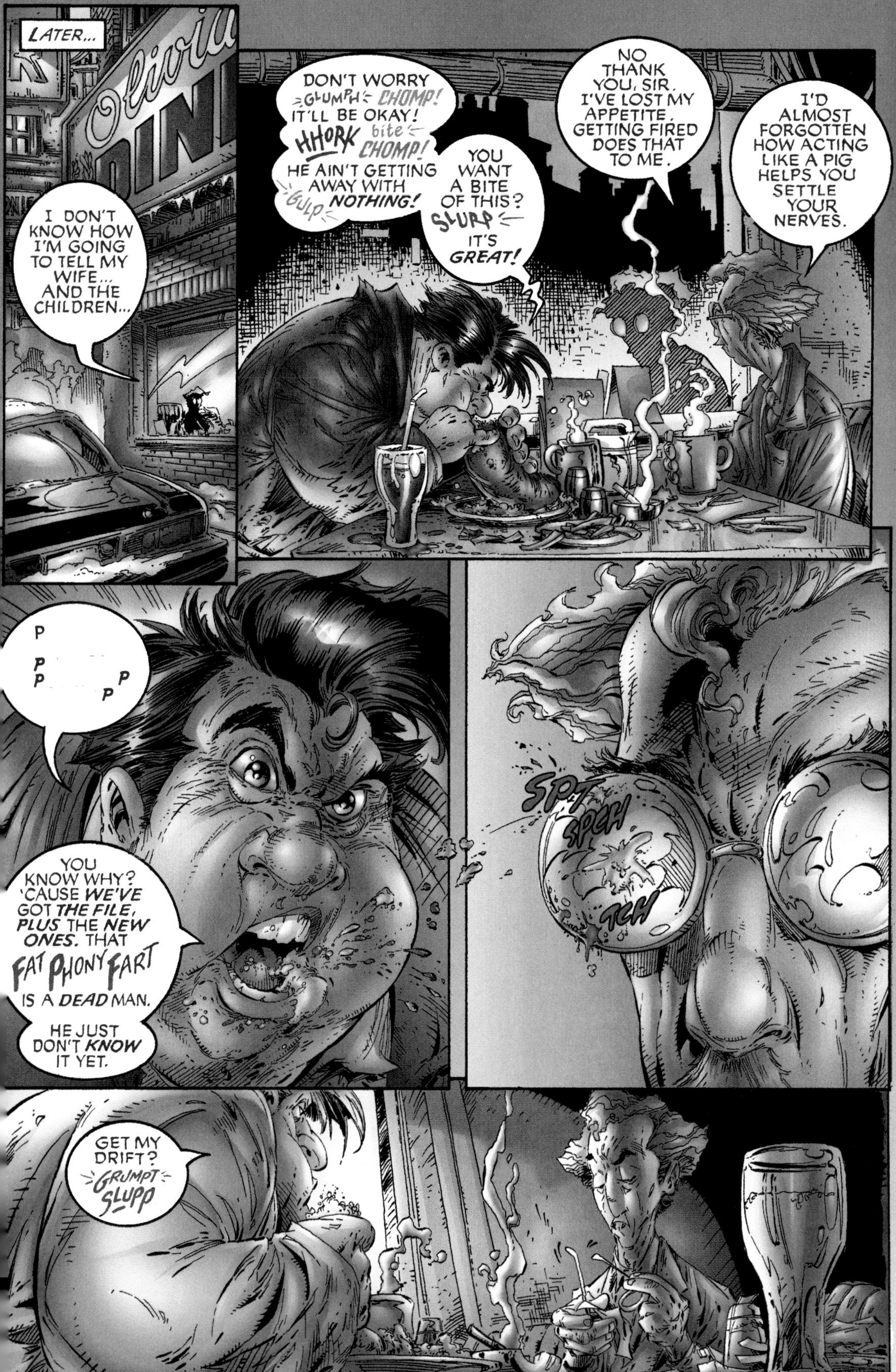

LATER...
Olivia DIN
I DON'T KNOW HOW I'M GOING TO TELL MY WIFE... AND THE CHILDREN...
DON'T WORRY GLUMPH CHOMP! IT'LL BE OKAY! HHORK bite CHOMP! HE AIN'T GETTING AWAY WITH NOTHING! GULP
YOU WANT A BITE OF THIS? SLURP IT'S GREAT!
NO THANK YOU, SIR. I'VE LOST MY APPETITE. GETTING FIRED DOES THAT TO ME.
I'D ALMOST FORGOTTEN HOW ACTING LIKE A PIG HELPS YOU SETTLE YOUR NERVES.
P P P P P
YOU KNOW WHY? 'CAUSE WE'VE GOT THE FILE, PLUS THE NEW ONES. THAT FAT PHONY FART IS A DEAD MAN.
HE JUST DON'T KNOW IT YET.
SPT SPCH TCH
GET MY DRIFT? GRUMPT SLUPP

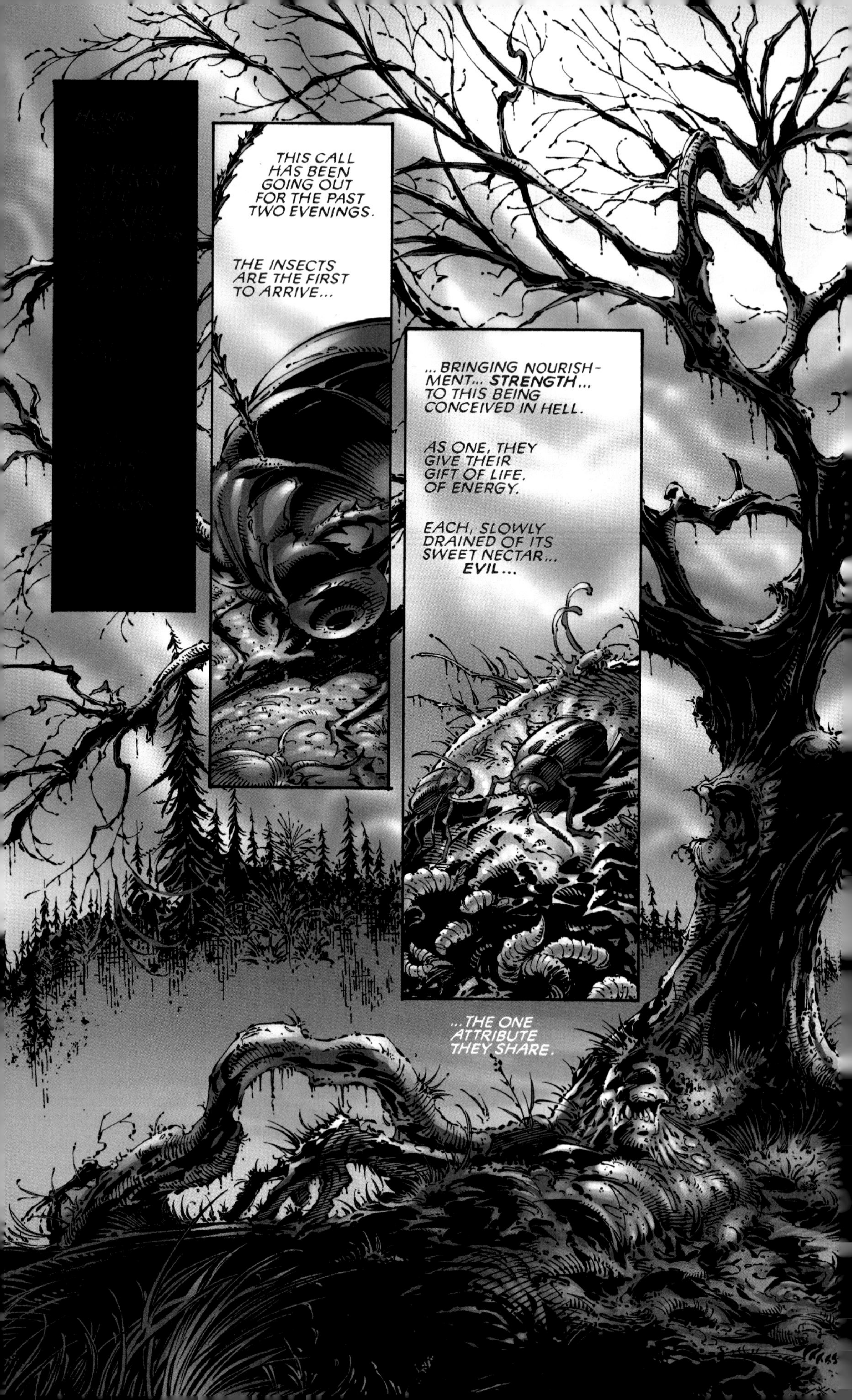
[redacted]
THIS CALL HAS BEEN GOING OUT FOR THE PAST TWO EVENINGS.
THE INSECTS ARE THE FIRST TO ARRIVE...
...BRINGING NOURISHMENT... STRENGTH... TO THIS BEING CONCEIVED IN HELL.
AS ONE, THEY GIVE THEIR GIFT OF LIFE, OF ENERGY.
EACH, SLOWLY DRAINED OF ITS SWEET NECTAR... EVIL...
...THE ONE ATTRIBUTE THEY SHARE.

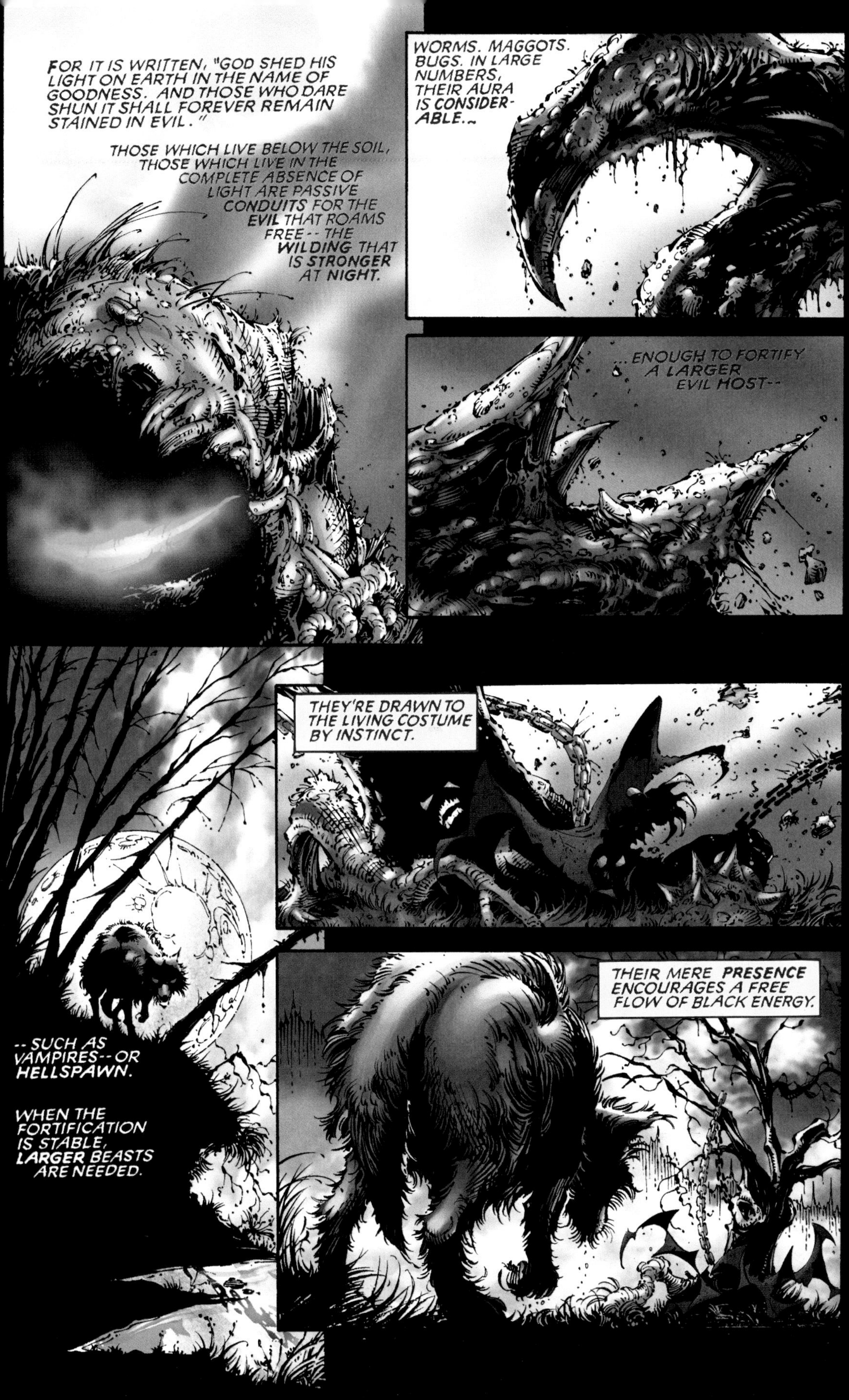
FOR IT IS WRITTEN, "GOD SHED HIS LIGHT ON EARTH IN THE NAME OF GOODNESS. AND THOSE WHO DARE SHUN IT SHALL FOREVER REMAIN STAINED IN EVIL."
THOSE WHICH LIVE BELOW THE SOIL, THOSE WHICH LIVE IN THE COMPLETE ABSENCE OF LIGHT ARE PASSIVE CONDUITS FOR THE EVIL THAT ROAMS FREE-- THE WILDING THAT IS STRONGER AT NIGHT.
WORMS. MAGGOTS. BUGS. IN LARGE NUMBERS, THEIR AURA IS CONSIDER-ABLE..
...ENOUGH TO FORTIFY A LARGER EVIL HOST--
--SUCH AS VAMPIRES--OR HELLSPAWN.
WHEN THE FORTIFICATION IS STABLE, LARGER BEASTS ARE NEEDED.
THEY'RE DRAWN TO THE LIVING COSTUME BY INSTINCT.
THEIR MERE PRESENCE ENCOURAGES A FREE FLOW OF BLACK ENERGY.

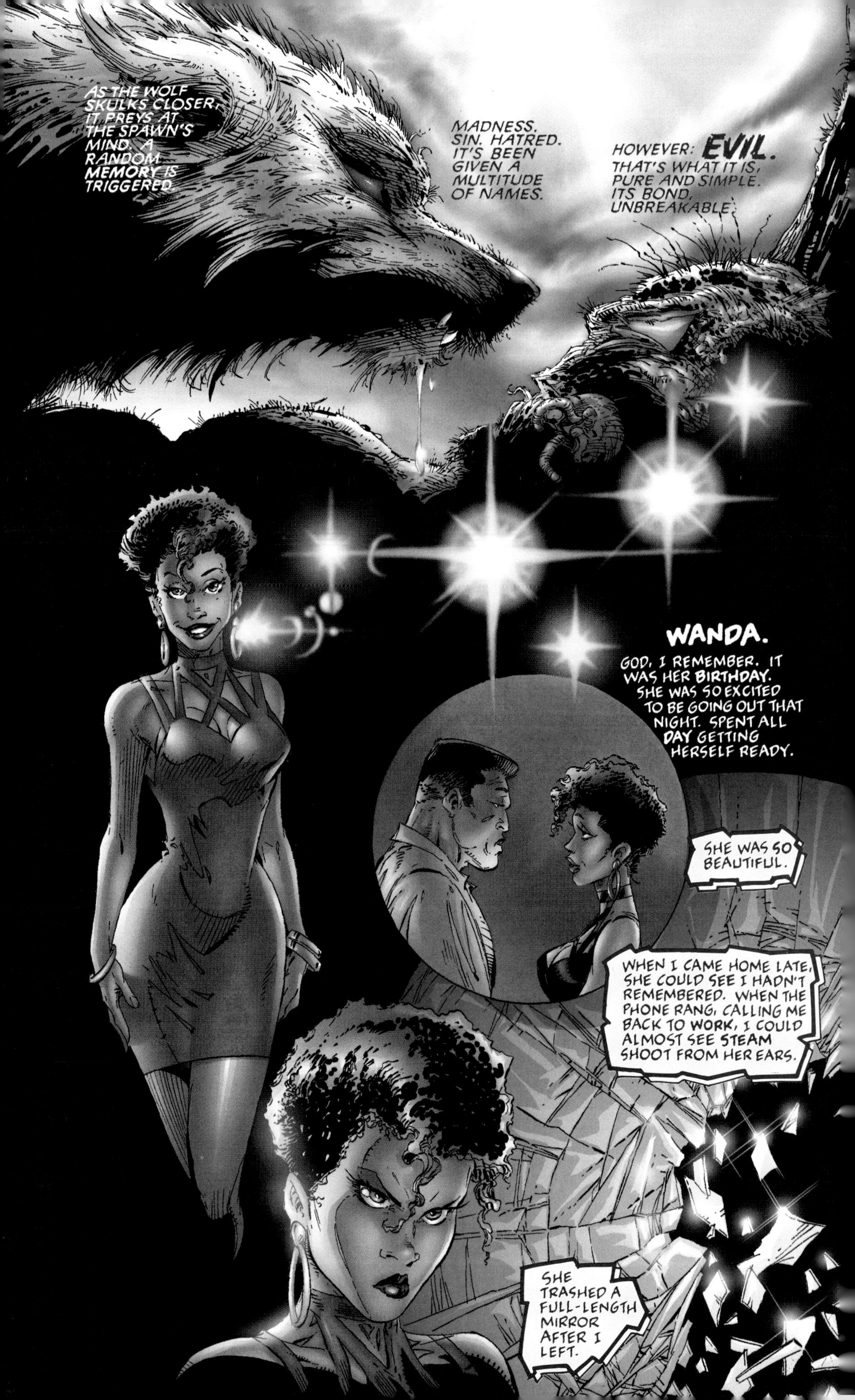
AS THE WOLF SKULKS CLOSER, IT PREYS AT THE SPAWN'S MIND. A RANDOM MEMORY IS TRIGGERED.
MADNESS. SIN. HATRED. IT'S BEEN GIVEN A MULTITUDE OF NAMES.
HOWEVER: EVIL. THAT'S WHAT IT IS, PURE AND SIMPLE. ITS BOND, UNBREAKABLE.
WANDA.
GOD, I REMEMBER. IT WAS HER BIRTHDAY. SHE WAS SO EXCITED TO BE GOING OUT THAT NIGHT. SPENT ALL DAY GETTING HERSELF READY.
SHE WAS SO BEAUTIFUL.
WHEN I CAME HOME LATE, SHE COULD SEE I HADN'T REMEMBERED. WHEN THE PHONE RANG, CALLING ME BACK TO WORK, I COULD ALMOST SEE STEAM SHOOT FROM HER EARS.
SHE TRASHED A FULL-LENGTH MIRROR AFTER I LEFT.

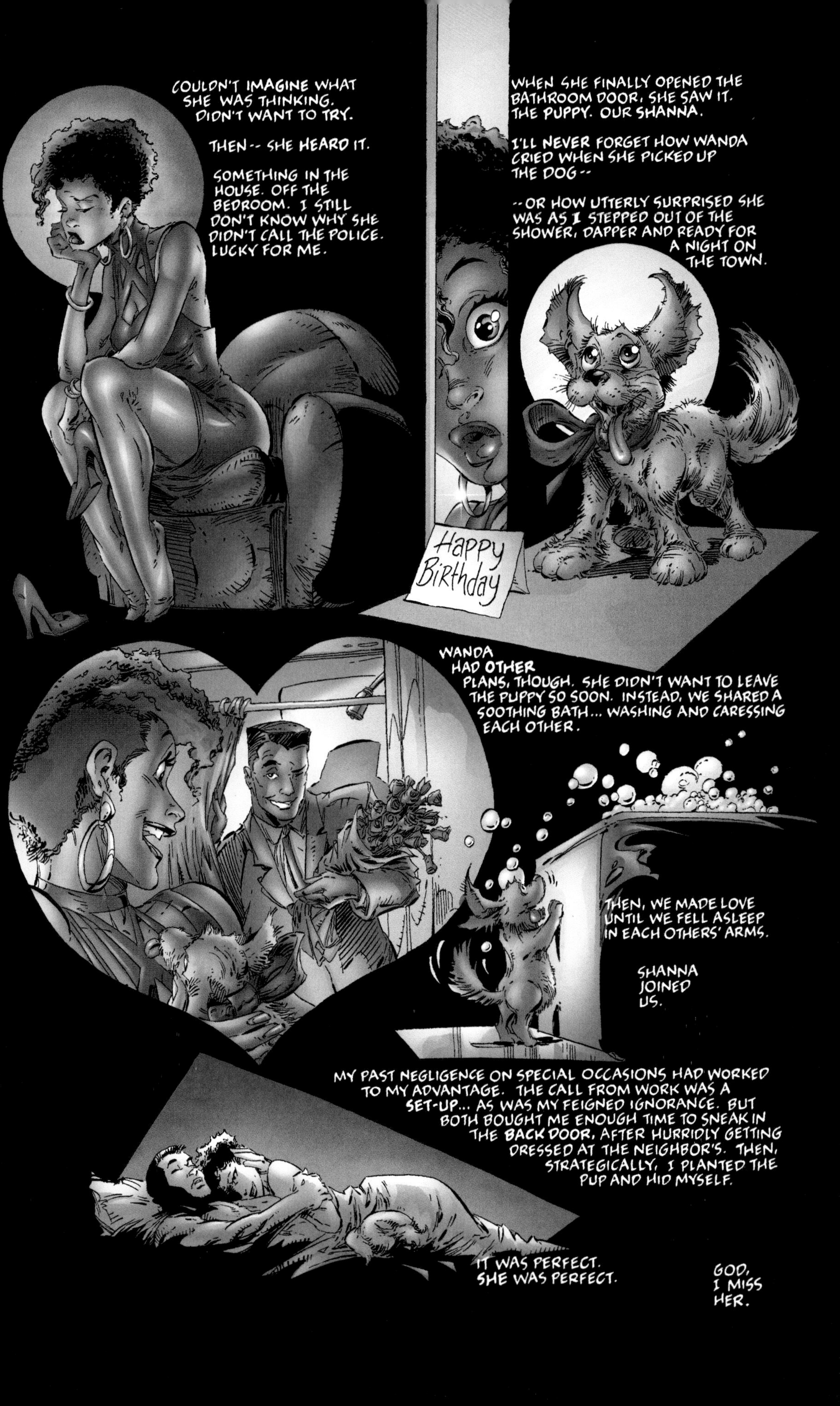

COULDN'T IMAGINE WHAT SHE WAS THINKING. DIDN'T WANT TO TRY.
THEN -- SHE HEARD IT.
SOMETHING IN THE HOUSE. OFF THE BEDROOM. I STILL DON'T KNOW WHY SHE DIDN'T CALL THE POLICE. LUCKY FOR ME.
WHEN SHE FINALLY OPENED THE BATHROOM DOOR, SHE SAW IT. THE PUPPY. OUR SHANNA.
I'LL NEVER FORGET HOW WANDA CRIED WHEN SHE PICKED UP THE DOG --
-- OR HOW UTTERLY SURPRISED SHE WAS AS I STEPPED OUT OF THE SHOWER, DAPPER AND READY FOR A NIGHT ON THE TOWN.
Happy Birthday
WANDA HAD OTHER PLANS, THOUGH. SHE DIDN'T WANT TO LEAVE THE PUPPY SO SOON. INSTEAD, WE SHARED A SOOTHING BATH... WASHING AND CARESSING EACH OTHER.
THEN, WE MADE LOVE UNTIL WE FELL ASLEEP IN EACH OTHERS' ARMS.
SHANNA JOINED US.
MY PAST NEGLIGENCE ON SPECIAL OCCASIONS HAD WORKED TO MY ADVANTAGE. THE CALL FROM WORK WAS A SET-UP... AS WAS MY FEIGNED IGNORANCE. BUT BOTH BOUGHT ME ENOUGH TIME TO SNEAK IN THE BACK DOOR, AFTER HURRIDLY GETTING DRESSED AT THE NEIGHBOR'S. THEN, STRATEGICALLY, I PLANTED THE PUP AND HID MYSELF.
IT WAS PERFECT. SHE WAS PERFECT.
GOD, I MISS HER.

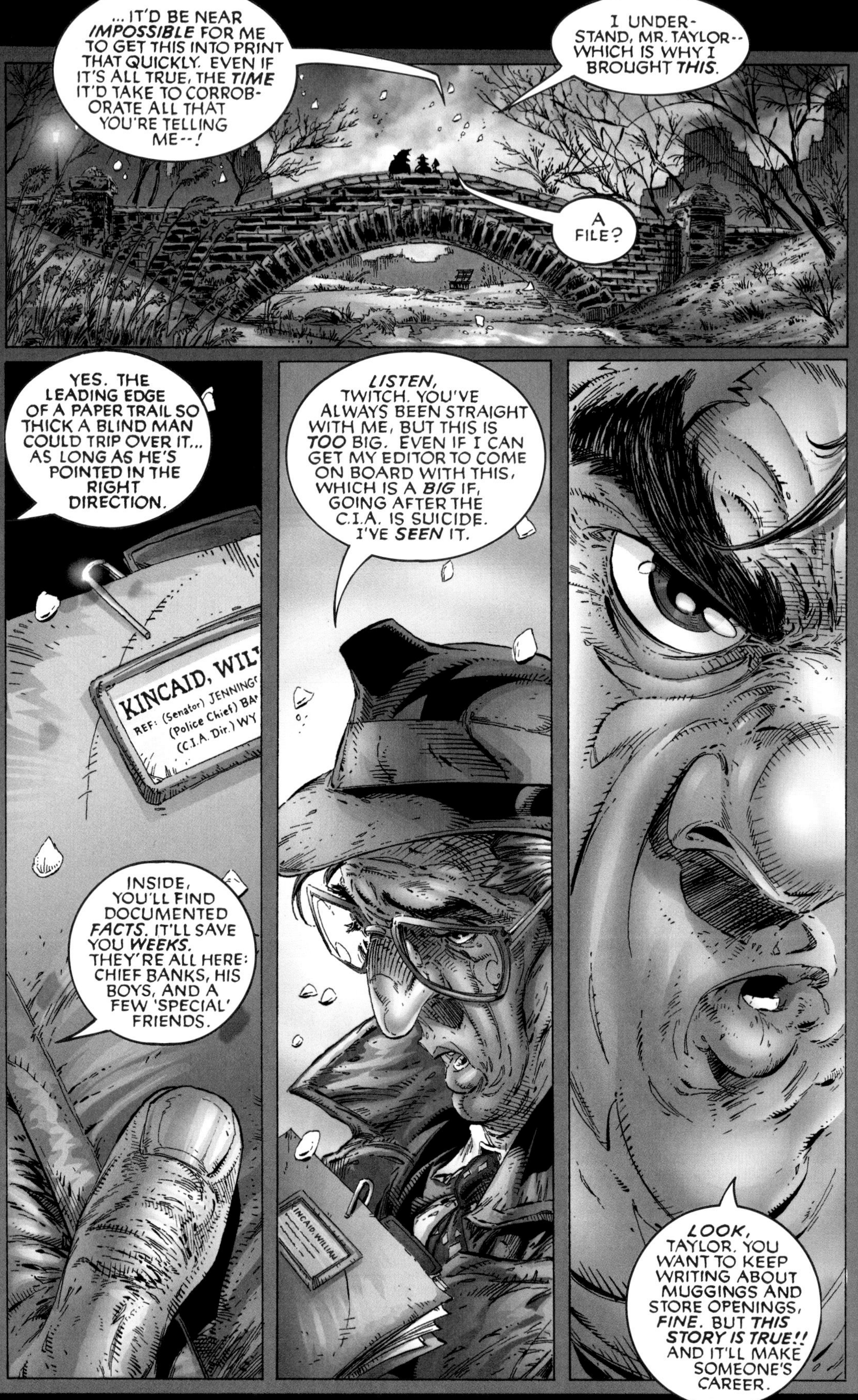

... IT'D BE NEAR *IMPOSSIBLE* FOR ME TO GET THIS INTO PRINT THAT QUICKLY. EVEN IF IT'S ALL TRUE, THE *TIME* IT'D TAKE TO CORROBORATE ALL THAT YOU'RE TELLING ME--!
I UNDERSTAND, MR. TAYLOR-- WHICH IS WHY I BROUGHT *THIS*.
A FILE?
YES. THE LEADING EDGE OF A PAPER TRAIL SO THICK A BLIND MAN COULD TRIP OVER IT... AS LONG AS HE'S POINTED IN THE RIGHT DIRECTION.
INSIDE, YOU'LL FIND DOCUMENTED *FACTS*. IT'LL SAVE YOU *WEEKS*. THEY'RE ALL HERE: CHIEF BANKS, HIS BOYS, AND A FEW 'SPECIAL' FRIENDS.
LISTEN, TWITCH. YOU'VE ALWAYS BEEN STRAIGHT WITH ME, BUT THIS IS *TOO* BIG. EVEN IF I CAN GET MY EDITOR TO COME ON BOARD WITH THIS, WHICH IS A *BIG* IF, GOING AFTER THE C.I.A. IS SUICIDE. I'VE *SEEN* IT.
LOOK, TAYLOR. YOU WANT TO KEEP WRITING ABOUT MUGGINGS AND STORE OPENINGS, *FINE*. BUT *THIS STORY IS TRUE!!* AND IT'LL MAKE SOMEONE'S CAREER.

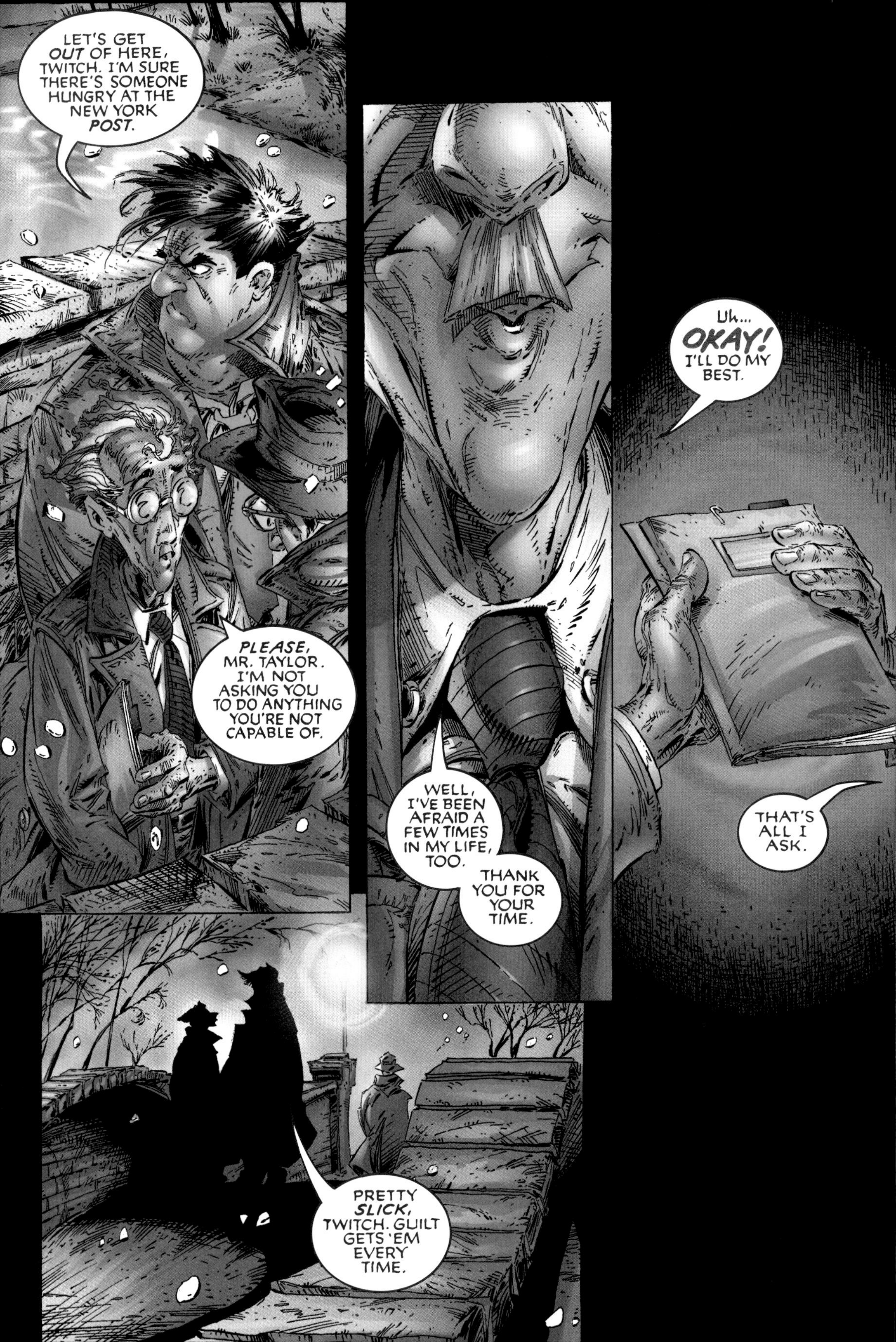

LET'S GET OUT OF HERE, TWITCH. I'M SURE THERE'S SOMEONE HUNGRY AT THE NEW YORK POST.
PLEASE, MR. TAYLOR. I'M NOT ASKING YOU TO DO ANYTHING YOU'RE NOT CAPABLE OF.
WELL, I'VE BEEN AFRAID A FEW TIMES IN MY LIFE, TOO.
THANK YOU FOR YOUR TIME.
Uh... OKAY! I'LL DO MY BEST.
THAT'S ALL I ASK.
PRETTY SLICK, TWITCH. GUILT GETS 'EM EVERY TIME.

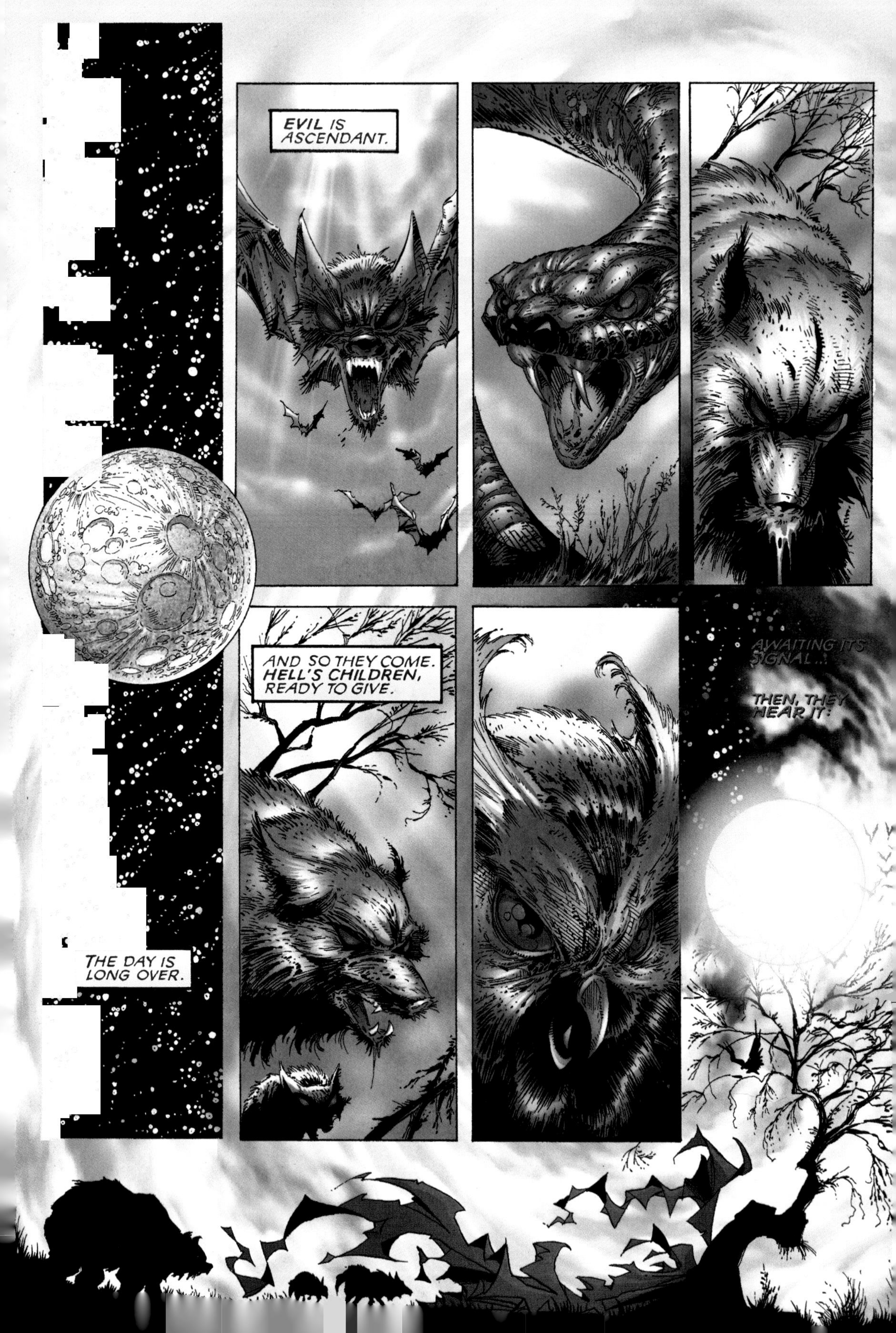
THE DAY IS LONG OVER.
EVIL IS ASCENDANT.
AND SO THEY COME. HELL'S CHILDREN, READY TO GIVE.
AWAITING ITS SIGNAL...
THEN, THEY HEAR IT:

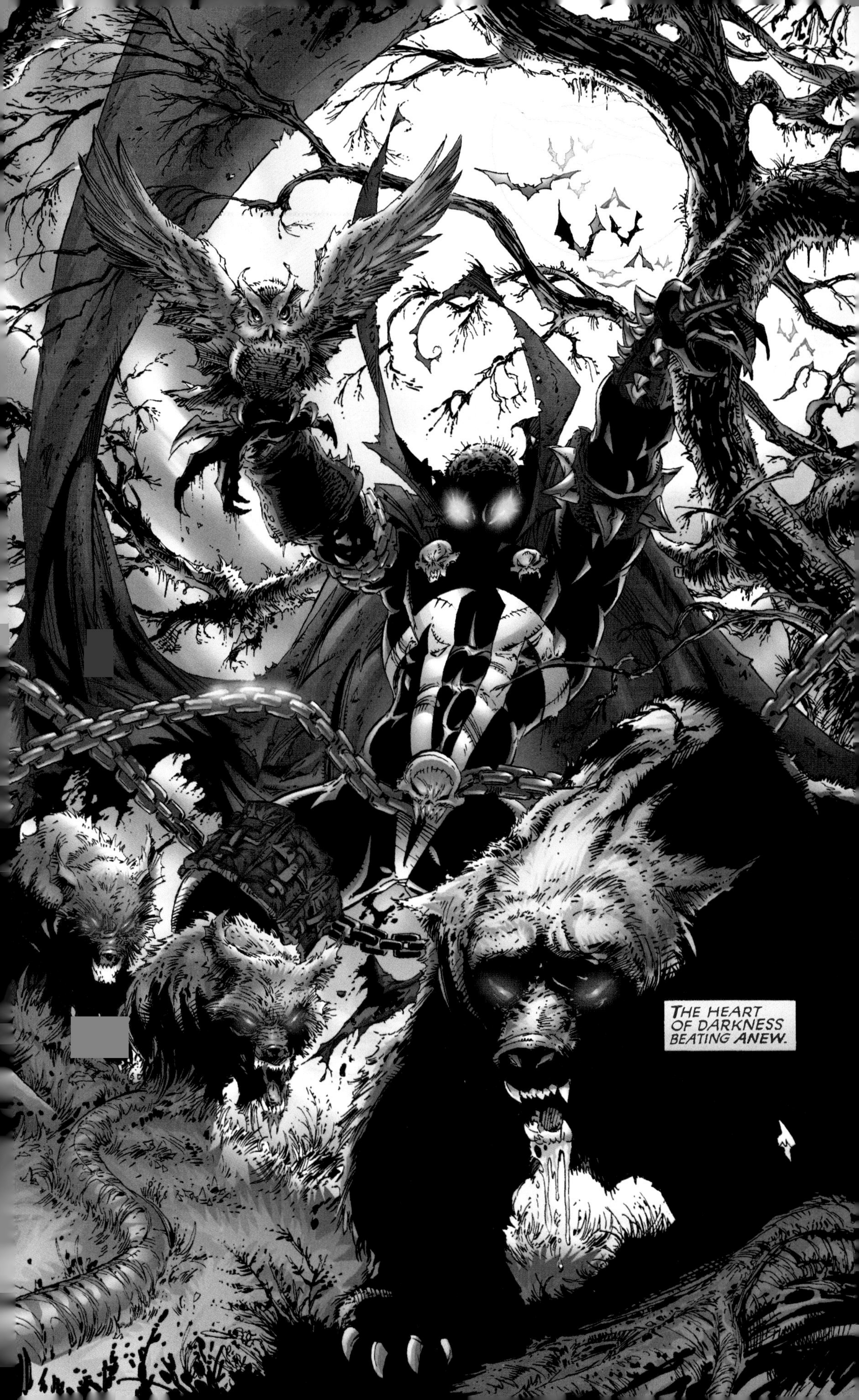
THE HEART OF DARKNESS BEATING ANEW.

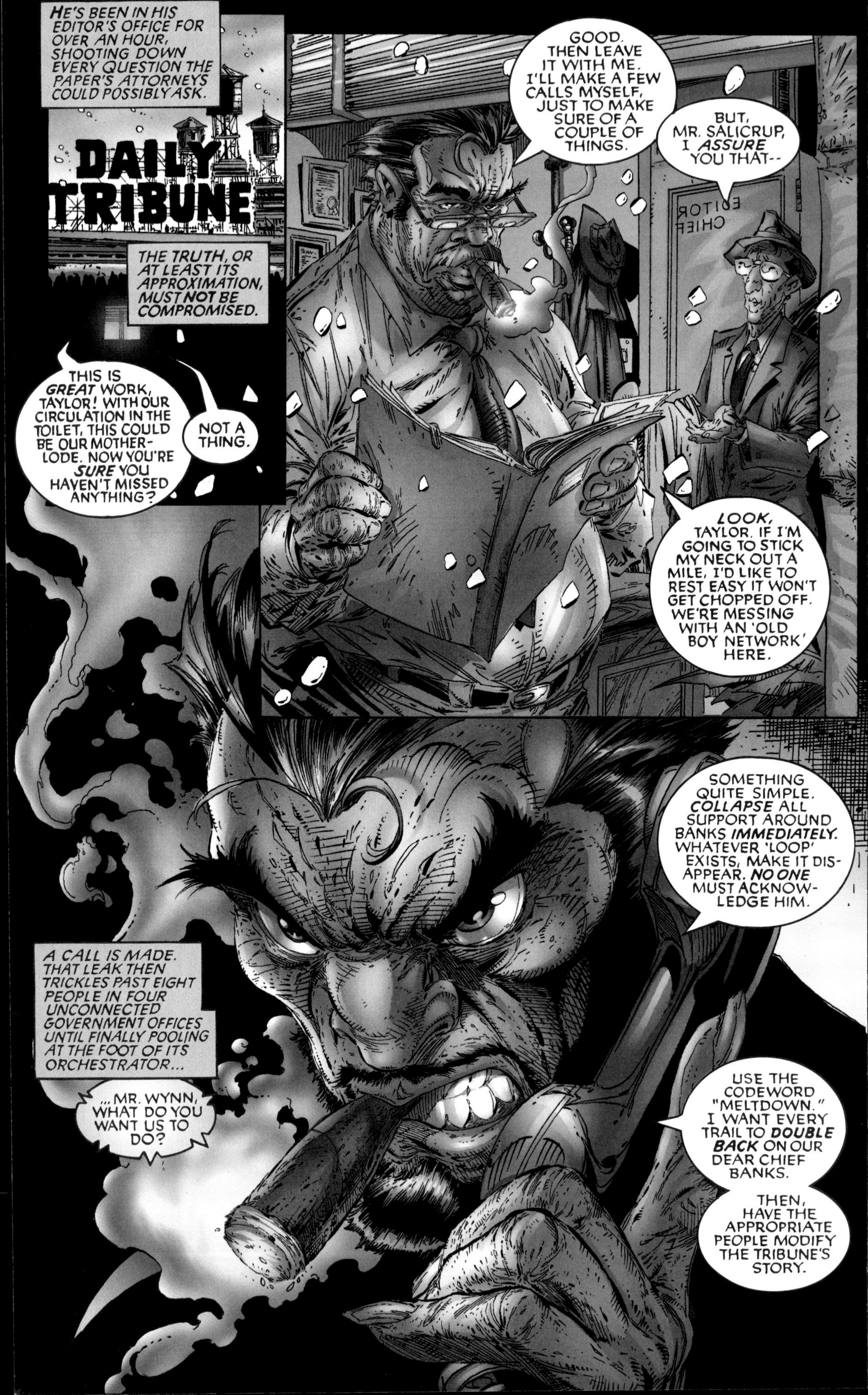
HE'S BEEN IN HIS EDITOR'S OFFICE FOR OVER AN HOUR, SHOOTING DOWN EVERY QUESTION THE PAPER'S ATTORNEYS COULD POSSIBLY ASK.
DAILY TRIBUNE
THE TRUTH, OR AT LEAST ITS APPROXIMATION, MUST NOT BE COMPROMISED.
THIS IS GREAT WORK, TAYLOR! WITH OUR CIRCULATION IN THE TOILET, THIS COULD BE OUR MOTHER-LODE. NOW YOU'RE SURE YOU HAVEN'T MISSED ANYTHING?
NOT A THING.
GOOD. THEN LEAVE IT WITH ME. I'LL MAKE A FEW CALLS MYSELF, JUST TO MAKE SURE OF A COUPLE OF THINGS.
BUT, MR. SALICRUP, I ASSURE YOU THAT--
EDITOR CHIEF
LOOK, TAYLOR. IF I'M GOING TO STICK MY NECK OUT A MILE, I'D LIKE TO REST EASY IT WON'T GET CHOPPED OFF. WE'RE MESSING WITH AN 'OLD BOY NETWORK' HERE.
A CALL IS MADE. THAT LEAK THEN TRICKLES PAST EIGHT PEOPLE IN FOUR UNCONNECTED GOVERNMENT OFFICES UNTIL FINALLY POOLING AT THE FOOT OF ITS ORCHESTRATOR...
...MR. WYNN, WHAT DO YOU WANT US TO DO?
SOMETHING QUITE SIMPLE. COLLAPSE ALL SUPPORT AROUND BANKS IMMEDIATELY. WHATEVER 'LOOP' EXISTS, MAKE IT DIS-APPEAR. NO ONE MUST ACKNOW-LEDGE HIM.
USE THE CODEWORD "MELTDOWN." I WANT EVERY TRAIL TO DOUBLE BACK ON OUR DEAR CHIEF BANKS.
THEN, HAVE THE APPROPRIATE PEOPLE MODIFY THE TRIBUNE'S STORY.

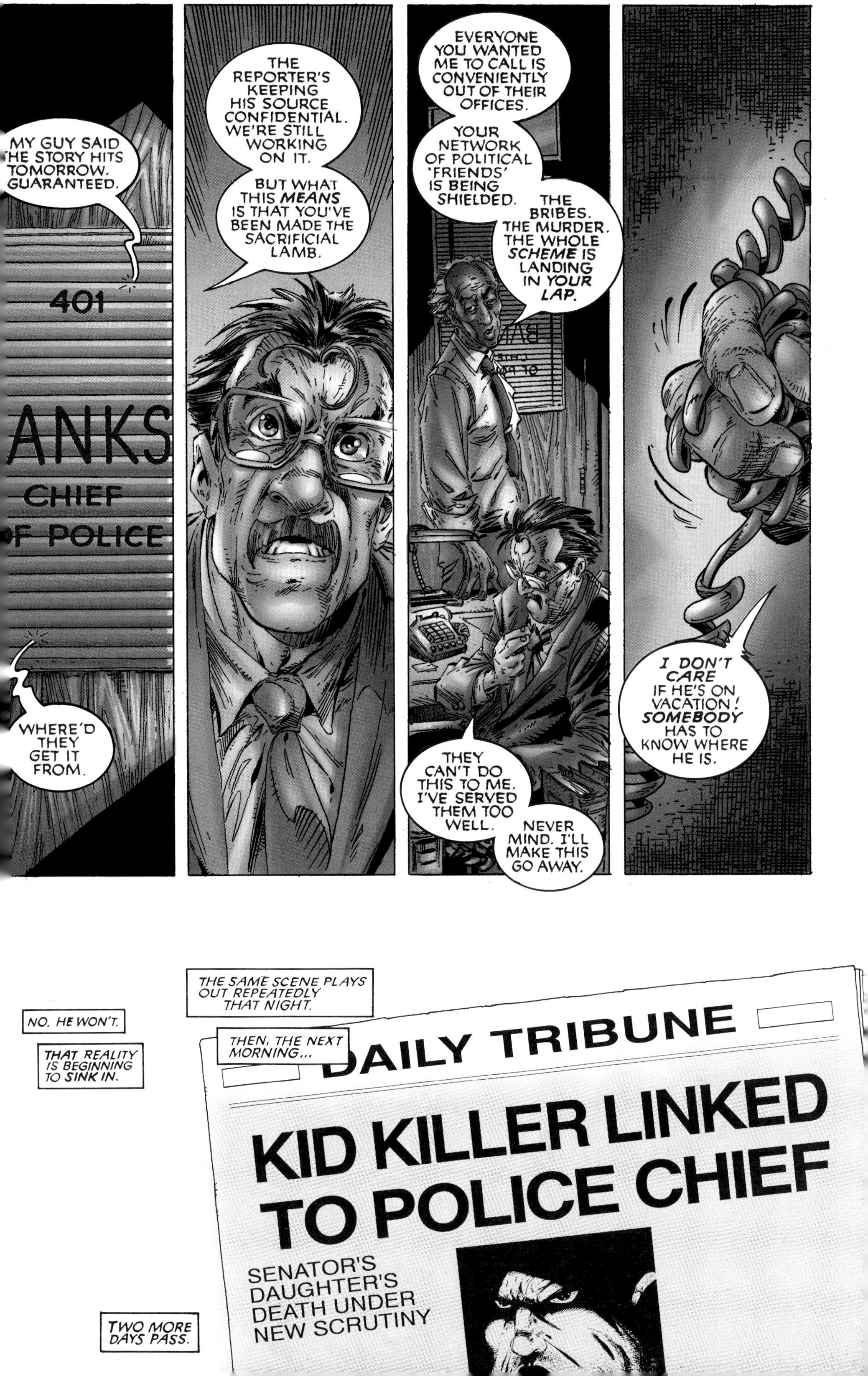

MY GUY SAID HE STORY HITS TOMORROW. GUARANTEED.
401
ANKS
CHIEF
F POLICE
WHERE'D THEY GET IT FROM.
THE REPORTER'S KEEPING HIS SOURCE CONFIDENTIAL. WE'RE STILL WORKING ON IT.
BUT WHAT THIS *MEANS* IS THAT YOU'VE BEEN MADE THE SACRIFICIAL LAMB.
EVERYONE YOU WANTED ME TO CALL IS CONVENIENTLY OUT OF THEIR OFFICES.
YOUR NETWORK OF POLITICAL 'FRIENDS' IS BEING SHIELDED.
THE BRIBES. THE MURDER. THE WHOLE *SCHEME* IS LANDING IN *YOUR LAP*.
THEY CAN'T DO THIS TO ME. I'VE SERVED THEM TOO WELL.
NEVER MIND. I'LL MAKE THIS GO AWAY.
I DON'T CARE IF HE'S ON VACATION! *SOMEBODY* HAS TO KNOW WHERE HE IS.
NO. HE WON'T.
THAT REALITY IS BEGINNING TO *SINK IN*.
THE SAME SCENE PLAYS OUT REPEATEDLY THAT NIGHT.
THEN, THE NEXT MORNING...
DAILY TRIBUNE
KID KILLER LINKED TO POLICE CHIEF
SENATOR'S DAUGHTER'S DEATH UNDER NEW SCRUTINY
TWO MORE DAYS PASS.

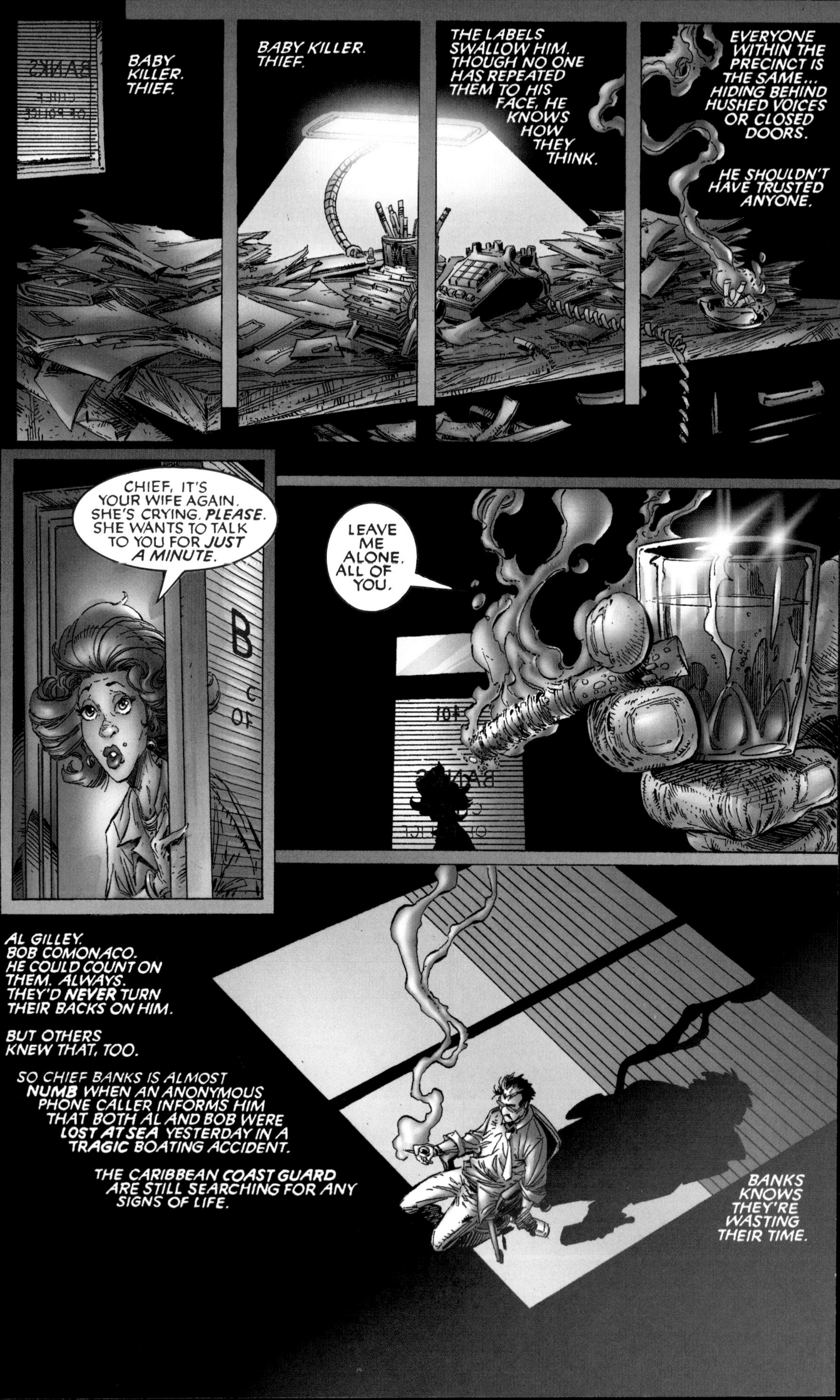

BABY KILLER. THIEF.

BABY KILLER. THIEF.

THE LABELS SWALLOW HIM. THOUGH NO ONE HAS REPEATED THEM TO HIS FACE, HE KNOWS HOW THEY THINK.

EVERYONE WITHIN THE PRECINCT IS THE SAME... HIDING BEHIND HUSHED VOICES OR CLOSED DOORS.

HE SHOULDN'T HAVE TRUSTED ANYONE.

CHIEF, IT'S YOUR WIFE AGAIN. SHE'S CRYING. *PLEASE.* SHE WANTS TO TALK TO YOU FOR *JUST A MINUTE.*

LEAVE ME ALONE, ALL OF YOU.

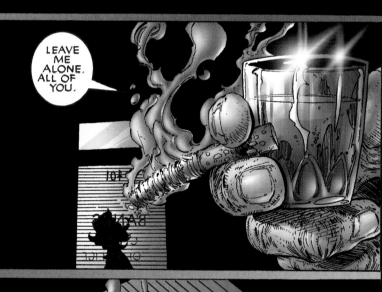

AL GILLEY. BOB COMONACO. HE COULD COUNT ON THEM, ALWAYS. THEY'D *NEVER* TURN THEIR BACKS ON HIM.

BUT OTHERS KNEW THAT, TOO.

SO CHIEF BANKS IS ALMOST *NUMB* WHEN AN ANONYMOUS PHONE CALLER INFORMS HIM THAT BOTH AL AND BOB WERE *LOST AT SEA* YESTERDAY IN A *TRAGIC* BOATING ACCIDENT.

THE CARIBBEAN COAST GUARD ARE STILL SEARCHING FOR ANY SIGNS OF LIFE.

BANKS KNOWS THEY'RE WASTING THEIR TIME.

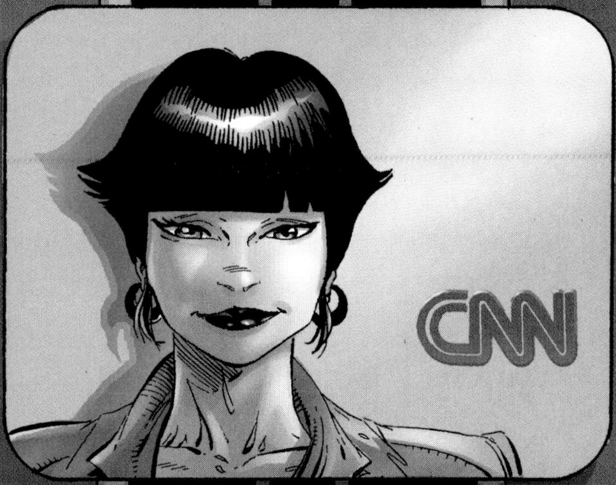
CNN

...THE SITUATION DEFIES EASY ANALYSIS. WHAT'S CLEAR IS THAT ***LOUIS BANKS,*** POLICE CHIEF OF NEW YORK CITY'S 12TH PRECINCT, HAS BEEN TIED TO EVENTS WHICH LED SEVERAL YEARS AGO TO THE DEATH OF 8-YEAR-OLD AMANDA JENNINGS, DAUGHTER OF D.C. APPROPRIATIONS SENATOR PAUL JENNINGS. BANKS' NAME WAS CONNECTED WITH THE AFFAIR WHEN A SUSPECT, ***WILLIAM KINCAID,*** WAS FOUND DEAD IN BANKS' OFFICE, AN UNSOLVED CRIME FOR WHICH BANKS WAS NOT ACCUSED.

BANKS, WHOSE PRECINCT INCLUDES THE BOWERY, HELD A NUMBER OF JOBS BEFORE BEING APPOINTED POLICE CHIEF, FROM SHERIFF IN A SMALL COUNTY IN DELAWARE TO HEAD OF A PRIVATE SECURITY FIRM IN WASHINGTON, D.C. HIS CONNECTION WITH JENNINGS DATES FROM THAT TIME, WHEN HIS FIRM WAS DISMISSED FOR JOB PERFORMANCE IRREGULARITIES. SKETCHY DETAILS SUGGEST HE THEN HELD AN INTELLIGENCE POSITION IN THE NATION'S CAPITOL BEFORE THE UNEXPLAINED MOVE UP TO THE CHIEF'S JOB.

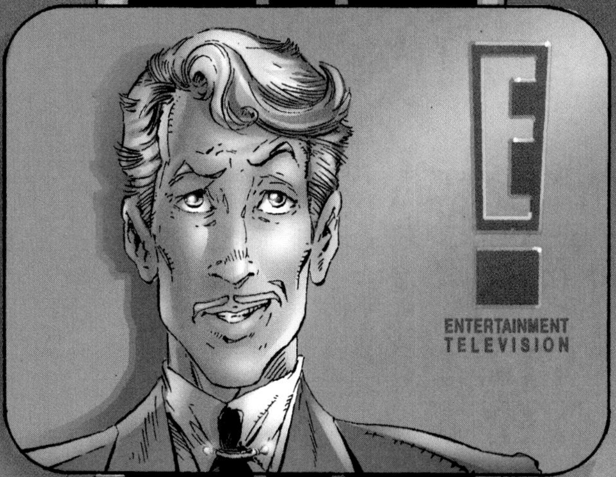
E!
ENTERTAINMENT TELEVISION

THIS FLAP OVER A CRIMINAL COVERUP IN THE BOWERY IS JUST THE MOST RECENT INDICATION THAT OFFICIAL CORRUPTION IN THIS CITY IS OUT OF CONTROL. A PERSON CAN'T HELP BUT BE NOSTALGIC FOR THE TIME WHEN SCANDALS WERE BREAKING OUT ON THE UPPER WEST SIDE OR GRAMMERCY PARK. ***THOSE*** REGIONS KNEW HOW IT WAS DONE, WITH SUBTLETY, STYLE, AND A WINK. IF THE FORCES OF JUSTICE WERE ACCOUNTABLE, ***THESE*** AFFAIRS WOULD BE GIVEN THE PUBLIC AIRING THEY DESEVE, RATHER THAN BEING HUSHED UP BY THE NEW MONEY IN TOWN. INSTEAD, WE'RE LEFT WITH MISERABLE CRIMES AGAINST CHILDREN FROM THE POOREST QUARTERS OF TOWN.

THE ONLY INTERESTING THING ABOUT THE WHOLE AFFAIR IS THE TRAGEDY OF CHIEF BANKS, A MAN WHO'S MOVED FROM JOB TO WELL-UNIFORMED JOB, ONLY TO END UP SCRAPING BOTTOM WEARING SUITS OFF THE RACK FROM WOOLWORTH'S.

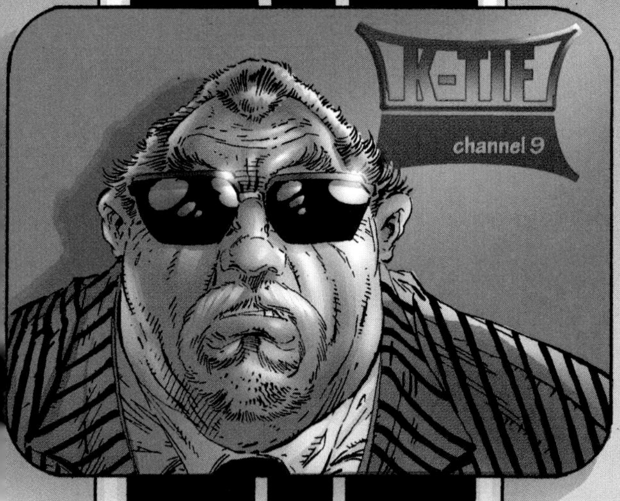
K-TIE
channel 9

SO THIS CITY'S TOP DOGS ARE HOLDING A CLOSED SESSION TO FIGURE WHAT TO TELL US PO' FOLK ABOUT A POLICE CHIEF WHO ***MIGHT*** HAVE ABETTED A ***CHILD MURDERER?*** A ***MASS*** CHILD MURDERER?!? I LOVE THIS TOWN!

LET'S SEE HOW THE FACTS LINE UP. CHIEF BANKS, FORMERLY SHERIFF BANKS, FORMERLY RENT-A-COP BANKS, FORMERLY R.O.T.C SECOND-LIEUTENANT BANKS, COMES OUT OF ***NOWHERE*** AND IS APPOINTED FOR NO APPARENT REASON TO THE MOST OBSCURE PRECINCT IN MANHATTAN. NOW WE'RE TOLD THERE'S A DIRECT LINK BETWEEN HIM, THE ***DEAD CHILD*** OF A ***SENATOR,*** AND ***KIDDIE KILLER KINCAID.*** AND WAIT-- HE ALSO HELD A JOB IN ***INTELLIGENCE?*** HEY, ARE WE SUPPOSED TO BELIEVE HE WAS DEMOTED FROM THE C.I.A. TO RIDING HERD ON ***DRUNKS,*** AND THEN TOOK HIS FRUSTRATIONS OUT ON THE SENATOR'S KID WHEN THE AGENCY HAD THEIR ***BUDGET*** SLASHED? OF COURSE, THIS SUGGESTS THE SPOOKS ARE CONTROLLING THE COPS... NAH. ***THAT*** WOULD BE ***ILLEGAL.***

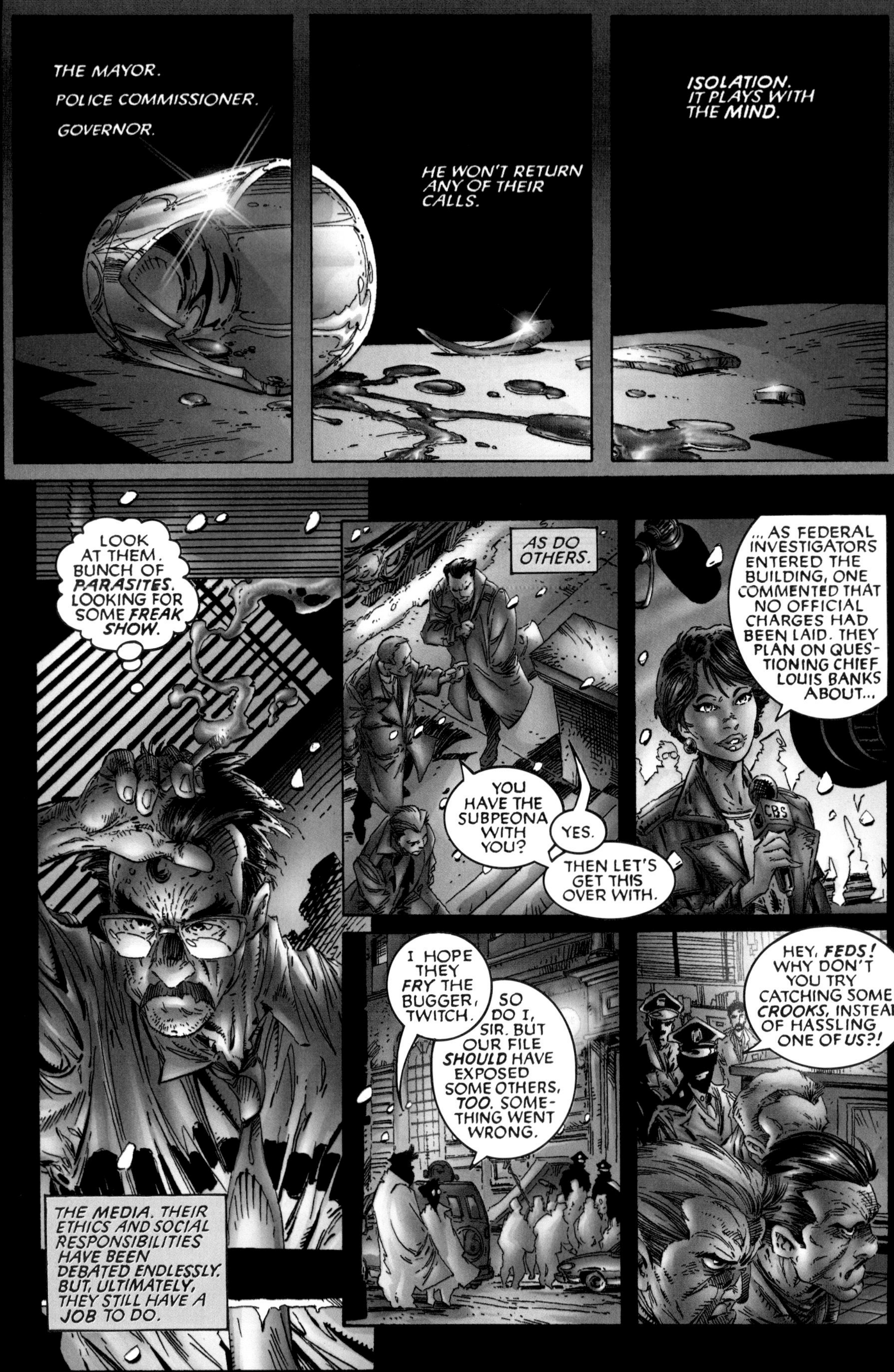
THE MAYOR.
POLICE COMMISSIONER.
GOVERNOR.
HE WON'T RETURN ANY OF THEIR CALLS.
ISOLATION. IT PLAYS WITH THE MIND.
LOOK AT THEM. BUNCH OF PARASITES. LOOKING FOR SOME FREAK SHOW.
THE MEDIA. THEIR ETHICS AND SOCIAL RESPONSIBILITIES HAVE BEEN DEBATED ENDLESSLY. BUT, ULTIMATELY, THEY STILL HAVE A JOB TO DO.
AS DO OTHERS.
YOU HAVE THE SUBPEONA WITH YOU?
YES.
THEN LET'S GET THIS OVER WITH.
...AS FEDERAL INVESTIGATORS ENTERED THE BUILDING, ONE COMMENTED THAT NO OFFICIAL CHARGES HAD BEEN LAID. THEY PLAN ON QUESTIONING CHIEF LOUIS BANKS ABOUT...
CBS
I HOPE THEY FRY THE BUGGER, TWITCH.
SO DO I, SIR. BUT OUR FILE SHOULD HAVE EXPOSED SOME OTHERS, TOO. SOMETHING WENT WRONG.
HEY, FEDS! WHY DON'T YOU TRY CATCHING SOME CROOKS, INSTEAD OF HASSLING ONE OF US?!

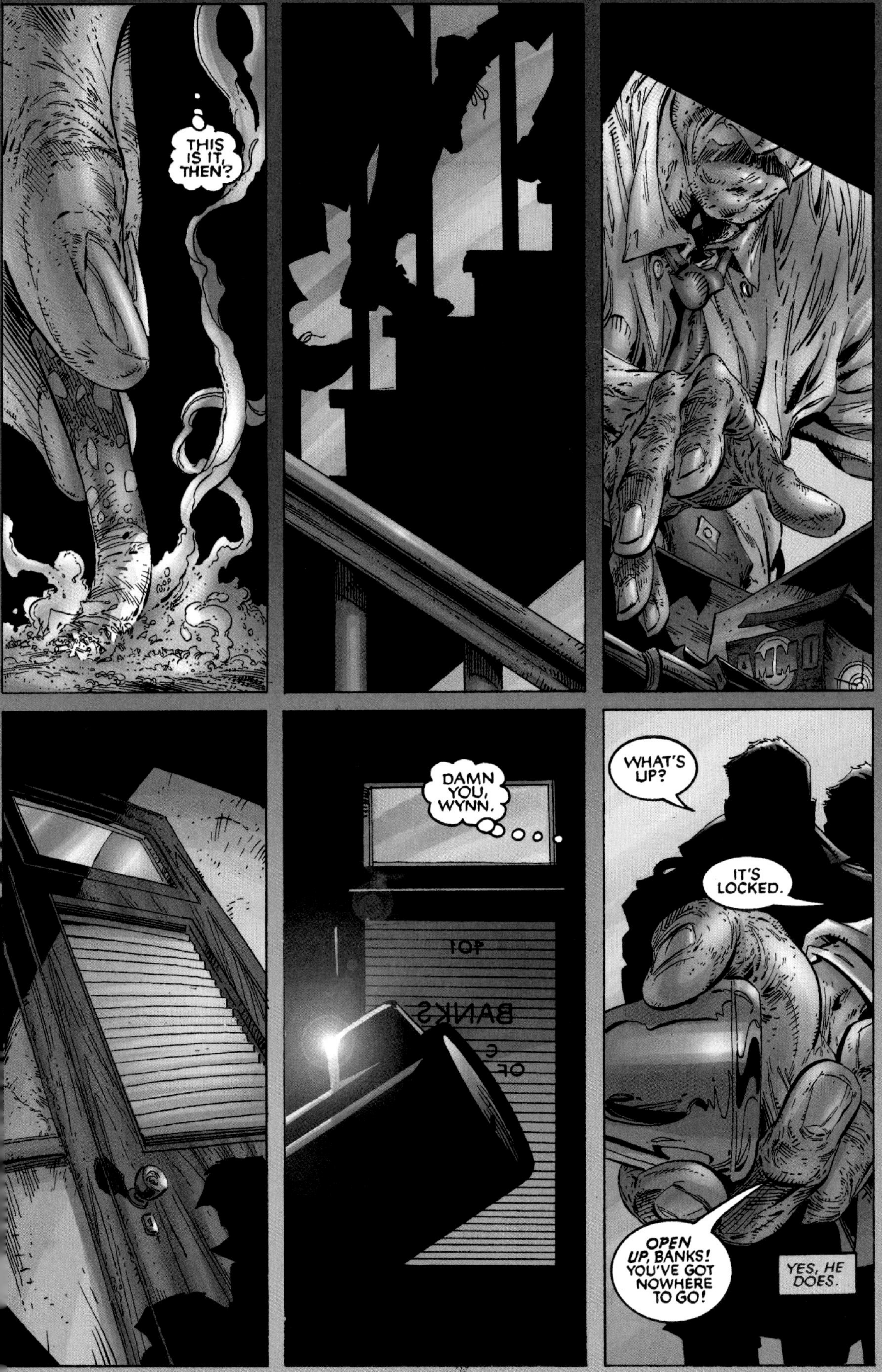
THIS IS IT, THEN?
DAMN YOU, WYNN.
WHAT'S UP?
IT'S LOCKED.
OPEN UP, BANKS! YOU'VE GOT NOWHERE TO GO!
YES, HE DOES.

BLAM

ANOTHER
BLACK ROSE
BLOOMS IN HELL
TONIGHT.

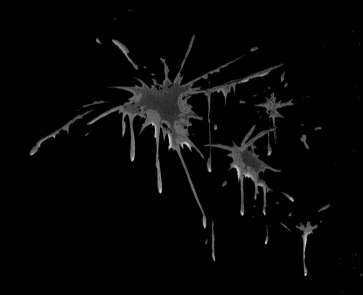

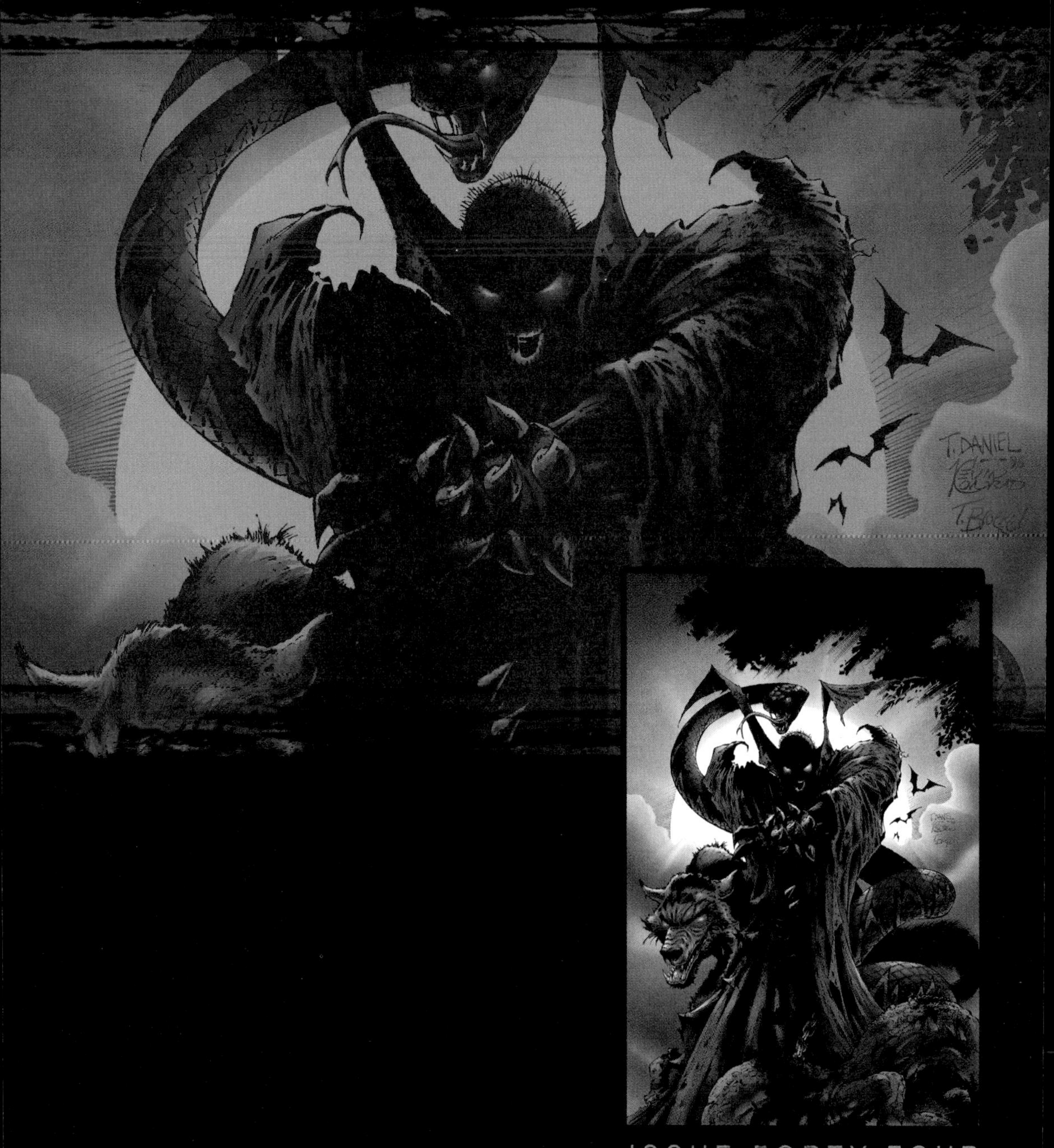
T. DANIEL

ISSUE FORTY-FOUR

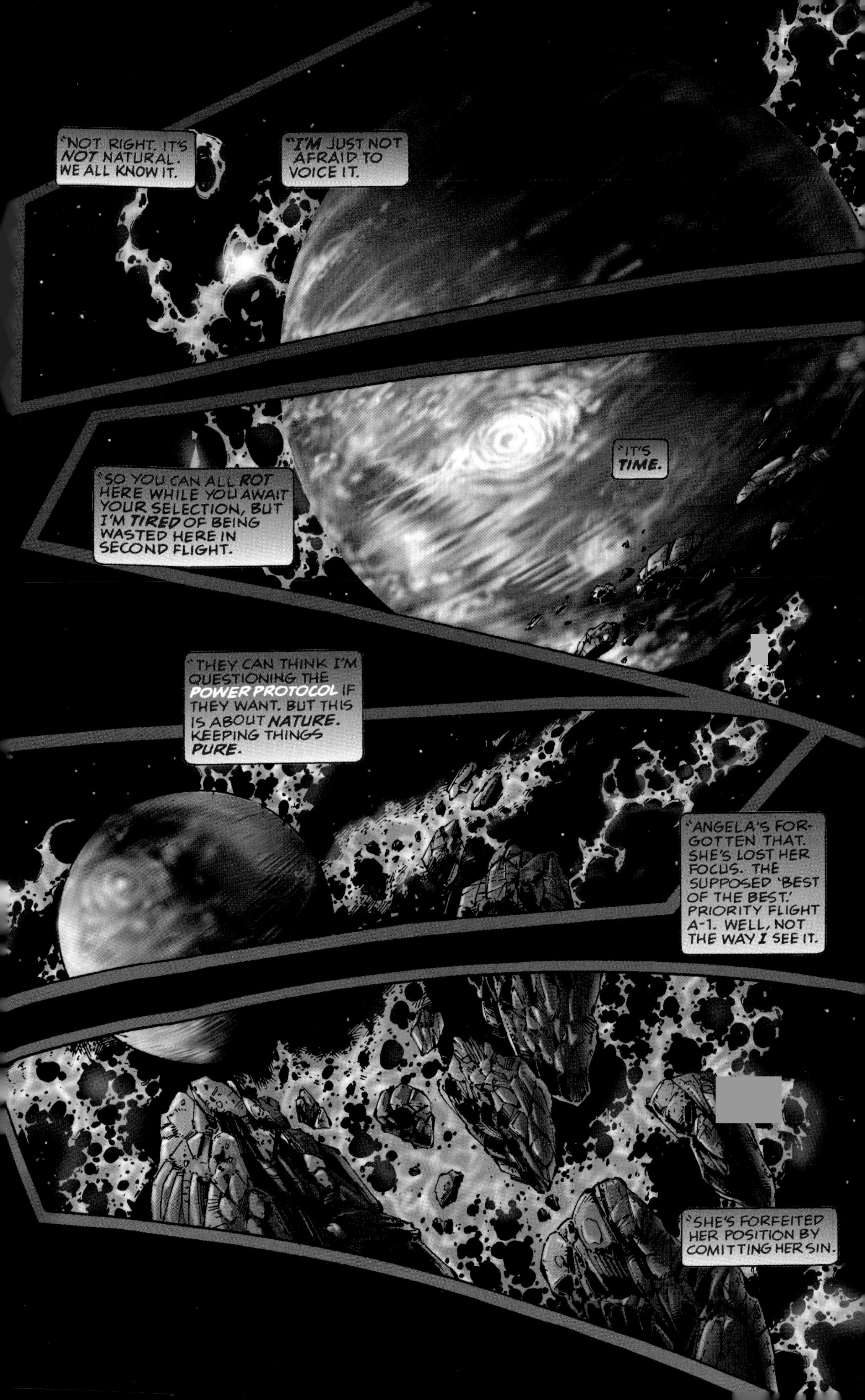
"NOT RIGHT. IT'S NOT NATURAL. WE ALL KNOW IT.
"I'M JUST NOT AFRAID TO VOICE IT.
"SO YOU CAN ALL ROT HERE WHILE YOU AWAIT YOUR SELECTION, BUT I'M TIRED OF BEING WASTED HERE IN SECOND FLIGHT.
"IT'S TIME.
"THEY CAN THINK I'M QUESTIONING THE POWER PROTOCOL IF THEY WANT. BUT THIS IS ABOUT NATURE. KEEPING THINGS PURE.
"ANGELA'S FORGOTTEN THAT. SHE'S LOST HER FOCUS. THE SUPPOSED 'BEST OF THE BEST.' PRIORITY FLIGHT A-1. WELL, NOT THE WAY I SEE IT.
"SHE'S FORFEITED HER POSITION BY COMITTING HER SIN.

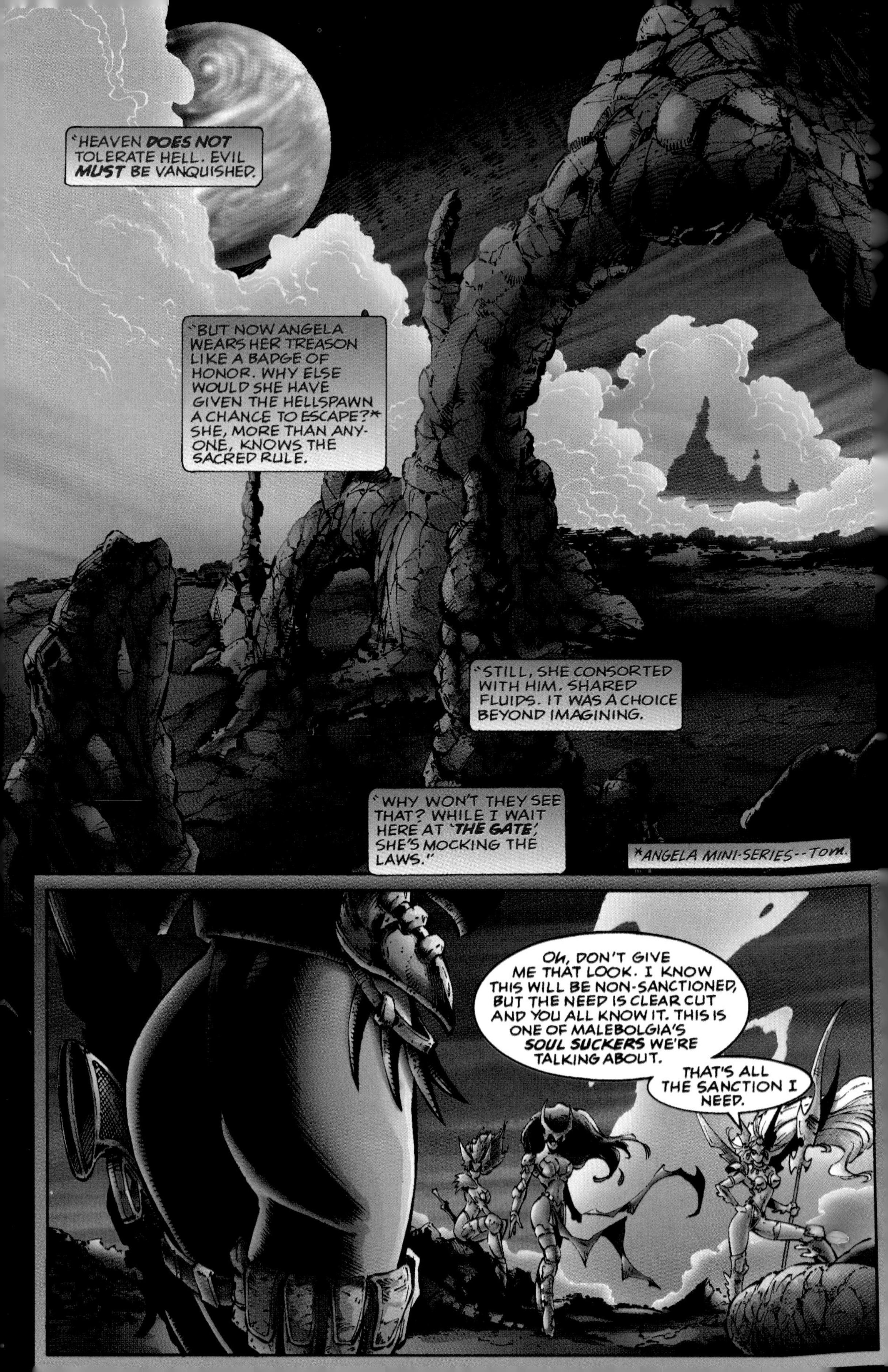
"HEAVEN **DOES NOT** TOLERATE HELL. EVIL **MUST** BE VANQUISHED.
"BUT NOW ANGELA WEARS HER TREASON LIKE A BADGE OF HONOR. WHY ELSE WOULD SHE HAVE GIVEN THE HELLSPAWN A CHANCE TO ESCAPE?* SHE, MORE THAN ANY-ONE, KNOWS THE SACRED RULE.
"STILL, SHE CONSORTED WITH HIM. SHARED FLUIDS. IT WAS A CHOICE BEYOND IMAGINING.
"WHY WON'T THEY SEE THAT? WHILE I WAIT HERE AT '**THE GATE**,' SHE'S MOCKING THE LAWS."
*ANGELA MINI-SERIES--Tom.
OH, DON'T GIVE ME THAT LOOK. I KNOW THIS WILL BE NON-SANCTIONED, BUT THE NEED IS CLEAR CUT AND YOU ALL KNOW IT. THIS IS ONE OF MALEBOLGIA'S **SOUL SUCKERS** WE'RE TALKING ABOUT.
THAT'S ALL THE SANCTION I NEED.

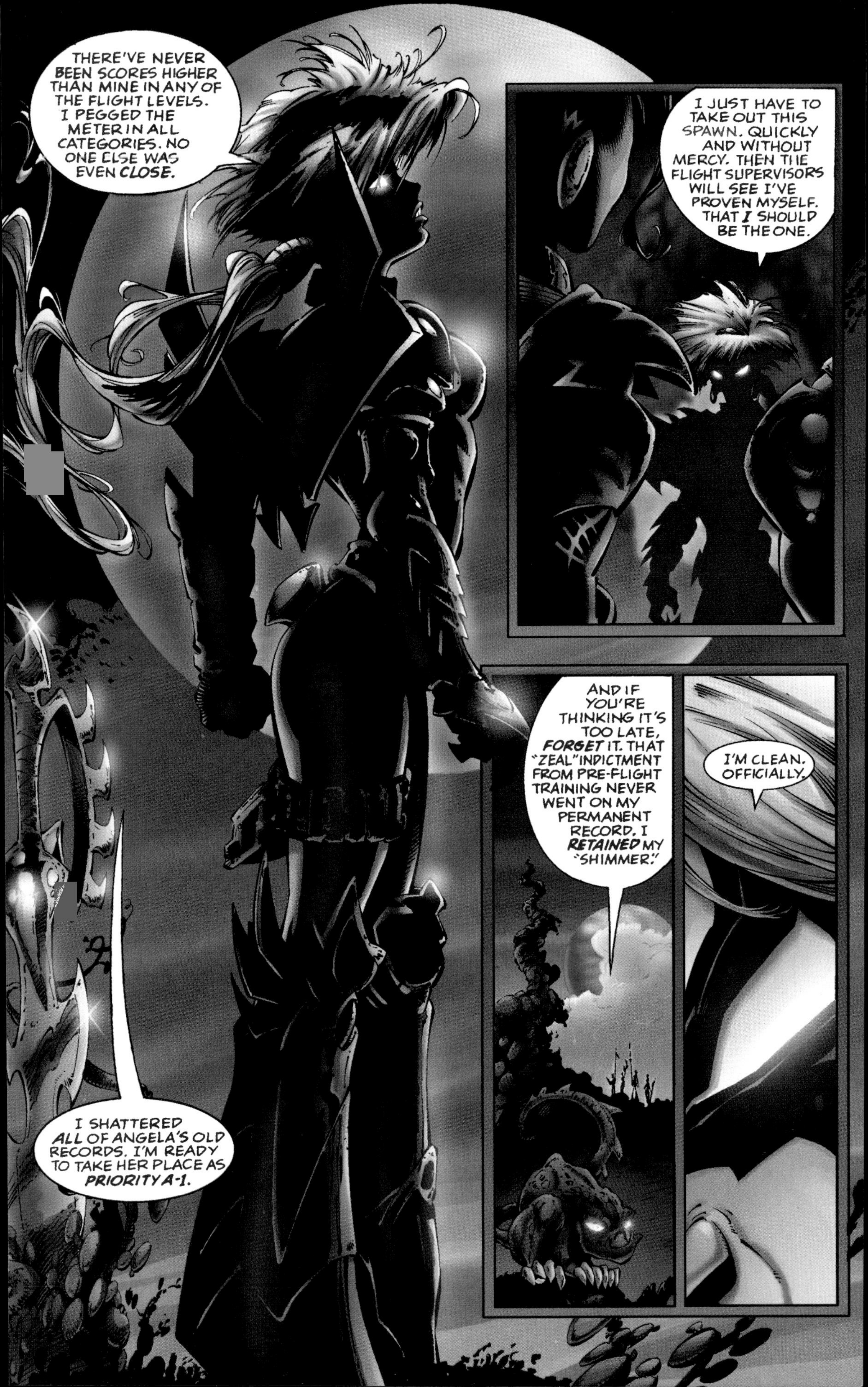
THERE'VE NEVER BEEN SCORES HIGHER THAN MINE IN ANY OF THE FLIGHT LEVELS. I PEGGED THE METER IN ALL CATEGORIES. NO ONE ELSE WAS EVEN *CLOSE.*
I SHATTERED *ALL* OF ANGELA'S OLD RECORDS. I'M READY TO TAKE HER PLACE AS *PRIORITY A-1.*
I JUST HAVE TO TAKE OUT THIS SPAWN. QUICKLY AND WITHOUT MERCY. THEN THE FLIGHT SUPERVISORS WILL SEE I'VE PROVEN MYSELF. THAT *I* SHOULD BE THE ONE.
AND IF YOU'RE THINKING IT'S TOO LATE, *FORGET* IT. THAT "ZEAL" INDICTMENT FROM PRE-FLIGHT TRAINING NEVER WENT ON MY PERMANENT RECORD. I *RETAINED* MY "SHIMMER."
I'M CLEAN. OFFICIALLY.

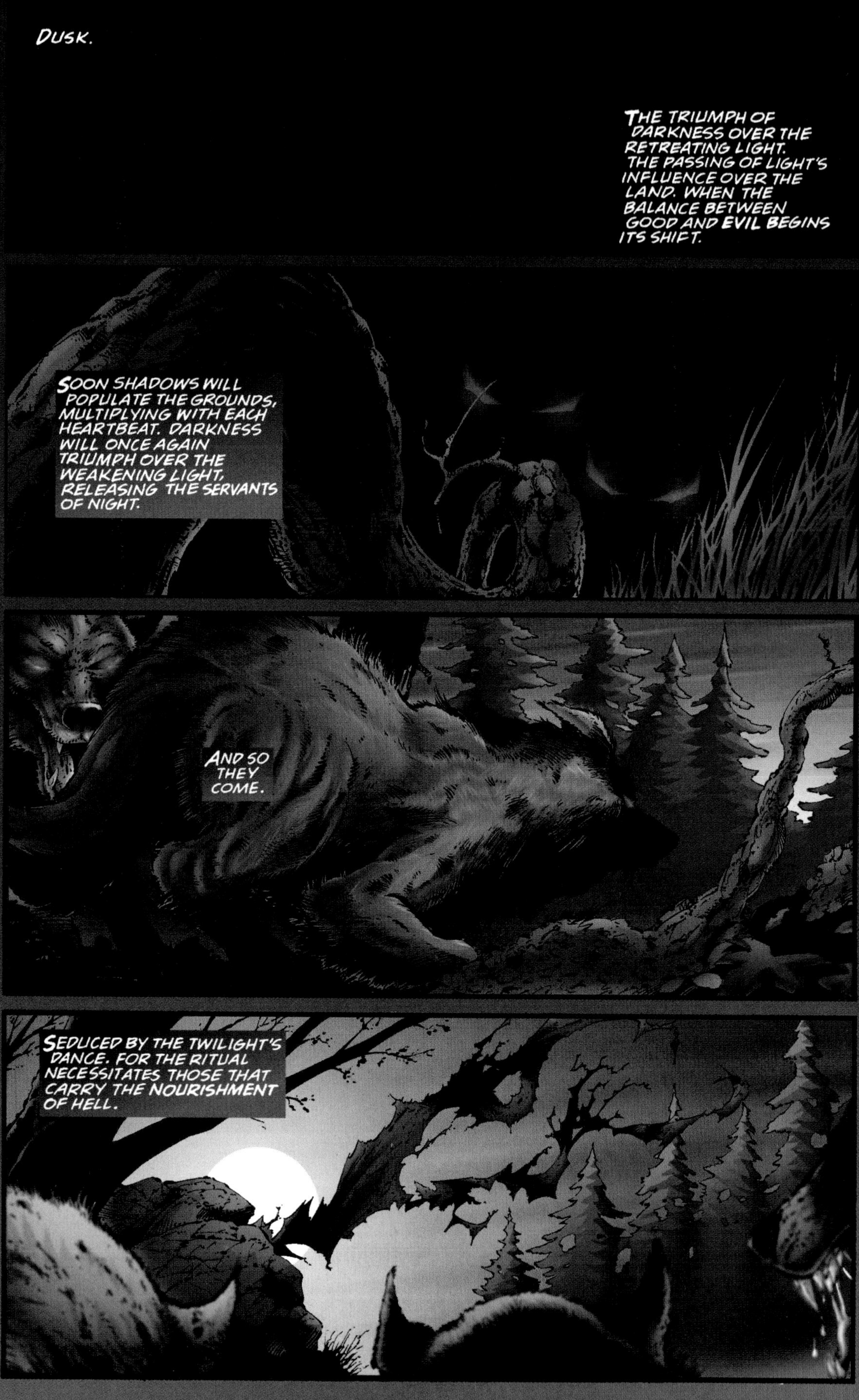
DUSK.
THE TRIUMPH OF DARKNESS OVER THE RETREATING LIGHT. THE PASSING OF LIGHT'S INFLUENCE OVER THE LAND. WHEN THE BALANCE BETWEEN GOOD AND EVIL BEGINS ITS SHIFT.
SOON SHADOWS WILL POPULATE THE GROUNDS, MULTIPLYING WITH EACH HEARTBEAT. DARKNESS WILL ONCE AGAIN TRIUMPH OVER THE WEAKENING LIGHT, RELEASING THE SERVANTS OF NIGHT.
AND SO THEY COME.
SEDUCED BY THE TWILIGHT'S DANCE. FOR THE RITUAL NECESSITATES THOSE THAT CARRY THE NOURISHMENT OF HELL.

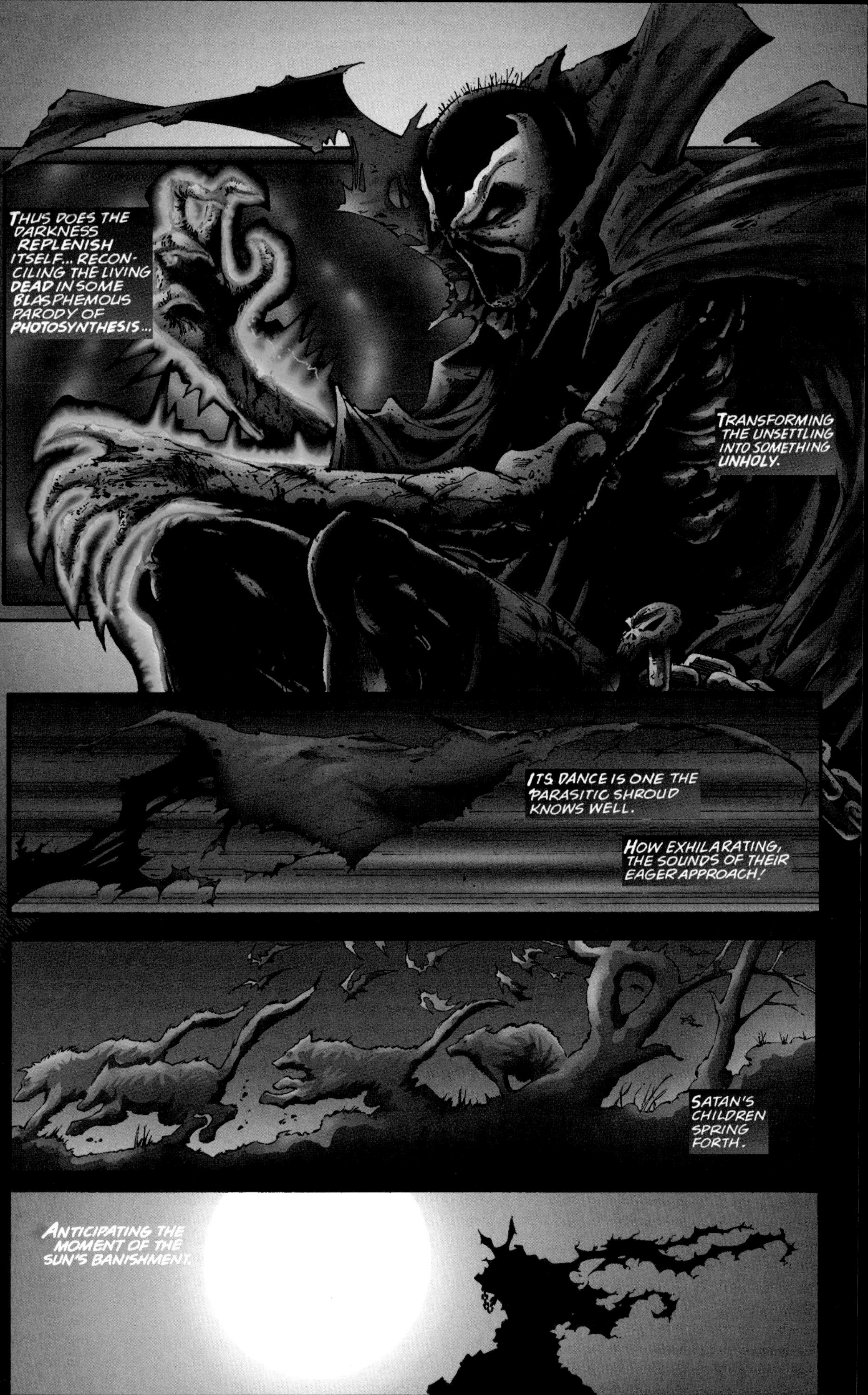

THUS DOES THE DARKNESS REPLENISH ITSELF... RECONCILING THE LIVING DEAD IN SOME BLASPHEMOUS PARODY OF PHOTOSYNTHESIS...
TRANSFORMING THE UNSETTLING INTO SOMETHING UNHOLY.
ITS DANCE IS ONE THE PARASITIC SHROUD KNOWS WELL.
HOW EXHILARATING, THE SOUNDS OF THEIR EAGER APPROACH!
SATAN'S CHILDREN SPRING FORTH.
ANTICIPATING THE MOMENT OF THE SUN'S BANISHMENT.

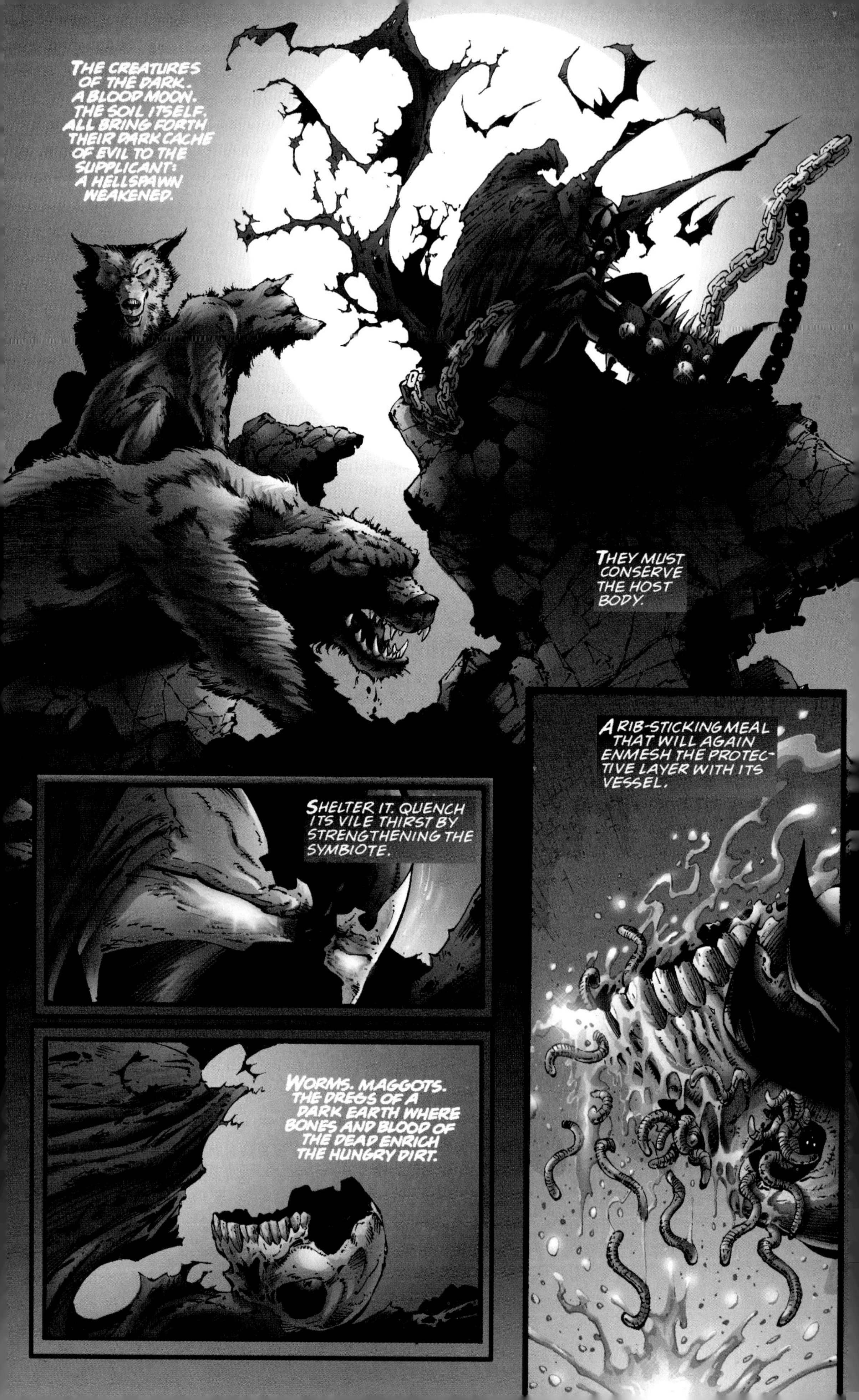
THE CREATURES OF THE DARK. A BLOOD MOON. THE SOIL ITSELF. ALL BRING FORTH THEIR DARK CACHE OF EVIL TO THE SUPPLICANT: A HELLSPAWN WEAKENED.
THEY MUST CONSERVE THE HOST BODY.
SHELTER IT. QUENCH ITS VILE THIRST BY STRENGTHENING THE SYMBIOTE.
WORMS. MAGGOTS. THE DREGS OF A DARK EARTH WHERE BONES AND BLOOD OF THE DEAD ENRICH THE HUNGRY DIRT.
A RIB-STICKING MEAL THAT WILL AGAIN ENMESH THE PROTECTIVE LAYER WITH ITS VESSEL.

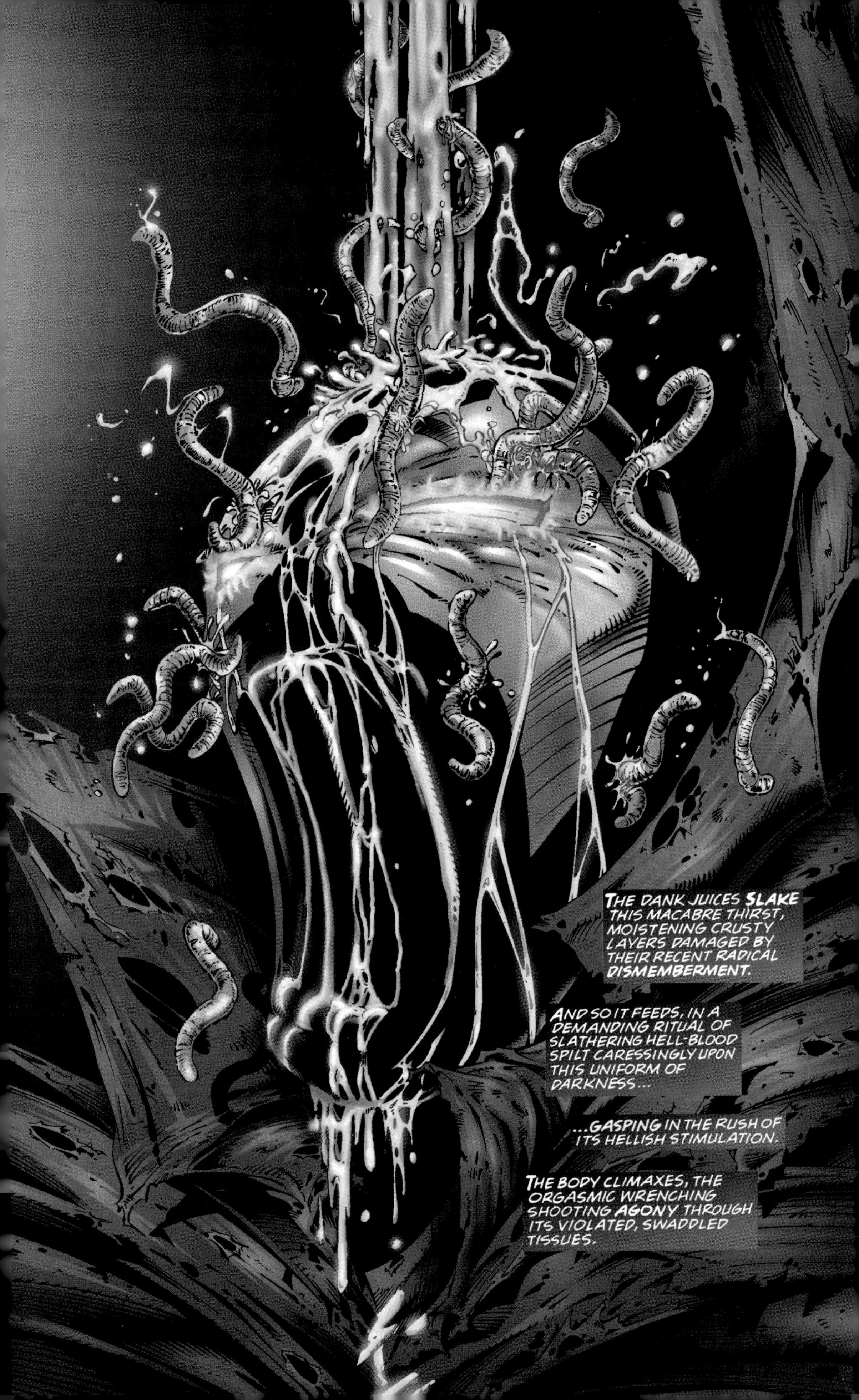
THE DANK JUICES SLAKE THIS MACABRE THIRST, MOISTENING CRUSTY LAYERS DAMAGED BY THEIR RECENT RADICAL DISMEMBERMENT.
AND SO IT FEEDS, IN A DEMANDING RITUAL OF SLATHERING HELL-BLOOD SPILT CARESSINGLY UPON THIS UNIFORM OF DARKNESS...
...GASPING IN THE RUSH OF ITS HELLISH STIMULATION.
THE BODY CLIMAXES, THE ORGASMIC WRENCHING SHOOTING AGONY THROUGH ITS VIOLATED, SWADDLED TISSUES.

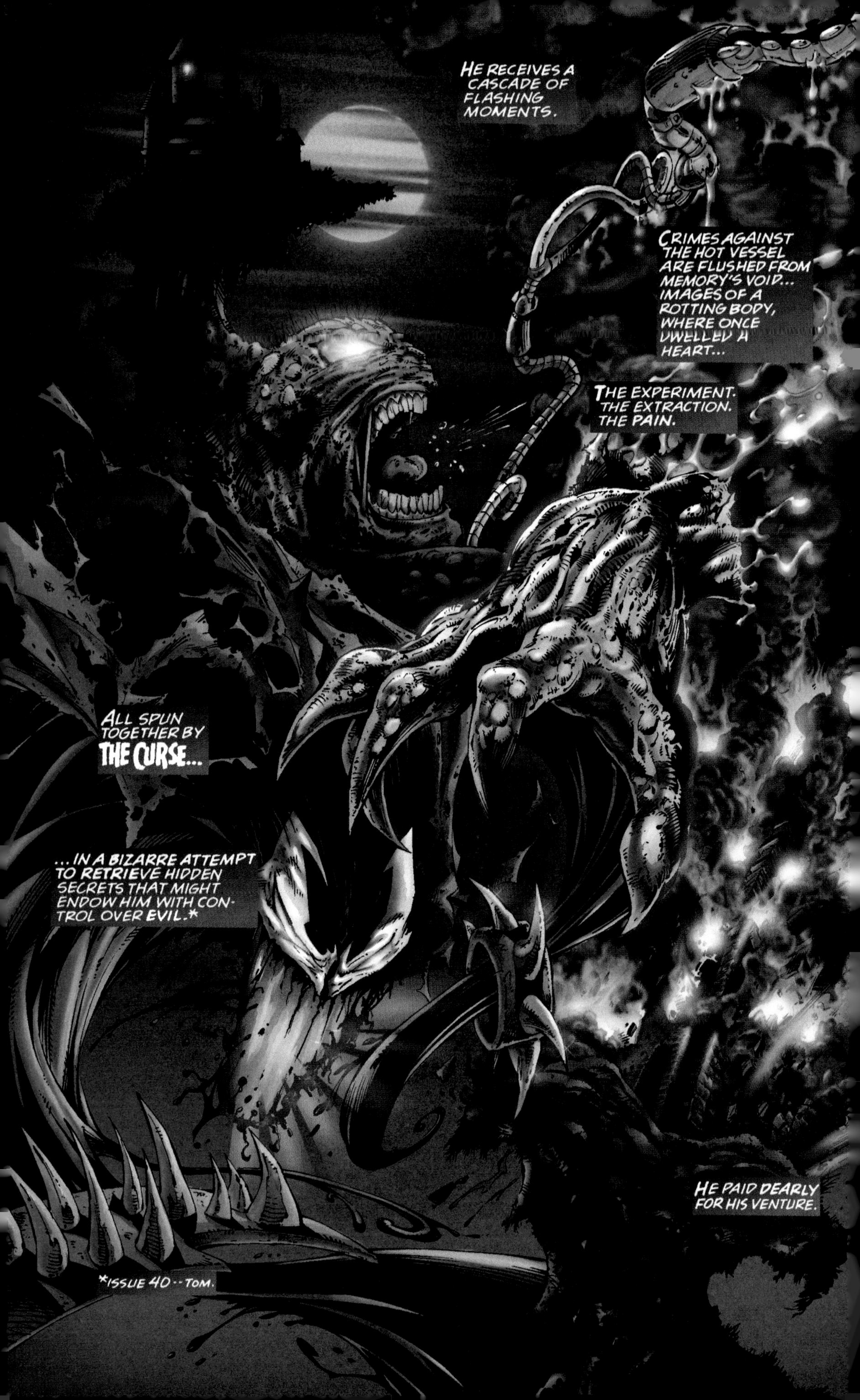
HE RECEIVES A CASCADE OF FLASHING MOMENTS.
CRIMES AGAINST THE HOT VESSEL ARE FLUSHED FROM MEMORY'S VOID... IMAGES OF A ROTTING BODY, WHERE ONCE DWELLED A HEART...
THE EXPERIMENT. THE EXTRACTION. THE PAIN.
ALL SPUN TOGETHER BY THE CURSE...
...IN A BIZARRE ATTEMPT TO RETRIEVE HIDDEN SECRETS THAT MIGHT ENDOW HIM WITH CONTROL OVER EVIL.*
HE PAID DEARLY FOR HIS VENTURE.
*ISSUE 40--TOM.

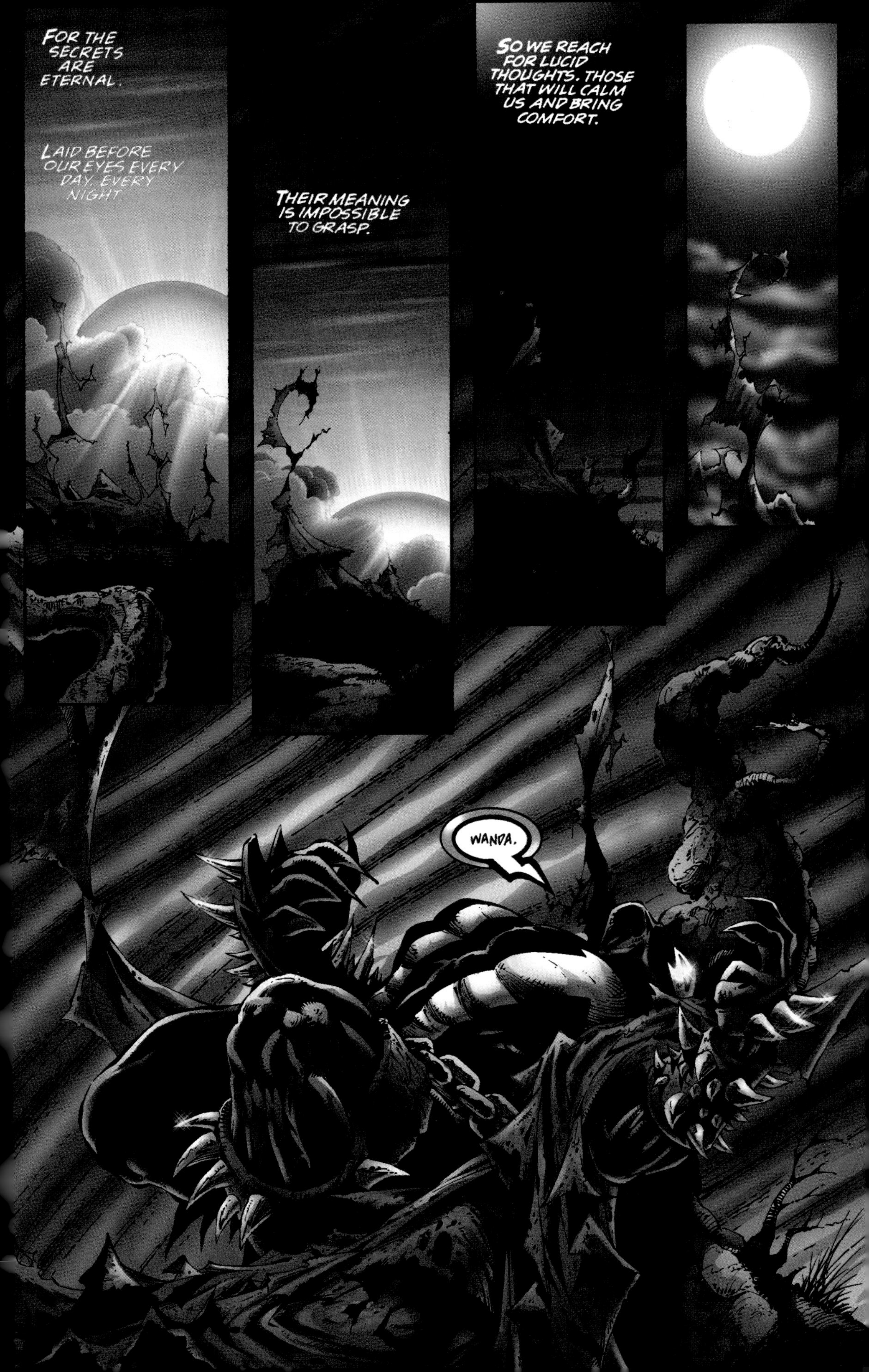
FOR THE SECRETS ARE ETERNAL.
LAID BEFORE OUR EYES EVERY DAY, EVERY NIGHT.
THEIR MEANING IS IMPOSSIBLE TO GRASP.
SO WE REACH FOR LUCID THOUGHTS. THOSE THAT WILL CALM US AND BRING COMFORT.
WANDA.

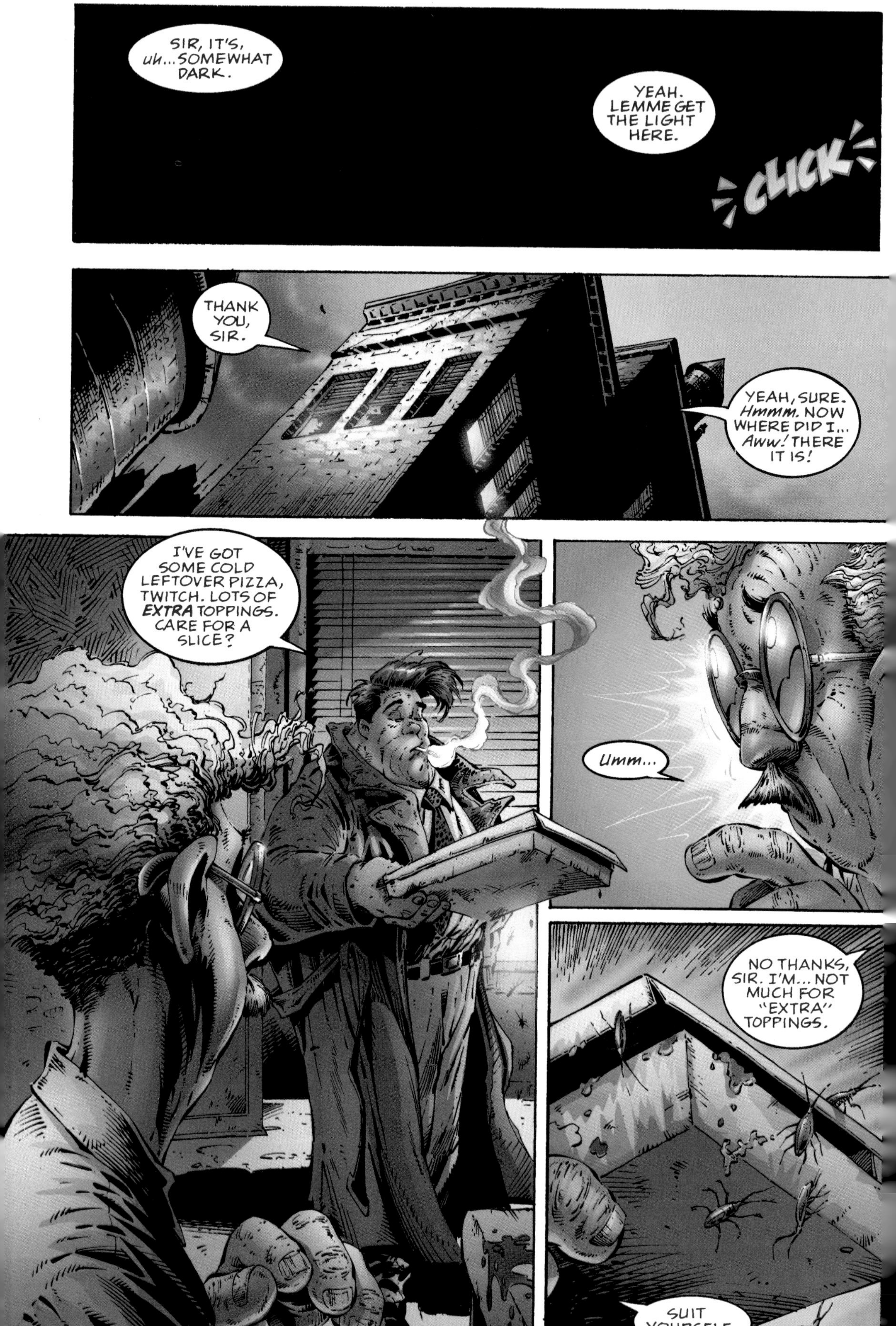
SIR, IT'S, uh... SOMEWHAT DARK.
YEAH. LEMME GET THE LIGHT HERE.
CLICK
THANK YOU, SIR.
YEAH, SURE. Hmmm. NOW WHERE DID I... Aww! THERE IT IS!
I'VE GOT SOME COLD LEFTOVER PIZZA, TWITCH. LOTS OF EXTRA TOPPINGS. CARE FOR A SLICE?
Umm...
NO THANKS, SIR. I'M... NOT MUCH FOR "EXTRA" TOPPINGS.
SUIT YOURSELF.

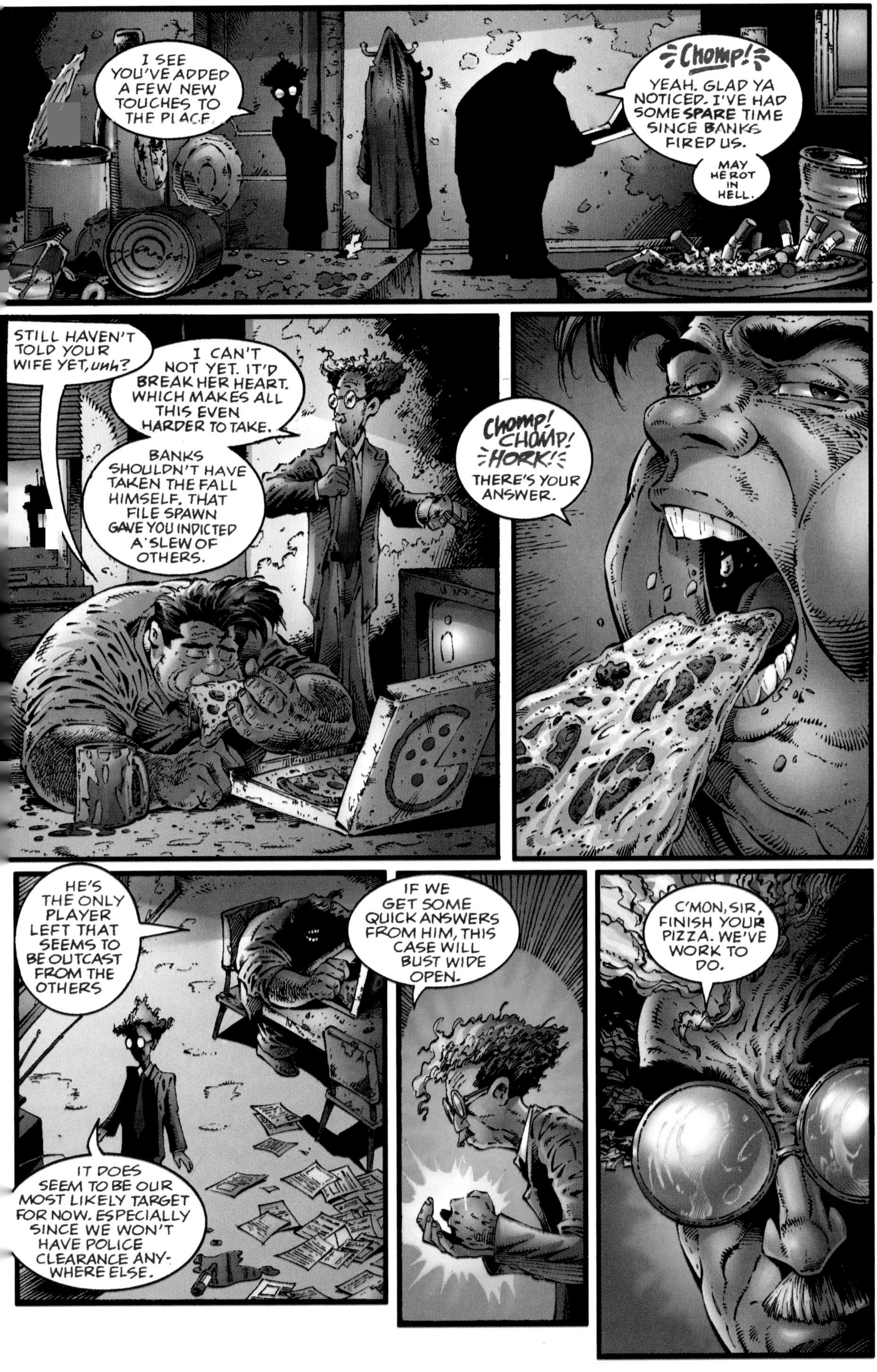
I SEE YOU'VE ADDED A FEW NEW TOUCHES TO THE PLACE.
CHOMP!
YEAH. GLAD YA NOTICED. I'VE HAD SOME **SPARE** TIME SINCE BANKS FIRED US.
MAY HE ROT IN HELL.
STILL HAVEN'T TOLD YOUR WIFE YET, *unh*?
I CAN'T NOT YET. IT'D BREAK HER HEART. WHICH MAKES ALL THIS EVEN HARDER TO TAKE.
BANKS SHOULDN'T HAVE TAKEN THE FALL HIMSELF. THAT FILE SPAWN GAVE YOU INDICTED A SLEW OF OTHERS.
CHOMP! CHOMP! HORK!
THERE'S YOUR ANSWER.
HE'S THE ONLY PLAYER LEFT THAT SEEMS TO BE OUTCAST FROM THE OTHERS
IT DOES SEEM TO BE OUR MOST LIKELY TARGET FOR NOW. ESPECIALLY SINCE WE WON'T HAVE POLICE CLEARANCE ANYWHERE ELSE.
IF WE GET SOME QUICK ANSWERS FROM HIM, THIS CASE WILL BUST WIDE OPEN.
C'MON, SIR, FINISH YOUR PIZZA. WE'VE WORK TO DO.

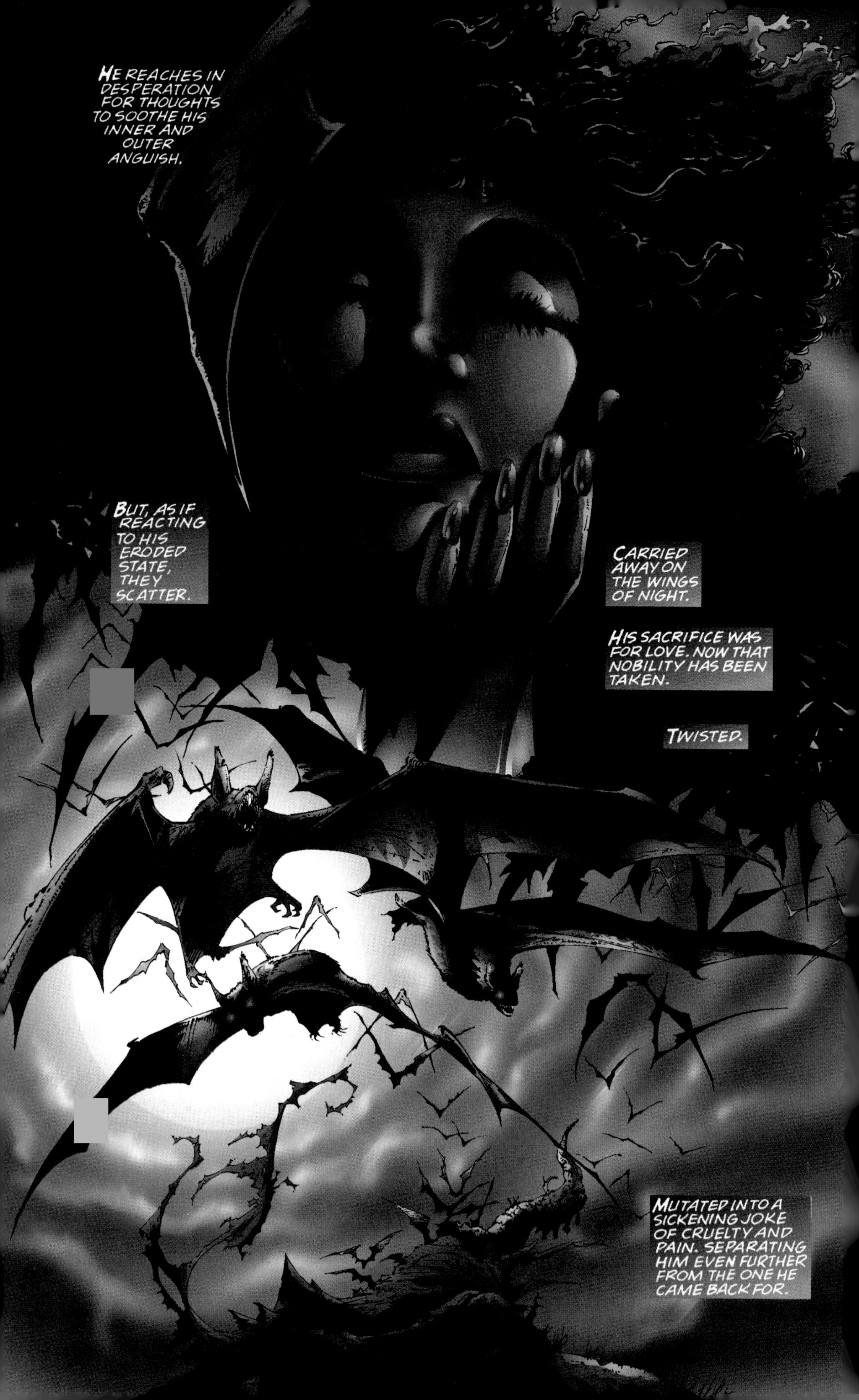
HE REACHES IN DESPERATION FOR THOUGHTS TO SOOTHE HIS INNER AND OUTER ANGUISH.
BUT, AS IF REACTING TO HIS ERODED STATE, THEY SCATTER.
CARRIED AWAY ON THE WINGS OF NIGHT.
HIS SACRIFICE WAS FOR LOVE. NOW THAT NOBILITY HAS BEEN TAKEN.
TWISTED.
MUTATED INTO A SICKENING JOKE OF CRUELTY AND PAIN. SEPARATING HIM EVEN FURTHER FROM THE ONE HE CAME BACK FOR.

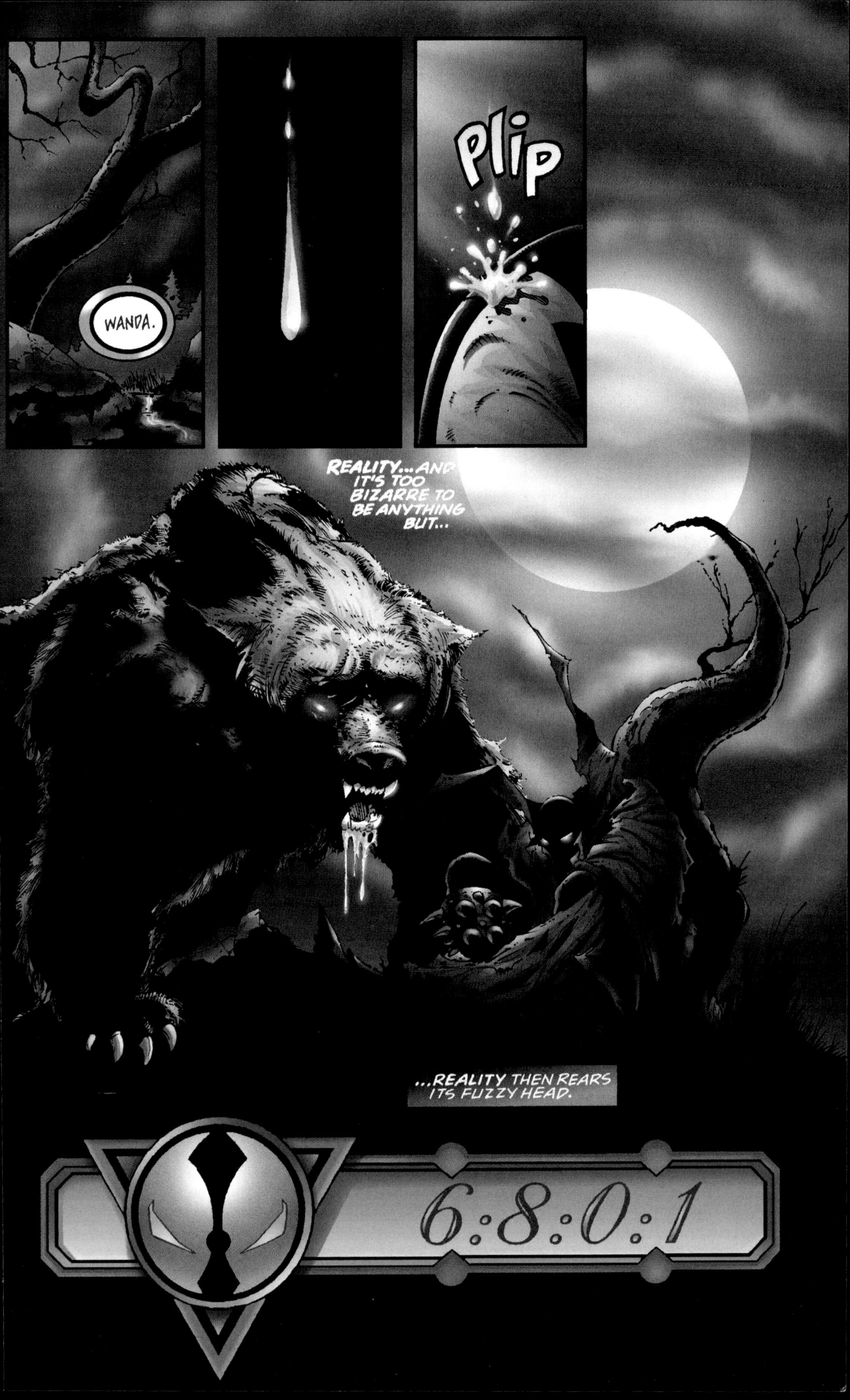
WANDA.
PLIP
REALITY...AND IT'S TOO BIZARRE TO BE ANYTHING BUT...
...REALITY THEN REARS ITS FUZZY HEAD.
6:8:0:1

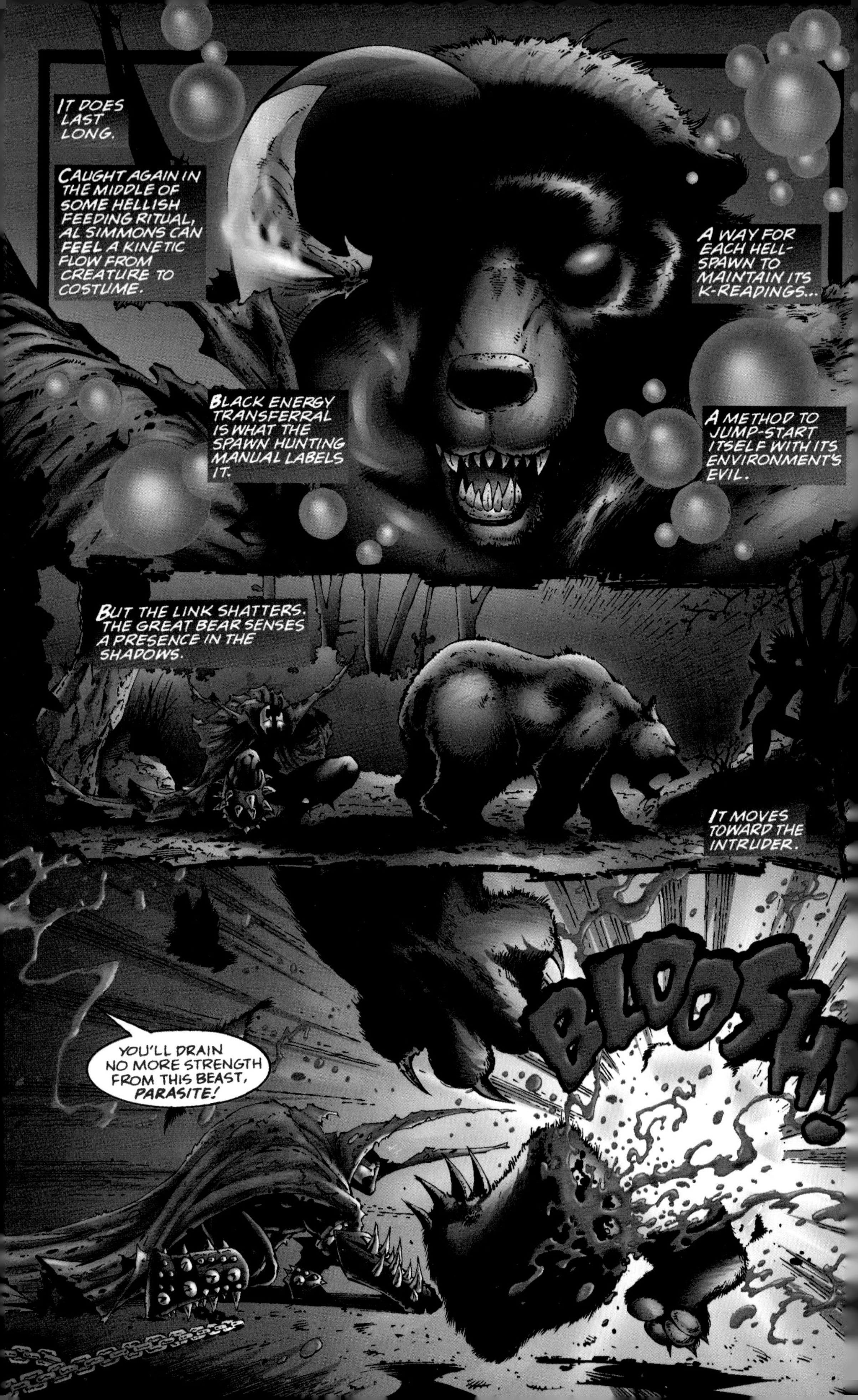
IT DOES LAST LONG.
CAUGHT AGAIN IN THE MIDDLE OF SOME HELLISH FEEDING RITUAL, AL SIMMONS CAN FEEL A KINETIC FLOW FROM CREATURE TO COSTUME.
A WAY FOR EACH HELL-SPAWN TO MAINTAIN ITS K-READINGS...
BLACK ENERGY TRANSFERRAL IS WHAT THE SPAWN HUNTING MANUAL LABELS IT.
A METHOD TO JUMP-START ITSELF WITH ITS ENVIRONMENT'S EVIL.
BUT THE LINK SHATTERS. THE GREAT BEAR SENSES A PRESENCE IN THE SHADOWS.
IT MOVES TOWARD THE INTRUDER.
YOU'LL DRAIN NO MORE STRENGTH FROM THIS BEAST, PARASITE!
BLOOSH!

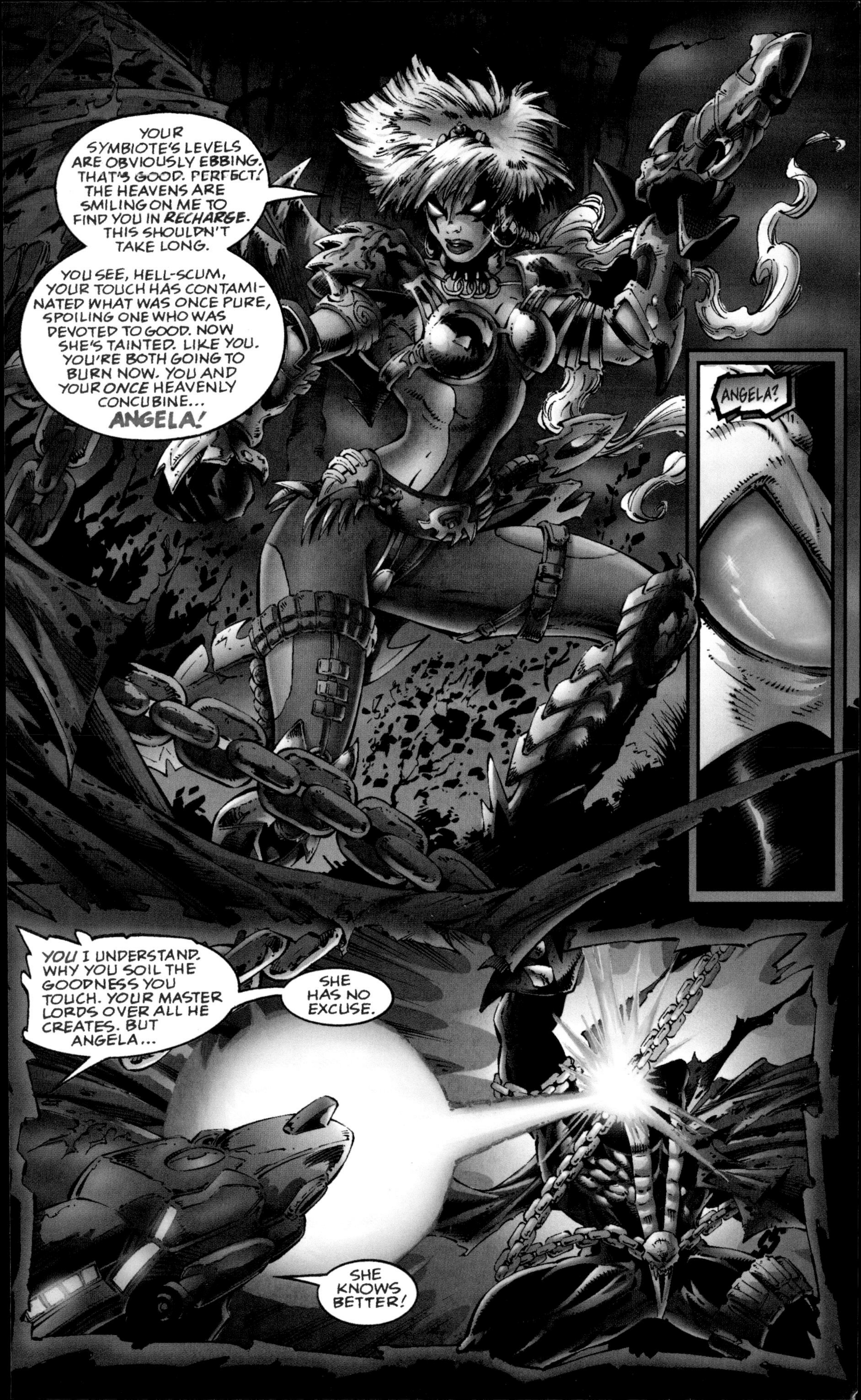
YOUR SYMBIOTE'S LEVELS ARE OBVIOUSLY EBBING. THAT'S GOOD. PERFECT! THE HEAVENS ARE SMILING ON ME TO FIND YOU IN RECHARGE. THIS SHOULDN'T TAKE LONG.
YOU SEE, HELL-SCUM, YOUR TOUCH HAS CONTAMINATED WHAT WAS ONCE PURE, SPOILING ONE WHO WAS DEVOTED TO GOOD. NOW SHE'S TAINTED. LIKE YOU. YOU'RE BOTH GOING TO BURN NOW. YOU AND YOUR ONCE HEAVENLY CONCUBINE... ANGELA!
ANGELA?
YOU I UNDERSTAND. WHY YOU SOIL THE GOODNESS YOU TOUCH. YOUR MASTER LORDS OVER ALL HE CREATES. BUT ANGELA...
SHE HAS NO EXCUSE.
SHE KNOWS BETTER!

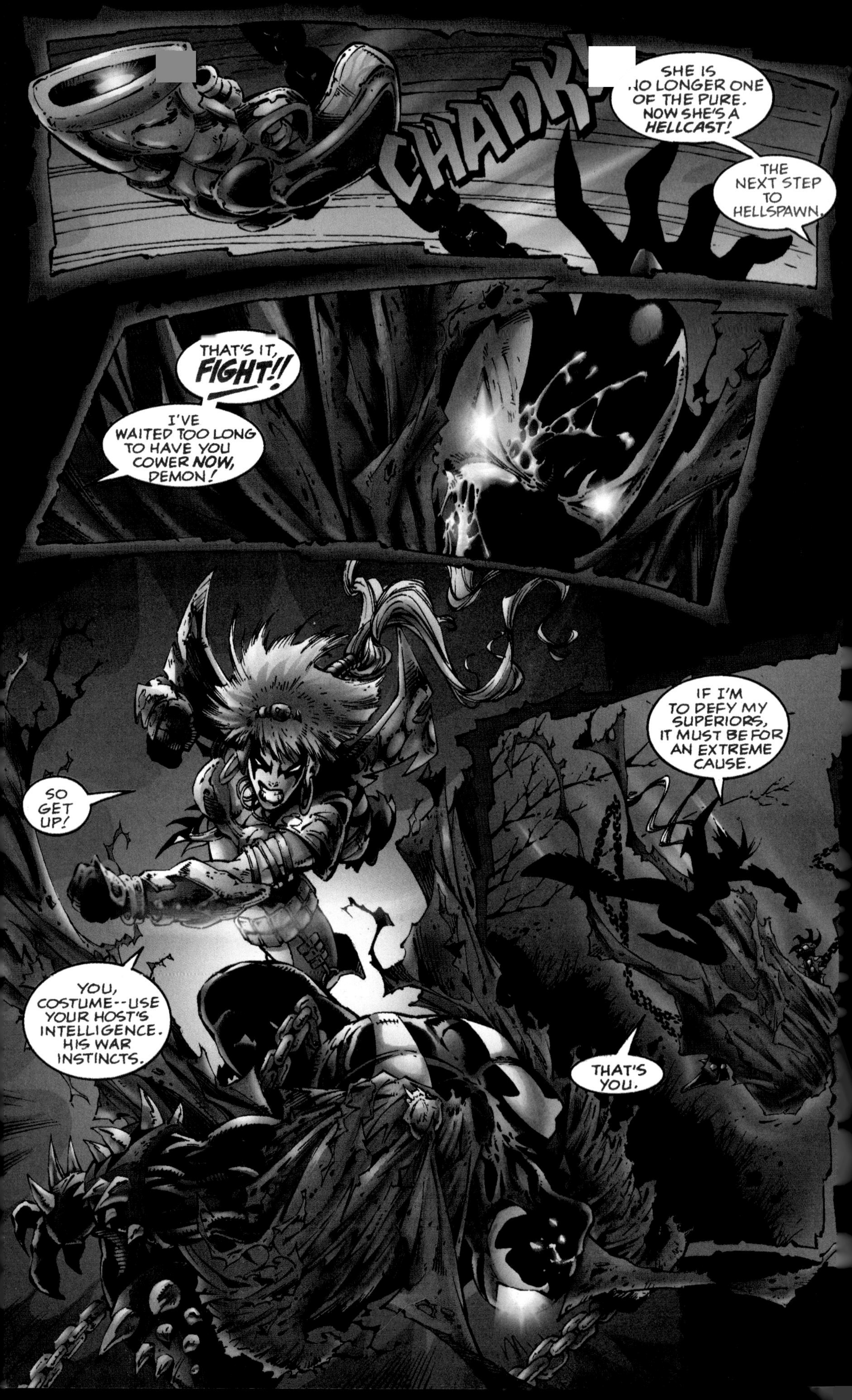
CHANK!
SHE IS NO LONGER ONE OF THE PURE. NOW SHE'S A HELLCAST!
THE NEXT STEP TO HELLSPAWN.
THAT'S IT, FIGHT!!
I'VE WAITED TOO LONG TO HAVE YOU COWER NOW, DEMON!
SO GET UP!
IF I'M TO DEFY MY SUPERIORS, IT MUST BE FOR AN EXTREME CAUSE.
YOU, COSTUME--USE YOUR HOST'S INTELLIGENCE. HIS WAR INSTINCTS.
THAT'S YOU.

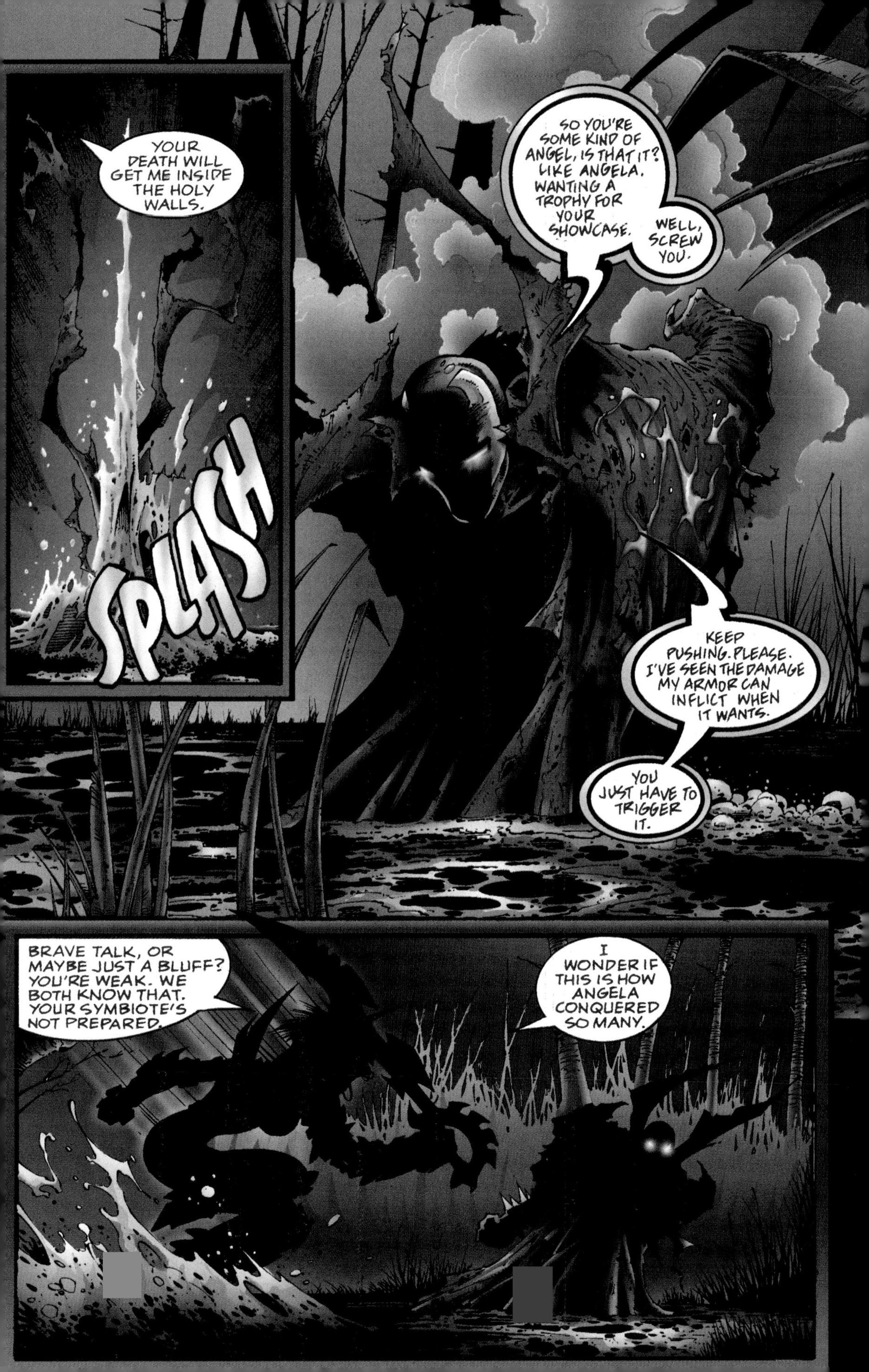
YOUR DEATH WILL GET ME INSIDE THE HOLY WALLS.
SPLASH
SO YOU'RE SOME KIND OF ANGEL, IS THAT IT? LIKE ANGELA. WANTING A TROPHY FOR YOUR SHOWCASE.
WELL, SCREW YOU.
KEEP PUSHING. PLEASE. I'VE SEEN THE DAMAGE MY ARMOR CAN INFLICT WHEN IT WANTS.
YOU JUST HAVE TO TRIGGER IT.
BRAVE TALK, OR MAYBE JUST A BLUFF? YOU'RE WEAK. WE BOTH KNOW THAT. YOUR SYMBIOTE'S NOT PREPARED.
I WONDER IF THIS IS HOW ANGELA CONQUERED SO MANY.

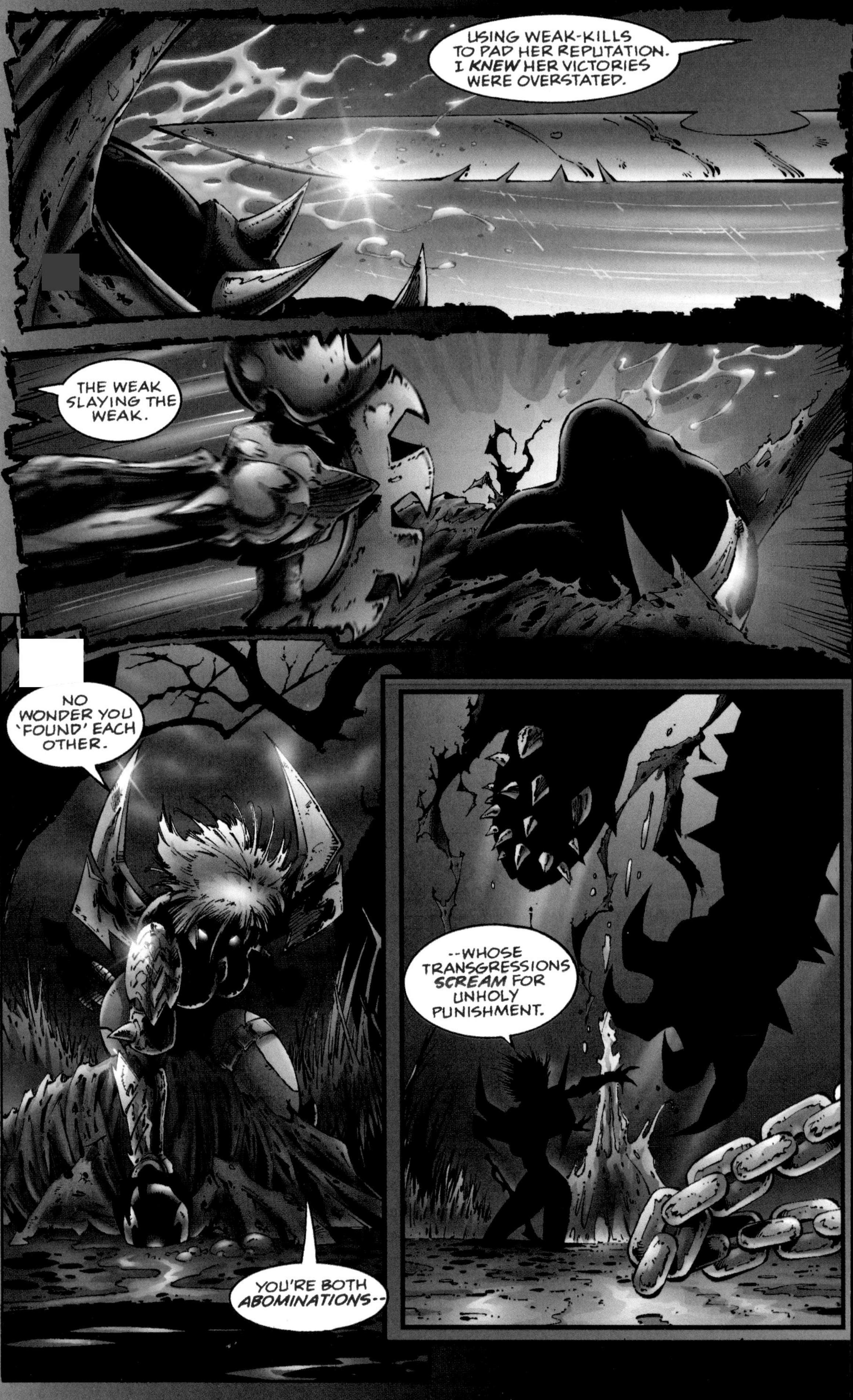
USING WEAK-KILLS TO PAD HER REPUTATION. I KNEW HER VICTORIES WERE OVERSTATED.
THE WEAK SLAYING THE WEAK.
NO WONDER YOU 'FOUND' EACH OTHER.
YOU'RE BOTH ABOMINATIONS--
--WHOSE TRANSGRESSIONS SCREAM FOR UNHOLY PUNISHMENT.

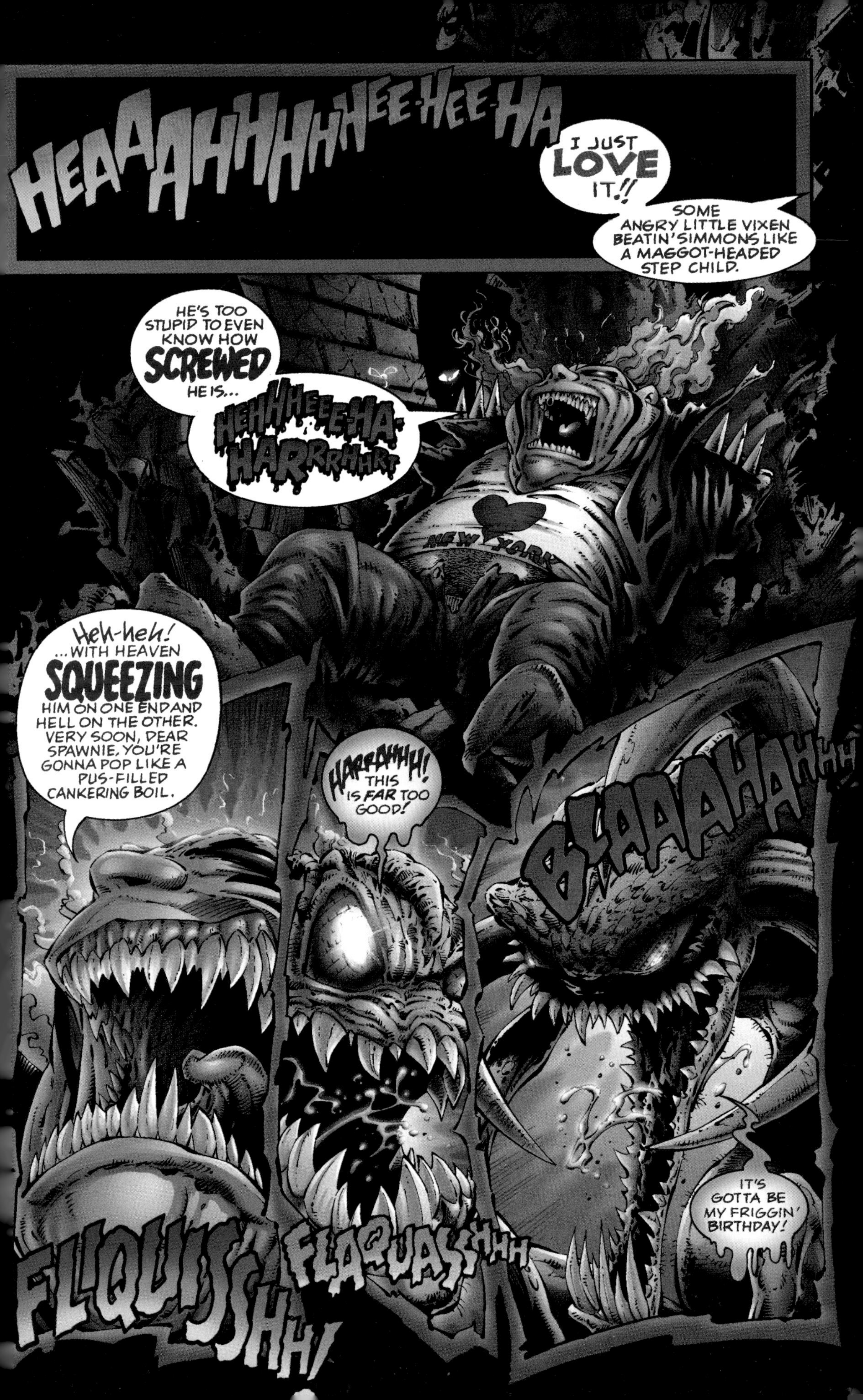
HEAAAAHHHHHHEE-HEE-HA
I JUST LOVE IT!!
SOME ANGRY LITTLE VIXEN BEATIN' SIMMONS LIKE A MAGGOT-HEADED STEP CHILD.
HE'S TOO STUPID TO EVEN KNOW HOW SCREWED HE IS... HEHHHEEE-HA-HARRRHHRT
Heh-heh! ...WITH HEAVEN SQUEEZING HIM ON ONE END AND HELL ON THE OTHER. VERY SOON, DEAR SPAWNIE, YOU'RE GONNA POP LIKE A PUS-FILLED CANKERING BOIL.
HARRAHHH! THIS IS FAR TOO GOOD!
BLAAAAHAHHH
IT'S GOTTA BE MY FRIGGIN' BIRTHDAY!
FLQUISSHH!
FLAQUASSHHH

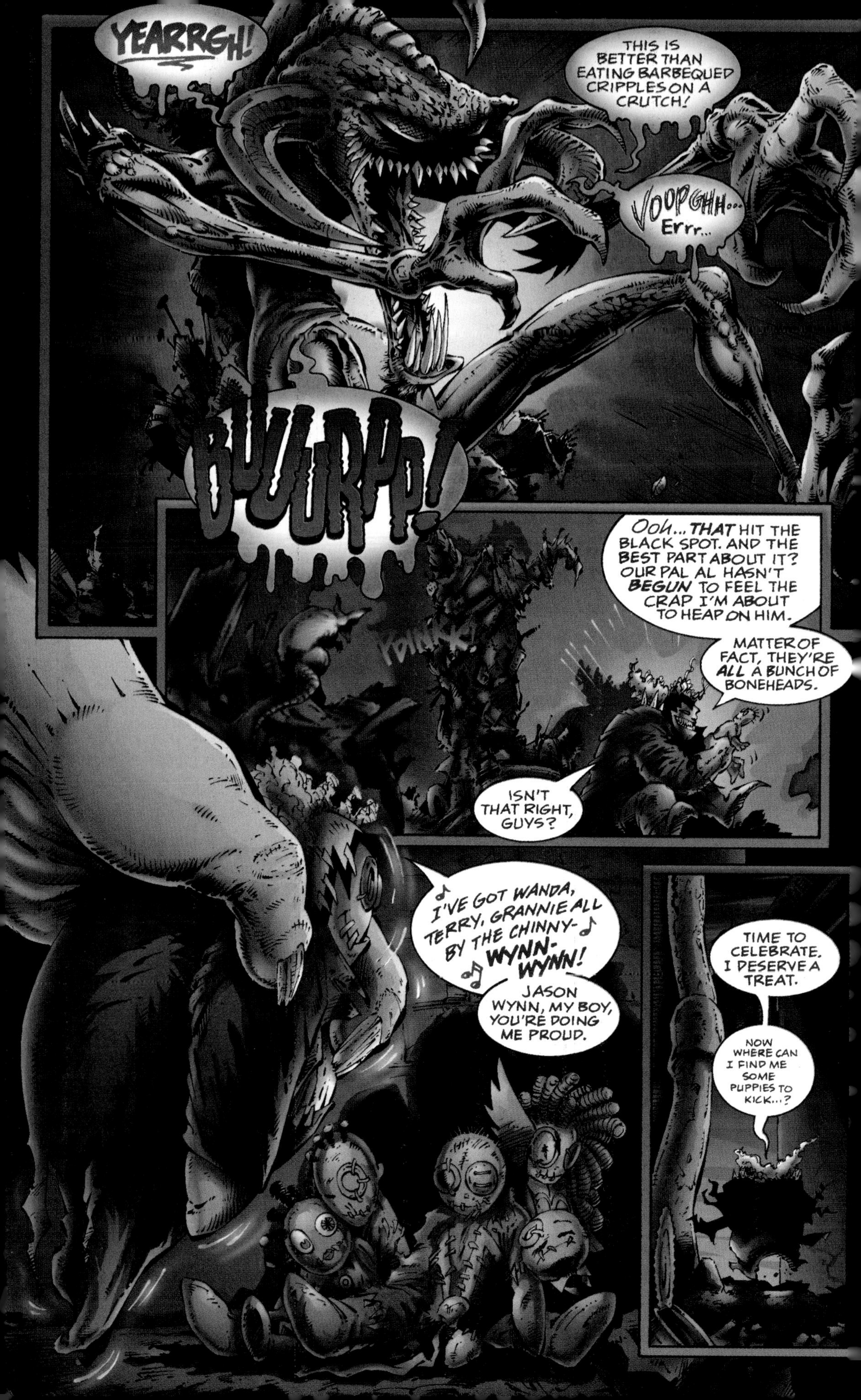
YEARRGH!
THIS IS BETTER THAN EATING BARBEQUED CRIPPLES ON A CRUTCH!
VOOPGHH... Errr...
BUURPP!
Ooh... THAT HIT THE BLACK SPOT. AND THE BEST PART ABOUT IT? OUR PAL AL HASN'T BEGUN TO FEEL THE CRAP I'M ABOUT TO HEAP ON HIM.
MATTER OF FACT, THEY'RE ALL A BUNCH OF BONEHEADS.
ISN'T THAT RIGHT, GUYS?
I'VE GOT WANDA, TERRY, GRANNIE ALL BY THE CHINNY-WYNN-WYNN!
JASON WYNN, MY BOY, YOU'RE DOING ME PROUD.
TIME TO CELEBRATE. I DESERVE A TREAT.
NOW WHERE CAN I FIND ME SOME PUPPIES TO KICK...?

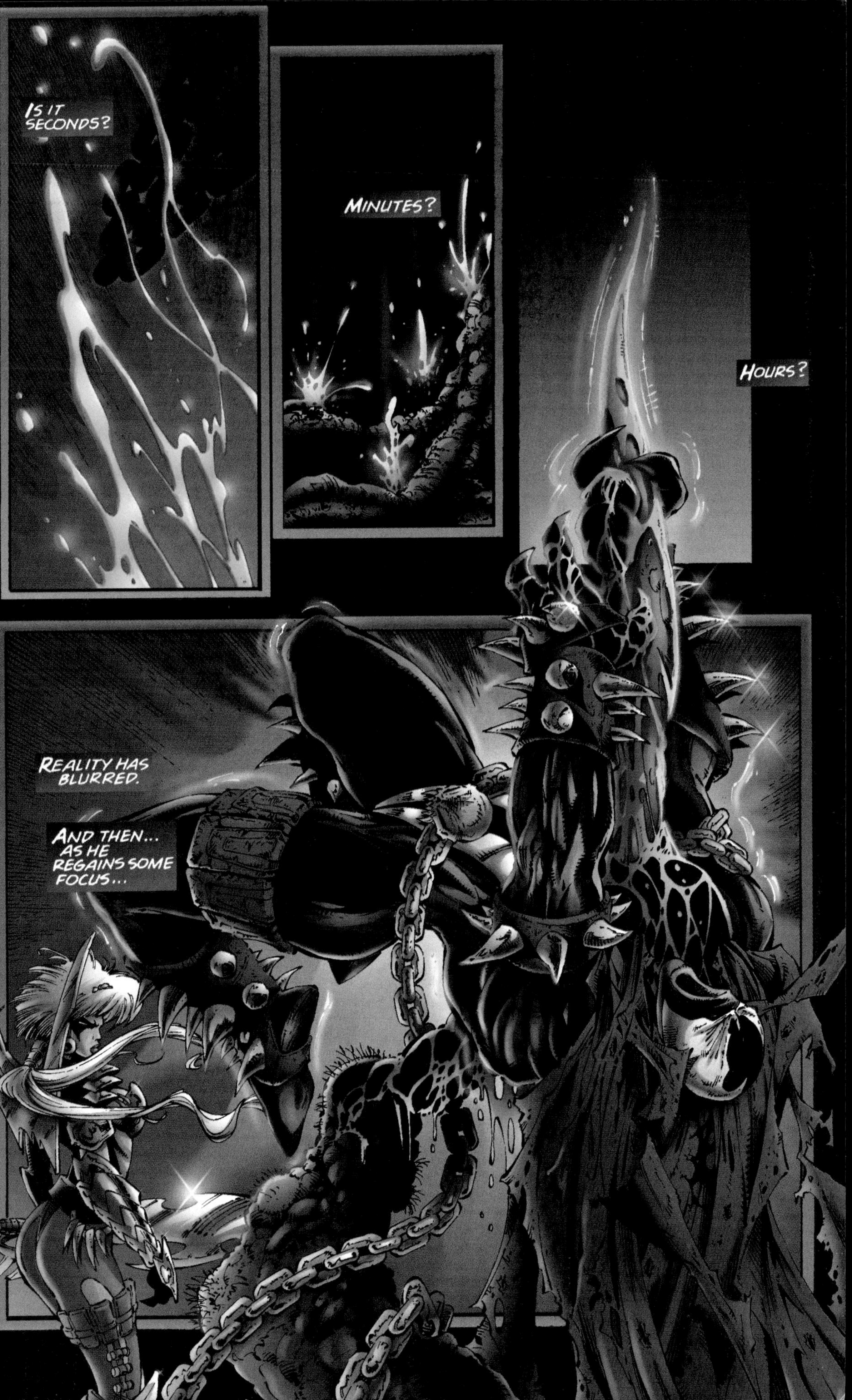
IS IT SECONDS?
MINUTES?
HOURS?
REALITY HAS BLURRED.
AND THEN... AS HE REGAINS SOME FOCUS...

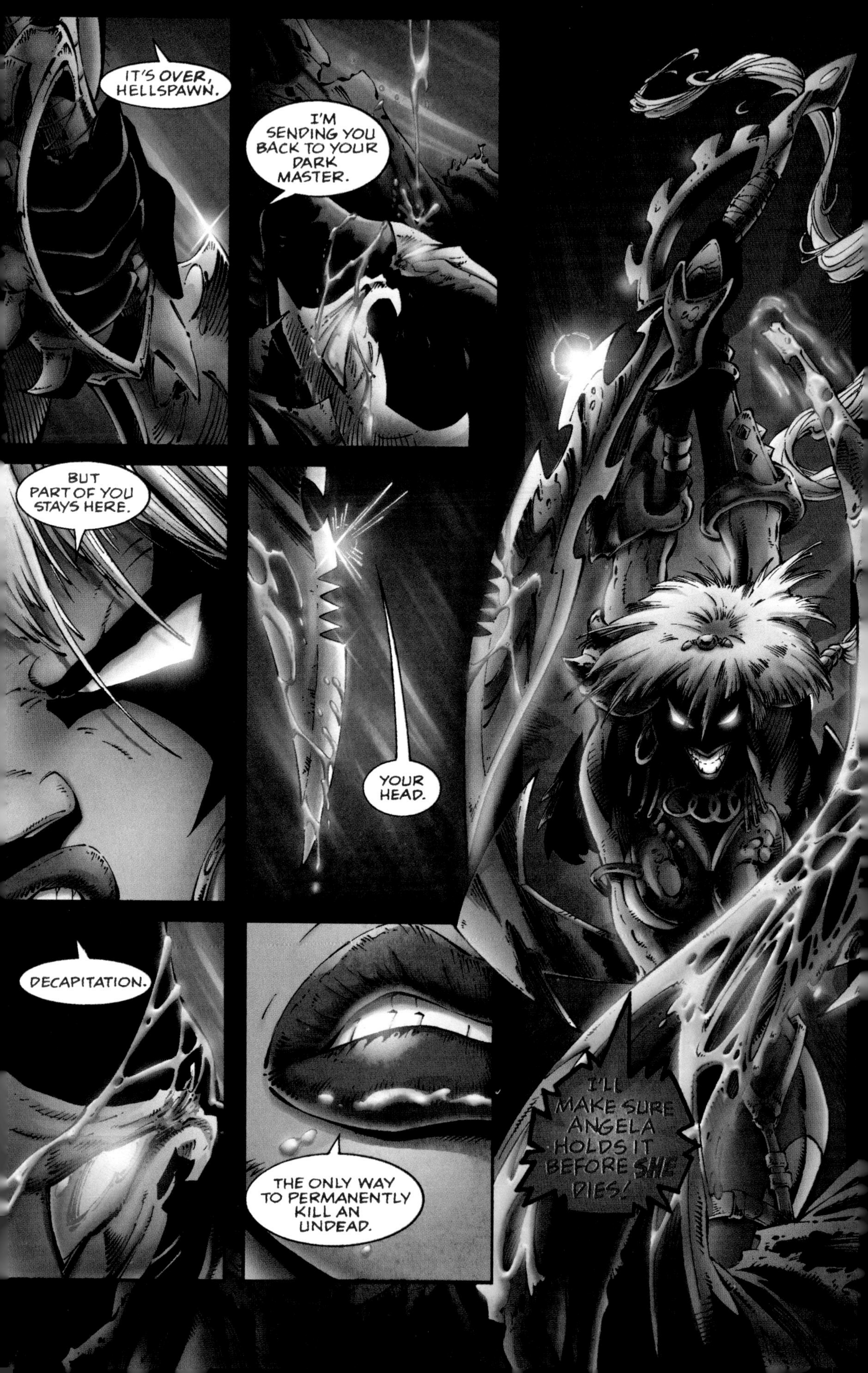
IT'S OVER, HELLSPAWN.
I'M SENDING YOU BACK TO YOUR DARK MASTER.
BUT PART OF YOU STAYS HERE.
YOUR HEAD.
DECAPITATION.
THE ONLY WAY TO PERMANENTLY KILL AN UNDEAD.
I'LL MAKE SURE ANGELA HOLDS IT BEFORE SHE DIES!

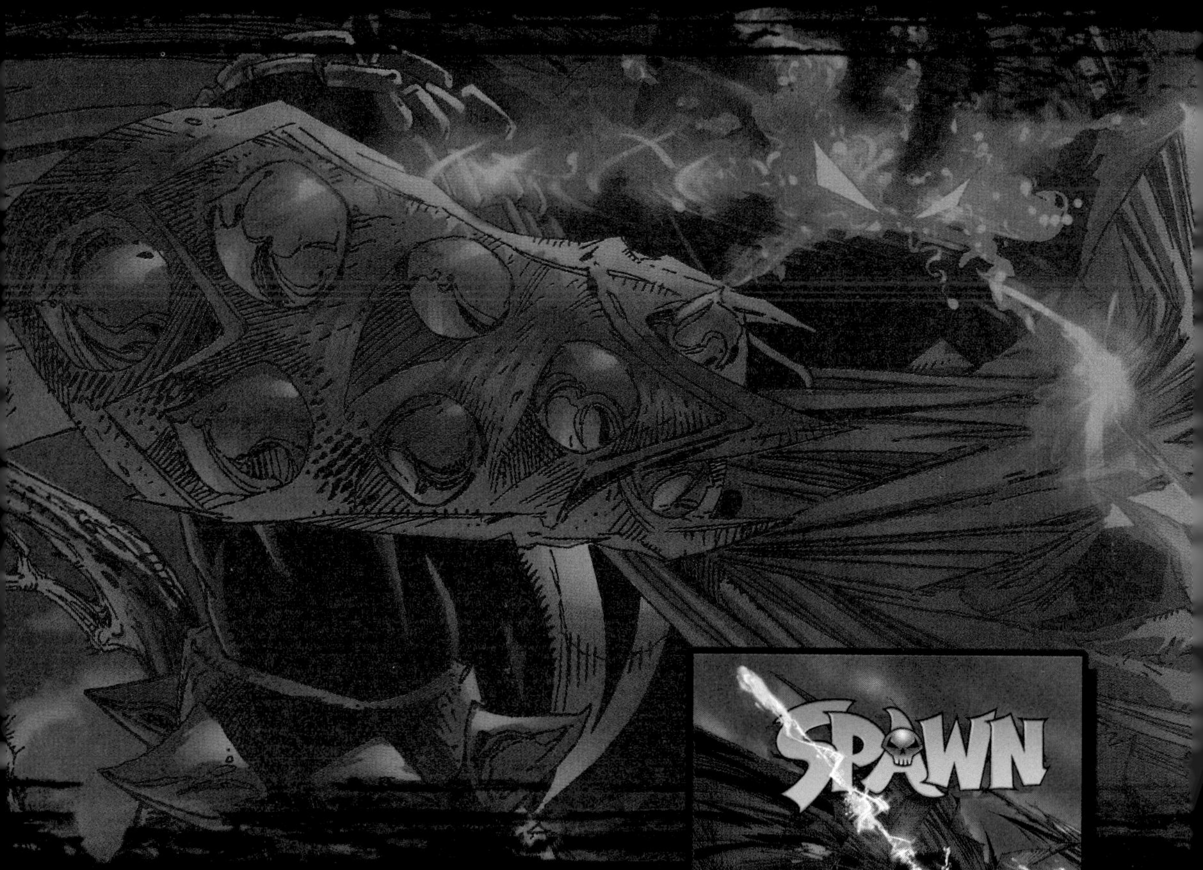

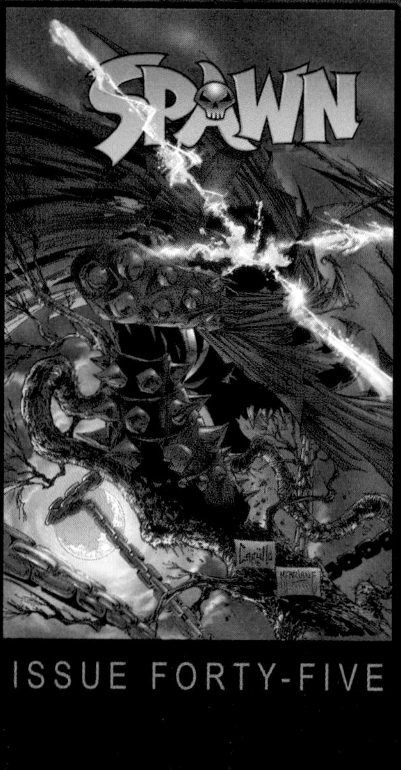
SPAWN

ISSUE FORTY-FIVE

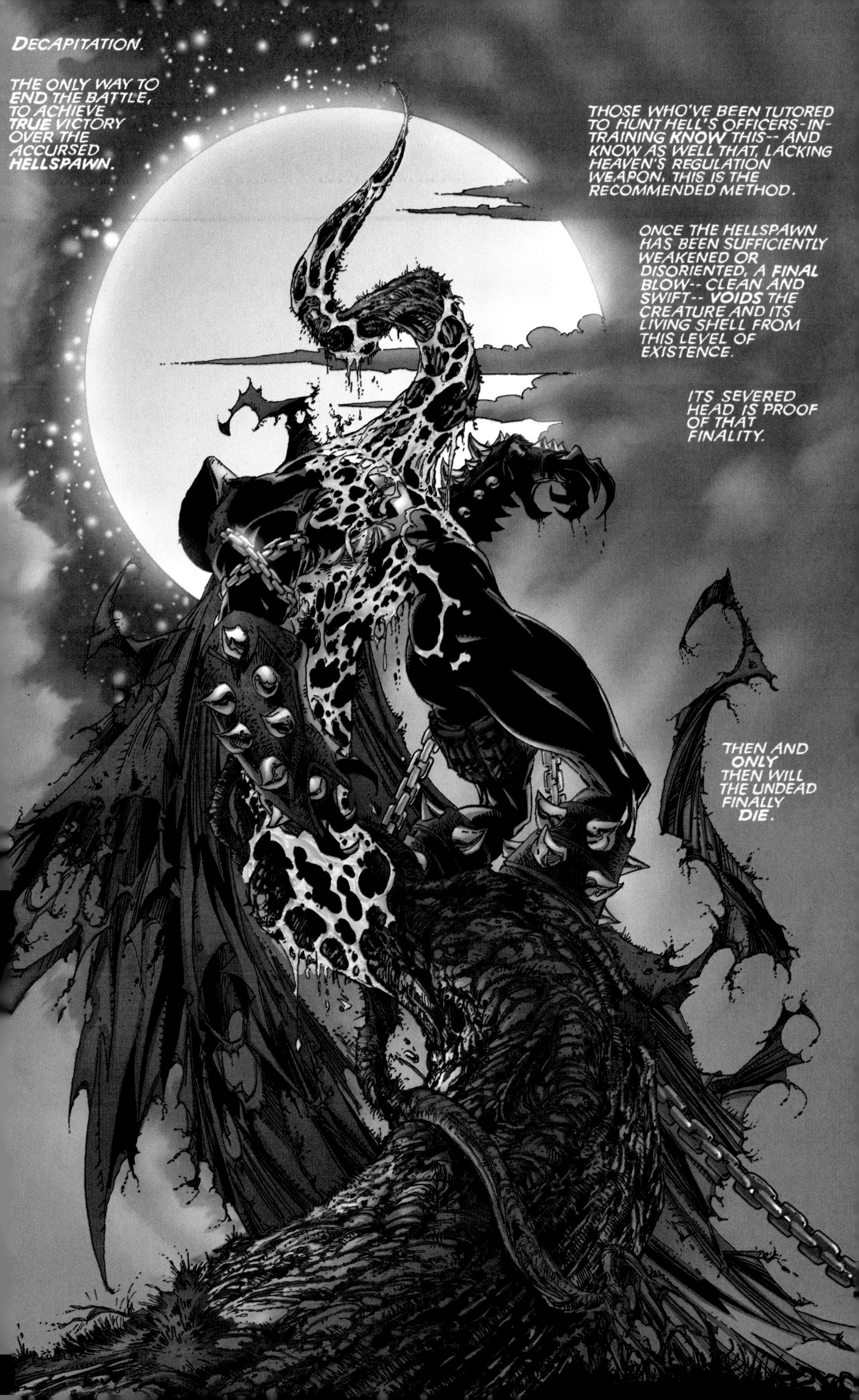
DECAPITATION.
THE ONLY WAY TO END THE BATTLE, TO ACHIEVE TRUE VICTORY OVER THE ACCURSED HELLSPAWN.
THOSE WHO'VE BEEN TUTORED TO HUNT HELL'S OFFICERS-IN-TRAINING KNOW THIS-- AND KNOW AS WELL THAT, LACKING HEAVEN'S REGULATION WEAPON, THIS IS THE RECOMMENDED METHOD.
ONCE THE HELLSPAWN HAS BEEN SUFFICIENTLY WEAKENED OR DISORIENTED, A FINAL BLOW-- CLEAN AND SWIFT-- VOIDS THE CREATURE AND ITS LIVING SHELL FROM THIS LEVEL OF EXISTENCE.
ITS SEVERED HEAD IS PROOF OF THAT FINALITY.
THEN AND ONLY THEN WILL THE UNDEAD FINALLY DIE.

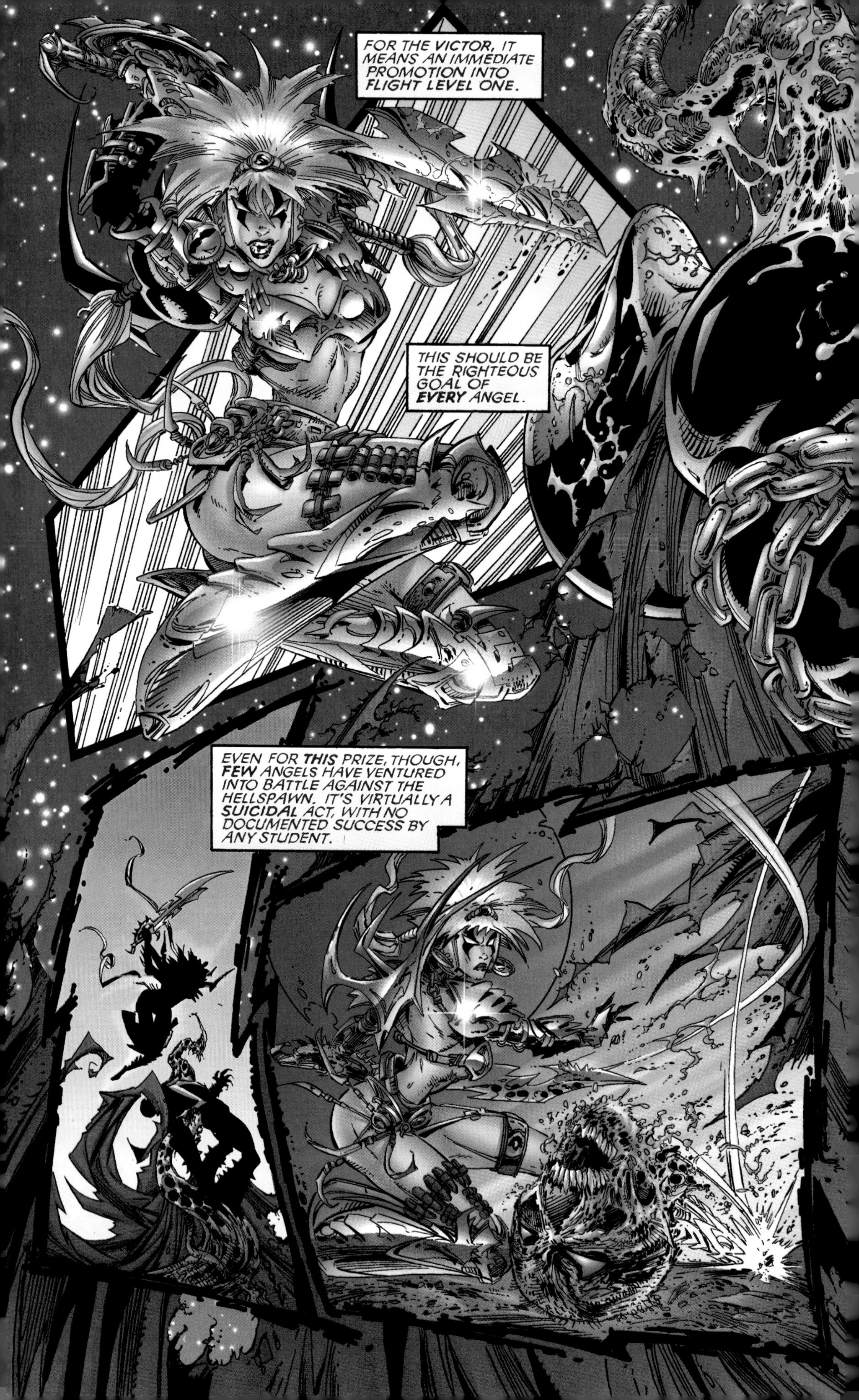
FOR THE VICTOR, IT MEANS AN IMMEDIATE PROMOTION INTO FLIGHT LEVEL ONE.
THIS SHOULD BE THE RIGHTEOUS GOAL OF EVERY ANGEL.
EVEN FOR THIS PRIZE, THOUGH, FEW ANGELS HAVE VENTURED INTO BATTLE AGAINST THE HELLSPAWN. IT'S VIRTUALLY A SUICIDAL ACT, WITH NO DOCUMENTED SUCCESS BY ANY STUDENT.

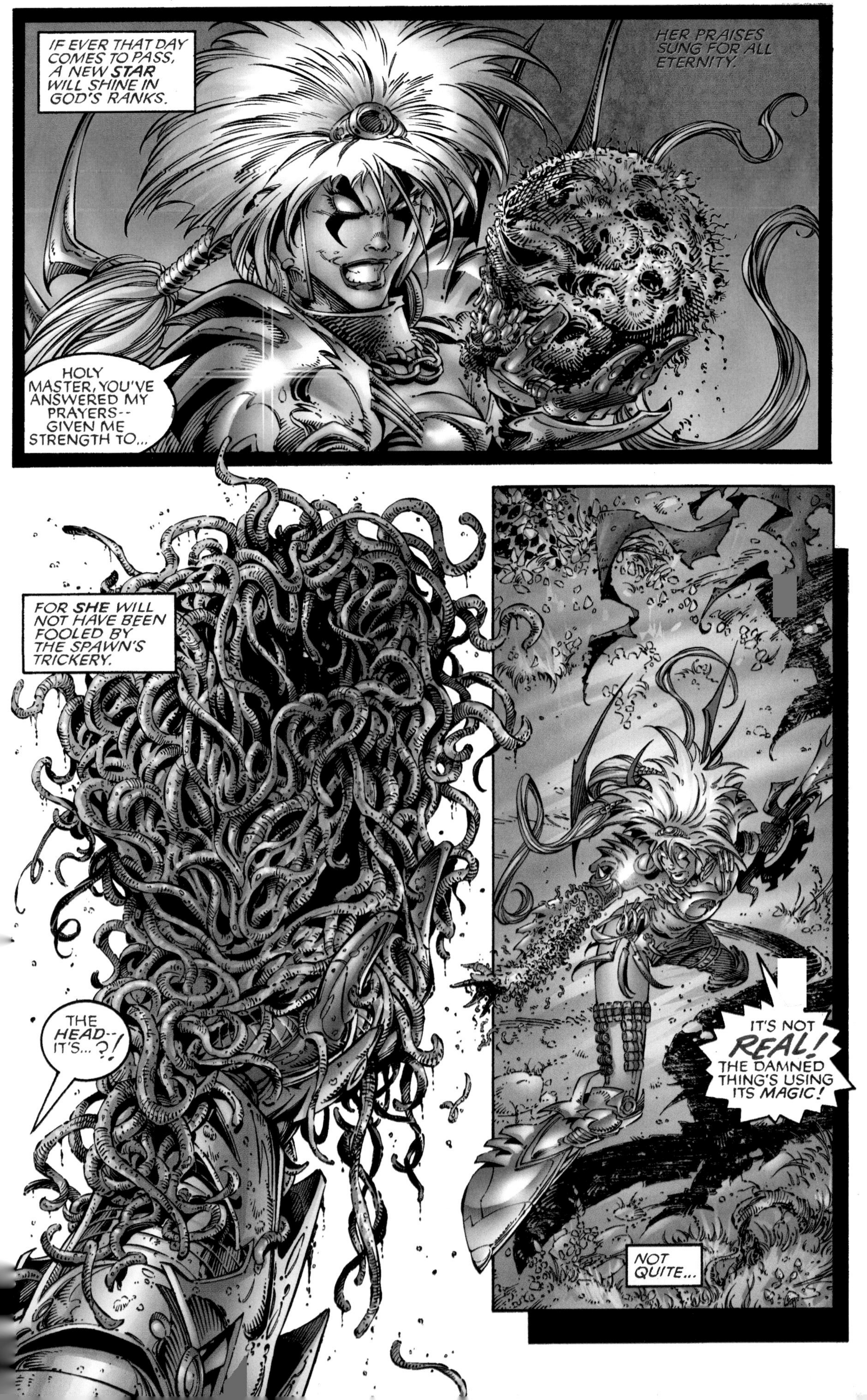
IF EVER THAT DAY COMES TO PASS, A NEW **STAR** WILL SHINE IN GOD'S RANKS.
HER PRAISES SUNG FOR ALL ETERNITY.
HOLY MASTER, YOU'VE ANSWERED MY PRAYERS-- GIVEN ME STRENGTH TO...
FOR **SHE** WILL NOT HAVE BEEN FOOLED BY THE SPAWN'S TRICKERY.
THE *HEAD*-- IT'S...?!
IT'S NOT ***REAL!*** THE DAMNED THING'S USING ITS *MAGIC!*
NOT QUITE...

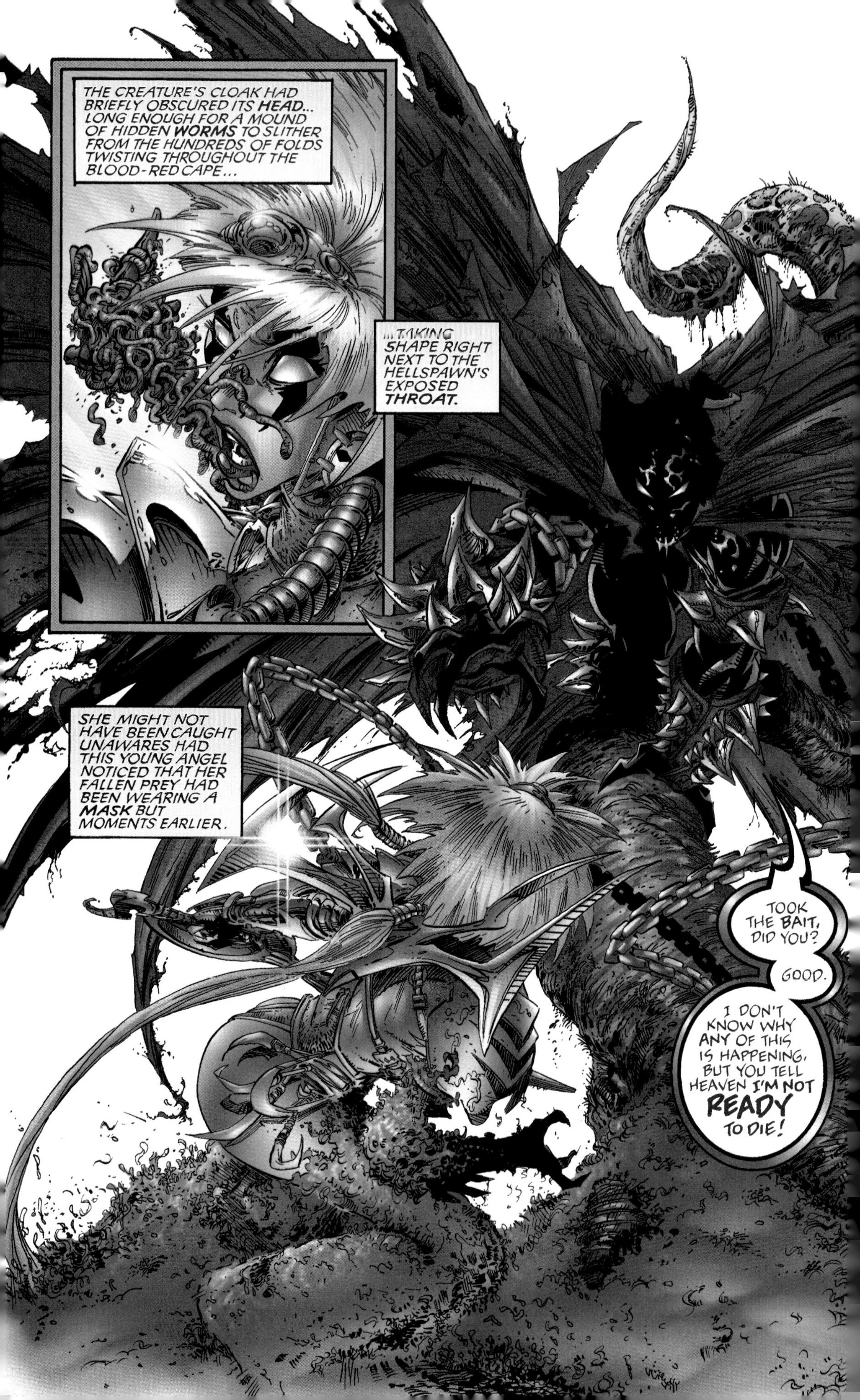
THE CREATURE'S CLOAK HAD BRIEFLY OBSCURED ITS **HEAD**... LONG ENOUGH FOR A MOUND OF HIDDEN **WORMS** TO SLITHER FROM THE HUNDREDS OF FOLDS TWISTING THROUGHOUT THE BLOOD-RED CAPE...
...TAKING **SHAPE** RIGHT NEXT TO THE HELLSPAWN'S EXPOSED **THROAT**.
SHE MIGHT NOT HAVE BEEN CAUGHT UNAWARES HAD THIS YOUNG ANGEL NOTICED THAT HER FALLEN PREY HAD BEEN WEARING A **MASK** BUT MOMENTS EARLIER.
TOOK THE **BAIT**, DID YOU?
GOOD.
I DON'T KNOW WHY ANY OF THIS IS HAPPENING, BUT YOU TELL HEAVEN **I'M NOT READY** TO DIE!

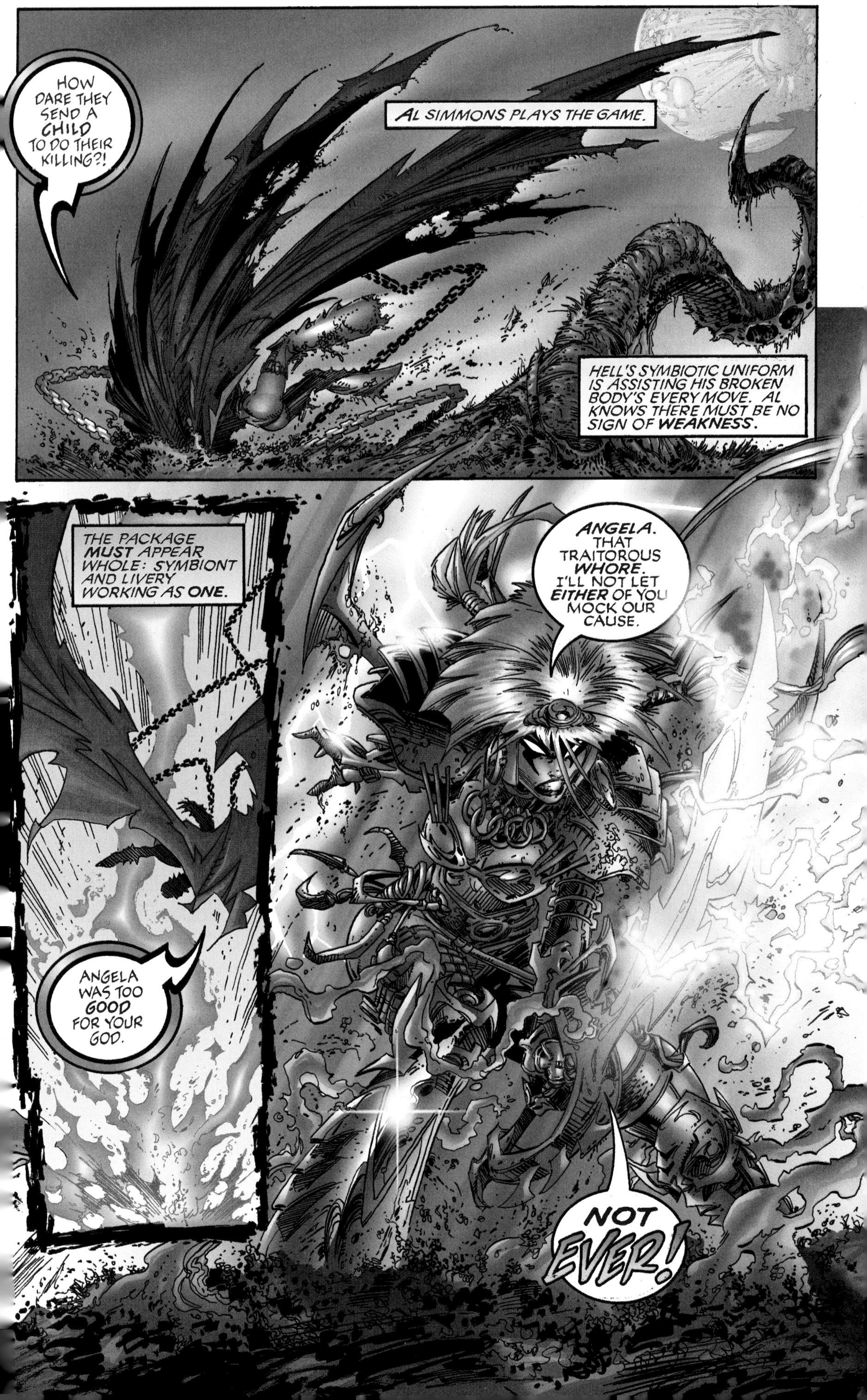
HOW DARE THEY SEND A CHILD TO DO THEIR KILLING?!
AL SIMMONS PLAYS THE GAME.
HELL'S SYMBIOTIC UNIFORM IS ASSISTING HIS BROKEN BODY'S EVERY MOVE. AL KNOWS THERE MUST BE NO SIGN OF WEAKNESS.
THE PACKAGE MUST APPEAR WHOLE: SYMBIONT AND LIVERY WORKING AS ONE.
ANGELA WAS TOO GOOD FOR YOUR GOD.
ANGELA. THAT TRAITOROUS WHORE. I'LL NOT LET EITHER OF YOU MOCK OUR CAUSE.
NOT EVER!

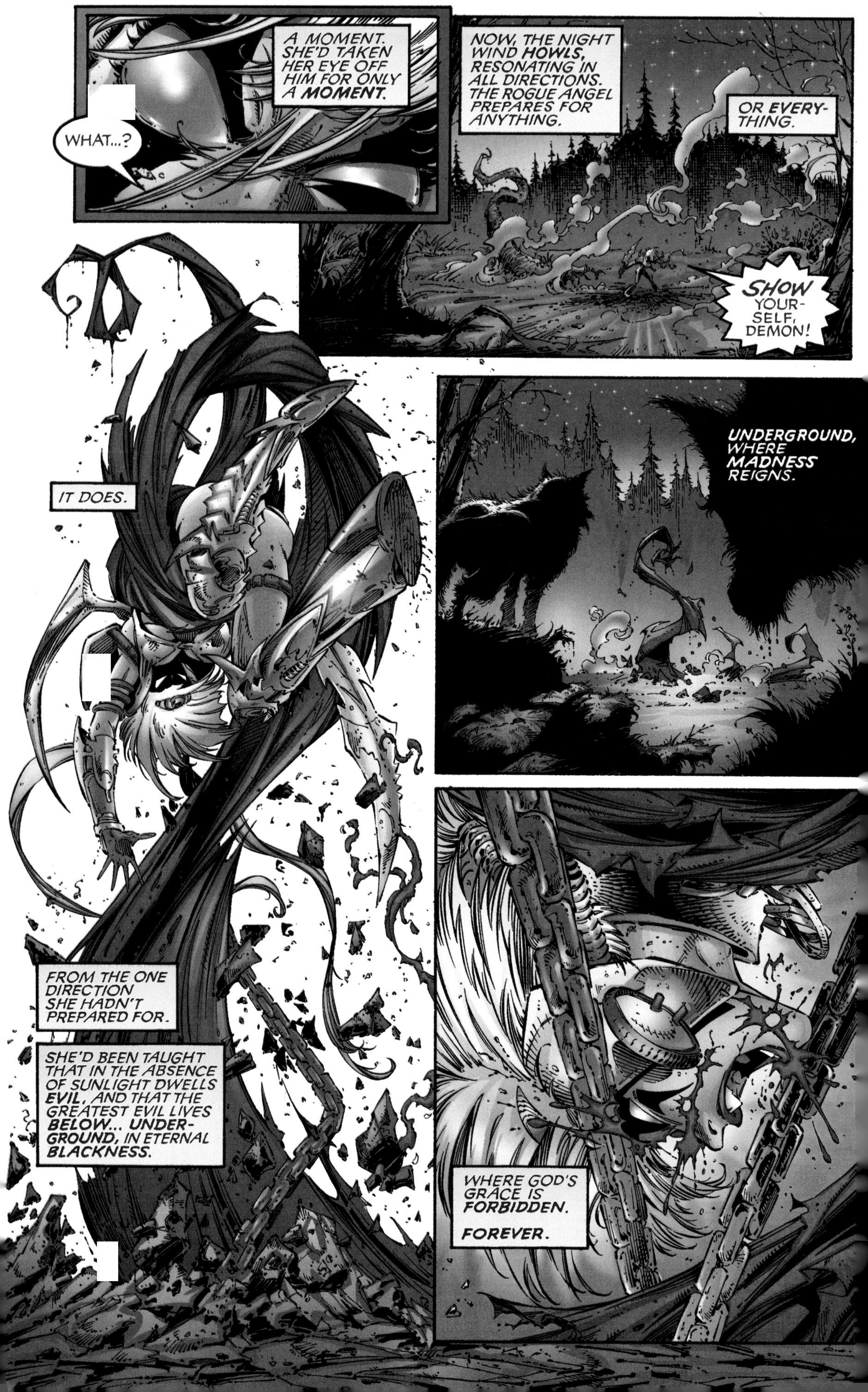
A MOMENT. SHE'D TAKEN HER EYE OFF HIM FOR ONLY A **MOMENT**.
WHAT...?
NOW, THE NIGHT WIND **HOWLS**, RESONATING IN ALL DIRECTIONS. THE ROGUE ANGEL PREPARES FOR ANYTHING.
OR **EVERY-THING**.
SHOW YOUR-SELF, DEMON!
IT DOES.
FROM THE ONE DIRECTION SHE HADN'T PREPARED FOR.
SHE'D BEEN TAUGHT THAT IN THE ABSENCE OF SUNLIGHT DWELLS **EVIL**, AND THAT THE GREATEST EVIL LIVES **BELOW**... **UNDER-GROUND**, IN ETERNAL **BLACKNESS**.
UNDERGROUND, WHERE **MADNESS** REIGNS.
WHERE GOD'S GRACE IS **FORBIDDEN**.
FOREVER.

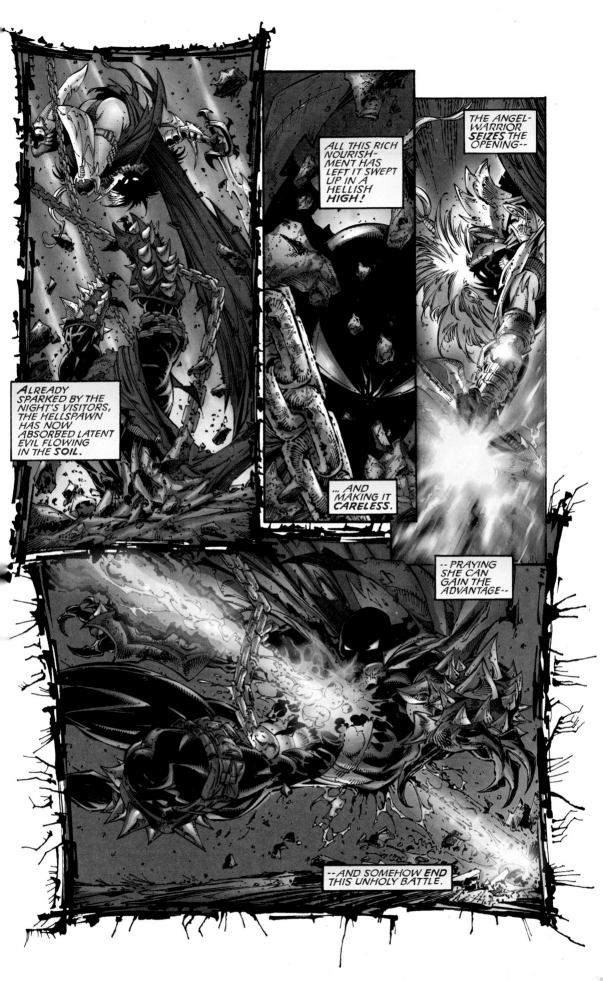

ALREADY SPARKED BY THE NIGHT'S VISITORS, THE HELLSPAWN HAS NOW ABSORBED LATENT EVIL FLOWING IN THE SOIL.

ALL THIS RICH NOURISHMENT HAS LEFT IT SWEPT UP IN A HELLISH HIGH!

"...AND MAKING IT CARELESS.

THE ANGEL-WARRIOR SEIZES THE OPENING--

--PRAYING SHE CAN GAIN THE ADVANTAGE--

--AND SOMEHOW END THIS UNHOLY BATTLE.

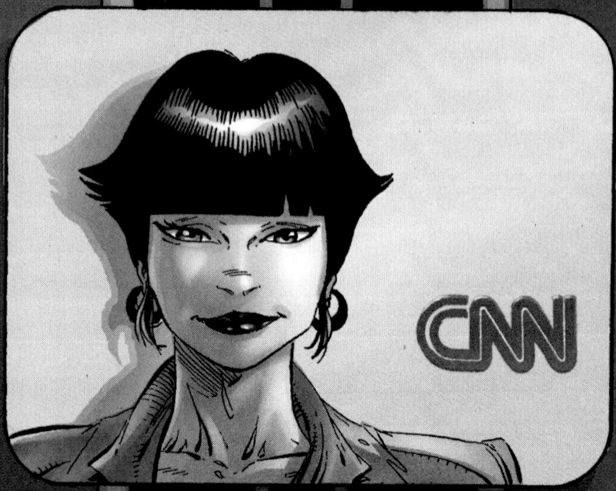
CNN

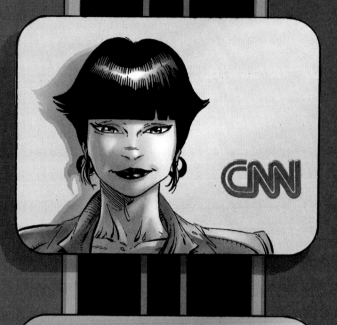

...FUNERAL OF LOUIS BANKS, CHIEF OF NEW YORK CITY'S 12TH PRECINCT. A LONE MOTOR-CYCLE ESCORT WAS THE TOKEN HONOR GUARD FOR THIS CONTROVERSIAL FIGURE.

HIS FREQUENT CAREER SHIFTS --PRIVATE SECURITY OPERATOR, CENTRAL INTELLIGENCE OPERATIVE, POLICE COMMANDER --SHOW A MAN OF RARE AMBITION. INFORMATION LEAKED JUST BEFORE HIS SUICIDE, HOW-EVER, RAISED ALLEGATIONS OF LONG-STANDING TIES TO ORGANIZED CRIME.

SEVERAL DRAMATIC EVENTS HAVE BEEN TIED TO BANKS. AN ATTACK MONTHS AGO ON THE C.I.A.'S NEW YORK OFFICES IS SEEN AS A REVENGE ATTACK ON HIS FORMER EMPLOY-ERS. THE BOMBING MINUTES LATER OF A NEIGHBORING SECURITIES BROKERAGE WAS THEN INTENDED TO ASSIST HIS AGENTS IN THEIR ESCAPE. THE CHILD-KILLING SPREE OF WILLIAM KINCAID HAS BEEN IDENTIFIED AS PART OF AN EXTORTION SCHEME.

THE N.Y.P.D.'S OFFICE OF INTERNAL AFFAIRS HAS LAUNCHED AN INVESTIGATION, QUIETING FOR NOW THE POINTED QUESTIONS RAISED BY SOME MEDIA OUTLETS.

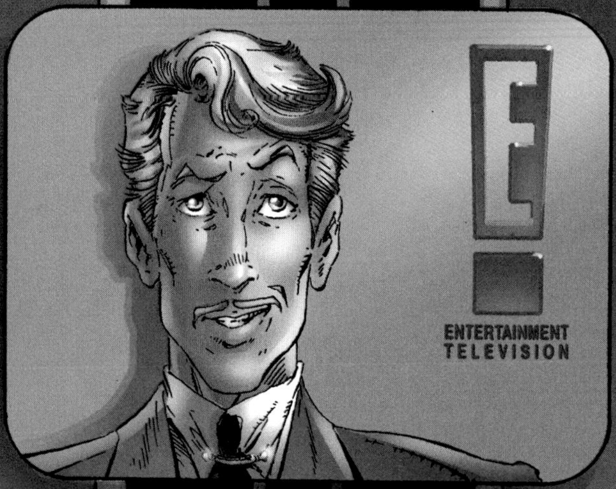
E!
ENTERTAINMENT
TELEVISION

NOTHING SAYS 'NEW YORK' MORE THAN A POIGNANT DISPLAY. OF *COURSE* I'M TALK-ING ABOUT FUNERALS. THE BOYS IN BLUE BURIED THEIR DARKEST KNIGHT YESTERDAY, IN THE FORM OF THE BOWERY'S CHIEF LOUIS BANKS.

IN CLEVER COUNTERPOINT TO HIS SHORT-COMINGS WITH PROCESSES OF *JUSTICE,* BANKS' SEND-OFF WAS THE *MODEL* OF RESTRAINT. THE PROCESSION WAS LED BY A SOLITARY OFFICER ON A MOTORCYCLE... A SIGHT MORE HEART-RENDING THAN TWO COPS IN A SQUAD CAR COULD *POSSIBLY* HAVE BEEN AND PROBABLY EASIER TO ASSIGN. BRINGING UP THE REAR WAS THE HEARSE ITSELF, CAR-RYING ONLY THE FUNERAL DIRECTOR, THE LATE CHIEF, AND HIS WIDOW. WHAT *TASTE!*

MY SOURCES TELL ME THE DECEASED WORE BLACK.

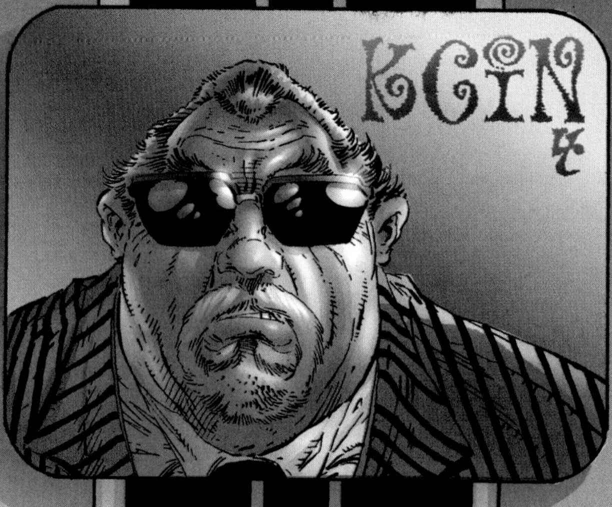
KGIN

HERE'S ONE FOR THE BOOKS. IN THE CAT-EGORY *"DECEASED WILD MEN WHO DIDN'T KNOW HOW OR WHEN TO STOP,"* COULD *ANY* NOMINEE BE MORE OF A SHOO-IN THAN OUR OWN *CHIEF BANKS?* NOT *ONLY* WAS HE AT ONE TIME OR ANOTHER A MEMBER OF EVERY SECURITY OR POLICING SERVICE KNOWN TO *MAN,* BUT, IF ALL OF OFFICIALDOM IS TO BE BELIEVED, HE WAS *AT THE SAME TIME* MAS-TERMINDING CRIMINAL AND TRAITOROUS ACTS AFFECTING EVERYONE SOUTH OF WESTCHES-TER COUNTY! CHIEF BANKS, *YOU THE MAN!*

MY CONFIDENCE IN HIS NOMINATION IS BACKED UP BY THE UNANIMINITY OF THE *FINGER-POINTING.* THE WORD ON THE STREET AND IN THE EXECUTIVE OFFICES IS THAT OUR MAN BANKS *SINGLE-HANDEDLY* RAISED THE *MONEY,* PROCURED THE *ORDINANCE,* RECRUITED *AND* TRAINED HIS OWN *PRIVATE ARMY,* AND CARRIED OUT *SEVERAL* SUCCESSFUL OPERATIONS WHILE IN THE EMPLOY OF NEW YORK'S FINEST. OF *COURSE* HE DIED CHILDLESS. WHEN WOULD HE HAVE FOUND THE TIME TO RAISE KIDS *AND* AN ARMY?

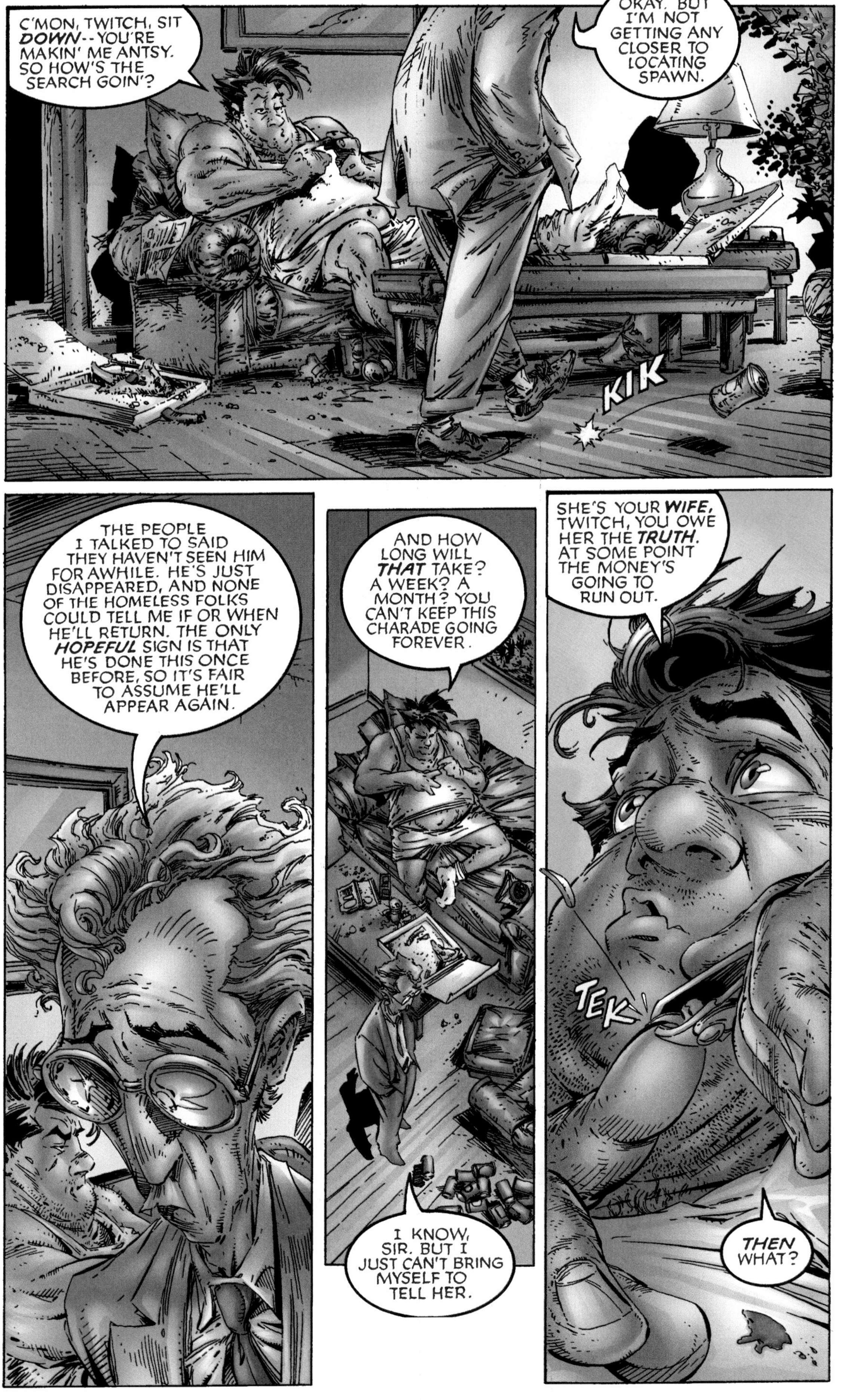

C'MON, TWITCH, SIT *DOWN*--YOU'RE MAKIN' ME ANTSY. SO HOW'S THE SEARCH GOIN'?
OKAY. BUT I'M NOT GETTING ANY CLOSER TO LOCATING SPAWN.
KIK
THE PEOPLE I TALKED TO SAID THEY HAVEN'T SEEN HIM FOR AWHILE. HE'S JUST DISAPPEARED, AND NONE OF THE HOMELESS FOLKS COULD TELL ME IF OR WHEN HE'LL RETURN. THE ONLY *HOPEFUL* SIGN IS THAT HE'S DONE THIS ONCE BEFORE, SO IT'S FAIR TO ASSUME HE'LL APPEAR AGAIN.
AND HOW LONG WILL *THAT* TAKE? A WEEK? A MONTH? YOU CAN'T KEEP THIS CHARADE GOING FOREVER.
I KNOW, SIR. BUT I JUST CAN'T BRING MYSELF TO TELL HER.
SHE'S YOUR *WIFE*, TWITCH, YOU OWE HER THE *TRUTH*. AT SOME POINT THE MONEY'S GOING TO RUN OUT.
TEK!
THEN WHAT?

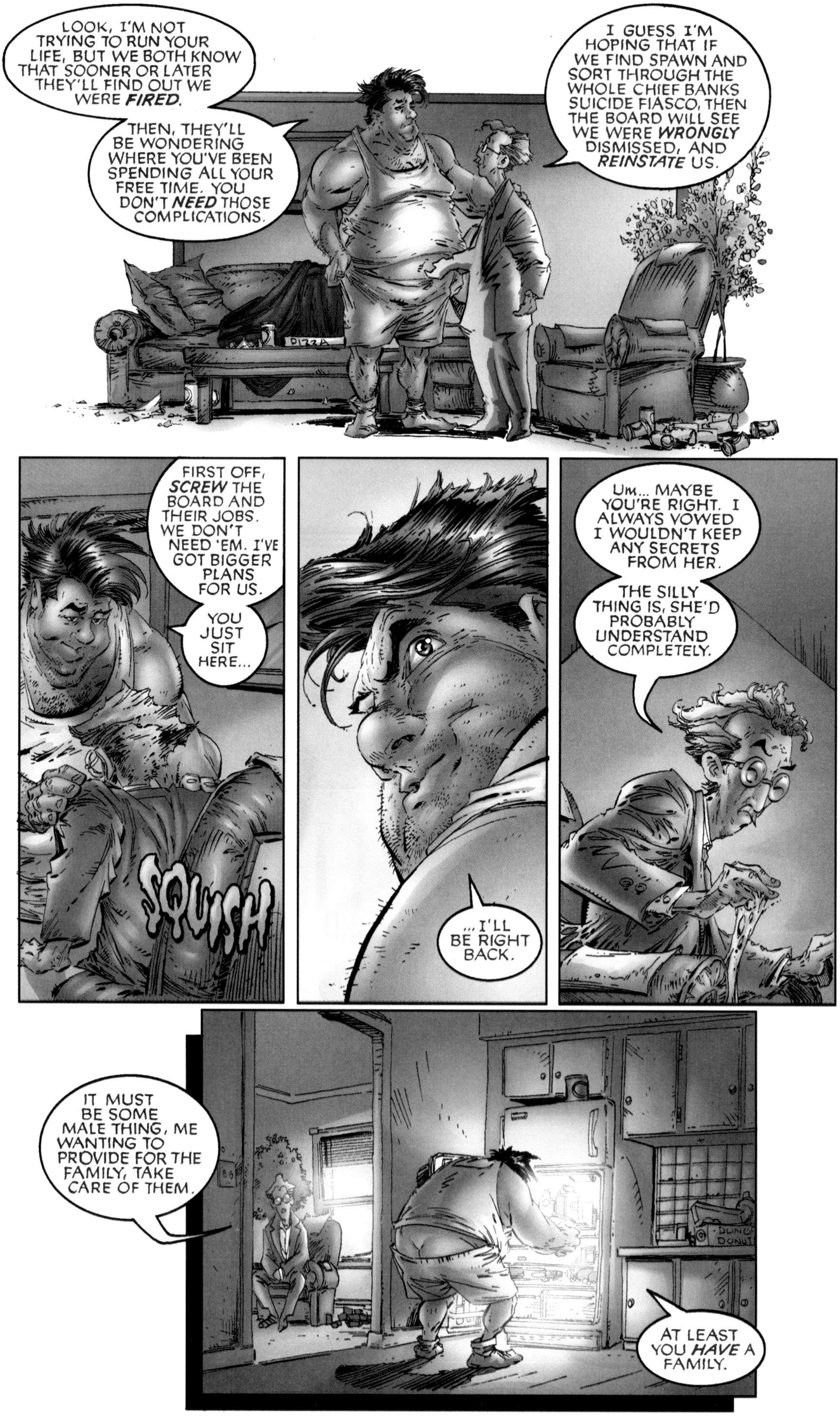
LOOK, I'M NOT TRYING TO RUN YOUR LIFE, BUT WE BOTH KNOW THAT SOONER OR LATER THEY'LL FIND OUT WE WERE *FIRED*.
THEN, THEY'LL BE WONDERING WHERE YOU'VE BEEN SPENDING ALL YOUR FREE TIME. YOU DON'T *NEED* THOSE COMPLICATIONS.
I GUESS I'M HOPING THAT IF WE FIND SPAWN AND SORT THROUGH THE WHOLE CHIEF BANKS SUICIDE FIASCO, THEN THE BOARD WILL SEE WE WERE *WRONGLY* DISMISSED, AND *REINSTATE* US.
PIZZA
FIRST OFF, *SCREW* THE BOARD AND THEIR JOBS. WE DON'T NEED 'EM. I'VE GOT BIGGER PLANS FOR US.
YOU JUST SIT HERE...
SQUISH
...I'LL BE RIGHT BACK.
Um... MAYBE YOU'RE RIGHT. I ALWAYS VOWED I WOULDN'T KEEP ANY SECRETS FROM HER.
THE SILLY THING IS, SHE'D PROBABLY UNDERSTAND COMPLETELY.
IT MUST BE SOME MALE THING, ME WANTING TO PROVIDE FOR THE FAMILY, TAKE CARE OF THEM.
AT LEAST YOU *HAVE* A FAMILY.

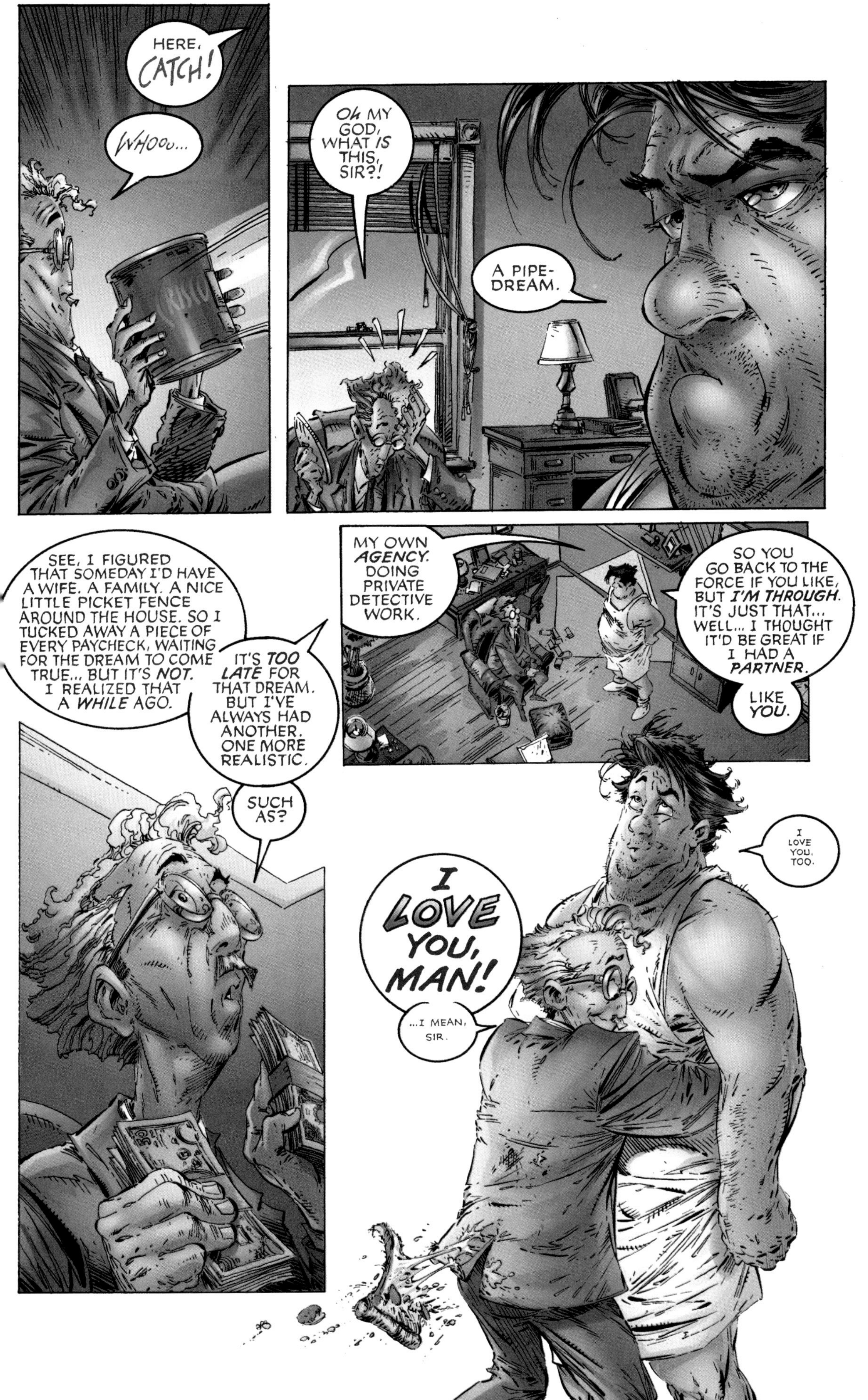
HERE, CATCH!
WHOOO...
OH MY GOD, WHAT IS THIS, SIR?!
A PIPE-DREAM.
SEE, I FIGURED THAT SOMEDAY I'D HAVE A WIFE. A FAMILY. A NICE LITTLE PICKET FENCE AROUND THE HOUSE. SO I TUCKED AWAY A PIECE OF EVERY PAYCHECK, WAITING FOR THE DREAM TO COME TRUE... BUT IT'S NOT. I REALIZED THAT A WHILE AGO.
IT'S TOO LATE FOR THAT DREAM. BUT I'VE ALWAYS HAD ANOTHER. ONE MORE REALISTIC.
SUCH AS?
MY OWN AGENCY. DOING PRIVATE DETECTIVE WORK.
SO YOU GO BACK TO THE FORCE IF YOU LIKE, BUT I'M THROUGH. IT'S JUST THAT... WELL... I THOUGHT IT'D BE GREAT IF I HAD A PARTNER.
LIKE YOU.
I LOVE YOU, MAN!
...I MEAN, SIR.
I LOVE YOU, TOO.

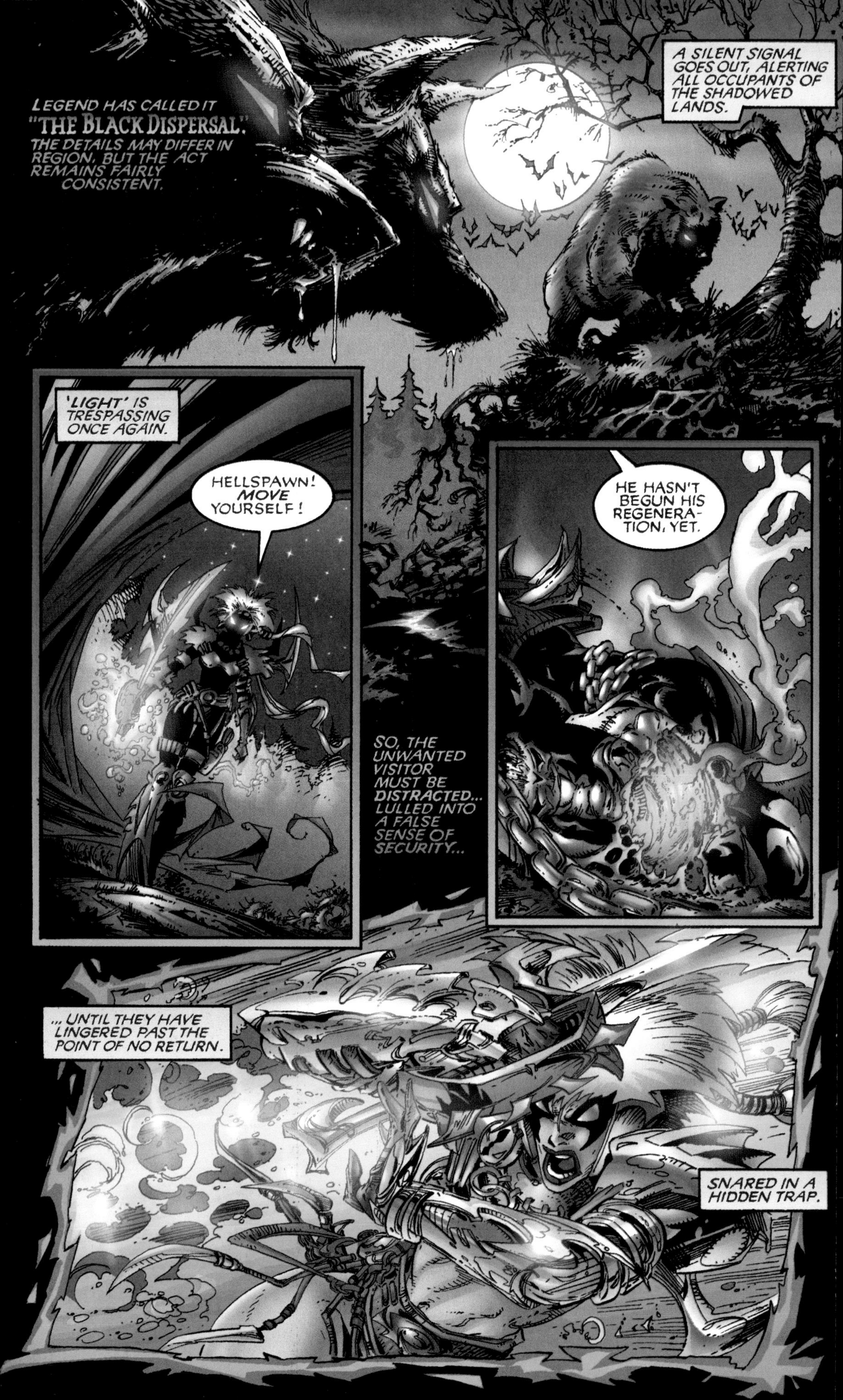
LEGEND HAS CALLED IT "THE BLACK DISPERSAL". THE DETAILS MAY DIFFER IN REGION, BUT THE ACT REMAINS FAIRLY CONSISTENT.
A SILENT SIGNAL GOES OUT, ALERTING ALL OCCUPANTS OF THE SHADOWED LANDS.
'LIGHT' IS TRESPASSING ONCE AGAIN.
HELLSPAWN! MOVE YOURSELF!
SO, THE UNWANTED VISITOR MUST BE DISTRACTED... LULLED INTO A FALSE SENSE OF SECURITY...
HE HASN'T BEGUN HIS REGENERA-TION, YET.
...UNTIL THEY HAVE LINGERED PAST THE POINT OF NO RETURN.
SNARED IN A HIDDEN TRAP.

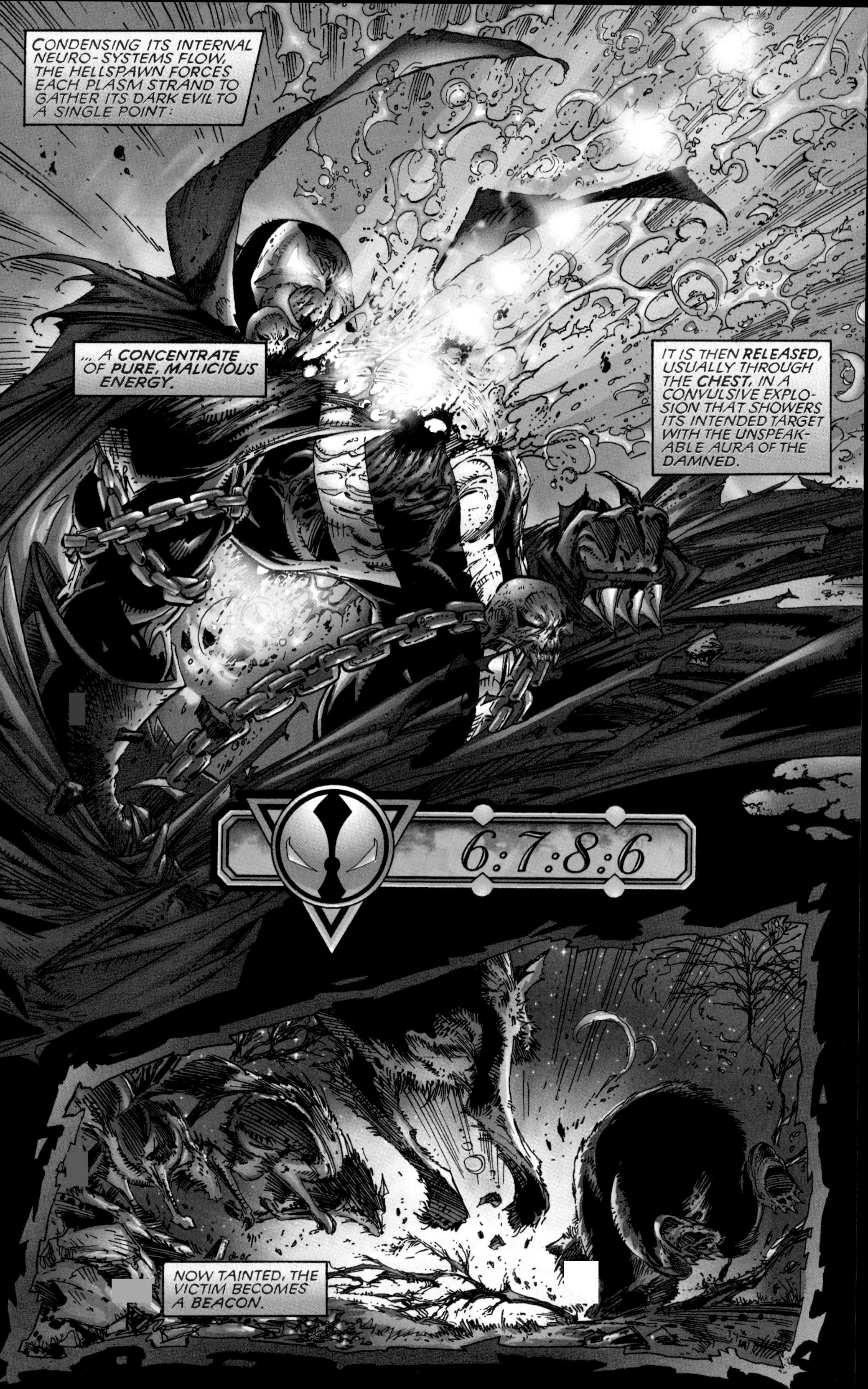
CONDENSING ITS INTERNAL NEURO-SYSTEMS FLOW, THE HELLSPAWN FORCES EACH PLASM STRAND TO GATHER ITS DARK EVIL TO A SINGLE POINT:
...A CONCENTRATE OF PURE, MALICIOUS ENERGY.
IT IS THEN RELEASED, USUALLY THROUGH THE CHEST, IN A CONVULSIVE EXPLOSION THAT SHOWERS ITS INTENDED TARGET WITH THE UNSPEAKABLE AURA OF THE DAMNED.
6:7:8:6
NOW TAINTED, THE VICTIM BECOMES A BEACON.

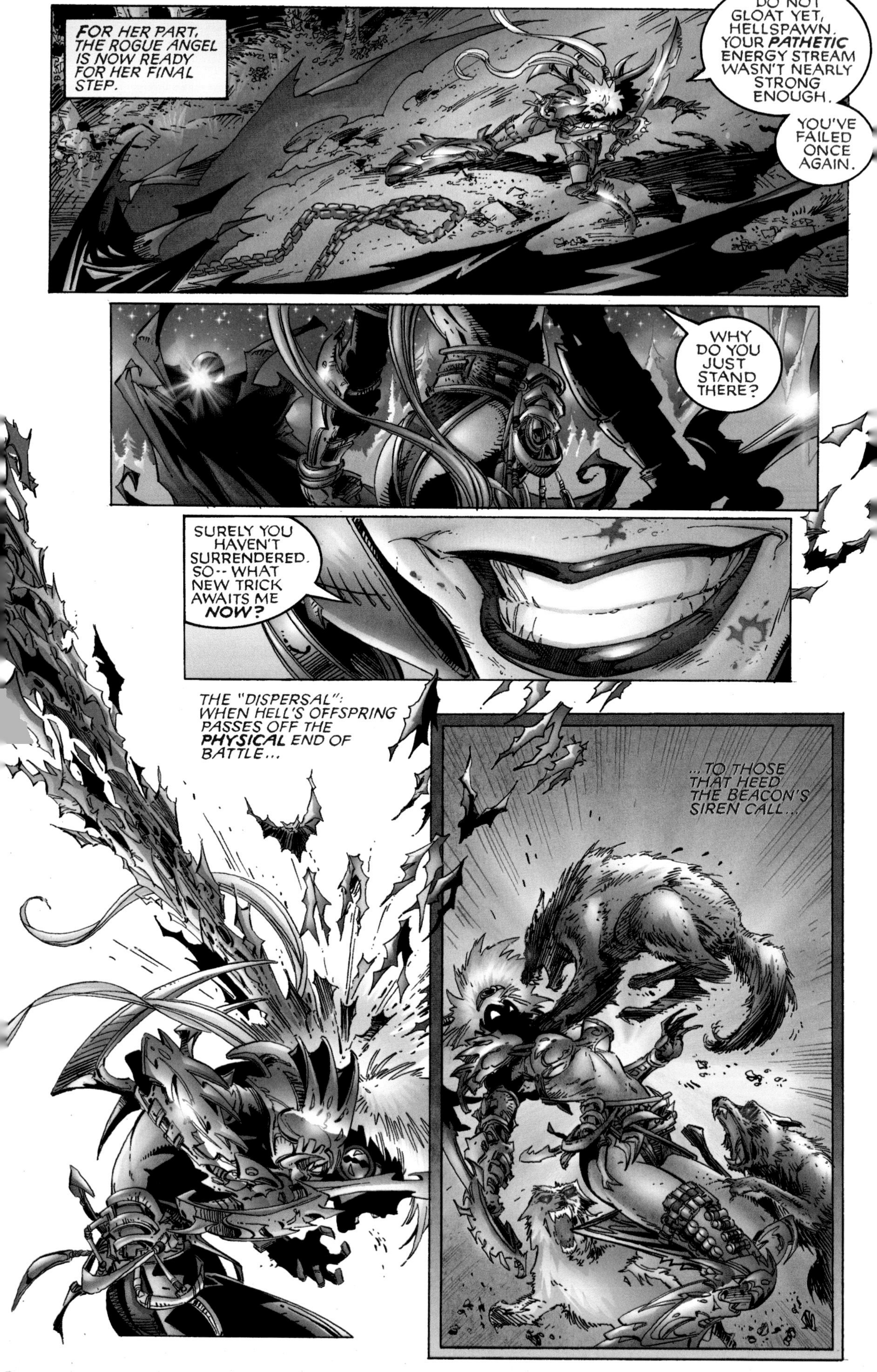
FOR HER PART, THE ROGUE ANGEL IS NOW READY FOR HER FINAL STEP.
DO NOT GLOAT YET, HELLSPAWN. YOUR PATHETIC ENERGY STREAM WASN'T NEARLY STRONG ENOUGH.
YOU'VE FAILED ONCE AGAIN.
WHY DO YOU JUST STAND THERE?
SURELY YOU HAVEN'T SURRENDERED. SO-- WHAT NEW TRICK AWAITS ME NOW?
THE "DISPERSAL": WHEN HELL'S OFFSPRING PASSES OFF THE PHYSICAL END OF BATTLE...
...TO THOSE THAT HEED THE BEACON'S SIREN CALL...

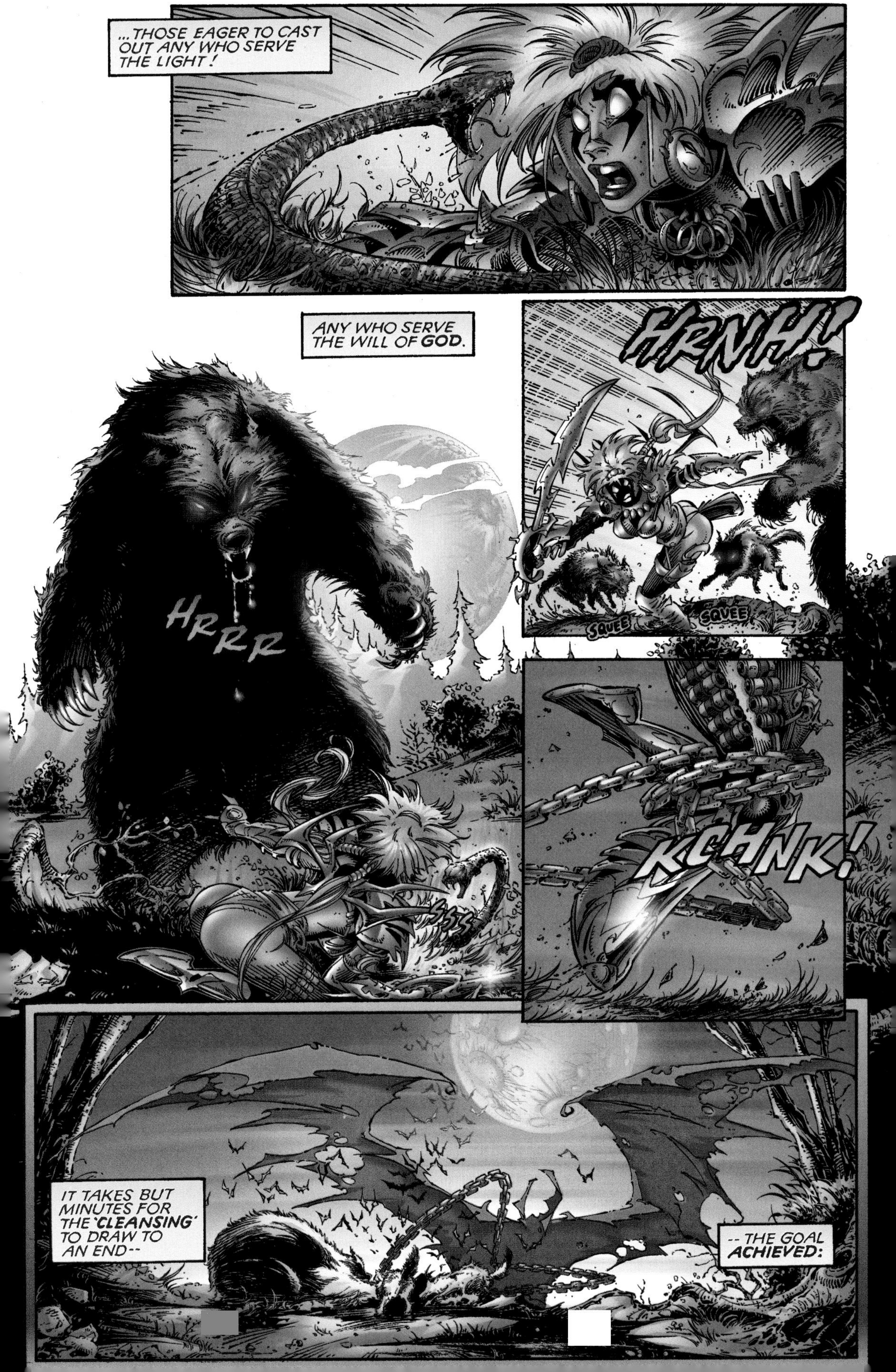
...THOSE EAGER TO CAST OUT ANY WHO SERVE THE LIGHT!
ANY WHO SERVE THE WILL OF GOD.
HRRR
HRNH!
SQUEE
SQUEE
KCHNK!
IT TAKES BUT MINUTES FOR THE 'CLEANSING' TO DRAW TO AN END--
-- THE GOAL ACHIEVED:

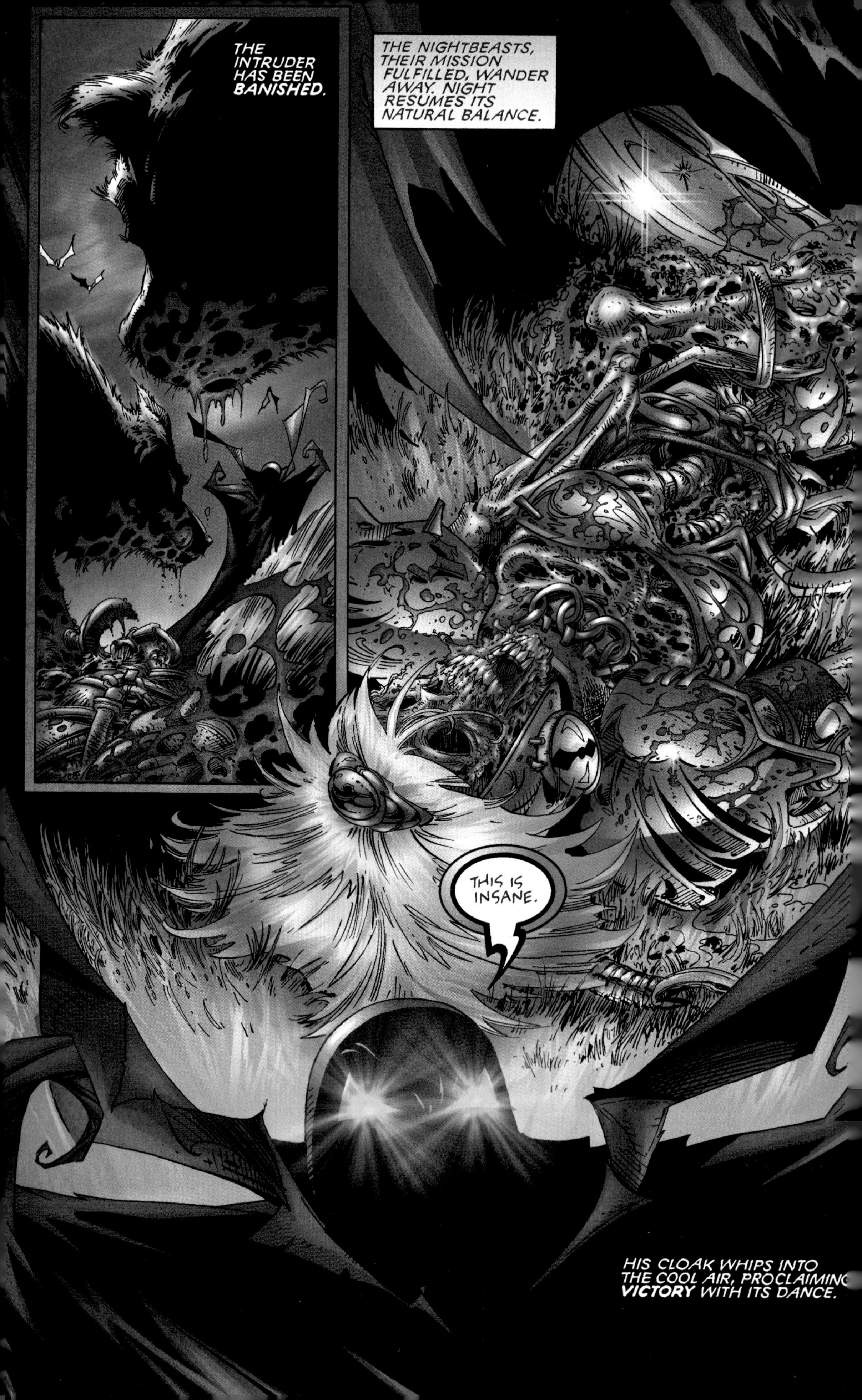
THE INTRUDER HAS BEEN BANISHED.
THE NIGHTBEASTS, THEIR MISSION FULFILLED, WANDER AWAY. NIGHT RESUMES ITS NATURAL BALANCE.
THIS IS INSANE.
HIS CLOAK WHIPS INTO THE COOL AIR, PROCLAIMING VICTORY WITH ITS DANCE.

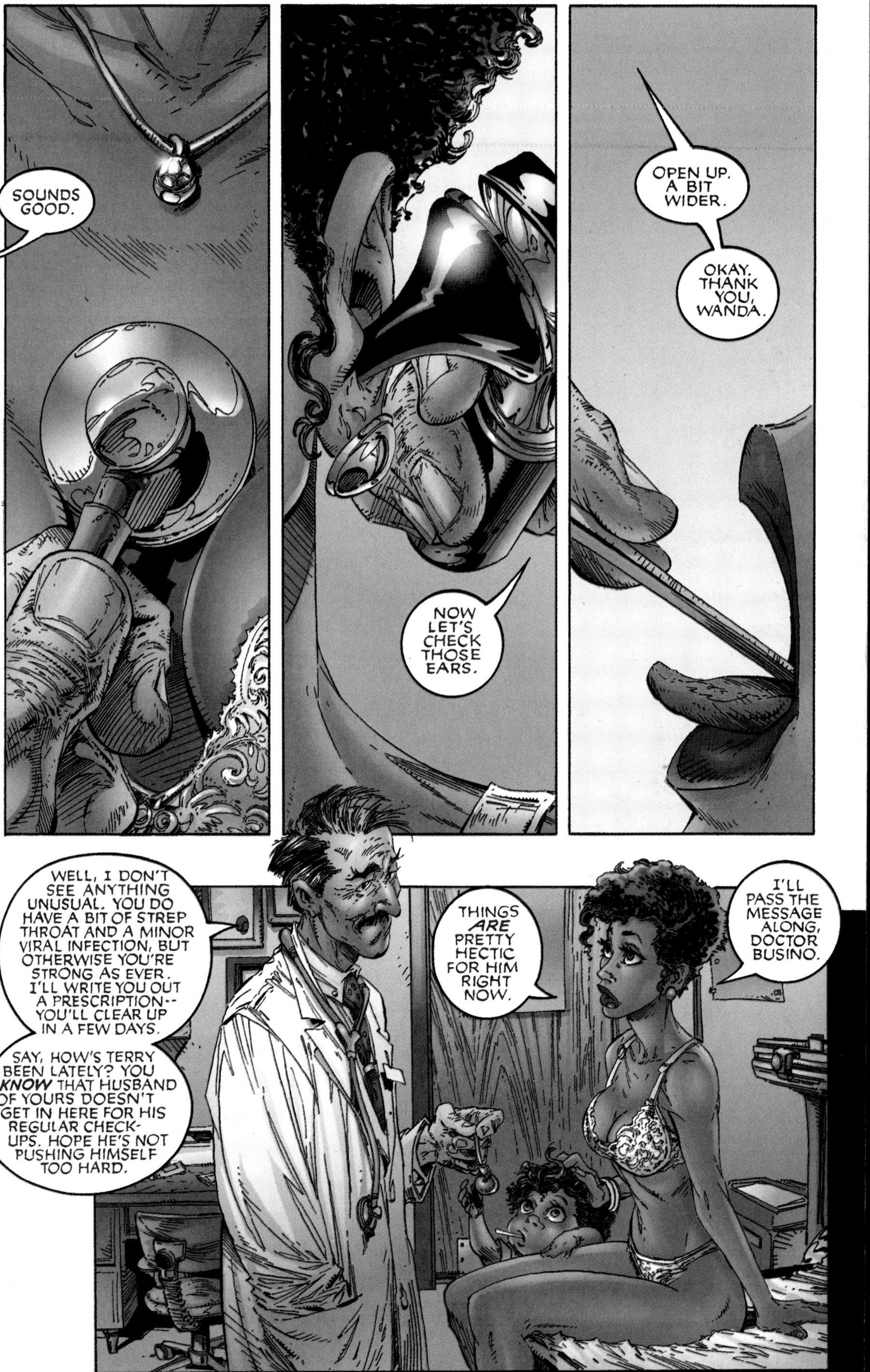
SOUNDS GOOD.
NOW LET'S CHECK THOSE EARS.
OPEN UP. A BIT WIDER.
OKAY. THANK YOU, WANDA.
WELL, I DON'T SEE ANYTHING UNUSUAL. YOU DO HAVE A BIT OF STREP THROAT AND A MINOR VIRAL INFECTION, BUT OTHERWISE YOU'RE STRONG AS EVER. I'LL WRITE YOU OUT A PRESCRIPTION-- YOU'LL CLEAR UP IN A FEW DAYS.
SAY, HOW'S TERRY BEEN LATELY? YOU KNOW THAT HUSBAND OF YOURS DOESN'T GET IN HERE FOR HIS REGULAR CHECK-UPS. HOPE HE'S NOT PUSHING HIMSELF TOO HARD.
THINGS ARE PRETTY HECTIC FOR HIM RIGHT NOW.
I'LL PASS THE MESSAGE ALONG, DOCTOR BUSINO.

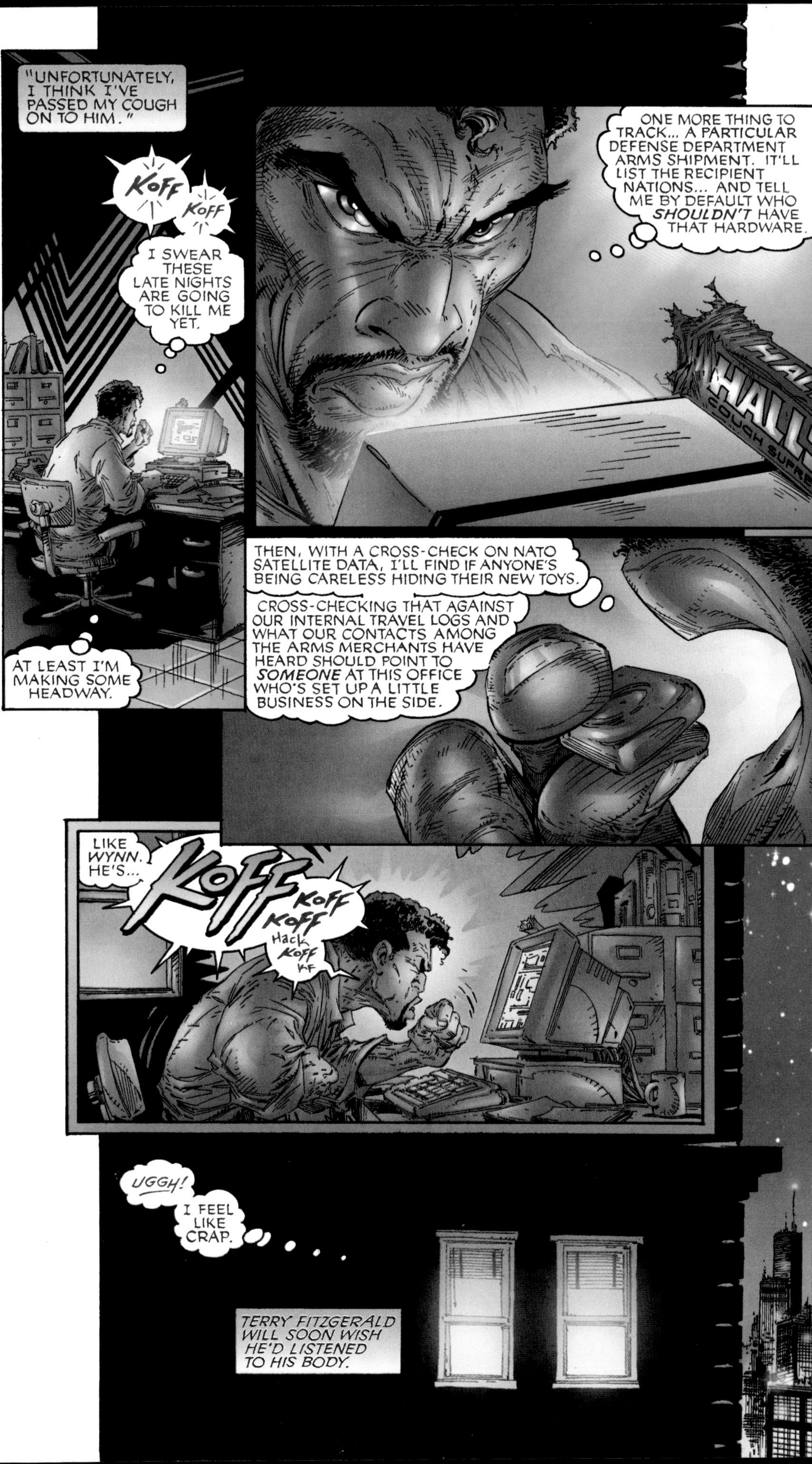
"UNFORTUNATELY, I THINK I'VE PASSED MY COUGH ON TO HIM."
KOFF
KOFF
I SWEAR THESE LATE NIGHTS ARE GOING TO KILL ME YET.
AT LEAST I'M MAKING SOME HEADWAY.
ONE MORE THING TO TRACK... A PARTICULAR DEFENSE DEPARTMENT ARMS SHIPMENT. IT'LL LIST THE RECIPIENT NATIONS... AND TELL ME BY DEFAULT WHO *SHOULDN'T* HAVE THAT HARDWARE.
HALLS
COUGH SUPPRE
THEN, WITH A CROSS-CHECK ON NATO SATELLITE DATA, I'LL FIND IF ANYONE'S BEING CARELESS HIDING THEIR NEW TOYS.
CROSS-CHECKING THAT AGAINST OUR INTERNAL TRAVEL LOGS AND WHAT OUR CONTACTS AMONG THE ARMS MERCHANTS HAVE HEARD SHOULD POINT TO *SOMEONE* AT THIS OFFICE WHO'S SET UP A LITTLE BUSINESS ON THE SIDE.
LIKE *WYNN.* HE'S...
KOFF
KOFF
KOFF
Hack
KOFF
KF
UGGH!
I FEEL LIKE CRAP.
TERRY FITZGERALD WILL SOON WISH HE'D LISTENED TO HIS BODY.

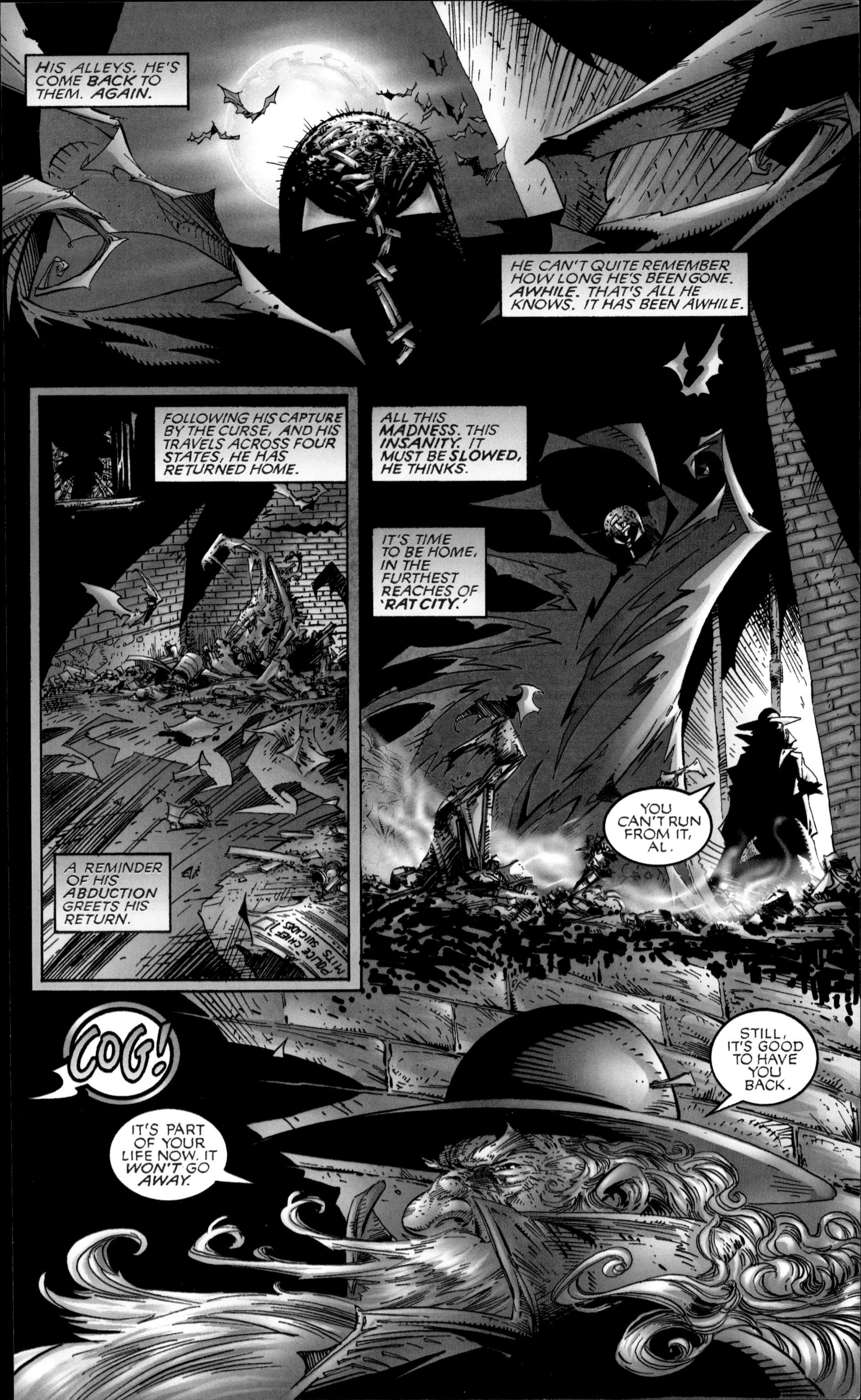
HIS ALLEYS. HE'S COME BACK TO THEM. AGAIN.
HE CAN'T QUITE REMEMBER HOW LONG HE'S BEEN GONE. AWHILE. THAT'S ALL HE KNOWS. IT HAS BEEN AWHILE.
FOLLOWING HIS CAPTURE BY THE CURSE, AND HIS TRAVELS ACROSS FOUR STATES, HE HAS RETURNED HOME.
A REMINDER OF HIS ABDUCTION GREETS HIS RETURN.
ALL THIS MADNESS. THIS INSANITY. IT MUST BE SLOWED, HE THINKS.
IT'S TIME TO BE HOME, IN THE FURTHEST REACHES OF 'RAT CITY.'
YOU CAN'T RUN FROM IT, AL.
COG!
IT'S PART OF YOUR LIFE NOW. IT WON'T GO AWAY.
STILL, IT'S GOOD TO HAVE YOU BACK.

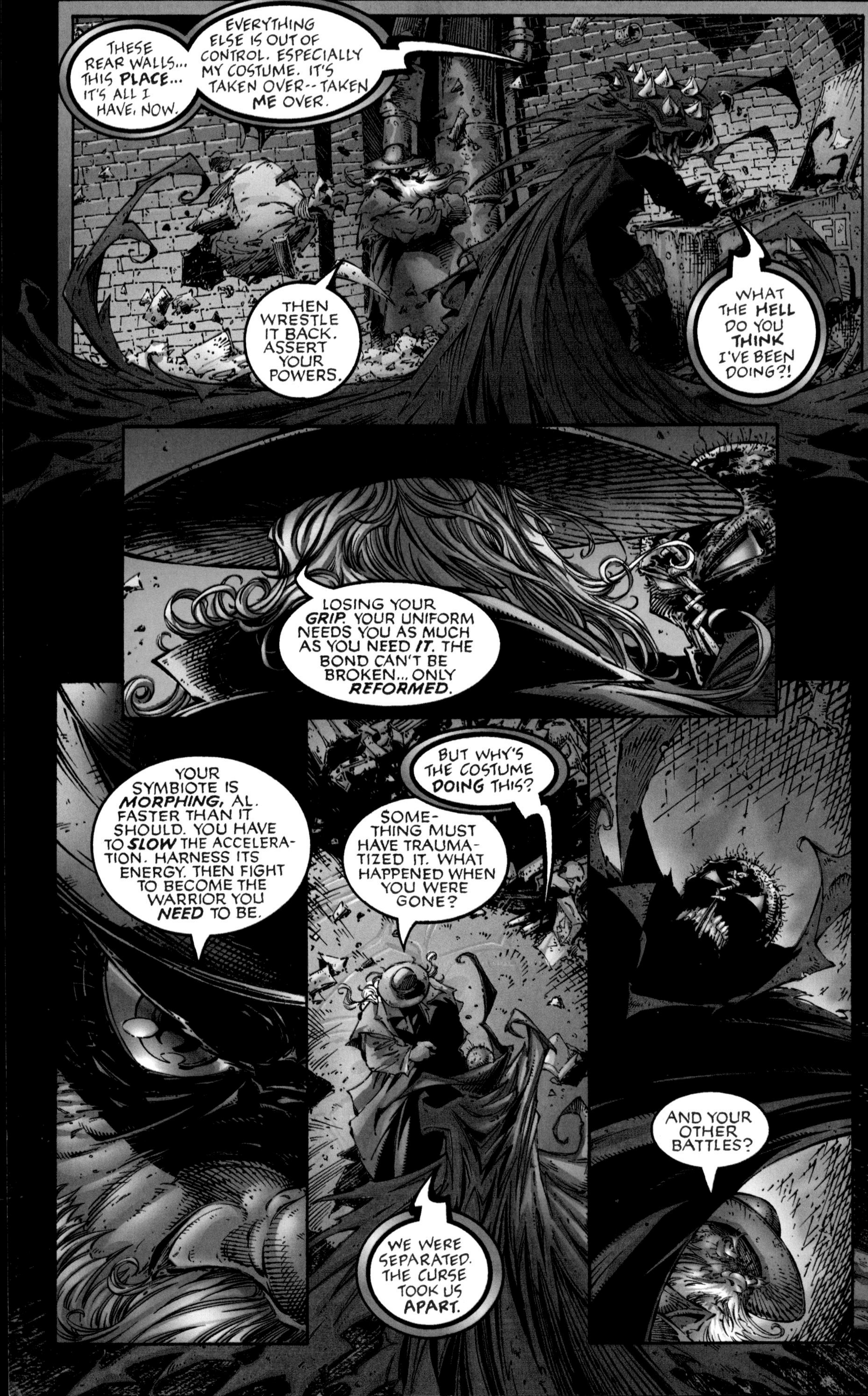
THESE REAR WALLS... THIS PLACE... IT'S ALL I HAVE, NOW.
EVERYTHING ELSE IS OUT OF CONTROL. ESPECIALLY MY COSTUME. IT'S TAKEN OVER--TAKEN ME OVER.
THEN WRESTLE IT BACK. ASSERT YOUR POWERS.
WHAT THE HELL DO YOU THINK I'VE BEEN DOING?!
LOSING YOUR GRIP. YOUR UNIFORM NEEDS YOU AS MUCH AS YOU NEED IT. THE BOND CAN'T BE BROKEN... ONLY REFORMED.
YOUR SYMBIOTE IS MORPHING, AL. FASTER THAN IT SHOULD. YOU HAVE TO SLOW THE ACCELERATION. HARNESS ITS ENERGY. THEN FIGHT TO BECOME THE WARRIOR YOU NEED TO BE.
BUT WHY'S THE COSTUME DOING THIS?
SOMETHING MUST HAVE TRAUMATIZED IT. WHAT HAPPENED WHEN YOU WERE GONE?
WE WERE SEPARATED. THE CURSE TOOK US APART.
AND YOUR OTHER BATTLES?

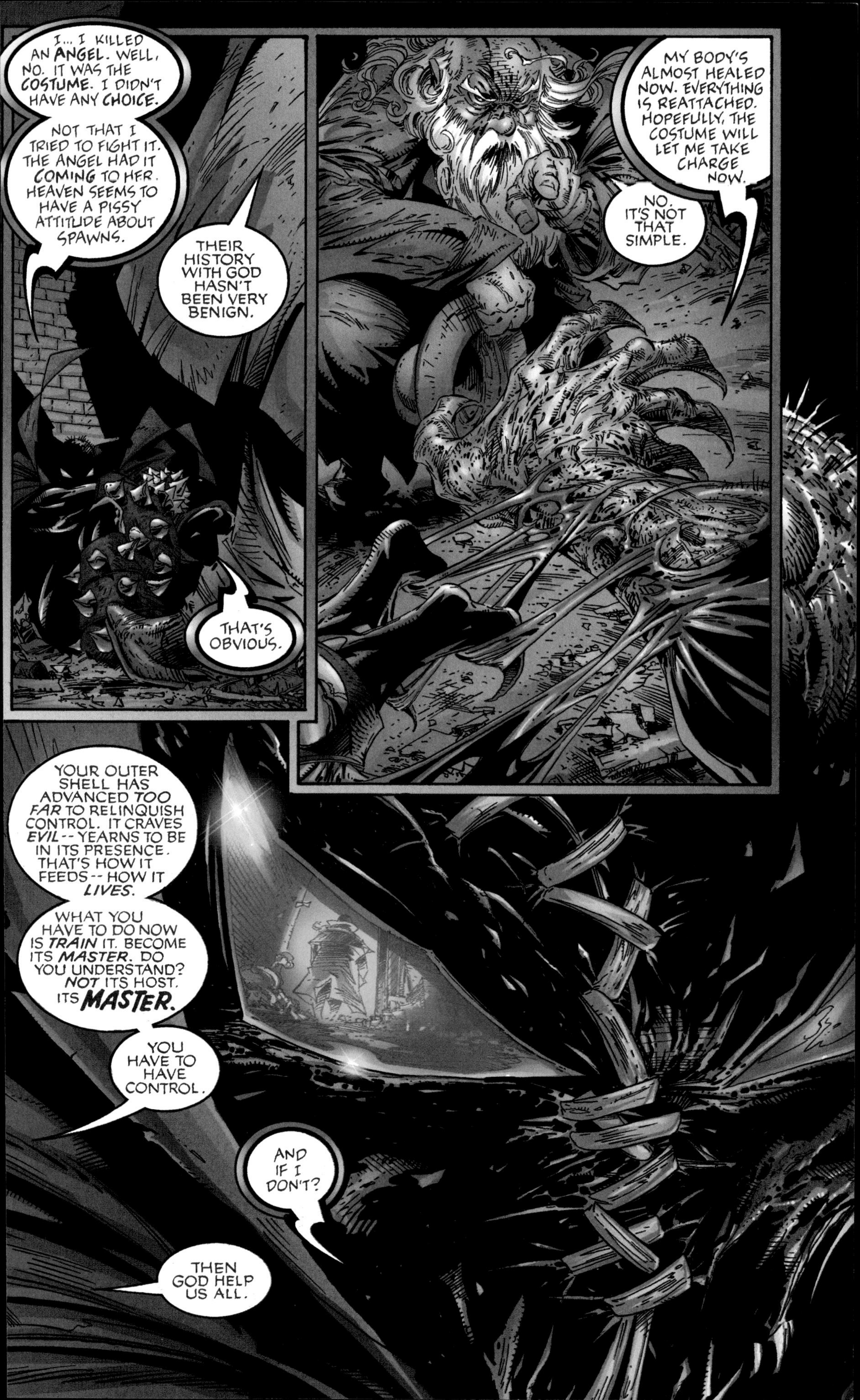
I... I KILLED AN ANGEL. WELL, NO. IT WAS THE COSTUME. I DIDN'T HAVE ANY CHOICE.
NOT THAT I TRIED TO FIGHT IT. THE ANGEL HAD IT COMING TO HER. HEAVEN SEEMS TO HAVE A PISSY ATTITUDE ABOUT SPAWNS.
THEIR HISTORY WITH GOD HASN'T BEEN VERY BENIGN.
THAT'S OBVIOUS.
MY BODY'S ALMOST HEALED NOW. EVERYTHING IS REATTACHED. HOPEFULLY, THE COSTUME WILL LET ME TAKE CHARGE NOW.
NO. IT'S NOT THAT SIMPLE.
YOUR OUTER SHELL HAS ADVANCED TOO FAR TO RELINQUISH CONTROL. IT CRAVES EVIL -- YEARNS TO BE IN ITS PRESENCE. THAT'S HOW IT FEEDS -- HOW IT LIVES.
WHAT YOU HAVE TO DO NOW IS TRAIN IT. BECOME ITS MASTER. DO YOU UNDERSTAND? NOT ITS HOST. ITS MASTER.
YOU HAVE TO HAVE CONTROL.
AND IF I DON'T?
THEN GOD HELP US ALL.

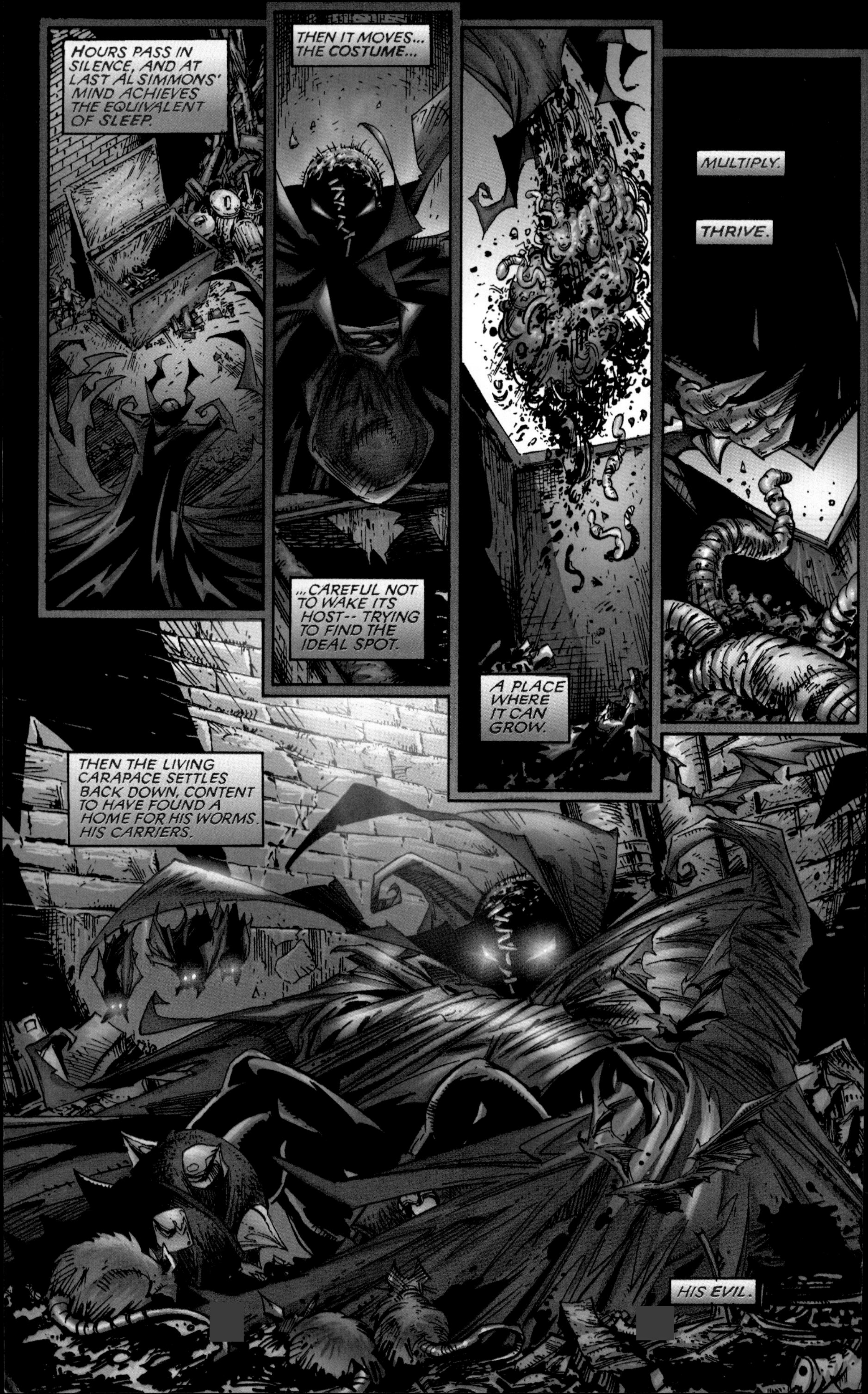
HOURS PASS IN SILENCE, AND AT LAST AL SIMMONS' MIND ACHIEVES THE EQUIVALENT OF SLEEP.
THEN IT MOVES... THE COSTUME...
...CAREFUL NOT TO WAKE ITS HOST-- TRYING TO FIND THE IDEAL SPOT.
A PLACE WHERE IT CAN GROW.
MULTIPLY.
THRIVE.
THEN THE LIVING CARAPACE SETTLES BACK DOWN, CONTENT TO HAVE FOUND A HOME FOR HIS WORMS. HIS CARRIERS.
HIS EVIL.

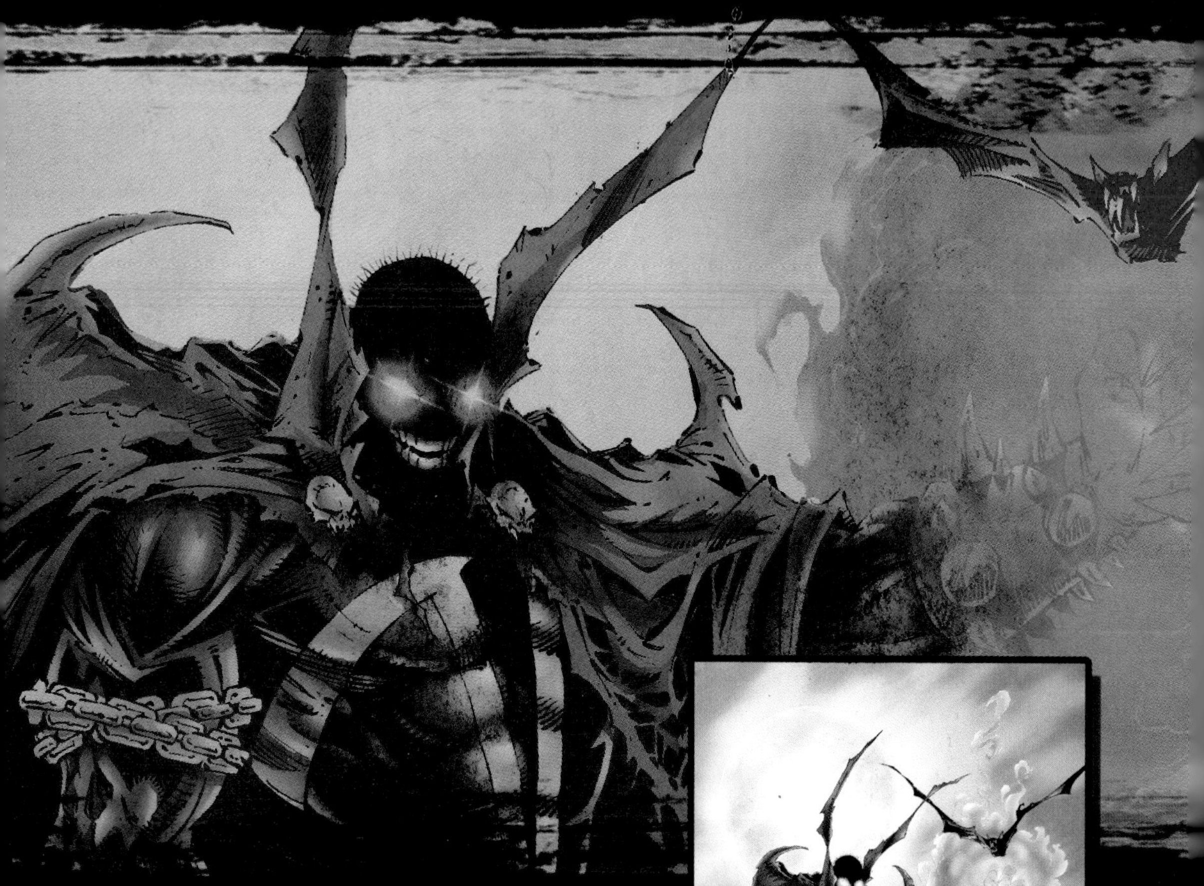

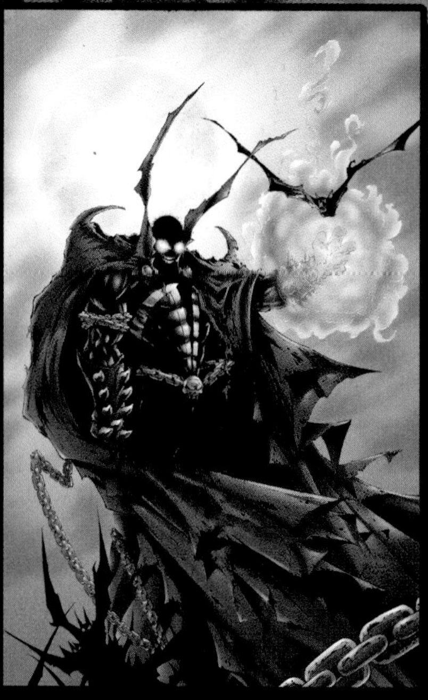

ISSUE FORTY-SIX

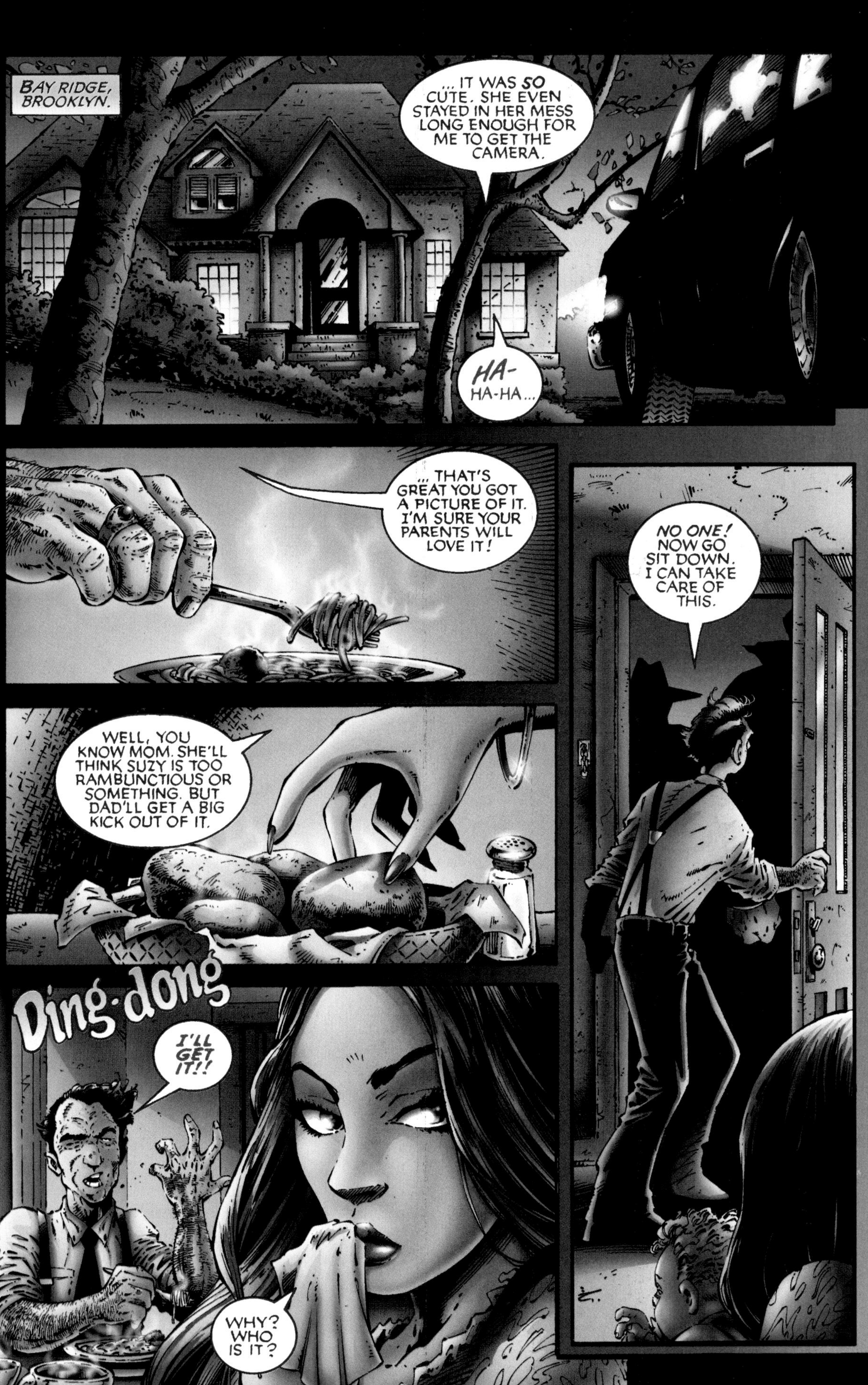
BAY RIDGE, BROOKLYN.
...IT WAS SO CUTE. SHE EVEN STAYED IN HER MESS LONG ENOUGH FOR ME TO GET THE CAMERA.
HA-HA-HA...
...THAT'S GREAT YOU GOT A PICTURE OF IT. I'M SURE YOUR PARENTS WILL LOVE IT!
WELL, YOU KNOW MOM. SHE'LL THINK SUZY IS TOO RAMBUNCTIOUS OR SOMETHING. BUT DAD'LL GET A BIG KICK OUT OF IT.
Ding-dong
I'LL GET IT!!
WHY? WHO IS IT?
NO ONE! NOW GO SIT DOWN. I CAN TAKE CARE OF THIS.

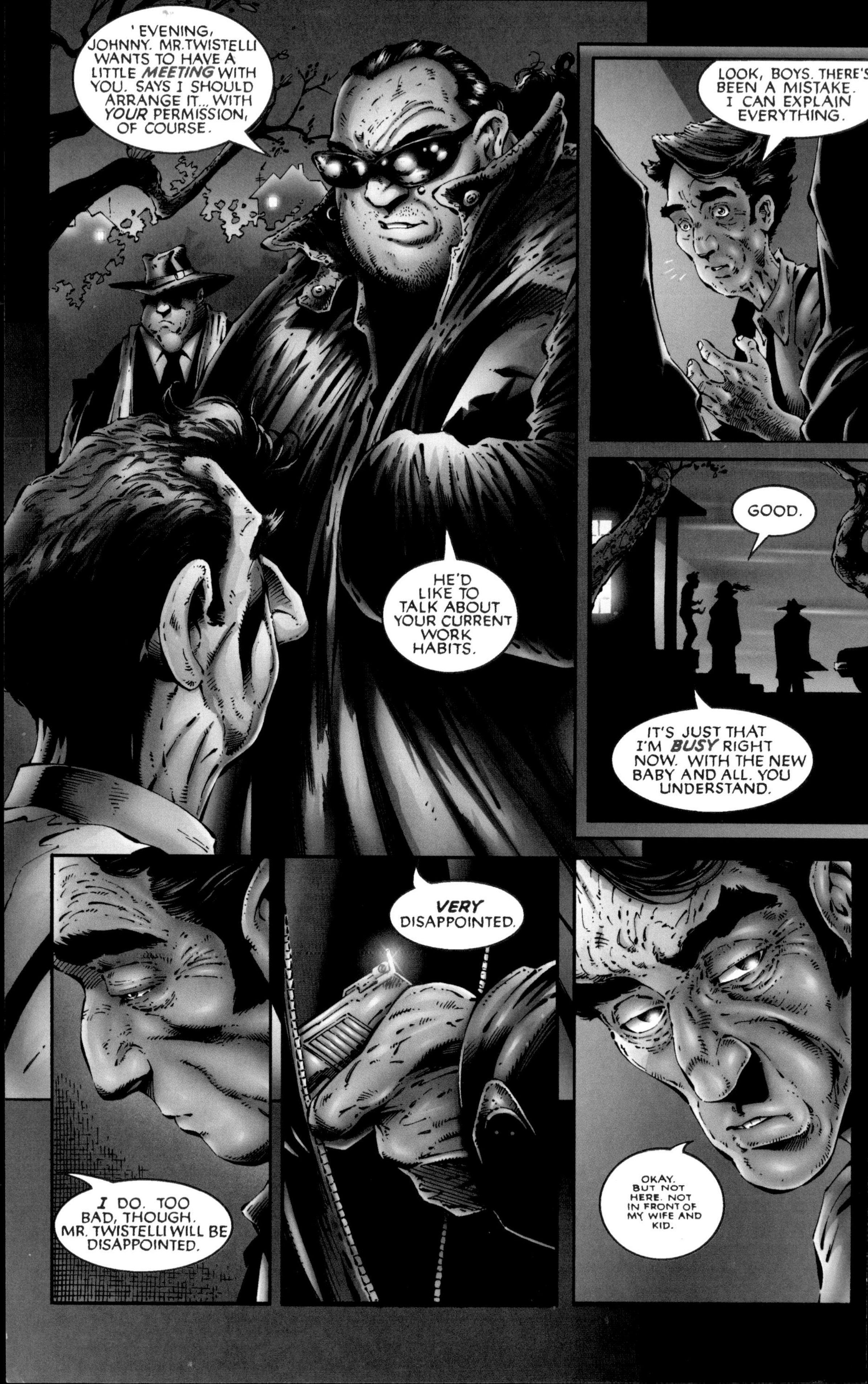
'EVENING, JOHNNY. MR.TWISTELLI WANTS TO HAVE A LITTLE MEETING WITH YOU. SAYS I SHOULD ARRANGE IT... WITH YOUR PERMISSION, OF COURSE.
HE'D LIKE TO TALK ABOUT YOUR CURRENT WORK HABITS.
LOOK, BOYS. THERE'S BEEN A MISTAKE. I CAN EXPLAIN EVERYTHING.
GOOD.
IT'S JUST THAT I'M BUSY RIGHT NOW. WITH THE NEW BABY AND ALL. YOU UNDERSTAND.
I DO. TOO BAD, THOUGH. MR. TWISTELLI WILL BE DISAPPOINTED.
VERY DISAPPOINTED.
OKAY. BUT NOT HERE. NOT IN FRONT OF MY WIFE AND KID.

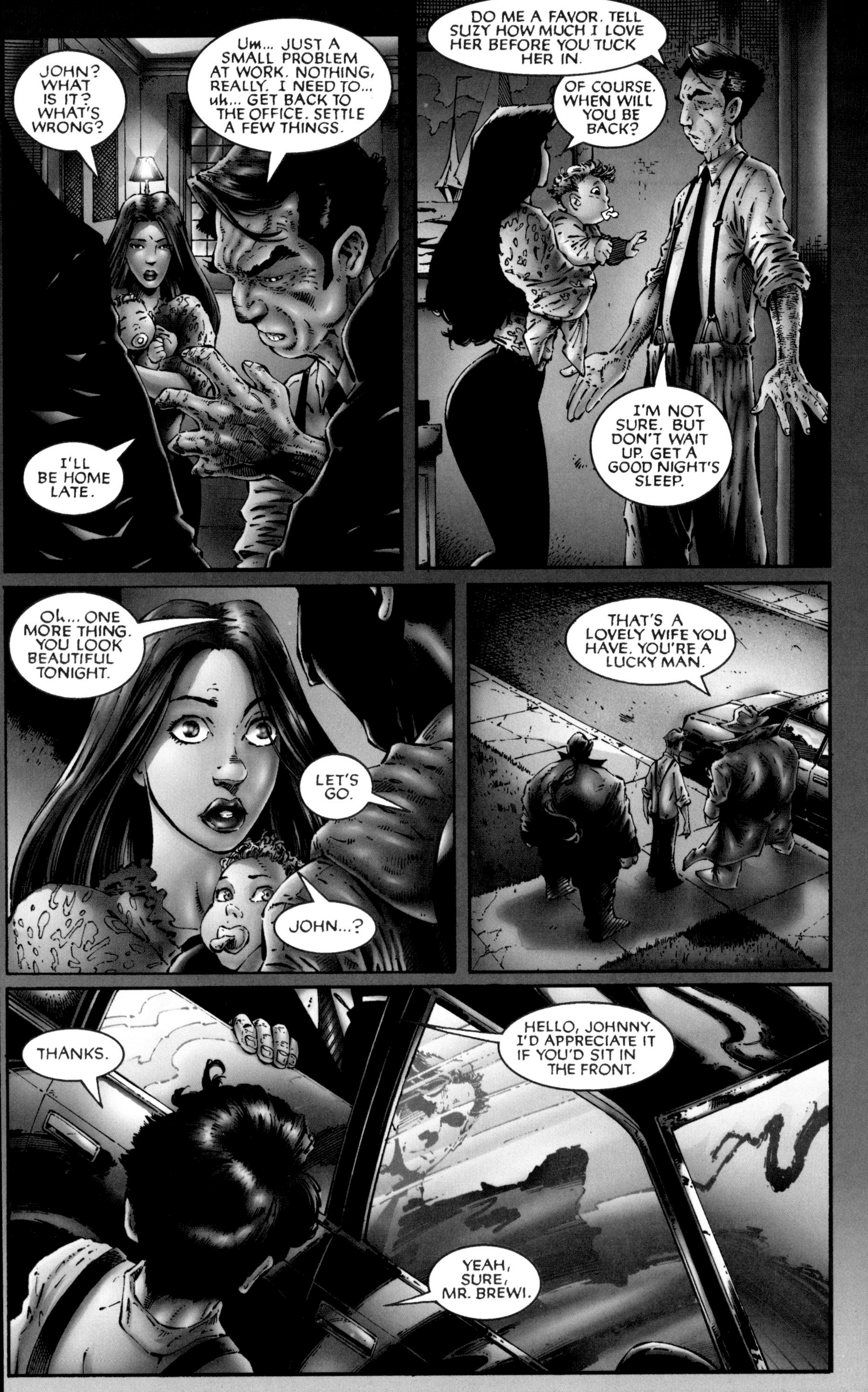
JOHN? WHAT IS IT? WHAT'S WRONG?
Um... JUST A SMALL PROBLEM AT WORK. NOTHING, REALLY. I NEED TO... uh... GET BACK TO THE OFFICE. SETTLE A FEW THINGS.
I'LL BE HOME LATE.
DO ME A FAVOR. TELL SUZY HOW MUCH I LOVE HER BEFORE YOU TUCK HER IN.
OF COURSE. WHEN WILL YOU BE BACK?
I'M NOT SURE. BUT DON'T WAIT UP. GET A GOOD NIGHT'S SLEEP.
Oh... ONE MORE THING. YOU LOOK BEAUTIFUL TONIGHT.
LET'S GO.
JOHN...?
THAT'S A LOVELY WIFE YOU HAVE. YOU'RE A LUCKY MAN.
THANKS.
HELLO, JOHNNY. I'D APPRECIATE IT IF YOU'D SIT IN THE FRONT.
YEAH, SURE, MR. BREWI.

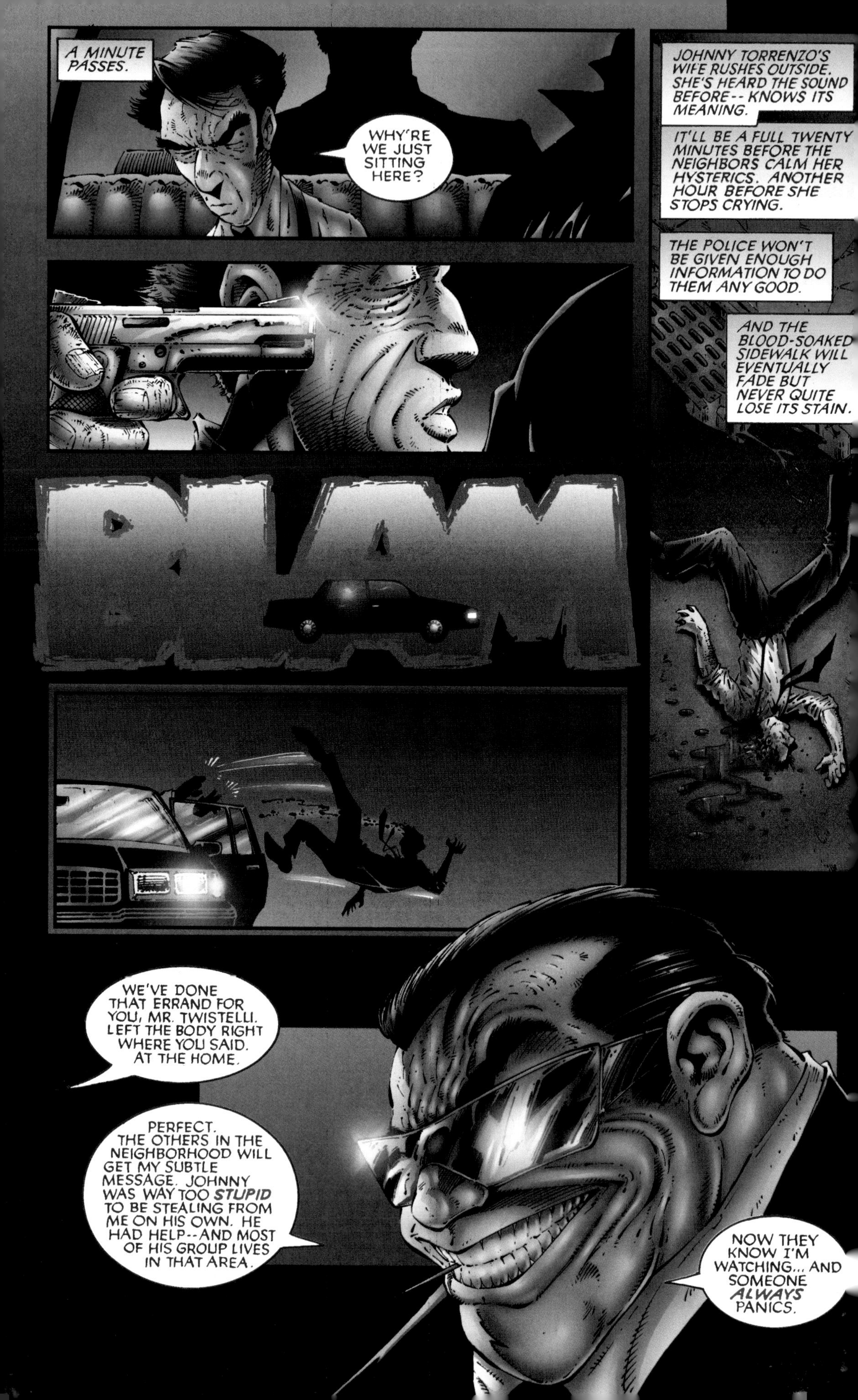
A MINUTE PASSES.
WHY'RE WE JUST SITTING HERE?
BLAM
JOHNNY TORRENZO'S WIFE RUSHES OUTSIDE. SHE'S HEARD THE SOUND BEFORE-- KNOWS ITS MEANING.
IT'LL BE A FULL TWENTY MINUTES BEFORE THE NEIGHBORS CALM HER HYSTERICS. ANOTHER HOUR BEFORE SHE STOPS CRYING.
THE POLICE WON'T BE GIVEN ENOUGH INFORMATION TO DO THEM ANY GOOD.
AND THE BLOOD-SOAKED SIDEWALK WILL EVENTUALLY FADE BUT NEVER QUITE LOSE ITS STAIN.
WE'VE DONE THAT ERRAND FOR YOU, MR. TWISTELLI. LEFT THE BODY RIGHT WHERE YOU SAID. AT THE HOME.
PERFECT. THE OTHERS IN THE NEIGHBORHOOD WILL GET MY SUBTLE MESSAGE. JOHNNY WAS WAY TOO ***STUPID*** TO BE STEALING FROM ME ON HIS OWN. HE HAD HELP--AND MOST OF HIS GROUP LIVES IN THAT AREA.
NOW THEY KNOW I'M WATCHING... AND SOMEONE ***ALWAYS*** PANICS.

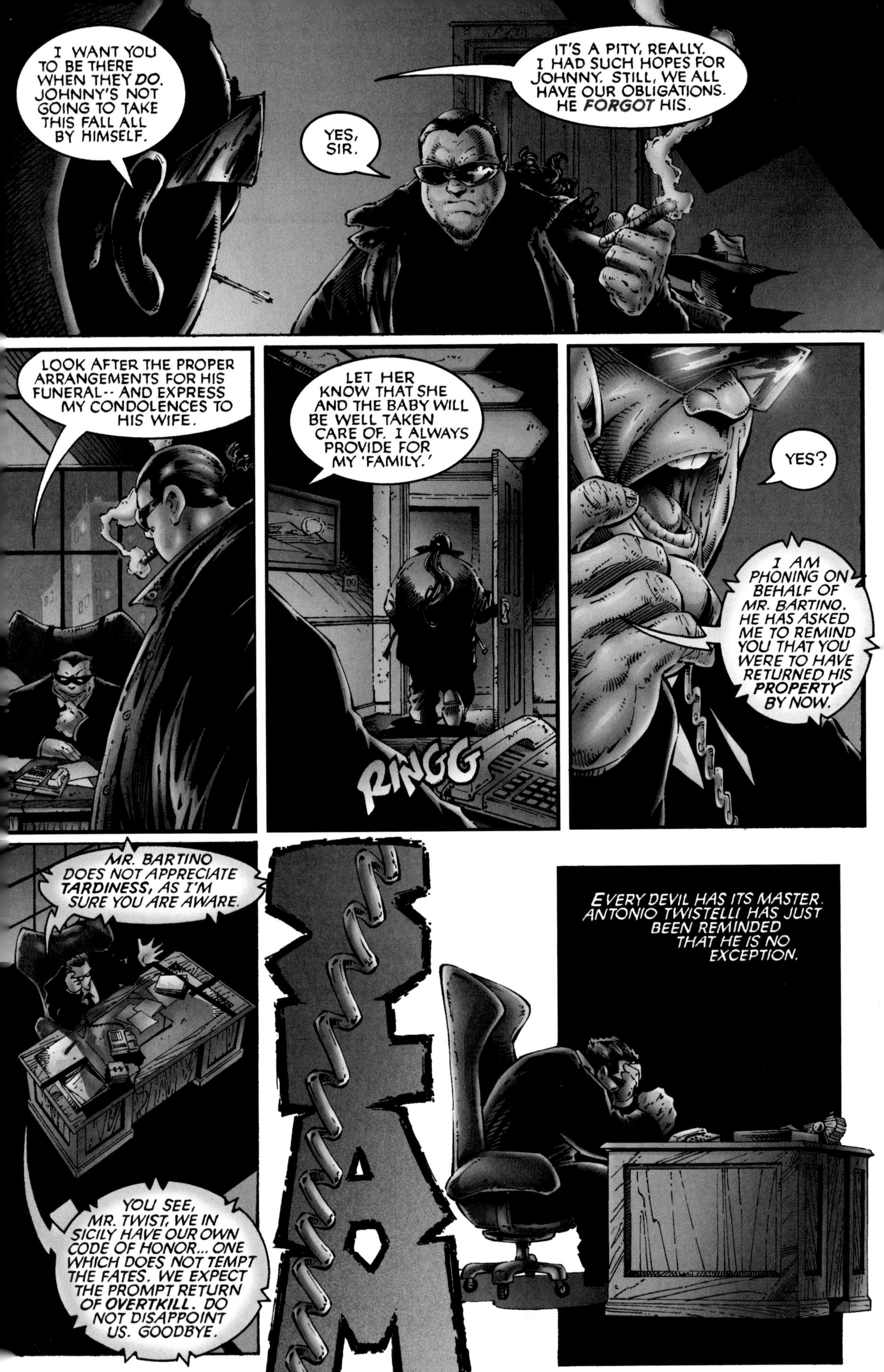
I WANT YOU TO BE THERE WHEN THEY *DO*. JOHNNY'S NOT GOING TO TAKE THIS FALL ALL BY HIMSELF.
YES, SIR.
IT'S A PITY, REALLY. I HAD SUCH HOPES FOR JOHNNY. STILL, WE ALL HAVE OUR OBLIGATIONS. HE ***FORGOT*** HIS.
LOOK AFTER THE PROPER ARRANGEMENTS FOR HIS FUNERAL-- AND EXPRESS MY CONDOLENCES TO HIS WIFE.
LET HER KNOW THAT SHE AND THE BABY WILL BE WELL TAKEN CARE OF. I ALWAYS PROVIDE FOR MY 'FAMILY.'
RINGG
YES?
*I AM PHONING ON BEHALF OF MR. BARTINO. HE HAS ASKED ME TO REMIND YOU THAT YOU WERE TO HAVE RETURNED HIS **PROPERTY** BY NOW.*
*MR. BARTINO DOES NOT APPRECIATE **TARDINESS,** AS I'M SURE YOU ARE AWARE.*
*YOU SEE, MR. TWIST, WE IN SICILY HAVE OUR OWN CODE OF HONOR... ONE WHICH DOES NOT TEMPT THE FATES. WE EXPECT THE PROMPT RETURN OF **OVERTKILL**. DO NOT DISAPPOINT US. GOODBYE.*
EVERY DEVIL HAS ITS MASTER. ANTONIO TWISTELLI HAS JUST BEEN REMINDED THAT HE IS NO EXCEPTION.

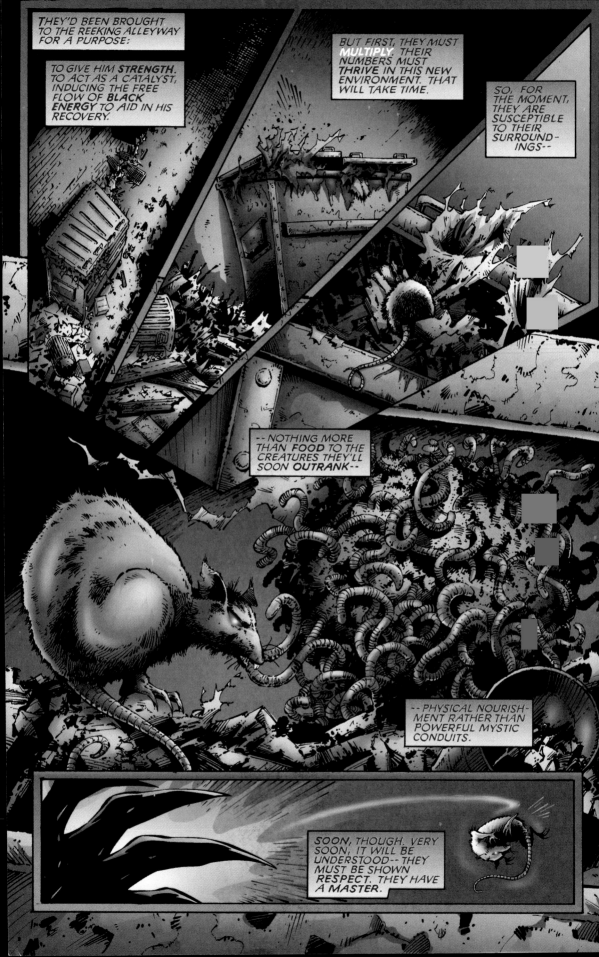

THEY'D BEEN BROUGHT TO THE REEKING ALLEYWAY FOR A PURPOSE:

TO GIVE HIM **STRENGTH**. TO ACT AS A CATALYST, INDUCING THE FREE FLOW OF **BLACK ENERGY** TO AID IN HIS RECOVERY.

BUT FIRST, THEY MUST **MULTIPLY**. THEIR NUMBERS MUST **THRIVE** IN THIS NEW ENVIRONMENT. THAT WILL TAKE TIME.

SO, FOR THE MOMENT, THEY ARE SUSCEPTIBLE TO THEIR SURROUND-INGS--

-- NOTHING MORE THAN **FOOD** TO THE CREATURES THEY'LL SOON **OUTRANK**--

--PHYSICAL NOURISH-MENT RATHER THAN POWERFUL MYSTIC CONDUITS.

SOON, THOUGH. VERY SOON, IT WILL BE UNDERSTOOD-- THEY MUST BE SHOWN **RESPECT**. THEY HAVE A **MASTER**.

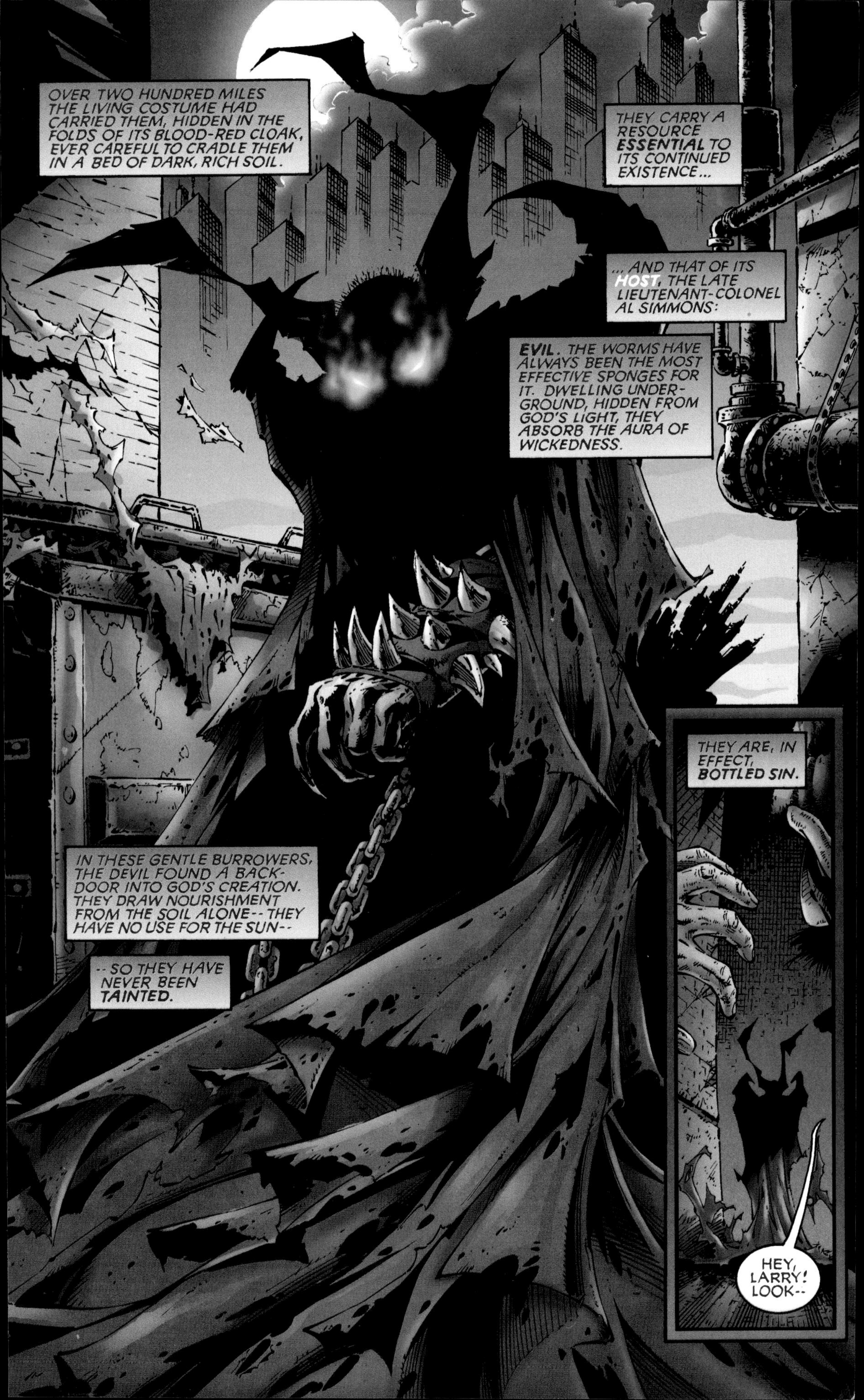
OVER TWO HUNDRED MILES THE LIVING COSTUME HAD CARRIED THEM, HIDDEN IN THE FOLDS OF ITS BLOOD-RED CLOAK, EVER CAREFUL TO CRADLE THEM IN A BED OF DARK, RICH SOIL.
THEY CARRY A RESOURCE ESSENTIAL TO ITS CONTINUED EXISTENCE...
...AND THAT OF ITS HOST, THE LATE LIEUTENANT-COLONEL AL SIMMONS:
EVIL. THE WORMS HAVE ALWAYS BEEN THE MOST EFFECTIVE SPONGES FOR IT. DWELLING UNDER-GROUND, HIDDEN FROM GOD'S LIGHT, THEY ABSORB THE AURA OF WICKEDNESS.
IN THESE GENTLE BURROWERS, THE DEVIL FOUND A BACK-DOOR INTO GOD'S CREATION. THEY DRAW NOURISHMENT FROM THE SOIL ALONE--THEY HAVE NO USE FOR THE SUN--
--SO THEY HAVE NEVER BEEN TAINTED.
THEY ARE, IN EFFECT, BOTTLED SIN.
HEY, LARRY! LOOK--

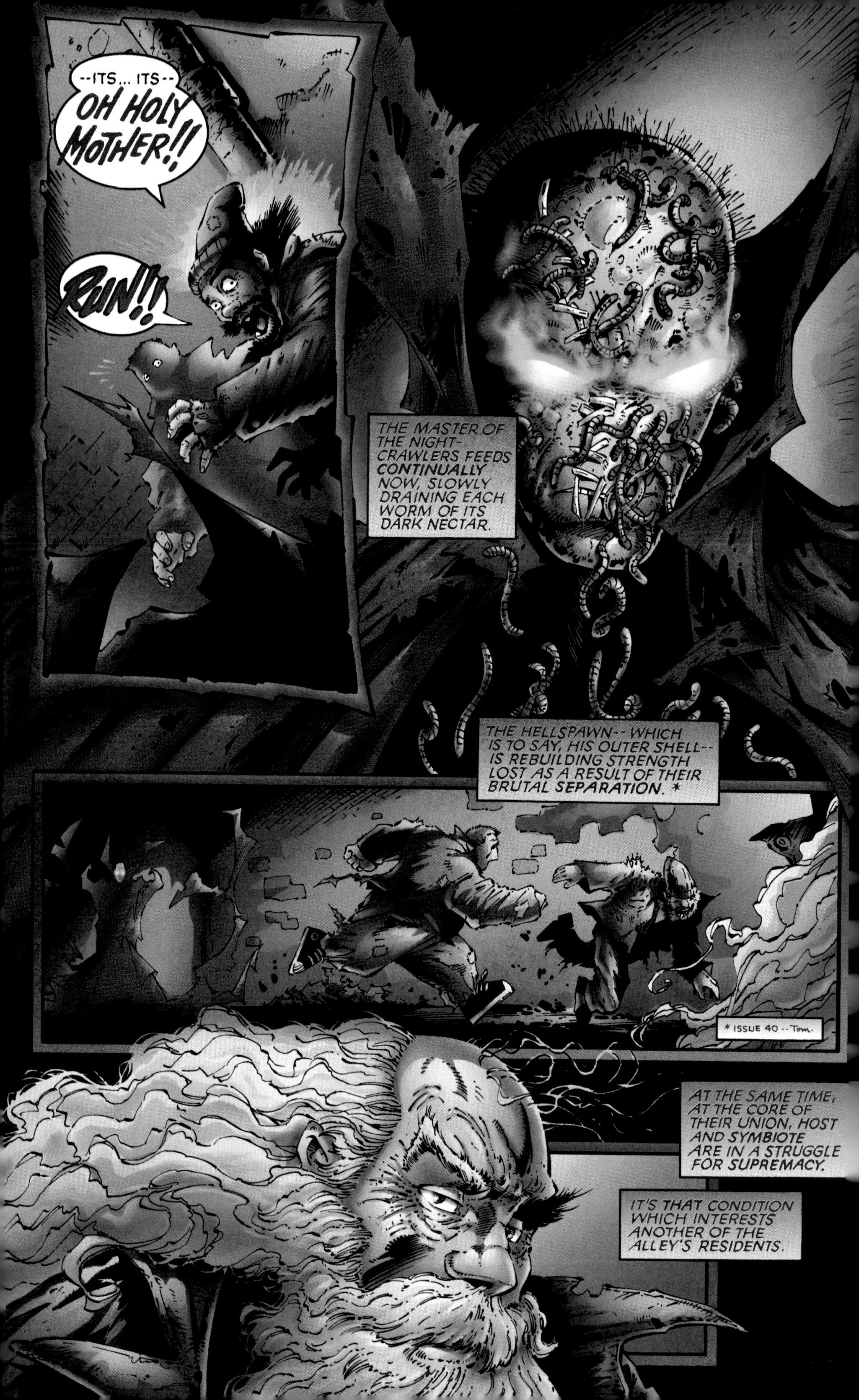
--ITS... ITS--
OH HOLY MOTHER!!
RUN!!
THE MASTER OF THE NIGHT-CRAWLERS FEEDS CONTINUALLY NOW, SLOWLY DRAINING EACH WORM OF ITS DARK NECTAR.
THE HELLSPAWN-- WHICH IS TO SAY, HIS OUTER SHELL-- IS REBUILDING STRENGTH LOST AS A RESULT OF THEIR BRUTAL SEPARATION. *
* ISSUE 40 --Tom.
AT THE SAME TIME, AT THE CORE OF THEIR UNION, HOST AND SYMBIOTE ARE IN A STRUGGLE FOR SUPREMACY.
IT'S THAT CONDITION WHICH INTERESTS ANOTHER OF THE ALLEY'S RESIDENTS.

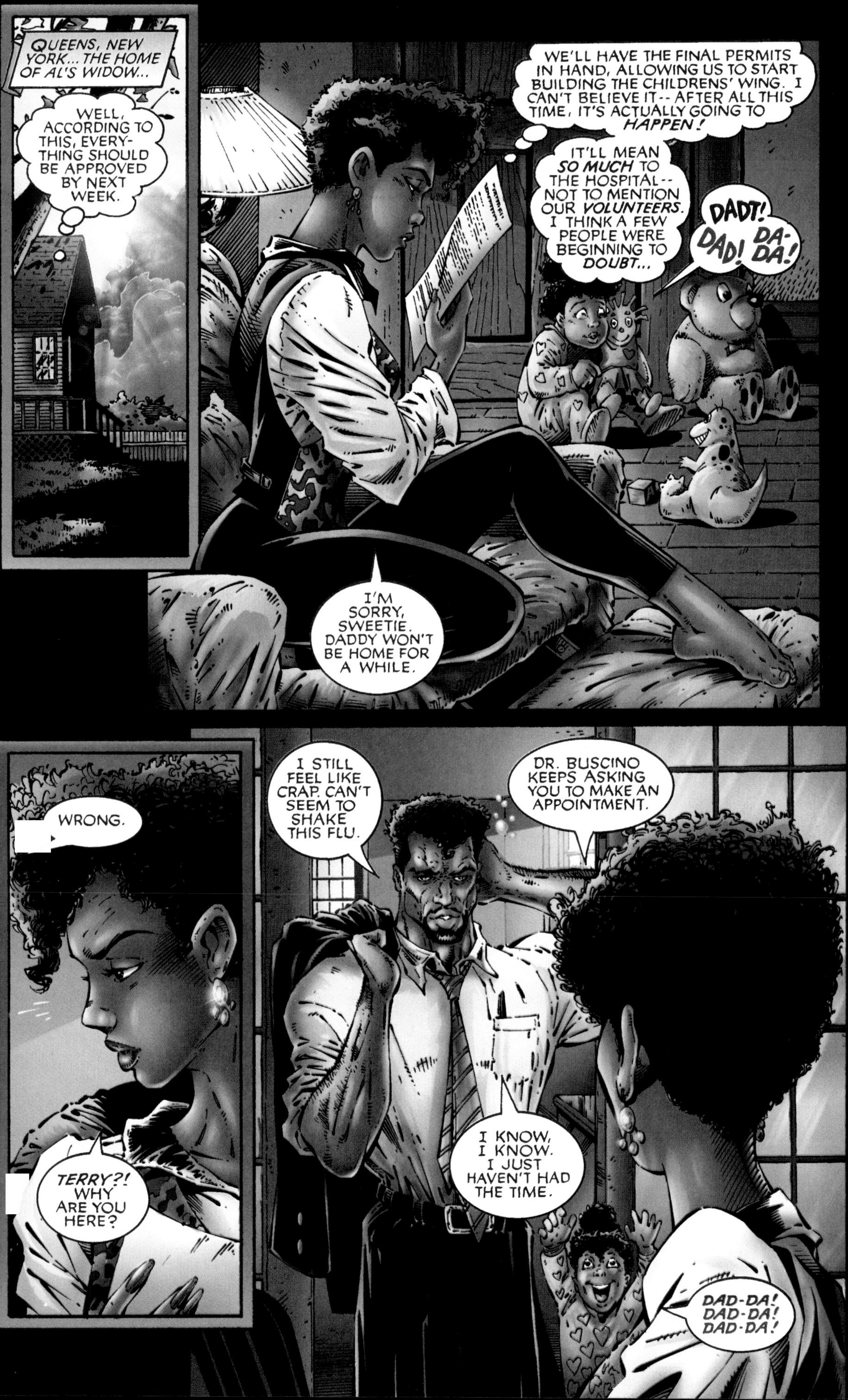
QUEENS, NEW YORK... THE HOME OF AL'S WIDOW...
WELL, ACCORDING TO THIS, EVERYTHING SHOULD BE APPROVED BY NEXT WEEK.
WE'LL HAVE THE FINAL PERMITS IN HAND, ALLOWING US TO START BUILDING THE CHILDRENS' WING. I CAN'T BELIEVE IT-- AFTER ALL THIS TIME, IT'S ACTUALLY GOING TO HAPPEN!
IT'LL MEAN SO MUCH TO THE HOSPITAL-- NOT TO MENTION OUR VOLUNTEERS. I THINK A FEW PEOPLE WERE BEGINNING TO DOUBT...
DADT! DAD! DA-DA!
I'M SORRY, SWEETIE. DADDY WON'T BE HOME FOR A WHILE.
WRONG.
TERRY?! WHY ARE YOU HERE?
I STILL FEEL LIKE CRAP. CAN'T SEEM TO SHAKE THIS FLU.
DR. BUSCINO KEEPS ASKING YOU TO MAKE AN APPOINTMENT.
I KNOW, I KNOW. I JUST HAVEN'T HAD THE TIME.
DAD-DA! DAD-DA! DAD-DA!

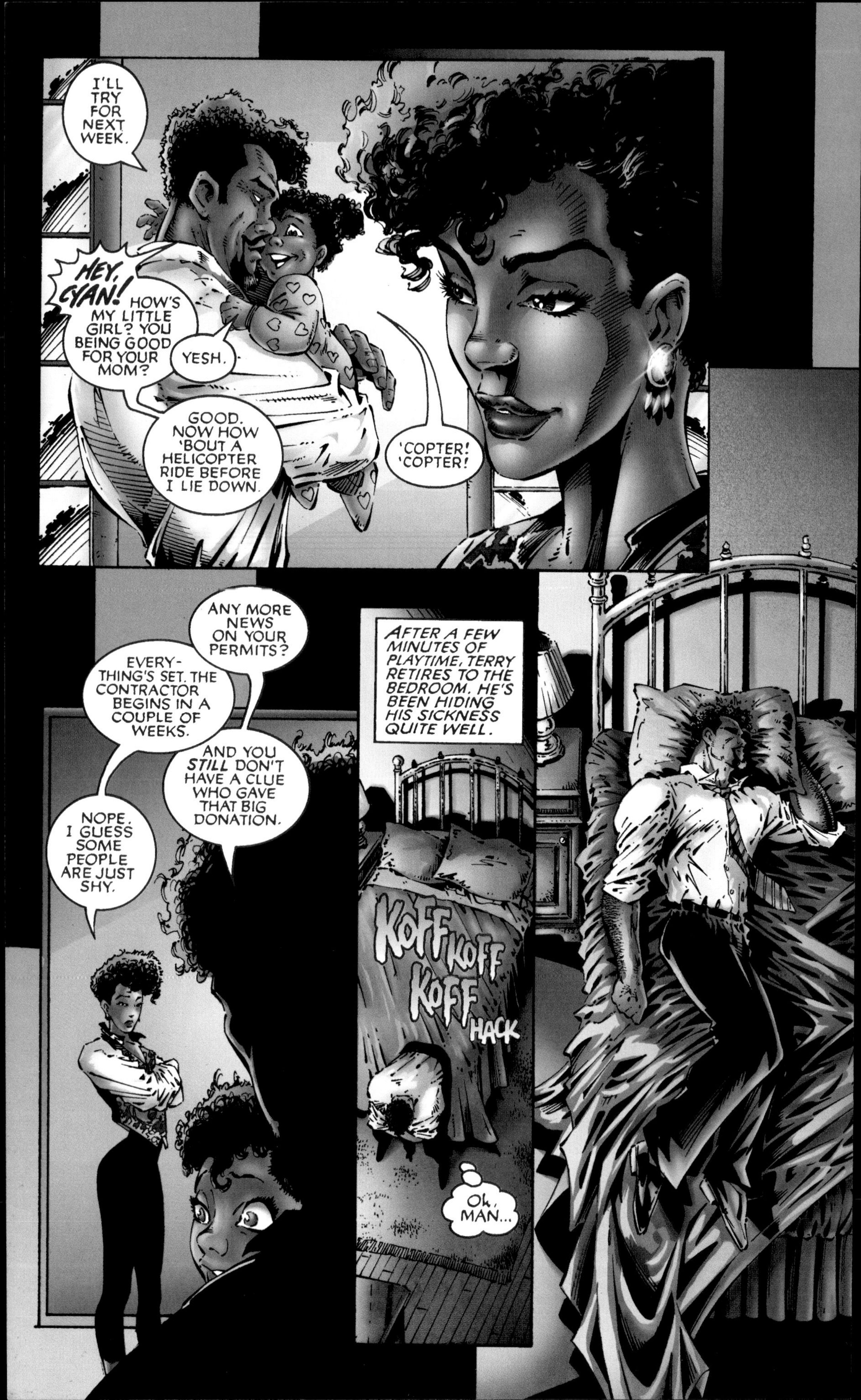
I'LL TRY FOR NEXT WEEK.
HEY, CYAN! HOW'S MY LITTLE GIRL? YOU BEING GOOD FOR YOUR MOM?
YESH.
GOOD. NOW HOW 'BOUT A HELICOPTER RIDE BEFORE I LIE DOWN.
'COPTER! 'COPTER!
ANY MORE NEWS ON YOUR PERMITS?
EVERY-THING'S SET. THE CONTRACTOR BEGINS IN A COUPLE OF WEEKS.
AND YOU STILL DON'T HAVE A CLUE WHO GAVE THAT BIG DONATION.
NOPE. I GUESS SOME PEOPLE ARE JUST SHY.
AFTER A FEW MINUTES OF PLAYTIME, TERRY RETIRES TO THE BEDROOM. HE'S BEEN HIDING HIS SICKNESS QUITE WELL.
KOFF KOFF KOFF HACK
Oh, MAN...

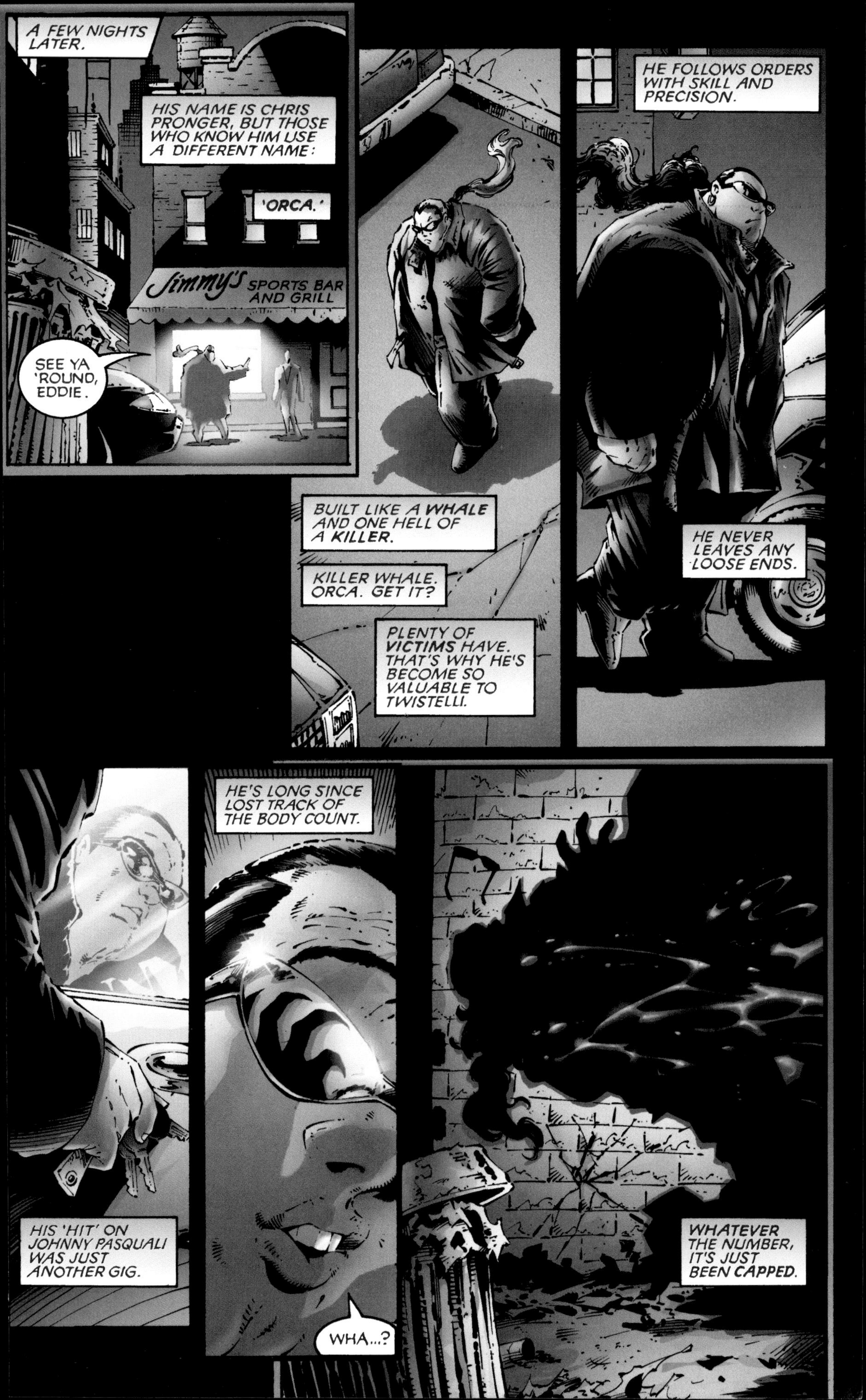
A FEW NIGHTS LATER.
HIS NAME IS CHRIS PRONGER, BUT THOSE WHO KNOW HIM USE A DIFFERENT NAME:
'ORCA.'
Jimmy's SPORTS BAR AND GRILL
SEE YA 'ROUND, EDDIE.
BUILT LIKE A **WHALE** AND ONE HELL OF A **KILLER**.
KILLER WHALE. ORCA. GET IT?
PLENTY OF **VICTIMS** HAVE. THAT'S WHY HE'S BECOME SO VALUABLE TO TWISTELLI.
HE FOLLOWS ORDERS WITH SKILL AND PRECISION.
HE NEVER LEAVES ANY **LOOSE ENDS**.
HIS 'HIT' ON JOHNNY PASQUALI WAS JUST ANOTHER GIG.
HE'S LONG SINCE LOST TRACK OF THE BODY COUNT.
WHA...?
WHATEVER THE NUMBER, IT'S JUST BEEN **CAPPED**.

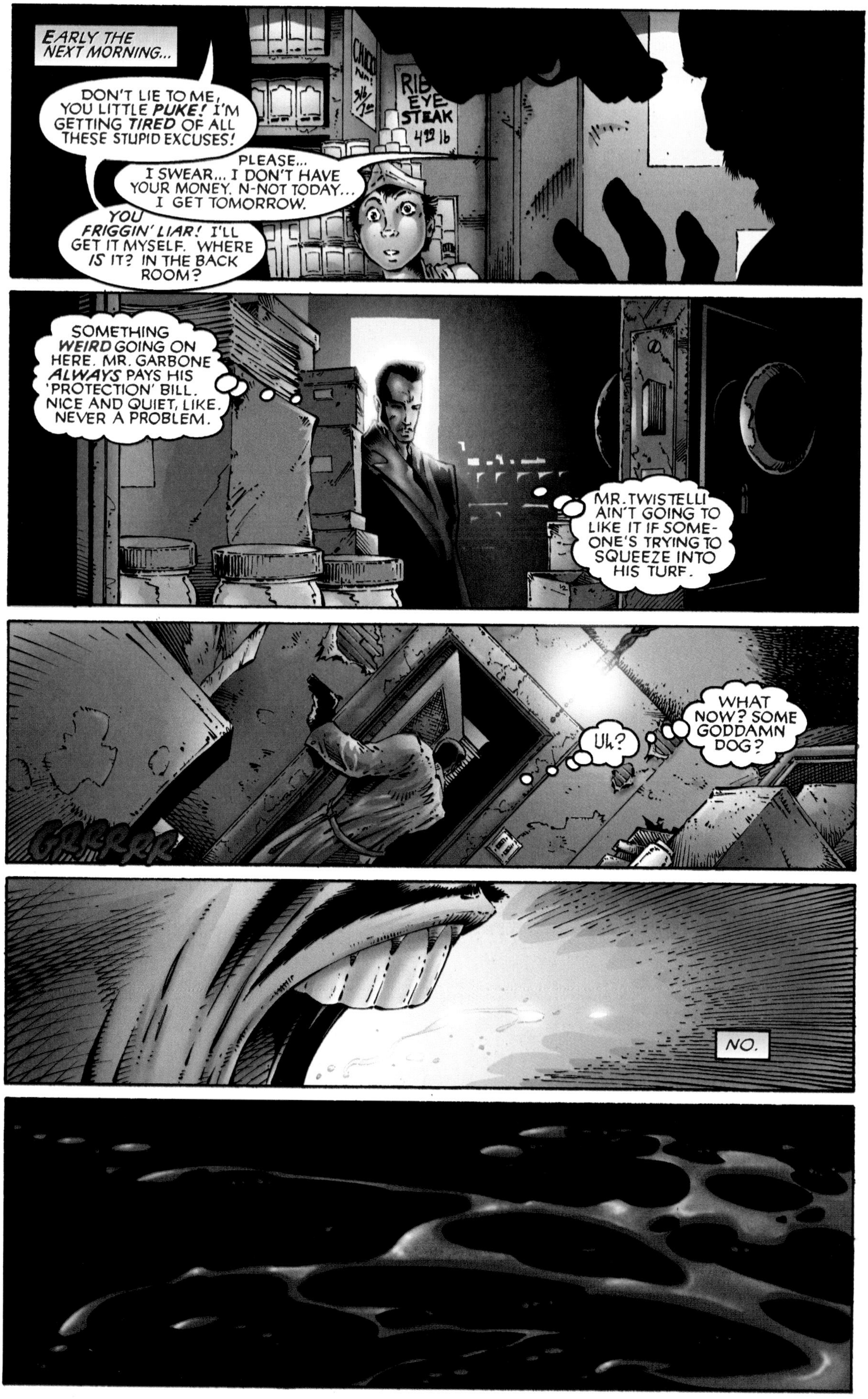
EARLY THE NEXT MORNING...
DON'T LIE TO ME, YOU LITTLE PUKE! I'M GETTING TIRED OF ALL THESE STUPID EXCUSES!
PLEASE... I SWEAR... I DON'T HAVE YOUR MONEY. N-NOT TODAY... I GET TOMORROW.
YOU FRIGGIN' LIAR! I'LL GET IT MYSELF. WHERE IS IT? IN THE BACK ROOM?
RIB EYE STEAK 4.99 lb
SOMETHING WEIRD GOING ON HERE. MR. GARBONE ALWAYS PAYS HIS 'PROTECTION' BILL. NICE AND QUIET, LIKE. NEVER A PROBLEM.
MR. TWISTELLI AIN'T GOING TO LIKE IT IF SOME-ONE'S TRYING TO SQUEEZE INTO HIS TURF.
GRRRRR
Uh?
WHAT NOW? SOME GODDAMN DOG?
NO.

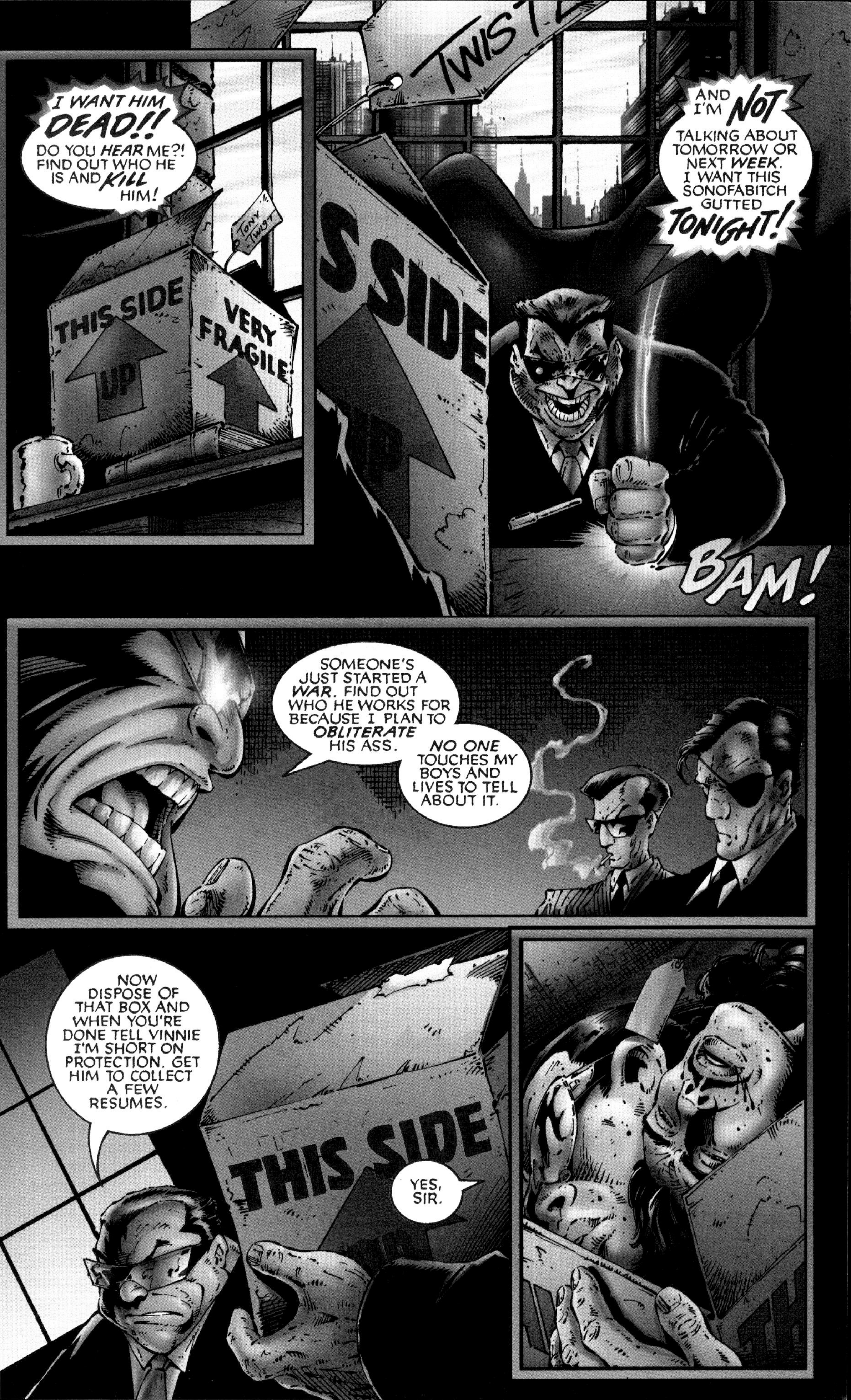
TWIST
I WANT HIM DEAD!! DO YOU HEAR ME?! FIND OUT WHO HE IS AND KILL HIM!
TONY TWIST
THIS SIDE UP
VERY FRAGILE
S SIDE UP
AND I'M NOT TALKING ABOUT TOMORROW OR NEXT WEEK. I WANT THIS SONOFABITCH GUTTED TONIGHT!
BAM!
SOMEONE'S JUST STARTED A WAR. FIND OUT WHO HE WORKS FOR BECAUSE I PLAN TO OBLITERATE HIS ASS.
NO ONE TOUCHES MY BOYS AND LIVES TO TELL ABOUT IT.
NOW DISPOSE OF THAT BOX AND WHEN YOU'RE DONE TELL VINNIE I'M SHORT ON PROTECTION. GET HIM TO COLLECT A FEW RESUMES.
THIS SIDE
YES, SIR.

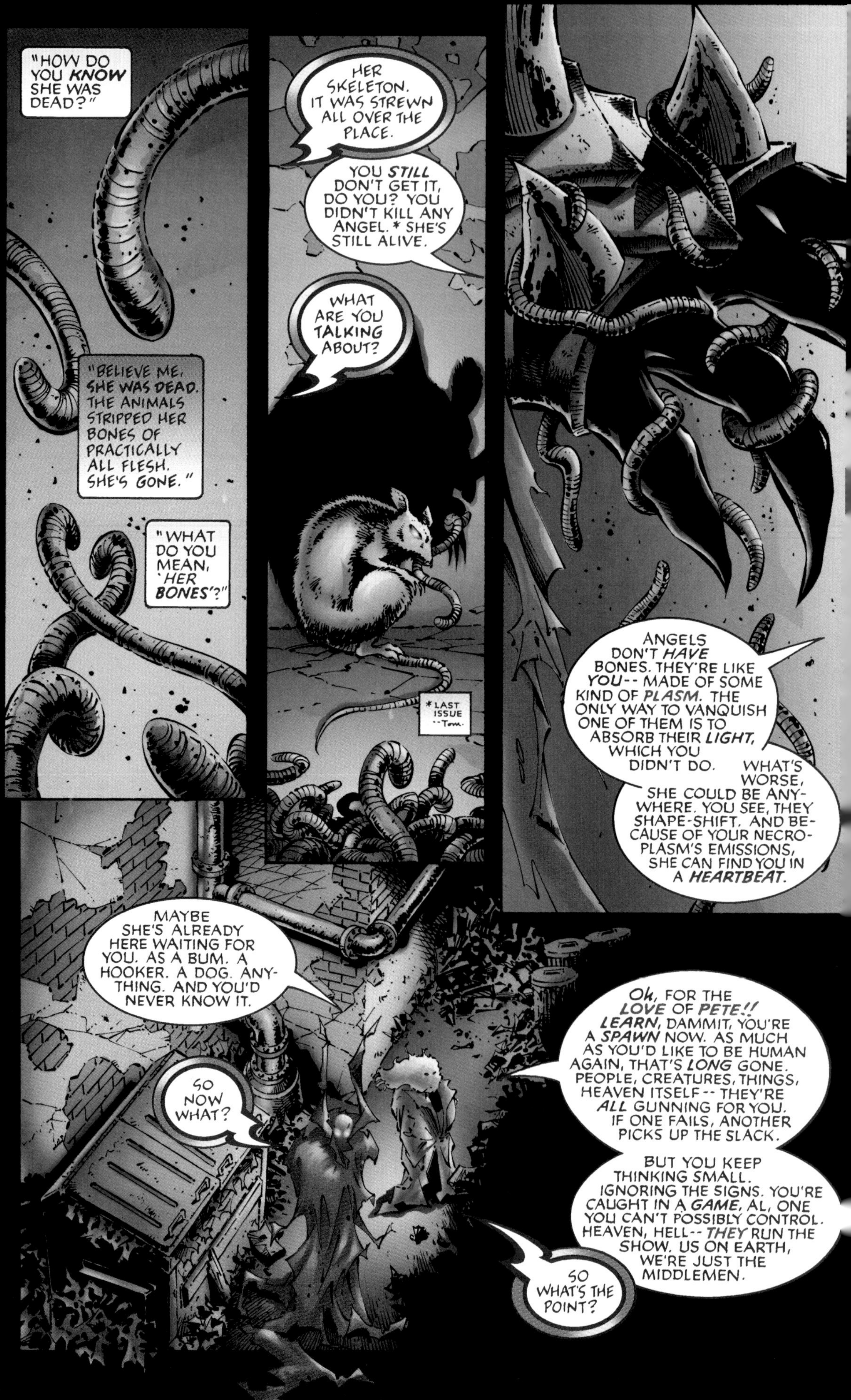
"HOW DO YOU KNOW SHE WAS DEAD?"
"BELIEVE ME, SHE WAS DEAD. THE ANIMALS STRIPPED HER BONES OF PRACTICALLY ALL FLESH. SHE'S GONE."
"WHAT DO YOU MEAN, 'HER BONES'?"
HER SKELETON. IT WAS STREWN ALL OVER THE PLACE.
YOU STILL DON'T GET IT, DO YOU? YOU DIDN'T KILL ANY ANGEL.* SHE'S STILL ALIVE.
WHAT ARE YOU TALKING ABOUT?
*LAST ISSUE --Tom.
ANGELS DON'T HAVE BONES. THEY'RE LIKE YOU-- MADE OF SOME KIND OF PLASM. THE ONLY WAY TO VANQUISH ONE OF THEM IS TO ABSORB THEIR LIGHT, WHICH YOU DIDN'T DO.
WHAT'S WORSE, SHE COULD BE ANYWHERE. YOU SEE, THEY SHAPE-SHIFT. AND BECAUSE OF YOUR NECROPLASM'S EMISSIONS, SHE CAN FIND YOU IN A HEARTBEAT.
MAYBE SHE'S ALREADY HERE WAITING FOR YOU. AS A BUM. A HOOKER. A DOG. ANYTHING. AND YOU'D NEVER KNOW IT.
SO NOW WHAT?
Oh, FOR THE LOVE OF PETE!! LEARN, DAMMIT. YOU'RE A SPAWN NOW. AS MUCH AS YOU'D LIKE TO BE HUMAN AGAIN, THAT'S LONG GONE. PEOPLE, CREATURES, THINGS, HEAVEN ITSELF-- THEY'RE ALL GUNNING FOR YOU. IF ONE FAILS, ANOTHER PICKS UP THE SLACK.
BUT YOU KEEP THINKING SMALL. IGNORING THE SIGNS. YOU'RE CAUGHT IN A GAME, AL, ONE YOU CAN'T POSSIBLY CONTROL. HEAVEN, HELL-- THEY RUN THE SHOW. US ON EARTH, WE'RE JUST THE MIDDLEMEN.
SO WHAT'S THE POINT?

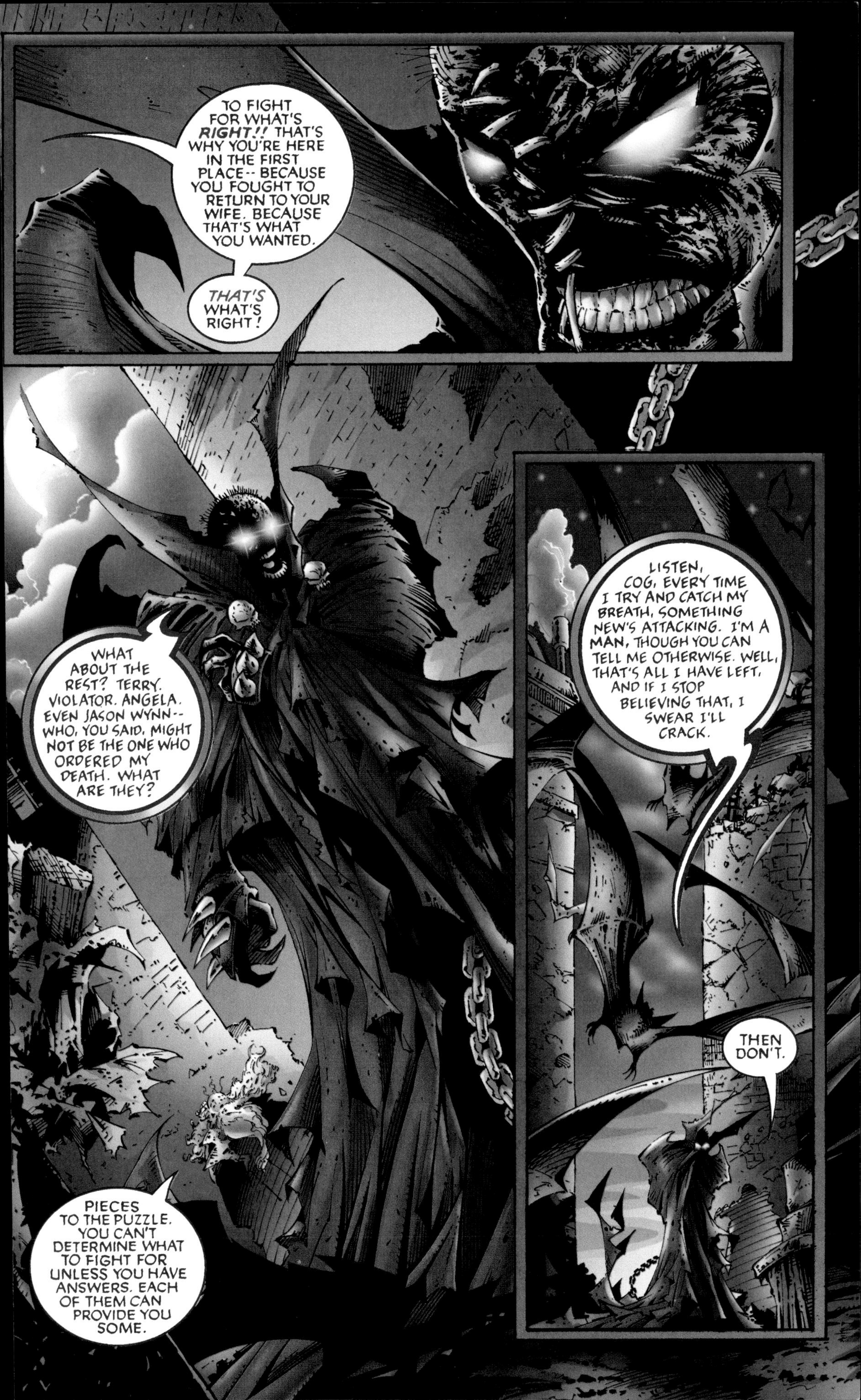
TO FIGHT FOR WHAT'S *RIGHT!!* THAT'S WHY YOU'RE HERE IN THE FIRST PLACE-- BECAUSE YOU FOUGHT TO RETURN TO YOUR WIFE. BECAUSE THAT'S WHAT YOU WANTED.
THAT'S WHAT'S RIGHT!
WHAT ABOUT THE REST? TERRY. VIOLATOR. ANGELA. EVEN JASON WYNN-- WHO, YOU SAID, MIGHT NOT BE THE ONE WHO ORDERED MY DEATH. WHAT ARE THEY?
PIECES TO THE PUZZLE. YOU CAN'T DETERMINE WHAT TO FIGHT FOR UNLESS YOU HAVE ANSWERS. EACH OF THEM CAN PROVIDE YOU SOME.
LISTEN, COG, EVERY TIME I TRY AND CATCH MY BREATH, SOMETHING NEW'S ATTACKING. I'M A MAN, THOUGH YOU CAN TELL ME OTHERWISE. WELL, THAT'S ALL I HAVE LEFT, AND IF I STOP BELIEVING THAT, I SWEAR I'LL CRACK.
THEN DON'T.

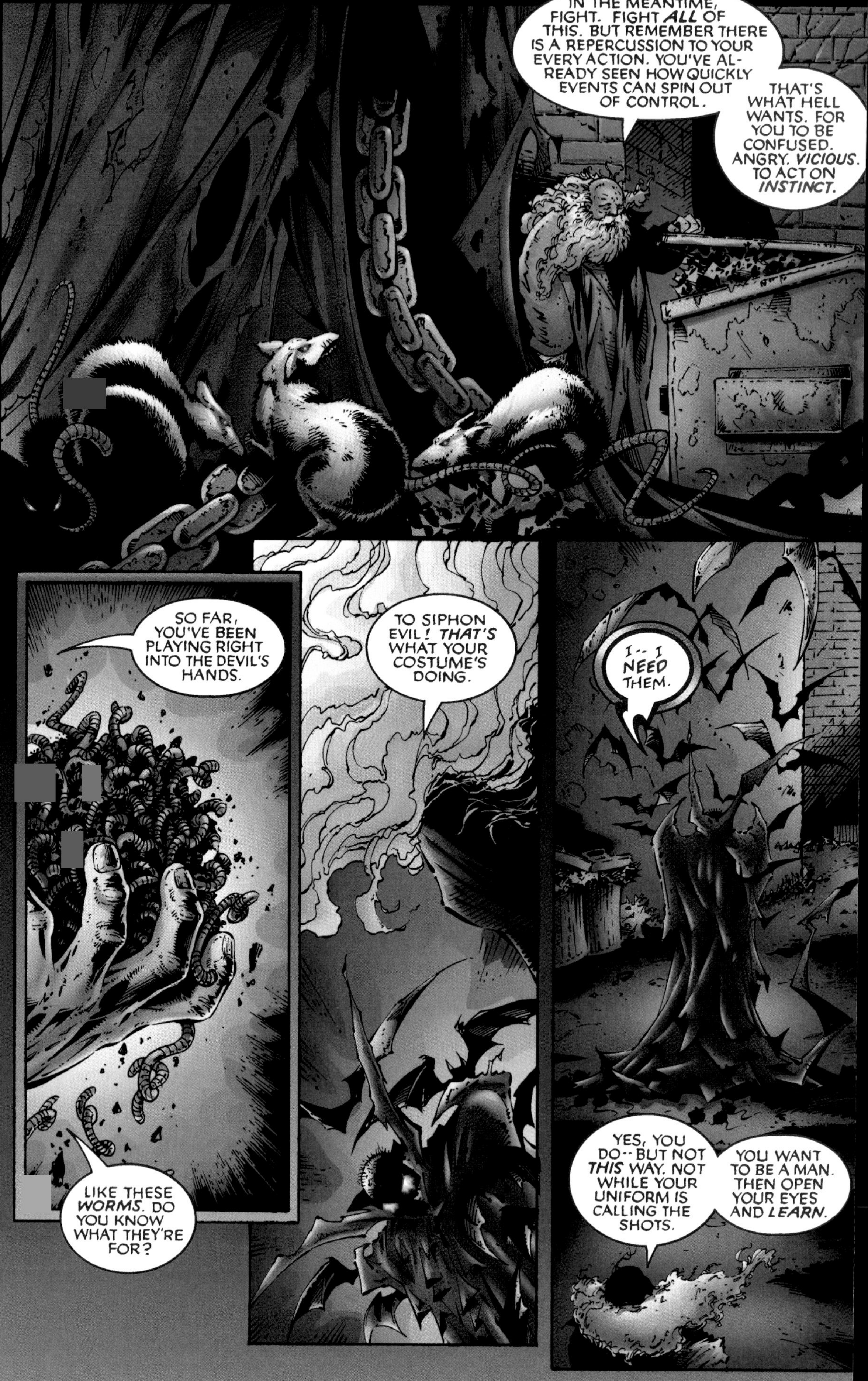
IN THE MEANTIME, FIGHT. FIGHT *ALL* OF THIS. BUT REMEMBER THERE IS A REPERCUSSION TO YOUR EVERY ACTION. YOU'VE ALREADY SEEN HOW QUICKLY EVENTS CAN SPIN OUT OF CONTROL.
THAT'S WHAT HELL WANTS. FOR YOU TO BE CONFUSED. ANGRY. *VICIOUS*. TO ACT ON *INSTINCT*.
SO FAR, YOU'VE BEEN PLAYING RIGHT INTO THE DEVIL'S HANDS.
LIKE THESE *WORMS*. DO YOU KNOW WHAT THEY'RE FOR?
TO SIPHON EVIL! *THAT'S* WHAT YOUR COSTUME'S DOING.
I-- I *NEED* THEM.
YES, YOU DO-- BUT NOT *THIS WAY*. NOT WHILE YOUR UNIFORM IS CALLING THE SHOTS.
YOU WANT TO BE A MAN. THEN OPEN YOUR EYES AND *LEARN*.

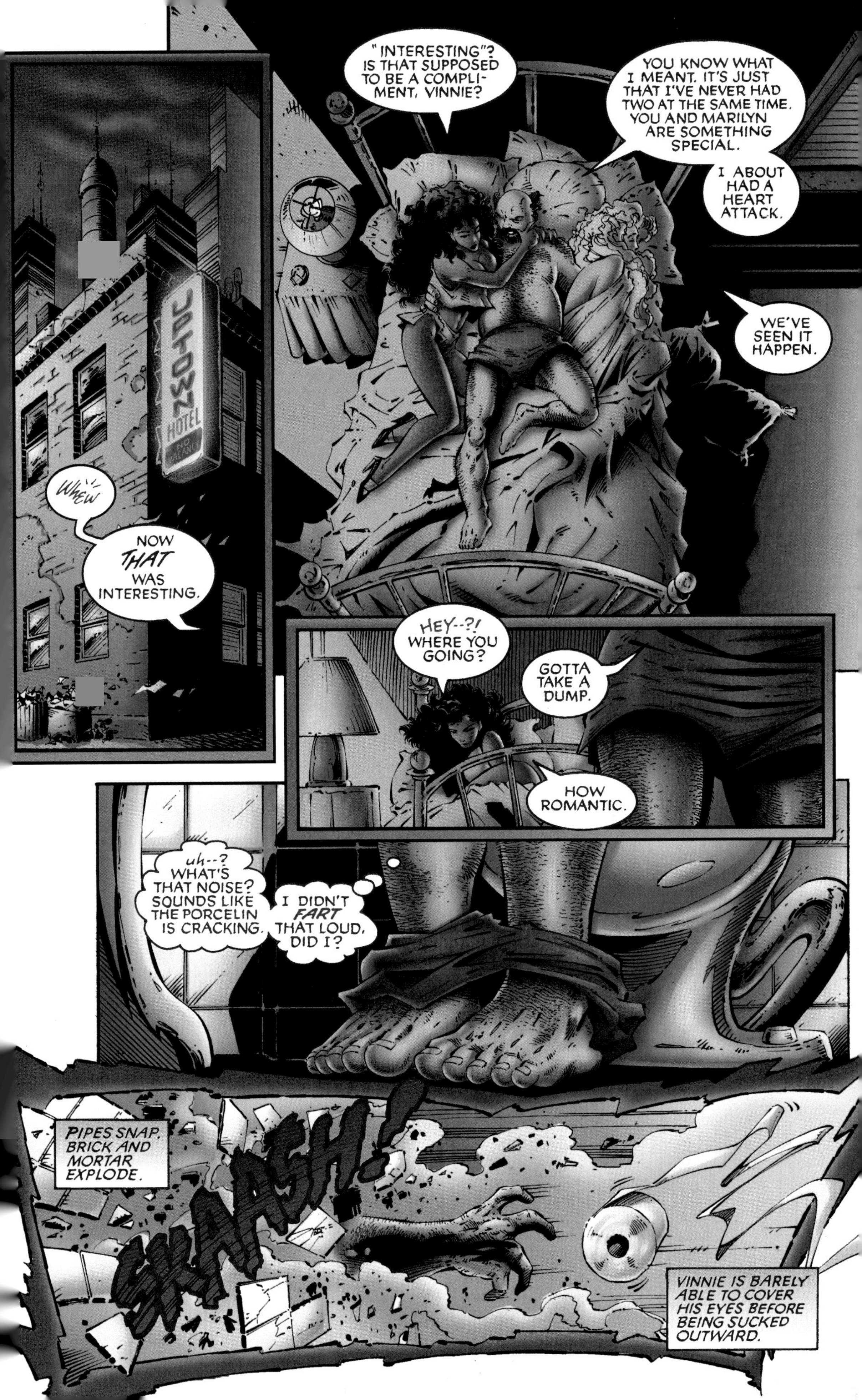
UPTOWN HOTEL
WHEW
NOW THAT WAS INTERESTING.
"INTERESTING"? IS THAT SUPPOSED TO BE A COMPLIMENT, VINNIE?
YOU KNOW WHAT I MEANT. IT'S JUST THAT I'VE NEVER HAD TWO AT THE SAME TIME. YOU AND MARILYN ARE SOMETHING SPECIAL.
I ABOUT HAD A HEART ATTACK.
WE'VE SEEN IT HAPPEN.
HEY--?! WHERE YOU GOING?
GOTTA TAKE A DUMP.
HOW ROMANTIC.
uh--? WHAT'S THAT NOISE? SOUNDS LIKE THE PORCELIN IS CRACKING.
I DIDN'T FART THAT LOUD, DID I?
PIPES SNAP. BRICK AND MORTAR EXPLODE.
SKLASH!
VINNIE IS BARELY ABLE TO COVER HIS EYES BEFORE BEING SUCKED OUTWARD.

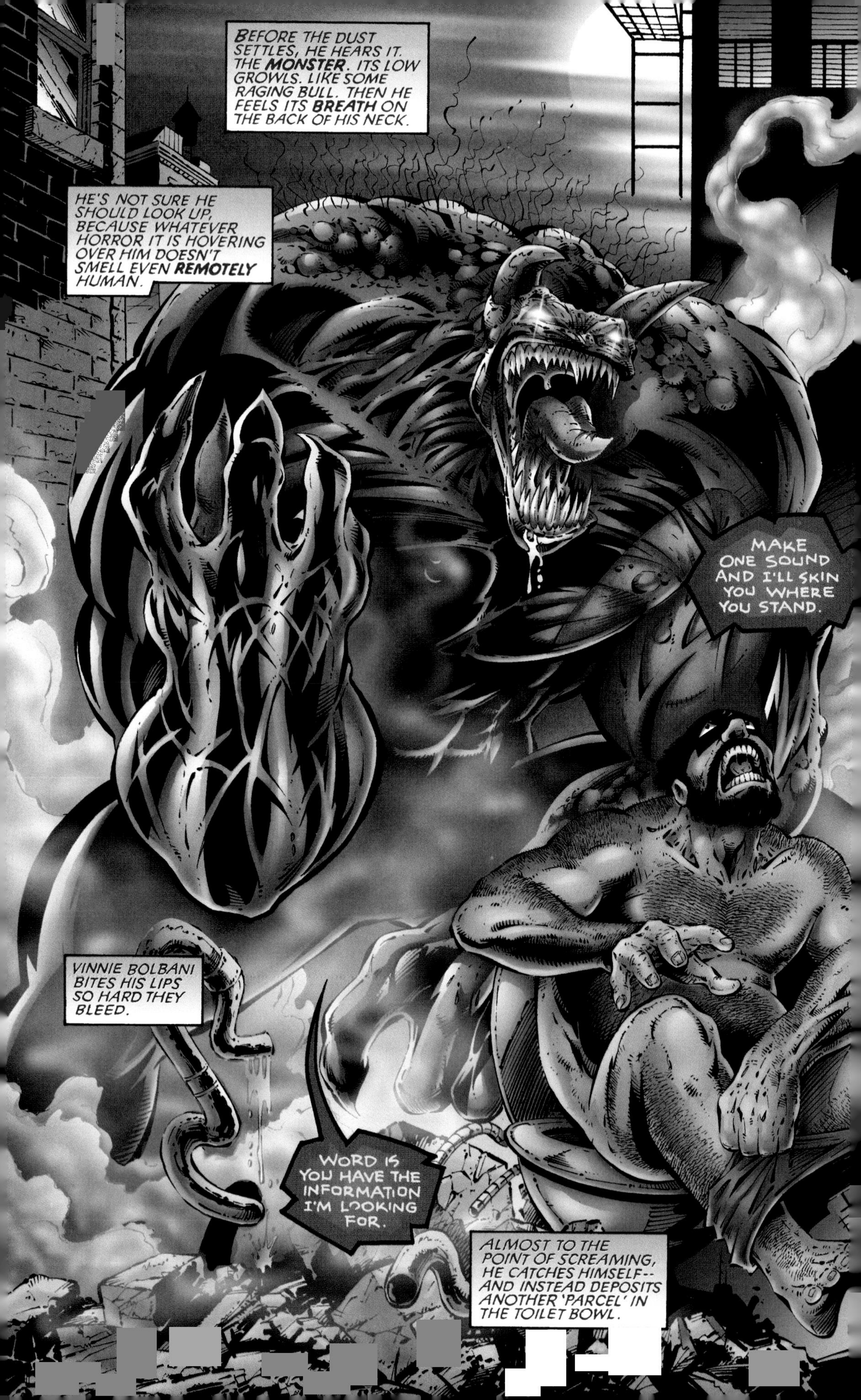
BEFORE THE DUST SETTLES, HE HEARS IT. THE MONSTER. ITS LOW GROWLS. LIKE SOME RAGING BULL. THEN HE FEELS ITS BREATH ON THE BACK OF HIS NECK.
HE'S NOT SURE HE SHOULD LOOK UP, BECAUSE WHATEVER HORROR IT IS HOVERING OVER HIM DOESN'T SMELL EVEN REMOTELY HUMAN.
MAKE ONE SOUND AND I'LL SKIN YOU WHERE YOU STAND.
VINNIE BOLBANI BITES HIS LIPS SO HARD THEY BLEED.
WORD IS YOU HAVE THE INFORMATION I'M LOOKING FOR.
ALMOST TO THE POINT OF SCREAMING, HE CATCHES HIMSELF-- AND INSTEAD DEPOSITS ANOTHER 'PARCEL' IN THE TOILET BOWL.

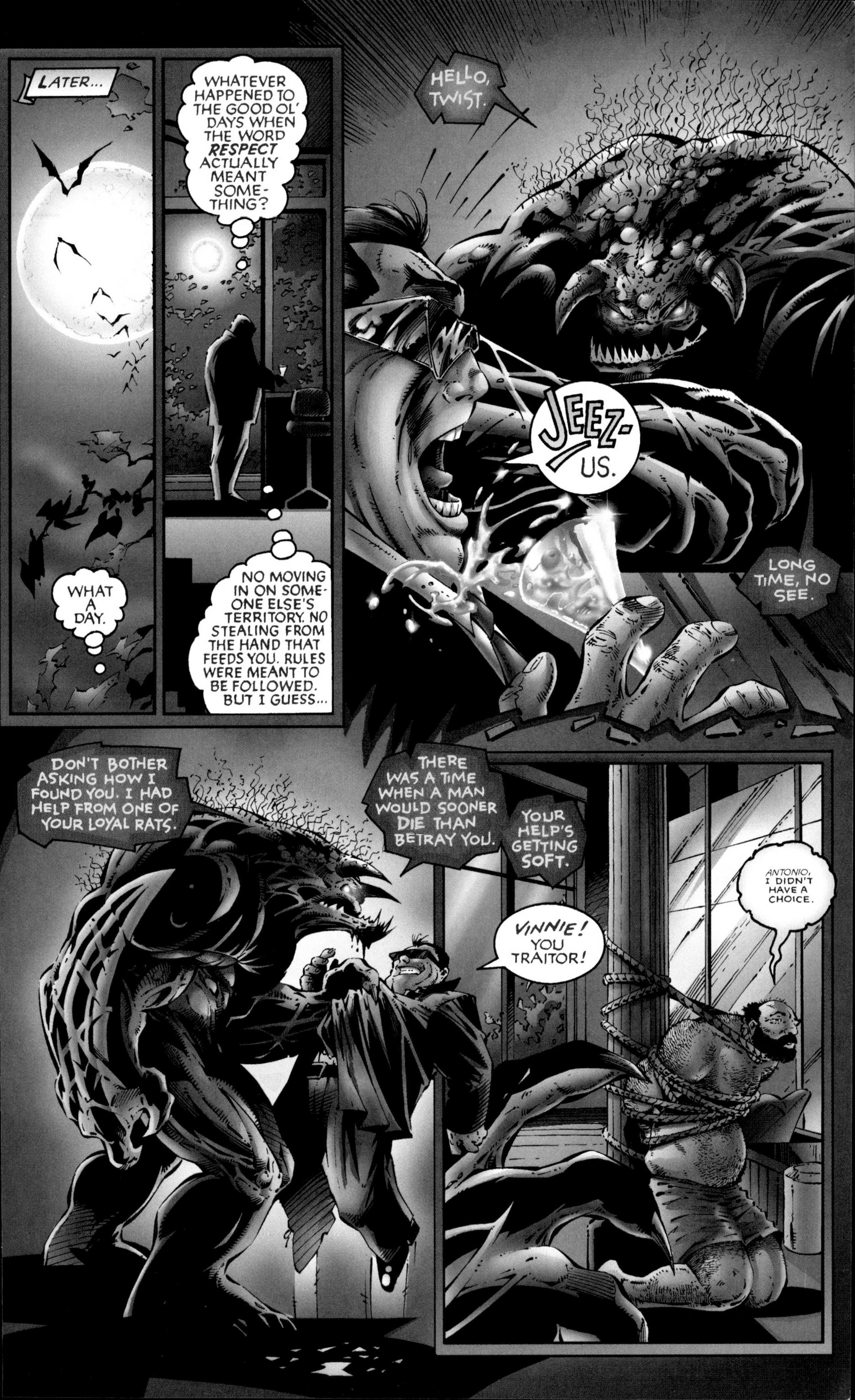
LATER...
WHAT A DAY.
WHATEVER HAPPENED TO THE GOOD OL' DAYS WHEN THE WORD RESPECT ACTUALLY MEANT SOMETHING?
NO MOVING IN ON SOMEONE ELSE'S TERRITORY. NO STEALING FROM THE HAND THAT FEEDS YOU. RULES WERE MEANT TO BE FOLLOWED. BUT I GUESS...
HELLO, TWIST.
JEEZ-US.
LONG TIME, NO SEE.
DON'T BOTHER ASKING HOW I FOUND YOU. I HAD HELP FROM ONE OF YOUR LOYAL RATS.
THERE WAS A TIME WHEN A MAN WOULD SOONER DIE THAN BETRAY YOU.
YOUR HELP'S GETTING SOFT.
VINNIE! YOU TRAITOR!
ANTONIO, I DIDN'T HAVE A CHOICE.

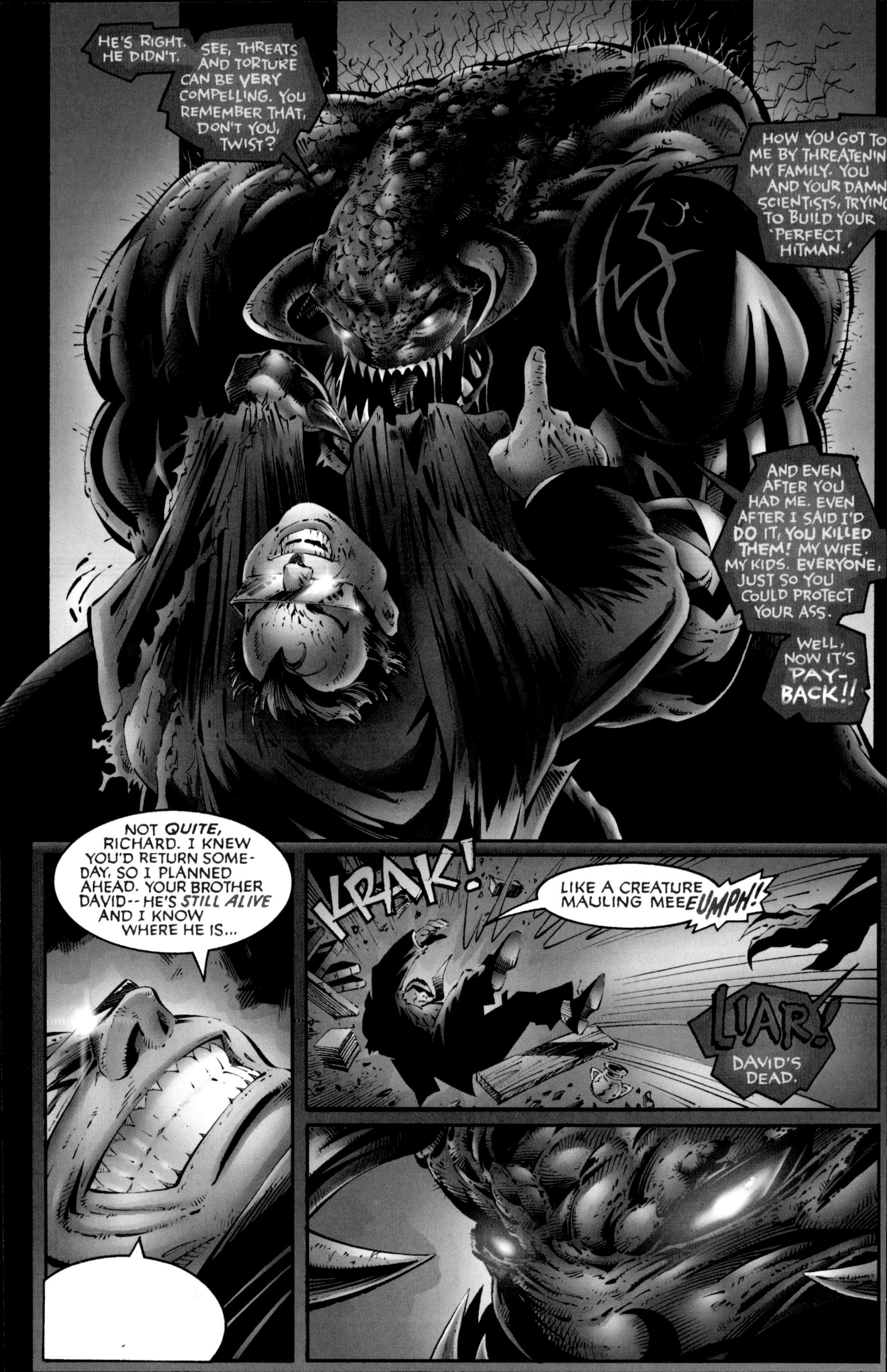
HE'S RIGHT. HE DIDN'T.
SEE, THREATS AND TORTURE CAN BE VERY COMPELLING. YOU REMEMBER THAT, DON'T YOU, TWIST?
HOW YOU GOT TO ME BY THREATENIN MY FAMILY. YOU AND YOUR DAMN SCIENTISTS, TRYING TO BUILD YOUR 'PERFECT HITMAN.'
AND EVEN AFTER YOU HAD ME. EVEN AFTER I SAID I'D DO IT, YOU KILLED THEM! MY WIFE. MY KIDS. EVERYONE, JUST SO YOU COULD PROTECT YOUR ASS.
WELL, NOW IT'S PAY-BACK!!
NOT QUITE, RICHARD. I KNEW YOU'D RETURN SOME-DAY, SO I PLANNED AHEAD. YOUR BROTHER DAVID-- HE'S STILL ALIVE AND I KNOW WHERE HE IS...
KRAK!
LIKE A CREATURE MAULING MEEEUMPH!!
LIAR!
DAVID'S DEAD.

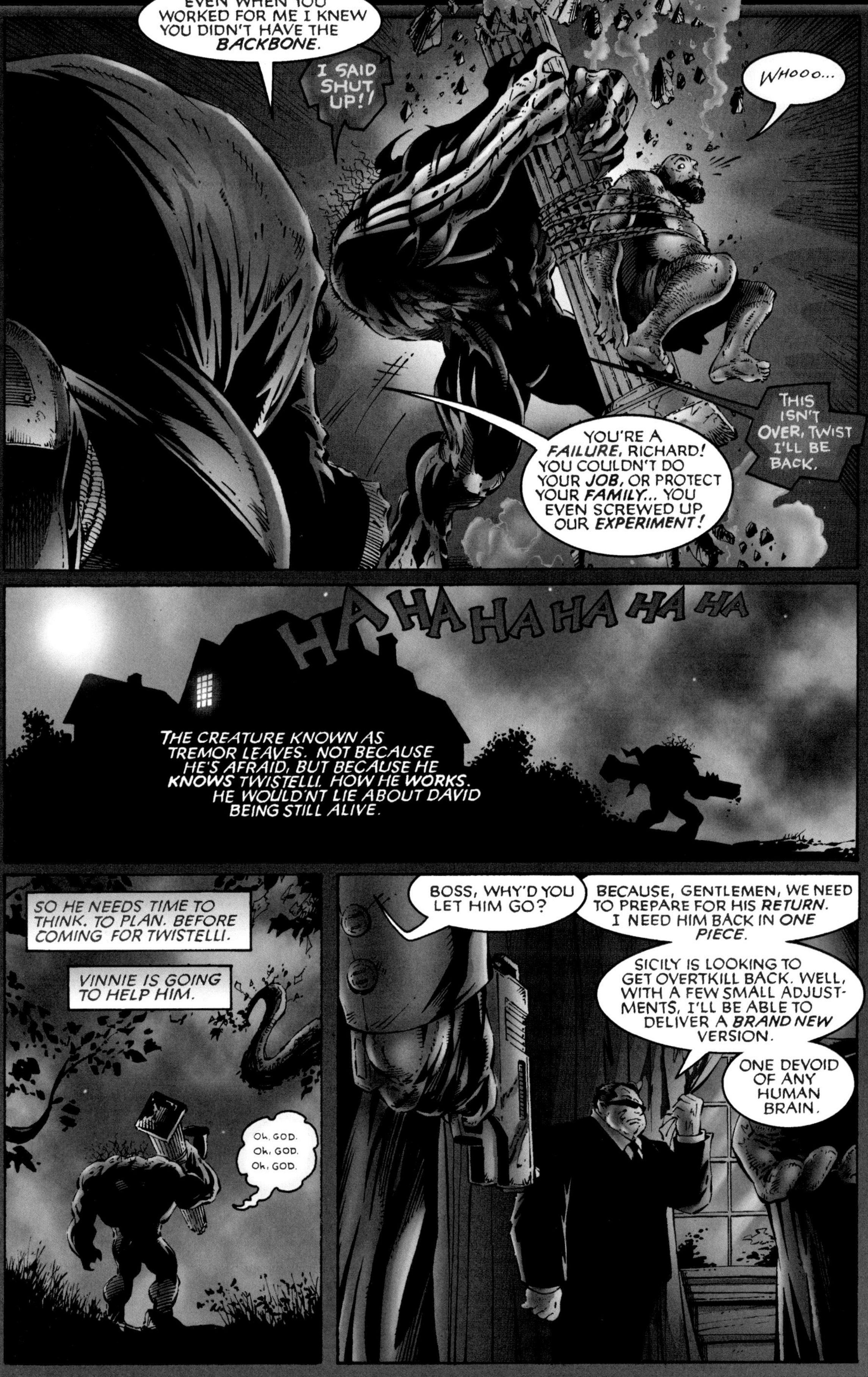
EVEN WHEN YOU WORKED FOR ME I KNEW YOU DIDN'T HAVE THE BACKBONE.
I SAID SHUT UP!!
WHOOO...
YOU'RE A FAILURE, RICHARD! YOU COULDN'T DO YOUR JOB, OR PROTECT YOUR FAMILY... YOU EVEN SCREWED UP OUR EXPERIMENT!
THIS ISN'T OVER, TWIST I'LL BE BACK.
HA HA HA HA HA HA HA
THE CREATURE KNOWN AS TREMOR LEAVES. NOT BECAUSE HE'S AFRAID, BUT BECAUSE HE KNOWS TWISTELLI. HOW HE WORKS. HE WOULD'NT LIE ABOUT DAVID BEING STILL ALIVE.
SO HE NEEDS TIME TO THINK. TO PLAN. BEFORE COMING FOR TWISTELLI.
VINNIE IS GOING TO HELP HIM.
Oh, GOD. Oh, GOD. Oh, GOD.
BOSS, WHY'D YOU LET HIM GO?
BECAUSE, GENTLEMEN, WE NEED TO PREPARE FOR HIS RETURN. I NEED HIM BACK IN ONE PIECE.
SICILY IS LOOKING TO GET OVERTKILL BACK. WELL, WITH A FEW SMALL ADJUST-MENTS, I'LL BE ABLE TO DELIVER A BRAND NEW VERSION.
ONE DEVOID OF ANY HUMAN BRAIN.

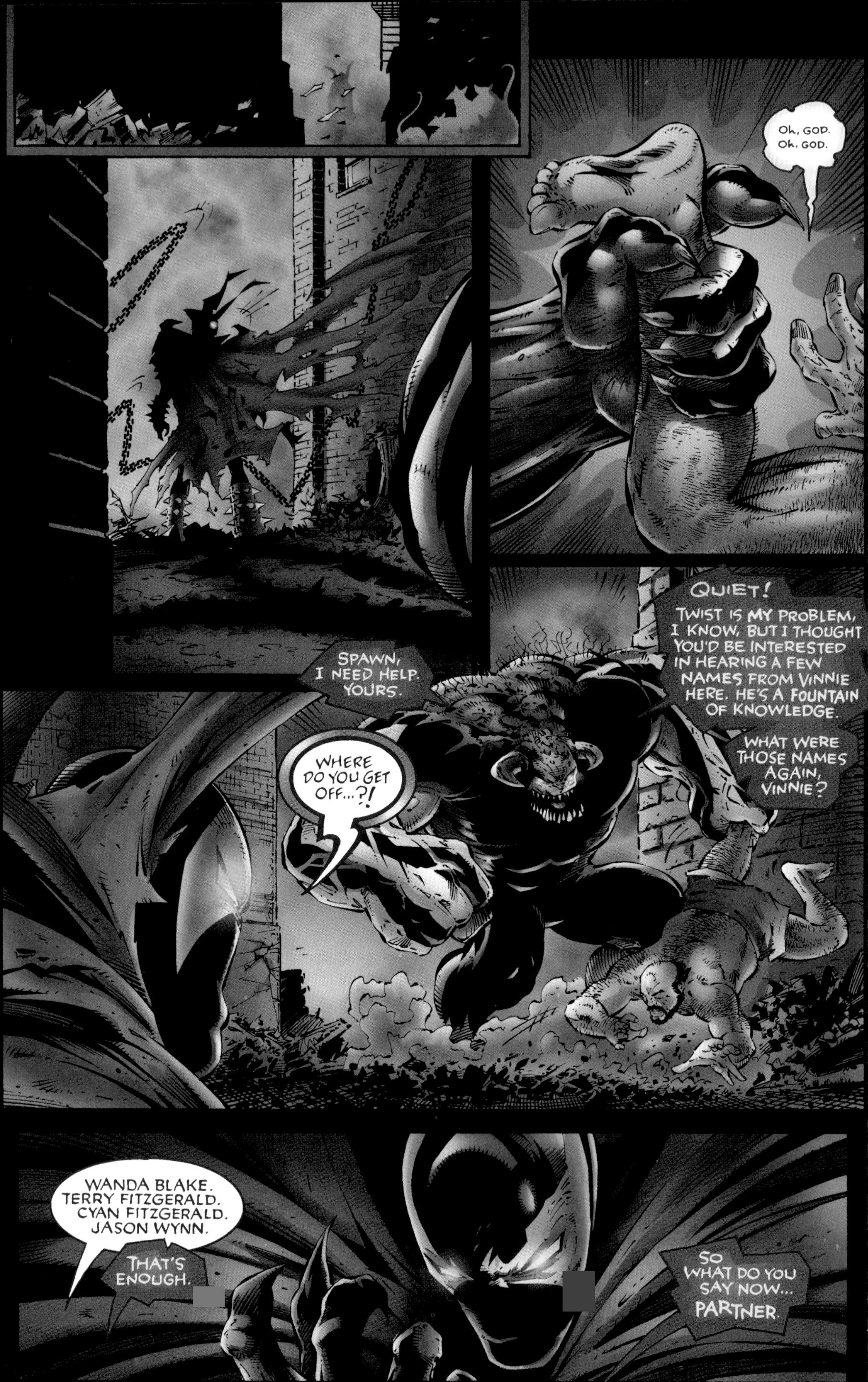
Oh, GOD. Oh, GOD.
SPAWN, I NEED HELP. YOURS.
QUIET!
TWIST IS MY PROBLEM, I KNOW, BUT I THOUGHT YOU'D BE INTERESTED IN HEARING A FEW NAMES FROM VINNIE HERE. HE'S A FOUNTAIN OF KNOWLEDGE.
WHERE DO YOU GET OFF...?!
WHAT WERE THOSE NAMES AGAIN, VINNIE?
WANDA BLAKE. TERRY FITZGERALD. CYAN FITZGERALD. JASON WYNN.
THAT'S ENOUGH.
SO WHAT DO YOU SAY NOW... PARTNER.

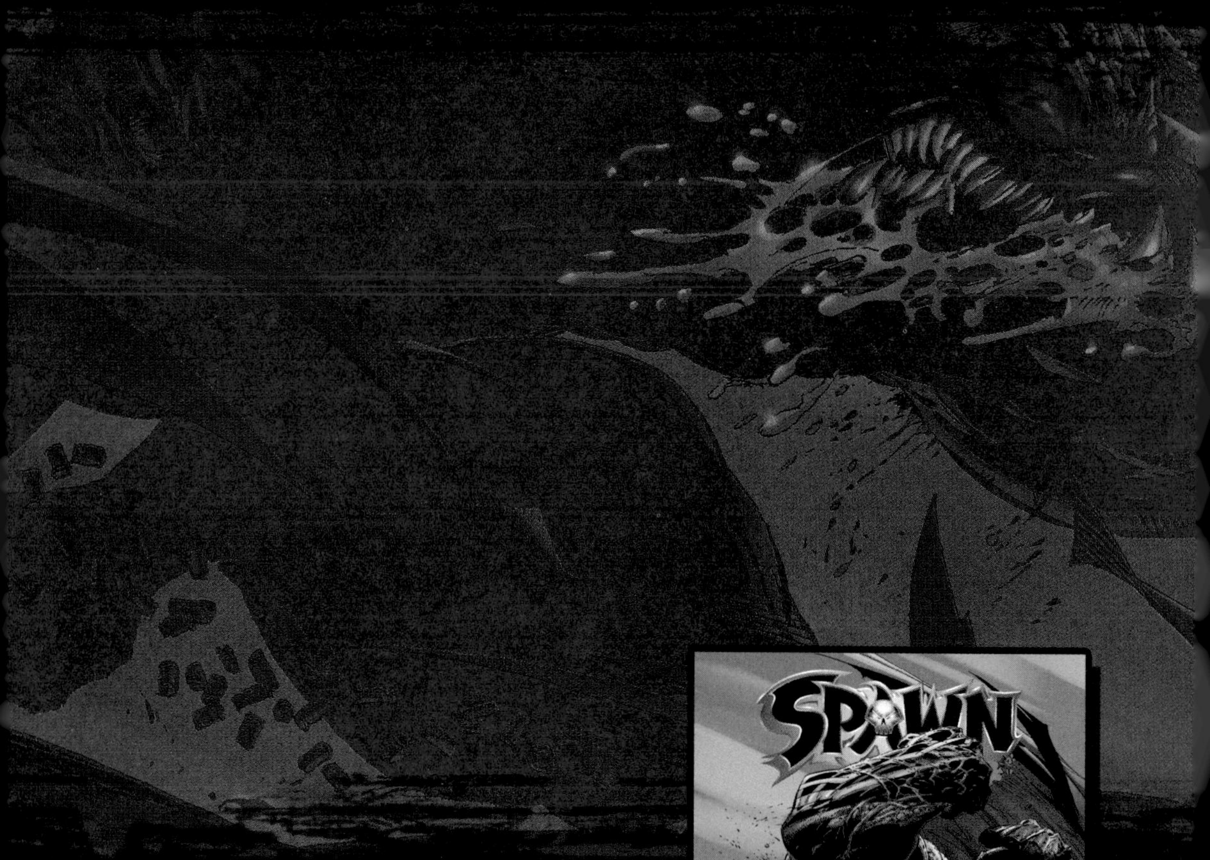

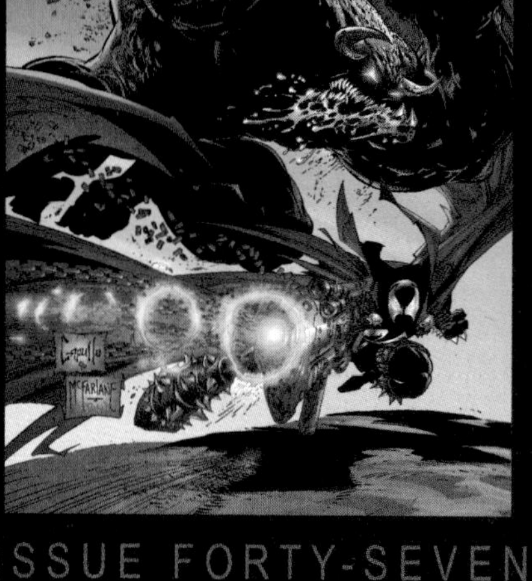
SPAWN

ISSUE FORTY-SEVEN

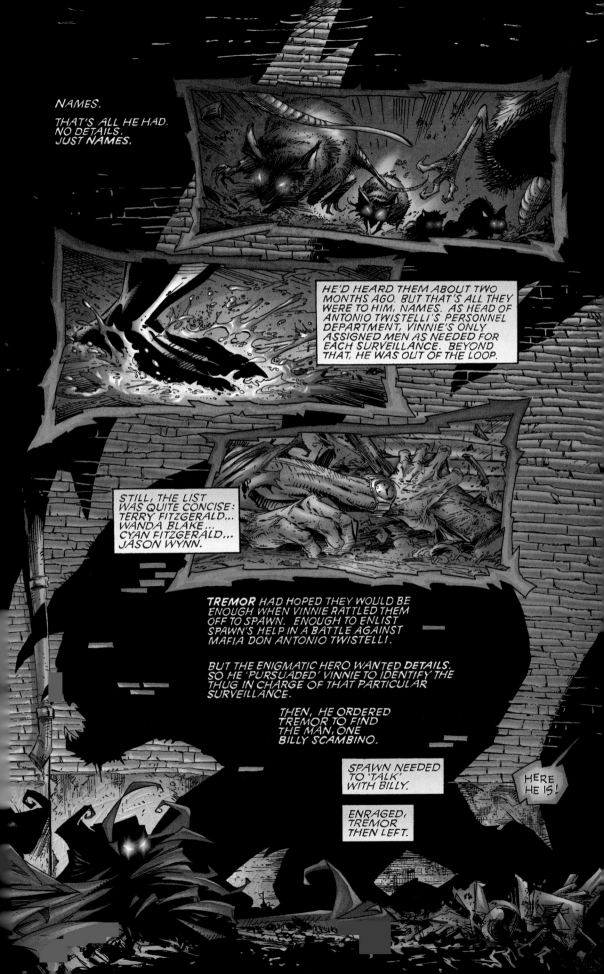

NAMES.
THAT'S ALL HE HAD.
NO DETAILS.
JUST NAMES.

HE'D HEARD THEM ABOUT TWO MONTHS AGO. BUT THAT'S ALL THEY WERE TO HIM, NAMES. AS HEAD OF ANTONIO TWISTELLI'S PERSONNEL DEPARTMENT, VINNIE'S ONLY ASSIGNED MEN AS NEEDED FOR EACH SURVEILLANCE. BEYOND THAT, HE WAS OUT OF THE LOOP.

STILL, THE LIST WAS QUITE CONCISE: TERRY FITZGERALD... WANDA BLAKE... CYAN FITZGERALD... JASON WYNN.

TREMOR HAD HOPED THEY WOULD BE ENOUGH WHEN VINNIE RATTLED THEM OFF TO SPAWN. ENOUGH TO ENLIST SPAWN'S HELP IN A BATTLE AGAINST MAFIA DON ANTONIO TWISTELLI.

BUT THE ENIGMATIC HERO WANTED DETAILS. SO HE 'PURSUADED' VINNIE TO IDENTIFY THE THUG IN CHARGE OF THAT PARTICULAR SURVEILLANCE.

THEN, HE ORDERED TREMOR TO FIND THE MAN, ONE BILLY SCAMBINO.

SPAWN NEEDED TO 'TALK' WITH BILLY.

HERE HE IS!

ENRAGED, TREMOR THEN LEFT.

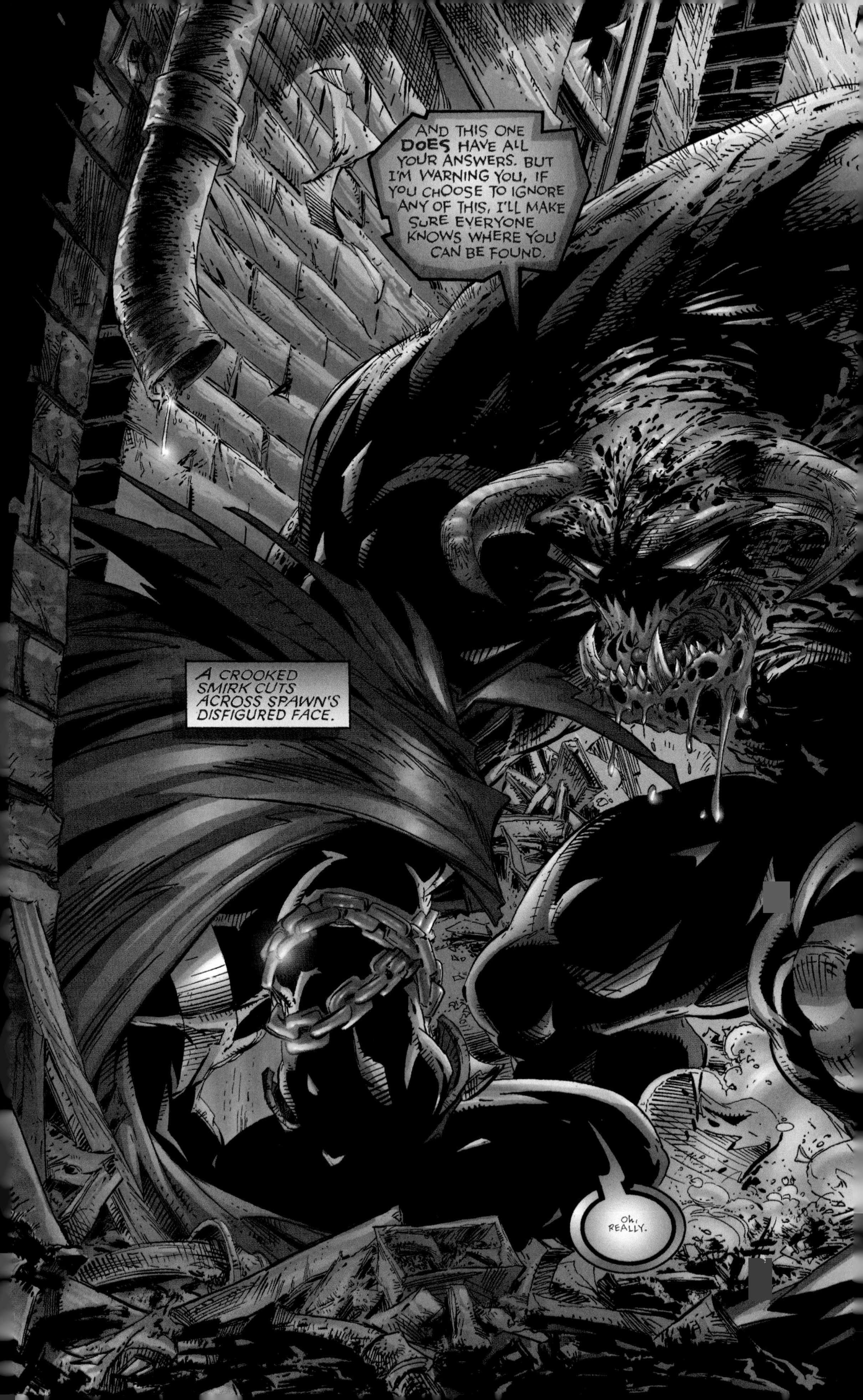
AND THIS ONE DOES HAVE ALL YOUR ANSWERS. BUT I'M WARNING YOU, IF YOU CHOOSE TO IGNORE ANY OF THIS, I'LL MAKE SURE EVERYONE KNOWS WHERE YOU CAN BE FOUND.
A CROOKED SMIRK CUTS ACROSS SPAWN'S DISFIGURED FACE.
OH, REALLY.

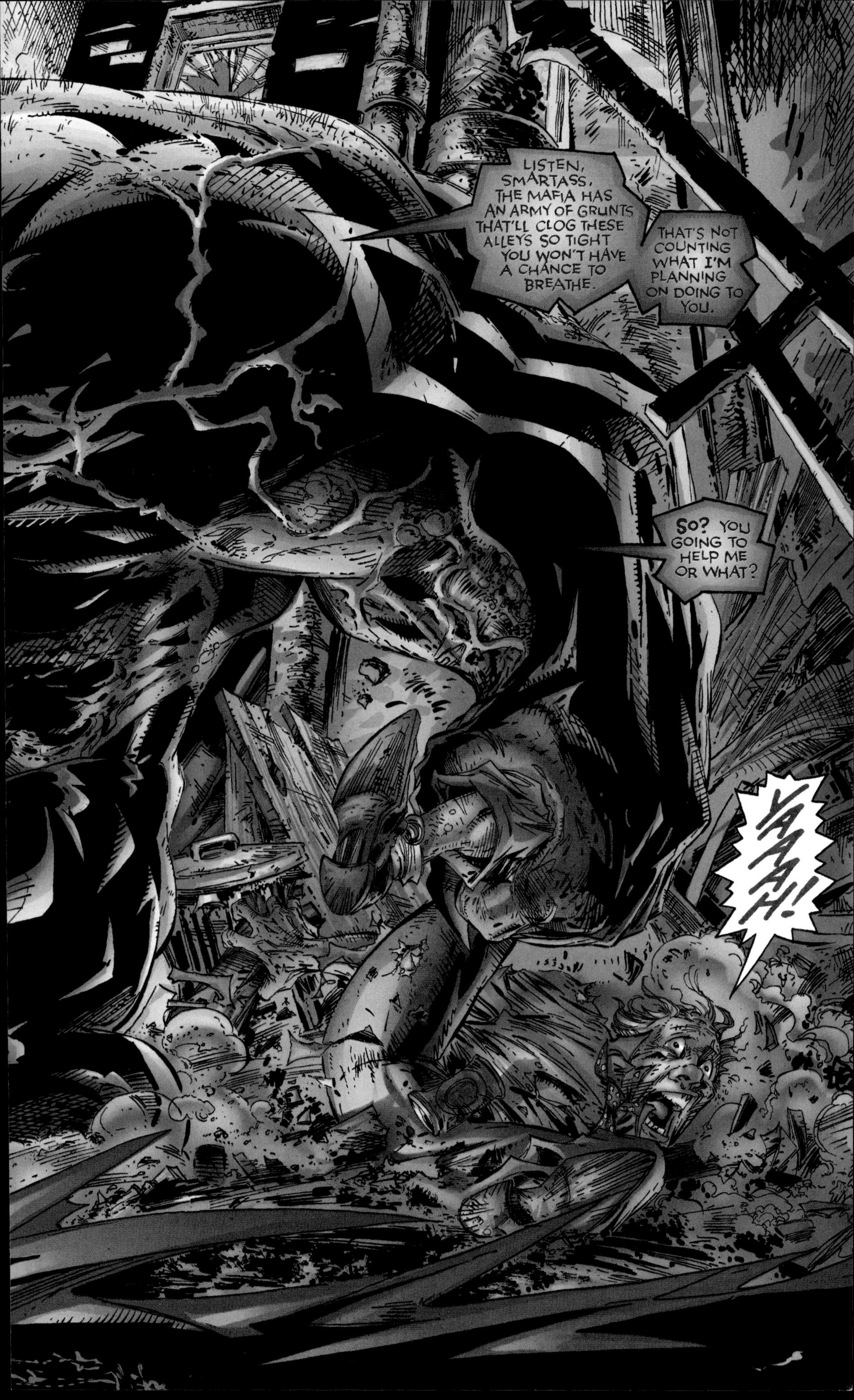
LISTEN, SMARTASS, THE MAFIA HAS AN ARMY OF GRUNTS THAT'LL CLOG THESE ALLEYS SO TIGHT YOU WON'T HAVE A CHANCE TO BREATHE.
THAT'S NOT COUNTING WHAT I'M PLANNING ON DOING TO YOU.
SO? YOU GOING TO HELP ME OR WHAT?
YAAAAH!

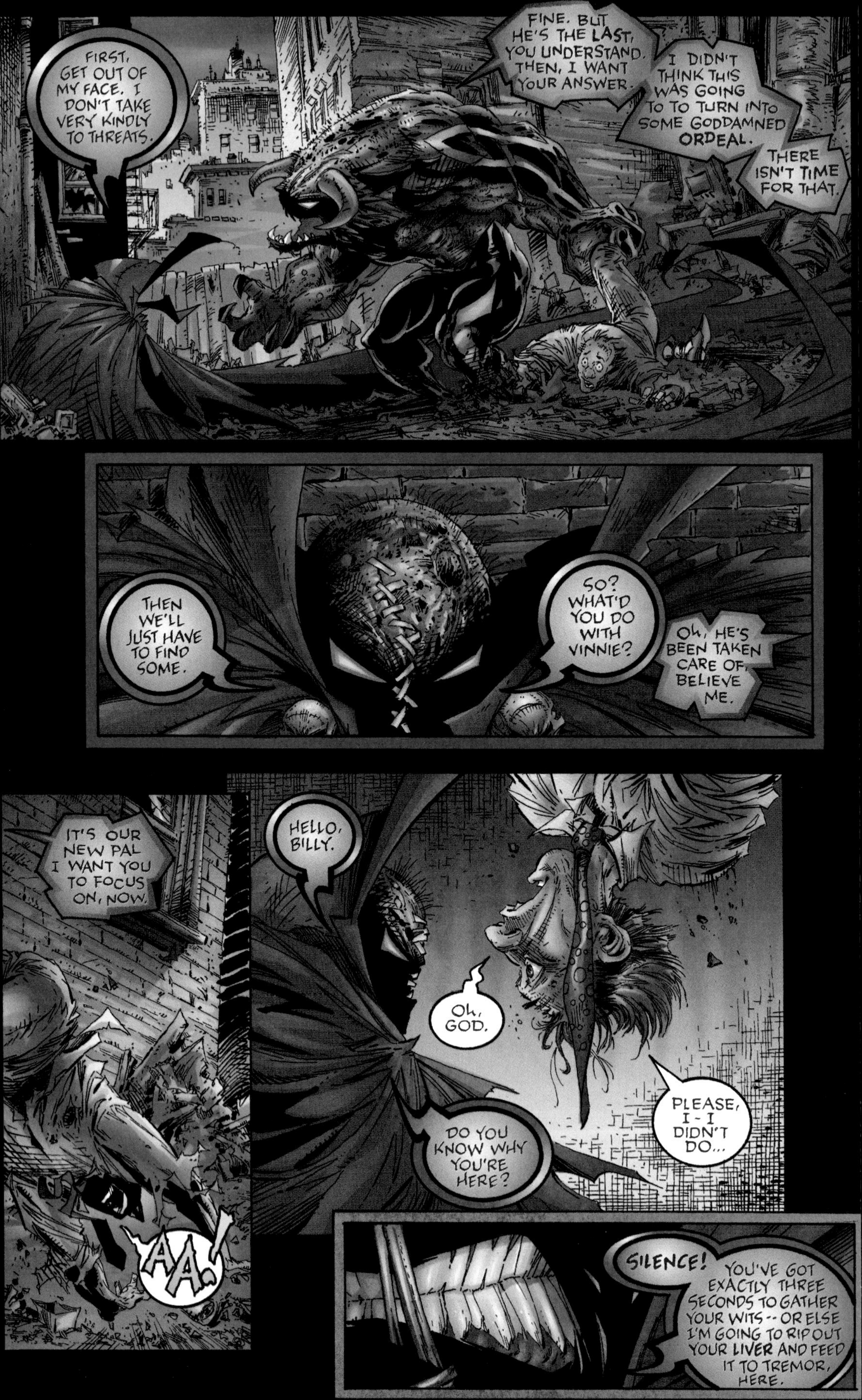
FIRST, GET OUT OF MY FACE. I DON'T TAKE VERY KINDLY TO THREATS.
FINE. BUT HE'S THE LAST, YOU UNDERSTAND. THEN, I WANT YOUR ANSWER.
I DIDN'T THINK THIS WAS GOING TO TO TURN INTO SOME GODDAMNED ORDEAL.
THERE ISN'T TIME FOR THAT.
THEN WE'LL JUST HAVE TO FIND SOME.
SO? WHAT'D YOU DO WITH VINNIE?
OH, HE'S BEEN TAKEN CARE OF. BELIEVE ME.
IT'S OUR NEW PAL I WANT YOU TO FOCUS ON, NOW.
AA..!
HELLO, BILLY.
OH, GOD.
DO YOU KNOW WHY YOU'RE HERE?
PLEASE, I - I DIDN'T DO...
SILENCE! YOU'VE GOT EXACTLY THREE SECONDS TO GATHER YOUR WITS -- OR ELSE I'M GOING TO RIP OUT YOUR LIVER AND FEED IT TO TREMOR, HERE.

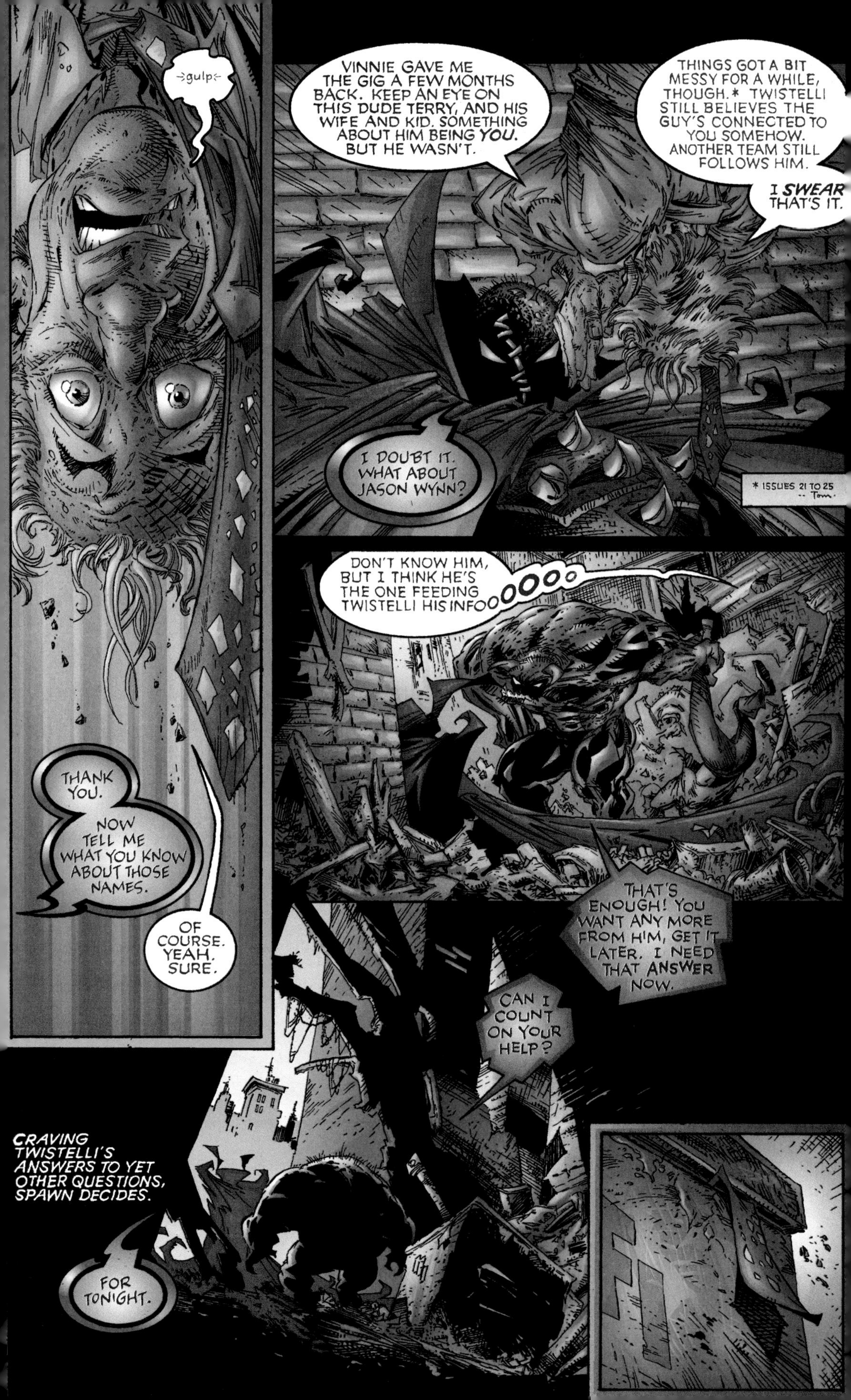

-gulp-
THANK YOU.
NOW TELL ME WHAT YOU KNOW ABOUT THOSE NAMES.
OF COURSE. YEAH. SURE.
VINNIE GAVE ME THE GIG A FEW MONTHS BACK. KEEP AN EYE ON THIS DUDE TERRY, AND HIS WIFE AND KID. SOMETHING ABOUT HIM BEING *YOU.* BUT HE WASN'T.
THINGS GOT A BIT MESSY FOR A WHILE, THOUGH.* TWISTELLI STILL BELIEVES THE GUY'S CONNECTED TO YOU SOMEHOW. ANOTHER TEAM STILL FOLLOWS HIM.
I ***SWEAR*** THAT'S IT.
I DOUBT IT. WHAT ABOUT JASON WYNN?
* ISSUES 21 TO 25 -- Tom
DON'T KNOW HIM, BUT I THINK HE'S THE ONE FEEDING TWISTELLI HIS INFOoOOOo
THAT'S ENOUGH! YOU WANT ANY MORE FROM HIM, GET IT LATER. I NEED THAT ANSWER NOW.
CAN I COUNT ON YOUR HELP?
CRAVING TWISTELLI'S ANSWERS TO YET OTHER QUESTIONS, SPAWN DECIDES.
FOR TONIGHT.

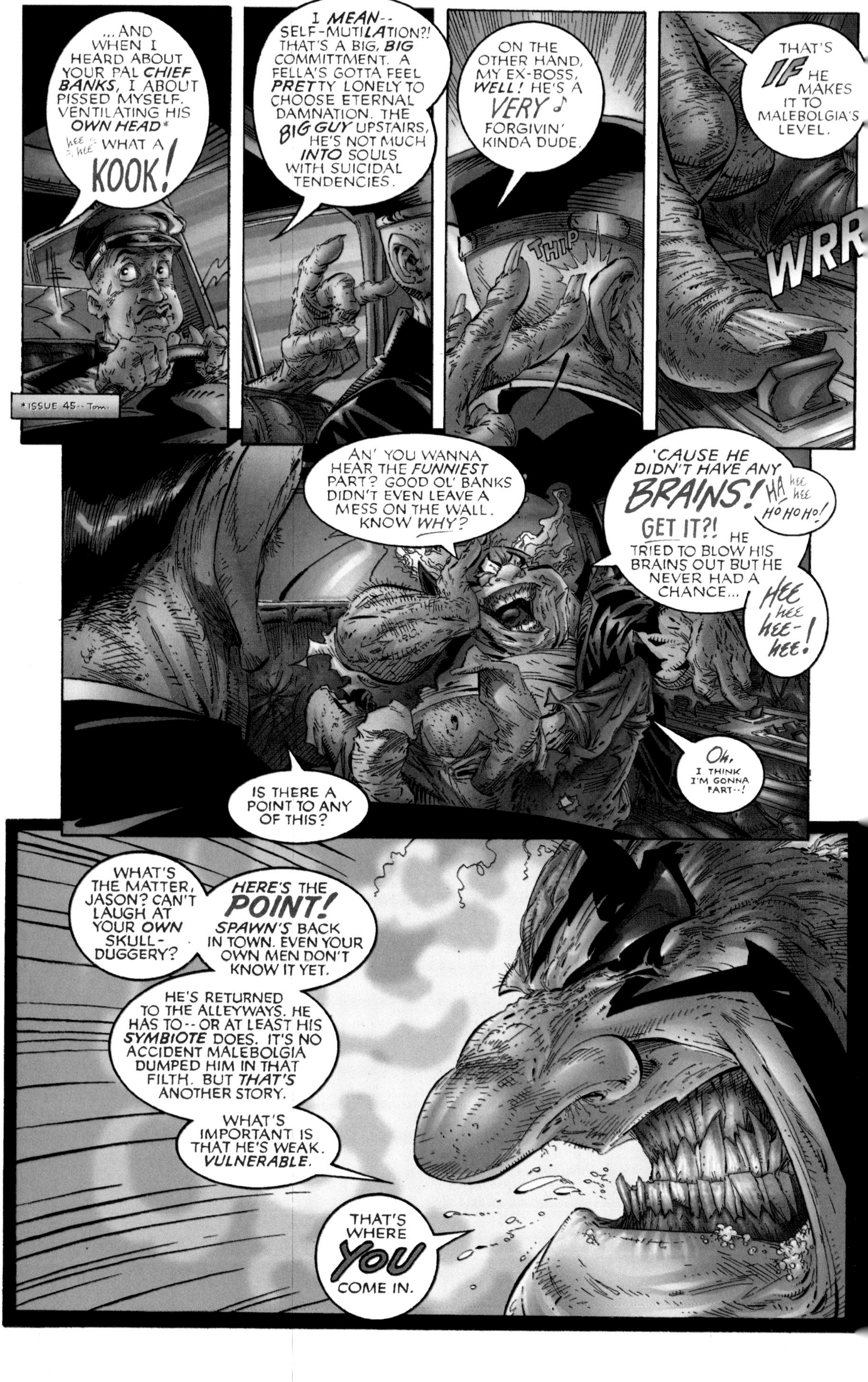
...AND WHEN I HEARD ABOUT YOUR PAL CHIEF BANKS, I ABOUT PISSED MYSELF. VENTILATING HIS OWN HEAD* hee hee hee WHAT A KOOK!
*ISSUE 45--Tom.
I MEAN-- SELF-MUTILATION?! THAT'S A BIG, BIG COMMITTMENT. A FELLA'S GOTTA FEEL PRETTY LONELY TO CHOOSE ETERNAL DAMNATION. THE BIG GUY UPSTAIRS, HE'S NOT MUCH INTO SOULS WITH SUICIDAL TENDENCIES.
ON THE OTHER HAND, MY EX-BOSS, WELL! HE'S A VERY ♪ FORGIVIN' KINDA DUDE.
THIP
THAT'S IF HE MAKES IT TO MALEBOLGIA'S LEVEL.
WRR
AN' YOU WANNA HEAR THE FUNNIEST PART? GOOD OL' BANKS DIDN'T EVEN LEAVE A MESS ON THE WALL. KNOW WHY?
'CAUSE HE DIDN'T HAVE ANY BRAINS! HA hee hee HO HO HO!
GET IT?! HE TRIED TO BLOW HIS BRAINS OUT BUT HE NEVER HAD A CHANCE... HEE hee hee-hee!
IS THERE A POINT TO ANY OF THIS?
Oh, I THINK I'M GONNA FART--!
WHAT'S THE MATTER, JASON? CAN'T LAUGH AT YOUR OWN SKULL-DUGGERY?
HERE'S THE POINT! SPAWN'S BACK IN TOWN. EVEN YOUR OWN MEN DON'T KNOW IT YET.
HE'S RETURNED TO THE ALLEYWAYS. HE HAS TO--OR AT LEAST HIS SYMBIOTE DOES. IT'S NO ACCIDENT MALEBOLGIA DUMPED HIM IN THAT FILTH. BUT THAT'S ANOTHER STORY.
WHAT'S IMPORTANT IS THAT HE'S WEAK. VULNERABLE.
THAT'S WHERE YOU COME IN.

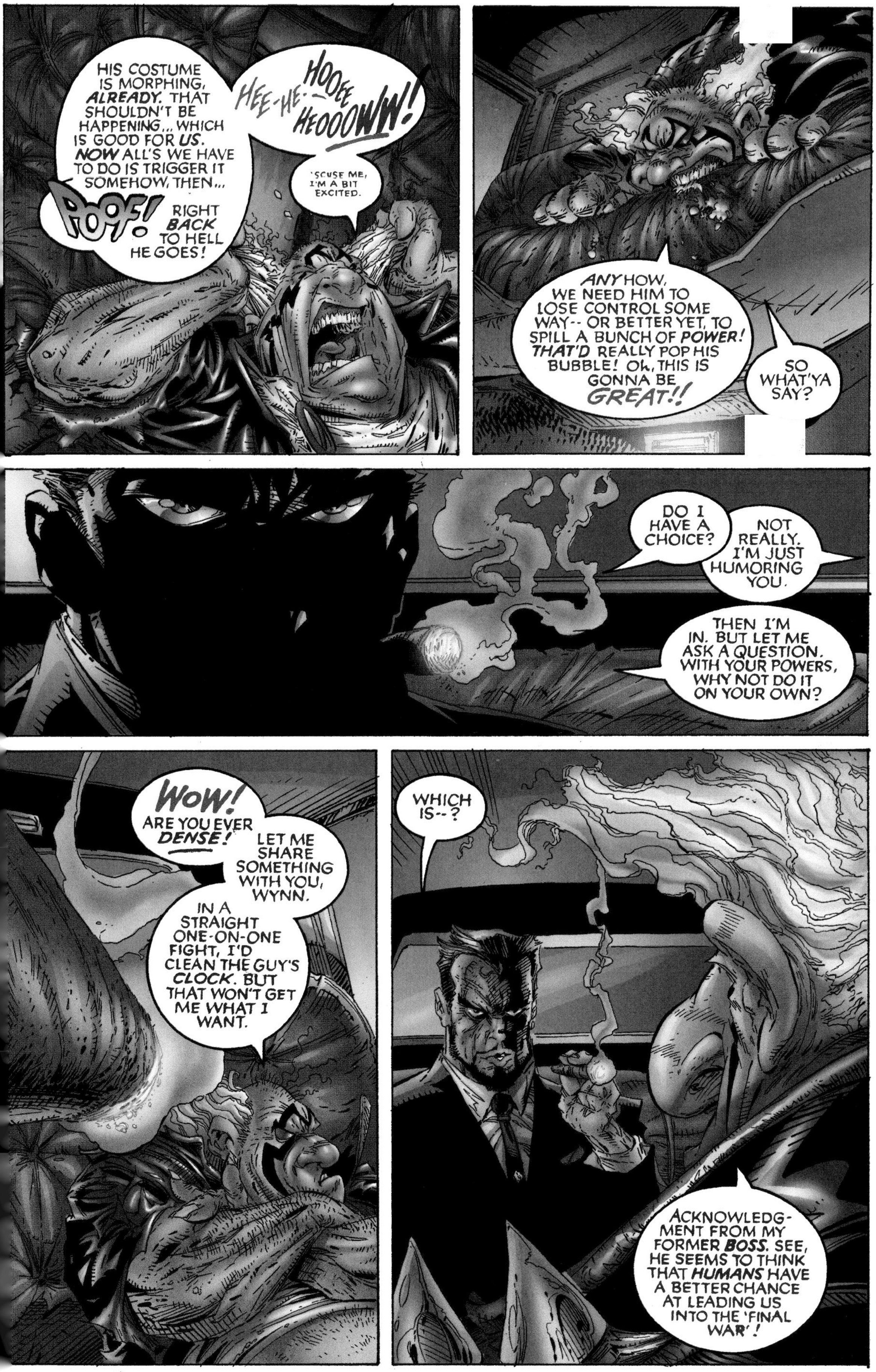
HIS COSTUME IS MORPHING, ALREADY. THAT SHOULDN'T BE HAPPENING... WHICH IS GOOD FOR US. NOW ALL'S WE HAVE TO DO IS TRIGGER IT SOMEHOW, THEN... POOF! RIGHT BACK TO HELL HE GOES!
HEE-HE-HOOEE HEOOOWW!
'SCUSE ME, I'M A BIT EXCITED.
ANYHOW, WE NEED HIM TO LOSE CONTROL SOME WAY-- OR BETTER YET, TO SPILL A BUNCH OF POWER! THAT'D REALLY POP HIS BUBBLE! Oh, THIS IS GONNA BE GREAT!!
SO WHAT'YA SAY?
DO I HAVE A CHOICE?
NOT REALLY. I'M JUST HUMORING YOU.
THEN I'M IN. BUT LET ME ASK A QUESTION. WITH YOUR POWERS, WHY NOT DO IT ON YOUR OWN?
WOW! ARE YOU EVER DENSE!
LET ME SHARE SOMETHING WITH YOU, WYNN.
IN A STRAIGHT ONE-ON-ONE FIGHT, I'D CLEAN THE GUY'S CLOCK. BUT THAT WON'T GET ME WHAT I WANT.
WHICH IS--?
ACKNOWLEDG-MENT FROM MY FORMER BOSS. SEE, HE SEEMS TO THINK THAT HUMANS HAVE A BETTER CHANCE AT LEADING US INTO THE 'FINAL WAR'!

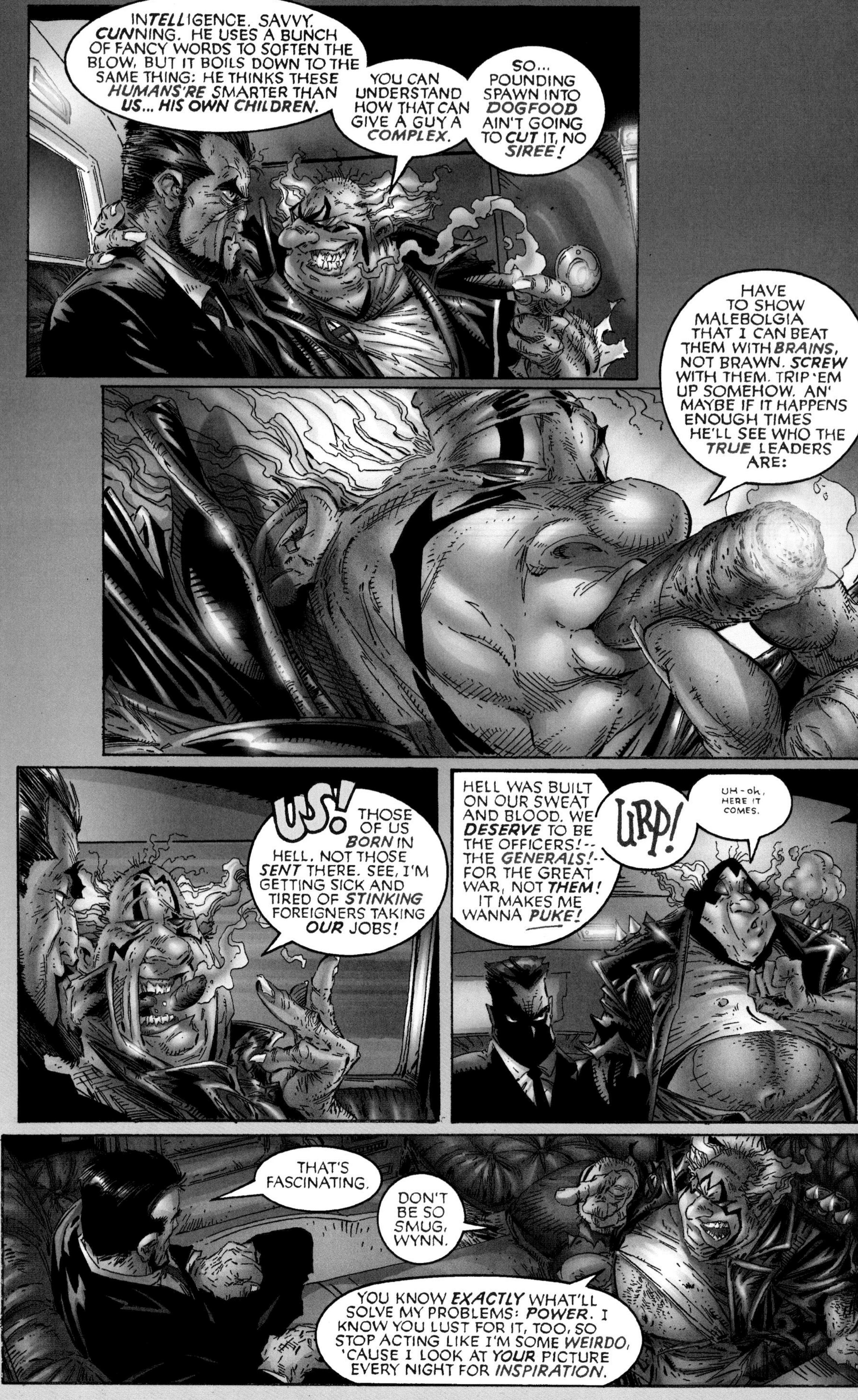
INTELLIGENCE. SAVVY. CUNNING. HE USES A BUNCH OF FANCY WORDS TO SOFTEN THE BLOW. BUT IT BOILS DOWN TO THE SAME THING: HE THINKS THESE HUMANS'RE SMARTER THAN US... HIS OWN CHILDREN.
YOU CAN UNDERSTAND HOW THAT CAN GIVE A GUY A COMPLEX.
SO... POUNDING SPAWN INTO DOGFOOD AIN'T GOING TO CUT IT, NO SIREE!
HAVE TO SHOW MALEBOLGIA THAT I CAN BEAT THEM WITH BRAINS, NOT BRAWN. SCREW WITH THEM. TRIP 'EM UP SOMEHOW. AN' MAYBE IF IT HAPPENS ENOUGH TIMES HE'LL SEE WHO THE TRUE LEADERS ARE:
US! THOSE OF US BORN IN HELL. NOT THOSE SENT THERE. SEE, I'M GETTING SICK AND TIRED OF STINKING FOREIGNERS TAKING OUR JOBS!
HELL WAS BUILT ON OUR SWEAT AND BLOOD. WE DESERVE TO BE THE OFFICERS! -- THE GENERALS! -- FOR THE GREAT WAR, NOT THEM! IT MAKES ME WANNA PUKE!
URP!
UH-oh, HERE IT COMES.
THAT'S FASCINATING.
DON'T BE SO SMUG, WYNN.
YOU KNOW EXACTLY WHAT'LL SOLVE MY PROBLEMS: POWER. I KNOW YOU LUST FOR IT, TOO, SO STOP ACTING LIKE I'M SOME WEIRDO, 'CAUSE I LOOK AT YOUR PICTURE EVERY NIGHT FOR INSPIRATION.

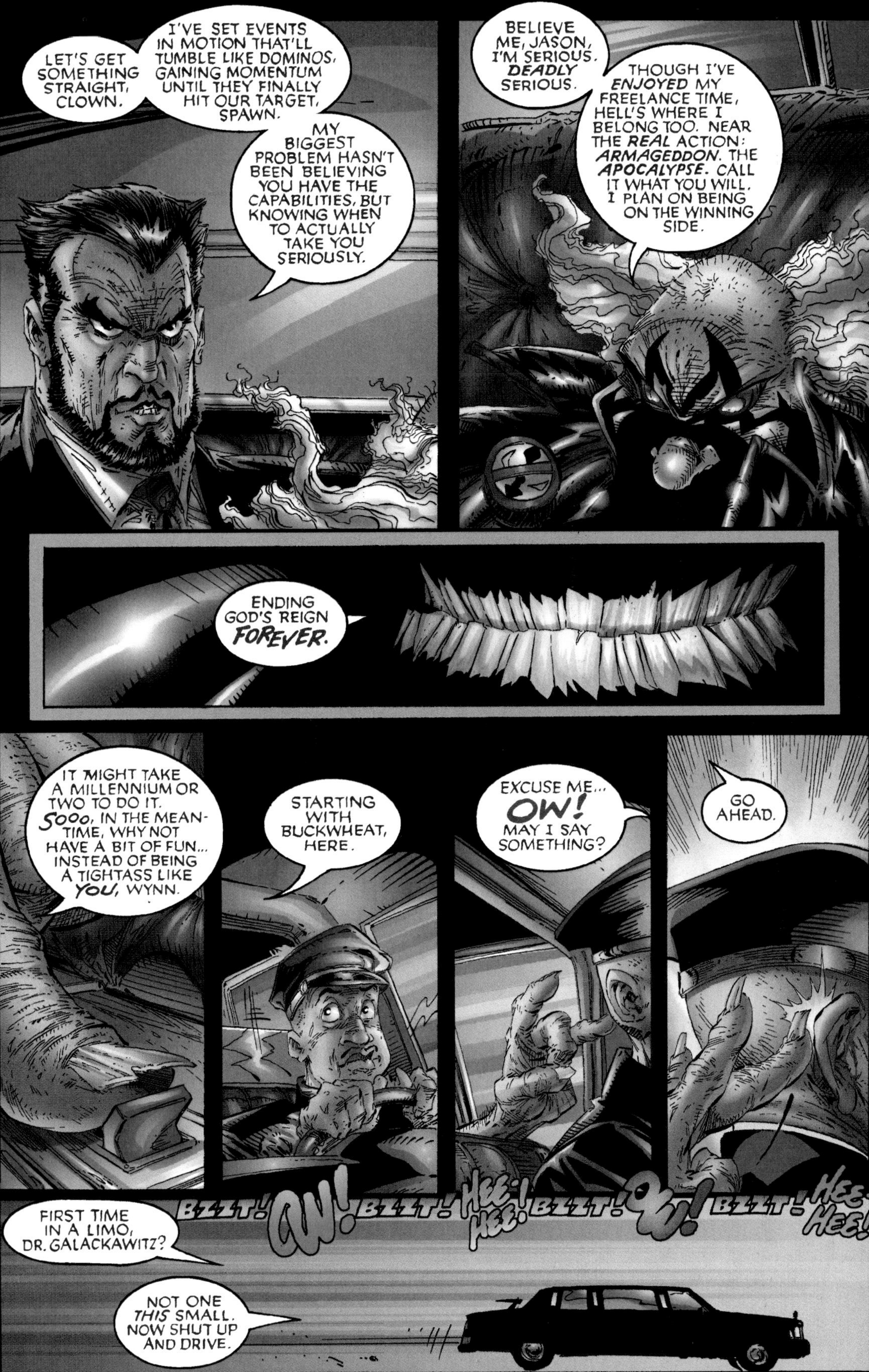
LET'S GET SOMETHING STRAIGHT, CLOWN.
I'VE SET EVENTS IN MOTION THAT'LL TUMBLE LIKE DOMINOS, GAINING MOMENTUM UNTIL THEY FINALLY HIT OUR TARGET, SPAWN.
MY BIGGEST PROBLEM HASN'T BEEN BELIEVING YOU HAVE THE CAPABILITIES, BUT KNOWING WHEN TO ACTUALLY TAKE YOU SERIOUSLY.
BELIEVE ME, JASON, I'M SERIOUS. DEADLY SERIOUS.
THOUGH I'VE ENJOYED MY FREELANCE TIME, HELL'S WHERE I BELONG TOO. NEAR THE REAL ACTION: ARMAGEDDON. THE APOCALYPSE. CALL IT WHAT YOU WILL. I PLAN ON BEING ON THE WINNING SIDE.
ENDING GOD'S REIGN FOREVER.
IT MIGHT TAKE A MILLENNIUM OR TWO TO DO IT. SOOO, IN THE MEAN-TIME, WHY NOT HAVE A BIT OF FUN... INSTEAD OF BEING A TIGHTASS LIKE YOU, WYNN.
STARTING WITH BUCKWHEAT, HERE.
EXCUSE ME... OW! MAY I SAY SOMETHING?
GO AHEAD.
BZZT! OW! BZZT! HEE-HEE! BZZT! OW! BZZT! HEE-HEE!
FIRST TIME IN A LIMO, DR. GALACKAWITZ?
NOT ONE THIS SMALL. NOW SHUT UP AND DRIVE.

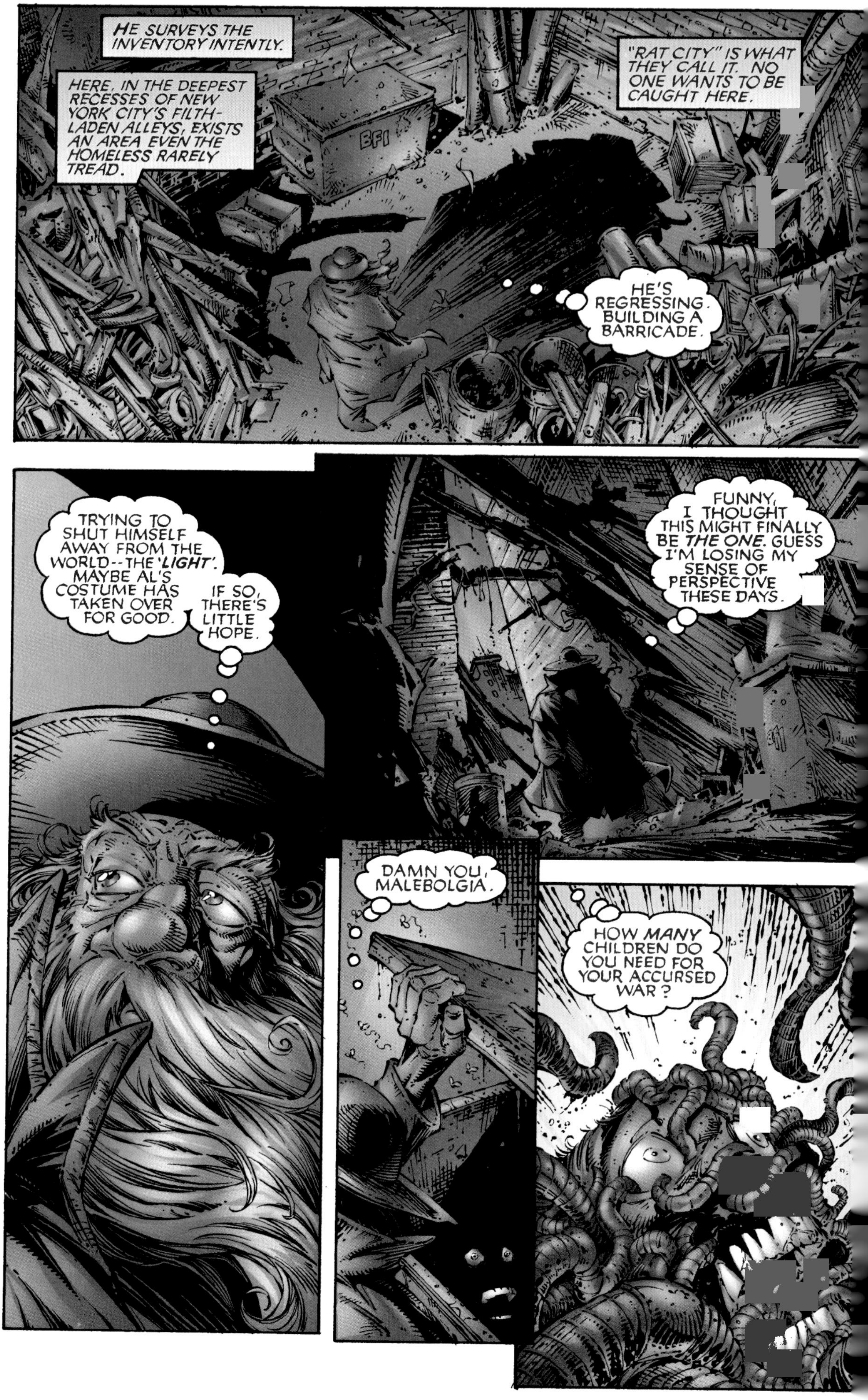
HE SURVEYS THE INVENTORY INTENTLY.
HERE, IN THE DEEPEST RECESSES OF NEW YORK CITY'S FILTH-LADEN ALLEYS, EXISTS AN AREA EVEN THE HOMELESS RARELY TREAD.
"RAT CITY" IS WHAT THEY CALL IT. NO ONE WANTS TO BE CAUGHT HERE.
BFI
HE'S REGRESSING. BUILDING A BARRICADE.
TRYING TO SHUT HIMSELF AWAY FROM THE WORLD--THE '*LIGHT*'. MAYBE AL'S COSTUME HAS TAKEN OVER FOR GOOD.
IF SO, THERE'S LITTLE HOPE.
FUNNY, I THOUGHT THIS MIGHT FINALLY BE *THE ONE*. GUESS I'M LOSING MY SENSE OF PERSPECTIVE THESE DAYS.
DAMN YOU, MALEBOLGIA.
HOW *MANY* CHILDREN DO YOU NEED FOR YOUR ACCURSED WAR?

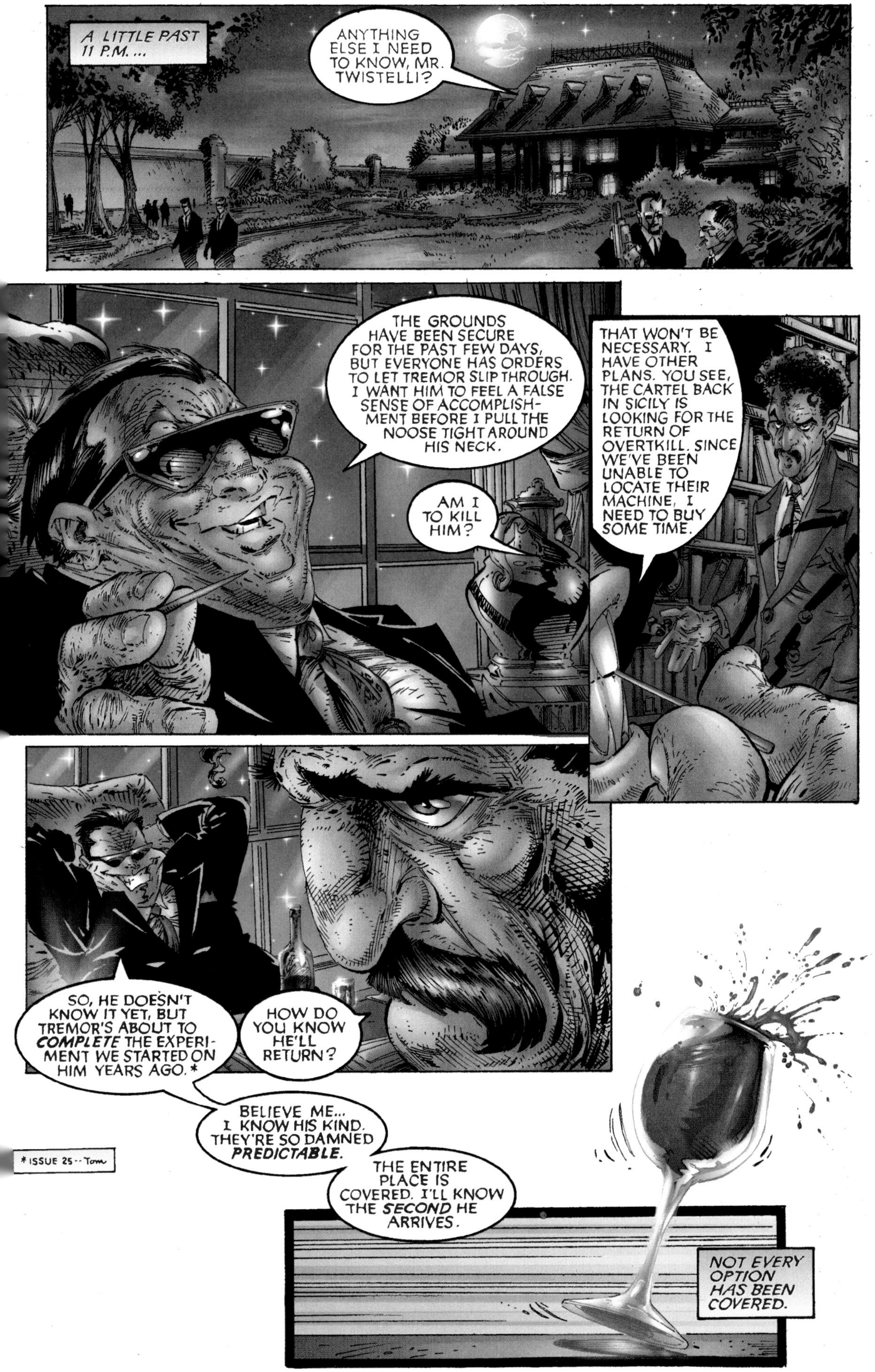

A LITTLE PAST 11 P.M. ...
ANYTHING ELSE I NEED TO KNOW, MR. TWISTELLI?
THE GROUNDS HAVE BEEN SECURE FOR THE PAST FEW DAYS, BUT EVERYONE HAS ORDERS TO LET TREMOR SLIP THROUGH. I WANT HIM TO FEEL A FALSE SENSE OF ACCOMPLISHMENT BEFORE I PULL THE NOOSE TIGHT AROUND HIS NECK.
AM I TO KILL HIM?
THAT WON'T BE NECESSARY. I HAVE OTHER PLANS. YOU SEE, THE CARTEL BACK IN SICILY IS LOOKING FOR THE RETURN OF OVERTKILL. SINCE WE'VE BEEN UNABLE TO LOCATE THEIR MACHINE, I NEED TO BUY SOME TIME.
SO, HE DOESN'T KNOW IT YET, BUT TREMOR'S ABOUT TO *COMPLETE* THE EXPERIMENT WE STARTED ON HIM YEARS AGO.*
HOW DO YOU KNOW HE'LL RETURN?
BELIEVE ME... I KNOW HIS KIND. THEY'RE SO DAMNED ***PREDICTABLE***.
*ISSUE 25 -- Tom
THE ENTIRE PLACE IS COVERED. I'LL KNOW THE *SECOND* HE ARRIVES.
NOT EVERY OPTION HAS BEEN COVERED.

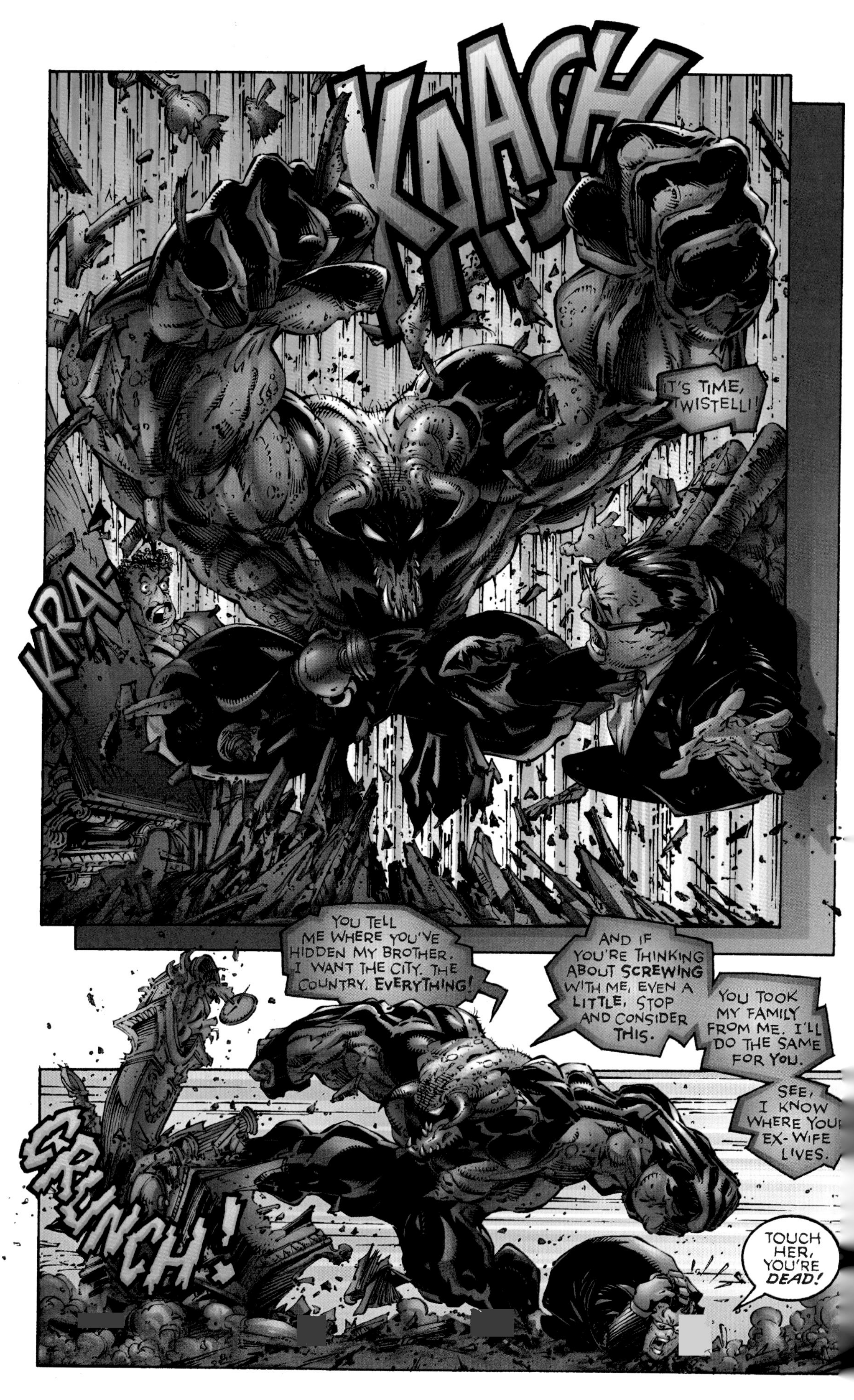
KRASH
IT'S TIME, TWISTELLI!
KRA-
YOU TELL ME WHERE YOU'VE HIDDEN MY BROTHER. I WANT THE CITY. THE COUNTRY. **EVERYTHING**!
AND IF YOU'RE THINKING ABOUT **SCREWING** WITH ME, EVEN A **LITTLE**, STOP AND CONSIDER **THIS**.
YOU TOOK MY FAMILY FROM ME. I'LL DO THE SAME FOR **YOU**.
SEE, I KNOW WHERE YOUR EX-WIFE LIVES.
CRUNCH!
TOUCH HER, YOU'RE ***DEAD!***

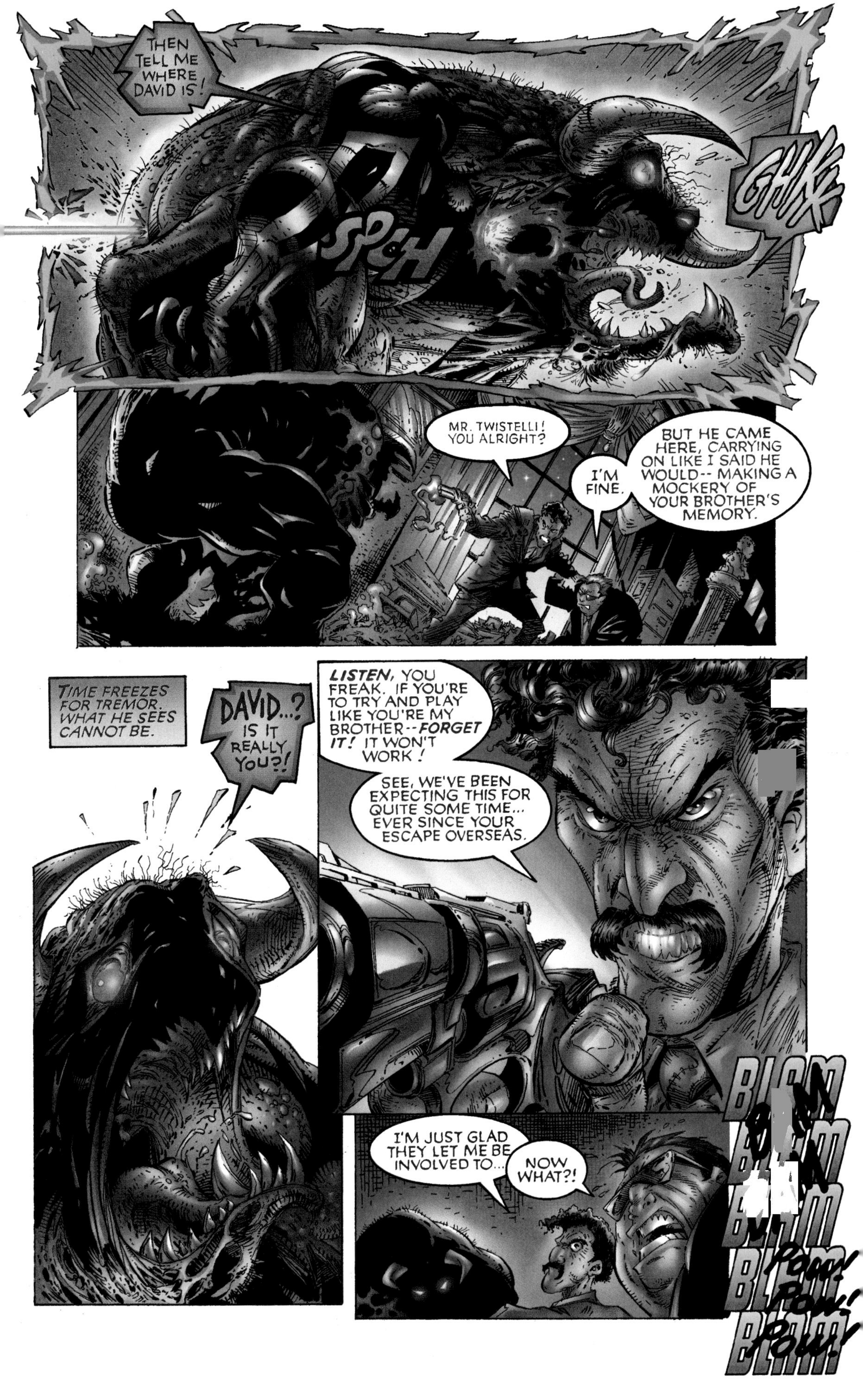
THEN TELL ME WHERE DAVID IS!
GHK
MR. TWISTELLI! YOU ALRIGHT?
I'M FINE.
BUT HE CAME HERE, CARRYING ON LIKE I SAID HE WOULD-- MAKING A MOCKERY OF YOUR BROTHER'S MEMORY.
TIME FREEZES FOR TREMOR. WHAT HE SEES CANNOT BE.
DAVID...? IS IT REALLY YOU?!
LISTEN, YOU FREAK. IF YOU'RE TO TRY AND PLAY LIKE YOU'RE MY BROTHER--***FORGET IT!*** IT WON'T WORK!
SEE, WE'VE BEEN EXPECTING THIS FOR QUITE SOME TIME... EVER SINCE YOUR ESCAPE OVERSEAS.
I'M JUST GLAD THEY LET ME BE INVOLVED TO...
NOW WHAT?!
BLAM BLAM BLAM BLAM BLAM
POW! POW! POW!

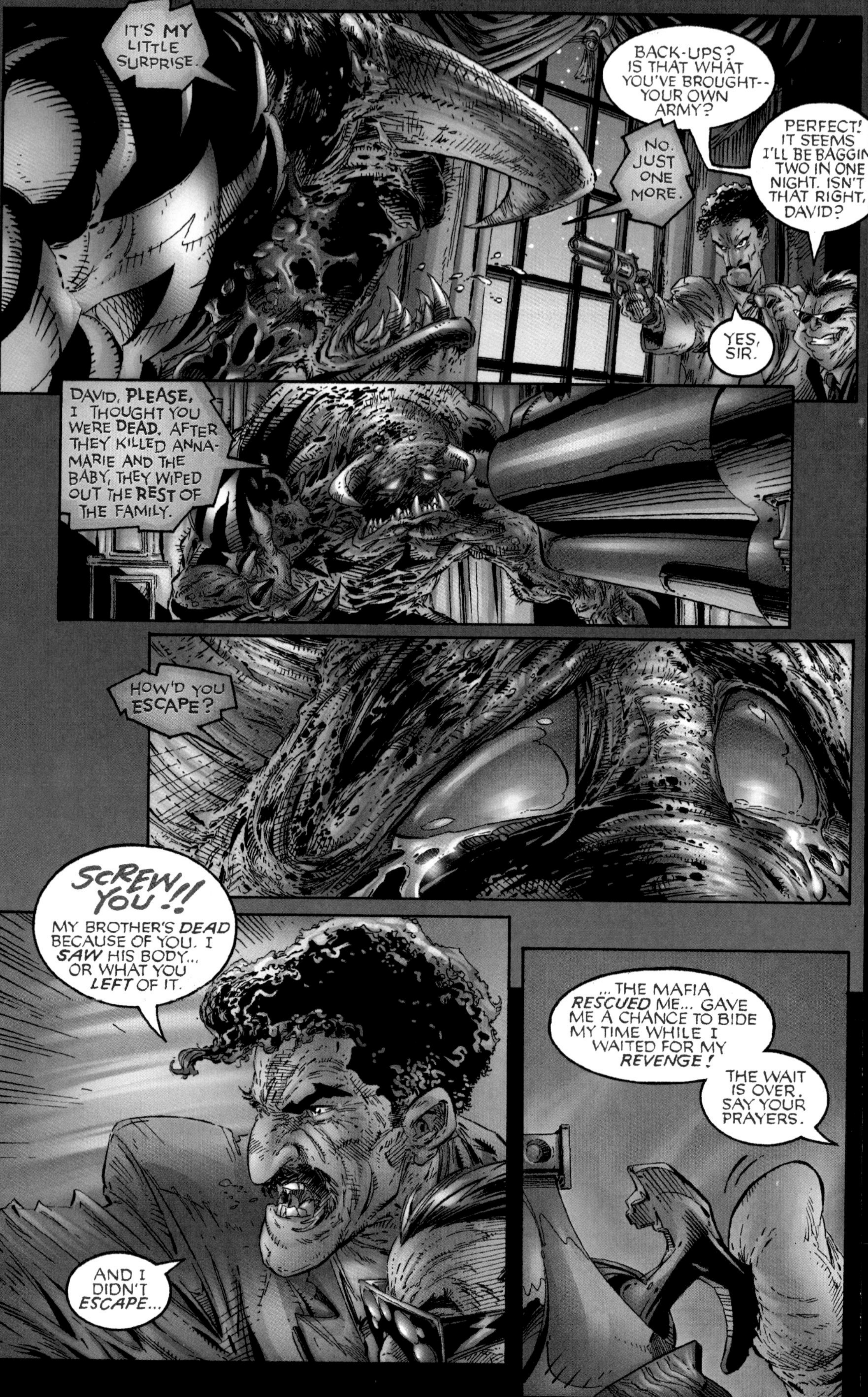

IT'S MY LITTLE SURPRISE.
BACK-UPS? IS THAT WHAT YOU'VE BROUGHT-- YOUR OWN ARMY?
NO. JUST ONE MORE.
PERFECT! IT SEEMS I'LL BE BAGGIN TWO IN ONE NIGHT. ISN'T THAT RIGHT, DAVID?
YES, SIR.
DAVID, PLEASE, I THOUGHT YOU WERE DEAD. AFTER THEY KILLED ANNA-MARIE AND THE BABY, THEY WIPED OUT THE REST OF THE FAMILY.
HOW'D YOU ESCAPE?
SCREW YOU!!
MY BROTHER'S DEAD BECAUSE OF YOU. I SAW HIS BODY... OR WHAT YOU LEFT OF IT.
AND I DIDN'T ESCAPE...
...THE MAFIA RESCUED ME... GAVE ME A CHANCE TO BIDE MY TIME WHILE I WAITED FOR MY REVENGE!
THE WAIT IS OVER. SAY YOUR PRAYERS.

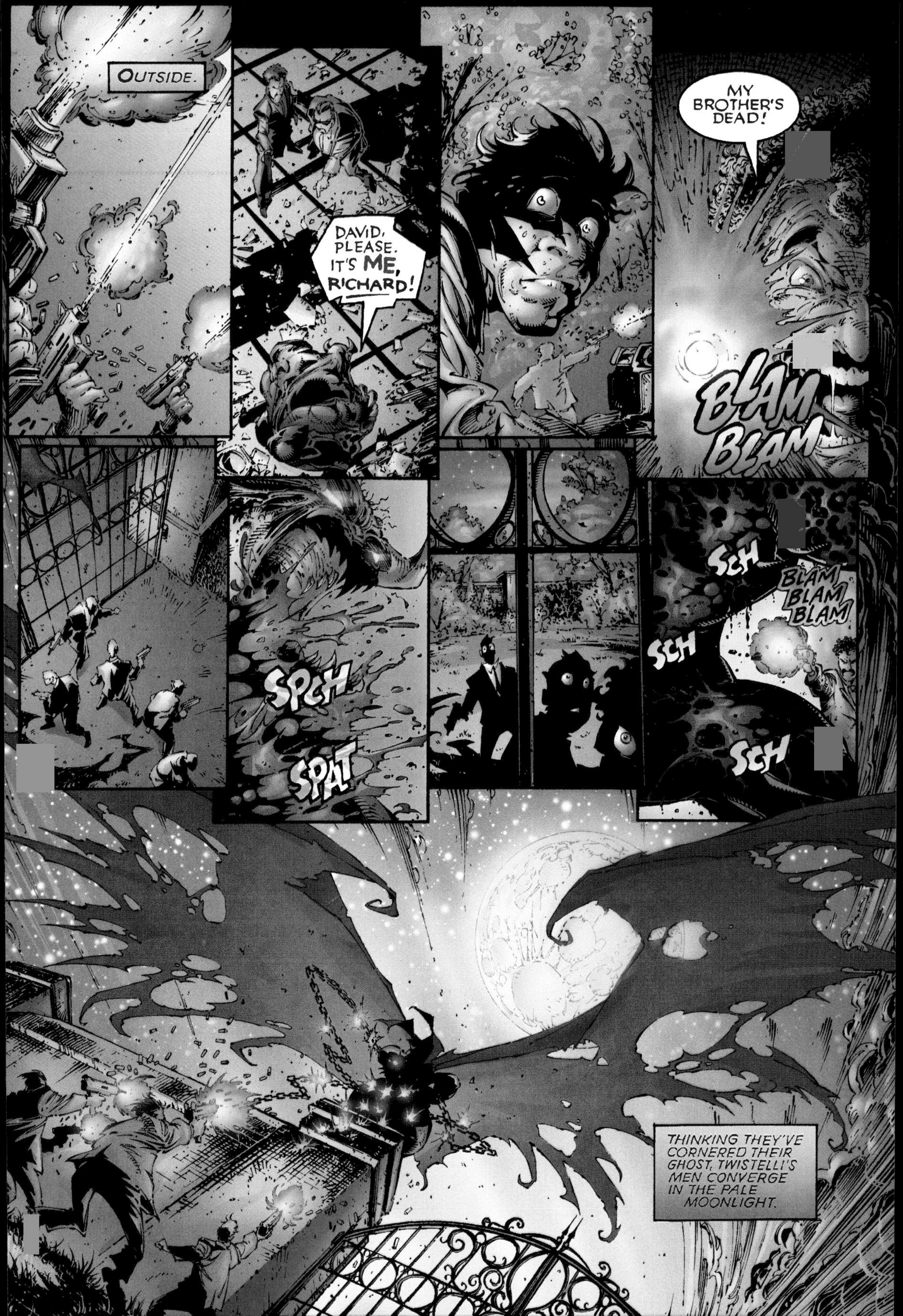
OUTSIDE.
DAVID, PLEASE. IT'S ME, RICHARD!
MY BROTHER'S DEAD!
BLAM BLAM
SPCH
SPAT
SCH
BLAM BLAM BLAM
SCH
SCH
THINKING THEY'VE CORNERED THEIR GHOST, TWISTELLI'S MEN CONVERGE IN THE PALE MOONLIGHT.

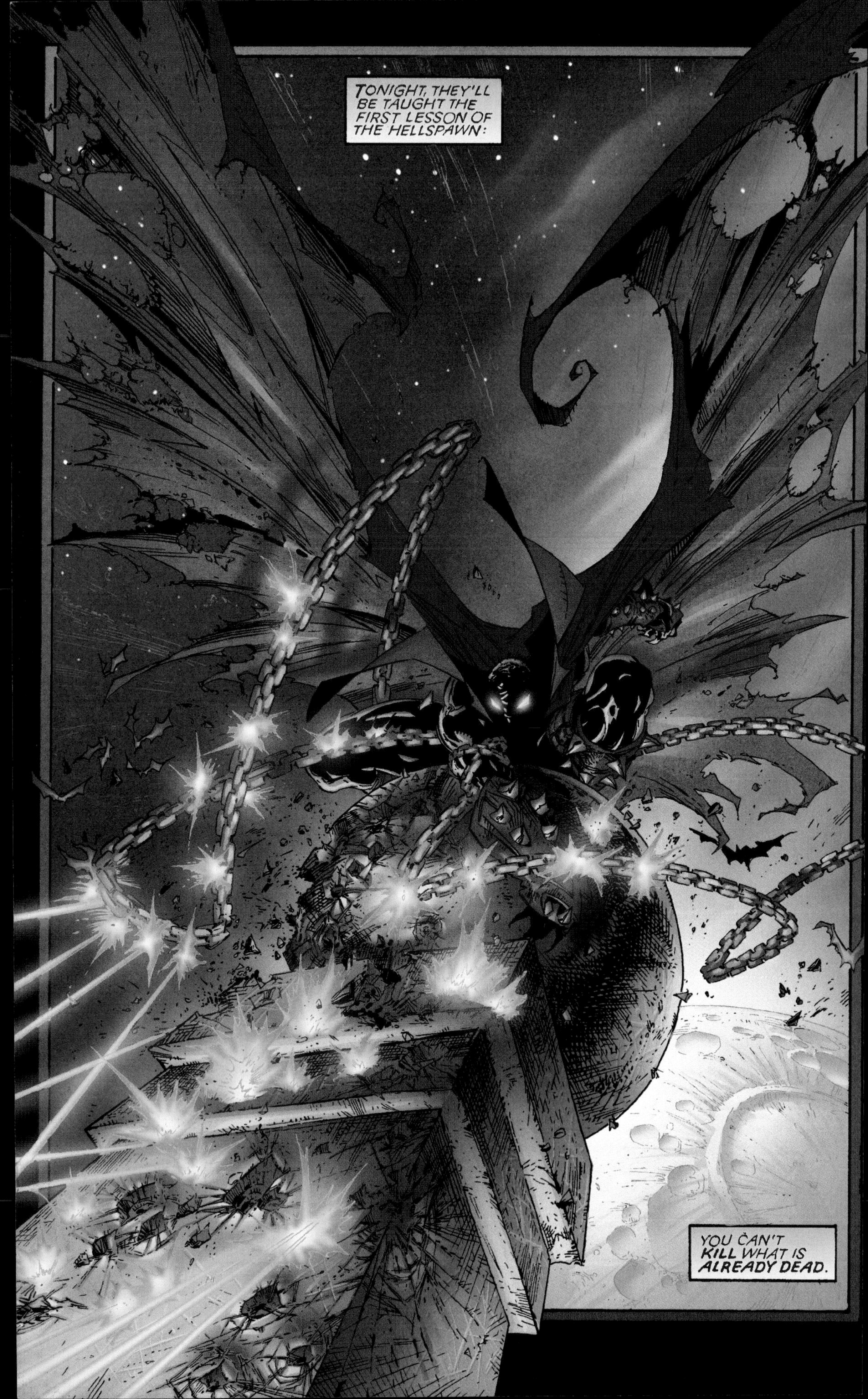
TONIGHT, THEY'LL BE TAUGHT THE FIRST LESSON OF THE HELLSPAWN:
YOU CAN'T **KILL** WHAT IS **ALREADY DEAD**.

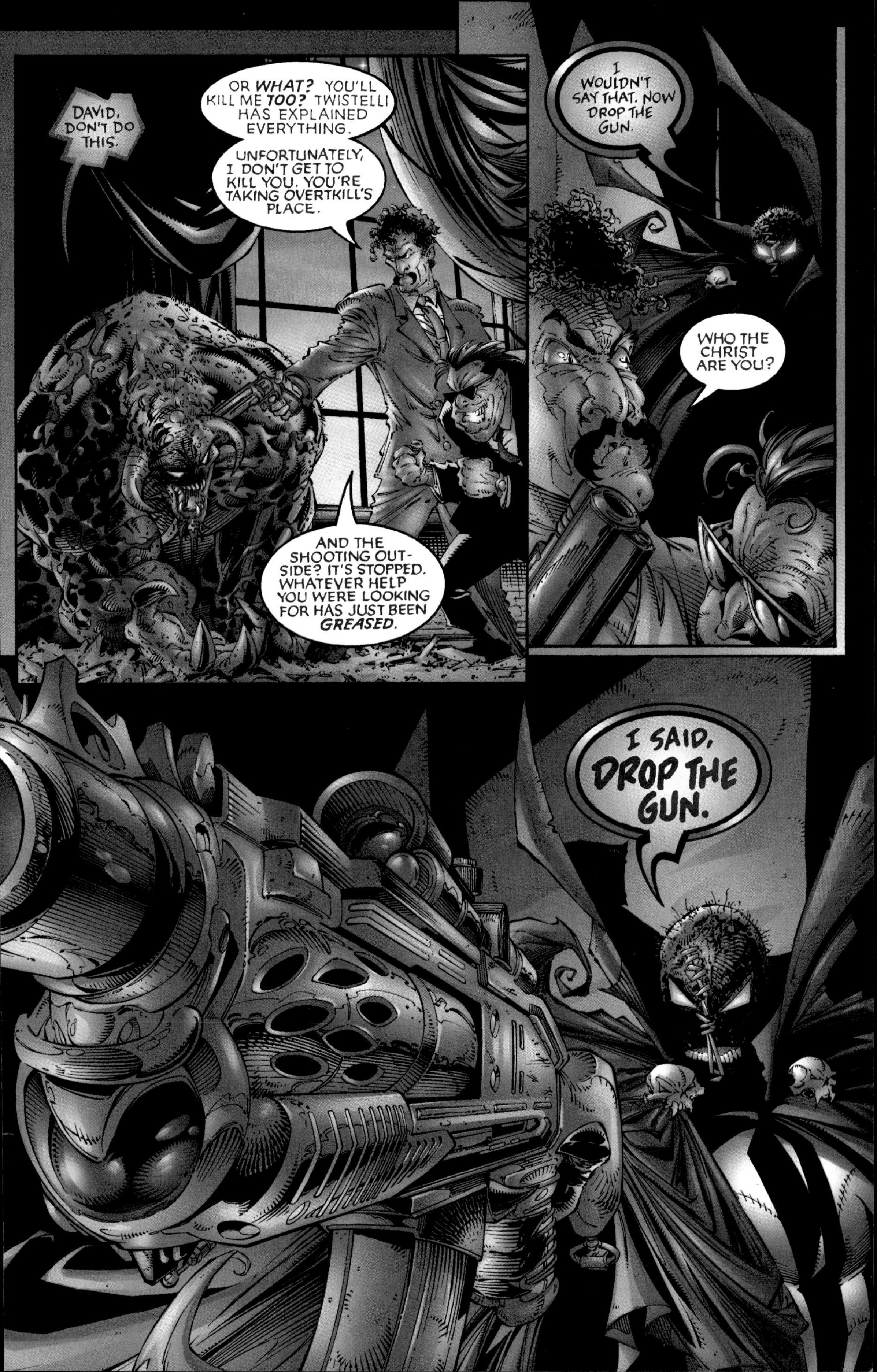
DAVID, DON'T DO THIS.
OR WHAT? YOU'LL KILL ME TOO? TWISTELLI HAS EXPLAINED EVERYTHING.
UNFORTUNATELY, I DON'T GET TO KILL YOU. YOU'RE TAKING OVERTKILL'S PLACE.
AND THE SHOOTING OUT-SIDE? IT'S STOPPED. WHATEVER HELP YOU WERE LOOKING FOR HAS JUST BEEN GREASED.
I WOULDN'T SAY THAT. NOW DROP THE GUN.
WHO THE CHRIST ARE YOU?
I SAID, DROP THE GUN.

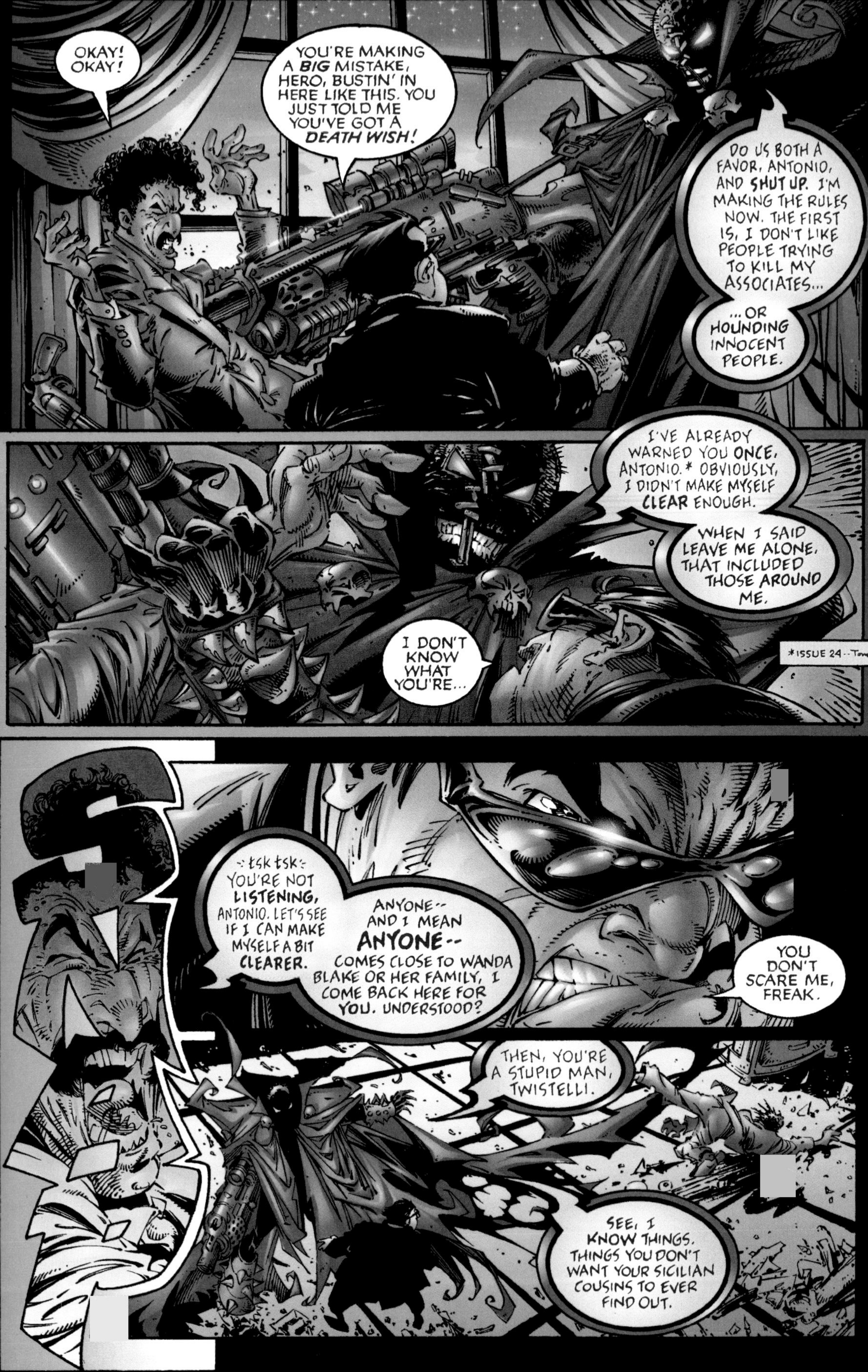
OKAY! OKAY!
YOU'RE MAKING A BIG MISTAKE, HERO, BUSTIN' IN HERE LIKE THIS. YOU JUST TOLD ME YOU'VE GOT A DEATH WISH!
DO US BOTH A FAVOR, ANTONIO, AND SHUT UP. I'M MAKING THE RULES NOW. THE FIRST IS, I DON'T LIKE PEOPLE TRYING TO KILL MY ASSOCIATES...
...OR HOUNDING INNOCENT PEOPLE.
I'VE ALREADY WARNED YOU ONCE, ANTONIO.* OBVIOUSLY, I DIDN'T MAKE MYSELF CLEAR ENOUGH.
WHEN I SAID LEAVE ME ALONE, THAT INCLUDED THOSE AROUND ME.
I DON'T KNOW WHAT YOU'RE...
*ISSUE 24--
tsk tsk YOU'RE NOT LISTENING, ANTONIO. LET'S SEE IF I CAN MAKE MYSELF A BIT CLEARER.
ANYONE-- AND I MEAN ANYONE-- COMES CLOSE TO WANDA BLAKE OR HER FAMILY, I COME BACK HERE FOR YOU. UNDERSTOOD?
YOU DON'T SCARE ME, FREAK.
THEN, YOU'RE A STUPID MAN, TWISTELLI.
SEE, I KNOW THINGS. THINGS YOU DON'T WANT YOUR SICILIAN COUSINS TO EVER FIND OUT.

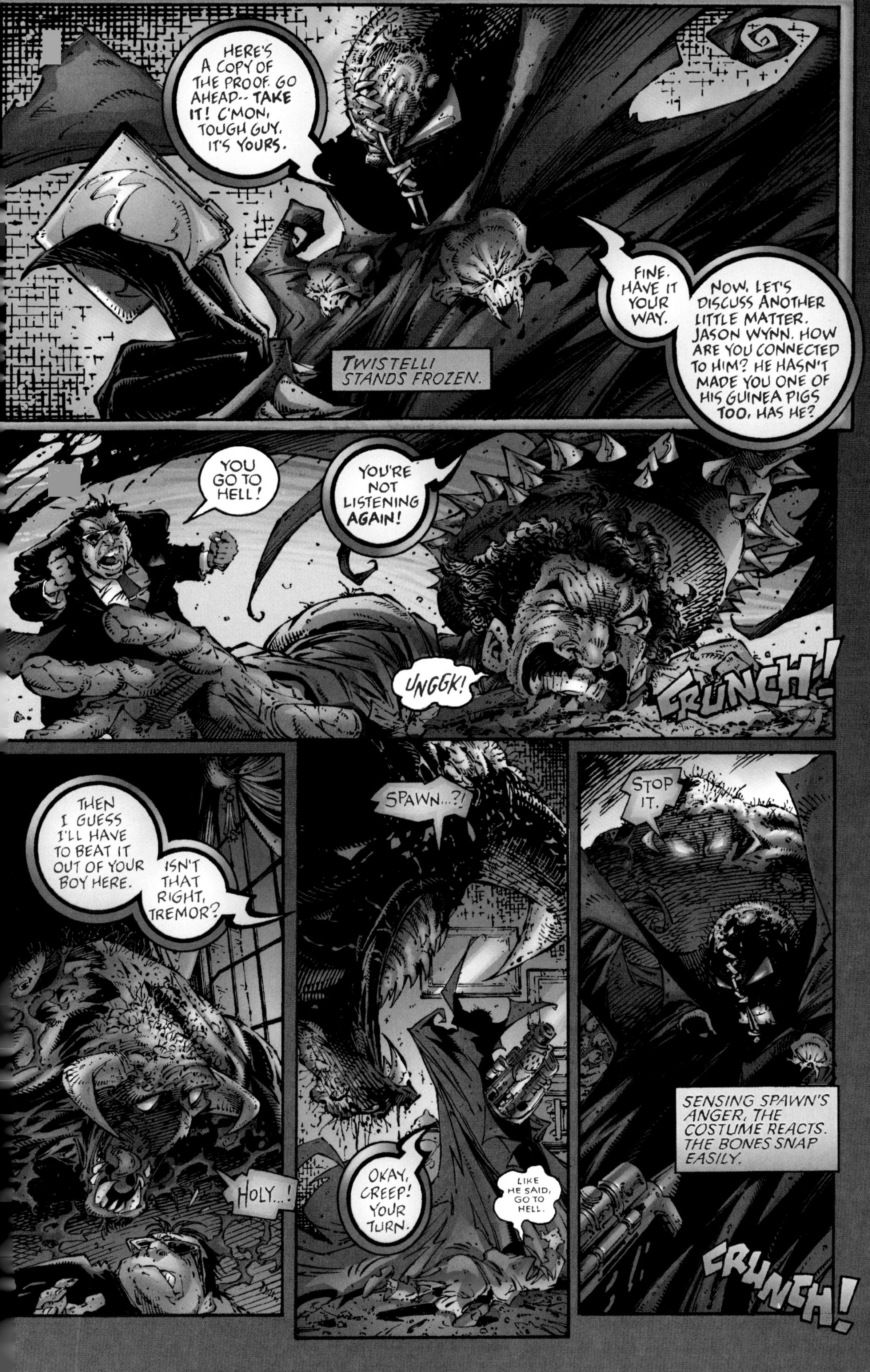
HERE'S A COPY OF THE PROOF. GO AHEAD-- TAKE IT! C'MON, TOUGH GUY. IT'S YOURS.
TWISTELLI STANDS FROZEN.
FINE. HAVE IT YOUR WAY.
NOW, LET'S DISCUSS ANOTHER LITTLE MATTER. JASON WYNN. HOW ARE YOU CONNECTED TO HIM? HE HASN'T MADE YOU ONE OF HIS GUINEA PIGS TOO, HAS HE?
YOU GO TO HELL!
YOU'RE NOT LISTENING AGAIN!
UNGGK!
CRUNCH!
THEN I GUESS I'LL HAVE TO BEAT IT OUT OF YOUR BOY HERE.
ISN'T THAT RIGHT, TREMOR?
HOLY...!
SPAWN...?!
OKAY, CREEP! YOUR TURN.
LIKE HE SAID, GO TO HELL.
STOP IT.
SENSING SPAWN'S ANGER, THE COSTUME REACTS. THE BONES SNAP EASILY.
CRUNCH!

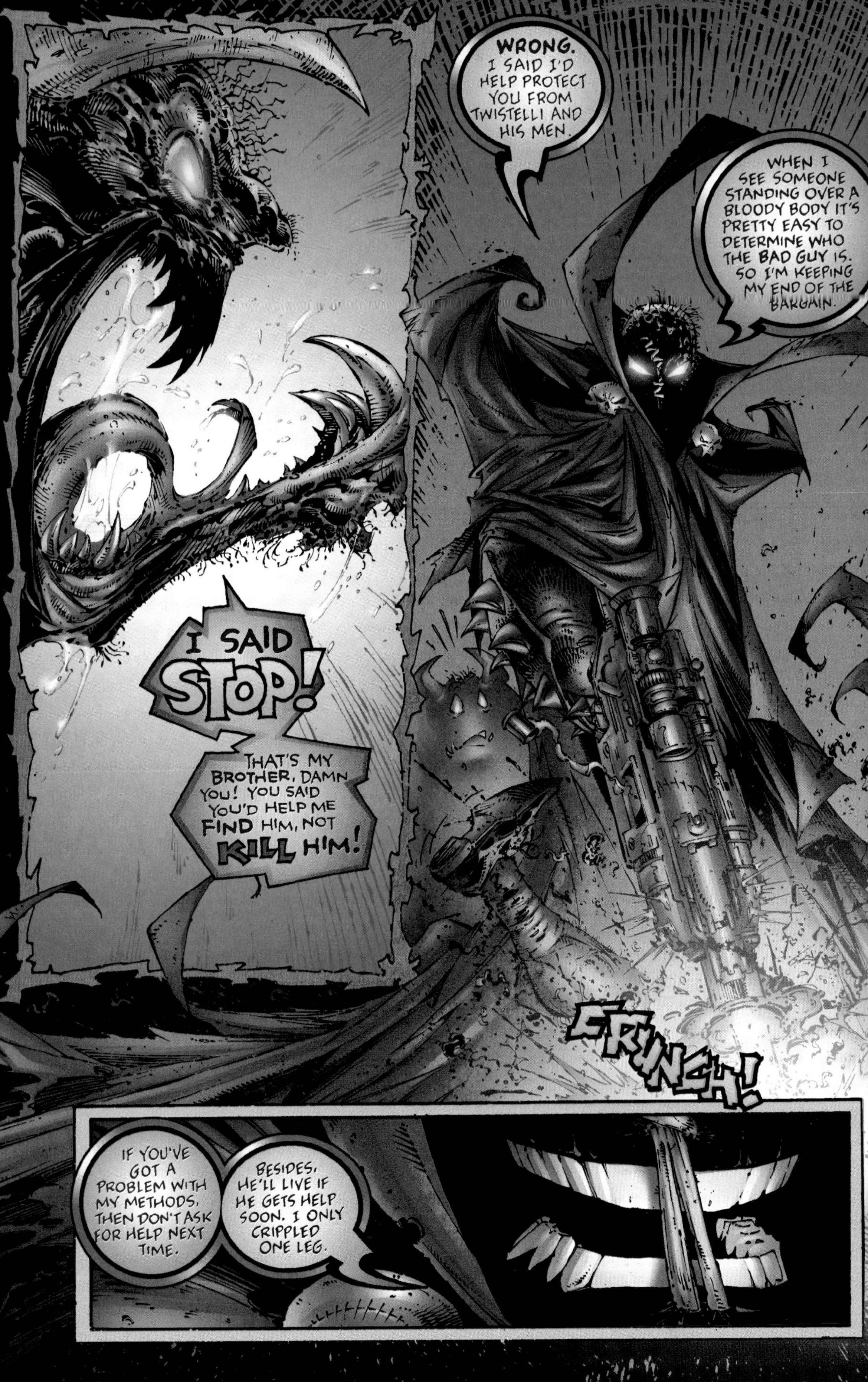
I SAID STOP!
THAT'S MY BROTHER, DAMN YOU! YOU SAID YOU'D HELP ME FIND HIM, NOT KILL HIM!
WRONG. I SAID I'D HELP PROTECT YOU FROM TWISTELLI AND HIS MEN.
WHEN I SEE SOMEONE STANDING OVER A BLOODY BODY IT'S PRETTY EASY TO DETERMINE WHO THE BAD GUY IS. SO I'M KEEPING MY END OF THE BARGAIN.
CRUNCH!
IF YOU'VE GOT A PROBLEM WITH MY METHODS, THEN DON'T ASK FOR HELP NEXT TIME.
BESIDES, HE'LL LIVE IF HE GETS HELP SOON. I ONLY CRIPPLED ONE LEG.

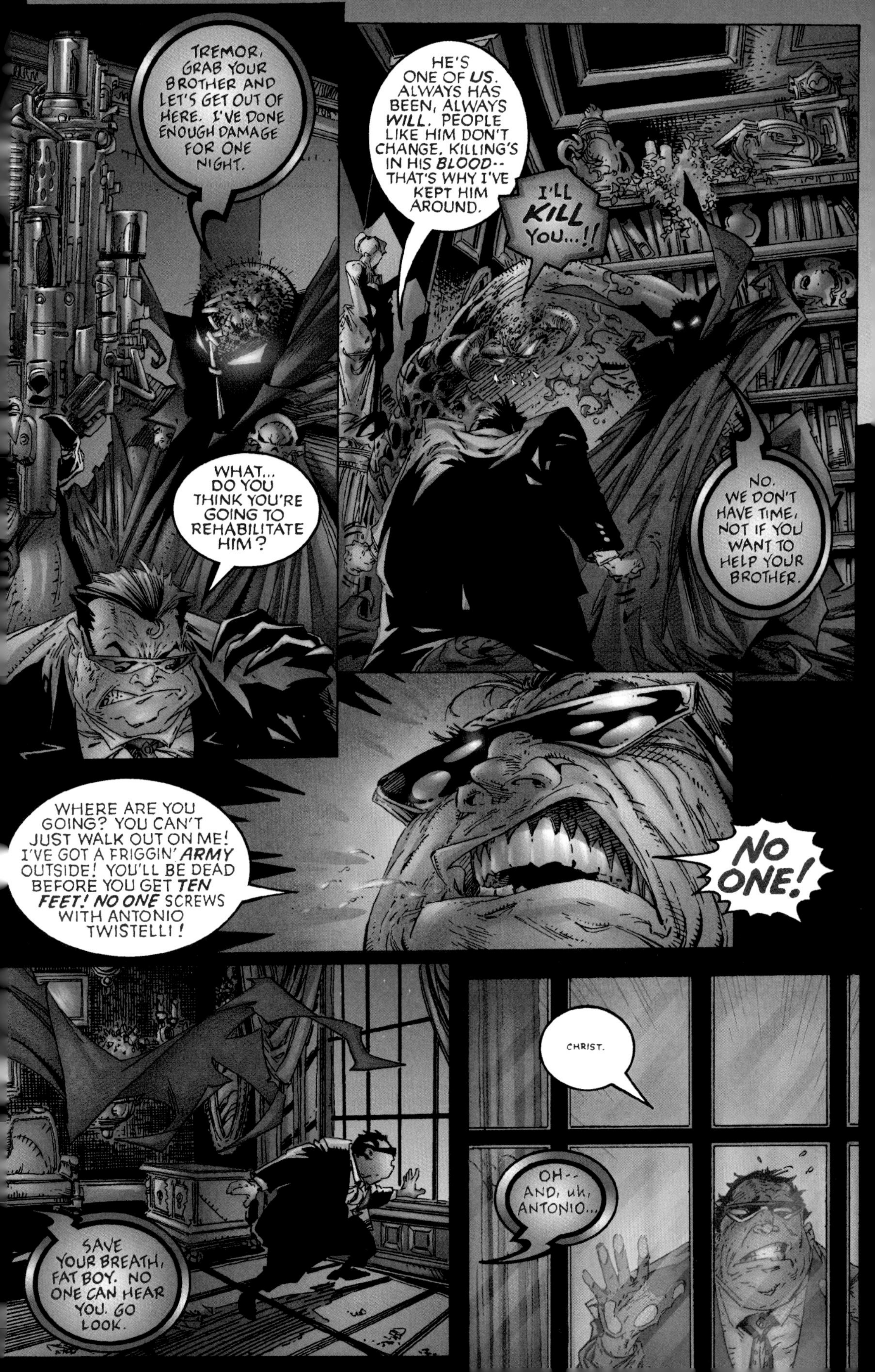
TREMOR, GRAB YOUR BROTHER AND LET'S GET OUT OF HERE. I'VE DONE ENOUGH DAMAGE FOR ONE NIGHT.
WHAT... DO YOU THINK YOU'RE GOING TO REHABILITATE HIM?
HE'S ONE OF US. ALWAYS HAS BEEN, ALWAYS WILL. PEOPLE LIKE HIM DON'T CHANGE. KILLING'S IN HIS BLOOD-- THAT'S WHY I'VE KEPT HIM AROUND.
I'LL KILL YOU...!!
NO. WE DON'T HAVE TIME, NOT IF YOU WANT TO HELP YOUR BROTHER.
WHERE ARE YOU GOING? YOU CAN'T JUST WALK OUT ON ME! I'VE GOT A FRIGGIN' ARMY OUTSIDE! YOU'LL BE DEAD BEFORE YOU GET TEN FEET! NO ONE SCREWS WITH ANTONIO TWISTELLI!
NO ONE!
SAVE YOUR BREATH, FAT BOY. NO ONE CAN HEAR YOU. GO LOOK.
CHRIST.
OH-- AND, uh, ANTONIO...

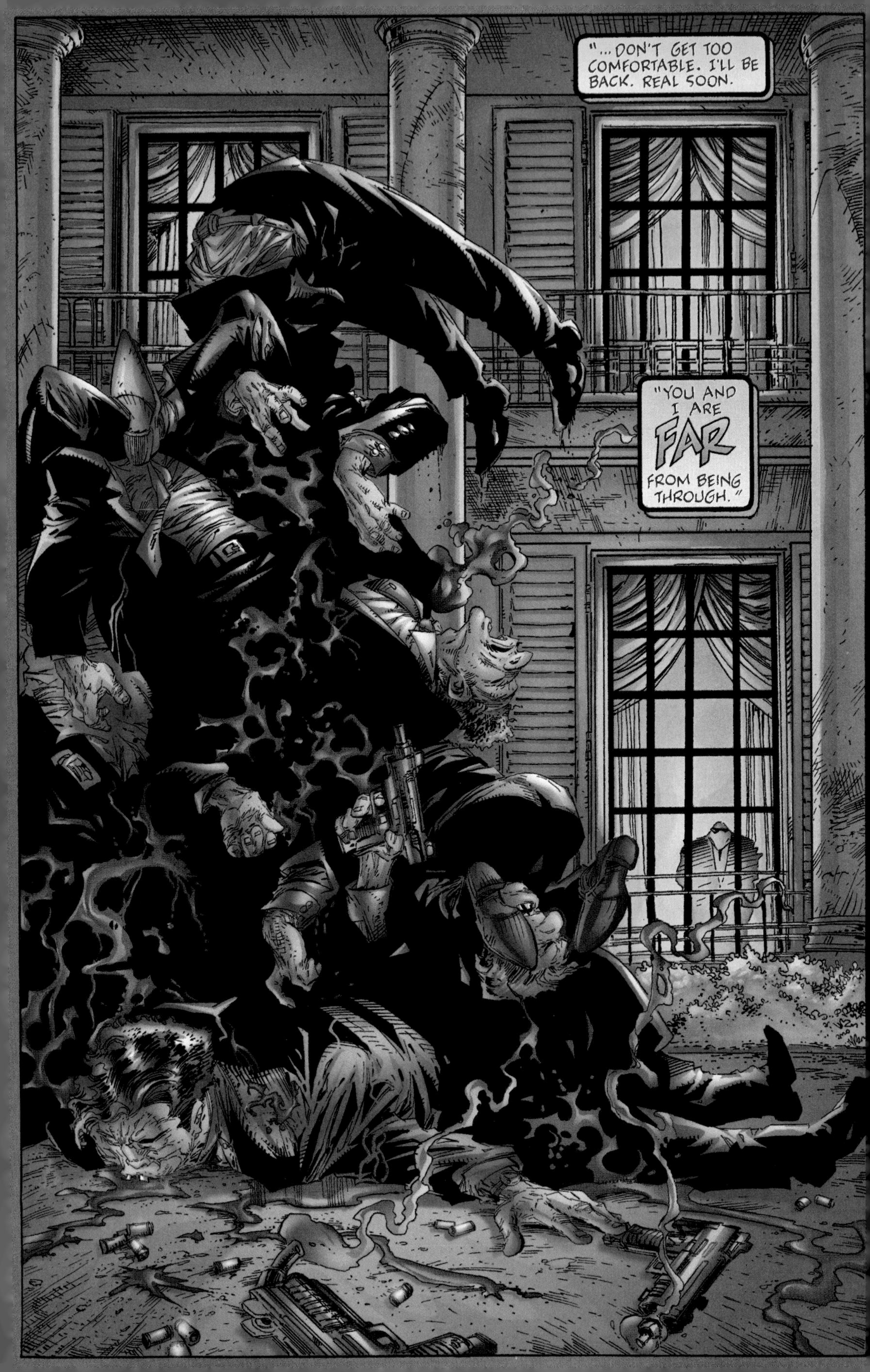
"...DON'T GET TOO COMFORTABLE. I'LL BE BACK. REAL SOON.
"YOU AND I ARE FAR FROM BEING THROUGH."

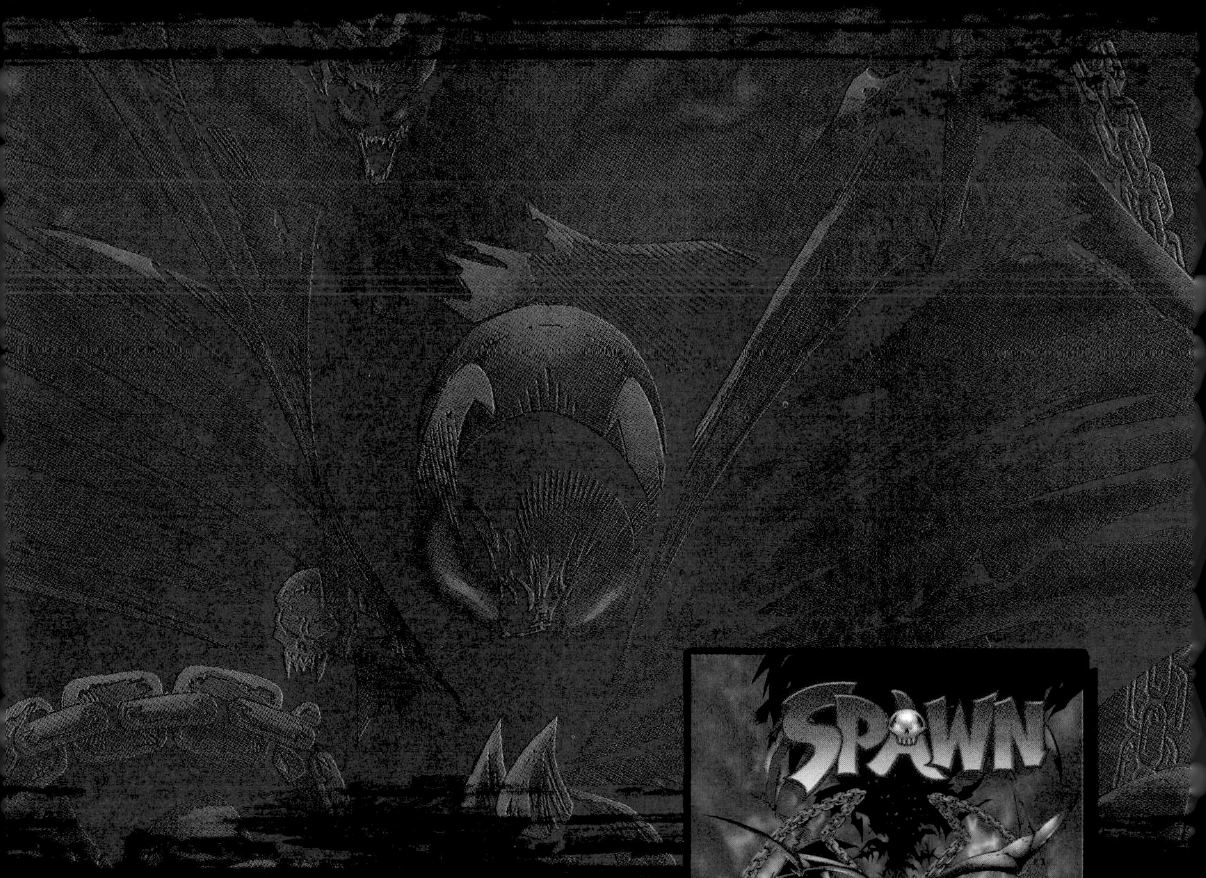

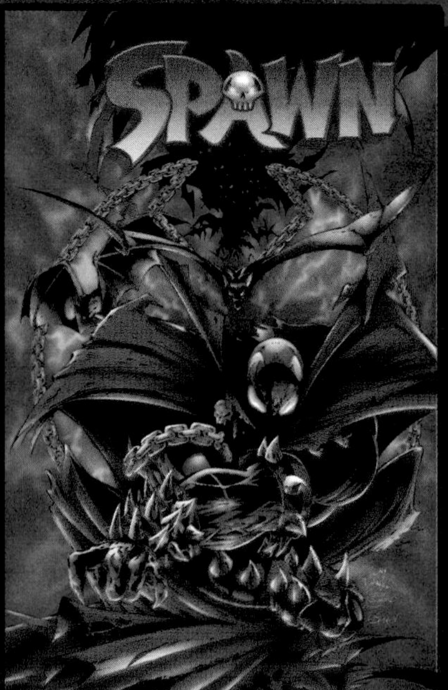
SPAWN

ISSUE FORTY-EIGHT

AT EIGHTEEN FEET, THE OFFICE CEILINGS ARE IMPRESSIVE, GIVING THE ROOM AN IMMENSE *DEPTH*. THE WALL PANELS ARE IMPORTED CHERRY-WOOD; BEHIND THEM, BANKS OF RETRIEVAL, SURVEILLANCE AND SECURITY SYSTEMS. FEATURED IN THE DECOR ARE STATUARY AND FURNITURE OF A PATRICIAN, VAGUELY *CONDESCENDING* STYLE, LAID UPON LUSH ORIENTAL CARPETING.

VERY FEW OFFICES CAN MATCH IT. BEING A CLOSE CONFIDANT TO THE PRESIDENT AND OTHER WORLD LEADERS DOES CARRY FRINGE BEN-EFITS. UNLIKE OTHER GOVERNMENTAL OFFICES BUILT TO THE SAME SPECIFI-CATIONS, THIS ONE BELIES ITS PURPOSE. RATHER THAN GIVING A SENSE OF HIGH PRESENCE AND ELEGANCE, THE LIGHTING HAS BEEN MODIFIED TO ILLUMINATE ONLY THE *NECESSI-TIES*. DEPENDING ON THE TIME OF DAY, IT APPEARS ALMOST AS A CANDLE-LIT FUNERAL PARLOR... OR AT NIGHT, A *BLACK HOLE*.

C.I.A. SECURITY HEAD JASON WYNN *LIKES* IT THAT WAY.

WE'VE PUT THE PROPER DOCUMENTS TOGETHER, ALONG WITH DENIABLY SUBSTANCIATED EVIDENCE. EVERYTHING TIES INTO A COHESIVE PRESENTA-TION THAT SHOULD CON-VINCE THE RECIPIENTS THAT IT'S *ALL* FACTUAL.

WE PLAN ON MAKING THE DROP LATER TODAY.

EXCELLENT. AND OUR OTHER INTERESTS...?

THE *GUATEMALAN* EMBASSY IS PREPARED TO HONOR YOUR REQUESTS. GENERAL HORTAS AND HIS STAFF ARE IN LINE WITH YOUR POSITION TO DEFY THE DEPOSED, TERRORIST LEADER. ADDITIONALLY, IN LIGHT OF THEIR PAST ENCOUNTERS WITH HIM, THE GENERAL HAS MADE READY *EXTRA* AIR SUPPORT FOR YOUR AGENTS.

IN *FRANCE*, SEVERAL OUTPOSTS OF THE RADICAL "PEOPLE FOR A NEW MONARCHY" HAVE BEEN...

THE LAUNDRY LIST OF RECENT U.S. INTELLIGENCE ACTIVI-TIES CONTINUES FOR ANOTHER HOUR.

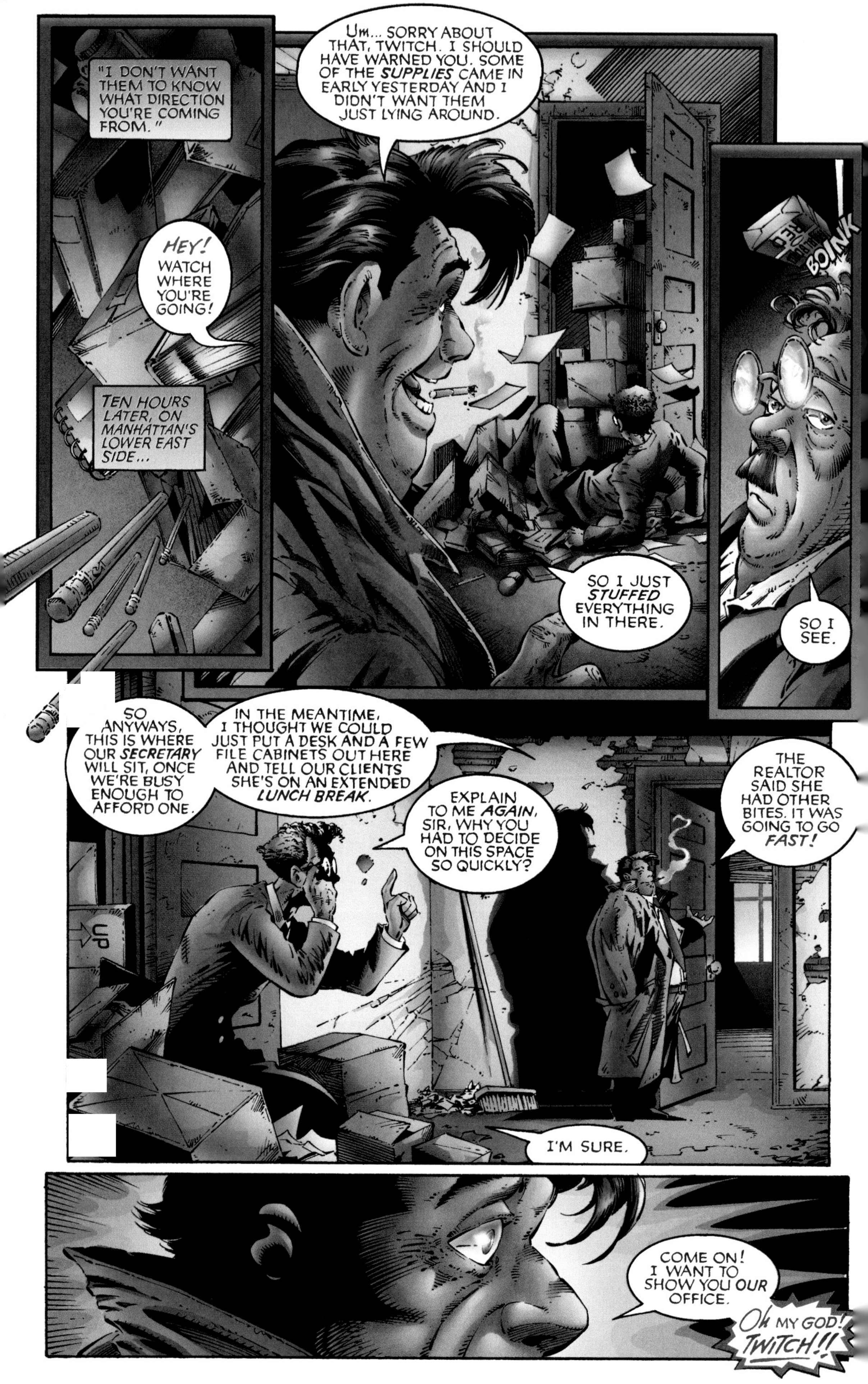
"I DON'T WANT THEM TO KNOW WHAT DIRECTION YOU'RE COMING FROM."
HEY! WATCH WHERE YOU'RE GOING!
TEN HOURS LATER, ON MANHATTAN'S LOWER EAST SIDE...
Um... SORRY ABOUT THAT, TWITCH. I SHOULD HAVE WARNED YOU. SOME OF THE SUPPLIES CAME IN EARLY YESTERDAY AND I DIDN'T WANT THEM JUST LYING AROUND.
SO I JUST STUFFED EVERYTHING IN THERE.
BOINK
SO I SEE.
SO ANYWAYS, THIS IS WHERE OUR SECRETARY WILL SIT, ONCE WE'RE BUSY ENOUGH TO AFFORD ONE.
IN THE MEANTIME, I THOUGHT WE COULD JUST PUT A DESK AND A FEW FILE CABINETS OUT HERE AND TELL OUR CLIENTS SHE'S ON AN EXTENDED LUNCH BREAK.
EXPLAIN TO ME AGAIN, SIR, WHY YOU HAD TO DECIDE ON THIS SPACE SO QUICKLY?
THE REALTOR SAID SHE HAD OTHER BITES. IT WAS GOING TO GO FAST!
UP
I'M SURE.
COME ON! I WANT TO SHOW YOU OUR OFFICE.
Oh MY GOD! TWITCH!!

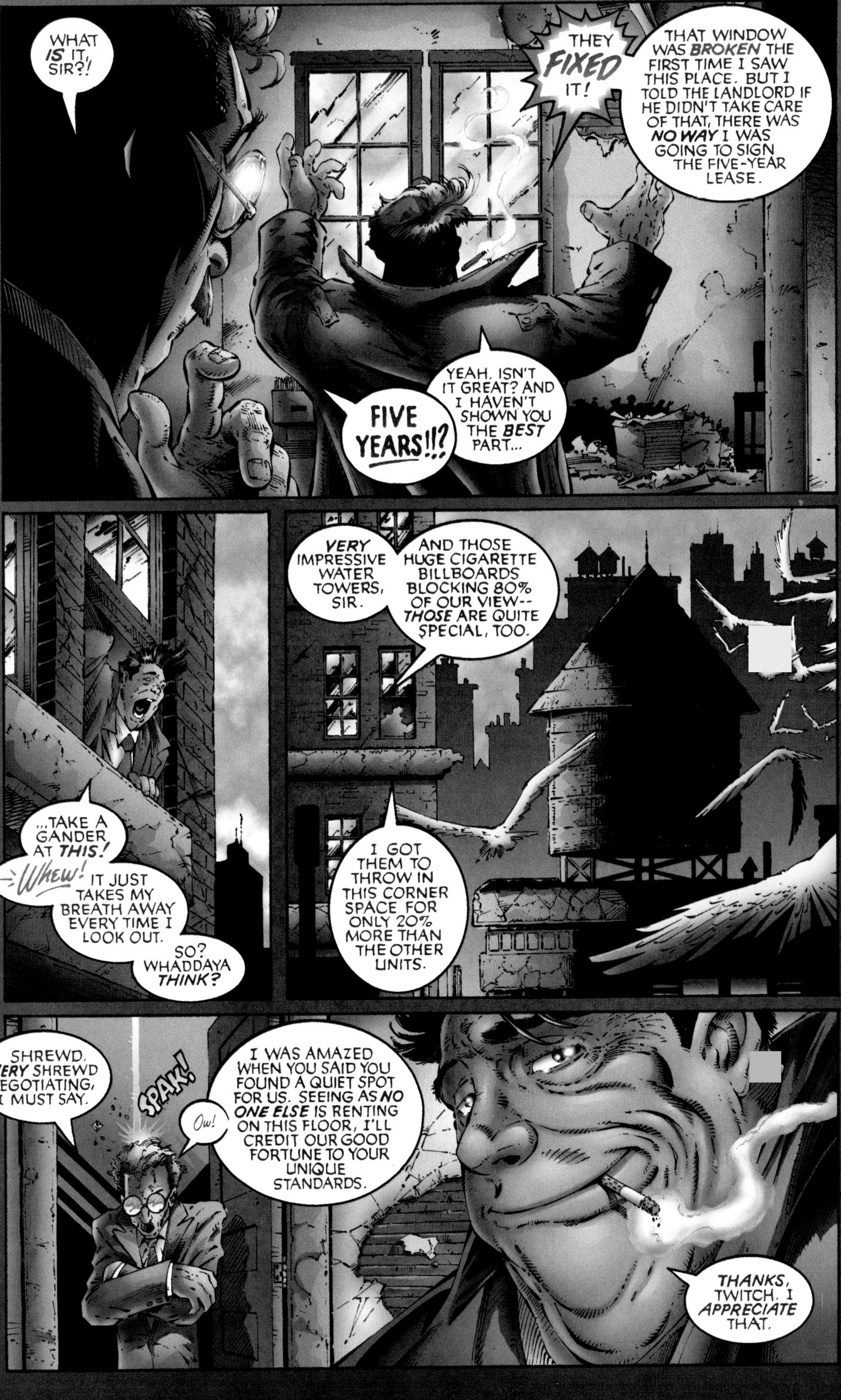

WHAT *IS* IT, SIR?!
THEY *FIXED* IT!
THAT WINDOW WAS *BROKEN* THE FIRST TIME I SAW THIS PLACE. BUT I TOLD THE LANDLORD IF HE DIDN'T TAKE CARE OF THAT, THERE WAS *NO WAY* I WAS GOING TO SIGN THE FIVE-YEAR LEASE.
FIVE YEARS!!?
YEAH. ISN'T IT GREAT? AND I HAVEN'T SHOWN YOU THE *BEST* PART...
...TAKE A GANDER AT *THIS!*
WHEW!
IT JUST TAKES MY BREATH AWAY EVERY TIME I LOOK OUT.
SO? WHADDAYA *THINK?*
VERY IMPRESSIVE WATER TOWERS, SIR.
AND THOSE HUGE CIGARETTE BILLBOARDS BLOCKING 80% OF OUR VIEW-- *THOSE* ARE QUITE SPECIAL, TOO.
I GOT THEM TO THROW IN THIS CORNER SPACE FOR ONLY 20% MORE THAN THE OTHER UNITS.
SHREWD. *VERY* SHREWD NEGOTIATING, I MUST SAY.
SPAK!
Ow!
I WAS AMAZED WHEN YOU SAID YOU FOUND A QUIET SPOT FOR US. SEEING AS *NO ONE ELSE* IS RENTING ON THIS FLOOR, I'LL CREDIT OUR GOOD FORTUNE TO YOUR UNIQUE STANDARDS.
THANKS, TWITCH. I *APPRECIATE* THAT.

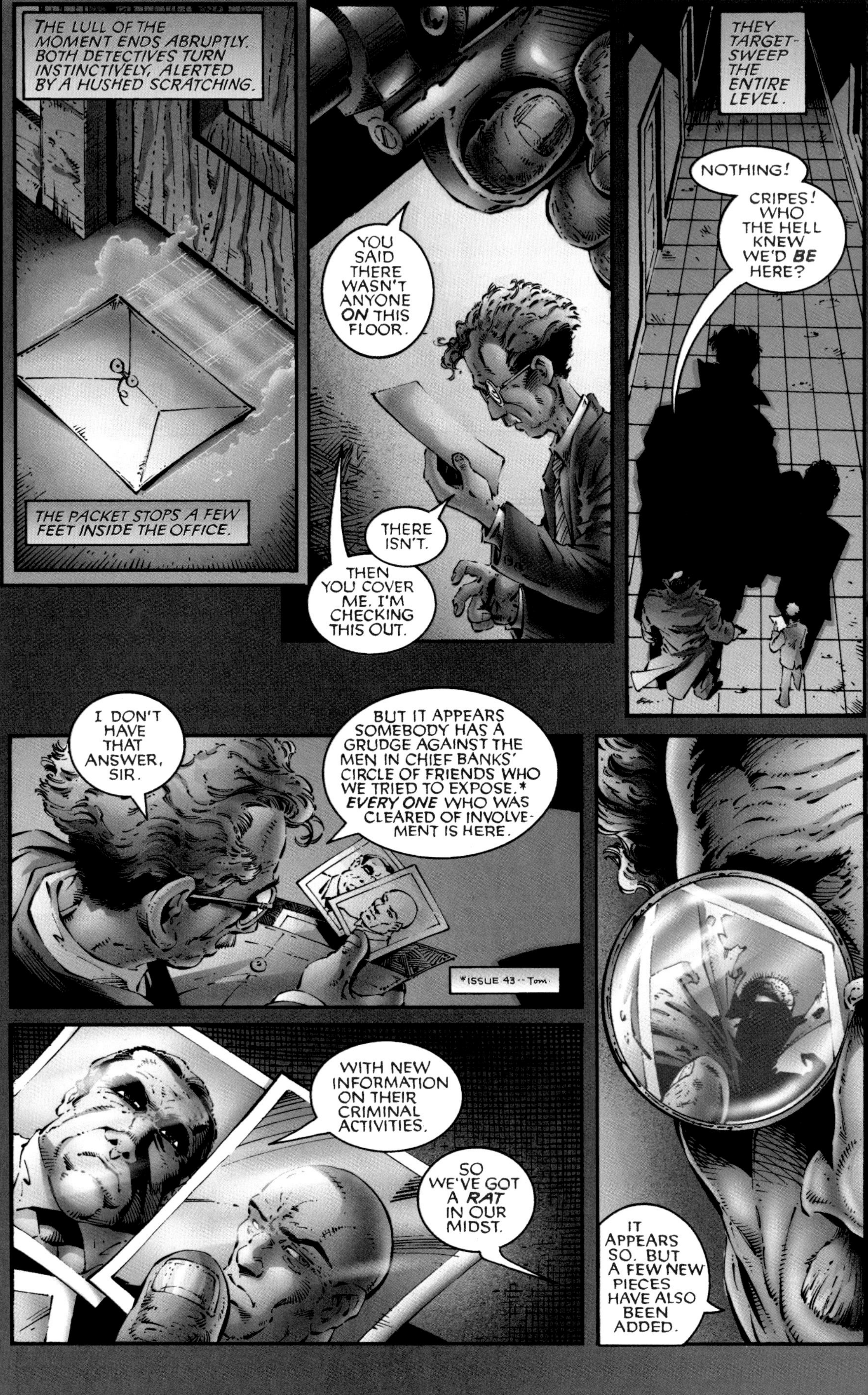

THE LULL OF THE MOMENT ENDS ABRUPTLY. BOTH DETECTIVES TURN INSTINCTIVELY, ALERTED BY A HUSHED SCRATCHING.
THE PACKET STOPS A FEW FEET INSIDE THE OFFICE.
YOU SAID THERE WASN'T ANYONE ON THIS FLOOR.
THERE ISN'T.
THEN YOU COVER ME. I'M CHECKING THIS OUT.
THEY TARGET-SWEEP THE ENTIRE LEVEL.
NOTHING!
CRIPES! WHO THE HELL KNEW WE'D BE HERE?
I DON'T HAVE THAT ANSWER, SIR.
BUT IT APPEARS SOMEBODY HAS A GRUDGE AGAINST THE MEN IN CHIEF BANKS' CIRCLE OF FRIENDS WHO WE TRIED TO EXPOSE.* EVERY ONE WHO WAS CLEARED OF INVOLVEMENT IS HERE.
*ISSUE 43 -- Tom.
WITH NEW INFORMATION ON THEIR CRIMINAL ACTIVITIES.
SO WE'VE GOT A RAT IN OUR MIDST.
IT APPEARS SO. BUT A FEW NEW PIECES HAVE ALSO BEEN ADDED.

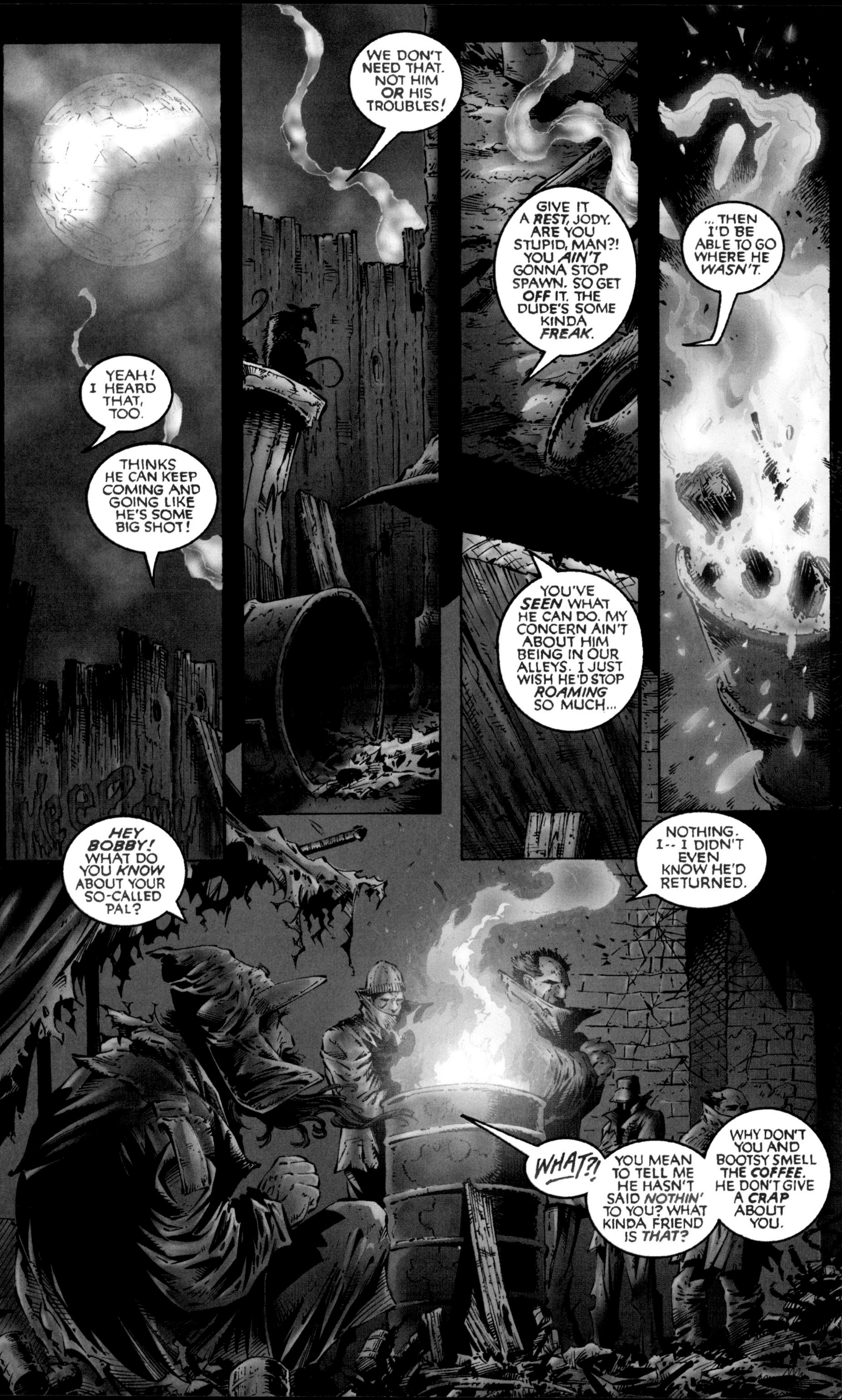
YEAH! I HEARD THAT, TOO.
THINKS HE CAN KEEP COMING AND GOING LIKE HE'S SOME BIG SHOT!
WE DON'T NEED THAT. NOT HIM OR HIS TROUBLES!
GIVE IT A REST, JODY. ARE YOU STUPID, MAN?! YOU AIN'T GONNA STOP SPAWN. SO GET OFF IT. THE DUDE'S SOME KINDA FREAK.
YOU'VE SEEN WHAT HE CAN DO. MY CONCERN AIN'T ABOUT HIM BEING IN OUR ALLEYS. I JUST WISH HE'D STOP ROAMING SO MUCH...
...THEN I'D BE ABLE TO GO WHERE HE WASN'T.
HEY BOBBY! WHAT DO YOU KNOW ABOUT YOUR SO-CALLED PAL?
NOTHING. I-- I DIDN'T EVEN KNOW HE'D RETURNED.
WHAT?!
YOU MEAN TO TELL ME HE HASN'T SAID NOTHIN' TO YOU? WHAT KINDA FRIEND IS THAT?
WHY DON'T YOU AND BOOTSY SMELL THE COFFEE. HE DON'T GIVE A CRAP ABOUT YOU.

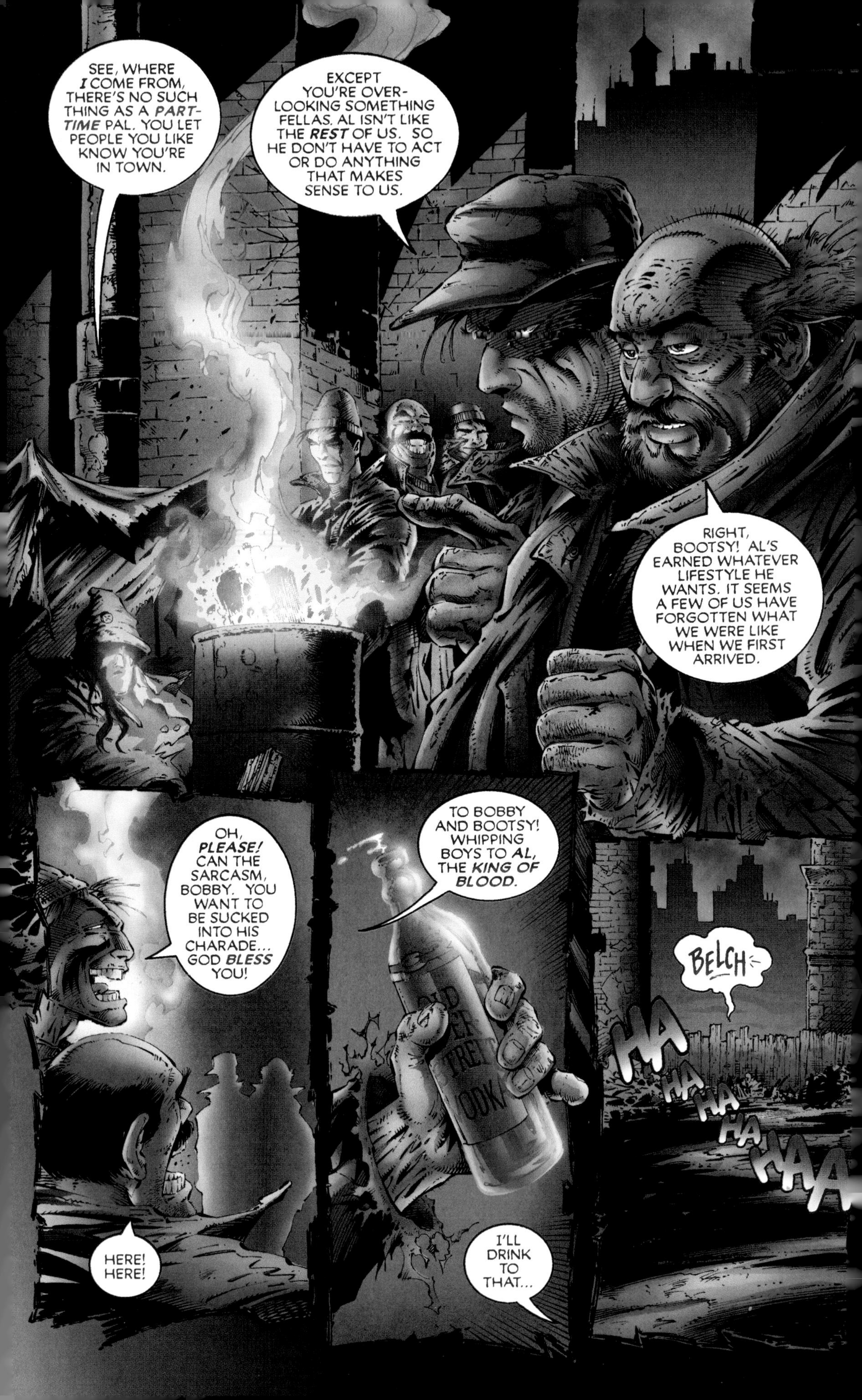
SEE, WHERE *I* COME FROM, THERE'S NO SUCH THING AS A *PART-TIME* PAL. YOU LET PEOPLE YOU LIKE KNOW YOU'RE IN TOWN.
EXCEPT YOU'RE OVER-LOOKING SOMETHING FELLAS. AL ISN'T LIKE THE *REST* OF US. SO HE DON'T HAVE TO ACT OR DO ANYTHING THAT MAKES SENSE TO US.
RIGHT, BOOTSY! AL'S EARNED WHATEVER LIFESTYLE HE WANTS. IT SEEMS A FEW OF US HAVE FORGOTTEN WHAT WE WERE LIKE WHEN WE FIRST ARRIVED.
OH, *PLEASE!* CAN THE SARCASM, BOBBY. YOU WANT TO BE SUCKED INTO HIS CHARADE... GOD *BLESS* YOU!
HERE! HERE!
TO BOBBY AND BOOTSY! WHIPPING BOYS TO *AL*, THE *KING OF BLOOD*.
I'LL DRINK TO THAT...
BELCH
HA HA HA HA HAA

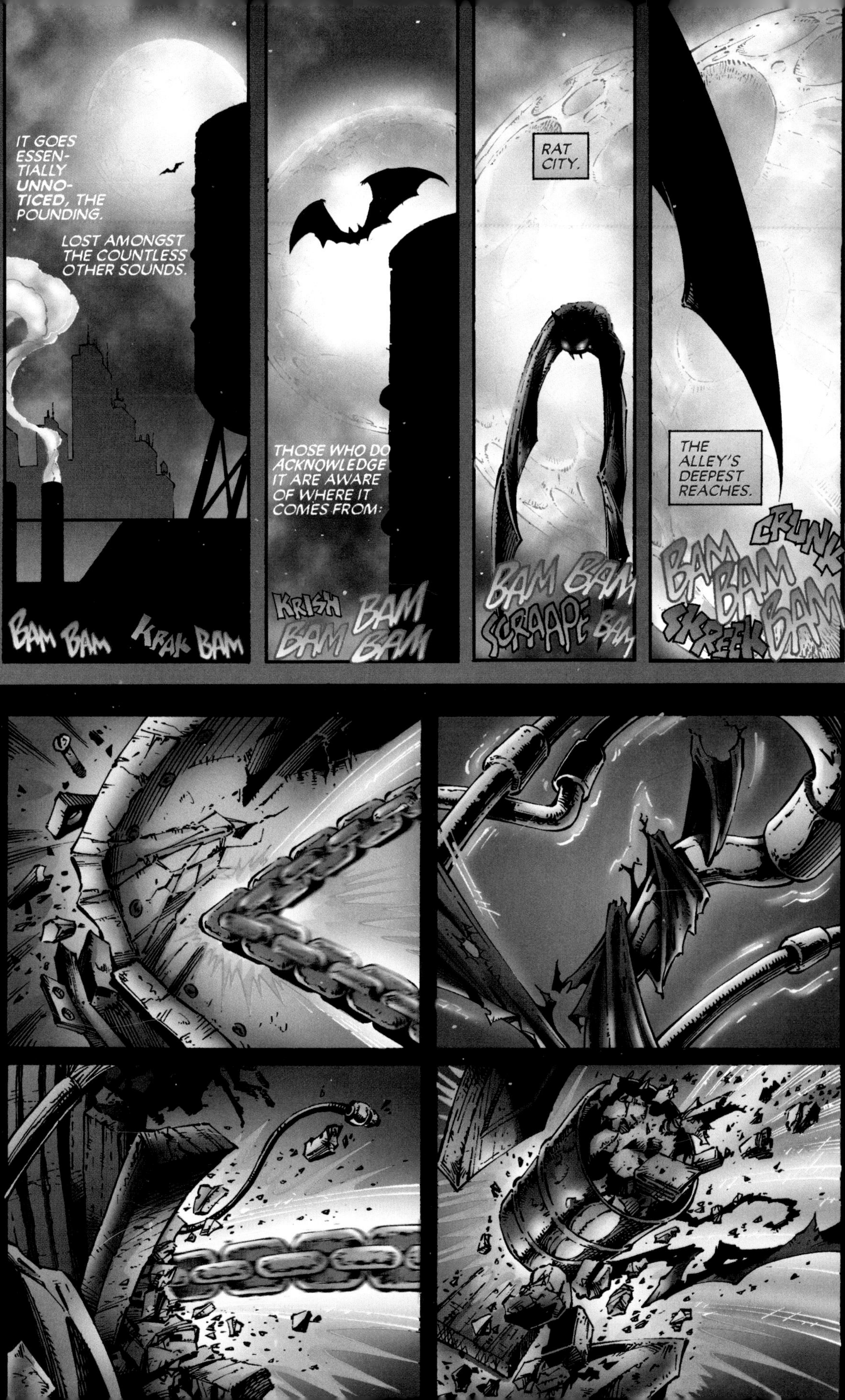
IT GOES ESSENTIALLY UNNOTICED, THE POUNDING.
LOST AMONGST THE COUNTLESS OTHER SOUNDS.
BAM BAM KRAK BAM
THOSE WHO DO ACKNOWLEDGE IT ARE AWARE OF WHERE IT COMES FROM:
KRISH BAM BAM BAM
RAT CITY.
BAM BAM SCRAAPE BAM
THE ALLEY'S DEEPEST REACHES.
CRUNK BAM BAM SKREEK BAM

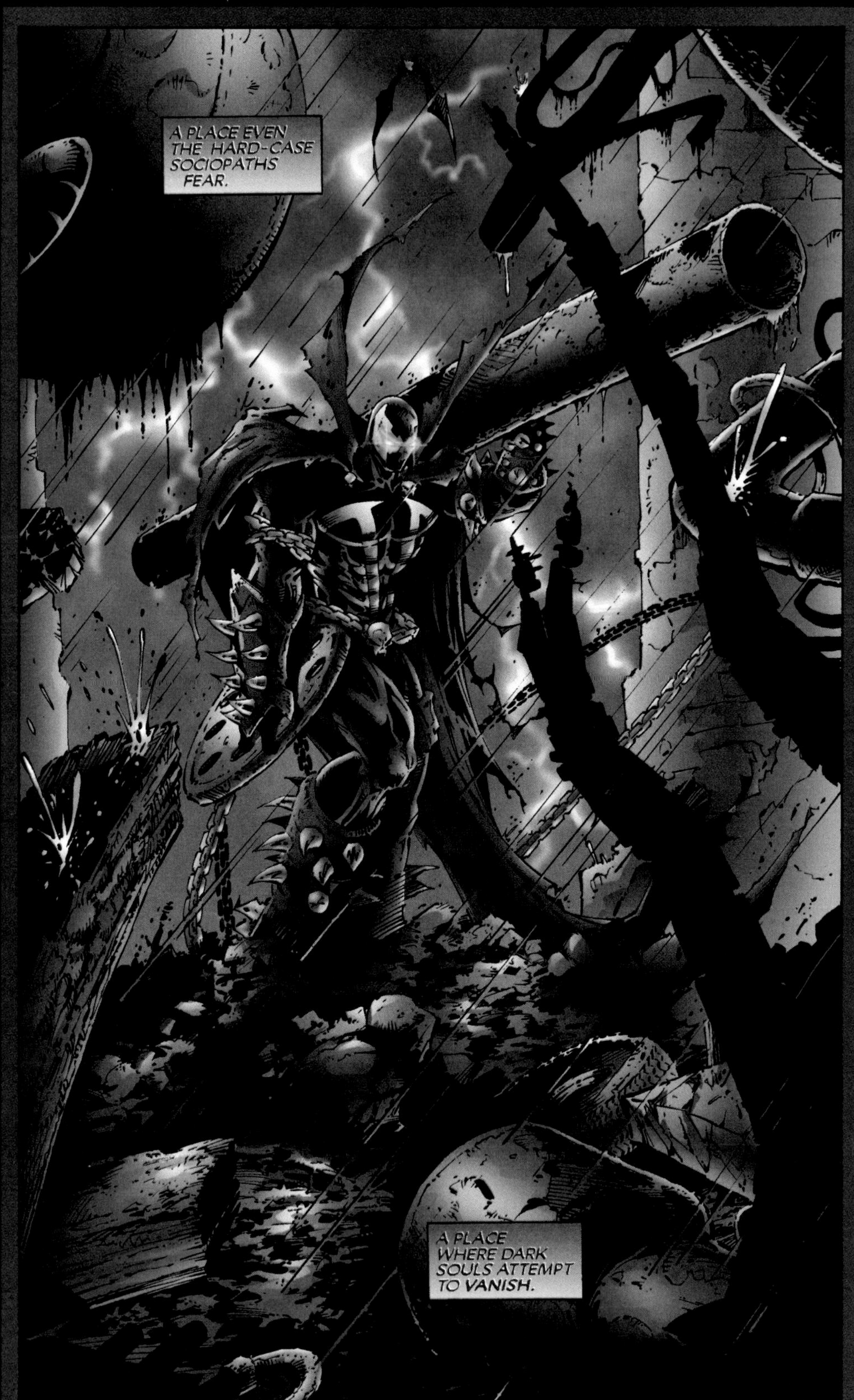
A PLACE EVEN THE HARD-CASE SOCIOPATHS FEAR.
A PLACE WHERE DARK SOULS ATTEMPT TO VANISH.

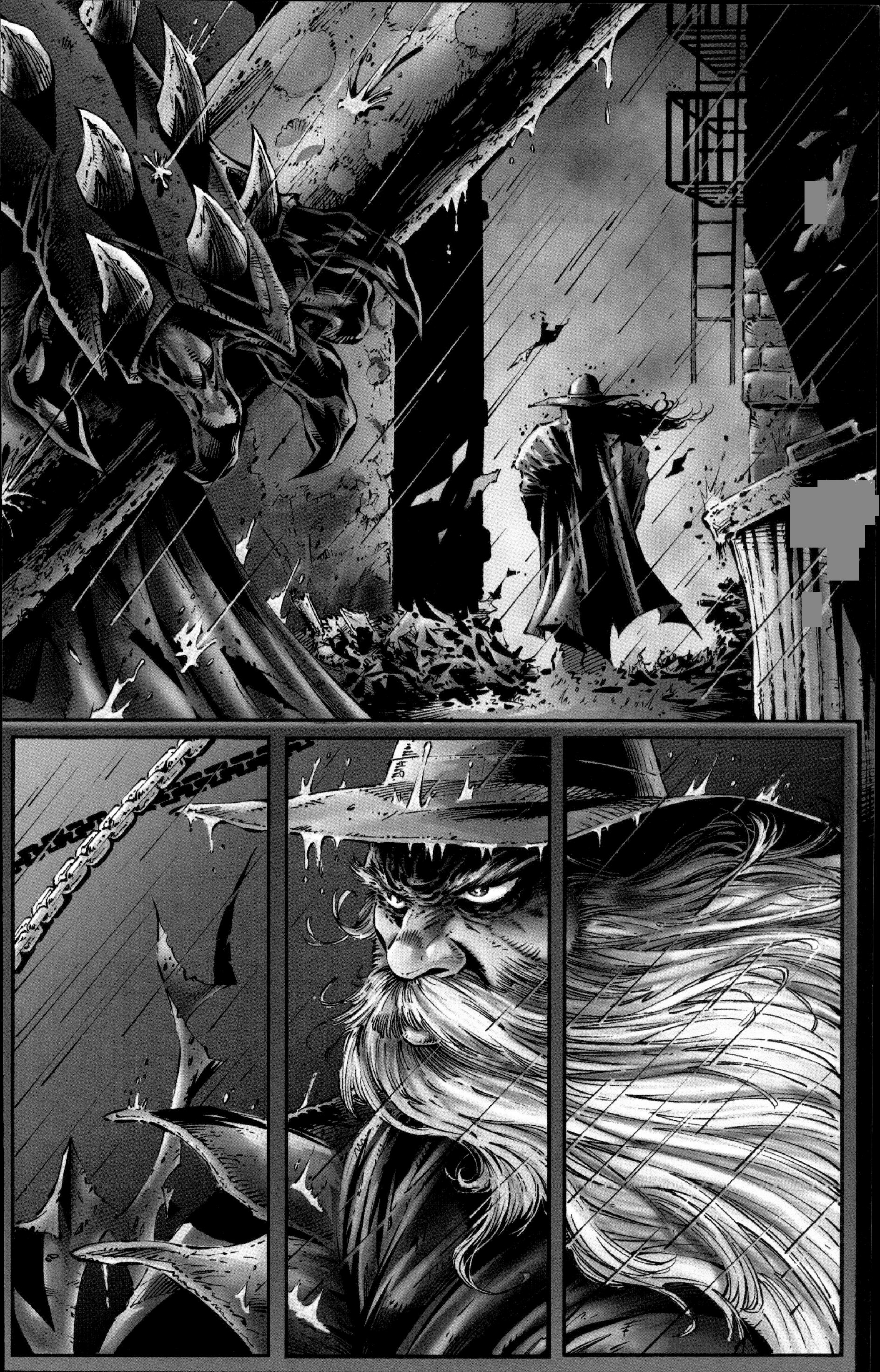

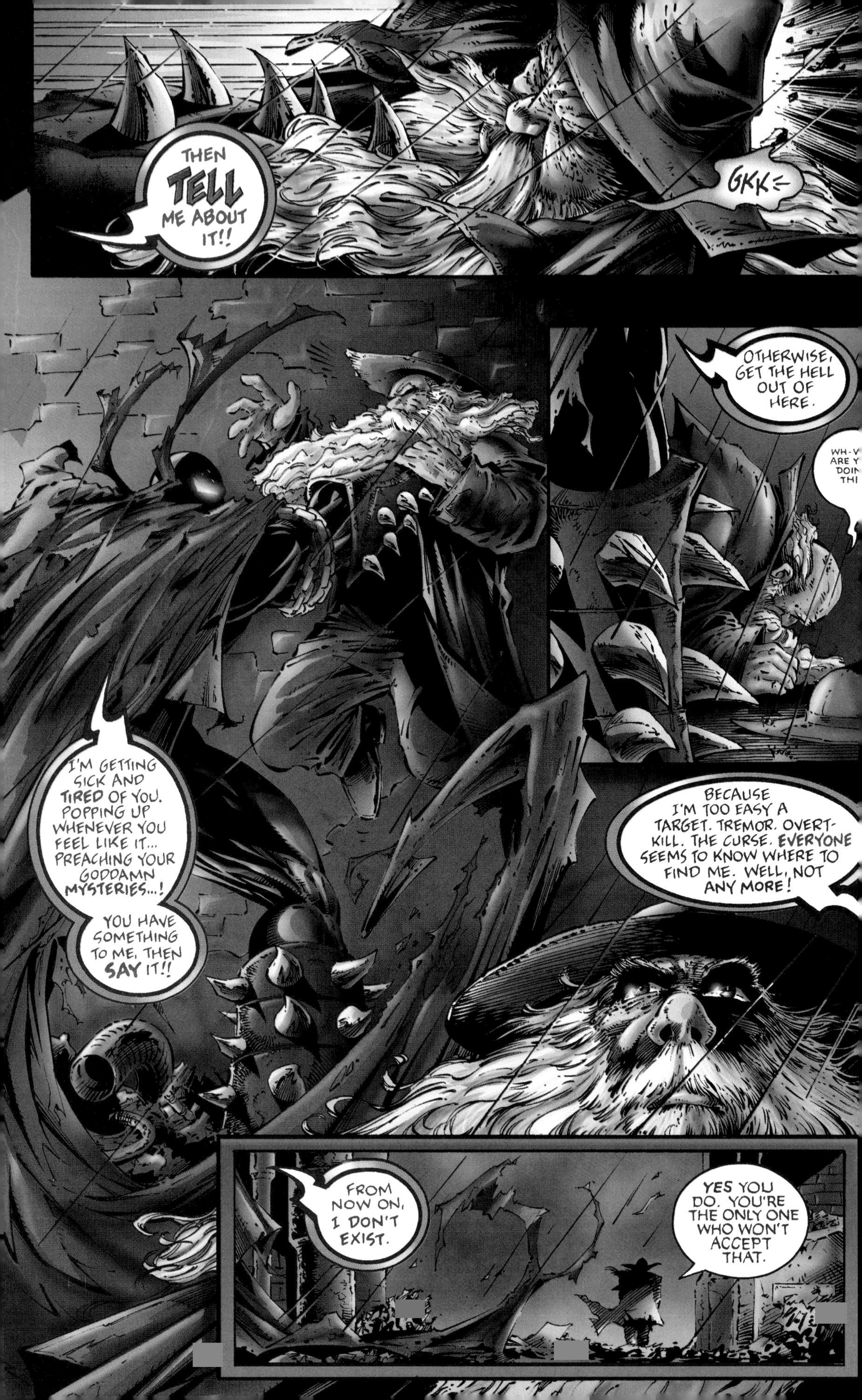
THEN TELL ME ABOUT IT!!
GKK
OTHERWISE, GET THE HELL OUT OF HERE.
I'M GETTING SICK AND TIRED OF YOU. POPPING UP WHENEVER YOU FEEL LIKE IT... PREACHING YOUR GODDAMN MYSTERIES...!
YOU HAVE SOMETHING TO ME, THEN SAY IT!!
BECAUSE I'M TOO EASY A TARGET. TREMOR. OVERT-KILL. THE CURSE. EVERYONE SEEMS TO KNOW WHERE TO FIND ME. WELL, NOT ANY MORE!
FROM NOW ON, I DON'T EXIST.
YES YOU DO. YOU'RE THE ONLY ONE WHO WON'T ACCEPT THAT.

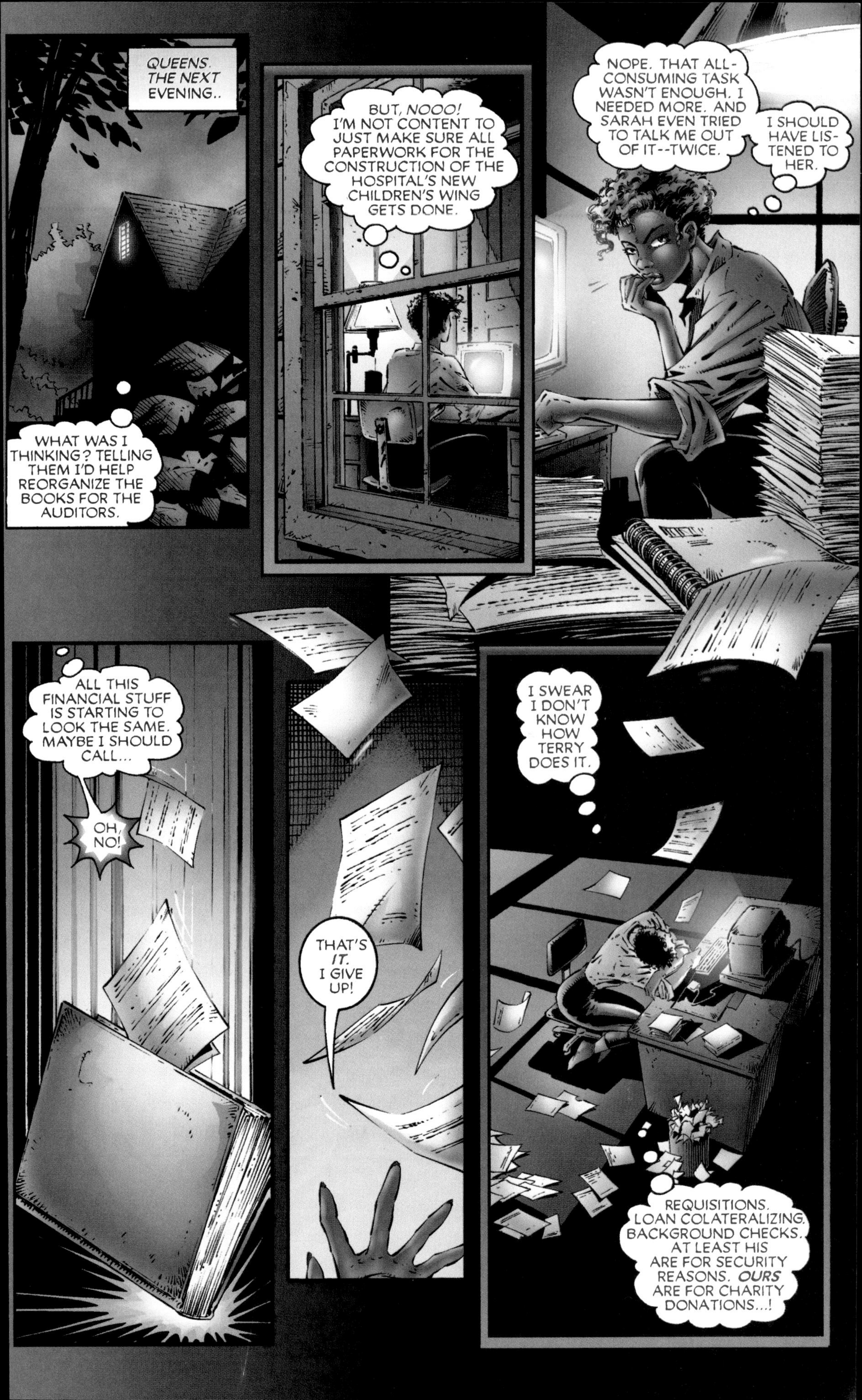
QUEENS. THE NEXT EVENING..
WHAT WAS I THINKING? TELLING THEM I'D HELP REORGANIZE THE BOOKS FOR THE AUDITORS.
BUT, NOOO! I'M NOT CONTENT TO JUST MAKE SURE ALL PAPERWORK FOR THE CONSTRUCTION OF THE HOSPITAL'S NEW CHILDREN'S WING GETS DONE.
NOPE. THAT ALL-CONSUMING TASK WASN'T ENOUGH. I NEEDED MORE. AND SARAH EVEN TRIED TO TALK ME OUT OF IT--TWICE.
I SHOULD HAVE LISTENED TO HER.
ALL THIS FINANCIAL STUFF IS STARTING TO LOOK THE SAME. MAYBE I SHOULD CALL...
OH, NO!
THAT'S IT. I GIVE UP!
I SWEAR I DON'T KNOW HOW TERRY DOES IT.
REQUISITIONS. LOAN COLATERALIZING. BACKGROUND CHECKS. AT LEAST HIS ARE FOR SECURITY REASONS. OURS ARE FOR CHARITY DONATIONS...!

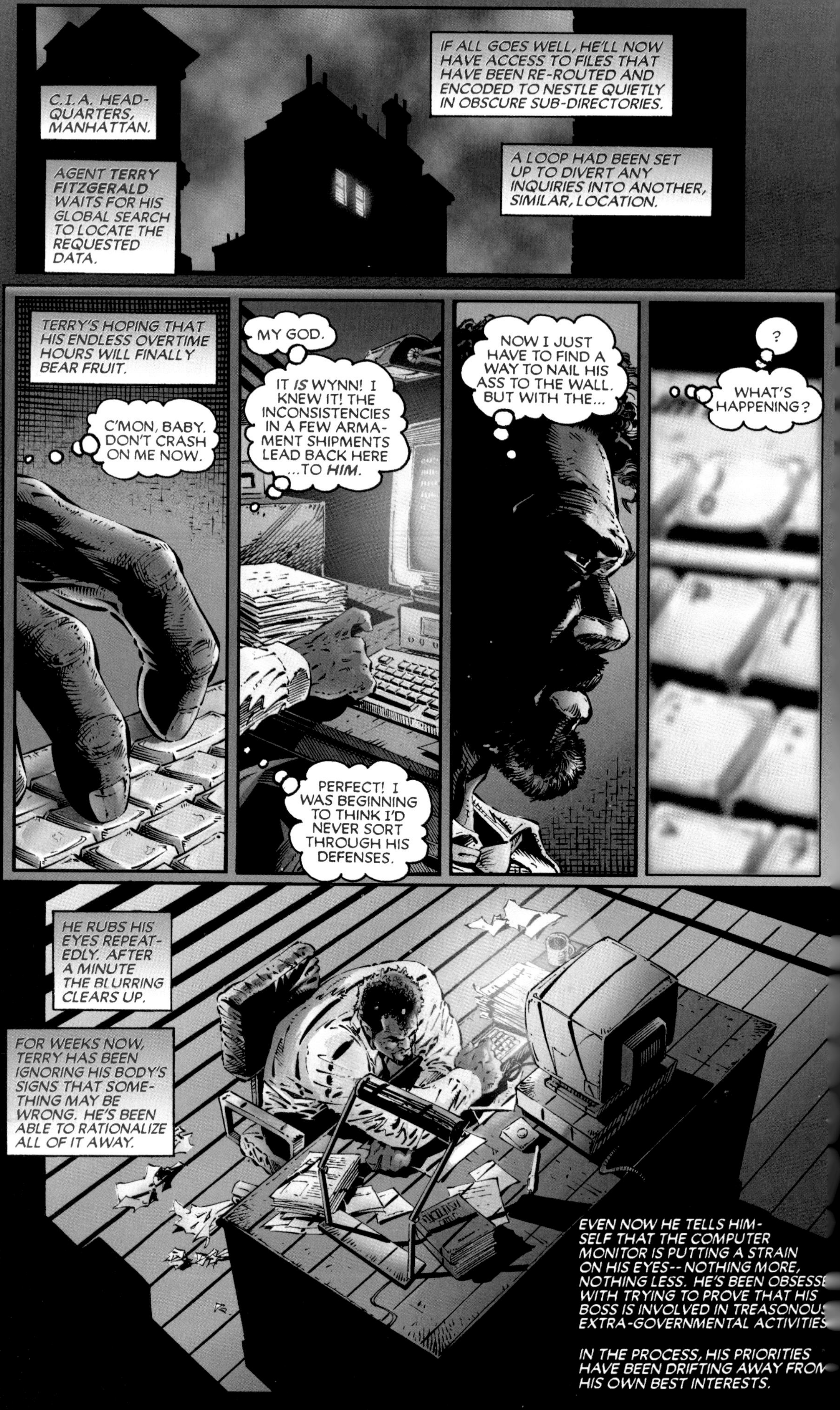

C.I.A. HEAD-QUARTERS, MANHATTAN.
AGENT TERRY FITZGERALD WAITS FOR HIS GLOBAL SEARCH TO LOCATE THE REQUESTED DATA.
IF ALL GOES WELL, HE'LL NOW HAVE ACCESS TO FILES THAT HAVE BEEN RE-ROUTED AND ENCODED TO NESTLE QUIETLY IN OBSCURE SUB-DIRECTORIES.
A LOOP HAD BEEN SET UP TO DIVERT ANY INQUIRIES INTO ANOTHER, SIMILAR, LOCATION.
TERRY'S HOPING THAT HIS ENDLESS OVERTIME HOURS WILL FINALLY BEAR FRUIT.
C'MON, BABY. DON'T CRASH ON ME NOW.
MY GOD.
IT *IS* WYNN! I KNEW IT! THE INCONSISTENCIES IN A FEW ARMA-MENT SHIPMENTS LEAD BACK HERE ...TO *HIM*.
PERFECT! I WAS BEGINNING TO THINK I'D NEVER SORT THROUGH HIS DEFENSES.
NOW I JUST HAVE TO FIND A WAY TO NAIL HIS ASS TO THE WALL. BUT WITH THE...
?
WHAT'S HAPPENING?
HE RUBS HIS EYES REPEAT-EDLY. AFTER A MINUTE THE BLURRING CLEARS UP.
FOR WEEKS NOW, TERRY HAS BEEN IGNORING HIS BODY'S SIGNS THAT SOME-THING MAY BE WRONG. HE'S BEEN ABLE TO RATIONALIZE ALL OF IT AWAY.
EVEN NOW HE TELLS HIM-SELF THAT THE COMPUTER MONITOR IS PUTTING A STRAIN ON HIS EYES-- NOTHING MORE, NOTHING LESS. HE'S BEEN OBSESSE WITH TRYING TO PROVE THAT HIS BOSS IS INVOLVED IN TREASONOU EXTRA-GOVERNMENTAL ACTIVITIES
IN THE PROCESS, HIS PRIORITIES HAVE BEEN DRIFTING AWAY FROM HIS OWN BEST INTERESTS.

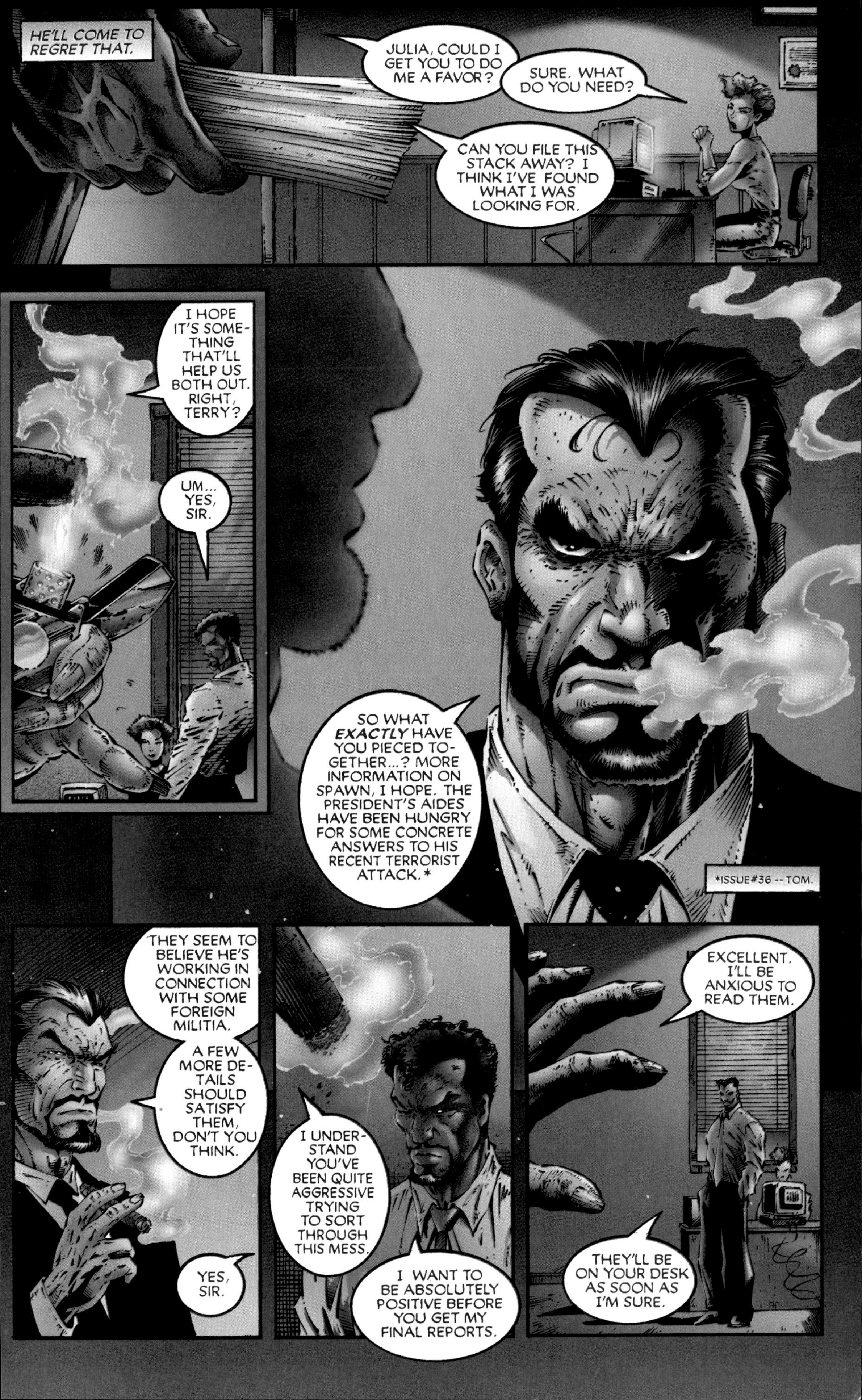
HE'LL COME TO REGRET THAT.
JULIA, COULD I GET YOU TO DO ME A FAVOR?
SURE. WHAT DO YOU NEED?
CAN YOU FILE THIS STACK AWAY? I THINK I'VE FOUND WHAT I WAS LOOKING FOR.
I HOPE IT'S SOMETHING THAT'LL HELP US BOTH OUT. RIGHT, TERRY?
UM... YES, SIR.
SO WHAT EXACTLY HAVE YOU PIECED TOGETHER...? MORE INFORMATION ON SPAWN, I HOPE. THE PRESIDENT'S AIDES HAVE BEEN HUNGRY FOR SOME CONCRETE ANSWERS TO HIS RECENT TERRORIST ATTACK.*
*ISSUE#36 -- TOM.
THEY SEEM TO BELIEVE HE'S WORKING IN CONNECTION WITH SOME FOREIGN MILITIA.
A FEW MORE DETAILS SHOULD SATISFY THEM, DON'T YOU THINK.
YES, SIR.
I UNDERSTAND YOU'VE BEEN QUITE AGGRESSIVE TRYING TO SORT THROUGH THIS MESS.
I WANT TO BE ABSOLUTELY POSITIVE BEFORE YOU GET MY FINAL REPORTS.
EXCELLENT. I'LL BE ANXIOUS TO READ THEM.
THEY'LL BE ON YOUR DESK AS SOON AS I'M SURE.

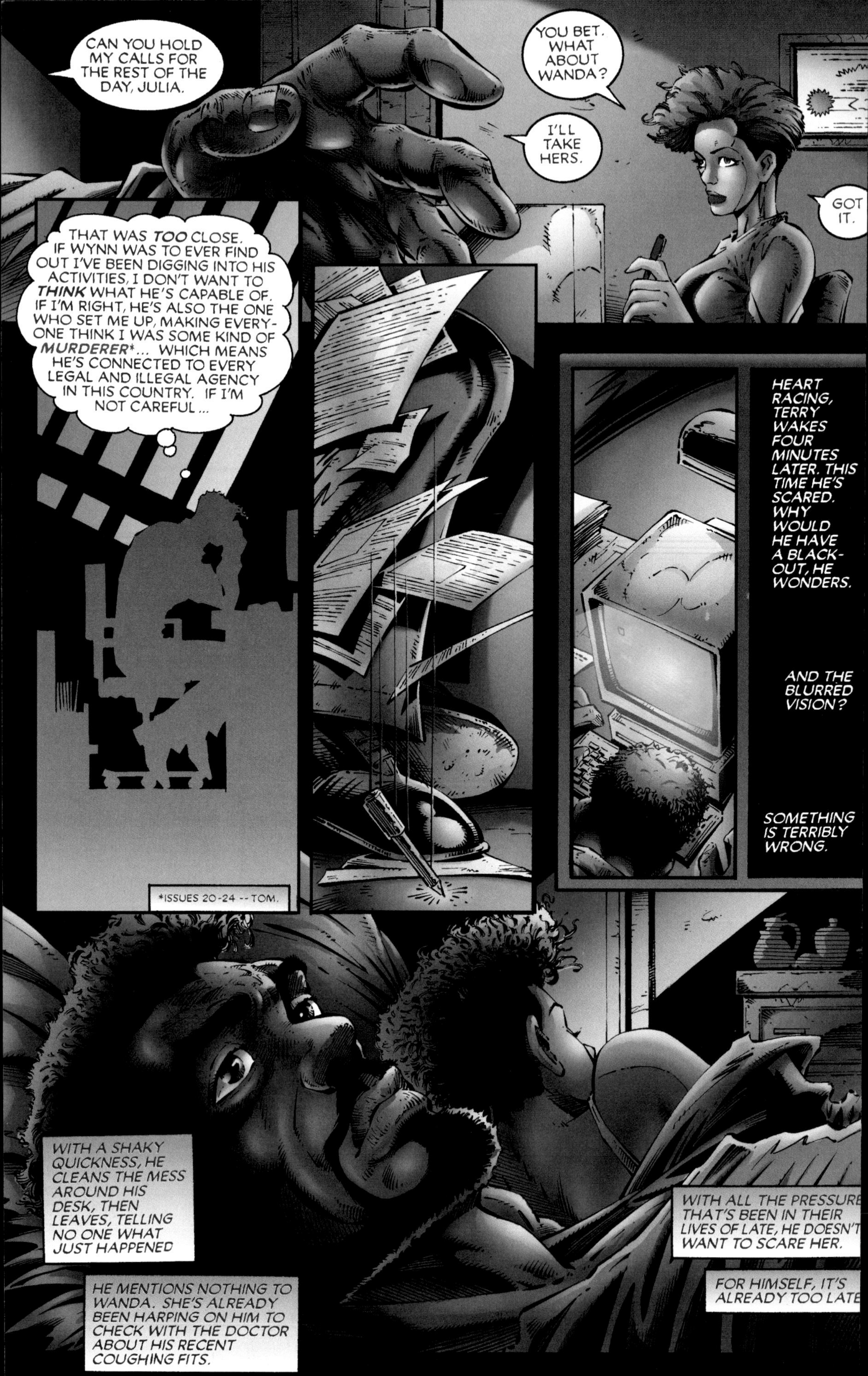

CAN YOU HOLD MY CALLS FOR THE REST OF THE DAY, JULIA.
YOU BET. WHAT ABOUT WANDA?
I'LL TAKE HERS.
GOT IT.
THAT WAS TOO CLOSE. IF WYNN WAS TO EVER FIND OUT I'VE BEEN DIGGING INTO HIS ACTIVITIES, I DON'T WANT TO THINK WHAT HE'S CAPABLE OF. IF I'M RIGHT, HE'S ALSO THE ONE WHO SET ME UP, MAKING EVERY-ONE THINK I WAS SOME KIND OF MURDERER*... WHICH MEANS HE'S CONNECTED TO EVERY LEGAL AND ILLEGAL AGENCY IN THIS COUNTRY. IF I'M NOT CAREFUL...
*ISSUES 20-24 -- TOM.
HEART RACING, TERRY WAKES FOUR MINUTES LATER. THIS TIME HE'S SCARED. WHY WOULD HE HAVE A BLACK-OUT, HE WONDERS.
AND THE BLURRED VISION?
SOMETHING IS TERRIBLY WRONG.
WITH A SHAKY QUICKNESS, HE CLEANS THE MESS AROUND HIS DESK, THEN LEAVES, TELLING NO ONE WHAT JUST HAPPENED
HE MENTIONS NOTHING TO WANDA. SHE'S ALREADY BEEN HARPING ON HIM TO CHECK WITH THE DOCTOR ABOUT HIS RECENT COUGHING FITS.
WITH ALL THE PRESSURE THAT'S BEEN IN THEIR LIVES OF LATE, HE DOESN'T WANT TO SCARE HER.
FOR HIMSELF, IT'S ALREADY TOO LATE

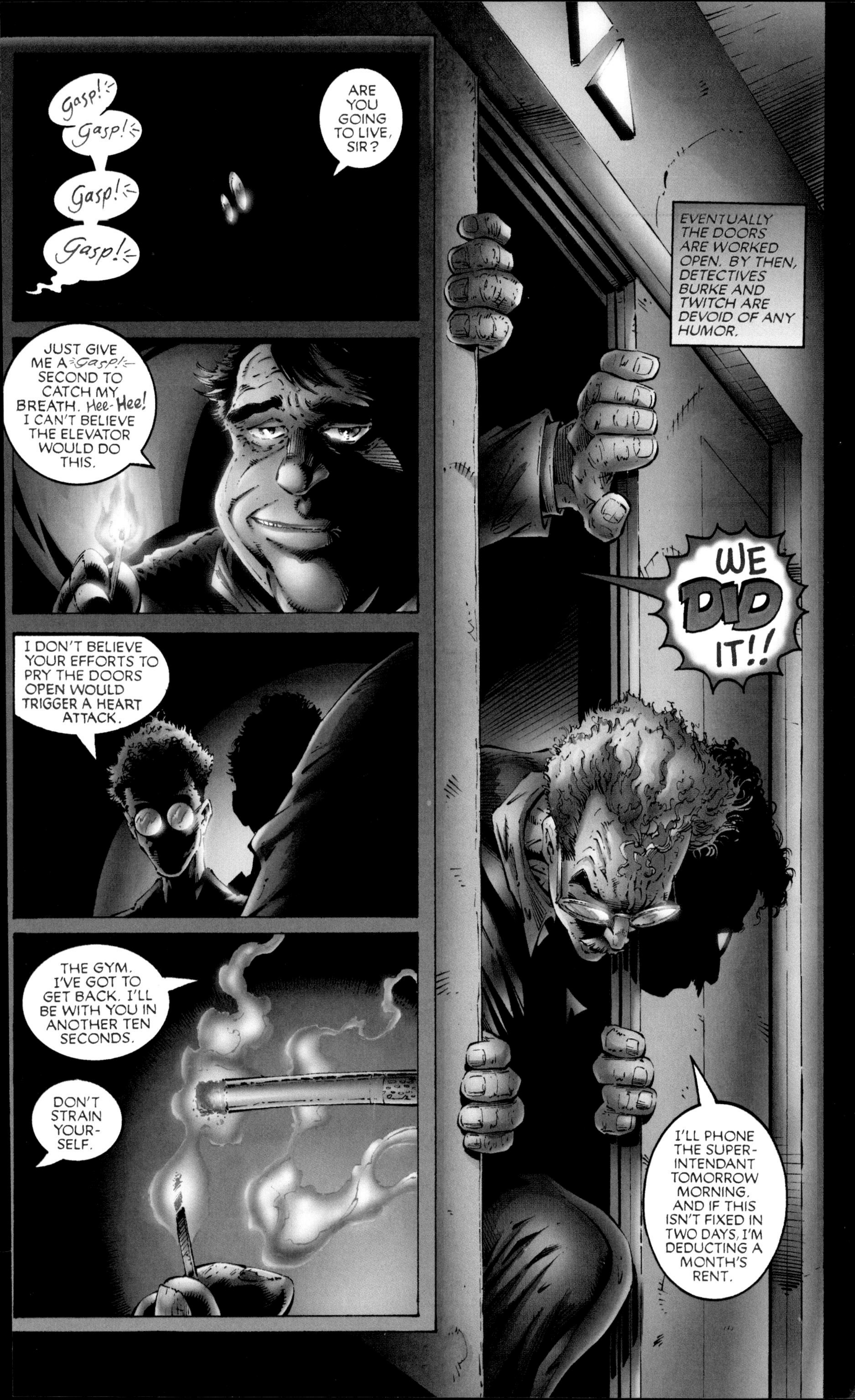
Gasp! Gasp! Gasp! Gasp!
ARE YOU GOING TO LIVE, SIR?
JUST GIVE ME A Gasp! SECOND TO CATCH MY BREATH. Hee-Hee! I CAN'T BELIEVE THE ELEVATOR WOULD DO THIS.
I DON'T BELIEVE YOUR EFFORTS TO PRY THE DOORS OPEN WOULD TRIGGER A HEART ATTACK.
THE GYM. I'VE GOT TO GET BACK. I'LL BE WITH YOU IN ANOTHER TEN SECONDS.
DON'T STRAIN YOURSELF.
EVENTUALLY THE DOORS ARE WORKED OPEN. BY THEN, DETECTIVES BURKE AND TWITCH ARE DEVOID OF ANY HUMOR.
WE DID IT!!
I'LL PHONE THE SUPERINTENDANT TOMORROW MORNING. AND IF THIS ISN'T FIXED IN TWO DAYS, I'M DEDUCTING A MONTH'S RENT.

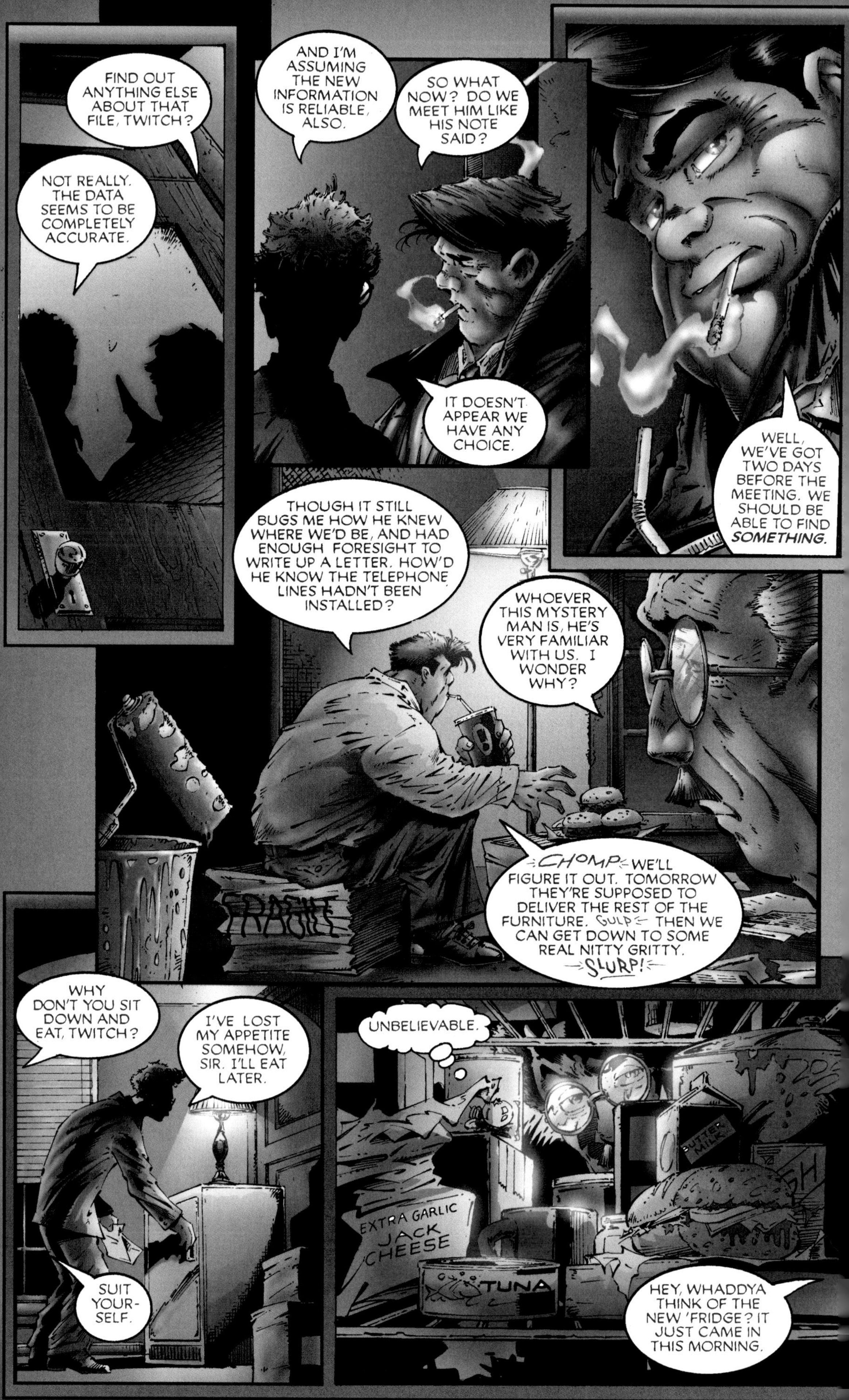
FIND OUT ANYTHING ELSE ABOUT THAT FILE, TWITCH?
NOT REALLY. THE DATA SEEMS TO BE COMPLETELY ACCURATE.
AND I'M ASSUMING THE NEW INFORMATION IS RELIABLE, ALSO.
SO WHAT NOW? DO WE MEET HIM LIKE HIS NOTE SAID?
IT DOESN'T APPEAR WE HAVE ANY CHOICE.
WELL, WE'VE GOT TWO DAYS BEFORE THE MEETING. WE SHOULD BE ABLE TO FIND SOMETHING.
THOUGH IT STILL BUGS ME HOW HE KNEW WHERE WE'D BE, AND HAD ENOUGH FORESIGHT TO WRITE UP A LETTER. HOW'D HE KNOW THE TELEPHONE LINES HADN'T BEEN INSTALLED?
WHOEVER THIS MYSTERY MAN IS, HE'S VERY FAMILIAR WITH US. I WONDER WHY?
CHOMP WE'LL FIGURE IT OUT. TOMORROW THEY'RE SUPPOSED TO DELIVER THE REST OF THE FURNITURE. GULP THEN WE CAN GET DOWN TO SOME REAL NITTY GRITTY. SLURP!
FRAGILE
WHY DON'T YOU SIT DOWN AND EAT, TWITCH?
I'VE LOST MY APPETITE SOMEHOW, SIR. I'LL EAT LATER.
SUIT YOURSELF.
UNBELIEVABLE.
EXTRA GARLIC JACK CHEESE
TUNA
BUTTER MILK
HEY, WHADDYA THINK OF THE NEW 'FRIDGE? IT JUST CAME IN THIS MORNING.

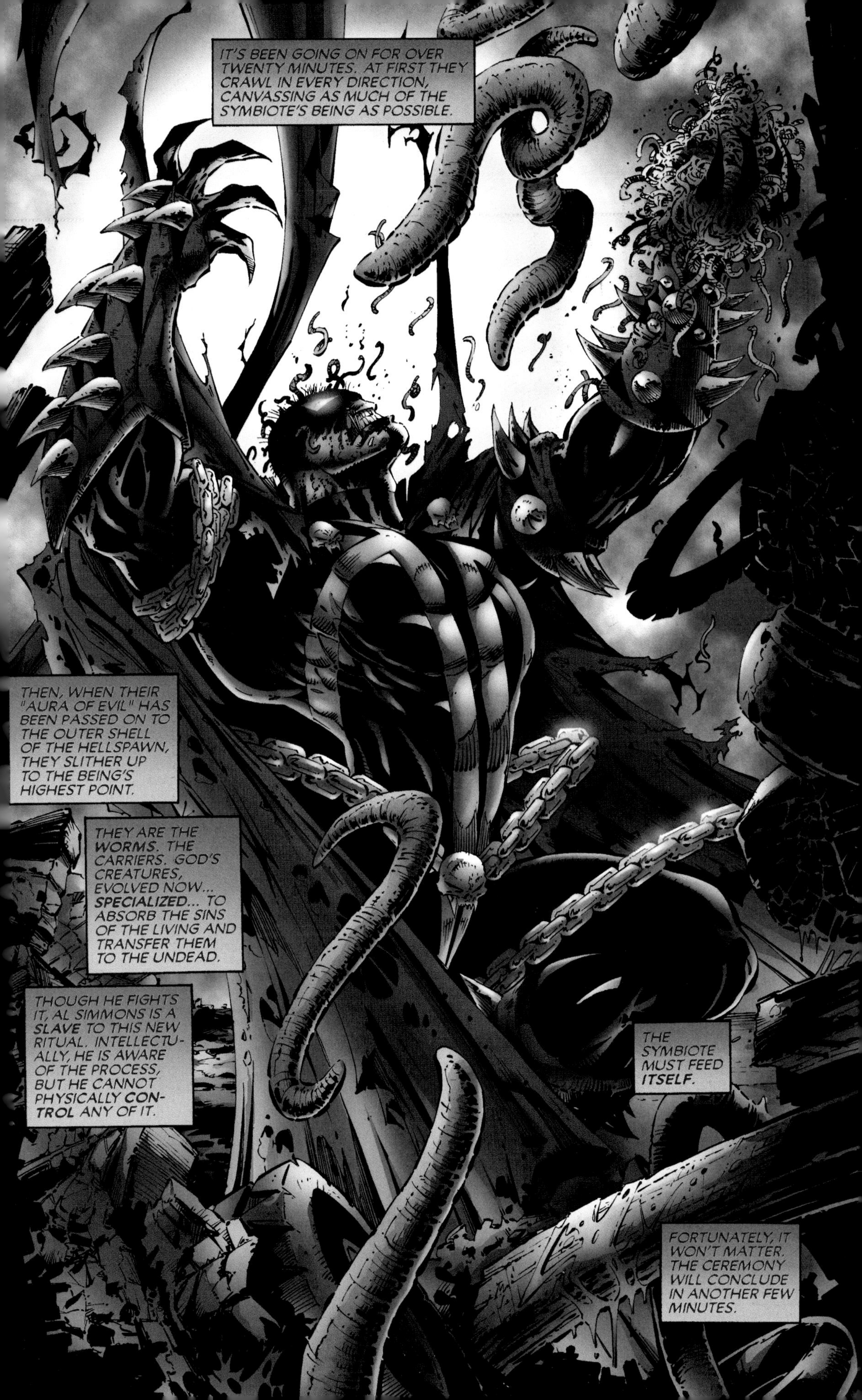
IT'S BEEN GOING ON FOR OVER TWENTY MINUTES. AT FIRST THEY CRAWL IN EVERY DIRECTION, CANVASSING AS MUCH OF THE SYMBIOTE'S BEING AS POSSIBLE.
THEN, WHEN THEIR "AURA OF EVIL" HAS BEEN PASSED ON TO THE OUTER SHELL OF THE HELLSPAWN, THEY SLITHER UP TO THE BEING'S HIGHEST POINT.
THEY ARE THE WORMS. THE CARRIERS. GOD'S CREATURES, EVOLVED NOW... SPECIALIZED... TO ABSORB THE SINS OF THE LIVING AND TRANSFER THEM TO THE UNDEAD.
THOUGH HE FIGHTS IT, AL SIMMONS IS A SLAVE TO THIS NEW RITUAL. INTELLECTUALLY, HE IS AWARE OF THE PROCESS, BUT HE CANNOT PHYSICALLY CONTROL ANY OF IT.
THE SYMBIOTE MUST FEED ITSELF.
FORTUNATELY, IT WON'T MATTER. THE CEREMONY WILL CONCLUDE IN ANOTHER FEW MINUTES.

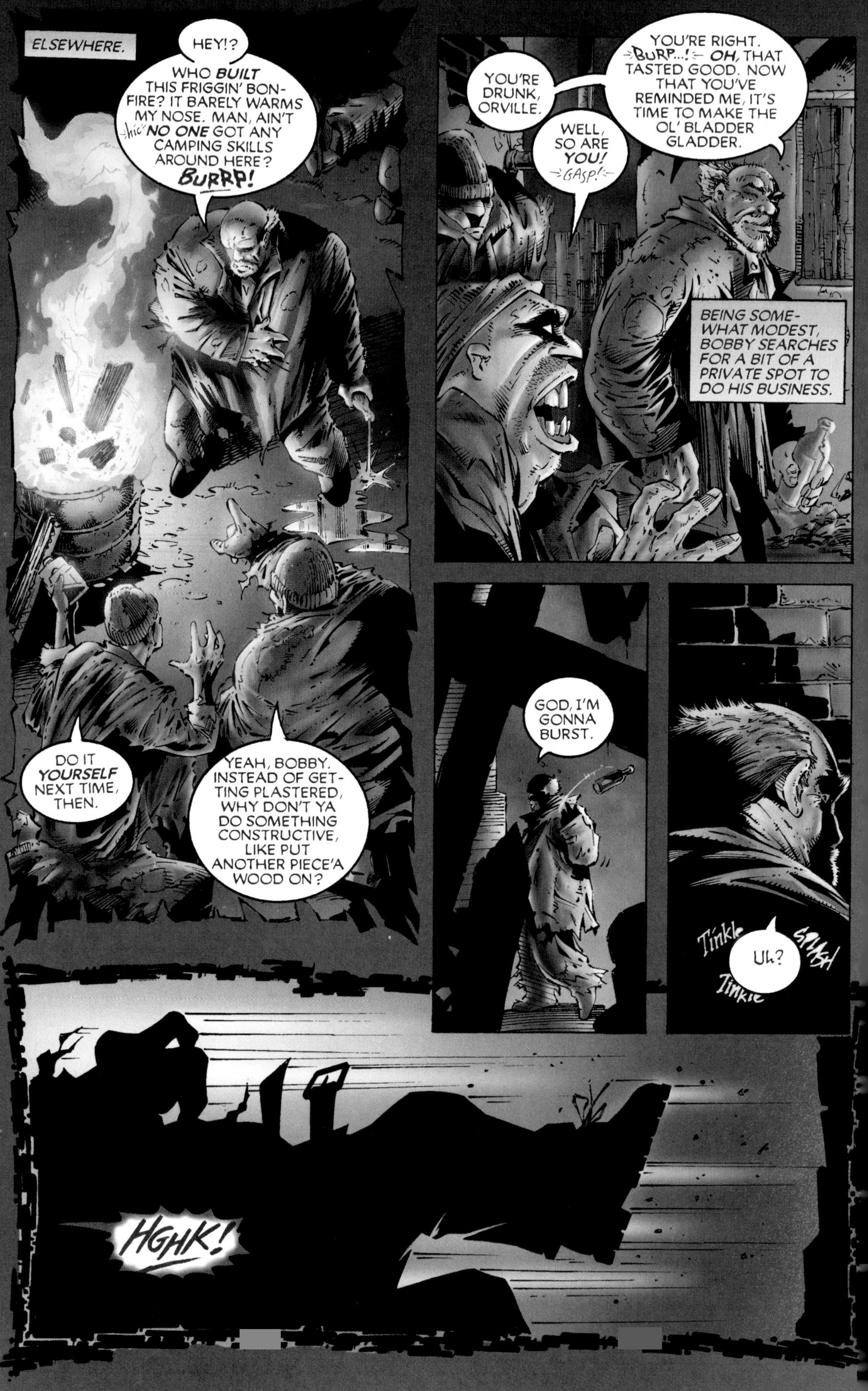
ELSEWHERE.
HEY!?
WHO BUILT THIS FRIGGIN' BONFIRE? IT BARELY WARMS MY NOSE. MAN, AIN'T *hic* NO ONE GOT ANY CAMPING SKILLS AROUND HERE? BURRP!
DO IT YOURSELF NEXT TIME, THEN.
YEAH, BOBBY. INSTEAD OF GETTING PLASTERED, WHY DON'T YA DO SOMETHING CONSTRUCTIVE, LIKE PUT ANOTHER PIECE'A WOOD ON?
YOU'RE DRUNK, ORVILLE.
WELL, SO ARE YOU! GASP!
YOU'RE RIGHT. BURP...! OH, THAT TASTED GOOD. NOW THAT YOU'VE REMINDED ME, IT'S TIME TO MAKE THE OL' BLADDER GLADDER.
BEING SOMEWHAT MODEST, BOBBY SEARCHES FOR A BIT OF A PRIVATE SPOT TO DO HIS BUSINESS.
GOD, I'M GONNA BURST.
Tinkle
SPLASH
Tinkle
Uh?
HGHK!

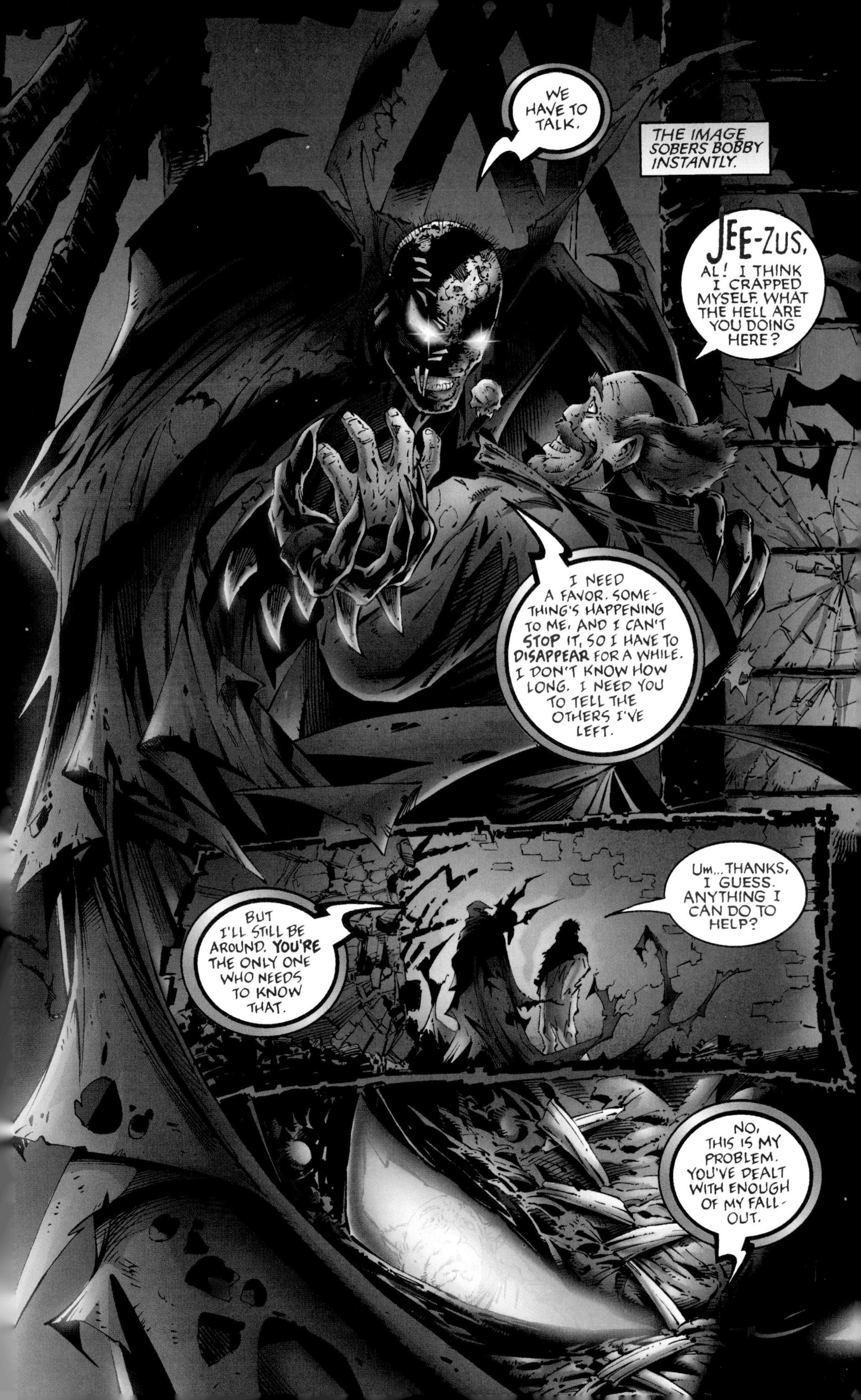
WE HAVE TO TALK.
THE IMAGE SOBERS BOBBY INSTANTLY.
JEE-ZUS, AL! I THINK I CRAPPED MYSELF. WHAT THE HELL ARE YOU DOING HERE?
I NEED A FAVOR. SOMETHING'S HAPPENING TO ME, AND I CAN'T STOP IT, SO I HAVE TO DISAPPEAR FOR A WHILE. I DON'T KNOW HOW LONG. I NEED YOU TO TELL THE OTHERS I'VE LEFT.
BUT I'LL STILL BE AROUND. YOU'RE THE ONLY ONE WHO NEEDS TO KNOW THAT.
Um... THANKS, I GUESS. ANYTHING I CAN DO TO HELP?
NO, THIS IS MY PROBLEM. YOU'VE DEALT WITH ENOUGH OF MY FALL-OUT.

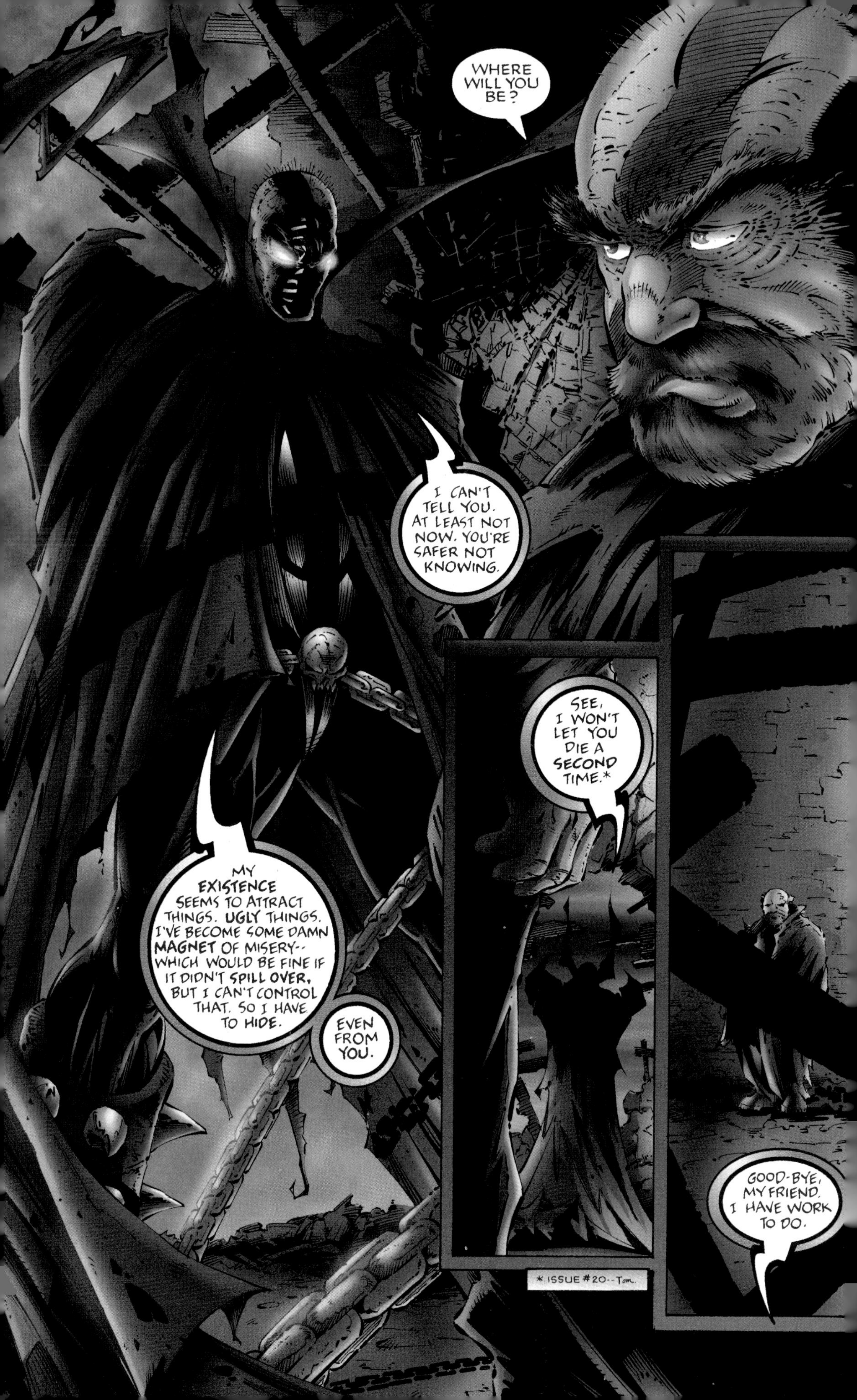
WHERE WILL YOU BE?
I CAN'T TELL YOU. AT LEAST NOT NOW. YOU'RE SAFER NOT KNOWING.
MY EXISTENCE SEEMS TO ATTRACT THINGS. UGLY THINGS. I'VE BECOME SOME DAMN MAGNET OF MISERY-- WHICH WOULD BE FINE IF IT DIDN'T SPILL OVER, BUT I CAN'T CONTROL THAT. SO I HAVE TO HIDE.
EVEN FROM YOU.
SEE, I WON'T LET YOU DIE A SECOND TIME.*
*ISSUE #20--Tom.
GOOD-BYE, MY FRIEND. I HAVE WORK TO DO.

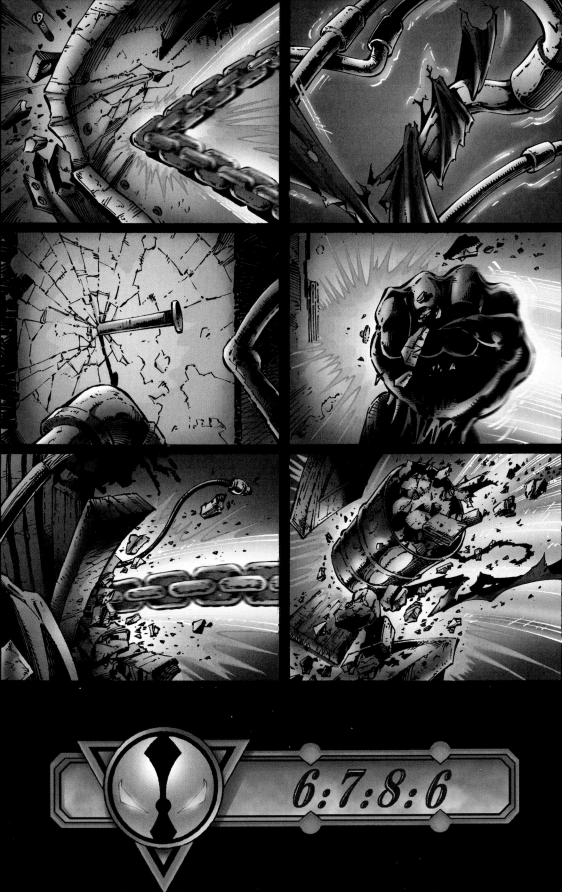

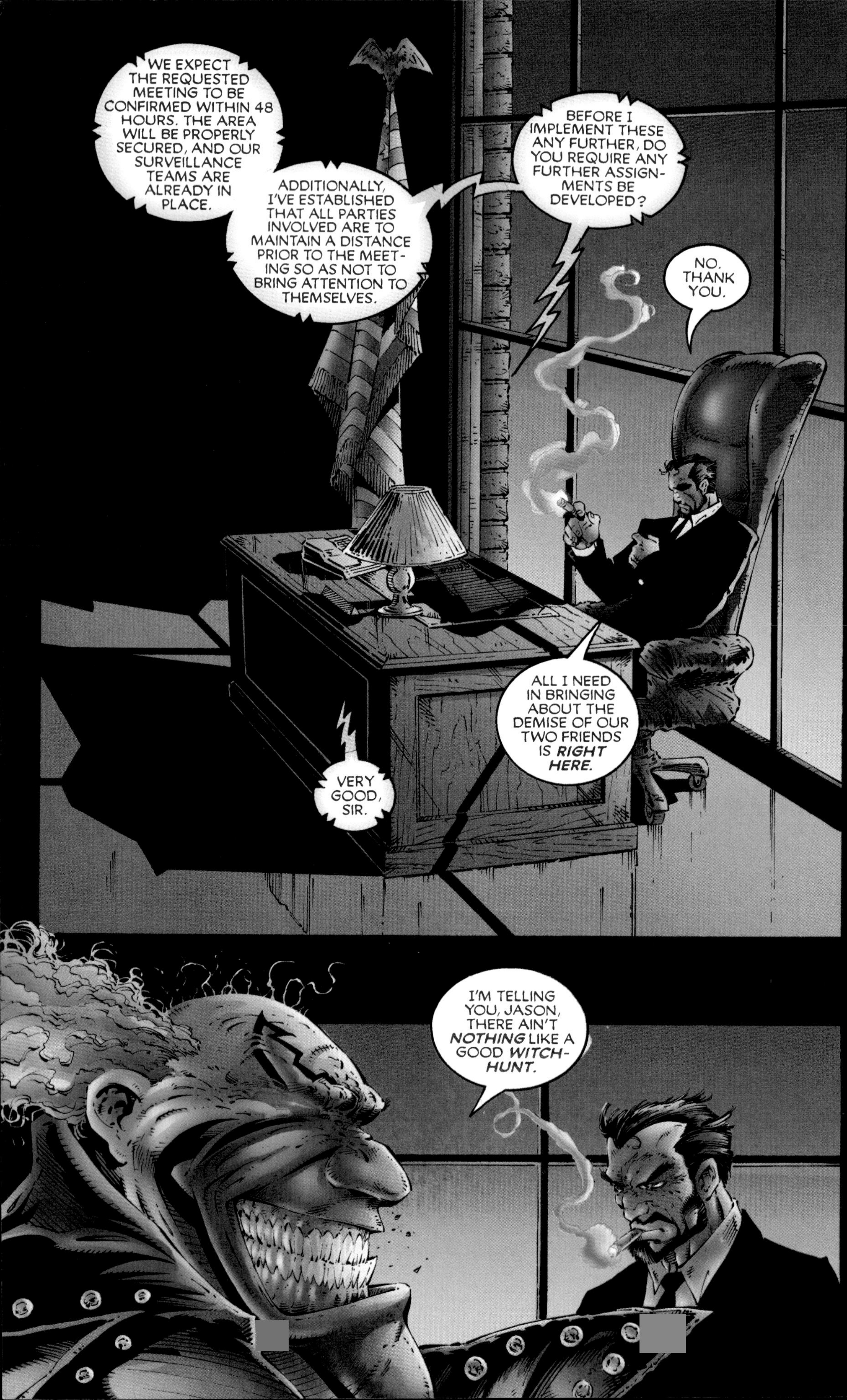
WE EXPECT THE REQUESTED MEETING TO BE CONFIRMED WITHIN 48 HOURS. THE AREA WILL BE PROPERLY SECURED, AND OUR SURVEILLANCE TEAMS ARE ALREADY IN PLACE.
ADDITIONALLY, I'VE ESTABLISHED THAT ALL PARTIES INVOLVED ARE TO MAINTAIN A DISTANCE PRIOR TO THE MEET-ING SO AS NOT TO BRING ATTENTION TO THEMSELVES.
BEFORE I IMPLEMENT THESE ANY FURTHER, DO YOU REQUIRE ANY FURTHER ASSIGN-MENTS BE DEVELOPED?
NO. THANK YOU.
ALL I NEED IN BRINGING ABOUT THE DEMISE OF OUR TWO FRIENDS IS ***RIGHT HERE.***
VERY GOOD, SIR.
I'M TELLING YOU, JASON, THERE AIN'T ***NOTHING*** LIKE A GOOD ***WITCH-HUNT.***

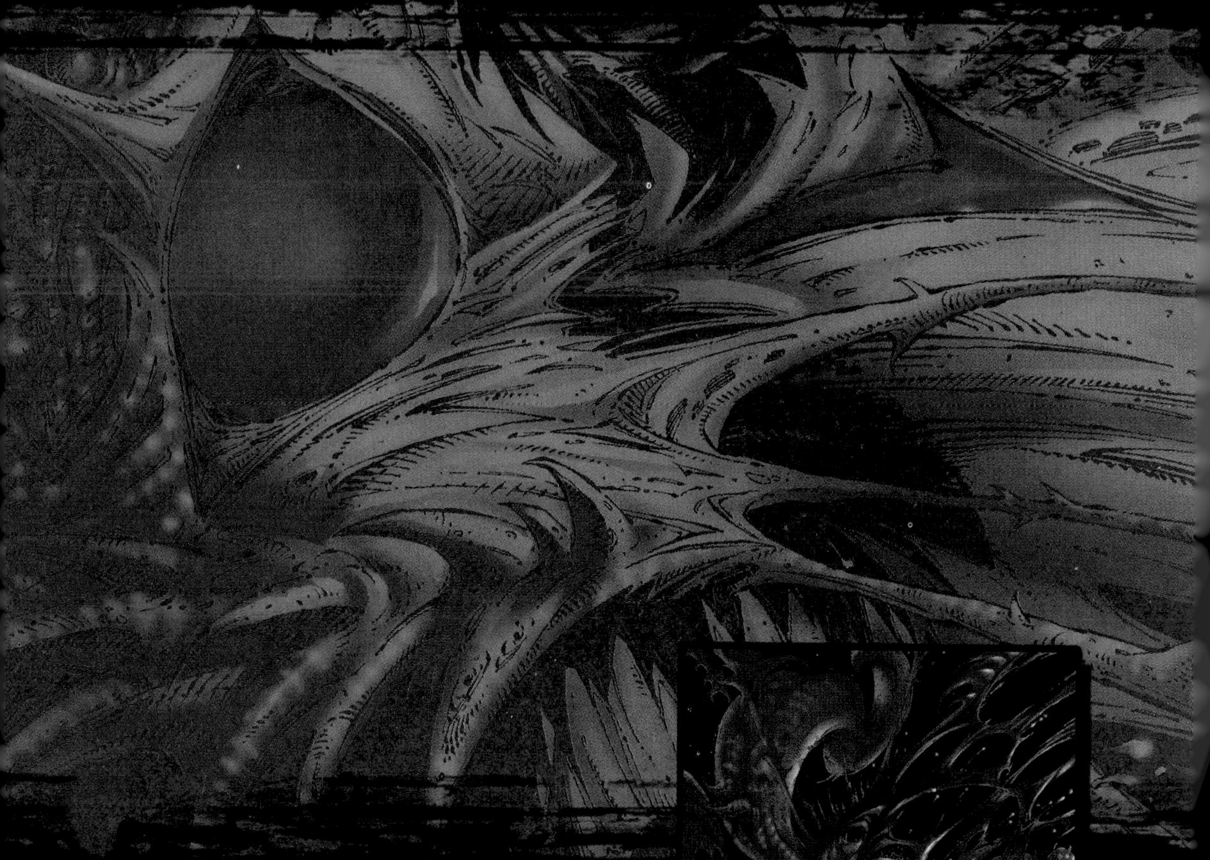

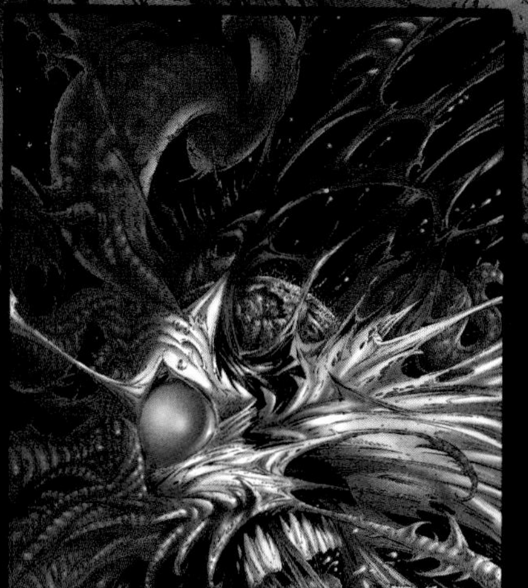

ISSUE FORTY-NINE

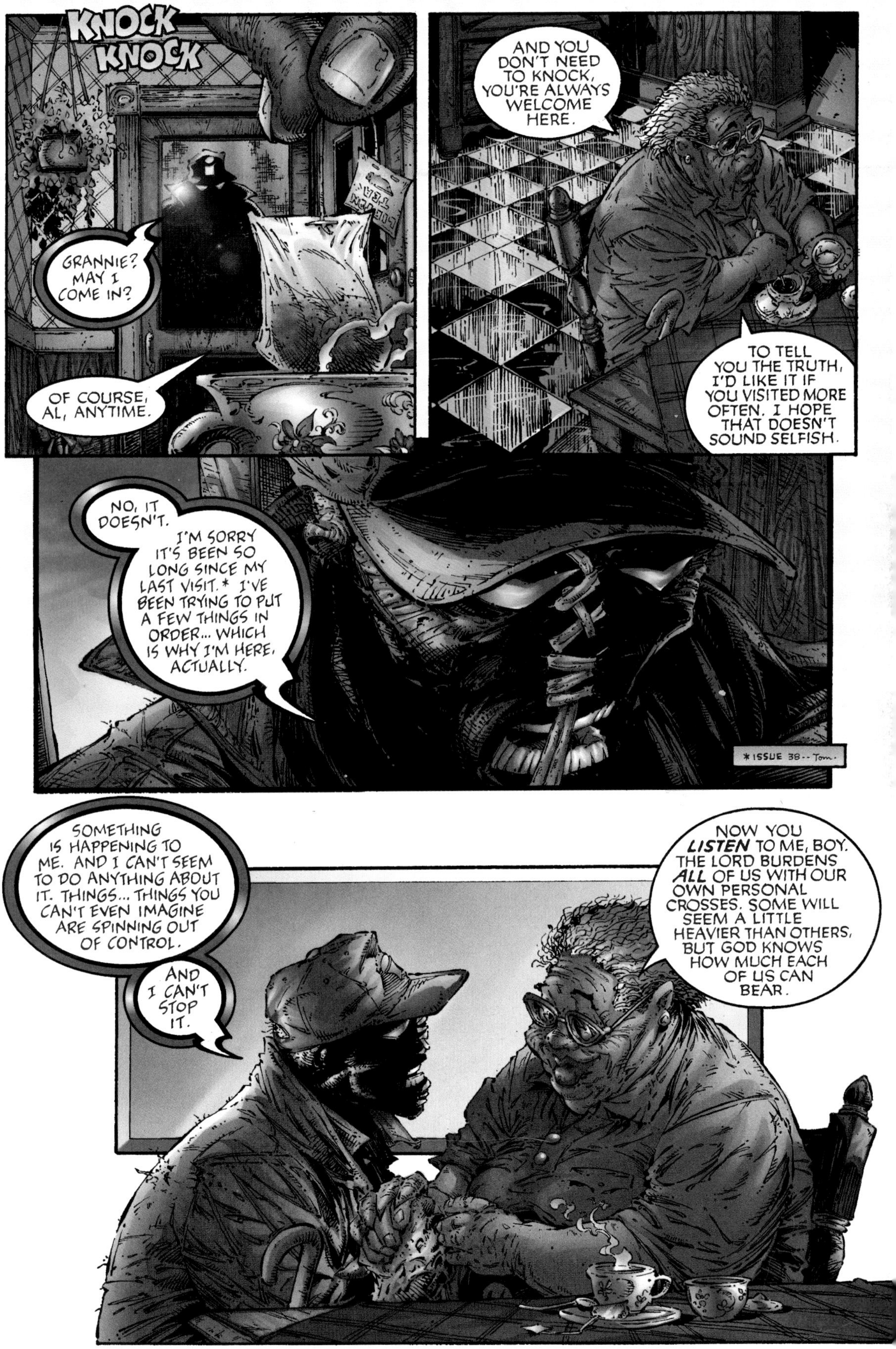
KNOCK KNOCK
GRANNIE? MAY I COME IN?
OF COURSE, AL, ANYTIME.
AND YOU DON'T NEED TO KNOCK, YOU'RE ALWAYS WELCOME HERE.
TO TELL YOU THE TRUTH, I'D LIKE IT IF YOU VISITED MORE OFTEN. I HOPE THAT DOESN'T SOUND SELFISH.
NO, IT DOESN'T.
I'M SORRY IT'S BEEN SO LONG SINCE MY LAST VISIT.* I'VE BEEN TRYING TO PUT A FEW THINGS IN ORDER... WHICH IS WHY I'M HERE, ACTUALLY.
*ISSUE 38 --Tom-
SOMETHING IS HAPPENING TO ME. AND I CAN'T SEEM TO DO ANYTHING ABOUT IT. THINGS... THINGS YOU CAN'T EVEN IMAGINE ARE SPINNING OUT OF CONTROL.
AND I CAN'T STOP IT.
NOW YOU LISTEN TO ME, BOY. THE LORD BURDENS ALL OF US WITH OUR OWN PERSONAL CROSSES. SOME WILL SEEM A LITTLE HEAVIER THAN OTHERS, BUT GOD KNOWS HOW MUCH EACH OF US CAN BEAR.

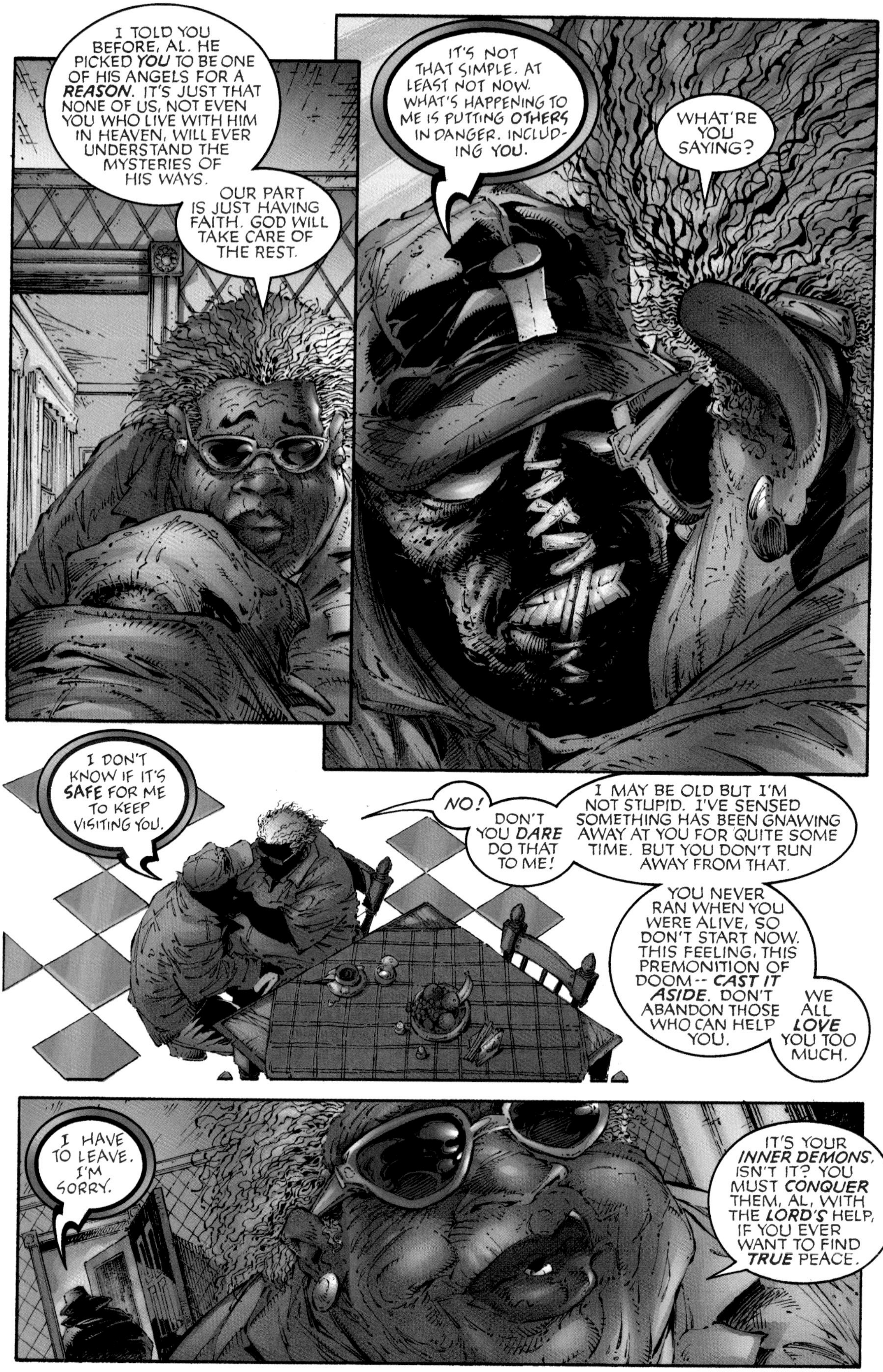
I TOLD YOU BEFORE, AL. HE PICKED YOU TO BE ONE OF HIS ANGELS FOR A REASON. IT'S JUST THAT NONE OF US, NOT EVEN YOU WHO LIVE WITH HIM IN HEAVEN, WILL EVER UNDERSTAND THE MYSTERIES OF HIS WAYS.
OUR PART IS JUST HAVING FAITH. GOD WILL TAKE CARE OF THE REST.
IT'S NOT THAT SIMPLE. AT LEAST NOT NOW. WHAT'S HAPPENING TO ME IS PUTTING OTHERS IN DANGER. INCLUDING YOU.
WHAT'RE YOU SAYING?
I DON'T KNOW IF IT'S SAFE FOR ME TO KEEP VISITING YOU.
NO!
DON'T YOU DARE DO THAT TO ME!
I MAY BE OLD BUT I'M NOT STUPID. I'VE SENSED SOMETHING HAS BEEN GNAWING AWAY AT YOU FOR QUITE SOME TIME. BUT YOU DON'T RUN AWAY FROM THAT.
YOU NEVER RAN WHEN YOU WERE ALIVE, SO DON'T START NOW. THIS FEELING, THIS PREMONITION OF DOOM-- CAST IT ASIDE. DON'T ABANDON THOSE WHO CAN HELP YOU.
WE ALL LOVE YOU TOO MUCH.
I HAVE TO LEAVE. I'M SORRY.
IT'S YOUR INNER DEMONS, ISN'T IT? YOU MUST CONQUER THEM, AL, WITH THE LORD'S HELP, IF YOU EVER WANT TO FIND TRUE PEACE.

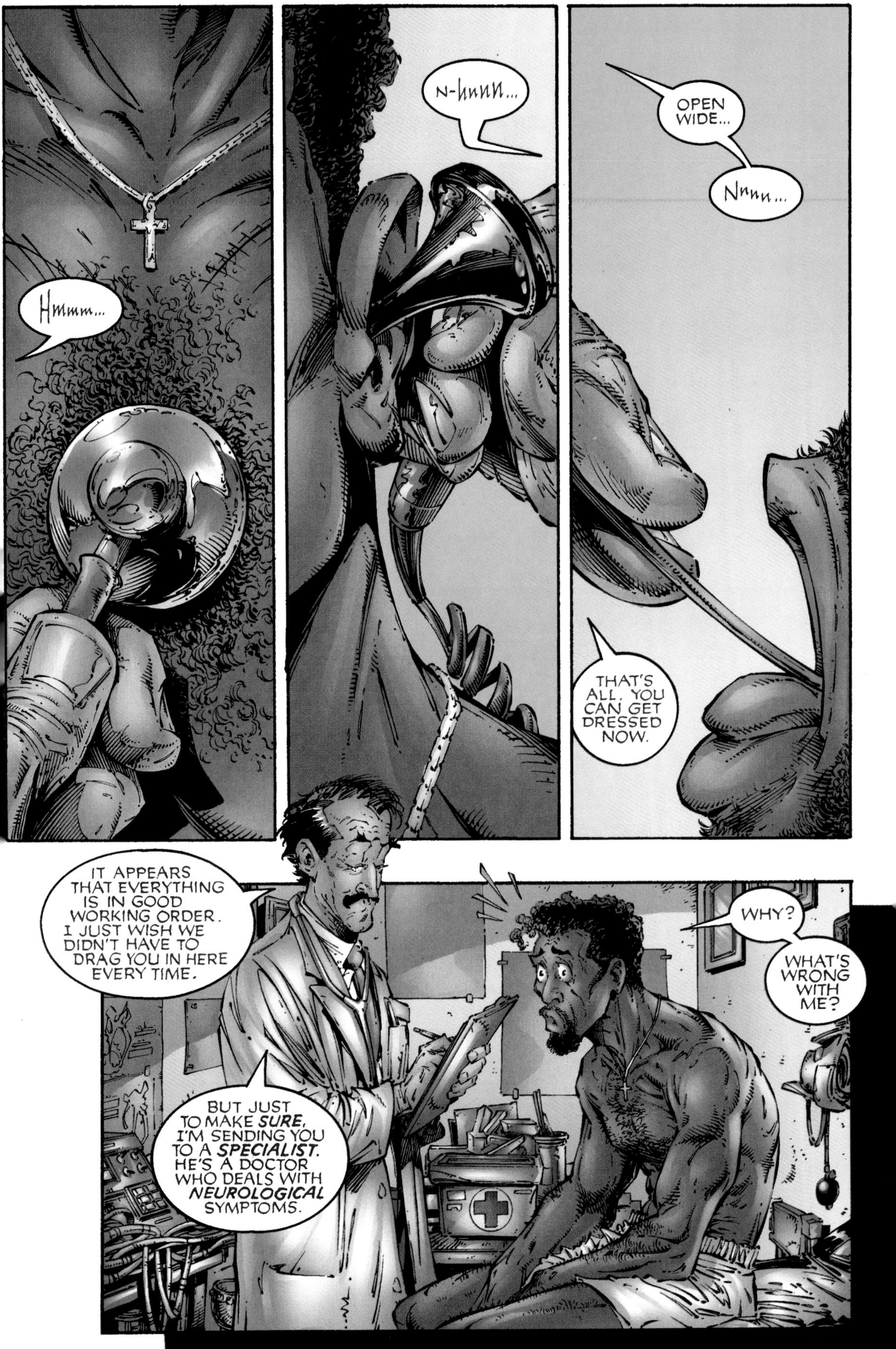
Hmmm...
N-hnnn...
OPEN WIDE...
Nnnn...
THAT'S ALL. YOU CAN GET DRESSED NOW.
IT APPEARS THAT EVERYTHING IS IN GOOD WORKING ORDER. I JUST WISH WE DIDN'T HAVE TO DRAG YOU IN HERE EVERY TIME.
BUT JUST TO MAKE SURE, I'M SENDING YOU TO A SPECIALIST. HE'S A DOCTOR WHO DEALS WITH NEUROLOGICAL SYMPTOMS.
WHY?
WHAT'S WRONG WITH ME?

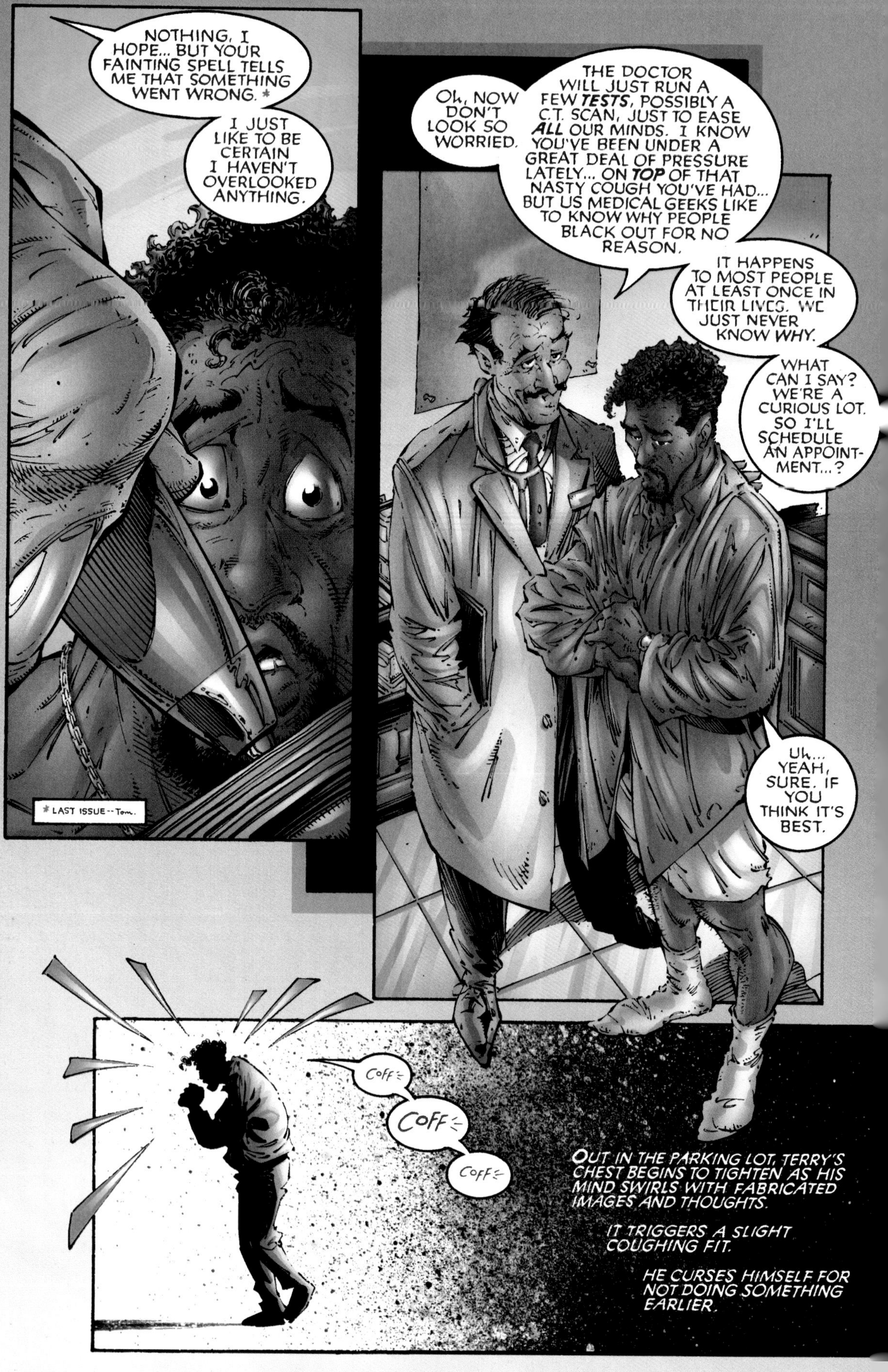
NOTHING, I HOPE... BUT YOUR FAINTING SPELL TELLS ME THAT SOMETHING WENT WRONG.*
I JUST LIKE TO BE CERTAIN I HAVEN'T OVERLOOKED ANYTHING.
* LAST ISSUE--Tom.
Oh, NOW DON'T LOOK SO WORRIED.
THE DOCTOR WILL JUST RUN A FEW TESTS, POSSIBLY A C.T. SCAN, JUST TO EASE ALL OUR MINDS. I KNOW YOU'VE BEEN UNDER A GREAT DEAL OF PRESSURE LATELY... ON TOP OF THAT NASTY COUGH YOU'VE HAD... BUT US MEDICAL GEEKS LIKE TO KNOW WHY PEOPLE BLACK OUT FOR NO REASON.
IT HAPPENS TO MOST PEOPLE AT LEAST ONCE IN THEIR LIVES. WE JUST NEVER KNOW WHY.
WHAT CAN I SAY? WE'RE A CURIOUS LOT. SO I'LL SCHEDULE AN APPOINT-MENT...?
Uh... YEAH, SURE. IF YOU THINK IT'S BEST.
COFF
COFF
COFF
OUT IN THE PARKING LOT, TERRY'S CHEST BEGINS TO TIGHTEN AS HIS MIND SWIRLS WITH FABRICATED IMAGES AND THOUGHTS.
IT TRIGGERS A SLIGHT COUGHING FIT.
HE CURSES HIMSELF FOR NOT DOING SOMETHING EARLIER.

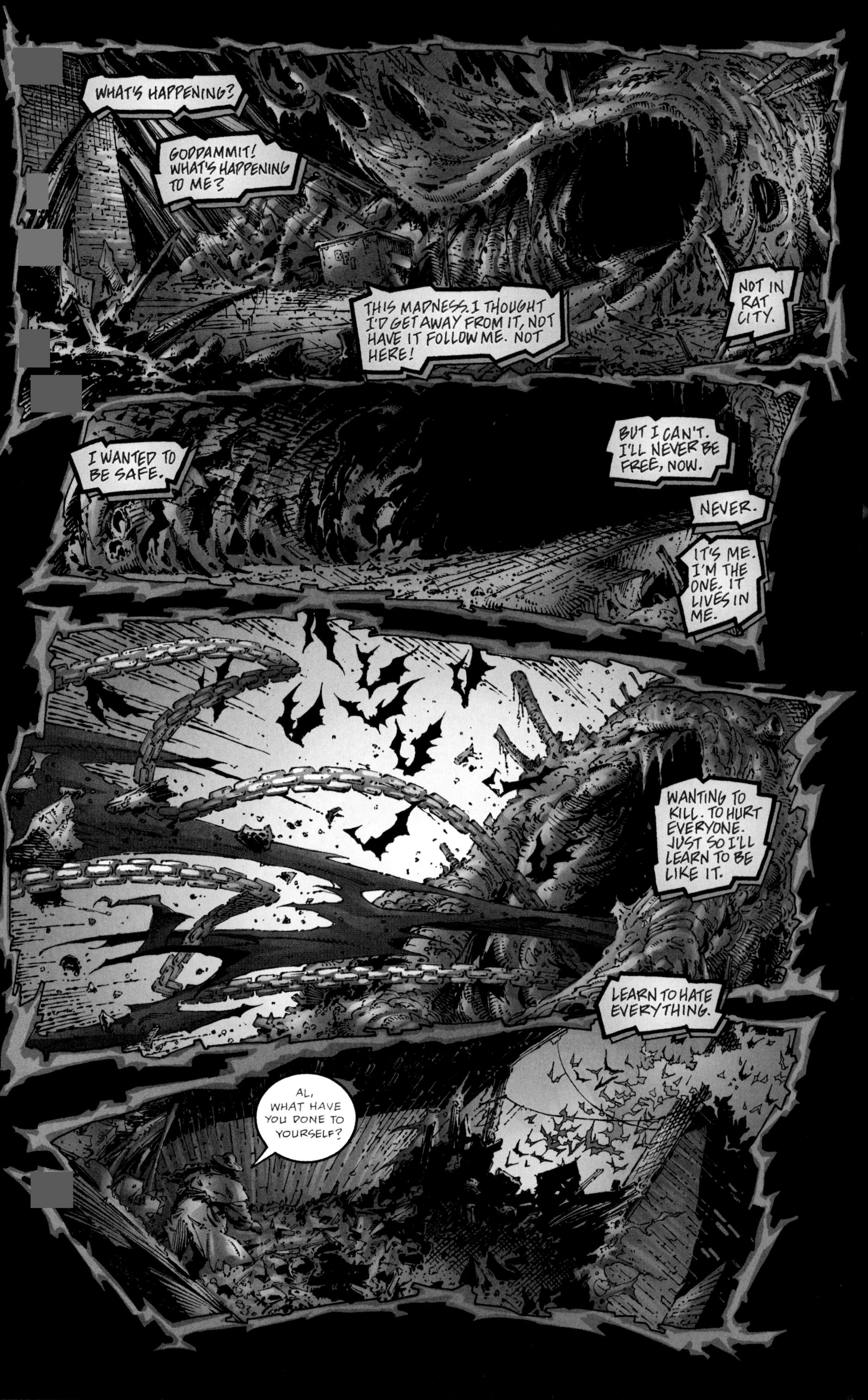
WHAT'S HAPPENING?
GODDAMMIT! WHAT'S HAPPENING TO ME?
THIS MADNESS. I THOUGHT I'D GET AWAY FROM IT, NOT HAVE IT FOLLOW ME. NOT HERE!
NOT IN RAT CITY.
I WANTED TO BE SAFE.
BUT I CAN'T. I'LL NEVER BE FREE, NOW.
NEVER.
IT'S ME. I'M THE ONE. IT LIVES IN ME.
WANTING TO KILL. TO HURT EVERYONE. JUST SO I'LL LEARN TO BE LIKE IT.
LEARN TO HATE EVERYTHING.
AL, WHAT HAVE YOU DONE TO YOURSELF?

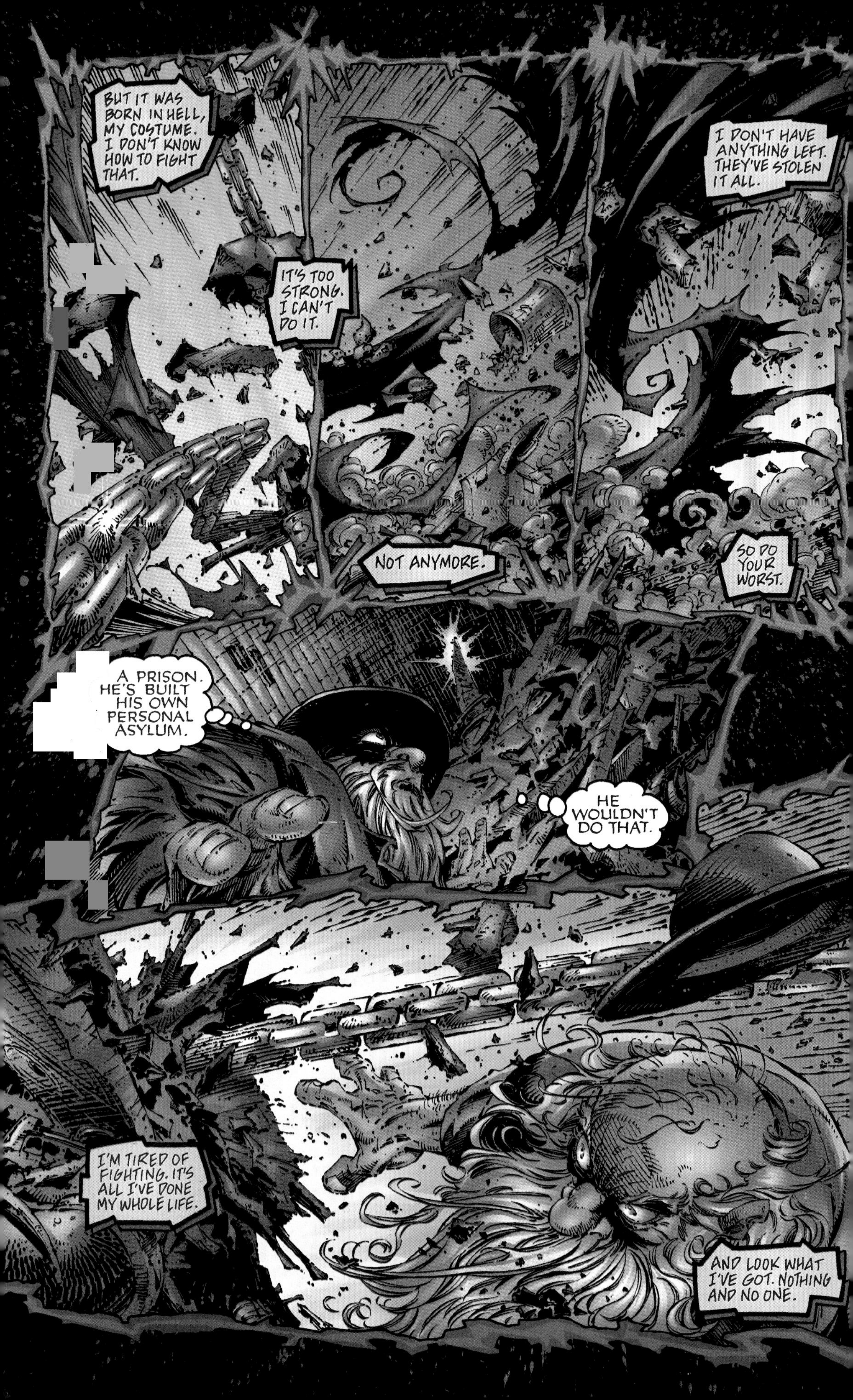
BUT IT WAS BORN IN HELL, MY COSTUME. I DON'T KNOW HOW TO FIGHT THAT.
IT'S TOO STRONG. I CAN'T DO IT.
I DON'T HAVE ANYTHING LEFT. THEY'VE STOLEN IT ALL.
NOT ANYMORE.
SO DO YOUR WORST.
A PRISON. HE'S BUILT HIS OWN PERSONAL ASYLUM.
HE WOULDN'T DO THAT.
I'M TIRED OF FIGHTING. IT'S ALL I'VE DONE MY WHOLE LIFE.
AND LOOK WHAT I'VE GOT. NOTHING AND NO ONE.

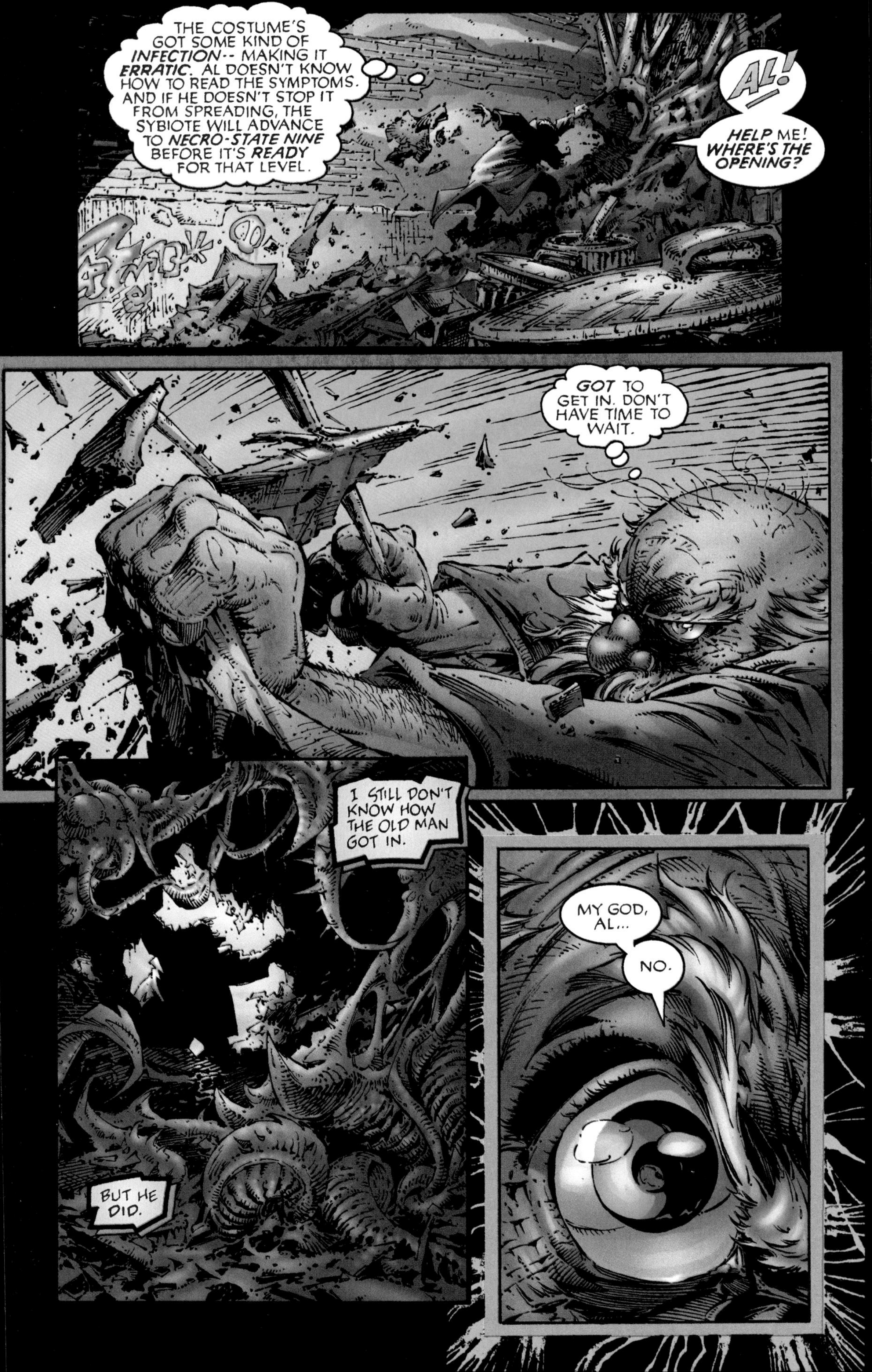
THE COSTUME'S GOT SOME KIND OF *INFECTION*-- MAKING IT *ERRATIC*. AL DOESN'T KNOW HOW TO READ THE SYMPTOMS. AND IF HE DOESN'T STOP IT FROM SPREADING, THE SYBIOTE WILL ADVANCE TO *NECRO-STATE NINE* BEFORE IT'S *READY* FOR THAT LEVEL.
AL!
HELP ME! *WHERE'S THE OPENING?*
GOT TO GET IN. DON'T HAVE TIME TO WAIT.
I STILL DON'T KNOW HOW THE OLD MAN GOT IN.
BUT HE DID.
MY GOD, AL...
NO.

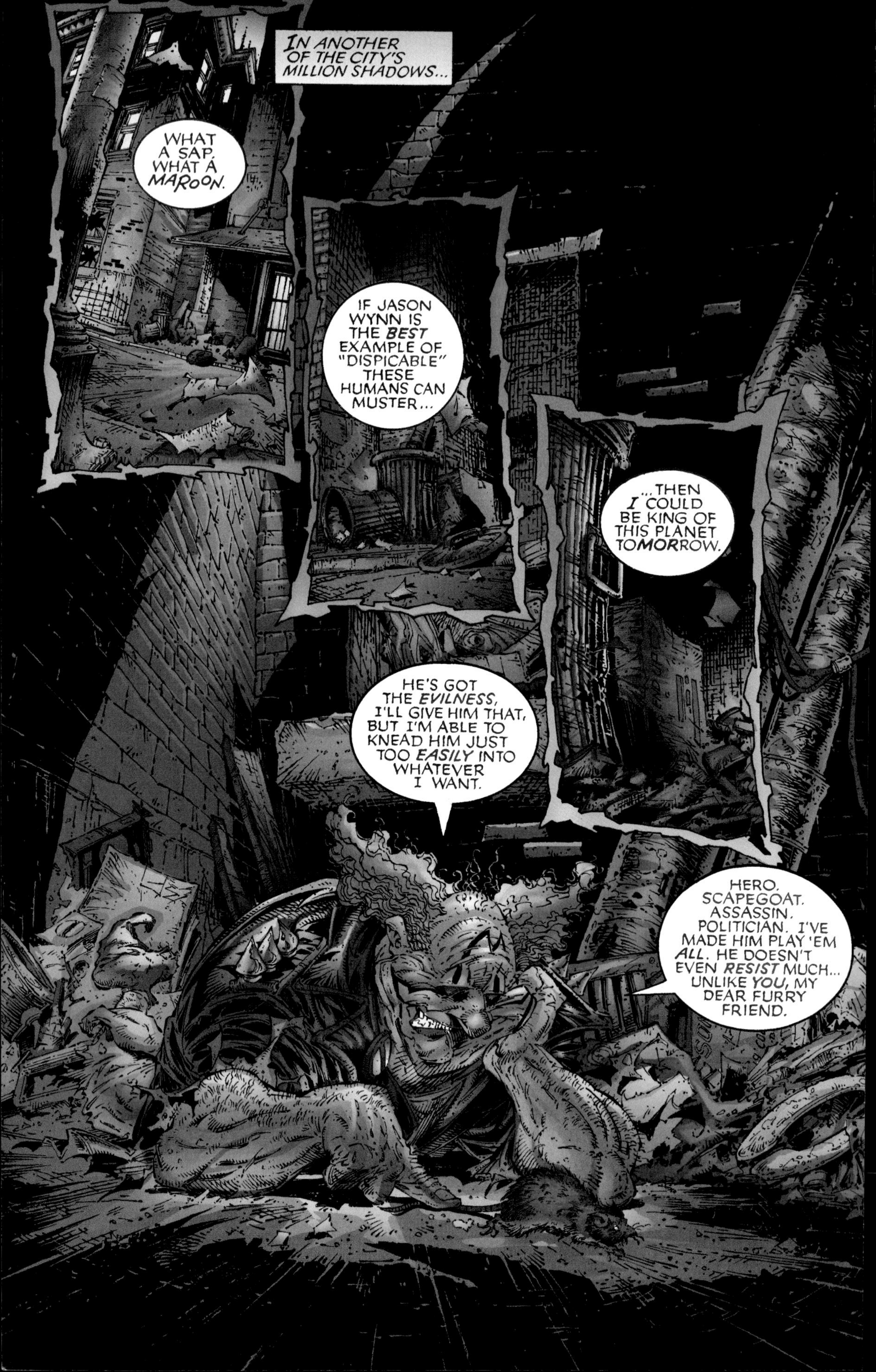
IN ANOTHER OF THE CITY'S MILLION SHADOWS...
WHAT A SAP. WHAT A MAROON.
IF JASON WYNN IS THE BEST EXAMPLE OF "DISPICABLE" THESE HUMANS CAN MUSTER...
...THEN I COULD BE KING OF THIS PLANET TOMORROW.
HE'S GOT THE EVILNESS, I'LL GIVE HIM THAT, BUT I'M ABLE TO KNEAD HIM JUST TOO EASILY INTO WHATEVER I WANT.
HERO. SCAPEGOAT. ASSASSIN. POLITICIAN. I'VE MADE HIM PLAY 'EM ALL. HE DOESN'T EVEN RESIST MUCH... UNLIKE YOU, MY DEAR FURRY FRIEND.

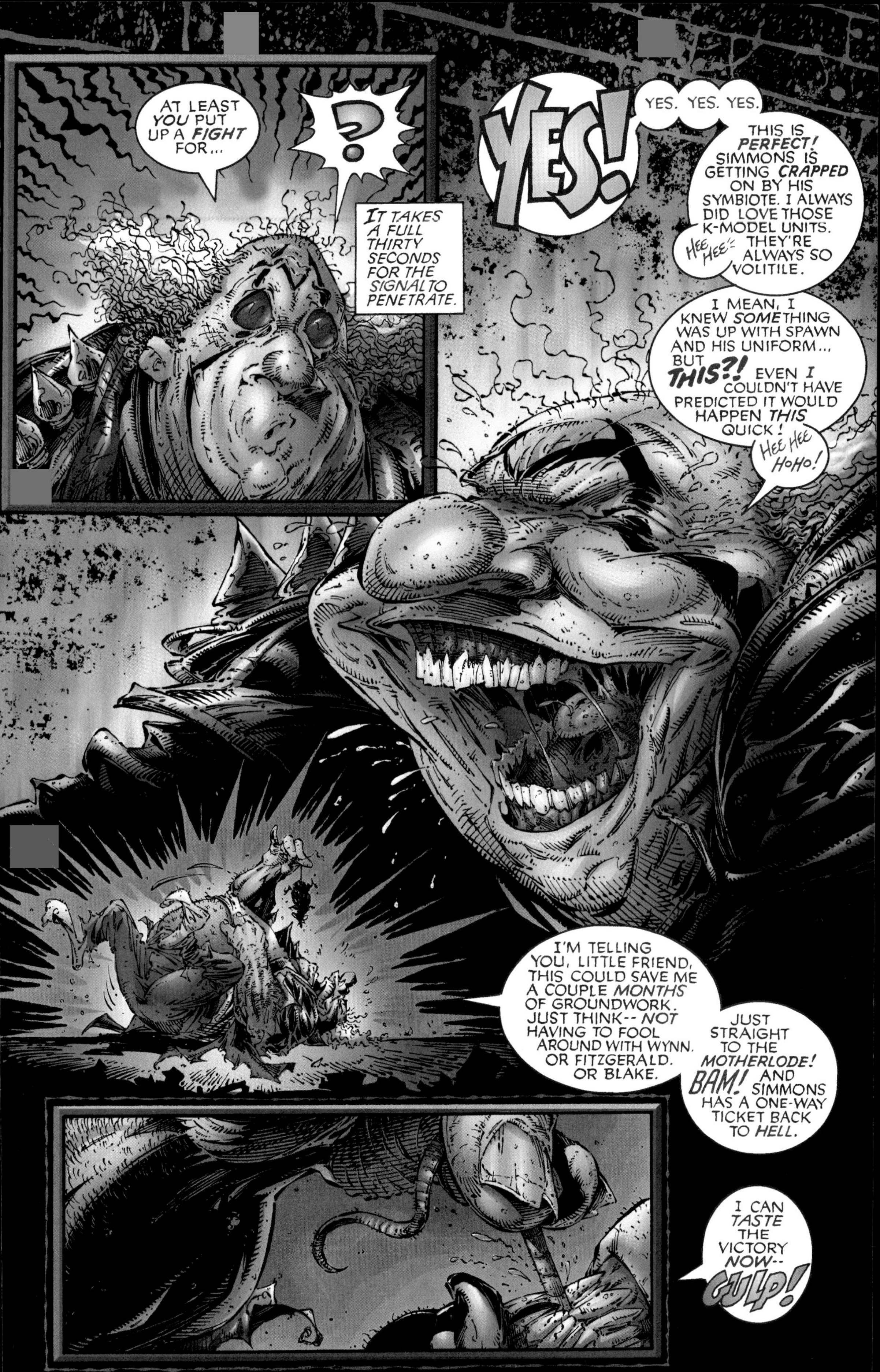
AT LEAST YOU PUT UP A FIGHT FOR...
?
IT TAKES A FULL THIRTY SECONDS FOR THE SIGNAL TO PENETRATE.
YES!
YES. YES. YES.
THIS IS PERFECT! SIMMONS IS GETTING CRAPPED ON BY HIS SYMBIOTE. I ALWAYS DID LOVE THOSE K-MODEL UNITS. THEY'RE ALWAYS SO VOLITILE.
HEE HEE
I MEAN, I KNEW SOMETHING WAS UP WITH SPAWN AND HIS UNIFORM... BUT THIS?! EVEN I COULDN'T HAVE PREDICTED IT WOULD HAPPEN THIS QUICK!
HEE HEE HOHO!
I'M TELLING YOU, LITTLE FRIEND, THIS COULD SAVE ME A COUPLE MONTHS OF GROUNDWORK. JUST THINK-- NOT HAVING TO FOOL AROUND WITH WYNN. OR FITZGERALD. OR BLAKE.
JUST STRAIGHT TO THE MOTHERLODE! BAM! AND SIMMONS HAS A ONE-WAY TICKET BACK TO HELL.
I CAN TASTE THE VICTORY NOW--
GULP!

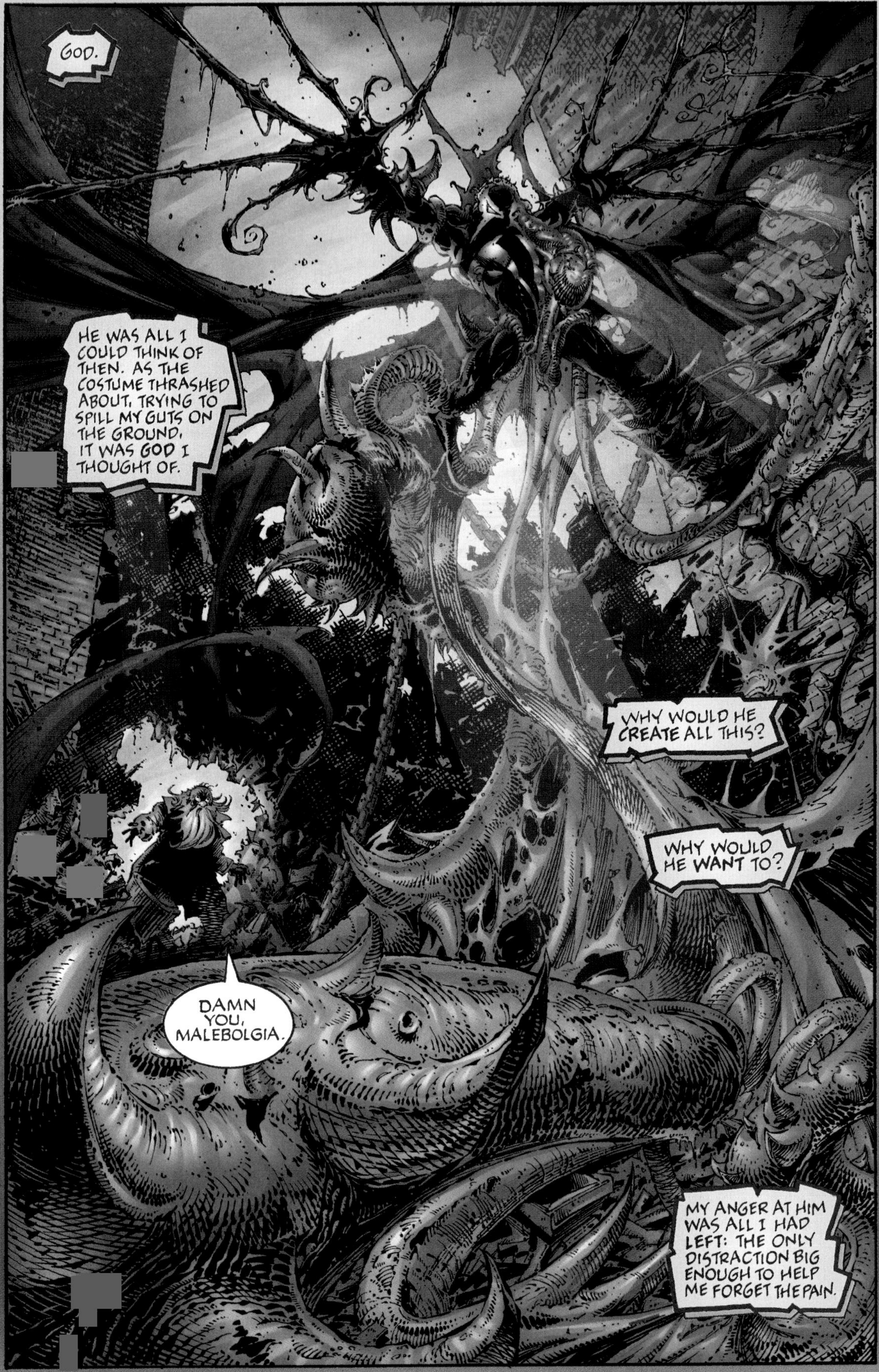
GOD.
HE WAS ALL I COULD THINK OF THEN. AS THE COSTUME THRASHED ABOUT, TRYING TO SPILL MY GUTS ON THE GROUND, IT WAS GOD I THOUGHT OF.
WHY WOULD HE CREATE ALL THIS?
WHY WOULD HE WANT TO?
DAMN YOU, MALEBOLGIA.
MY ANGER AT HIM WAS ALL I HAD LEFT: THE ONLY DISTRACTION BIG ENOUGH TO HELP ME FORGET THE PAIN.

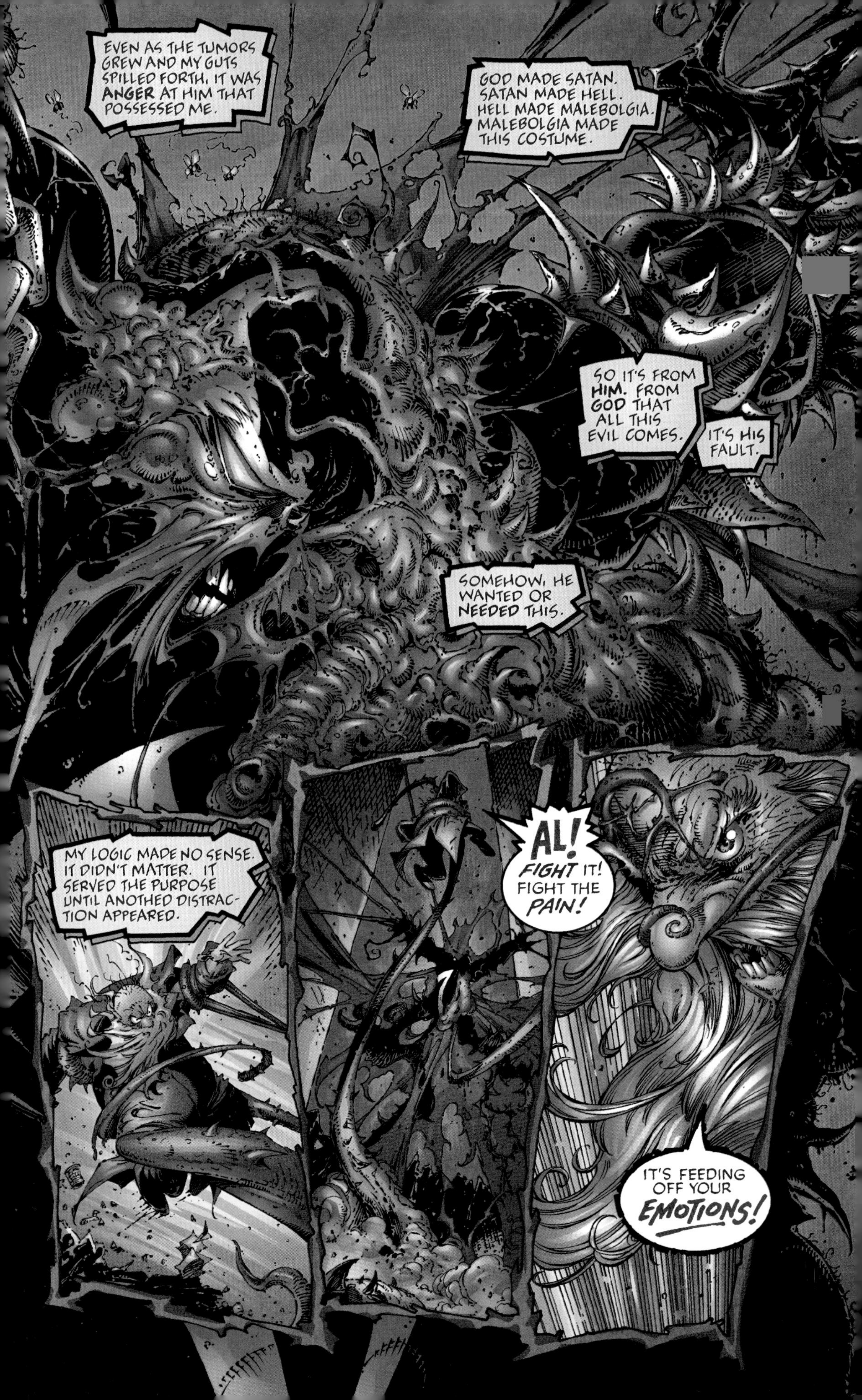
EVEN AS THE TUMORS GREW AND MY GUTS SPILLED FORTH, IT WAS **ANGER** AT HIM THAT POSSESSED ME.
GOD MADE SATAN. SATAN MADE HELL. HELL MADE MALEBOLGIA. MALEBOLGIA MADE THIS COSTUME.
SO IT'S FROM **HIM.** FROM **GOD** THAT ALL THIS EVIL COMES.
IT'S HIS FAULT.
SOMEHOW, HE WANTED OR **NEEDED** THIS.
MY LOGIC MADE NO SENSE. IT DIDN'T MATTER. IT SERVED THE PURPOSE UNTIL ANOTHED DISTRACTION APPEARED.
AL! ***FIGHT*** IT! FIGHT THE ***PAIN!***
IT'S FEEDING OFF YOUR ***EMOTIONS!***

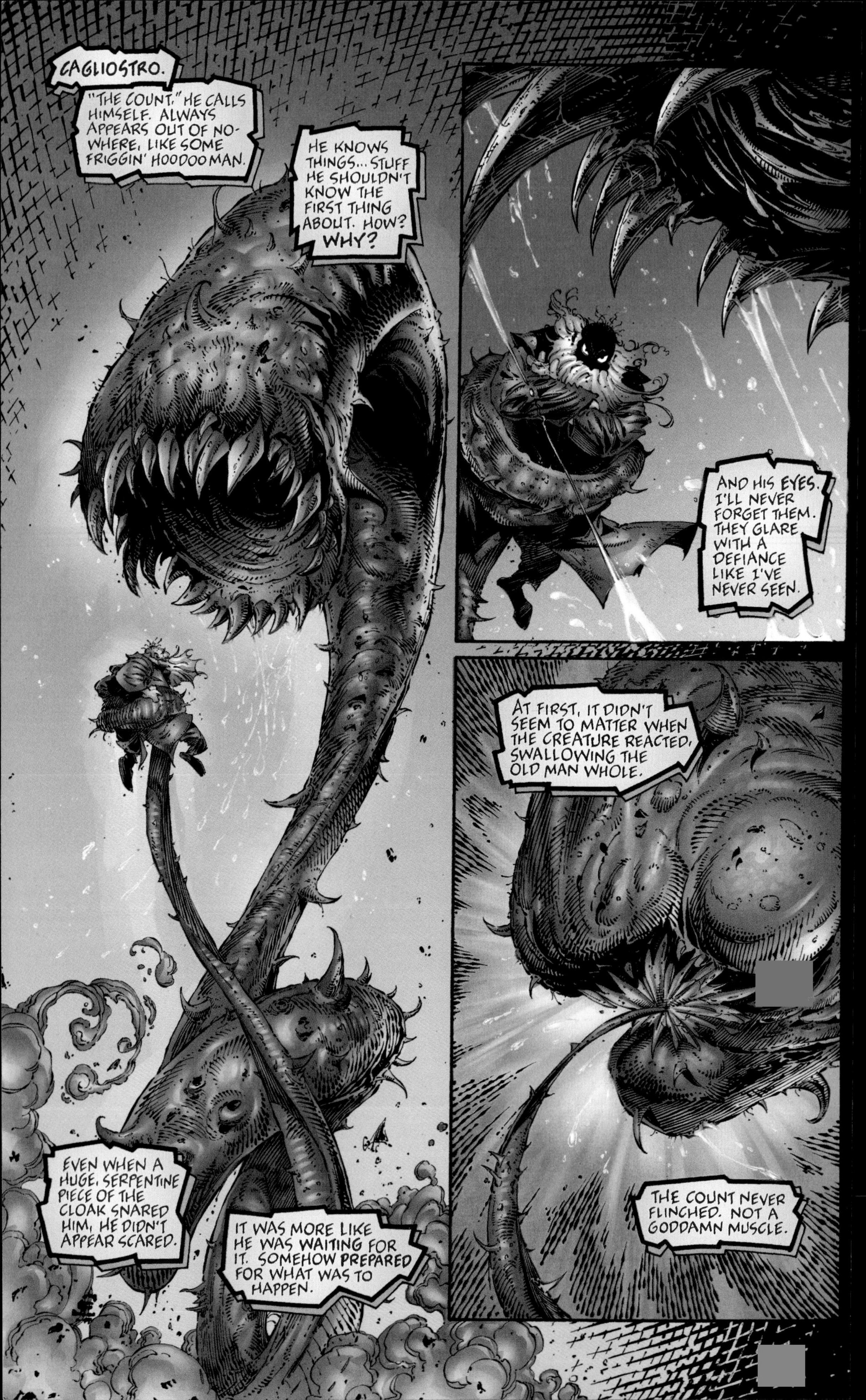
CAGLIOSTRO.
"THE COUNT," HE CALLS HIMSELF. ALWAYS APPEARS OUT OF NO-WHERE, LIKE SOME FRIGGIN' HOODOO MAN.
HE KNOWS THINGS... STUFF HE SHOULDN'T KNOW THE FIRST THING ABOUT. HOW? WHY?
EVEN WHEN A HUGE, SERPENTINE PIECE OF THE CLOAK SNARED HIM, HE DIDN'T APPEAR SCARED.
IT WAS MORE LIKE HE WAS WAITING FOR IT. SOMEHOW PREPARED FOR WHAT WAS TO HAPPEN.
AND HIS EYES. I'LL NEVER FORGET THEM. THEY GLARE WITH A DEFIANCE LIKE I'VE NEVER SEEN.
AT FIRST, IT DIDN'T SEEM TO MATTER WHEN THE CREATURE REACTED, SWALLOWING THE OLD MAN WHOLE.
THE COUNT NEVER FLINCHED. NOT A GODDAMN MUSCLE.

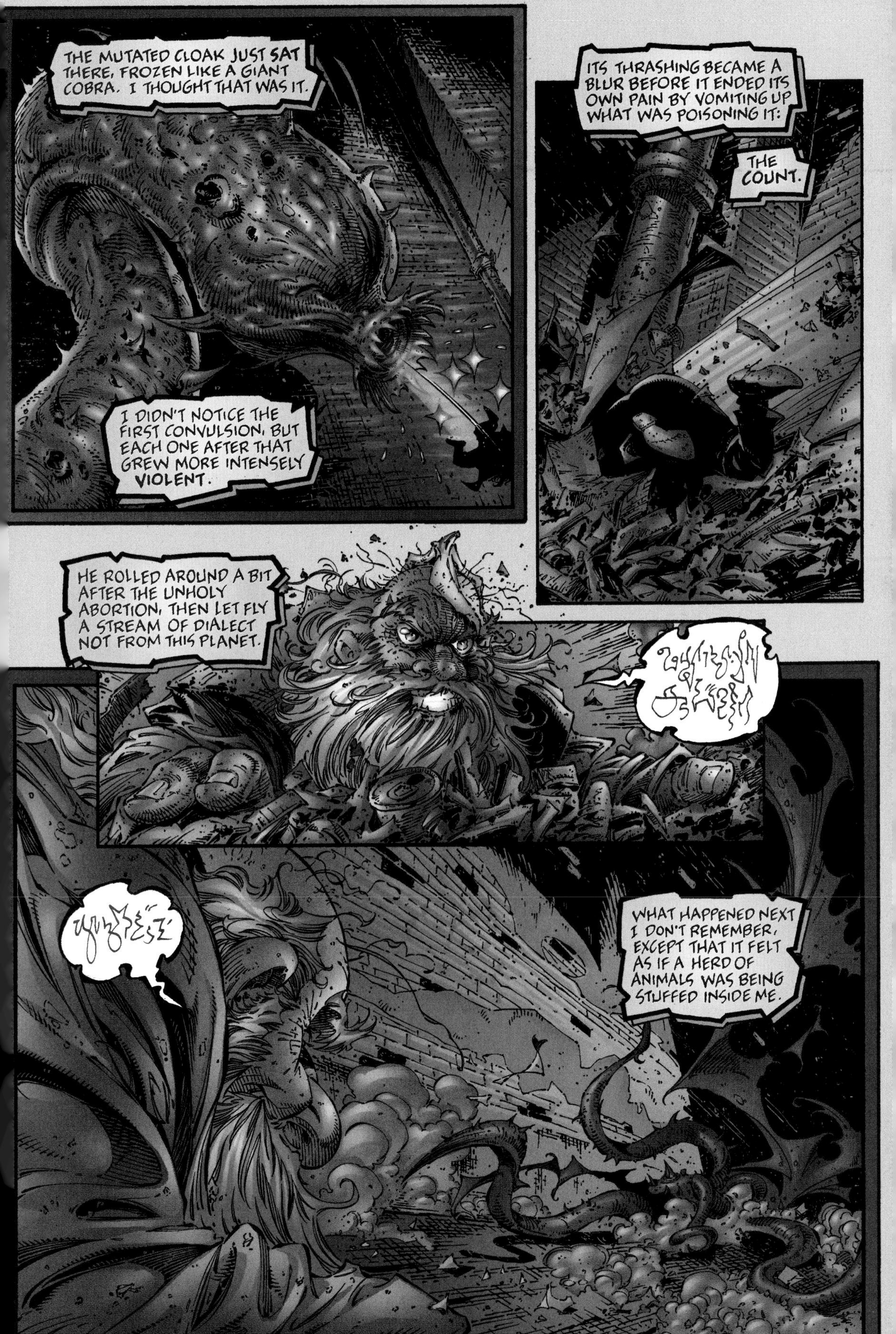
THE MUTATED CLOAK JUST SAT THERE, FROZEN LIKE A GIANT COBRA. I THOUGHT THAT WAS IT.
I DIDN'T NOTICE THE FIRST CONVULSION, BUT EACH ONE AFTER THAT GREW MORE INTENSELY VIOLENT.
ITS THRASHING BECAME A BLUR BEFORE IT ENDED ITS OWN PAIN BY VOMITING UP WHAT WAS POISONING IT:
THE COUNT.
HE ROLLED AROUND A BIT AFTER THE UNHOLY ABORTION, THEN LET FLY A STREAM OF DIALECT NOT FROM THIS PLANET.
WHAT HAPPENED NEXT I DON'T REMEMBER, EXCEPT THAT IT FELT AS IF A HERD OF ANIMALS WAS BEING STUFFED INSIDE ME.

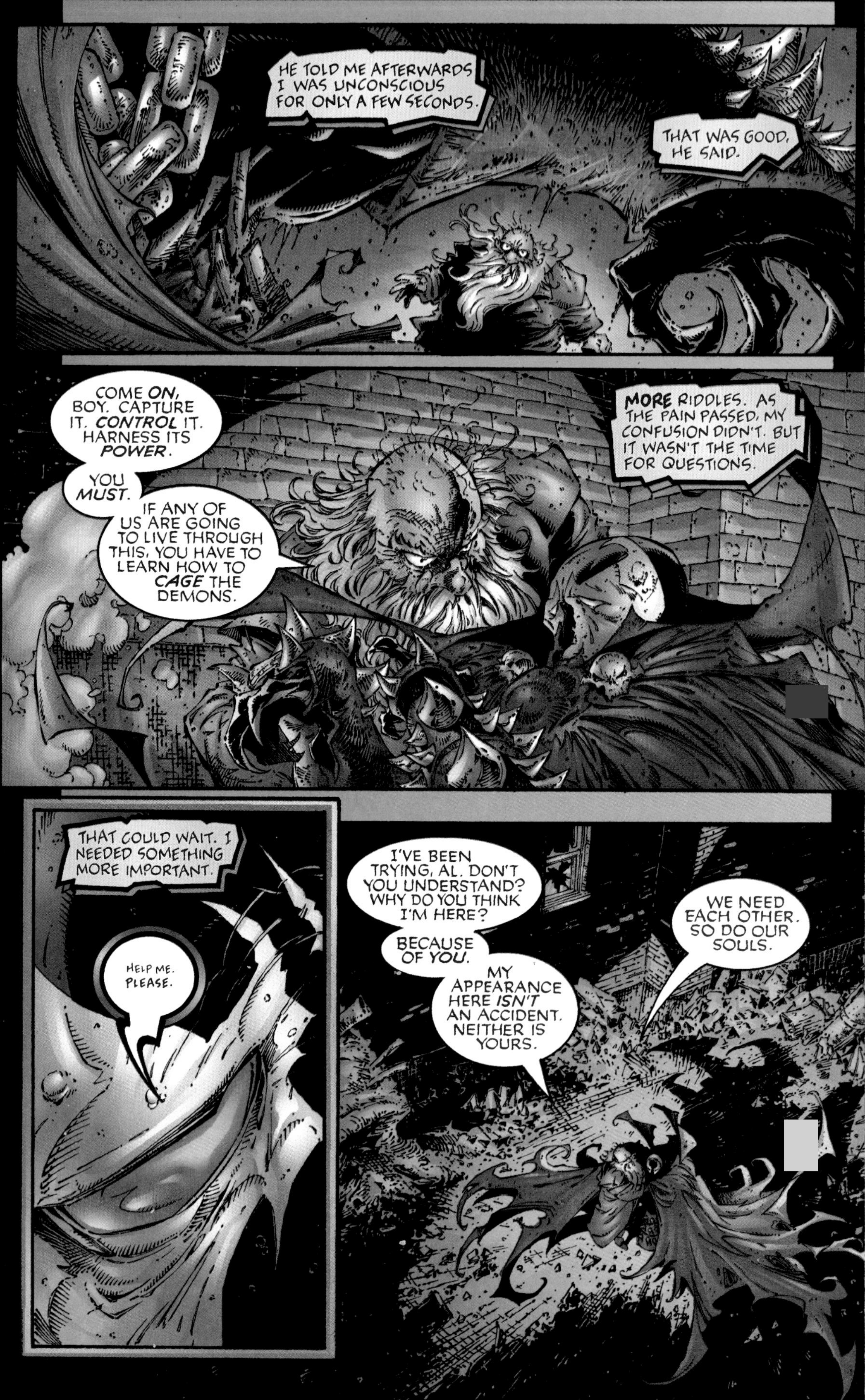
HE TOLD ME AFTERWARDS I WAS UNCONSCIOUS FOR ONLY A FEW SECONDS.
THAT WAS GOOD, HE SAID.
COME ON, BOY. CAPTURE IT. CONTROL IT. HARNESS ITS POWER.
YOU MUST.
IF ANY OF US ARE GOING TO LIVE THROUGH THIS, YOU HAVE TO LEARN HOW TO CAGE THE DEMONS.
MORE RIDDLES. AS THE PAIN PASSED, MY CONFUSION DIDN'T. BUT IT WASN'T THE TIME FOR QUESTIONS.
THAT COULD WAIT. I NEEDED SOMETHING MORE IMPORTANT.
HELP ME. PLEASE.
I'VE BEEN TRYING, AL. DON'T YOU UNDERSTAND? WHY DO YOU THINK I'M HERE?
BECAUSE OF YOU.
MY APPEARANCE HERE ISN'T AN ACCIDENT. NEITHER IS YOURS.
WE NEED EACH OTHER. SO DO OUR SOULS.

DR. ROLLINS
NEUROLOGIST
SUITE 209
THEY'RE HIDING SOMETHING, I *KNOW* THEY ARE. I CAN SEE IT IN HIS FACE.
IF I'VE GOT A PROBLEM, WHY DON'T THEY JUST SPIT IT OUT? ALL THIS WAITING IS KILLING ME. I'D RATHER HAVE BAD NEWS THAN *NO* NEWS.
mmmHmm
TAP TAP TAP
I'VE GOT TO GET OUT OF HERE. THIS IS CRAZY. I'M PERFECTLY FINE.
tic tic tic
THEY SAID THIS HAPPENS TO EVERYONE. SO, I SHOULD JUST GO. THAT'S IT! I'M OUTTA HERE.
WELL, MR. FITZGERALD, YOUR CHART APPEARS TO BE IN ORDER. IT LOOKS LIKE DR. BUSINO JUST WANTS ME TO RUN SOME STANDARD TESTS.
NOTHING TO GET EXCITED ABOUT.
I'M DYING. I'M DYING. I'M DYING.
THAT'D BE FINE. WHATEVER YOU NEED, DOCTOR.

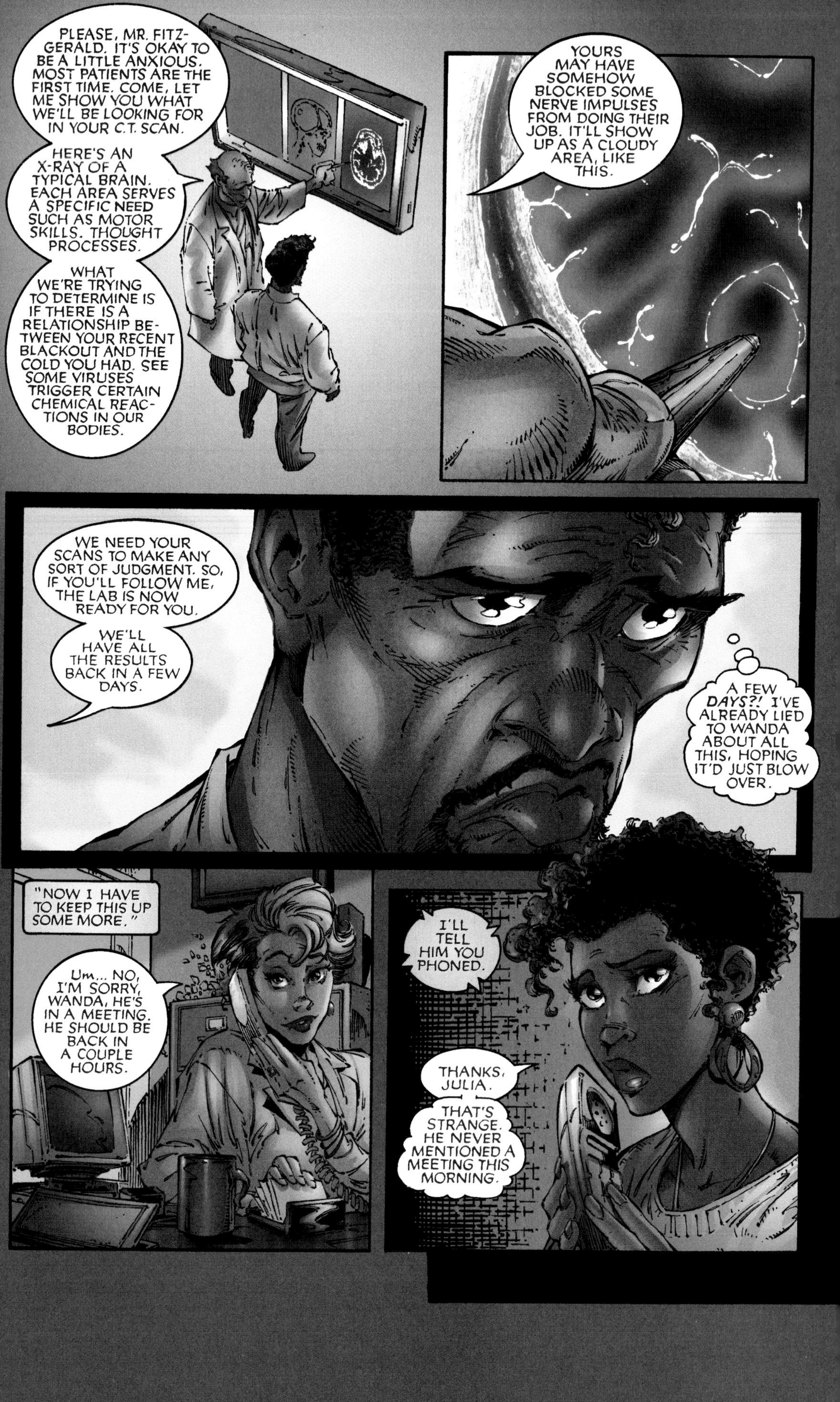
PLEASE, MR. FITZ-GERALD. IT'S OKAY TO BE A LITTLE ANXIOUS. MOST PATIENTS ARE THE FIRST TIME. COME, LET ME SHOW YOU WHAT WE'LL BE LOOKING FOR IN YOUR C.T. SCAN.
HERE'S AN X-RAY OF A TYPICAL BRAIN. EACH AREA SERVES A SPECIFIC NEED SUCH AS MOTOR SKILLS. THOUGHT PROCESSES.
WHAT WE'RE TRYING TO DETERMINE IS IF THERE IS A RELATIONSHIP BE-TWEEN YOUR RECENT BLACKOUT AND THE COLD YOU HAD. SEE SOME VIRUSES TRIGGER CERTAIN CHEMICAL REAC-TIONS IN OUR BODIES.
YOURS MAY HAVE SOMEHOW BLOCKED SOME NERVE IMPULSES FROM DOING THEIR JOB. IT'LL SHOW UP AS A CLOUDY AREA, LIKE THIS.
WE NEED YOUR SCANS TO MAKE ANY SORT OF JUDGMENT. SO, IF YOU'LL FOLLOW ME, THE LAB IS NOW READY FOR YOU.
WE'LL HAVE ALL THE RESULTS BACK IN A FEW DAYS.
A FEW DAYS?! I'VE ALREADY LIED TO WANDA ABOUT ALL THIS, HOPING IT'D JUST BLOW OVER.
"NOW I HAVE TO KEEP THIS UP SOME MORE."
Um... NO, I'M SORRY, WANDA, HE'S IN A MEETING. HE SHOULD BE BACK IN A COUPLE HOURS.
I'LL TELL HIM YOU PHONED.
THANKS, JULIA.
THAT'S STRANGE. HE NEVER MENTIONED A MEETING THIS MORNING.

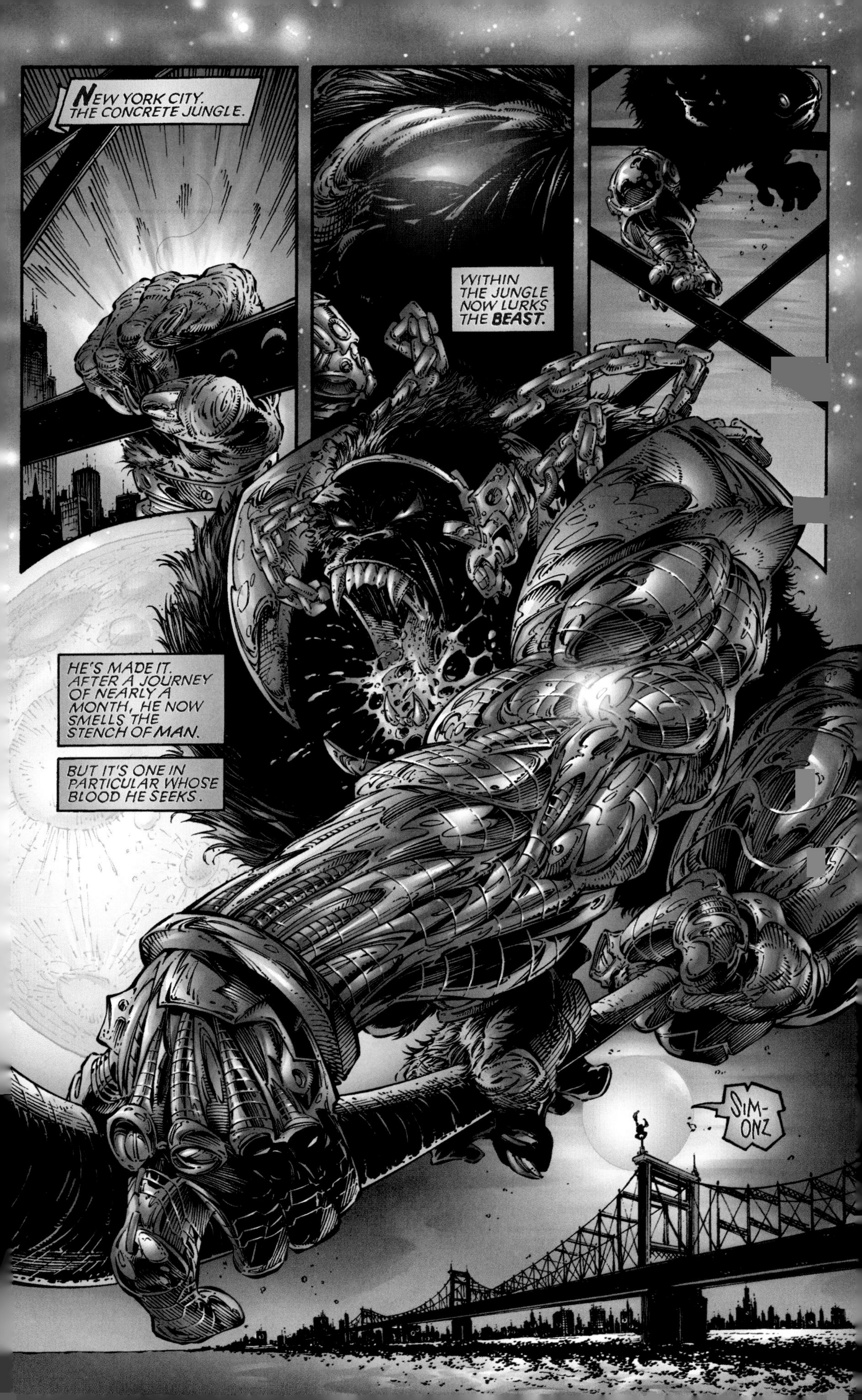
NEW YORK CITY. THE CONCRETE JUNGLE.
WITHIN THE JUNGLE NOW LURKS THE BEAST.
HE'S MADE IT. AFTER A JOURNEY OF NEARLY A MONTH, HE NOW SMELLS THE STENCH OF MAN.
BUT IT'S ONE IN PARTICULAR WHOSE BLOOD HE SEEKS.
SIM-ONZ

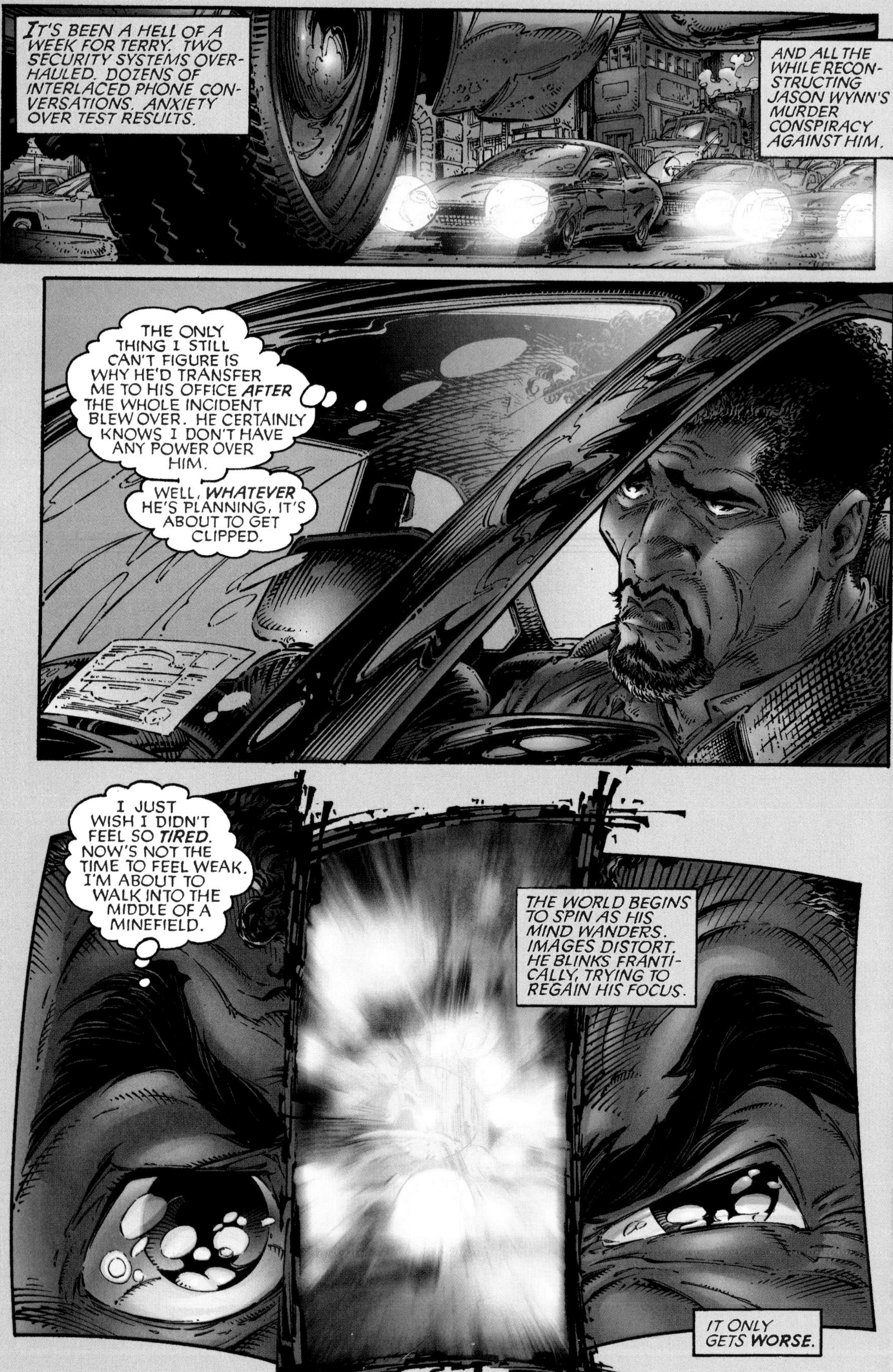
IT'S BEEN A HELL OF A WEEK FOR TERRY. TWO SECURITY SYSTEMS OVER-HAULED. DOZENS OF INTERLACED PHONE CON-VERSATIONS. ANXIETY OVER TEST RESULTS.
AND ALL THE WHILE RECON-STRUCTING JASON WYNN'S MURDER CONSPIRACY AGAINST HIM.
THE ONLY THING I STILL CAN'T FIGURE IS WHY HE'D TRANSFER ME TO HIS OFFICE AFTER THE WHOLE INCIDENT BLEW OVER. HE CERTAINLY KNOWS I DON'T HAVE ANY POWER OVER HIM.
WELL, WHATEVER HE'S PLANNING, IT'S ABOUT TO GET CLIPPED.
I JUST WISH I DIDN'T FEEL SO TIRED. NOW'S NOT THE TIME TO FEEL WEAK. I'M ABOUT TO WALK INTO THE MIDDLE OF A MINEFIELD.
THE WORLD BEGINS TO SPIN AS HIS MIND WANDERS. IMAGES DISTORT. HE BLINKS FRANTI-CALLY, TRYING TO REGAIN HIS FOCUS.
IT ONLY GETS WORSE.

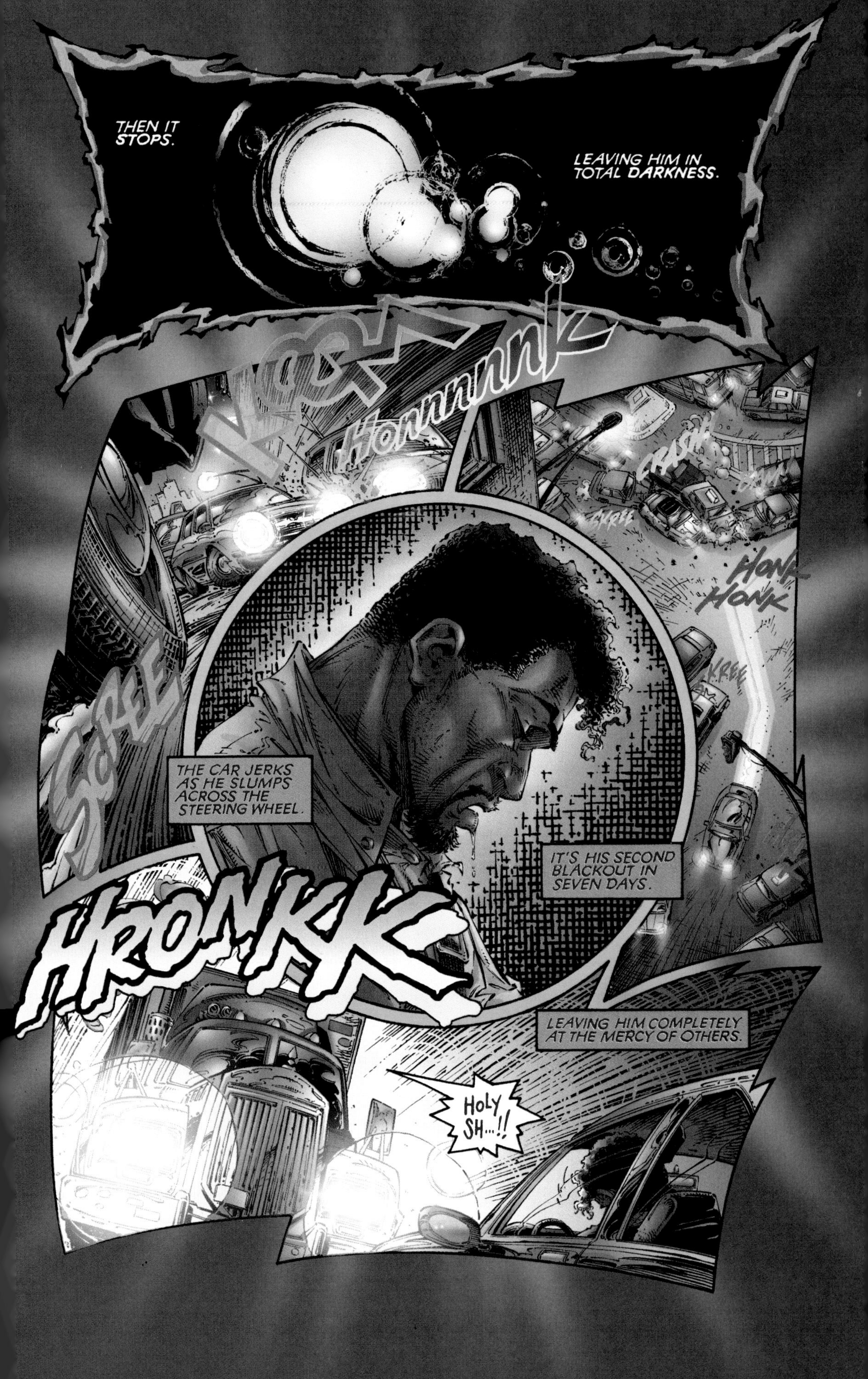
THEN IT STOPS.
LEAVING HIM IN TOTAL DARKNESS.
Honnnnnk
CRASH
HONK HONK
THE CAR JERKS AS HE SLUMPS ACROSS THE STEERING WHEEL.
IT'S HIS SECOND BLACKOUT IN SEVEN DAYS.
HRONKK
LEAVING HIM COMPLETELY AT THE MERCY OF OTHERS.
HOLY SH...!!

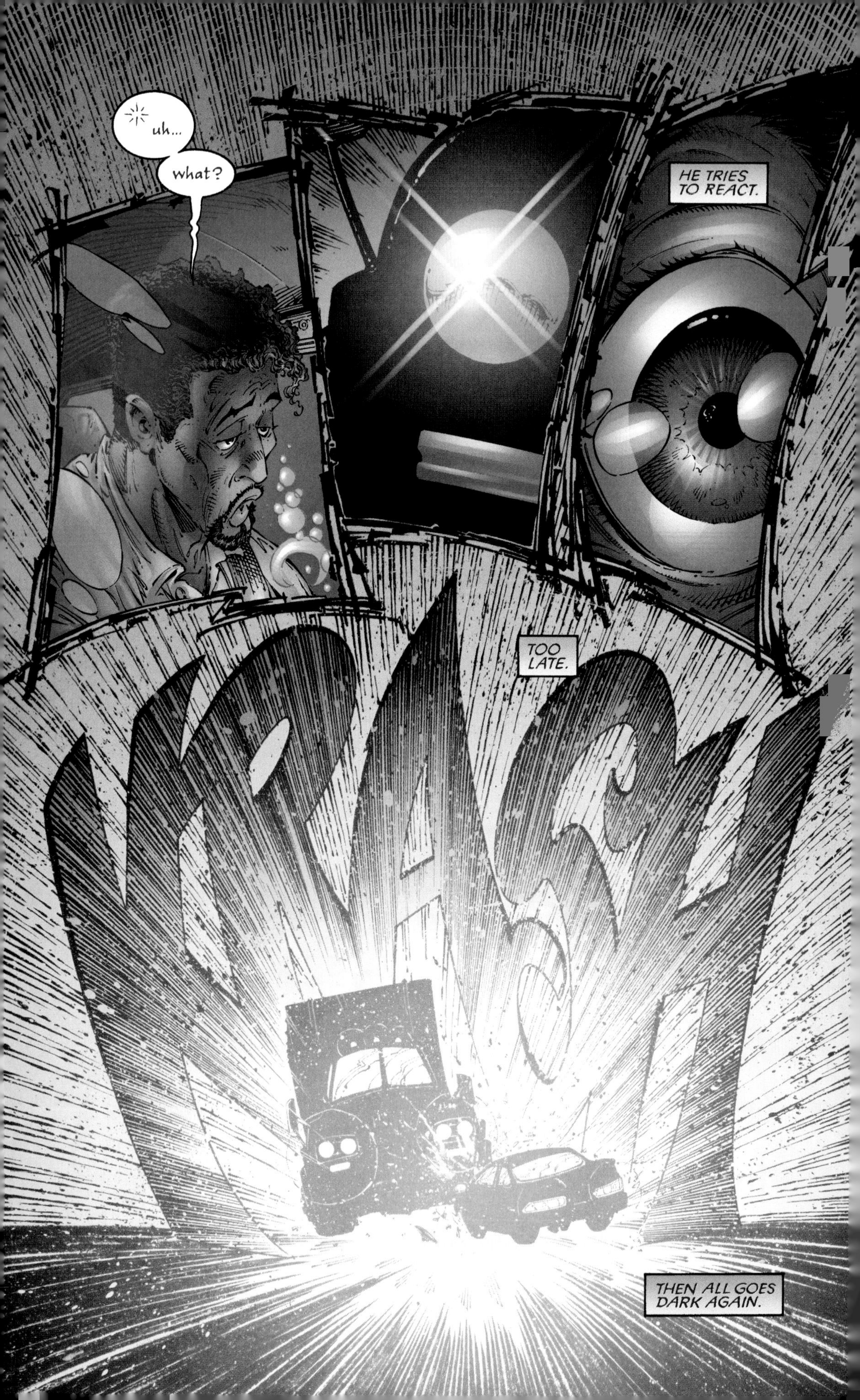
uh... what?
HE TRIES TO REACT.
TOO LATE.
THEN ALL GOES DARK AGAIN.

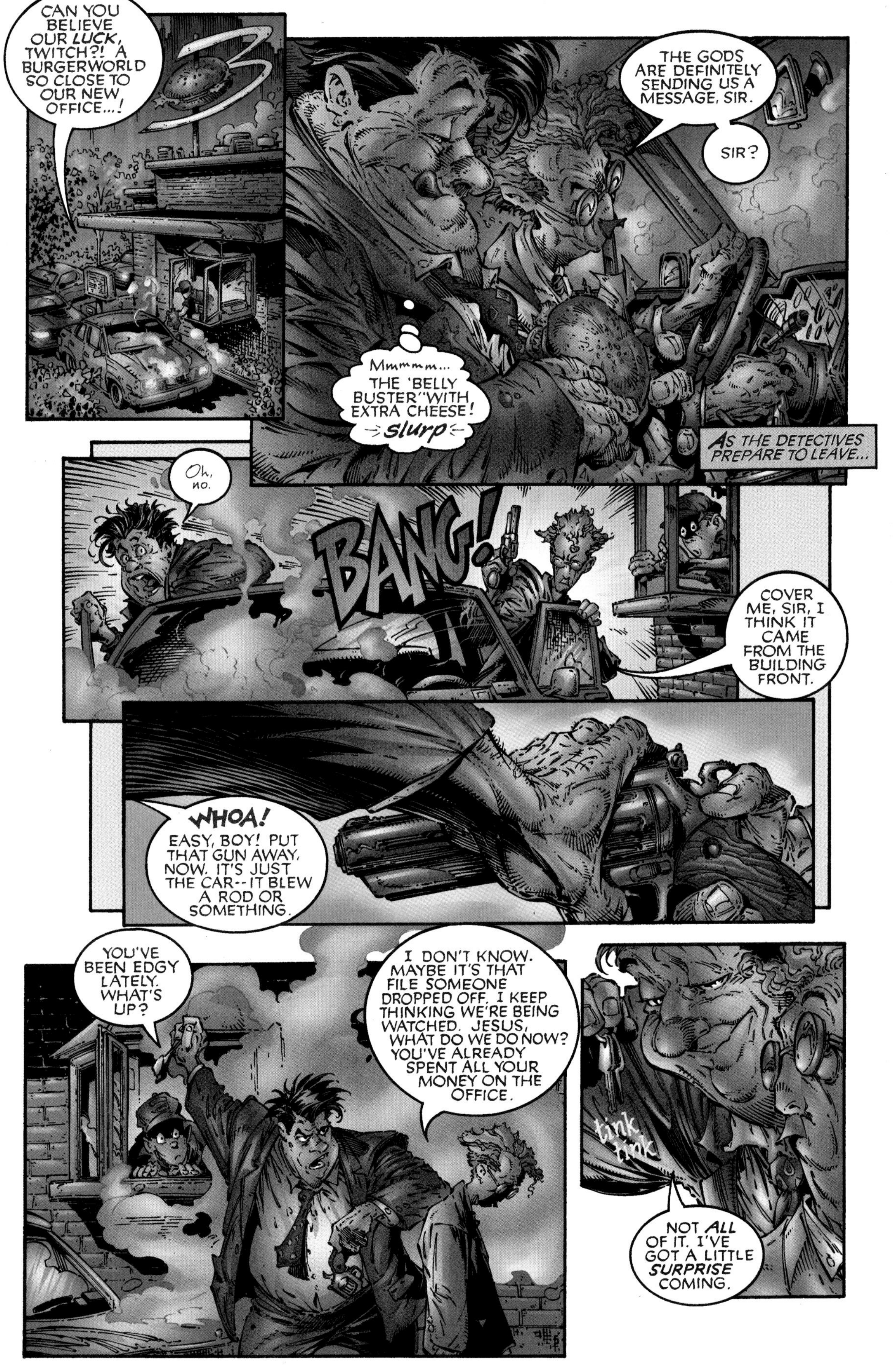
CAN YOU BELIEVE OUR *LUCK*, TWITCH?! A BURGERWORLD SO CLOSE TO OUR NEW OFFICE...!
THE GODS ARE DEFINITELY SENDING US A MESSAGE, SIR.
SIR?
Mmmmm... THE 'BELLY BUSTER" WITH EXTRA CHEESE! slurp
AS THE DETECTIVES PREPARE TO LEAVE...
Oh, no.
BANG!
COVER ME, SIR, I THINK IT CAME FROM THE BUILDING FRONT.
WHOA! EASY, BOY! PUT THAT GUN AWAY, NOW. IT'S JUST THE CAR--IT BLEW A ROD OR SOMETHING.
YOU'VE BEEN EDGY LATELY. WHAT'S UP?
I DON'T KNOW. MAYBE IT'S THAT FILE SOMEONE DROPPED OFF. I KEEP THINKING WE'RE BEING WATCHED. JESUS, WHAT DO WE DO NOW? YOU'VE ALREADY SPENT ALL YOUR MONEY ON THE OFFICE.
tink tink
NOT *ALL* OF IT. I'VE GOT A LITTLE *SURPRISE* COMING.

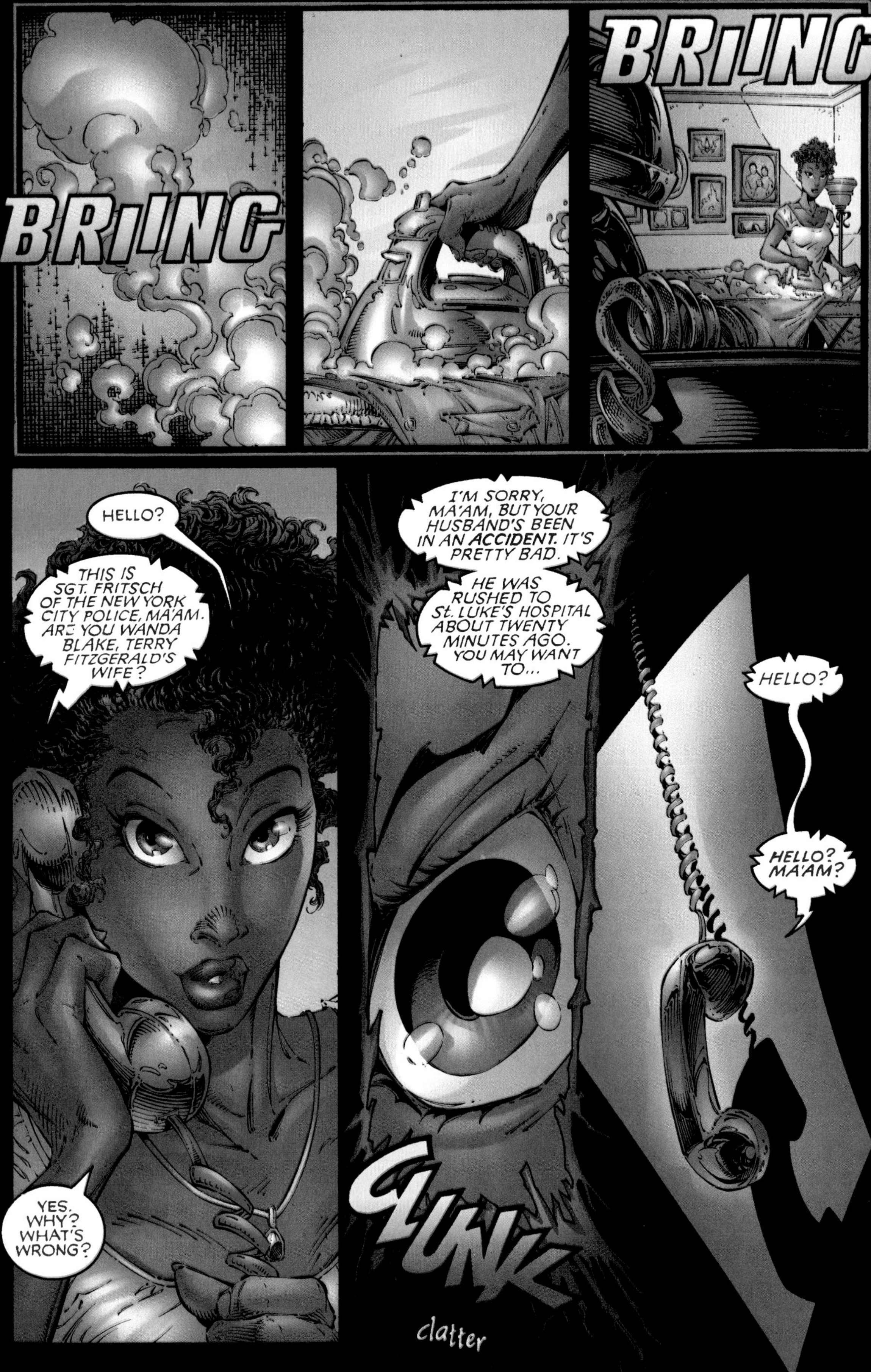
BRIING
BRIING
HELLO?
THIS IS SGT. FRITSCH OF THE NEW YORK CITY POLICE, MA'AM. ARE YOU WANDA BLAKE, TERRY FITZGERALD'S WIFE?
YES. WHY? WHAT'S WRONG?
I'M SORRY, MA'AM, BUT YOUR HUSBAND'S BEEN IN AN ACCIDENT. IT'S PRETTY BAD.
HE WAS RUSHED TO St. LUKE'S HOSPITAL ABOUT TWENTY MINUTES AGO. YOU MAY WANT TO...
CLUNK
clatter
HELLO?
HELLO? MA'AM?

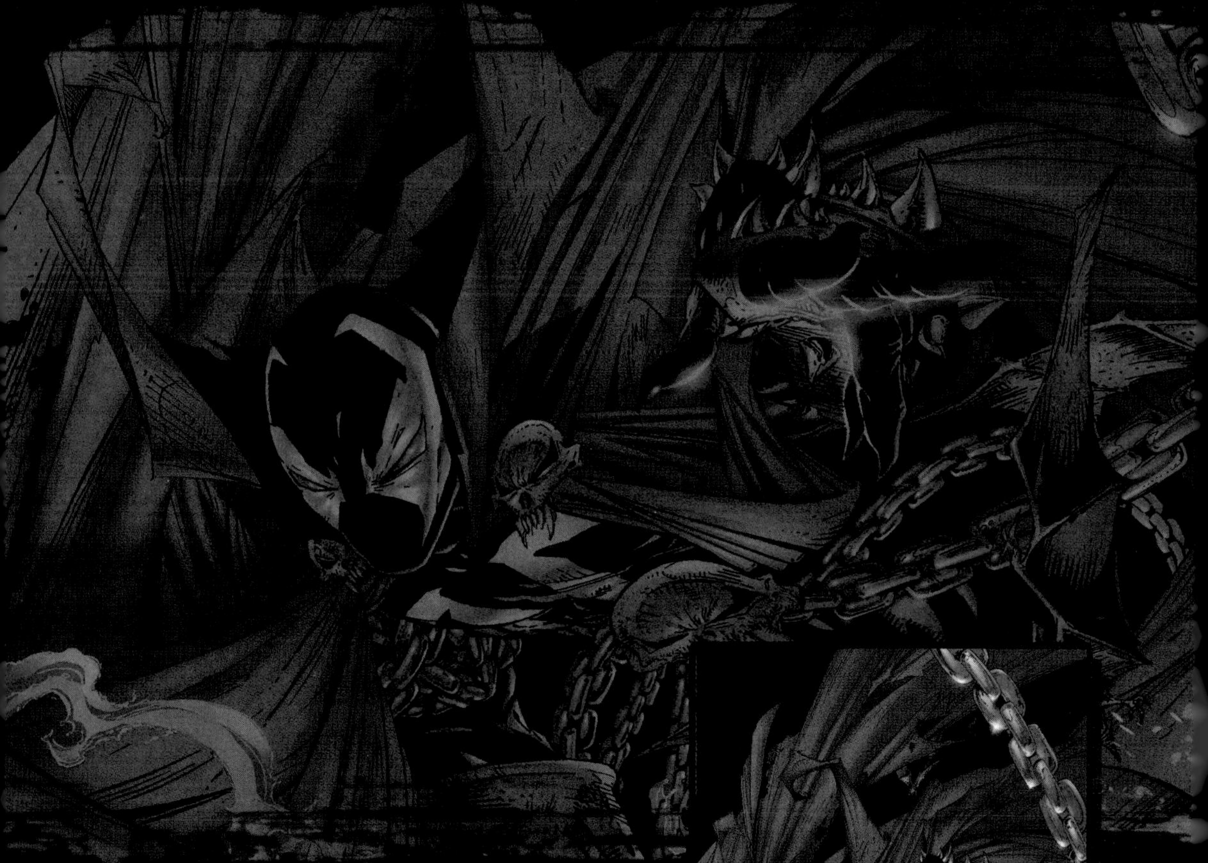

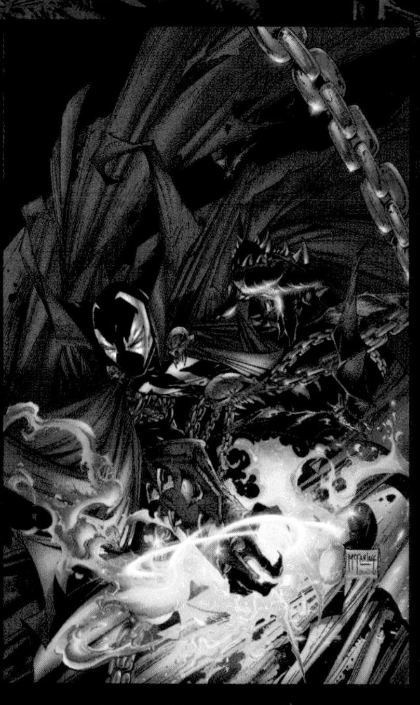

ISSUE FIFTY
Part One

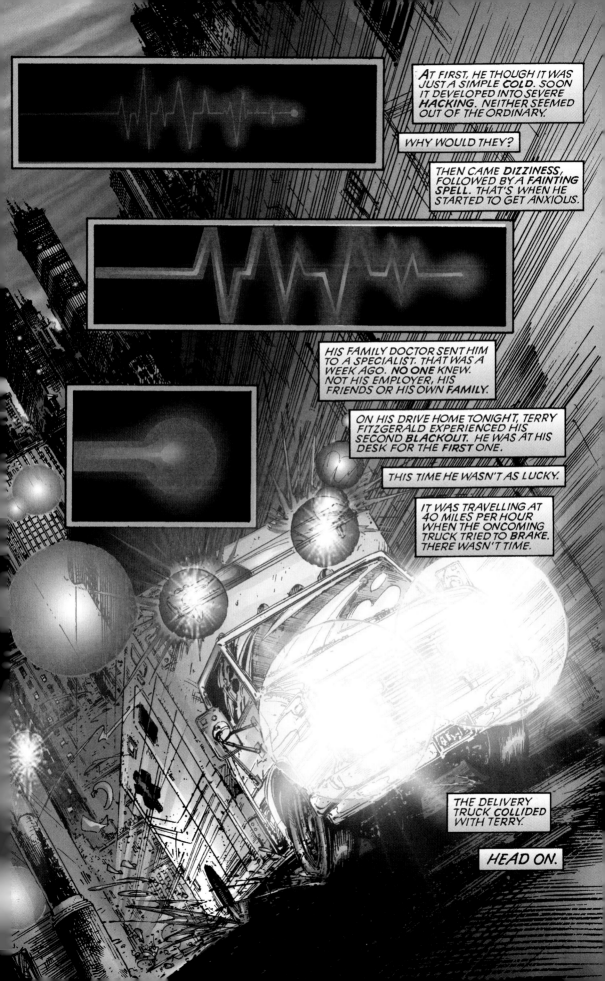

AT FIRST, HE THOUGH IT WAS JUST A SIMPLE **COLD.** SOON IT DEVELOPED INTO SEVERE **HACKING.** NEITHER SEEMED OUT OF THE ORDINARY.

WHY WOULD THEY?

THEN CAME **DIZZINESS,** FOLLOWED BY A **FAINTING SPELL.** THAT'S WHEN HE STARTED TO GET ANXIOUS.

HIS FAMILY DOCTOR SENT HIM TO A SPECIALIST. THAT WAS A WEEK AGO. **NO ONE** KNEW. NOT HIS EMPLOYER, HIS FRIENDS OR HIS OWN **FAMILY.**

ON HIS DRIVE HOME TONIGHT, TERRY FITZGERALD EXPERIENCED HIS SECOND **BLACKOUT.** HE WAS AT HIS DESK FOR THE **FIRST** ONE.

THIS TIME HE WASN'T AS LUCKY.

IT WAS TRAVELLING AT 40 MILES PER HOUR WHEN THE ONCOMING TRUCK TRIED TO BRAKE. THERE WASN'T TIME.

THE DELIVERY TRUCK COLLIDED WITH TERRY.

HEAD ON.

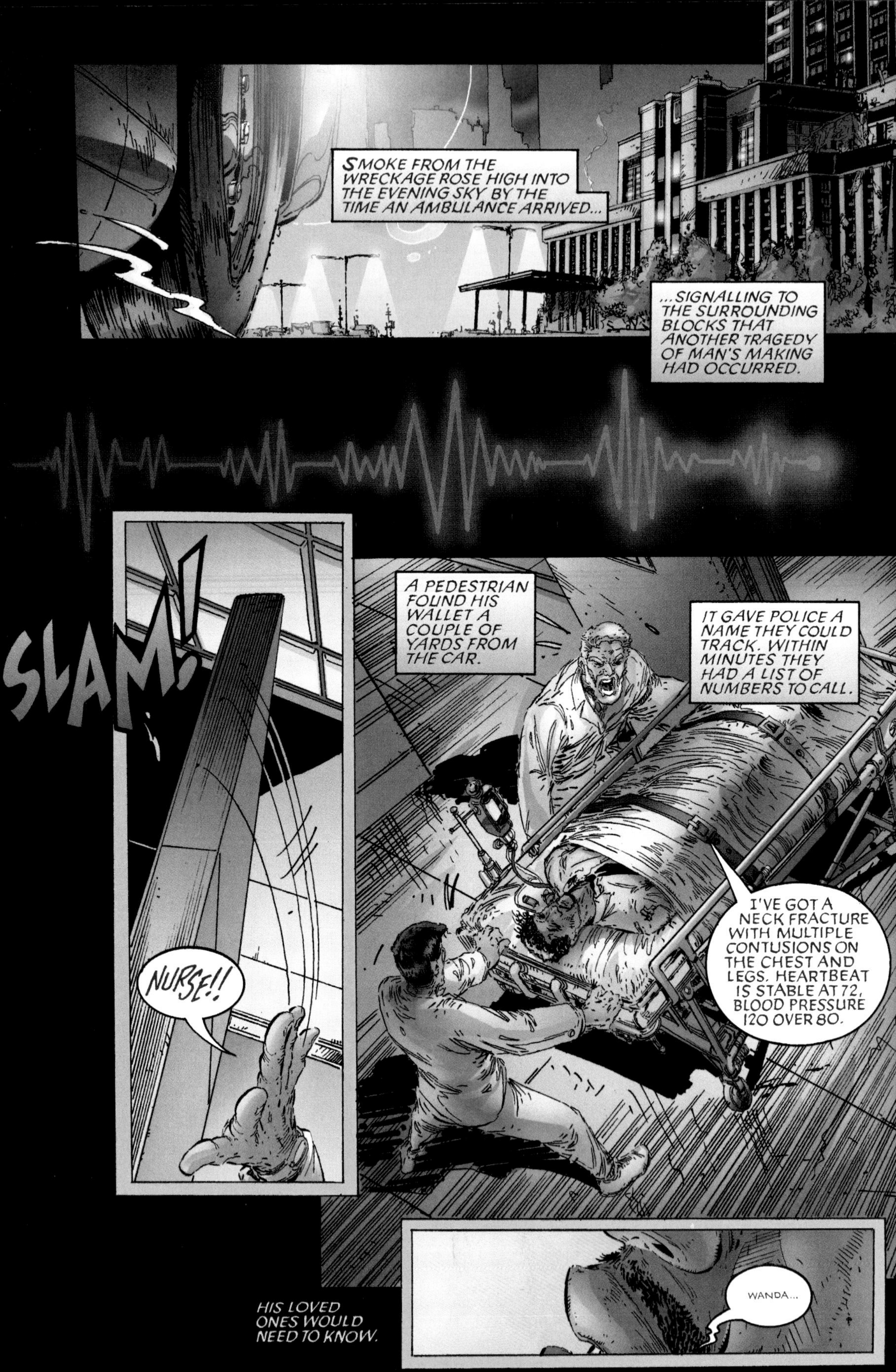
SMOKE FROM THE WRECKAGE ROSE HIGH INTO THE EVENING SKY BY THE TIME AN AMBULANCE ARRIVED...
...SIGNALLING TO THE SURROUNDING BLOCKS THAT ANOTHER TRAGEDY OF MAN'S MAKING HAD OCCURRED.
SLAM!
NURSE!!
A PEDESTRIAN FOUND HIS WALLET A COUPLE OF YARDS FROM THE CAR.
IT GAVE POLICE A NAME THEY COULD TRACK. WITHIN MINUTES THEY HAD A LIST OF NUMBERS TO CALL.
I'VE GOT A NECK FRACTURE WITH MULTIPLE CONTUSIONS ON THE CHEST AND LEGS. HEARTBEAT IS STABLE AT 72, BLOOD PRESSURE 120 OVER 80.
HIS LOVED ONES WOULD NEED TO KNOW.
WANDA...

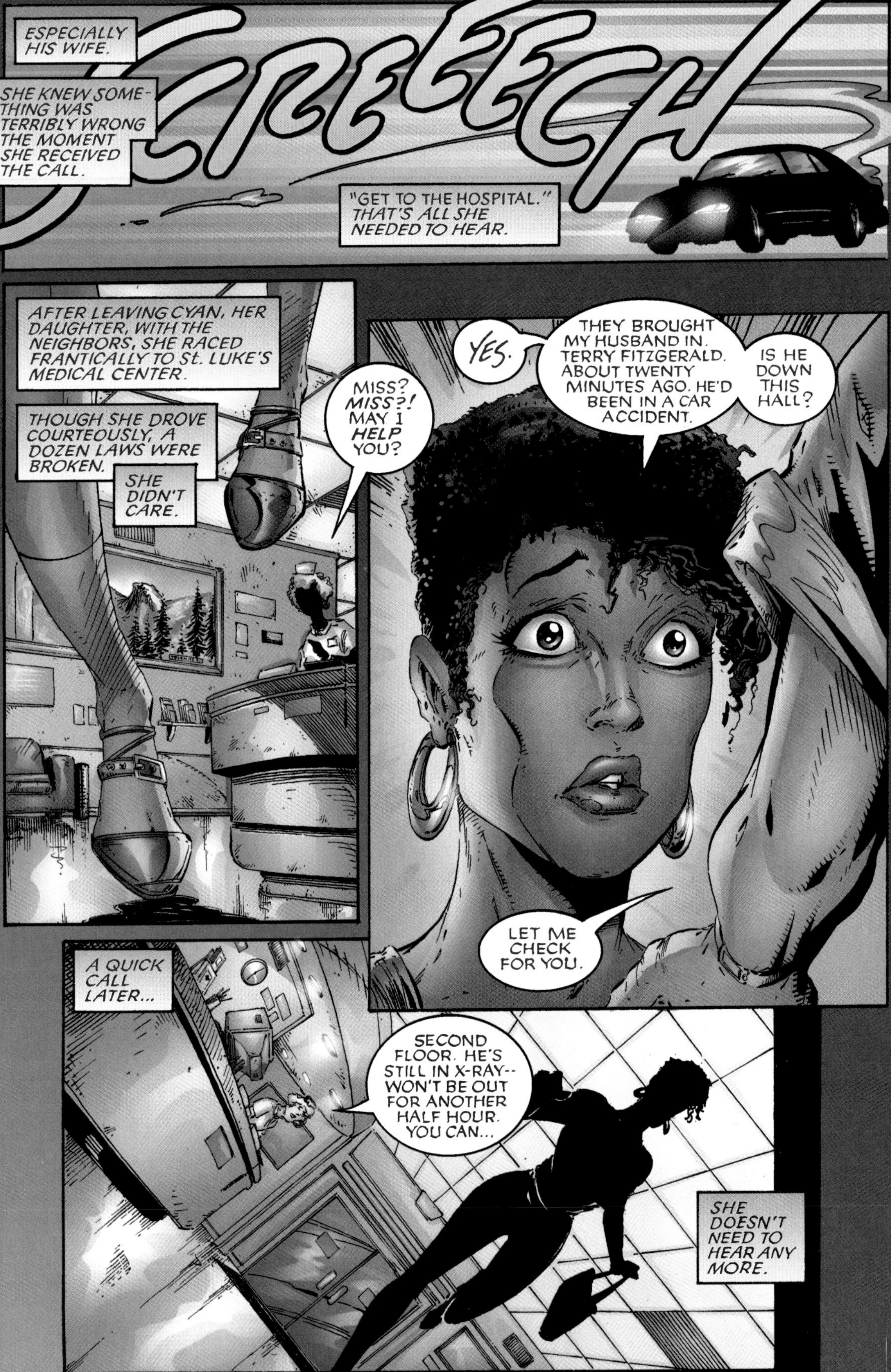
ESPECIALLY HIS WIFE.
SCREEECH
SHE KNEW SOMETHING WAS TERRIBLY WRONG THE MOMENT SHE RECEIVED THE CALL.
"GET TO THE HOSPITAL." THAT'S ALL SHE NEEDED TO HEAR.
AFTER LEAVING CYAN, HER DAUGHTER, WITH THE NEIGHBORS, SHE RACED FRANTICALLY TO St. LUKE'S MEDICAL CENTER.
THOUGH SHE DROVE COURTEOUSLY, A DOZEN LAWS WERE BROKEN.
SHE DIDN'T CARE.
MISS? MISS?! MAY I HELP YOU?
YES.
THEY BROUGHT MY HUSBAND IN. TERRY FITZGERALD. ABOUT TWENTY MINUTES AGO. HE'D BEEN IN A CAR ACCIDENT.
IS HE DOWN THIS HALL?
LET ME CHECK FOR YOU.
A QUICK CALL LATER...
SECOND FLOOR. HE'S STILL IN X-RAY-- WON'T BE OUT FOR ANOTHER HALF HOUR. YOU CAN...
SHE DOESN'T NEED TO HEAR ANY MORE.

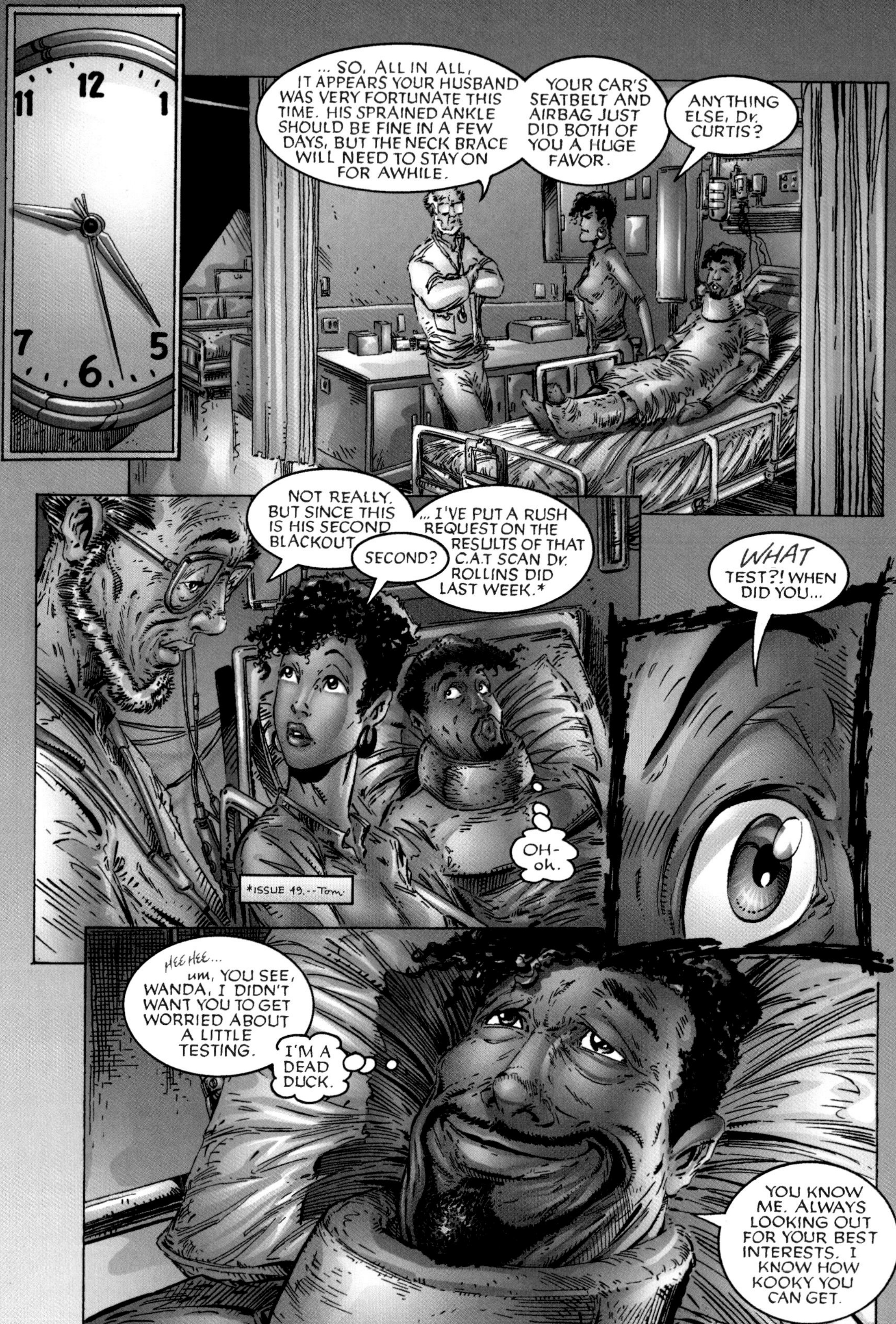
... SO, ALL IN ALL, IT APPEARS YOUR HUSBAND WAS VERY FORTUNATE THIS TIME. HIS SPRAINED ANKLE SHOULD BE FINE IN A FEW DAYS, BUT THE NECK BRACE WILL NEED TO STAY ON FOR AWHILE.
YOUR CAR'S SEATBELT AND AIRBAG JUST DID BOTH OF YOU A HUGE FAVOR.
ANYTHING ELSE, Dr. CURTIS?
NOT REALLY. BUT SINCE THIS IS HIS SECOND BLACKOUT...
SECOND?
... I'VE PUT A RUSH REQUEST ON THE RESULTS OF THAT C.A.T SCAN Dr. ROLLINS DID LAST WEEK.*
OH-oh.
*ISSUE 49.--Tom.
WHAT TEST?! WHEN DID YOU...
HEE HEE... um, YOU SEE, WANDA, I DIDN'T WANT YOU TO GET WORRIED ABOUT A LITTLE TESTING.
I'M A DEAD DUCK.
YOU KNOW ME. ALWAYS LOOKING OUT FOR YOUR BEST INTERESTS. I KNOW HOW KOOKY YOU CAN GET.

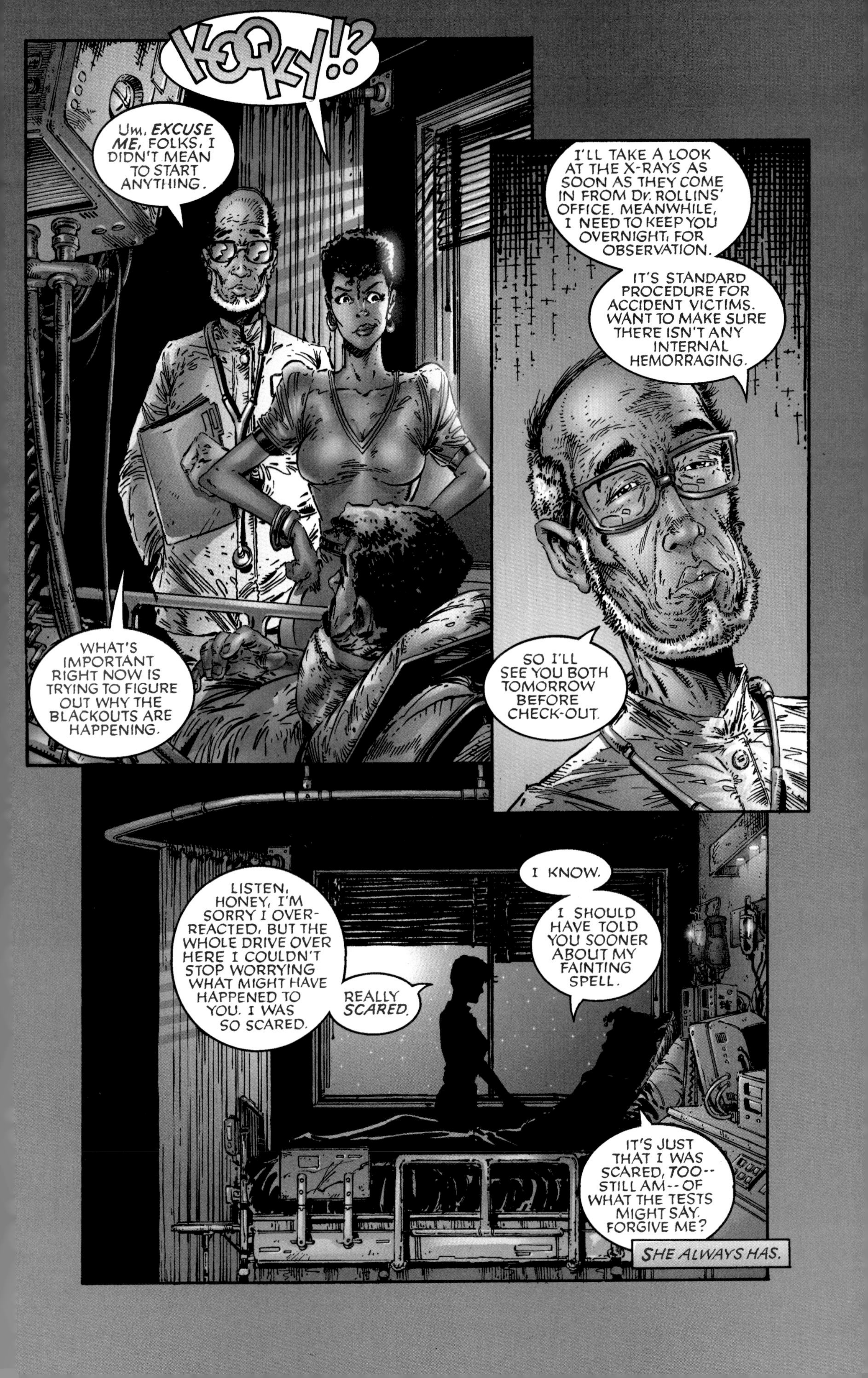
KOOKY!?
Um, EXCUSE ME, FOLKS, I DIDN'T MEAN TO START ANYTHING.
WHAT'S IMPORTANT RIGHT NOW IS TRYING TO FIGURE OUT WHY THE BLACKOUTS ARE HAPPENING.
I'LL TAKE A LOOK AT THE X-RAYS AS SOON AS THEY COME IN FROM Dr. ROLLINS' OFFICE. MEANWHILE, I NEED TO KEEP YOU OVERNIGHT, FOR OBSERVATION.
IT'S STANDARD PROCEDURE FOR ACCIDENT VICTIMS. WANT TO MAKE SURE THERE ISN'T ANY INTERNAL HEMORRAGING.
SO I'LL SEE YOU BOTH TOMORROW BEFORE CHECK-OUT.
LISTEN, HONEY, I'M SORRY I OVER-REACTED, BUT THE WHOLE DRIVE OVER HERE I COULDN'T STOP WORRYING WHAT MIGHT HAVE HAPPENED TO YOU. I WAS SO SCARED.
REALLY SCARED.
I KNOW.
I SHOULD HAVE TOLD YOU SOONER ABOUT MY FAINTING SPELL.
IT'S JUST THAT I WAS SCARED, TOO-- STILL AM-- OF WHAT THE TESTS MIGHT SAY. FORGIVE ME?
SHE ALWAYS HAS.

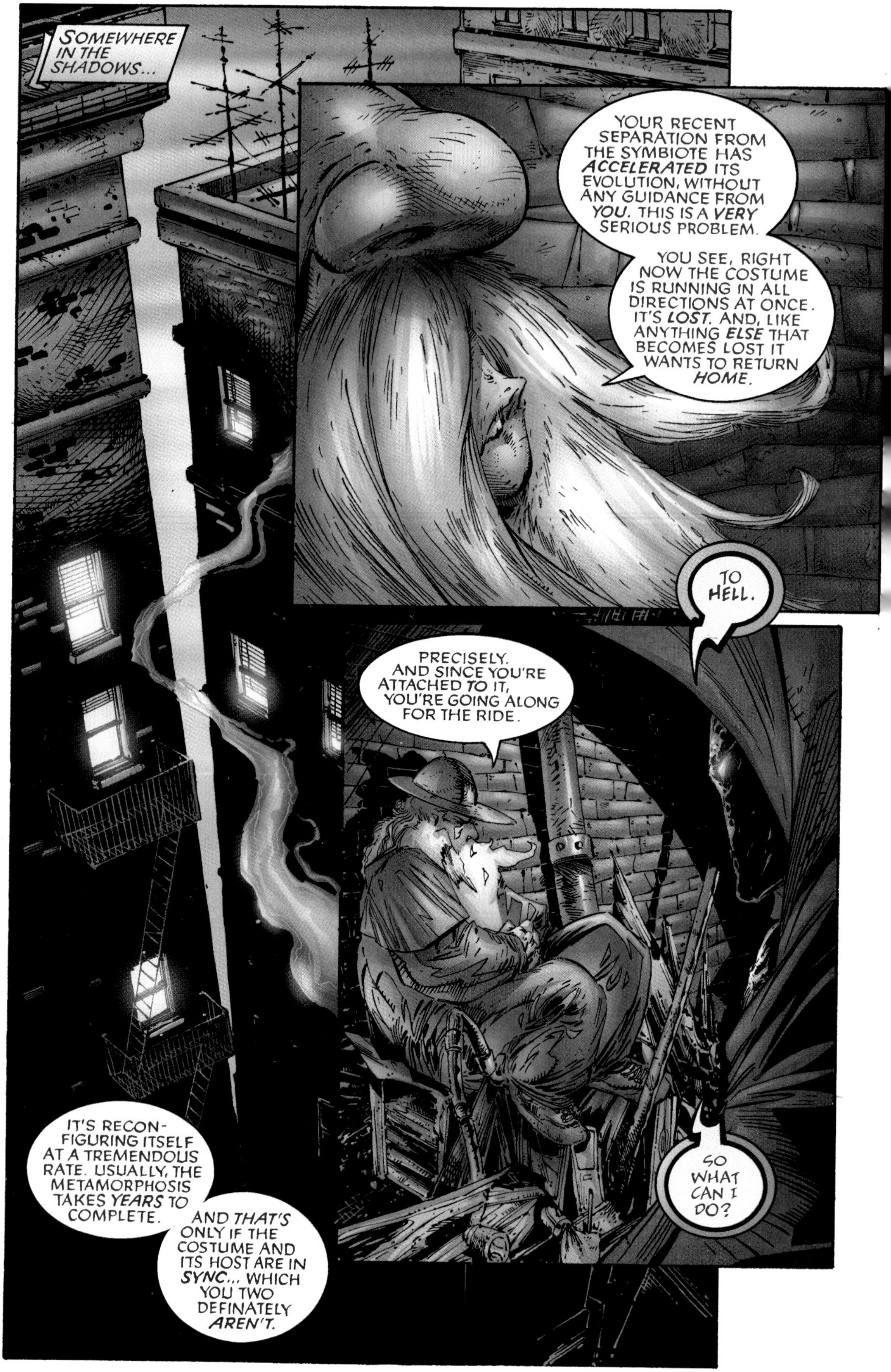
SOMEWHERE IN THE SHADOWS...
YOUR RECENT SEPARATION FROM THE SYMBIOTE HAS ACCELERATED ITS EVOLUTION, WITHOUT ANY GUIDANCE FROM YOU. THIS IS A VERY SERIOUS PROBLEM.
YOU SEE, RIGHT NOW THE COSTUME IS RUNNING IN ALL DIRECTIONS AT ONCE. IT'S LOST. AND, LIKE ANYTHING ELSE THAT BECOMES LOST IT WANTS TO RETURN HOME.
TO HELL.
PRECISELY. AND SINCE YOU'RE ATTACHED TO IT, YOU'RE GOING ALONG FOR THE RIDE.
SO WHAT CAN I DO?
IT'S RECON-FIGURING ITSELF AT A TREMENDOUS RATE. USUALLY, THE METAMORPHOSIS TAKES YEARS TO COMPLETE.
AND THAT'S ONLY IF THE COSTUME AND ITS HOST ARE IN SYNC... WHICH YOU TWO DEFINATELY AREN'T.

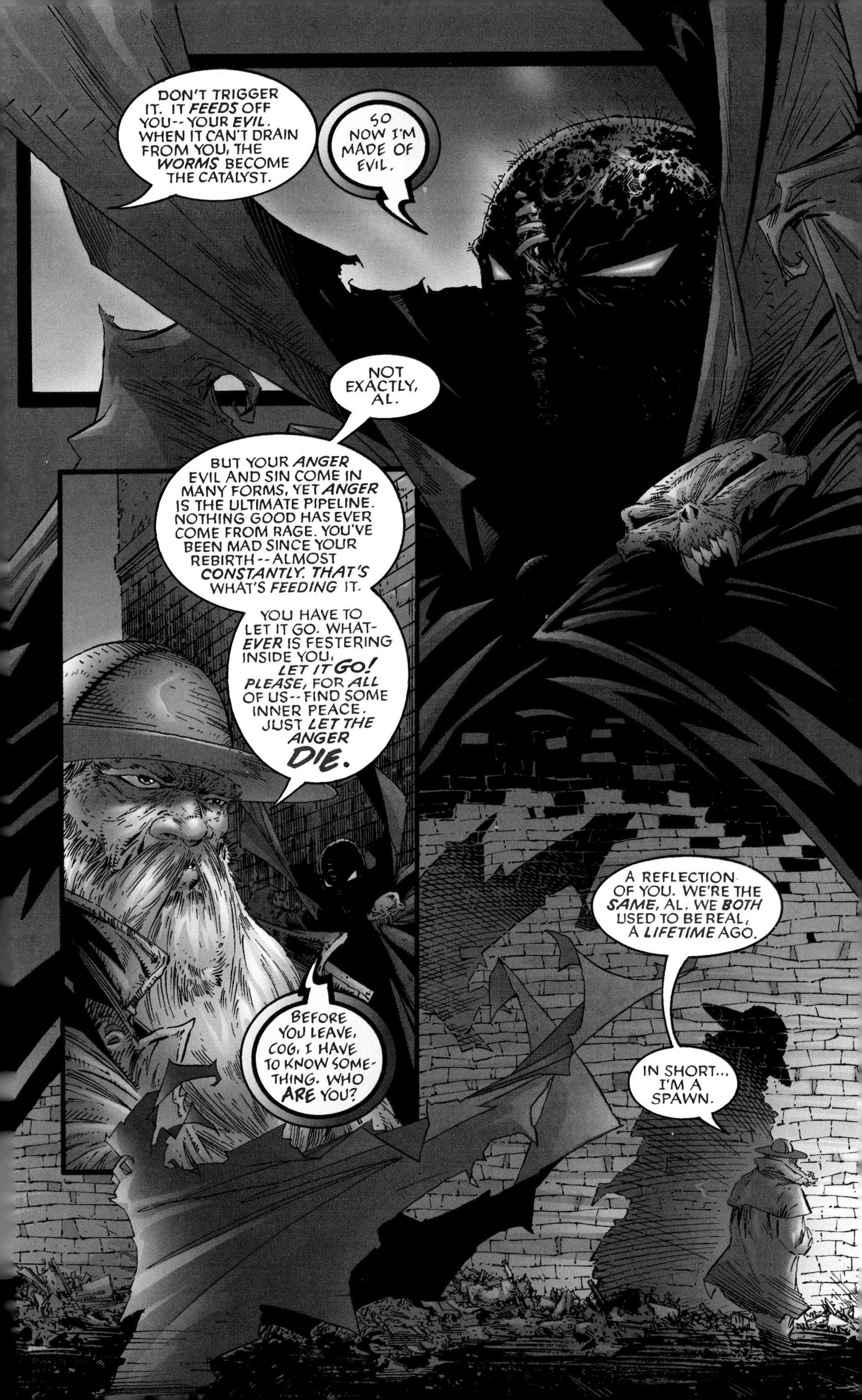
DON'T TRIGGER IT. IT FEEDS OFF YOU--YOUR EVIL. WHEN IT CAN'T DRAIN FROM YOU, THE WORMS BECOME THE CATALYST.
SO NOW I'M MADE OF EVIL.
NOT EXACTLY, AL.
BUT YOUR ANGER EVIL AND SIN COME IN MANY FORMS, YET ANGER IS THE ULTIMATE PIPELINE. NOTHING GOOD HAS EVER COME FROM RAGE. YOU'VE BEEN MAD SINCE YOUR REBIRTH--ALMOST CONSTANTLY. THAT'S WHAT'S FEEDING IT.
YOU HAVE TO LET IT GO. WHAT-EVER IS FESTERING INSIDE YOU, LET IT GO! PLEASE, FOR ALL OF US--FIND SOME INNER PEACE. JUST LET THE ANGER DIE.
BEFORE YOU LEAVE, COG. I HAVE TO KNOW SOME-THING. WHO ARE YOU?
A REFLECTION OF YOU. WE'RE THE SAME, AL. WE BOTH USED TO BE REAL, A LIFETIME AGO.
IN SHORT... I'M A SPAWN.

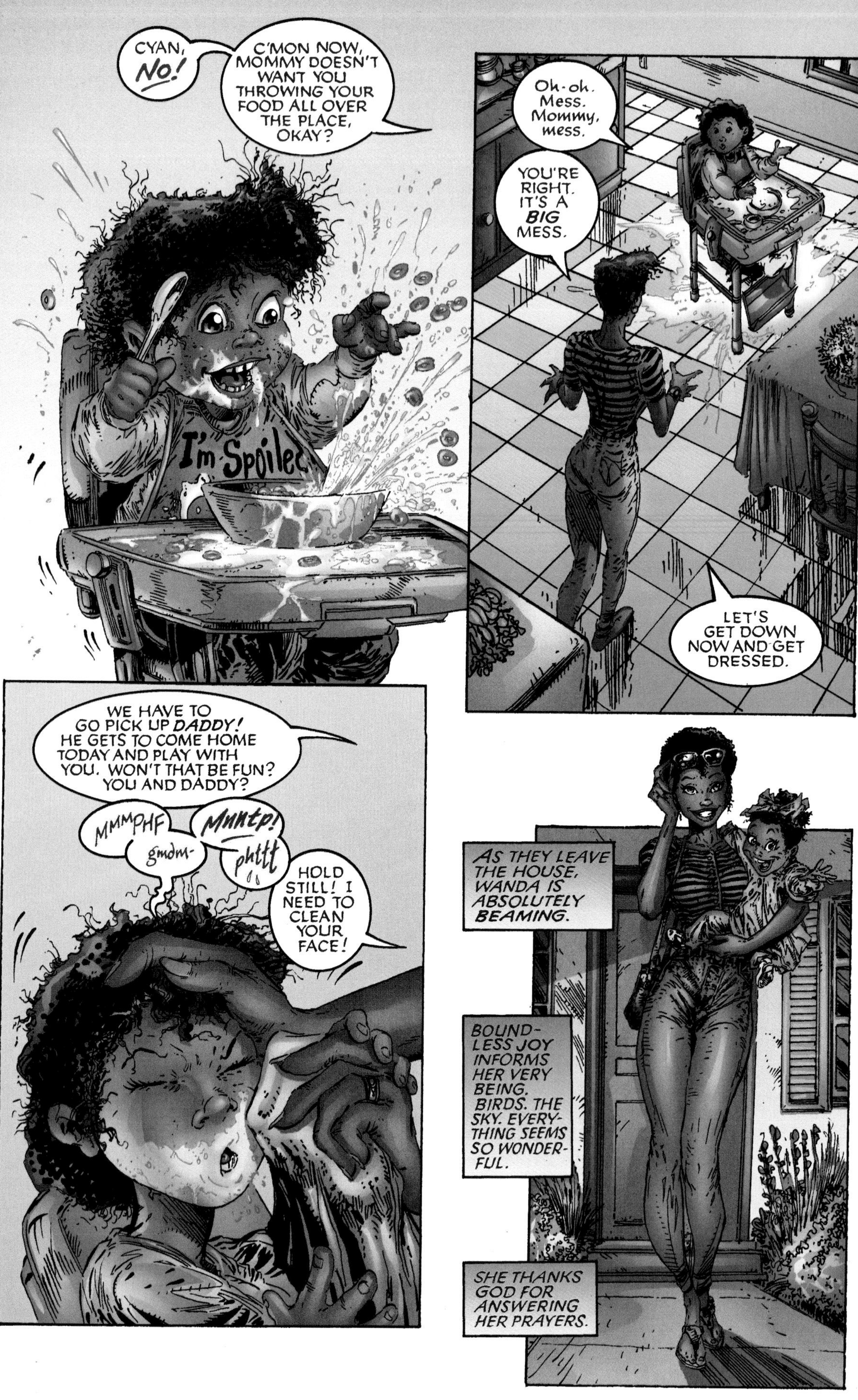
CYAN, No!
C'MON NOW, MOMMY DOESN'T WANT YOU THROWING YOUR FOOD ALL OVER THE PLACE, OKAY?
I'm Spoiled
Oh-oh. Mess. Mommy, mess.
YOU'RE RIGHT. IT'S A BIG MESS.
LET'S GET DOWN NOW AND GET DRESSED.
WE HAVE TO GO PICK UP DADDY! HE GETS TO COME HOME TODAY AND PLAY WITH YOU. WON'T THAT BE FUN? YOU AND DADDY?
MMMPHF
gmdm-
Mnntp!
phttt
HOLD STILL! I NEED TO CLEAN YOUR FACE!
AS THEY LEAVE THE HOUSE, WANDA IS ABSOLUTELY BEAMING.
BOUNDLESS JOY INFORMS HER VERY BEING. BIRDS. THE SKY. EVERYTHING SEEMS SO WONDERFUL.
SHE THANKS GOD FOR ANSWERING HER PRAYERS.

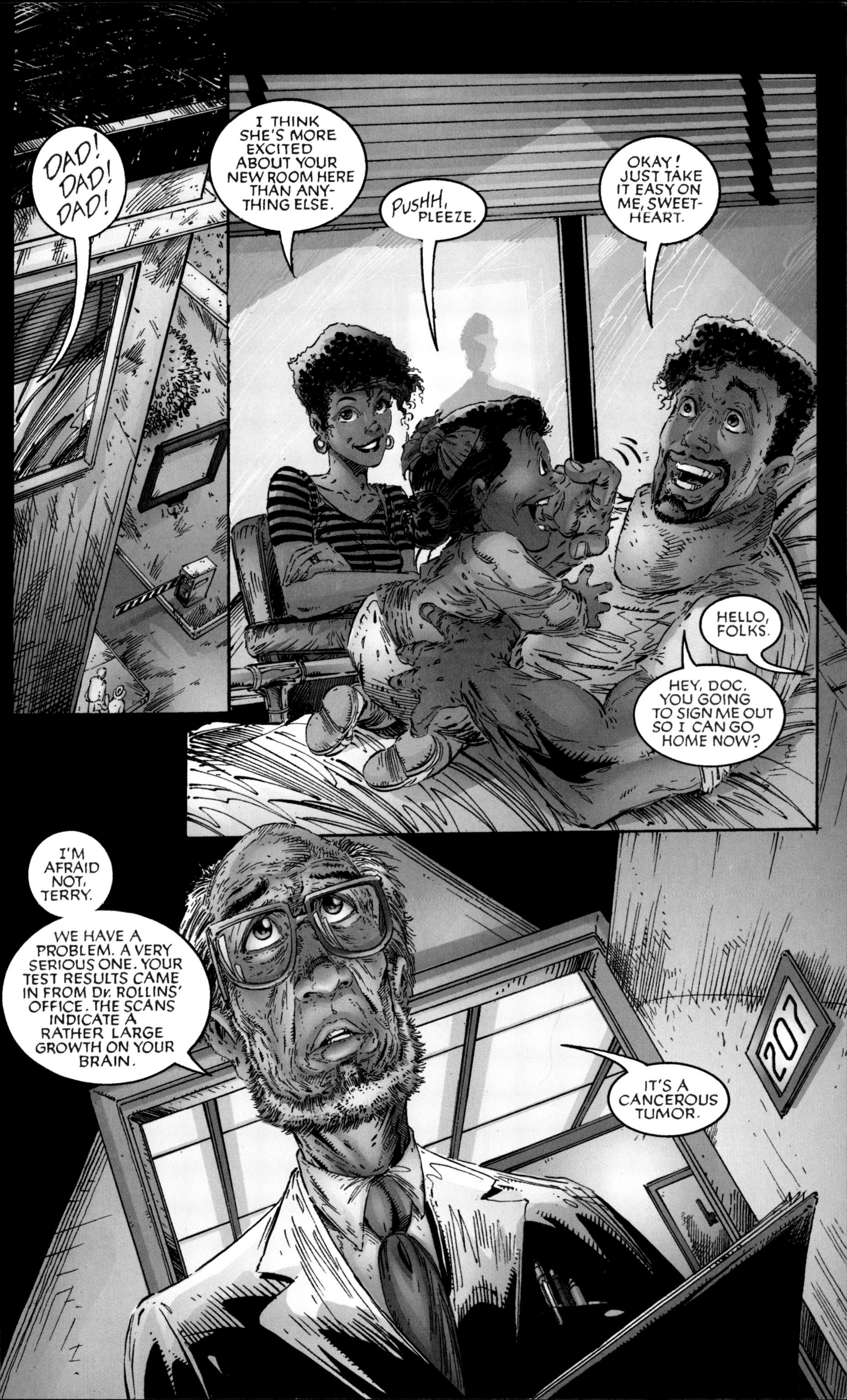
DAD! DAD! DAD!
I THINK SHE'S MORE EXCITED ABOUT YOUR NEW ROOM HERE THAN ANY-THING ELSE.
PUSHH, PLEEZE.
OKAY! JUST TAKE IT EASY ON ME, SWEET-HEART.
HELLO, FOLKS.
HEY, DOC, YOU GOING TO SIGN ME OUT SO I CAN GO HOME NOW?
I'M AFRAID NOT, TERRY.
WE HAVE A PROBLEM. A VERY SERIOUS ONE. YOUR TEST RESULTS CAME IN FROM Dr. ROLLINS' OFFICE. THE SCANS INDICATE A RATHER LARGE GROWTH ON YOUR BRAIN.
IT'S A CANCEROUS TUMOR.
207

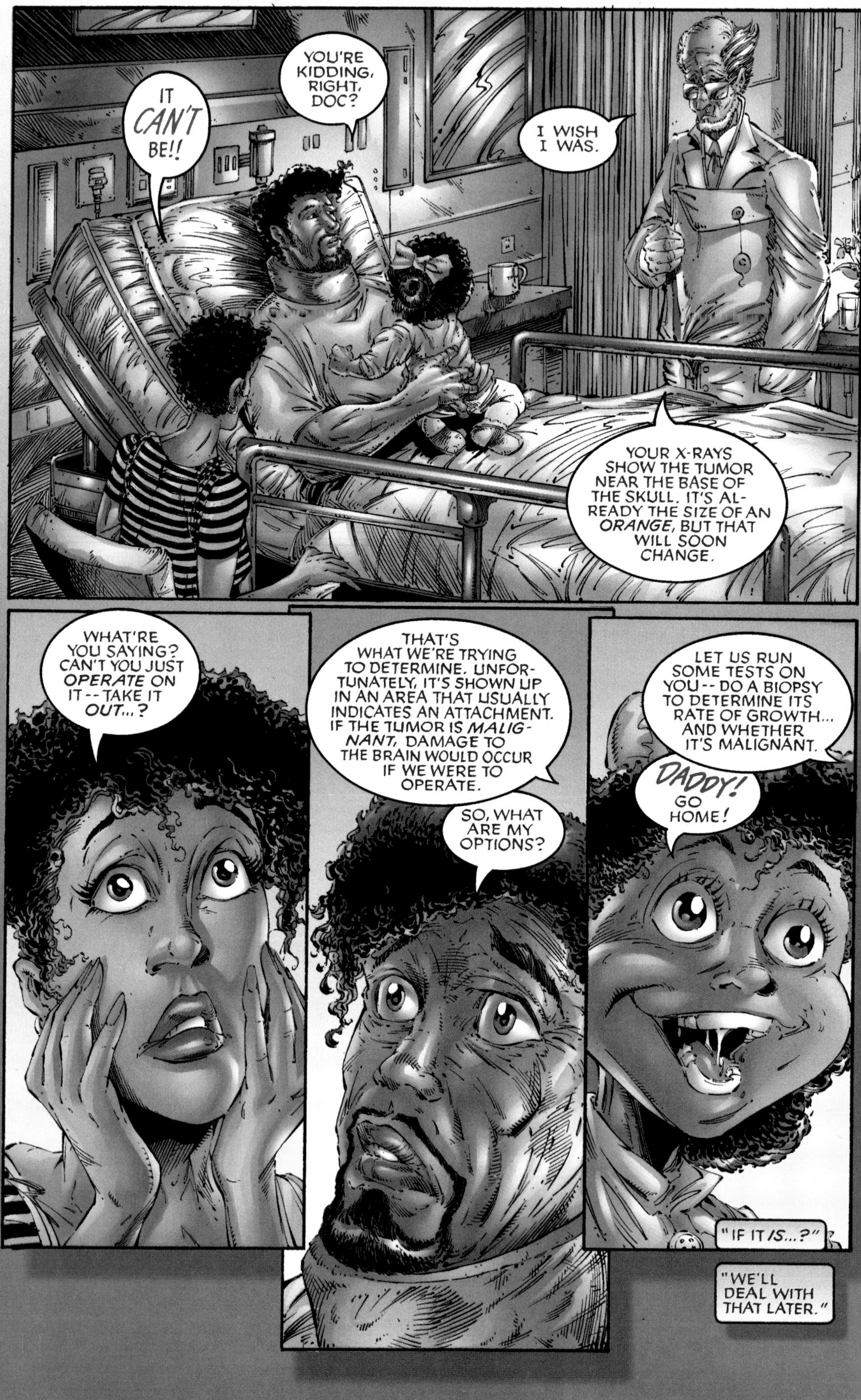
IT CAN'T BE!!
YOU'RE KIDDING, RIGHT, DOC?
I WISH I WAS.
YOUR X-RAYS SHOW THE TUMOR NEAR THE BASE OF THE SKULL. IT'S AL-READY THE SIZE OF AN *ORANGE*, BUT THAT WILL SOON CHANGE.
WHAT'RE YOU SAYING? CAN'T YOU JUST *OPERATE* ON IT -- TAKE IT *OUT*...?
THAT'S WHAT WE'RE TRYING TO DETERMINE. UNFOR-TUNATELY, IT'S SHOWN UP IN AN AREA THAT USUALLY INDICATES AN ATTACHMENT. IF THE TUMOR IS *MALIG-NANT,* DAMAGE TO THE BRAIN WOULD OCCUR IF WE WERE TO OPERATE.
SO, WHAT ARE MY OPTIONS?
LET US RUN SOME TESTS ON YOU -- DO A BIOPSY TO DETERMINE ITS RATE OF GROWTH... AND WHETHER IT'S MALIGNANT.
DADDY! GO HOME!
"IF IT *IS*...?"
"WE'LL DEAL WITH THAT LATER."

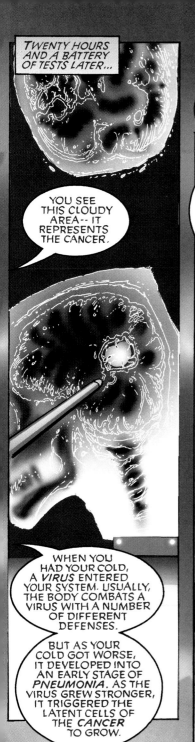

TWENTY HOURS AND A BATTERY OF TESTS LATER...

YOU SEE THIS CLOUDY AREA-- IT REPRESENTS THE CANCER.

WHEN YOU HAD YOUR COLD, A *VIRUS* ENTERED YOUR SYSTEM. USUALLY, THE BODY COMBATS A VIRUS WITH A NUMBER OF DIFFERENT DEFENSES.

BUT AS YOUR COLD GOT WORSE, IT DEVELOPED INTO AN EARLY STAGE OF *PNEUMONIA*. AS THE VIRUS GREW STRONGER, IT TRIGGERED THE LATENT CELLS OF THE *CANCER* TO GROW.

MEANING YOU'VE ALWAYS HAD THIS IN YOU, JUST IN A DORMANT STATE. YOU, LIKE MILLIONS OF OTHERS, WERE PROBABLY BORN WITH IT.

UNFORTUNATELY, ITS POSITIONING MAKES IT IMPOSSIBLE FOR US TO OPERATE. TO REMOVE IT *ALL*, I'D HAVE TO REMOVE PART OF THE BRAIN, *TOO*. THIS IS COMPOUNDED BY THE FACT THAT THE TUMOR IS *MALIGNANT*.

MALIGNANT.

TERRY SQUEEZES WANDA EVEN HARDER.

SO IT'D JUST GROW BACK, EVEN IF YOU *COULD* REMOVE IT.

YES.

MEANING I'M GOING TO *DIE*. ISN'T THAT RIGHT, DOCTOR? H-HOW MUCH TIME DO I HAVE?

AT ITS CURRENT RATE OF GROWTH, ABOUT TWO MONTHS, BUT THERE IS A SERIES OF PROCEDURES THAT CAN SLOW THE SPEAD OF IT.

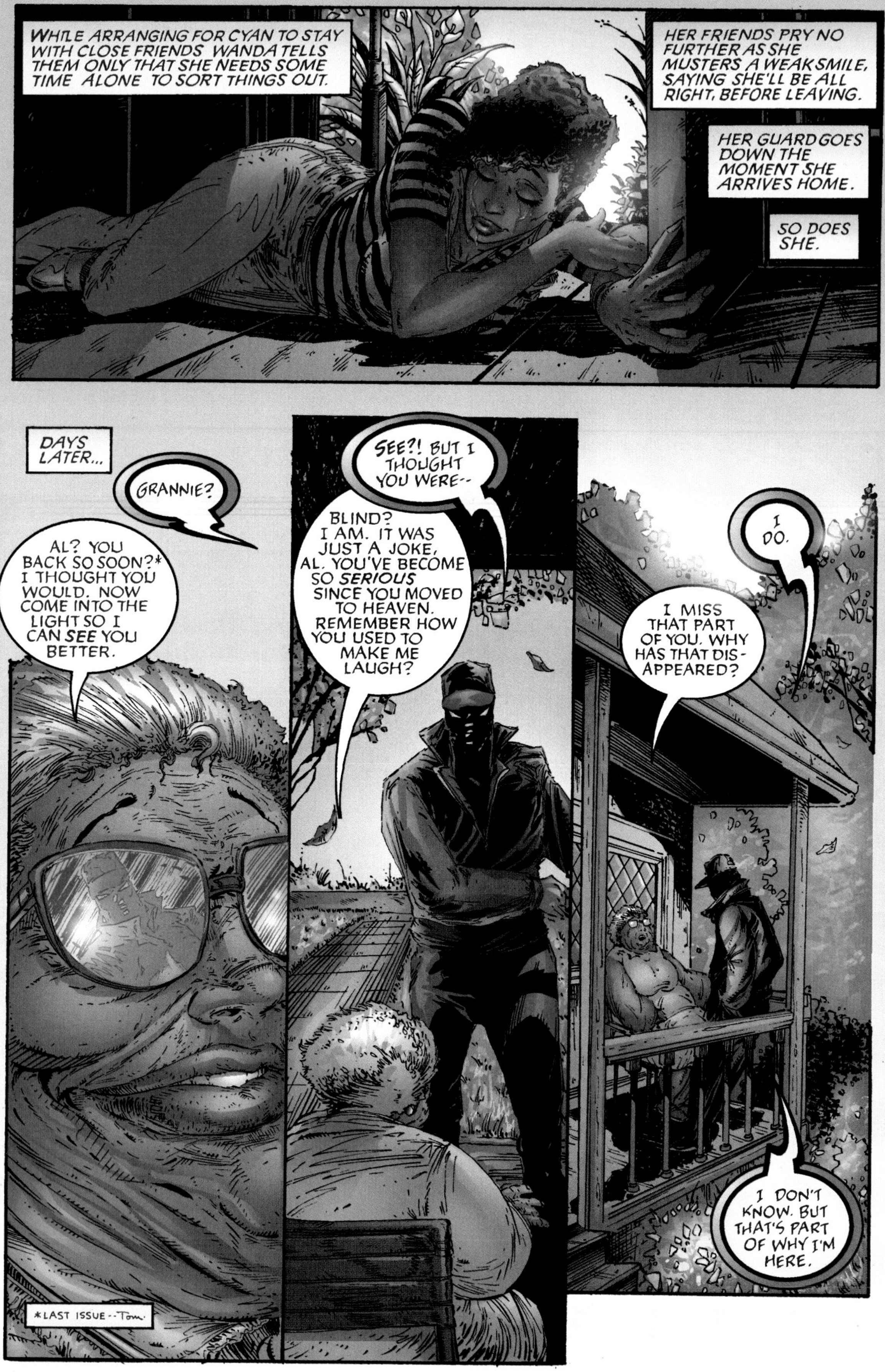
WHILE ARRANGING FOR CYAN TO STAY WITH CLOSE FRIENDS WANDA TELLS THEM ONLY THAT SHE NEEDS SOME TIME ALONE TO SORT THINGS OUT.
HER FRIENDS PRY NO FURTHER AS SHE MUSTERS A WEAK SMILE, SAYING SHE'LL BE ALL RIGHT, BEFORE LEAVING.
HER GUARD GOES DOWN THE MOMENT SHE ARRIVES HOME.
SO DOES SHE.
DAYS LATER...
GRANNIE?
AL? YOU BACK SO SOON?* I THOUGHT YOU WOULD. NOW COME INTO THE LIGHT SO I CAN SEE YOU BETTER.
*LAST ISSUE--Tom.
SEE?! BUT I THOUGHT YOU WERE--
BLIND? I AM. IT WAS JUST A JOKE, AL. YOU'VE BECOME SO SERIOUS SINCE YOU MOVED TO HEAVEN. REMEMBER HOW YOU USED TO MAKE ME LAUGH?
I DO.
I MISS THAT PART OF YOU. WHY HAS THAT DIS-APPEARED?
I DON'T KNOW. BUT THAT'S PART OF WHY I'M HERE.

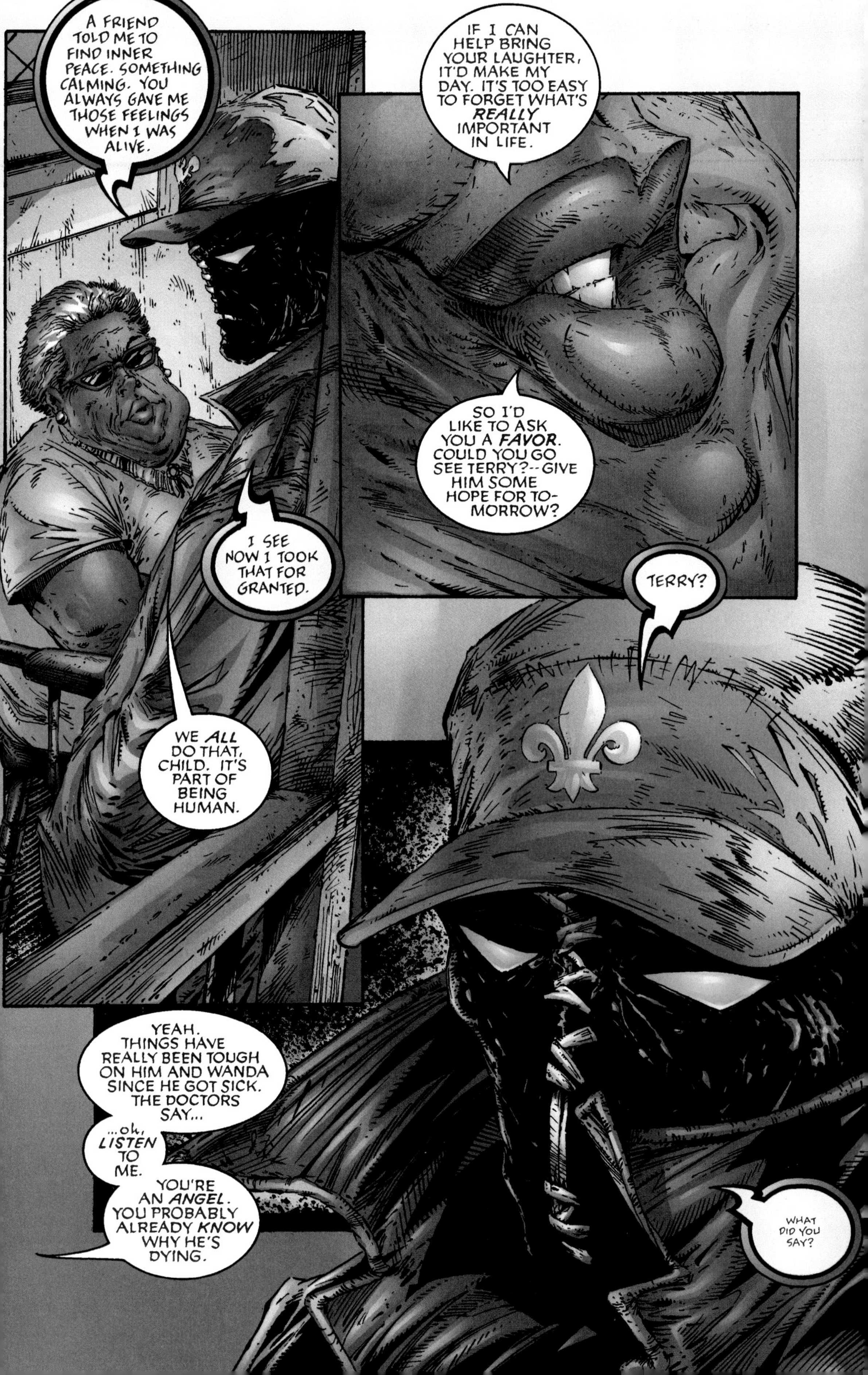
A FRIEND TOLD ME TO FIND INNER PEACE. SOMETHING CALMING. YOU ALWAYS GAVE ME THOSE FEELINGS WHEN I WAS ALIVE.
I SEE NOW I TOOK THAT FOR GRANTED.
WE ALL DO THAT, CHILD. IT'S PART OF BEING HUMAN.
IF I CAN HELP BRING YOUR LAUGHTER, IT'D MAKE MY DAY. IT'S TOO EASY TO FORGET WHAT'S REALLY IMPORTANT IN LIFE.
SO I'D LIKE TO ASK YOU A FAVOR. COULD YOU GO SEE TERRY?--GIVE HIM SOME HOPE FOR TO-MORROW?
TERRY?
YEAH. THINGS HAVE REALLY BEEN TOUGH ON HIM AND WANDA SINCE HE GOT SICK. THE DOCTORS SAY...
...oh, LISTEN TO ME.
YOU'RE AN ANGEL. YOU PROBABLY ALREADY KNOW WHY HE'S DYING.
WHAT DID YOU SAY?

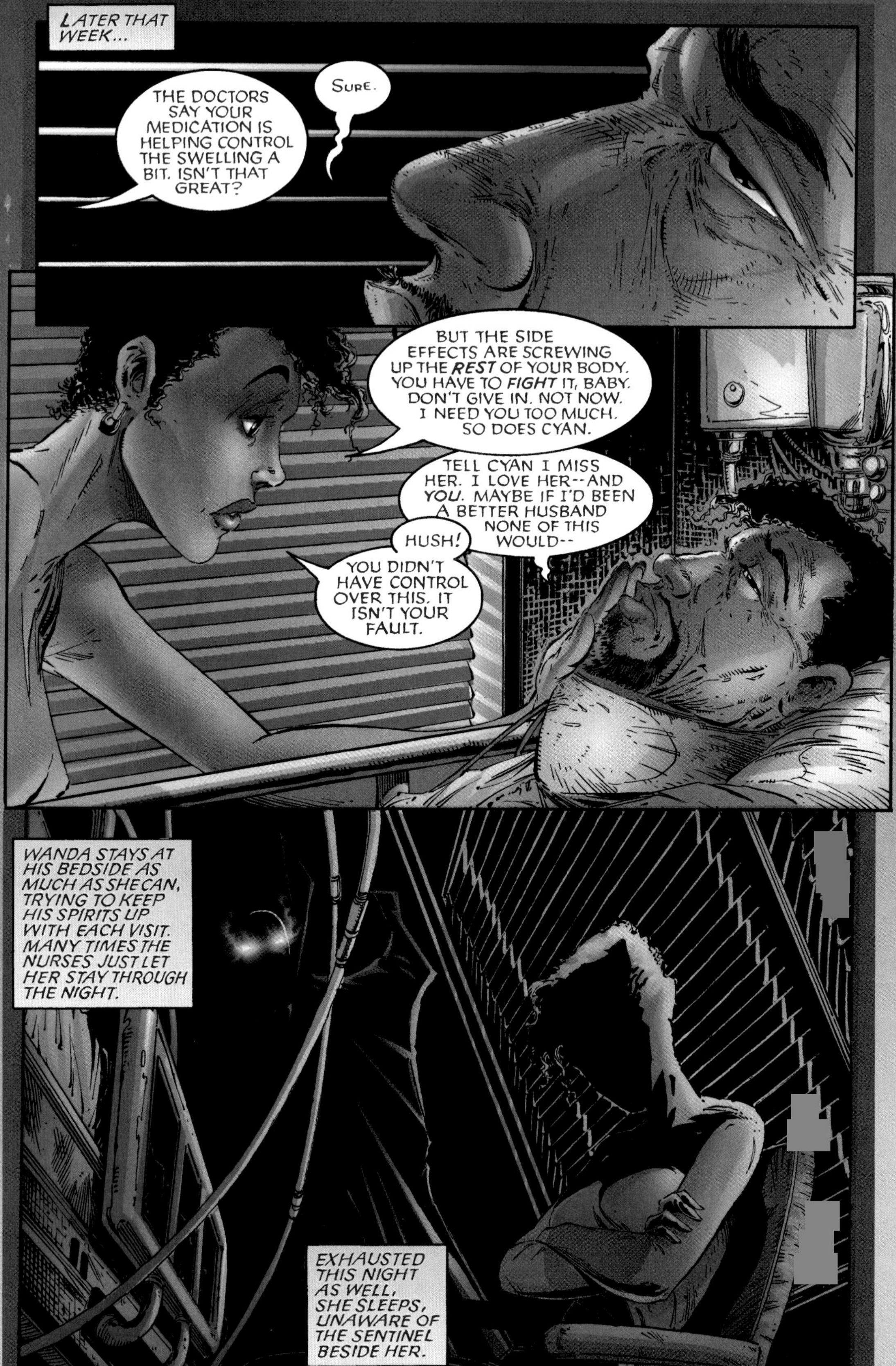
LATER THAT WEEK...
THE DOCTORS SAY YOUR MEDICATION IS HELPING CONTROL THE SWELLING A BIT. ISN'T THAT GREAT?
SURE.
BUT THE SIDE EFFECTS ARE SCREWING UP THE REST OF YOUR BODY. YOU HAVE TO FIGHT IT, BABY. DON'T GIVE IN. NOT NOW. I NEED YOU TOO MUCH. SO DOES CYAN.
TELL CYAN I MISS HER. I LOVE HER--AND YOU. MAYBE IF I'D BEEN A BETTER HUSBAND NONE OF THIS WOULD--
HUSH!
YOU DIDN'T HAVE CONTROL OVER THIS. IT ISN'T YOUR FAULT.
WANDA STAYS AT HIS BEDSIDE AS MUCH AS SHE CAN, TRYING TO KEEP HIS SPIRITS UP WITH EACH VISIT. MANY TIMES THE NURSES JUST LET HER STAY THROUGH THE NIGHT.
EXHAUSTED THIS NIGHT AS WELL, SHE SLEEPS, UNAWARE OF THE SENTINEL BESIDE HER.

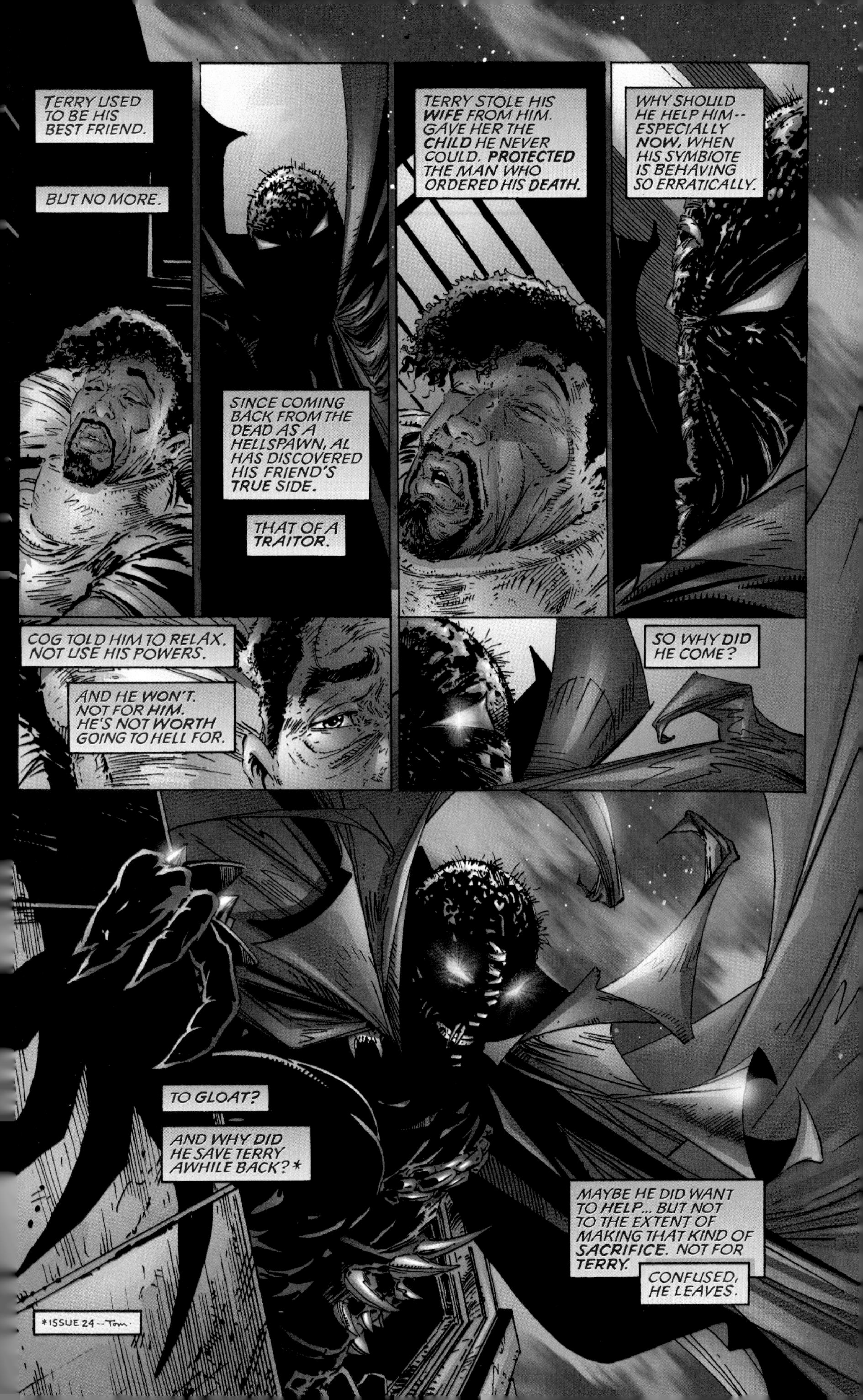

TERRY USED TO BE HIS BEST FRIEND.
BUT NO MORE.
SINCE COMING BACK FROM THE DEAD AS A HELLSPAWN, AL HAS DISCOVERED HIS FRIEND'S TRUE SIDE.
THAT OF A TRAITOR.
TERRY STOLE HIS WIFE FROM HIM. GAVE HER THE CHILD HE NEVER COULD. PROTECTED THE MAN WHO ORDERED HIS DEATH.
WHY SHOULD HE HELP HIM-- ESPECIALLY NOW, WHEN HIS SYMBIOTE IS BEHAVING SO ERRATICALLY.
COG TOLD HIM TO RELAX. NOT USE HIS POWERS.
AND HE WON'T. NOT FOR HIM. HE'S NOT WORTH GOING TO HELL FOR.
SO WHY DID HE COME?
TO GLOAT?
AND WHY DID HE SAVE TERRY AWHILE BACK?*
MAYBE HE DID WANT TO HELP... BUT NOT TO THE EXTENT OF MAKING THAT KIND OF SACRIFICE. NOT FOR TERRY.
CONFUSED, HE LEAVES.
*ISSUE 24 --Tom

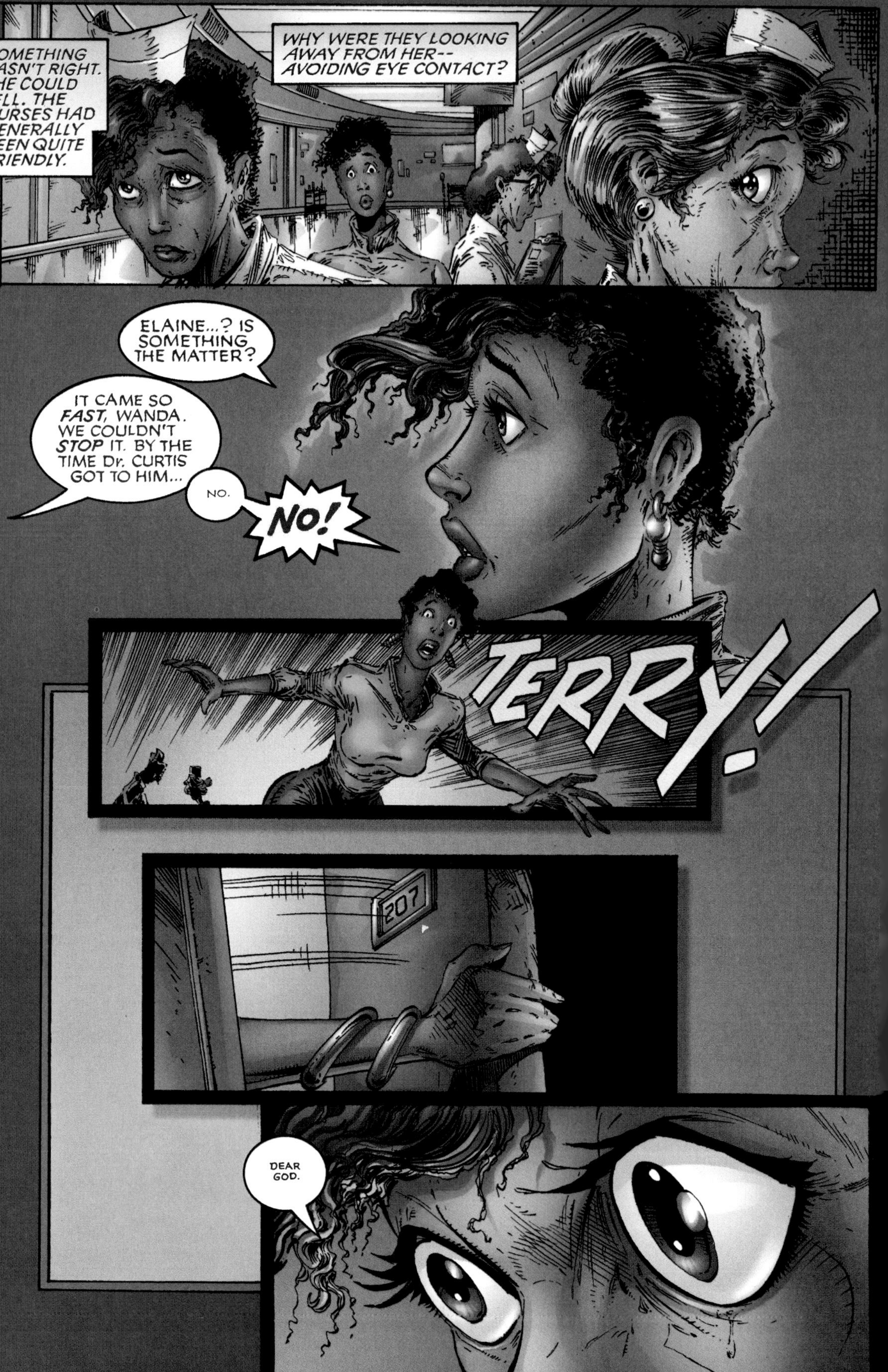
SOMETHING WASN'T RIGHT. SHE COULD TELL. THE NURSES HAD GENERALLY BEEN QUITE FRIENDLY.
WHY WERE THEY LOOKING AWAY FROM HER-- AVOIDING EYE CONTACT?
ELAINE...? IS SOMETHING THE MATTER?
IT CAME SO FAST, WANDA. WE COULDN'T STOP IT. BY THE TIME Dr. CURTIS GOT TO HIM...
NO.
NO!
TERRY!
207
DEAR GOD.

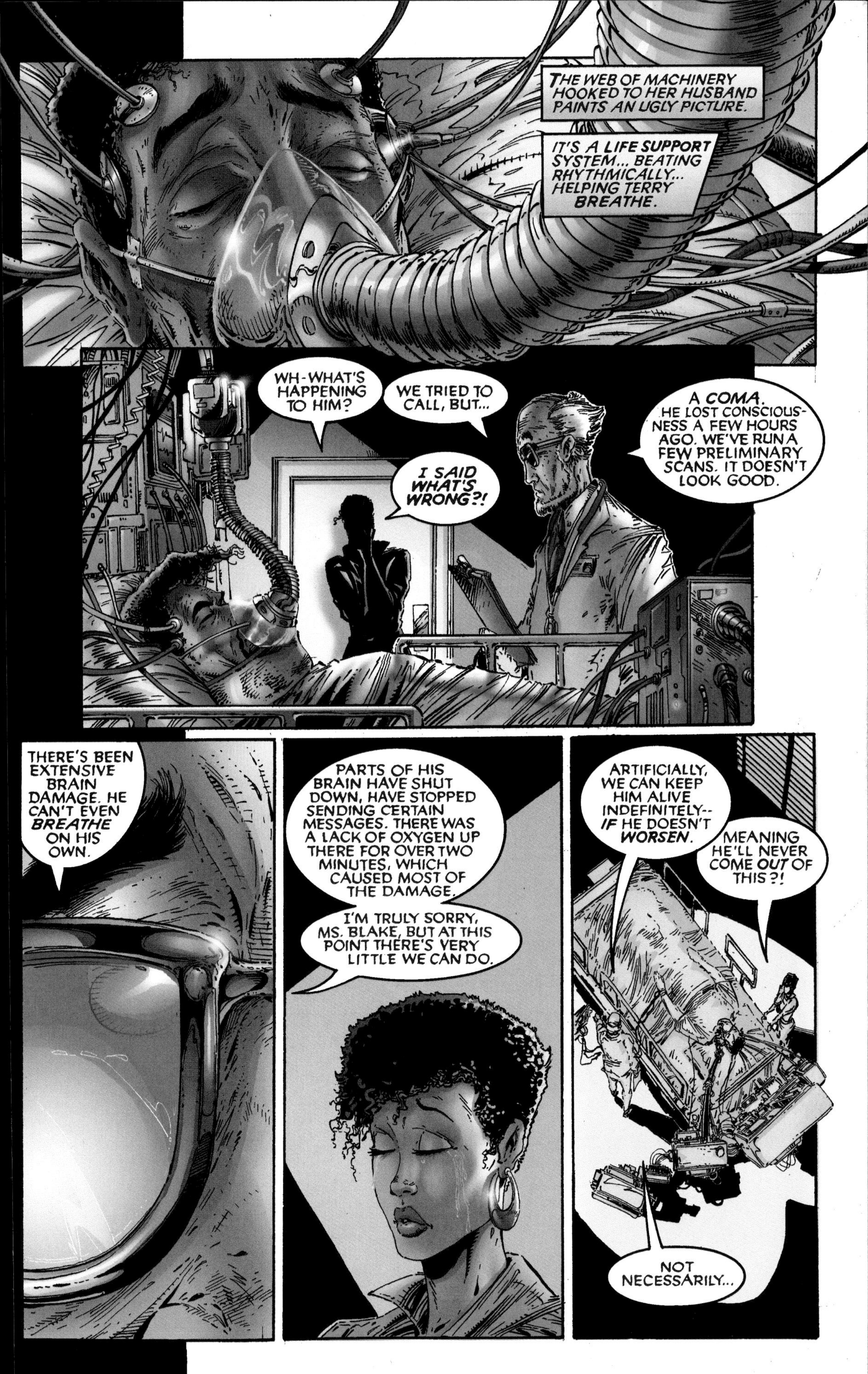

THE WEB OF MACHINERY HOOKED TO HER HUSBAND PAINTS AN UGLY PICTURE.
IT'S A LIFE SUPPORT SYSTEM... BEATING RHYTHMICALLY... HELPING TERRY BREATHE.
WH-WHAT'S HAPPENING TO HIM?
WE TRIED TO CALL, BUT...
I SAID WHAT'S WRONG?!
A COMA. HE LOST CONSCIOUSNESS A FEW HOURS AGO. WE'VE RUN A FEW PRELIMINARY SCANS. IT DOESN'T LOOK GOOD.
THERE'S BEEN EXTENSIVE BRAIN DAMAGE. HE CAN'T EVEN BREATHE ON HIS OWN.
PARTS OF HIS BRAIN HAVE SHUT DOWN, HAVE STOPPED SENDING CERTAIN MESSAGES. THERE WAS A LACK OF OXYGEN UP THERE FOR OVER TWO MINUTES, WHICH CAUSED MOST OF THE DAMAGE.
I'M TRULY SORRY, MS. BLAKE, BUT AT THIS POINT THERE'S VERY LITTLE WE CAN DO.
ARTIFICIALLY, WE CAN KEEP HIM ALIVE INDEFINITELY-- IF HE DOESN'T WORSEN.
MEANING HE'LL NEVER COME OUT OF THIS?!
NOT NECESSARILY...

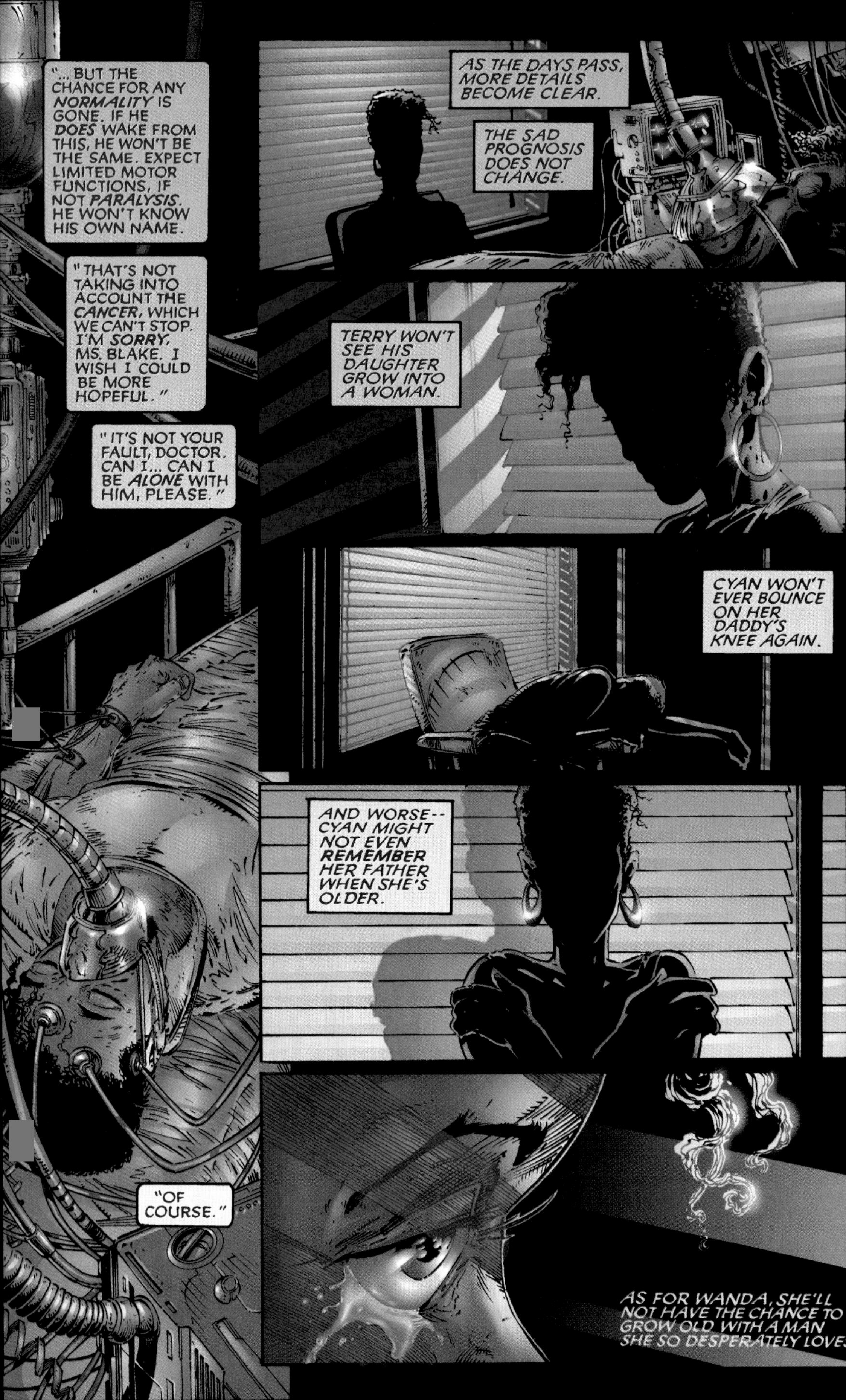
"... BUT THE CHANCE FOR ANY NORMALITY IS GONE. IF HE DOES WAKE FROM THIS, HE WON'T BE THE SAME. EXPECT LIMITED MOTOR FUNCTIONS, IF NOT PARALYSIS. HE WON'T KNOW HIS OWN NAME.
"THAT'S NOT TAKING INTO ACCOUNT THE CANCER, WHICH WE CAN'T STOP. I'M SORRY, MS. BLAKE. I WISH I COULD BE MORE HOPEFUL."
"IT'S NOT YOUR FAULT, DOCTOR. CAN I... CAN I BE ALONE WITH HIM, PLEASE."
"OF COURSE."
AS THE DAYS PASS, MORE DETAILS BECOME CLEAR.
THE SAD PROGNOSIS DOES NOT CHANGE.
TERRY WON'T SEE HIS DAUGHTER GROW INTO A WOMAN.
CYAN WON'T EVER BOUNCE ON HER DADDY'S KNEE AGAIN.
AND WORSE-- CYAN MIGHT NOT EVEN REMEMBER HER FATHER WHEN SHE'S OLDER.
AS FOR WANDA, SHE'LL NOT HAVE THE CHANCE TO GROW OLD WITH A MAN SHE SO DESPERATELY LOVES.

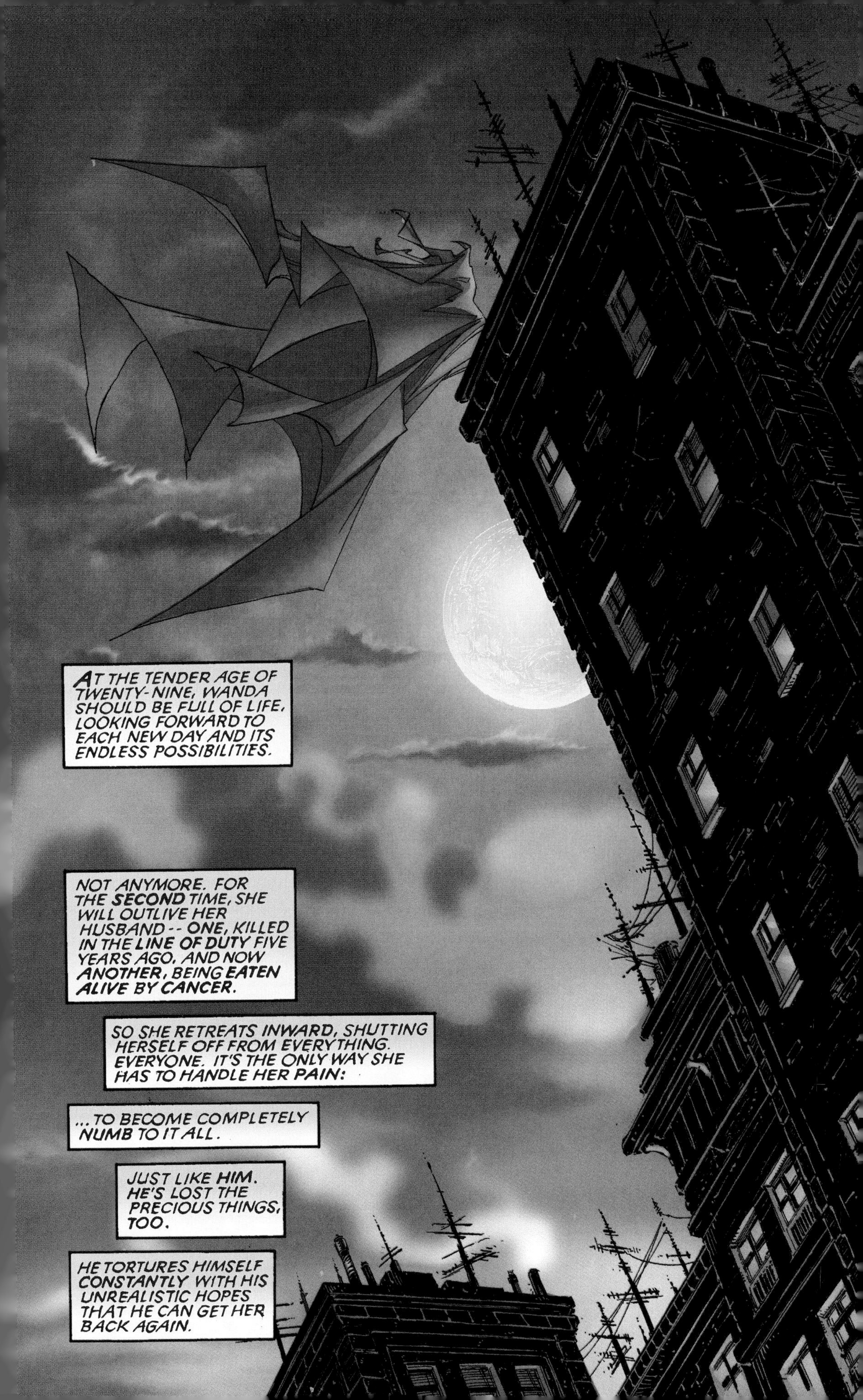
AT THE TENDER AGE OF TWENTY-NINE, WANDA SHOULD BE FULL OF LIFE, LOOKING FORWARD TO EACH NEW DAY AND ITS ENDLESS POSSIBILITIES.
NOT ANYMORE. FOR THE SECOND TIME, SHE WILL OUTLIVE HER HUSBAND -- ONE, KILLED IN THE LINE OF DUTY FIVE YEARS AGO, AND NOW ANOTHER, BEING EATEN ALIVE BY CANCER.
SO SHE RETREATS INWARD, SHUTTING HERSELF OFF FROM EVERYTHING. EVERYONE. IT'S THE ONLY WAY SHE HAS TO HANDLE HER PAIN:
...TO BECOME COMPLETELY NUMB TO IT ALL.
JUST LIKE HIM. HE'S LOST THE PRECIOUS THINGS, TOO.
HE TORTURES HIMSELF CONSTANTLY WITH HIS UNREALISTIC HOPES THAT HE CAN GET HER BACK AGAIN.

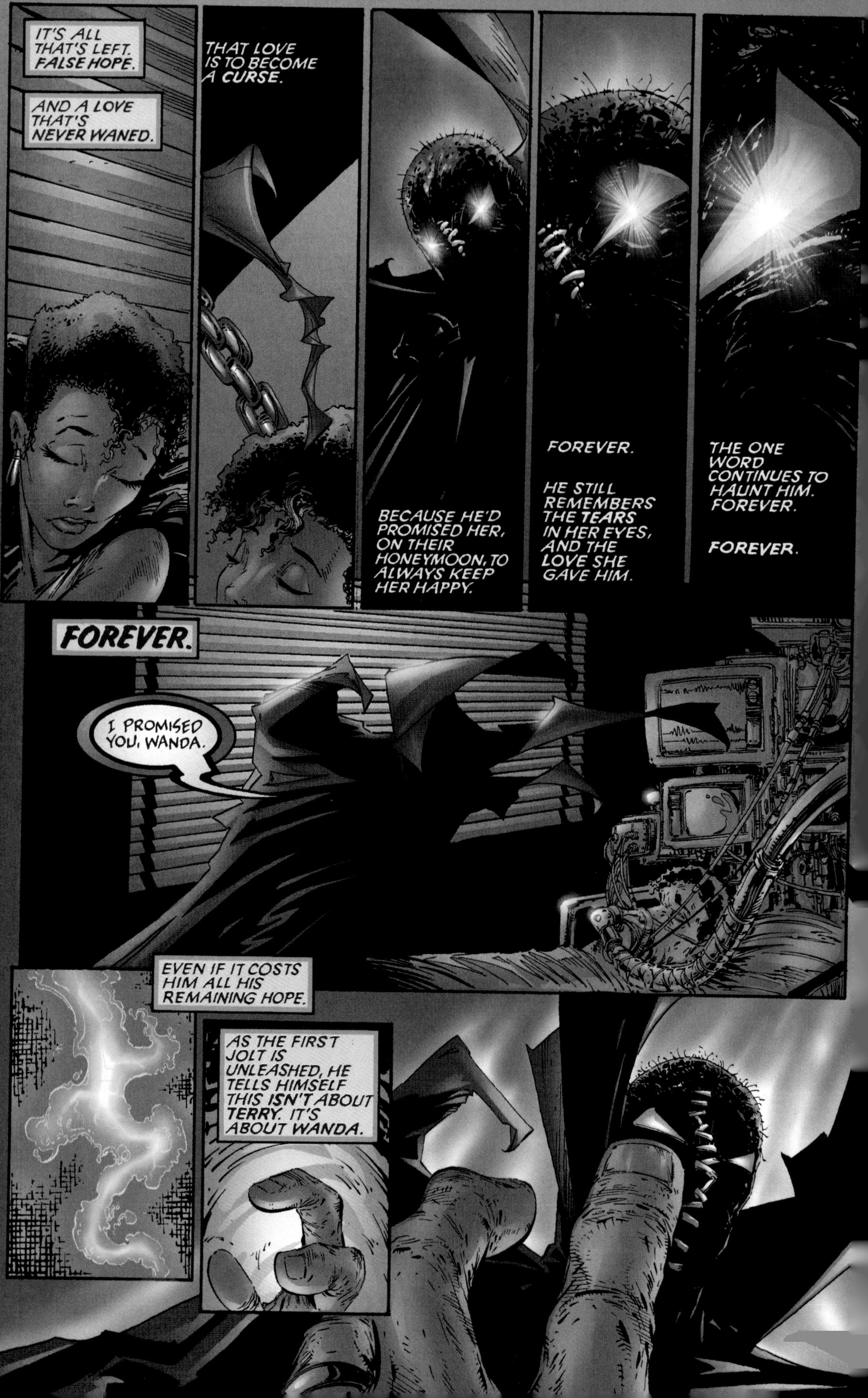
IT'S ALL THAT'S LEFT. FALSE HOPE.
AND A LOVE THAT'S NEVER WANED.
THAT LOVE IS TO BECOME A CURSE.
BECAUSE HE'D PROMISED HER, ON THEIR HONEYMOON, TO ALWAYS KEEP HER HAPPY.
FOREVER.
HE STILL REMEMBERS THE TEARS IN HER EYES, AND THE LOVE SHE GAVE HIM.
THE ONE WORD CONTINUES TO HAUNT HIM. FOREVER.
FOREVER.
FOREVER.
I PROMISED YOU, WANDA.
EVEN IF IT COSTS HIM ALL HIS REMAINING HOPE.
AS THE FIRST JOLT IS UNLEASHED, HE TELLS HIMSELF THIS ISN'T ABOUT TERRY. IT'S ABOUT WANDA.

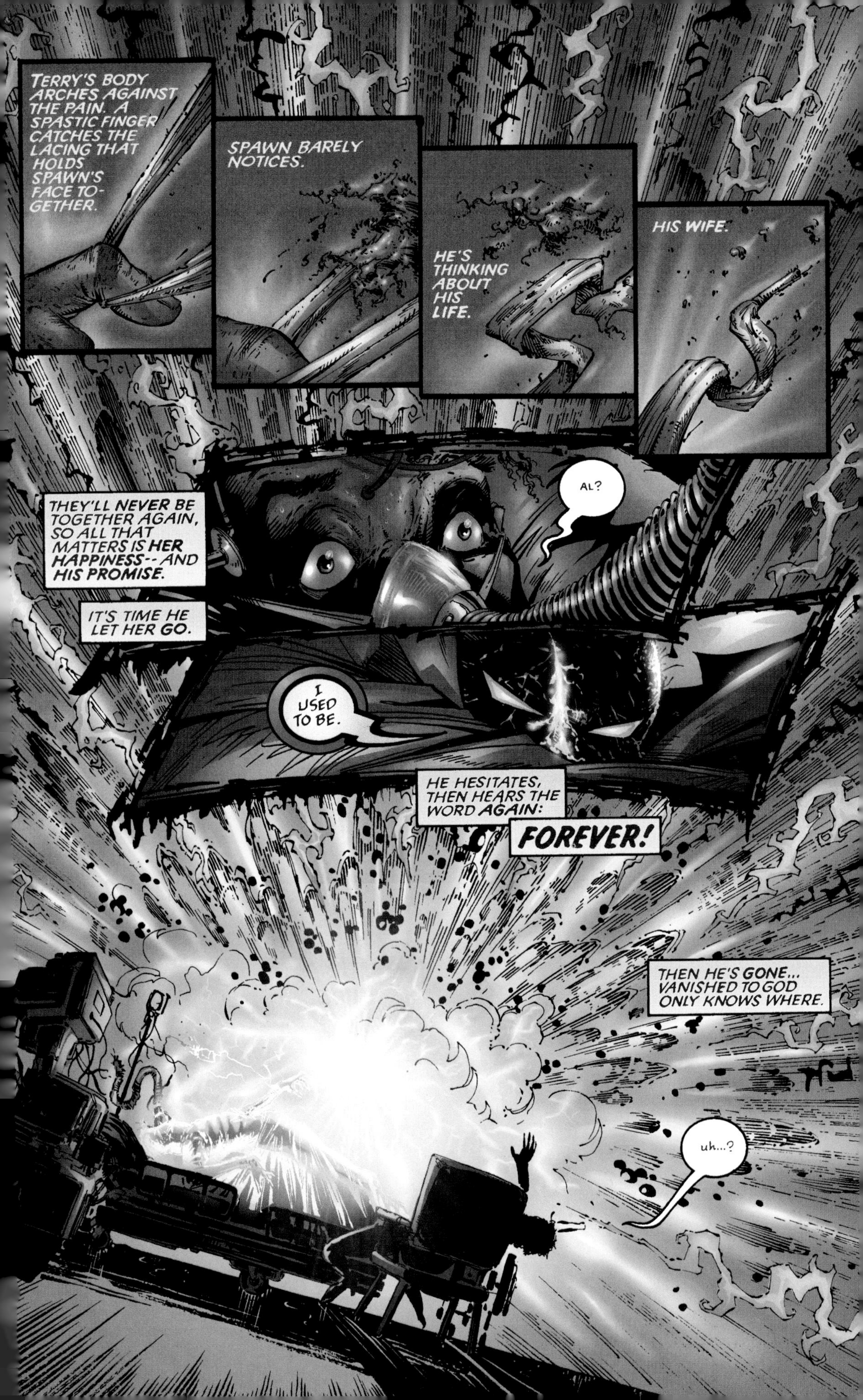
TERRY'S BODY ARCHES AGAINST THE PAIN. A SPASTIC FINGER CATCHES THE LACING THAT HOLDS SPAWN'S FACE TO-GETHER.
SPAWN BARELY NOTICES.
HE'S THINKING ABOUT HIS LIFE.
HIS WIFE.
THEY'LL NEVER BE TOGETHER AGAIN, SO ALL THAT MATTERS IS HER HAPPINESS-- AND HIS PROMISE.
AL?
IT'S TIME HE LET HER GO.
I USED TO BE.
HE HESITATES, THEN HEARS THE WORD AGAIN:
FOREVER!
THEN HE'S GONE... VANISHED TO GOD ONLY KNOWS WHERE.
uh...?

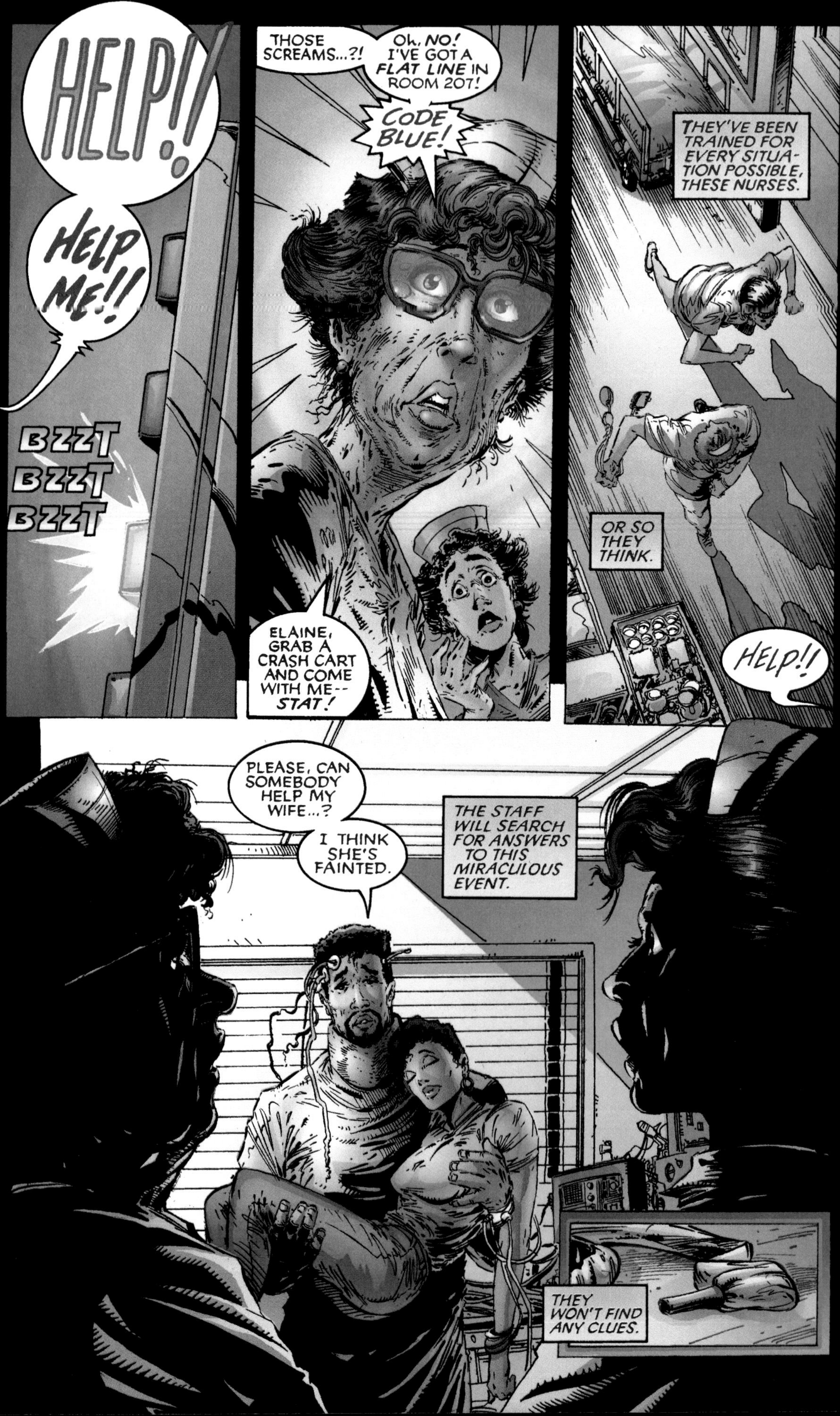
HELP!!
HELP ME!!
BZZT BZZT BZZT
THOSE SCREAMS...?!
Oh, NO! I'VE GOT A FLAT LINE IN ROOM 207!
CODE BLUE!
ELAINE, GRAB A CRASH CART AND COME WITH ME-- STAT!
THEY'VE BEEN TRAINED FOR EVERY SITUATION POSSIBLE, THESE NURSES.
OR SO THEY THINK.
HELP!!
PLEASE, CAN SOMEBODY HELP MY WIFE...?
I THINK SHE'S FAINTED.
THE STAFF WILL SEARCH FOR ANSWERS TO THIS MIRACULOUS EVENT.
THEY WON'T FIND ANY CLUES.

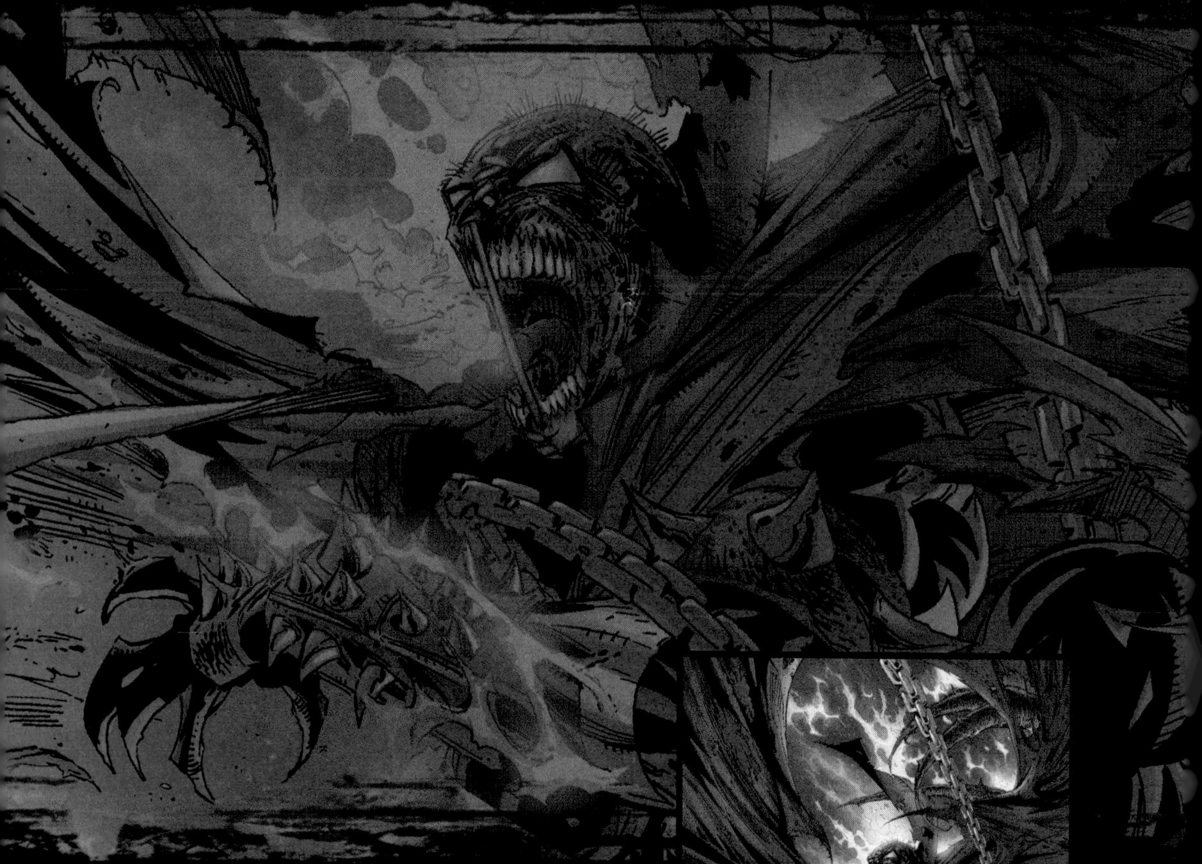

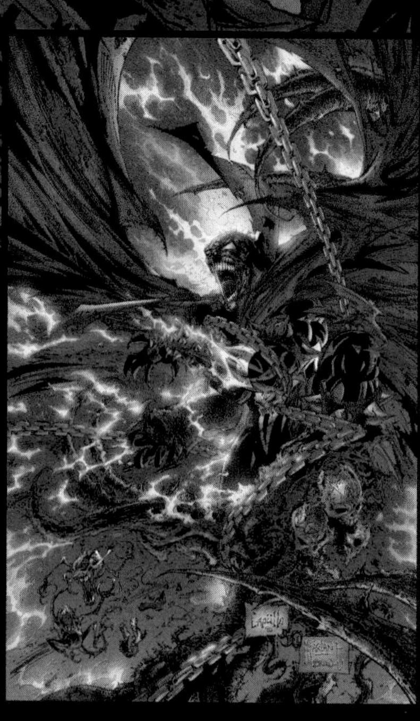

ISSUE FIFTY
Part Two

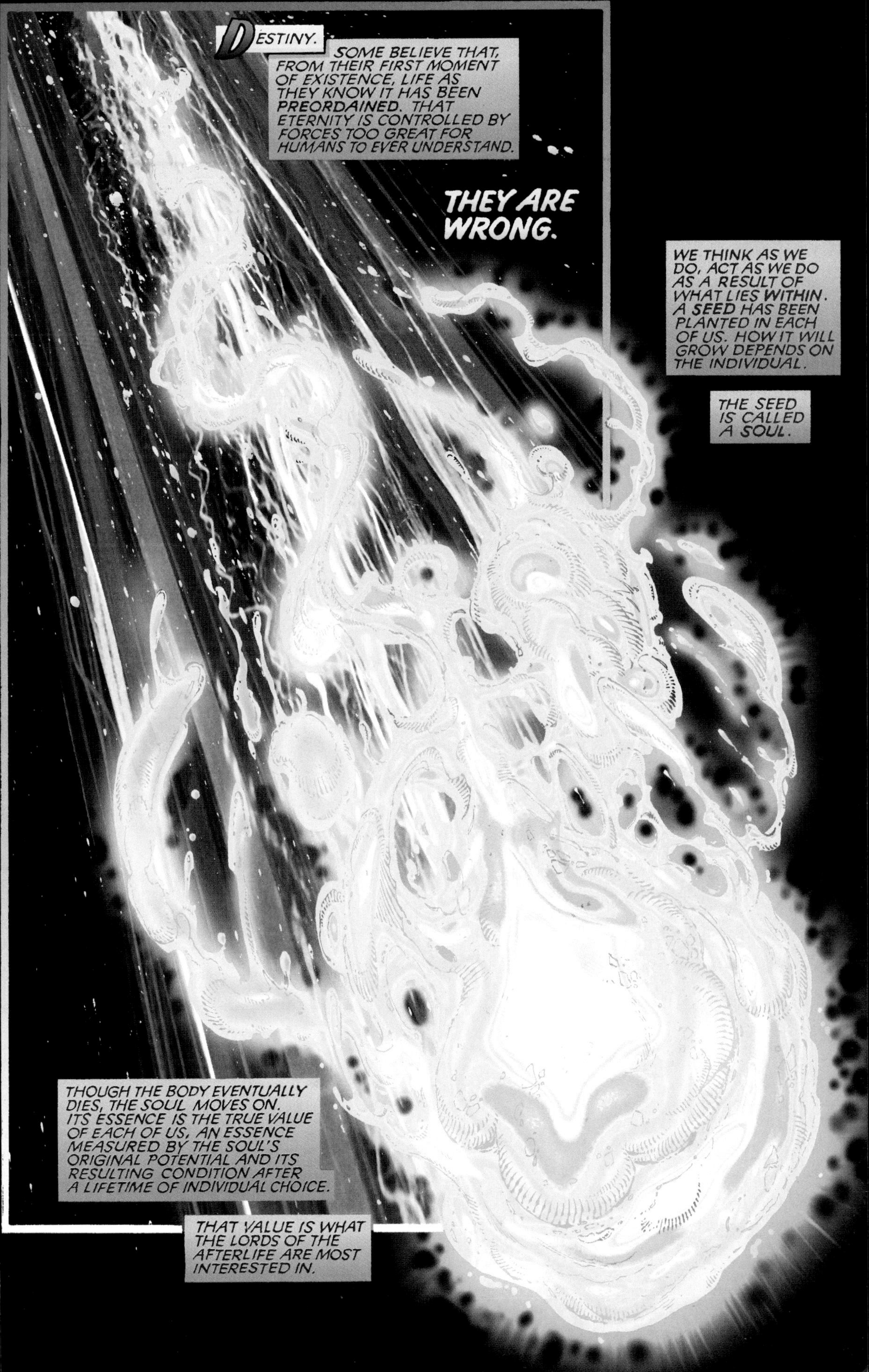
DESTINY. SOME BELIEVE THAT, FROM THEIR FIRST MOMENT OF EXISTENCE, LIFE AS THEY KNOW IT HAS BEEN PREORDAINED. THAT ETERNITY IS CONTROLLED BY FORCES TOO GREAT FOR HUMANS TO EVER UNDERSTAND.
THEY ARE WRONG.
WE THINK AS WE DO, ACT AS WE DO AS A RESULT OF WHAT LIES WITHIN. A SEED HAS BEEN PLANTED IN EACH OF US. HOW IT WILL GROW DEPENDS ON THE INDIVIDUAL.
THE SEED IS CALLED A SOUL.
THOUGH THE BODY EVENTUALLY DIES, THE SOUL MOVES ON. ITS ESSENCE IS THE TRUE VALUE OF EACH OF US, AN ESSENCE MEASURED BY THE SOUL'S ORIGINAL POTENTIAL AND ITS RESULTING CONDITION AFTER A LIFETIME OF INDIVIDUAL CHOICE.
THAT VALUE IS WHAT THE LORDS OF THE AFTERLIFE ARE MOST INTERESTED IN.

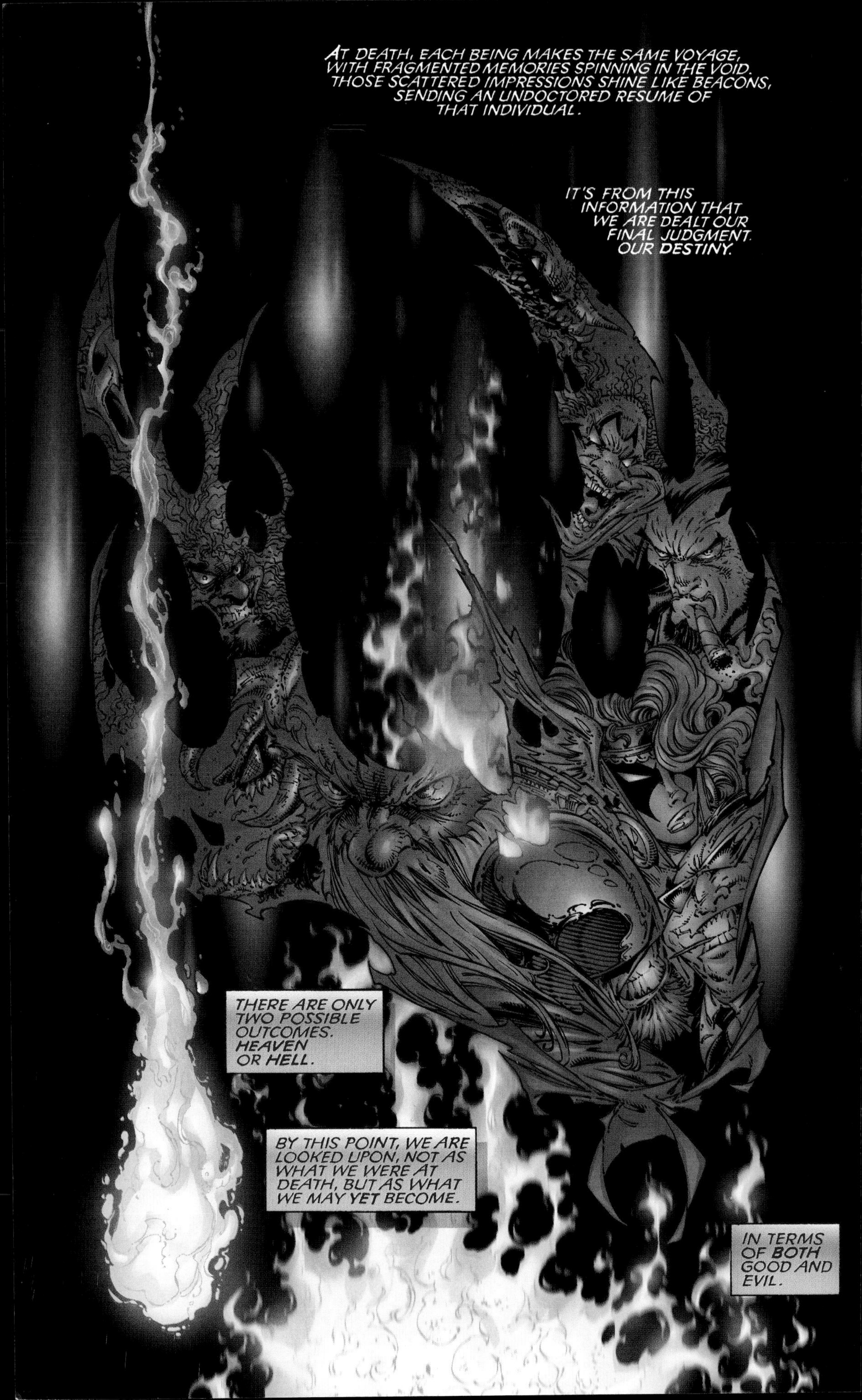
AT DEATH, EACH BEING MAKES THE SAME VOYAGE, WITH FRAGMENTED MEMORIES SPINNING IN THE VOID. THOSE SCATTERED IMPRESSIONS SHINE LIKE BEACONS, SENDING AN UNDOCTORED RESUME OF THAT INDIVIDUAL.
IT'S FROM THIS INFORMATION THAT WE ARE DEALT OUR FINAL JUDGMENT. OUR DESTINY.
THERE ARE ONLY TWO POSSIBLE OUTCOMES. HEAVEN OR HELL.
BY THIS POINT, WE ARE LOOKED UPON, NOT AS WHAT WE WERE AT DEATH, BUT AS WHAT WE MAY YET BECOME.
IN TERMS OF BOTH GOOD AND EVIL.

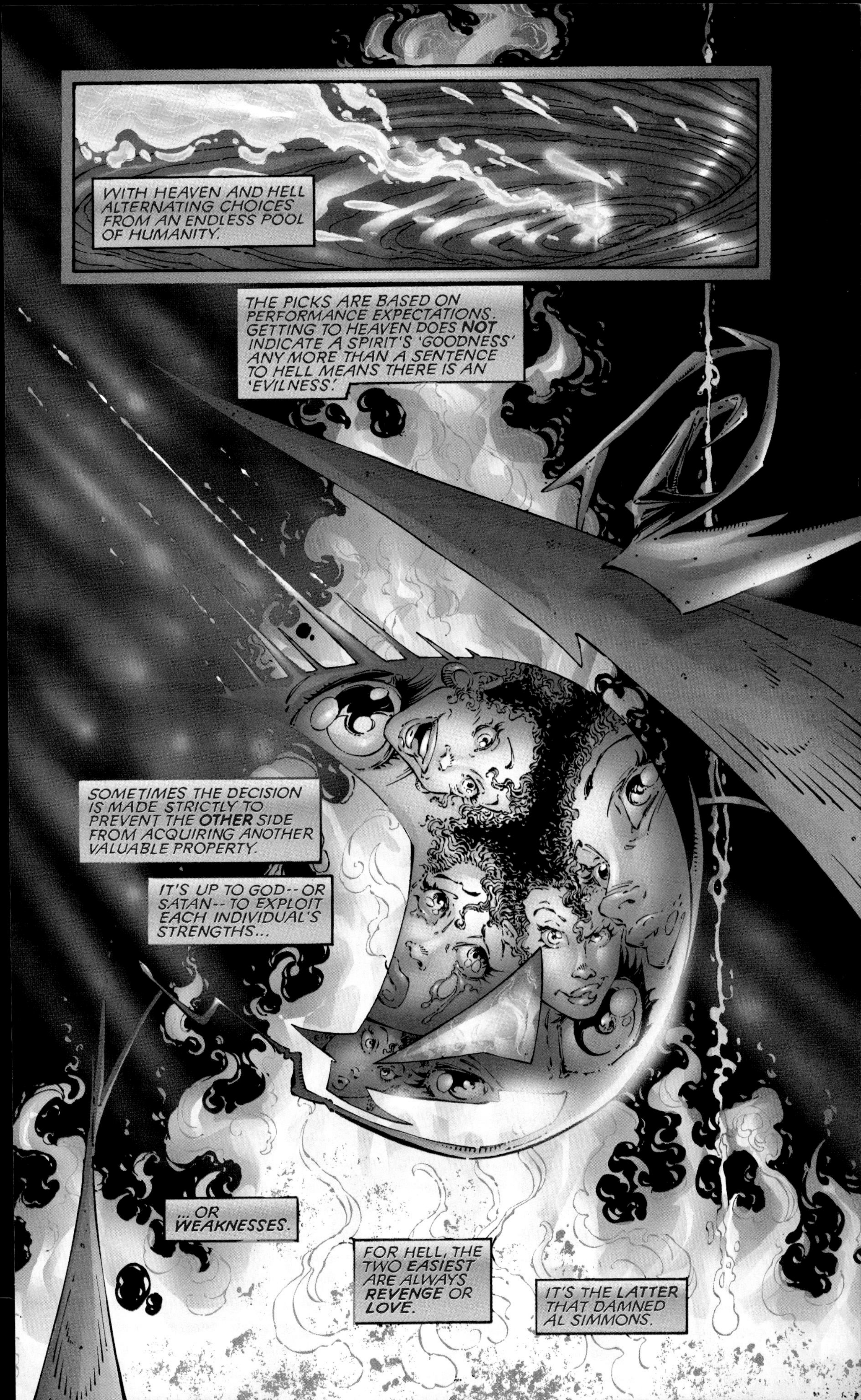
WITH HEAVEN AND HELL ALTERNATING CHOICES FROM AN ENDLESS POOL OF HUMANITY.
THE PICKS ARE BASED ON PERFORMANCE EXPECTATIONS. GETTING TO HEAVEN DOES **NOT** INDICATE A SPIRIT'S 'GOODNESS' ANY MORE THAN A SENTENCE TO HELL MEANS THERE IS AN 'EVILNESS.'
SOMETIMES THE DECISION IS MADE STRICTLY TO PREVENT THE **OTHER** SIDE FROM ACQUIRING ANOTHER VALUABLE PROPERTY.
IT'S UP TO GOD-- OR SATAN-- TO EXPLOIT EACH INDIVIDUAL'S STRENGTHS...
...OR **WEAKNESSES**.
FOR HELL, THE TWO **EASIEST** ARE ALWAYS **REVENGE** OR **LOVE**.
IT'S THE **LATTER** THAT DAMNED AL SIMMONS.

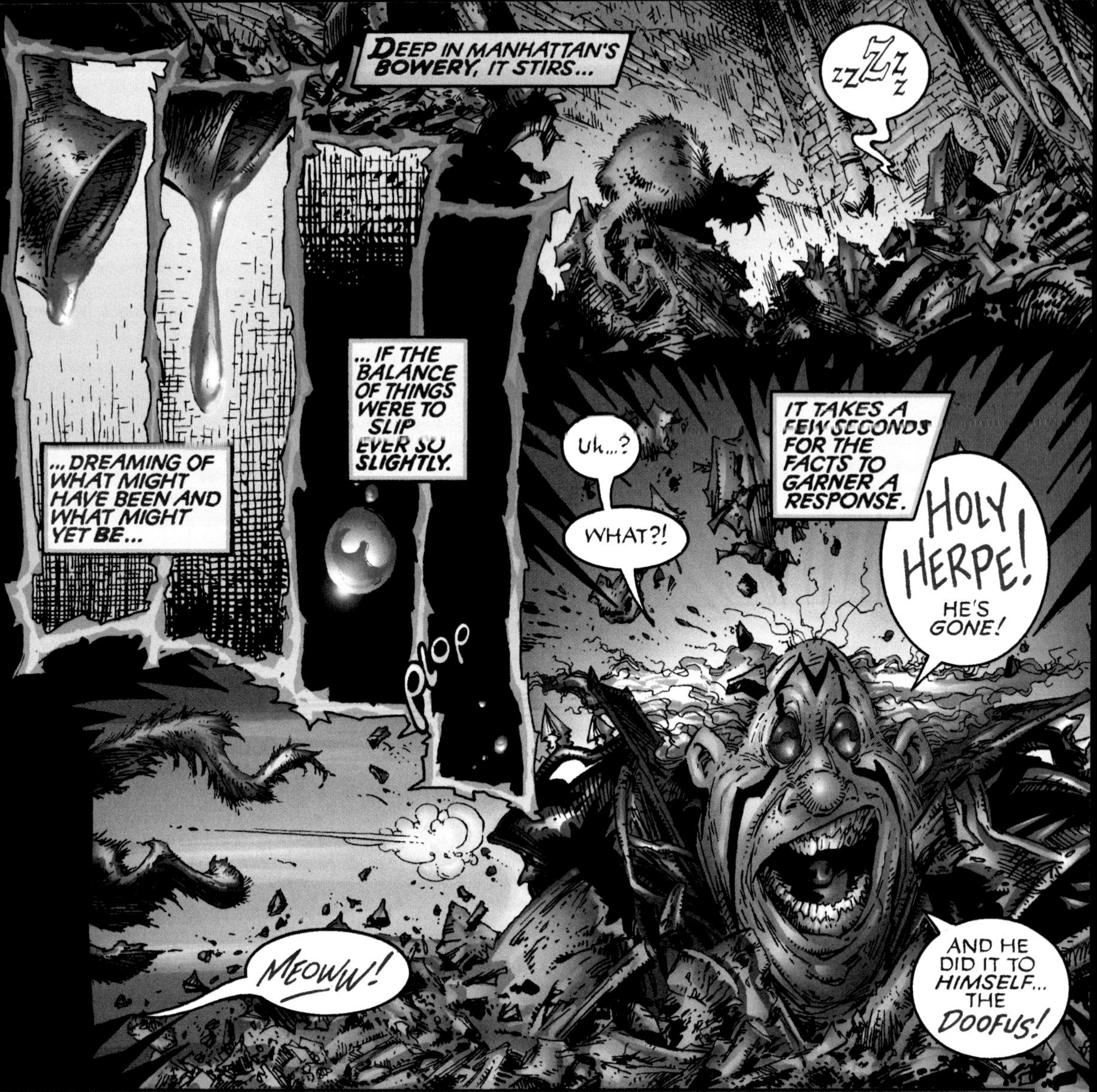
DEEP IN MANHATTAN'S BOWERY, IT STIRS...
zzZzz
...DREAMING OF WHAT MIGHT HAVE BEEN AND WHAT MIGHT YET BE...
...IF THE BALANCE OF THINGS WERE TO SLIP EVER SO SLIGHTLY.
PLOP
Uh...?
WHAT?!
IT TAKES A FEW SECONDS FOR THE FACTS TO GARNER A RESPONSE.
HOLY HERPE! HE'S GONE!
MEOWW!
AND HE DID IT TO HIMSELF... THE DOOFUS!

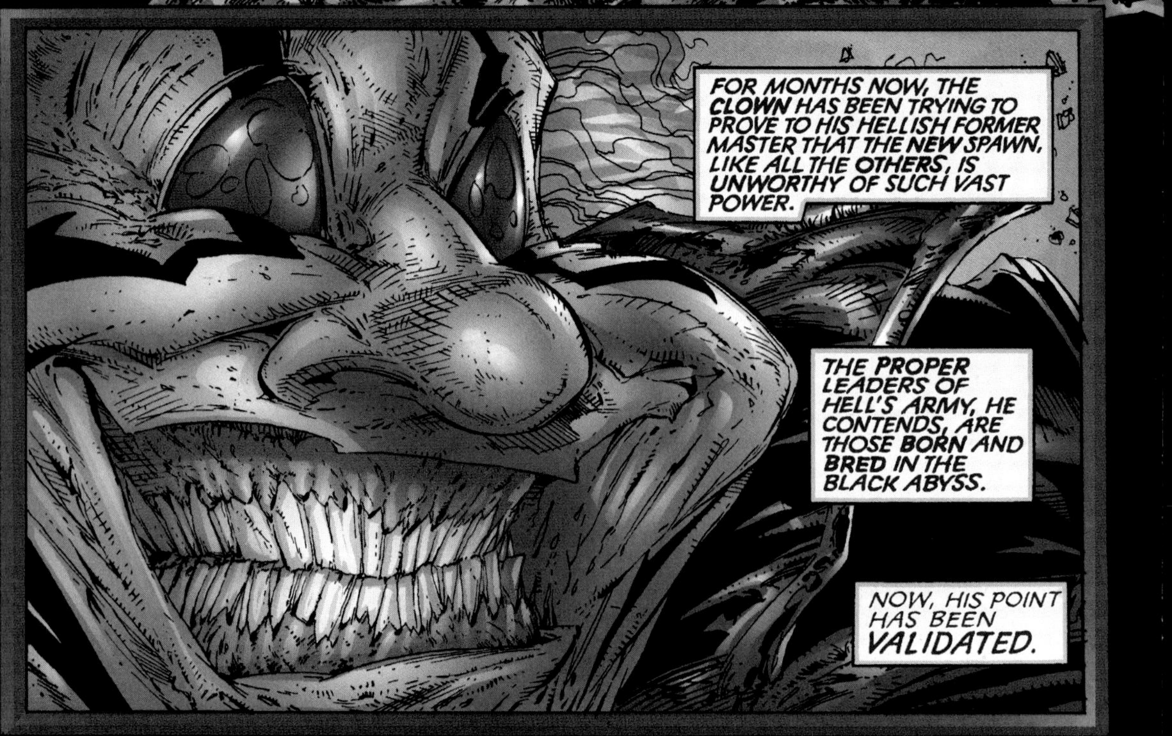
FOR MONTHS NOW, THE CLOWN HAS BEEN TRYING TO PROVE TO HIS HELLISH FORMER MASTER THAT THE NEW SPAWN, LIKE ALL THE OTHERS, IS UNWORTHY OF SUCH VAST POWER.
THE PROPER LEADERS OF HELL'S ARMY, HE CONTENDS, ARE THOSE BORN AND BRED IN THE BLACK ABYSS.
NOW, HIS POINT HAS BEEN VALIDATED.

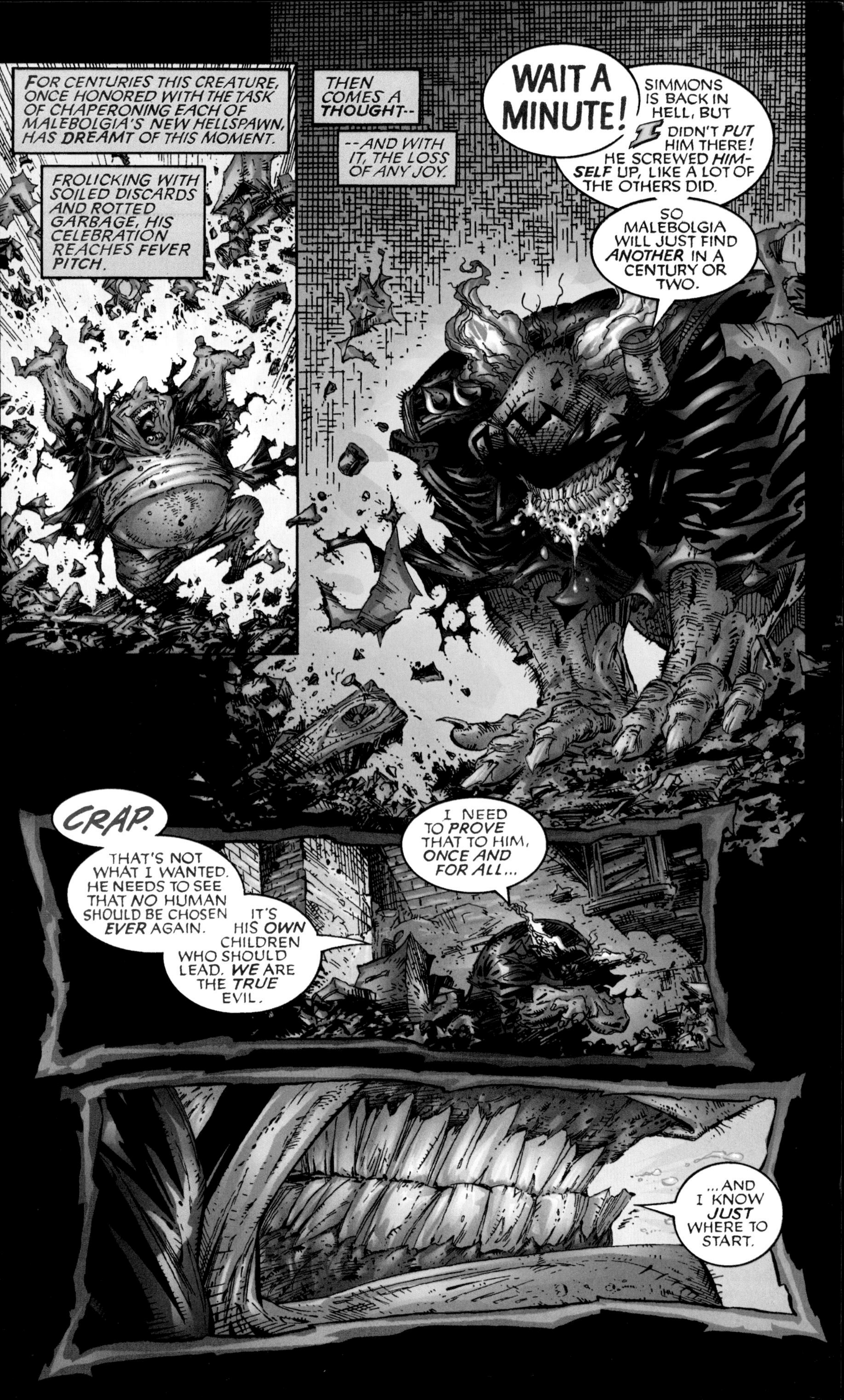
FOR CENTURIES THIS CREATURE, ONCE HONORED WITH THE TASK OF CHAPERONING EACH OF MALEBOLGIA'S NEW HELLSPAWN, HAS DREAMT OF THIS MOMENT.
FROLICKING WITH SOILED DISCARDS AND ROTTED GARBAGE, HIS CELEBRATION REACHES FEVER PITCH.
THEN COMES A THOUGHT--
--AND WITH IT, THE LOSS OF ANY JOY.
WAIT A MINUTE!
SIMMONS IS BACK IN HELL, BUT I DIDN'T PUT HIM THERE! HE SCREWED HIMSELF UP, LIKE A LOT OF THE OTHERS DID.
SO MALEBOLGIA WILL JUST FIND ANOTHER IN A CENTURY OR TWO.
CRAP.
THAT'S NOT WHAT I WANTED. HE NEEDS TO SEE THAT NO HUMAN SHOULD BE CHOSEN EVER AGAIN.
IT'S HIS OWN CHILDREN WHO SHOULD LEAD. WE ARE THE TRUE EVIL.
I NEED TO PROVE THAT TO HIM, ONCE AND FOR ALL...
...AND I KNOW JUST WHERE TO START.

A FEW DAYS LATER...

OUTPATIENT REGISTRATION

AFTERNOON, MS. BLAKE.

HELLO, DOCTOR. YOU SAID YOU WANTED TO SEE ME.

YES. I JUST RECEIVED THE RESULTS OF THE LATEST TESTS. AND TO BE QUITE HONEST, THIS WHOLE SITUATION HAS EVERYONE COMPLETELY STUMPED.

THERE'S NO MORE EVIDENCE OF CANCER *ANYWHERE* IN HIS BODY. AS A MATTER OF FACT, THE AREA OF HIS HEAD WHICH WAS AFFECTED IS CLEANER THAN NORMAL. WE'VE RUN EVERY DIAGNOSTIC I CAN THINK OF. EACH RESULT IS *NEGATIVE*.

SO WHAT DOES THAT MEAN?

CALL IT A MIRACLE, BUT TERRY IS 100% CURED. SO, UNLESS EITHER ONE OF YOU HAS ANY OBJECTIONS...

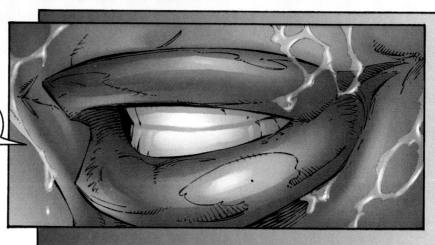

... I'M RELEASING HIM TOMORROW. IT'S TIME HE WENT HOME TO HIS FAMILY.

THANK YOU, DOCTOR. AND IF YOU DON'T MIND, I'D LIKE TO TELL HIM MYSELF.

OF COURSE.

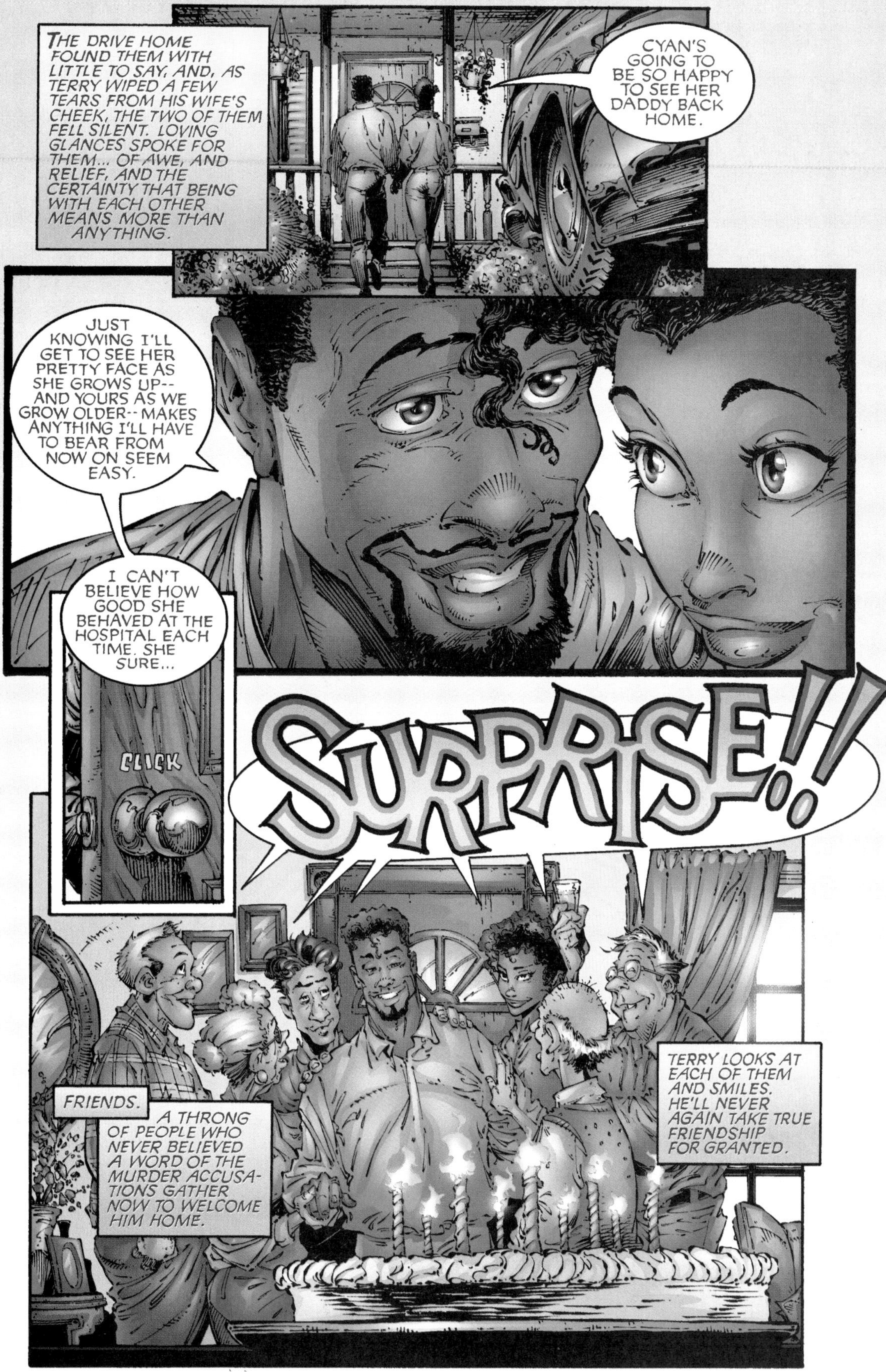
THE DRIVE HOME FOUND THEM WITH LITTLE TO SAY, AND, AS TERRY WIPED A FEW TEARS FROM HIS WIFE'S CHEEK, THE TWO OF THEM FELL SILENT. LOVING GLANCES SPOKE FOR THEM... OF AWE, AND RELIEF, AND THE CERTAINTY THAT BEING WITH EACH OTHER MEANS MORE THAN ANYTHING.
CYAN'S GOING TO BE SO HAPPY TO SEE HER DADDY BACK HOME.
JUST KNOWING I'LL GET TO SEE HER PRETTY FACE AS SHE GROWS UP-- AND YOURS AS WE GROW OLDER-- MAKES ANYTHING I'LL HAVE TO BEAR FROM NOW ON SEEM EASY.
I CAN'T BELIEVE HOW GOOD SHE BEHAVED AT THE HOSPITAL EACH TIME. SHE SURE...
CLICK
SURPRISE!!
FRIENDS.
A THRONG OF PEOPLE WHO NEVER BELIEVED A WORD OF THE MURDER ACCUSATIONS GATHER NOW TO WELCOME HIM HOME.
TERRY LOOKS AT EACH OF THEM AND SMILES. HE'LL NEVER AGAIN TAKE TRUE FRIENDSHIP FOR GRANTED.

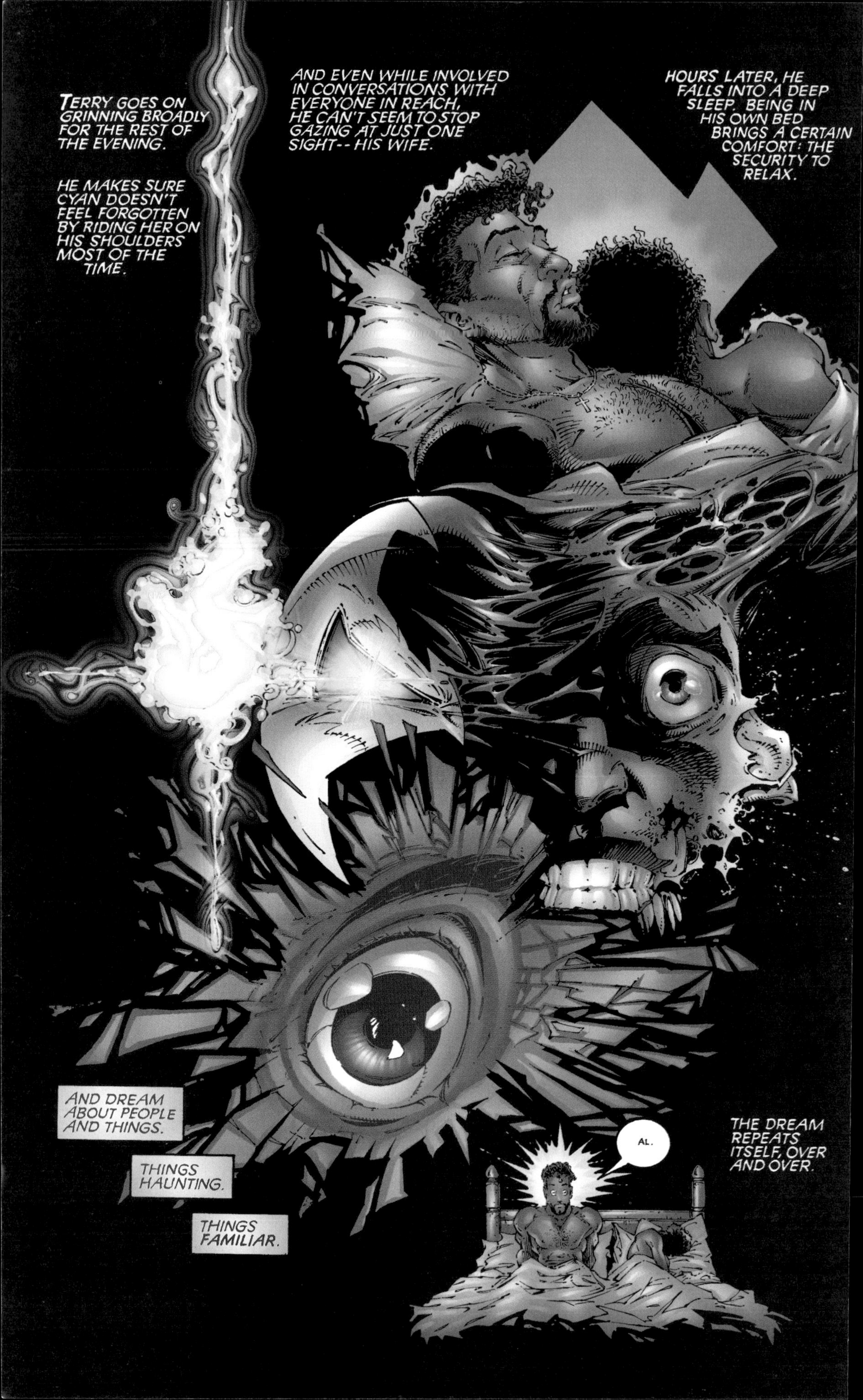
TERRY GOES ON GRINNING BROADLY FOR THE REST OF THE EVENING.
HE MAKES SURE CYAN DOESN'T FEEL FORGOTTEN BY RIDING HER ON HIS SHOULDERS MOST OF THE TIME.
AND EVEN WHILE INVOLVED IN CONVERSATIONS WITH EVERYONE IN REACH, HE CAN'T SEEM TO STOP GAZING AT JUST ONE SIGHT-- HIS WIFE.
HOURS LATER, HE FALLS INTO A DEEP SLEEP. BEING IN HIS OWN BED BRINGS A CERTAIN COMFORT: THE SECURITY TO RELAX.
AND DREAM ABOUT PEOPLE AND THINGS.
THINGS HAUNTING.
THINGS FAMILIAR.
AL.
THE DREAM REPEATS ITSELF, OVER AND OVER.

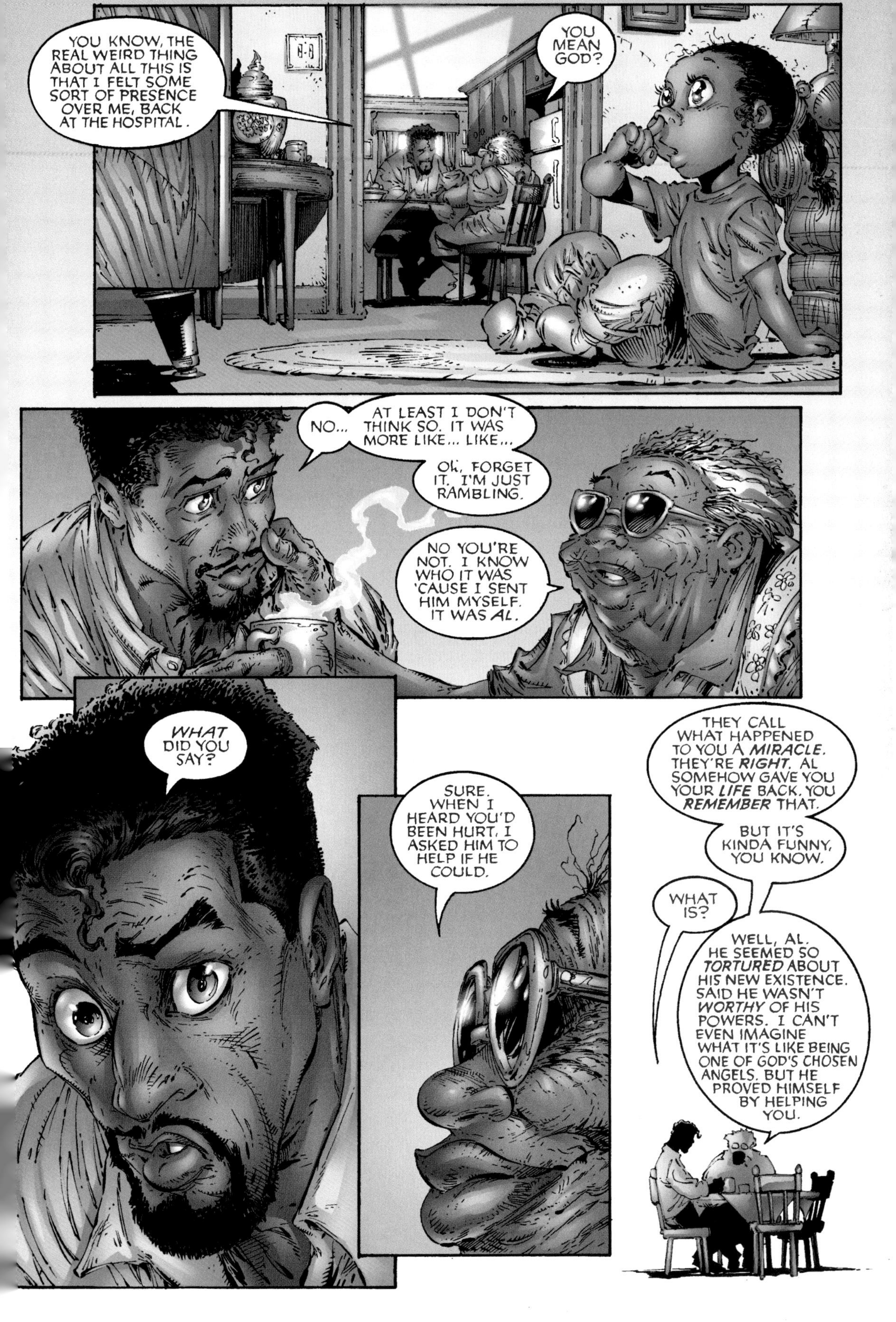
YOU KNOW, THE REAL WEIRD THING ABOUT ALL THIS IS THAT I FELT SOME SORT OF PRESENCE OVER ME, BACK AT THE HOSPITAL.
YOU MEAN GOD?
NO...
AT LEAST I DON'T THINK SO. IT WAS MORE LIKE... LIKE...
OH, FORGET IT. I'M JUST RAMBLING.
NO YOU'RE NOT. I KNOW WHO IT WAS 'CAUSE I SENT HIM MYSELF. IT WAS AL.
WHAT DID YOU SAY?
SURE. WHEN I HEARD YOU'D BEEN HURT, I ASKED HIM TO HELP IF HE COULD.
THEY CALL WHAT HAPPENED TO YOU A MIRACLE. THEY'RE RIGHT. AL SOMEHOW GAVE YOU YOUR LIFE BACK. YOU REMEMBER THAT.
BUT IT'S KINDA FUNNY, YOU KNOW.
WHAT IS?
WELL, AL. HE SEEMED SO TORTURED ABOUT HIS NEW EXISTENCE. SAID HE WASN'T WORTHY OF HIS POWERS. I CAN'T EVEN IMAGINE WHAT IT'S LIKE BEING ONE OF GOD'S CHOSEN ANGELS. BUT HE PROVED HIMSELF BY HELPING YOU.

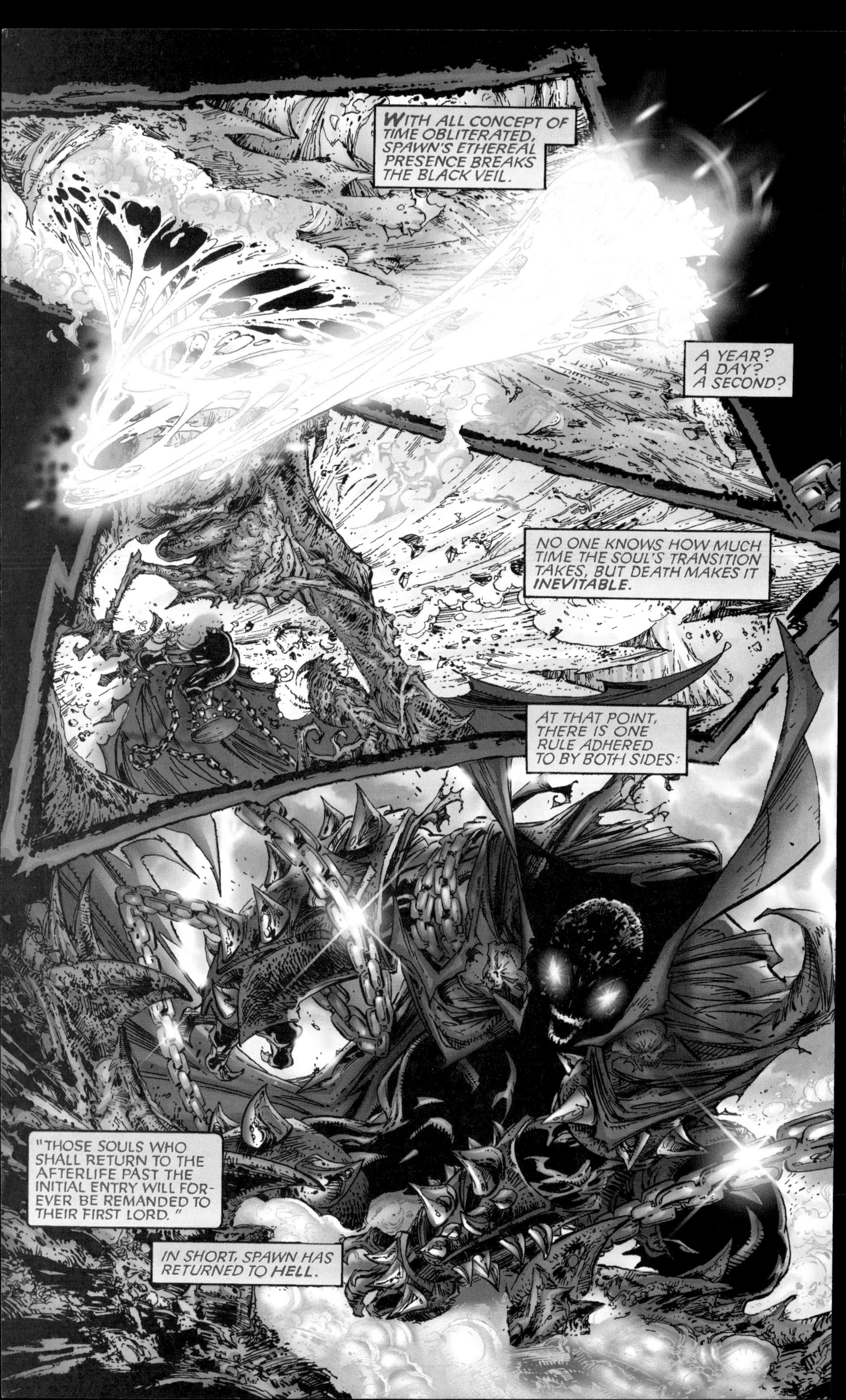
WITH ALL CONCEPT OF TIME OBLITERATED, SPAWN'S ETHEREAL PRESENCE BREAKS THE BLACK VEIL.
A YEAR? A DAY? A SECOND?
NO ONE KNOWS HOW MUCH TIME THE SOUL'S TRANSITION TAKES, BUT DEATH MAKES IT INEVITABLE.
AT THAT POINT, THERE IS ONE RULE ADHERED TO BY BOTH SIDES:
"THOSE SOULS WHO SHALL RETURN TO THE AFTERLIFE PAST THE INITIAL ENTRY WILL FOREVER BE REMANDED TO THEIR FIRST LORD."
IN SHORT, SPAWN HAS RETURNED TO HELL.

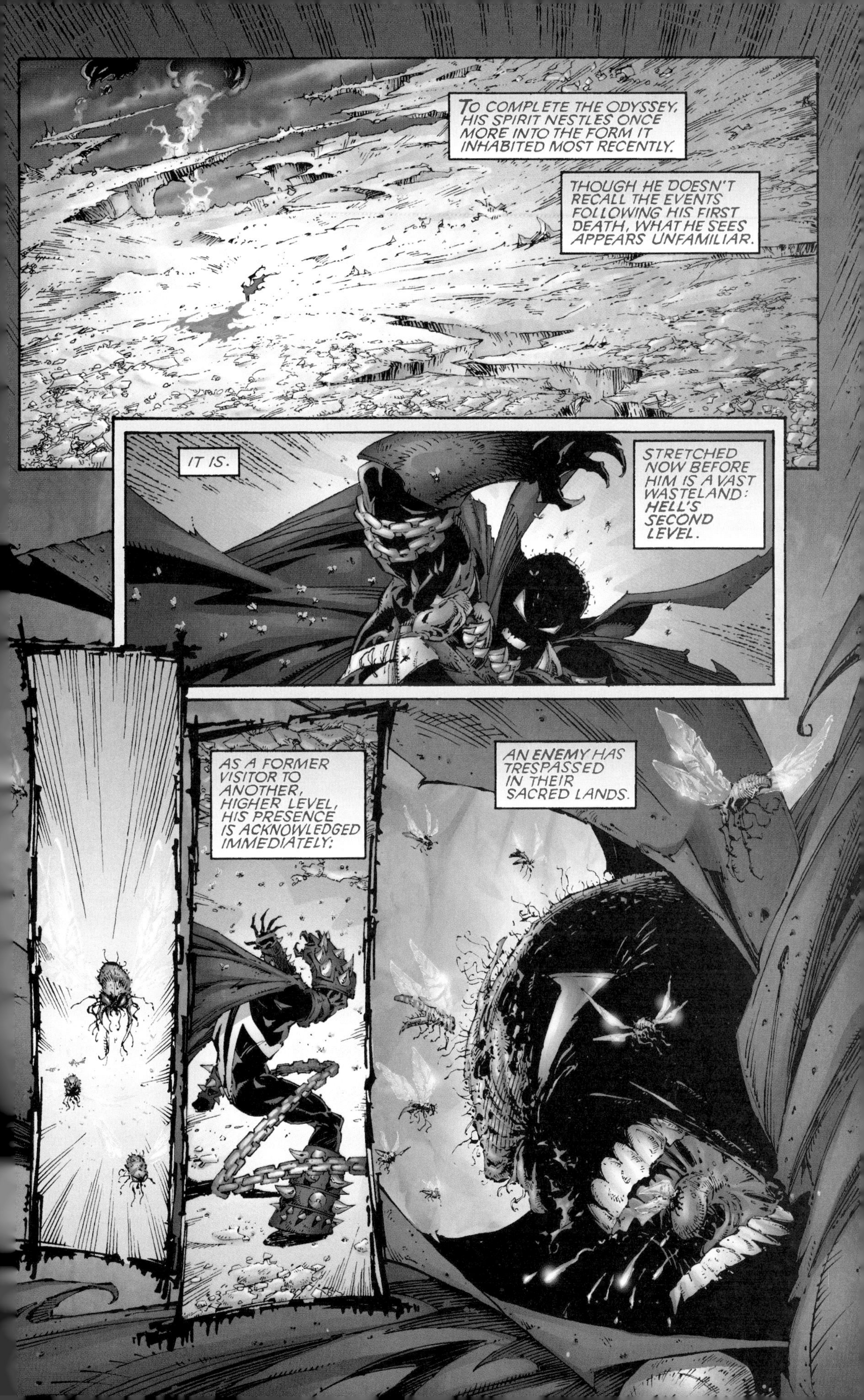
TO COMPLETE THE ODYSSEY, HIS SPIRIT NESTLES ONCE MORE INTO THE FORM IT INHABITED MOST RECENTLY.
THOUGH HE DOESN'T RECALL THE EVENTS FOLLOWING HIS FIRST DEATH, WHAT HE SEES APPEARS UNFAMILIAR.
IT IS.
STRETCHED NOW BEFORE HIM IS A VAST WASTELAND: HELL'S SECOND LEVEL.
AS A FORMER VISITOR TO ANOTHER, HIGHER LEVEL, HIS PRESENCE IS ACKNOWLEDGED IMMEDIATELY:
AN ENEMY HAS TRESPASSED IN THEIR SACRED LANDS.

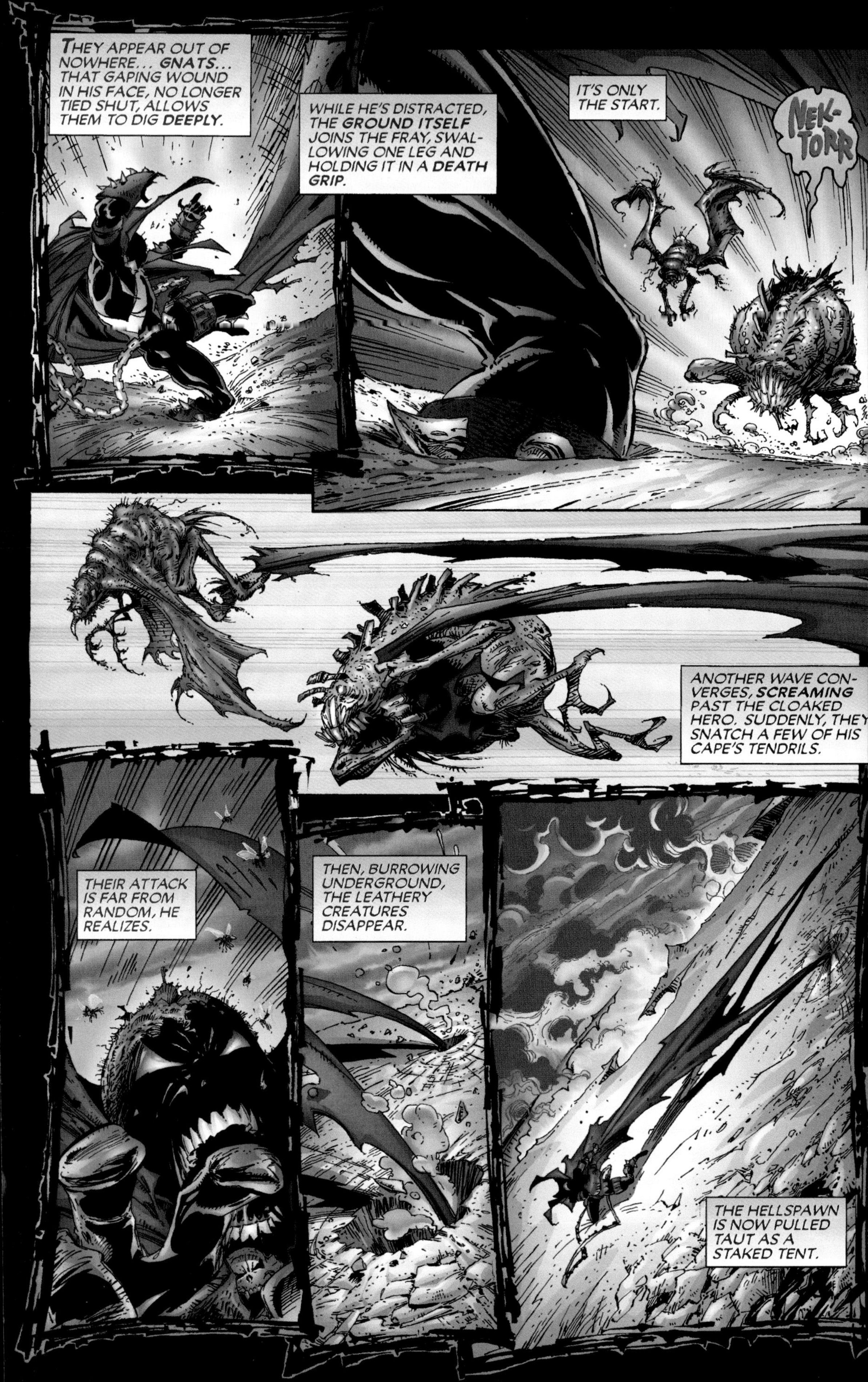
THEY APPEAR OUT OF NOWHERE... GNATS... THAT GAPING WOUND IN HIS FACE, NO LONGER TIED SHUT, ALLOWS THEM TO DIG DEEPLY.
WHILE HE'S DISTRACTED, THE GROUND ITSELF JOINS THE FRAY, SWALLOWING ONE LEG AND HOLDING IT IN A DEATH GRIP.
IT'S ONLY THE START.
NEK-TORR
ANOTHER WAVE CONVERGES, SCREAMING PAST THE CLOAKED HERO. SUDDENLY, THEY SNATCH A FEW OF HIS CAPE'S TENDRILS.
THEIR ATTACK IS FAR FROM RANDOM, HE REALIZES.
THEN, BURROWING UNDERGROUND, THE LEATHERY CREATURES DISAPPEAR.
THE HELLSPAWN IS NOW PULLED TAUT AS A STAKED TENT.

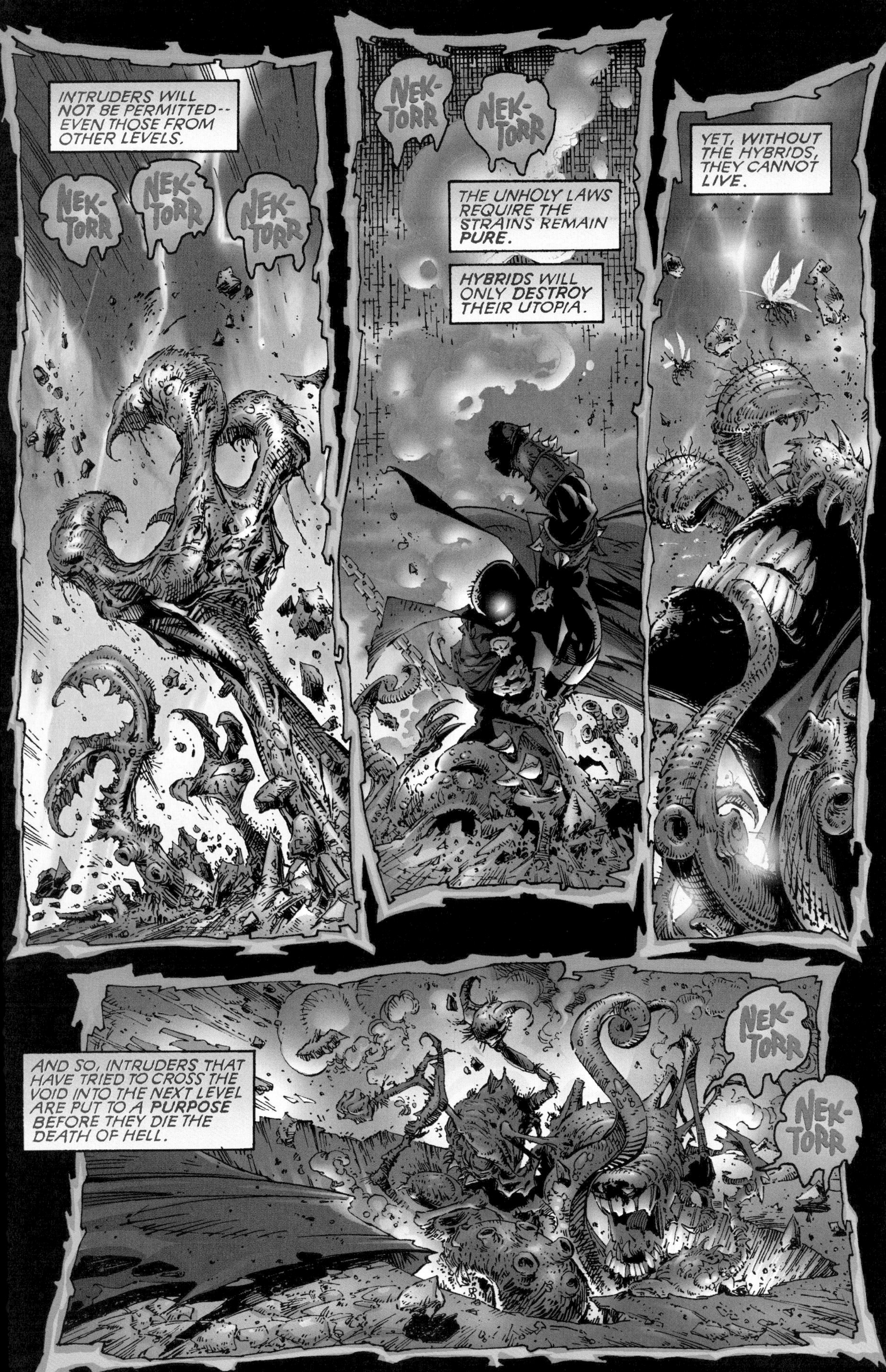
INTRUDERS WILL NOT BE PERMITTED-- EVEN THOSE FROM OTHER LEVELS.
NEK-TORR
NEK-TORR
NEK-TORR
NEK-TORR
NEK-TORR
THE UNHOLY LAWS REQUIRE THE STRAINS REMAIN **PURE**.
HYBRIDS WILL ONLY **DESTROY** THEIR UTOPIA.
YET, WITHOUT THE HYBRIDS, THEY CANNOT **LIVE**.
AND SO, INTRUDERS THAT HAVE TRIED TO CROSS THE VOID INTO THE NEXT LEVEL ARE PUT TO A **PURPOSE** BEFORE THEY DIE THE DEATH OF HELL.
NEK-TORR
NEK-TORR

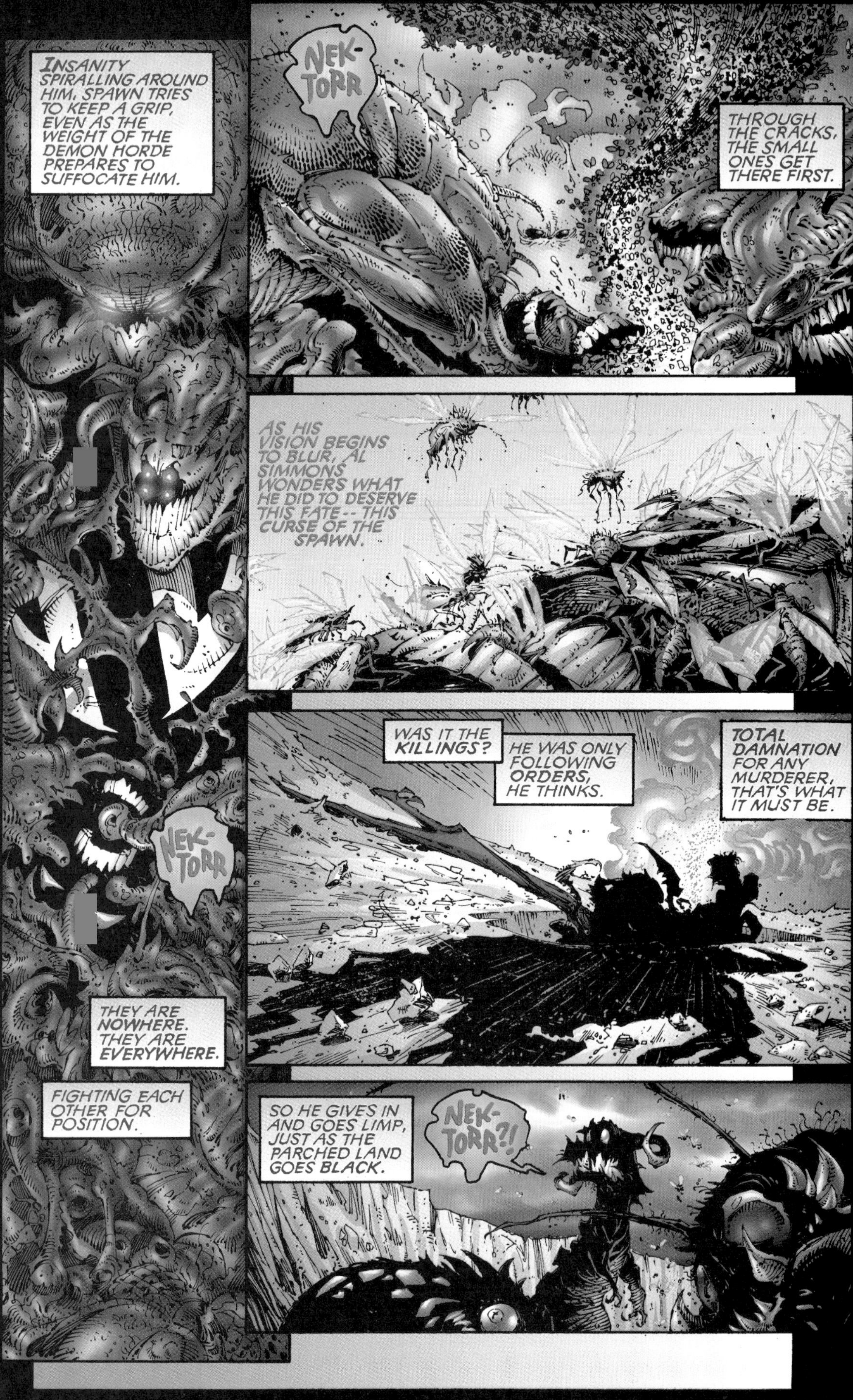

INSANITY SPIRALLING AROUND HIM, SPAWN TRIES TO KEEP A GRIP, EVEN AS THE WEIGHT OF THE DEMON HORDE PREPARES TO SUFFOCATE HIM.
NEK-TORR
THEY ARE NOWHERE. THEY ARE EVERYWHERE.
FIGHTING EACH OTHER FOR POSITION.
NEK-TORR
THROUGH THE CRACKS, THE SMALL ONES GET THERE FIRST.
AS HIS VISION BEGINS TO BLUR, AL SIMMONS WONDERS WHAT HE DID TO DESERVE THIS FATE -- THIS CURSE OF THE SPAWN.
WAS IT THE KILLINGS?
HE WAS ONLY FOLLOWING ORDERS, HE THINKS.
TOTAL DAMNATION FOR ANY MURDERER, THAT'S WHAT IT MUST BE.
SO HE GIVES IN AND GOES LIMP, JUST AS THE PARCHED LAND GOES BLACK.
NEK-TORR?!

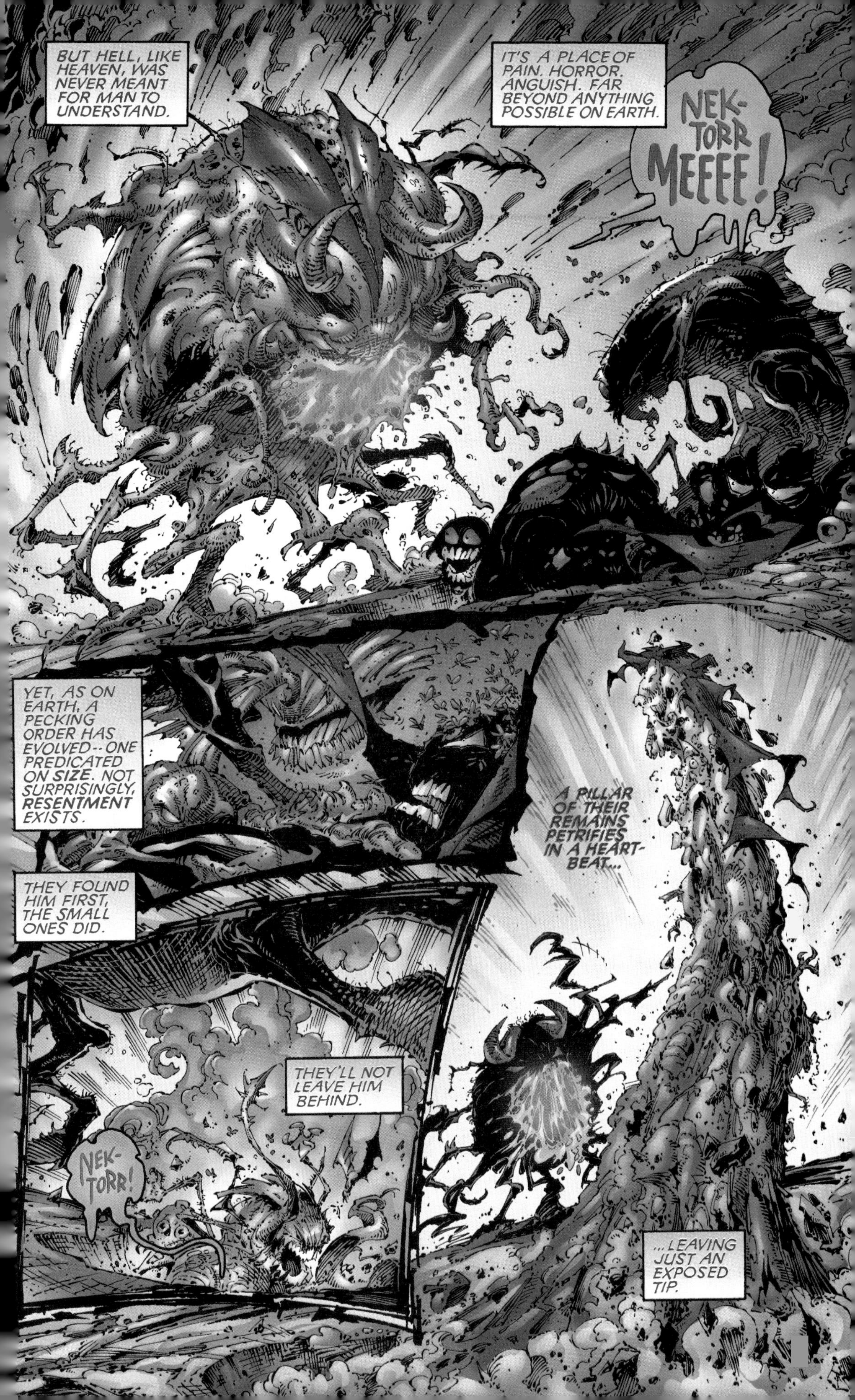
BUT HELL, LIKE HEAVEN, WAS NEVER MEANT FOR MAN TO UNDERSTAND.
IT'S A PLACE OF PAIN. HORROR. ANGUISH. FAR BEYOND ANYTHING POSSIBLE ON EARTH.
NEK-TORR MEEEE!
YET, AS ON EARTH, A PECKING ORDER HAS EVOLVED--ONE PREDICATED ON **SIZE**. NOT SURPRISINGLY, **RESENTMENT** EXISTS.
THEY FOUND HIM FIRST, THE SMALL ONES DID.
THEY'LL NOT LEAVE HIM BEHIND.
NEK-TORR!
A PILLAR OF THEIR REMAINS PETRIFIES IN A HEART-BEAT...
...LEAVING JUST AN EXPOSED TIP.

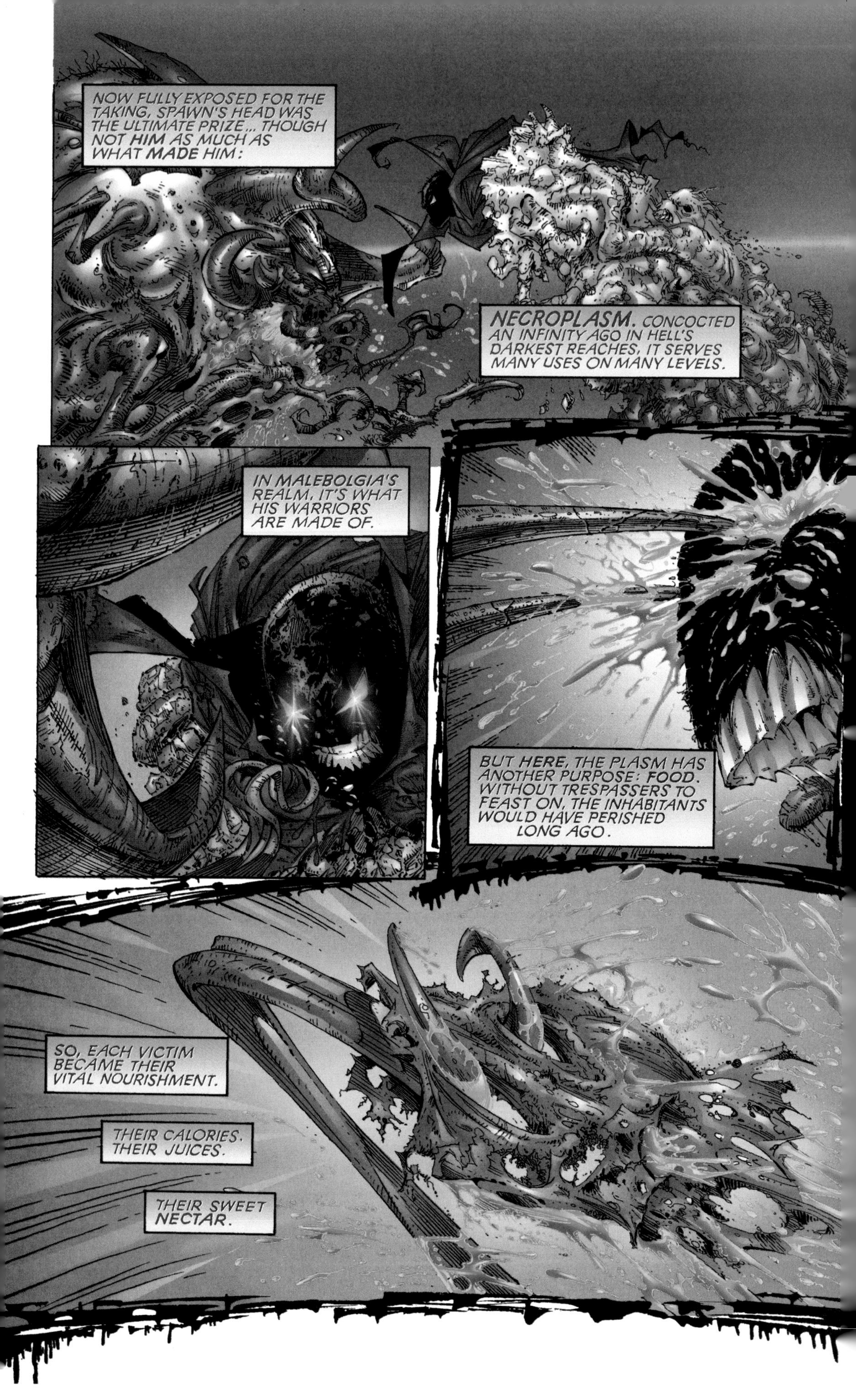
NOW FULLY EXPOSED FOR THE TAKING, SPAWN'S HEAD WAS THE ULTIMATE PRIZE... THOUGH NOT HIM AS MUCH AS WHAT MADE HIM:
NECROPLASM. CONCOCTED AN INFINITY AGO IN HELL'S DARKEST REACHES, IT SERVES MANY USES ON MANY LEVELS.
IN MALEBOLGIA'S REALM, IT'S WHAT HIS WARRIORS ARE MADE OF.
BUT HERE, THE PLASM HAS ANOTHER PURPOSE: FOOD. WITHOUT TRESPASSERS TO FEAST ON, THE INHABITANTS WOULD HAVE PERISHED LONG AGO.
SO, EACH VICTIM BECAME THEIR VITAL NOURISHMENT.
THEIR CALORIES. THEIR JUICES.
THEIR SWEET NECTAR.

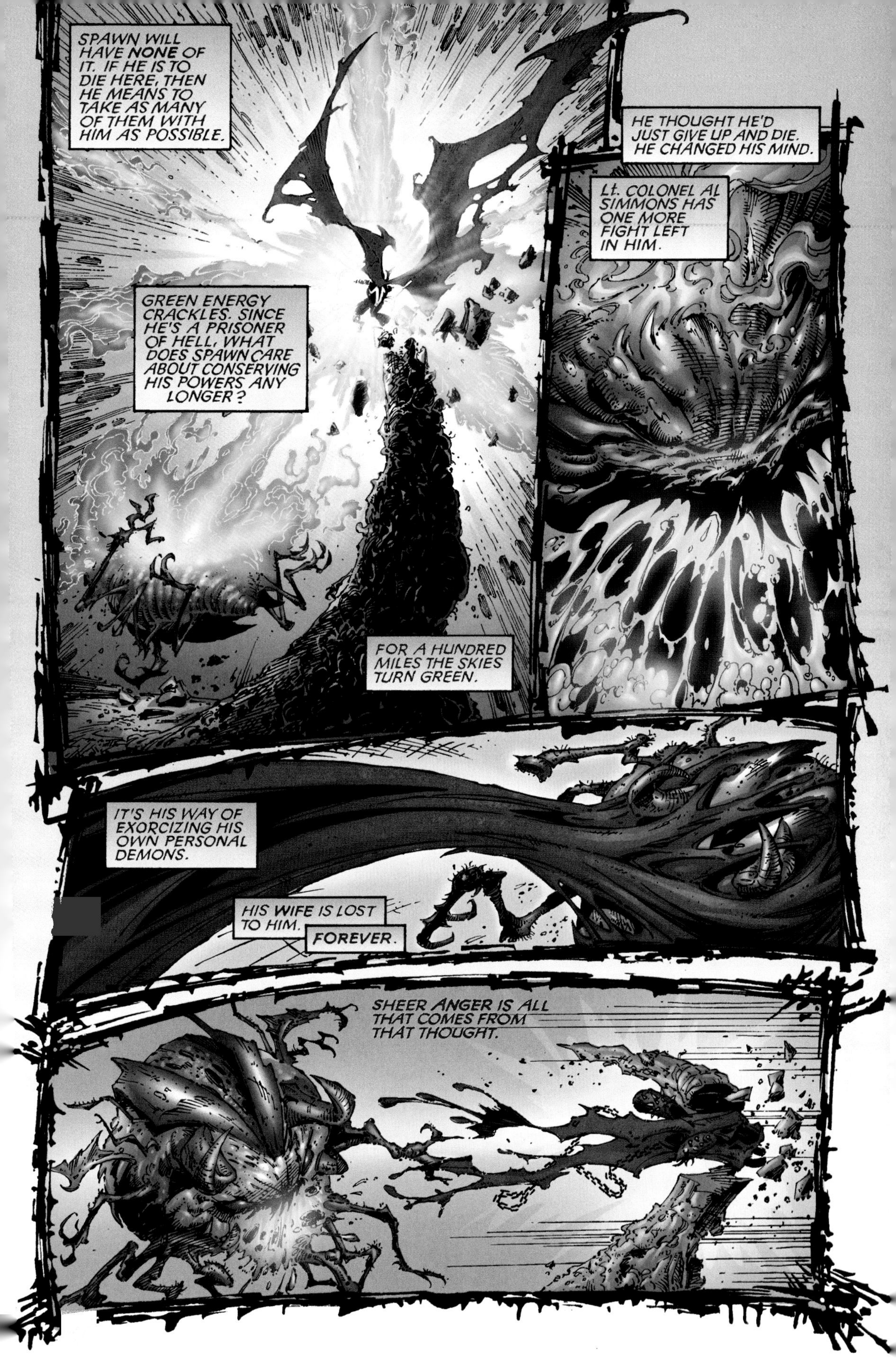
SPAWN WILL HAVE **NONE** OF IT. IF HE IS TO DIE HERE, THEN HE MEANS TO TAKE AS MANY OF THEM WITH HIM AS POSSIBLE.
GREEN ENERGY CRACKLES. SINCE HE'S A PRISONER OF HELL, WHAT DOES SPAWN CARE ABOUT CONSERVING HIS POWERS ANY LONGER?
FOR A HUNDRED MILES THE SKIES TURN GREEN.
HE THOUGHT HE'D JUST GIVE UP AND DIE. HE CHANGED HIS MIND.
Lt. COLONEL AL SIMMONS HAS ONE MORE FIGHT LEFT IN HIM.
IT'S HIS WAY OF EXORCIZING HIS OWN PERSONAL DEMONS.
HIS **WIFE** IS LOST TO HIM.
FOREVER.
SHEER **ANGER** IS ALL THAT COMES FROM THAT THOUGHT.

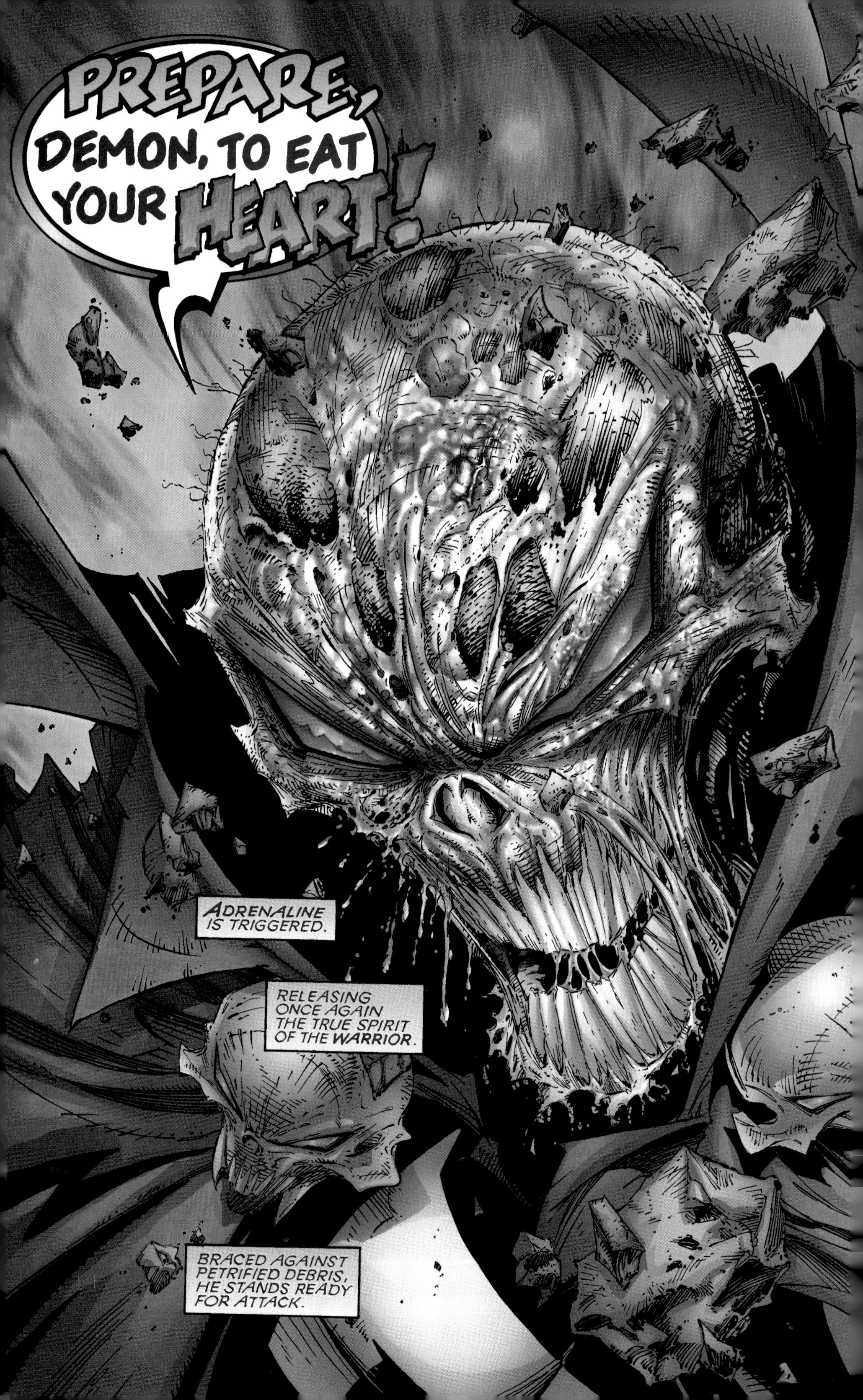
PREPARE, DEMON, TO EAT YOUR HEART!
ADRENALINE IS TRIGGERED.
RELEASING ONCE AGAIN THE TRUE SPIRIT OF THE WARRIOR.
BRACED AGAINST PETRIFIED DEBRIS, HE STANDS READY FOR ATTACK.

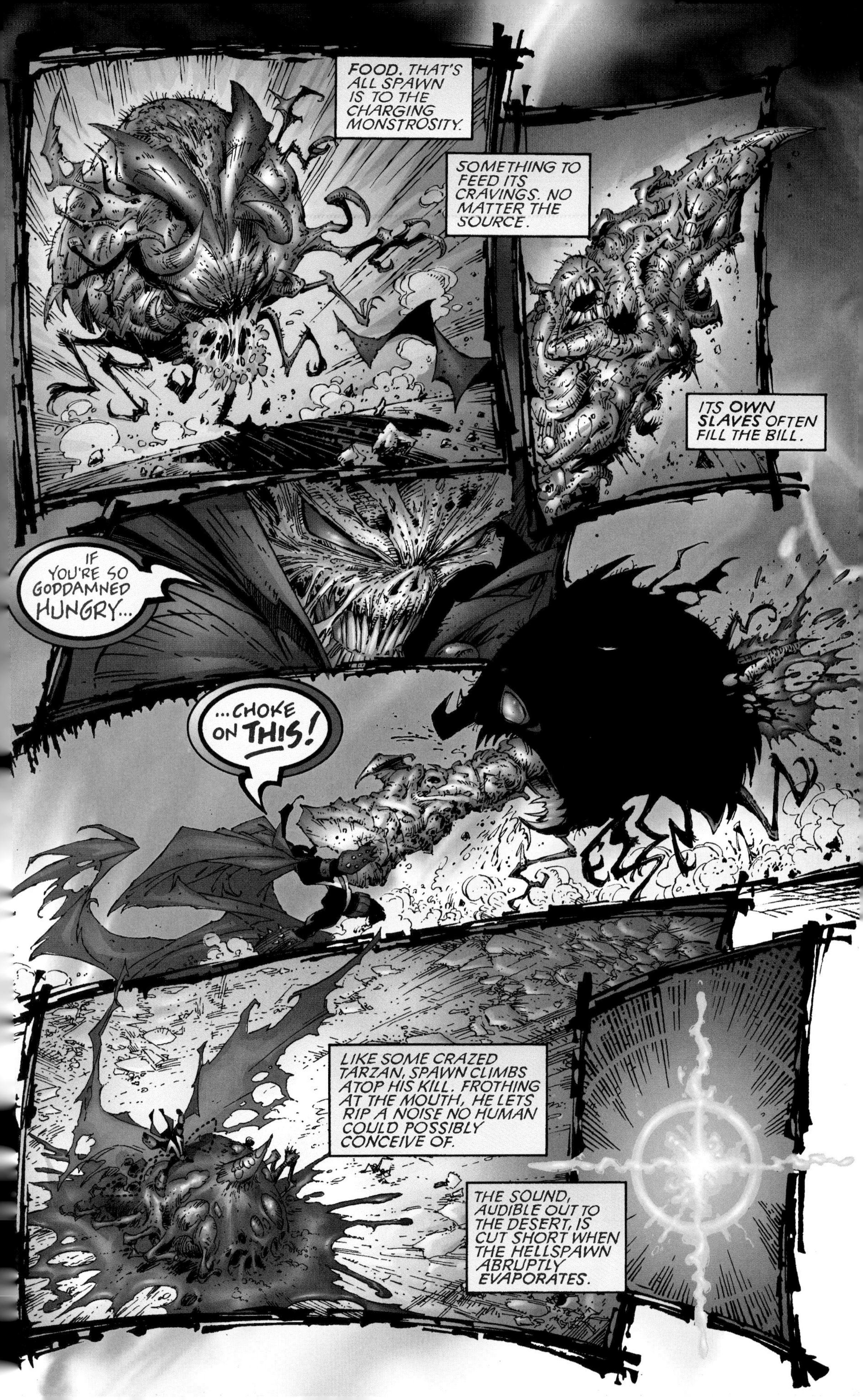
FOOD. THAT'S ALL SPAWN IS TO THE CHARGING MONSTROSITY.
SOMETHING TO FEED ITS CRAVINGS. NO MATTER THE SOURCE.
ITS OWN SLAVES OFTEN FILL THE BILL.
IF YOU'RE SO GODDAMNED HUNGRY...
...CHOKE ON THIS!
LIKE SOME CRAZED TARZAN, SPAWN CLIMBS ATOP HIS KILL. FROTHING AT THE MOUTH, HE LETS RIP A NOISE NO HUMAN COULD POSSIBLY CONCEIVE OF.
THE SOUND, AUDIBLE OUT TO THE DESERT, IS CUT SHORT WHEN THE HELLSPAWN ABRUPTLY EVAPORATES.

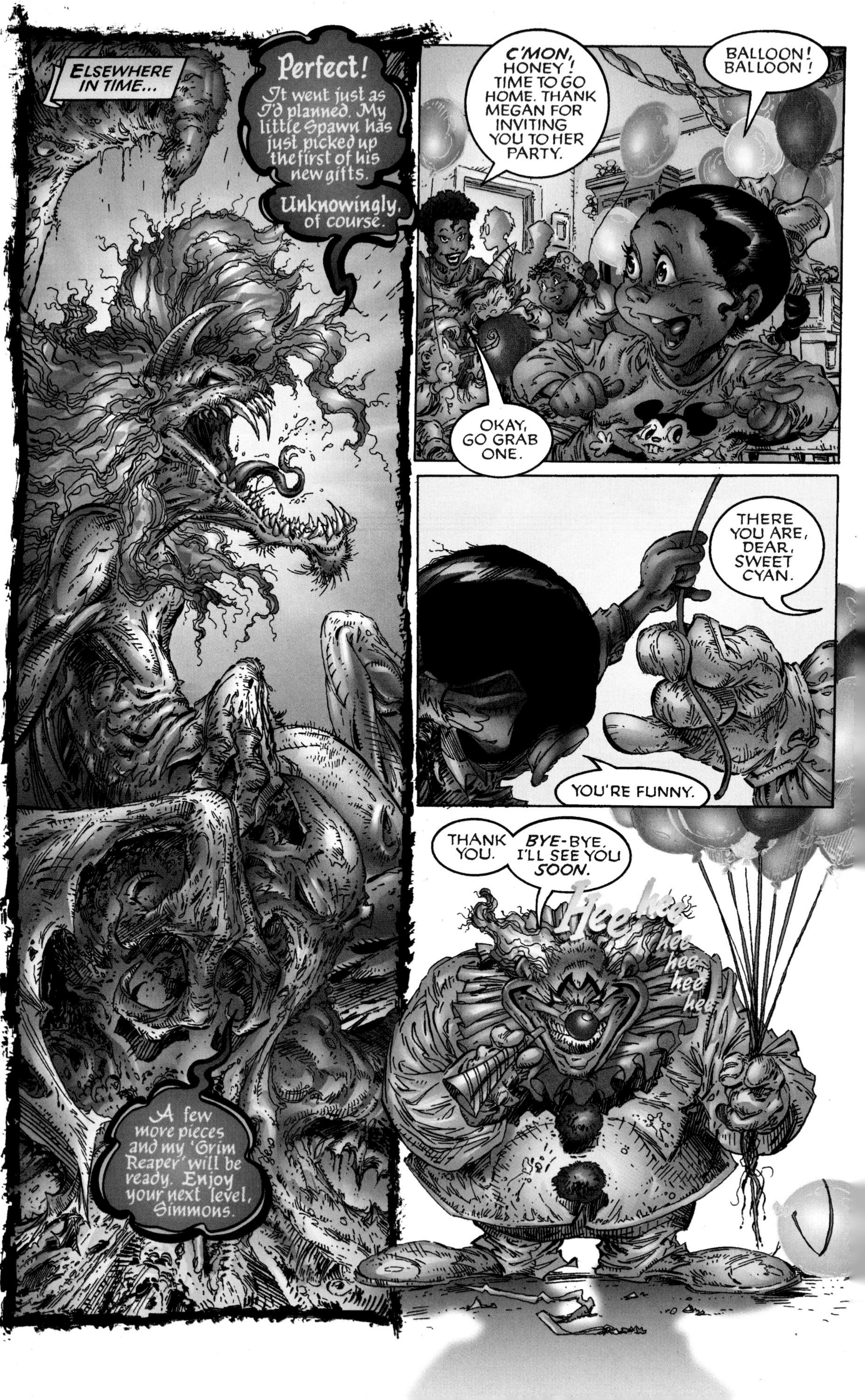
ELSEWHERE IN TIME...
Perfect! It went just as I'd planned. My little Spawn has just picked up the first of his new gifts.
Unknowingly, of course.
A few more pieces and my 'Grim Reaper' will be ready. Enjoy your next level, Simmons.
C'MON, HONEY! TIME TO GO HOME. THANK MEGAN FOR INVITING YOU TO HER PARTY.
BALLOON! BALLOON!
OKAY, GO GRAB ONE.
THERE YOU ARE, DEAR, SWEET CYAN.
YOU'RE FUNNY.
THANK YOU.
BYE-BYE. I'LL SEE YOU SOON.
Hee hee hee hee hee

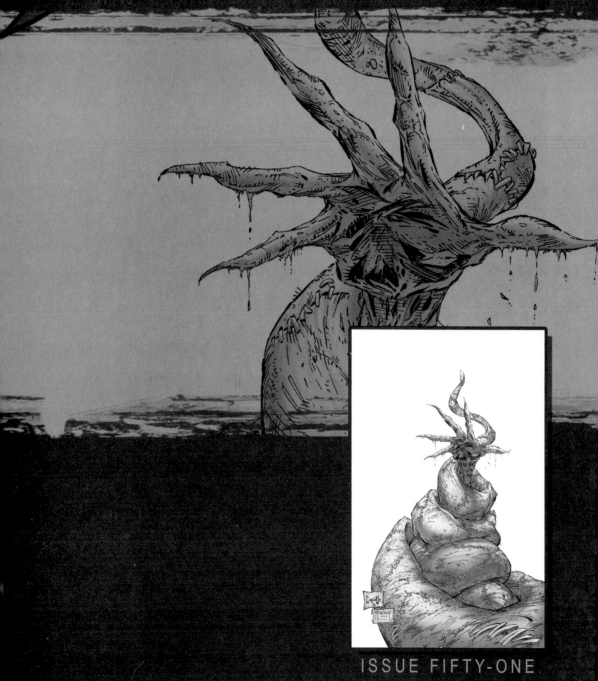

ISSUE FIFTY-ONE

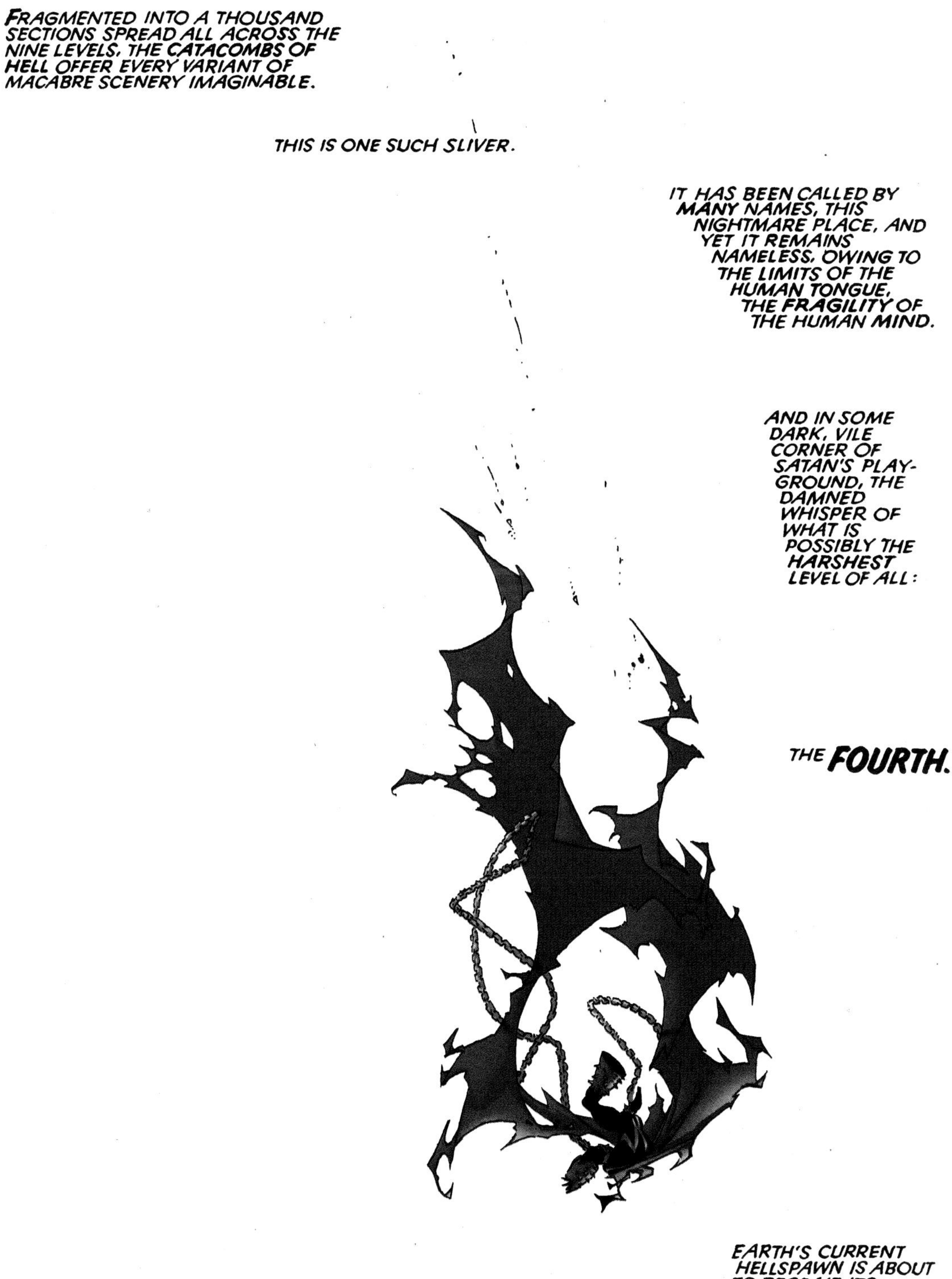
FRAGMENTED INTO A THOUSAND SECTIONS SPREAD ALL ACROSS THE NINE LEVELS, THE CATACOMBS OF HELL OFFER EVERY VARIANT OF MACABRE SCENERY IMAGINABLE.
THIS IS ONE SUCH SLIVER.
IT HAS BEEN CALLED BY MANY NAMES, THIS NIGHTMARE PLACE, AND YET IT REMAINS NAMELESS, OWING TO THE LIMITS OF THE HUMAN TONGUE, THE FRAGILITY OF THE HUMAN MIND.
AND IN SOME DARK, VILE CORNER OF SATAN'S PLAY-GROUND, THE DAMNED WHISPER OF WHAT IS POSSIBLY THE HARSHEST LEVEL OF ALL:
THE FOURTH.
EARTH'S CURRENT HELLSPAWN IS ABOUT TO BECOME ITS NEWEST VICTIM.

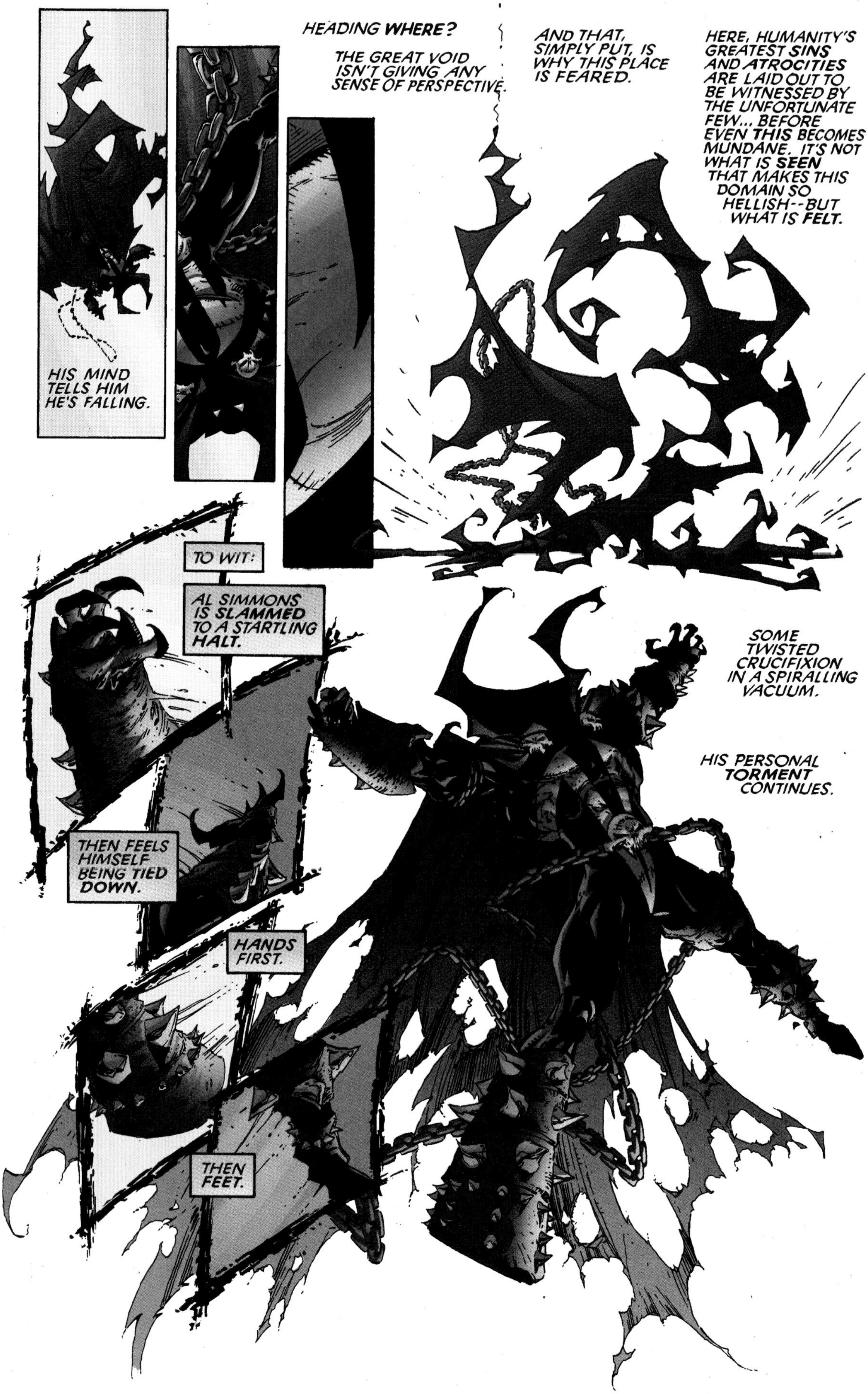
HIS MIND TELLS HIM HE'S FALLING.
HEADING WHERE?
THE GREAT VOID ISN'T GIVING ANY SENSE OF PERSPECTIVE.
AND THAT, SIMPLY PUT, IS WHY THIS PLACE IS FEARED.
HERE, HUMANITY'S GREATEST SINS AND ATROCITIES ARE LAID OUT TO BE WITNESSED BY THE UNFORTUNATE FEW... BEFORE EVEN THIS BECOMES MUNDANE. IT'S NOT WHAT IS SEEN THAT MAKES THIS DOMAIN SO HELLISH--BUT WHAT IS FELT.
TO WIT:
AL SIMMONS IS SLAMMED TO A STARTLING HALT.
THEN FEELS HIMSELF BEING TIED DOWN.
HANDS FIRST.
THEN FEET.
SOME TWISTED CRUCIFIXION IN A SPIRALLING VACUUM.
HIS PERSONAL TORMENT CONTINUES.

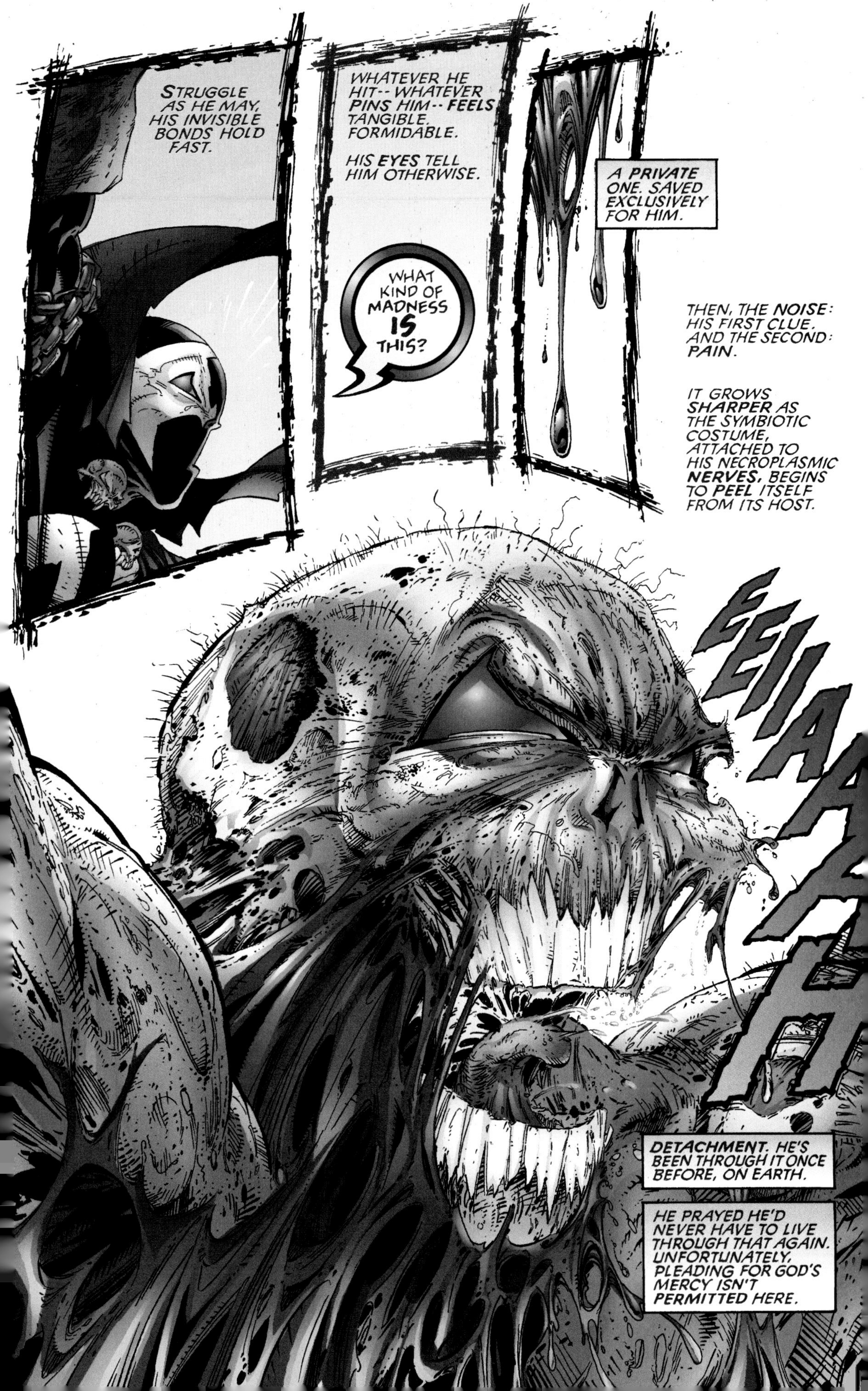
STRUGGLE AS HE MAY, HIS INVISIBLE BONDS HOLD FAST.
WHATEVER HE HIT-- WHATEVER PINS HIM-- FEELS TANGIBLE. FORMIDABLE.
HIS EYES TELL HIM OTHERWISE.
WHAT KIND OF MADNESS IS THIS?
A PRIVATE ONE. SAVED EXCLUSIVELY FOR HIM.
THEN, THE NOISE: HIS FIRST CLUE. AND THE SECOND: PAIN.
IT GROWS SHARPER AS THE SYMBIOTIC COSTUME, ATTACHED TO HIS NECROPLASMIC NERVES, BEGINS TO PEEL ITSELF FROM ITS HOST.
EEIIAAAH
DETACHMENT. HE'S BEEN THROUGH IT ONCE BEFORE, ON EARTH.
HE PRAYED HE'D NEVER HAVE TO LIVE THROUGH THAT AGAIN. UNFORTUNATELY, PLEADING FOR GOD'S MERCY ISN'T PERMITTED HERE.

NOT IN ANY SHAPE OR FORM.

BUT OTHERS ARE **GLAD** FOR THE ENTERTAINMENT-- SUCH AS THE **LATEST** UNHOLY RULER OF THIS TERRITORY.

AWWWH... **THERE** YOU ARE!

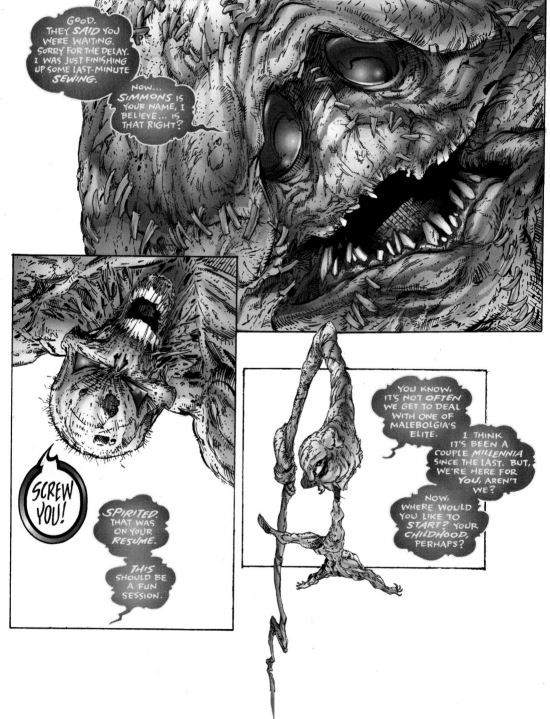

GOOD. THEY **SAID** YOU WERE WAITING. SORRY FOR THE DELAY. I WAS JUST FINISHING UP SOME LAST-MINUTE **SEWING.**

NOW... **SIMMONS** IS YOUR NAME, I BELIEVE... IS THAT RIGHT?

SCREW YOU!

SPIRITED. THAT WAS ON YOUR **RESUME.**

THIS SHOULD BE A FUN SESSION.

YOU KNOW, IT'S NOT **OFTEN** WE GET TO DEAL WITH ONE OF MALEBOLGIA'S ELITE. I THINK IT'S BEEN A COUPLE **MILLENNIA** SINCE THE LAST. BUT, WE'RE HERE FOR **YOU,** AREN'T WE?

NOW, WHERE WOULD YOU LIKE TO **START?** YOUR **CHILDHOOD,** PERHAPS?

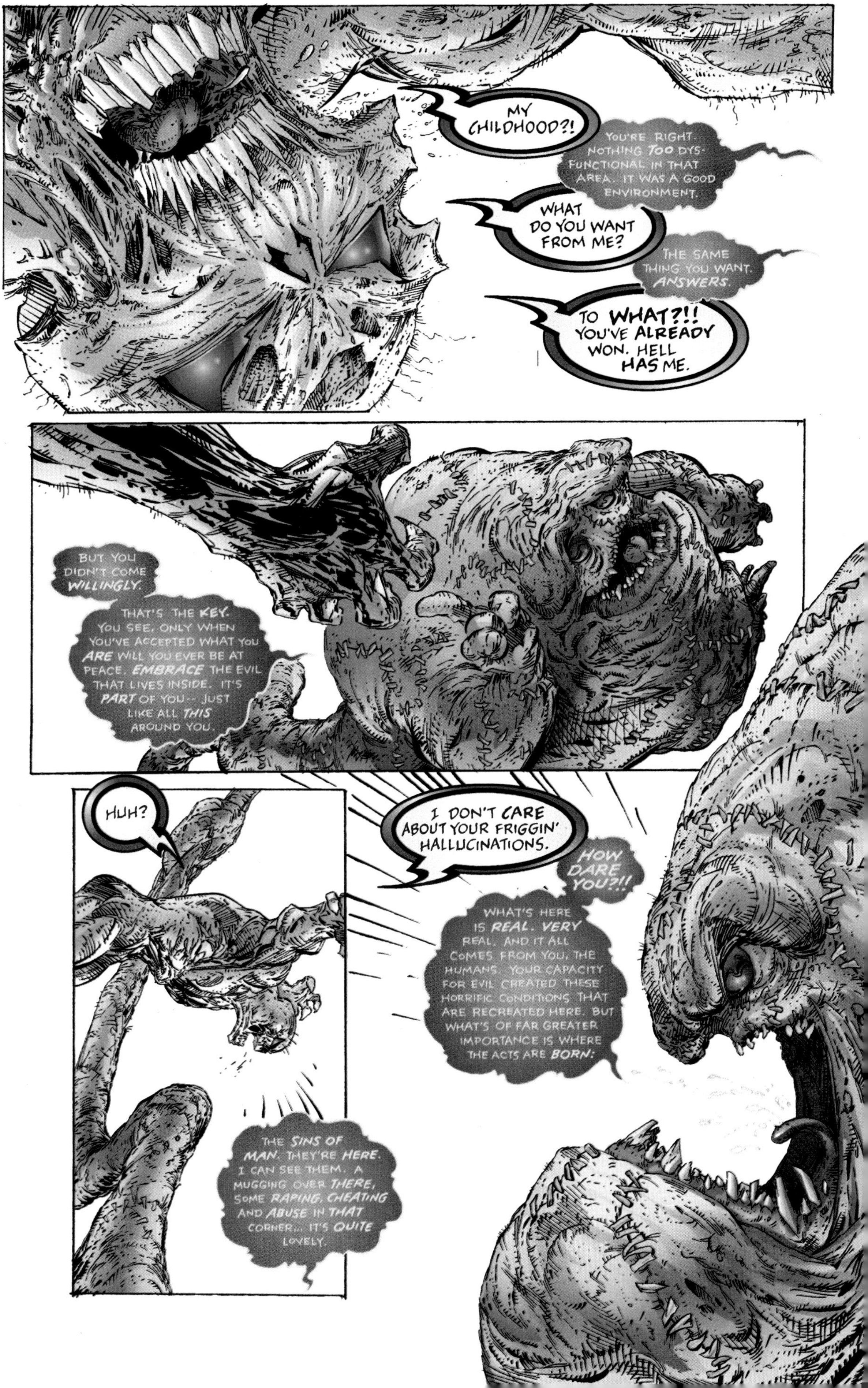

MY CHILDHOOD?!
YOU'RE RIGHT. NOTHING TOO DYS-FUNCTIONAL IN THAT AREA. IT WAS A GOOD ENVIRONMENT.
WHAT DO YOU WANT FROM ME?
THE SAME THING YOU WANT. ANSWERS.
TO WHAT?!! YOU'VE ALREADY WON. HELL HAS ME.
BUT YOU DIDN'T COME WILLINGLY.
THAT'S THE KEY. YOU SEE, ONLY WHEN YOU'VE ACCEPTED WHAT YOU ARE WILL YOU EVER BE AT PEACE. EMBRACE THE EVIL THAT LIVES INSIDE. IT'S PART OF YOU-- JUST LIKE ALL THIS AROUND YOU.
HUH?
THE SINS OF MAN. THEY'RE HERE. I CAN SEE THEM. A MUGGING OVER THERE, SOME RAPING, CHEATING AND ABUSE IN THAT CORNER... IT'S QUITE LOVELY.
I DON'T CARE ABOUT YOUR FRIGGIN' HALLUCINATIONS.
HOW DARE YOU?!!
WHAT'S HERE IS REAL. VERY REAL. AND IT ALL COMES FROM YOU, THE HUMANS. YOUR CAPACITY FOR EVIL CREATED THESE HORRIFIC CONDITIONS THAT ARE RECREATED HERE. BUT WHAT'S OF FAR GREATER IMPORTANCE IS WHERE THE ACTS ARE BORN:

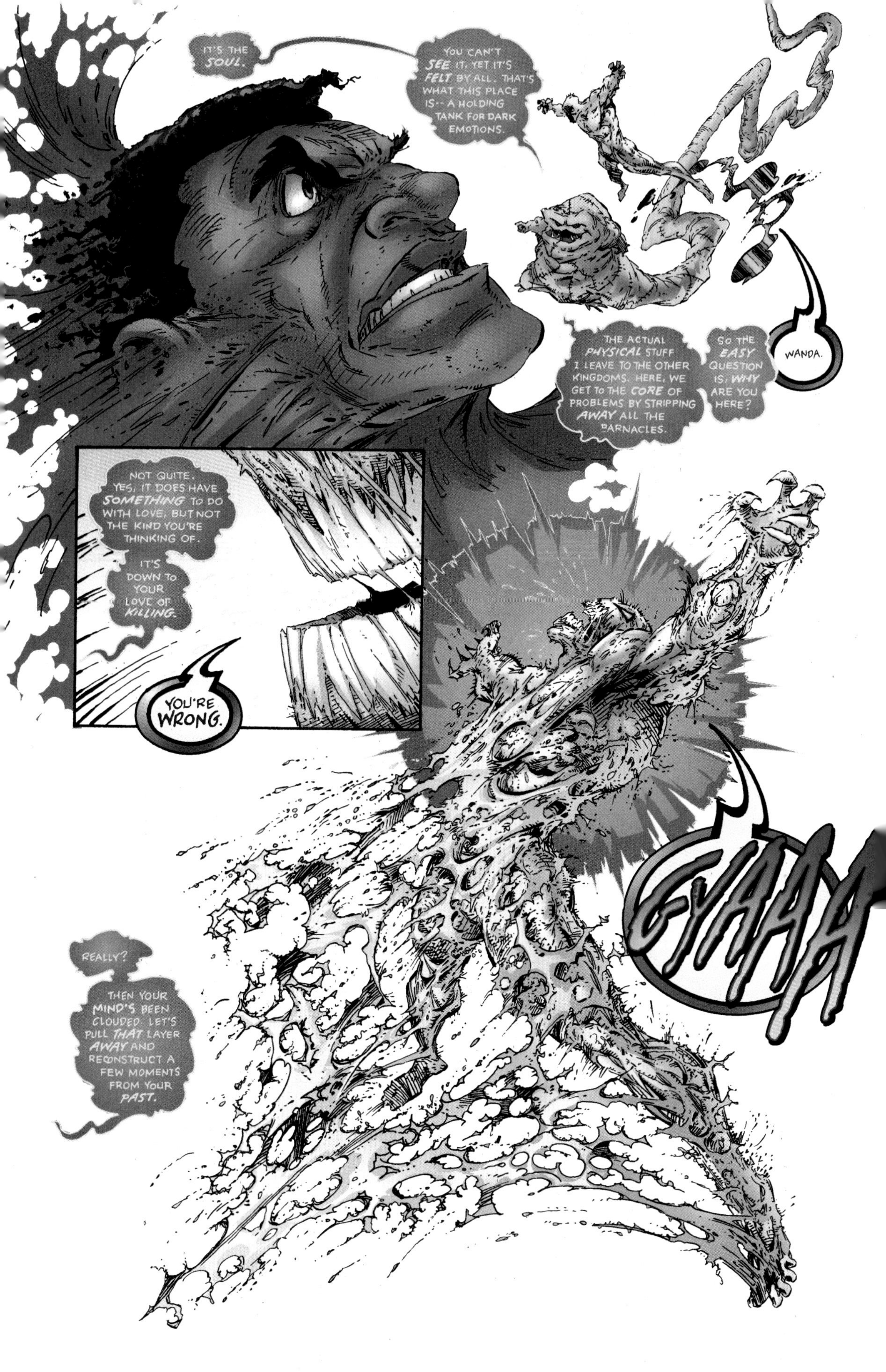
IT'S THE SOUL.
YOU CAN'T SEE IT, YET IT'S FELT BY ALL. THAT'S WHAT THIS PLACE IS-- A HOLDING TANK FOR DARK EMOTIONS.
THE ACTUAL PHYSICAL STUFF I LEAVE TO THE OTHER KINGDOMS. HERE, WE GET TO THE CORE OF PROBLEMS BY STRIPPING AWAY ALL THE BARNACLES.
SO THE EASY QUESTION IS, WHY ARE YOU HERE?
WANDA.
NOT QUITE. YES, IT DOES HAVE SOMETHING TO DO WITH LOVE, BUT NOT THE KIND YOU'RE THINKING OF.
IT'S DOWN TO YOUR LOVE OF KILLING.
YOU'RE WRONG.
GYAAA
REALLY?
THEN YOUR MIND'S BEEN CLOUDED. LET'S PULL THAT LAYER AWAY AND RECONSTRUCT A FEW MOMENTS FROM YOUR PAST.

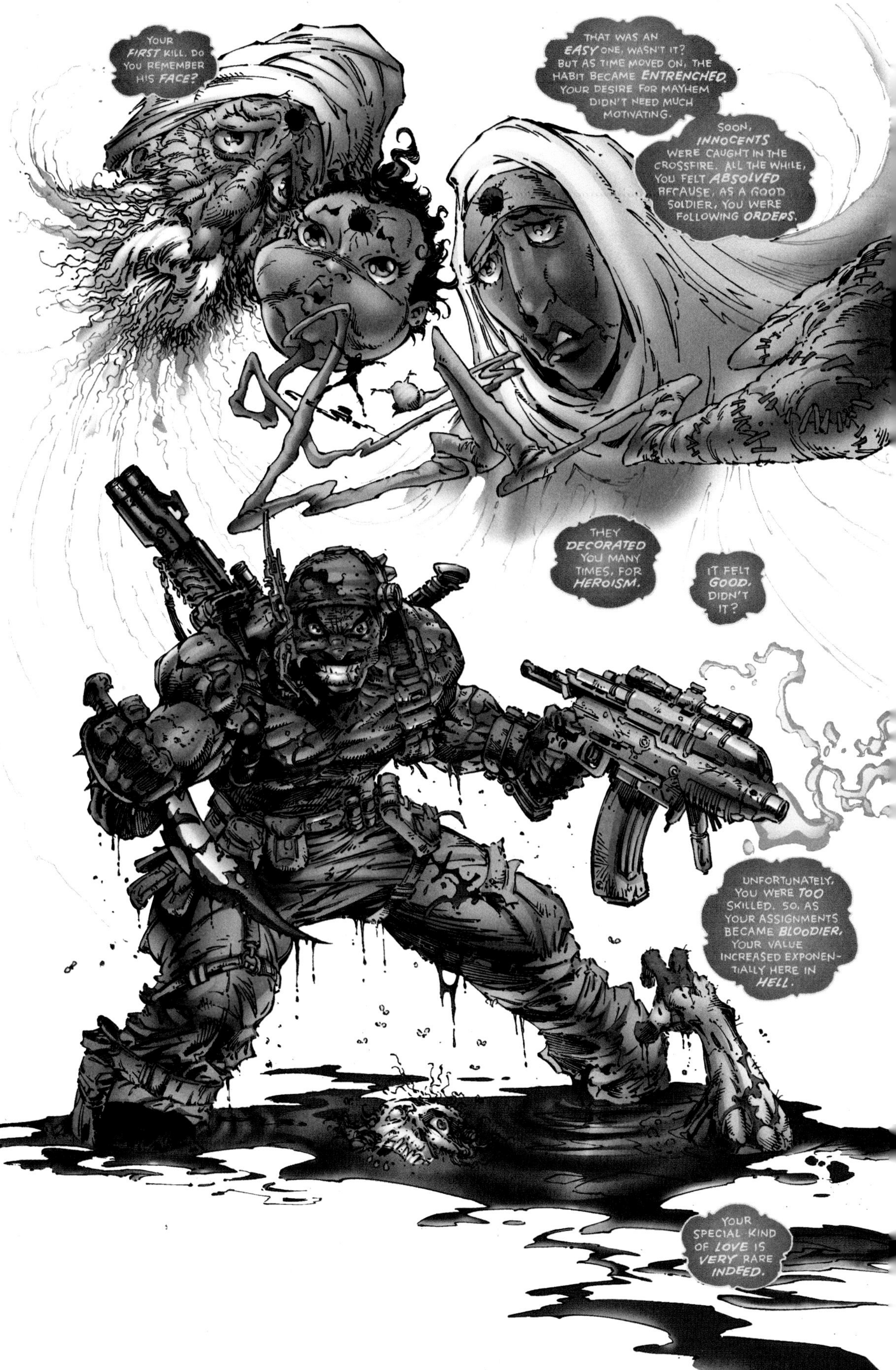
YOUR FIRST KILL. DO YOU REMEMBER HIS FACE?
THAT WAS AN EASY ONE, WASN'T IT? BUT AS TIME MOVED ON, THE HABIT BECAME ENTRENCHED. YOUR DESIRE FOR MAYHEM DIDN'T NEED MUCH MOTIVATING.
SOON, INNOCENTS WERE CAUGHT IN THE CROSSFIRE. ALL THE WHILE, YOU FELT ABSOLVED BECAUSE, AS A GOOD SOLDIER, YOU WERE FOLLOWING ORDERS.
THEY DECORATED YOU MANY TIMES, FOR HEROISM.
IT FELT GOOD, DIDN'T IT?
UNFORTUNATELY, YOU WERE TOO SKILLED. SO, AS YOUR ASSIGNMENTS BECAME BLOODIER, YOUR VALUE INCREASED EXPONENTIALLY HERE IN HELL.
YOUR SPECIAL KIND OF LOVE IS VERY RARE INDEED.

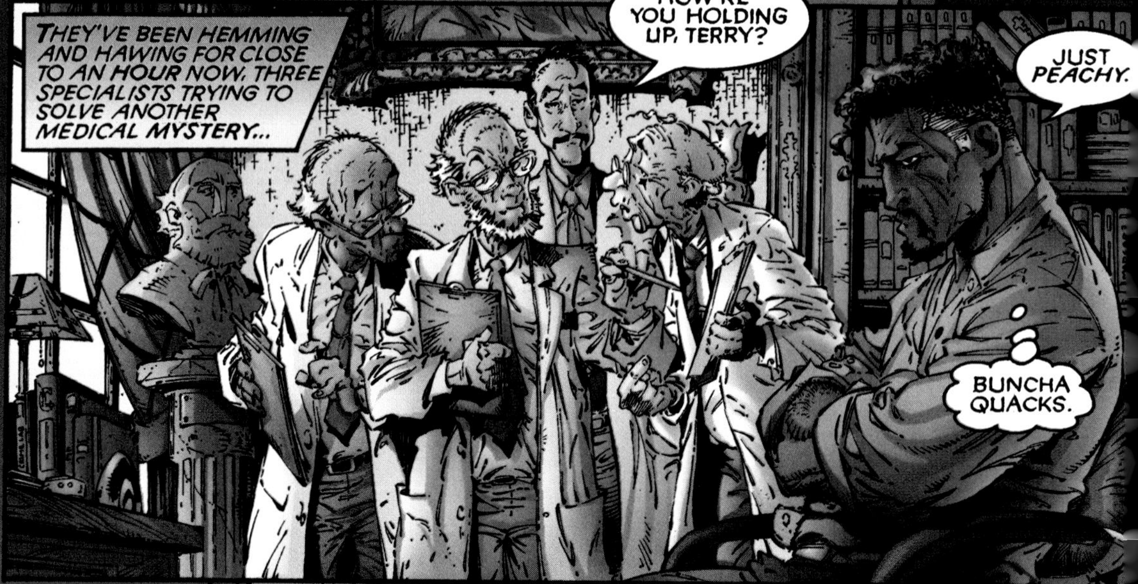
THEY'VE BEEN HEMMING AND HAWING FOR CLOSE TO AN HOUR NOW. THREE SPECIALISTS TRYING TO SOLVE ANOTHER MEDICAL MYSTERY...
HOW'RE YOU HOLDING UP, TERRY?
JUST PEACHY.
BUNCHA QUACKS.

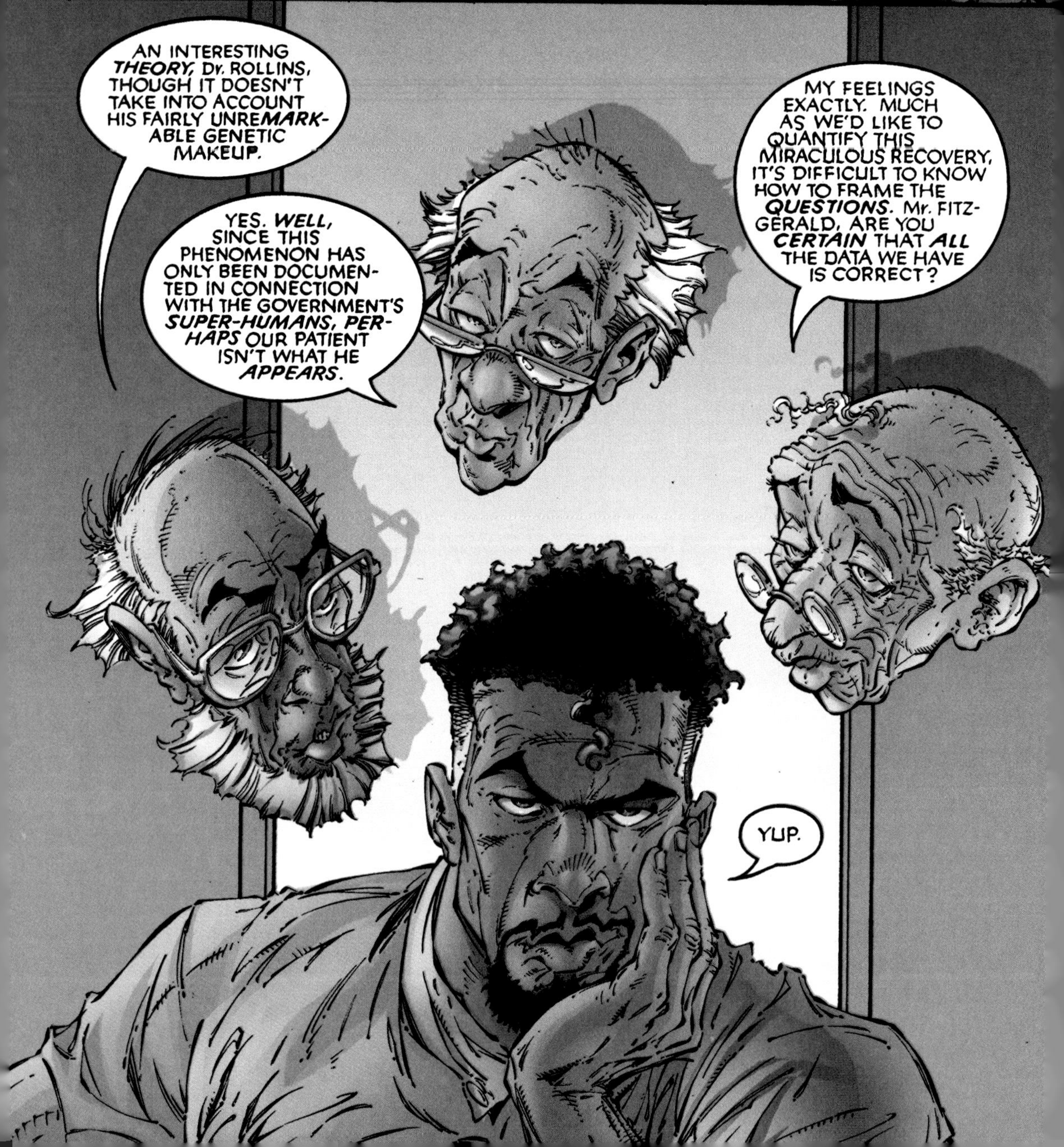
AN INTERESTING THEORY, Dr. ROLLINS, THOUGH IT DOESN'T TAKE INTO ACCOUNT HIS FAIRLY UNREMARKABLE GENETIC MAKEUP.
YES. WELL, SINCE THIS PHENOMENON HAS ONLY BEEN DOCUMENTED IN CONNECTION WITH THE GOVERNMENT'S SUPER-HUMANS, PERHAPS OUR PATIENT ISN'T WHAT HE APPEARS.
MY FEELINGS EXACTLY. MUCH AS WE'D LIKE TO QUANTIFY THIS MIRACULOUS RECOVERY, IT'S DIFFICULT TO KNOW HOW TO FRAME THE QUESTIONS. Mr. FITZGERALD, ARE YOU CERTAIN THAT ALL THE DATA WE HAVE IS CORRECT?
YUP.

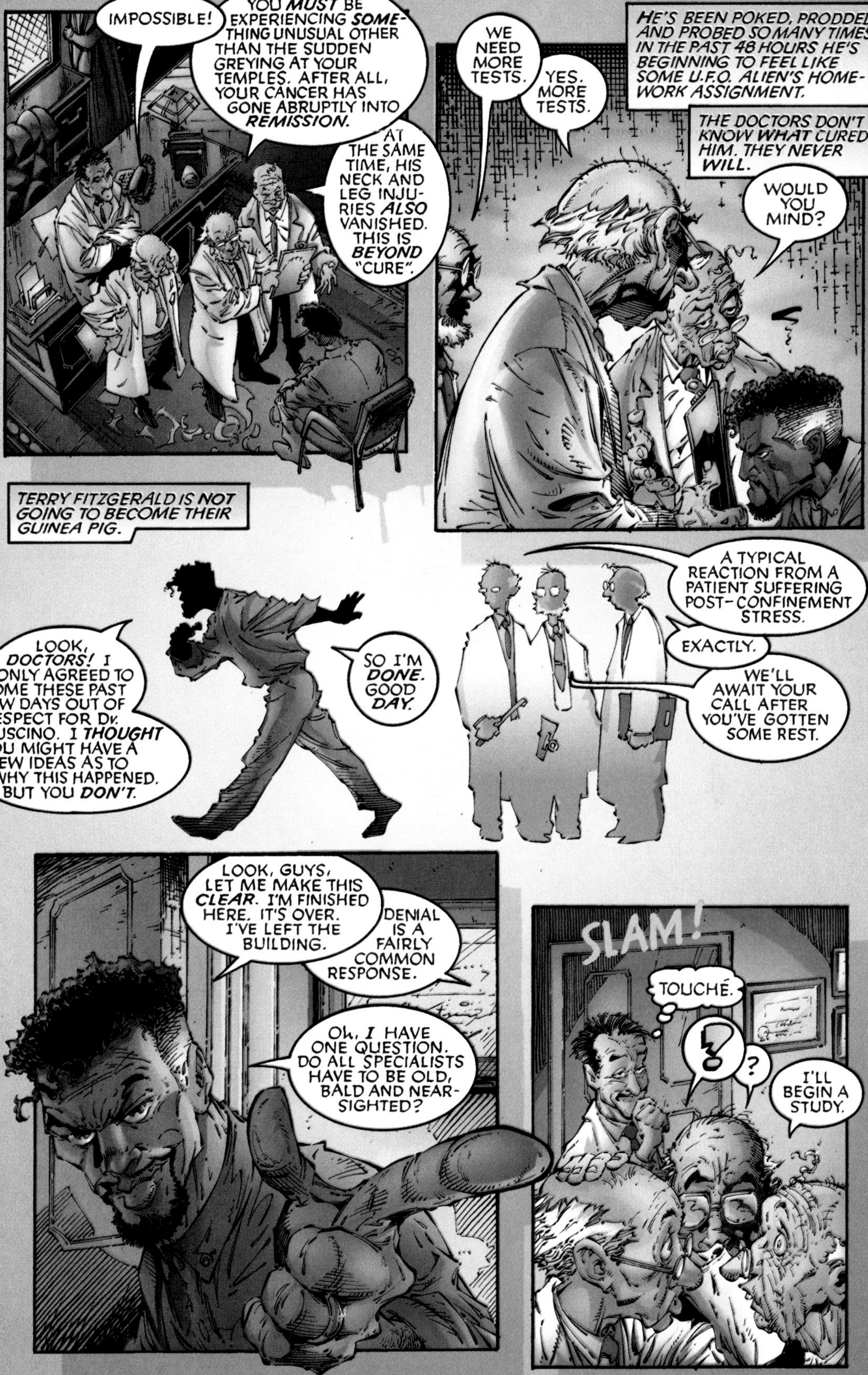
IMPOSSIBLE!
YOU MUST BE EXPERIENCING SOMETHING UNUSUAL OTHER THAN THE SUDDEN GREYING AT YOUR TEMPLES. AFTER ALL, YOUR CANCER HAS GONE ABRUPTLY INTO REMISSION.
AT THE SAME TIME, HIS NECK AND LEG INJURIES ALSO VANISHED. THIS IS BEYOND "CURE".
TERRY FITZGERALD IS NOT GOING TO BECOME THEIR GUINEA PIG.
WE NEED MORE TESTS.
YES. MORE TESTS.
HE'S BEEN POKED, PRODDED AND PROBED SO MANY TIMES IN THE PAST 48 HOURS HE'S BEGINNING TO FEEL LIKE SOME U.F.O. ALIEN'S HOMEWORK ASSIGNMENT.
THE DOCTORS DON'T KNOW WHAT CURED HIM. THEY NEVER WILL.
WOULD YOU MIND?
LOOK, DOCTORS! I ONLY AGREED TO COME THESE PAST FEW DAYS OUT OF RESPECT FOR Dr. BUSCINO. I THOUGHT YOU MIGHT HAVE A FEW IDEAS AS TO WHY THIS HAPPENED. BUT YOU DON'T.
SO I'M DONE. GOOD DAY.
A TYPICAL REACTION FROM A PATIENT SUFFERING POST-CONFINEMENT STRESS.
EXACTLY.
WE'LL AWAIT YOUR CALL AFTER YOU'VE GOTTEN SOME REST.
LOOK, GUYS, LET ME MAKE THIS CLEAR. I'M FINISHED HERE. IT'S OVER. I'VE LEFT THE BUILDING.
DENIAL IS A FAIRLY COMMON RESPONSE.
Oh, I HAVE ONE QUESTION. DO ALL SPECIALISTS HAVE TO BE OLD, BALD AND NEAR-SIGHTED?
SLAM!
TOUCHÉ.
?
I'LL BEGIN A STUDY.

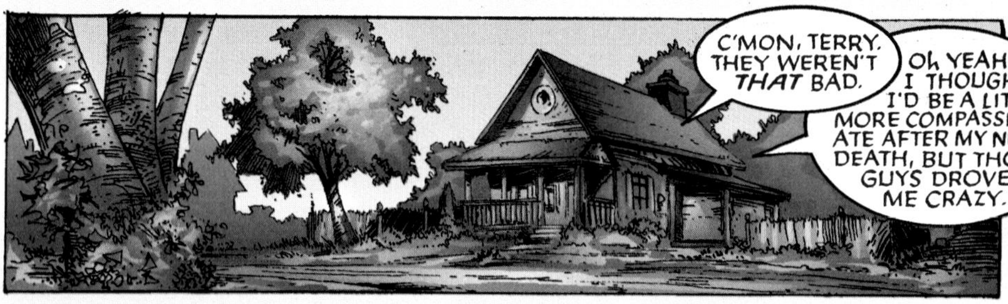
C'MON, TERRY. THEY WEREN'T *THAT* BAD.
Oh YEAH?! I THOUGHT I'D BE A LITTLE MORE COMPASSION-ATE AFTER MY NEAR-DEATH, BUT THOSE GUYS DROVE ME CRAZY.
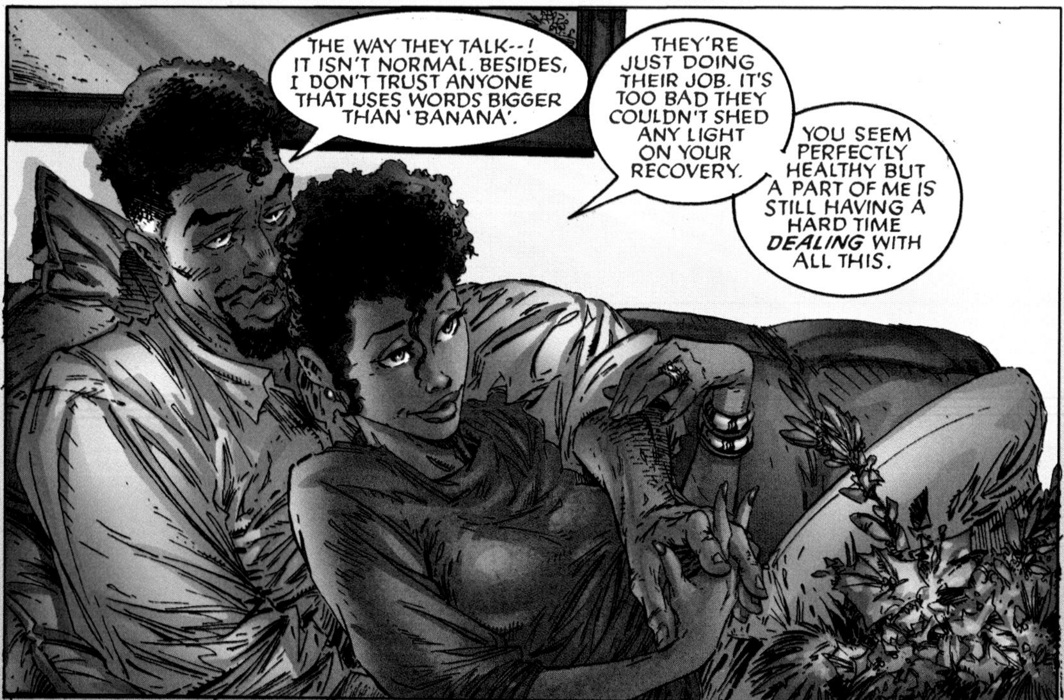
THE WAY THEY TALK--! IT ISN'T NORMAL. BESIDES, I DON'T TRUST ANYONE THAT USES WORDS BIGGER THAN 'BANANA'.
THEY'RE JUST DOING THEIR JOB. IT'S TOO BAD THEY COULDN'T SHED ANY LIGHT ON YOUR RECOVERY.
YOU SEEM PERFECTLY HEALTHY BUT A PART OF ME IS STILL HAVING A HARD TIME *DEALING* WITH ALL THIS.
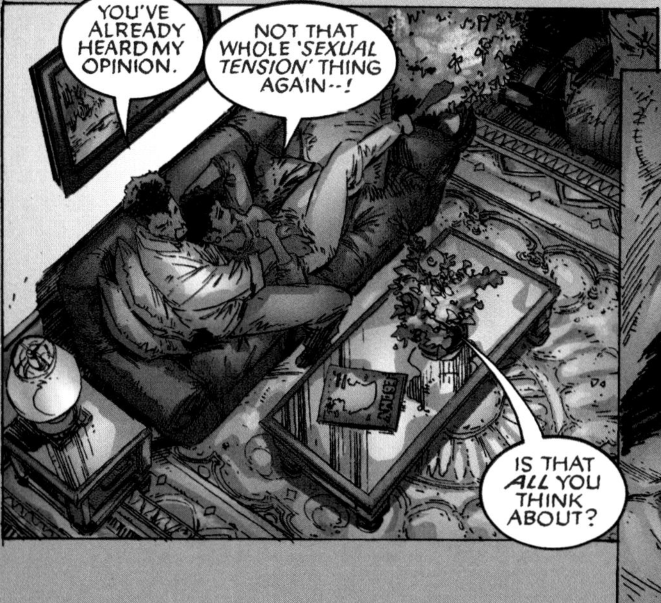
YOU'VE ALREADY HEARD MY OPINION.
NOT THAT WHOLE '*SEXUAL TENSION*' THING AGAIN--!
IS THAT *ALL* YOU THINK ABOUT?
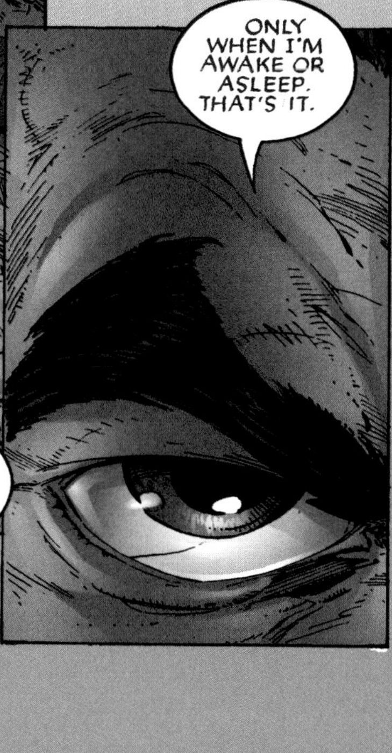
ONLY WHEN I'M AWAKE OR ASLEEP. THAT'S IT.

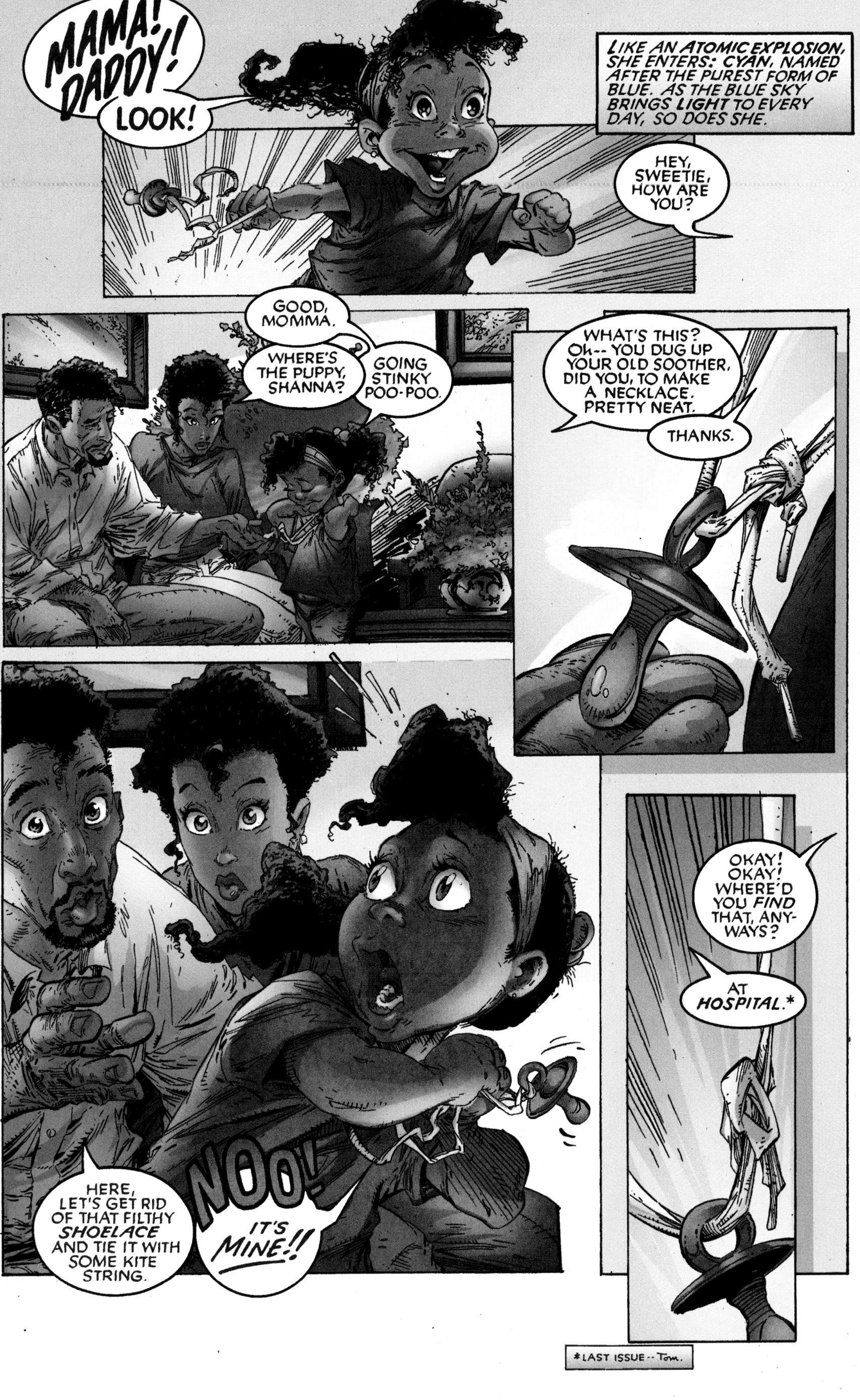
MAMA! DADDY!
LOOK!
LIKE AN ATOMIC EXPLOSION, SHE ENTERS: CYAN, NAMED AFTER THE PUREST FORM OF BLUE. AS THE BLUE SKY BRINGS LIGHT TO EVERY DAY, SO DOES SHE.
HEY, SWEETIE, HOW ARE YOU?
GOOD, MOMMA.
WHERE'S THE PUPPY, SHANNA?
GOING STINKY POO-POO.
WHAT'S THIS? Oh-- YOU DUG UP YOUR OLD SOOTHER, DID YOU, TO MAKE A NECKLACE. PRETTY NEAT.
THANKS.
HERE, LET'S GET RID OF THAT FILTHY SHOELACE AND TIE IT WITH SOME KITE STRING.
NOO!
IT'S MINE!!
OKAY! OKAY! WHERE'D YOU FIND THAT, ANYWAYS?
AT HOSPITAL.*
*LAST ISSUE -- Tom.

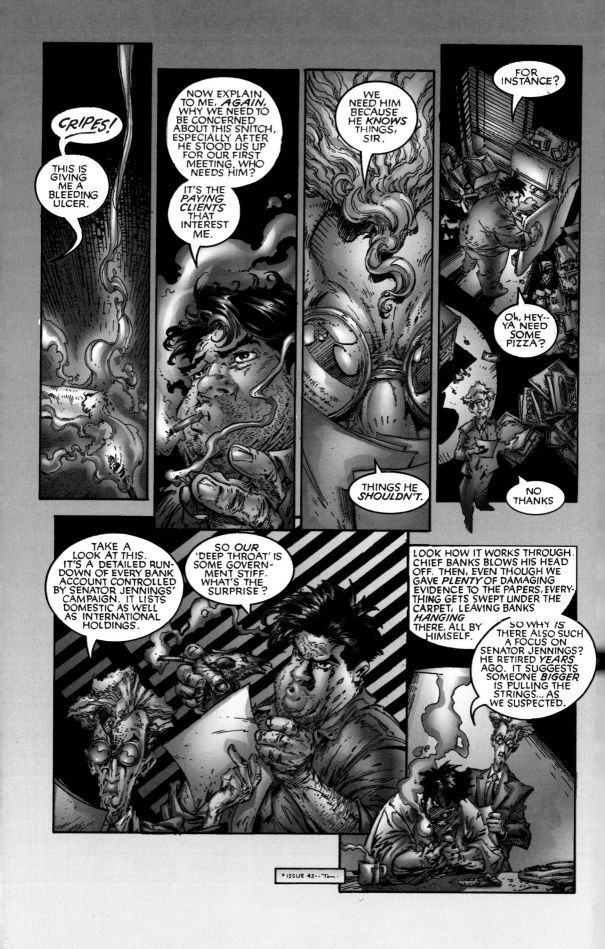

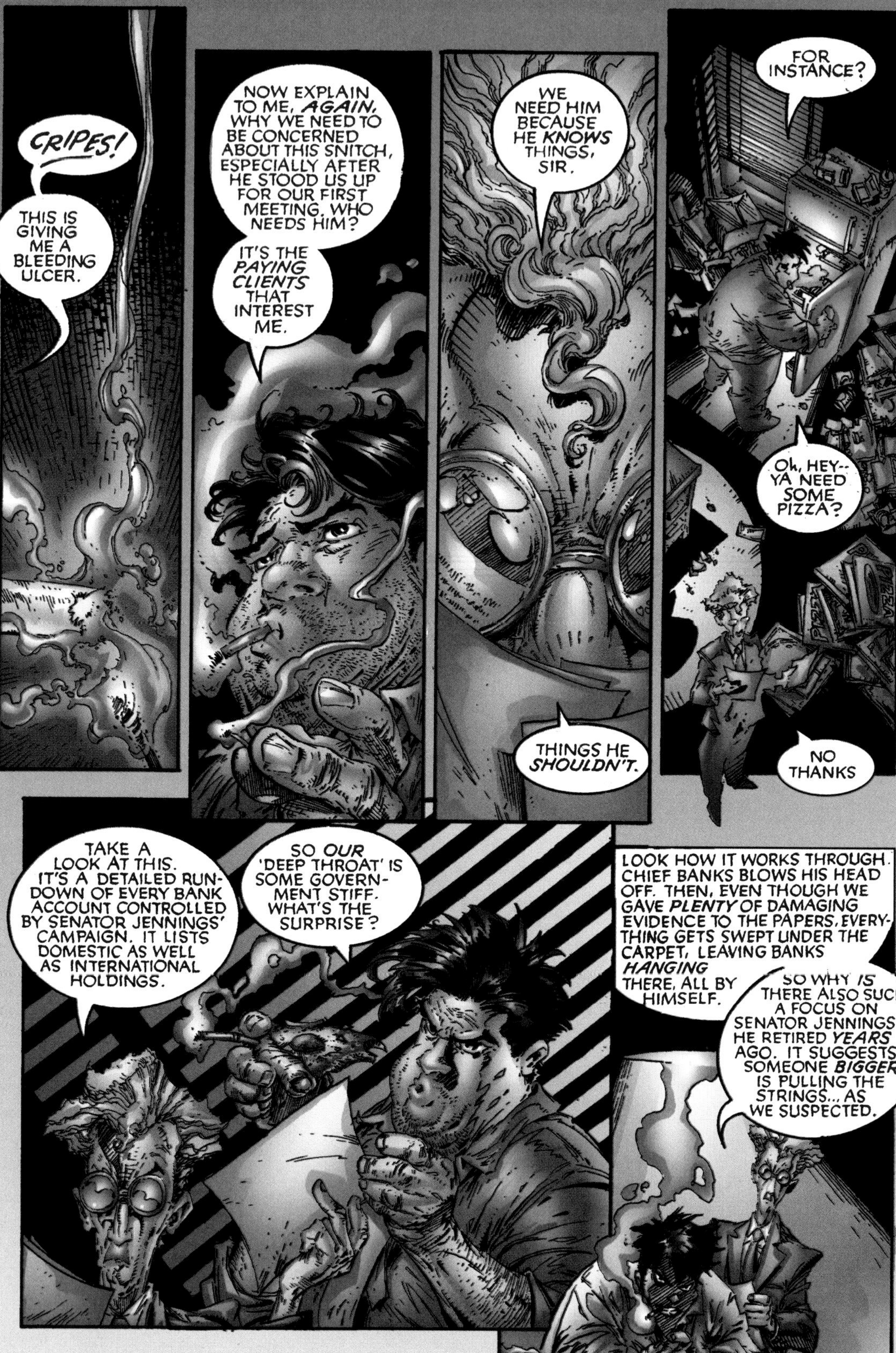
CRIPES!
THIS IS GIVING ME A BLEEDING ULCER.
NOW EXPLAIN TO ME, AGAIN, WHY WE NEED TO BE CONCERNED ABOUT THIS SNITCH, ESPECIALLY AFTER HE STOOD US UP FOR OUR FIRST MEETING. WHO NEEDS HIM?
IT'S THE PAYING CLIENTS THAT INTEREST ME.
WE NEED HIM BECAUSE HE KNOWS THINGS, SIR.
THINGS HE SHOULDN'T.
FOR INSTANCE?
Oh, HEY-- YA NEED SOME PIZZA?
NO THANKS
TAKE A LOOK AT THIS. IT'S A DETAILED RUN-DOWN OF EVERY BANK ACCOUNT CONTROLLED BY SENATOR JENNINGS' CAMPAIGN. IT LISTS DOMESTIC AS WELL AS INTERNATIONAL HOLDINGS.
SO OUR 'DEEP THROAT' IS SOME GOVERNMENT STIFF. WHAT'S THE SURPRISE?
LOOK HOW IT WORKS THROUGH. CHIEF BANKS BLOWS HIS HEAD OFF. THEN, EVEN THOUGH WE GAVE PLENTY OF DAMAGING EVIDENCE TO THE PAPERS, EVERYTHING GETS SWEPT UNDER THE CARPET, LEAVING BANKS HANGING THERE, ALL BY HIMSELF.
SO WHY IS THERE ALSO SUCH A FOCUS ON SENATOR JENNINGS? HE RETIRED YEARS AGO. IT SUGGESTS SOMEONE BIGGER IS PULLING THE STRINGS... AS WE SUSPECTED.
*ISSUE 43-- Tom.

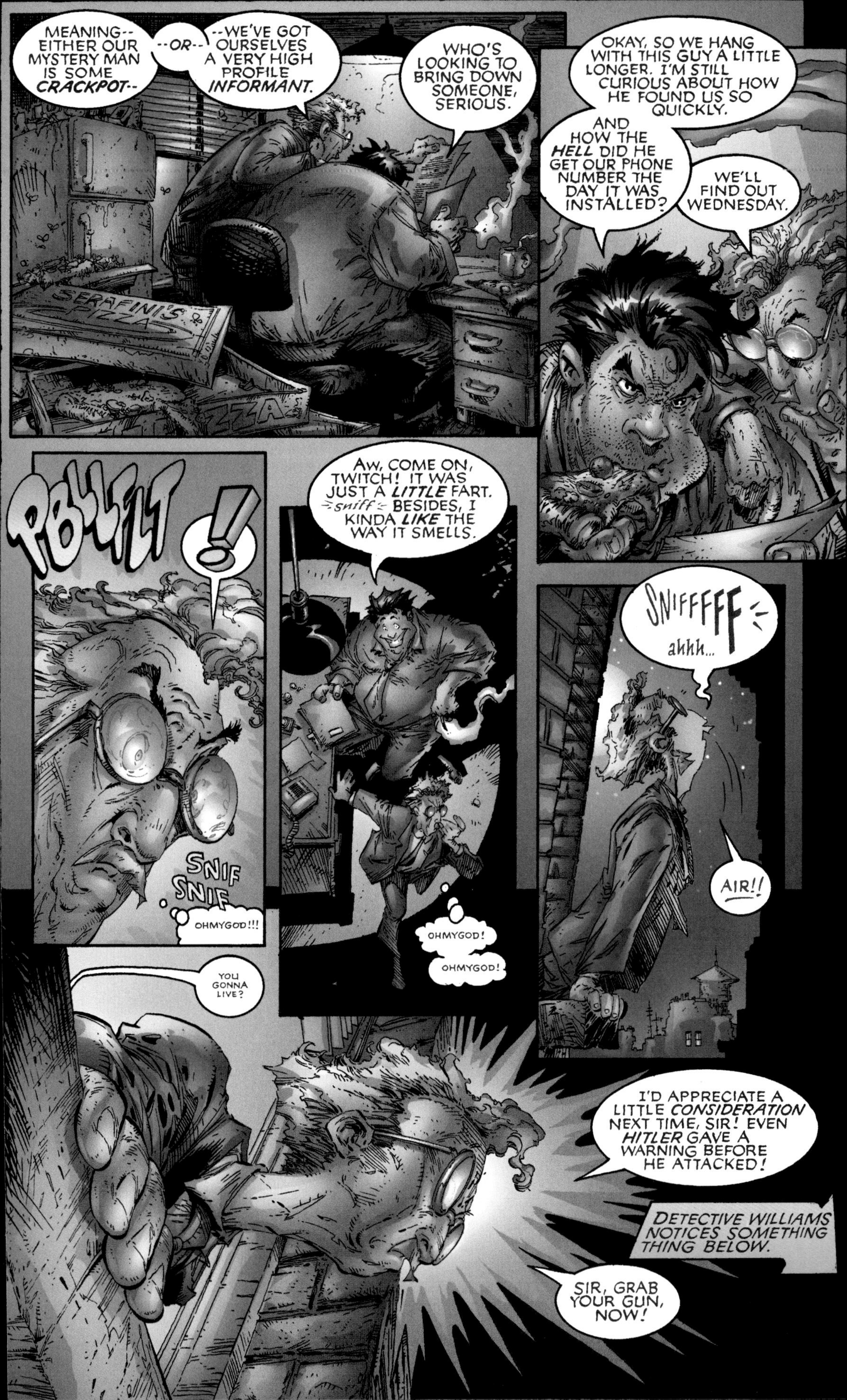
MEANING-- EITHER OUR MYSTERY MAN IS SOME CRACKPOT--
--OR--
--WE'VE GOT OURSELVES A VERY HIGH PROFILE INFORMANT.
WHO'S LOOKING TO BRING DOWN SOMEONE, SERIOUS.
SERAFINI'S PIZZA
OKAY, SO WE HANG WITH THIS GUY A LITTLE LONGER. I'M STILL CURIOUS ABOUT HOW HE FOUND US SO QUICKLY.
AND HOW THE HELL DID HE GET OUR PHONE NUMBER THE DAY IT WAS INSTALLED?
WE'LL FIND OUT WEDNESDAY.
PBLLLT
!
SNIF SNIF
OHMYGOD!!!
AW, COME ON, TWITCH! IT WAS JUST A LITTLE FART. sniff BESIDES, I KINDA LIKE THE WAY IT SMELLS.
OHMYGOD!
OHMYGOD!
SNIFFFFF ahhh...
AIR!!
YOU GONNA LIVE?
I'D APPRECIATE A LITTLE CONSIDERATION NEXT TIME, SIR! EVEN HITLER GAVE A WARNING BEFORE HE ATTACKED!
DETECTIVE WILLIAMS NOTICES SOMETHING THING BELOW.
SIR, GRAB YOUR GUN, NOW!

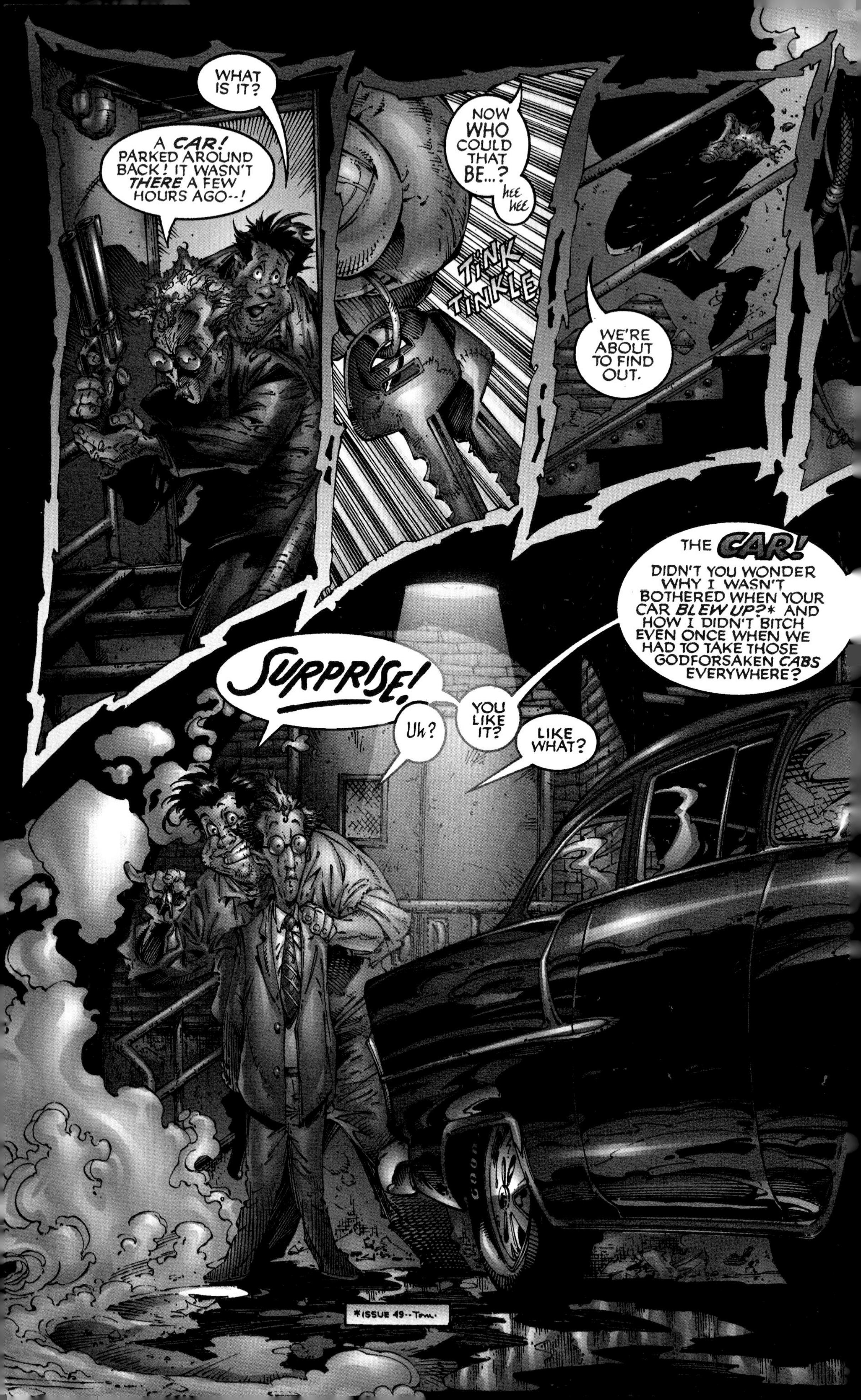
WHAT IS IT?
A CAR! PARKED AROUND BACK! IT WASN'T THERE A FEW HOURS AGO--!
NOW WHO COULD THAT BE...?
HEE HEE
TINK TINKLE
WE'RE ABOUT TO FIND OUT.
SURPRISE!
Uh?
YOU LIKE IT?
LIKE WHAT?
THE CAR! DIDN'T YOU WONDER WHY I WASN'T BOTHERED WHEN YOUR CAR BLEW UP?* AND HOW I DIDN'T BITCH EVEN ONCE WHEN WE HAD TO TAKE THOSE GODFORSAKEN CABS EVERYWHERE?
*ISSUE 49--Tom.

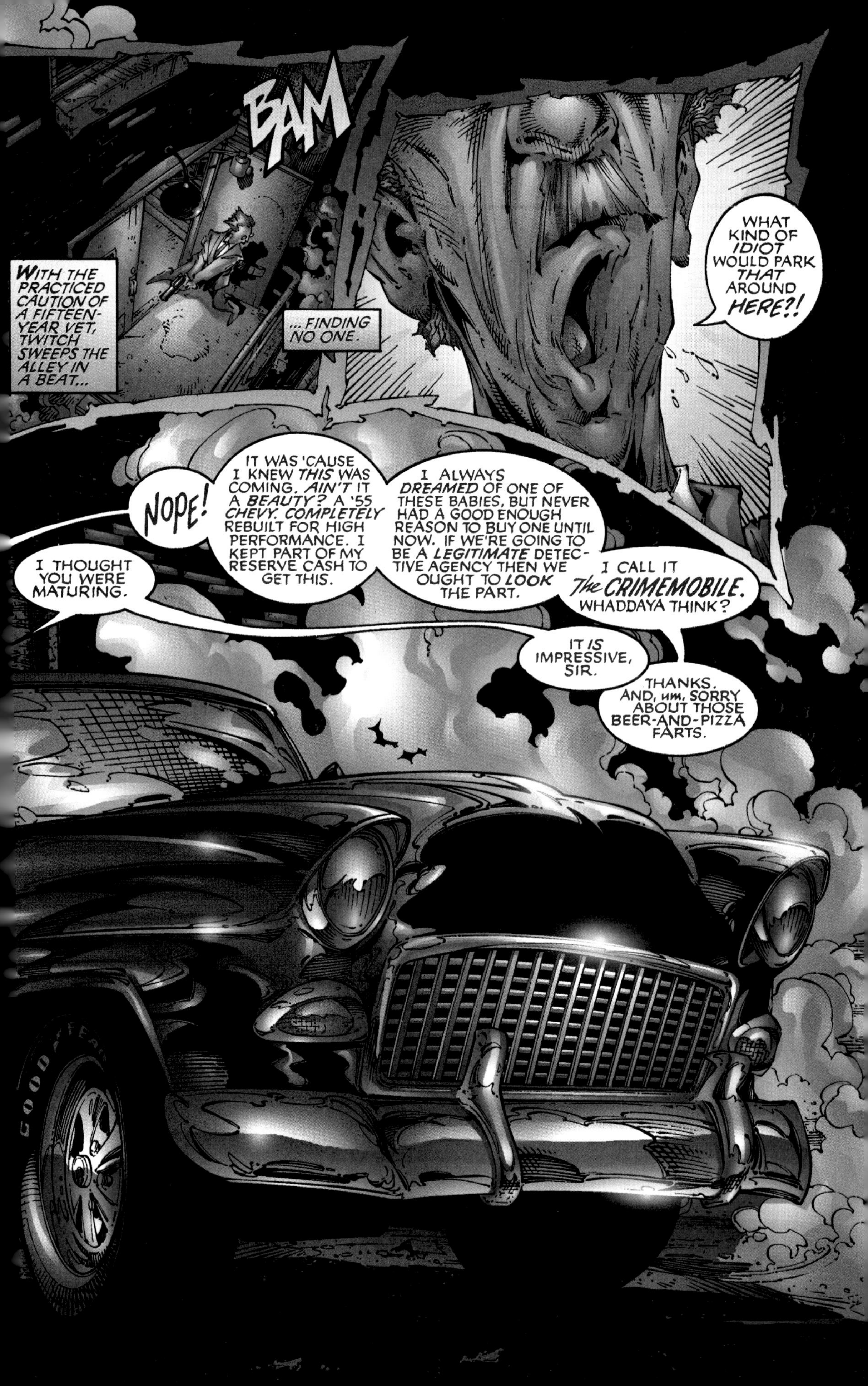
BAM
WITH THE PRACTICED CAUTION OF A FIFTEEN-YEAR VET, TWITCH SWEEPS THE ALLEY IN A BEAT...
...FINDING NO ONE.
WHAT KIND OF IDIOT WOULD PARK THAT AROUND HERE?!
I THOUGHT YOU WERE MATURING.
NOPE!
IT WAS 'CAUSE I KNEW THIS WAS COMING. AIN'T IT A BEAUTY? A '55 CHEVY. COMPLETELY REBUILT FOR HIGH PERFORMANCE. I KEPT PART OF MY RESERVE CASH TO GET THIS.
I ALWAYS DREAMED OF ONE OF THESE BABIES, BUT NEVER HAD A GOOD ENOUGH REASON TO BUY ONE UNTIL NOW. IF WE'RE GOING TO BE A LEGITIMATE DETECTIVE AGENCY THEN WE OUGHT TO LOOK THE PART.
I CALL IT The CRIMEMOBILE. WHADDAYA THINK?
IT IS IMPRESSIVE, SIR.
THANKS. AND, um, SORRY ABOUT THOSE BEER-AND-PIZZA FARTS.
GOODYEAR

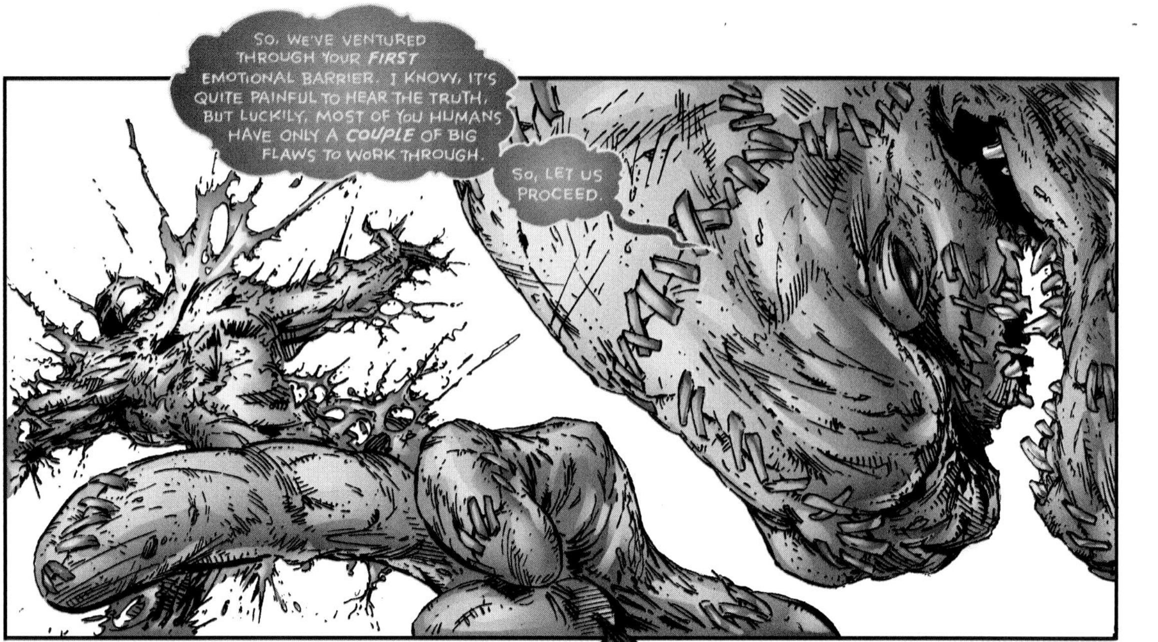
SO, WE'VE VENTURED THROUGH YOUR FIRST EMOTIONAL BARRIER. I KNOW, IT'S QUITE PAINFUL TO HEAR THE TRUTH, BUT LUCKILY, MOST OF YOU HUMANS HAVE ONLY A COUPLE OF BIG FLAWS TO WORK THROUGH.
SO, LET US PROCEED.
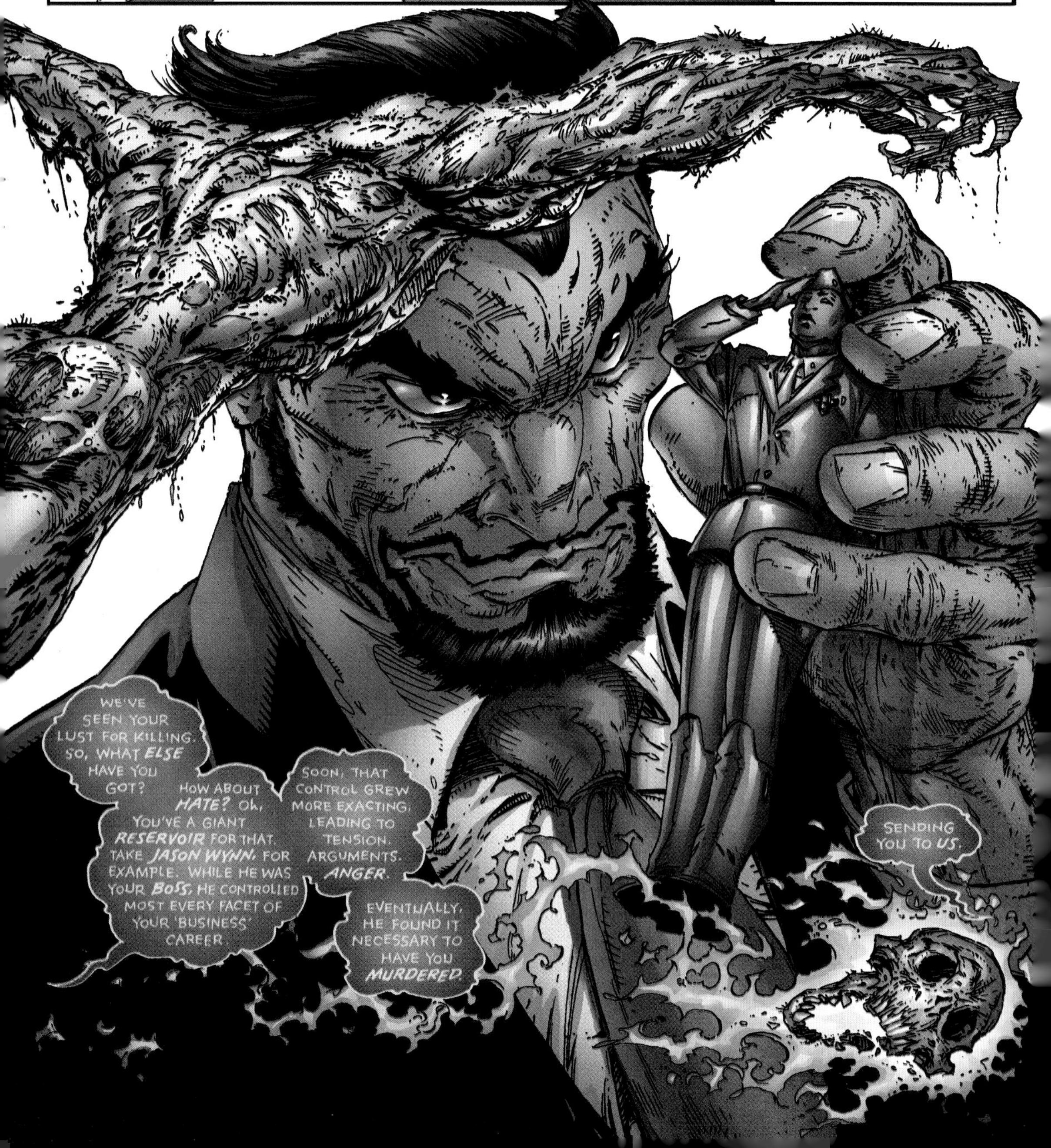
WE'VE SEEN YOUR LUST FOR KILLING. SO, WHAT ELSE HAVE YOU GOT?
HOW ABOUT HATE? OH, YOU'VE A GIANT RESERVOIR FOR THAT. TAKE JASON WYNN, FOR EXAMPLE. WHILE HE WAS YOUR BOSS, HE CONTROLLED MOST EVERY FACET OF YOUR 'BUSINESS' CAREER.
SOON, THAT CONTROL GREW MORE EXACTING, LEADING TO TENSION. ARGUMENTS. ANGER.
EVENTUALLY, HE FOUND IT NECESSARY TO HAVE YOU MURDERED.
SENDING YOU TO US.

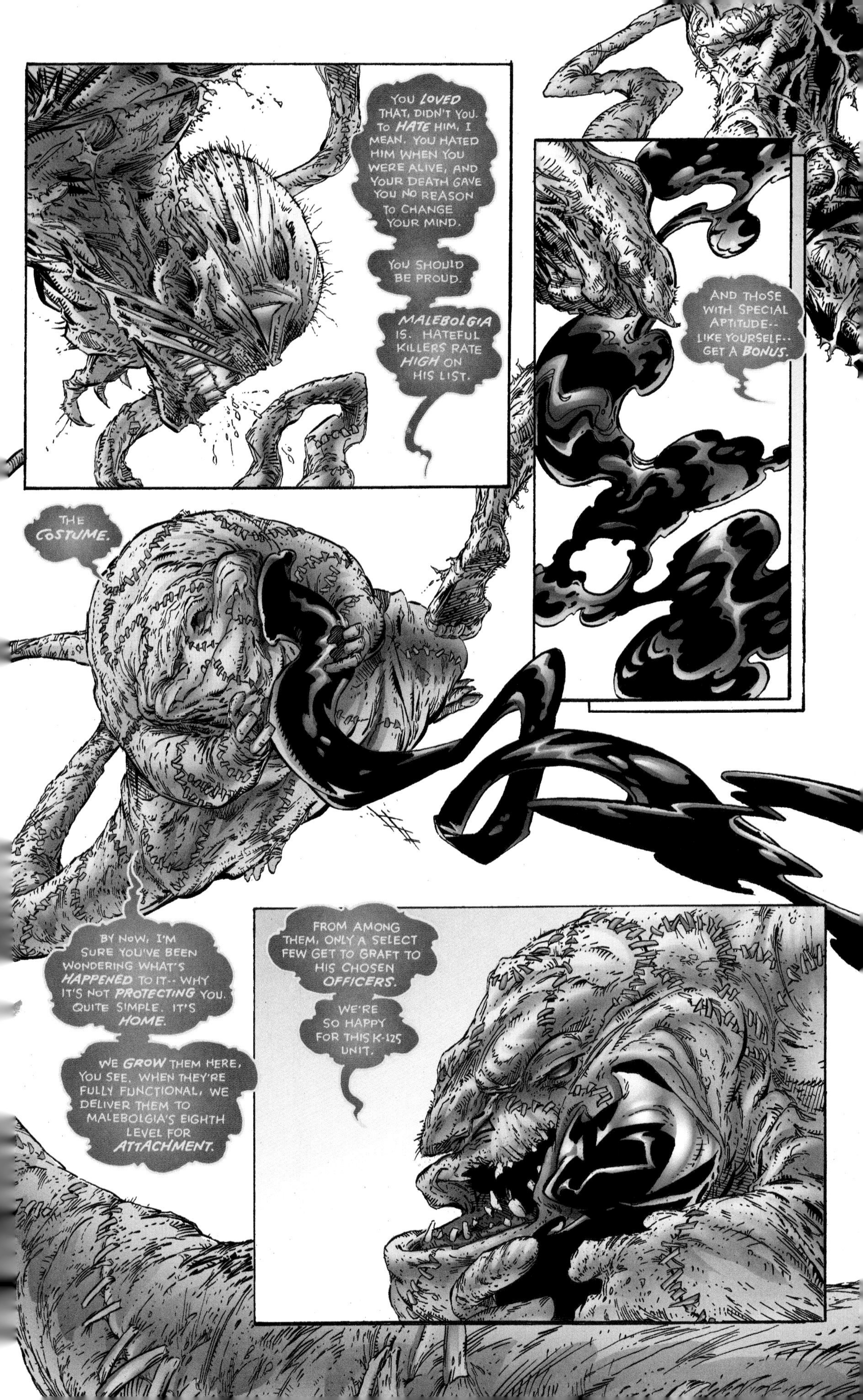
YOU LOVED THAT, DIDN'T YOU. TO HATE HIM, I MEAN. YOU HATED HIM WHEN YOU WERE ALIVE, AND YOUR DEATH GAVE YOU NO REASON TO CHANGE YOUR MIND.
YOU SHOULD BE PROUD.
MALEBOLGIA IS. HATEFUL KILLERS RATE HIGH ON HIS LIST.
AND THOSE WITH SPECIAL APTITUDE-- LIKE YOURSELF-- GET A BONUS.
THE COSTUME.
BY NOW, I'M SURE YOU'VE BEEN WONDERING WHAT'S HAPPENED TO IT-- WHY IT'S NOT PROTECTING YOU. QUITE SIMPLE. IT'S HOME.
WE GROW THEM HERE, YOU SEE. WHEN THEY'RE FULLY FUNCTIONAL, WE DELIVER THEM TO MALEBOLGIA'S EIGHTH LEVEL FOR ATTACHMENT.
FROM AMONG THEM, ONLY A SELECT FEW GET TO GRAFT TO HIS CHOSEN OFFICERS.
WE'RE SO HAPPY FOR THIS K-125 UNIT.

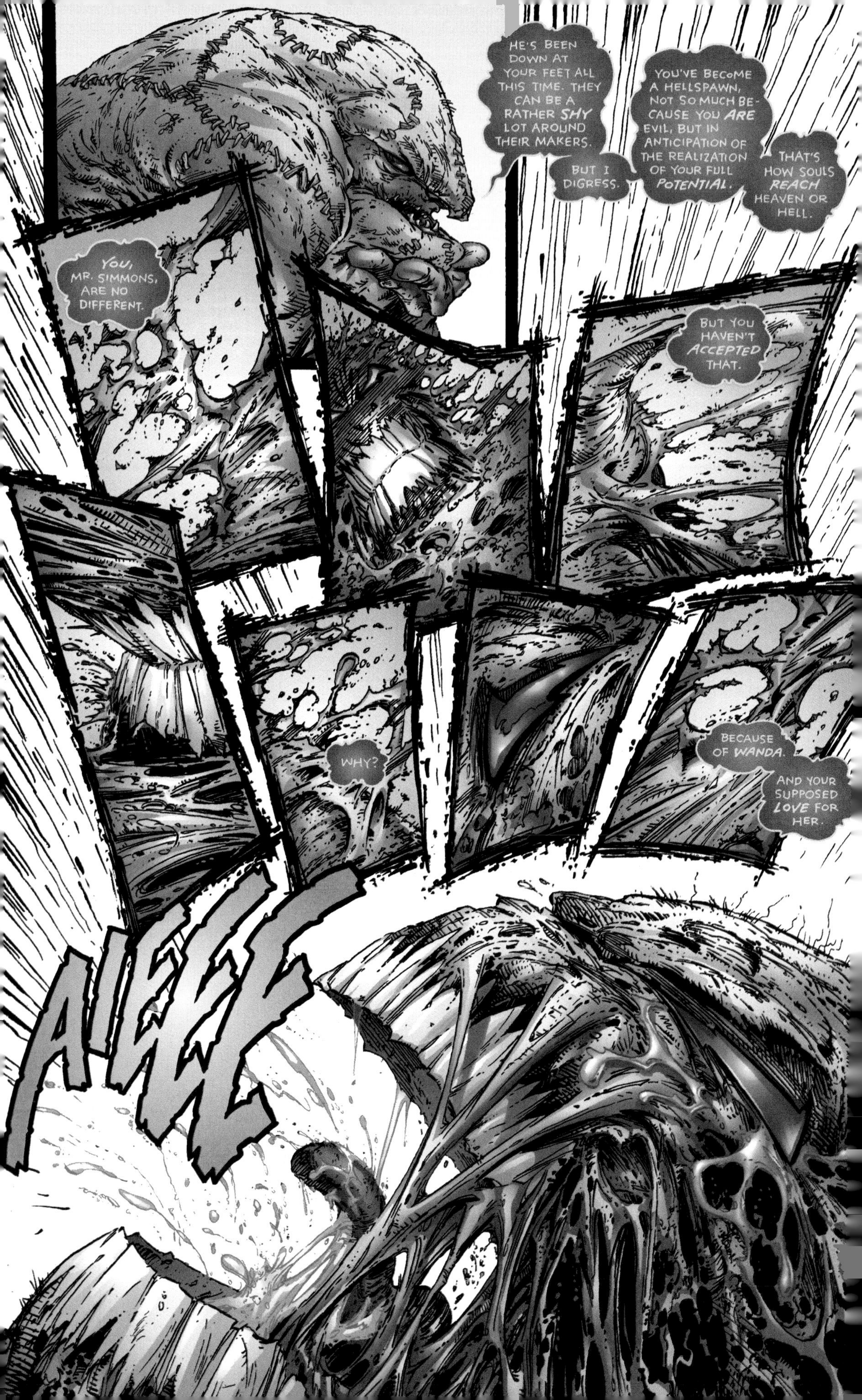
HE'S BEEN DOWN AT YOUR FEET ALL THIS TIME. THEY CAN BE A RATHER SHY LOT AROUND THEIR MAKERS.
BUT I DIGRESS.
YOU'VE BECOME A HELLSPAWN, NOT SO MUCH BECAUSE YOU ARE EVIL, BUT IN ANTICIPATION OF THE REALIZATION OF YOUR FULL POTENTIAL.
THAT'S HOW SOULS REACH HEAVEN OR HELL.
YOU, MR. SIMMONS, ARE NO DIFFERENT.
BUT YOU HAVEN'T ACCEPTED THAT.
WHY?
BECAUSE OF WANDA.
AND YOUR SUPPOSED LOVE FOR HER.
AIEE

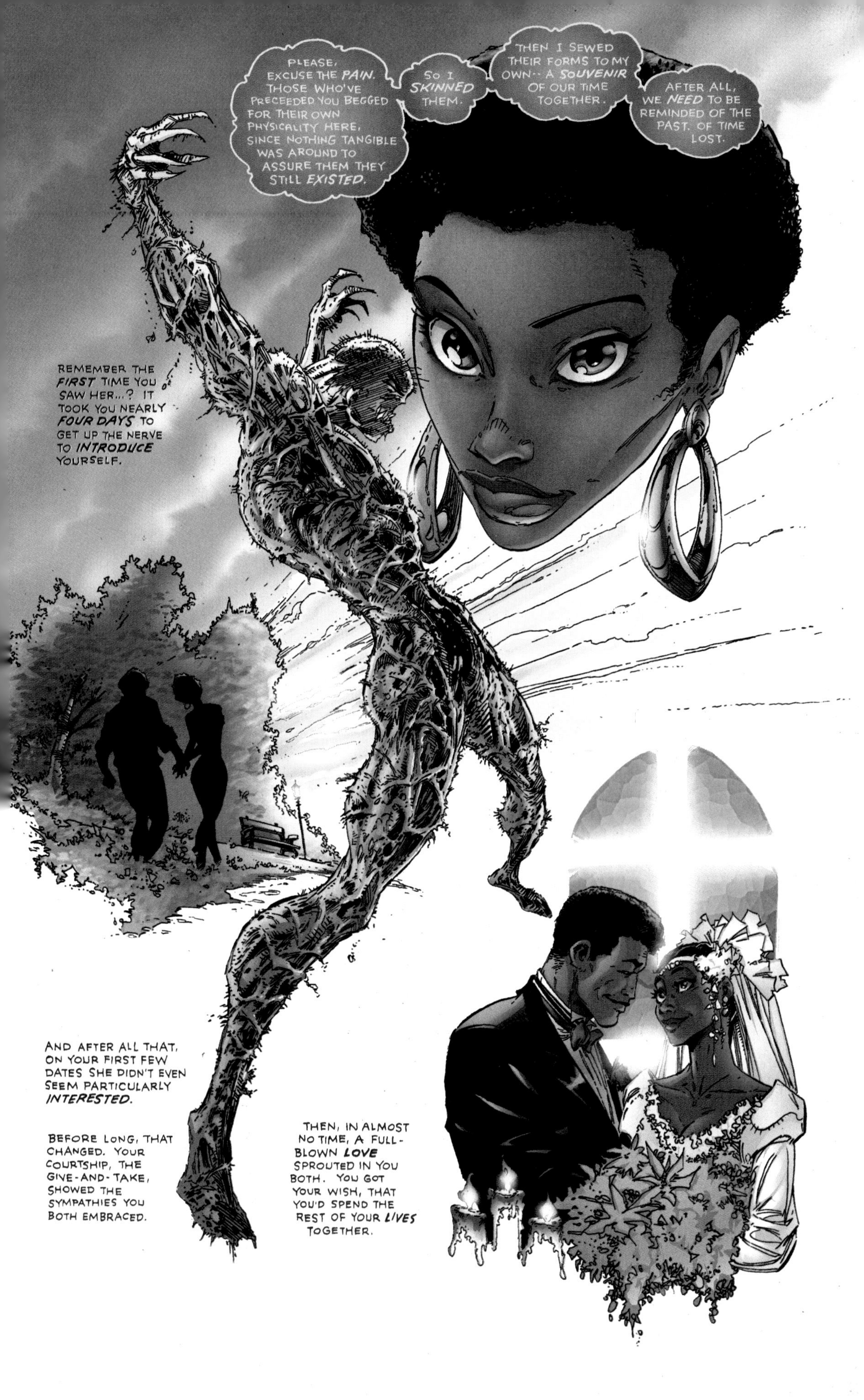
PLEASE, EXCUSE THE PAIN. THOSE WHO'VE PRECEEDED YOU BEGGED FOR THEIR OWN PHYSICALITY HERE, SINCE NOTHING TANGIBLE WAS AROUND TO ASSURE THEM THEY STILL EXISTED.
SO I SKINNED THEM.
THEN I SEWED THEIR FORMS TO MY OWN-- A SOUVENIR OF OUR TIME TOGETHER.
AFTER ALL, WE NEED TO BE REMINDED OF THE PAST. OF TIME LOST.
REMEMBER THE FIRST TIME YOU SAW HER...? IT TOOK YOU NEARLY FOUR DAYS TO GET UP THE NERVE TO INTRODUCE YOURSELF.
AND AFTER ALL THAT, ON YOUR FIRST FEW DATES SHE DIDN'T EVEN SEEM PARTICULARLY INTERESTED.
BEFORE LONG, THAT CHANGED. YOUR COURTSHIP, THE GIVE-AND-TAKE, SHOWED THE SYMPATHIES YOU BOTH EMBRACED.
THEN, IN ALMOST NO TIME, A FULL-BLOWN LOVE SPROUTED IN YOU BOTH. YOU GOT YOUR WISH, THAT YOU'D SPEND THE REST OF YOUR LIVES TOGETHER.

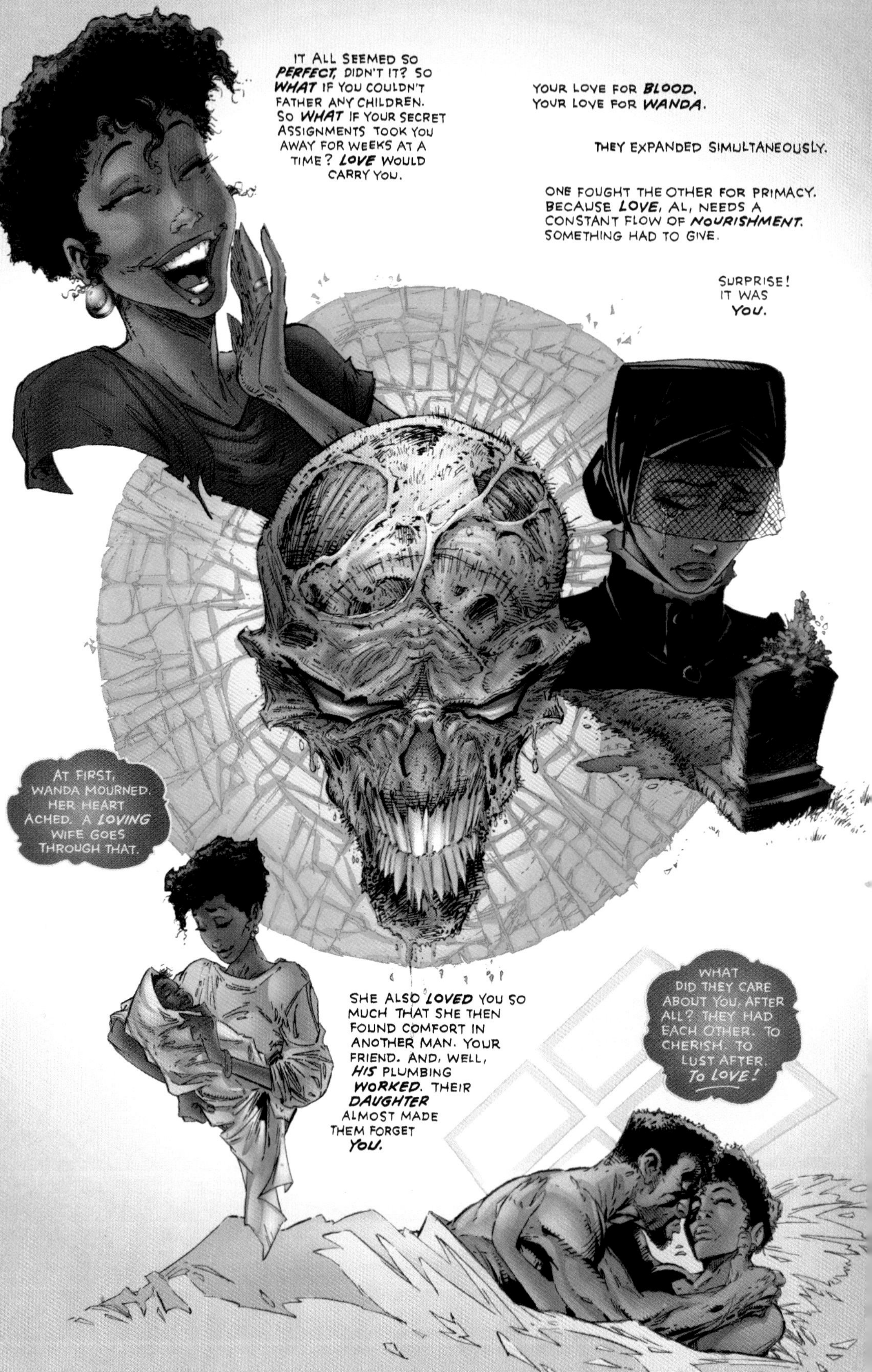
IT ALL SEEMED SO PERFECT, DIDN'T IT? SO WHAT IF YOU COULDN'T FATHER ANY CHILDREN. SO WHAT IF YOUR SECRET ASSIGNMENTS TOOK YOU AWAY FOR WEEKS AT A TIME? LOVE WOULD CARRY YOU.
YOUR LOVE FOR BLOOD. YOUR LOVE FOR WANDA.
THEY EXPANDED SIMULTANEOUSLY.
ONE FOUGHT THE OTHER FOR PRIMACY. BECAUSE LOVE, AL, NEEDS A CONSTANT FLOW OF NOURISHMENT. SOMETHING HAD TO GIVE.
SURPRISE! IT WAS YOU.
AT FIRST, WANDA MOURNED. HER HEART ACHED. A LOVING WIFE GOES THROUGH THAT.
SHE ALSO LOVED YOU SO MUCH THAT SHE THEN FOUND COMFORT IN ANOTHER MAN. YOUR FRIEND. AND, WELL, HIS PLUMBING WORKED. THEIR DAUGHTER ALMOST MADE THEM FORGET YOU.
WHAT DID THEY CARE ABOUT YOU, AFTER ALL? THEY HAD EACH OTHER. TO CHERISH. TO LUST AFTER. TO LOVE!

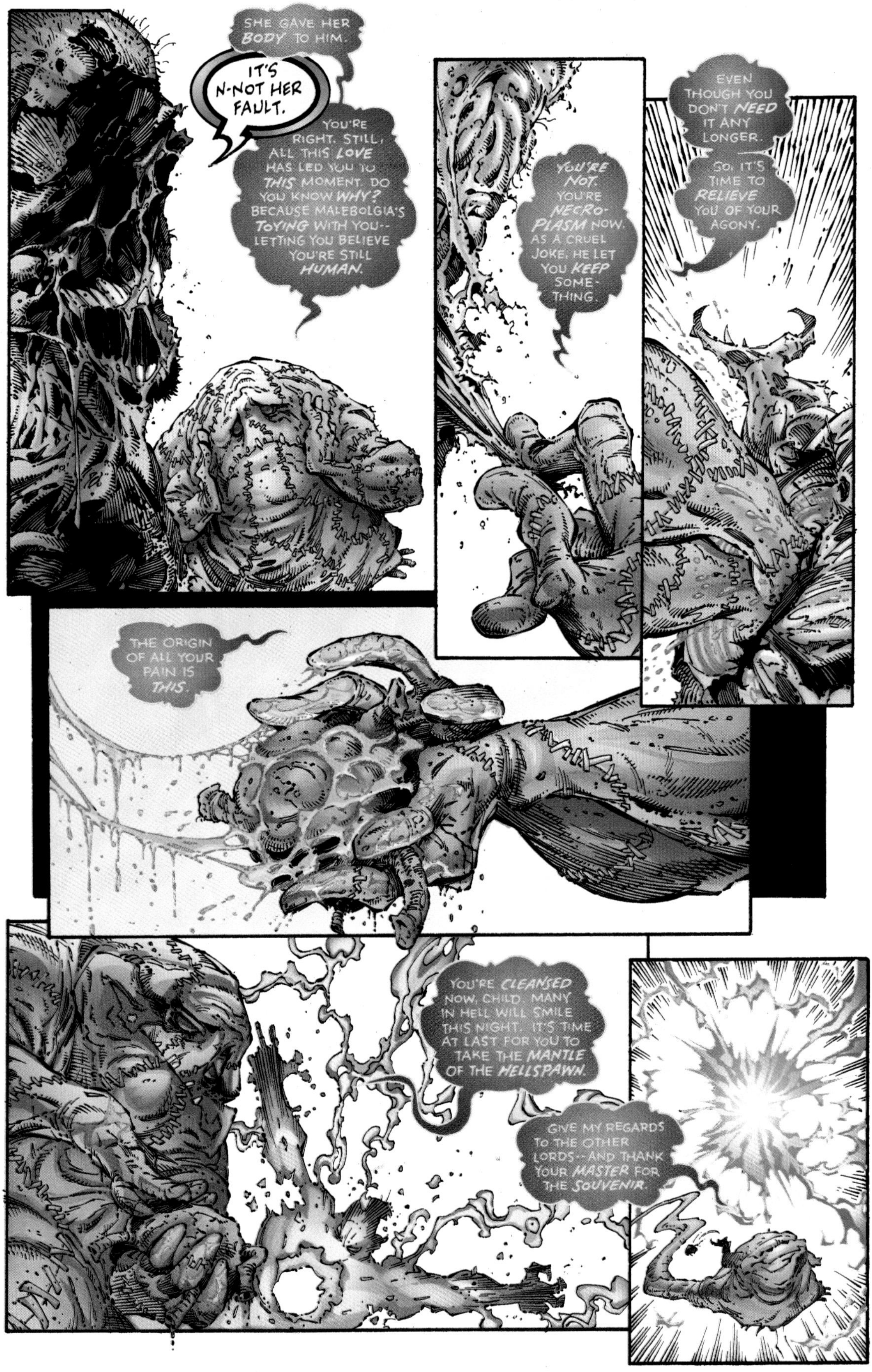
SHE GAVE HER *BODY* TO HIM.
IT'S N-NOT HER FAULT.
YOU'RE RIGHT. STILL, ALL THIS *LOVE* HAS LED YOU TO *THIS* MOMENT. DO YOU KNOW *WHY?* BECAUSE MALEBOLGIA'S *TOYING* WITH YOU-- LETTING YOU BELIEVE YOU'RE STILL *HUMAN*.
YOU'RE NOT. YOU'RE *NECRO-PLASM* NOW. AS A CRUEL JOKE, HE LET YOU *KEEP* SOME-THING.
EVEN THOUGH YOU DON'T *NEED* IT ANY LONGER.
SO, IT'S TIME TO *RELIEVE* YOU OF YOUR AGONY.
THE ORIGIN OF ALL YOUR PAIN IS *THIS*.
YOU'RE *CLEANSED* NOW, CHILD. MANY IN HELL WILL SMILE THIS NIGHT. IT'S TIME AT LAST FOR YOU TO TAKE THE *MANTLE* OF THE *HELLSPAWN*.
GIVE MY REGARDS TO THE OTHER LORDS--AND THANK YOUR *MASTER* FOR THE *SOUVENIR*.

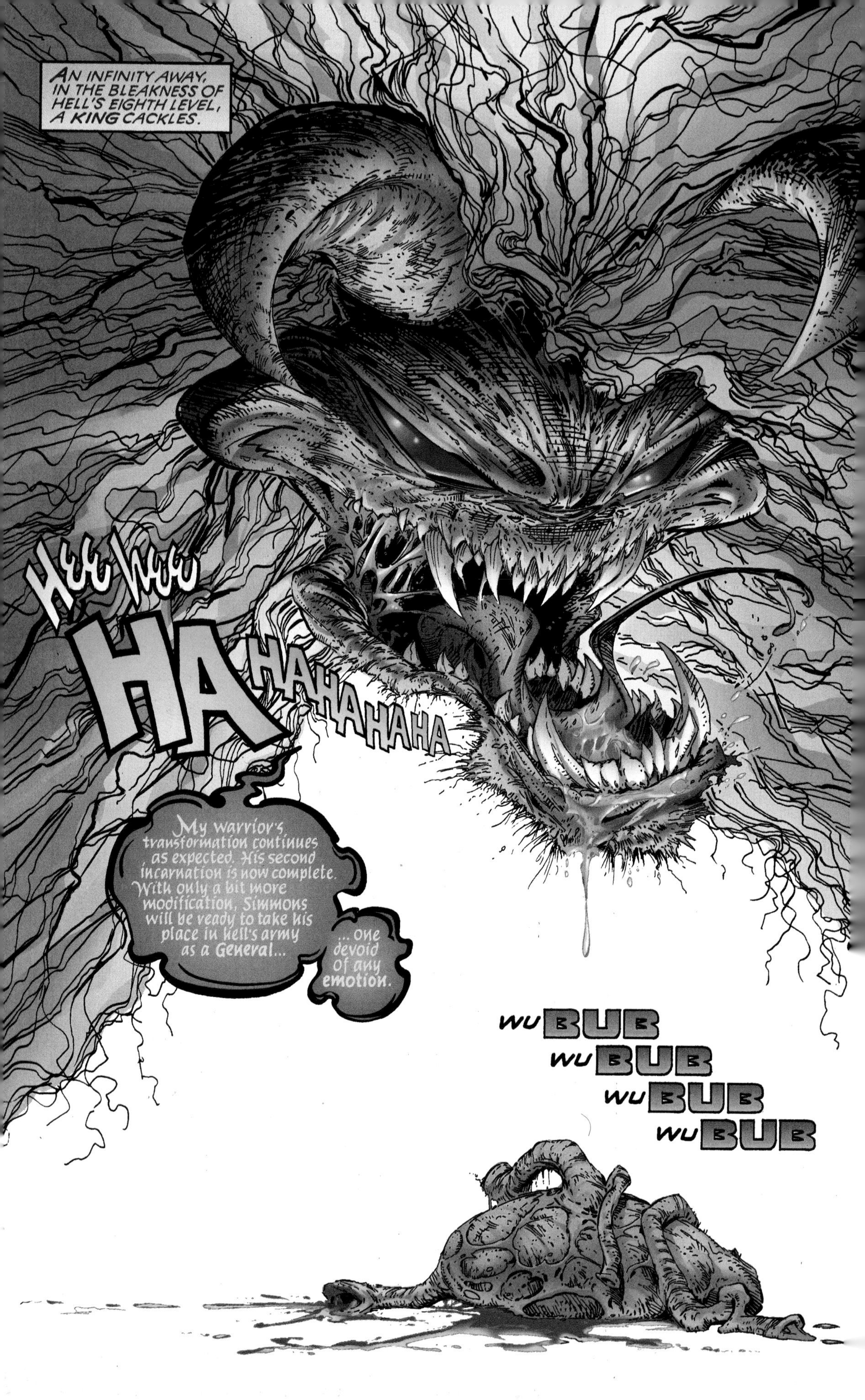

AN INFINITY AWAY, IN THE BLEAKNESS OF HELL'S EIGHTH LEVEL, A KING CACKLES.
Hee hee HA HAHAHAHAHA
My warrior's transformation continues as expected. His second incarnation is now complete. With only a bit more modification, Simmons will be ready to take his place in hell's army as a General...
...one devoid of any emotion.
WUBUB WUBUB WUBUB WUBUB

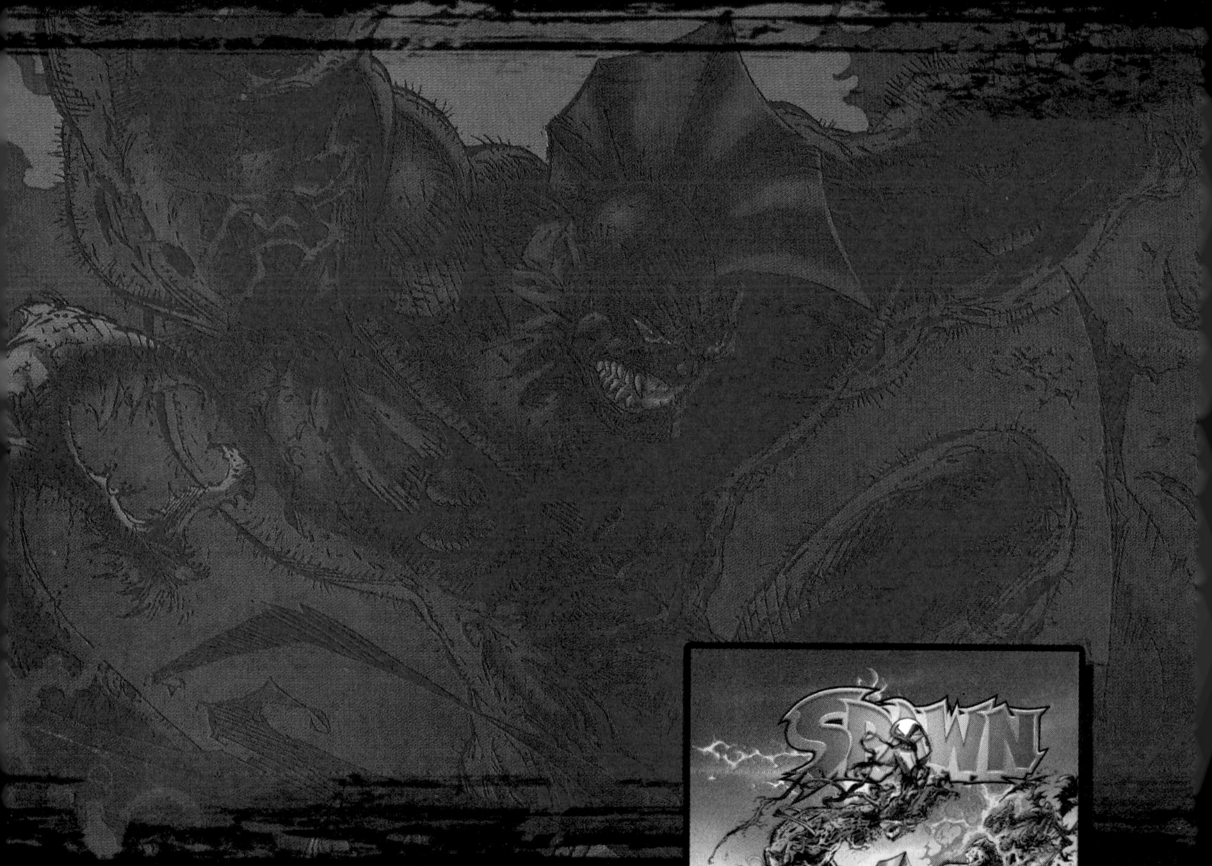

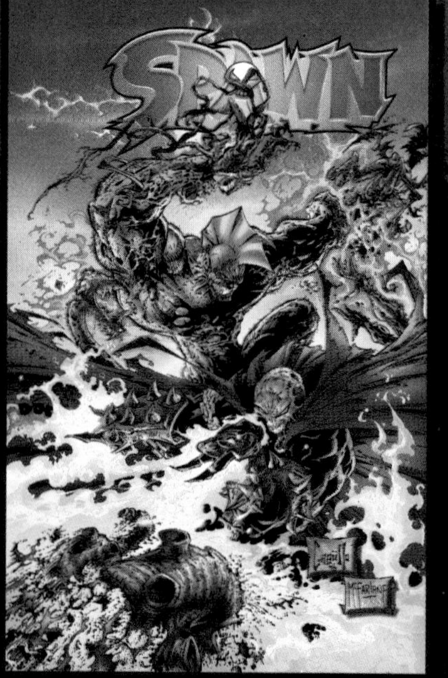
SPAWN

ISSUE FIFTY-TWO

THROUGH THE CENTURIES IT'S TOUCHED LITERALLY **MILLIONS** OF LIVES-- SOME THROUGH **DIRECT** CONTACT, OTHERS MERELY THE VICTIMS OF FALLOUT THEY WEREN'T EVEN *AWARE* OF. IT'S MERE *EXISTENCE* HAS CAUSED A RIPPLE EFFECT THAT SWALLOWED MANY **WORTHY** OF DEATH AND THOUSANDS OF INNOCENTS WHOSE ONLY 'CRIME' WAS TO BE CAUGHT IN ITS **WAKE**.

ITS TIME HAS COME AGAIN. IT IS NOW IN EVIDENCE FOR THE FIRST TIME IN NEARLY **TWO HUNDRED YEARS**:

THE HELLSPAWN. AND THE CURSE HE BRINGS WITH HIM.

AT FIRST, THE CREATURE IS DISORIENTED FROM THE **TRANSFORMATION** AND HAS ONLY LIMITED UNDERSTANDING OF THE **IMPLICATIONS**. AS A RESULT, THE NEW SPAWN WARRIOR THINKS OF THINGS ON A PERSONAL LEVEL EXCLUSIVELY, TRYING **DESPERATELY** TO MAKE SENSE OF HIS RETURN FROM THE GRAVE. IT'S AT THIS TIME THE METAPHORICAL **PEBBLE** HITS THE WATER AND THE OUTWARD RIPPLING BEGINS. HELL **SMILES**, ANTICIPATING THE AVALANCHE OF SOULS TO BE DELIVERED SOON TO THE FLAMING PITS-- GROWING THE **ARMIES** WHICH WILL ONE DAY **OPPOSE** HEAVEN.

THE **OFFICER-IN-TRAINING GRASPS NONE OF THIS**, AS HE IS CONSUMED BY THE URGE TO REGAIN A LIFE NOW FOREVER LOST.

ALL OF WHICH BRINGS US NOW TO THIS QUIET, NONDESCRIPT HOUSE-- WHICH, AT FIRST GLANCE, APPEARS TO BE JUST LIKE THE **OTHER** HOUSES ON THE BLOCK. **AND**, IN FACT, IT **IS**. THOSE WHO **LIVE** WITHIN ITS WALLS ARE WHAT MAKE IT DIFFERENT. ARE WHAT MAKE IT **CURSED**.

FOR THEY HAVE **ALL** BEEN TOUCHED.

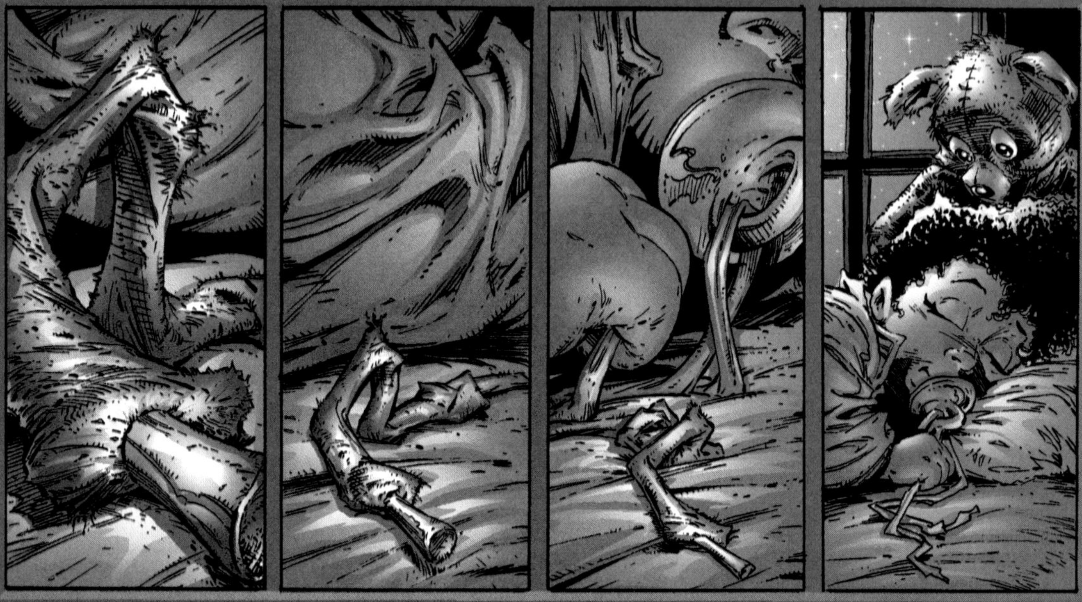

THIS ONE HAS BEEN AT THE **GREATEST** DISTANCE FROM THE CREATURE. SHE HAS HAD BUT A BRIEF ENCOUNTER WITH THE SPAWN WHILE HE WAS IN THE GUISE OF ANOTHER. IT'S HER **MOTHER AND FATHER** WHO'VE BEEN ENMESHED IN THE TRAUMA OF HELL'S NEW WARRIOR.

THAT SITUATION HAS CHANGED.

WHEN SHE FOUND IT AT THE HOSPITAL, SHE FELT THE SAME AS WHEN SHE'S GOTTEN PRESENTS AT CHRISTMAS. WHY? SHE DIDN'T KNOW. IT WAS ONLY A **DIRTY OLD SHOELACE**, BUT SHE FELT COMPELLED TO TURN IT INTO SOME KIND OF **TREASURE**. SO, SHE DUG OUT A **SOOTHER** SHE HADN'T USED IN OVER FOURTEEN MONTHS AND MADE HERSELF A NECKLACE. TONIGHT, SHE WENT BACK TO SUCKING THE SOOTHER, FEELING AN **ATTACHMENT** TO HER NEWFOUND GIFT--

--THE SHOELACE--

--THE UNSUSPECTED **EVIDENCE** THAT **SOMETHING** OR **SOMEONE** HAD INTERVENED AGAINST HER FATHER'S IRREVERSABLE ILLNESS.

JUST DOWN THE HALL RESTS HER MOTHER. SHE WAS ONCE MARRIED TO A MAN NAMED **AL SIMMONS**. HE DIED OVER FIVE YEARS AGO, "IN DEFENSE OF HIS COUNTRY"... OR SO SHE WAS **TOLD**. AT HIS GRAVESITE, THEY GAVE HER AN AMERICAN FLAG AS A TOKEN OF HIS NATION'S GRATITUDE. THOUGH THANKFUL FOR IT, SHE HELD IN HER FIST A MOMENTO OF FAR **GREATER** VALUE:

HER WEDDING BAND.

IT WAS NEARLY A YEAR BEFORE SHE PUT IT ASIDE, AT THE TIME WHEN SHE STARTED DATING ANOTHER MAN, **TERRY FITZGERALD... AL'S BEST FRIEND**. TERRY BROUGHT HAPPINESS INTO HER LIFE. THEY MARRIED ANOTHER YEAR LATER. AND YET, HER FIRST RING STILL SITS NO MORE THAN ARM'S-LENGTH AWAY--FOREVER KEEPING AL'S MEMORY ALIVE.

SHE IS UNAWARE THAT THE THING CALLED **"SPAWN"** -- THE CREATURE WHO FILLS HER WITH FEAR AND ANXIETY--IS HER FORMER LOVE, **RETURNED FROM THE DEAD**.

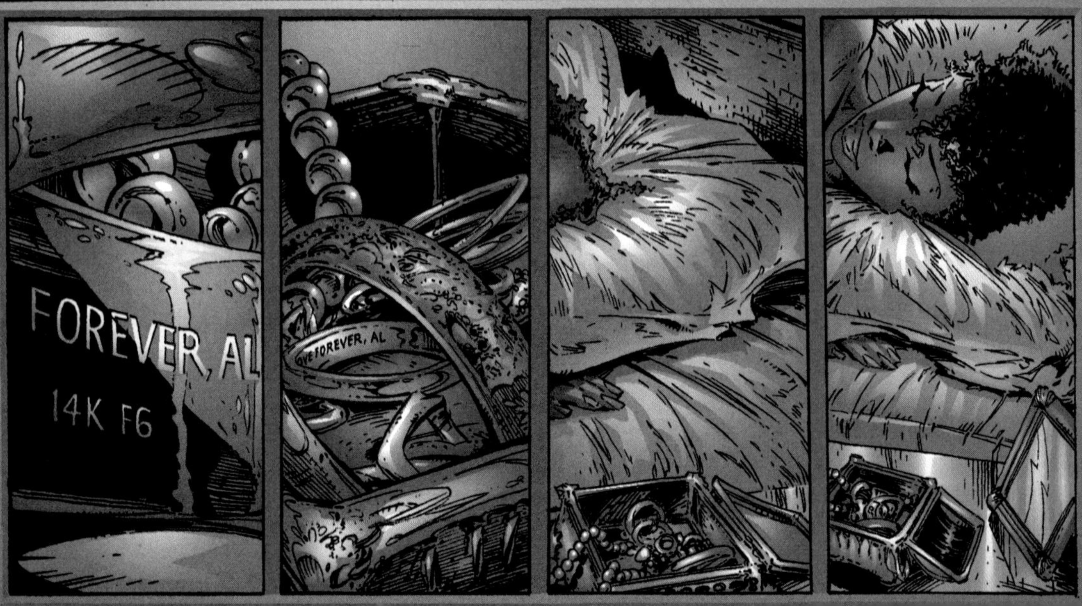
FOREVER, AL
14K F6

IT'S BEEN OVER THREE HOURS SINCE HE CLOSED HIS EYES, YET THE *SLEEP* HE SO DESPERATELY WANTS CONTINUES TO EVADE HIM. SINCE HIS "MIRACULOUS" *CURE* FROM *CANCER*, REST HASN'T COME EASY. THE DREAMS... OR ARE THEY *NIGHTMARES?*... CREEP INTO HIS SUBCONSCIOUS, FLASHING RANDOM, *SENSELESS* IMAGES. FRUSTRATED BY THEIR *AMBIGUITY*, TERRY LIES THERE IN THE DARK, TRYING TO PIECE THIS PUZZLE TOGETHER.

THE ONLY PHYSICAL CLUE TO HIS RECOVERY -- THE BIZARRE, OVERLOOKED *DETAIL* -- LIES NOW IN A *CRIB*, NEXT TO HIS DAUGHTER: THE SHOELACE *RIPPED FROM THE VISAGE OF THE HELLSPAWN* DURING THE MOMENT OF THAT CREATURE'S UNWILLING, LIFESAVING GESTURE.

TO CURE TERRY. OUT OF LOVE FOR *WANDA.*

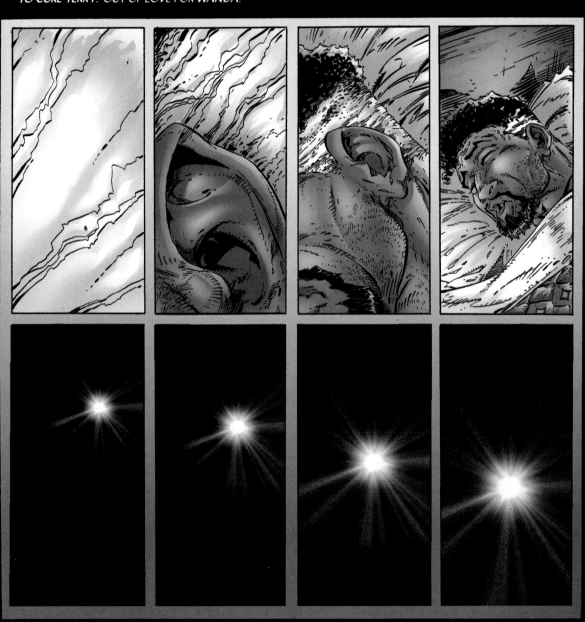

HE'D BEEN WARNED, THE HELLSPAWN HAD, AGAINST USING SUCH A *SUDDEN* BURST OF ENERGY. GIVEN THE *UNSTABLE* STATE OF SPAWN'S *SYMBIOTIC COSTUME*, THE *NEXT* ABRUPT DRAIN WOULD TRIGGER THE EJECTION OF THE WARRIOR FROM THIS EARTH AND INTO AN EXPEDITION THROUGH *HELL.*

GREEN NECROPLASMIC ENERGY EXPENDED IN THE CAUSE OF *GOOD* HAS ONCE AGAIN ADDED TO SPAWN'S MISERY. THE ONLY HOPE REMAINING FOR THE FORMER AL SIMMONS IS AN ETHEREAL *CONNECTION* TO HIS FRIEND. THOUGH NEITHER IS AWARE OF IT ON ANY LEVEL, THE GREYING AT TERRY'S TEMPLES IS PROOF THE TWO HAD BEEN IN CONTACT...

...THAT, AND THE SCRAMBLED IMAGES TRYING TO SPEAK TO TERRY AT NIGHT.

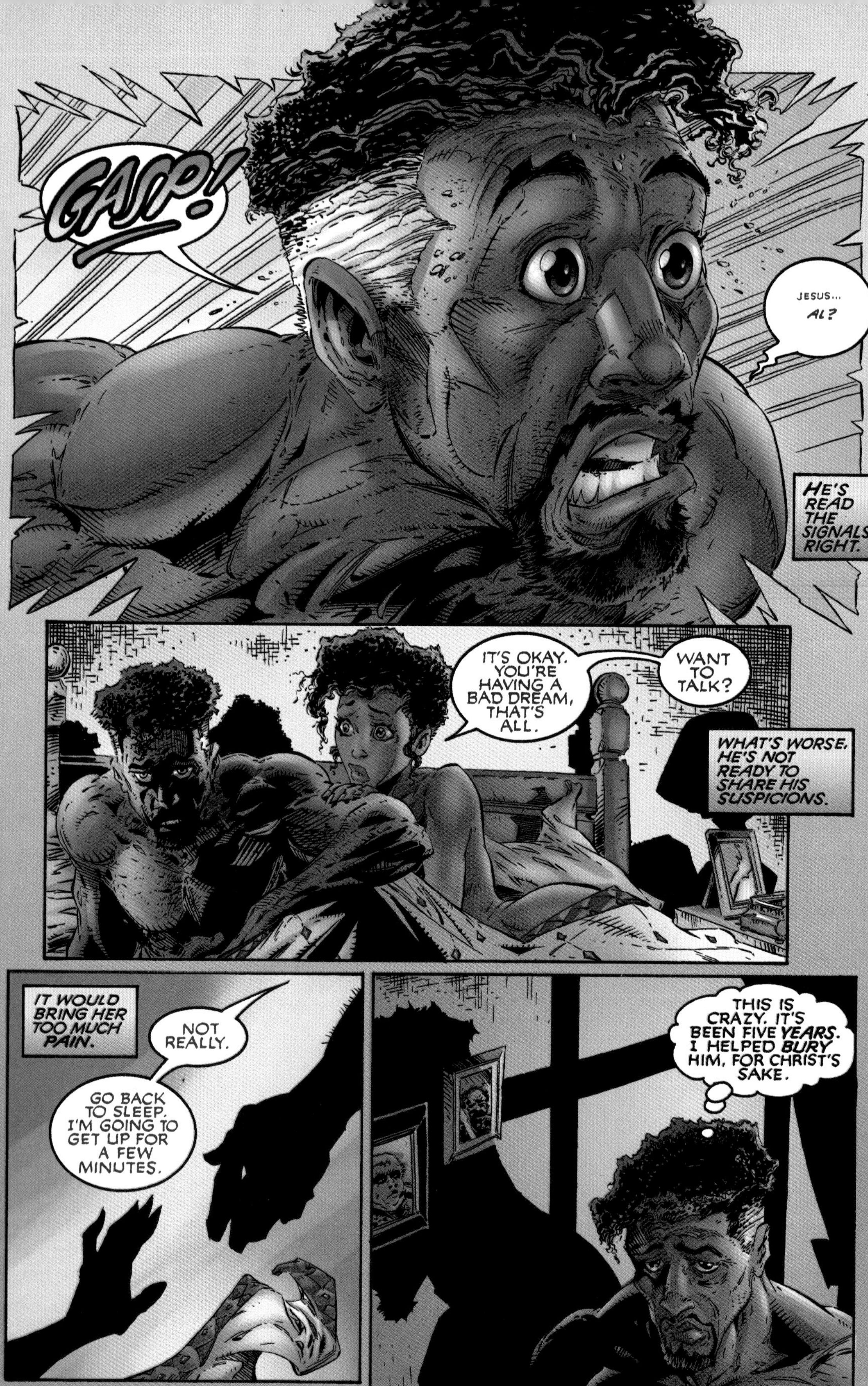
GASP!
JESUS... AL?
HE'S READ THE SIGNALS RIGHT.
IT'S OKAY. YOU'RE HAVING A BAD DREAM, THAT'S ALL.
WANT TO TALK?
WHAT'S WORSE, HE'S NOT READY TO SHARE HIS SUSPICIONS.
IT WOULD BRING HER TOO MUCH PAIN.
NOT REALLY.
GO BACK TO SLEEP. I'M GOING TO GET UP FOR A FEW MINUTES.
THIS IS CRAZY. IT'S BEEN FIVE YEARS. I HELPED BURY HIM, FOR CHRIST'S SAKE.

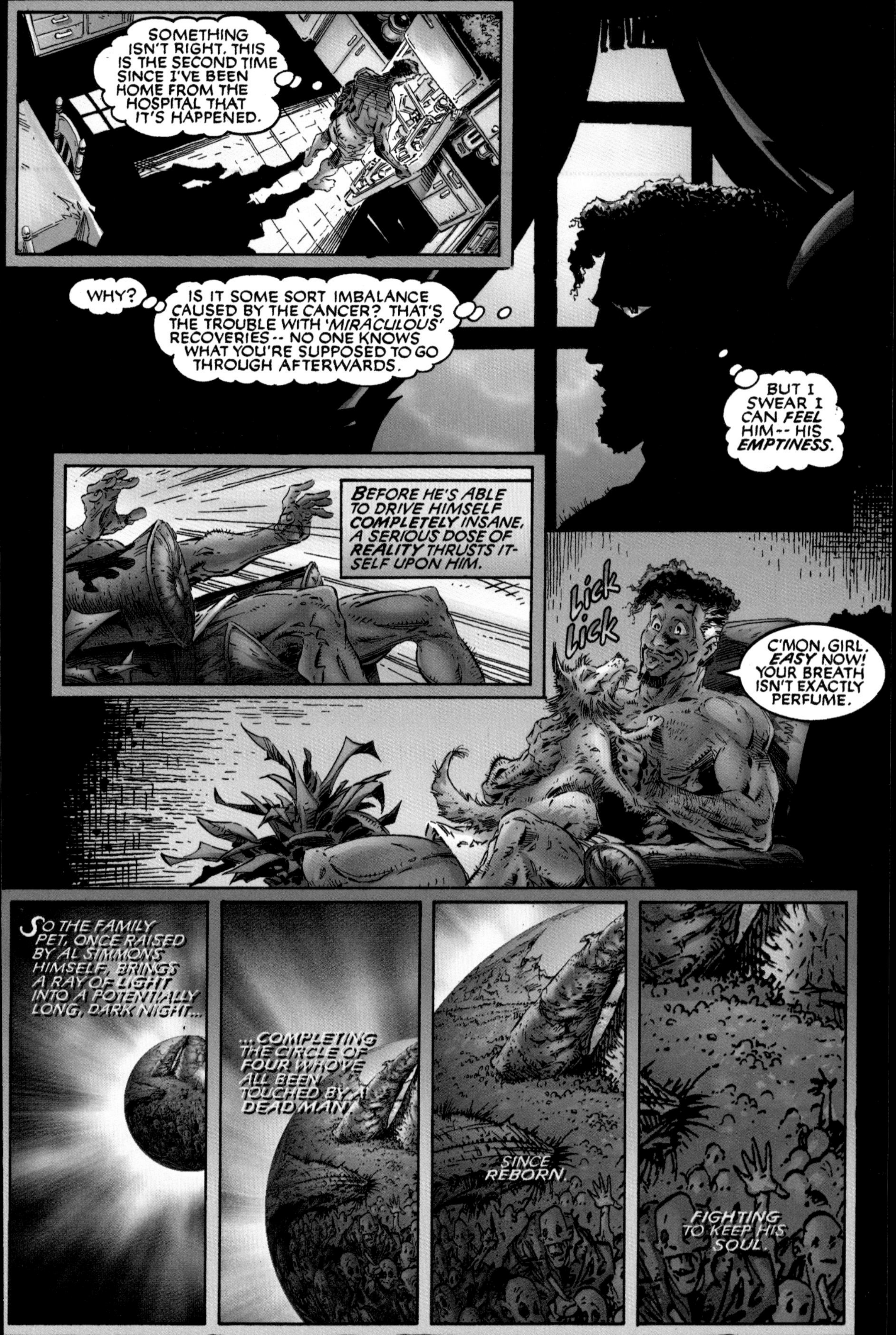
SOMETHING ISN'T RIGHT. THIS IS THE SECOND TIME SINCE I'VE BEEN HOME FROM THE HOSPITAL THAT IT'S HAPPENED.
WHY?
IS IT SOME SORT IMBALANCE CAUSED BY THE CANCER? THAT'S THE TROUBLE WITH '*MIRACULOUS*' RECOVERIES -- NO ONE KNOWS WHAT YOU'RE SUPPOSED TO GO THROUGH AFTERWARDS.
BUT I SWEAR I CAN *FEEL* HIM -- HIS *EMPTINESS.*
BEFORE HE'S ABLE TO DRIVE HIMSELF *COMPLETELY* INSANE, A SERIOUS DOSE OF *REALITY* THRUSTS IT-SELF UPON HIM.
LICK LICK
C'MON, GIRL, *EASY* NOW! YOUR BREATH ISN'T EXACTLY PERFUME.
SO THE FAMILY PET, ONCE RAISED BY AL SIMMONS HIMSELF, BRINGS A RAY OF LIGHT INTO A POTENTIALLY LONG, DARK NIGHT...
...COMPLETING THE CIRCLE OF FOUR WHO'VE ALL BEEN TOUCHED BY A DEADMAN.
SINCE REBORN.
FIGHTING TO KEEP HIS SOUL.

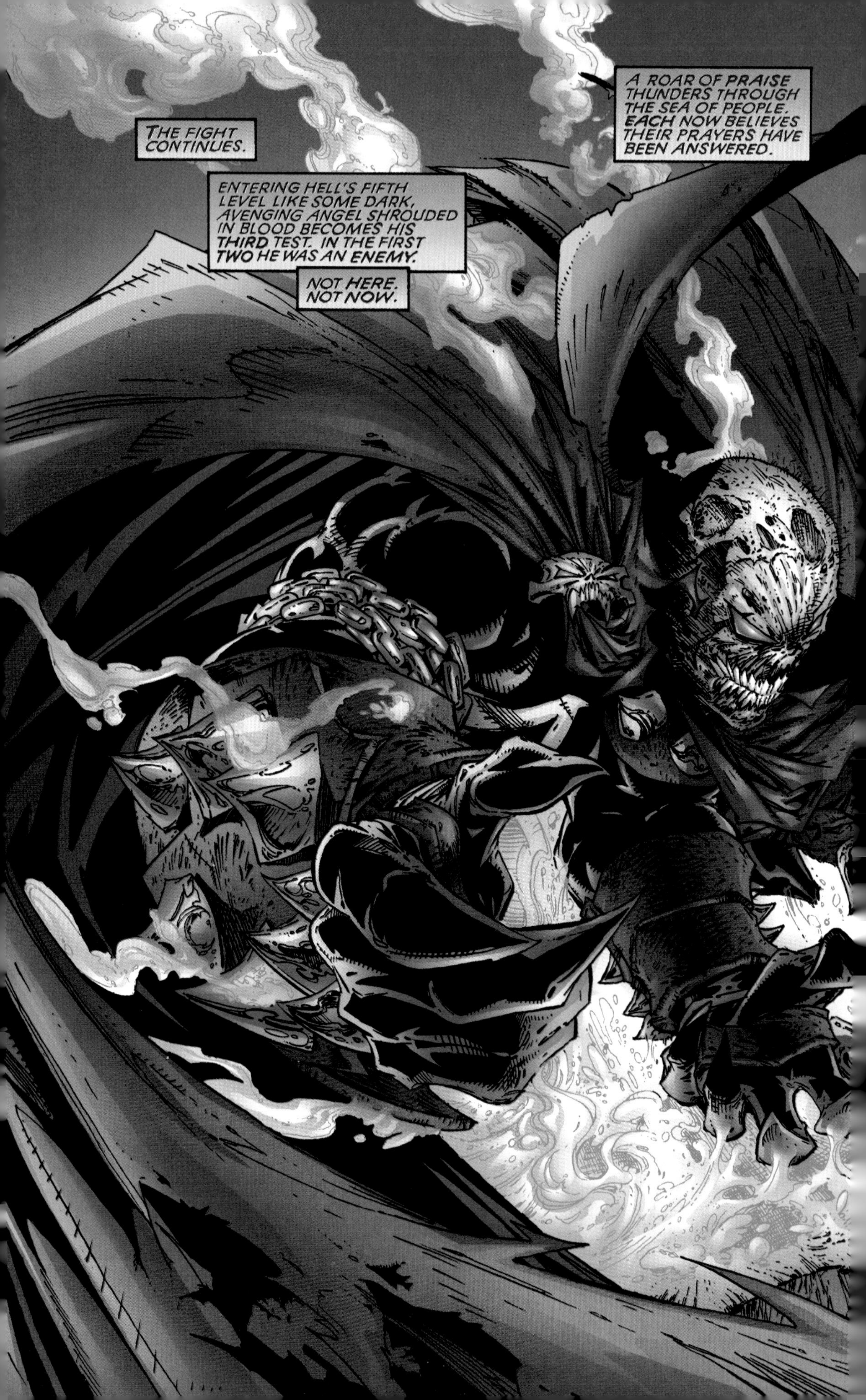
THE FIGHT CONTINUES.
ENTERING HELL'S FIFTH LEVEL LIKE SOME DARK, AVENGING ANGEL SHROUDED IN BLOOD BECOMES HIS THIRD TEST. IN THE FIRST TWO HE WAS AN ENEMY.
NOT HERE. NOT NOW.
A ROAR OF PRAISE THUNDERS THROUGH THE SEA OF PEOPLE. EACH NOW BELIEVES THEIR PRAYERS HAVE BEEN ANSWERED.

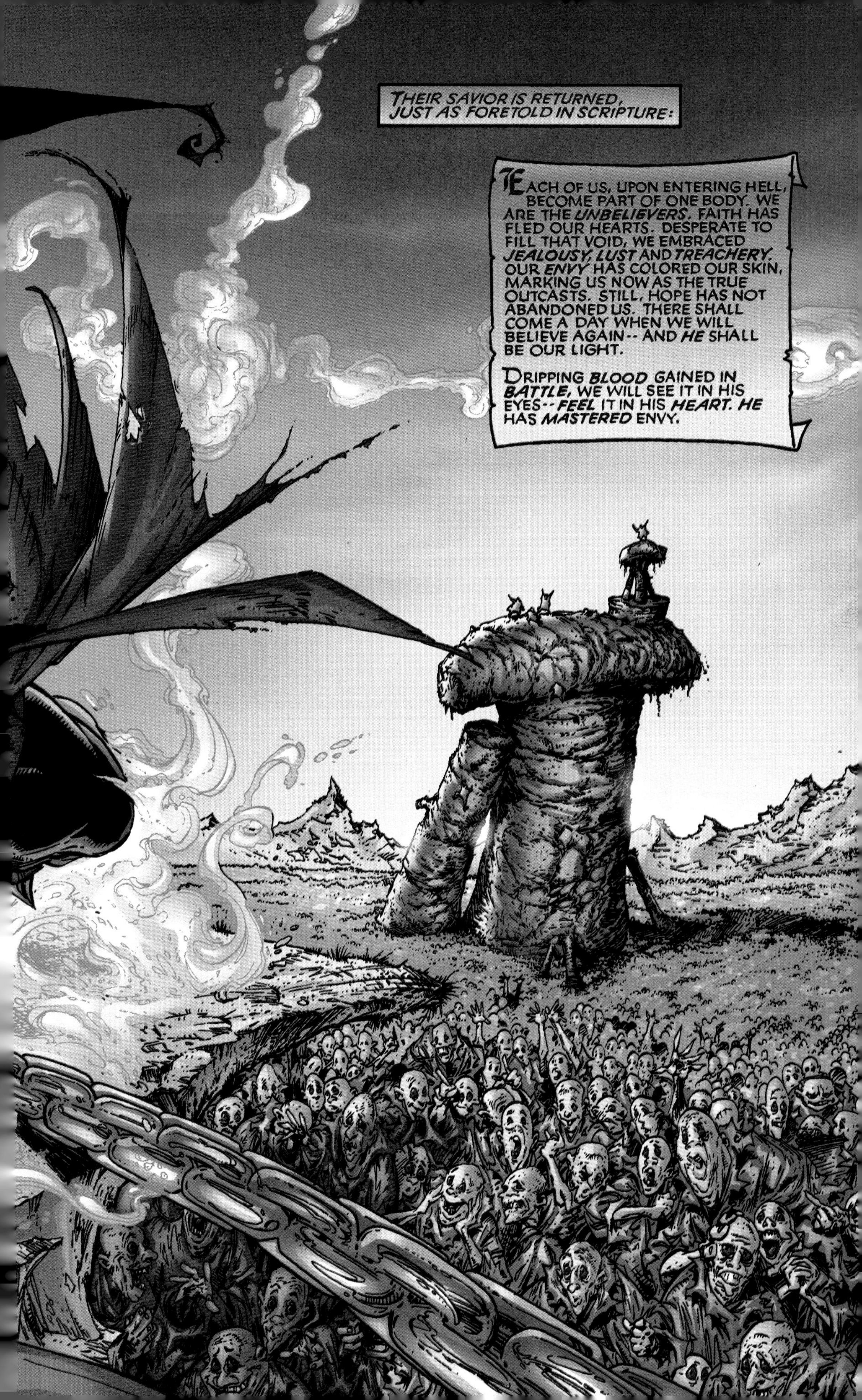
THEIR SAVIOR IS RETURNED, JUST AS FORETOLD IN SCRIPTURE:
EACH OF US, UPON ENTERING HELL, BECOME PART OF ONE BODY. WE ARE THE UNBELIEVERS. FAITH HAS FLED OUR HEARTS. DESPERATE TO FILL THAT VOID, WE EMBRACED JEALOUSY, LUST AND TREACHERY. OUR ENVY HAS COLORED OUR SKIN, MARKING US NOW AS THE TRUE OUTCASTS. STILL, HOPE HAS NOT ABANDONED US. THERE SHALL COME A DAY WHEN WE WILL BELIEVE AGAIN -- AND HE SHALL BE OUR LIGHT.
DRIPPING BLOOD GAINED IN BATTLE, WE WILL SEE IT IN HIS EYES -- FEEL IT IN HIS HEART. HE HAS MASTERED ENVY.

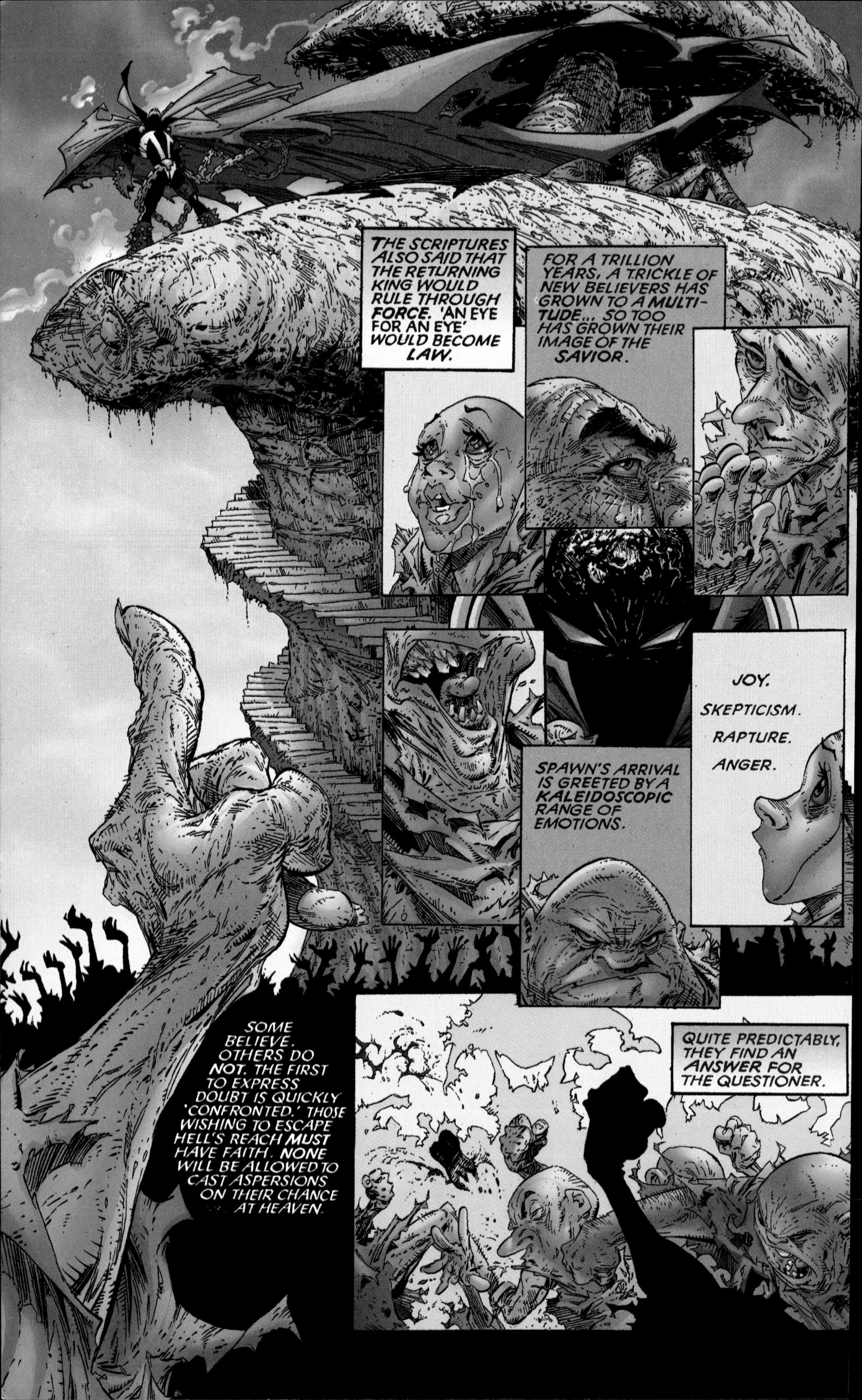
THE SCRIPTURES ALSO SAID THAT THE RETURNING KING WOULD RULE THROUGH FORCE. 'AN EYE FOR AN EYE' WOULD BECOME LAW.
FOR A TRILLION YEARS, A TRICKLE OF NEW BELIEVERS HAS GROWN TO A MULTITUDE... SO TOO HAS GROWN THEIR IMAGE OF THE SAVIOR.
SPAWN'S ARRIVAL IS GREETED BY A KALEIDOSCOPIC RANGE OF EMOTIONS.
JOY.
SKEPTICISM.
RAPTURE.
ANGER.
SOME BELIEVE. OTHERS DO NOT. THE FIRST TO EXPRESS DOUBT IS QUICKLY 'CONFRONTED.' THOSE WISHING TO ESCAPE HELL'S REACH MUST HAVE FAITH. NONE WILL BE ALLOWED TO CAST ASPERSIONS ON THEIR CHANCE AT HEAVEN.
QUITE PREDICTABLY, THEY FIND AN ANSWER FOR THE QUESTIONER.

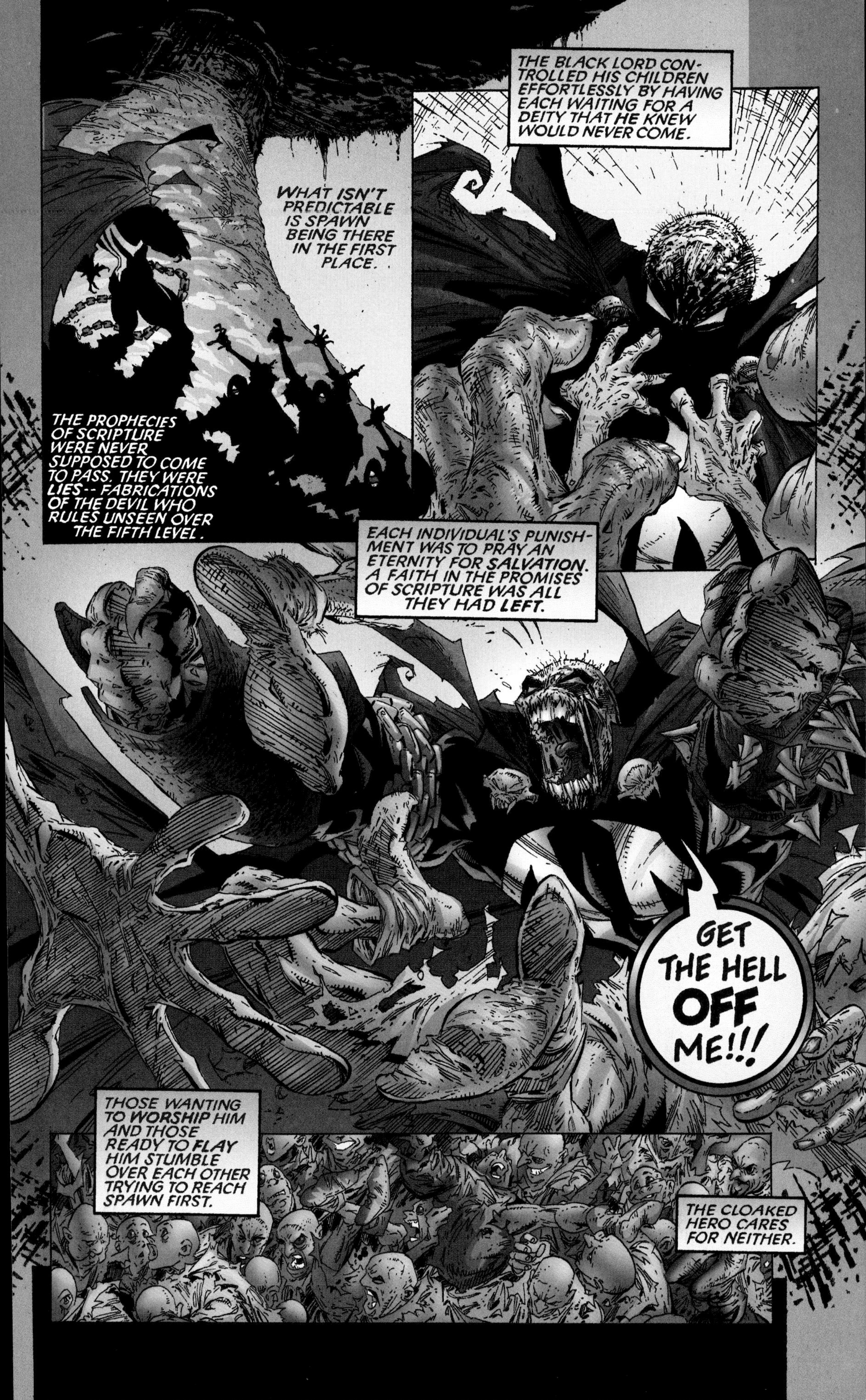
WHAT ISN'T PREDICTABLE IS SPAWN BEING THERE IN THE FIRST PLACE.
THE PROPHECIES OF SCRIPTURE WERE NEVER SUPPOSED TO COME TO PASS. THEY WERE LIES-- FABRICATIONS OF THE DEVIL WHO RULES UNSEEN OVER THE FIFTH LEVEL.
THE BLACK LORD CONTROLLED HIS CHILDREN EFFORTLESSLY BY HAVING EACH WAITING FOR A DEITY THAT HE KNEW WOULD NEVER COME.
EACH INDIVIDUAL'S PUNISHMENT WAS TO PRAY AN ETERNITY FOR SALVATION. A FAITH IN THE PROMISES OF SCRIPTURE WAS ALL THEY HAD LEFT.
GET THE HELL OFF ME!!!
THOSE WANTING TO WORSHIP HIM AND THOSE READY TO FLAY HIM STUMBLE OVER EACH OTHER TRYING TO REACH SPAWN FIRST.
THE CLOAKED HERO CARES FOR NEITHER.

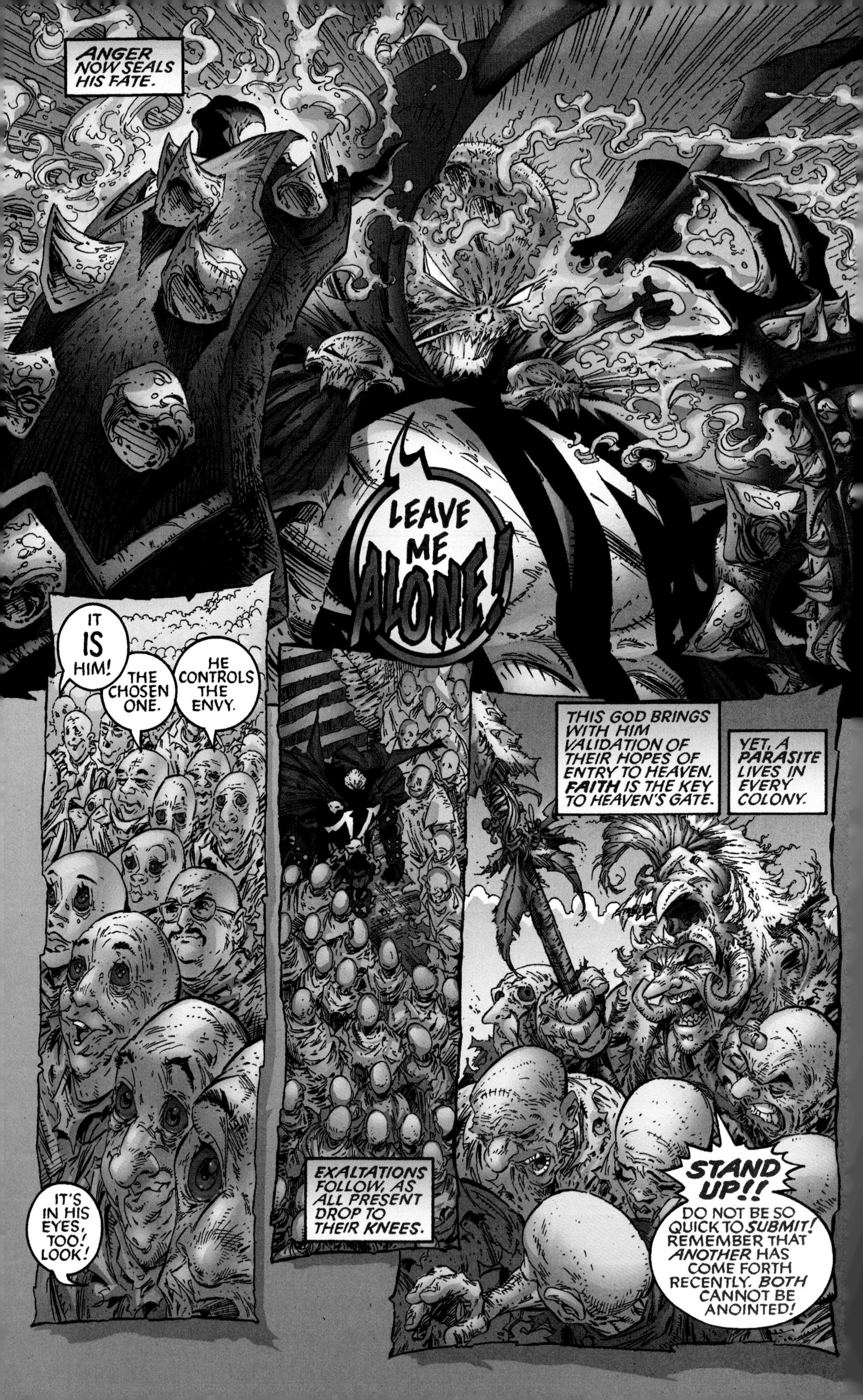
ANGER NOW SEALS HIS FATE.
LEAVE ME ALONE!
IT IS HIM!
THE CHOSEN ONE.
HE CONTROLS THE ENVY.
IT'S IN HIS EYES, TOO! LOOK!
EXALTATIONS FOLLOW, AS ALL PRESENT DROP TO THEIR KNEES.
THIS GOD BRINGS WITH HIM VALIDATION OF THEIR HOPES OF ENTRY TO HEAVEN. FAITH IS THE KEY TO HEAVEN'S GATE.
YET, A PARASITE LIVES IN EVERY COLONY.
STAND UP!!
DO NOT BE SO QUICK TO SUBMIT! REMEMBER THAT ANOTHER HAS COME FORTH RECENTLY. BOTH CANNOT BE ANOINTED!

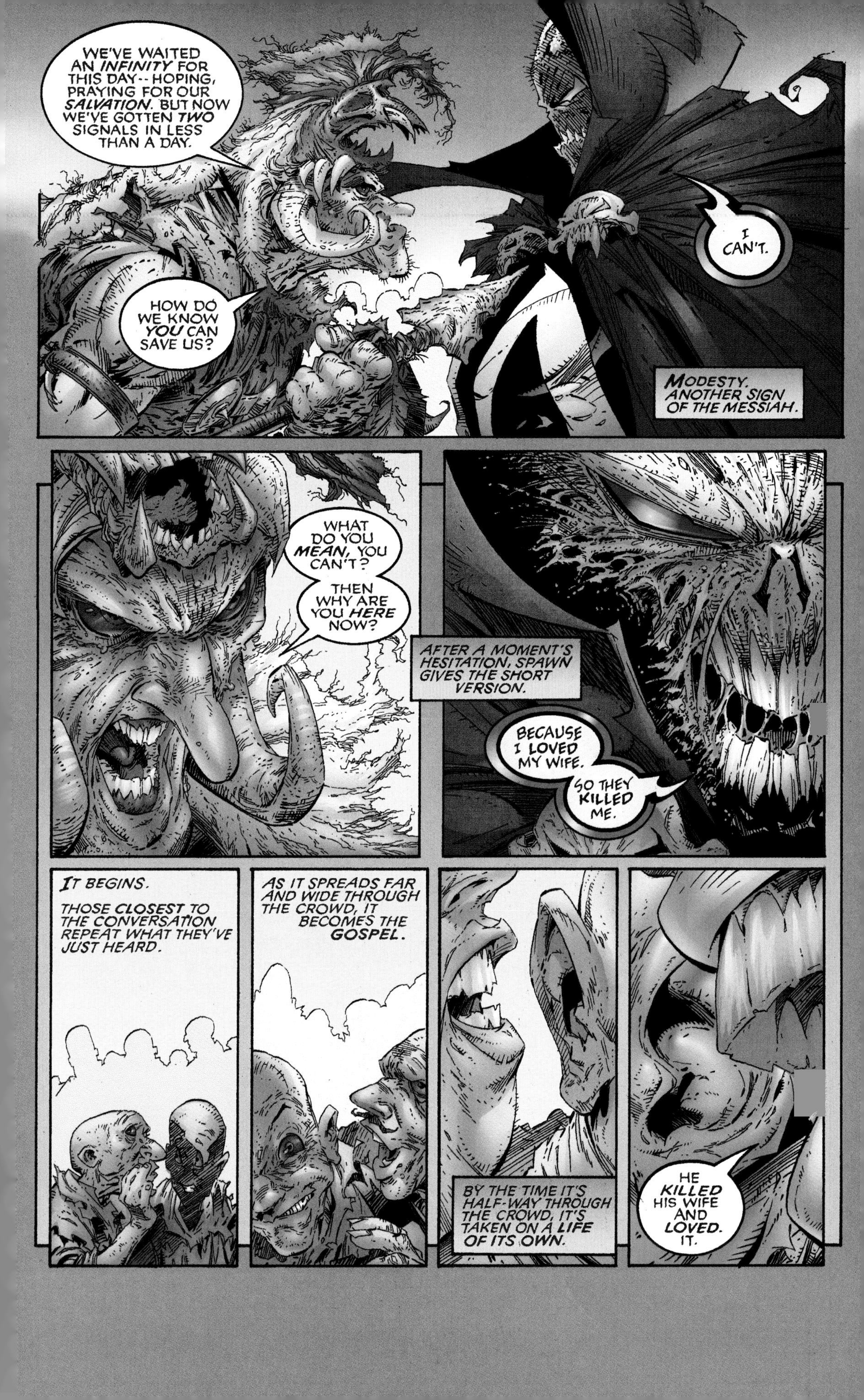

WE'VE WAITED AN *INFINITY* FOR THIS DAY-- HOPING, PRAYING FOR OUR *SALVATION*. BUT NOW WE'VE GOTTEN *TWO* SIGNALS IN LESS THAN A DAY.
HOW DO WE KNOW *YOU* CAN SAVE US?
I CAN'T.
MODESTY. ANOTHER SIGN OF THE MESSIAH.
WHAT DO YOU *MEAN*, YOU CAN'T?
THEN WHY ARE YOU *HERE* NOW?
AFTER A MOMENT'S HESITATION, SPAWN GIVES THE SHORT VERSION.
BECAUSE I **LOVED** MY WIFE.
SO THEY **KILLED** ME.
IT BEGINS.
THOSE **CLOSEST** TO THE CONVERSATION REPEAT WHAT THEY'VE JUST HEARD.
AS IT SPREADS FAR AND WIDE THROUGH THE CROWD, IT BECOMES THE **GOSPEL**.
BY THE TIME IT'S HALF-WAY THROUGH THE CROWD, IT'S TAKEN ON A **LIFE OF ITS OWN**.
HE **KILLED** HIS WIFE AND **LOVED**. IT.

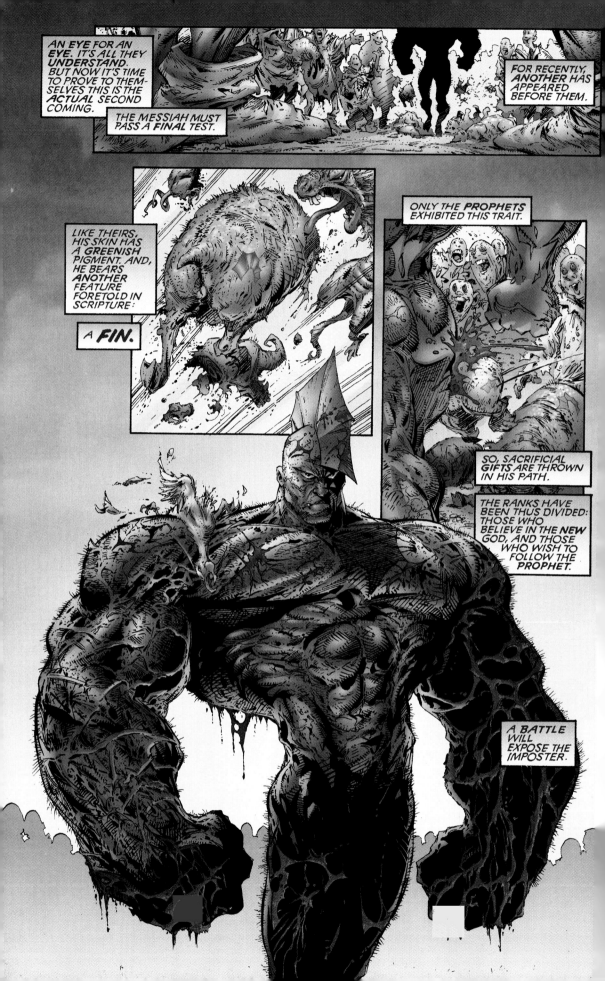

AN EYE FOR AN EYE. IT'S ALL THEY UNDERSTAND. BUT NOW IT'S TIME TO PROVE TO THEMSELVES THIS IS THE ACTUAL SECOND COMING.

THE MESSIAH MUST PASS A FINAL TEST.

FOR RECENTLY, ANOTHER HAS APPEARED BEFORE THEM.

LIKE THEIRS, HIS SKIN HAS A GREENISH PIGMENT. AND, HE BEARS ANOTHER FEATURE FORETOLD IN SCRIPTURE:

A FIN.

ONLY THE PROPHETS EXHIBITED THIS TRAIT.

SO, SACRIFICIAL GIFTS ARE THROWN IN HIS PATH.

THE RANKS HAVE BEEN THUS DIVIDED: THOSE WHO BELIEVE IN THE NEW GOD, AND THOSE WHO WISH TO FOLLOW THE PROPHET.

A BATTLE WILL EXPOSE THE IMPOSTER.

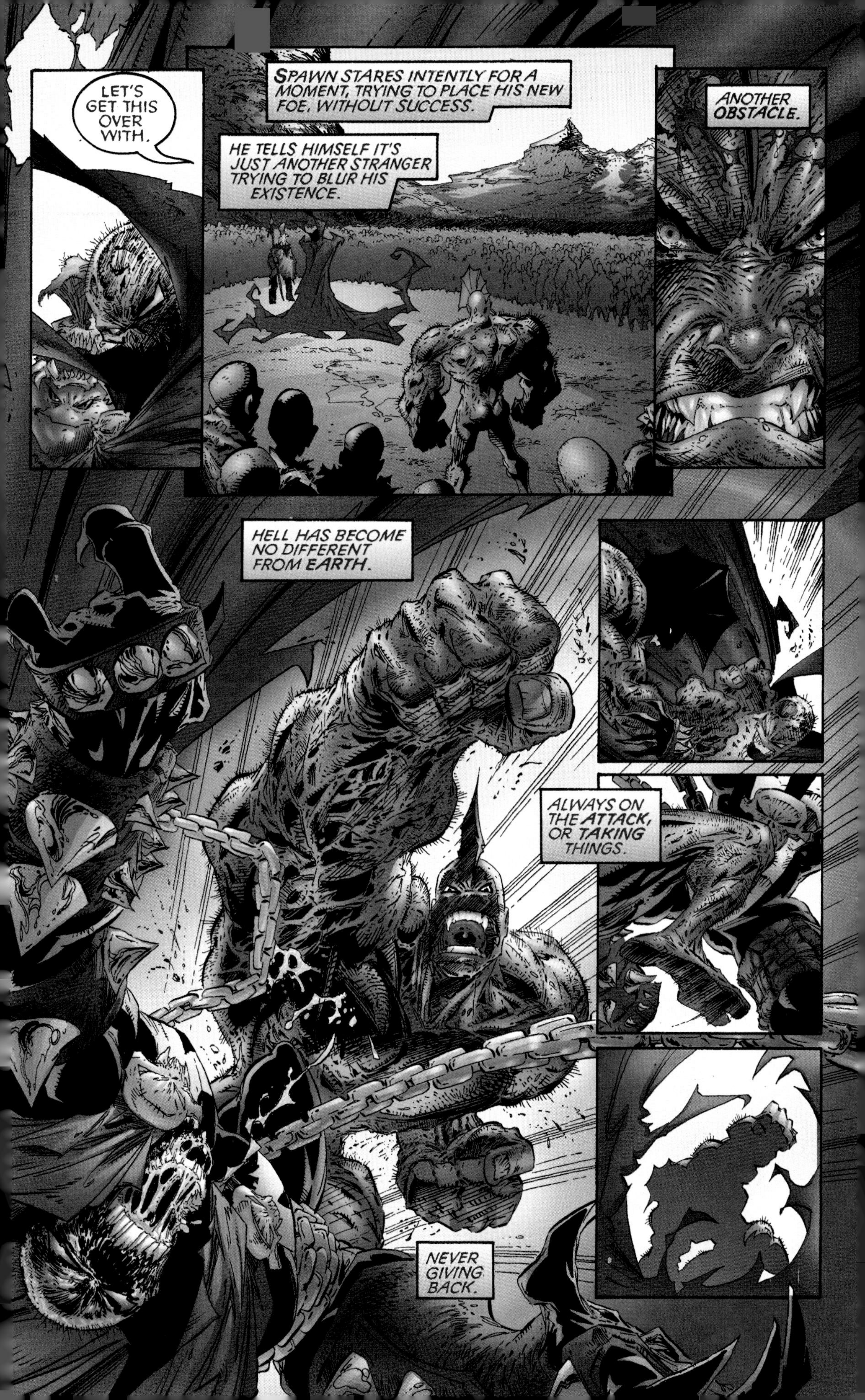
LET'S GET THIS OVER WITH.
SPAWN STARES INTENTLY FOR A MOMENT, TRYING TO PLACE HIS NEW FOE, WITHOUT SUCCESS.
HE TELLS HIMSELF IT'S JUST ANOTHER STRANGER TRYING TO BLUR HIS EXISTENCE.
ANOTHER OBSTACLE.
HELL HAS BECOME NO DIFFERENT FROM EARTH.
ALWAYS ON THE ATTACK, OR TAKING THINGS.
NEVER GIVING BACK.

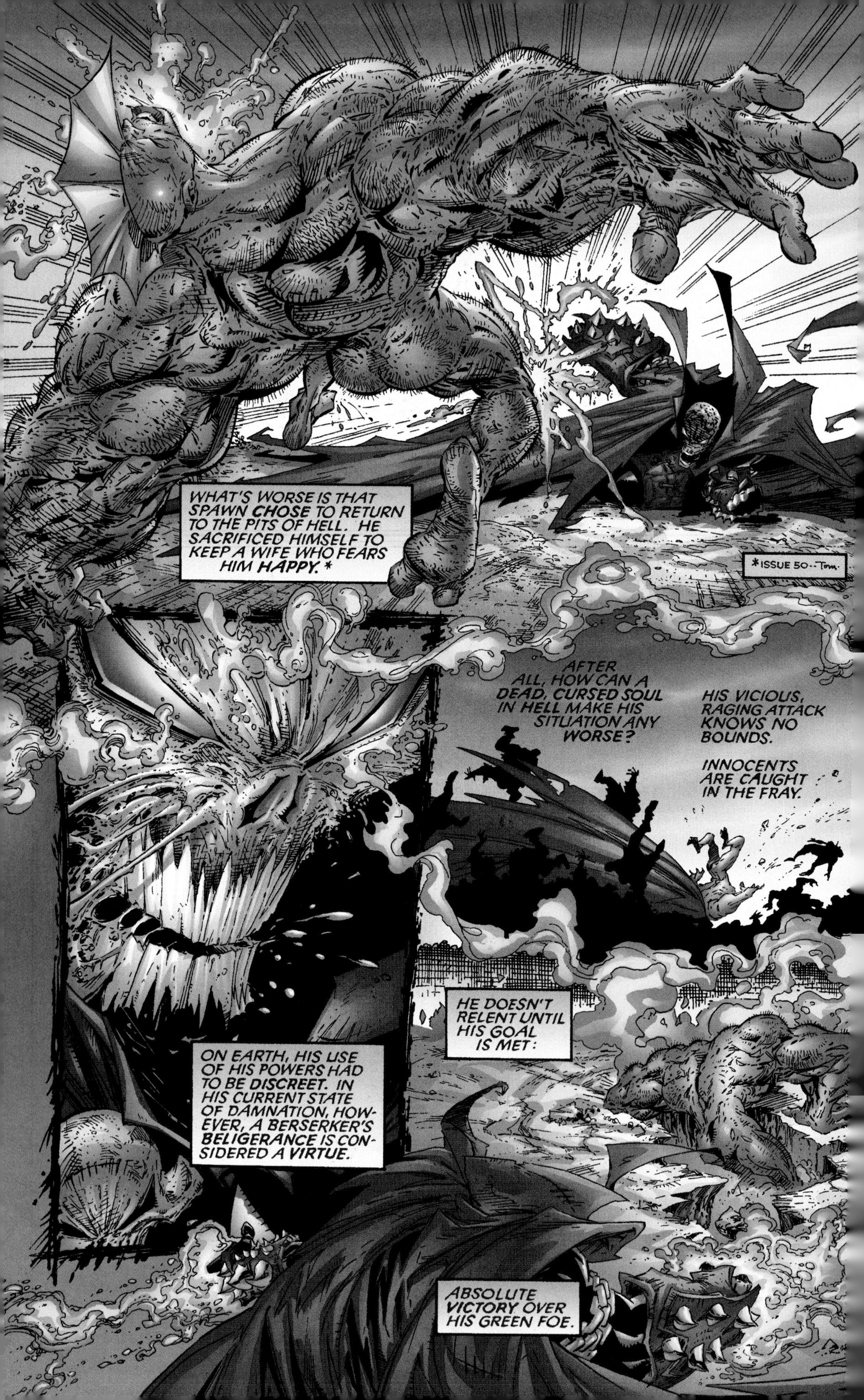
WHAT'S WORSE IS THAT SPAWN CHOSE TO RETURN TO THE PITS OF HELL. HE SACRIFICED HIMSELF TO KEEP A WIFE WHO FEARS HIM HAPPY.*
*ISSUE 50--Tom
ON EARTH, HIS USE OF HIS POWERS HAD TO BE DISCREET. IN HIS CURRENT STATE OF DAMNATION, HOWEVER, A BERSERKER'S BELIGERANCE IS CONSIDERED A VIRTUE.
AFTER ALL, HOW CAN A DEAD, CURSED SOUL IN HELL MAKE HIS SITUATION ANY WORSE?
HIS VICIOUS, RAGING ATTACK KNOWS NO BOUNDS.
INNOCENTS ARE CAUGHT IN THE FRAY.
HE DOESN'T RELENT UNTIL HIS GOAL IS MET:
ABSOLUTE VICTORY OVER HIS GREEN FOE.

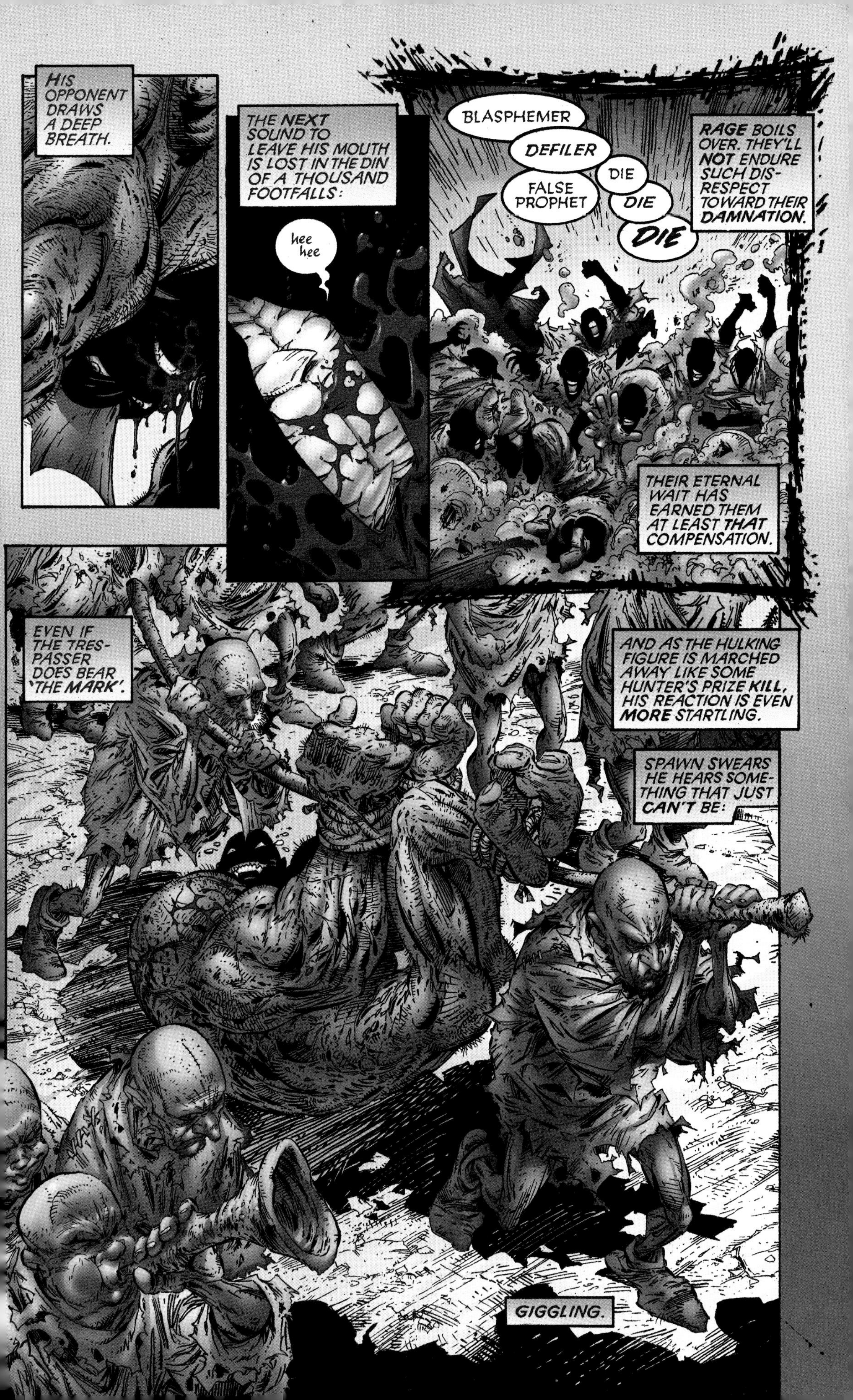
HIS OPPONENT DRAWS A DEEP BREATH.
THE NEXT SOUND TO LEAVE HIS MOUTH IS LOST IN THE DIN OF A THOUSAND FOOTFALLS:
hee hee
BLASPHEMER
DEFILER
FALSE PROPHET
DIE
DIE
DIE
RAGE BOILS OVER. THEY'LL NOT ENDURE SUCH DIS-RESPECT TOWARD THEIR DAMNATION.
THEIR ETERNAL WAIT HAS EARNED THEM AT LEAST THAT COMPENSATION.
EVEN IF THE TRES-PASSER DOES BEAR 'THE MARK'.
AND AS THE HULKING FIGURE IS MARCHED AWAY LIKE SOME HUNTER'S PRIZE KILL, HIS REACTION IS EVEN MORE STARTLING.
SPAWN SWEARS HE HEARS SOME-THING THAT JUST CAN'T BE:
GIGGLING.

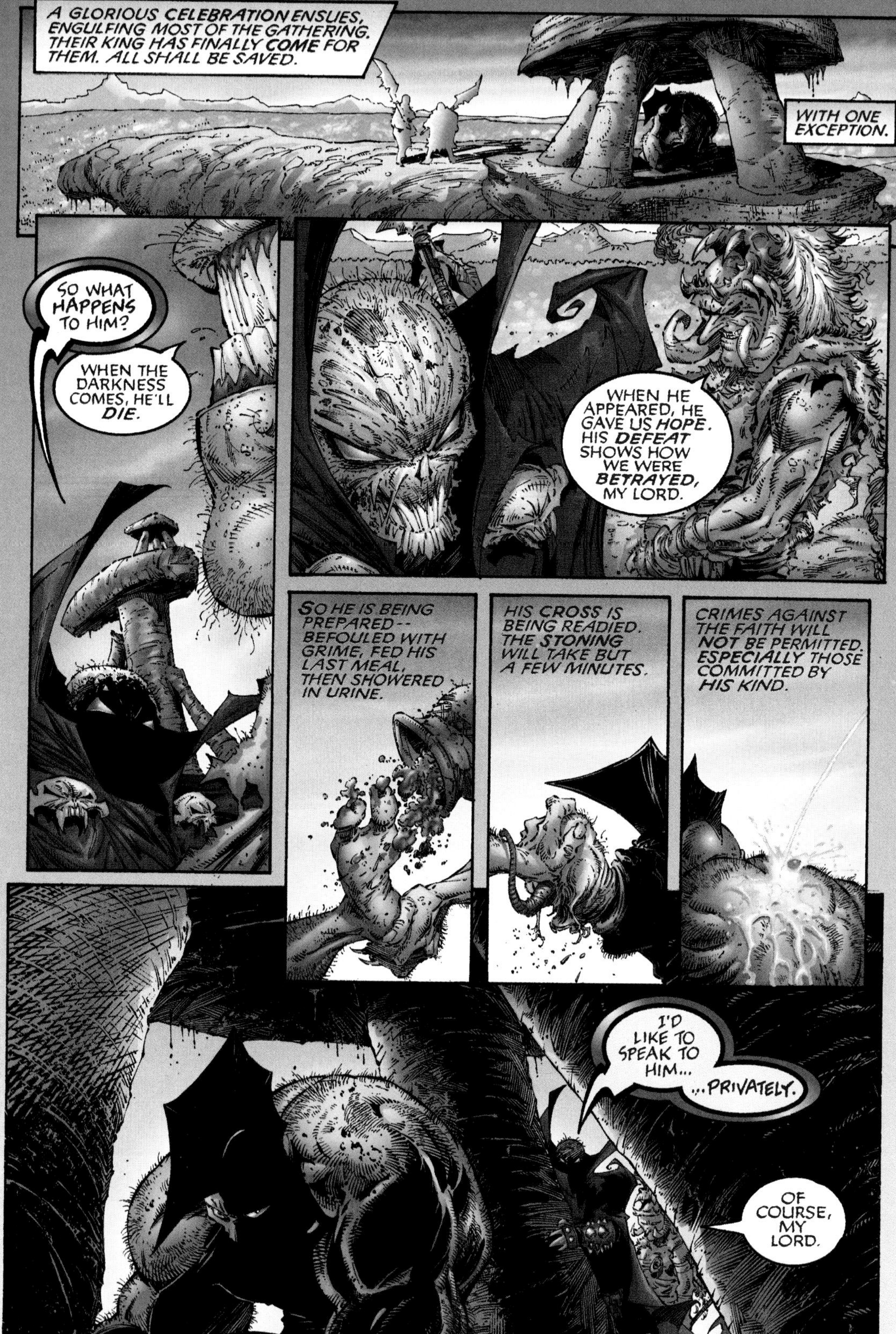
A GLORIOUS CELEBRATION ENSUES, ENGULFING MOST OF THE GATHERING. THEIR KING HAS FINALLY COME FOR THEM. ALL SHALL BE SAVED.
WITH ONE EXCEPTION.
SO WHAT HAPPENS TO HIM?
WHEN THE DARKNESS COMES, HE'LL DIE.
WHEN HE APPEARED, HE GAVE US HOPE. HIS DEFEAT SHOWS HOW WE WERE BETRAYED, MY LORD.
SO HE IS BEING PREPARED-- BEFOULED WITH GRIME, FED HIS LAST MEAL, THEN SHOWERED IN URINE.
HIS CROSS IS BEING READIED. THE STONING WILL TAKE BUT A FEW MINUTES.
CRIMES AGAINST THE FAITH WILL NOT BE PERMITTED. ESPECIALLY THOSE COMMITTED BY HIS KIND.
I'D LIKE TO SPEAK TO HIM...
...PRIVATELY.
OF COURSE, MY LORD.

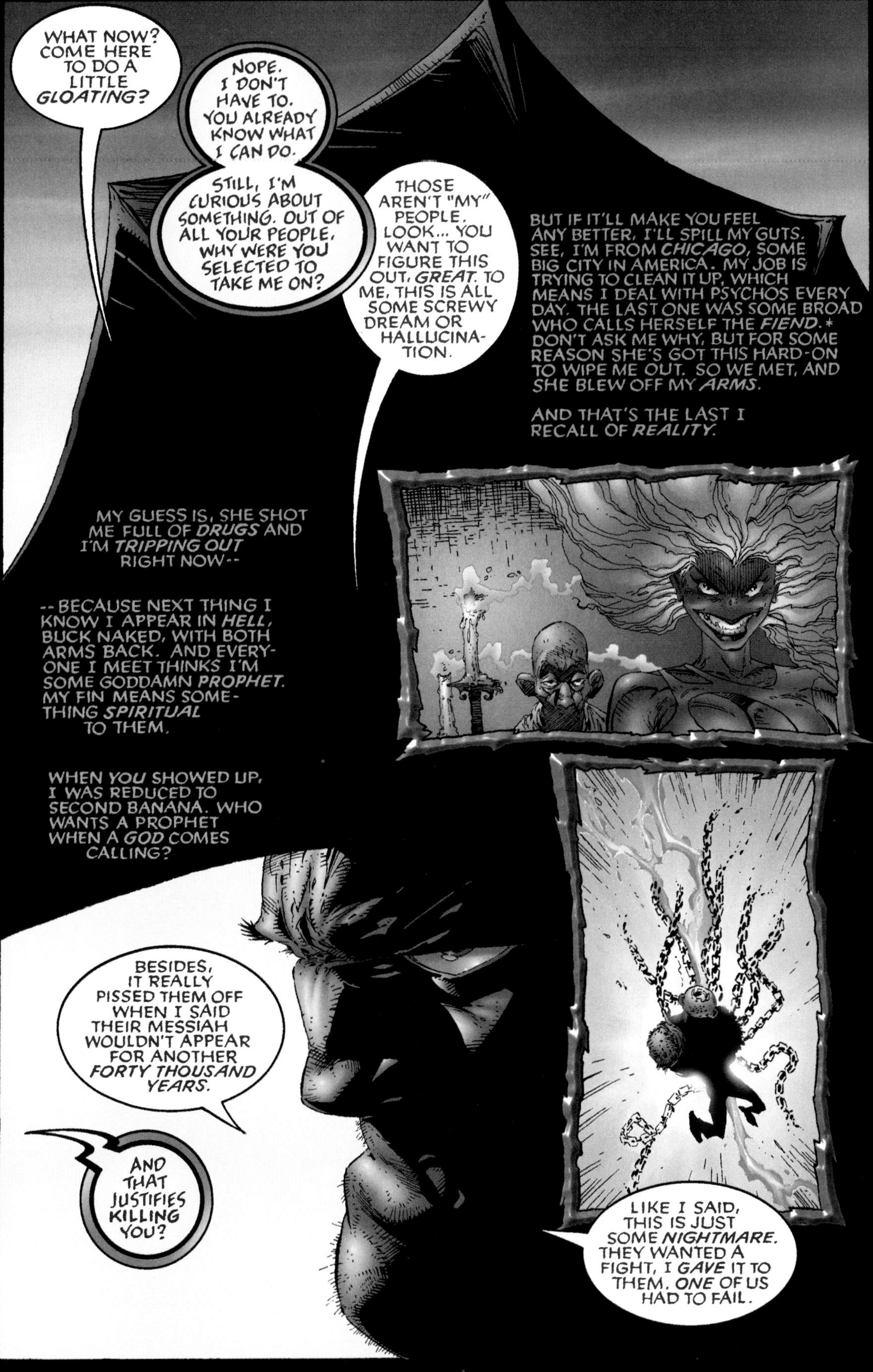
WHAT NOW? COME HERE TO DO A LITTLE GLOATING?
NOPE. I DON'T HAVE TO. YOU ALREADY KNOW WHAT I CAN DO.
STILL, I'M CURIOUS ABOUT SOMETHING. OUT OF ALL YOUR PEOPLE, WHY WERE YOU SELECTED TO TAKE ME ON?
THOSE AREN'T "MY" PEOPLE. LOOK... YOU WANT TO FIGURE THIS OUT, GREAT. TO ME, THIS IS ALL SOME SCREWY DREAM OR HALLUCINATION.
BUT IF IT'LL MAKE YOU FEEL ANY BETTER, I'LL SPILL MY GUTS. SEE, I'M FROM CHICAGO, SOME BIG CITY IN AMERICA. MY JOB IS TRYING TO CLEAN IT UP, WHICH MEANS I DEAL WITH PSYCHOS EVERY DAY. THE LAST ONE WAS SOME BROAD WHO CALLS HERSELF THE FIEND.* DON'T ASK ME WHY, BUT FOR SOME REASON SHE'S GOT THIS HARD-ON TO WIPE ME OUT. SO WE MET, AND SHE BLEW OFF MY ARMS.
AND THAT'S THE LAST I RECALL OF REALITY.
MY GUESS IS, SHE SHOT ME FULL OF DRUGS AND I'M TRIPPING OUT RIGHT NOW--
--BECAUSE NEXT THING I KNOW I APPEAR IN HELL, BUCK NAKED, WITH BOTH ARMS BACK. AND EVERYONE I MEET THINKS I'M SOME GODDAMN PROPHET. MY FIN MEANS SOMETHING SPIRITUAL TO THEM.
WHEN YOU SHOWED UP, I WAS REDUCED TO SECOND BANANA. WHO WANTS A PROPHET WHEN A GOD COMES CALLING?
BESIDES, IT REALLY PISSED THEM OFF WHEN I SAID THEIR MESSIAH WOULDN'T APPEAR FOR ANOTHER FORTY THOUSAND YEARS.
AND THAT JUSTIFIES KILLING YOU?
LIKE I SAID, THIS IS JUST SOME NIGHTMARE. THEY WANTED A FIGHT, I GAVE IT TO THEM. ONE OF US HAD TO FAIL.

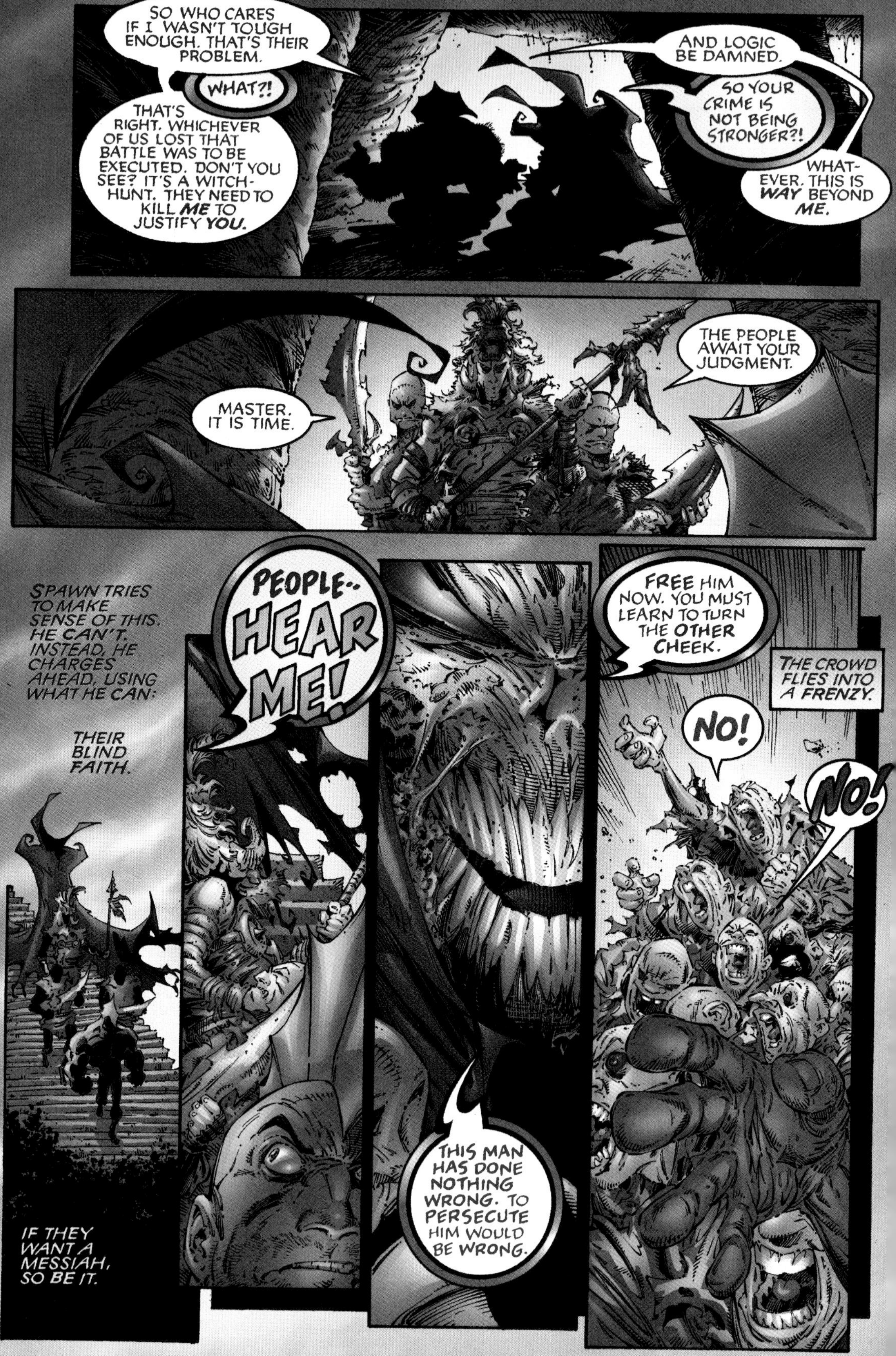

SO WHO CARES IF I WASN'T TOUGH ENOUGH. THAT'S THEIR PROBLEM.
WHAT?!
THAT'S RIGHT. WHICHEVER OF US LOST THAT BATTLE WAS TO BE EXECUTED. DON'T YOU SEE? IT'S A WITCH-HUNT. THEY NEED TO KILL **ME** TO JUSTIFY **YOU.**
AND LOGIC BE DAMNED.
SO YOUR CRIME IS NOT BEING STRONGER?!
WHAT-EVER. THIS IS **WAY** BEYOND **ME.**
MASTER. IT IS TIME.
THE PEOPLE AWAIT YOUR JUDGMENT.
SPAWN TRIES TO MAKE SENSE OF THIS. HE **CAN'T.** INSTEAD, HE CHARGES AHEAD, USING WHAT HE **CAN:**
THEIR BLIND **FAITH.**
IF THEY WANT A MESSIAH, SO BE IT.
PEOPLE.. HEAR ME!
THIS MAN HAS DONE **NOTHING WRONG.** TO **PERSECUTE** HIM WOULD BE **WRONG.**
FREE HIM NOW. YOU MUST LEARN TO TURN THE **OTHER CHEEK.**
THE CROWD FLIES INTO A **FRENZY.**
NO!
NO!

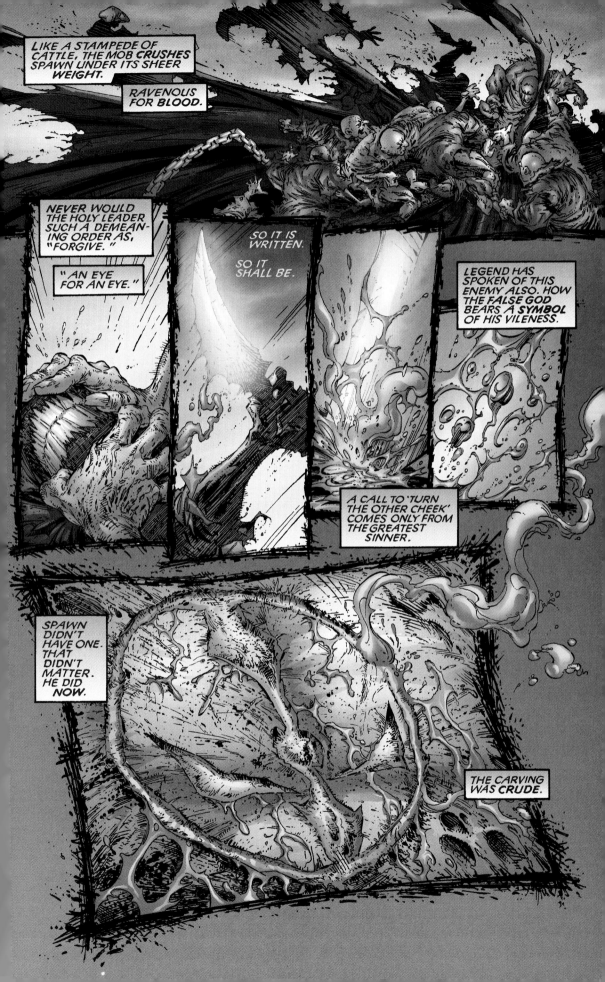

LIKE A STAMPEDE OF CATTLE, THE MOB CRUSHES SPAWN UNDER ITS SHEER WEIGHT.

RAVENOUS FOR BLOOD.

NEVER WOULD THE HOLY LEADER SUCH A DEMEANING ORDER AS, "FORGIVE."

"AN EYE FOR AN EYE."

SO IT IS WRITTEN.

SO IT SHALL BE.

LEGEND HAS SPOKEN OF THIS ENEMY ALSO. HOW THE FALSE GOD BEARS A SYMBOL OF HIS VILENESS.

A CALL TO 'TURN THE OTHER CHEEK' COMES ONLY FROM THE GREATEST SINNER.

SPAWN DIDN'T HAVE ONE. THAT DIDN'T MATTER. HE DID NOW.

THE CARVING WAS CRUDE.

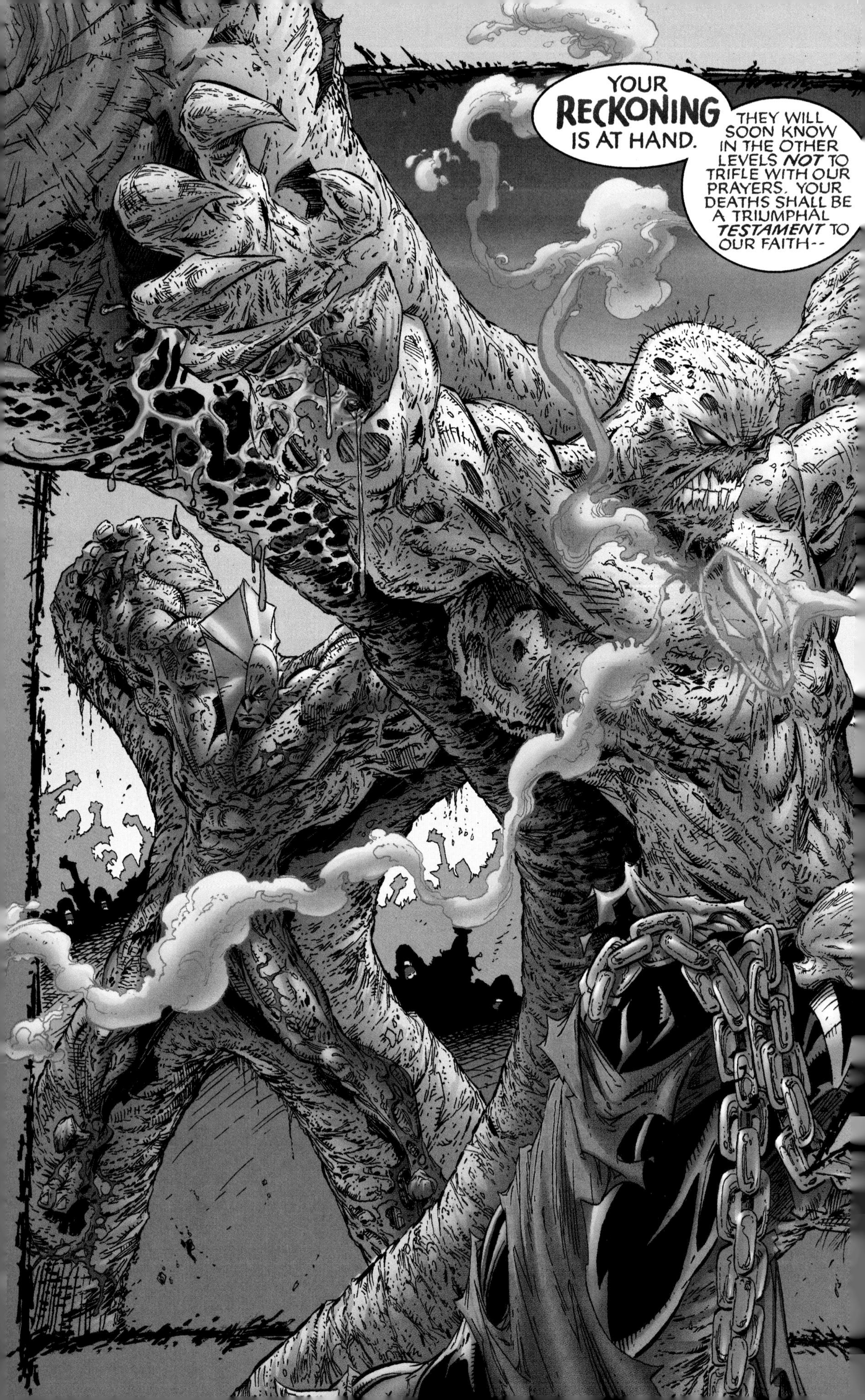
YOUR RECKONING IS AT HAND.
THEY WILL SOON KNOW IN THE OTHER LEVELS *NOT* TO TRIFLE WITH OUR PRAYERS. YOUR DEATHS SHALL BE A TRIUMPHAL *TESTAMENT* TO OUR FAITH--

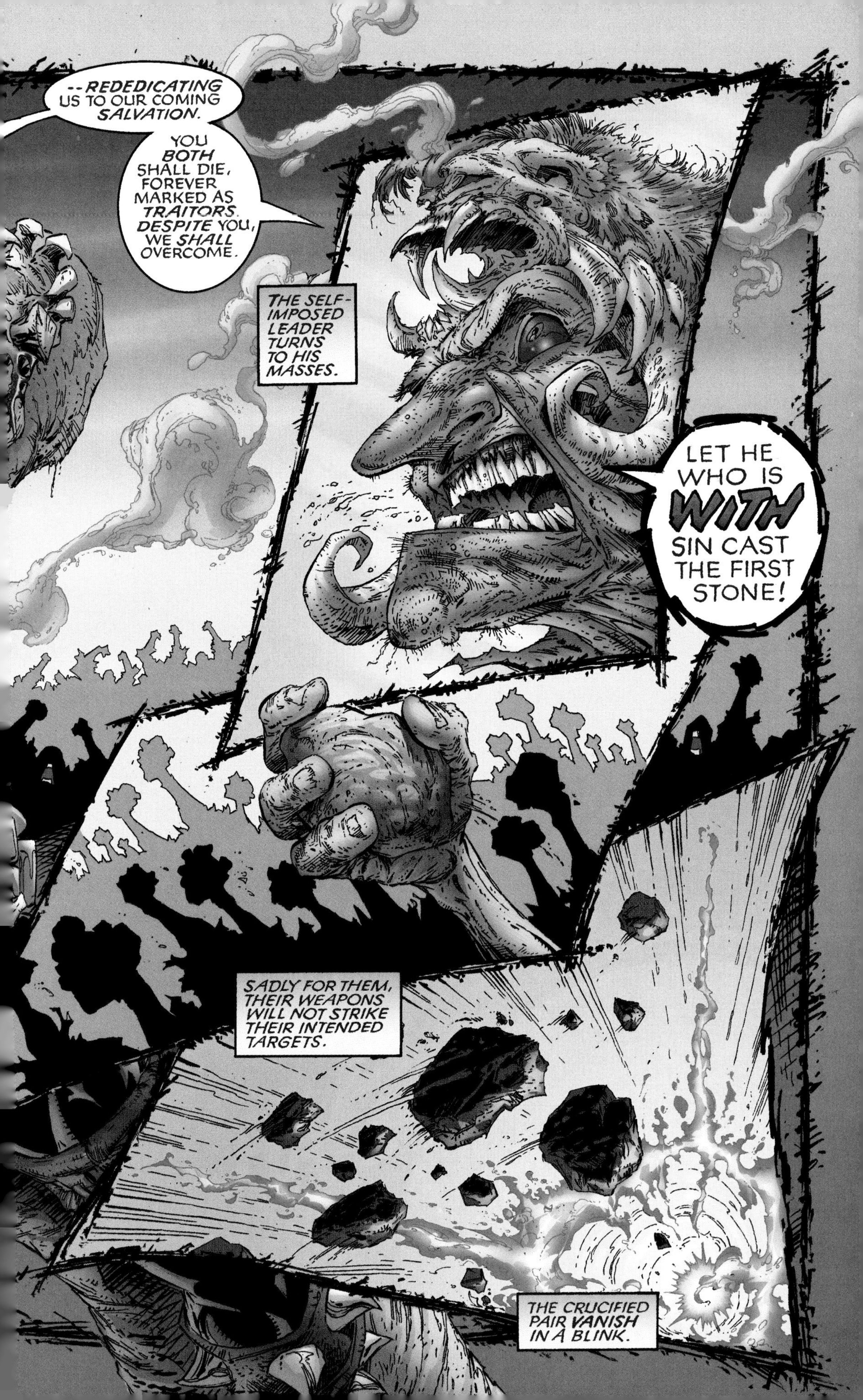
--REDEDICATING US TO OUR COMING SALVATION.
YOU BOTH SHALL DIE, FOREVER MARKED AS TRAITORS. DESPITE YOU, WE SHALL OVERCOME.
THE SELF-IMPOSED LEADER TURNS TO HIS MASSES.
LET HE WHO IS WITH SIN CAST THE FIRST STONE!
SADLY FOR THEM, THEIR WEAPONS WILL NOT STRIKE THEIR INTENDED TARGETS.
THE CRUCIFIED PAIR VANISH IN A BLINK.

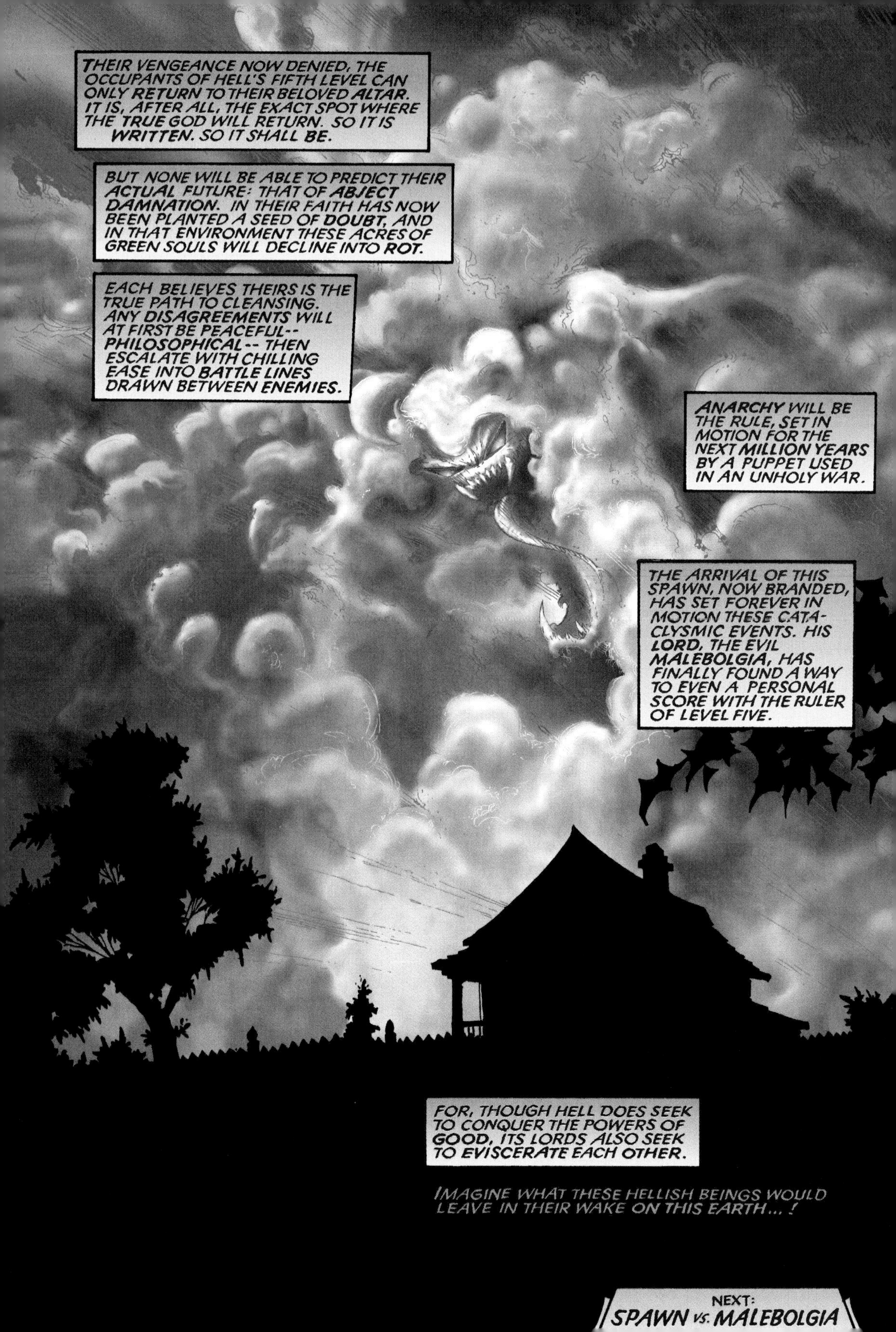
THEIR VENGEANCE NOW DENIED, THE OCCUPANTS OF HELL'S FIFTH LEVEL CAN ONLY RETURN TO THEIR BELOVED ALTAR. IT IS, AFTER ALL, THE EXACT SPOT WHERE THE TRUE GOD WILL RETURN. SO IT IS WRITTEN. SO IT SHALL BE.
BUT NONE WILL BE ABLE TO PREDICT THEIR ACTUAL FUTURE: THAT OF ABJECT DAMNATION. IN THEIR FAITH HAS NOW BEEN PLANTED A SEED OF DOUBT, AND IN THAT ENVIRONMENT THESE ACRES OF GREEN SOULS WILL DECLINE INTO ROT.
EACH BELIEVES THEIRS IS THE TRUE PATH TO CLEANSING. ANY DISAGREEMENTS WILL AT FIRST BE PEACEFUL-- PHILOSOPHICAL -- THEN ESCALATE WITH CHILLING EASE INTO BATTLE LINES DRAWN BETWEEN ENEMIES.
ANARCHY WILL BE THE RULE, SET IN MOTION FOR THE NEXT MILLION YEARS BY A PUPPET USED IN AN UNHOLY WAR.
THE ARRIVAL OF THIS SPAWN, NOW BRANDED, HAS SET FOREVER IN MOTION THESE CATACLYSMIC EVENTS. HIS LORD, THE EVIL MALEBOLGIA, HAS FINALLY FOUND A WAY TO EVEN A PERSONAL SCORE WITH THE RULER OF LEVEL FIVE.
FOR, THOUGH HELL DOES SEEK TO CONQUER THE POWERS OF GOOD, ITS LORDS ALSO SEEK TO EVISCERATE EACH OTHER.
IMAGINE WHAT THESE HELLISH BEINGS WOULD LEAVE IN THEIR WAKE ON THIS EARTH... !
NEXT: SPAWN VS. MALEBOLGIA

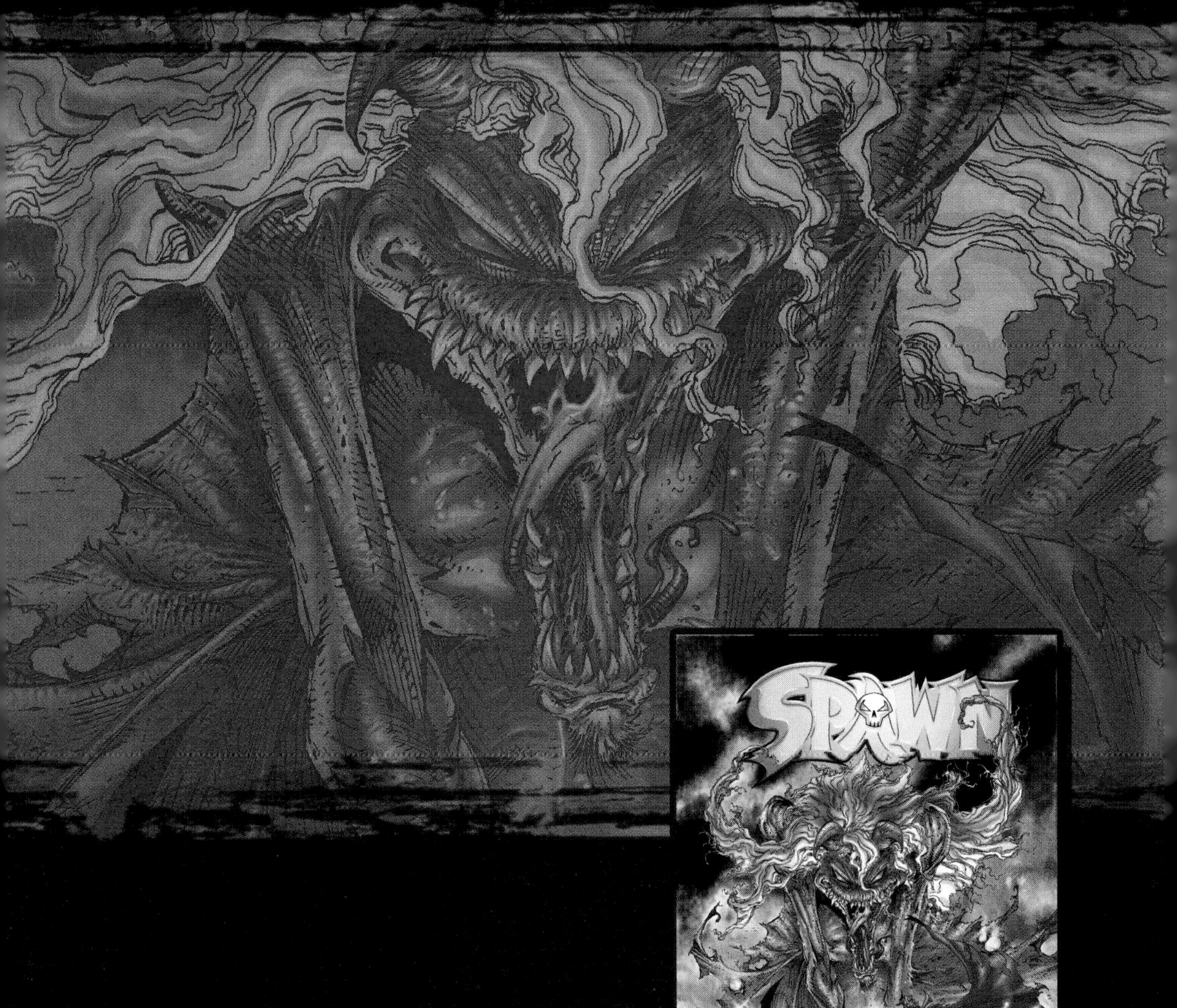
SPAWN

ISSUE FIFTY-THREE

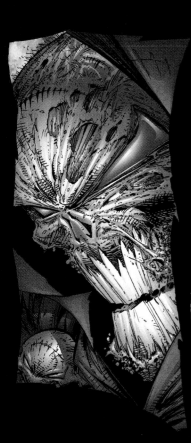

The ABYSS. A HARSH BLACKNESS SO
DENSE NO **LIGHT** HAS EVER INTRUDED
HERE. WHILE GOD WAS CREATING THE
COSMOS, GIVING LIFE TO EVERY CORNER, HIS
OMNISCIENT PRESENCE CAST A **SHADOW**.
PLANTED THERE AS WELL WAS A SEED. IT
GREW STEADILY IN THE COLD PALL
OF THE ALMIGHTY.

THIS PATCH OF INFINITY, JUST TO
THE LEFT OF THE PRECIOUS LIGHT,
IS NOW A **HARVEST GROUND** FOR
THE DIVINELY THWARTED SEED.

SEED WE NOW
CALL **SIN**.

IT GERMINATES IN
MEN OF **WEAKNESS**.
LUST, GREED, AND
THE OTHER DEADLY
SINS TAKE ROOT
IN THEM.

EMBEDDED NOW IN
THIS DARK LOAM IS
A MAN CONDEMNED
BY HIS OWN ACTS
UPON HUMANITY:

Lt. COLONEL AL SIMMONS.

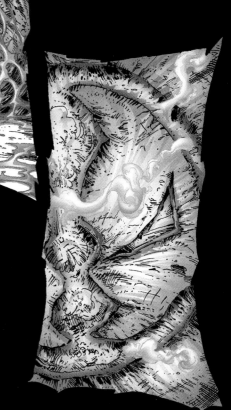

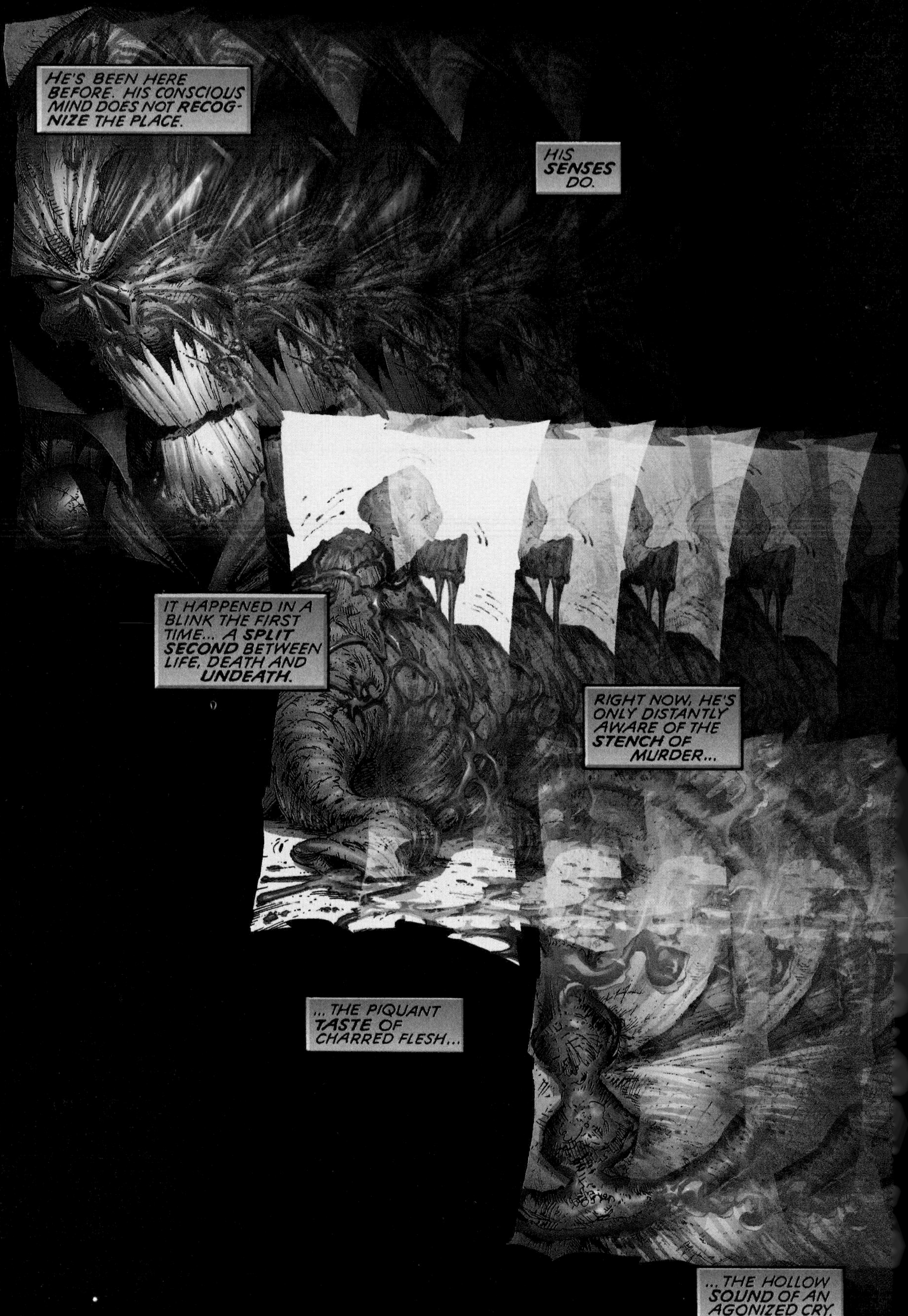
HE'S BEEN HERE BEFORE. HIS CONSCIOUS MIND DOES NOT RECOGNIZE THE PLACE.
HIS SENSES DO.
IT HAPPENED IN A BLINK THE FIRST TIME... A SPLIT SECOND BETWEEN LIFE, DEATH AND UNDEATH.
RIGHT NOW, HE'S ONLY DISTANTLY AWARE OF THE STENCH OF MURDER...
...THE PIQUANT TASTE OF CHARRED FLESH...
...THE HOLLOW SOUND OF AN AGONIZED CRY.

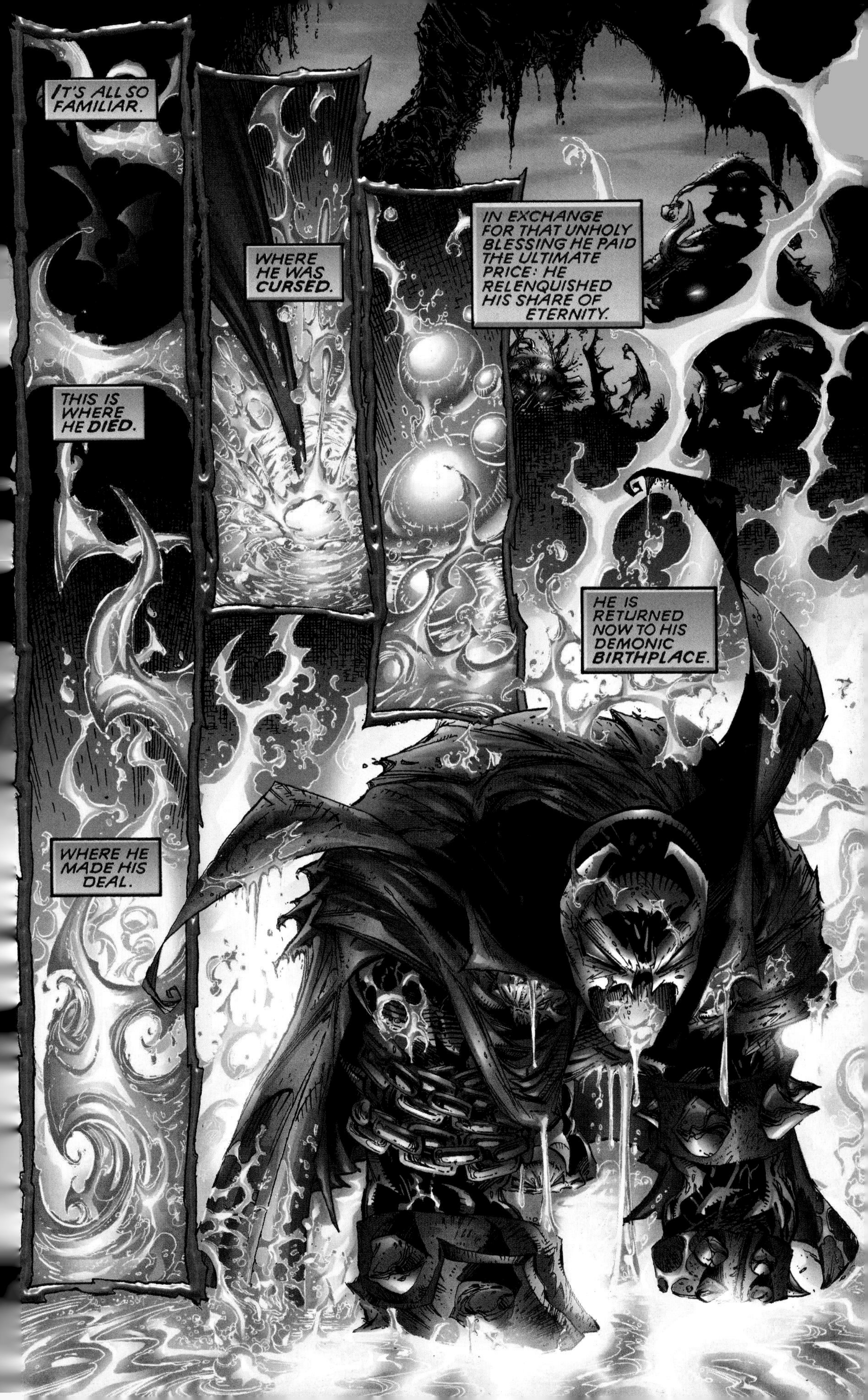
IT'S ALL SO FAMILIAR.
THIS IS WHERE HE DIED.
WHERE HE MADE HIS DEAL.
WHERE HE WAS CURSED.
IN EXCHANGE FOR THAT UNHOLY BLESSING HE PAID THE ULTIMATE PRICE: HE RELENQUISHED HIS SHARE OF ETERNITY.
HE IS RETURNED NOW TO HIS DEMONIC BIRTHPLACE.

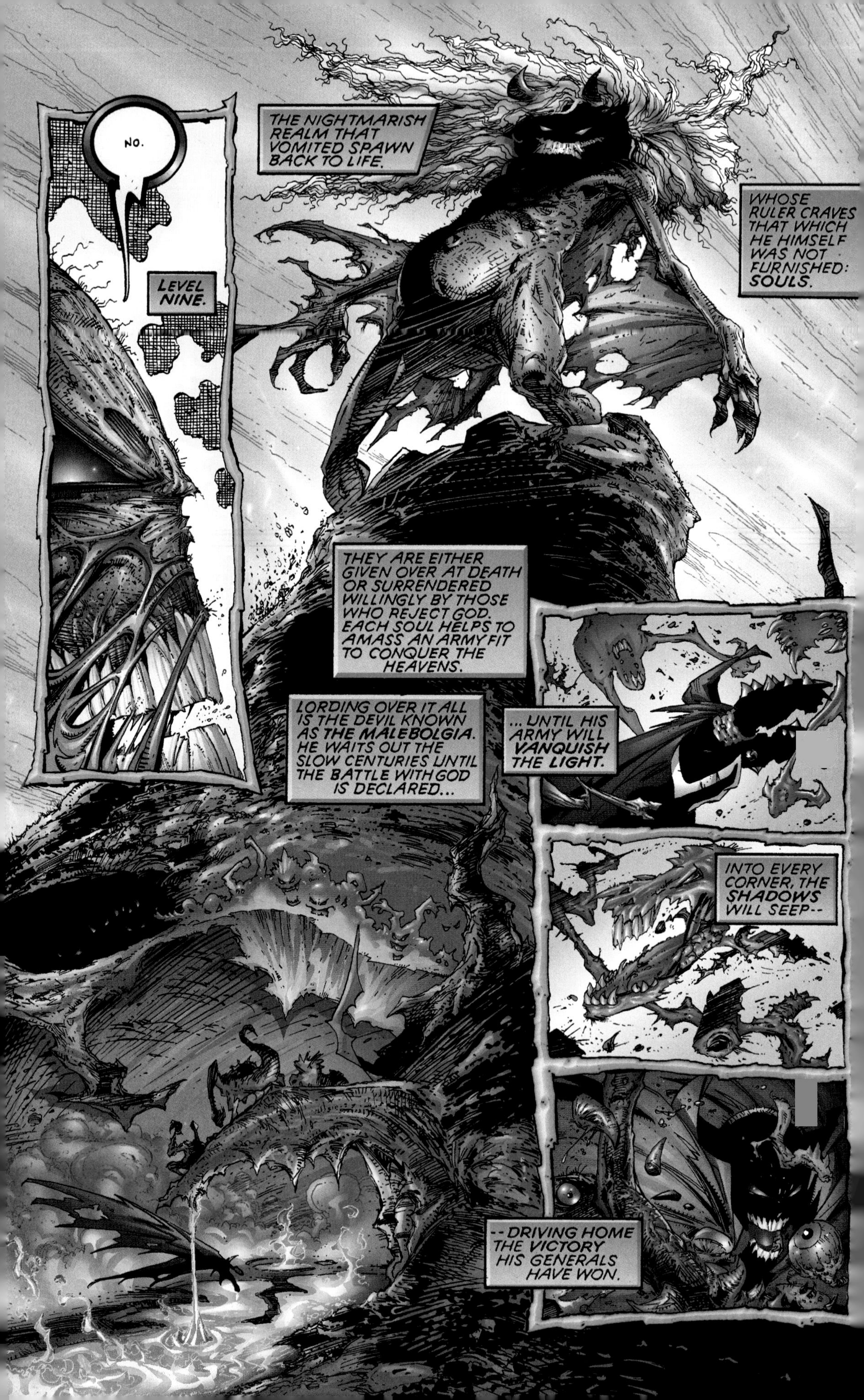
NO.
LEVEL NINE.
THE NIGHTMARISH REALM THAT VOMITED SPAWN BACK TO LIFE.
WHOSE RULER CRAVES THAT WHICH HE HIMSELF WAS NOT FURNISHED: SOULS.
THEY ARE EITHER GIVEN OVER AT DEATH OR SURRENDERED WILLINGLY BY THOSE WHO REJECT GOD. EACH SOUL HELPS TO AMASS AN ARMY FIT TO CONQUER THE HEAVENS.
LORDING OVER IT ALL IS THE DEVIL KNOWN AS THE MALEBOLGIA. HE WAITS OUT THE SLOW CENTURIES UNTIL THE BATTLE WITH GOD IS DECLARED...
...UNTIL HIS ARMY WILL VANQUISH THE LIGHT.
INTO EVERY CORNER, THE SHADOWS WILL SEEP--
--DRIVING HOME THE VICTORY HIS GENERALS HAVE WON.

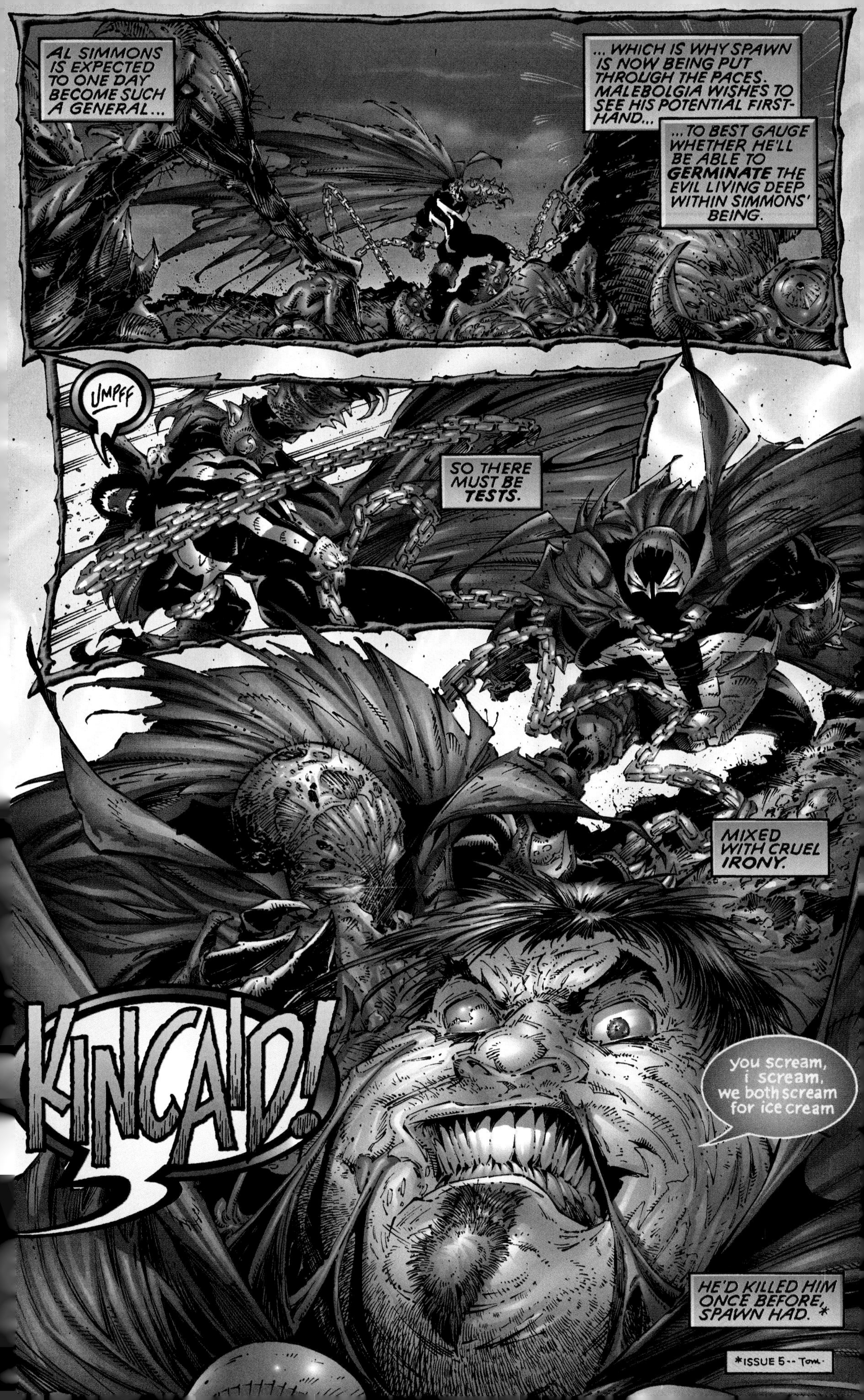
AL SIMMONS IS EXPECTED TO ONE DAY BECOME SUCH A GENERAL...
...WHICH IS WHY SPAWN IS NOW BEING PUT THROUGH THE PACES. MALEBOLGIA WISHES TO SEE HIS POTENTIAL FIRST-HAND...
...TO BEST GAUGE WHETHER HE'LL BE ABLE TO GERMINATE THE EVIL LIVING DEEP WITHIN SIMMONS' BEING.
UMPFF
SO THERE MUST BE TESTS.
MIXED WITH CRUEL IRONY.
KINCAID!
you scream, i scream, we both scream for ice cream
HE'D KILLED HIM ONCE BEFORE, SPAWN HAD.*
*ISSUE 5--Tom.

BUT THIS IS HELL.
THIS IS NOW.

LOGIC ISN'T ACCORDED
ANY FAVORS. INSTINC-
TIVELY, SPAWN KNOWS
THIS. MORE IMPOR-
TANTLY, HE ACCEPTS IT
WITHOUT QUESTION.

ON EARTH, BILLY
KINCAID HAD FALLEN
TO THE LOWEST
POSSIBLE LEVEL
KNOWN TO MAN: A
MURDERING
PEDOPHILE.

STRIPPING CHILDREN
OF THEIR INNOCENCE...
AND SOCIETY OF ITS
CHILDREN.

THE HELLSPAWN
DISEMBOWELS HIM A
SECOND TIME WHILE
WISHING THAT KINCAID
WILL TRY TO GET UP SO
HE CAN GUT HIM AGAIN.

AND SO,
SPAWN HAS
PASSED
THIS TEST.

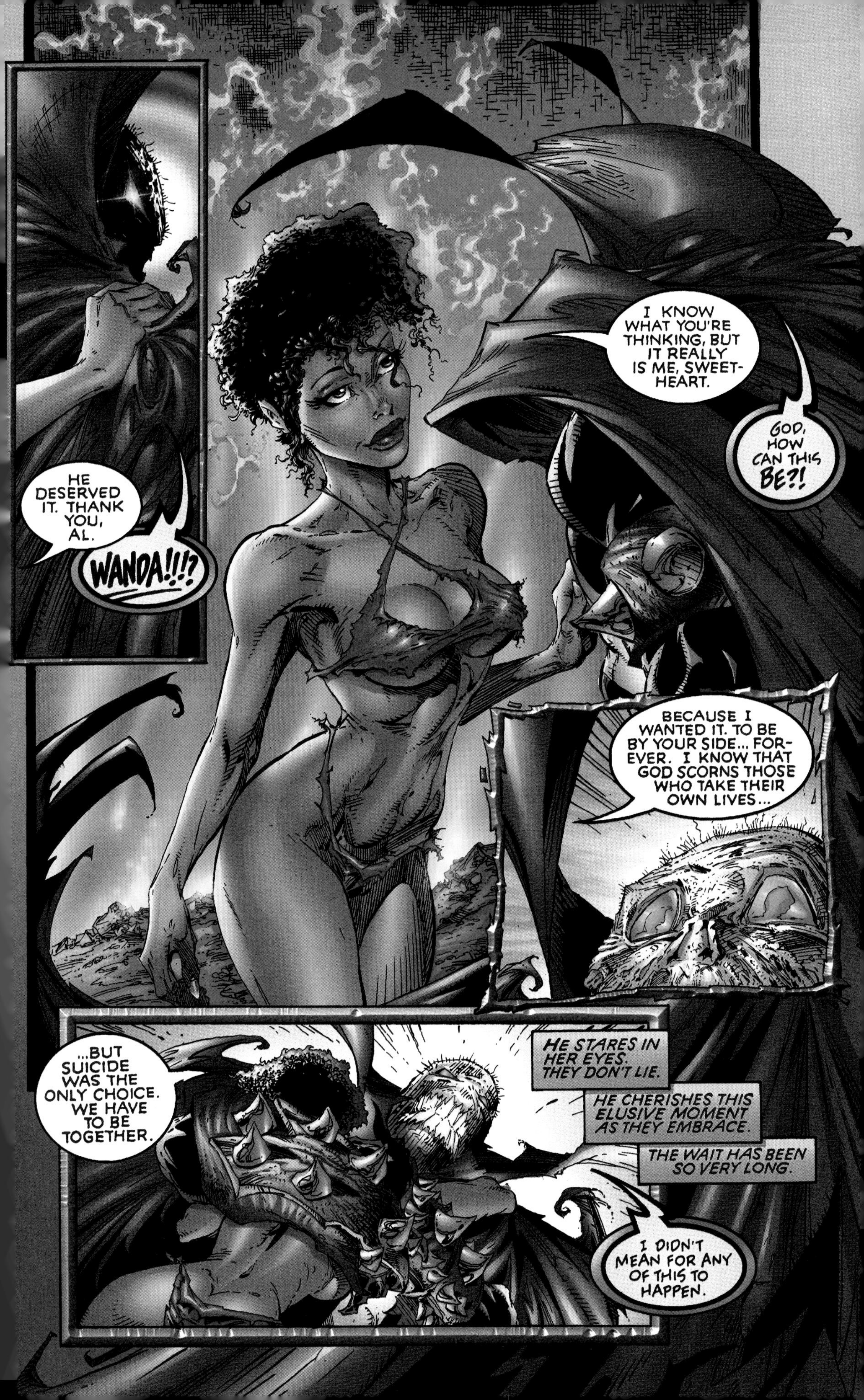
HE DESERVED IT. THANK YOU, AL.
WANDA!!!?
I KNOW WHAT YOU'RE THINKING, BUT IT REALLY IS ME, SWEET-HEART.
GOD, HOW CAN THIS BE?!
BECAUSE I WANTED IT. TO BE BY YOUR SIDE... FOR-EVER. I KNOW THAT GOD SCORNS THOSE WHO TAKE THEIR OWN LIVES...
...BUT SUICIDE WAS THE ONLY CHOICE. WE HAVE TO BE TOGETHER.
HE STARES IN HER EYES. THEY DON'T LIE.
HE CHERISHES THIS ELUSIVE MOMENT AS THEY EMBRACE.
THE WAIT HAS BEEN SO VERY LONG.
I DIDN'T MEAN FOR ANY OF THIS TO HAPPEN.

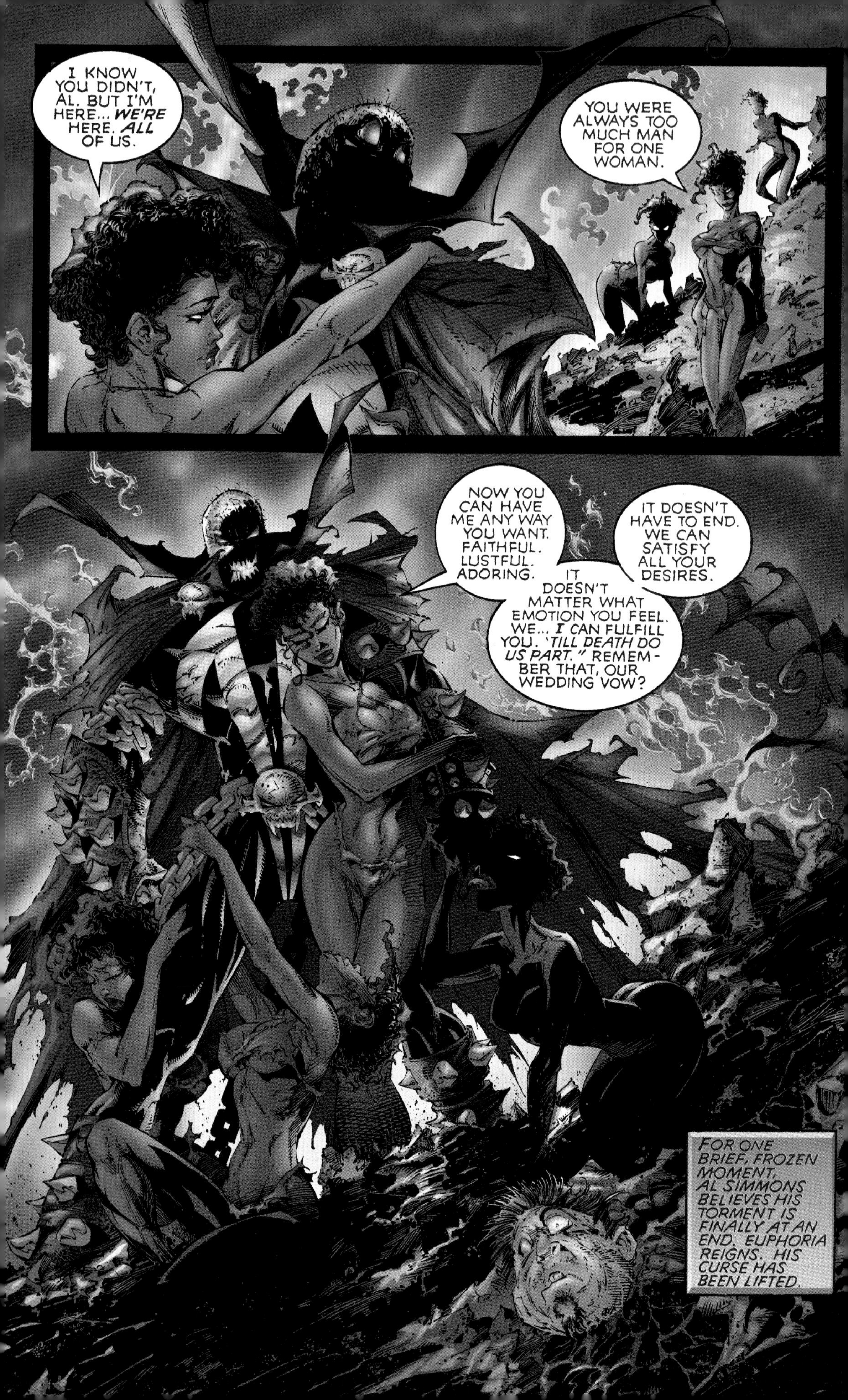
I KNOW YOU DIDN'T, AL. BUT I'M HERE... *WE'RE* HERE. *ALL* OF US.
YOU WERE ALWAYS TOO MUCH MAN FOR ONE WOMAN.
NOW YOU CAN HAVE ME ANY WAY YOU WANT. FAITHFUL. LUSTFUL. ADORING.
IT DOESN'T HAVE TO END. WE CAN SATISFY ALL YOUR DESIRES.
IT DOESN'T MATTER WHAT EMOTION YOU FEEL. WE... *I* CAN FULFILL YOU. '*TILL DEATH DO US PART.*" REMEMBER THAT, OUR WEDDING VOW?
FOR ONE BRIEF, FROZEN MOMENT, AL SIMMONS BELIEVES HIS TORMENT IS FINALLY AT AN END. EUPHORIA REIGNS. HIS CURSE HAS BEEN LIFTED.

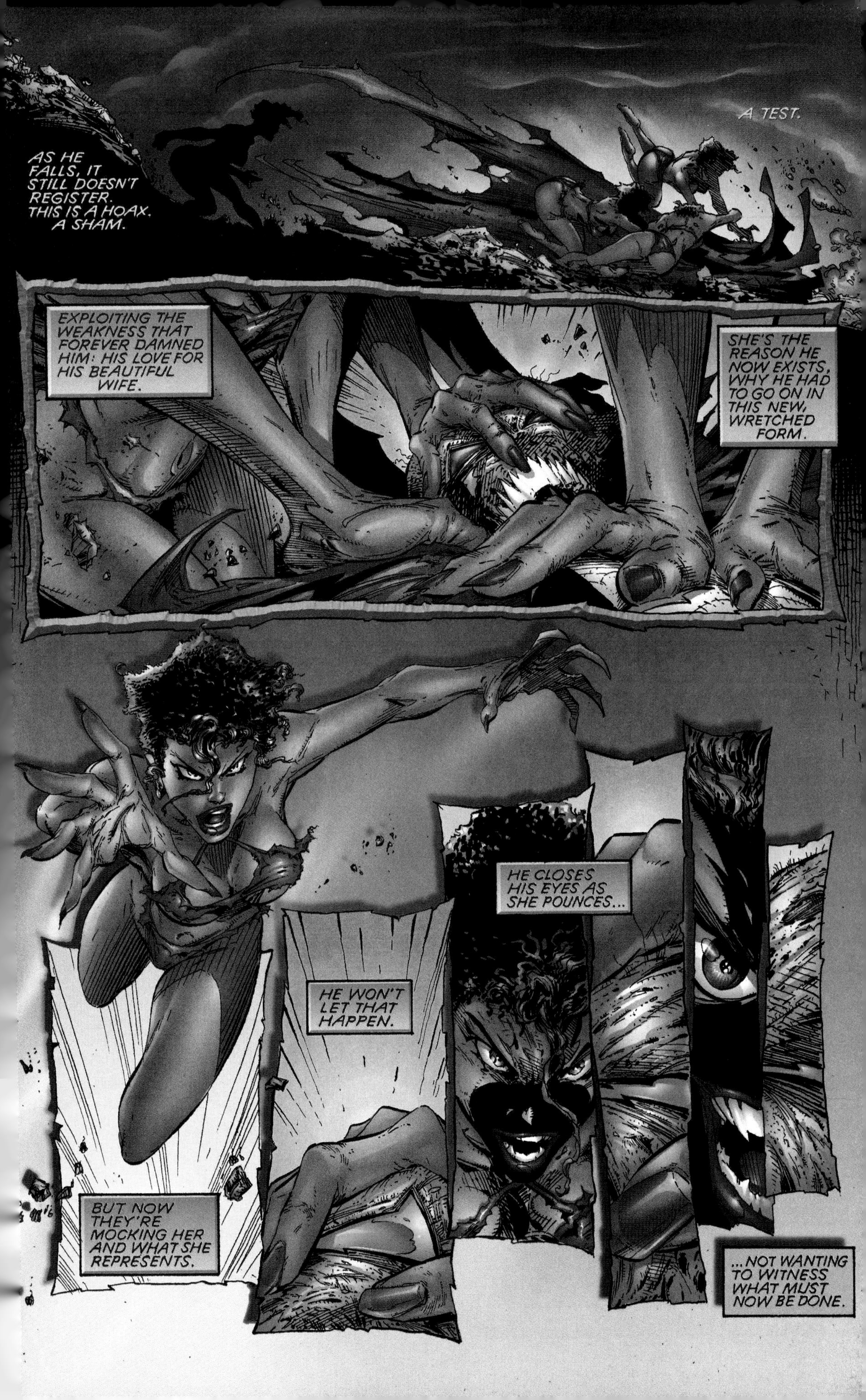
AS HE FALLS, IT STILL DOESN'T REGISTER. THIS IS A HOAX. A SHAM.
A TEST.
EXPLOITING THE WEAKNESS THAT FOREVER DAMNED HIM: HIS LOVE FOR HIS BEAUTIFUL WIFE.
SHE'S THE REASON HE NOW EXISTS, WHY HE HAD TO GO ON IN THIS NEW, WRETCHED FORM.
BUT NOW THEY'RE MOCKING HER AND WHAT SHE REPRESENTS.
HE WON'T LET THAT HAPPEN.
HE CLOSES HIS EYES AS SHE POUNCES...
...NOT WANTING TO WITNESS WHAT MUST NOW BE DONE.

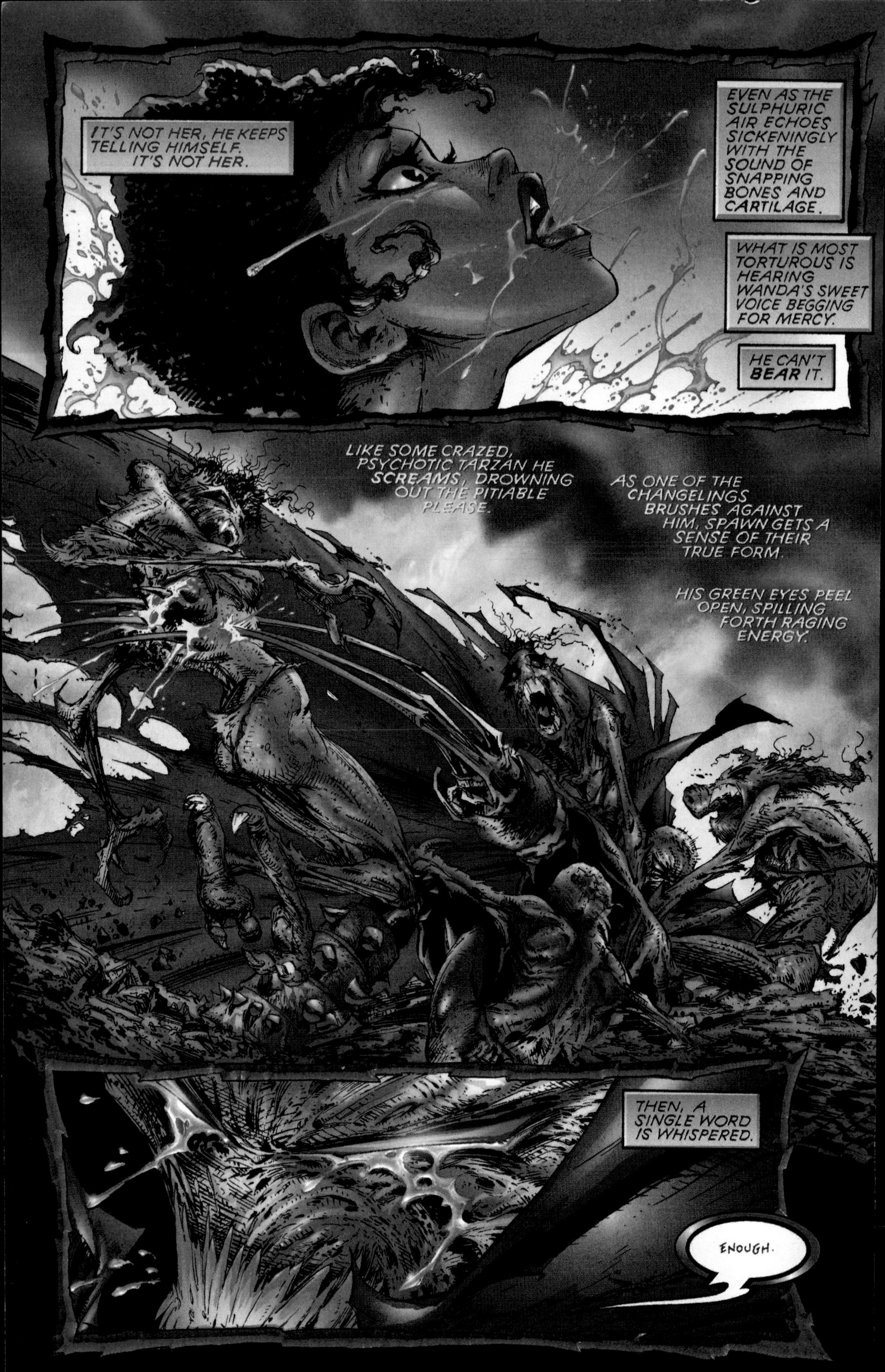
IT'S NOT HER, HE KEEPS TELLING HIMSELF. IT'S NOT HER.
EVEN AS THE SULPHURIC AIR ECHOES SICKENINGLY WITH THE SOUND OF SNAPPING BONES AND CARTILAGE.
WHAT IS MOST TORTUROUS IS HEARING WANDA'S SWEET VOICE BEGGING FOR MERCY.
HE CAN'T BEAR IT.
LIKE SOME CRAZED, PSYCHOTIC TARZAN HE SCREAMS, DROWNING OUT THE PITIABLE PLEASE.
AS ONE OF THE CHANGELINGS BRUSHES AGAINST HIM, SPAWN GETS A SENSE OF THEIR TRUE FORM.
HIS GREEN EYES PEEL OPEN, SPILLING FORTH RAGING ENERGY.
THEN, A SINGLE WORD IS WHISPERED.
ENOUGH.

GODDAMMIT, I'VE SUFFERED ENOUGH!
MALEBOLGIA WANTS A WAR, HE'S GOT IT! I DON'T GIVE A CRAP ANYMORE.
SEND YOUR PUPPETS! EVERY LAST ONE OF THEM. I'LL TAKE 'EM.
YOU WANT ME TO BE LIKE YOU, FINE. I'LL BE VICIOUS, EVIL, SOULLESS!! AFTER I'VE RIPPED YOUR THROAT OUT.
YOU BASTARD. THIS IS GOING TO END.

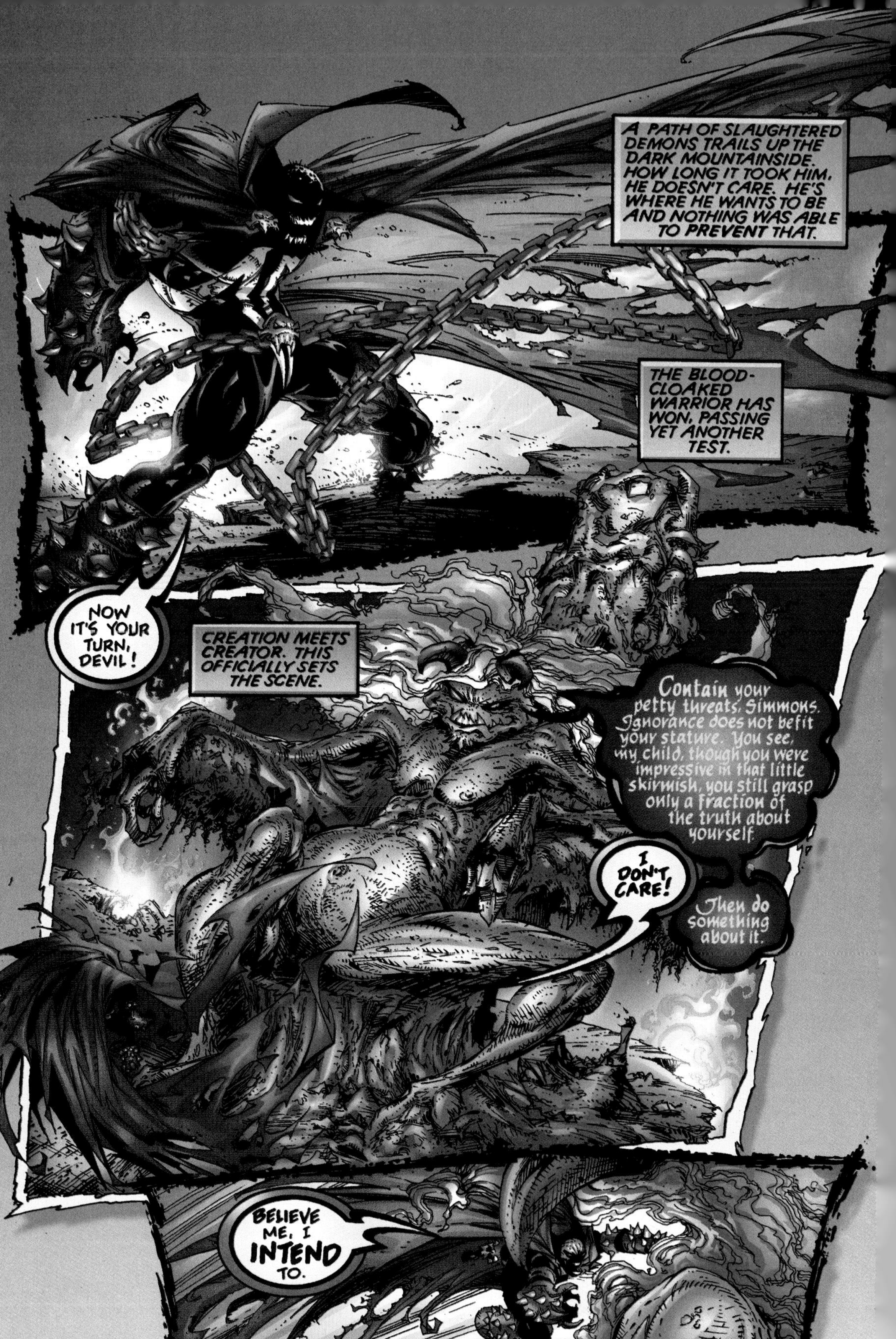
A PATH OF SLAUGHTERED DEMONS TRAILS UP THE DARK MOUNTAINSIDE. HOW LONG IT TOOK HIM, HE DOESN'T CARE. HE'S WHERE HE WANTS TO BE AND NOTHING WAS ABLE TO PREVENT THAT.
THE BLOOD-CLOAKED WARRIOR HAS WON, PASSING YET ANOTHER TEST.
NOW IT'S YOUR TURN, DEVIL!
CREATION MEETS CREATOR. THIS OFFICIALLY SETS THE SCENE.
Contain your petty threats, Simmons. Ignorance does not befit your stature. You see, my child, though you were impressive in that little skirmish, you still grasp only a fraction of the truth about yourself.
I DON'T CARE!
Then do something about it.
BELIEVE ME, I INTEND TO.

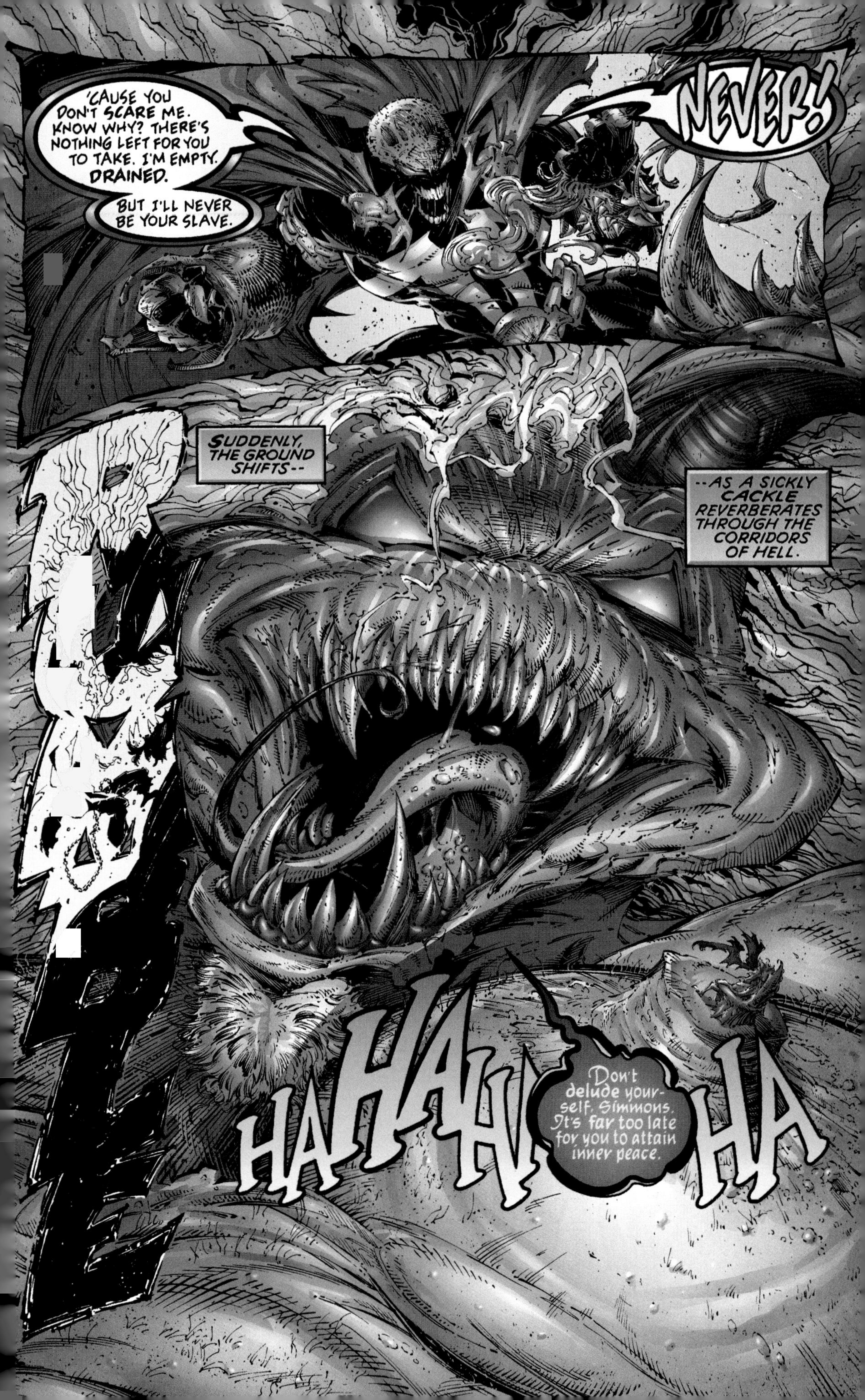
'CAUSE YOU DON'T SCARE ME. KNOW WHY? THERE'S NOTHING LEFT FOR YOU TO TAKE. I'M EMPTY. DRAINED.
BUT I'LL NEVER BE YOUR SLAVE.
NEVER!
SUDDENLY, THE GROUND SHIFTS--
--AS A SICKLY CACKLE REVERBERATES THROUGH THE CORRIDORS OF HELL.
HAHAH HA
Don't delude yourself, Simmons. It's far too late for you to attain inner peace.

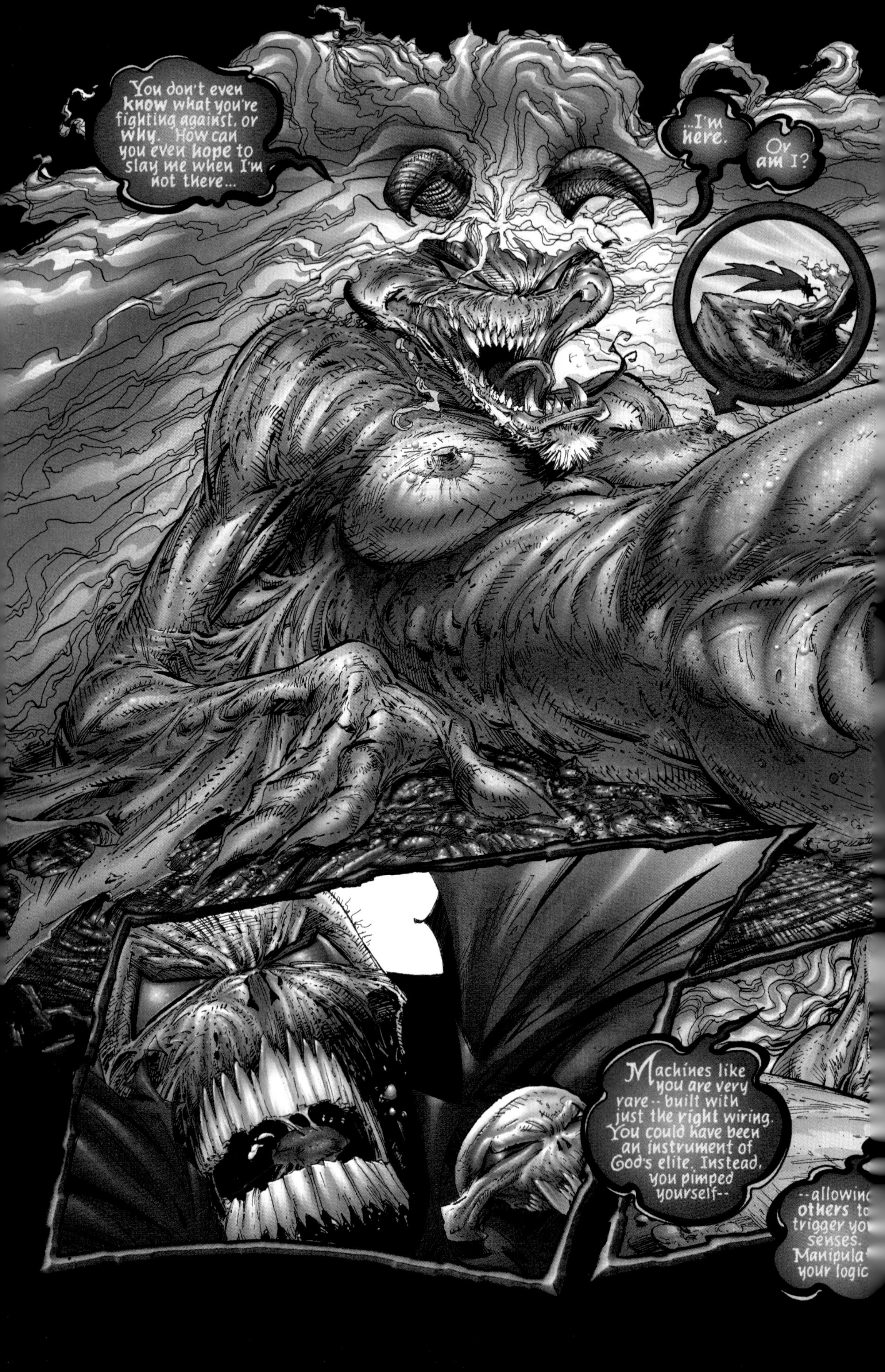

You don't even know what you're fighting against, or why. How can you even hope to slay me when I'm not there...
...I'm here.
Or am I?
Machines like you are very rare-- built with just the right wiring. You could have been an instrument of God's elite. Instead, you pimped yourself--
--allowing others to trigger your senses. Manipula your logic

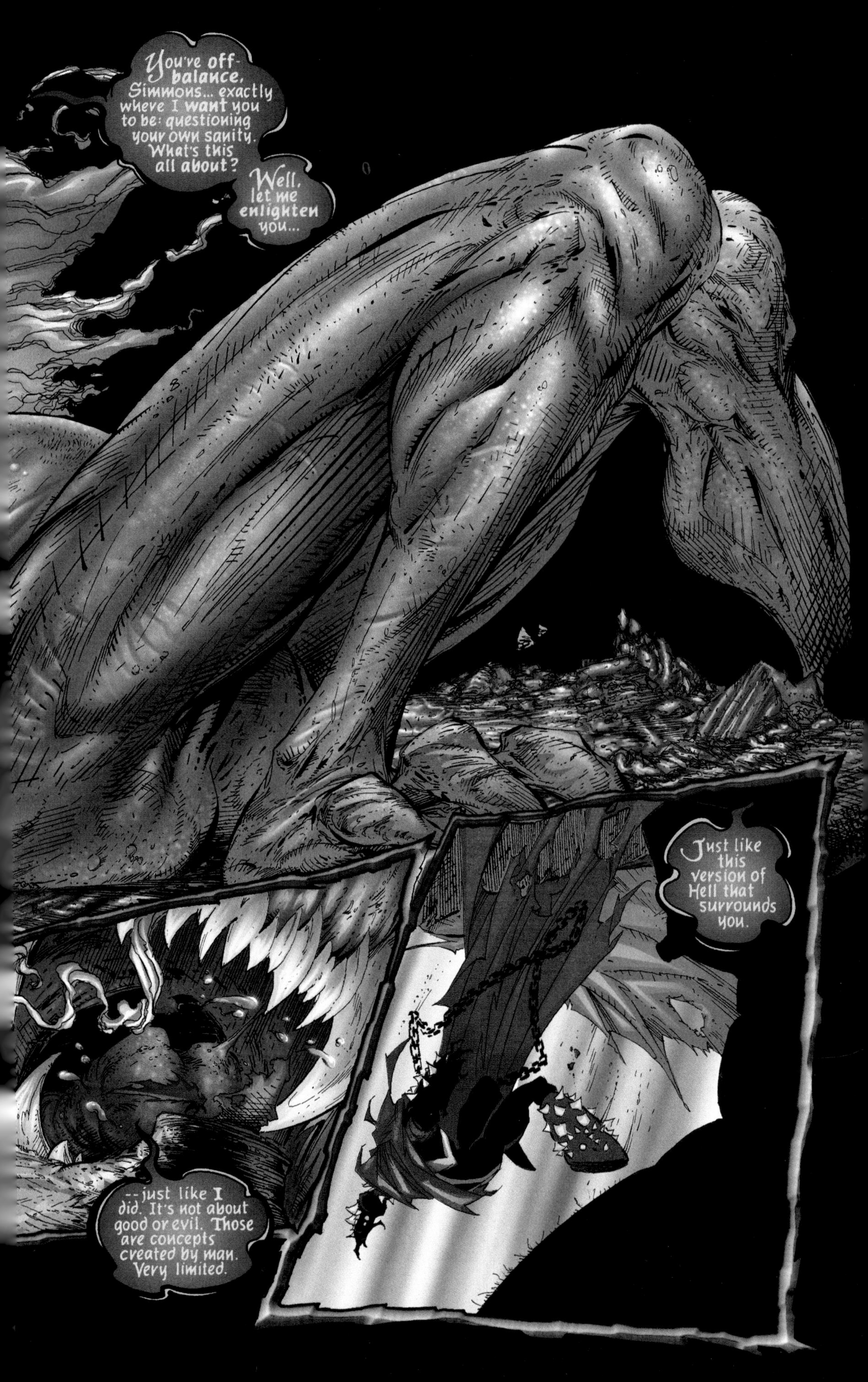

You're off-balance, Simmons... exactly where I want you to be: questioning your own sanity. What's this all about?
Well, let me enlighten you...
Just like this version of Hell that surrounds you.
--just like I did. It's not about good or evil. Those are concepts created by man. Very limited.

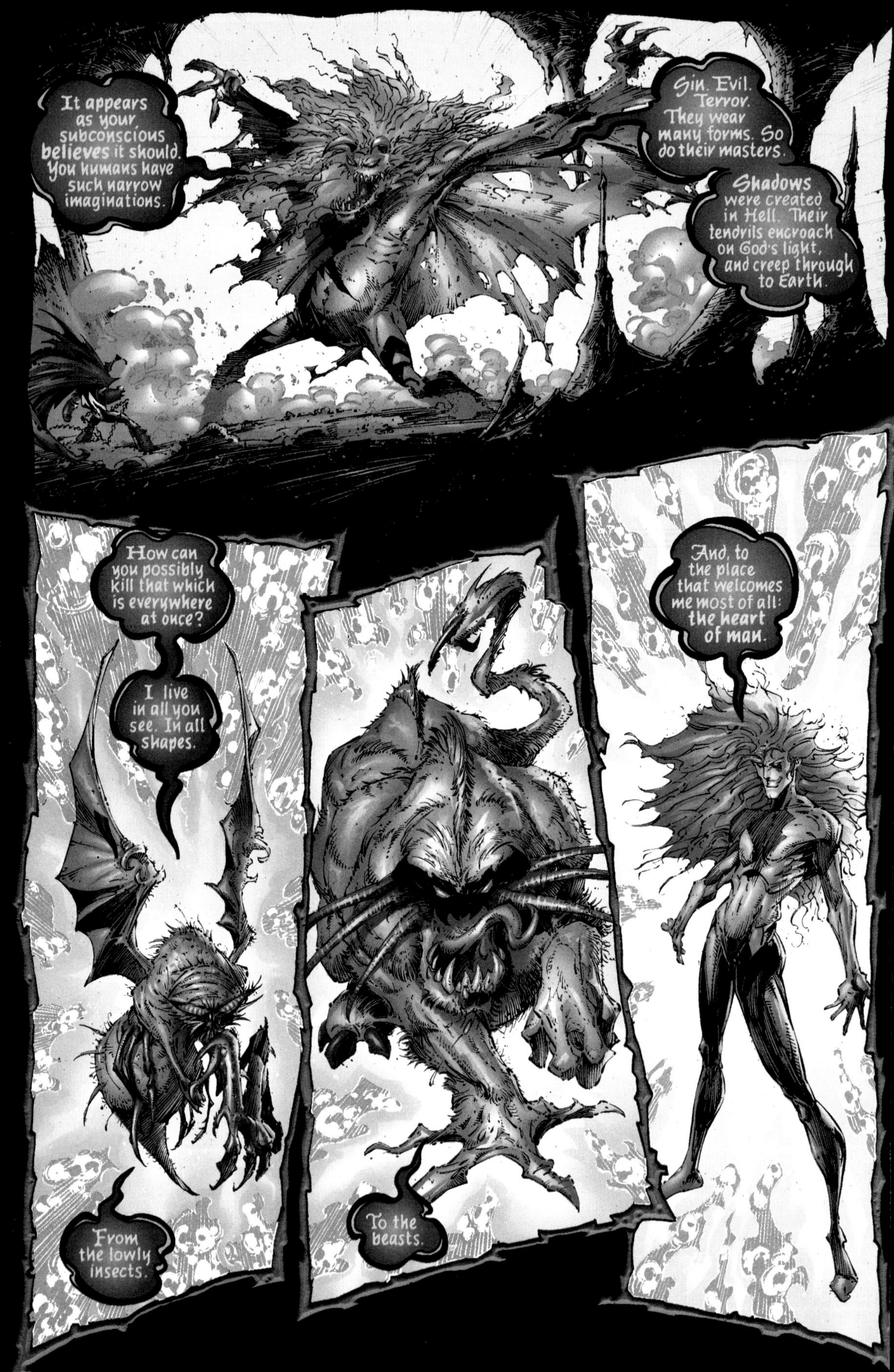
It appears as your subconscious **believes** it should. You humans have such narrow imaginations.
Sin. Evil. Terror. They wear many forms. So do their masters.
Shadows were created in Hell. Their tendrils encroach on God's light, and creep through to Earth.
How can you possibly kill that which is everywhere at once?
I live in all you see. In all shapes.
From the lowly insects.
To the beasts.
And, to the place that welcomes me most of all: **the heart of man.**

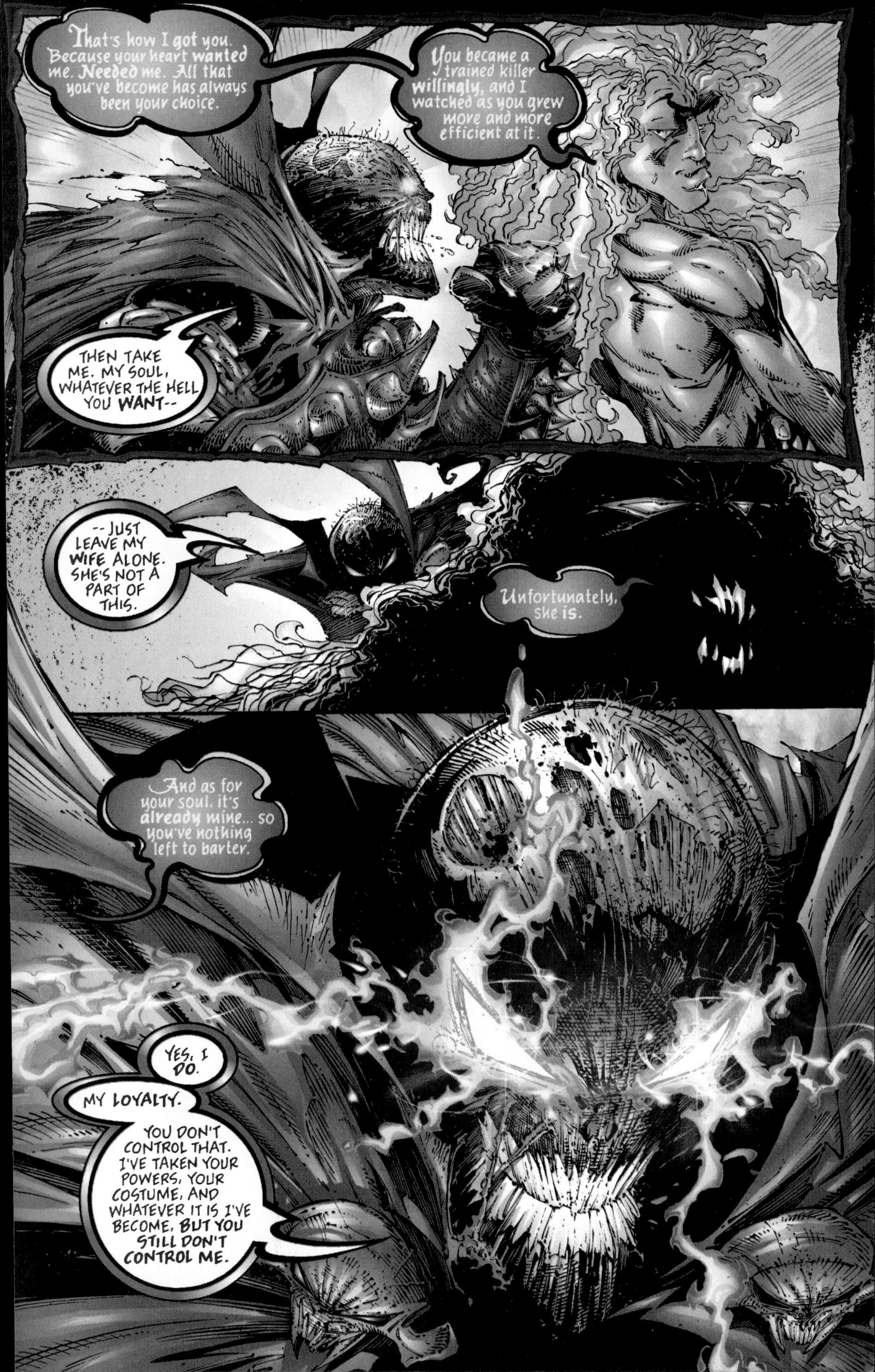
That's how I got you. Because your heart wanted me. Needed me. All that you've become has always been your choice.
You became a trained killer willingly, and I watched as you grew more and more efficient at it.
THEN TAKE ME. MY SOUL, WHATEVER THE HELL YOU WANT--
--JUST LEAVE MY WIFE ALONE. SHE'S NOT A PART OF THIS.
Unfortunately, she is.
And as for your soul, it's already mine... so you've nothing left to barter.
YES, I DO.
MY LOYALTY.
YOU DON'T CONTROL THAT. I'VE TAKEN YOUR POWERS, YOUR COSTUME, AND WHATEVER IT IS I'VE BECOME. BUT YOU STILL DON'T CONTROL ME.

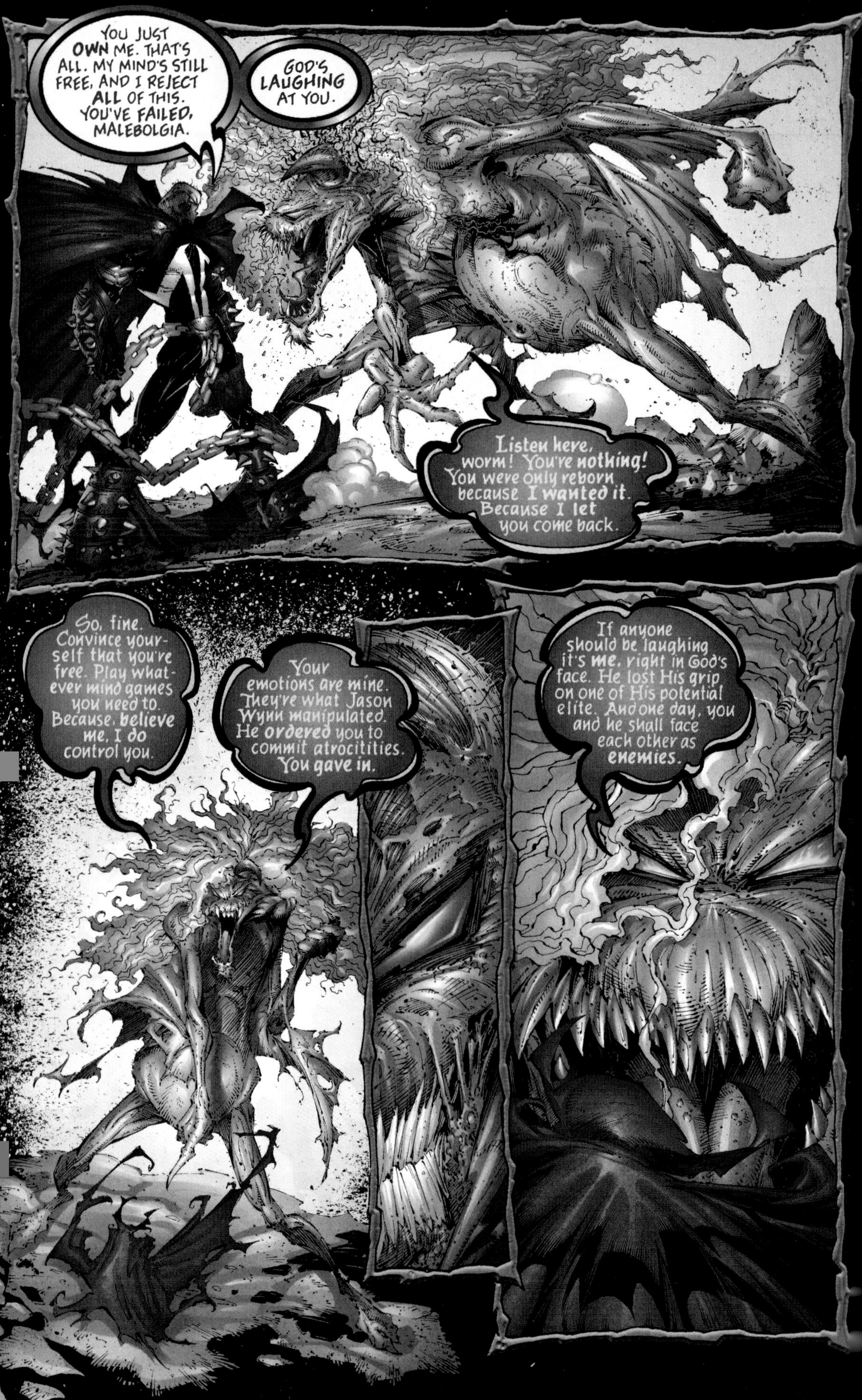

YOU JUST OWN ME. THAT'S ALL. MY MIND'S STILL FREE, AND I REJECT ALL OF THIS. YOU'VE FAILED, MALEBOLGIA.
GOD'S LAUGHING AT YOU.
Listen here, worm! You're nothing! You were only reborn because I wanted it. Because I let you come back.
So, fine. Convince your-self that you're free. Play what-ever mind games you need to. Because, believe me, I do control you.
Your emotions are mine. They're what Jason Wynn manipulated. He ordered you to commit atrocities. You gave in.
If anyone should be laughing it's me, right in God's face. He lost His grip on one of His potential elite. And one day, you and he shall face each other as enemies.

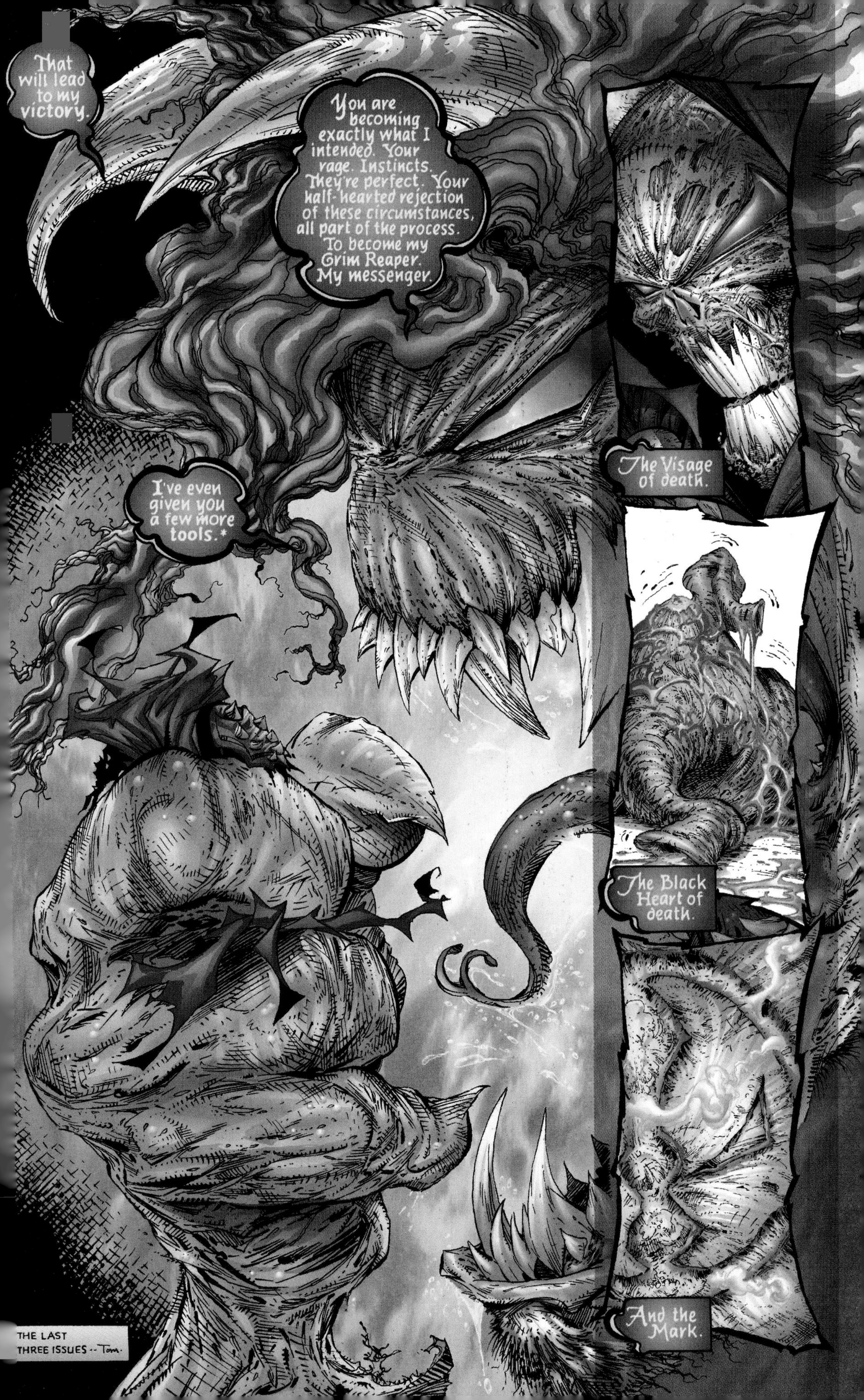
That will lead to my victory.
You are becoming exactly what I intended. Your rage. Instincts. They're perfect. Your half-hearted rejection of these circumstances, all part of the process. To become my Grim Reaper. My messenger.
I've even given you a few more tools.*
THE LAST THREE ISSUES -- Tom.
The Visage of death.
The Black Heart of death.
And the Mark.

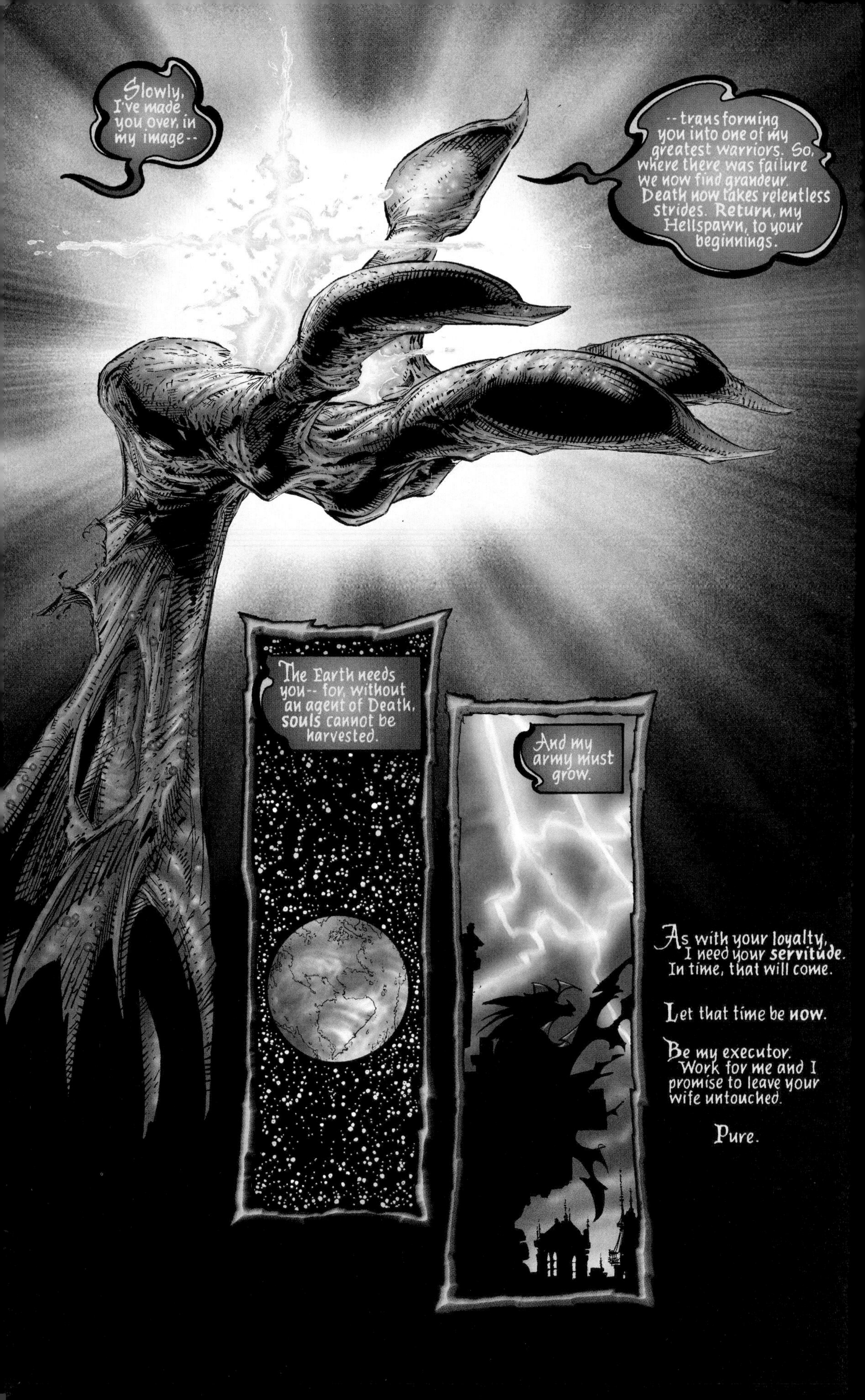
Slowly, I've made you over, in my image--
--transforming you into one of my greatest warriors. So, where there was failure we now find grandeur. Death now takes relentless strides. Return, my Hellspawn, to your beginnings.
The Earth needs you-- for, without an agent of Death, souls cannot be harvested.
And my army must grow.
As with your loyalty, I need your servitude. In time, that will come.
Let that time be now.
Be my executor. Work for me and I promise to leave your wife untouched.
Pure.

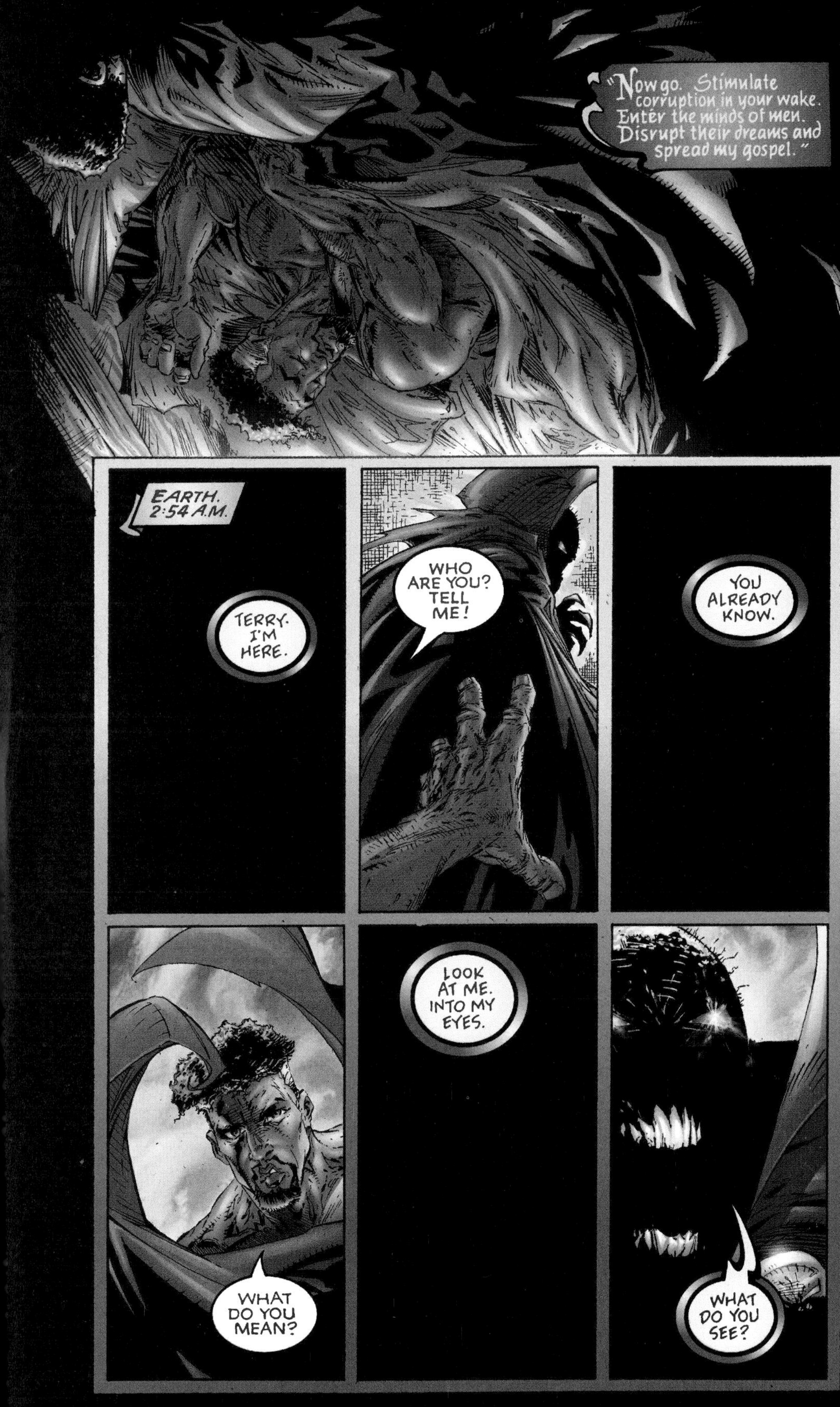
"Now go. Stimulate corruption in your wake. Enter the minds of men. Disrupt their dreams and spread my gospel."
EARTH. 2:54 A.M.
TERRY. I'M HERE.
WHO ARE YOU? TELL ME!
YOU ALREADY KNOW.
WHAT DO YOU MEAN?
LOOK AT ME. INTO MY EYES.
WHAT DO YOU SEE?

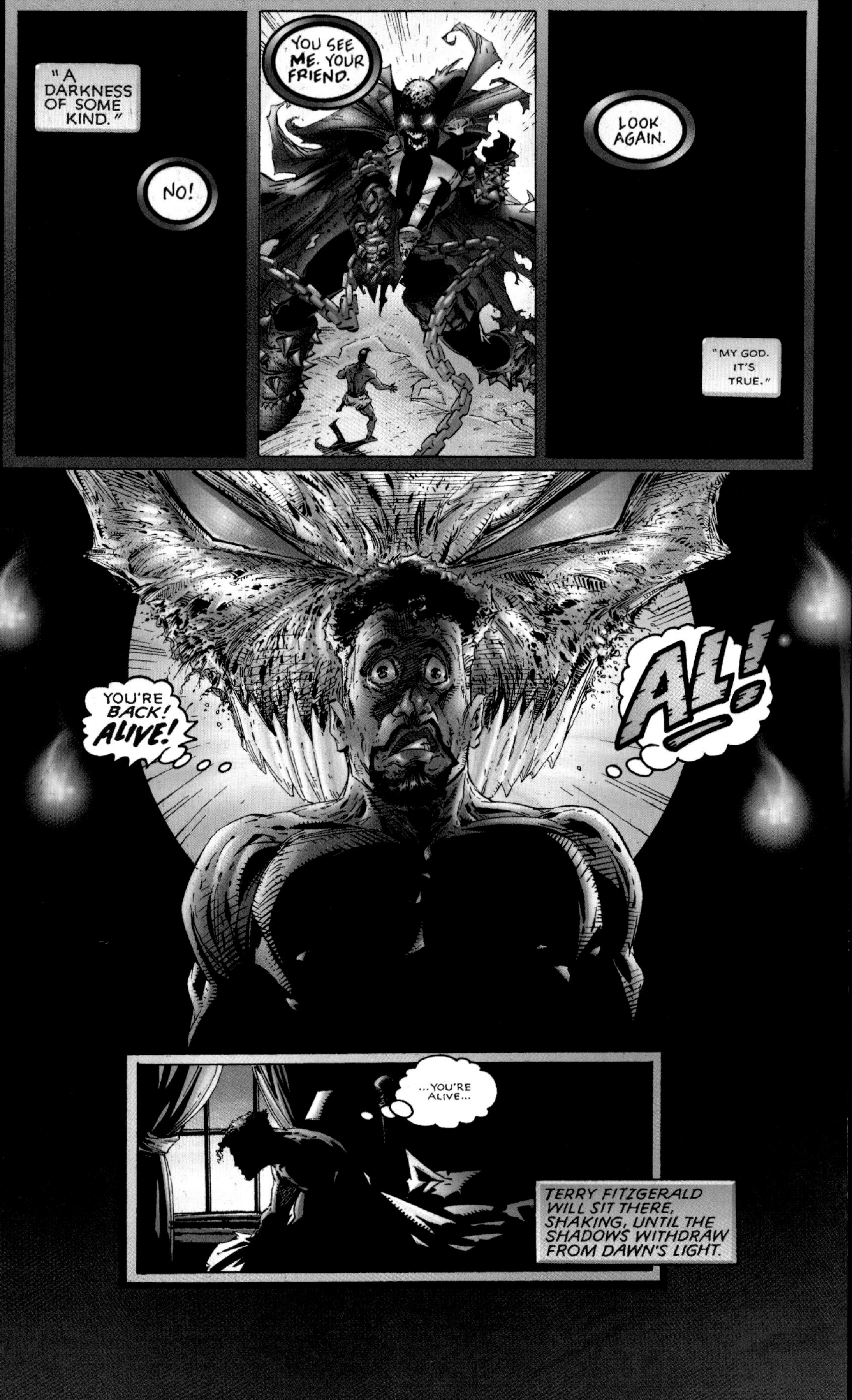
"A DARKNESS OF SOME KIND."
NO!
YOU SEE ME. YOUR FRIEND.
LOOK AGAIN.
"MY GOD. IT'S TRUE."
YOU'RE BACK! ALIVE!
AL!
...YOU'RE ALIVE...
TERRY FITZGERALD WILL SIT THERE, SHAKING, UNTIL THE SHADOWS WITHDRAW FROM DAWN'S LIGHT.

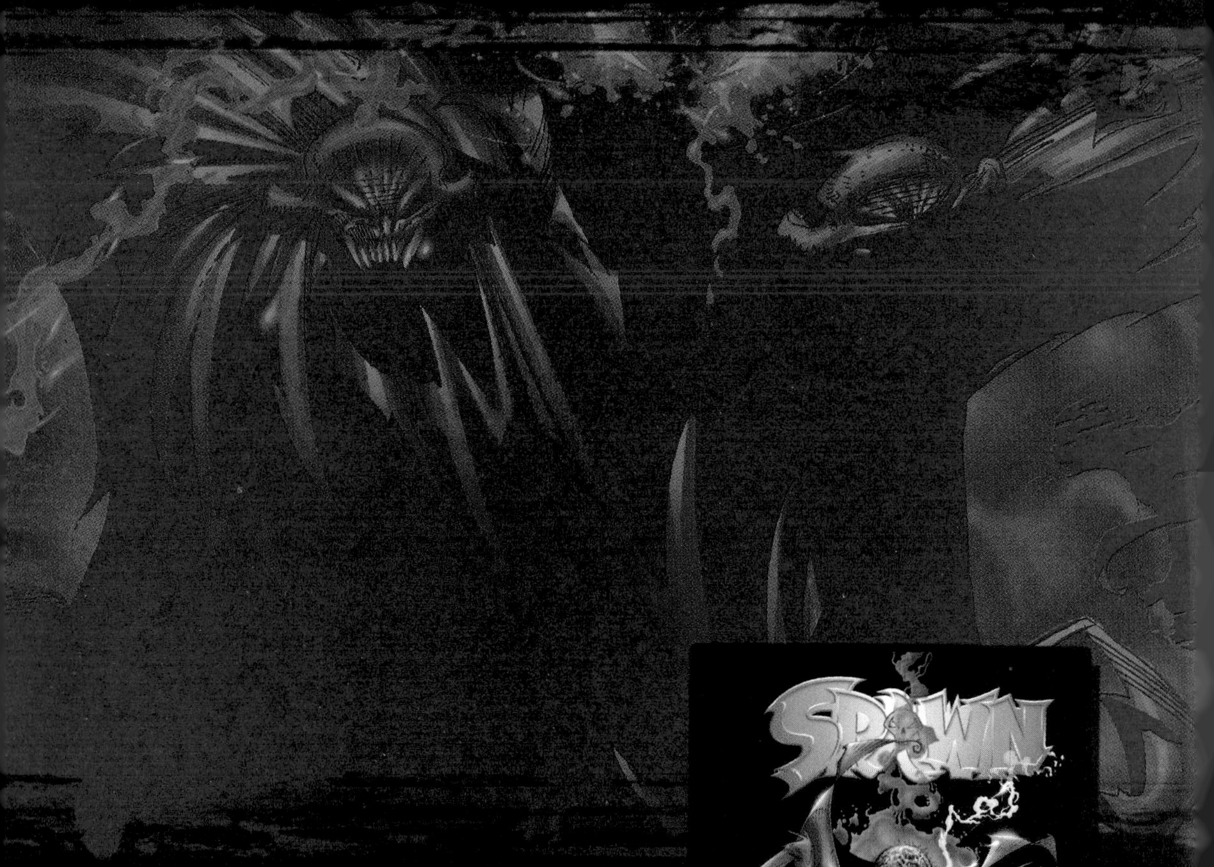

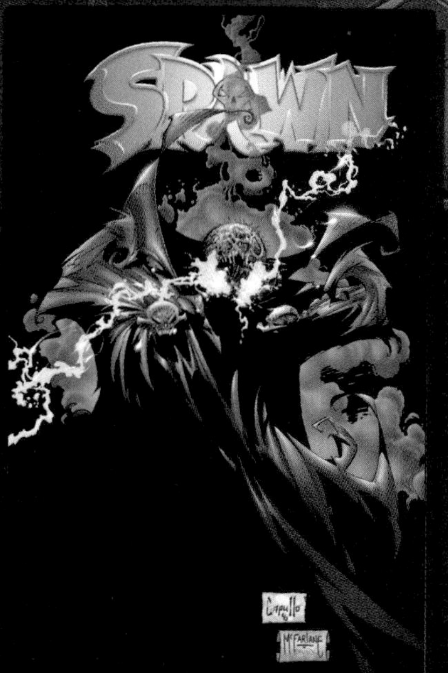

ISSUE FIFTY-FOUR

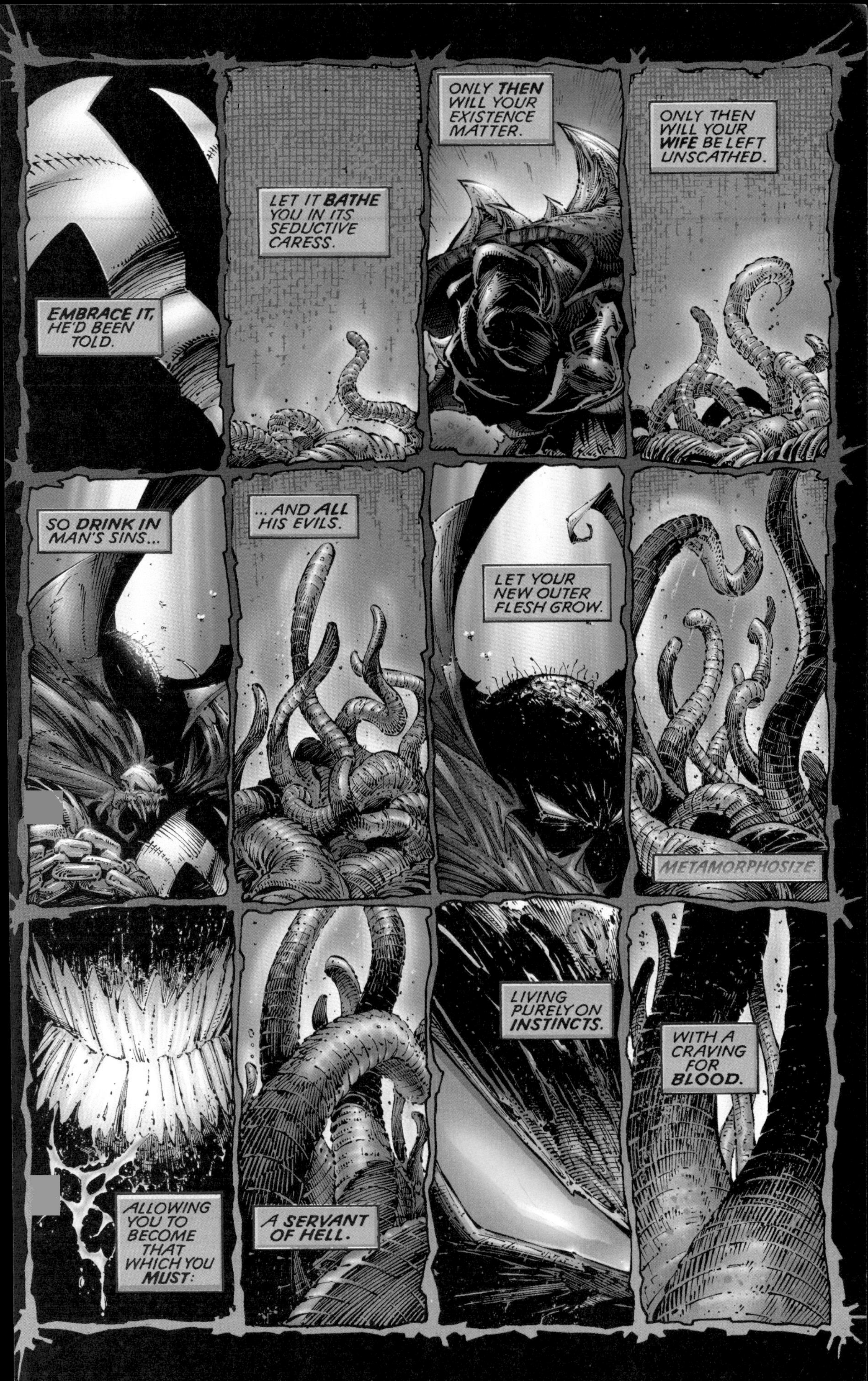
EMBRACE IT, HE'D BEEN TOLD.
LET IT BATHE YOU IN ITS SEDUCTIVE CARESS.
ONLY THEN WILL YOUR EXISTENCE MATTER.
ONLY THEN WILL YOUR WIFE BE LEFT UNSCATHED.
SO DRINK IN MAN'S SINS...
...AND ALL HIS EVILS.
LET YOUR NEW OUTER FLESH GROW.
METAMORPHOSIZE.
ALLOWING YOU TO BECOME THAT WHICH YOU MUST:
A SERVANT OF HELL.
LIVING PURELY ON INSTINCTS.
WITH A CRAVING FOR BLOOD.

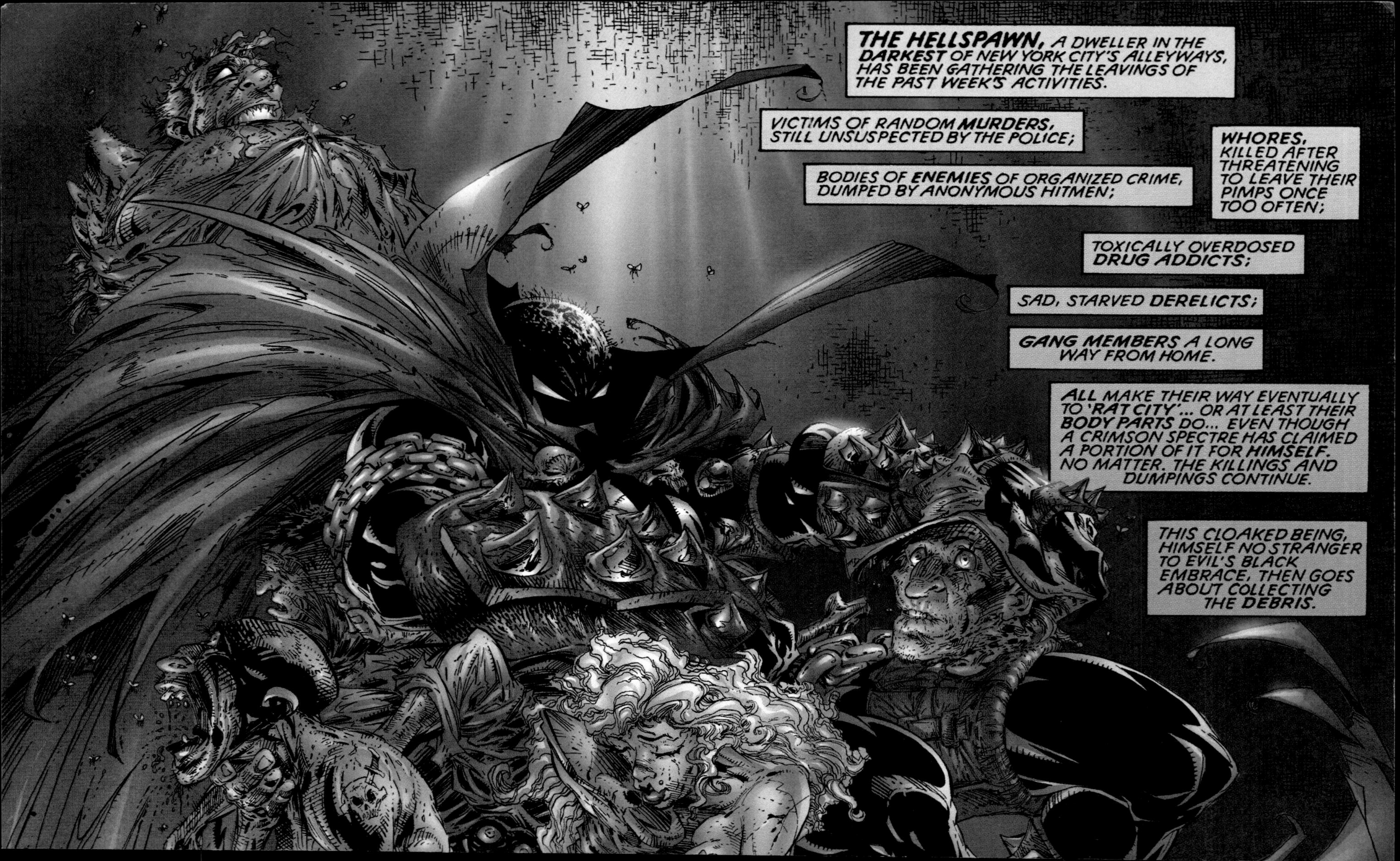
THE HELLSPAWN, A DWELLER IN THE DARKEST OF NEW YORK CITY'S ALLEYWAYS, HAS BEEN GATHERING THE LEAVINGS OF THE PAST WEEK'S ACTIVITIES.
VICTIMS OF RANDOM MURDERS, STILL UNSUSPECTED BY THE POLICE;
BODIES OF ENEMIES OF ORGANIZED CRIME, DUMPED BY ANONYMOUS HITMEN;
WHORES, KILLED AFTER THREATENING TO LEAVE THEIR PIMPS ONCE TOO OFTEN;
TOXICALLY OVERDOSED DRUG ADDICTS;
SAD, STARVED DERELICTS;
GANG MEMBERS A LONG WAY FROM HOME.
ALL MAKE THEIR WAY EVENTUALLY TO 'RAT CITY'... OR AT LEAST THEIR BODY PARTS DO... EVEN THOUGH A CRIMSON SPECTRE HAS CLAIMED A PORTION OF IT FOR HIMSELF. NO MATTER. THE KILLINGS AND DUMPINGS CONTINUE.
THIS CLOAKED BEING, HIMSELF NO STRANGER TO EVIL'S BLACK EMBRACE, THEN GOES ABOUT COLLECTING THE DEBRIS.

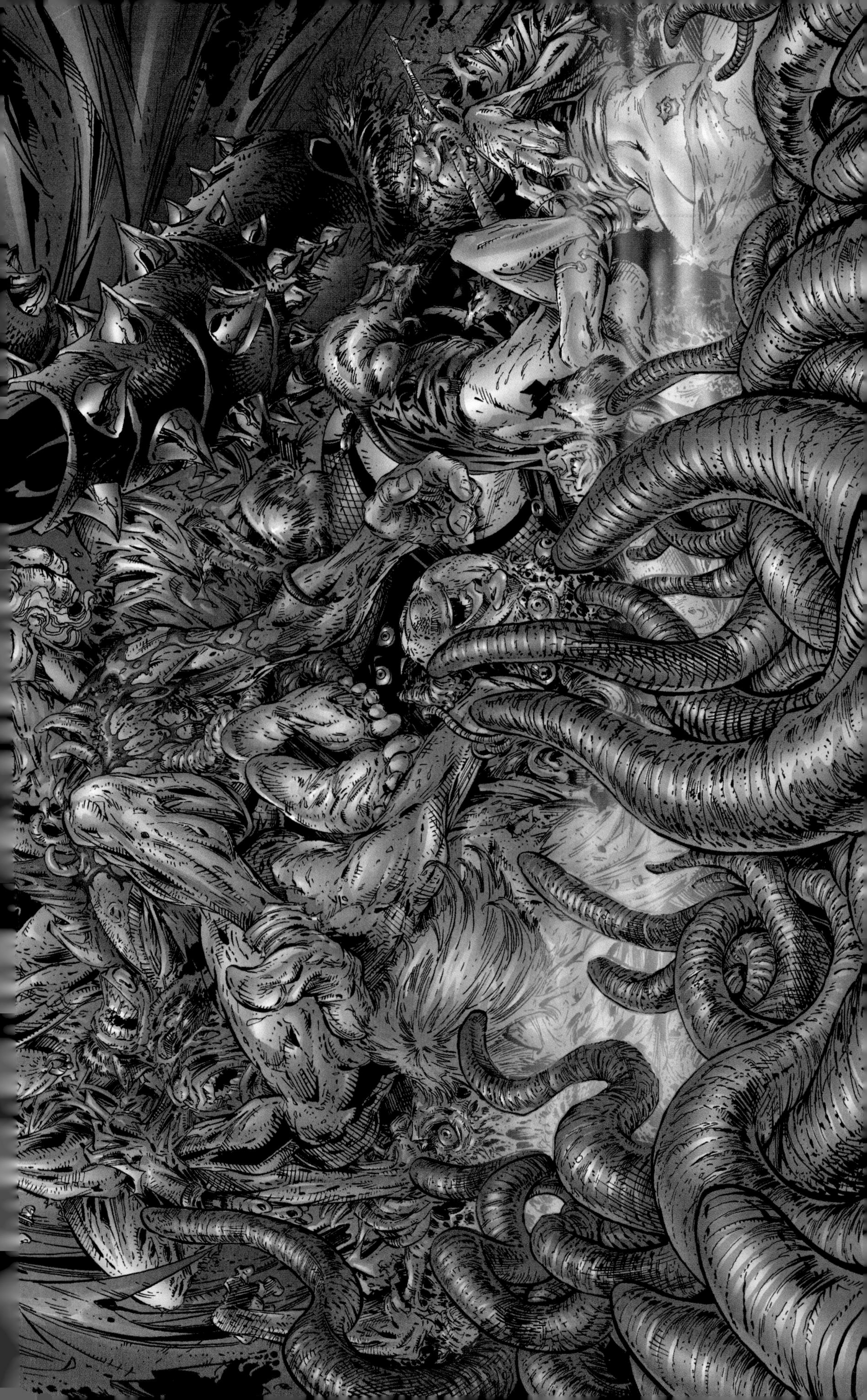

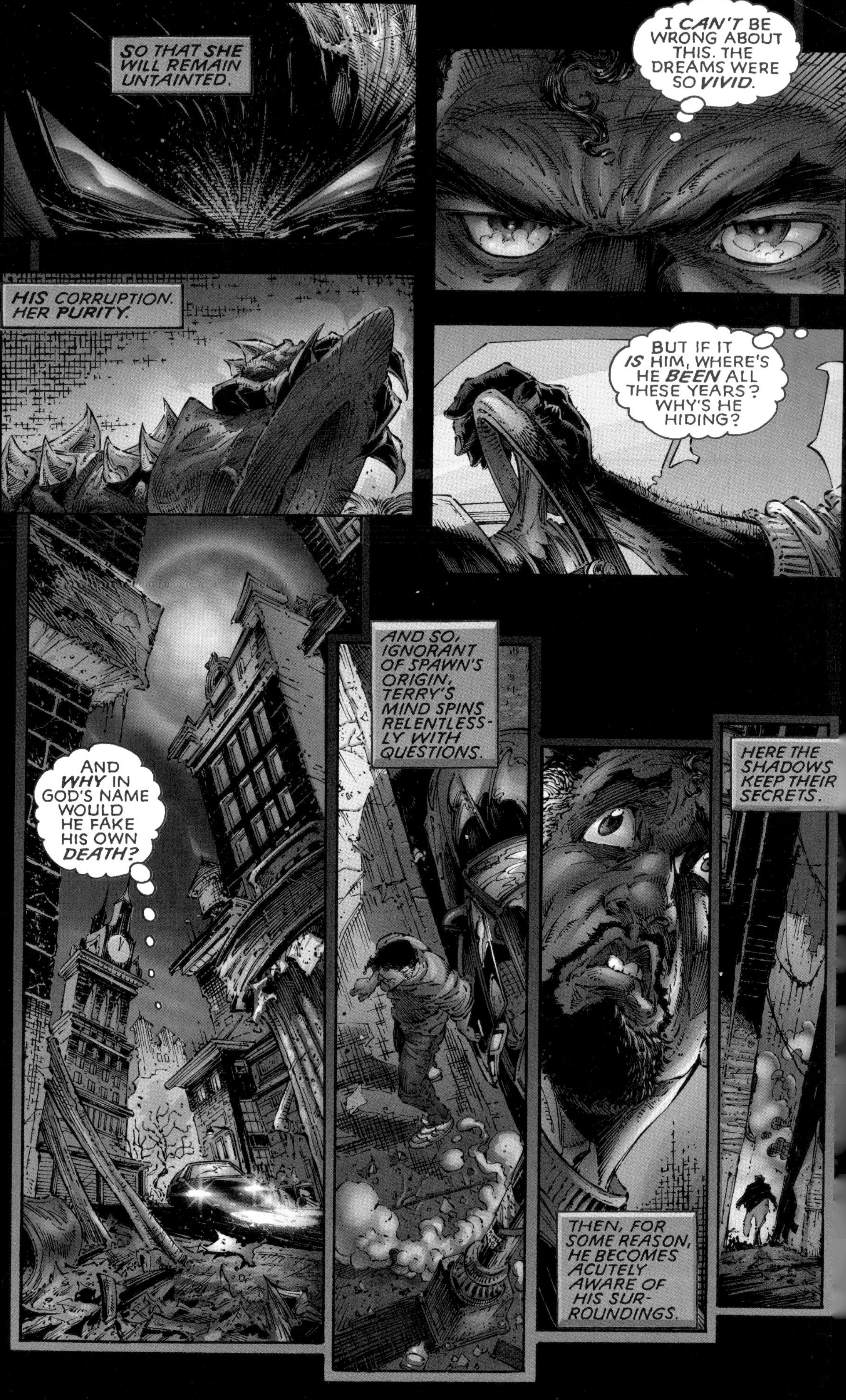
SO THAT SHE WILL REMAIN UNTAINTED.
I CAN'T BE WRONG ABOUT THIS. THE DREAMS WERE SO VIVID.
HIS CORRUPTION. HER PURITY.
BUT IF IT IS HIM, WHERE'S HE BEEN ALL THESE YEARS? WHY'S HE HIDING?
AND WHY IN GOD'S NAME WOULD HE FAKE HIS OWN DEATH?
AND SO, IGNORANT OF SPAWN'S ORIGIN, TERRY'S MIND SPINS RELENTLESS-LY WITH QUESTIONS.
THEN, FOR SOME REASON, HE BECOMES ACUTELY AWARE OF HIS SUR-ROUNDINGS.
HERE THE SHADOWS KEEP THEIR SECRETS.

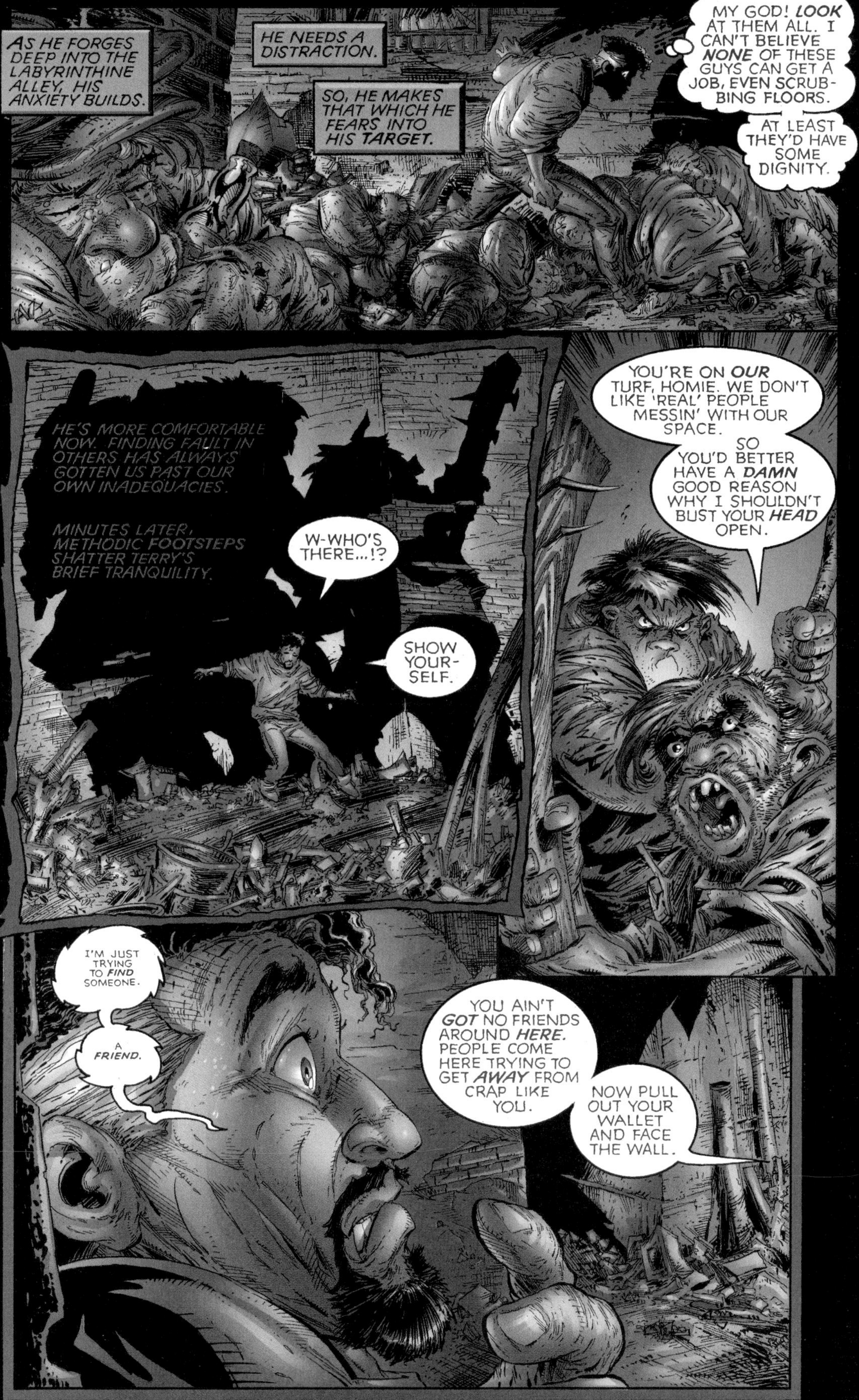

AS HE FORGES DEEP INTO THE LABYRINTHINE ALLEY, HIS ANXIETY BUILDS.
HE NEEDS A DISTRACTION.
SO, HE MAKES THAT WHICH HE FEARS INTO HIS TARGET.
MY GOD! LOOK AT THEM ALL. I CAN'T BELIEVE NONE OF THESE GUYS CAN GET A JOB, EVEN SCRUB-BING FLOORS.
AT LEAST THEY'D HAVE SOME DIGNITY.
HE'S MORE COMFORTABLE NOW. FINDING FAULT IN OTHERS HAS ALWAYS GOTTEN US PAST OUR OWN INADEQUACIES.
MINUTES LATER, METHODIC FOOTSTEPS SHATTER TERRY'S BRIEF TRANQUILITY.
W-WHO'S THERE...!?
SHOW YOUR-SELF.
YOU'RE ON OUR TURF, HOMIE. WE DON'T LIKE 'REAL' PEOPLE MESSIN' WITH OUR SPACE.
SO YOU'D BETTER HAVE A DAMN GOOD REASON WHY I SHOULDN'T BUST YOUR HEAD OPEN.
I'M JUST TRYING TO FIND SOMEONE.
A FRIEND.
YOU AIN'T GOT NO FRIENDS AROUND HERE. PEOPLE COME HERE TRYING TO GET AWAY FROM CRAP LIKE YOU.
NOW PULL OUT YOUR WALLET AND FACE THE WALL.

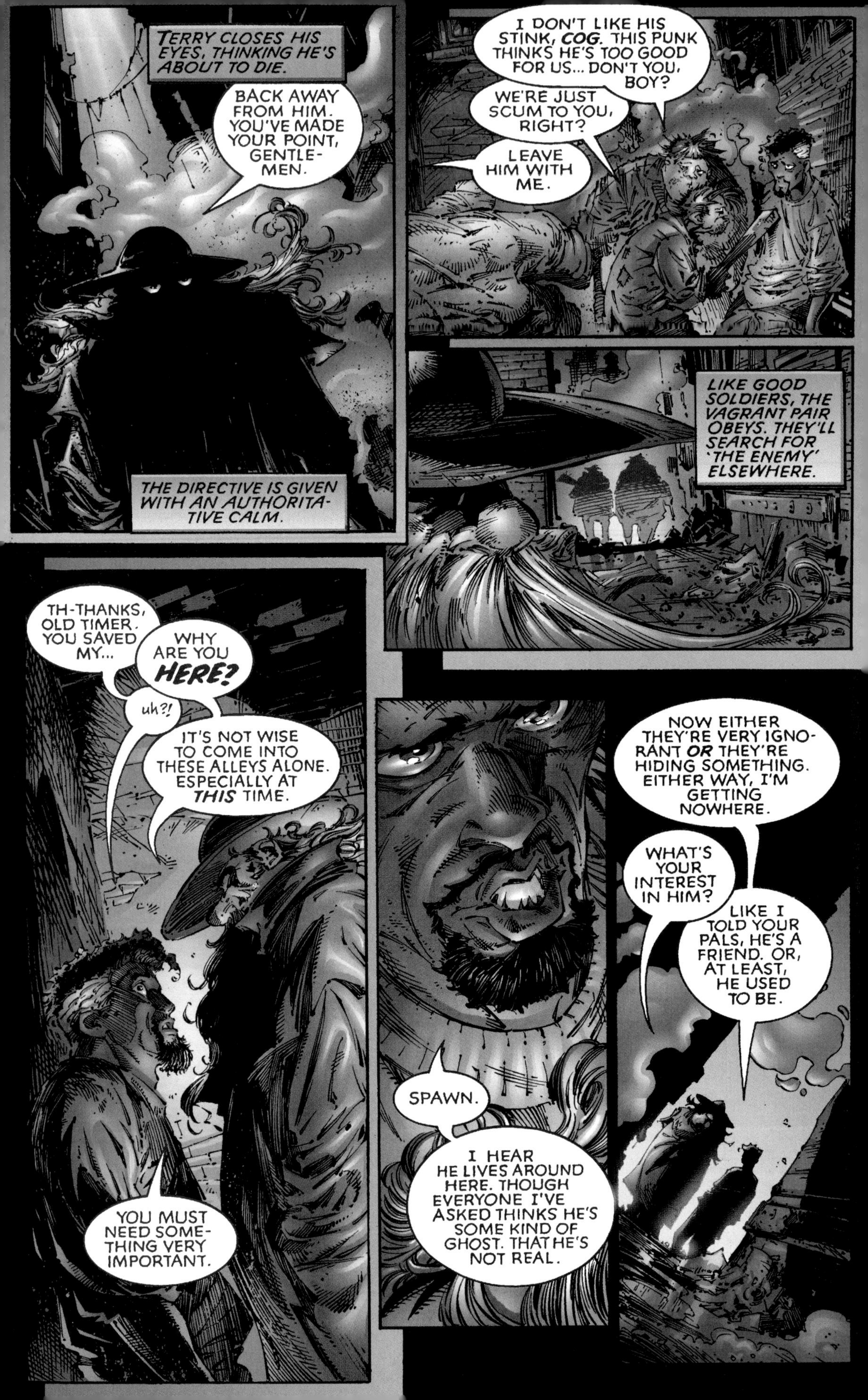
TERRY CLOSES HIS EYES, THINKING HE'S ABOUT TO DIE.
BACK AWAY FROM HIM. YOU'VE MADE YOUR POINT, GENTLE-MEN.
THE DIRECTIVE IS GIVEN WITH AN AUTHORITA-TIVE CALM.
I DON'T LIKE HIS STINK, COG. THIS PUNK THINKS HE'S TOO GOOD FOR US... DON'T YOU, BOY?
WE'RE JUST SCUM TO YOU, RIGHT?
LEAVE HIM WITH ME.
LIKE GOOD SOLDIERS, THE VAGRANT PAIR OBEYS. THEY'LL SEARCH FOR 'THE ENEMY' ELSEWHERE.
TH-THANKS, OLD TIMER. YOU SAVED MY...
WHY ARE YOU HERE?
uh?!
IT'S NOT WISE TO COME INTO THESE ALLEYS ALONE. ESPECIALLY AT THIS TIME.
YOU MUST NEED SOME-THING VERY IMPORTANT.
SPAWN.
I HEAR HE LIVES AROUND HERE. THOUGH EVERYONE I'VE ASKED THINKS HE'S SOME KIND OF GHOST. THAT HE'S NOT REAL.
NOW EITHER THEY'RE VERY IGNO-RANT OR THEY'RE HIDING SOMETHING. EITHER WAY, I'M GETTING NOWHERE.
WHAT'S YOUR INTEREST IN HIM?
LIKE I TOLD YOUR PALS, HE'S A FRIEND. OR, AT LEAST, HE USED TO BE.

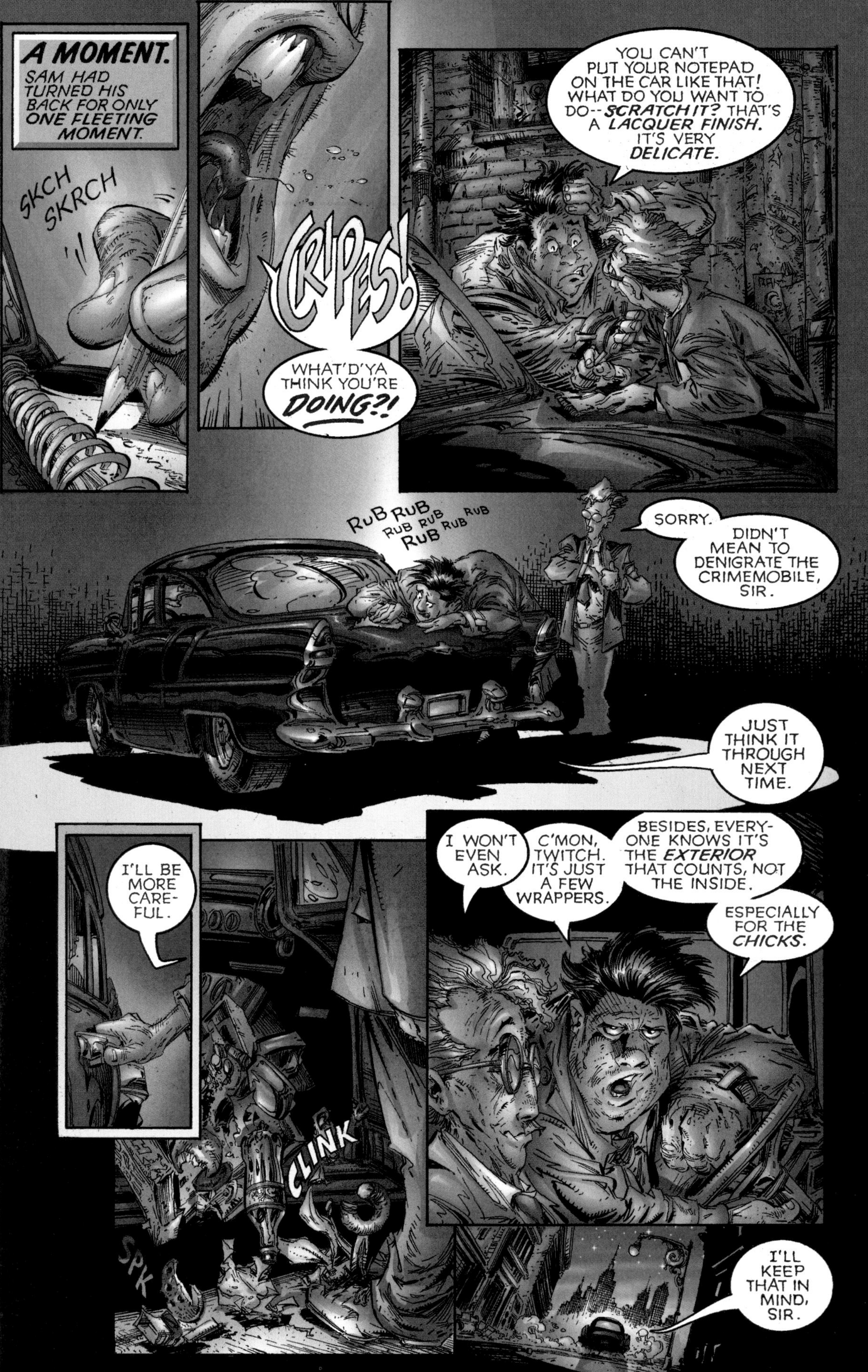
A MOMENT.
SAM HAD TURNED HIS BACK FOR ONLY ONE FLEETING MOMENT.
SKCH SKRCH
CRIPES!
WHAT'D'YA THINK YOU'RE DOING?!
YOU CAN'T PUT YOUR NOTEPAD ON THE CAR LIKE THAT! WHAT DO YOU WANT TO DO--SCRATCH IT? THAT'S A LACQUER FINISH. IT'S VERY DELICATE.
RUB RUB RUB RUB RUB RUB RUB
SORRY.
DIDN'T MEAN TO DENIGRATE THE CRIMEMOBILE, SIR.
JUST THINK IT THROUGH NEXT TIME.
I'LL BE MORE CARE-FUL.
I WON'T EVEN ASK.
C'MON, TWITCH. IT'S JUST A FEW WRAPPERS.
BESIDES, EVERY-ONE KNOWS IT'S THE EXTERIOR THAT COUNTS, NOT THE INSIDE.
ESPECIALLY FOR THE CHICKS.
CLINK
SPK
I'LL KEEP THAT IN MIND, SIR.

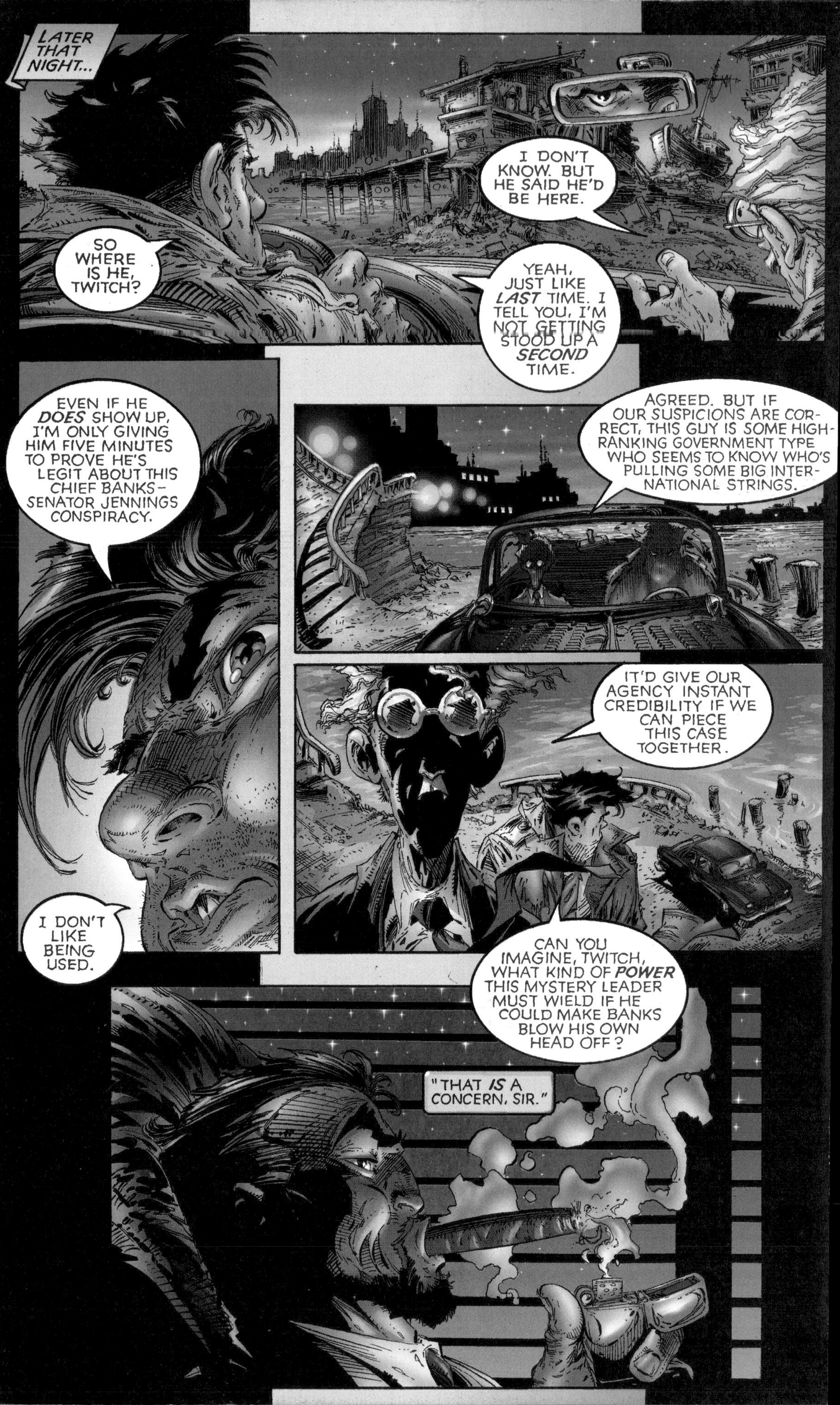
LATER THAT NIGHT...
SO WHERE IS HE, TWITCH?
I DON'T KNOW. BUT HE SAID HE'D BE HERE.
YEAH, JUST LIKE *LAST* TIME. I TELL YOU, I'M NOT GETTING STOOD UP A *SECOND* TIME.
EVEN IF HE *DOES* SHOW UP, I'M ONLY GIVING HIM FIVE MINUTES TO PROVE HE'S LEGIT ABOUT THIS CHIEF BANKS-SENATOR JENNINGS CONSPIRACY.
I DON'T LIKE BEING USED.
AGREED. BUT IF OUR SUSPICIONS ARE CORRECT, THIS GUY IS SOME HIGH-RANKING GOVERNMENT TYPE WHO SEEMS TO KNOW WHO'S PULLING SOME BIG INTERNATIONAL STRINGS.
IT'D GIVE OUR AGENCY INSTANT CREDIBILITY IF WE CAN PIECE THIS CASE TOGETHER.
CAN YOU IMAGINE, TWITCH, WHAT KIND OF *POWER* THIS MYSTERY LEADER MUST WIELD IF HE COULD MAKE BANKS BLOW HIS OWN HEAD OFF?
"THAT *IS* A CONCERN, SIR."

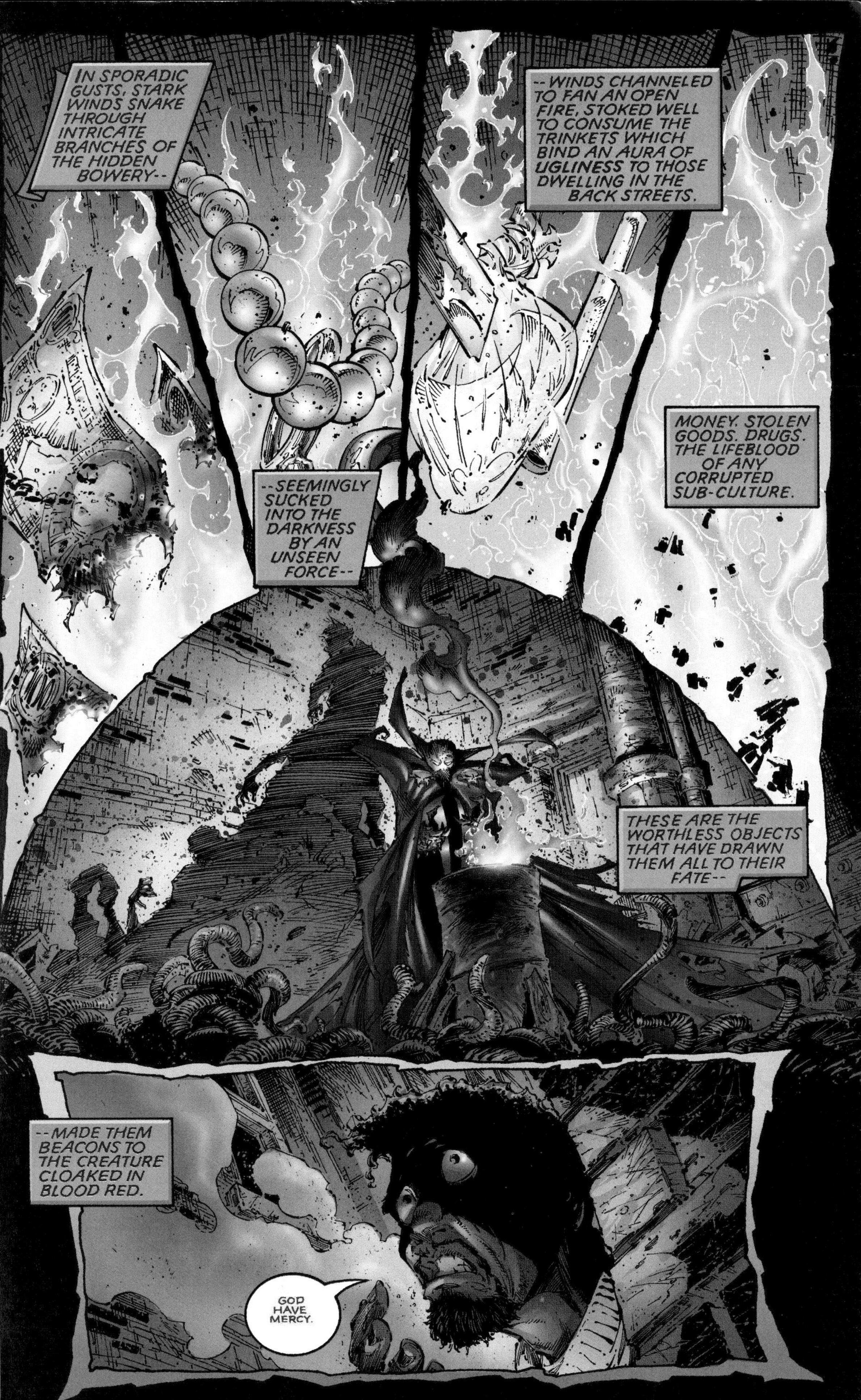
IN SPORADIC GUSTS, STARK WINDS SNAKE THROUGH INTRICATE BRANCHES OF THE HIDDEN BOWERY--
--WINDS CHANNELED TO FAN AN OPEN FIRE, STOKED WELL TO CONSUME THE TRINKETS WHICH BIND AN AURA OF UGLINESS TO THOSE DWELLING IN THE BACK STREETS.
--SEEMINGLY SUCKED INTO THE DARKNESS BY AN UNSEEN FORCE--
MONEY. STOLEN GOODS. DRUGS. THE LIFEBLOOD OF ANY CORRUPTED SUB-CULTURE.
THESE ARE THE WORTHLESS OBJECTS THAT HAVE DRAWN THEM ALL TO THEIR FATE--
--MADE THEM BEACONS TO THE CREATURE CLOAKED IN BLOOD RED.
GOD HAVE MERCY.

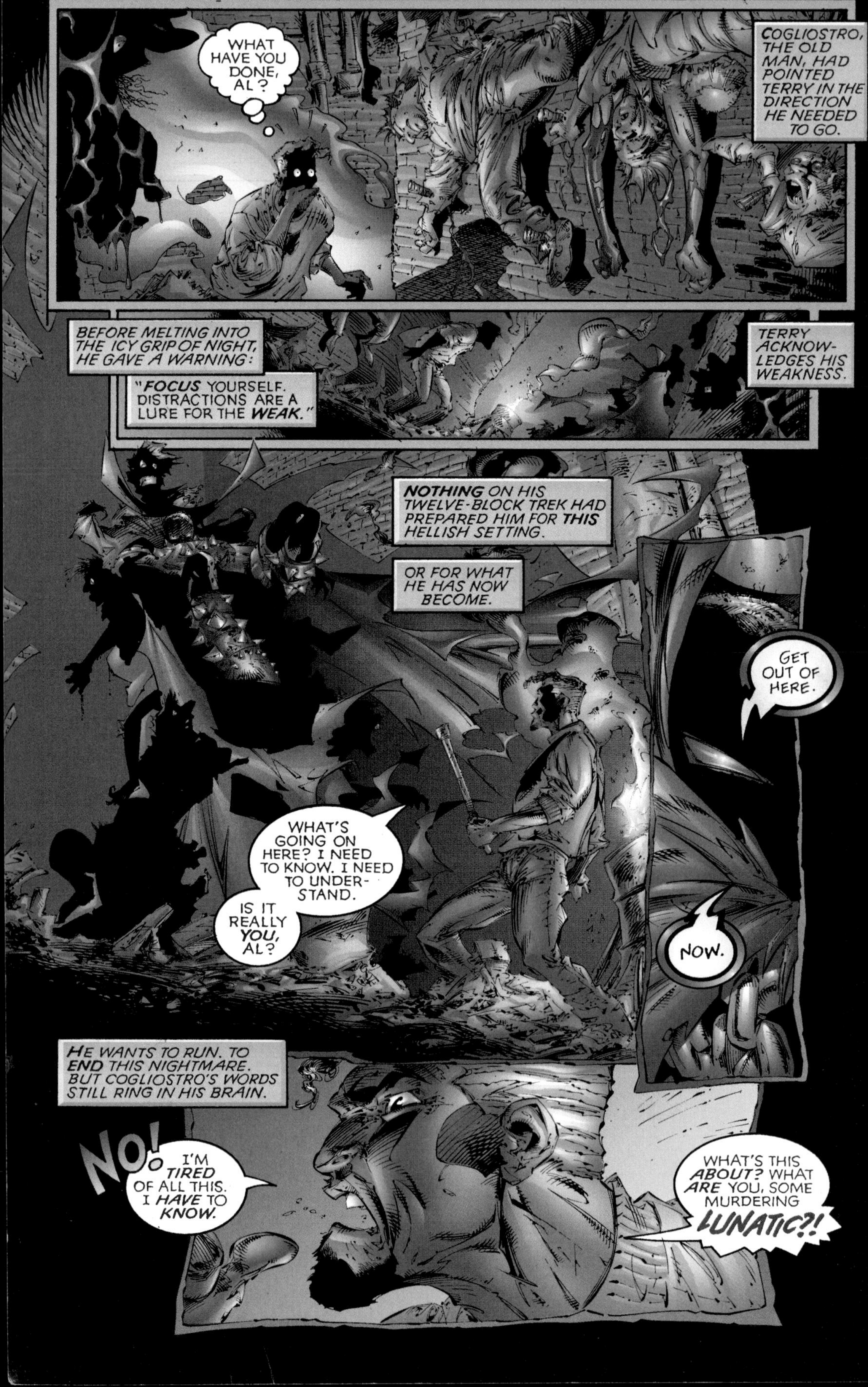
WHAT HAVE YOU DONE, AL?
COGLIOSTRO, THE OLD MAN, HAD POINTED TERRY IN THE DIRECTION HE NEEDED TO GO.
BEFORE MELTING INTO THE ICY GRIP OF NIGHT, HE GAVE A WARNING:
"FOCUS YOURSELF. DISTRACTIONS ARE A LURE FOR THE WEAK."
TERRY ACKNOWLEDGES HIS WEAKNESS.
NOTHING ON HIS TWELVE-BLOCK TREK HAD PREPARED HIM FOR THIS HELLISH SETTING.
OR FOR WHAT HE HAS NOW BECOME.
WHAT'S GOING ON HERE? I NEED TO KNOW. I NEED TO UNDERSTAND.
IS IT REALLY YOU, AL?
GET OUT OF HERE.
NOW.
HE WANTS TO RUN. TO END THIS NIGHTMARE. BUT COGLIOSTRO'S WORDS STILL RING IN HIS BRAIN.
NO!
I'M TIRED OF ALL THIS. I HAVE TO KNOW.
WHAT'S THIS ABOUT? WHAT ARE YOU, SOME MURDERING LUNATIC?!

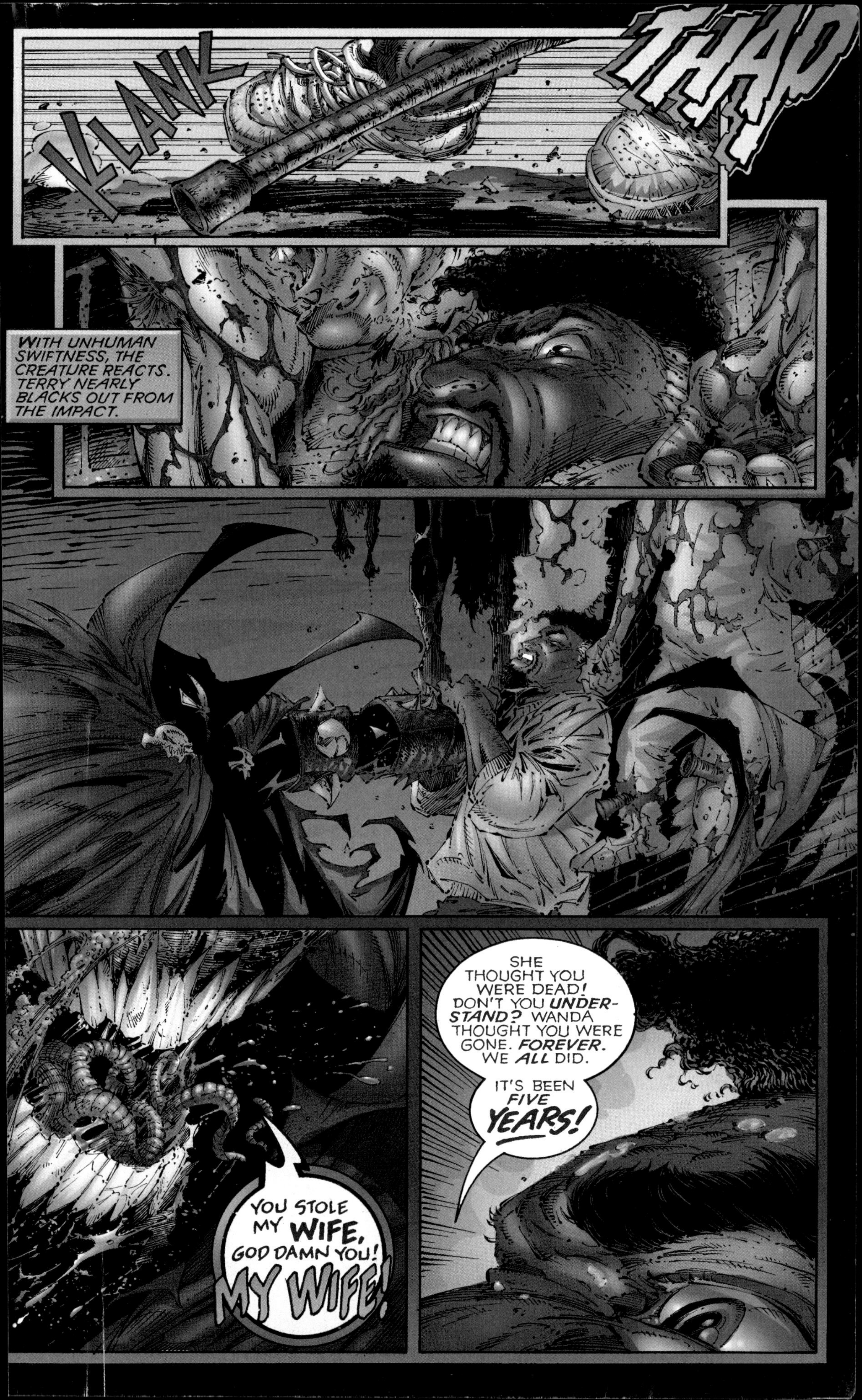
KLANK
THAP
WITH UNHUMAN SWIFTNESS, THE CREATURE REACTS. TERRY NEARLY BLACKS OUT FROM THE IMPACT.
YOU STOLE MY WIFE, GOD DAMN YOU! MY WIFE!
SHE THOUGHT YOU WERE DEAD! DON'T YOU UNDER-STAND? WANDA THOUGHT YOU WERE GONE. FOREVER. WE ALL DID.
IT'S BEEN FIVE YEARS!

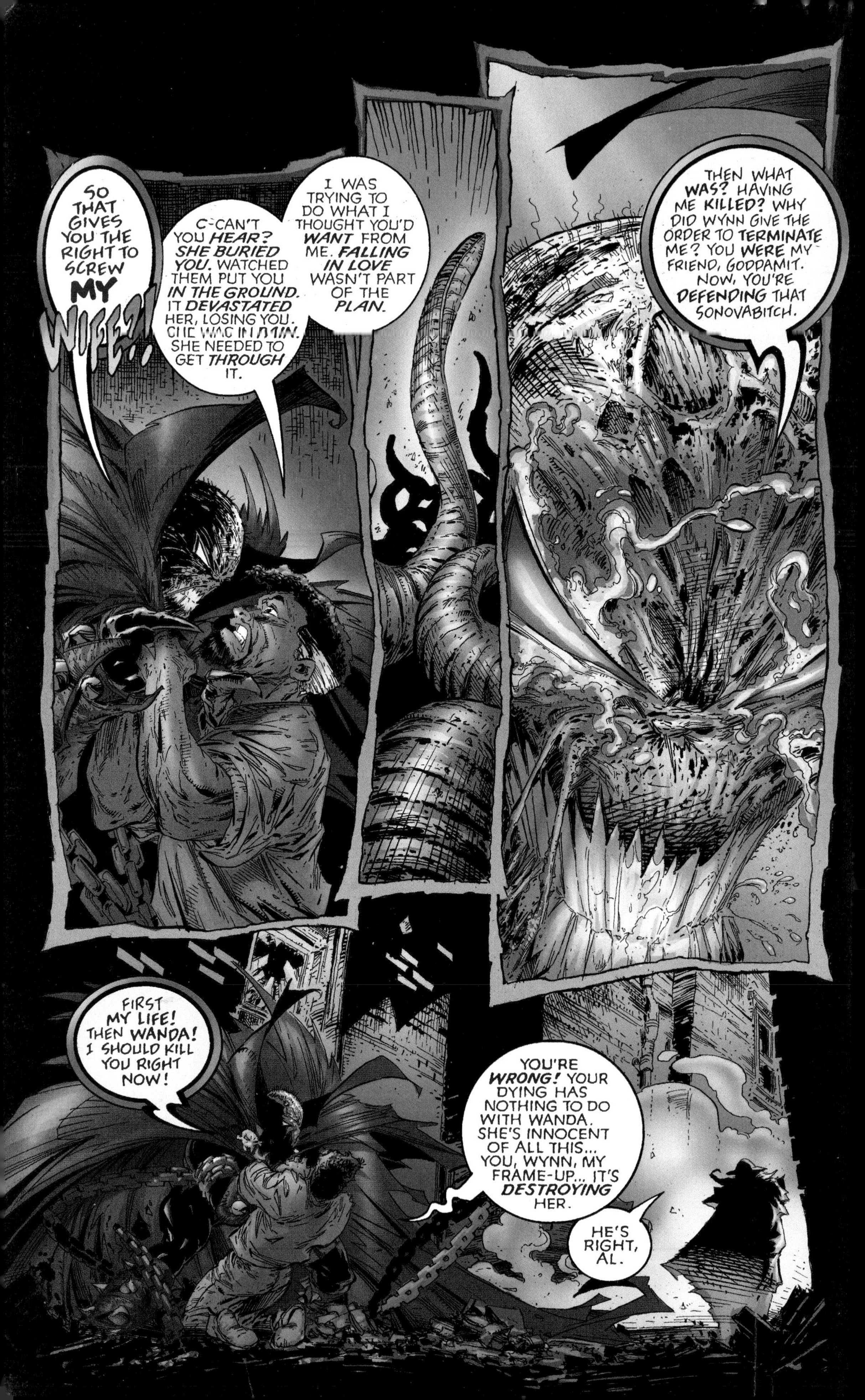
SO THAT GIVES YOU THE RIGHT TO SCREW MY WIFE?!
C-CAN'T YOU HEAR? SHE BURIED YOU. WATCHED THEM PUT YOU IN THE GROUND. IT DEVASTATED HER, LOSING YOU. SHE WAS IN PAIN. SHE NEEDED TO GET THROUGH IT.
I WAS TRYING TO DO WHAT I THOUGHT YOU'D WANT FROM ME. FALLING IN LOVE WASN'T PART OF THE PLAN.
THEN WHAT WAS? HAVING ME KILLED? WHY DID WYNN GIVE THE ORDER TO TERMINATE ME? YOU WERE MY FRIEND, GODDAMIT. NOW, YOU'RE DEFENDING THAT SONOVABITCH.
FIRST MY LIFE! THEN WANDA! I SHOULD KILL YOU RIGHT NOW!
YOU'RE WRONG! YOUR DYING HAS NOTHING TO DO WITH WANDA. SHE'S INNOCENT OF ALL THIS... YOU, WYNN, MY FRAME-UP... IT'S DESTROYING HER.
HE'S RIGHT, AL.

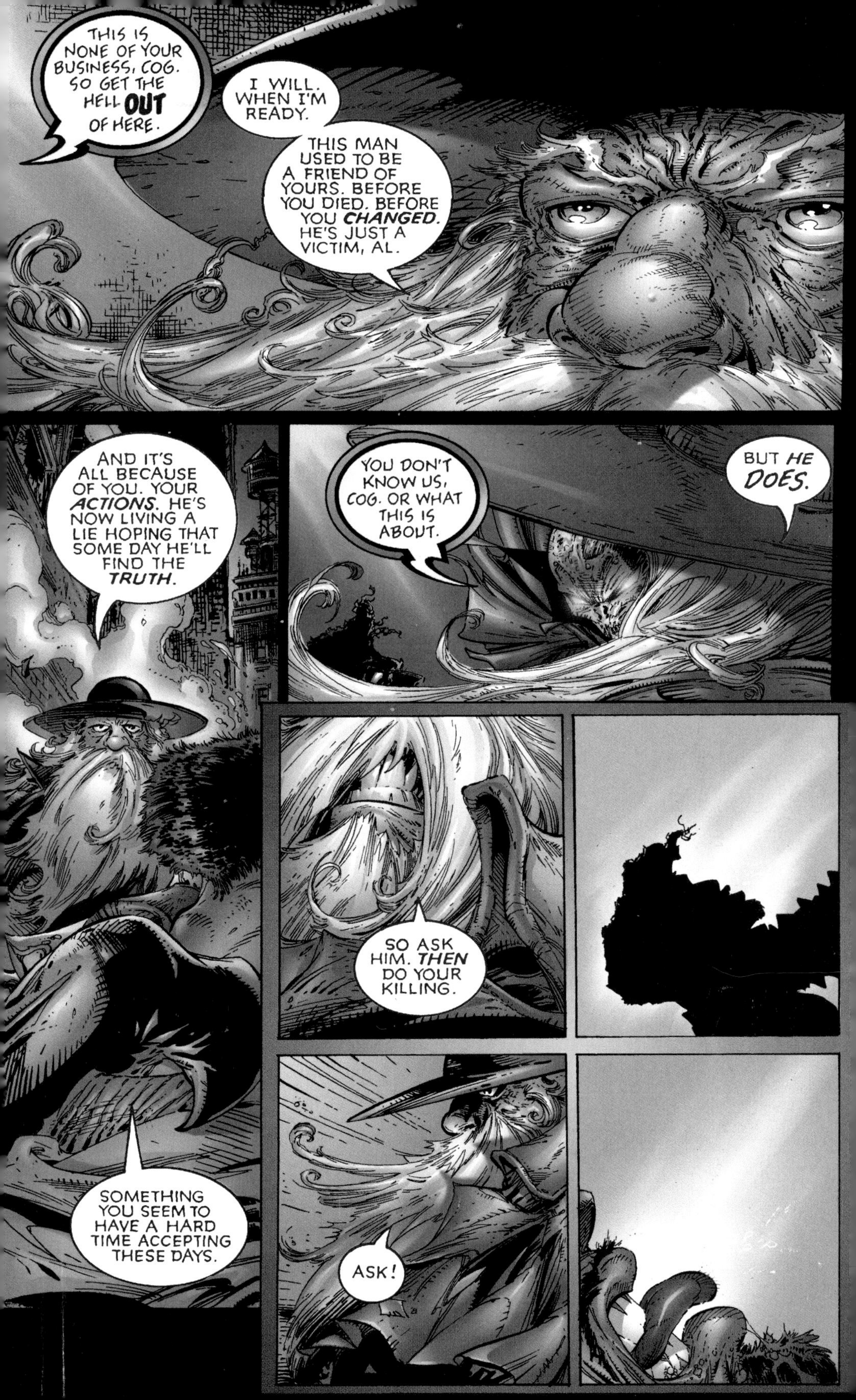
THIS IS NONE OF YOUR BUSINESS, COG. SO GET THE HELL OUT OF HERE.
I WILL. WHEN I'M READY.
THIS MAN USED TO BE A FRIEND OF YOURS. BEFORE YOU DIED. BEFORE YOU CHANGED. HE'S JUST A VICTIM, AL.
AND IT'S ALL BECAUSE OF YOU. YOUR ACTIONS. HE'S NOW LIVING A LIE HOPING THAT SOME DAY HE'LL FIND THE TRUTH.
SOMETHING YOU SEEM TO HAVE A HARD TIME ACCEPTING THESE DAYS.
YOU DON'T KNOW US, COG. OR WHAT THIS IS ABOUT.
BUT HE DOES.
SO ASK HIM. THEN DO YOUR KILLING.
ASK!

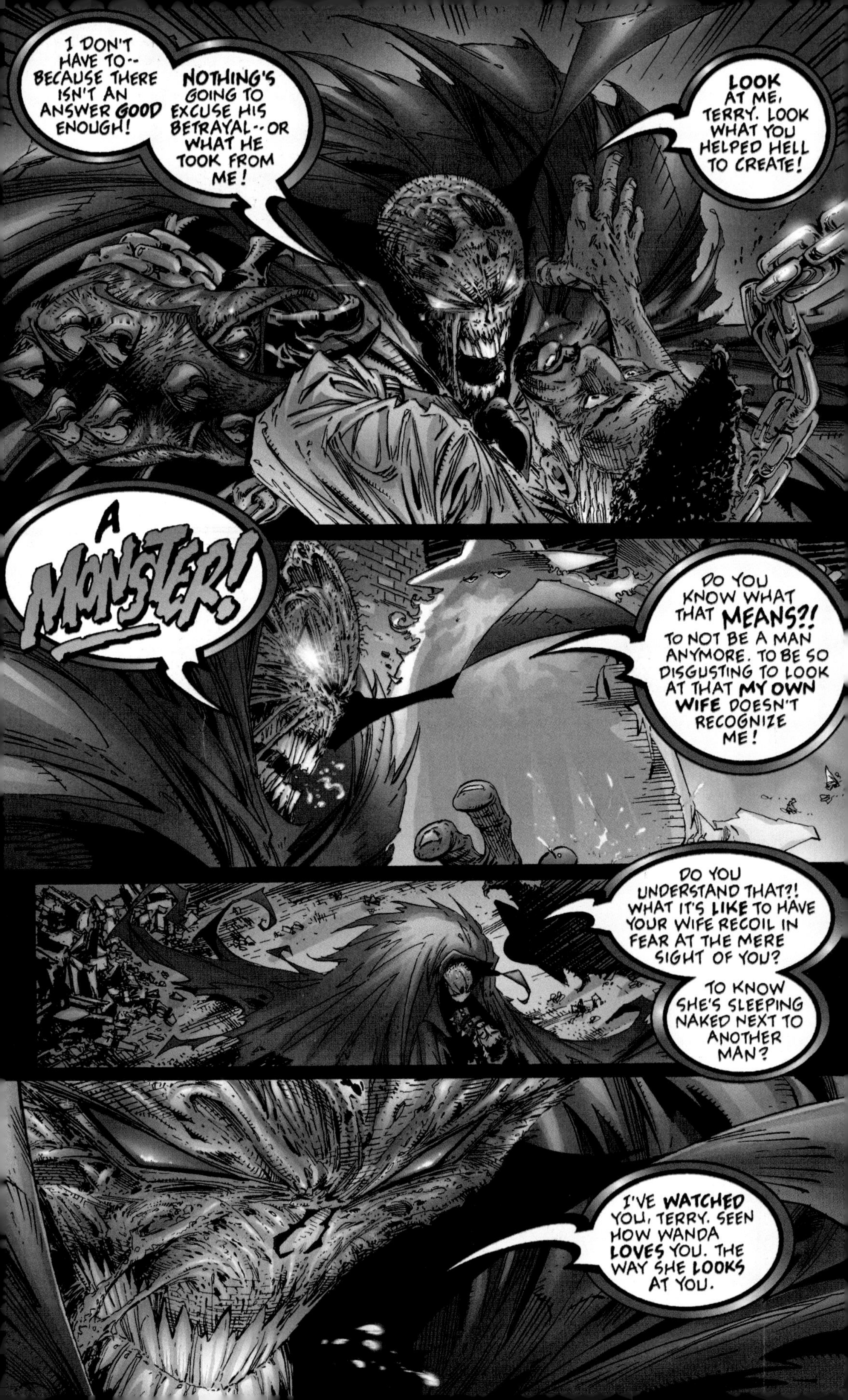
I DON'T HAVE TO-- BECAUSE THERE ISN'T AN ANSWER GOOD ENOUGH!
NOTHING'S GOING TO EXCUSE HIS BETRAYAL--OR WHAT HE TOOK FROM ME!
LOOK AT ME, TERRY. LOOK WHAT YOU HELPED HELL TO CREATE!
A MONSTER!
DO YOU KNOW WHAT THAT MEANS?! TO NOT BE A MAN ANYMORE. TO BE SO DISGUSTING TO LOOK AT THAT MY OWN WIFE DOESN'T RECOGNIZE ME!
DO YOU UNDERSTAND THAT?! WHAT IT'S LIKE TO HAVE YOUR WIFE RECOIL IN FEAR AT THE MERE SIGHT OF YOU?
TO KNOW SHE'S SLEEPING NAKED NEXT TO ANOTHER MAN?
I'VE WATCHED YOU, TERRY. SEEN HOW WANDA LOVES YOU. THE WAY SHE LOOKS AT YOU.

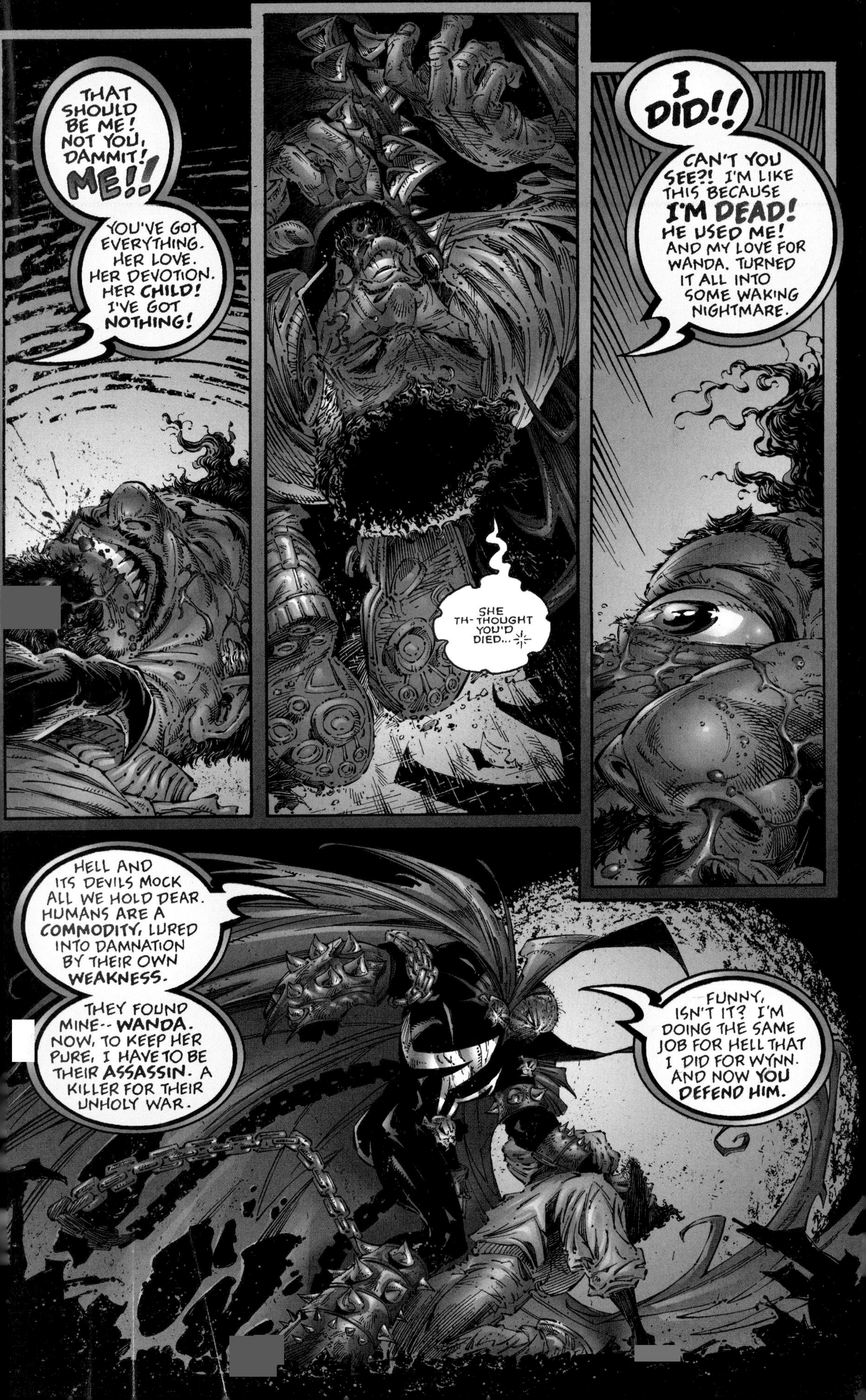
THAT SHOULD BE ME! NOT YOU, DAMMIT! ME!!
YOU'VE GOT EVERYTHING. HER LOVE. HER DEVOTION. HER CHILD! I'VE GOT NOTHING!
SHE TH-THOUGHT YOU'D DIED...
I DID!!
CAN'T YOU SEE?! I'M LIKE THIS BECAUSE I'M DEAD! HE USED ME! AND MY LOVE FOR WANDA. TURNED IT ALL INTO SOME WAKING NIGHTMARE.
HELL AND ITS DEVILS MOCK ALL WE HOLD DEAR. HUMANS ARE A COMMODITY, LURED INTO DAMNATION BY THEIR OWN WEAKNESS.
THEY FOUND MINE-- WANDA. NOW, TO KEEP HER PURE, I HAVE TO BE THEIR ASSASSIN. A KILLER FOR THEIR UNHOLY WAR.
FUNNY, ISN'T IT? I'M DOING THE SAME JOB FOR HELL THAT I DID FOR WYNN. AND NOW YOU DEFEND HIM.

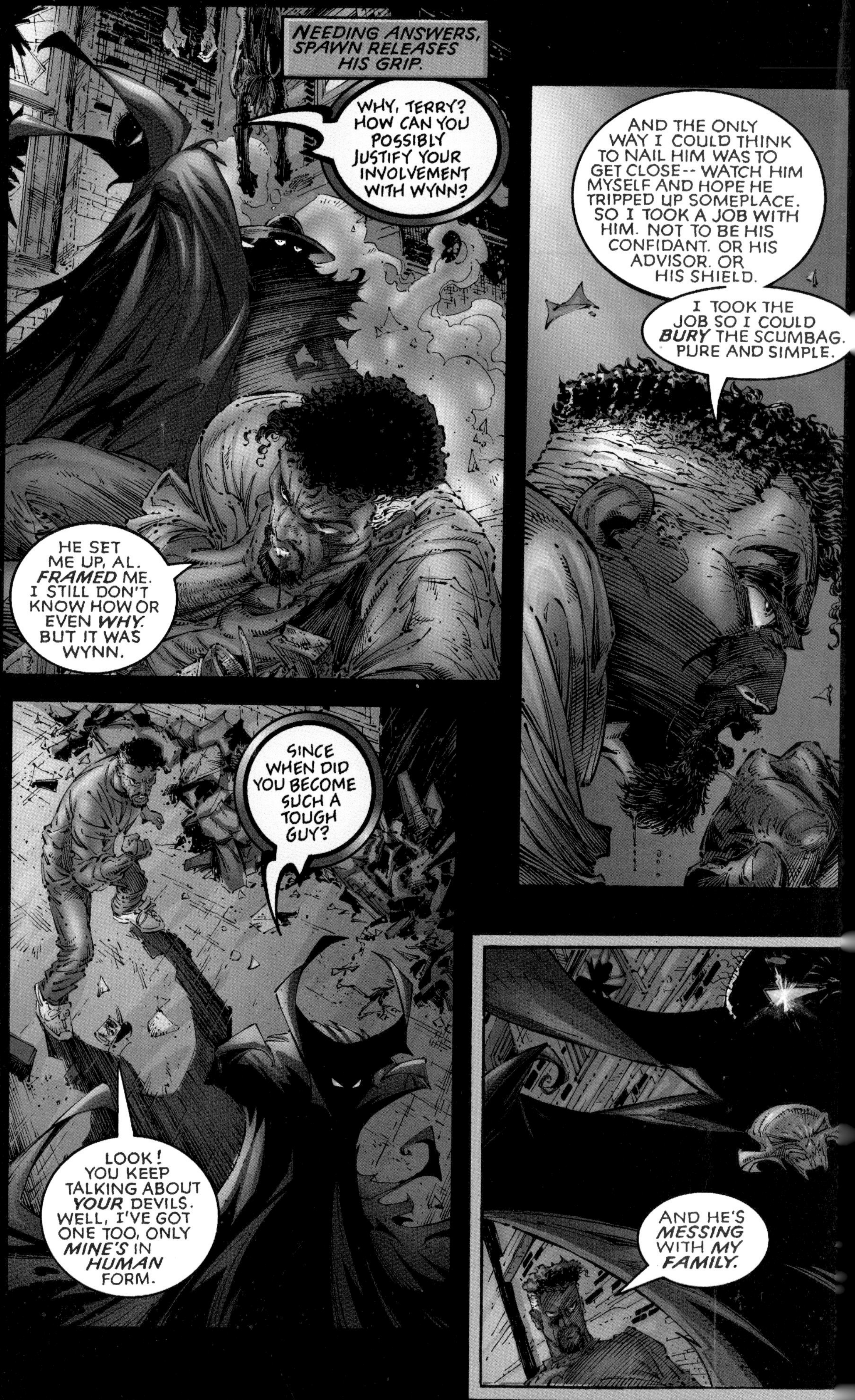
NEEDING ANSWERS, SPAWN RELEASES HIS GRIP.
WHY, TERRY? HOW CAN YOU POSSIBLY JUSTIFY YOUR INVOLVEMENT WITH WYNN?
HE SET ME UP, AL. FRAMED ME. I STILL DON'T KNOW HOW OR EVEN WHY. BUT IT WAS WYNN.
AND THE ONLY WAY I COULD THINK TO NAIL HIM WAS TO GET CLOSE-- WATCH HIM MYSELF AND HOPE HE TRIPPED UP SOMEPLACE. SO I TOOK A JOB WITH HIM. NOT TO BE HIS CONFIDANT. OR HIS ADVISOR. OR HIS SHIELD.
I TOOK THE JOB SO I COULD BURY THE SCUMBAG. PURE AND SIMPLE.
SINCE WHEN DID YOU BECOME SUCH A TOUGH GUY?
LOOK! YOU KEEP TALKING ABOUT YOUR DEVILS. WELL, I'VE GOT ONE TOO, ONLY MINE'S IN HUMAN FORM.
AND HE'S MESSING WITH MY FAMILY.

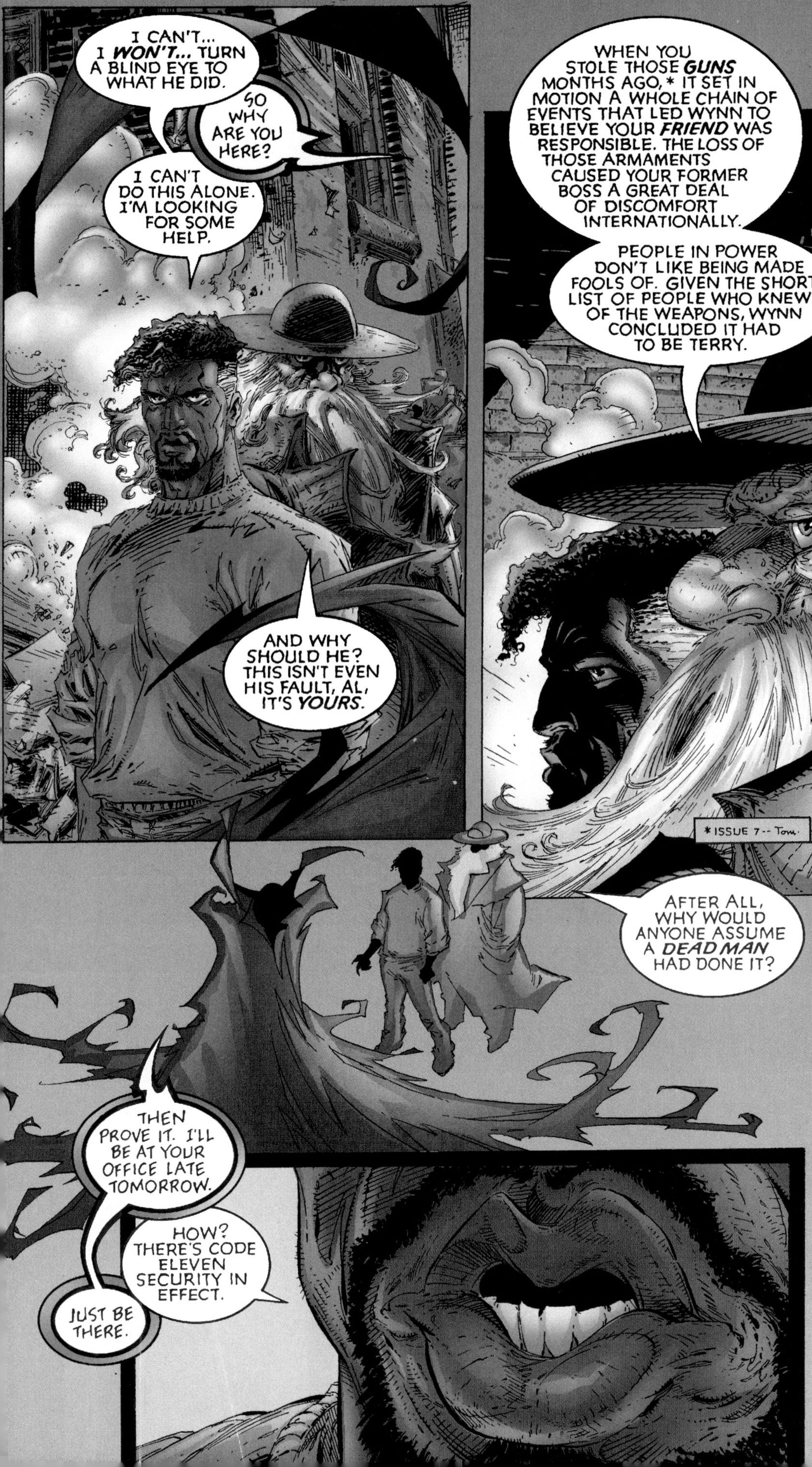
I CAN'T... I WON'T... TURN A BLIND EYE TO WHAT HE DID.
SO WHY ARE YOU HERE?
I CAN'T DO THIS ALONE. I'M LOOKING FOR SOME HELP.
AND WHY SHOULD HE? THIS ISN'T EVEN HIS FAULT, AL, IT'S YOURS.
WHEN YOU STOLE THOSE GUNS MONTHS AGO,* IT SET IN MOTION A WHOLE CHAIN OF EVENTS THAT LED WYNN TO BELIEVE YOUR FRIEND WAS RESPONSIBLE. THE LOSS OF THOSE ARMAMENTS CAUSED YOUR FORMER BOSS A GREAT DEAL OF DISCOMFORT INTERNATIONALLY.
PEOPLE IN POWER DON'T LIKE BEING MADE FOOLS OF. GIVEN THE SHORT LIST OF PEOPLE WHO KNEW OF THE WEAPONS, WYNN CONCLUDED IT HAD TO BE TERRY.
*ISSUE 7 -- Tom.
AFTER ALL, WHY WOULD ANYONE ASSUME A DEAD MAN HAD DONE IT?
THEN PROVE IT. I'LL BE AT YOUR OFFICE LATE TOMORROW.
HOW? THERE'S CODE ELEVEN SECURITY IN EFFECT.
JUST BE THERE.

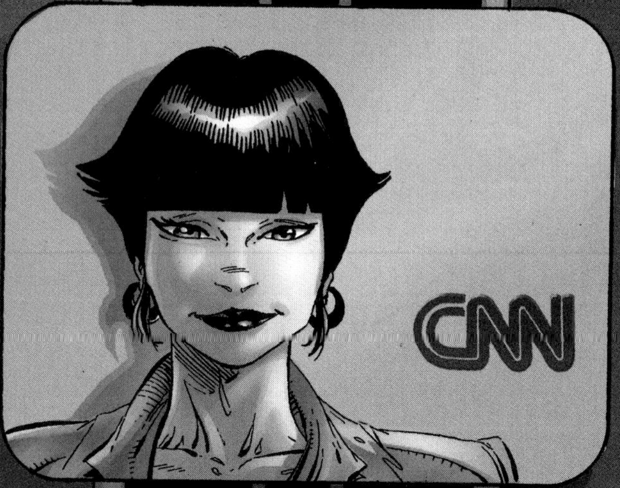
CNN

IN SAN FRANCISCO, THE DRUG ENFORCEMENT AGENCY HAS ARRESTED A PAIR OF MAJOR COCAINE IMPORTERS. NORVIN BLANDON AND DANILO MENESES, TWO COLUMBIAN NATIONALS, ARE BELIEVED TO HAVE DISTRIBUTED SEVERAL TONS OF COCAINE THROUGH BAY AREA STREET GANGS.

PROFITS ARE ALLEGED TO HAVE BEEN FUNNELLED TO A GUERILLA ARMY WHOSE LEADERS WERE GRADUATES OF THE C.I.A.-RUN "SCHOOL OF THE AMERICAS." BOTH MENESES AND BLANDON HAD BEEN EMPLOYED BY THE C.I.A. AS CIVILIAN LEADERS OF ANTI-COMMUNIST MILITIAS. THE HOUSE INTELLIGENCE COMMITTEE IS INVESTIGATING ANY POSSIBLE LINKS THERE, AS WELL AS WITH PARAMILITARY GROUPS IN TURKEY AND IRELAND, ACCORDING TO AN UNNAMED STATE DEPARTMENT SOURCE.

THE PAIR HAD FALLEN INTO DISFAVOR WITH THEIR COLUMBIAN SUPPLIERS OVER UNPAID DEBTS, ACCORDING TO THE SAME SOURCE.

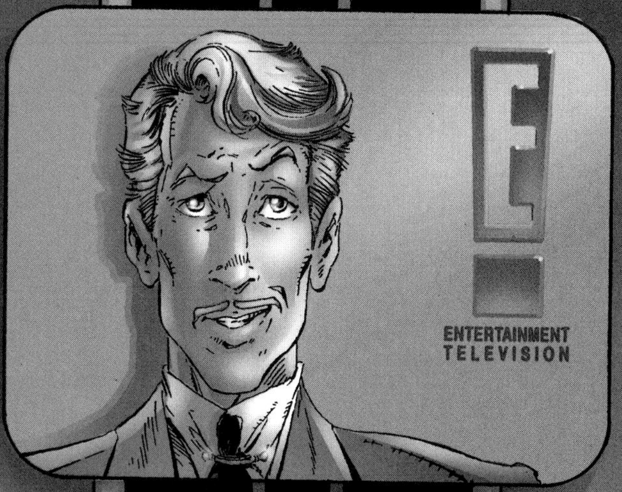
E!
ENTERTAINMENT TELEVISION

REGULAR VIEWERS KNOW MY FEELINGS ABOUT THE C.I.A. -- HOW I'VE BEGGED AND ***PLEADED*** WITH OUR GOVERNMENT TO PUT A LEASH ON THEM. THE AGENCY'S BLATANT MANIPULATION OF OUR OVERSEAS INTERESTS WILL HAVE REPERCUSSIONS WELL INTO OUR ***GRANDKIDS'*** LIFETIMES, ASSUMING THEY LIVE SO LONG AND EVEN HEAR ABOUT IT. THE ***BIGGEST*** CRISIS OF ALL IS THAT OUR EVER-DWINDLING CABAL OF ***MEDIA OUTLETS*** FOLLOWS THEIR LEAD IN THE SHIFTING PRIORITIES OF INTELLIGENCE GATHERING.

IN OTHER WORDS, ***OUR SPIES KEEP SWITCHING ENEMIES.*** IT'S AS THOUGH THEY'RE BEING LED BY A RING THROUGH THEIR SPECIAL INTERESTS. POLITICAL? MILITARY? WHAT DAY IS THIS?

IT'S BAD ***ENOUGH*** THAT NATIONAL SECRETS ARE BEING BOUGHT AND SOLD LIKE SOME CHEAP WATCH IN A PAWN SHOP. MY PROBLEM IS THAT THE PAWN SHOP KEEPS ***CHANGING MANAGEMENT.***

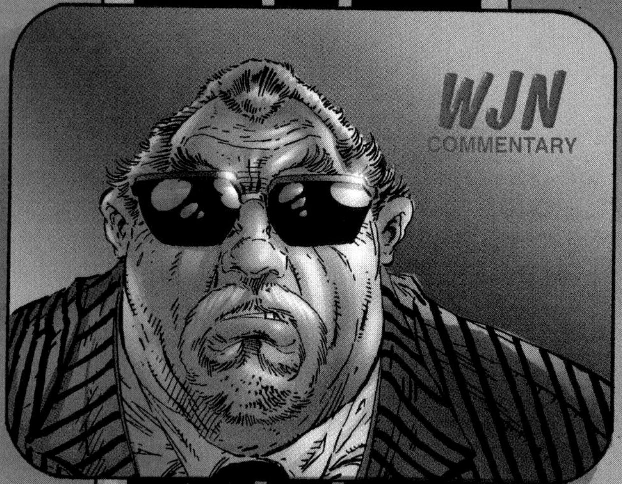
WJN
COMMENTARY

NOTED DOCUMENTARY FILMMAKER DUNCAN LEVIN, JUST BACK FROM NORTHERN IRELAND, IS FURIOUS WITH THE ***EMBASSY*** THERE. HIS FILM CREW, PERMITS IN HAND, WERE DENIED ACCESS TO A REMOTE VILLAGE NEAR THE CITY OF HEMTORG. AS THEY PRESSED THE ISSUE, THEY WERE ***'REMOVED'*** BY LOCALS. WHEN LEVIN BROUGHT THE MATTER TO THE EMBASSY, THE U.S. AMBASSADOR SUPPORTED THE ACTIONS OF THE LOCALS.

LEVIN SUSPECTS THE EMBASSY WAS PRESSURED BY THE C.I.A. DUE TO REBEL ACTIVITY IN THE AREA. THIS IS BORNE OUT BY EMBASSY RECOMMENDATIONS THAT, "FOR POLITICAL REASONS," THE PROJECT BE "REWORKED" FOR FILMING IN THE SOUTHERN PART OF THE COUNTRY.

ON A SADDER NOTE, I REGRET TO REPORT THE DEATH OF HAROLD CASE, A VETERAN INVESTIGATIVE REPORTER WITH NBC. HE WAS ON SPECIAL ASSIGNMENT IN ISTANBUL WHEN HE DIED IN A TRAGIC ***CAR ACCIDENT.*** HE WAS 61.

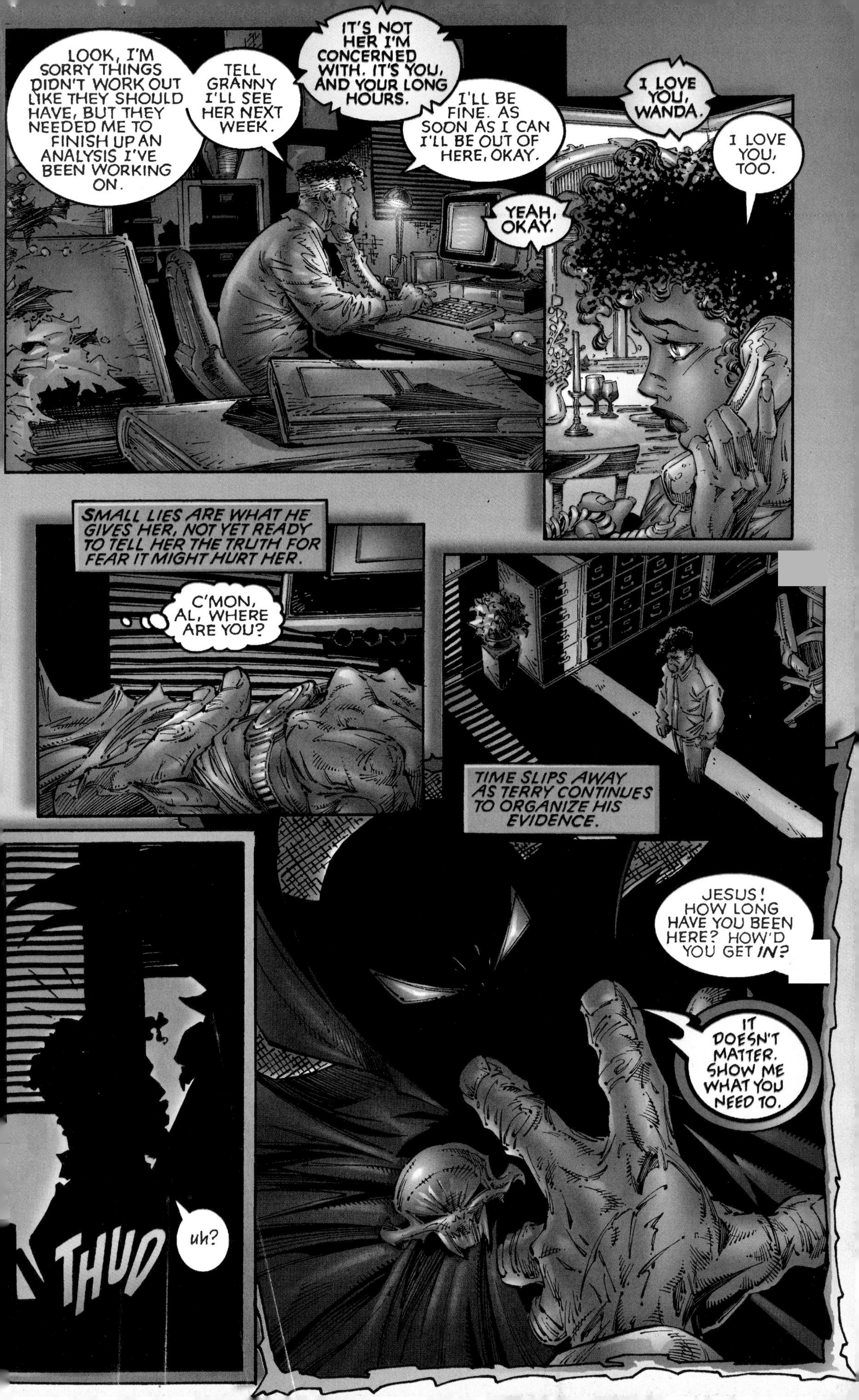
LOOK, I'M SORRY THINGS DIDN'T WORK OUT LIKE THEY SHOULD HAVE, BUT THEY NEEDED ME TO FINISH UP AN ANALYSIS I'VE BEEN WORKING ON.
TELL GRANNY I'LL SEE HER NEXT WEEK.
IT'S NOT HER I'M CONCERNED WITH. IT'S YOU, AND YOUR LONG HOURS.
I'LL BE FINE. AS SOON AS I CAN I'LL BE OUT OF HERE, OKAY.
YEAH, OKAY.
I LOVE YOU, WANDA.
I LOVE YOU, TOO.
SMALL LIES ARE WHAT HE GIVES HER, NOT YET READY TO TELL HER THE TRUTH FOR FEAR IT MIGHT HURT HER.
C'MON, AL, WHERE ARE YOU?
TIME SLIPS AWAY AS TERRY CONTINUES TO ORGANIZE HIS EVIDENCE.
THUD
uh?
JESUS! HOW LONG HAVE YOU BEEN HERE? HOW'D YOU GET IN?
IT DOESN'T MATTER. SHOW ME WHAT YOU NEED TO.

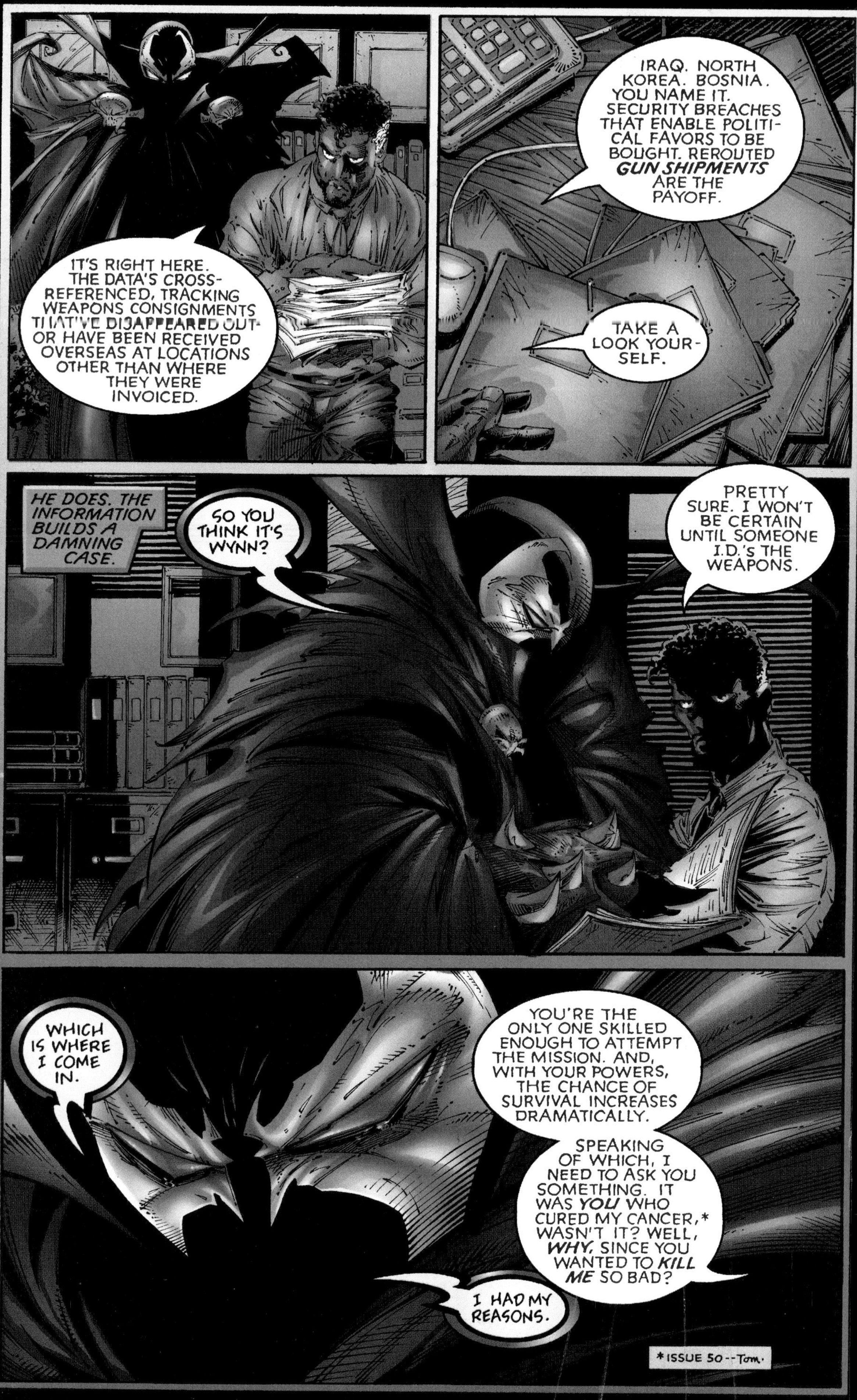
IT'S RIGHT HERE. THE DATA'S CROSS-REFERENCED, TRACKING WEAPONS CONSIGNMENTS THAT'VE DISAPPEARED OUT-OR HAVE BEEN RECEIVED OVERSEAS AT LOCATIONS OTHER THAN WHERE THEY WERE INVOICED.
IRAQ. NORTH KOREA. BOSNIA. YOU NAME IT. SECURITY BREACHES THAT ENABLE POLITICAL FAVORS TO BE BOUGHT. REROUTED GUN SHIPMENTS ARE THE PAYOFF.
TAKE A LOOK YOURSELF.
HE DOES. THE INFORMATION BUILDS A DAMNING CASE.
SO YOU THINK IT'S WYNN?
PRETTY SURE. I WON'T BE CERTAIN UNTIL SOMEONE I.D.'s THE WEAPONS.
WHICH IS WHERE I COME IN.
YOU'RE THE ONLY ONE SKILLED ENOUGH TO ATTEMPT THE MISSION. AND, WITH YOUR POWERS, THE CHANCE OF SURVIVAL INCREASES DRAMATICALLY.
SPEAKING OF WHICH, I NEED TO ASK YOU SOMETHING. IT WAS YOU WHO CURED MY CANCER,* WASN'T IT? WELL, WHY, SINCE YOU WANTED TO KILL ME SO BAD?
I HAD MY REASONS.
*ISSUE 50--Tom.

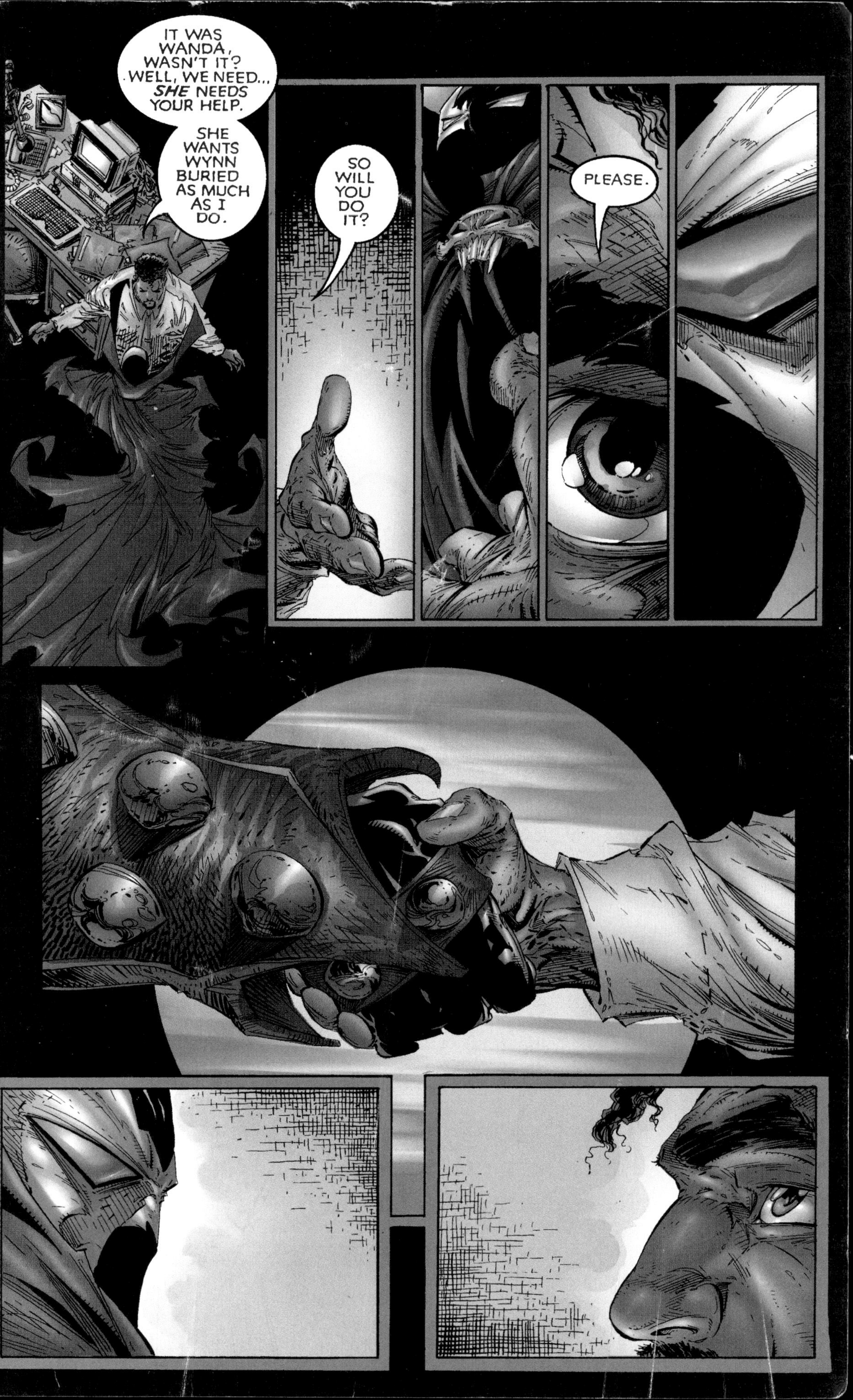
IT WAS WANDA, WASN'T IT? WELL, WE NEED... *SHE* NEEDS YOUR HELP.
SHE WANTS WYNN BURIED AS MUCH AS I DO.
SO WILL YOU DO IT?
PLEASE.

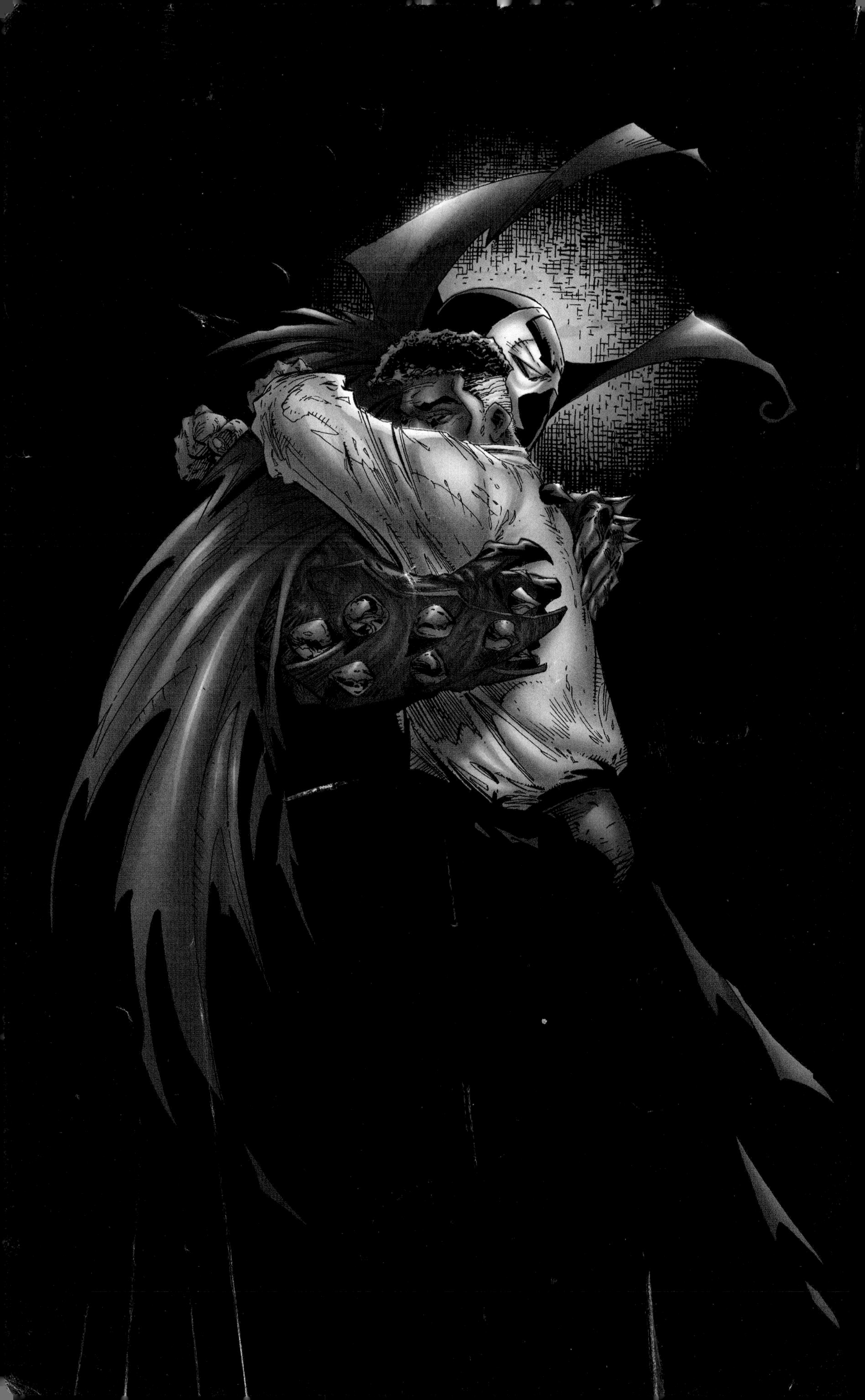

COMPLETE YOUR SPAWN LIBRARY!

HELLSPAWN
THE ASHLEY WOOD COLLECTION

SAM AND TWITCH
DO NOT
THE BRIAN MICHAEL BENDIS COLLECTION VOL. 1

SPAWN
TODD MCFARLANE

CREECH RAGE AGAINST DEATH TP.... $9.95

(ISBN: 1-58240-100-4)

HELLSPAWN ASHLEY WOOD COLLECTION TP.... $24.95

(ISBN: 1-58240-598-0)

SAM & TWITCH BRIAN MICHAEL BENDIS COLLECTION VOL 1 TP.... $24.95

(ISBN: 1-580240-583-2)

SPAWN COLLECTION VOL 1 TP.... $19.95

(ISBN: 1-58240-563-8)

SPAWN COLLECTION VOL 2 TP....29.95

(ISBN: 1-58240-610-3)

SPAWN MANGA VOL 1 TP....$9.99

(ISBN: 1-58240-571-9)

SPAWN MANGA VOL 2 TP $9.99

(ISBN: 1-58240-542-5)

SPAWN MANGA VOL 3 TP....$9.99

(ISBN: 1-58240-576-X)

THE BEST OF CURSE OF THE SPAWN....16.99

(ISBN: 1-58240-616-2)

For a comic store near you, call 1-888-comicbook

TODD McFARLANE PRODUCTIONS spawn.com